D1198978

Life Skills for the 21st Century

Building a Foundation for Success

Teacher's Wraparound Edition

Betsy Newberry

Prentice Hall

Boston • Columbus • Indianapolis • New York • San Francisco • Upper Saddle River
Amsterdam • Cape Town • Dubai • London • Madrid • Milan • Munich • Paris • Montreal • Toronto
Delhi • Mexico City • Sao Paulo • Sydney • Hong Kong • Seoul • Singapore • Taipei • Tokyo

Photo Acknowledgments

p. 461 © Andy Crawford & Steve Gorton/Dorling Kindersley Media Library

p. 461 © Dorling Kindersley Media Library

p. 461 © Steve Tanner/Dorling Kindersley Media Library

All other images courtesy of Shutterstock.com.

Executive Editor: Sande L. Johnson
Editorial Assistant: Clara Ciminelli
Director of Marketing: David Gesell
Campaign Marketing Manager:
  Leigh Ann Sims
Curriculum Marketing Manager:
  Thomas Hayward
Marketing Assistant: Les Roberts
Associate Managing Editor:
  Alexandrina Benedicto Wolf
Project Manager: Emergent Learning, LLC
Senior Operations Supervisor: Pat Tonneman
Operations Specialist: Deidra Schwartz

Web Content Specialist: Terri Mitchell
Text Designer: Vanessa Moore
Cover Designer: Keithley & Associates, Inc.
Cover Images: Shutterstock
Manager, Rights and Permissions: Zina Arabia
Image Permission Coordinator: Craig Jones
Full-Service Project Management:
  Emergent Learning, LLC
Composition: Vanessa Moore
Printer/Binder: Courier Kendallville
Cover Printer: Moore Langen,
  a Courier Company
Text Font: 10.5/12 Minion

Credits and acknowledgments borrowed from other sources and reproduced, with permission, in this textbook appear on appropriate page within text.

10 9 8 7 6 5 4 3 2 1

Prentice Hall
an imprint of

PearsonSchool.com/careertech

ISBN-10:   0-13-704531-X

ISBN-13: 978-0-13-704531-0

Contents

Introduction

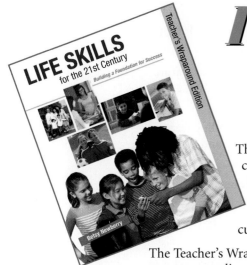

The Teacher's Wraparound Edition for *Life Skills for the 21st Century* is a comprehensive guide to the student edition text. In addition to providing instructors with essential information about how to use the student edition in the classroom, it includes exclusive material such as additional activities, vocabulary, discussion topics, and suggestions for ways to customize lessons for tiered learning.

The Teacher's Wraparound Edition presents instructors with teaching tips and other relevant content directly alongside the full-page view of the student edition text. Instructors can see exactly what the student sees while referencing the information they need to manage the classroom and promote learning.

To make it easy for teachers to access information relating to the current content, the Teacher's Wraparound Edition uses the following features and elements:

Overview: Each chapter starts with an overview that presents the main topics covered in the chapter.

Advance Preparation: A table on the opening page of each chapter lists suggestions for steps instructors may take to prepare for the class.

Customized Instruction Overview: A table that lists the pages where teachers can look for instruction materials customized for different levels of learning.

Focus and Engage: Each chapter begins with a "bell-ringer" activity to start the class off and to help focus the students' attention on the content to come. Corresponding text in the teacher's wrap helps teachers expand on that activity.

Introduce the Section: A list of important facts covered in the chapter that can be used to introduce content to come.

Vocabulary: A list of key terms and definitions introduced on the current page.

Discuss: Discussion topics that relate directly and indirectly to the content on the current page.

Reinforce and Review: Topics covered in the previous section, or in previous chapters, that instructors may want to review before continuing.

Teaching Tips: Bullet items that help explain the contain and provide additional information for instructors to use in the classroom.

Customized Instruction boxes: These include accommodations and additional activities for More Advanced, Less Advanced, ESOL, Special Needs, and At-Risk Students.

Student Activity boxes: Original activities that are not in the student edition textbook.

Critical Thinking Activity boxes: Original activities designed to encourage students to use critical thinking skills.

Teamwork Activity boxes: Original activities designed to promote teamwork, cooperation, and leadership skills.

Apply It boxes: These include hands-on activities where students can apply the skills that they are learning.

Figure Focus: Every figure in the student edition has a corresponding Figure Focus feature in the Teacher's Wraparound Edition. They give answers to the figure prompts and questions and provide additional information for discussion and instruction.

Feature Focuses: Every feature and box in the student edition has a corresponding feature in the Teacher's Wraparound Edition, to provide answers, discussion prompts, and additional teaching tips.

End-of-Chapter Activities: Answers, additional teaching tips, discussion points, and supplemental activities relating to the end of chapter activities.

Teacher Companion Web Site

The *Life Skills for the 21st Century: Building a Foundation for Success* Teacher Access Web site includes answer keys to the Web essay questions and additional material to support the textbook. To access the Teacher Access Companion Web site, visit www.phschool.com and enter the Web code GEF-1234.

Part 1

Self Discovery

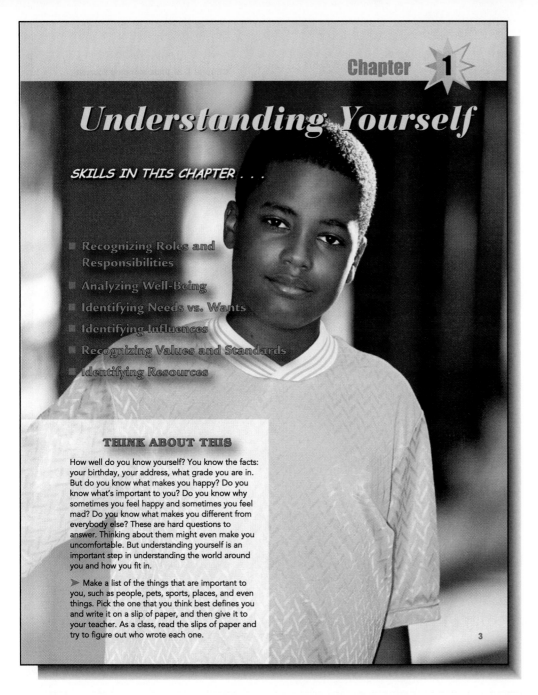

Chapter 1

Understanding Yourself

SKILLS IN THIS CHAPTER . . .

- Recognizing Roles and Responsibilities
- Analyzing Well-Being
- Identifying Needs vs. Wants
- Identifying Influences
- Recognizing Values and Standards
- Identifying Resources

THINK ABOUT THIS

How well do you know yourself? You know the facts: your birthday, your address, what grade you are in. But do you know what makes you happy? Do you know what's important to you? Do you know why sometimes you feel happy and sometimes you feel mad? Do you know what makes you different from everybody else? These are hard questions to answer. Thinking about them might even make you uncomfortable. But understanding yourself is an important step in understanding the world around you and how you fit in.

➤ Make a list of the things that are important to you, such as people, pets, sports, places, and even things. Pick the one that you think best defines you and write it on a slip of paper, and then give it to your teacher. As a class, read the slips of paper and try to figure out who wrote each one.

3

Chapter 1 Overview

In this chapter, students explore the many influences that shape their personalities and affect their behavior.

Recognizing Roles and Responsibilities By identifying the roles they play in specific situations, students gain a better understanding of what their families, friends, teachers, and employers expect of them.

Analyzing Well-Being Students discover that they can control how things go in their lives.

Identifying Needs vs. Wants Human *needs* are basic, but our *wants* and how we go about getting them have an important bearing on our personalities.

Identifying Influences Knowing the people and events that affect the way you think and act can help you better understand yourself.

Recognizing Values and Standards Students learn to identify what is important to them and how to measure the satisfaction it provides.

Identifying Resources Knowing what you can use to get something else helps you make decisions, solve problems, and achieve goals.

Focus and Engage

Bell-Ringer: Think About This

Students are asked to make a list of things that are important to them and then to pick one from the list that best defines them. Students will turn these in and then, as a class, try to figure out who wrote each one. Make sure students are specific enough so that others have a reasonable chance of identifying them. For example, writing "my brother" probably will not give other students enough information to identify the person who wrote it. Instead, the student might write "my older brother who taught me how to play basketball."

ADVANCE PREPARATION	
Review	*Life Skills for the 21st Century* textbook, Chapter 1.
Prepare	Students will need paper and pencil for some activities.
	Colored pencils or markers for drawing.
	Scissors and newspapers and magazines from which they can cut advertisements.
	Box labeled "Hot Topics."

CUSTOMIZED INSTRUCTION OVERVIEW				
Less Advanced Students	More Advanced Students	ESOL Students	Special Needs Students	At-Risk Students
Pages 6, 12, 14, 19	Pages 5, 10, 16	Pages 4, 10, 17	Pages 5, 8, 12, 14	Pages 4, 6, 9, 14, 16, 19

Introduce the Section

Explain that each of us fills many different roles every day of our lives, and that each role demands that we take on different responsibilities. In this section, students are introduced to the main areas in their lives in which they have roles.

Vocabulary

Peers: People your own age.
Responsibility: Something you are expected to do, or that you must accomplish.
Role: The way in which you behave in a specific situation.
Unique: One of a kind.

Teaching Tips

Make sure students can distinguish between a "role" and a "responsibility." A role is the individual function you fill; a responsibility is what you are accountable for doing or accomplishing in that role.

Discuss

Discuss roles that students might fill, in addition to the ones mentioned in the text. For example, older siblings often fill the role of mentor to younger siblings. Some children may have to fill the role of caretaker for an ill parent or older relative. More advanced students may fill the role of tutor to other students or assistant to teachers and other school staff. Helping students understand the important roles they play will increase their self-esteem.

Recognizing Roles and Responsibilities

You have roles in life that help you know how to act in different situations.

An actor might play one role in a movie and a different role on television. In real life, you play different roles, too. That doesn't mean you pretend to be someone you are not—it just means you act differently depending on who you are with and what you are doing.

A **role** is the way you behave in a specific situation. As a student, teachers expect you to behave a certain way in school, but that's not the same way a coach expects you to behave as an athlete in practice.

You have responsibilities in each role. A **responsibility** is something people expect you to do, or something you must accomplish. As a student your teachers expect you to come to class and do your homework. As an athlete, your coach expects you to come to practice and work hard. Responsibilities help define the way people interact and communicate with each other in different circumstances. When you live up to your responsibilities, you are successful in your role.

Different Roles = Different Responsibilities

You have roles in five main areas of your life: at home, with your **peers**—people your own age, in school, at work, and in your community. You also have a role as an individual—a **unique**—or one of a kind—person.

You relate to people in each area in different ways. For example, you probably use different words when you talk to your friends than you do when you talk to your parents or teachers. You might dress differently, too. Hanging around at home, you might wear sweats, but at school or work you want to express your style.

Responsibilities are different in each role:

- As a family member, you might be responsible for making your bed.
- As a friend, you might be responsible for being a good listener.
- As a student, you might be responsible for completing your assignments.
- As an employee, you might be responsible for showing up on time.
- As a neighbor, you might be responsible for picking up trash in front of your house.

Customized Instruction: ESOL Students

Have students say the vocabulary words in the primary language. Ask if the terms mean the same thing in both the primary language and English.

Customized Instruction: At-Risk Students

Have students develop a list of what they consider their responsibilities as a student. Be prepared to provide feedback on their lists. For example, do their lists include completing assignments on time, following student conduct rules, coming to class prepared, etc.?

Assigned Roles vs. Acquired Roles

Many of our roles happen because of who we are. Take the role of family member, for example. We don't choose to be a brother or sister or son or daughter. These roles are assigned to us.

Some roles we choose for ourselves. For example,

- You might want to be a musician, so you learn to play an instrument and audition for a band.
- You might want to be a member of the student government, so you campaign for office.
- You might want to work in a restaurant, so you apply for a job.
- You might want to contribute to your community, so you volunteer at a senior center.

Not everyone chooses the same roles. We choose certain roles because they are important to us. The roles we choose are the ones that make us unique—different from other people.

Roles and Responsibilities Change

Roles change depending on your **stage of life**, or how old you are. (There's more about stages of life in Chapter 6.) Right now, you are a son or daughter. Someday, you might be a parent. Right now, you are a friend. Someday, you might be a husband or wife.

Like roles, responsibilities change over time or in different situations.

- Now, you might be responsible for watching your little brother in the afternoon. Someday, you might be responsible for driving him to a friend's house.
- Now, you might be responsible for making your own lunch. Someday, you might be responsible for preparing dinner for your whole family.

Just because the role and responsibility are the same for you as for someone else doesn't mean you will both behave the same way. Everyone in your math class is responsible for doing the homework, but one person might do it every morning on the bus, while you meet with a classmate to do it after school.

The way we meet our responsibilities is unique, because we are unique. When you understand your roles and responsibilities, you understand more about yourself and why you behave the way you do in a certain situation.

Who Am I Now?

Your roles vary depending on the five main areas of your life:

Family

Son or daughter

Brother or sister

Niece or nephew

Cousin

Grandchild

Peers

Friend

Rival

Teammate

School

Student

Classmate

Work

Employee

Co-worker

Community

Neighbor

Volunteer

Consumer

Teaching Tips

Make sure students can distinguish between assigned roles and acquired roles. You are assigned the role of member of a community; you might acquire the role of being a member of a community sports team. Assigned roles are inherent, or in place without your having the choice to fill them or not. Acquired roles are those you choose to fill.

STUDENT ACTIVITY

Have students develop a comprehensive list of roles they fill in the five main areas of their lives, similar to the "Who Am I Now?" list. When they have completed the list, have them write beside each role if it is an "assigned" role or an "acquired" role.

Vocabulary

Stage of life: How old you are.

Discuss

There are nine stages of life:

- Infant: birth to 1 year old
- Toddler: 2–3 years old
- Early childhood: 3–6 years old
- Middle childhood: 6–11 years old
- Adolescence: 11–21 years old
- Young adulthood: 20s and 30s
- Middle adulthood: 40s and 50s
- Senior adulthood: 60s and 70s
- Old age: 80s and beyond

Ask students to give examples of people they know in the various stages of life. Then, ask them to identify a role that a person fills at that stage of his or her life. How is the role different from the roles the student now fills?

Customized Instruction: More Advanced Students

Have students prepare a list of their "acquired" roles. Then have them describe their responsibilities for each role.

Customized Instruction: Special Needs Students

Have students draw a picture of themselves in one of their assigned roles; i.e., a student in a classroom; a son or daughter with a parent; a brother or sister to a sibling.

Reinforce and Review

Remind students that responsibilities are those things for which you are accountable for doing or accomplishing.

Teaching Tips

Make sure students understand the word "respect" as it relates to fulfilling their responsibilities. When people respect you, they feel admiration for you and hold you in high esteem. When you behave responsibly in the roles you fill, people will respect you.

Discuss

Ask students what they think it means to be responsible. Responses might include:

- Doing what needs to be done without having to be asked.
- Not blaming others when things do not get done, or are done incorrectly.
- Demonstrating good judgment and following the rules to fulfill a responsibility.
- Considering how others will be affected by the manner in which you act.

No Excuses!

Ask students to consider their responsibilities in one of their acquired roles. What would happen if they did not fulfill their responsibilities? How would other people be affected?

Vocabulary

Rule: A written or unwritten statement about how something is supposed to be done.

TEAMWORK ACTIVITY

Have each team of students develop a list of rules that should be followed when with their peers. The list might include:

- Do not interrupt when someone else is talking.
- Do not criticize others.
- Respect the opinions of others.
- Respect the property of others.
- Be considerate of different cultural, social, and religious practices.

Figure Focus

Have students make a list of their responsibilities as a student and as a classmate. Compile a list on the board of the different responsibilities students come up with. Which role has more responsibilities?

No Excuses!

Being good at something doesn't mean you can ignore your responsibilities. Even the captain of the basketball team has to meet expectations—or end up sitting on the bench.

👎 Skipping practice

👎 Showing up late for games

👎 Laughing at other players

👍 Always trying your best

👍 Setting a positive example

👍 Cheering on the team

What problems might come from not living up to your responsibilites?

"In school, I'm both a student and a classmate. What responsibilities do I have in each role?"

Fulfilling Your Responsibilities

You might think responsibilities are a burden. After all, why should you care what other people expect from you? But, people treat you with more respect if you fulfill your responsibilities.

- They trust you.
- They take you seriously.
- They enjoy being with you.

If you do not fulfill your responsibilities, people stop expecting very much from you. They think you are immature.

- People feel you let them down.
- They see you as a slacker.
- They find someone else who will meet their expectations.

Rules and Responsibilities

Living up to your responsibilities means playing by the rules. A **rule** is a written or unwritten statement about how something is supposed to be done. Rules are meant to protect people and to help people live together in communities. When you follow the rules, you show people that you are responsible.

There are rules in every area of your life—home, school, in the community, at work, and even when you are with your peers.

- At home, you may have to be in bed at a certain time. You may not be able to watch television or use your phone until your homework is complete.
- In school, you may have to sit in assigned seats. You may have to raise your hand to speak in class.
- In your community, you may have to turn off your phone in a movie. You may have to wait for the signal to cross a street.

When you break the rules, you show that you are not responsible. There may be consequences for breaking the rules.

- If you come home too late, your parents may not let you go out next weekend.
- If you use your phone during a movie, the usher may ask you to leave.

Customized Instruction: Less Advanced/At-Risk Students

Have students tell three rules that apply in school. Ask them to describe how school would be different if these rules were not in effect.

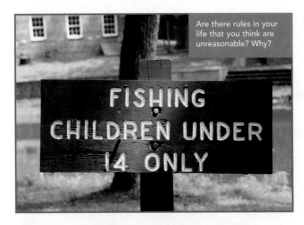

Are there rules in your life that you think are unreasonable? Why?

Different Rules for Different People

If you think that there are different rules for different people, you are right—there are. Many rules are meant to protect people, such as rules for wearing a seatbelt or a motorcycle helmet. Some rules vary depending on your age.

- When you are 15 your parents probably let you stay up later than when you were 10.
- When you are 18 you can vote.

Some families make their own rules, based on tradition, culture, and values. Many families traditionally set different rules for girls and boys. For example, parents might tell their daughter she can't date until she is a certain age but allow their son to date when he is younger.

If you think a rule is unreasonable, try to find out why the rule is in place. Once you understand the reason for the rule, you might understand why it is important not to break it.

You may be able to change some rules. For example, if you show your parents you are responsible and can be trusted to make smart decisions, your parents might agree to change a strict rule.

What's the Compromise?

At some point you will come across a rule that you think is unreasonable. You might be able to think of a **compromise**—*a solution—that makes everyone happy. What if your parents won't let you watch television on school nights?*

★ *Maybe they'll let you watch television if you finish all of your homework, first.*

★ *Maybe you could watch one television show a night.*

★ *Maybe you could record shows to watch another time.*

★ *Maybe you could watch television together.*

Remaining calm and proving you are responsible are the best ways to convince your parents they can trust you. Are there any rules in your house you would like to change?

Ask students why the sign shown in the figure might be considered unreasonable. Ask students why they think this sign was posted. The reason might be that many states require people age 14 or older to have a fishing license. This sign relieves the owner from having to check for valid fishing licenses. What other rules do students think are unreasonable? Make sure students explain why they think a rule is unreasonable.

Discuss

Encourage students to talk about rules in school. Are there different rules that apply to different grade levels? For example, maybe juniors and seniors are allowed to leave the school premises for lunch, but lower-level grades are not.

Teaching Tips

Make sure you steer any discussion about "unreasonable" rules in the direction of why they might exist in the first place. As the text states, some rules are established for our protection. Others are established because of individual traditions and values. Still others exist because governing bodies require them. For example, a city government might set a rule that requires pets to be on a leash at all times in city parks and on city-owned property. Point out to students how important it is to understand why the rule exists before they label it as "unreasonable."

What's the Compromise?

Explain to students that a *compromise* is an agreement between two or more parties in which all sides make concessions and usually accept less than what they originally wanted. Have students discuss rules at home they would like to change. Ask them to suggest a compromise that would help execute the change.

Introduce the Section

This section covers the concept of well-being. Most people think of "well-being" as a state in which they are healthy and comfortable. Things are going right in their lives, and conflicts of any type—interpersonal, economic, political—are at a minimum. Students are introduced to the idea that they are in control of their own well-being.

Vocabulary

Well-being: The feeling and understanding that everything is going right in your life.

Figure Focus

Ask students to identify the factors that they consider important to their well-being. Some general responses might be:

- Good health
- Safe environment
- Financial stability
- Achieving goals
- Contributing to success
- Enjoyment

Point out to students that identifying the factors that detract from their well-being is as important as knowing which ones contribute to it. For example, staying up late every night can detract from your physical well-being. Ask students to provide examples of factors that can get in the way of their well-being. How do they affect their ability to meet their responsibilities?

Teaching Tips

Stress to students that they are responsible for their own well-being. The state of their well-being has significant effects on their behavior and the manner in which they fill their roles and handle their responsibilities.

Analyzing Well-Being

When you are happy and well, you are able to meet your responsibilities.

Well-being is the feeling and understanding that everything is going right in your life. It is when you have a positive outlook about yourself and the people and things around you. You are happy, healthy, confident, and satisfied. Often, well-being has a lot to do with how well you meet your responsibilities.

You are responsible for your own well-being. It is not up to other people to make sure you are happy and confident. You can take steps to do things that contribute to your well-being and to avoid things that get in the way of your well-being.

Lots of things get in the way of well-being. You might feel tired or sick. You might be mad at your sister for hogging the bathroom, or sad that your mom has to miss your game because she is working the late shift.

Problems in one area of well-being can affect the other areas. If you're tired, you might have less patience with your sister and get mad faster. If you're sad about your mom missing your game, you might not play your best, and then you'll be dissatisfied with your performance.

Well-Being: Four Ways

Four areas of your life contribute to your well-being, and when all four work together successfully, you experience an overall feeling of well-being.

- **Emotional well-being** depends on your ability to deal with problems and stress.
- **Physical well-being** depends on your health.
- **Social well-being** depends on how you get along with other people.
- **Personal well-being** depends on how satisfied and confident you are with yourself.

Customized Instruction: Special Needs Students

There may be students in the class who have chronic health concerns, such as asthma or allergies. They might feel comfortable discussing in class the extra measures they must take to ensure their physical well-being.

Promote Your Own Well-Being

To promote your own well-being, you can be aware of what makes you happy and satisfied, and then take the action you need to make it happen. You can take action about a specific problem that is interfering with your well-being, such as finding time to be with your mom.

You might want to make general changes that will promote overall well-being, such as getting more exercise or being a better friend.

- To promote emotional well-being, you can start writing your thoughts, fears, worries, and concerns in a journal.
- To promote physical well-being, you can make sure you get enough sleep.
- To promote social well-being, you can join a club or student organization.
- To promote personal well-being, you can be honest with yourself and the people around you.

Your Well-Being Might Not Be My Well-Being

Things that contribute to your well-being might not be the same things that contribute to someone else's well-being. Because we are all unique individuals, our well-being is unique, too.

- Does missing the coming attractions before a movie annoy you? Maybe not, but it might make your friend mad.
- Is your brother grumpy unless he gets eight hours of sleep at night? You might be fine with only seven.
- Are you satisfied with one really good friend? Someone else might need a whole crowd.

"Exercising promotes my physical well-being. What can I do to promote well-being in the other areas of my life?"

Whose Well-Being Is More Important?

Sometimes, looking out for your own well-being could actually interfere with the well-being of others. While some people such as your parents might be willing to put your well-being first, you cannot expect that from everyone. What if you want to sleep late in the morning?

★ *Your sister has to get up earlier because she must use the bathroom first.*

★ *Your brother has to walk the dog because you don't have time.*

★ *Your mother has to drive you to school because you miss the bus.*

Is your action fair to everyone else in your family? What could you do so that your well-being does not interfere with the well-being of the others?

21st Century Skills

What Happens Next?

Both Charles and Danny decide to campaign for election as a representative to the student council. Candidates must give a speech before the voting; if they do not give a speech, they cannot be elected.

Charles has always had an interest in politics. He might want to study government in college and maybe even run for office himself someday.

Danny thinks he has enough friends to elect him for anything. He considered running for class president last year, but decided it would take too much time away from sports and fun. This election will be quick, and the meetings are held at night, and only once a month.

Charles puts up posters around the school and starts giving out buttons he made himself that say "Vote for Charles." On Tuesday, Charles finds some of his posters ripped down. He hears a lot of laughing and sees Danny's friends paying students $1 each for the "Vote for Charles" buttons.

Charles considers his options. He wants to be on the student council, but not if people are going to laugh at him.

What happens next? Using your 21st Century Skills—such as decision making, goal setting, and problem solving—write an ending to the story. Read it to the class, or form a small group and present it as a skit.

Customized Instruction: At-Risk Students

Ask students to describe how school contributes to their well-being. Be prepared with prompts, such as: "School is a safe place so it contributes to emotional well-being"; "School offers a healthy lunch and opportunities to exercise so it contributes to physical well-being"; and so forth.

Reinforce and Review

Emphasize to students that they can manage their own well-being if they understand what factors contribute to it and what detracts from it.

Figure Focus

Have students list the things they do each day to ensure well-being in each of the four areas of their lives. For example:

- Emotional well-being: "I talk about any problems with my parents instead of trying to deal with them on my own."
- Physical well-being: "I eat a healthy breakfast every morning."
- Social well-being: "I avoid people with negative attitudes and bad behavior."
- Personal well-being: "I try my best on everything I do."

21st Century Skills

What Happens Next?

Students should write what they think Charles will do about the student council election. Student responses will vary, but possible options may include:

- Charles will decide to drop out of the election to avoid the ridicule and antics of Danny and his supporters.
- Charles will consult with a teacher or other school administrator to see if they can put a stop to what Danny and his friends are doing.
- Charles will come up with a new campaign strategy that does not include posters or buttons.
- Charles will confront Danny and convince him to run a fair campaign.

Whose Well-Being Is More Important?

Ask students to consider a factor that contributes to their well-being, but which might be disruptive to someone else. For example, having your friends over after school every day contributes to your social well-being, but how does it affect other siblings who are trying to concentrate on their homework?

Introduce the Section

It is common for people to confuse wants and needs. In this section, wants and needs are defined, and students learn to identify what is a necessity in their lives and what is simply something they desire.

Vocabulary

Goal: A plan to obtain something.
Motivator: Something that can encourage you to set goals and make decisions that will lead to your happiness and well-being.
Need: Something you cannot live without.
Want: Something you desire.

Focus and Engage

Ask students to identify what they need to survive; for example, food, water, and shelter. Then, ask them to identify what they believe would improve their existence; for example, regular visits to their favorite fast-food restaurant, bottled water, and a nicely furnished home with cable TV.

Figure Focus

Ask students what they think the photo illustrates. The boy has a number of electronic gadgets, which represent things he wants or desires. Ask students to name two to three things they strongly desire at this point in their lives.

What Will You Do to Get It?

Discuss measures students might take to get what they want. Encourage them to talk about both material things and things that don't carry a price tag, such as a higher grade point average or a winning soccer season. How will they achieve their goal? Encourage them to elaborate on the specific plans they have for achieving the goal.

Identifying Needs vs. Wants

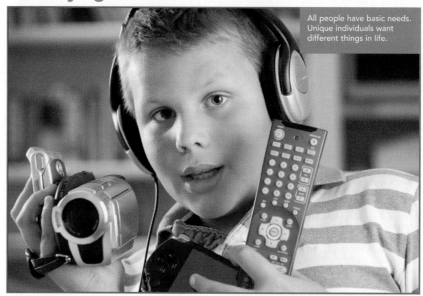

All people have basic needs. Unique individuals want different things in life.

When you say that you absolutely, positively need a new video game, you're wrong. You might *want* a new video game. But you don't *need* it.

- A **need** is a something you can't live without.
- A **want** is something you desire.

Humans *need* certain basic items in order to survive. We *want* things to improve our quality of life. All people have the same needs. What we want makes us different and unique. Recognizing the difference between things you need and things you want is one way you show that you understand yourself.

What Will You Do to Get It?

Wanting or needing something can be a strong **motivator**, which means it can encourage you to set goals and make decisions that will lead to your happiness and well-being.

- On the up side, wanting or needing something can motivate you to act responsible and smart in a way that will lead to your happiness and well-being. You might have to get a job and save money for a long time to buy a red convertible.
- On the down side, wanting or needing something might make you act irresponsible and stupid. You might decide the fastest way to get the car is to steal it.

A **goal** is a plan to obtain something. You might set a goal to obtain a specific thing—such as a new jacket or a motorbike. You might set a goal to achieve a position—such as soloist in the chorus or team captain. Goals help you focus on what is really important to you and what you are willing to work for.

Customized Instruction: More Advanced Students

Have students map out a plan to get the two to three things they most desire at this point in their lives. Will they ask their parents for money? Will they get a job to earn money to buy it themselves? Make sure their plans include a timeline.

Customized Instruction: ESOL Students

What are the words for "want" and "need" in the primary language? Are they used as both nouns and verbs in the primary language?

But I Want It!

Wants are things that are not necessary for survival. They are things that you think will make you happy and contribute to your well-being—and they might. But, you can make do without them.

There are some things most people want, such as entertainment and dessert. Some wants are very personal and help define us as individuals. You might want that red convertible to cruise around town, while someone else might want a blue bicycle.

Human Needs

Human needs can be divided into two basic categories: physical and psychological. Both are vital for well-being.

- **Physical needs** include the basic items all people need to survive, such as food, water, shelter, and clothing.
- **Psychological needs** are more difficult to define, because they include the things that affect the way you think and feel, and they are different for different people. For example, safety, security, love, acceptance, and respect are psychological needs.

Different People, Different Needs

Some needs aren't actually required to survive. For example, you could survive without friendship, but it would be an unhappy existence. Other needs are qualified by where you live or what standards you live by. In many countries, people survive without indoor plumbing, but in the United States we consider a flush toilet and a shower basic needs for survival.

Can you think of other things that we think of as needs that people in other countries consider wants? Individually or with a partner, come up with one item and make a magazine ad for it, or a video commerical.

N U M B E R S
G A M E

Your mother needs milk. She gives you $7.00 and sends you to the store to buy a gallon. The milk costs $3.50. She says you can spend the change on anything you want. How much will you have left to spend?

To figure it out, you must subtract the cost of the milk from the amount of money you have. Make sure you line up the decimal points so the answer comes out right!

Decimals are part of a whole. When you are working with dollars, decimals are parts of a dollar, or cents. The decimal point is the dot between the whole number and the parts.

How much would you have left over if your mom gave you $10.00 and asked you to buy milk for $3.50 and eggs for $2.75?

Psychological Needs

Psychological needs include the things that affect the way we think and feel. They include:

✔ Safety

✔ Acceptance

✔ Love

✔ Respect

✔ Recognition

✔ Achievement

✔ Friendship

✔ Self-esteem

No Excuses!

Wanting something that will promote your well-being shows that you are responsible. Interfering with the well-being of others in order to get what you want is not.

👎 Taking credit for someone else's achievement

👎 Stealing someone else's belongings

👎 Putting someone down to make you look better

👍 Working hard to achieve your goal

Can you think of responsible ways to identify and achieve your wants and needs?

N U M B E R S   G A M E

The amount left over from the $7 is $3.50. The amount left over from the $10 is $3.75. Explain to students that they will need to total the amounts for the milk and eggs first. Then, they should subtract that total from the $10. When subtracting, make sure they understand to line up the decimal points.

Reinforce and Review

Make sure students can distinguish the difference between wants and needs. Wants are the things we desire and that *appear* to be instrumental to our well-being. Needs are the things that *really* are instrumental to our well-being.

Teaching Tips

Discuss how an individual's "wants" help define his or her character and personality. For example, one 12-year-old boy's biggest desire is to get a trampoline for his backyard. His 12-year-old friend really wants an easel and paints. You might deduce that the boy who wants the trampoline depends on a lot of physical activity to maintain his well-being, while the other boy relies on solitude and being creative for his well-being.

Vocabulary

Physical needs: Basic items all people need to survive, such as food, water, shelter, and clothing.

Psychological needs: Things that affect the way you think and feel, and which vary from person to person.

Psychological Needs

Ask students if their psychological needs are similar to the list in the text. Do they have other needs? Encourage them to expand upon the list. Some others might include: independence, autonomy (feeling that you're acting on your own choices and are happy with those choices), competence, and relatedness (sense of closeness with others).

 ### Different People, Different Needs

Students are asked to prepare an ad or video commercial on something we consider a need but which people in another country would consider a want. Some examples include freezers for preserving food and making ice; air conditioning; and automobiles.

No Excuses!

Explain to students that pursuing what we want is conducive to setting goals and going the extra mile to achieve them, but not if it violates the rights of others. Students should also consider that what they want might occasionally turn out to be their downfall. For example, wanting certain types of food could lead to weight problems; wanting to play video games for hours a day could lead to poor performance in school; and so forth.

Introduce the Section

This section discusses the influences that affect our behavior and dictate the way we live our lives. Virtually everything we see, hear, feel, taste, and smell influences us in some manner.

Vocabulary

Influence: Something that affects the way you think and act.

Figure Focus

Discuss ways in which friends influence us. Are we influenced by their study habits? The clothes they wear? Their religious beliefs? Their ethnicity? Their physical appearance? Ask students to consider how much they are influenced by their friends. Do they ever think it is too much?

Discuss

Discuss things other than those covered in the text that influence students. For example, the state of the national economy might influence the way they shop. War and conflict overseas might influence their opinion of other cultures. A new job might influence their decision about college.

CRITICAL THINKING ACTIVITY

Ask students how *they* are an influence on other people, such as their friends, family, and teachers. Encourage them to think about anything they do or say that affects the way other people think and act.

Identifying Influences

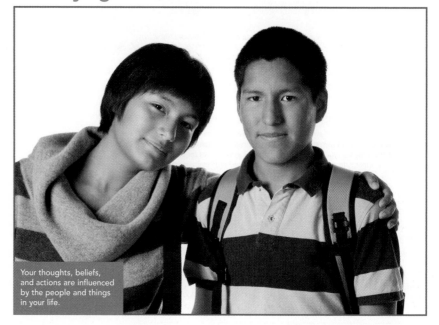

Your thoughts, beliefs, and actions are influenced by the people and things in your life.

An **influence** is something that affects the way you think and act. You are influenced by pretty much everything in your life.

When you are young, your biggest influence is your family. That's who you spend the most time with and who teaches you about life. As you grow older, you are influenced by a wider range of people and information, including friends, teachers, current events, advertising, and celebrities.

Understanding Influence

Recognizing the things that influence you can help you understand yourself better. When you know where influence comes from, you can make up your own mind about whether the influence would be positive—a good influence—or negative—a bad influence.

There are major influences in all areas of your life. You are influenced by your family and friends, by your culture and community. You may be influenced by things you read or see on television. You may be influenced by the behavior of athletes and celebrities you don't even know.

A lot of influence happens without your even knowing it.

- For example, just living in a certain neighborhood can influence you and your opinions of others. In a friendly neighborhood, you might feel safe and spend a lot of time outside, but in a less friendly neighborhood, you might be wary and stay indoors.
- The media—television, radio, magazines, and the Internet—can influence you. For example, you see pictures of pretty, happy people in an ad for a particular store, and you want to shop in that store so you can be pretty and happy, too.

Customized Instruction: Less Advanced/Special Needs Students

Have students cut out an ad in a newspaper or magazine that appeals to them. Ask them to explain what words or parts of the ad influenced their decision to pick it.

Good Influence or Bad Influence?

Sometimes it's pretty easy to tell whether an influence is positive or negative.

■ If something influences you in a way that promotes your well-being, it's a good bet the influence is positive.

■ If something influences you to break the law, or risk your life or health—or someone else's life or health—it's a good bet the influence is negative.

Sometimes it's not so easy to tell a positive influence from a negative influence. A friend might want you to join a club or organization—usually that's a positive influence. But it's still a good idea to check out the club first and make sure it is right for you.

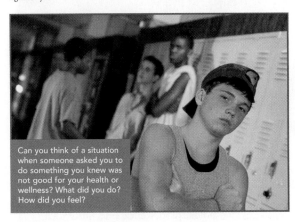

Can you think of a situation when someone asked you to do something you knew was not good for your health or wellness? What did you do? How did you feel?

Influence As a Roadblock

A **roadblock** is something that gets in the way and interferes with your progress. Sometimes influences can interfere with your well-being. For example, the behavior of the people around you can be a roadblock to your personal and emotional well-being.

■ Your family members might fight a lot, causing you stress.

■ Your teachers might have unrealistic expectations of what you can accomplish.

■ Your friends might want you to participate in risky behavior.

Things you see in the movies or magazines can be a roadblock to your physical well-being:

■ You might be influenced by ultra-thin models to try to lose weight.

■ You might be influenced by violence in movies to act violent yourself.

Understanding influences helps you to recognize the roadblocks and make healthy decisions that are in your own best interest.

What Influences You?

Your thoughts, beliefs, and actions are influenced by the people and things in your life. Major influences include:

✔ *Family*   ✔ *Friends*
✔ *Culture*   ✔ *Community*
✔ *Current Events* ✔ *Media*

Positive or Negative?

Sometimes influences that seem positive at the time turn out to have a negative effect. Your parents might be overprotective.

👎 You never have a chance to make your own decisions.

👎 You expect other people to take care of your well-being.

👎 You have trouble identifying your own needs and wants.

👍 You talk to your parents about your concerns and they give you more responsibility.

Can you think of influences in your life that seem positive but might be negative in the long run?

Discuss

Discuss with students the things that can have a positive influence on their day. A good night's sleep and a healthy breakfast can contribute positively to their physical well-being. Or, walking to school with a friend, paying a compliment to someone, or organizing your room can also have positive influences. Then, explore how not doing these things can have a negative influence on their day, or cause a roadblock.

What Influences You?

Ask students to provide an example of how each major influence affects their lives. For example, a current event, such as an economic recession, might contribute to job loss within the family, thereby affecting the family's financial situation.

Figure Focus

Students may be reluctant to elaborate on a situation in which someone asked them to do something that was not good for them. Encourage them to share by providing examples from your own personal experiences or others, such as:

■ Getting in a car driven by an inexperienced driver.

■ Staying out past curfew.

■ Drinking alcohol or smoking cigarettes.

Be sure to ask students how giving in to a bad influence made them feel.

Positive or Negative?

Students are asked to think of influences that seem positive at first, but turn out to be negative later on. Getting an after-school job, for example, has a positive influence on your personal well-being in that you have your own money to spend and also have a sense of commitment and responsibility. But in the long run, it has a negative influence on the amount of time you can commit to your school work, your family, and your friends. Does the positive outweigh the negative, or vice versa?

Stay in School

What influences students to drop out of school? Some experts believe a major influence is boredom or a disconnect between what is relevant to the student and what they are exposed to in school. Explain to students that school equips them with the tools they need to succeed in life, such as:

■ Language and writing skills to communicate effectively.

■ Math skills to compute and calculate.

■ Social skills to build and nurture relationships.

These skills are relevant to students regardless of their family, social, or academic situation. Further, explain to students that the cure for boredom is to become involved in extracurricular activities and school functions. Discuss with students the various activities available in school and through school.

Introduce the Section

In this section, students are introduced to the concepts of values and standards. They learn to identify the things—tangible and intangible—that are important to them, and they determine what standards or guidelines to use to measure value.

Figure Focus

The photo depicts a girl and her grandmother looking through a photo album. Ask students what values this activity demonstrates. Responses might include family history, relationships, or spending time with family.

Vocabulary

Monetary value: The dollars and cents cost of something of importance.

Personal values: Thoughts, ideas, and actions that are important to you.

Sentimental value: The emotional or personal reason that something is important to you.

Standards: Guidelines for whether or not something meets expectations.

Value: Something that is important to you.

Teaching Tips

Make sure students understand the difference between monetary values, sentimental values, and personal values. Monetary value refers to how much something is worth in dollars and cents, such as your stereo system. Sentimental value refers to the emotional association to something, such as a favorite stuffed animal. Personal value refers to the principals or ideals that are important to you, such as honesty and respect.

Recognizing Values and Standards

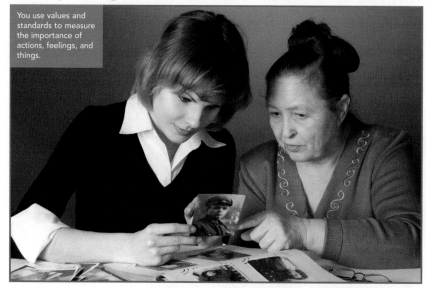

You use values and standards to measure the importance of actions, feelings, and things.

If something is important to you, it has **value**. Some things have **monetary value**, which means they cost money. Other things have **sentimental value**, which means they are important for emotional or personal reasons.

When thoughts, ideas, and actions are important to you, they have value, too. You might not be able to put a dollar price on them, but you can use them to gauge or evaluate the people and things in your life. They are called your **personal values**.

Standards are really just guidelines for whether or not something meets expectations. We use standards to measure performance on everything from how many miles per gallon a car gets, to how well students do in a class. We also use standards to judge behavior.

You probably know when someone is judging you to see if you meet his or her standards: A teacher gives you a test or a parent comments on your table manners. You might not realize that you set standards, too, and you use them to measure whether people and things meet your expectations.

Developing Values and Standards

You develop values by figuring out what is important to you. The influences in your life help you develop values. When you are young, your values might reflect the values of the people in your life. For example, you might value the same things your parents and friends value.

As you grow and learn more about the world around you, you can develop your own values. Your parents might not value an MP3 player the way you do, or your friends might not value physical exercise as much as you do.

We use values to set standards. Setting a high standard shows you value something a lot; a lower standard shows you don't value it so much. For example, your parents might set a high standard for your grades in school because they value education a lot.

Customized Instruction: Less Advanced/Special Needs Students

Provide students with a list of words, such as *cell phone, video games, love, family photographs, friendship, bicycle, car, diploma,* etc. Ask them to place a dollar sign ($) beside the things that have monetary value, an "S" beside the things that have sentimental value, and a "P" beside the things that have personal value.

Customized Instruction: At-Risk Students

Provide students with a list of words that relate to school and education, such as *books, "A" on a test, diploma, teacher, computer,* etc. Ask them to place a "Y" for yes if it holds value for them, and an "N" for no if it does not.

Types of Values

Something has **instrumental value** if it is important for acquiring something else. For example, money has instrumental value because you use it to buy other things. A car has instrumental value because you use it to drive to school or work. Clothes and an education also have instrumental value.

Something has **intrinsic value** if it is important in and of itself. Things with intrinsic value may be hard to explain. They might include emotions or feelings. For example, happiness, love, respect, justice, and beauty have intrinsic value.

As soon as you are old enough to tell right from wrong, you develop **moral values**. Moral values help us judge behavior based on what we think is good compared to what we think is wrong. Moral values usually include honesty, respect, justice, and responsibility.

Not everyone values the same things. Your family might value dinner time together, while your friend's family might not think dinner together is important at all. It is important to be able to respect other people's values even if you don't agree with them.

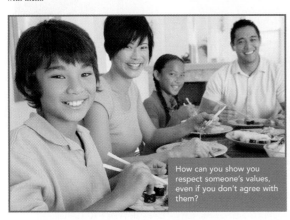

How can you show you respect someone's values, even if you don't agree with them?

Displaying Values

You show your values by the way you act and the things you say. If you value kindness, you act kindly to others. If you value friendship, you are a good friend. If you value your clothes, you keep them clean and in good repair.

You can also show your values by the choices you make in life. If you value health, you can choose to eat a healthy diet. If you value the environment, you can choose to recycle.

Even when people value the same things, they might show their values in different ways. For example, people of different religions might all value faith, but they have different ways of showing it. One person might wear a necklace with a religious symbol on it, while another might not want to wear a religious symbol as jewelry. It doesn't mean one person has more faith than the other.

No Excuses

Saying you value something means very little. Showing you value something by the way you live your life means a lot.

👎 Complaining about the trash in your neighborhood

👍 Organizing a community clean-up

👎 Watching a senior citizen struggle to carry a heavy bag

👍 Offering to carry the bag

How do you show that something is important to you?

Myth Once you develop a value, it stays with you for life.

Truth Like roles and responsibilities, values change over time. Things that are important to you when you are young might become less important as you grow older.

TEAMWORK ACTIVITY

Have students pair up and identify one value they see in each other and to explain how they were able to identify that value. For example, one student might recognize that his or her partner gets good grades, so therefore places high value on education.

Vocabulary

Instrumental value: Being important for acquiring something else.
Intrinsic value: Being important in and of itself.
Moral values: Help us judge behavior based on what we think is right compared to what we think is wrong.

Teaching Tips

Students may have trouble distinguishing between instrumental and intrinsic values. Point out that something is instrumentally valuable if it is the means by which something else good is obtained. For example, a computer has instrumental value because you can use it to obtain information. An intrinsically valuable thing is worth having for itself. Think of it as "isolated" from everything else. If it is still deemed to be good, then it has intrinsic value.

Moral values are derived from personal conscience and are based on what you think is right and wrong.

Figure Focus

Students are asked to consider how to show respect for someone's values when they do not agree with them. For example, ask students how they would show respect for a friend who places high value on winning a game at any cost when they feel that having fun is of higher value. Students should demonstrate problem-solving skills in their responses.

No Excuses

Remind students of the old saying, "Actions speak louder than words." Ask them what actions they could take to show something is important to them.

Myth/Truth

Have students consider how their values have changed from the time they were in elementary school to the present. For example, in elementary school, they might have placed high value on recess. Now, they might place high value on getting homework done in study hall. What do they value now that might not be so important in adulthood? For example, socializing with friends might be important now, but in adulthood, family and work commitments may be more important.

Reinforce and Review

Students should understand that what they value is reflected in the way they act and behave.

Discuss

Make sure students understand that it is normal to have conflicting values of their own and with others. What an individual values is part of what makes that person unique.

"Quote Box"

Elaborate on the quote by explaining that a person's fingerprints are their unique identifier. Likewise, the things you value and the way you demonstrate their value to you help define your individuality. Explain to students that Elvis Presley was one of the best-selling solo artists in the history of popular music and was referred to as the "King of Rock and Roll." Some of his greatest hits were "Hound Dog," "Suspicious Minds," and "Jailhouse Rock." He died in 1977.

Showing Values in Different Ways

Students are asked if they think two people with different values can be friends. Ask them to give an example of a value they share with a friend. Then ask them to explain the differences in how they show that value. For example, you both value money. You show that value by donating extra money to a charity; your friend shows that value by spending extra money on things for herself.

Figure Focus

Students are asked to think of a time when they had to choose between conflicting values. Ask them to elaborate on the considerations that led to the choice they made.

Reinforce and Review

Review the definition of "standard." Standards are guidelines for whether or not something meets expectations.

Conflicting Values

Sometimes your values might conflict with each other. For example, on Saturday morning you might have the opportunity to sleep late or to go out for breakfast with your dad. Your value of extra sleep conflicts with your value of time with your dad. You will have to decide which you value more.

Sometimes your values might conflict with the values of other people. Your parents might think you should spend your afternoons studying, because they place a high value on good grades. You might think you should have an after-school job, because you place a high value on earning money. You might have to work out a compromise that respects the values of everyone involved.

> " Values are like fingerprints. Nobody's are the same, but you leave 'em all over everything you do. "
>
> — *Elvis Presley, American music icon*

Showing Values in Different Ways

People have different ways of showing what they value. What if you value animals? Does everyone who values animals show it in the same way?

★ *You might volunteer at an animal shelter.*

★ *You might take care of your own pet.*

★ *You might walk your neighbor's dog.*

★ *You might eat a vegetarian diet.*

★ *You might not wear clothes made from animal products.*

Showing values in different ways doesn't mean one person is right and the other is wrong. Do you think two people with different values can be friends?

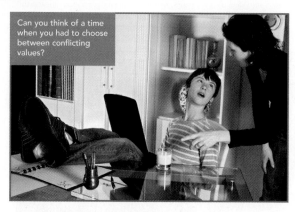

Can you think of a time when you had to choose between conflicting values?

Identifying Standards

Some standards—such as miles per gallon or points on a test—are easy to define and measure. There might be government regulations, such as a speed limit, or a rubric that identifies exactly what you have to do to meet the standards.

Some standards are less easy to define and measure. These are the standards based on how much you value something.

Because people value different things, not everyone has the same standards.

■ You might value neatness, so you make your bed every day.

■ Your brother does not care about being neat, so he never makes his bed.

Society sets standards, too, based on generally accepted behavior. That's why people wait patiently in a checkout line at the market instead of knocking each other over to be first; society expects people will be polite and wait their turn.

Customized Instruction: At-Risk Students

Have students talk about conflicting values they might have with teachers and administrators. For example, teachers might place a high value on homework, whereas students think it is valuable to have time to complete assignments during the school day, thus leaving them more free time after school to do what they want. Be prepared to suggest ways to compromise; for example, maybe teachers do not give homework over weekends.

Customized Instruction: More Advanced Students

Students hear a lot about academic standards. Have students write a paragraph on how academic standards help measure the performance or quality of their education.

Are Your Standards Flexible?

Sometimes, having different standards can cause conflicts—disagreements. If you share a room with your brother, and you have different standards of neatness, you might fight about it.

One way to avoid such conflict is to have **flexible standards**—standards that you can adapt to different situations.

- Could you lower your neatness standard so you will be happy if your brother makes his bed when you have friends over?
- Could you lower your neatness standard so just throwing a blanket over the unmade bed is enough?

Having flexible standards shows you are **tolerant**, or willing to consider the opinions of others.

Understanding Ethics

Your values and standards are also influenced by your **ethics**. Ethics are a set of beliefs about what is right and what is wrong.

- Some ethics are established by society. They determine how people are supposed to behave, usually in terms of human rights, responsibilities, and justice. They may be based on customs or on law.
- Some ethics are established by groups of people, such as the members of certain professions. For example, doctors and lawyers must abide by strict ethical standards, or they can lose their licenses to practice.
- Some ethics are personal and usually measure **virtues**—or positive character traits—such as honesty, compassion, and loyalty.

People don't always agree on what is ethical. One student may think it is ethical to let a friend copy his homework, while another student may think it is unethical.

Even when there are laws defining what is ethical, some people still don't agree. For example, one person might think it is ethical to download movies or share music files, even though it is illegal.

 How does it feel when you know you don't measure up to someone else's standards?

 "People will yell at me if I cut to the front of the line. What else do I do because of society's standards?"

Standards Around the World

Societies have different standards of behavior, just as individuals do. In the United States, people (other than athletes) rarely spit in public—and if they do, others think they are gross. In some countries, like China, people spit everywhere. They even blow their noses without using a tissue!

Individually or with a partner, research some societal values that vary by region. Make a poster or chart comparing the differences.

Vocabulary

Ethics: Set of beliefs about what is right and what is wrong.

Flexible standards: Standards that you can adapt to different situations.

Tolerant: Willing to consider the opinion of others.

Figure Focus

Students are asked how it feels when they don't measure up to someone else's standards. Some might answer that they are embarrassed, humiliated, or uncomfortable. Be prepared to offer suggestions on how to deal with those feelings. For example, make sure you understand what exactly the standard measures. If your boss says your customer service skills need to be improved, find out specifically what his good customer service standards are. Be sure to emphasize that some standards represent merely the opinions of others and that your opinions may vary widely.

Standards Around the World

Students are asked to create a poster or chart that compares societal values between regions in the world. Some values that students might explore are women in the workplace, legal driving age, or dining etiquette.

Discuss

Students learned earlier in the chapter that moral values help people judge behavior based on what is right compared to what is wrong. Ethics is a set of beliefs about what is right and what is wrong. Your ethics influence your morals. Ask students to give examples of organizations to which they belong that have a code of ethics. For example, the Boy Scouts of America has a code of ethics that outlines the acceptable behavior and responsibilities given to members.

Figure Focus

Ask students to give examples of societal standards that determine their behavior. Examples might include:

- Throwing trash in a waste receptacle.
- Practicing good hygiene.
- Recycling.

Introduce the Section

In this section, students learn what resources are, where to find them, and how to manage them. Explain that resources are the tools we use to get something else or achieve goals.

Figure Focus

Ask students to identify resources in the photo. Examples are:

- Water, air, and trees (natural resources).
- People on whom you depend for things, such as friendship, love, and protection (human resources).
- Car and clothes (non-human or material resources).

Vocabulary

Human resources: Resources that people provide, such as knowledge, talent, and time, which things cannot provide.

Resources: Things you use to get something else; a source of help or information.

Teaching Tips

Explain that resources can be found everywhere and in every facet of our daily routine: water to take a shower, money to buy lunch, schools to help educate, and so forth. Make sure students understand that some resources are abundant, such as air and knowledge, but others are limited in supply, such as money and petroleum.

Discuss

Ask students to name resources available to them now. What resources are *not* available to them now, but which they would like to have available in the future? Point out that they will need some resources throughout the duration of their lives. For example, they will always need air, water, and food to survive. Most likely, they will also always need money.

TEAMWORK ACTIVITY

Have teams of students consider the resources available to them in school. Ask each team to compile a list and to identify the resource as natural, human, or non-human. Then, ask them to decide as a team which resources they could do without. Allow time to discuss their choices.

Identifying Resources

Resources are things and ideas that we use to achieve our goals.

Resources are things you can use to get something else. We need resources to help us achieve our goals.

- Some resources are things, such as money, cars, and computers.
- Some resources are thoughts, ideas, and abilities, such as talent, friendship, and knowledge.

Some resources are available to everyone, such as air and water. Other resources may be available only to some people, such as artistic ability or talent.

When you can recognize the resources that are available to you, you can use them to help you make decisions, solve problems, and achieve your goals in life.

Lots of resources can be used by more than one person at a time. A family shares a home. In school, a whole class shares one teacher. A whole community shares the public library. The whole United States—and even people from other countries—share the national parks.

Available Resources

The types of resources you have available depend on your current role and your stage of life. For example, you might not have money if you're too young to have a job. You might have more physical strength and energy than your grandparents.

You can develop your resources in order to make sure you have them available when you need them.

- You can eat well and exercise to develop your health.
- You can work and save money to develop financial security.
- You can practice to develop a skill or talent.

Types of Resources

You can categorize resources into seven main groups:

- **Human resources** are the resources people provide that things cannot. Human resources include knowledge, talent, physical and mental abilities, time, energy, and even personal character. You are the source of your own human resources, and so are all the other people in your life.
- **Non-human resources** include things, such as money and material possessions.
- **Technological resources** have a great impact on your life. They include everything from computers to automated teller machines to medical equipment.
- **Community resources** are services that the government provides, such as public parks, public schools, libraries, and police and fire departments. Some businesses contribute to community resources as well. For example, a company might sponsor a softball team.
- **Natural resources** are things that exist in nature and are available for everyone. Natural resources include air, water, wildlife, minerals, and plants.
- **Renewable resources** are natural resources that can be recreated in unlimited quantities, such as air and sunlight.
- **Nonrenewable resources** are natural resources that are available in limited quantities and may one day be used up. Coal is a nonrenewable resource.

Managing Resources

It's also hard not to worry if you don't have as many resources as someone else, or if you have different resources. You can make the most out of the resources you have by managing them. That means making sure you use your resources at the right time and for the right purpose.

For example, a day has only 24 hours, which makes time a valuable resource. You can spend your time in many ways—with your family, with your friends, studying, reading, participating in sports, volunteering, cleaning your room, cooking a meal, shopping, and so on. How will you manage your resource of time?

To make that decision, you consider your values, standards, and ethics, and figure out what's most important to you. Is it more important to spend time sleeping—which contributes to your physical well-being—or to spend time with your dad—which contributes to your emotional well-being?

Managing your resources shows that you are responsible and can make good decisions. You learn more about making decisions in Chapter 2.

MONEY MADNE$$

Money is a resource we use to acquire things we need or want. We work to earn money so we can spend it on needs such as food, shelter, and transportation as well as on wants such as video games, cell phones, and MP3 players.

For most people, money is a limited resource—we do not have an unending supply. That means we have to make decisions about how we use money. If we spend it all on wants, we won't be able to pay for our needs.

Your parents agreed to upgrade your cell service to include unlimited calls and texting if you pay the difference between the current plan and the new plan. The current plan costs $65.75 per month. The new plan costs $84.25. How much will you have to pay? If you earn $8.00 an hour, how many hours will you have to work to earn enough money?

Making the Most of What You Have

Not everyone has access to the same resources. What if you want to play guitar in a band but cannot afford lessons?

★ *You could get a job and earn the money you need.*

★ *You could offer to do chores for the guitar teacher in exchange for lessons.*

★ *You could borrow a guitar lesson book from the library and teach yourself.*

Sometimes you might have to be creative in order to manage your resources to achieve your goals. Can you think of creative ways you could manage your resources?

Myth Money is the most important resource.

Truth Money is important if you want to buy something. Other resources are important for achieving different goals. If you want to run a race, you need your health more than you need money. If you want to make a new friend, you need a sense of humor more than you need money.

Customized Instruction: Less Advanced/At-Risk Students

Ask students to list on paper the resources they could use to complete a homework assignment. Be prepared to offer suggestions, such as the paper and pencil, textbook, library, computer, and teacher.

Vocabulary

Community resources: Services that government provides, such as public parks, public schools, libraries, and police and fire departments.

Natural resources: Things that exist in nature and are available for everyone, including air, water, wildlife, minerals, and plants.

Non-human resources: Things such as money and material possessions.

Nonrenewable resources: Natural resources that are available in limited quantities and may one day be used up.

Renewable resources: Natural resources that can be recreated in unlimited quantities, such as air and sunlight.

Technological resources: Things such as computers, software, and medical equipment that automate tasks and allow us to execute functions quickly and accurately.

Making the Most of What You Have

Students are asked to think of ways to manage their resources in order to achieve their goals. You might provide the following example: Kate wants to go to the mall with her friends on Saturday afternoon, but she does not have any money and she needs to work on a school project that is due on Monday over the weekend. She decides to take a babysitting job on Friday night to earn some money. After she puts the kids to bed, she will work on her school project instead of watching TV or talking on the phone with friends.

Myth/Truth

Ask students if they think there is any single resource that can be considered the most important. Their answers should be "no." Every individual needs to have a variety of resources available to survive and to succeed.

MONEY MADNE$$

To solve the problem, students must first find the difference between the cost of the current plan and the cost of the new plan. They should subtract $65.75 from $84.25. Remind them to line up the decimals. The answer is $18.50 per month. If their job pays $8 an hour, they will have to work 2.3 hours more per month to cover the cost of the upgrade. Ask them to figure out the cost of the upgrade for an entire year. The answer is $222. Ask students if they would use their money resources for this upgrade.

End-of-Chapter Activities

Case Study

Mary's behavior was influenced by her desire to be with her friends, and possibly see the boy she likes.

Mary's actions interfered with Sarah's well-being because Sarah was late to the senior center, and some of the residents were angry. It also affected the well-being of the seniors, and even Sarah's sister, who drove Sarah.

Mary showed that she values being social and meeting boys more than she values her time volunteering at the senior center. Her actions also show she does not value her relationship with Sarah very much, because she lied and then never showed up. Sarah showed that she values her commitments and volunteer work more than she values being social at a party. These values may change in time.

Sounding Off!

1. Help students develop a list of the things that are similar among them and the things that differ from student to student. Similarities might include education, language, and political beliefs. Differences would include appearance, interests, and ethnicity.

2. Help the class develop a list of class resources. These would include books and teaching aids, such as overhead transparencies and videos; desks and chairs; supplies such as paper and pencils; and you, the instructor.

Case Study

Every Friday at 5:30, Mary and her mom pick up Sarah to go volunteer at the senior center. The senior citizens look forward to their visit.

One week, both girls are invited to the same party on a Friday night. Mary really wants to go to the party because she thinks the boy she likes will be there. Sarah would rather go to the senior center. Mary tells Sarah she will skip the party and will pick her up as she usually does.

On Friday, Sarah is ready at the usual time and waits at the door for Mary and her mom. After 20 minutes, she asks her sister to drive her to the senior center. The seniors are annoyed that she is late. Some have left the common area and gone back to their own rooms. Mary never shows up. She is at the party.

■ What influenced Mary's behavior?
■ Did Mary's actions interfere with Sarah's well-being?
■ What conflicting values did the girls show?

Sounding Off!

❶ Are you similar to your classmates or different? Discuss the things that make you the same and the things that make you different.

❷ Do you share resources with your classmates? Do you think everyone respects the shared resources and manages them cooperatively for the good of the whole class? Discuss ways you could more effectively manage your class resources.

1. What are the five main areas of your life that define your roles and responsibilities?
2. What are the four areas of well-being?
3. What is the difference between a need and a want?
4. List four physical needs and four psychological needs.
5. What are the six major influence factors?
6. What is the difference between monetary value and sentimental value?
7. How can you develop values?
8. What are flexible standards?
9. What are ethics?
10. List six types of resources.

FAQ

1. The fine main areas are at home, with your peers, in school, at work, and in your community.

2. Emotional well-being depends on your ability to deal with problems and stress. Physical well-being depends on your health. Social well-being depends on how you get along with other people. Personal well-being depends on how satisfied and confident you are with yourself.

3. A need is a fundamental requirement. A want is something you desire.

4. Physical needs are food, water, shelter, and clothing. Psychological needs are safety, security, love, acceptance, and respect.

5. Factors are family, friends, culture, community, current events, and media.

6. Some things have monetary value, which means they cost money. Other things have sentimental value, which means they are important for emotional or personal reasons.

7. You develop values by figuring out what is important to you. The influences in your life help you develop values.

8. Flexible standards are standards that you can adapt to different situations.

9. Ethics are a set of beliefs about what is right and what is wrong.

10. ■ Human resources are the resources people provide that things cannot.

   ■ Non-human resources include things, such as money and material possessions.

   ■ Technological resources include everything from computers to automated teller machines to medical equipment.

   ■ Community resources are services that the government provides. Some businesses contribute to community resources as well.

   ■ Natural resources are things that exist in nature and are available for everyone.

   ■ Renewable resources are natural resources that can be recreated in unlimited quantities, such as air and sunlight.

   ■ Nonrenewable resources are natural resources that are available in limited quantities and may one day be used up.

The purpose of advertising is to influence people to buy a certain product, use a certain service, or even think a certain way. In a small group, select an advertisement from a magazine, the Internet, or television and look at it closely to figure out how it influences people. Answer the following questions:

■ What is being advertised?
■ Who is doing the advertising?
■ What methods does the ad use to exert influence?
■ Is the ad effective?

Then, pick a product, service, or idea and create your own advertisement. It might be a poster, video, presentation, or even a song. Work together as a team to complete the project, using cooperation, compromise, and teamwork to achieve your goal.

Hot Topics

Do conflicting values pose a problem for you? They may be internal—pitting your own values against each other—or they may be external—pitting your values against someone else's.

Take this opportunity to write about how conflicting values affect you. You can vent about the problems they cause and how they interfere with your well-being. Use a word processor and do not sign your name. It will be anonymous, so you can be honest and open. Print the document and put it in your class Hot Topics box.

As a class, read the anonymous entries and discuss them.

| Web Extra ▼ |

Use the Internet to locate information about community resources in your area. Are there state parks? National parks? How about libraries or museums? As a class, collect the information into a booklet or Web page, and make it available in your school library or Web site.

Problem Solver

We take human rights for granted in the United States. In fact, they are written into our Constitution. But not every country of the world agrees. Some countries treat women as second-class citizens. Some countries force children to work instead of going to school.

Do you think it matters whether other countries do not have the same standards of human rights as we do? Do you think there is anything American students can do to promote human rights around the world? Working with a partner or in small groups, research a human rights issue. Make a plan of how you would raise awareness of the issue, and then present it to your class.

Team Players

Divide students appropriately into teams. They are asked to critique an advertisement and then to create their own advertisement for a product, service, or idea of their choice. Be sure that each member of the team has an opportunity to voice his or her opinion and to contribute to the project.

Hot Topics

Before the first class, create a "Hot Topics" box. This can be any shape or size; you can even cover a cereal box with plain paper and use that. Make sure students understand that they can turn in their papers anonymously. Encourage them to be open and honest about their conflicting values and how such conflicts interfere with their well-being. In the discussion about the entries, encourage students to offer suggestions on how the conflict could be resolved.

Web Extra

Students are to identify resources in their community and surrounding area and compile a booklet or Web page that describes them. Remind them that community resources are services that the government provides, such as public parks, public schools, libraries, and police and fire departments. Businesses and other nongovernment organizations provide community resources as well, such as a garden and landscape business that might donate services or products to beautify a community's green spaces.

Problem Solver

Students are to work with a partner or in small groups to research a human rights issue and develop a plan on how to raise awareness of it. Discuss the concept of "grass roots," which can be defined as a group of local people working together to solve problems within their community. Their work may gain momentum and notoriety, allowing them to expand to other communities. Eventually, their effort is being duplicated in other states and thereafter, other countries. The concept can be applied to raising worldwide awareness of human rights issues.

Write Now

Students are asked to write an essay on a role they fill that they believe is most important. Remind them that a role is the way they behave in a specific situation. Make sure they address the responsibilities their chosen role carries with it.

Be Involved!

Students create a poster or collage about themselves that includes five things they value, five things they need, and five things they want. Remind students that a need is something they cannot live without; a want is something they desire; and something of value is important to them. Also, introduce students to the Family, Career and Community Leaders of America (FCCLA), a national nonprofit organization for young men and women in Family and Consumer Sciences education in public and private school through grade 12. This organization and others are discussed in *Appendix B Joining a Career Technical Student Organization* starting on page 525 of the student text.

The Power of One program is divided into the following five units:

- A Better You—Improve personal traits
- Family Ties—Get along better with family members
- Working on Working—Explore work options, prepare for a career, or sharpen skills useful in business
- Take the Lead—Develop leadership qualities
- Speak Out for FCCLA—Tell others about positive experiences in FCCLA

Students are to include a goal from each of the areas above on their poster or collage.

Social Networking

Students are asked to research the topic of animal testing and using animals for research, and to create a chart that lists the reasons why it might be considered ethically right on the one hand and ethically wrong on the other. How does the majority of the class feel on the topic? How might an individual's values affect his or her opinion on the topic?

Write Now

Think about your roles and responsibilities. What roles do you play in your family, with your peers, at school, at work, and in your community? Is one role more important to you?

Write a personal essay describing the role you think is most important and why. Be sure to contrast it to some of your other roles that you think are less important.

Be Involved!

www.fcclainc.org

Collect pictures and text that you can use to make a poster or collage about yourself. The collage should include your name, at least five things that you value, five things that you need, and five things that you want. You should also include goals in each of the FCCLA Power of One areas: A Better You, Family Ties, Working on Working, Take the Lead, and Speak out for FCCLA.

You can cut the content from magazines or newspapers, print Web pages (with permission), bring in photos, or create the content yourself—such as drawings or poems.

When your collage is complete, explain it in a written essay or an oral presentation. Be sure to point out each required element.

Social Networking

Using animals for research is an ethically complex issue. Some people think it is necessary for the good of humans, while others think it is a cruel and inhumane. Some people think it is right when the research is for medical purposes, such as to find a cure for cancer, but they think it is wrong when the research is used for testing cosmetics and other consumer products. Use the Internet to research the topic. After learning about testing on animals, make a chart that lists reasons animal testing might be ethically right on one side, and reasons it might be ethically wrong on the other. Discuss the topic as a class.

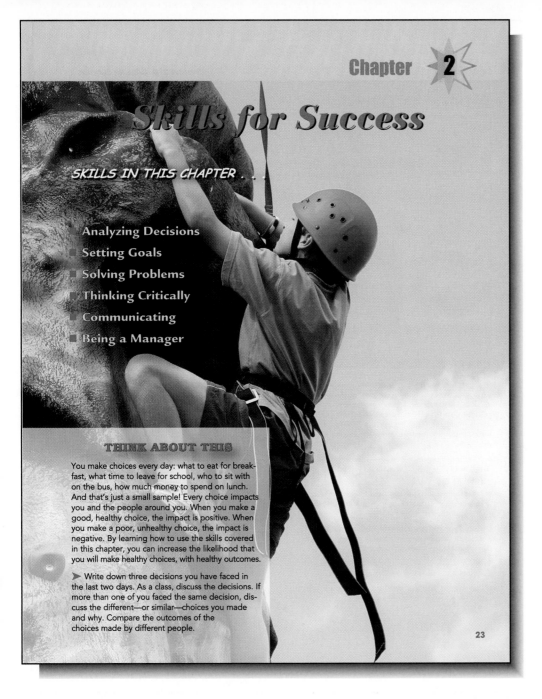

Chapter 2

Skills for Success

SKILLS IN THIS CHAPTER . . .

- Analyzing Decisions
- Setting Goals
- Solving Problems
- Thinking Critically
- Communicating
- Being a Manager

THINK ABOUT THIS

You make choices every day: what to eat for breakfast, what time to leave for school, who to sit with on the bus, how much money to spend on lunch. And that's just a small sample! Every choice impacts you and the people around you. When you make a good, healthy choice, the impact is positive. When you make a poor, unhealthy choice, the impact is negative. By learning how to use the skills covered in this chapter, you can increase the likelihood that you will make healthy choices, with healthy outcomes.

➤ Write down three decisions you have faced in the last two days. As a class, discuss the decisions. If more than one of you faced the same decision, discuss the different—or similar—choices you made and why. Compare the outcomes of the choices made by different people.

23

Chapter 2 Overview

In this chapter, students explore the complexities of decision-making, goal-setting, problem-solving, and communicating. They also learn tips for how to use these critical-thinking skills to further develop their roles and fulfill their responsibilities.

Analyzing Decisions Understanding why you make the decisions you do will help you better control the consequences and outcomes of those decisions.

Setting Goals Students discover that setting goals helps them focus their energy on what they feel is important to obtain. It also affects the decisions they make.

Solving Problems With strong problem-solving skills, you are able to recognize when a problem exists and then take proper action to solve it.

Thinking Critically Being able to make honest, rational, and open-minded judgments plays an important role in strengthening decision-making skills.

Communicating Students learn the value of being able to effectively communicate their thoughts, ideas, and opinions in both verbal and nonverbal forms.

Being a Manager By sharpening their decision-making, problem-solving, critical-thinking, and communication skills, students will be better prepared to successfully manage their day-to-day activities.

Focus and Engage

Bell-Ringer: Think About This

Students are asked to write down three decisions they have faced in the last two days. Encourage students to list decisions that forced them to earnestly consider the consequences of the decision. For example, deciding whether to have a bagel or toast for breakfast will not lead to a constructive class discussion about decision-making. On the other hand, deciding whether you should make breakfast for your younger brother or ignore him and go about your business might stimulate a more productive discussion. If a student decides to share a particularly poor decision he or she made, make sure all the circumstances surrounding the decision are understood. It is very important that students are not angered, embarrassed, or humiliated over what they share with the class.

ADVANCE PREPARATION

Review	*Life Skills for the 21st Century* textbook, Chapter 2.
Prepare	Students will need paper and pencil for some activities. Colored pencils or markers for drawing. Colored beads or blocks. Money—$5, $10, or $20 bill. Box labeled "Hot Topics."

CUSTOMIZED INSTRUCTION OVERVIEW

Less Advanced Students	More Advanced Students	ESOL Students	Special Needs Students	At-Risk Students
Pages 24, 32, 38, 39	Pages 28, 39	Pages 35, 36	Pages 24, 27, 34	Pages 26, 30, 37, 39

Introduce the Section

This section discusses how the decisions we make, whether big or small, give us power and control over our lives.

Figure Focus

The girl in the photo is trying to make a decision about which shirt to buy. Ask students what considerations will probably factor into the girl's decision. Some possible answers include the cost, color, brand name, or the type of fabric. What about peer pressure? Ask students if they think her decision might be affected by what her friends or peers would think of the shirt.

Vocabulary

Consequences: Results of a decision.
Decision: Act of choosing one option over another.

Discuss

Some experts say that the average adult living in the United States makes about 35,000 decisions a day! Discuss with students the many decisions they make during every waking hour of the day—what to eat, what to wear, what to say, who to ask, which way to go, and so on. Decisions can be simple, such as picking up your clothes or leaving them on the floor. Or, they can be life-changing, such as buckling up a seatbelt that prevents you from being injured in a car accident.

Teaching Tips

The text states that decisions give us power and control over our lives. Make sure students understand that it is still all right for them to rely on others—their parents, an older relative, a mentor, or a teacher—to make decisions for them or to be heavily involved in their decision-making process.

Customized Instruction: Less Advanced/Special Needs Students

Hold up a $5, $10, or $20 bill. Ask students to write down what they would do with the money if you gave it to them. Write their responses on the board. Have them discuss why they made the choice they did.

Analyzing Decisions

Knowing how and why you make decisions gives you control over your life.

Any time you make up your mind about something, or choose one option over another, you are making a **decision**. Some decisions are simple—what time will I leave for school? Some are more difficult—should I tell my friend I don't like her hair style? The results—or **consequences**—of your decisions affect you in big and small ways.

- If the consequences of a decision are positive and contribute to your well-being, it means you made a healthy—or good—choice.
- If the consequences are negative and interfere with your well-being, well, that means you made an unhealthy—or poor—choice.

Decisions give you power and control over your life. When you make a decision, you are showing yourself and others that you are independent and responsible.

- When you are young, your mother might decide what clothes you wear.
- As you grow older, you can select your own wardrobe and use it to express your unique style.

Every Decision Is Unique

Clearly, not everyone will make the same decision in the same situation. That's because we each use our own character qualities, values, and available resources when we make a choice.

You and a friend might both decide to join your community's recycling action committee, but you might have different reasons for doing so. You might be disgusted by the trash you see along the road, but your friend might want to meet new people. A third friend might choose not to join the committee at all.

Stay in School

Students decide to drop out of school for many reasons. Some are bored and believe that what they learn in school is irrelevant to their well-being. Others are unmotivated and just don't feel like going to school. Some have struggled with their studies all along and have no confidence they will ever graduate. Many, unfortunately, are ostracized and drop out because they feel like outcasts.

Whatever the reason, emphasize that students who drop out of school are making a life-changing decision that will have negative consequences. Explain to students that high school dropouts earn about 35 percent less than those with a high school degree, and can expect to make $250,000 to $300,000 less over the course of their lifetime. And that's if they are lucky enough to even be in the labor force. Dropouts tend to be in worse health than those who have graduated. Furthermore, dropouts make up a disproportionately higher percentage of prison inmates.

Six Steps to a Decision

You can take some of the uncertainty and doubt out of decision-making by turning it into a process. A process is a series of steps that leads to a conclusion.

1. *Identify the decision to be made.* Make sure you recognize and understand the choice. Define the decision as a goal—what do I want to achieve with this choice?
2. *Consider all possible options.* You usually have lots of options for each decision. Try to think of as many as you can, and write them down. Don't just consider the obvious choice; some of the best options might seem pretty bizarre at first. Consider your available resources, and what you are trying to achieve.
3. *Identify the consequences of each option.* Each option will have consequences—some positive and some negative; some long-term and some short-term. Recognizing all the consequences will help you predict the outcome of your decision.
4. *Select the best option.* Once you consider the options and identify the consequences, you have the information you need to make your decision.
5. *Make and implement a plan of action.* Making the decision is not the end of the process. You must take steps to make it happen. Until you do, the decision is just an idea or thought in your head.
6. *Evaluate the decision, process, and outcome.* After you have acted on your decision, you can look back and evaluate it, based on your values and standards. Did you achieve the goal you defined in step 1? Did you miss any possible options? Did you correctly identify the consequences? Did you make use of your resources? Was the outcome what you hoped for?

Overwhelmed by Options

Decision-making can be stressful. Even simple choices can seem overwhelming at times. For example, should you wear jeans or khakis to the party Saturday night?

Once you make a decision, you might second-guess yourself, which means doubting your own choice. You wore the jeans, but the whole ride to the party you wonder whether the khakis would have looked better.

- If you are indecisive—unable to make a decision—you might think about what will happen if you choose one option over another, and never make a decision at all.
- If you are **impulsive**—inclined to act without thinking—you might make a snap decision without considering the consequences.

Myth All healthy choices lead to positive consequences.

Truth Sometimes even the best decisions lead to negative consequences. Life is unpredictable. When that happens, we have to try to learn from the experience, and make the best possible choices going forward.

Some people take a long time to make a decision, some make snap decisions, and others are thoughtful and deliberate. What type of decision-maker are you?

Influences

Things that influence your decisions:

✔ *Values*
✔ *Goals*
✔ *Standards*
✔ *Ethics*
✔ *Roles*
✔ *Stage in life*
✔ *Other people*
✔ *Resources*
✔ *Experience*
✔ *Knowledge*

Influences

Review the terms on the list that were defined in Chapter 1:

- **Values:** Things that are important to you.
- **Goals:** Things you want to achieve.
- **Standards:** Guidelines for whether or not something meets expectations.
- **Ethics:** Set of beliefs about what is right and what is wrong.
- **Roles:** The ways in which you behave in a specific situation.
- **Stage in life:** How old you are.
- **Resources:** Things you use to get something else; a source of help or information.

Come up with a topic on which a decision needs to be made and lead students through the six steps explained in the text.

1. **Identify the decision.** For example, a group of students has held a number of fundraisers during the course of the year and has a sizable amount of money to spend on something school-related. They need to decide on what to spend the money.
2. **Consider options.** One option is to create a land lab on school grounds that will give students the opportunity to study habitats and nature and to gain an appreciation for the environment. Another option is to sponsor a school dance.
3. **Identify consequences.** Have students list the pros and cons of each option.
4. **Select the best option.** Have students vote on the best option. Make sure they understand that the option with the most votes will be considered the class's choice.
5. **Develop a plan of action.** Have students brainstorm the steps they will take to implement the decision made.
6. **Evaluate.** Ask students to predict if their goal will be met.

Myth/Truth

We've probably all heard someone say, "It seemed like a good idea at the time." We all make decisions that seemed right when we made them, but turned out to be wrong. For example, you take your dog to a dog park thinking it will be good exercise for him, but a larger dog gets too aggressive with him and scares him into not leaving your side.

Figure Focus

Students are asked to identify the type of decision-maker they are. Most people are probably a mix of both. We make snap decisions about certain things, like buying pizza for lunch instead of eating the packed lunch brought from home. We put more thought into decisions about other things, like what to spend your allowance on.

Reinforce and Review

Remind students that a consequence is simply the result of a choice made. When you are responsible enough to make a decision, you also must be responsible enough to deal with the consequences of your decision, whether they are positive or negative.

Teaching Tips

Make sure students distinguish between short-term and long-term. They should also understand that defining consequences as short-term or long-term is relative to the decision as a whole. Short term means lasting a relatively short period of time, while long term means affecting a time long into the future.

"Quote Box"

Students should understand that the President of the United States is faced with making decisions every day that affect millions of people. Ask students to consider decisions the president might make that affect only him. Does he decide what he eats for breakfast? Does he pick out his clothes? Does he decide how to have his hair cut?

Predicting Consequences

Students are asked to consider the consequences of buying a new red shirt. In addition to the ones listed in the text, some other possibilities are:

- You spent all your money on the shirt and therefore cannot afford to go out after school with your friends.

- Your friend is jealous that he/she cannot afford the same shirt so avoids talking to you all day.

Figure Focus

Ask students if anyone has ever advised them to "learn from their mistakes." Everyone can make a poor choice, but knowing how to avoid making the same poor choice a second time is an invaluable decision-making skill.

Myth/Truth

Point out that sometimes the decisions they make have a negative outcome that is not their fault. External factors can sometimes play a role in the consequences of a decision. Continuing with the dog example used for the *Myth/Truth* on the previous page, you decide to take your dog to the dog park because you think it will give him good exercise, but then another dog gets too aggressive and your dog won't leave your side. You have to deal with the consequences of someone else's poor decision. Ask students how they might turn a negative consequence into a positive. In this example, you could introduce yourself to the dog's owner, figure out a way to "reintroduce" your dogs, and perhaps make a new friend who has the common interest of dogs with you.

Predicting Consequences

Do you need a crystal ball to predict the long-term consequences of a decision? What about how your decisions affect others? What if you decide to wear your new red shirt to school today?

★ *Short-term consequence: You feel good all day.*

★ *Long-term consequence: You catch the eye of the new kid in Science class and start dating.*

★ *Consequence that affects others: Your friend likes the shirt and buys one after school.*

★ *Another consequence that affects others: The sales clerk who sells your friend the shirt earns a commission.*

Can you think of other consequences that might come from the simple decision to wear the red shirt?

"That might not have been my best decision. I wonder what I could do differently next time?"

Myth All poor choices lead to negative consequences.

Truth As luck would have it, sometimes things work out okay even when we make really stupid decisions. Just breathe a sigh of relief, recognize that we got away with something, and once again, make the best possible choices going forward.

More About Consequences

Consequences of our choices can be short-term or long-term. What you eat for breakfast might affect your energy level for a few hours. Whether you go to college can affect your whole life.

Most decisions actually have both long-term and short-term consequences. Long-term, what you eat for breakfast might affect your health and wellness. Short-term, it might affect how you do on a test.

Sometimes consequences have both positive and negative results. Take the breakfast decision: On the up side, a doughnut tastes good and gives you a sugar boost of energy. On the down side, a doughnut raises your cholesterol level, which might lead to a heart condition.

The good news is that you can learn how to make healthy decisions that turn out positive more often than they turn out negative.

If you make a decision that has negative consequences, what can you change next time in order to make a better choice?

> The only things that land on my desk are tough decisions. Because, if they were easy decisions, somebody down the food chain's already made them.
>
> — *Barack Obama, 44th U.S. President*

Did I Make the Best Choice?

How can your values, standards, and ethics help you make healthy choices?

We all make mistakes. Despite our best intentions, we make poor choices. Most of the time, it doesn't matter too much. If you cut your hair too short, it will grow. You can choose a different style next time, or even go to a different shop for the next haircut.

Sometimes, though, we must live with the consequences of our actions for a long time—maybe even our whole lives. It's part of the deal—if you are independent and responsible enough to make the decision, you're stuck with the results. For example, if you talk on the phone while driving and get into an accident, that's your responsibility.

But, even when we make a poor choice with long-term consequences, we can learn from our mistakes and try to make better choices going forward.

Customized Instruction: At-Risk Students

Present the following scenario to students: James flunked a math test because instead of studying, he watched his favorite television show. What can James learn from his mistake?

Can Your Decisions Be Hurtful?

How can you be sure your decisions won't interfere with the well-being of yourself and others? When you are evaluating your options while making a decision, consider these questions:

■ Is it hurtful to me?

■ Is it hurtful to someone else?

If the answer to the questions above is "Yes," you might want to look for other alternatives. If the answer to the following questions is "Yes," you are on the right track:

■ Is it fair?

■ Is it honest?

■ Is it legal?

■ Is it practical?

Can you think of other questions that might help you evaluate your options?

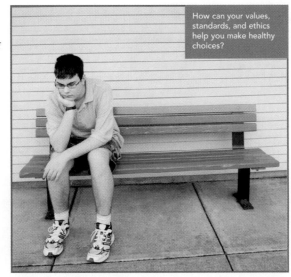

How can your values, standards, and ethics help you make healthy choices?

NUMBERS GAME

You can use **probability**—the chance that something will happen—to measure how likely it is that a particular outcome will occur. The **formula**—rule or method of doing something—for probability is the number of times the particular outcome occurs divided by the total number of possible outcomes. In fractional form, it looks like this:

$$\text{Probability} = \frac{\text{No. of particular outcomes}}{\text{Total no. of possible outcomes}}$$

As an example, consider a laundry basket full of socks. There are five blue socks, three white socks, one brown sock, and six black socks.

What is the probability that you pick a white sock your first time? Hint: Divide 3 (the number of white socks) by 15 (the total number of socks).

What is the probability that you pick a blue sock your first time? Hint: Divide 5 by 15.

Customized Instruction: Special Needs Students

Use colored beads or blocks to review probability with students. Put a collection of the beads or blocks in various colors in a bucket or box. Have students count the total number and then count the number of each individual color. Ask them the probability of picking one color over the others from the bucket or box.

Teaching Tips

Students do not always realize just how many people might be affected by the decisions they make. People are affected directly and indirectly by the decisions others make. For example, you decide to sit with a new group of kids at lunch instead of the friend you have sat with for the last few days. You know your friend is upset, but you decide not to do anything about it. She is directly affected by your decision. When the friend goes home after school, she is still upset and tells her mother how you hurt her feelings. Her mother feels bad for her and tries to comfort her. The friend's mother is indirectly affected by your decision.

Discuss

Discuss with students the meaning of "hurtful." If something causes emotional pain or suffering, it is hurtful.

Figure Focus

Students are asked how their values, standards, and ethics help them make healthy choices. Remind students that **values** are things that are important to them. **Standards** are guidelines for whether or not something meets expectations. **Ethics** are a set of beliefs about what is right and what is wrong.

Vocabulary

Formula: Rule or method for doing something.
Probability: The chance that something will happen.

NUMBERS GAME

Probability falls under the statistics branch of math. It is expressed as the ratio of the number of favorable outcomes in the set of outcomes divided by the total number of possible outcomes. It is often expressed as a percentage. For the white sock problem, 3 divided by 15 equals .2, or a 20% chance you will pick a white sock. For the blue sock problem, 5 divided by 15 equals .33, or a 33% chance you will pick a blue sock. The higher the percentage, the better your chance to pick the desired color sock. Therefore, the probability of picking a blue sock is higher than that for a white sock.

Introduce the Section

This section reviews the concept of goal-setting and developing a plan for achieving goals.

Vocabulary

Goal: Something you are trying to achieve.

Discuss

Discuss the goals students set for themselves every day. Goals can be simple, such as getting up on time so you do not miss the bus. Or, they can be more challenging, such as acing a math test. You probably set some goals subconsciously, meaning you set them without even being aware that you have set them. For example, you get your homework done early, allowing you time to watch TV.

Figure Focus

Ask students why setting goals will help them focus on what they want to achieve. Setting goals gives us direction. By nature, most humans strive to achieve—financial stability, good health, personal security, loving relationships, and so on. The goals you set for yourself shape the decisions you make and the actions you take.

Goals for Roles

Students are asked to list goals they strive to achieve in different areas of their lives. Remind students that they fill roles in five main areas: at home, with peers, in school, at work, and in their community. Some examples of goals that cross over into many areas are being organized, showing more patience, paying someone a compliment, or improving physical health.

Setting Goals

Setting goals helps you focus on what you want to achieve.

If you read Chapter 1, you know that a **goal** is something you are trying to achieve. Goals help direct your actions and guide your decision-making because they give you something to work toward. They help give your life meaning, because you know that there is a purpose in what you do. When you achieve a goal, you can be proud and express satisfaction.

If all you do is think about a goal, it's just a dream. You make goals real by deciding what you want to achieve and then planning how to get there. While you should set goals that are within reach, there is nothing wrong with challenging yourself to push harder.

Goals are not written in stone. As you progress through different stages of your life, you will learn more about yourself, your values, and your standards. Your resources will change. You can change your goals at any time, and develop new goals. Most people do.

Goals for Roles

You can set goals for all your roles in life, both individually and as part of a group or team. Do you think the goals you set for different roles in your life might ever overlap? What if you want to conserve energy?

- At home: Enlist your family members to shut off lights and take shorter showers.
- At school: Convince the school administrators to install low wattage light bulbs.
- With friends: Walk or bike with friends instead of driving.
- In your community: Encourage neighbors to recycle.
- At work: Turn off computers at the end of the day.
- As a consumer: Shop at businesses that are committed to energy conservation.

Can you think of other goals that have a place in many areas of your life? Make a list and discuss it in class.

Customized Instruction: More Advanced Students

Have students write about a goal they have as an individual that could also apply to a group of which they are a part. For example, a student might set a goal of being the soccer team's high scorer, and the team's goal is to score as many points as possible.

Five Steps to a Goal

There's a process you can use to help identify, assess, and set goals:

1. *Identify the goal.* Write down the goal using as much detail as you can. This helps you understand and recognize the goal. Be positive, not negative: I will attend the FCCLA meeting rather than I won't skip the FCCLA meeting.
2. *Assess whether the goal is something you really want.* It might be a fad, or something that sounds good, or even something someone else wants for you.
3. *Make a plan for achieving the goal.* This step will help you identify whether or not the goal is reasonable and attainable. What resources will you need? If you cannot come up with a plan that works, you may need to go back to step 1.
4. *Write down your action plan for achieving the goal,* being as specific as possible.
5. *Every once in a while, reevaluate your goals.* Make sure they are still important to you and, if so, that you are on track to achieve them.

Short-Term Goals and Long-Term Goals

When you want to achieve something quickly, you set **short-term goals**. You can accomplish short-term goals in the near future—maybe even today. For example, finishing your homework on time is a short-term goal. It is usually easy to define short-term goals because they are specific and not very complicated. If you keep a to-do list, it is full of short-term goals—meet friends at the mall, call your grandmother, make your bed.

A **long-term goal** is something you want to achieve in the more distant future—maybe a year from now, or maybe even more distant than that. Graduating from college is a long-term goal. So is buying a car.

Defining long-term goals may be more difficult than defining short-term goals. You might know you want to get married some day, but you don't know when or to whom. You might know you want to travel, but you don't know where or how.

Sometimes it's harder to stay focused on a long-term goal—it seems far away. Breaking the long-term goal down into a series of short-term goals—or milestones—makes it easier to stay on track. Becoming a nurse might be a long-term goal. To achieve that goal, you can set short-term goals of:

- Working part-time in a hospital
- Graduating from high school
- Attending college

Test IT Yourself!

How much does peer pressure influence decisions?

1. Think of a question you could ask your classmate, such as whether she wants a test on Thursday or Friday.
2. Ask five people the question, without saying anything else: "Do you want the test on Thursday or Friday?"
3. Ask five other people the question, but add a comment that indicates their peers have already made a choice: "Do you want the test on Thursday or Friday? Most people have been picking Thursday."
4. Make a chart comparing the results, and discuss it as a class.

Make a Plan

Just because a goal is short-term doesn't mean you can achieve it without a plan. What if you have a short-term goal to meet friends at the mall?

★ *Where will you meet?*

★ *What time will you meet?*

★ *How will you get there?*

★ *What time should you leave?*

Considering all of the factors helps you make decisions and form a realistic plan. The more specific the plan, the easier it will be to achieve your goal. How can you make a plan for long-term goals?

"I might not win this time, but I think I'll beat my personal best."

Test IT Yourself!

Explain to students that peer pressure is the social pressure put on an individual to adopt a type of behavior, dress, or attitude in order to be accepted as part of a group. To conduct this activity during the class period, have one student volunteer to ask the questions. Then have several (up to 10, if possible) student volunteers wait outside the classroom. Have the one student volunteer ask a simple question of half of the other volunteers by calling them in one at a time. Then, ask the embellished question one-by-one to the other volunteers. Write the results on the board. Ask students what they think about peer pressure.

Apply the five-step process outlined in the text to a goal the class as a whole would like to achieve. For example:

1. **Goal:** No behavior-related disruptions for an entire class period.
2. **Assess:** Convince students that the goal is one they should all strive for.
3. **Make a plan:** Ask students for suggestions on what is needed to meet the goal.
4. **Action plan:** Write on the board the suggestions students made for achieving the goal.
5. **Evaluate:** At the end of the class period, determine if the goal was met.

Make a Plan

Students should consider how to make a plan for long-term goals. Tell them they must consider the resources necessary to meet a long-term goal. They should also consider coming up with milestones—or significant or important events—that mark the journey toward meeting the goal.

Vocabulary

Long-term goals: Goals you want to achieve in the more distant future.

Short-term goals: Goals you want to achieve quickly or in the near future.

Teaching Tips

Help students distinguish between short-term and long-term goals, and point out that short-term goals may be milestones for long-term goals. For example, your long-term goal is to live to be 100 years old. Your short-term goals include cutting down on candy and soda pop and riding your bike to places you need to go instead of having your parents drive you. Meeting your short-term goals will help you meet your long-term goal.

Figure Focus

Ask students to comment on the goal the swimmer has set for himself. Some students might think that "not winning" means you have not achieved a goal. Point out that improving your time is a short-term goal that could lead to achieving a win.

Introduce the Section

This section explores how to identify a problem, recognize who owns the problem, and formulate a solution to the problem.

Figure Focus

Ask students what they think the boy in the picture is having problems with. Too much homework? Once they identify possible problems, ask them how the problems might be solved.

Vocabulary

Problem: A difficulty you must resolve before you can make progress; any barrier or obstacle between you and a goal.

Owning the Problem

The text states that generally the person who is blocked from a goal is the one who owns the problem. But what if circumstances out of your control have created the problem for you? For example, your community sponsors soccer teams for all age levels. You have played on the same team with kids in your grade for several years. But this year, the community recreation director decides to move you and a couple of other players to another team that does not have enough players. You want to continue playing with your old team because you know the coach and most of the players are your friends.

Someone else's decision has forced you to own this problem. How might you resolve it? One way is to be proactive and help recruit additional players for the other team. If that team has more players, they will not need you and you could continue to play with your old team.

Solving Problems

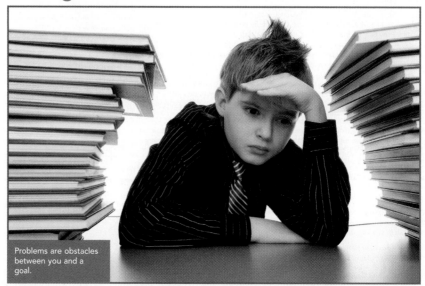

Problems are obstacles between you and a goal.

A problem—or challenge—is a difficulty that you must resolve before you can make progress. In other words, any barrier or obstacle between you and a goal is a problem.

Problems pop up all the time. Mostly, we come up with a solution without thinking too hard. Say you want to go to the movies Saturday night, but your mother says you can't go out until you clean your room. You have a problem: Your messy room is an obstacle between you and the movies. Solving the problem is easy: You clean your room.

Some problems sneak up on us over time, sometimes hidden by something else. You might want to do well in Social Studies, but you fall asleep in class every day. Is the problem that your teacher is boring, that your classroom is too warm, or is it that you are staying up late at night playing video games? Recognizing the real problem is the first step in solving it.

Owning the Problem

One difficulty with solving problems is figuring out whose problem it really is. Generally, the person who is blocked from a goal is the one who owns the problem.

■ If your friend loses his math book and wants to borrow yours, is it your problem or his? What if you loan him the book and he loses it?

■ If you forget your homework, and your mother does not have time to pick it up and drop it off at school, is it her problem or yours? Who should take responsibility for solving it?

If you own the problem, you are responsible for solving it. If someone else owns the problem, you may be able to help solve it, but ultimately it is not your responsibility.

Taking responsibility for your own problems, and working to find solutions, shows that you are independent and capable.

Customized Instruction: At-Risk Students

Ask students to identify any barriers or obstacles between them and success at school. Be prepared to discuss solutions or methods for overcoming the obstacles.

Six Steps to a Solution

When problems are harder to identify, or harder to solve, you can use the decision-making process to figure out the best solution:

1. *Identify the problem.* This is your chance to be honest, acknowledge the problem, and determine what goal it is blocking.

2. *Consider all possible solutions.* There may be one obvious solution, or there may be many possible solutions. Write down as many as you can think of. You will need to consider your values, standards, and resources, too. Some solutions might be harder to make happen, or take longer than others. Some might cost money and some might be free. Some might solve only part of the problem.

3. *Identify the consequences of each solution.* Like decisions, each solution will have consequences, and it is important to recognize how the consequences will affect you and others. Again, write them down.

4. *Select the best solution.* The best solution offers the best possible opportunity for you to continue your progress toward your goal.

5. *Make and implement a plan of action.* Recognizing and selecting a solution are only part of the process. You must take the necessary steps to make the solution real.

6. *Evaluate the solution, process, and outcome.* Did your solution work? Did you achieve your goal? Would you do anything differently if you had the same problem again?

What's Really the Problem?

Sometimes things can distract you from seeing the real problem. If you show up at your career counselor's office to ask her to fill out a reference form, and she is busy with another student, what is the problem?

👎 The counselor doesn't have time for you?

👎 The counselor doesn't like you?

👍 You forgot to make an appointment?

Since you can't go back in time to make an appointment, what steps can you take now to solve the problem?

MONEY MADNE$$

You have volunteered to buy the beverages for a class party. The teacher gave you a budget of $10.00. There are 23 students in the class.

At the market, you find a six-pack of soda in 12 oz. cans for $2.25, and a 2-liter bottle of the same soda for $1.15. The label on the bottle says it holds 67.62 ounces. You must decide what to buy. When making your decision, you should consider the cost and the amount of soda. But there may be other factors as well. Use the decision-making process and your math skills to decide what to buy.

Explain your decision.

MONEY MADNE$$

To make the decision, the student might calculate the per ounce cost of each option:

■ Cans: 6 cans × 12 ounces = 72 ounces.
  $2.25 ÷ 72 = $0.03 per ounce

■ Bottles: $1.15 ÷ 67.62 = $0.02 per ounce

They may also consider how many cans or bottles they will need for the whole class. If they want to provide one can per student, they must purchase four six-packs, which will cost $9.00. If they purchase four bottles, it will cost $4.60. Some of the other things to consider include the cost of cups and ice, and the convenience of transporting bottles vs. cans.

Discuss

Explain to students that the six steps to a solution are very similar to the steps they learned for making a decision on page 25 of the text. An example was supplied in the annotations on that page. You can modify the example to apply here:

1. **Identify the problem.** A group of students has held a number of fundraisers during the course of the year and has a sizable amount of money to spend on something school-related. Half the group wants to spend the money on a land lab that will give students the opportunity to study habitats and nature and to gain an appreciation for the environment. The other half wants to sponsor a school dance.

2. **Consider possible solutions.** Some solutions include:
   ■ Putting the two options up for the entire student body to vote on.
   ■ Exploring ways to divide the money so that both options are possible.
   ■ Asking teachers to decide.

3. **Identify consequences.** Have students list the consequences of each possible solution.

4. **Select the best solution.** Have students determine the best solution.

5. **Develop a plan of action.** Have students brainstorm the steps they will take to implement the solution.

6. **Evaluate.** Ask students to predict if their solution will work.

What's Really the Problem?

Students are asked what steps they can take to solve the problem with the counselor. Explain to students how important their critical-thinking skills are in helping them identify the real problem. If they use a rational, honest, and open-minded approach to assessing a problem, they will be more successful in understanding it and, therefore, better prepared to solve it.

Introduce the Section

In this section, students are introduced to the complex set of skills that help them to think critically. These skills include rationality, honesty, open-mindedness, and discipline.

Figure Focus

The term "thinking critically" implies deep, extremely important thoughts, which the boy in the photo appears to be contemplating. That can intimidate many students, but reassure them that thinking critically is something many of them may have already learned to do. If they have done something or made a decision using research, knowledge of historical context, and balanced judgment, then they have exhibited critical thinking skills.

Vocabulary

Critical thinking: Applying honesty, rationality, and open-mindedness when making decisions, setting goals, and solving problems.

Objective: Free of bias or prejudice; based on fact rather than opinions or emotions.

Subjective: Affected by existing opinions, feelings, and beliefs.

CRITICAL THINKING IN ACTION

Make sure students can distinguish between thinking objectively vs. thinking subjectively. Being objective means you are not influenced by outside factors, such as opinions or emotions. Being subjective means you are influenced by opinions, feelings, and emotions.

Thinking Critically

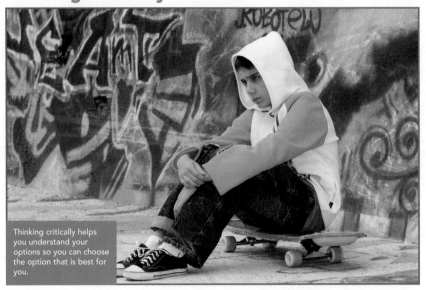

Thinking critically helps you understand your options so you can choose the option that is best for you.

Critical thinking can help you evaluate your options in many situations. You can use it when you are making decisions, setting goals, and solving problems. When you think critically, you are honest, rational, and open-minded about your options. You try not to let emotions get in the way of choosing the best course of action.

- Being honest means acknowledging selfish feeling and preexisting opinions.
- Being rational means relying on reason and thought instead of on emotion or impulse.
- Being open-minded means being willing to evaluate all possible options—even those that are unpopular.

Thinking critically doesn't mean you should ignore emotions, or any of the other influence factors. It just means you should consider all possibilities before rushing to judgment.

Critical Thinking in Action

You can think critically about a lot of things, not just decisions and problems. You don't have to believe everything you hear or read. You can question a news report, look deeper into the meaning of a magazine article, or investigate the truth behind a rumor.

When you think critically, you consider all possible options and other points of view. You look objectively at information. **Objective** means fairly, without emotion or prejudice. Then, you use your values, standards, and ethics to interpret the information subjectively. **Subjective** means affected by existing opinions, feelings, and beliefs.

Looking at things both objectively and subjectively can help you make choices that are right for you. For example, you can look at a candidate for class president objectively and see that she is smart, hard-working, and honest. Subjectively, you can disagree with everything she stands for, and vote for someone else.

Customized Instruction: Less Advanced Students

Read the labeling and other information found on a food or other packaged product. Ask students to decide what information is objective and what is subjective.

Are Emotions Always a Problem?

Emotions can affect critical thinking. That's not necessarily bad, but it's not necessarily good, either. Skipping class because you are angry about a low grade might seem like a good choice at the time, but the consequence might be more low grades.

If you think critically, you acknowledge that you are angry and are honest about why. Then, you can let the anger go and assess your options with a clear head. Maybe it would be better to go to class and ask the teacher what you can do to improve. The consequences might be better grades, an improved relationship with the teacher, and—best of all—no more anger.

Hearing a bit of gossip might be fun. It might be exciting, and you might get pleasure from hearing about someone's actions. It might make you feel superior. But, if you stop and think critically, you might realize that the news could not be true, or if it is true, it might be a difficult situation for that person. You can ask questions and learn more about the situation. Once you know all the facts, you can decide how you really feel about the situation and how you want to react.

Emotions can keep you from thinking with a clear head. Why is it important to have a clear head when you make decisions or solve problems?

Myth You can't trust your gut and think critically at the same time.

Truth Trusting your gut is not the same as being impulsive. Sometimes your gut—or that little voice inside your head—is really your values, standards, and ethics pointing you in the right direction. If you use the decision-making process and your gut is pointing out the best choice, go with it.

21st Century Skills

What Happens Next?

Katie is one of five students picked to participate in a student exchange weekend. It means traveling to a different state, staying with a host family, and participating in community activities. Katie thinks it will be a great experience, and she wants to go.

Her parents say they will sign the permission slip, but they cannot afford to give her the $75 she needs to pay for the bus. Katie has been saving her money to pay for a dress for the spring dance. She has $150 dollars in her savings account. She could afford the $75 for the bus, but then she would have only $75 left in her account.

Katie tells her best friend Shawna that she is thinking of using her dress money for the exchange weekend. Shawna thinks Katie is crazy and tells her so. She advises Katie to skip the exchange weekend. She assures Katie that a new dress is much more important.

Katie thinks about Shawna's advice. She really wants a new dress. She also really wants to go on the exchange weekend. She asks her parents again, but they say they cannot afford it right now.

Katie hands in the permission slip without the money. Her teacher says she has until the end of the week to pay, but then he will give her spot to someone else.

What problems and choices are facing Katie? What life skills can she use to find solutions and make decisions? Using your 21st Century Skills—such as decision making, goal setting, and problem solving—write an ending to the story. Read it to the class, or form a small group and present it as a skit.

Teaching Tips

Make sure students understand that while thinking critically requires an honest, rational, and open-minded approach to decision-making and problem-solving, it can tap their emotions and feelings as well. It is important to keep your feelings and emotions in check, allowing yourself the time to process what you know about the decision or the problem and to develop the best strategy for addressing it.

Figure Focus

The photo is intended to illustrate how emotions can cloud your ability to make reasonable decisions. Students are asked why it is important to keep this from happening. Some responses include:

- ■ Emotions might make you jump to the wrong conclusion.

- ■ Emotions that are negative can lead to denial and, therefore, prevent you from taking action to make a decision or solve a problem.

- ■ Emotions can sometimes make you act impulsively, meaning you act without thinking things through.

Myth/Truth

Students have probably often heard others talk about "trusting their instincts." Instincts and gut feelings play an important role in critical thinking. Your instincts represent natural, inborn behavioral characteristics, and your "gut" sometimes signals you to follow these instincts. For example, you see a neighbor's dog ready to cross the street just as a car pulls around the corner. Your instincts tell you to shout at the dog or at the car so as to avoid an accident.

21st Century Skills

What Happens Next?

Will Katie use her money to pay for the student exchange weekend or to buy a dress for the spring dance? Students are asked to write an ending to the story or prepare a skit that demonstrates the ending. Encourage students to consider all possible options for solving Katie's dilemma. Maybe she can afford to do both. She could narrow her search for a new dress to discount stores or those holding sales. Or, maybe she could find a way to add to her savings by babysitting or doing chores for family or neighbors.

Introduce the Section

In this section, students are introduced to communication skills. Students learn the value of being able to effectively communicate their thoughts, ideas, and opinions in both verbal and nonverbal forms.

Figure Focus

The photo illustrates a young man communicating with a handheld electronic device. Ask students to comment on this form of communication. How is it effective for sharing thoughts and ideas?

Vocabulary

Effective communication: When the receiver interprets the message the way the sender intended.

Ineffective communication: When the receiver misinterprets the message.

Discuss

Explain that communication is the exchange of information between individuals by means of speaking, writing, or using a system of signs or behavior. Ask students to discuss the methods other than writing and speaking that they use for communicating. Some examples are facial expressions, hand gestures, and other body language.

Communicating

Communicating lets you connect with other people to share thoughts and ideas.

Open and honest communication with other people helps you make healthy choices. Communication prevents misunderstandings. It gives you a way to share ideas. It even makes it easier for you to appreciate and respect other people's opinions.

At its most basic, communication is an exchange between a sender and a receiver. The sender transmits the message with a specific intent. The receiver interprets the message and responds.

Effective vs. Ineffective Communication

Effective communication is when the receiver interprets the message the way the sender intended. **Ineffective communication** is when the receiver misinterprets the message. Sometimes the sender thinks the message is clear, but in fact it might confuse or mislead the receiver.

In order to ensure effective communication:

- The message must be clear
- The sender must be able to deliver the message in a concise and accurate manner
- The receiver must be able to hear and receive the message
- The receiver must be able to interpret the message correctly

Customized Instruction: Hearing-Impaired or Visually-Impaired Students

Hearing-impaired and visually-impaired students may be comfortable sharing ways in which they communicate with others. Many hearing-impaired students read lips and use sign language. Visually-impaired students use Braille, large print, and other low vision aids. Computer-generated speech devices are helpful for hearing what others are seeing.

Using the Communication Process

You can communicate effectively by using a six-step process:

1. *Be clear.* The receiver is more likely to get your message if you deliver it in a way he can understand. Speak slowly. Consider who he is. You probably use different language when you talk to a teacher than when you talk to a friend. You might even use a completely different type of communication—face to face instead of a social networking site.

What message are you transmitting when you roll eyes and look away when someone talks to you?

2. *Be personal.* Use the other person's name—then he'll know you are communicating with him. Use an "I" statement—a statement that starts with the word "I"—to frame the statement in terms of you and your goals. An "I" statement indicates that you are taking responsibility for your thoughts and feelings. It helps the receiver understand your point of view and respond to you, instead of focusing on himself and how your statement affects him.
3. *Be positive.* Phrase your message in positive terms. Say what you want, not what you don't want.
4. *Get to the point.* Follow the "I" statement with an explanation of the message you are sending. Explain how or why you feel a certain way, or how or why you think a certain thing.
5. *Actively listen to the response.* Pay attention and make sure you hear the response.
6. *Think before you respond.* Make sure you understand the message. Repeat it, if necessary, and ask questions for clarification. Use critical thinking to make sure you are not letting emotions and preconceived ideas get in the way.

Verbal Communications

Verbal communication is the exchange of messages by speaking or writing. For most of us, verbal communication is the most common way we stay in touch with other people in our lives. We talk face to face or on the phone. We send text messages, e-mails, and instant messages. We write blogs, pass notes, and send cards.

Talking is usually a very effective form of verbal communication. When you speak clearly and use language the receiver understands, he or she almost always gets the message the way you intend it.

Nonverbal communication helps put words into context. This form of communication includes visual messages that the receiver can see, such as a smile when you are talking. It also includes physical messages, such as a pat on the back. During a conversation, the tone of your voice and the language you use combine to provide context for the words.

When you write, you lose some of the **context**, which can make the communication less effective. Exchanging written messages doesn't take place face to face. It might be across great distances. When the receiver can't hear your voice, he or she might misinterpret the message.

The Importance of Context

If you think people get the wrong message when you communicate, you might need to work on context. Context is the information surrounding your message that gives it meaning. What if people think you are kidding, even when you are being serious?

★ *Nervous laughter might make a serious message sound like a joke.*

★ *Rolling your eyes might distract the listener.*

★ *Making eye contact lets the other person know you are serious and attentive.*

★ *Adding smiley face icons, pictures, and extra punctuation makes a note or text seem light hearted.*

Context includes nonverbal communication, such as your tone of voice, expressions, and body language. It also includes an understanding or knowledge about you, the situation, and communications you might have had before. How can you improve your communication skills?

Customized Instruction: ESOL Students

Ask students to comment on facial expressions or gestures that provide context in their primary language.

Discuss

Review the six steps for communicating effectively listed in the text.

1. **Be clear.** Emphasize that the manner in which you send your message reflects your personality and has great impact on the impression you make on others. For example, if you fail to look a person in the eye when you are speaking to him or her, that person might think you have bad manners or are not interested in what is being said.
2. **Be personal.** People are more likely to respond to you in a positive way if you have taken the time to understand who you are communicating with and how they will be affected by the communication.
3. **Be positive.** Always stress the positive. People tend to put up their guard when they read or hear something negative.
4. **Get to the point.** Don't go off on tangents or topics that do not apply to the communication. Being concise and to the point helps eliminate confusion and miscommunication.
5. **Actively listen to the response.** Listening is key to effective communication.
6. **Think before you respond.** If you need time to formulate a response, ask for it.

Vocabulary

Context: Information surrounding a message that gives it meaning.

Nonverbal communication: Form of communication that includes visual messages that the receiver can see as well as physical messages, such as a thumbs-up or thumbs-down.

Verbal communication: Exchange of messages by speaking or writing.

Figure Focus

Ask students to consider the message the girl in the photo is sending with her facial expression and body language. She appears annoyed or bored. What about the woman talking to her? What is she communicating through body language?

The Importance of Context

Students are asked how they can improve their communication skills through a better understanding of context. Context is the words, phrases, or passages that surround the written word and help explain its full meaning. Context also encompasses the tone, facial expressions, and body language that accompany verbal communication.

Barriers to Communication

Explain that a barrier is something that obstructs the smooth flow of information exchange. Students are asked to think of barriers that get in the way of effective communication. Examples of barriers are a power outage that knocks out e-mail or phone service, or a distraction, such as the television, that prevents one individual from listening to another.

Vocabulary

Active listening: Paying attention to the speaker and making sure you hear and understand the message.

Figure Focus

Students are asked to consider the importance of eliminating distractions when someone is talking to them. Their responses should include the fact that the message can easily be misunderstood if they are distracted, thereby sabotaging the whole idea of effective communication.

 Cross-Cultural Communications

Students are asked to research how forms of communication vary from culture to culture. They should explore all types of verbal and nonverbal communication. If students have Internet access, they might find helpful information at the following Web sites:

- www.pbs.org/ampu/crosscult.html
- http://soc302.tripod.com/soc_302rocks/id6.html

Barriers to Communication

Barriers to communication cause a lot of misunderstandings. Your friend asked you to send her a homework assignment, but you never did. What might have blocked you from getting the message?

👎 The technology malfunctioned and your Internet connection went down.

👎 You were distracted by call waiting, a text message, or someone else in the room.

👎 She used an abbreviation or slang word you didn't recognize.

👎 She talked too fast.

👎 She was complaining about the assignment, so you stopped listening.

👍 When you didn't respond, your friend called again. She spoke slowly and clearly and made sure you understood what she was asking.

Recognizing barriers and eliminating them will help you be a better communicator, which will help you make more healthy choices. Can you think of other barriers that might get in the way of effective communication?

Active Listening

Active listening is an important part of effective communication. When you are an active listener, you pay attention to the speaker, and make sure you hear and understand the message.

Use these skills to be an active listener:

- Show interest using eye contact and positive nonverbal messages.
- Let the other person finish speaking before you respond.
- Ignore distractions such as cell phones and other people.
- Set your predetermined opinions and emotions aside.
- Repeat the message that you hear out loud, to make sure you received it correctly.

Active listening is a sign of respect. It shows you are willing to communicate and that you care about the speaker and the message. When you listen actively, the other person is more likely to listen when you speak, too.

Why is it important to not have distrctions when someone is trying to talk to you?

 Cross-Cultural Communications

Nonverbal communications can be tricky when you are communicating with people from different cultures. Personal space, touching, and gestures frequently mean different things depending on where in the world you live.

For instance, in the United States we call someone to us by bending our index finger. In Asian cultures, that gesture is used to call dogs and other animals and is considered insulting if used to a person.

Do you know of any other types of communication that mean different things to different people? Can you find examples on the Internet? Make a poster that shows an example and display it in your classroom.

Customized Instruction: ESOL Students

Ask students to share their thoughts on the following nonverbal communication behaviors:

- The proximity between people when interacting.
- Eye contact.
- The loudness or softness of your voice in a normal conversation.

Asking for and Giving Help

You do not have to make every decision or solve every problem on your own. You have many people around to help, including family, friends, and teachers.

You might think asking for help is a sign of weakness, but it's really a sign of strength. Recognizing that you need help shows that you are responsible. It proves that you understand your limitations. Face it—you don't know all the answers. Asking for help shows that you want to learn from the experience of others.

How can you recognize when you need to ask for help?

When someone comes to you for help, remember it is his or her problem to solve, not yours. With that in mind, you should listen carefully and critically, and then share your thoughts and opinions. Try not to make the decision yourself—it's not your responsibility. If you don't think you are qualified to help, say so, and then suggest someone who might be. You can probably help a friend decide what to wear on a date, but a parent, teacher or counselor might be better equipped to offer advice on how to prepare for a job interview.

TECH CONNECT

Technology can make effective communications easier by eliminating barriers. Take the combination of video cameras and voice over Internet Protocol (VoIP). You can use your computer to make a phone call and see the person you are talking to on your monitor—including gestures, facial expressions, and all those nonverbal messages that give context to words.

Can you think of other technologies that eliminate barriers to communication? Research one and prepare a report about it. You might start by searching for the key words *communication technology*. Share your report with your class.

Who Can Help?

There are people who can help you in all the areas of your life. What if an older student is teasing you on your walk to school each day?

★ Your parents can drive you to school.

★ Your brothers and sisters can walk with you.

★ Your friends can walk with you.

★ Your teachers can contact the older student's parents.

★ Your neighbors can look out for you when you pass by.

Can you think of a problem the people in your life helped you solve?

Discuss

Provide students with school and/or community resources that provide help or assistance. Select resources that students may not be aware of, such as the staff at the local library, a youth recreation center, or a homework assistance center sponsored by your school.

Figure Focus

Help students recognize the signs or symptoms of needing help. Some of these are:

■ Loss of interest in usual activities.

■ Decreased energy level or a feeling of being tired more often than usual.

■ Difficulties with making decisions or concentrating.

■ Change in eating or sleeping habits.

 TECH CONNECT

Students are asked to research and write about a technology that eliminates barriers to communication. Some technologies include cell phones, laptop computers, netbooks, and software applications.

Who Can Help?

Students are asked to think of a problem the people in their life helped them solve. Encourage students to discuss a problem of some magnitude; for example, maybe they loaned a friend some money and now the friend will not pay it back. Who would the student talk to about the problem?

Customized Instruction: At-Risk Students

Have students prepare a list of the people whom they would feel comfortable talking to about a problem.

Introduce the Section

The section discusses the skills that make for a successful and effective manager.

Vocabulary

Manager: Someone who makes decisions, solves problems, and uses resources to achieve specific goals.

Discuss

Make sure students understand the meaning of the term "manager" as it is used in the text. They might tend to think of a manager as someone who supervises other people. But, according to the text, everyone is a manager because we all make decisions, solve problems, and use resources to get what we want and need. People are effective managers when they utilize the appropriate skills at the appropriate times.

Figure Focus

Ask students how they define the term "manager." According to their definition, can everyone be a manager?

COMMUNITY SERVICE

Ask students who they think are effective managers within their community. Ask them to elaborate on why they think these people are effective. Encourage them to consider the person's use of their resources (time, energy, technology, and people), and their decision-making and problem-solving abilities.

Being a Manager

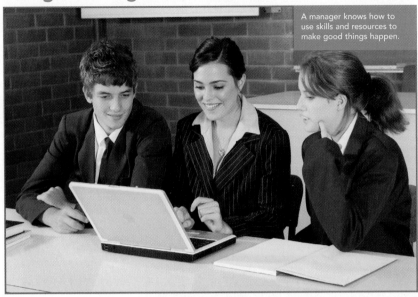

A manager knows how to use skills and resources to make good things happen.

You are already a manager. A **manager** is someone who makes decisions, solves problems, and uses resources to achieve specific goals. A manager thinks critically and communicates effectively.

Being a manager means that you are in control and responsible. You are willing to take the blame when something goes wrong, and you are willing to share the credit when something goes right.

What Makes a Manager Effective?

A manager is effective when he or she achieves a goal. An effective manager knows how to recognize and use available resources, including

- Time
- Energy
- Technology
- People

An effective manager knows how to make healthy choices in all areas of life. For example, an effective manager knows how to:

- Communicate with family members
- Think critically about friends and peers
- Set goals for school and career
- Solve problems in the community

Customized Instruction: Less Advanced Students

Ask students to draw a picture of themselves in the role of manager. They might draw pictures of themselves making breakfast, walking to school, or studying.

What a Manager Does

A good manager uses a three-step process to make thoughts and ideas become reality. He or she knows how to use goal-setting, decision-making, and critical thinking to find a way to get things done.

- First, you figure out what needs to be done. You set a goal. You consider your resources. You assess problems that might be in the way. And, you develop an action plan.
- Next, you put the plan into action. You monitor the plan to make sure it is going the way you expect. You might even need to make changes along the way.
- Finally, you look back to assess and evaluate. Did the plan work the way you expected? Did you achieve your goal?

What Makes a Leader?

Leaders exhibit positive qualities that other people respect, such as self-confidence. They use skills such as goal setting and critical thinking to make healthy decisions for the benefit of the group. If you are an effective leader you:

- Respect others
- Know how to compromise
- Know how to communicate

As a leader, you understand your own strengths and weaknesses. You also know how to accept responsibility when something goes wrong and how to give credit to others when something goes right. Finally, a strong leader is willing to take a stand, even if it's unpopular.

Be a Leader

A **leader** is a type of manager. A leader is someone who unites people to work toward common goals. If you are a leader, it means others trust you and trust your judgment.

Although you might have heard that someone is a "born leader," that's not usually the case. Becoming a leader takes time and patience. Leaders have to prove that they can make healthy decisions, set goals, and solve problems. They have to know how to use their resources to help others achieve their goals.

Leaders are successful in their different roles and meet their responsibilities. For example, at home you might show your siblings how to cooperate with each other. In school, you might listen to what peers and teacher have to say. At work, you might accept responsibility for new projects. In the community, you might attend meetings and help organize events.

How Can I Become a Leader?

Joining an organization such as the Family, Career and Community Leaders of America (FCCLA) helps you build leadership skills. You can:

✔ *Explore career opportunities*

✔ *Attend conferences*

✔ *Participate in competitions*

✔ *Access information about jobs, internships, and scholarships.*

If your school has an FCCLA chapter, become a member. If not, talk to your teacher about starting one. Learn more about FCCLA at www.fcclainc.org.

What skills and resources can you use to be an effective manager?

Reinforce and Review

Review the responsibilities of a manager. A manager determines the goal to achieve, develops a plan to achieve the goal, and evaluates the outcome of the plan.

Vocabulary

Leader: A type of manager who unites people to work toward a common goal.

Discuss

Discuss with students the people they consider leaders. Ask them to name characteristics of those leaders. Do the leaders share common characteristics?

How Can I Become a Leader?

Students are introduced to Family, Career and Community Leaders of America (FCCLA), a national nonprofit organization for young men and women in Family and Consumer Sciences education in public and private school through grade 12. FCCLA and other student organizations are discussed in *Appendix B Joining a Career Technical Student Organization*, which starts on page 525 of the student text. Other organizations that focus on youth leadership, such as Junior Achievement and Boys and Girls Clubs of America, are listed at the following Web site:

http://www.nhs.us/s_nhs/
   sec.asp?CID=118&DID=28339

Figure Focus

Students are asked what skills and resources will help them be effective managers. What skills or resources might the young man in the photo possess?

- Positive attitude
- Ability to motivate others
- Interpersonal communication skills

Customized Instruction: More Advanced Students

Have students pick a person in government who they consider a great leader. This can be someone in their local government, state government, or federal government. It could be a government leader in a foreign country. It can even be a person who is no longer living. Have them prepare a short report (one page or less) that describes the qualities the person exhibits that make him or her a great leader.

Customized Instruction: Less Advanced/At-Risk Students

Have students name a person in their lives who they consider a leader. Ask them to list words that describe the person. You should look for words such as smart, strong, nice, and caring.

End-of-Chapter Activities

Case Study

Jamal has to decide whether to join the wrestling team. Problems include conflicting schedules with his job at karate. Jamal can talk to his karate instructor to see if he can work out a different schedule. He may be able to manage his time so he can fit in both activities. If not, he will have to decide which activity he values more—working at the dojo or being on the wrestling team.

Answers to what Jamal should do will vary.

Web Extra

Encourage students to be specific about their goal. That will help focus their Internet search and lead to the Web sites with the most useful information.

Sounding Off!

Encourage students to consider all options for each scenario before making a decision. Remind them to consider the scenarios objectively.

FAQ

1. If the consequences of a decision are positive and contribute to your well-being, it means you made a healthy—or good—choice. If the consequences are negative and interfere with your well-being, that means you made an unhealthy—or poor—choice.

2. If you are impulsive, you are inclined to act without thinking.

3. Values, goals, standards, ethics, roles, stage in life, other people, resources, experience, and knowledge are examples of factors. (Students may think of others in addition to these.)

4. Identify the decision to be made. Consider all possible options. Identify the consequences of each option. Select the best option. Make and implement a plan of action. Evaluate the decision, process, and outcome.

5. You can accomplish short-term goals in the near future. A long-term goal is something you want to achieve in the more distant future.

6. Generally, the person who is blocked from a goal by the problem is the one who owns the problem.

7. Being honest, being rational, and being open-minded.

8. Not listening, being distracted, talking too fast, not understanding the language, and problems with technology are five possible barriers.

Case Study

Jamal has been taking karate classes after school since the age of eleven. Now he is a sophomore in high school. He has earned a first-degree black belt and works at the dojo (karate school) to earn money to pay for his lessons.

Jamal's friend has asked him to join the wrestling team at school. The practices are fun, and Jamal is good at wrestling. The coach thinks he can start on the varsity team if he works hard. The problem is, practices are at the same time that Jamal usually works at the dojo.

- What decision does Jamal have to make?
- Are there any problems he has to solve?
- What resources can Jamal use to make his decision?
- What do you think Jamal should do? Why?

 Sounding Off!

❶ You and a friend are walking home from school. You see an older boy yelling at a younger boy. What would you do?

❷ What if you saw a mother yelling at her son? Would you respond differently?

Web Extra

Use the Internet to locate information that might help you achieve a personal goal. Look for resources, suggestions, and stories about other people with similar goals. Bookmark the sites so you can refer to them as you work to achieve the goal.

F A Q

1. What is the difference between a healthy choice and an unhealthy choice?
2. What is the definition of impulsive?
3. What are five factors that influence our decisions?
4. What are the six steps in the decision-making process?
5. What is the difference between a short-term goal and a long-term goal?

6. How can you tell who owns a problem?
7. What are three qualities of critical thinking?
8. What are five possible barriers to communication?
9. What is the purpose of an "I" statement?
10. What are the qualities of an effective leader?

9. An "I" statement indicates that you are taking responsibility for your thoughts and feelings. It helps the receiver understand your point of view and respond to you, instead of focusing on himself and how your statement affects him.

10. An effective leader uses skills such as goal setting and critical thinking to make healthy decisions for the benefit of the group. Effective leaders respect others, know how to compromise, know how to communicate, and understand their own strengths and weaknesses. They know how to accept responsibility when something goes wrong and how to give credit to others when something goes right. A strong leader is willing to take a stand, even if it is unpopular.

What would you do if you caught your little sister smoking cigarettes? In a small group, use decision making, problem solving, communication, and critical thinking to come up with a solution. Work cooperatively, and compromise when necessary. Perform a skit for your class that illustrates your solution.

Hot Topics

What do think you are going to do after high school? Do you have a goal? Are there obstacles between you and that goal?

Take this opportunity to write about some of your long-term goals. You can write them on paper or print them with a word processing program, and then drop them into your classroom's Hot Topics Box. It's your chance to put your goals in writing and to address the obstacles that might be in your way. It's all anonymous, so you can be honest and open.

As a class, read the anonymous entries and discuss them. See if you can come up with solutions for overcoming obstacles, identify different obstacles, and suggest an action plan for achieving the goal.

Problem Solver

Some people claim that the flap of a butterfly's wings affects the climate around the globe. What do you think that statement means? Think of something you do that might have an impact around the globe. For example, what happens to the soda can you throw in the trash, or to the paper you put in the recycle bin? Working with a partner or in small groups, make a presentation that shows how even a single person can affect the whole world.

Team Players

Divide students appropriately into teams. They are asked to perform a skit, so be sure that each team includes at least one student who is comfortable speaking in front of a group.

Hot Topics

Make sure students understand that they can turn in their papers anonymously. Encourage them to be open and honest about their goals and their concerns about achieving them. In the discussion about the entries, offer concrete solutions that students can realistically apply.

Problem Solver

Students are to work with a partner or in small groups to develop a presentation on how a single person can affect the whole world. Make sure they do not confuse "single person" with a person like the President of the United States or the Pope, both of whom are empowered to do things that can affect the whole world.

Write Now

Students are asked to provide definitions of the idioms listed. Following are sample definitions:

- **Go with your gut.** Follow your instincts or personal intuition.
- **Look before you leap.** Do not rush into something before considering all possible results.
- **Look through my window.** See things from my perspective.
- **Walk a mile in his shoes.** Consider how you would feel if you were in his place.
- **Reach for the stars.** Set no limits on achieving your goals.

Be Involved!

The class develops a list of long-term self-improvement projects. Review the five steps to meeting a goal:

1. Identify the goal.
2. Assess whether the goal is something you really want.
3. Make a plan for achieving the goal.
4. Write down your action plan for achieving the goal.
5. Reevaluate the goal, making sure it is still important to you.

Social Networking

Students are asked to create a poster or brochure that explains the problem-solving process to either a group of kids in daycare or to elderly citizens at a senior center. Their work should illustrate in some manner the six steps below:

1. Identify the problem.
2. Consider all possible solutions.
3. Identify the consequences of each solution.
4. Select the best solution.
5. Make and implement a plan of action.
6. Evaluate the solution, process, and outcome.

Write Now

Go with your gut. Look before you leap. Look through my window. Walk a mile in his shoes. Reach for the stars. These are all **idioms**—expressions that mean something different from what the words actually say. Idioms are particularly difficult for non-native speakers to understand, because the literal translation is different from the meaning. Working alone or with a partner, write definitions for each of these idioms that you could give to someone just learning to speak English. Include examples of each idiom. Share your definitions and examples with the class.

Be Involved!

www.fcclainc.org

As a class, develop a list of long-term self-improvement projects, such as improving grades, becoming physically fit, learning a new skill, or maintaining an exercise program. Individually or with your teacher or advisor, use the five-step goal-setting process to select one of the projects that interests you. You might also consider a project that was not discussed by the class.

Define the project as a goal, make an action plan for achieving the goal—including a timeframe, assess the plan to make sure it is reasonable and attainable, and then put the plan into action to achieve your goal.

As you work toward your goal, keep a journal to record your progress, and collect documentation that you can use to show what you have achieved. At the end of the set timeframe, use the documentation to make a poster or presentation. Write a report explaining what you learned, whether you were successful or not, and what you would do differently if you were going to start the project all over again.

How might stressful decisions interfere with your well-being?

Social Networking

Sometimes, the way people communicate depends on their age. Think about how you would explain the problem-solving process to a first-grader.

Would it be different if you were explaining it to a grandmother? Alone or in pairs, create an age-appropriate poster or brochure for a day care or senior center in your area, explaining the process. Contact the center and arrange a time when you can visit and share the information.

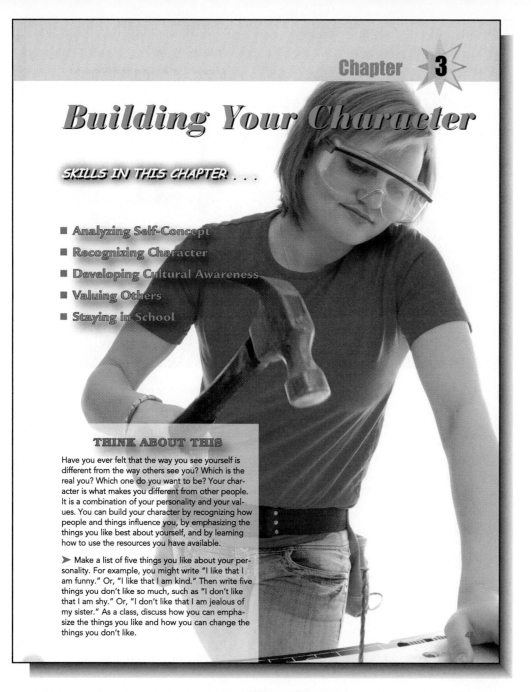

Building Your Character

Chapter 3

SKILLS IN THIS CHAPTER . . .

- Analyzing Self-Concept
- Recognizing Character
- Developing Cultural Awareness
- Valuing Others
- Staying in School

THINK ABOUT THIS

Have you ever felt that the way you see yourself is different from the way others see you? Which is the real you? Which one do you want to be? Your character is what makes you different from other people. It is a combination of your personality and your values. You can build your character by recognizing how people and things influence you, by emphasizing the things you like best about yourself, and by learning how to use the resources you have available.

➤ Make a list of five things you like about your personality. For example, you might write "I like that I am funny." Or, "I like that I am kind." Then write five things you don't like so much, such as "I don't like that I am shy." Or, "I don't like that I am jealous of my sister." As a class, discuss how you can emphasize the things you like and how you can change the things you don't like.

Chapter 3 Overview

This chapter looks at what it means to "build character." Students are introduced to the idea that doing positive things for themselves and for others and developing a positive outlook will emphasize their strengths and empower them to address their weaknesses.

Analyzing Self-Concept Numerous factors contribute to an individual's self-concept, from self-esteem to body image. Students learn to identify these factors and distinguish their impact on overall character.

Recognizing Character Students learn to identify both their positive traits and negative traits.

Developing Cultural Awareness Understanding the attitudes, values, and behaviors that typify your culture helps you develop self-awareness. Recognizing how they differentiate your culture from other cultures helps you appreciate human diversity.

Valuing Others Students discover that most people they interact with fill some type of role in their daily routine. Being respectful and courteous toward them demonstrates that you value the role they fill.

Staying in School Students learn that dropping out of school has negative effects on their physical, emotional, and financial well-being. They also learn to identify the risk factors that are common among dropouts.

Focus and Engage

Bell-Ringer: Think About This

Students are asked to write down five things about their personality they like and five things they are not crazy about. Emphasize that they are to write about personality or character traits, *not* physical traits. For example, writing that you have crooked teeth is not an example of something you dislike about your personality. During the class discussion, provide suggestions on how to emphasize the things students like about themselves. For example, you could spend more time doing things that utilize your strong traits. If patience is something you like about yourself, look for opportunities to instruct or train others. On the other hand, if impatience is something you don't like about yourself, then avoid situations in which you have to instruct or train others, or find another resource to do it.

ADVANCE PREPARATION

Review	*Life Skills for the 21st Century* textbook, Chapter 3.
Prepare	Magazines and newspapers from which students can cut pictures or text.
	Paper and pencil for some activities.
	Index cards.
	Cups and a pitcher of water.
	Box labeled "Hot Topics."

CUSTOMIZED INSTRUCTION OVERVIEW

Less Advanced Students	More Advanced Students	ESOL Students	Special Needs Students	At-Risk Students
Pages 44, 51, 54	Pages 48, 57	Pages 46, 53	Pages 44, 51, 54	Pages 45, 54, 57

Introduce the Section

This section defines self-concept as a composite of the ideas, feelings, and attitudes a person has about him- or herself. Students explore their strengths and weaknesses and take a close look at the factors they use to develop and form their self-concept.

Figure Focus

As the photo illustrates, looking in a mirror reflects your physical traits, but not your personality traits, or your thoughts and feelings, or your values and standards. Explain that you must consider all these things in order to understand your self-concept.

Vocabulary

Healthy self-concept: Having an appreciation for your strengths and acceptance of your weaknesses.

Ideal self: The person you would like to be.

Public self: The person other people think you are.

Real self: What you really think of yourself.

Realistic self-concept: When your ideal self, public self, and real self are similar.

Self-concept or self-image: The way you see yourself that takes into account your physical appearance; your abilities, beliefs, values, and feelings; and the way you think other people see you.

Discuss

Review the three components of self-concept: ideal self, real self, and public self. Distinguish among the three by using yourself or a student volunteer as an example.

STUDENT ACTIVITY

Have students create a chart with three columns. In the first column, they should write about their ideal self; in the second column, their real self; and in the third column, their public self. Collect their charts. Read what each student wrote in the public self column and ask the class to guess who wrote it.

Analyzing Self-Concept

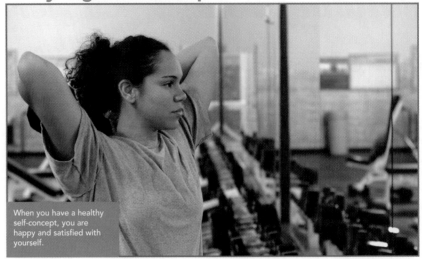

When you have a healthy self-concept, you are happy and satisfied with yourself.

When you look in the mirror, what do you see? You see the color of your hair, skin, and eyes. You see if you have pimples, or if there are shadows under your eyes from too little sleep. You see your smile, dimples, and freckles. But do you see your personality? Do you see whether you are shy or outgoing, enthusiastic or quiet?

Your **self-concept**—or **self-image**—is the way you see yourself. It includes your physical appearance, as well as how you see your character, abilities, values, feelings, and beliefs. It also includes what you think other people see when they look at you.

A **healthy self-concept** means that you appreciate your strengths and accept your weaknesses. It means, for example, that you know you are very good in math, but that you have to work very hard to do well in history.

Your self-concept can change from day to day—even from minute to minute. It changes based on your current role, as well as on your changing values and standards. You might be confident in music class, but unsure in history.

Three Components of Self-Concept

Your self-concept has three parts:

- The person you would like to be—your **ideal self**
- The person other people think you are—your **public self**
- What you really think of yourself—your **real self**

When these three parts are similar, you have a **realistic self-concept**. You see yourself the way others see you; you are honest about your strengths and weaknesses. Having a realistic self-concept is healthy. You are comfortable with the way others see you. You can set realistic goals.

Can you think of conflicts that might come up if your real self is different from your public self? What if your public self is different from your ideal self?

Customized Instruction: Less Advanced/Special Needs Students

Have students cut pictures from magazines or newspapers that portray something they feel is important about themselves. These could be pictures of families doing something together, a sports or other type of activity or event that illustrates the student's participation or interest, or even products or scenery. Have them write a sentence or two that describes what the picture portrays.

What About Self-Esteem?

Self-esteem is the pride you feel for yourself—your self-respect.

- When you have high self-esteem, you feel good about yourself. You are satisfied and proud of the person you are. High self-esteem gives you confidence to make decisions and solve problems. It helps you cope with mistakes and setbacks.
- When you have low self-esteem, you do not feel good about yourself. You are unhappy with yourself as a person. You may not feel confident. You may not want to be with other people, because you think they won't like you. You may have trouble trusting your decisions and meeting your goals.

Self-concept and self-esteem influence each other. If you have a healthy self-concept, you are likely to have high self-esteem. If you have an unhealthy self-concept, you are likely to have low self-esteem.

Self-Esteem or Self-Conceit?

Self-conceit—or just conceit—is a false or exaggerated pride in your own accomplishments. You might know someone you think is conceited. He probably has an unrealistic self-concept. He thinks he is better than everyone else. He thinks only his opinion matters. He thinks he is always right.

One way people develop self-conceit is by receiving praise when they don't deserve it. They also develop an unrealistic self-concept. People who have an unrealistic self-concept might have trouble setting realistic goals, because they see themselves as having better abilities and more resources than they really have.

> "My parents always told me I was better than everyone else. Why wasn't I elected class president?"

21st Century Skills — What Happens Next?

Jackson lives in the city with his parents and two sisters. Jackson has always been busy with sports. He plays soccer in the fall, basketball in the winter, and lacrosse in the spring. Some seasons, he is on more than one team at a time. His dad likes to be involved and usually coaches at least one team each season.

Most of Jackson's friends play sports, too. They always seem to be going to practice or to games and rarely have time for any social activities that don't involve the teams.

Jackson's older sister, Janie, is very musical. She plays piano, has a pretty singing voice, and is in the choir. Most of her friends are also musical.

One day, Janie and her friends are hanging around the house. They sing together. One boy plays the guitar. Jackson listens in. He thinks the guitar is pretty cool.

Jackson asks his parents if he can take guitar lessons. His dad thinks there is not enough time between games and practices. Jackson says he is willing to give up a sport.

What problems and choices are facing Jackson? What life skills can he use to find solutions and make decisions? Using your 21st Century Skills—such as decision making, goal setting, and problem solving—write an ending to the story. Read it to the class, or form a small group and present it as a skit.

Make a Good First Impression

A **first impression** is the opinion someone forms about you the first time you meet. What contributes to a positive first impression?

- 👎 Not making eye-contact when you speak to someone for the first time
- 👎 Having dirty teeth and bad breath
- 👎 Negative body language, such as slouching
- 👍 Smiling and shaking hands as a greeting
- 👍 Keeping your fingernails clean and trimmed
- 👍 Having clean, combed hair

Although you might be able to overcome a negative first impression, it is much easier if you start off on the right foot by making a positive first impression. What steps can you take to make a positive first impression?

Customized Instruction: At-Risk Students

Tape a label to a box, basket, or bucket that says, "It's All About Me!" Write each student's name on a slip of paper, fold it, and put it in the container. Have students pick a paper from the container and then write something nice (on the same paper) about the person whose name is on it. Have students return their papers to the container. Read the student's name and what was written about him or her to the class.

Make a Good First Impression

Ask students to think about their public self as they consider the steps they can take to make a positive first impression. Remind them that your public self is the person other people think you are. First impressions can have a significant impact on an individual's public self.

Vocabulary

First impression: The opinion someone forms about you the first time you meet.

Self-conceit: A false or exaggerated pride in your own accomplishments.

Self-esteem: The pride you feel for yourself; your self-respect.

Teaching Tips

Explain that self-esteem is a measure of how you feel about yourself. Having high self-esteem means you are confident and are happy with yourself. Having low self-esteem means you are not as confident and not as happy.

Discuss

Some students might find their self-esteem is higher when the important adults in their lives openly exhibit acceptance, concern, and interest in them, while it is lower when this is not the case. Engage students in a discussion about the influence of others on their self-esteem. How much influence does another's opinion of them have?

Figure Focus

Ask students why they think the girl's parents would have told her she was better than everyone else. Explain that most parents want their children to have a healthy self-esteem, but sometimes their methods of fostering this are taken out of context or misinterpreted. In this case, the end result was a daughter with a case of self-conceit. Ask students what the girl's parents could have told her instead. An example: "We will support you and be proud of you no matter how the election turns out."

21st Century Skills

What Happens Next?

Students are asked to write an ending to the story or present a skit. Their endings should identify Jackson's problem, which is having to give up something to make time for guitar lessons. Some students might also think that convincing his father that he can make time for lessons is a problem for Jackson. Students should also list the choices Jackson must make. Which sport will he give up? Their endings should include the six steps to making a decision:

- Identify the decision to be made.
- Consider all possible options.
- Identify the consequences of each option.
- Select the best option.
- Create a plan to execute the best option.
- Evaluate the decision.

Vocabulary

Self-awareness: Sense of self.

Discuss

Explain that being self-aware means you have a balanced and honest view of yourself. You understand your strengths, but you also acknowledge that you have weaknesses. You have a realistic self-concept.

Others Affect Our Sense of Self

As much as we might like to argue that another person's opinion of us doesn't matter, the truth is, it really does! Whether consciously or subconsciously, humans seek approval for their actions. Approval can come in many forms, including someone's opinion of what you say or do. Students are asked how the opinions of others influence their sense of self. Follow up by asking them how they think their opinions can have a positive or negative influence on someone.

Figure Focus

A keen sense of self is characterized by your ability to make the most of your strengths. But it also means acknowledging your weaknesses. Knowing your strengths and weaknesses guides you in the decisions you make. If punctuality is one of your strengths, then you will decide to set your alarm so you get up and arrive at work on time. If punctuality is one of your weaknesses, then you will decide to set your alarm 15 minutes earlier than necessary, allowing yourself extra time to get to work.

Others Affect Our Sense of Self

The way other people treat us and react to us is an important part of our own self-concept. When people have positive opinions of us, we see ourselves in a positive way. When people have negative opinions of us, we might see ourselves in a negative way. Their opinions influence our opinions.

👍 If someone thinks you are smart, you think you are smart.

👍 If someone thinks you are pretty, you think you are pretty.

👎 If someone thinks you are clumsy, you think you are clumsy.

How do the positive opinions of peers and other people affect your sense of self? What if their opinions are not so positive?

Your Sense of Self

Your sense of self—or **self-awareness**—is a combination of things, including self-concept and self-esteem. Developing self-awareness helps you set goals that are right for you, no matter what others think.

Some of the strongest influences come from our family. A positive sense of self develops from:

- Supportive parents and siblings
- Respect among family members
- Parents who allow children to assume responsibility

When you are young, your sense of self depends a lot on how other people treat you. For example, your parents might treat your brother as the "smart one" and you as the "athletic one."

As you get older and more self-aware, your self-concept is influenced by your own experience. You might think that the way others see you is not how you really are. You might want to make up your own mind about yourself.

For example, even though your parents don't think you are athletic, you might try a new sport, and be proud of your abilities.

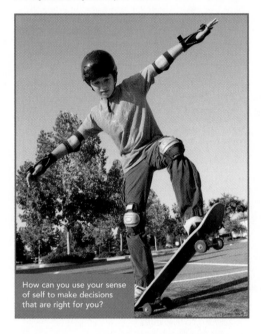

How can you use your sense of self to make decisions that are right for you?

Customized Instruction: ESOL Students

Ask students to write on the board common first names in their primary language. Ask them to translate the names to English, if possible.

What's Body Image?

The opinion you have of your physical appearance is your **body image**. A positive body image means you feel good about the way you look. A negative body image means you feel bad about the way you look. Often, the way you feel about your body image has a lot to do with your self-esteem.

Sometimes we create our body image by comparing ourselves to others. You might think you have nicer hair than your sister, or that your nose is bigger than your friend's nose. We also compare ourselves to pictures we see in magazines, movies, and on television. You might want to be as thin as a model, or as muscular as a movie star.

When your body changes as you grow, your body image will probably change, too. Finding a way to keep a positive body image helps you have positive self-esteem.

How can comparing yourself to people in magazines, movies, and on television give you an unrealistic or negative body image? What can you do to stay positive about your body image?

Image vs. Identity

Are your image and your identity the same?

- Image is the way you express yourself and how you present yourself to others.
- Identity is the person you really are.

Have you ever tried to present an image that is different from who you really are? What were the circumstances? Were you successful? How did it make you feel?

Does the Way You Look Matter?

The way you take care of your physical appearance sends a message to the people around you. If you are clean and neat, the message is that you think highly of yourself and that it is important to you to look your best. Your grooming shows you are responsible and considerate. If you are dirty or leave the house without combing your hair, the message is that you don't care what you look like. People assume that if you don't care about yourself, you probably don't care about other things, either.

Do you think presenting a good appearance depends on your physical beauty?

Myth People are supposed to look like the models and actors we see on TV and in magazines.

Truth People come in all shapes and sizes, and most do not look like models and actors. Even the models and actors don't usually look like the pictures! Pictures can be changed to remove problems such as pimples and uneven skin tone. Lighting and special effects can make people look different—taller, shorter, fatter, or thinner.

TECH CONNECT

Have you heard the expression "Photoshop It?" It means using a software program such as Adobe Photoshop to edit or change a picture. Maybe you've used such a program to change a picture of yourself or your friends.

Even basic photo editing software lets you change colors, crop edges, and even delete parts of pictures. Sophisticated programs make it possible to drastically alter backgrounds, faces, and other important parts of a photo. This raises all sort of questions about whether photos you see in magazines, on television, or the Internet are "real" or altered.

Do you think it matters if a picture is edited? Is it ethical to edit a picture? Are there some situations when it is okay and some when it is not? Write an essay explaining your opinion, and then discuss the topic as a class.

 TECH CONNECT

Students are asked to write an essay on picture editing and whether or not it is ethical. A number of Web sites show before and after photos of celebrities and models. You might allow students time to browse these, but note that some of the photos are provocative (although no different from the magazine covers you might see on grocery store shelves). You might want to review them first. Three of these are listed below:

- http://www.hemmy.net/2007/12/01/celebrity-photoshop/#more-1434
- http://funfever.blogspot.com/2008/10/celebrities-before-and-after-photoshop.html
- http://www.nextnature.net/?p=2227

Vocabulary

Body image: The opinion you have of your physical appearance.

Teaching Tips

Be aware that body image can be a sensitive subject for some students. Steer the discussion to what students can do to stay positive about their body image. Encourage them to focus on what they like about their bodies; for example, nice skin, straight teeth, or good muscle tone. Then, be prepared to offer suggestions on how to deal with the things they would like to improve. For example, exercising can tone muscles.

Discuss

Explain the difference between image and identity. Image is what you see, while identity is who you are. You can't change your identity, but you can change your image. Ask students to share stories about changing their image or about people they know who changed their image. Why did they do it and were they successful?

Figure Focus

Students are asked if a good appearance depends on physical beauty. A good appearance does not depend solely on a person's physical qualities. Explain that it has a lot to do with the way in which a person speaks, postures, and acts toward others. For example, you are introduced to someone who you think is very attractive, but during the introduction, the person turns around and makes an offensive remark to another person standing nearby. Would you think he or she made a good appearance?

Myth/Truth

Many studies have been done about the unhealthy comparisons people make between themselves and the people they see in magazines, in movies, and on television. Many people in the public eye spend ghastly sums of money on their image. Furthermore, expensive computer technology and airbrushing are almost always used to hide flaws and alter images. Explain that such comparisons can lead to anxiety and a distorted perception of reality.

Introduce the Section

This section discusses character and the qualities that make each person unique.

Figure Focus

The way people act and the things they say define their character. Ask students to describe the character traits of the youth in the photo. Their descriptions will be based on how the person is dressed and the facial expression and posturing. Some responses might be brash, carefree, lighthearted, and confident.

Vocabulary

Character: Personal qualities or traits that make you unique.

Virtues: Positive character qualities that make you feel good about yourself and contribute to your well-being.

Recognizing Character

Your personal character qualities combine to make you a unique individual.

Your **character** is the personal qualities or traits that make you unique. You show your character qualities by the way you act and the things you say. Most people have both positive and not-so-positive character traits.

These character traits combine to make you the type of person you are. You might be kind, helpful, or considerate. You might be stubborn, sad, or mean.

Your character traits influence the way other people see you and the way you see yourself. They can contribute to your self-esteem and your well-being. You are not stuck with the same character traits for your whole life. You might change some traits, and you might gain new ones.

Benefits of Character Qualities

Positive character qualities—or **virtues**—make you feel good about yourself and contribute to your well-being.

- People recognize your character is positive, and they respect you for it. This contributes to your social well-being.
- Positive character qualities also make you feel proud of yourself and confident in your abilities. This contributes to your personal well-being.
- When people think your character is negative, they don't trust or respect you. This interferes with your social well-being.

Customized Instruction: More Advanced Students

Give students ten index cards or have them tear a piece of paper into ten strips. Have them write a word or phrase that describes themselves on each. Ask students to arrange the traits from which they like most to which they like least. Now, ask them to give up one trait. How does taking that trait away affect their character in general? Have them take away additional traits. After giving up half of them, ask students again what they think of their character without those traits.

Developing Your Character

You develop character qualities over time as you come to understand what is important to you. You can also work to develop character qualities. For example, you can decide you want to be more compassionate.

■ Can you show compassion by walking dogs at an animal shelter?

■ Can you show compassion by stocking shelves at the food pantry?

■ Can you show compassion by speaking up when someone is mean to another person?

Another way to develop character qualities is to find someone who has the character you admire and then try to **emulate**—or copy in a respectful manner—his or her behavior.

Sometimes, your character traits show up only in certain situations. You might be shy in class but outgoing when you are with your family and friends. You might be lazy when you have homework to do but enthusiastic when you play soccer.

Recognizing Your Character

Sometimes it is hard to recognize your own character qualities. You might be embarrassed to think about your positive traits. People might think you are bragging or conceited.

You might be unwilling to think about your negative traits. You might not want to admit you can sometimes be mean or stubborn.

The more you understand about yourself, the easier it is to identify all of your traits. You can accept both the good and the bad, and understand how you might try to improve.

One way to tell a positive character trait from a negative character trait is to ask yourself whether you would like that trait in someone else. For example, do you like it when someone else is rude? Do you like it when someone else is bossy? If not, you might not want to show those character traits yourself, either.

You are waiting your turn to buy an ice cream cone. A woman with a little girl walks into the shop and starts ordering before you. What character traits is she showing? What lesson might the little girl learn from the woman's behavior?

Positive Character Qualities

Positive character qualities contribute to your well-being. Some common positive traits include:

✔ *Enthusiasm*

✔ *Thoughtfulness*

✔ *Compassion*

✔ *Trustworthiness*

✔ *Tolerance*

✔ *Kindness*

"Maybe I need to develop more positive character qualities. What positive character qualities do I already have?"

Negative Character Qualities

Negative character qualities interfere with your well-being. Some common negative traits include:

✔ *Laziness*

✔ *Indifference (lack of concern)*

✔ *Dishonesty*

✔ *Intolerance (prejudice)*

✔ *Meanness*

✔ *Stubbornness*

CRITICAL THINKING ACTIVITY

Recognizing your negative character traits is as important to building character as knowing your positive ones. Ask students to provide examples of the negative character qualities listed in the text.

Vocabulary

Emulate: Copy in a respectful manner.

Discuss

Discuss ways in which students can develop positive character qualities. Simply doing the things that make you feel good about yourself is one way. For example, walking your younger sister home from school makes you feel trustworthy and responsible. Likewise, doing things that make others feel good can also help build character. For example, befriending someone who looks, thinks, and acts differently from you and your other friends makes you feel tolerant and open minded.

Positive Character Qualities

Help students understand the meaning of the qualities listed:

■ **Enthusiasm:** Having a passionate interest in or eagerness to do something.

■ **Thoughtfulness:** Treating people in a kind and considerate way.

■ **Compassion:** Sympathy for the suffering of others with a desire to help them.

■ **Trustworthiness:** Reliability.

■ **Tolerance:** Acceptance of others with differing views.

■ **Kindness:** Showing sympathy or compassion.

Figure Focus

Write a list of positive character qualities on the board. You can write the ones listed in the text or ones of your own, such as Fairness, Respect, Citizenship, and Friendship. Ask students to write about an instance in which they exercised that trait.

Negative Character Qualities

Review the meaning of the qualities listed:

■ **Laziness:** Unwillingness to work.

■ **Indifference:** Lack of interest, care, or concern.

■ **Dishonesty:** Use of lies or deceit.

■ **Intolerance:** Unwillingness or refusal to accept people who are different from you.

■ **Meanness:** Unkindness or maliciousness.

■ **Stubbornness:** Unreasonably determined to persevere or prevail.

Vocabulary

Attitude: The way you think, feel, or behave, particularly when you are with other people.

Positive attitude: When your personal view is happy, confident, and satisfied.

Myth/Truth

Ask students if they think they have more positive character qualities than negative. Follow up by asking if they know someone with more negative qualities than positive. Ask if that's a person they like to be around.

Appearance and Attitude

We've all heard the saying, "Don't judge a book by its cover." With regard to the people we meet, this means we shouldn't judge a person by the way he or she looks. But face it, we all do. We decide whether or not to buy a book based on what we read or see on its cover just as we form an opinion of someone based on his or her outward appearance. And that includes both physical attributes as well as attitude. Students are asked how they can convey a positive attitude. Some suggestions include:

- Smiling, which is probably the expression you see the most in a positive person.
- Looking people in the eye and leaning forward or tilting your head slightly, which indicates you are actively listening.
- Standing or sitting up straight and with your shoulders back, which indicates you are confident.

Figure Focus

Students are asked to consider how their attitudes affect the people around them. If they have trouble giving examples, reword the question as, "How do the attitudes of my friends, family, and teachers affect me?"

Test IT Yourself!

Students are asked to conduct a test with classmates to determine optimism vs. pessimism. Many students may already be familiar with the glass half full or half empty test. You can find many more quizzes at Web sites such as FunQuizCards.com and About.com. Explain to students that an optimist is someone who is hopeful or positive and a pessimist is someone who always expects the worst to happen. Being an optimist and having a positive attitude can help you cope with disappointment. When you are able to move past disappointments, you can focus on the things that provide satisfaction, thus helping your self-concept and well-being.

Myth A person has either all positive or all negative character qualities.

Truth Most people have both positive and negative character qualities. To be a good person, you might want to try to have more positive qualities than negative ones.

Appearance and Attitude

Do people judge your attitude based on your appearance? It might be a bias or a prejudice, but it happens all the time. Can you convey an attitude by the way you look or dress?

- 👎 Scowling and slouching
- 👎 Wearing all black clothing
- 👎 Wearing heavy dark makeup and black nail polish
- 👍 Smiling
- 👍 Wearing a variety of colors
- 👍 Making eye contact

Do you think people should judge you by the way you look and dress? How can you convey a positive attitude no matter what you look like?

A Positive Attitude

Attitude is the way you think, feel, or behave, particularly when you are with other people. If you have a **positive attitude**, you are happy, you think life is good, and you have confidence in yourself and the people around you. If you have a negative attitude, you are unhappy, you think life is unfair, and you have little confidence in yourself and others. When you have a positive attitude, people want to be around you.

Attitude changes depending on your situation. You might have a positive attitude about school and a negative attitude about your family. You might have a positive attitude about language arts class and a negative attitude about social studies.

You can develop a positive attitude by developing positive character traits. You can pay attention to the good things in your life and learn how to let the bad things go, so they don't bother you or make you sad.

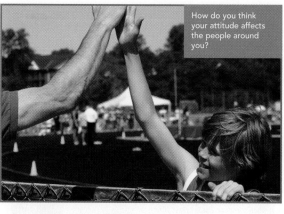

How do you think your attitude affects the people around you?

Test IT Yourself!

Are you an **optimist**—someone who has a positive attitude—or a **pessimist**—someone who has a negative attitude?

1. Fill a glass full of water and then pour out half.
2. Show the glass to a classmate and ask the question, "Is the glass half full or half empty?"

An optimist sees the glass as half full. A pessimist sees the glass as half empty.

Perform the experiment with at least ten classmates and then graph your results. As a class, discuss the difference between an optimist and a pessimist and how a positive attitude can help your self-concept and well-being.

Your Reputation

Your **reputation** is the way your peers see you. It is usually based on your behavior and on the personal character traits they think you have. Most teens worry about their reputation; they want to be liked, and they want their peers to respect them.

It can be frustrating if you don't think your reputation is correct. Maybe it is based on one event or on something that happened in the past.

- You might have cried at school in the first grade, and people still think of you as a crybaby.
- You might have forgotten to bring a snack for a class party, and now people think you are irresponsible.

Maybe your reputation is deserved. Maybe you show certain character qualities, even though you don't mean to.

- You might be shy, but your peers see you as snobby.
- You might be confident, but your peers see you as conceited, or stuck up.

It can be hard to change your reputation, so it's important to always show others your best qualities.

"For every one of us that succeeds, it's because there's somebody there to show you the way out. For me it was teachers and school."

— Oprah Winfrey, Talk show host

MONEY MADNE$$

Research shows that high school dropouts in the United States earn a lot less than high school graduates. In fact, they earn 35% less. What exactly does that mean? It means that if a high school graduate working as a chef earns $27,000.00 a year, a high school dropout would only earn $17,550.00.

How much more does the grad earn? To find the **difference**, or how much more the grad earns than the dropout, subtract the dropout's salary from the graduate's salary.

What could you do with that much more money a year?

What if the grad earns $32,000.00 a year? To find the dropout's salary, you multiply the grad's salary by 35% and then subtract the answer from 32,000.00. If you have a calculator, press 32000 × 35%. Then subtract the result from 32000 to get the amount of the dropout's salary.

If you don't have a calculator, convert the percentage to a decimal so you can multiply it by the grad's salary. To convert to a decimal, divide the percent by 100: 35/100 = 0.35.

Myth You cannot change your reputation.

Truth It might take work to change your reputation, but you can do it. Take steps to develop and show the character qualities you want people to know you have.

Customized Instruction: Less Advanced/Special Needs Students

Develop a list of fictional characters that students will be familiar with. Some examples are Harry Potter, Cinderella, the Grinch, Indiana Jones, Big Bird, Darth Vader, Bart Simpson, the Rugrats' Angelica, and Shrek. Ask students to indicate if these characters have a good reputation or a bad reputation and to explain why.

Myth/Truth

Ask students to discuss things you can do to change your reputation. Some options are:

- Identify the image you want to project and determine the changes to your appearance and attitude you must make to achieve it.

- Write down the qualities or traits you want to convey. You may already possess them—they might just need a little polishing.

- Seek support from your friends and family. Make sure they understand how important it is for you to execute this change. It may take a while, but the word will spread.

Vocabulary

Reputation: The way your peers see you; usually based on your behavior and on the personal character traits they think you have.

Discuss

Discuss with students what contributes to an individual's reputation. The things they say and do and the way they behave have a lot to do with it. If you are always willing to help others with their homework assignments, then you might have a reputation for being generous. If you are always misplacing things, you might have a reputation for being absentminded.

STUDENT ACTIVITY

Ask students to consider the saying, "Your reputation precedes you." Simply put, the saying means that people have heard about you or know something about you before ever meeting you. Have students write about a quality or trait they would like someone to know about them before they ever meet.

"Quote Box"

Ask students to consider the quote from Oprah Winfrey. Explain that Oprah Winfrey was born in 1954 to a family that struggled to make ends meet. Today, she is a billionaire. She founded Oprah's Angel Network, a charity aimed at making a difference in the lives of others who are underprivileged that includes a number of educational initiatives, and started a Leadership Academy for Girls in South Africa.

Figure Focus

Ask students to comment on what is happening in the photo. Do they think a bad reputation is given to someone, or does a person acquire it on his or her own? Have they ever felt they have been given a bad reputation? Ask students to share specific examples.

MONEY MADNE$$

To determine how much more the high school graduate makes, subtract the dropout's salary from the graduate's salary:

$27,000 − $17,550 = $9,450

To determine the dropout's salary if the grad earns $32,000 a year:

$32,000 × 35% (or .35) = $11,200

$32,000 − $11,200 = $20,800

Introduce the Section

Students learn about the many variables that define the culture to which they belong. The section covers the concept of cultural diversity and the importance of acceptance and respect of those with different cultural backgrounds.

Teaching Tips

Help students distinguish between culture, race, and ethnicity.

- **Culture** refers to a group of people whose shared beliefs and practices identify the particular place, class, or time to which they belong. All students belong to the American culture. They may have ancestors who belonged to an ancient European culture.

- **Ethnicity** refers to the national, racial, linguistic, or religious heritage shared by a group of people who may or may not reside in the same country. For example, you may belong to the American culture, but your grandparents emigrated from Germany, so you are of German ethnicity. It could also be said that you are part of the German-American culture.

- **Race** refers to a group of humans who share the same genetically transmitted physical characteristics, such as skin color. For example, you belong to the American culture, are of German ethnicity, and a member of the Caucasian race.

Figure Focus

Ask students to reflect on the cultures to which they belong. Ask them to describe their ethnicity by identifying things such as attire, foods, and traditions that set it apart.

Vocabulary

Cultural diversity: When people of many cultures live together.

Culture: The attitudes, values, and behaviors that are common to a particular group of people.

Developing Cultural Awareness

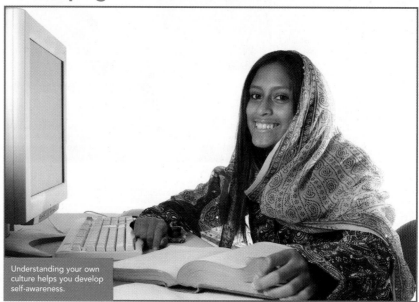

Understanding your own culture helps you develop self-awareness.

Culture is the attitudes, values, and behaviors that are common to a particular group of people. Culture develops over long periods of time. It includes knowledge, experience, language, beliefs, traditions, and celebrations.

Every person belongs to a culture. You may belong to more than one. For example, you are part of the American culture. You go to American schools, live in an American city, have American friends, and watch American television. You might also be part of a culture based on your heritage or religion. If your family came to America from an African country, you might be part of the African-American culture. If your family came from Mexico, you might be Hispanic-American. You might be Native American, Asian, or Latino.

Understanding your own culture can help you develop self awareness. Understanding the culture of others helps you communicate with people of all backgrounds. It also helps you develop the positive character qualities of open-mindedness and tolerance.

Cultural Diversity

Have you ever heard America described as a "salad bowl"? The term means that people from all over the world come here and make it their home. They take on some of the culture of Americans, and they keep some of their own culture.

When people of many cultures live together as they do in America, a country has **cultural diversity**. Our country is a more interesting place to live because it contains people with different experiences, traditions, and points of view.

Where Does Culture Come From?

Many cultures are based on nationality, religion, and heritage—traditions that are passed down through families. For example, people who live in Ireland share a culture based on nationality and religion, but Irish culture is different from the culture of people who live in Cambodia.

Even within the U.S., people have different cultures based on where they live.

■ Foods commonly eaten in the south might seem unusual to people in the north.

■ People from Louisiana might have trouble understanding the language and manner of speaking of someone from New York.

■ If you live in the city, you have a culture different from someone who lives on a farm.

The neighborhood where you live or the school you attend might have a particular culture. Your neighborhood might have traditions such as block parties. Your school might have a uniform or a mascot.

Some cultures form around people with common values and beliefs, even if they are from different places or have different religions. People of similar ages are often part of a **generational culture**. Generational cultures are shaped by shared music, current events, and experiences. **Baby Boomers** are people born between 1946 and 1964. **Generation X** includes people born between 1965 and 1976. **Generation Y**—or **Millennials**—includes people born between 1977 and 1998. **Generation Z** refers to people born in the mid-1990s to late 2000s.

Bias and Prejudice

You might have some thoughts about people from different cultures, even before you meet them. These thoughts are **biases**—opinions based on something you think you know, not on the truth. When your bias is negative, it is called **prejudice**.

For example, you might think that all Chinese people are good at math. That is a bias. You might think Chinese people are not as friendly as Americans. That is prejudice. Both are **generalizations**, which means you are assigning one character trait to an entire culture. When you meet a Chinese person, you might learn that he is friendly and better at social studies than he is at math. You might meet another Chinese person and learn that she is a little mean and really good at science. How might biases and prejudices influence the way you treat new neighbors?

Self-Concept and Culture

Your self-concept can be affected by your association with a culture. If you are proud of your culture, it will positively affect your self-concept. If you are ashamed, the impact will be negative.

As a child, you probably don't notice the culture you are raised in. You take for granted the celebrations, the food, the language, the attitudes, and the beliefs. It is only when you start to see your culture through the eyes of other people that you might notice whether your culture makes you like other people, or different from them.

What cultural traditions do you have that might be different from the cultural traditions of your peers? Present the class with an example of your traditions and discuss why it makes you proud.

Leadership and Diversity

Can cultural awareness help you be a better leader? What if you are working in a group with someone from a different culture?

★ Respect the differences.

★ Listen carefully to avoid misunderstandings.

★ Speak clearly and to the point.

★ Be open-minded, even if others in the group are not.

★ Avoid making generalizations.

★ Recognize your own biases.

What can you do as an effective leader to help everyone in the group accept and respect each other?

NUMBERS GAME

Even though the United States is big and diverse, you can drive to every state except Hawaii. You can use the **odometer**—a device that measures the distance traveled in a vehicle—in your car to calculate how many miles you drive.

At the beginning of the trip, the odometer shows the starting mileage.

At the end of the trip, it shows the ending mileage.

Subtract the starting mileage from the ending mileage to calculate how many miles you drove.

For example, if you drive to visit your aunt and uncle, and the starting mileage on your odometer is

and the ending mileage is

| 5 | 3 | 7 | 6 | 5 | 7 |

how far did you drive?

53765.7 − 53452.3 = 313.4

What if the starting mileage is 53452.3 and the ending mileage is 53972.2?

Vocabulary

Baby Boomers: Group of people born between 1946 and 1964.

Biases: Opinions based on something you think you know instead of on the truth.

Generalizations: Assigning one character trait to an entire culture.

Generational culture: A group of people of similar ages who share music, current events, and experiences.

Generation X: Group of people born between 1965 and 1976.

Generation Y or Millennials: Group of people born between 1977 and 1998.

Generation Z: Group of people born in the mid-1990s to late 2000s.

Prejudice: A negative bias.

Leadership and Diversity

Being culturally aware demonstrates strong leadership skills for several reasons:

■ When you are respectful and accepting of the beliefs and practices of another culture, you can more easily unite people to work toward a common goal.

■ When others of varying backgrounds see you demonstrate cultural awareness, they are more likely to trust you and your judgment.

■ You recognize the vast resources that people of different cultures bring to the table.

NUMBERS GAME

Students should be familiar with an odometer, but you might point out that it is commonly built into the dashboard of a vehicle. Students should subtract 53452.3 from 53972.2. The answer is 519.9. Remind students to line up decimals when they subtract.

Self-Concept and Culture

Students are asked to discuss their cultural traditions and how these traditions might differ from those of their peers. Remind them that cultural traditions include the way in which they celebrate holidays, birthdays, and weddings, but cultural traditions can also be the types of games or sports they play, the special foods they eat, and the clothes they wear.

Customized Instruction: ESOL Students

Ask students to discuss things in the American culture that seem strange or unusual to them; for example, Americans' love for air conditioning.

Introduce the Section

In this section, students explore how to recognize the role other people play in their well-being.

Reinforce and Review

Remind students that your public self is the person other people think you are. Your public self is defined in part by your image, attitude, reputation, and character traits. It also is largely affected by the way you value other people.

Figure Focus

Ask students how the two people in the photo are showing that they value each other. The delivery man is performing a valuable service by personally delivering the fragile package to the girl's front door. The girl is demonstrating how she values and appreciates his attention to customer service. Discuss the fallout effect this simple exchange might have on a community. For example, the girl is so pleased with the delivery service that she tells other people about it. These people start using the service, helping the delivery business to grow and expand, thus necessitating the need to hire more employees, resulting in new jobs in the community.

Valuing Others

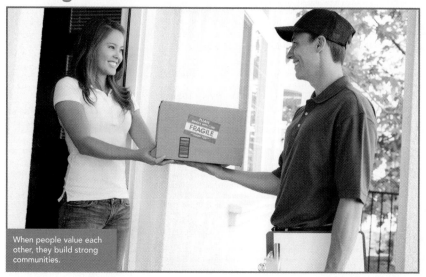

When people value each other, they build strong communities.

Valuing other people shows that you recognize and appreciate the role they play in your life. It is not the same as loving them, being their friend, or even liking them. You do not have to love the bus driver, but you can value the role she plays in making sure you travel safely and on time between home and school.

Other people help meet your needs for support, respect, love, and friendship. They are also a resource you may need to meet your goals. For example, you need the bus driver to help you meet a goal of doing well in school.

When people value each other, it shows that they care about each other's successes and failures. They help and support each other.

Common Courtesy

Courtesy is behavior that makes other people feel comfortable and appreciated. When you are discourteous, your behavior negatively affects others. For example, when you talk in a movie theater, you distract the people around you and prevent them from enjoying the show.

Courteous people are polite and have good manners. When you are polite, you:

- Say please, thank you, and excuse me
- Remove your headphones or ear buds when someone is talking to you
- Show up on time
- Answer invitations promptly
- Pay your fair share
- Write thank-you notes
- Dress appropriately
- Dispose of your trash appropriately

Courtesy shows other people that you value them. When you are courteous, people will treat you with courtesy in return.

Customized Instruction: Less Advanced/At-Risk Students

Have students create a list of people who have played a role in their lives up to that point in the day. Urge them to make the list comprehensive. It should include not only family members, but also those who played a role in getting them to school (bus driver, crossing guard, traffic cop, etc.), and those who play a role in their lives at school (teacher, principal, custodian, librarian, etc.).

Customized Instruction: Special Needs Students

Some students might be willing to discuss a special aid or assistant who plays a valuable role in their lives; for example, a hearing-impaired student's sign language interpreter.

Is It Personal?

Some people play a very *personal role* in your life. They contribute to your personal growth and development. They meet your needs for love and belonging.

Obviously, your family and friends are at the top of this list. You do, in fact, love them. And they love you back. Some teachers, doctors, coaches, and members of the clergy play an important, personal role in your life. These people know you well, care about you, and value you.

People you meet in casual, less personal ways play a *functional role* in your life. They may help you meet certain goals, and they may help you meet some basic needs, but they probably don't contribute directly to your well-being.

You might not even know the names of people who play a functional role in your life. Sometimes, you might not notice them at all.

The bus driver might fit in this category. So do salespeople who help you at a store as well as police officers in your neighborhood.

Valuing the Opinions of Others

You can value someone's opinion but not agree with it. For example, you might like the Disney Channel and your friend might like Nickelodeon. You can appreciate his opinion even if you don't agree with it. People are different and have different values, standards, and opinions.

- You can respect what others say.
- You can respect what others think is important.
- You can be considerate of the feelings of others.

When you take someone else's opinion into consideration, you might learn something new. You might see your own opinion from a different view. You might even change your mind. Valuing someone else's opinion contributes to your social well-being and helps you develop positive character qualities, such as tolerance and understanding.

Recognizing Common Bonds

Even people from different cultures have common bonds with each other. When you look for common bonds, you focus on the things that make you like someone else. You do not spend time worrying about what makes you different.

Experience, environment, culture, and current events are things that people might share. These are the things we talk about the first time we meet someone, and they help us see right away what we have in common.

- We might both live in the city.
- We might both have pets.
- We might both have brothers.
- We might both have parents who are divorced.

Finding the common bonds helps us communicate and understand each other. They help us appreciate each other.

Show You Value Others

You can show others you value them by:

✔ Listening to what they have to say

✔ Asking for their opinion

✔ Accepting their differences

✔ Spending time with them

✔ Saying "Thank you"

"Am I a freak with this pimple? What do I have in common with everyone else?"

Things Teens Worry About

No matter where they live, most teens have common concerns.

✔ Am I dressed right?

✔ Does anyone like me?

✔ Do I fit in?

✔ Am I popular?

✔ Why do I have pimples?

✔ Will I get good grades?

✔ What are they saying about me?

✔ What will I be in the future?

Discuss

Help students understand the difference between the people who play a personal role vs. a functional role in their lives. Those in a personal role contribute significantly in some way to your well-being. Remind students that well-being is the feeling and understanding that everything is going right in your life. Those people who play a functional role help you meet basic needs and contribute in some way to your daily routine, but they probably do not have an impact on your well-being.

Teaching Tips

In the discussion about opinions, expand upon the topic of Disney Channel vs. Nickelodeon. Ask individual students to give their opinions and then ask others if they agree or disagree, and why. Take note of students who show consideration in their responses and those who fail to.

Show You Value Others

Ask students to write down an instance in which they practiced each of the five methods listed for showing you value someone.

Figure Focus

Have students pair up and interview each other for a few minutes. Their questions should focus on family, friends, interests, and hobbies. When they are done, have each team report what they found they had in common with each other.

Things Teens Worry About

The concerns listed are common among teens. But increasingly, many youngsters are faced with much bigger concerns that grow out of the current social, political, and economic climate. "Will my brother who enlisted in the Army be sent to fight in a war?" "Will my mother lose her job?" "Will my grandmother get the treatment she needs for her illness?" Ask students to share concerns they have other than those listed in the text.

Introduce the Section

This section discusses the negative effects on your self-concept and well-being of dropping out of school.

Figure Focus

Ask students to comment on the positive character qualities and resources you develop in school. Some qualities include: tolerance, dependability, trustworthiness, and conscientiousness. Resources would include people who educate and coach, books and computers, and knowledge.

Vocabulary

Dropout: Someone who leaves school without receiving a degree.

Staying in School

Staying in school helps you build positive character qualities and develop resources.

What do you think dropping out of school has to do with well-being? For starters, studies show that people who stay in school have higher self-esteem, better physical health, and a more positive attitude. They are more likely to have a job, and they earn a lot more money.

A **dropout**—someone who leaves school without receiving a degree—is more likely to be poor, receive assistance from the government, and be a single parent. Dropouts are more likely to commit crimes and go to jail, to suffer from depression, and to have substance abuse problems.

Why School Is Cool

School is an opportunity. When you stay in school, you can learn new things, meet new people, and try new activities. You can practice skills you will need to get by when you graduate, such as getting along with others, speaking up for yourself, and being on time for appointments.

You might think dropping out of school to get a job is a good idea. Maybe you need money. Maybe you are tired of going to class. Maybe you think you are ready to live like a grownup. When you are not in school, you will be expected to pay your own rent, pay for your own transportation, and pay for your own food.

Stay in School

Many kids who drop out of school share a common character trait: apathy. Apathy is the lack of interest in anything, or the absence of a wish or desire to do anything.

You often hear of "voter apathy," where people decline to vote in an election because they do not care about its outcome or believe their vote will not affect the outcome. Student apathy is much the same. Students do not care about what they're being taught, and often they don't believe it is doing anything to prepare them for the real world.

For students who demonstrate apathy, consider "higher order" activities, or those that encourage them to look at the big picture. Have students research an issue in their individual community. For example, does the community have an animal shelter and is it effective?

Who Drops Out?

Do you think the "cool kids" are the ones who drop out? How about the "popular kids"? Is it the jocks or the goths or the nerds or the band geeks? Do you think you can tell by looking at someone whether he or she will someday drop out?

Studies show that most people who drop out of school have similar **risk factors**—characteristics that show they are more likely to drop out than other people.

- Most dropouts are from low-income families where there are fewer resources.
- They are more likely to have physical, emotional, or learning disabilities.
- Students of Hispanic and African-American heritage are more likely than white students to drop out.
- Students who do not get good grades, who repeat a grade, or who are older than their classmates are more likely to drop out.
- Students who have low self-esteem and who think they are not good enough to get a good job anyway are more likely to drop out.

> If you were an employer, what characteristics would you look for in someone you were going to hire? Would you rather hire a graduate or a dropout?

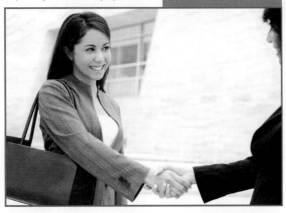

Does that mean that anyone with these characteristics is definitely going to drop out? Of course not! If you can identify the risk factors, you can take control and make healthy decisions that are in your best interest.

School and Employment

Think about this: Most companies will not hire an employee who has not graduated from high school. Some will not hire an employee who has not graduated from college. If a company does hire dropouts, it usually pays them less than it pays graduates. Even for the same jobs.

Employers assume that graduates have certain characteristics that dropouts don't have. If a graduate and a dropout apply for the same job, the employer thinks that the graduate:

- Knows how to read and write
- Understands basic math
- Can communicate with others
- Knows how to solve problems
- Has a good work ethic
- Has a positive attitude
- Is self-disciplined
- Is motivated to succeed

Why Students Say They Drop Out

Students who drop out often have a negative self-image. They don't think they deserve help. Sometimes all it takes is a request for help to keep someone from dropping out. Teachers and counselors are excellent resources for anyone who feels overwhelmed by school. Some common reasons students say they drop out include:

- ✔ I was failing and couldn't keep up with the work.
- ✔ No one cared whether I stayed or left.
- ✔ I didn't feel safe in school.
- ✔ I had to get a job to earn money.
- ✔ I decided to get married and have a baby.
- ✔ I had a substance abuse problem.

Vocabulary

Risk factors: Characteristics that increase the probability of harm to a person's health.

Teaching Tips

The risk factors listed are only general indicators of who is more likely to drop out of school. Reassure students that even if they fall into one of these categories, it does not mean they are on course to drop out. Remind students that most people who fall within these categories do *not* drop out.

Figure Focus

Recent statistics indicate that the unemployment rate for high school dropouts is roughly 60 percent higher than that of high school graduates and about 75 percent higher than that of college graduates. Not only is a high school diploma crucial to getting a job, it is a critical step to avoiding poverty. A college degree is instrumental in obtaining a well-paying job.

Teaching Tips

Students often respond more to their peers then to their instructors. Encourage dialogue on this topic between your advanced students and those at risk to drop out.

Why Students Say They Drop Out

Discuss with students the resources at your school that can keep them on the right track to graduation. List on the board the school's extracurricular activities, school-sponsored groups and organizations, and homework and other assistance programs.

Customized Instruction: More Advanced/At-Risk Students

Pair up an advanced student with an at-risk student and have them research a school-based or community-based group or program in which they could both be involved. These could range from the school chorus to the community drop-in center. Have students gather information on the program's focus, its meeting times and location, requirements to be involved, etc. They should prepare a one-page report on the program or group they chose and share it with the class. Encourage students to take the next step and become involved together.

End-of-Chapter Activities

Case Study

Answers to the first bullet will vary, but should indicate that Sophia is not right about quitting school.

Problems Sophia must deal with include moving to a new city and a new school, missing her old school and friends, having trouble keeping up in school, and teachers thinking she is not trying. To solve these problems, she could make an appointment to talk to her teachers or the guidance counselor about how she can do better. She can also join clubs or organizations in school to make new friends.

Sounding Off!

1. Self-esteem is the pride you feel for yourself, whereas self-conceit is a false or exaggerated sense of pride in yourself. When someone has high self-esteem, he shows confidence, happiness, and satisfaction. When someone is self-conceited, she acts arrogant, superior, and condescending.

2. Student answers will vary but should express their feelings about someone close moving away.

FAQ

1. The three parts are:
   - The person you would like to be—your ideal self.
   - The person other people think you are—your public self.
   - What you really think of yourself—your real self.

2. Five things are to make eye contact, smile, shake hands, be clean and neat, stand up straight, and speak up.

3. Body image is the opinion you have of your physical appearance.

4. Positive character qualities include being kind, helpful, considerate, enthusiastic, thoughtful, compassionate, trustworthy, and tolerant. Students may think of others.

5. Negative character qualities are laziness, indifference, dishonesty, intolerance, meanness, and stubbornness. Students may think of others.

6. You develop character qualities over time as you come to understand what is important to you. You can also work to develop character qualities. Another way to develop character qualities is to find someone who has the character you admire and then try to emulate—or copy in a respectful manner—his or her behavior.

7. An optimist is someone who has a positive attitude.

Case Study

Sophia moved to a new city three months ago and started at a new school. She thinks the work is much harder than at her old school, and she is having trouble keeping up. Sophia's teachers think she is not trying very hard. One told her that if she didn't improve, she would have to repeat the grade. She misses her old school and her old friends. She has made only one good friend in her new neighborhood—Selena—but Selena goes to a different school. Sophia will be 16 in three months. She is thinking about getting a job and quitting school.

- Do you think Sophia is right about getting a job and quitting school?
- What problems does she have to deal with?
- What can she do to solve the problems?

Sounding Off!

1. What's the difference between self-esteem and conceit? Discuss the different behaviors associated with each, and why you might like someone with high self-esteem, but not someone who is conceited.

2. How would you feel if someone who plays a personal role in your life moved away?

1. What are the three parts that make up your self-concept?
2. What are five things you can do to make a good impression?
3. What is body image?
4. List five positive character qualities.
5. List five negative character qualities.
6. What is one way you can develop or change your character?
7. What is an optimist?
8. What is prejudice?
9. List five ways you can show others you value them.
10. List four factors that indicate a person might be at risk of dropping out of school.

8. Prejudice is a negative bias.

9. Ways you can show others you value them:
   - Say please, thank you, and excuse me.
   - Listen to what they have to say.
   - Ask for their opinion.
   - Accept their differences.
   - Spend time with them.
   - Remove your ear buds or headphones when someone is talking to you.
   - Show up on time.
   - Answer invitations promptly.
   - Pay your fair share.
   - Write thank-you notes.
   - Dress appropriately.
   - Dispose of your trash appropriately.

10. Factors that indicate a person might be at risk of dropping out of school are:
    - Most dropouts are from low-income families where there are fewer resources.
    - They are more likely to have physical, emotional, or learning disabilities.
    - Students of Hispanic and African-American heritage are more likely than white students to drop out.
    - Students who do not get good grades, who repeat a grade, or who are older than their classmates are more likely to drop out.
    - Students who have low self-esteem and who think they are not good enough to get a good job anyway are more likely to drop out.

Form small groups to act as a company that specializes in helping people make good first impressions. Brainstorm scenarios when it is important to make a good first impression, such as a first date, a job interview, or the first day of school. Select a scenario and make a list of things that might cause a negative impression and things that might cause a positive impression. Create a presentation advertising how your company would help a client make a positive impression in your selected scenario.

Team Players

Divide students appropriately into teams. They are asked to develop a list of scenarios in which making a good first impression is important. Then they are to create a presentation that advertises how their company would help a client make a positive impression. Their presentations should cover the factors that contribute to a good first impression:

- Making eye contact
- Neat, clean appearance
- Good posture, both standing and sitting
- Smiling and shaking hands

Hot Topics

Are you proud of your culture? Do you find any of your culture's traditions embarrassing?

Take this opportunity to write about the aspects of your culture that make you proud, as well as those that embarrass you. Use a word processor and do not sign your name. It will be anonymous, so you can be honest and open. Print the document and drop it in your class Hot Topics box.

As a class, read the anonymous entries and discuss them. See if others find your traditions embarrassing, too, or if they find them interesting.

```
Web Extra  ▼
```
Use the Internet to locate information about a country you would like to visit. For example, you might research the capital city, tourist attractions, and weather. As a class, collect the information and make a travel brochure.

Hot Topics

Make sure students understand that they can turn in their papers anonymously. Encourage them to be open and honest about the aspects of their culture.

Web Extra

Students are to create a brochure about a country they would like to visit. Their brochures should include major attractions, transportation, climate, and customs and traditions.

Problem Solver

Have you ever seen or heard someone being rude? Did you think it was funny? Did it make you uncomfortable? Individually or in pairs, discuss situations when people might be rude. Think of reasons they might be rude and ways others might react. Come up with a plan that you might use to discourage someone from being rude. Make a poster illustrating your plan and share it with your class.

Problem Solver

Students are asked to consider situations in which people behave rudely. Explain that people can be rude intentionally, such as by cutting in line. Or, they can be rude accidentally, such as by forgetting to turn off their cell phone in the movie theater. Students are to create a poster that illustrates a plan for discouraging rude behavior.

Write Now

Students are to write an essay on the qualities they have that might make them a role model, or the qualities that make someone a role model for them. Review the elements of a personal essay. It should have a beginning in which the character and setting are introduced, a body in which the plot is developed or supported with details, and an ending in which you summarize or wrap up your thoughts and the information presented. Emphasize the importance of relating personal experiences and feelings and providing readers with specific examples as opposed to sweeping generalizations.

Be Involved!

Students are to create a work of art on one of the six pillars of character:

- **Trustworthiness:** Reliability.
- **Respect:** Feeling or attitude of admiration.
- **Responsibility:** The state, fact, or position of being accountable to somebody for something.
- **Fairness:** Condition of being just or impartial.
- **Caring:** Showing concern or compassion for others.
- **Citizenship:** Duties and responsibilities that come with being part of a community.

Social Networking

Students are to organize a World of Food event in which they gather and share recipes and/or dishes from different cultures. They are to create a cookbook as well as posters and pictures of the food and the culture they represent.

Write Now

A **role model** is someone who shows you how to behave in a specific situation. He or she exhibits the qualities others expect, and meets the responsibilities of the role. Role models influence the thoughts and behaviors of others, and the influence might be positive or negative.

What personal qualities do you have that might make you a role model? What qualities might make someone a role model for you? Write a personal essay answering one of these two questions.

Be Involved!

www.fcclainc.org

As a class, discuss the six pillars of character as defined by FCCLA: trustworthiness, respect, responsibility, fairness, caring, and citizenship.

Individually or in small groups, create a work of art illustrating one of the six pillars of character. Use only symbols and pictures—no words or text. For example, you might draw or paint a picture, make a collage, build a sculpture or piece of fabric art, or make a mobile. Present your piece to the class, or at an FCCLA meeting. Explain what it means, and how it relates to character.

Social Networking

Food is an excellent way to learn about different cultures. As a class, organize a World of Food event. Students can select a culture and bring in a recipe of a traditional food, or you can invite people from different cultures to bring in a recipe. Create a cookbook from the recipes.

Set up a table in the cafeteria during lunch or at a school event. Display the cookbook as well as posters and pictures of the cultures and the food. If possible, prepare a few of the recipes so people can taste them.

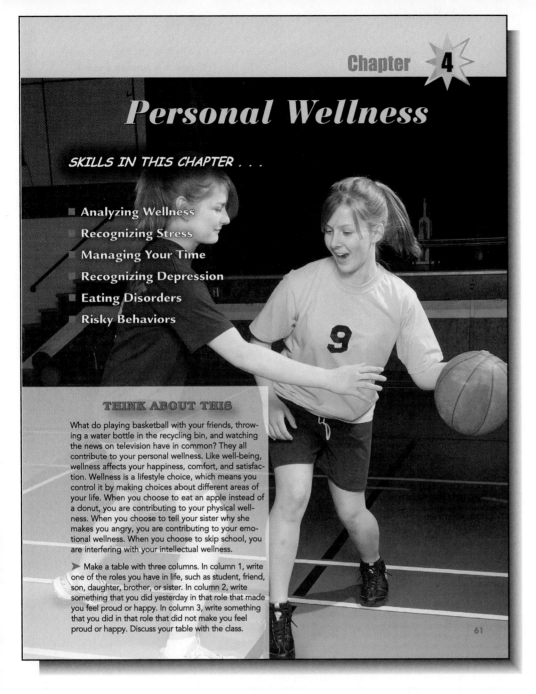

Chapter **4**

Personal Wellness

SKILLS IN THIS CHAPTER . . .

- Analyzing Wellness
- Recognizing Stress
- Managing Your Time
- Recognizing Depression
- Eating Disorders
- Risky Behaviors

THINK ABOUT THIS

What do playing basketball with your friends, throwing a water bottle in the recycling bin, and watching the news on television have in common? They all contribute to your personal wellness. Like well-being, wellness affects your happiness, comfort, and satisfaction. Wellness is a lifestyle choice, which means you control it by making choices about different areas of your life. When you choose to eat an apple instead of a donut, you are contributing to your physical wellness. When you choose to tell your sister why she makes you angry, you are contributing to your emotional wellness. When you choose to skip school, you are interfering with your intellectual wellness.

➤ Make a table with three columns. In column 1, write one of the roles you have in life, such as student, friend, son, daughter, brother, or sister. In column 2, write something that you did yesterday in that role that made you feel proud or happy. In column 3, write something that you did in that role that did not make you feel proud or happy. Discuss your table with the class.

61

Chapter 4 Overview

Students analyze factors affecting their wellness, including risky behavior and stress.

Analyzing Wellness   Students discover that wellness is a balance of all areas of their lifestyles. They learn the difference between wants and needs, and how to make smart decisions.

Recognizing Stress   By identifying the role stress plays, students learn how to cope with their emotional and physical reactions to it.

Managing Your Time   Students learn how to prioritize their activities according to goals and deadlines. Effective time management can help relieve stress.

Recognizing Depression   Students identify the difference between sadness and depression, as well as ways to confront a peer who may be suicidal.

Eating Disorders   Recognizing the role of food in daily life is pivotal to understanding physical wellness. Students learn the causes and symptoms of eating disorders.

Risky Behaviors   Students identify dangerous activities and negative consequences.

Focus and Engage

Bell-Ringer: Think About This

Students are asked to create a three-column table. In column 1, they are to list one of the roles they have in life; in column 2, they are to write something they did yesterday in that role that made them feel proud or happy; and in column 3, they are to write something they did in that role that didn't make them happy or proud. Encourage students to be open and honest. If you sense they are uncomfortable sharing with the class, then consider allowing them to turn in their tables anonymously, in which case, you can read them to the class. For the items in column 3, ask students to suggest what could have been done instead to contribute to personal wellness instead of detracting from it.

ADVANCE PREPARATION	
Review	*Life Skills for the 21st Century* textbook, Chapter 4.
Prepare	Paper and pencil.
	Poster board and glue.
	Newspapers and magazines from which students can cut.
	Box labeled "Hot Topics."

CUSTOMIZED INSTRUCTION OVERVIEW				
Less Advanced Students	**More Advanced Students**	**ESOL Students**	**Special Needs Students**	**At-Risk Students**
Pages 64, 70, 72, 77	Pages 63, 68, 74	Pages 62, 68, 75	Pages 63, 66, 70, 72	Pages 62, 64, 70, 72, 74, 77

Introduce the Section

Ask students what wellness means to them. Everyone has a different definition of what makes them happy, and defining it for yourself will give you the drive and focus to stay on track to achieve goals.

Figure Focus

Wellness doesn't just mean being athletic and eating well. It can also mean knowing when your schedule is too busy, and learning when to relax and reassess how your time is spent.

Vocabulary

Environmental wellness: Feeling safe and confident in the social and cultural environment that shapes your life.

Intellectual wellness: The way you think and learn.

Lifestyle: The way you think and behave every day that reflects your attitudes and values.

Wellness: When all of the areas of your life are working together to make you healthy, happy, and confident.

Discuss

Ask students to give examples of behaviors that are commonly accepted but may have negative effects. Give examples such as being involved in too many extracurricular activities or staying up late on a regular basis to study. Then, ask students how they might change these counter-productive behaviors.

Analyzing Wellness

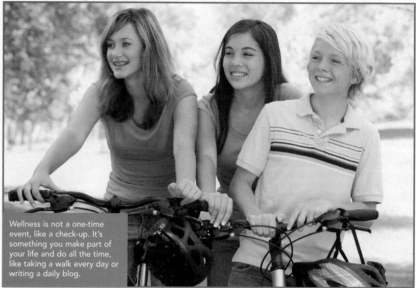

Wellness is not a one-time event, like a check-up. It's something you make part of your life and do all the time, like taking a walk every day or writing a daily blog.

Wellness is when all of the areas of your life are working together to make you healthy, happy, and confident. Wellness is not an accident. It happens when you make healthy choices about the way you live your life.

When you make wellness part of your **lifestyle**—the way you think and behave every day—you take control of your health and well-being. Instead of letting other people determine what is best for you, you accept responsibility for your health and happiness.

Six Areas of Wellness

Six areas of your life contribute to your complete well-being. The first four are the same areas of well-being that you read about in Chapter 1.

- Physical
- Emotional
- Social
- Personal

There are two more areas of wellness. **Intellectual wellness** has to do with the way you think and learn. **Environmental wellness** has to do with the environment in which you live.

Customized Instruction: ESOL Students

Have students say the vocabulary words in their primary language. Ask if the terms mean the same thing in both the primary language and English.

Customized Instruction: At-Risk Students

Have students develop a list of what they consider to be activities that may hurt their well-being, and ask that they write what they could do instead to help their well-being. Be prepared to provide feedback on their lists. For example, do their lists include watching TV instead of doing assigned homework?

Physical Wellness

Being physically fit makes you alert and energetic. You can focus when you are at school or work and have lots of energy for enjoying your friends and other activities. Things that contribute to physical fitness include:

- Routine medical care
- Getting enough sleep
- Eating right
- Regular exercise

Physical activity is one of the best things you can do to promote your own wellness. It keeps your heart and other muscles strong, increases your energy level, improves self-esteem, and—best of all—it's fun.

Emotional Wellness

Being emotionally healthy makes you confident and enthusiastic. You can think clearly and critically, set realistic goals, and make healthy choices. Things that contribute to emotional wellness include:

- High self-esteem
- Positive self-concept
- A way to express thoughts and feelings
- A positive attitude

You are angry because your brother is hogging the computer. How might anger affect your emotional wellness? What can you do to reduce your anger?

TECH CONNECT

A **pedometer** is a small electronic device that counts the number of steps you take. Most models also tell you the number of miles or kilometers you walk and calculate how many calories you burn. Advanced models store data for days and can connect to a computer or other device so you can export the data into a spreadsheet program for analysis.

Walking is one of the easiest, cheapest, and most convenient means of being physically active. Wearing a pedometer encourages you to set fitness goals, because it keeps track of your progress and motivates you to succeed.

Do you know of any other technologies that might help motivate you to be physically active?

Roadblocks to Wellness

Sometimes, the way you think or act in a situation can affect your wellness. Positive thoughts and actions contribute to wellness; negative thoughts and attitudes are roadblocks to wellness.

- 👎 Low self-esteem
- 👎 Conflicting values
- 👎 Inflexible standards
- 👎 Unrealistic goals
- 👎 Risky decisions
- 👍 High self-esteem
- 👍 Positive values
- 👍 Flexible standards
- 👍 Realistic goals
- 👍 Healthy decisions

How can you use critical thinking to identify whether a factor will contribute to wellness or interfere with it?

Discuss

Make sure students understand how physical and emotional wellness relate to one another. For example, sleep deprivation can cause a student to feel cranky and irritable at school the next day. Have students brainstorm 10- to 15-minute activities to help their emotional and physical wellness. For example, they could write in a journal, listen to music, go on a walk, or sit outside to find solitude on a busy day.

Teaching Tips

Make sure students can distinguish between physical wellness and emotional wellness. Physical wellness means you respect your body's uniqueness and avoid habits that may have long-term consequences. Emotional wellness means maintaining a positive attitude, high self-esteem, and a strong self-image.

Roadblocks to Wellness

Additional roadblocks may include "quick fixes." We hear about people using liposuction, fad diets, and drugs as quick fixes all the time. Remind students that critical thinking means to apply honesty, rationality, and open-mindedness when making decisions and setting goals. Ask them to consider how they measure their own physical and emotional wellness. Do they have daily habits that support their wellness?

TECH CONNECT

Ask students to think of technologies that would help motivate them to be more active. Start the class thinking with the example of playing sports through electronic video games. Ask them to make a chart about the technology. The name of the technology would be in column 1, how it motivates them to work out in column 2, and how they can work it into their schedules in column 3.

Customized Instruction: More Advanced Students

Have students prepare a list of activities they have done today and yesterday and have them explain how these activities fit into the subcategories of physical and emotional wellness. For example, running every day is regular exercise, writing in a journal is an example of expressing thoughts and feelings, etc.

Customized Instruction: Special Needs Students

Ask students to draw a picture of themselves doing something that contributes to their physical or emotional wellness, and describe what they are doing.

STUDENT ACTIVITY

Ask students to develop a list of extracurricular activities in which they are involved. Have them write a realistic and unrealistic goal for each activity. For instance, scoring a goal in every game would be an unrealistic goal for playing soccer. However, scoring three goals in a season may be realistic.

Reinforce and Review

Ask students how they feel a sense of belonging in their community. Are they on sports teams, do they volunteer, or do they spend time with friends? Why is it important to feel that you belong to a group? Explain to students that your personal wellness can positively affect social wellness. Being self-aware gives you the confidence to assert yourself and participate in group activities.

Teaching Tips

Explain the difference between social wellness and personal wellness. Social wellness is the ability to communicate, have meaningful relationships, and feel connected to your community. Personal wellness means you are personally satisfied and happy with yourself.

Wellness Factors

Laughing is another example of a wellness factor. Studies show that laughing often boosts the immune system and is a characteristic seen in people who live longer. How often do you laugh in a day? Ask students to keep a running count of how often they laugh in one day. Ask them to consider if laughing changes their mood or the mood of someone they are around.

Figure Focus 1

Write the word "unique" on the board, and ask students what it means. Unique means that you are different from others in a way that makes you special and noteworthy. Ask students what it is that makes them unique. For example, maybe a student can fluently speak a language other than English. Have students consider uniqueness in respect to tolerance. A person's ethnicity, interests, hobbies, and physical traits all lend to their uniqueness. Stress the importance of respecting others because of their unique qualities.

Figure Focus 2

Remind students that intellectual wellness has to do with the way you think and learn. If you are motivated to learn and think critically when making decisions and solving problems, then you are most likely intellectually fit.

Wellness Factors

Factors that influence your wellness include:

✔ *Self-esteem*

✔ *Values*

✔ *Standards*

✔ *Goals*

✔ *Health*

✔ *Safety*

✔ *Decision-making*

Social Wellness

Being socially fit makes you comfortable and relaxed. You can communicate effectively with others and have fun with your friends. Things that contribute to social wellness include:

- An open-minded attitude towards others
- Acceptance and respect from others
- A sense of belonging
- Effective communication skills

Your friends don't understand why you want to eat lunch with the new kid in school. How can you communicate that it is important to you?

Being tolerant of people who are different from you contributes to your social wellness.

"I am intellectually fit even though I don't get all As."

Personal Wellness

Being personally fit makes you happy and satisfied with yourself. You understand your own strengths and weaknesses, and you recognize the things that influence you. Things that contribute to personal wellness include:

- Self-awareness
- A realistic self-concept
- Having flexible standards
- Setting realistic goals

It is important to you to go to your friend's birthday party, but you know her parents are not going to be home. How can you resolve your conflicting values?

Customized Instruction: Less Advanced/At-Risk Students

Have students tell three things they do to respect the diversity of others.

Intellectual Wellness

Being intellectually fit helps you be open-minded about other people and new situations. You can think critically and make reasonable decisions. Things that contribute to your intellectual wellness include:

- Staying in school
- Listening to other people's thoughts and opinions
- Experiencing new things
- Being a leader

Student organizations provide opportunities to travel, compete, and meet new people. How can you become involved?

Environmental Wellness

Being environmentally fit ensures that you feel safe in your community. You have respect for the natural environment, and you appreciate your own home and neighborhood. Things that contribute to your environmental wellness include:

- Keeping your home clean and organized
- Knowing the people in your neighborhood and community
- Recycling
- Being aware of how your actions affect your environment

A big, scary dog is chained to a fence that you pass on your way to school. He barks and runs at you every day. How does this affect your environmental wellness? What can you do to improve the situation?

How can you contribute to environmental wellness in your home and community?

21st Century Skills

What Happens Next?

Mark is worried about his parents. They have been fighting more than usual since his mother lost her job, and they have not been paying much attention to Mark and his younger brothers. Sometimes Mark has to make sure all the kids do their homework and eat something for dinner. He helps them find clean clothes when their mom forgets to do the wash.

At school, Mark is finding it hard to concentrate in class. He has been very tired, and sometimes he has headaches. He usually gets pretty good grades, but lately there have been more Cs than Bs. One teacher asked him if something was on his mind, but Mark said no. He didn't think that he should discuss his parents' troubles with anyone outside the family.

Mark's friends have noticed a change, too. Mark is spending less time with them and more time with his brothers. He makes excuses when he doesn't answer their text messages, but they are starting to think he just doesn't like them anymore.

One friend, Miguel, invites Mark to go camping. Miguel says it is Mark's last chance to show he still wants to be friends. If Mark doesn't come, then Miguel will know their friendship is over.

Mark doesn't know what to do. He misses his friends and wants to go camping, but he thinks he needs to be home for his brothers.

What problems and choices are facing Mark? What life skills can he use to find solutions and make decisions? Using your 21st Century Skills—such as decision making, goal setting, and problem solving—write an ending to the story. Read it to the class, or form a small group and present it as a skit.

Discuss

Explain that intellectual wellness involves using creative and stimulating activities to broaden your horizons and to discover the world around you. Environmental wellness involves learning from your surroundings and contributing to the health of the planet.

Figure Focus

What ways can students contribute to their environmental wellness by helping in the community? Some possibilities are recycling, printing on both sides of the paper, or helping at a community center.

Teaching Tips

Make sure students understand that intellectual wellness doesn't mean just taking in knowledge but also communicating their own knowledge through creativity and sharing.

21st Century Skills

What Happens Next?

Discuss with the class who Mark should talk to about his problems at home, and how taking responsibility for his little brothers may be a disservice to both his brothers and himself. If he were to tell his teachers, friends, or even his parents about what he was feeling, could there be a positive outcome? Students are to write about the problems and choices Mark is facing—should he go camping or stay home to look after his brothers? How can he deal with the problems with his parents?

CRITICAL THINKING ACTIVITY

Brainstorm with the class what has changed in the last 100 years in the way we interact with our environment; for example, the use of solar power, wind turbines, hybrid cars, etc. What will the next 100 years look like?

Introduce the Section

In this section, students learn about stress. Stress can be a response to changing events, as well as an ongoing or long-term event. Students explore the causes of stress and how it affects their physical and emotional wellness.

Figure Focus

Stress has both emotional and physical side effects. Extreme stressors can have effects varying from a change in eating habits and impulsive behaviors to neck or back pain, stomach aches, dizziness, and dry mouth.

Vocabulary

Stress: The body's reaction to a difficult or demanding situation.

Stressor: An activity or event that causes stress.

Discuss

Go around the room and ask each student to tell the class what might be stressing him or her out at the moment. Explain to students that many times we think we are the only ones feeling overwhelmed, when in reality, everyone has some kind of stress in their lives.

Teaching Tips

Emphasize the difference between good stress, which can motivate you to remember your lines before a speech, and bad stress, which can have physical and emotional symptoms. Signs of excessive stress may include sadness, depression, anxiety, sleep deprivation, irritability, moodiness, chest pain, headaches, and panic attacks.

Reinforce and Review

Have students review things they can do to keep their stress under control. Some options are to not over-schedule themselves, be realistic, and exercise.

Recognizing Stress

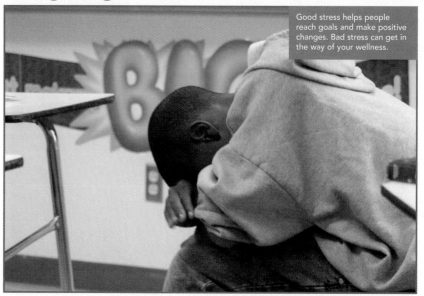

Good stress helps people reach goals and make positive changes. Bad stress can get in the way of your wellness.

Stress is the way your body reacts to a difficult or demanding situation. You might feel stress in both good situations and in bad. For example:

- You might feel stress at a birthday party because you have to talk to lots of people and make sure everyone is having a good time.
- You might feel stress when you start a new school or meet new people.

Stress can have positive or negative results. Competition usually causes stress. For some people, the stress is good, while for others it is bad. For example:

- You might try harder when you are in a real game than when you are in practice. It might bring out the best in you.
- Your friend might hate competition. It might give him a headache or a stomachache.

Some stress is normal, but too much stress can cause problems and interfere with your overall wellness.

What Causes Stress?

Any event or situation that is unfamiliar or demanding can be a **stressor**—a cause of stress. A situation that is threatening to your basic needs can be a stressor, such as hunger or noise that keeps you awake. A physical or lifestyle condition such as a speech impairment or an unsafe neighborhood can also be a stressor.

- Stress can come from serious, life-changing events. Death, divorce, changing jobs, and moving to a new town are all major events that can cause stress.
- Stress can also come from small, everyday events. Missing the school bus, meeting the principal, and losing your lunch money are all common events that can cause stress.

Some stressors affect most people. For example, speaking in front of an audience makes pretty much everyone feel stress. Some events might cause one person to feel stress, but not affect a different person at all. For example, you might enjoy talking to your teacher, but it might make your friend feel a lot of stress.

Customized Instruction: Special Needs Students

Some students might feel comfortable talking about stressors unique to them. For example, if a student is wheelchair-bound, does he or she constantly have to worry about wheelchair access before going somewhere?

Signs of Stress

When you experience stress, your body responds as if you are in danger—your heart beats faster, you breathe faster, and you might have a burst of energy.

Sometimes, people react to stress emotionally. You might become sad or depressed. You might have mood swings, which means you quickly change from being happy to sad or from confident to timid. You might be tense and angry.

Sometimes, people react to stress physically. You might have headaches, back pain, and an upset stomach. You might have trouble sleeping, or trouble staying awake.

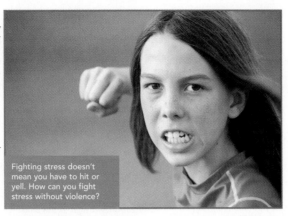

Fighting stress doesn't mean you have to hit or yell. How can you fight stress without violence?

Fight or Flight?

The way you react to stress depends on a lot of things, such as how much stress there is, how long the stress lasts, your personality, and how you are feeling. For example, if you are tired, you might have a stronger reaction to a stressful situation than if you are well-rested.

Physically, stress produces a similar response in all people, including faster heart beat, faster breathing, and sweating. Sometimes the way your body reacts to stress is called the **fight-or-flight response**. That's how people react when they are faced with danger; they choose to fight it or take flight—run away from it.

Fighting stress doesn't mean hitting, kicking, or yelling. It means taking action to solve the problem that is causing the stress, or to learn to cope with it. For example, if your sister borrows your favorite shirt without asking, it might make you feel tense. Instead of yelling at her, you could explain why it makes you tense and set some rules for sharing clothes.

Running away might make you feel better for the moment, but it doesn't solve the problem causing the stress. For example, you might feel tense because you are not prepared for a math test. Playing with your friends might make you feel better for a while, but only studying for the test will solve the problem causing the stress.

The Stress of War

War causes stress in many ways. The people living in the place where there is fighting feel stress. The people doing the fighting feel stress. And the families of the people who are fighting feel stress, even when they are safe at home.

There are wars and fighting in many countries around the world. Some involve the United States, and some do not. Using the Internet, newspapers, or magazines, look up someplace in the world where there is war now. Write a letter to a child who might be affected by that war, offering advice on how to cope with the stress.

Common Stressors

Common stressors—or events that cause stress—include:

✔ Fighting in the family

✔ Divorce or separation

✔ Death of a friend or family member

✔ Dating

✔ A physical impairment

✔ An outstanding achievement

✔ A change in financial status

✔ A change in social status

✔ Over scheduling

✔ Competition

✔ Overwhelming pressure to succeed

✔ Being bullied

TEAMWORK ACTIVITY

Have students form teams. Give each team a current newspaper and have them search for a photograph of a tense situation. Have them reflect on their own emotional responses to the photograph. Ask them to predict the behavior and emotional responses the people in the photo may have from the situation. Encourage students to discuss how emotions affect decision-making in stressful situations.

Reinforce and Review

Explain to students that expressing their feelings is one of the best ways to alleviate stress and confront their problems. If they don't feel comfortable speaking to someone else, they can use writing in a journal (therapeutic writing) as a tool to relieve stress.

Common Stressors

Review the list of stressors and ask students to raise their hand if it is currently a stressor in their life. Keep a tally, and after you have gone through the list, determine the top five. Discuss ways students might deal with those stressors.

Vocabulary

Fight-or-flight response: Physiological changes, such as increased heart rate, sweating, and muscle tension, that prepare you for immediate action whether it be to flee, freeze, or fight.

Figure Focus

Explain to students that instead of fighting stress with violence, you can build resilience to it by changing your mindset. Emphasize that they should think of changes as a normal part of life, setbacks as temporary and solvable, and success as always attainable. Building strong relationships with family and friends can help offset stress, and a support system is good when you need to ask for help. Last, by making an effort to relax and have fun, you can release stress without noticing.

The Stress of War

Students are asked to write their advice to a child affected by war. Some responses might be:

■ Stay close with your family and friends to maintain a support network.

■ Talk about your feelings to someone you trust, or write about them in a journal.

■ Recognize symptoms of stress that you may be showing, and find ways to relieve it through exercising or thinking positively.

Causing Your Own Stress

Explain to students that there are basically two types of stress: Bad sstress arises from too many negative demands, while good stress stems from the challenges of an activity you enjoy but have to work hard at. Whether it is good or bad stress, you need to learn how to manage it, and not allow it to get in the way of your wellness.

Discuss

- Ask the class how many of them play sports. Then, ask how many of them feel stress before an upcoming sports game or event. Can nervousness be bad stress, good stress, or both? What are ways to turn bad stress into good stress? For example, imagining yourself scoring the winning point may help you turn bad stress into a positive feeling.

- Some studies suggest that an increase in teen stress is associated with a greater likelihood of being overweight or obese. Why do you think that is? Ask students to talk about a time when they ate more than they needed to because they were stressed.

Figure Focus

Ask students to think of special foods or drinks they instinctually want or crave when they're feeling stressed. Is it healthy or unhealthy?

Manage Your Stress

It is unrealistic to think you can remove stress from your life. But, because stress is a problem, you can use problem solving skills to manage it.

1. *Identify the stressor.* Admit you are feeling stress, and figure out the cause. If there is more than one cause, identify each one.

2. *Consider all possible solutions for removing or minimizing the stress.* Make sure your solutions are realistic. Do you have the resources you will need?

3. *Identify the consequences of each solution.* Will they cause more stress for you or others?

4. *Select the best solution.* Look for the solution that will be most effective and give you the best chance to succeed.

5. *Make and implement an action plan.*

6. *Evaluate the results.* Did your plan work? Were there any consequences you did not expect?

Causing Your Own Stress

You can cause your own stress by setting unrealistic goals, putting yourself into situations that you cannot handle, or worrying about things that are beyond your control.

- 👎 Needing all As on your report card

- 👎 Scoring the most points on your basketball team

- 👎 Volunteering to run a bake sale the same week you have a report due

- 👎 Worrying about an asteroid hitting Earth

- 👍 Recognizing that you do not have to be perfect, or meet unreasonable expectations, or solve everyone's problems

Has anyone ever wanted you to do something you thought would cause you stress? What can you do in that situation to protect your personal wellness?

Stress and Food

Sometimes stress changes the way people eat. It can make you eat too little or too much. You might make unhealthy choices about food because you are in a hurry or because you are thinking about other things instead of good nutrition.

Some food choices can affect stress. Some foods might increase stress, because they make you feel anxious, nervous, or sick to your stomach. Foods that may increase stress usually contain caffeine, sugar, alcohol, salt, or too much protein. Some foods decrease stress, because they make you feel calm or satisfied. Foods that may lessen stress usually contain carbohydrates, such as a baked potato, brown rice, and whole wheat spaghetti.

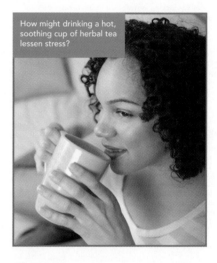

How might drinking a hot, soothing cup of herbal tea lessen stress?

Customized Instruction: More Advanced Students

Have students create a collage of pictures they have found in magazines or newspapers that represent a stressful moment. Then, have them describe why the pictures illustrate a stressful situation.

Customized Instruction: ESOL Students

What is the word for *stress* in the student's primary language? Is there a word for *good stress* in the language?

Learn to Cope

Sometimes, you cannot solve the problem causing the stress. You cannot stop your parents from fighting. You cannot cure a relative's cancer. **Coping skills** help you deal with or overcome problems and difficulties that you might not be able to solve. Here are some coping skills you can use to relieve stress and make yourself feel better:

- Relax. Sit or lie down in a quiet place. Breathe deeply.
- Do something you enjoy with people you like.
- Stretch your muscles to relieve tension, or be physically active.
- **Prioritize.** That means ranking items in order of importance, so you can decide what you need to do now and what can wait for later. If stressors are piling up, you can deal with one now and another one later.
- Accept what you cannot change.
- Have a positive attitude.
- Express your feelings. Write down your thoughts in a journal or blog.
- Take steps to avoid situations you know cause you stress.
- Talk to someone you trust.

Have you ever had problems or stressors piling up? If you are faced with more than one stressor at a time, how can you decide which one to deal with first?

Test IT Yourself!

Do coping skills really help relieve stress?

Keep a stress diary for one week. Write down the date, time, and stressor whenever you feel stress. Rate your level of stress on a scale of 1 to 10, with 1 being very mild and 10 being very severe.

On each occasion, select a coping skill that is supposed to relieve stress, such as taking deep breaths, stretching, or being physically active, and apply it to see if it helps. Write down the result.

Did the coping skills relieve your stress? Did one work better than the others? Draw a picture illustrating the experiment. Discuss it with the class.

Prepare for Stress

If you cannot avoid a stressful situation, you can at least be ready for it. When you know you will be doing something new or scary, practice.

- Think about what you will say when you meet the principal.
- Practice the presentation you must give to the class.
- Rehearse the words you will use to tell your mother you failed a test.

Most things get easier with practice or experience. A situation that is stressful the first time may be easier to cope with the second time.

Defense Mechanisms

Some people use **defense mechanisms** to cope with difficult or stressful situations. A defense mechanism changes the situation in your mind so that it is easier to deal with. This might work in the short term, but in the long term, the problem goes unsolved. For example, you could use a defense mechanism to cope with being unprepared for a test, but that won't help you learn the subject or get a good grade.

👎 **Rationalization.** You explain away the situation. "I'd rather be popular than smart."

👎 **Identification.** You look for acceptance from a person or group. "None of the kids I hang out with care about the test."

👎 **Compensation.** You substitute one goal for another. "It is more important to learn my lines for the school play than to do well on the test."

👎 **Projection.** You blame someone or something else. "I'll fail anyway because the teacher doesn't like me."

👎 **Denial.** You refuse to recognize the situation. "I'm ready to do well on the test."

👍 You recognize that if you prepare for the test, you will do fine. You study and ask the teacher for extra help.

Have you used a defense mechanism to relieve stress? Did it help you cope? Did it solve the problem?

APPLY IT

Show students how progressive muscle relaxation works. Have students close their eyes and get comfortable. Give them a minute to relax, while you tell them to take deep breaths slowly in through their nose and out through their mouth. Have them shift their attention to their right foot and take a moment to focus on the way it feels. Tell them to slowly tense the muscles in the foot, and count up to ten while they squeeze the muscles harder. When you reach ten, tell them to slowly relax it until it becomes limp and loose. Have them continue breathing deeply and slowly as you do the same with the other foot, and then their hands. When you tell them to open their eyes, ask them how they feel.

Reinforce and Review

Review with students that stress comes in many forms and can attack your positive outlook if you let it. You can learn to manage stress by employing certain coping skills.

Discuss

Ask students to discuss coping skills of their own that are different from those listed in the text. For example, do they listen to certain music when they're feeling stressed? Or, maybe they have a pet whose companionship helps relieve stress.

Vocabulary

Coping skills: Help you deal with or overcome problems and difficulties that you might not be able to solve.

Defense mechanisms: Means of avoiding emotional distress, destructive impulses, or a threat to self-esteem.

Prioritize: Ranking items in order of importance.

Test IT Yourself!

Students are to keep a stress diary for a week in which they report stressors, select a coping skill, and then assess whether it worked or not. Before students start their diaries, have them develop a list of coping techniques they would realistically use. They can use those listed in the text or ones of their own. As a class, discuss the techniques. One student may have a coping technique that another thinks could work for him or her.

Teaching Tips

Emphasize the benefits of relaxation techniques, which include better circulation, ease of muscle tension, a better outlook, and most important, the release of stress.

Defense Mechanisms

In addition to those discussed in the text, you can mention the following defense mechanisms:

- **Regression:** Choosing not to engage in everyday activities at all, and often refusing to leave your bed.
- **Acting out:** Showing extreme behavior to express thoughts that are difficult to communicate, possibly by throwing a book instead of discussing your anger.
- **Dissociation:** Acting as if you are somewhere else or someone else so you don't have to deal with the emotions of stress. By doing this, you are putting off the inevitable.
- **Intellectualization:** Focusing on the details of a stressful situation in order to put off your emotional reaction to it.

Introduce the Section

In this section, students learn the importance of managing their time resource. They explore ways to prioritize their activities and to identify the activities that can cause stress.

Schedule It!

Ask students for a show of hands on who keeps a daily, weekly, or monthly planner. What types of things do they keep track of in the planner? Some things might be homework assignments, meetings, upcoming events, and people to contact. Ask for a show of hands on who makes to-do lists. What things might you make a to-do list for? Some things might be a big school project or a party you are planning.

STUDENT ACTIVITY

Ask students to write about their preferences when doing homework. Is there a certain time of day they prefer to do it? Do they like to do it on their own or with a group? Are they sitting or lying down? Is music playing? Do they prefer to be in a warm room or one that's cooler? Does understanding these preferences help them with scheduling the time to do their homework and study?

Figure Focus

Discuss the concept of procrastination and how it can contribute to poor time management. Procrastination is the postponement of doing something, especially as a regular practice. People procrastinate for many reasons. You might feel overwhelmed, that there is too much to do so you can't do anything. Or, you might think you need to wait for the right mood to hit you. Or, you cannot decide on what to do, so you put off doing anything. Discuss ways to counteract procrastination. These might include writing to-do lists, keeping a calendar or planner, or breaking something into smaller, more manageable tasks.

Managing Your Time

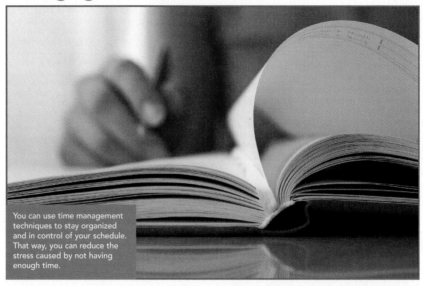

You can use time management techniques to stay organized and in control of your schedule. That way, you can reduce the stress caused by not having enough time.

One common cause of stress is not having enough time. Think about what you do every day: eating, studying, sleeping, talking to friends, taking a shower, fixing your hair, texting, using your computer, traveling to and from school, watching television, and talking to your family. You might have work, sports, religious activities, and community service responsibilities.

Most of your time is already planned. From Monday to Friday, you spend about 8 hours each day in school, and about 8 hours sleeping. So, 16 out of 24 hours a day are already booked. That leaves 8 hours for everything else. How on earth are you going to get it all done?

Time management techniques include figuring out exactly how you currently spend your time, creating a weekly schedule, making to-do lists, and ranking list items in order of importance.

Schedule It!

Scheduling helps you plan ahead, so you know when you will do something, and you can be ready for it. You can schedule by any time period, but the most useful are by month, week, and day. For example, a monthly schedule can help you plan your science project. You can schedule the time you need to meet with your lab partner, conduct the experiment, and prepare the poster. If you don't have a schedule, you might find yourself in the stressful situation of trying to complete the whole project in just a few days.

Making a to-do list every morning can help you plan your time for that day. Prioritize the items on the list—rank them in order of importance—so you know what you should do first. If something doesn't get done, put it at the top of the to-do list for the next day.

Have you ever been late for or missed an appointment or event because you forgot about it? How did that make you feel? How can you use a schedule to keep track of your responsibilities?

Customized Instruction: Less Advanced/Special Needs/At-Risk Students

Provide students with a calendar for the week. You can create this in your word processor or print one out from a scheduling or calendar software application. Have students write in their homework assignments and tests as well as any activities or events that are scheduled for the week. Do they feel that they are over-scheduled at any time?

Make a Time Journal

To figure out how you spend your time, keep a time journal for one week. Record how you spend every hour of the day. Highlight the activities you do at the same time each week. For example, you might visit your grandmother at 10:00 on Sunday morning, or babysit at 4:00 on Friday afternoon.

After one week, you will have a schedule that shows how you are spending your time. You will see both your regular activities and the things you do once in a while. The schedule will show if you are wasting time, and where there is room to make better use of your time. It will also show you your free time, which you can spend any way you want.

How do you spend most of the hours in your day? How do you spend your free time?

Goals and Time Management

Combining goal-setting with time management is a very effective way to make sure you get things done. Each time you set a goal, include a realistic time frame. You might set a goal to finish your reading book by Sunday, or to practice the guitar for one hour every day.

Setting specific goals is also effective. It helps you know how much time you should schedule. For example, setting a goal to study is not very specific. You don't know how much time you will need. You could study for ten minutes or for two hours. Setting a goal to learn your spelling words or to do ten math problems is more specific. You might know it takes you one hour to do ten math problems, or 45 minutes to learn your spelling words.

NUMBERS GAME

Elapsed time is the amount of time that has passed from one time to another. You find the amount of elapsed time by subtracting the earlier time from the later time.

For example, to find out how long it took you to do your homework, you subtract the time you started from the time you finished.

If you start doing your homework at 6:30 and finish at 7:10, how long did it take?

If you know the time now, and you know how long it will take you to do something, you can calculate the **future time**, which is the time it will be when you finish. You find the future time by adding the time it will take to do something to the current time.

For example, to find out when you will be finished with your homework, you add the time it takes you to do your homework to the time it is now.

It's 3:10 on Saturday afternoon. Your friend wants you to come over to play video games. First, you must clean your room. It usually takes you 55 minutes to clean your room. What time will you be able to leave for your friend's?

Can you think of other ways knowing how to tell time and compute with hours and minutes can help you cope with your responsibilities?

How can managing your time help you achieve your goals?

Obstacles to Time Management

Things that can cause us to waste time include:

✔ *Procrastination, which means putting off the things you need to do*

✔ *Interruptions, which means letting someone or something distract you from what you need to do*

✔ *Not knowing what to do first, which can happen if you don't prioritize*

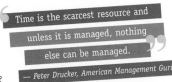

" Time is the scarcest resource and unless it is managed, nothing else can be managed. "

— *Peter Drucker, American Management Guru*

NUMBERS GAME

If you start doing your homework at 6:30 and finish at 7:10, it took you 40 minutes to finish it.

If it is 3:10 and you will need 55 minutes to clean your room before you can play video games with a friend, you will be able to leave at 4:05.

Explain that by knowing how to tell time and compute with hours and minutes, you can more effectively schedule assignments and extracurricular activities and end up with more free time for other things you enjoy doing.

Discuss

Setting goals is an integral part of wellness, stress reduction, and a feeling of personal success. By setting goals and including timeframes for achieving them, you are, in essence, effectively managing your time.

Figure Focus

Students are asked how managing their time effectively can help them achieve their goals. An effective time-management tool is segmenting. Breaking the goal down into a series of mini or short-term goals and determining how much time it will take to complete each can help you better determine how much time you will need to achieve the overall goal. Furthermore, by meeting these short-term goals, you feel a sense of achievement in small doses, which reduces stress and contributes to your wellness.

Obstacles to Time Management

Discuss ways to overcome obstacles to time management. For example, focus on the positive rather than the negative. This will motivate you to execute rather than procrastinate. Identify interruptions and determine how to eliminate them. Prioritize by due dates and importance.

"Quote Box"

Explain to students that Peter Drucker, who died in 2005, was considered one of the world's most influential business leaders because of his visionary philosophies on corporate management. Ask them what they think the quote by him means. One interpretation is that if you cannot manage your time effectively, you cannot manage your other resources, including people, money, and knowledge. For example, if you consider your relationships with friends a top priority, but fail to schedule time to devote to that priority, then you are ineffectively managing your resources.

Vocabulary

Elapsed time: The measured time while an event is occurring.

Future time: The time it will be when you finish something.

Procrastination: To delay an activity until an opportunity is lost.

Introduce the Section

In this section, students learn the differences between sadness and depression.

Figure Focus

The picture depicts a person who is alone. How can comforting a friend who is sad or depressed help him or her? Ask students to think about times when they felt sad. What were the physical effects of feeling this way? Did it make them feel tired? Did they lose their appetite? Was their physical appearance affected?

Discuss

Discuss the concept of grief. Grief is a feeling of intense sadness. Explain that many psychologists believe there are several things that characterize grief:

- **Denial:** Refusing to acknowledge what is causing the grief.
- **Anger:** Showing outrage or extreme annoyance over trivial things.
- **Bargaining:** Making a deal to give up something in return for a specific end result.
- **Depression:** State of unhappiness or hopelessness.
- **Acceptance:** Learning to live with grief while focusing on your own wellness.

Vocabulary

Depression: The condition of prolonged sadness that causes emotional withdrawal.

Teaching Tips

Make sure students understand the difference between sadness and depression. Sadness is feeling or showing unhappiness, grief, or sorrow. It is part of being human and is a natural reaction to painful experiences. However, depression is more than unhappy moods. There isn't always a logical reason for feeling depressed. Stress to students that it is important to tell someone about feelings of depression.

Recognizing Depression

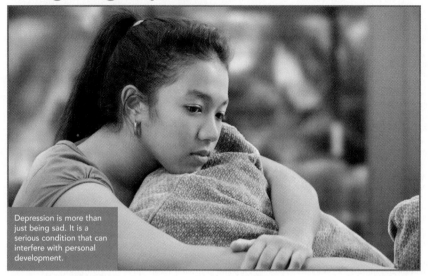

Depression is more than just being sad. It is a serious condition that can interfere with personal development.

Everyone feels sad or blue once in awhile. But, if sadness continues for a long time or for no reason, you may be depressed. **Depression** is a state of extreme sadness. People who are depressed usually have low self-esteem and feel that they are not worthy of anything good.

Lots of things can cause depression, such as anxiety, physical problems or changes, or stress. Changes in your lifestyle such as moving to a new town, breaking up with a boyfriend or girlfriend, the birth of a new sibling, or a divorce in your family can cause depression.

Depression can interfere with personal wellness. If you recognize and understand depression, you can get help to overcome it.

Identifying Depression

Depression may be caused by something that seems small to other people, such as not getting a lead in the school play. It may be caused by something big, such as moving to a new neighborhood.

The symptoms are different for everyone. Some of the common symptoms include:

- Changes in the way you usually sleep or eat
- Extreme tiredness
- Aches and pains for no reason
- A loss of interest in activities and friends
- Neglect of personal appearance
- Changes in personality
- Difficulty concentrating
- Feelings of hopelessness, helplessness, and worthlessness

It can be difficult to recognize depression because most of the symptoms are also symptoms of other problems, such as stress or illness. Also, not everyone will experience all of the symptoms. In fact, most people will have only a few.

Customized Instruction: Less Advanced/Special Needs Students

Ask students to consider the last time they were sad about something. Then, have them draw a picture of what would help alleviate or eliminate their feelings of sadness.

Customized Instruction: At-Risk Students

Have students write responses to the following situation: Jeremy's parents recently divorced, and he is feeling very upset about their split. He stopped calling his friends, his grades have gotten worse, and he feels sad often. As a friend, what can you do to help?

Coping with Depression

If you or someone you know has symptoms of depression, you should take it seriously. Whatever the cause, depression is not a sign of weakness, or a mood that will pass. It is a problem affecting your wellness and interfering with your ability to achieve your goals. You must take action to end it.

You can use your problem-solving skills to tackle depression:

- Start by identifying the problem. See if you can figure out the reason you are depressed. If there is more than one reason, take on one at a time.
- Look critically at all possible solutions.
- Consider the consequence of each solution.
- Select the best solution.
- Make and implement a plan of action.
- Evaluate the results.

You may not be able to solve depression on your own. Don't hesitate to get help! Tell your family, your teachers, a guidance counselor, a nurse or doctor, or your other friends.

Depression and Suicide

Suicide means killing oneself. It is a frightening, desperate act. It leaves family, friends, and the community confused, sad, angry, and filled with guilt.

In addition to being depressed, people usually show signs when they are thinking about suicide:

- They might talk about suicide or threaten to commit suicide.
- They might give or throw away their personal belongings.
- They might talk a lot about death.
- They might talk about being a bad person or about feeling bad inside.
- They might read books about suicide, or spend time looking at Web sites about suicide.
- They might say goodbye to people, or refer to a time when they will not be around.
- They might attempt suicide one or more times.

Sometimes, two or more people enter into a **suicide pact**, which is an agreement that they will commit suicide together. They might think it will be easier if they are not acting alone, or they might be trying to escape from the same bad feelings.

Anyone considering suicide needs help immediately. The pain they feel is very real, but they are wrong to think it is their only option.

"She seems really depressed. I will go with her to talk to the guidance counselor."

 Myth If you hear someone talking about suicide, you should ignore it, or turn it into a joke.

Truth If you or someone you know is considering suicide, you must get help from a parent or professional, such as doctor, guidance counselor, or clergy member. You should not be afraid to talk about it. There are Web sites and hotlines that provide advice, such as National Suicide Hotlines USA at suicide-hotlines.com; 1-800-784-2433.

There Is Another Solution

Someone considering suicide usually feels more pain than he or she can bear and has unrealistic thoughts. The pain might be caused by depression, but there might be other causes. A person considering suicide might think:

- 👎 He is facing a problem that has no solution.
- 👎 She made an unhealthy decision that resulted in consequences that are unbearable.
- 👎 No one will understand or be forgiving.
- 👎 He has no resources available to help.
- 👍 There must be a way to ease the pain without committing suicide.
- 👍 Talking to a trusted friend or adult will help her cope with a painful situation.
- 👍 Calling a suicide hotline will give him support and help him find an alternative.

What would you tell a friend who says she's thinking about suicide?

Reinforce and Review

Emphasize that suicide is often the last resort for someone suffering from extreme depression. Stress the importance of recognizing the signs of depression, and make sure students understand that even if someone exhibits only a few of the symptoms, it should send up a red flag.

Discuss

Discuss the causes of depression. The causes are wide-ranging but include the significant loss of someone or something, disappointment, perceived failure, or negative thinking. Sometimes, overcoming depression can be as easy as changing your daily habits. For example, devoting 30 minutes a day to exercise has been proven to lessen the effects of depression. Volunteering or becoming involved in group activities can help you focus on things other than your personal feelings. Be sure to review the symptoms of depression with students. It will help them learn to identify it in themselves and in others.

Vocabulary

Suicide: Killing oneself.

Suicide pact: An agreement between two or more people that they will commit suicide together.

Myth/Truth

Make sure students understand the risk factors that have been associated with suicide victims:

- They may have attempted suicide previously.
- They have low self-esteem.
- They suffer from depression.
- They have been abused or neglected.
- They drink alcohol or take drugs.
- They are perfectionists.
- They struggle with sexual orientation.
- They live with dysfunctional families.

There Is Another Solution

Students are asked what they would tell a friend who is thinking about suicide. Some suggestions are:

- Be supportive and patient, letting the person know you are concerned.
- Encourage the person to seek professional help.

Figure Focus

The photo shows a girl feeling depressed and a friend trying to be supportive. Remind students that they should be supportive if a friend is acting depressed. Emphasize that it is also all right to go to an adult when they fear a friend is seriously depressed. An adult can intervene without the friend ever knowing you consulted someone else.

Introduce the Section

This section discusses different types of eating disorders. Students learn how to recognize the symptoms of an eating disorder and what can cause an eating disorder.

Discuss

Ask students what they know about eating disorders and their causes. How have they heard about them? Make sure they understand that an eating disorder is an illness that usually requires medical treatment.

Figure Focus

Body image is how you perceive your body. Stress that an eating disorder is less about what you look like, and more about the perception you have of your body. Concerns about weight and body image play a role in eating disorders, but other things, such as peer pressure, family issues, personality disorders, major life transitions, and biologic factors also play a role.

Teaching Tips

Explain to students that eating disorders can have lasting effects on an individual's body. It can cause slowness of thought, erosion of teeth and gums, osteoporosis, stunted growth, infertility, heart attacks, and shrinkage of the brain, to name a few.

Vocabulary

Eating disorder: An illness that causes a severe disturbance in eating habits.

TEAMWORK ACTIVITY

Have students break into groups of three to five. Have them come up with examples of how the media contributes to the development of eating disorders. Give them magazines and newspapers to review and allow them time to search the Internet if access is available. Some examples are diet commercials and advertisements, glamorization of thin celebrities and models, reports on who has gained or lost weight, etc.

Eating Disorders

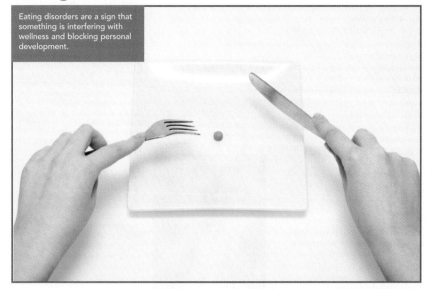

Eating disorders are a sign that something is interfering with wellness and blocking personal development.

Eating disorders are a sign of problems that are interfering with all areas of wellness. An eating disorder is not just eating too much or too little, or eating too many sweets, or not enough protein. An eating disorder is an illness. It is diagnosed by doctors, and treated by doctors.

Just because someone is thin does not mean she has an eating disorder. For someone to be diagnosed with an eating disorder, her condition and behavior must meet the medical description outlined by the American Psychiatric Association's (APA) Diagnostic and Statistical Manual of Mental Disorders (DSM-IV).

Recognizing an Eating Disorder

People who have eating disorders are not likely to admit it. In fact, one symptom is being unable to recognize the problem in oneself. It is up to other people to recognize the problem and help the sufferer get help.

Family members and friends can look for the following signs:

- Depression
- Abnormal weight loss or a pattern of losing and gaining weight
- Vomiting without any other signs of illness
- Excessive physical activity
- A refusal to eat
- Eating extremely large quantities of food at one sitting
- Always rushing to the bathroom immediately after eating
- Avoiding social gatherings where food is served

Customized Instruction: At-Risk Students

Have students draw a picture of what they see when they look at themselves in the mirror, including their clothing and distinguishing features. Have them describe what they think they look like.

Customized Instruction: More Advanced Students

Divide students into three groups, assigning one of the following eating disorders to each group: anorexia nervosa, bulimia, and binge eating. Students are to create a fictional teenage character who suffers from the eating disorder assigned to their group. They should research the common characteristics of people who are at high risk of developing the disorder. The group will prepare a description of their character and appoint a spokesperson to present the description to the class. The descriptions should include the character's name, age, and gender; the type of relationships he or she has with family and friends, and the warning signs he or she exhibits that indicate an eating disorder.

Anorexia Nervosa

People who have anorexia nervosa are so fearful of being overweight that they develop an unrealistic view of their own weight; they think they are overweight when they are, in fact, very thin. Most people with this disease are girls, but it also affects boys. It is a very serious illness and can cause death. Sufferers may fast (not eat at all), eat only minimal calories, or eliminate certain food groups.

Anorexia nervosa is deadly because the body is starving. People with anorexia nervosa are at great risk for heart problems and severe stomach problems.

Bulimia Nervosa

Someone suffering from bulimia nervosa uses food to **binge** and **purge**. During the binge, he or she eats an abnormal amount. During the purge, he or she vomits or uses laxatives to expel the food before it is digested. The sufferer may also use excessive exercise to burn off the calories.

When the sufferer is binging—eating too much—he or she feels unable to control the eating. During the purge, he or she feels guilt. Bulimia nervosa is even more common than anorexia nervosa, but less deadly. Many people who have bulimia nervosa also have anorexia nervosa. Bulimia can lead to serious problems with the heart, stomach, and esophagus. It can cause tooth erosion, staining and decay, as well as mouth sores, and swelling of the cheeks or jaw area.

Other Eating Disorders

Binge eating disorder is when someone has the first part of bulimia nervosa—the binge eating—but not the purging part. Individuals who have it tend to be obese—extremely overweight—and may describe their relationship with food as an **addiction**—a compulsion or uncontrollable urge.

Chronic dieting is a common form of disordered eating, but it is not necessarily an eating disorder. With chronic dieting, the person consistently and successfully follows a diet to maintain an average or below-average body weight. People who diet chronically may be at risk for poor health and nutrition, and may participate in another type of disordered eating, **yo-yo dieting**, which means he or she repeatedly loses and gains weight.

Treatments for Eating Disorders

There are different ways to treat eating disorders, including learning how to change behavior and undergoing psychological treatment. What if you think someone you know has an eating disorder?

- She could participate in individual counseling.
- She could join group counseling sessions.
- He could undergo treatment to try to change his behavior.
- She could participate in a nutrition study.
- He could try to reduce stress with activities such as yoga, meditation, or exercise.
- He could take medication.
- In extreme cases, she could be hospitalized.

Treatment is considered a "success" when the harmful behaviors cease and when the patient learns new ways to deal with the emotions or psychological events that trigger the behavior in the first place.

"My wellness depends on eating a well-balanced, nutritious diet."

Causes of Eating Disorders

Many factors contribute to the development of an eating disorder, including:

✔ *Pressure from family and friends to be thin*

✔ *Low self-esteem or feelings of inadequacy*

✔ *Depression, anger, anxiety, or loneliness*

✔ *Seeing unrealistic media images of overly thin models*

✔ *A problem with the chemicals that control hunger, appetite, or digestion*

Vocabulary

Addiction: A compulsion or uncontrollable urge.

Anorexia nervosa: An eating disorder characterized by the fear of becoming fat, a distorted body image, and excessive dieting.

Binge eating disorder: A disorder characterized by eating excessive amounts at irregular intervals.

Bulimia nervosa: An eating disorder characterized by frequently eating excessive amounts of food and self-induced vomiting to avert weight gain.

Chronic dieting: Consistently and successfully following a diet to maintain an average or below-average body weight.

Causes of Eating Disorders

Explain that athletes often fall victim to eating disorders. Weight may be emphasized in sports such as gymnastics, wrestling, and track and field. Christy Henrich was one of the world's top gymnasts, representing the United States in the 1989 World Championships. Although she was on the road to great gymnastics success, a judge at an international meet told her bluntly that she was fat and needed to lose weight. She took the "advice" to heart. She became anorexic and bulimic to control her weight until it controlled her life. Her weight plummeted to 47 pounds and she eventually died of multiple organ failure at the age of 22.

Figure Focus

Many health organizations have long contended that there's a link between the thinness of models seen in fashion magazines and the number of eating disorders among the readers of those magazines. In fact, some government officials have publicly spoken about instituting weight requirements for modeling. What would be the benefits of instituting a weight requirement for models, both for the models and society?

Customized Instruction: ESOL Students

Have students explain what the word "beauty" means in their primary language.

Introduce the Section

This section examines risky and dangerous activities and the negative consequences of engaging in them.

Figure Focus

Research has concluded that teenagers often seek out risky behavior because brain functions involved in decision-making occur at different times. The part of the brain involved in emotional and social interactions becomes active, while the part for regulating behavior develops later. This may explain why peer pressure can be such a big influence on teenage behavior.

Identifying Risky Behavior

Research indicates that teenagers who engaged in risky behaviors were more likely to believe that they would die younger than those who did not. Ask the class why teenagers would act so recklessly if they believed doing so would result in them dying young.

Vocabulary

Risky behavior: An activity that puts your health and wellness in danger.

Teaching Tips

Explain to students that risk-taking usually occurs in new or unfamiliar situations, the outcome is unknown, and it can result in physical and emotional harm. Have students give examples of when risk-taking can be positive. For example, running for class president involves the risk of losing the election, but by taking the risk, you might meet new people and strengthen your leadership skills.

Risky Behaviors

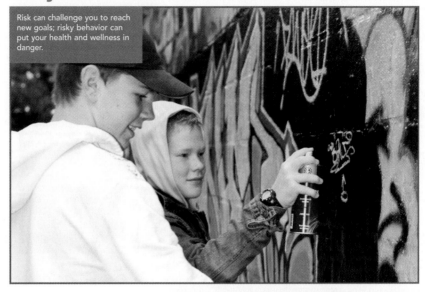

Risk can challenge you to reach new goals; risky behavior can put your health and wellness in danger.

Any activity that puts your health and wellness in danger is a **risky behavior**. Risky behaviors often look like fun, such as painting graffiti on a school wall. They might seem adventurous, such as jumping into a quarry at night. Maybe you know people doing them. Maybe those people seem brave, mature, and independent.

In reality, risky behaviors are simply risky. They put you in danger.

If you are caught painting graffiti on the school, you might be suspended or even arrested. You might have to repeat a grade. You might have a record that will keep colleges from offering you a scholarship. If you get hurt jumping into the quarry, you might drown.

When you make a choice to participate in risky behavior—and it is your choice—you are accepting the possibility of negative consequences.

Identifying Risky Behavior

Sometimes it is hard to tell if an activity will be risky or not. Is it risky to join your friends for a bonfire on the beach? It might not be risky at all. You might sit around singing songs and toasting marshmallows.

But, what if someone brings beer to the bonfire? What if some kids decide to go swimming? What if older kids show up and start putting their arms around you? What if another group of kids starts a fight?

When you know how to consider all possible options before you make a decision, you can avoid risky situations, or minimize the harmful consequences.

Is It Legal?

One really good way to identify a risky behavior is to ask yourself this: Is it legal? If the answer is no, it's a good bet it's risky, and the consequences are likely to be negative. Consider the following list of illegal activities:

- Stealing
- Driving a car without a license
- **Vandalism**—destroying property that belongs to someone else
- Using illegal drugs
- Using any medication prescribed for someone else
- Drinking alcoholic beverages when you are underage
- Smoking cigarettes or chewing tobacco when you are underage
- Engaging in sexual activity when you are underage

Are you willing to risk the consequences of illegal, risky behavior? What would happen if you were driving without a license and hit a pedestrian? What if you get caught shoplifting?

Isn't It Good to Take Risks?

Taking a risk means trying something when you are not sure if the outcome will be good or bad. When you taste a food you've never tried before, you are taking a risk. It might taste good. It might taste bad. Either way, it's no big deal. If you don't like it, you never have to eat it again.

Risk is different for different people. A person who has been playing soccer for eight years and is invited to try out for the team is not taking much of a risk. It is likely she will make the team. Someone who has never played before is taking a greater risk; she might make the team, but she might not.

Taking a risk means that you have the courage to face the possibility of failure. If you have a strong self-concept and understand your strengths and your weaknesses, you are more likely to recover quickly if the outcome is negative.

Risky behavior is not the same as taking a risk. You know the outcome of risky behavior is going to be negative.

You and a friend are going to bike to the store. He doesn't wear a bike helmet, so you don't either. Are you taking a risk, or participating in risky behavior?

Why Would I Abuse a Substance?

Substance abuse is when you eat, drink, smoke, or otherwise use substances—such as food, drugs, or alcohol—that are bad for your health and wellness. The substances can be legal—such as medicines you can buy at the supermarket. They can also be illegal—such as cocaine, heroin, marijuana, or ecstasy, or alcohol and tobacco products if you are underage.

Abused substances usually change the way you think and feel. They confuse your brain so you cannot tell right from wrong. You don't remember what's important to you. Things might seem to move faster or slower. You might feel light-headed. Sometimes you might feel calm and more focused. You might lose control over your body.

What Are Risky Behaviors?

Any decision that has consequences that put you in danger is a risky behavior, including:

✔ *Giving out your personal information online*

✔ *Going alone to meet an Internet buddy*

✔ *Smoking cigarettes or chewing tobacco*

✔ *Using anabolic steroids*

✔ *Drinking alcohol*

✔ *Engaging in sexual activity*

✔ *Using illegal drugs*

✔ *Abusing legal drugs*

✔ *Dropping out of school*

"I know I'm not supposed to climb this fence. Am I going to get into trouble now?"

Stay in School

Drug and alcohol abuse is considered one of the top reasons students fail to complete their high school education. Students use drugs and alcohol to relieve boredom, to feel grown-up, or to show their independence. But they also use them because they mistakenly believe drugs and alcohol will help them forget their troubles and ease the pains and pressures of growing up.

To discourage this type of behavior, consider starting a peer group that meets during the school day or before or after regular class hours. The members of the group would be responsible for encouraging positive behavior among their peers and helping classmates solve their problems. First and foremost, they would explore ways to manage the problems that at-risk students often say drive them to abuse drugs and alcohol.

Vocabulary

Substance abuse: Use of a substance, such as food, drugs, or alcohol, that is bad for your health and wellness.

What Are Risky Behaviors?

You might consider discussing sexting with students if it is relevant to your class. "Sexting" (*sex* and *texting*) is another example of risky behavior. It is the act of sending sexually explicit messages or photos electronically, primarily between cell phones. A person who sexts can be charged with child pornography whether they send, forward, or are in possession of illicit texts or photos.

Figure Focus

Risky behaviors may put teenagers at risk of injury to themselves and others. A recent survey indicated, fortunately, that risky behaviors among teenagers have declined in general since 1997. Injury-related behaviors, such as carrying a weapon or fighting, have decreased; however, the number of teens abusing drugs, alcohol, and tobacco remains high.

Discuss

Ask students what binge drinking means, and why someone would choose to do it. Binge drinking is the heavy consumption of alcohol over a short period of time. Risk factors of binge drinking include genetics; regular displays of impulsive, restless, and easily distractible behavior; psychiatric disorders; and suicidal behavior.

Customized Instruction: Less Advanced/At-Risk Students

Have students look up the definition of the word "clique" and write it down. A clique is defined as an exclusive group. Ask students if the following groups represent a clique:

- A group of young men playing a pickup game of basketball (*not a clique*)
- A group of athletes who stake their claim at the same table everyday at lunch (*clique*)
- A group of employees who form an alliance against an unpopular manager (*clique*)
- A group of volunteers cleaning up trash (*not a clique*)
- A group of students who hang out together because they all come from wealthy families (*clique*)

Vocabulary

Steroid: Artificial version of the hormone testosterone.

The Risks of Sex

Discuss the risks listed in the text. Point out to students that a recent survey of teens found that two out of three sexually experienced teens said they wished they had waited longer before having sex. Also mention that about one-sixth of all U.S. births are to teenage women.

Babies born to young teens have a higher risk of health problems.

Explain to students that you can become pregnant the first time you have unprotected sex. Ask students to discuss the things they would miss out on if they became a mother or father at this age.

Discuss

With everything we know about the dangers of tobacco and steroids, ask students why some teenagers still choose to use these substances. Discuss what the government is doing to regulate these substances. Examples include investigating steroid use in professional sports and increasing taxes on tobacco products.

Figure Focus

Explain to students the lasting effects that steroids can have. These include baldness, increased facial hair, changes in voice pitch, and accelerated skeletal changes. Talk about professional athletes who have illegally used steroids to enhance their performance. Examples are Olympic track star Marion Jones and Major League Baseball player Barry Bonds. Ask students if their opinion of these athletes has changed because of this.

The Risks of Sex

Sexual activity is highly risky behavior for teens. Some consequences include:

✔ *Disease. Sexually transmitted diseases—STDs—are diseases that are passed from person to person through sexual contact.*

✔ *Low self-esteem. You might recall from Chapter 3 that low self-esteem can put you at risk for other problems, such as depression.*

✔ *Pregnancy. Teens that get pregnant or cause a pregnancy are more likely to be depressed and to drop out of school.*

Most people abuse substances because they like the way those substances make them feel. It's fun and social, and everyone seems to have a good time. Some people abuse substances because of peer pressure—your friends are doing it and you want them to think you are cool. Some people start because they are curious, or because it helps relieve stress.

In the short term, substance abuse can cause you to hurt yourself or someone else. For example, you might be drunk and wander away from your friends. You might walk in the road at night and get hit by a car. You might have to go to the emergency room and have your stomach pumped out.

In the long term, you could become addicted to the substance. An addiction is a need to continue using the substance even though it has negative consequences. The best way to avoid substance abuse is abstinence—which means never using the substance at all. If you become addicted, you will need professional help to recover.

What would you do if you are invited to a party where you know there will be illegal substances?

What's Wrong with Steroids?

Steroids are artificial versions of the hormone testosterone. Testosterone brings out male sexual traits and promotes the growth of muscle. Steroids can make you a better or stronger athlete.

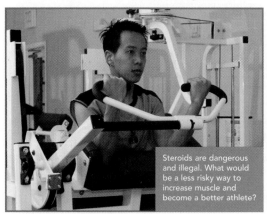

Steroids are dangerous and illegal. What would be a less risky way to increase muscle and become a better athlete?

Steroids are available legally only if you have a prescription from your doctor. They can be injected, taken by mouth, or rubbed on the skin in the form of gels or cream. They can cause many serious problems including heart attacks and liver cancer, which can result in death. Side effects of taking anabolic steroids include body odor, swollen feet, shaking, and red spots on the skin. They can also make you moody or aggressive—a condition known as "roid rage." They can cause acne. Males who take steroids have been known to stop making natural testosterone, which causes them to grow breasts and become sterile. Females might grow facial hair and stop menstruating.

Tobacco Stinks

According to the Centers for Disease Control, a government agency, smoking is bad for almost every organ in your body. It causes cancer in many parts of the body, including the lungs, mouth, bladder, and kidneys. It raises the risk of heart disease and stroke.

If that's not bad enough, smoking causes your skin to wrinkle, making you look old. It can stain your fingers and mouth brown. It gives you bad breath and makes your hair smell bad. It can burn your clothes. It can make you irritable and out of breath. It makes you cough and gives you a sore throat that won't go away. It costs a lot of money.

Chewing tobacco causes cancer, too, usually in the mouth and throat. It stains your teeth brown and can make them fall out. You have to spit out the tobacco juice all the time, which is gross.

Both tobacco and cigarettes are addictive, which means that once you start using them, it is really hard to stop.

What would you do if you stopped at the store with a friend, and he asked you for money to buy a pack of cigarettes?

Cyberspace Is a Risky Place

Most of the time, the Internet is fun. It's a place you can chat with friends, keep up with everything that's going on, learn new things, and share your ideas. Sometimes, though, it can lead to risk.

How much trouble can you get in sitting alone at your computer?

- How much do you really know about your new online friend? You can't see her. You can't hear her voice. **Predators**—adults who look for ways to mistreat children—know how to tell really believable lies. A man might say he is a boy. He might even say he is a girl! He will tell you secrets hoping that you will tell him secrets, too. He might want to meet you face to face. What dangerous consequences can come from not knowing who you are communicating with online?

- How much information do you want out there? Everything you put on the Internet is public. That means everyone can see it, including your friends, your parents, your teachers, and your boss. Before you write in your blog, or post a new picture, consider if it is something you want your grandparents to see. And remember, e-mail is the Internet, even when you are using your cell phone! What consequences might come from posting a message about someone you are mad at on your social networking page?

- How much control are you willing to give up? As soon as you put information online, you have lost control over it. You might send a picture to a friend, who sends it to someone else, who posts it on a Web page. What consequences might come from sending a picture of yourself in your pajamas to a friend?

Get Help

There are organizations that provide information, counseling, and advice for people struggling with problems they cannot solve by themselves. Some groups are specifically for adolescents and teens, and others are for anyone who needs help.

Your local community may have resources, including a teen center, a Boys and Girls Club, and other organizations that provide support. Your school may have groups such as Students Against Destructive Decisions (SADD).

Your parents, guidance counselor, or doctor can help you find these organizations. You can also find directories in your local library or on the Internet.

Unintended Consequences

One risk of risky behavior is that you can't foresee all possible consequences. What if you drink alcohol at a party?

★ *You might get sick.*

★ *You might make a fool of yourself.*

★ *You might say something you regret.*

★ *You might do something you regret.*

★ *Your parents might find out and ground you.*

★ *Police might raid the party and arrest you.*

★ *Someone might see that you are drunk and take advantage of you sexually.*

★ *You might lose control of your emotions and get in a fight.*

★ *You might decide to drive a car and cause an accident.*

The more consequences you can think of, the better you will be prepared to make decisions about risky behavior. Can you think of other consequences of drinking alcohol at a party?

Reinforce and Review

Review risky behaviors with students. Have students draw a line down the middle of a piece of paper. In the left column, have them list five risky behaviors they should avoid. In the right column, they should list five activities that would contribute to their wellness. Have students volunteer to share their lists with the class.

Figure Focus

The Internet can be a fun place to "hang out." Cyberspace is like a big city with plenty of places to learn and discover. However, as in any big city, there are dangers. Offer the following guidelines for being safe in cyberspace:

- Never give your address, phone number, name of your school, or any other information that could help someone determine your identity.

- Don't get together with someone you "meet" online, and if you feel it is necessary, talk to your parents about it.

- If you receive hostile, belligerent, or inappropriate e-mails or instant messages, don't respond. Sending a response only encourages the person.

Discuss

Ask students to discuss techniques they might have for turning down the invitation to do something risky. Here are some ideas:

- Blame it on your parents. "My parents won't let me out of the house tonight," or "My parents are making me babysit my little brother tonight."

- Talk about physical effects. "Smoke gives me a headache."

- Text your parents to call you, and pretend you have to go home right away.

- Suggest an alternative, such as, "Let's go to a movie instead."

- Stand your ground and just say, "No."

Unintended Consequences

Explain that alcohol alters your ability to think clearly. Alcohol may affect who you choose to "hook up" with, whether you use protection, and when to have an intimate relationship with someone. Have students consider the following:

- 55% of teens say that having sex while drinking or on drugs was a reason for unplanned teenage pregnancy.

- Nearly 50% of teenage girls who have sex for the first time before age 15 report having become pregnant, compared with almost 25% of girls age 15 or older.

- 7 out of 10 women who had intercourse before age 13 said it was unwanted or involuntary.

End-of-Chapter Activities

Case Study

Answers for the first two bullets may vary, but should be yes for both. For the third bullet, Patrice could be bulimic. She could be eating and purging.

Sounding Off

Student answers will vary.

FAQ

1. The six areas of wellness are physical, emotional, social, personal, intellectual, and environmental.

2. Being physically active makes you alert and energetic, it keeps your heart and other muscles strong, it improves your self-esteem, and it's fun.

3. Staying in school, listening to other people's thoughts and opinions, experiencing new things, and being a leader contribute to intellectual wellness.

4. Your heart beats faster, you breathe faster, and you might have a burst of energy. You might become sad or depressed. You might have mood swings. You might be tense and angry. You might have headaches, back pain, and an upset stomach. You might have trouble sleeping, or trouble staying awake.

5. Relax. Sit or lie down in a quiet place. Breathe deeply. Do something you enjoy with people you like. Stretch your muscles to relieve tension, or be physically active. Prioritize. Accept what you cannot change. Have a positive attitude. Express your feelings. Take steps to avoid situations you know cause you stress. Talk to someone you trust.

6. Procrastination, interruptions, and not knowing what to do first are obstacles to time management.

7. Symptoms of depression include changes in the way you usually sleep or eat, extreme tiredness, aches and pains for no reason, a loss of interest in activities and friends, neglect of personal appearance, changes in personality, difficulty concentrating, and feelings of hopelessness, helplessness, and worthlessness.

8. Eating disorders are anorexia nervosa, bulimia nervosa, binge eating, and chronic dieting.

9. Risky behavior is any activity that puts your health and wellness in danger.

10. SADD—Students Against Destructive Decisions—helps teens cope with risky behavior.

Case Study

Amy is worried that her friend Patrice may have an eating disorder. Patrice eats a lot but is very thin and never seems to gain any weight. Patrice always goes to the bathroom right after a meal. Recently, Patrice spent the night at Amy's house. Before bed, they made a pan of brownies. In the morning, all of the brownies were gone. Patrice said Amy's mom must have eaten them, but Amy's mom doesn't eat chocolate.

- Do you think Amy is right to be worried?
- Do you think Amy should talk to Patrice about it?
- What reasons could there be for Patrice's behavior?

Sounding Off!

1. Do you think one area of wellness is more important than the others? Discuss your opinion with your classmates.

2. Have you heard of comfort food? It is food that makes you feel good, and think about happy times. Discuss the types of foods you like to eat when you are feeling stress.

FAQ

1. What are the six areas of wellness?
2. What are four benefits of being active?
3. What are four things that contribute to intellectual wellness?
4. What are seven signs of stress?
5. What is one thing you can do to cope with stress?
6. What are three obstacles to time management?
7. List five symptoms of depression.
8. List two eating disorders.
9. What is risky behavior?
10. Name one organization that helps teens cope with risky behavior.

In small groups, discuss the six areas of wellness and how they contribute to your overall well-being. When you are finished with your discussion, play the following game, with each group working together as a team to compete against the other teams:

The teacher will write one area of wellness on the board, and each team will write down as many ways as they can think of to make it part of their lives. After three minutes, each team will read its list. One point is awarded for a unique idea—an idea that none of the other teams thought of. You will repeat the activity for each area of wellness, then add up the points. The team with the most points—the most unique ideas—wins.

Hot Topics

Is there one area of your life where things are interfering with your wellness? Maybe you are overweight or don't get enough exercise. Maybe your friends aren't supportive. Maybe you feel unsafe in school.

Take this opportunity to write anonymously about the problem. Use a word processor so no one recognizes your handwriting. Be honest and open. Put the paper in the class Hot Topics box.

As a class, read the anonymous entries and discuss them.

Web Extra ▼

Use the Internet to locate the contact information for organizations that help teens in trouble. As a class, collect the information and make a booklet that students can use as a resource if they need information.

Problem Solver

Which is worse, smoking cigarettes or chewing tobacco? Divide the class in half and hold a debate. One half will research the problems caused by smoking, and the other will research the problems caused by chewing tobacco. Both sides should consider factors such as health and cost, as well as other possible concerns such as the effect on the environment. The two sides will debate the topic to decide which is worse.

If possible, invite another class to watch and judge the debate.

Team Players

Review the six areas of wellness: physical, emotional, social, personal, intellectual, and environmental. Stress to the class that all answers are good answers, and that they should think about their daily routine. Wellness is a part of their walk to school, how they interact with friends between classes, and what they eat at lunch, for example.

Hot Topics

Again, review the six areas of wellness (see *Team Players* above). Make sure students understand that they can turn in their papers anonymously. Encourage them to be open and honest about their problem.

Web Extra

Make sure all class members contribute to the booklet. The contact information should include the organization's address, phone number, e-mail address, Web address, and contact name as well as a description of the programs and services it offers.

Problem Solver

If possible, have another class watch the debate and then provide feedback to both sides. After the debate is over, discuss why there is such a strong campaign against tobacco in general.

Write Now

Review examples of roadblocks such as low self-esteem, inflexible standards, and risky decisions. During the class discussion, stress that students should not make judgments about others' road-blocks. Also, try to find connections between students' roadblocks.

Be Involved!

Make sure students are realistic in the goals they list. Remind them to consider time constraints as well as their larger goals. If students do have larger goals (such as making a varsity sports team in high school), have them determine short-term goals that can help them reach the end goal.

Social Networking

Students are asked to find resources available online and within their community that would be helpful to someone with an eating disorder. They are to prepare a list to give to the school nurse to share with other students.

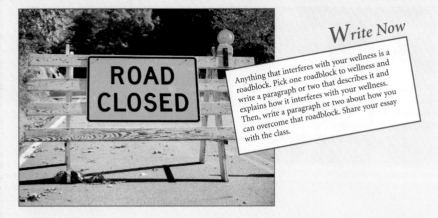

Write Now

Anything that interferes with your wellness is a roadblock. Pick one roadblock to wellness and write a paragraph or two that describes it and explains how it interferes with your wellness. Then, write a paragraph or two about how you can overcome that roadblock. Share your essay with the class.

Be Involved!

www.fcclainc.org

Make a table with four columns and 6 rows. Label column 1 Role, column 2 Goals, column 3 How Long?, and column 4 When?

In column 1, list areas of your life in which you can work for wellness, such as your family life, your school life, your social life, and your personal life. In column 2, list at least one specific goal for each area. For example, in your family life, you might want to fight less with your brother about watching television. In your personal life, you might want to improve your singing. In column 3, write how much time you want to spend on each goal. In column 4, write when during the week you will be able to spend the time. Use the table to schedule the time you need to achieve each goal. Keep a journal tracking your progress. If you achieve one goal, write a new one in its place.

Social Networking

There are many resources available online to provide people with eating disorders with information and support. There are also health centers that specialize in treating eating disorders.

Individually or in pairs, make a list of Web sites and other resources in your area that would be helpful to someone with an eating disorder. Write a brief description of each one to explain the service that it offers. Give the list to your school nurse to share with other students.

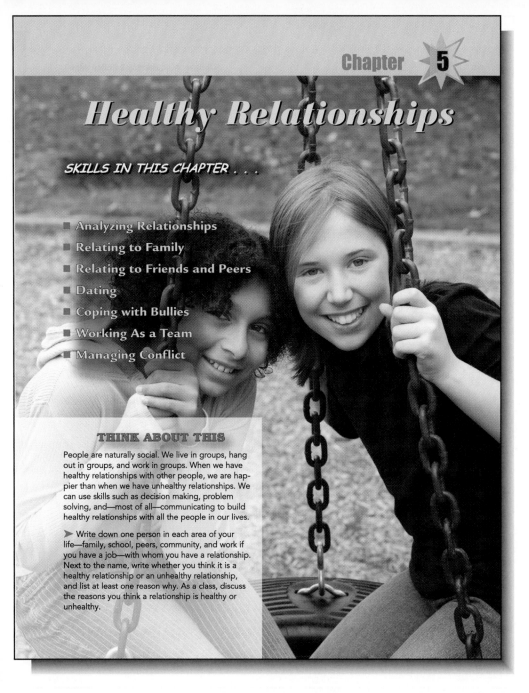

Chapter 5 Overview

This chapter examines the dynamics of relationships. Students learn about the types of relationships they develop at various stages in their lives and how these relationships affect their wellness and well-being.

Analyzing Relationships   Students explore the qualities of healthy relationships and unhealthy relationships. They also learn how relationships develop.

Relating to Family   Families play an integral role in an individual's ability to develop and maintain healthy relationships.

Relating to Friends and Peers   Students learn that the way they relate to friends and peers has a significant impact on their happiness and well-being. They explore what it takes to develop friendships and how to be a good friend.

Dating   The qualities of a healthy dating relationship are discussed. Students learn to distinguish between infatuations and true love and explore the challenges associated with dating.

Coping with Bullies   Students learn to identify bully behavior. Tips are provided on how to handle a bully and be assertive in a positive way.

Working As a Team   Students discover that being part of a team gives them access to valuable resources that would not be available if they work on their own.

Managing Conflict   Students learn that conflicts occur in all types of relationships. Taking positive steps to resolve conflicts will help you strengthen your relationships.

Focus and Engage

Bell-Ringer: Think About This

Students are asked to write down the name of one person with whom they have a relationship in each area of their life—home, school, peers, community, and work. Emphasize that the person does not have to be a friend or even someone they like. In fact, it will make for a better class discussion if they list a person or two about whom they do not feel strongly. They are to identify the relationship with each person as healthy or unhealthy and provide a reason why. Discuss the reasons students provide. What reason contributes most to a healthy relationship and which one to an unhealthy relationship?

Chapter 5

Healthy Relationships

SKILLS IN THIS CHAPTER . . .

- Analyzing Relationships
- Relating to Family
- Relating to Friends and Peers
- Dating
- Coping with Bullies
- Working As a Team
- Managing Conflict

THINK ABOUT THIS

People are naturally social. We live in groups, hang out in groups, and work in groups. When we have healthy relationships with other people, we are happier than when we have unhealthy relationships. We can use skills such as decision making, problem solving, and—most of all—communicating to build healthy relationships with all the people in our lives.

➤ Write down one person in each area of your life—family, school, peers, community, and work if you have a job—with whom you have a relationship. Next to the name, write whether you think it is a healthy relationship or an unhealthy relationship, and list at least one reason why. As a class, discuss the reasons you think a relationship is healthy or unhealthy.

ADVANCE PREPARATION	
Review	*Life Skills for the 21st Century* textbook, Chapter 5.
Prepare	Paper and pencil for some activities.
	Building blocks (optional).
	Box labeled "Hot Topics."

CUSTOMIZED INSTRUCTION OVERVIEW				
Less Advanced Students	More Advanced Students	ESOL Students	Special Needs Students	At-Risk Students
Pages 84, 88, 101, 103	Pages 91, 100, 107	Pages 95, 102	Pages 84, 88, 101, 103	Pages 86, 97, 105, 107

Introduce the Section

In this section, students identify different types of relationships they have with others and explore the qualities that characterize healthy and unhealthy relationships.

Vocabulary

Proximity relationship: Relationships with the people who are nearby.

Relationship: A connection between two or more people, especially as regards the way they behave toward and feel about one another.

Figure Focus

People in healthy relationships often have many things in common. They both like sports, or they both like going to movies, or they both enjoy art. Ask students to consider the things they have in common with one of their close friends.

Reinforce and Review

In Chapter 3, students learned the difference between the people who play a personal role vs. a functional role in their lives. Remind students that those people who fill a personal role contribute significantly in some way to their well-being. Those people who play a functional role may help students meet basic needs, but they probably do not have an impact on students' well-being.

Analyzing Relationships

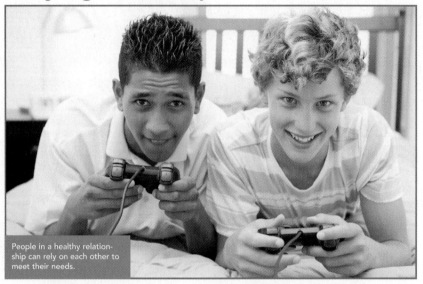

People in a healthy relationship can rely on each other to meet their needs.

You have a **relationship** with anyone you interact with, in all five areas of your life—home, school, peers, work, and community. It might be a brief or passing relationship, such as with a stranger who bumps into you and apologizes. It might be functional or recurring, such as with the mail carrier who delivers your mail. It might be personal, such as with your family and friends.

- If the relationship is satisfying and contributes to your well-being, it is healthy—or positive.
- If the relationship is unsatisfying and interferes with your well-being, it is unhealthy—or negative.

Relationships are important in every role of your life and at every stage of your life. They help you share and exchange resources and achieve common goals.

Building Relationships

Some relationships are part of your life whether you like it or not. For example, you don't get to decide who will be your brothers and sisters. As you get older, you get to choose your relationships. You can choose your friends, as well as your employer, your doctor, and your banker.

When you are young, you have **proximity relationships**—which are relationships with the people who are nearby. You might hang around with the kids who live next door. Your first employer might be the woman upstairs who asks you to walk her dog.

As you get older, you can develop personal relationships with people who have something in common with you. You might play on the same team, attend the same after-school program, or have the same culture.

You develop functional relationships with people who can meet your needs and who need something from you in return. You might start working at the local market so you can earn more money. You might volunteer for a local veterinarian because you enjoy helping animals.

Customized Instruction: Less Advanced/Special Needs Students

Have students create a table with three columns. They should write "Personal" in column 1, "Functional" in column 2, and "Proximity" in column 3. Have them write the names of people with whom they have relationships in the appropriate column. Encourage them to list all the people with whom they interact in a typical day; for example, family members, neighbors, friends, and teachers and school staff.

A Two-Way Street

All relationships are a two-way street. That means both people involved share the responsibility of keeping the relationship healthy.

When you have a relationship with someone, you exchange resources. That means you give and take. In personal relationships, you exchange resources such as time, attention, love, respect, and support. In functional relationships, you exchange resources such as time, attention, and respect. You might also exchange money or other items. When the exchange is unequal—you are either giving or receiving more than the other person—it may lead to conflict.

- If you only talk to a friend when you make the call or send the text, you are giving more to the relationship than you are receiving.
- If you don't have time to help your sister with her homework, but you expect her to help you do the dishes or clean your room, you are receiving more from the relationship than you are giving.

"We fight all the time. Maybe it's time to find a new friend."

Qualities of a Healthy Relationship

A functional relationship is healthy if both parties give and receive what they need. Your guidance counselor at school helps you find clubs and sports that fit your interests and life style. In return, you are a positive, active member of the school community.

A personal relationship is a bit more complicated, because emotions are involved. Both people care about each other. They support and depend on each other. They help meet each other's needs.

A healthy personal relationship has these important characteristics:

- Respect
- Honesty
- Open communication
- Trust
- Responsibility

Communicate, Communicate, Communicate!

Effective communication is the foundation for a healthy relationship. When you communicate openly and honestly, you understand each other. You avoid misunderstandings. (For a reminder about effective communications, look back at Chapter 2.)

- When you listen and respond to someone, you show respect.
- When you share your thoughts and feelings, you show trust.
- When you **honor a confidence**—listen to someone's private thoughts without telling anyone else—you show that you are trustworthy.
- When you are willing to discuss differences, you show openness.

Using communication to build a healthy relationship helps you enjoy being with other people. You are more likely to be comfortable and happy when you are with people who you respect and trust, and who respect and trust you.

Myth A healthy relationship will last forever.

Truth Sometimes even the best relationships come to an end. People change. Circumstances change. One person might move away. Both people might develop conflicting values. It is sad when a relationship ends, but we can use our understanding of what made the relationship so good to build new, healthy relationships.

Unhealthy Relationships

Relationships that are full of conflict or are not satisfying are unhealthy, or *dysfunctional*—not working correctly. Ways to tell if a relationship is unhealthy include:

✔ You are unhappy in the relationship.
✔ You feel like you cannot be yourself.
✔ You are afraid the other person will end the relationship.
✔ You are afraid the other person will hurt you—physically or emotionally.
✔ You do not trust the other person.
✔ You are dishonest.
✔ You cannot or will not talk about your feelings.
✔ You do not respect the other person.
✔ You fight a lot.

Unhealthy Relationships

Ask students to consider if they are currently involved in an unhealthy or dysfunctional relationship. Offer suggestions on how to end such a relationship. For example:

- Make sure the person is exhibiting characteristics that you find unhealthy or offensive and that her behavior is not something temporary, caused by trauma or some other serious event in her personal life.

- Determine if the other person is aware of a problem in the friendship.

- Be direct. Avoiding phone calls and contact with the person might send the message you want, but being upfront with him will help avoid bad feelings that could have lasting effects on both of you.

Discuss

Engage students in a conversation about what makes for a healthy relationship. Discuss the characteristics listed in the text:

- **Respect:** Feeling or attitude of admiration toward another person.
- **Trust:** Firm belief in the honesty and reliability of another person.
- **Honesty:** Condition of being fair, truthful, and morally upright.
- **Responsibility:** State of being accountable to somebody or for something.
- **Open communication:** Uninhibited exchange of information between people.

Ask students if they think they can have a healthy relationship with someone if one of these characteristics is missing.

Vocabulary

Dysfunctional relationship: Relationship that is full of conflict or is not satisfactory.
Honor a confidence: Listen to someone's private thoughts without telling anyone else.

Myth/Truth

Ask students to share reasons why a relationship of their own might have ended. Was there something they could have done to prevent it from ending?

Figure Focus

It's not unusual for friends to argue with each other. But at what point does a healthy relationship turn unhealthy? Tell students to consider the following signs, which might mean their friendship is coming to an end:

- Distant behavior and a lack of interest in staying in touch with each other.
- Sense of competition or jealousy between the two of you.
- Topic of conversation is never focused on you.
- Feeling of anger after seeing or talking with each other.
- Feeling of relief that your conversation or encounter with the person is over with.

Introduce the Section

This section discusses the relationships we have with members of our family. Students learn the importance of nurturing family relationships and how these relationships affect the way they get along with others in general.

Figure Focus

Ask students to comment on the things their families teach them about relationships. For example, when you are part of a family, you learn how to share, which is vital to any healthy relationship. You learn the importance of responsibility. You rely on your family to fill basic and other needs, and they rely on you for the same.

Vocabulary

Extended family: Grandparents, aunts, uncles, and cousins.

STUDENT ACTIVITY

Have students think about their extended family. An extended family is a network of relatives that makes up a close-knit community. Have students write a paragraph about the people who make up their extended family. Ask them to describe the things that extended family members do for them and which they might do for others.

Relating to Family

You learn a lot about relationships from your family.

The relationships you build with your family may be the most important throughout your life. They are the people who are with you at every stage. They know you better than anyone else. You share experiences, culture, and history that people outside your family may not understand.

- Parents meet your basic needs by providing food, shelter, security, and love. They know you from the beginning and understand your values, wants, and goals.
- You have unique bonds with your brothers and sisters that develop from sharing a family and a home.
- Your **extended family**—grandparents, aunts, uncles, and cousins—provide acceptance and support.

Your family relationships are the first relationships you have. From them, you learn about relationships in general and how to get along with others.

Brothers and Sisters

Your siblings are your first friends and playmates. When you have a healthy relationship with your brothers and sisters, you can fight without hurting each other. You can share resources, compromise, and even compete without becoming angry or hateful. A healthy relationship with your siblings can last your whole life.

When you have siblings:

- You learn how to share the bathroom in the morning and the computer at night.
- You compromise about the television shows you watch.
- You adjust your schedule of activities for each other.
- You compete to see who finishes chores faster.
- You can share clothes, books, and music.

When you trust your siblings, you can talk openly and honestly about issues that other people might not understand, including your relationship with your parents.

Customized Instruction: At-Risk Students

On a piece of paper, have students list some facts about their parents or guardians. Start with the basics, such as their full name, age, date of birth, names of parents and siblings, and their job. Then, have students list additional things about them, such as their favorite color or food, hobbies, and the names of their close friends. If students struggle with this, encourage them to get the information from their parents and bring it back to class.

Your Parents

Your first relationship is with your parents. When you have a healthy relationship with your parents, you know you are loved. You can talk about your goals and your problems, and you can ask them for advice. You know that even when you make a poor decision, they will help you find a way to move forward.

When you are a baby, your parents take care of you. You depend on them to make sure you have the basic things you need. By providing for you and loving you, they teach you how to trust other people. You learn about values and standards from your parents. You learn about your culture and traditions.

As you get older, your relationship with your parents changes. They are still an important part of your life, but now you have more resources. You are more independent, but your parents are still responsible for your care and your welfare.

- You have friends who care about you.
- You may have your own money to buy things.
- You have activities that don't include your parents, such as school clubs and teams.
- Your parents still provide for your basic needs, and set the rules for your family life.

Your parents expect you to spend every Friday night at home with them. Your friend invites you over to play video games. You assume your parents will say no, and never even ask them if you can go. Instead, you spend Friday night sulking angrily in your room. What could you have done differently?

"He might yell, and I might be grounded, but I know he loves me, doesn't he?"

MONEY MADNE$$

> **Y**our family is going bowling on Saturday afternoon. It costs $4.00 per person for each game and $2.00 to rent shoes. Drinks cost $1.50, and snacks such as popcorn, chips, or cookies cost $2.50.
>
> There are four people in your family. You all need to rent shoes. How much will it cost for the family to bowl four games? How much if you each have a drink and a snack?

I'm an Only Child

Only children have no brothers or sisters. They tend to receive a lot of attention from their parents. As a result, they may develop a strong sense of self and confidence. Alternatively, they may be lonely without siblings around and may relate better to adults than to peers. What if you are an only child?

★ *You do not have to modify your schedule to suit your siblings.*

★ *You may build strong bonds with peers to satisfy your need for friendship and acceptance.*

★ *You may be bored without other children in your home.*

★ *You may develop a close relationship with your parents.*

If you are a "one and only," do you wish you had siblings? If you have siblings, do you wish you were an only child? Why?

Discuss

Ask students to discuss the different roles their parents fill during the various stages of their life. For example, they fill the role of teacher and educator in all stages of childhood and even beyond. Do they also fill the role of friend, buddy, or confidante? What about disciplinarian?

In the last paragraph of the text, students are to consider a parent-child scenario. What is the danger of making assumptions about people? Explain that even the smallest incorrect assumptions can lead to major errors in judgment. For example, you assume your parents will say no when you ask them to go to your friend's house because you have always been expected to be at home on Friday night. That may lead you to form the opinion that your parents are unfair. But what if your parents assume you *want* to stay at home on Friday nights? By making assumptions, you and your parents have both created a communication barrier.

Figure Focus

Ask students to consider how a lack of discipline can affect a child's behavior. Many studies suggest that the biggest reason why kids misbehave is because their parents are unable to say "no" and constantly give in to their kids' demands.

MONEY MADNE$$

Students should understand that they will need to first multiply the cost of shoes, the cost of a game, the cost of a drink, and the cost of a snack by 4. So, it will cost $8 for shoes ($2.00 × 4 = $8.00) and $16 for four games ($4.00 × 4 = $16.00), so the total cost to bowl is $24. If each person gets a drink, that's an additional $6 ($1.50 × 4 = $6.00), plus another $10 for snacks ($2.50 × 4 = $10.00), so $16 more added on to the $24 for bowling equals $40.

I'm an Only Child

Determine who in the class is an only child. Encourage these students to discuss the advantages and disadvantages of being an only child. Ask the other students to comment on why they might want to be an only child.

Vocabulary

Immediate or nuclear family: Your parents and siblings.

Expecting Too Much

Ask students to discuss the resources that characterize a relationship. Remind them of basic human resources, such as knowledge, talent, physical and mental abilities, time, energy, and even personal character. A positive attitude and high self-esteem determine in large part your personal character. If you possess confidence and have a positive attitude, you have valuable resources to contribute to your relationships.

Figure Focus

Grandparents can often be instrumental in building the self-esteem of their grandchildren. Raising their own children has given them the experience and wisdom to recognize a child's strengths and weaknesses, maybe even quicker than the child's parents. Plus, grandparents are often retired and have the quality time available to spend with grandchildren, whereas parents are pulled in different directions by their jobs and other responsibilities.

 Extended Families Around the World

Students are to research cultures where extended families live in the same household. Some examples are Africans, Koreans, Middle Easterners, Jewish families of central Europe, Latin Americans, Indians, East Asians, and Pacific Islanders. Some benefits might be the delegation of duties, where everyone has responsibilities to fulfill, and the large network of human resources. Some drawbacks are less privacy and fewer non-human resources to spread around.

Expecting Too Much

Expecting too much means you are taking more than you are giving. You are too needy—you need more resources than you give in order to feel satisfied with the relationship. The other person might get tired of it, or annoyed, causing conflict.

- You expect others to listen to you complain all the time.
- You expect others to provide constant reassurance about your appearance, personality, and abilities.
- You expect others to put up with you even when you are dishonest, irresponsible, or disrespectful.
- You expect others to share your values and standards.
- You expect to exchange resources equally, and to give as much as you receive.

How can a positive attitude and high self-esteem help you build healthy relationships?

Extended Family

Your parents and siblings are part of your **immediate**, or **nuclear**, **family**. Your aunts, uncles, cousins, and grandparents are your extended family.

Members of your extended family can be a great source of support throughout your life. A healthy relationship with grandparents, aunts, and uncles provides unconditional love. While they care for you and your welfare, they are not responsible for you in the same way as your parents. They have more freedom to enjoy just spending time with you.

A healthy relationship with cousins can also be very satisfying. Cousins are usually close to your age, like brothers and sisters. You probably don't live together, which eliminates many of the things that cause conflict between you and your siblings.

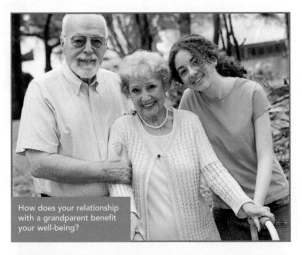

How does your relationship with a grandparent benefit your well-being?

 Extended Families Around the World

In the United States, the basic family unit is the immediate or nuclear family. In some cultures and communities, it is common for members of extended families to live in the same house. For example, in parts of Asia, children, parents, grandparents, uncles, aunts, and cousins often live in the same household.

Use books or the Internet to learn more about cultures where extended families live in the same household. What are the benefits? What are the drawbacks? Would you like to live with your extended family?

Customized Instruction: Less Advanced/Special Needs Students

Students will create a family tree. They should write their name, the name(s) of their parent(s), and any siblings on the trunk of the tree. They can draw branches to one side that represent their mother's parents and siblings and branches to the other side that represent their father's parents and siblings. From each parent's siblings, they should draw branches for their children (which represent the student's cousins). Reassure students that family trees can be simple, with only a few branches, or more elaborate, with many branches.

Blended Families

A **blended family** includes members originally from two separate families. For example, when people who already have children get married, they create a blended family. Since more than 50% of marriages in the United States end in divorce, there are a lot of blended families.

- If your mother marries a man who is not your father, he becomes your stepfather.
- If your father marries a woman who is not your mother, she becomes your stepmother.
- If the step-parent has children, they become your step-siblings.
- If either parent has a baby with the new spouse, the baby is your half-sibling.

Relationships in a blended family can be complicated. You find yourself in new and unfamiliar roles, with new and unfamiliar responsibilities. Rules that worked for the old family might not work for the new, blended family. For example, your family might have watched television during dinner, but the other family might have kept the television off.

Are you part of a blended family? What do you think are the advantages and disadvantages?

Test **IT** Yourself!

Cooking and eating together is a fun way to spend time with family and friends. Instead of buying salsa to serve the next time your friends come over to play video games, try making it yourself.

You will need:

3 cups of tomatoes, seeds removed and the tomatoes diced
¾ cup of onion, minced
½ cup green pepper, diced
2 cloves of garlic, minced
1 tablespoon cilantro, chopped
1 teaspoon oregano, chopped
The juice from two limes
1 jalapeno, seeds removed and the pepper minced
2 tablespoons olive oil
½ teaspoon ground black pepper
1 teaspoon salt

To make the salsa:

1. Combine all ingredients.
2. Adjust seasonings to taste.
3. Serve with chips and guacamole.

Roadblocks to Blended Relationships

A negative attitude, inflexible standards, and holding on to bad feelings might interfere with your personal and emotional well-being, and get in the way of building relationships in a blended family.

- 👎 Feeling resentment toward a stepparent
- 👎 Being jealous of a stepsibling
- 👎 Being angry that one parent is being replaced
- 👎 Feeling guilty about liking the stepparent
- 👎 Refusing to accept new rules
- 👎 Refusing to communicate with new family members
- 👍 Accepting a situation that you cannot change, and making an effort to find common bonds with your new family

The choice to create the blended family was not yours. Your choice is whether you are going to move forward in a positive way, doing your best to achieve wellness in your life. What can you do to build healthy relationships in a blended family?

Vocabulary

Blended family: Includes members originally from two separate families.

Discuss

Ask students to comment on how a blended family can affect their role at home. If they were once the oldest child in the family and now have an older sibling, then they now take on the new role of younger brother or sister. What changes in their responsibilities might result from this?

Roadblocks to Blended Relationships

Some studies indicate that at least one-third of all children in the United States will be part of a blended family before the age of 18. Ask for a show of hands of students who are part of a blended family. Ask students for suggestions on what they can do to build healthy relationships in a blended family. Some examples are:

- Making an attempt to find things in common with stepsiblings.
- Avoiding the temptation to make comparisons between their biological parent and stepparent.
- Actively participating in family activities.

Test **IT** Yourself!

Ask students to consider their family's favorite meal. Then, ask them to plan a week's worth of meals for their families. They should write down what each meal will include. Stress the importance of well-balanced meals, with food from different food groups. Encourage them to share the list of meals with their families and get their feedback. Will they prepare any of the meals?

Also, point out that many studies have been conducted on the benefits of family dinners on kids' behavior. According to one study, children and teens who have frequent family dinners are at 70 percent lower risk for substance abuse and likelier to get better grades in school than those who have fewer than three family dinners per week.

Introduce the Section

In this section, students explore the types of relationships they have with friends and peers. The text discusses the qualities of a good friend, and what differentiates a friend from a peer.

Figure Focus

Talk with students about the things they have in common with their friends. Do they play on the same sports teams, join the same clubs, and like the same music? Then, discuss the differences between them and their friends. Do they feel the same about education? What about risky behaviors?

Vocabulary

Socializing: Getting together with people to have fun and relax.

Relating to Friends and Peers

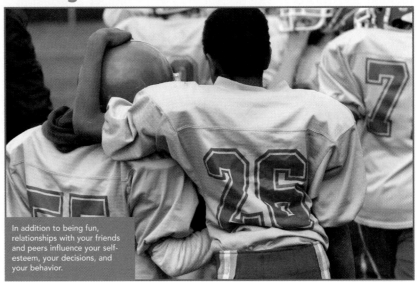

In addition to being fun, relationships with your friends and peers influence your self-esteem, your decisions, and your behavior.

At school you have relationships with peers, friends, teachers, school staff, and administrators. Some of these relationships are personal, such as with your friends. Some are functional, such as with a cafeteria worker.

You spend a lot of time at school. If you have healthy relationships with the people who are there, you are more likely to enjoy school. You look forward to seeing your friends. You have fun in class. Your teachers are helpful, concerned for your well-being, and supportive.

Healthy school relationships contribute to all areas of your wellness: social, personal, emotional, physical, intellectual, and environmental.

A Social Life

Socializing is when you get together with people to have fun and relax. You might sit around and talk, play a game, or participate in almost any activity that you all enjoy.

You can socialize with friends, peers, family members, co-workers, classmates, and neighbors. When you socialize, you learn about each other's character qualities. You discover the interests that you have in common and the things that make you different. Socializing is a good way to get to know new people and to keep up with those who are already part of your life.

Many people socialize online in social networking sites, forums, and chat rooms. These sites let you communicate with family and friends and meet new people who have similar interests.

Keep in mind that you do not always know the truth about people you socialize with online. They can be dishonest about their age, name, interests, and gender. Stay safe! Avoid giving out personal information or agreeing to meet someone by yourself. (Chapter 4 has more information about the risks of Cyberspace.)

Stay in School

Peer pressure can heavily impact students in middle school through high school. At those levels, students are socializing on a more regular basis and are gaining and asserting their independence. In fact, some experts believe that an adolescent's desire to be accepted by his or her peers might be the single biggest influence on behavior at that stage of his or her life. For this reason, peer pressure can be a contributing factor to a student's decision to drop out of school.

If a student is bullied or ostracized by peers, then he might decide to remove himself from such an environment. On the other hand, if dropping out of school is deemed "cool" by certain peers, then a student might be tempted to do so just to fit in with the crowd.

Suggest to students ways to handle this type of negative peer pressure:

■ Avoid situations that make you uncomfortable.

■ Avoid relationships with people who engage in risky behavior, such as dropping out of school.

■ Think about the consequences. High school dropouts make less, are more likely to end up incarcerated, and suffer more health problems than those who graduate.

■ Don't change your behavior, values, or standards just to fit in with a particular group.

Your Peers

Everyone wants to fit in. In fact, being part of a group is a basic need for most people. That's why relationships with people your own age are so important.

You relate to your peers in many ways. You share common bonds in school and out. Even if you are not friends, you may be:

- *Teammates.* You practice and compete together. You encourage each other to set and achieve goals.
- *Classmates.* You might not even know the name of the kid who has the locker next to yours, but you interact daily as you respect each other's personal space, or raise your eyebrows in a greeting.
- *Rivals.* You compete against each other academically, socially, and athletically. You might want the same spot in band, the same solo in chorus, or the same position on the baseball team. You might both want to have the highest grades in the class. You spur each other to do your best.
- *Lab partners.* You follow rules and procedures together. You share the responsibility for experiments and lab reports.

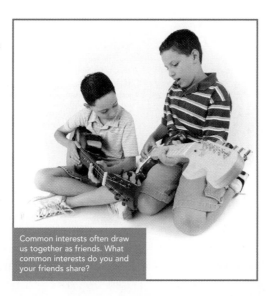

Common interests often draw us together as friends. What common interests do you and your friends share?

Developing Friendships

Your friends are different from your peers. You choose your friends based on shared interests and values. You are comfortable with them; they understand you, and you understand them. You like them, and they like you. You belong together. Friends make your life better.

Ways to meet people and develop friendships include:

- Socializing
- Asking people about their interests
- Trying new activities
- Volunteering
- Being friendly
- Being yourself
- Having fun

When you find ways to meet new people and develop new friendships, you contribute to your social wellness.

" When you're going through the good times, there are tons of people there. When you go through bad times, some people fade. Your friends are there with you every step of the way. "

— *Michael Phelps, U.S. Olympic Gold Medalist*

Discuss

Explain to students the difference between friends and peers. A peer is a person of equal standing with another. A peer is not always your friend. For example, in a speech competition, you will debate with your peers from other schools. And a friend is not always your peer. For example, you and your older neighbor are friends, but she is not your peer. In most instances, your friends are your peers. You live in the same community, go to the same school, and share other common bonds.

Figure Focus

Students are asked to consider the common interests they share with their friends. Ask them to comment also on the differences between them and their friends.

"Quote Box"

Ask students if they agree with the quote from Michael Phelps. Can they think of an instance when a friend disappointed them during a particularly bad time?

Michael Phelps was born in 1985 and won a record-breaking eight gold medals in swimming in the 2008 Summer Olympics in Beijing.

Customized Instruction: More Advanced Students

Have students develop a skit on how to make friends. Give them time to plan and assign roles. Have them perform the skit for the class. Some things their skit should touch upon include: 1) making eye contact and smiling when someone looks at you; 2) practicing what you will say before you approach someone; 3) checking that your appearance is neat and clean; 4) determining beforehand what you might have in common with others; and 5) speaking in a positive way without bragging about yourself.

Qualities of a Good Friend

Have students give an example of how friends exhibit each of the qualities listed. For example, a friend who gives up going out to a movie because you would rather stay home and rent a video is flexible. A friend who doesn't hold a grudge against you when you forget to call is forgiving.

Teaching Tips

Make sure students understand the difference between being a friend and being friendly. Being a friend means you are emotionally close to someone and trust each other. Being a friendly person means you are outgoing, sociable, and pleasant. Ask students to think of the people who are friendly to them in school.

Discuss

Discuss the concept of "best friend." Do the majority of students have a best friend, or do they have a number of good friends, all of whom they are equally fond of? What are the advantages and disadvantages of each situation?

Figure Focus

Emphasize that the middle and high school years are a period of change and adjustment for most adolescents. They might be starting their middle school or high school years in a new school. They are given more opportunities to join school clubs, organizations, and sports teams where they meet new people who obviously have something in common with them. When friendships wane because two people discover they don't have that much in common anymore, they can still remain friendly toward each other.

Vocabulary

Peer pressure: When your peers and friends influence you to do something.

Qualities of a Good Friend

In order to have good friends, you need to be a good friend. A good friend is:

✔ Fun
✔ Honest
✔ A good listener
✔ Flexible
✔ Supportive
✔ Trustworthy
✔ Loyal
✔ Understanding
✔ Forgiving

Being a Friend vs. Being Friendly

Being a friend is an honor and a responsibility. It's a bond between two people who trust, respect, and enjoy each other.

Being friendly is good manners. It's smiling at a cashier in the supermarket or holding the door for the person behind you.

There's no reason to try to be friends with everyone you meet, but there is good reason to be friendly. Friendly people usually have a positive attitude. They are happier than unfriendly people, and they are often treated better. There are even studies that show friendly people earn more money in the same jobs as unfriendly people. A friendly waitress is likely to get a bigger tip than an unfriendly waitress. Likewise, a friendly customer is likely to receive better service.

When Friendships End

Some friendships last a lifetime. Some don't. You have changed since elementary school. You might find that you have less in common with your friends than you used to. You might like to do different things on weekends or after school.

The friendship might not have to end. It might just change. Someone who was your best friend might become a good friend. You might not like to do the same things, but you still might trust each other and be able to talk about things that are important. Instead of spending every afternoon together, you might just send text messages, and get together once a month.

You feel as if you have outgrown an old friend, but she doesn't realize you have changed. Can you stay friends?

If you feel uncomfortable, though, you might have to let the friendship end. Your friend might be doing things that conflict with your values, or spending time with people you don't like. You might be putting more time or effort into the friendship than he is, making you feel hurt or resentful.

When a friendship stops being fun or when it makes you feel bad, it's time to let it go. Talk to your friend and explain how you feel. He or she might feel the same way.

Peer Pressure

Peer pressure is when your peers and friends influence you to do something. They might actively try to convince you to do something you haven't done before, or to stop doing something you are doing. For example, a friend who is a vegetarian might try to convince you to stop eating meat.

Or, you might decide to do something or stop doing something because of what you think your peers might think. For example, you might start drinking soda instead of juice because everyone else drinks soda. No one actually told you to drink soda, but you think you will fit in better and they will like you more if you do.

- Peer pressure can be positive if it contributes to your well-being and does not interfere with your values, standards, and beliefs. For example, a friend might love mountain biking, so you try mountain biking and find out you love it, too.
- Peer pressure can be negative. It might interfere with your well-being or go against your values. For example, you might know staying out past curfew is wrong, but your friends convince you to do it anyway.

Recognizing peer pressure can help you make healthy choices. You can decide for yourself whether it is positive or negative and whether you want it to influence you.

Peers away from School

You have relationships with peers outside of school, too. You know them from after school activities, the neighborhood, or the nursing home where you volunteer. They might be the sons and daughters of your parents' friends, who live in a different town. Some peers you relate to away from school include:

- *Co-workers.* You volunteer together or work for the same employer. You share an interest outside of school.
- *Neighbors.* You wait at the same bus stop, walk the same route to school, and play in the same streets.
- *Summer friends.* You go to the same summer camp or summer school. You go to the same place for vacations.

Your relationships with these groups give you opportunities to test how different people react to your personal qualities, values, and standards. When you are not thinking about the influence or attitudes of your school and friends and peers, you express yourself in a way that might be different from how you are at school. For example, your school friends might not know you like to go hiking or canoeing, but your summer friends do.

Good, Better, Best Friends

Not everyone has to be your best friend, and your friends don't have to be friends with each other. What if you have different friends for different situations?

★ *Your best friend might be the person you like to be with most of the time. You trust each other, share secrets, and have fun.*

★ *Your good friends might be a group you like to hang around with on weekends.*

★ *Your casual friends might be classmates or teammates. They might be the people you are comfortable sitting with on the bus or in the cafeteria when your good friends aren't around.*

★ *You might have friends you see only in the summer or during school vacations.*

★ *You might have neighborhood friends who go to different schools.*

★ *You might have friends in the band and friends on the soccer team.*

Having different types of friends is one way you learn about other people. What problems might come from having different friends who don't like each other?

Discuss

Discuss with students some of the grave consequences of caving in to peer pressure using examples such as these:

- Your friend found a lighter and talks you into experimenting with setting things on fire. You experiment with different things over a trash can and when you are done, you simply walk away. You don't get far when you notice that the trash can is on fire. If you call for help, you might get in trouble. If you don't, the fire could spread to nearby houses, and people could be inside.

- You go to a party and everyone there is drinking beer. You know they shouldn't be, but you don't want to be labeled a "goody two-shoes," so you have a beer. Then, you have another. The alcohol slows down your ability to think clearly and make decisions, so you accept a ride home from another partygoer. The driver gets pulled over for crossing the center line and is eventually given a DUI (driving under the influence). You are charged with underage drinking, fined $500, and ordered to attend an alcohol education program.

- A couple of your friends have decided they don't like the new kid in school. They ridicule and bully him at every opportunity. They pressure you into going along with the pranks. One day, they decide to sabotage the brakes on the student's bicycle. He's going down a hill toward an intersection, can't stop, gets hit by a car, and ends up in the hospital with serious injuries. Criminal charges are brought against you and your friends, and the student's parents have filed lawsuits against all your families.

Good, Better, Best Friends

Students are asked to consider what problems might arise from having different friends who don't like each other. One problem is that you have to avoid doing things in which all three of you would be together, such as a school basketball game. Another problem is that you might be forced to choose between the friends. At the school basketball game, which one will you sit with?

Introduce the Section

This section covers the topic of dating. Students learn to identify the different types of attractions that exist between two people and determine what makes for a healthy and unhealthy romantic relationship.

Vocabulary

Dating: When you socialize with another person as a couple.

Romantic: Relationship that is based on love.

Figure Focus

How do kids in your class view the idea of dating? Do they go out on dates or do they tend to be more casual about it and just "hang out"? Ask them what the difference is between dating and hanging out. Most will say that dating is more serious than hanging out and involves more of a commitment on two fronts: financially, because it usually means you have to spend money, and personally, because you tend to put yourself in a one-on-one situation with another person.

Discuss

Have students consider how they learn to date. Do they learn in school? From friends? From their parents? Explain that while dating might cause jitters or good stress, it really should be as natural and comfortable as other healthy relationships the student forms. If the qualities of respect, trust, honesty, responsibility, and communication are missing, then the dating relationship may be problematic.

Dating

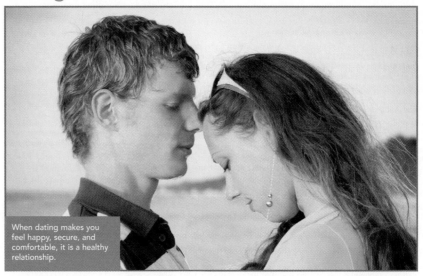

When dating makes you feel happy, secure, and comfortable, it is a healthy relationship.

Dating is when you socialize with another person as a couple. You might spend time alone, just the two of you, or with other couples. When you start dating, it is so you can get to know each other better without being distracted by other people. Once you know each other well, and the relationship becomes **romantic**, or based on love, you date because it gives you the chance to be alone and focus on each other.

The qualities of a healthy dating relationship are the same as for other relationships.

- Respect
- Trust
- Honesty
- Responsibility
- Communication

A healthy dating relationship is good for your self-esteem and your well-being. It helps you learn how to communicate with a partner and how to cope with conflict.

An unhealthy dating relationship can be risky. It can cause stress, depression, and even violence.

Why Do People Date?

Usually, people start dating because they feel an attraction to each other. The attraction could come from many things.

- It might be based on common interests: You might listen to the same music.
- It might be based on common values: You might volunteer at the same food pantry.
- It might be based on common goals: You might both want to become firefighters.

When you both feel an attraction and want to get to know each other better, you go on a date. If you have fun, you go on another date.

What Is Dating?

Dating means different things to different people. Sometimes "**going out**" is really going out—to the movies, for a meal, or to the mall. It also might mean that you talk on the phone, sit together on the bus, and exchange text messages on a regular basis.

Some people enjoy **casual dating**, which means you spend time one-on-one with a lot of different people. Casual dating gives you a chance to get to know more than one person. For example, you might like to skateboard with one person, but you like to eat lunch with someone else.

When two people decide they like each other better than they like anyone else, they might choose to be **exclusive**. Exclusive dating means you make a commitment to your partner and both agree not to date anyone else. It does not mean you cannot have other friends.

Is It a Crush, Infatuation, or True Love?

Dating someone new—or even just thinking about it—is very exciting. It usually comes with strong feelings that are both physical and emotional. Your heart might beat faster, you might sweat, and you might even feel a little lightheaded. You might be embarrassed.

You might be **infatuated**, or have a **crush**. When you are infatuated, you are not realistic. You see only the positive qualities of the other person, instead of *all* the qualities. You are subjective about your relationship and cannot be objective. Infatuation can be fun, but it usually doesn't last very long.

You might be in love. Love is hard to explain. Loving your family is not the same as loving a boyfriend or girlfriend. Loving a pet is not the same as loving ice cream.

Love is a strong, positive emotion. In general, it means you feel an attachment or commitment to someone. It means you care deeply about someone's well-being. Sometimes love starts out as infatuation. Sometimes it starts out as friendship. Love lasts a long time.

TECH CONNECT

The Internet provides many ways for people to meet and socialize online.

■ Social networking sites let you post information and pictures about yourself and your friends. You can join groups, exchange messages, and stay in touch.

■ Chat rooms let you discuss topics with people who have similar interests.

■ Text messaging keeps you in constant contact with friends and family.

■ RSS feeds lets you broadcast your thoughts and actions, as well as follow the thoughts and actions of others.

How can socializing online contribute to a healthy relationship? How can it create conflict?

When Should You Date?

There is no set age when people start to date. Some families have rules about how old you should be; some cultures have different dating traditions. What do you think are good reasons for starting to date?

👎 Everyone else is dating.

👎 Someone asks you on a date.

👎 You want to be the first one in your group to date.

👎 Your mother thinks it would be cute.

👍 You met someone special you would like to get to know better.

Only you know for sure when you are ready to date. You might start thinking about dating before you really want to date. You might talk about it with your friends, even pointing out who you might date.

You mention to a friend you think a classmate is cute. He tells someone else, and soon the whole school is saying you want to date that person. Should you ask that person out?

Vocabulary

Casual dating: Form of dating in which you spend time one-on-one with more than one person.

Exclusive dating: Form of dating in which two people make a commitment to each other and agree not to date anyone else.

Going out: Form of dating that involves literally going out together away from the home, or doing something together on a regular basis.

Infatuated or crush: To behave irrationally as a result of passion.

When Should You Date?

Ask students for their opinions on a good age to start dating. Have their parents set an age at which they can start dating? Do they think it is wise to start with one-on-one dates, or is a group date the best way to start? Point out to students that studies indicate the younger kids are when they begin dating, the younger they are when they start kissing and experimenting with sex. This, in turn, increases the likelihood of more teen pregnancies and more kids contracting STDs.

TECH CONNECT

Students are asked for their feedback on how socializing online can contribute to a healthy relationship and how it can create conflict. Some ideas on how it contributes are:

■ Many users find they can be more honest and open about their feelings, values, and interests when they are not face to face.

■ It can improve their cultural awareness, as they often socialize online with people from all different cultures and backgrounds. This can carry over to their in-person social skills.

■ They can interact with new groups of people who share the same interests, whereas these opportunities are more limited in their school and community lives.

On the other hand, socializing online can create conflict:

■ Anonymity empowers some users to insult and bully without being held accountable.

■ What you write can easily be misinterpreted. Without the benefit of facial expressions and body language, your true message can be misunderstood.

■ Cliques often form online, and whether you're in or out can depend on someone else's uninformed opinion of you.

Customized Instruction: ESOL Students

Have students create a poster that describes any customs, traditions, rituals, or gestures that relate to dating in their country of origin. What are the words in their primary language for "date," "group date," or "hanging out"?

Discuss

Ask students how they might determine if they are in a healthy romantic relationship with someone. Some indications are:

- You feel good, not worried, sad, scared, or angry.

- You feel that you are receiving as much from your partner as you are giving.

- You trust the other person with your secrets and, sometimes, even your welfare.

One-Sided Attraction

Students are asked to consider how to politely respond to an invitation they do not want to accept. The best option is to say, "Thank you for asking, but no." Avoid the long, drawn-out explanation of why you are declining. You don't owe the person a detailed explanation. Plus, the more you talk, the bigger the chance you have of saying something you didn't intend to. If the person persists, then you might have to be blunt: "No, I'm not interested." The important thing is to tell the truth. If you make something up, such as, "I'm not allowed to date," it's quite possible you'll be found out or, worse, seen out on a date! Save yourself and the other person the embarrassment.

Figure Focus

Students are asked how they show respect in a healthy relationship. Some ways are:

- Allowing the other person the freedom to be with other friends and to pursue their own interests.

- Respecting yourself and not bowing to pressures to change or do things you are uncomfortable with.

- Refraining from verbal and emotional abuse in the form of insults, jealousy, and indifference.

One-Sided Attraction

At some point, you might be attracted to someone who is not attracted back. That can be disappointing. You might also attract the attention of someone who does not interest you at all. What if someone asks you on a date but you don't want to go?

- ★ *Should you make excuses or tell a lie?*

- ★ *Should you feel guilty?*

- ★ *Should you feel ashamed?*

- ★ *Should you say yes because you feel bad for the other person?*

- ★ *Should you politely say "No. I'm not interested in dating at the moment."*

It doesn't matter why you don't want to go. How can you politely respond to an invitation that you don't want to accept?

Developing a Healthy Romantic Relationship

Even when you feel ready to date and want to date, it can be scary. Will we have something to talk about? Will we have fun? Will I wear the right clothes? Will she notice my pimple?

People aren't born knowing how to date, but it is something you can learn. One way to learn how to date is to watch people who are in a successful, healthy relationship. You can learn a lot watching how they interact:

- How do they show they care for each other?
- How do they show they respect each other?
- Do they share open and honest communications?
- What do they do to have fun?

Another way to learn about healthy relationships is to ask what makes their relationship successful. They might tell you that they know how to argue, which means they can have a fight and still be friends. They might also tell you that they allow each other a lot of room, which means they have other friends and interests and don't spend all their time together.

What About Physical Attraction?

A healthy romantic relationship is based on many elements, including shared values, interests, and goals; the ability to communicate; and physical attraction. As part of a healthy romantic relationship, you might express your affection by holding hands or kissing.

Some couples date only because they feel a physical attraction to each other. They might not care so much about common interests or values. They care only about the hand-holding and kissing.

All couples experience conflict at some point. When the only common bond is physical attraction, it may be easier to break up than to resolve the conflict. There is no other attachment between the couple, and they can simply find other people to date.

Dating Challenges

Communication is one of the most important challenges in all relationships. Expressing your thoughts and feelings is hard, but it is critical if you are going to create and maintain a lasting romantic relationship. Open, honest discussion and careful listening help you understand each other.

Breaking up is another challenge. You may decide the person you are dating is not right for you. Or, the person you are dating may decide you are not right for her or him. Breaking up is hard. It is a loss and will probably make you feel sad and lonely. It may make you feel insecure.

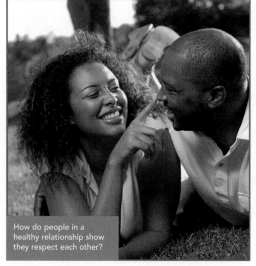

How do people in a healthy relationship show they respect each other?

You can cope with a breakup by spending time doing things that you value and that make you happy. You can find ways to build your self-esteem, and you can seek support from your friends and family.

Pressure to become involved in a physical relationship is a challenge, too. Sometimes, one partner may feel pressure to be physical in order to keep the relationship from ending, or to be cool, or because it's what other people are doing. No one has the right to pressure you into doing things that conflict with your values and standards, or make you feel ashamed or guilty.

Sexual behavior can lead to unwanted pregnancy and sexually transmitted disease. It can also cause depression, stress, and low self-esteem.

Many couples practice **abstinence**, which is a voluntary decision to avoid sexual behavior. Abstinence allows you to:

- Get to know each other in many ways before beginning a sexual relationship
- Take time to mature, to make better decisions, and to avoid unwanted problems
- Find other meaningful ways of being close, such as sharing deep personal thoughts

Recognizing Inappropriate Behavior

Inappropriate behavior in a relationship is any behavior that makes one person uncomfortable, afraid, or hurt—emotionally or physically. It can range from calling someone an unkind name to hitting or forcing unwanted sexual contact. It often involves threats. For example, one person might say "I'll kill myself if you leave me!" or "He did it because he loves me." or "I had to keep her in line." There are often attempts to control the other person. For instance, one person might tell the other not to see friends or family any more.

Sometimes it is hard to recognize inappropriate behavior because you think you are in love and that you care about each other. You might even think the behavior is caused by love. For example, you might think your boyfriend's jealousy is a sign of love. Sometimes your family and friends do not support your relationship because they recognize inappropriate behavior when you do not.

If you ever feel stress, depression, or conflict as the result of dating, you may need to seek help from a professional. If you are ever physically harmed by someone in a relationship, you must seek help. You can talk to your guidance counselor or family doctor about the situation. You can also contact an agency such as the Centers for Disease Control and Prevention (www.cdc.gov) or safeyouth.org. These agencies will help you locate resources in your community and find a way to talk to your parents.

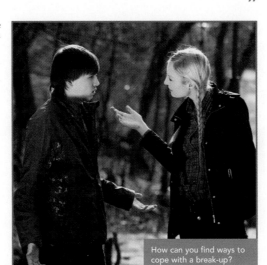

How can you find ways to cope with a break-up?

Unhealthy Dating Warning Signs

Signs that a dating relationship may be unhealthy include:

✔ Mistrust

✔ Jealousy

✔ Unequal exchange of resources

✔ Ineffective communication

✔ One partner trying to control the actions of the other

✔ Threats

✔ Violence

Customized Instruction: At-Risk Students

Research resources within your community that offer counseling and/or programs on teen dating violence. You can research on the Internet or contact your local government offices, or visit centers that are listed in the phone book. Create a brochure that lists the name of the resource and how to contact it, including a street address, Web address, phone number, and contact person, if available.

Discuss

Ask students to discuss some of the challenges they face in dating. Discuss socioeconomic factors such as:

- **Education:** Does a person's level of education or the school which he or she attends pose a challenge?
- **Occupation:** Does a person's job create conflicts?
- **Income level:** Does the relationship involve financial responsibilities or commitments that are beyond your means?
- **Health:** Does a person's physical, mental, and emotional health present challenges to overcome?
- **Culture, ethnicity, and race:** Are cultural, ethnic, and racial differences a source for conflict?

Vocabulary

Abstinence: Voluntary decision to avoid sexual behavior.

Inappropriate behavior: Any behavior that makes one person uncomfortable, afraid, or hurt, either emotionally or physically.

Figure Focus

Suggest the following ways to cope with a break-up:

- Allow yourself to feel the sadness, anger, or embarrassment of the break-up. Don't try to minimize the importance of the relationship by suppressing your feelings.
- Connect or reconnect with others. They can lend you the support you need to get through a difficult time.
- Consider what you have learned from the relationship as well as from the break-up and how you might apply it to future relationships.
- Try to follow your usual routine, but avoid the things that might bring back painful reminders.
- Re-examine your interests and hobbies and consider developing new ones.
- Do something to help others. Volunteer at a community center or get involved in a volunteer project.

Unhealthy Dating Warning Signs

Ask students to provide examples of how a person might exhibit each of the warning signs listed. For example, if your partner gets angry when you go out with other friends, he is being jealous. If your partner always decides where you will go and when, she is being controlling.

Introduce the Section

In this section, students learn to identify bully behavior. They also explore effective ways to handle a bully and how to assert themselves in a positive way.

Vocabulary

Bully: Someone who tries to regularly hurt others on purpose.

Figure Focus

Ask students to comment on some of the not-so-obvious ways students bully others. One example is gossiping or talking negatively about a person behind his or her back. There is no confrontation or physical contact, but it is still a form of bullying. Another subtle form of bullying is excluding an individual from being part of something. The person is not invited to join in, and if they decide to on his or her own, they are ignored.

STUDENT ACTIVITY

Students should determine if their school has a policy on bullying. If yes, have them obtain a copy of the written policy and write a summary of it. Their summaries should include the types of behavior that constitute bullying, the school's policy on dealing with bullies, and the methods by which the school will enforce the policies. If your school does not have a policy on bullying, have students as a class draft one that they can then present to school administrators for consideration.

Coping with Bullies

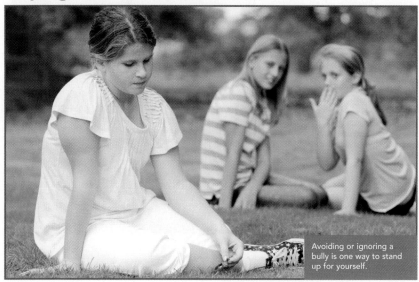

Avoiding or ignoring a bully is one way to stand up for yourself.

A **bully** is someone who tries to hurt others on purpose, not just once but over and over. Bullies can be boys or girls, big or small, young or old. Bullies can be found at school, but they can also turn up in other areas of your life, including in your neighborhood, at work, and even at home.

There are different reasons why bullies behave badly. Maybe they have low self-esteem and want to make themselves feel more important. Maybe they think it will impress their friends. Of course, if you are being bullied, you don't really care why the bully is a bully; you just want it to stop.

Bully Behavior

Bullies behave badly because it gets them attention. Bullies respond when witnesses laugh by bullying more. They respond when victims cry by bullying more. Some of the things bullies do include:

- Physically hurting others by tripping, pushing, kicking, pinching, or punching
- Calling people names
- Teasing people about the way they look, the way they act, or their values
- **Excluding** someone—leaving someone out
- Spreading rumors
- Stealing or breaking personal belongings
- Using threats or violence to make people do things they don't want to do

The more people react, the worse the bullying gets. When you are being bullied, it can make you feel scared, lonely, sad, embarrassed, and even sick. It contributes to stress and depression and interferes with every type of wellness.

How to Handle a Bully

Bullies tend to pick on kids who are smaller, kids who don't know how to stand up for themselves, kids who are easily upset, and kids who don't have a lot of friends. If you are being bullied, you need to take action right away.

- *Tell someone!* Pick someone you trust such as a parent, teacher, counselor, or older sibling and tell that person what is happening, or write him or her a note. If the first person you tell doesn't help, tell someone else.

- *Avoid the bully as much as you can.* That doesn't mean you have to hide or stay home from school. But you might be able to take a different route to class or to walk home instead of taking the bus.

- *Refuse to do what the bully says.* Say "No" in a loud, clear voice to get the attention of other people who might stand up for you, and then walk away.

- *Stand up for yourself!* Even if you don't feel brave, act as if you are.

It's hard, but you should also try not to react to the bully. Bullies like seeing that you are upset, and it might make them bully you even more. You also should try not to respond with anger or violence, because you'll probably get hurt, and might get in trouble.

Remember that you are a good person, with good qualities, and that you deserve to be safe and feel good about yourself. Surround yourself with people who will stand up for you, and let the bullies know you won't stand for it.

How can you show a bully you are brave?

21st Century Skills

What Happens Next?

Gina and Lizzie have been friends since kindergarten. They live on the same block, go to the same school, and their birthdays are even in the same month. They have been in the same Girl Scout troop and on the same soccer team for years.

The girls have a small group of close friends with whom they spend most of their free time. They all like to listen to music, read magazines, and talk about boys. They go to the mall to shop with each other, and they like to do each other's hair and nails.

This year they started 8th grade. For the first time, Gina and Lizzie were not in the same classes. One day, Gina noticed that kids at school were looking at her funny. They whispered when she walked by, and started to laugh. Lizzie did, too. Gina found out that Lizzie was sending around a really funny picture of Gina in a bikini she had taken last summer. Gina called Lizzie and asked her to delete the picture. Lizzie laughed and said it was too late. Everyone was forwarding it, and the whole school would have it soon.

The next day Gina heard that Lizzie was sending around another picture—even worse than the first. Gina was horrified and embarrassed.

What problems and choices are facing Gina and Lizzie? What life skills can they use to find solutions and make decisions? What resources do they have available? Using your 21st Century Skills—such as decision making, goal setting, and problem solving—write an ending to the story. Read it to the class, or form a small group and present it as a skit.

21st Century Skills

What Happens Next?

Students are asked to write or prepare a skit of the ending to the story about Gina and Lizzie. Their endings should address:

- The problems and choices the two girls are facing. Gina must decide whether she wants to continue doing things that will negatively affect her relationship with Lizzie. Lizzie must decide if she wants to continue her friendship with Gina. She also is faced with the problem of dealing with the bullying of others who have seen the unflattering pictures.

- The life skills they can use to find solutions and make decisions. These include thinking critically and communicating effectively.

- The resources they have available. These would include human, non-human, and technological resources.

Teaching Tips

Be aware that your class may include a student who has bullied or been bullied. Consider the consequences of asking these students pointed questions in front of the class about bullying, as it may only aggravate or intensify the situation.

Discuss

Discuss other ways to handle a bully. Some ideas are:

- Ask questions using bold, forceful words. "Why are you *criticizing* my clothes?" Often, the bully will not be able to answer intelligently because there is no intelligent answer.

- Repeat back to the bully what he said: "So you don't like my taste in clothes." This signals an end to the conversation.

- Ask for advice. "Where do you buy your clothes?" An unexpected response such as this will take the bully by surprise.

- Use humor. "Maybe it does look like I put this outfit together in the dark." Again, the element of surprise can silence the bully.

Figure Focus

Explain that showing courage when you are face-to-face with someone who wants to hurt you isn't easy, but *acting* brave can sometimes be enough. For example:

- Look your best. When your appearance is neat and clean, you feel confident about yourself, and others usually sense it.

- Stand up straight with your shoulders back.

- Look the person in the eye and hold the eye contact.

- Use a loud but calm voice. It's all right if others hear you talking back to a bully.

- Rein in your emotions. Take a deep breath, count by 2s to 100, or take some other measure to keep your emotions under control.

Don't Just Stand There

Students are asked to consider their responsibilities when they see someone being bullied. What are proactive things they can do to stop the bullying? Discuss with students the idea of Good Samaritan laws. In the United States, these laws or acts are designed to protect from liability those who choose to help or aid others who are injured or ill. They are intended to reduce a bystander's hesitation or reluctance to help someone in need because he or she is fearful of legal repercussions.

CRITICAL THINKING ACTIVITY

Ask students if they think a variation of the Good Samaritan law could be applied in their school, where students are rewarded for getting involved and taking a stand against bullying.

Figure Focus

Explain that while cyber bullying occurs less than in-person bullying, it can still result in victimization of an individual. Ask students to share any incidents in which they were cyber bullied.

NUMBERS GAME

Review with students how to calculate an average, which is the sum of two or more quantities divided by the number of quantities. The answer to the second calculation, 282 + 96 = 378 ÷ 4 = 94.5.

Don't Just Stand There

Seeing someone being bullied can make you feel bad, too. You might be scared or worried that the bully will turn on you, next. How should you act if you see someone being bullied?

👎 Laugh.

👎 Join in.

👎 Look down at the ground and sneak away as quietly as possible.

👍 Speak up and tell the bully to stop.

👍 Tell a teacher, parent, counselor, or older sibling about it.

At basketball tryouts, an older boy started pointing, whispering, and laughing at a skinny kid who was having trouble dribbling the ball. It made you feel uncomfortable. What could you do?

"Oh no! Should I show my parents this e-mail? Can this guy really hurt me?"

Bullies Online

Cyber bullies are bullies who use technology such as the Internet, cell phones, and interactive gaming devices to hurt others. They might:

- Send threatening or harassing messages
- Steal passwords and pretend to be someone else online
- Use blogs or social networking sites to spread rumors
- Send private pictures through e-mail or cell phones
- Create hurtful Web sites
- Distribute someone else's personal information

Cyber bullying can be tricky to stop, because it is anonymous and takes place away from school. If you are being cyber-bullied, you can take many of the same steps you would take with a face-to-face bully. In fact, it might be easier to not react and to avoid the cyber bully because you are not face to face. It's pretty easy just to delete a text message or an e-mail without reading it.

You can tell someone you trust right away, but if the cyber bully doesn't stop, you may have to report it to the Internet or telephone service provider. If the behavior is illegal, you may have to report it to the police.

NUMBERS GAME

Many people like to socialize by going to sporting events or talking about games. They often talk about averages when they compare teams or players. An **average** is the sum of two or more quantities divided by the number of quantities. For example, you can calculate the average number of points a team scores by adding the points scored in each game and dividing the sum by the number of games played.

If a basketball team played three games and scored 88 points, 95 points, and 99 points, what's the average number of points per game?

- First, add up the points: 88 + 95 + 99 = 282
- Next, divide the sum by the number of games: 282 ÷ 3 = 94

The team is averaging 94 points per game.

If they play another game and score 96 points, what would the average score per game be?

Hint: Add 96 to 282 and divide by 4.

Customized Instruction: More Advanced Students

Have students research their state's anti-bullying laws and legislation. If your state does not have such a law, have students pick another state that does. They should write a report that summarizes the law, includes examples of how the law is being enforced, and states their opinion on whether they think the law is effective.

Asserting Yourself

One positive way to cope with bullies is to be assertive. Being **assertive** means that you stand up for yourself. You express your feelings and thoughts with confidence, in a strong, honest, and direct way. When you are assertive, you show others that you have the right to:

- Be treated with respect
- Say no
- Ask for what you need

One negative way to cope with bullies is to be aggressive. Being **aggressive** means that you force your opinions on others. You express your feelings and thoughts in a hostile, or angry, way. When you are aggressive, you show others that you have no respect for their thoughts or feelings. Bullies are aggressive. If you respond with aggression, you might end up fighting, getting hurt, and getting in trouble.

Standing up for yourself and others is one way to defeat a bully. What are some other ways you can deal with a bully?

JOBS

Job Search

If you enjoy giving people relationship advice and helping people understand the risks and responsibilities of relationships, you might want to look for a career in counseling. Some types of counselors include marriage counselors, family therapists, licensed social workers, school counselors, clinical psychologists, and psychiatrists.

The educational requirements depend on the type of career; for example, some substance abuse counselors may need only an associate's degree, while a psychiatrist must be a licensed physician. Use the Internet, library, or school's guidance resources to learn more about a career in counseling. Write a job description, including the educational requirements, career pathway, and potential salary range.

Vocabulary

Aggressive: Forcing your opinions on others.

Assertive: Standing up for yourself; expressing your feelings and thoughts with confidence, in a strong, honest, and direct way.

Discuss

Make sure students can distinguish between aggressive, submissive, and assertive:

- Aggressive indicates a readiness to be mean or do harm. For example, "Move out of my seat, or I'll move you out myself."
- Submissive means giving in to the demands of others. For example, "All right, I'll move from your seat."
- Assertive means being strong. For example, "I'll be done in a minute and then you can have this seat."

Figure Focus

Discuss with students ways to be assertive:

- Use "I" instead of "you." This shows you are standing up for yourself.
- Tell a bully firmly and repeatedly what *you* want and need. This sends a signal that you will not back down.
- Just say "no" loudly and clearly. Practice it in the mirror, on family, and with your friends.

Job Search

Students are to research careers in counseling and then write a job description for a related position in which they might be interested. Make sure their job descriptions include the position title, educational requirements, experience needed, duties and responsibilities, and the salary range.

Customized Instruction: Less Advanced/Special Needs Students

Write on the board, "I feel _____ when you _____ because _____." Present the scenarios listed below to students and ask them to fill in the blanks in response. For the first blank, they should respond with a feeling; for the second blank, they should respond with a description of the action; for the third blank, they should respond with a reason why.

- A student is ignored at the lunch table. ("I feel *sad* when you *ignore me* because *I thought we were friends*.")
- A student is threatened with bodily harm if he doesn't share answers to a homework assignment. ("I feel *angry* when you *threaten me* because *you are breaking the rules*.")
- A student is tripped on purpose and everyone who sees it laughs. ("I feel *embarrassed* when you *laugh at me* because *it hurts to fall down and to be made fun of*.")

Introduce the Section

In this section, students discover that being part of a team gives them access to valuable resources that would not be available if they work on their own.

Vocabulary

Team: Any group that works together to achieve a common goal.

Figure Focus

In the course of a day, most students frequently participate in team activities, perhaps not even realizing it. Ask them to consider the teams to which they belong, both organized and those that are not so organized. For example, you and a few other students are responsible for collecting recycling bins from each classroom. You are part of the recycling collection team. You and a classmate work as a team to conduct an experiment in biology class. You are assigned to a volleyball team in gym class.

Discuss

Discuss the roles of members of a team. Explain that while a team is expected to work together as a whole, there are individual roles that members consciously, and sometimes subconsciously, fill. For example, a team might have a:

- Leader—either appointed or assumed.
- Creator or innovator—the person with the ideas.
- Manager—the person who organizes and manages resources.
- Finisher—the person who evaluates, concludes, and completes.

Note that many teams have more than one member filling these roles.

Working As a Team

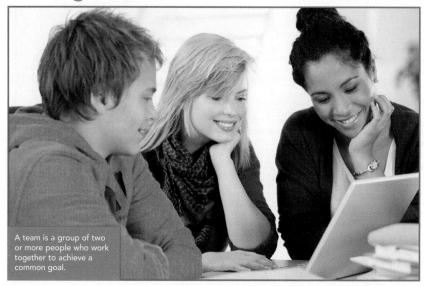

A team is a group of two or more people who work together to achieve a common goal.

Any group that works together to achieve a common goal is a **team**. When you are part of a team, you have access to all the knowledge, experience, and abilities of your teammates. Together you can have more ideas, achieve more goals, and solve more problems.

A successful team relationship depends on all team members working together. They depend on each other. They trust one another. If one team member does not do his or her share, the entire team suffers.

The challenges of a team relationship come from having different people working together. Even if everyone agrees on a common goal, they may not agree on how to achieve that goal. Your friends might agree to celebrate the end of the school year together, but:

- Some of you might want to go to the lake.
- Some might want to play Frisbee in the park.
- Some might want to have a picnic.

Types of Teams

You might think there are two types of teams—teams for sports and teams for work. In reality, there are teams in all areas of your life:

- Your family works together to maintain your home. You support each other and share tasks and responsibilities.
- Your class in school cooperates to complete projects and learn a subject. You organize events together and listen to each other in class.
- Your friends communicate to schedule group activities. You respect each other's thoughts and opinions.

All types of teams function in the same basic way. Team members must be able to communicate, set goals, and work together to solve problems.

A healthy relationship as a team member contributes to your self-esteem. Your teammates respect you and value your contribution to their success.

Customized Instruction: ESOL Students

What techniques might a team employ to overcome language barriers that exist between members? Have students create a list of guidelines for overcoming language barriers that any type of team could follow. Their list should address things such as making sure all team members understand the goal and their individual responsibilities in meeting the goal, speaking clearly (and more slowly, if necessary), keeping a translation dictionary close by, using an interpreter, and exercising patience and understanding if something needs to be repeated or explained in a different way.

Developing a Team Relationship

Teams are influenced by different things, including the personal qualities of the team members, the resources available, and the purpose or goals of the team.

When a team first forms, team members might feel nervous or uncomfortable. You might not know each other very well. You might wonder what to expect.

At first, you might misunderstand each other, or misinterpret communications. One teammate might say she can't come to a meeting, and you might think she means she doesn't want to be part of the team. Another teammate might have lots of plans and ideas, and the rest of you might think he is trying to take over and be the boss.

As you get to know each other, and learn how to communicate, you might feel a sense of belonging. You might develop common bonds. You might give your team a name and identify with your teammates. You will be able to work together to achieve your goal.

Who's the Boss?

Even when all members of a team have an equal role in decision-making and problem-solving, it is important to have a leader.

If you are the leader, you take on the responsibility for:

■ Organizing the team's activities
■ Encouraging everyone to share ideas and give opinions
■ Motivating all team members to work toward established goals

Being the leader does not mean you are always right. The leader's opinion does not count more than the opinions of the other team members. An effective leader keeps the team on track and focused on achieving its goals.

What About Team Members?

While a strong leader is important to the success of a team, team members must also be committed to the group's success. An effective team member helps teammates if they need help, does not blame teammates for problems or mistakes, and offers ideas and suggestions instead of criticism.

You are a good team member if you are:

■ Open minded   ■ Willing to compromise
■ Cooperative   ■ Friendly
■ Trustworthy

To be successful, a team needs all members to agree on how to achieve your goal. To have agreement, teams must be able to communicate. They must also be ready to resolve conflicts in an open and honest way. You and your friends might use your problem-solving skills to figure out how best to celebrate the end of the school year.

You might also have to make personal sacrifices for the success of the team. For example, if your friends decide the picnic is best, you might have to give up dinner with your family in order to celebrate with them.

You show up for a community clean-up day and are assigned to work in a group of four to clean up trash along a narrow, two-lane street. One team member is concerned about being hit by a car and is spending more time complaining about the assignment than picking up trash. What can you do as a team to calm her fears and clean up the street?

What If You Hate Your Team?

You might not want to be part of a team. Maybe you were placed on a team that you did not choose. Maybe you think you are the only one on the team who is making an effort. How can you help your team succeed, even if you don't like your teammates?

👎 Refuse to cooperate.

👎 Do not participate in team discussions.

👎 Do what you think is best, even if the rest of the team has a different plan.

👎 Yell at your teammates until they do what you want.

👍 Listen respectfully, keep a positive attitude, and present your opinions in a clear and concise way.

Sometimes being an effective member of a team does not depend on the actual outcome of the project. Sometimes it depends on how well you get along with your teammates and whether you give your teammates a chance to succeed.

"If I'm stuck with this group, I'd better figure out a way to make it work."

Reinforce and Review

Review the six steps for communicating effectively:

1. **Be clear.** The manner in which you send your message reflects your personality and has great impact on the impression you make on other team members. For example, if you fail to look a person in the eye when you are speaking to her, she might think you have bad manners or are distracted.

2. **Be personal.** People are more likely to respond to you in a positive way if you have taken the time to learn their names and know their special interests.

3. **Be positive.** Always stress the positive. People tend to put up their guard when they read or hear something negative.

4. **Get to the point.** Don't go off on tangents or topics that do not apply to the team's goals. Being concise and to the point helps eliminate confusion and miscommunication.

5. **Actively listen to the response.** Listening is key to effective communication.

6. **Think before you respond.** If you need time to formulate a response, ask for it.

What If You Hate Your Team?

Ask students for other ideas on how to make the most of a bad situation. Emphasize that it is always important to stay focused on the goal of the team, and to not let your personal agenda get in the way of achieving the goal. Concentrate on your responsibilities as a team member and remain objective. Being objective means you are free of bias or prejudice. You consider facts rather than thoughts or opinions.

Customized Instruction: Less Advanced/Special Needs Students

You will need at least five students for this activity. Students will work as a team to build a structure using building blocks or other random items found in the classroom (tissue box, ruler, books, etc.). Have the team assign one member as the "creator," one as the "manager," one as the "leader," and the remaining members as the "builders." The creator will build the structure, without the others being able to see it. The manager will draw a picture of the structure on paper, labeling its parts as necessary. Once the drawing is complete, the creator should disassemble the structure. Using the drawing, the leader will instruct the builders how to recreate the structure. When the structure is done, assess the team's performance.

Introduce the Section

In this section, students learn that conflicts occur in all types of relationships. They discover that taking positive steps to resolve conflicts will help them strengthen their relationships.

Vocabulary

Conflict: Disagreement between two or more people who have different ideas.

Figure Focus

Explain that conflicts arise between friends all the time. A healthy relationship can usually withstand conflict because you value the other person and recognize and appreciate the role he or she plays in your life. Ask students to comment on examples of conflict between them and their friends. How do they normally resolve these conflicts?

Discuss

Discuss with students the concept of "internal conflict." Inner conflict occurs when you have to make a difficult choice about something. For example, you committed to going shopping with your friend on Saturday night, but at the last minute, a guy you are interested in calls and asks you to go out on a date. What choice will you make? Remind students of the six steps to making a decision:

1. Identify the decision to be made.
2. Consider all possible options.
3. Identify the consequences of each option.
4. Select the best option.
5. Make a plan to implement the option.
6. Evaluate the outcome.

Managing Conflict

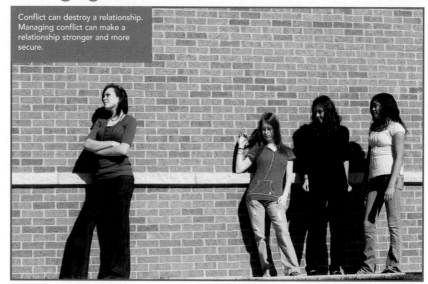

Conflict can destroy a relationship. Managing conflict can make a relationship stronger and more secure.

Conflict is a disagreement between two or more people who have different ideas. Conflict occurs in all relationships at one time or another.

- When a relationship is healthy, people talk about what is causing the conflict and work together to find a solution.
- When a relationship is not healthy, conflict can go unresolved. Unresolved conflict interferes with well-being and can cause stress, depression, anger, and resentment.

Managing conflict does not always mean eliminating the conflict completely. It means you are able to recognize what is causing the conflict, and that you can cope with it in an honest and respectful way.

Types of Conflict

There are different types of conflict. The way you respond to conflict depends on what it is and how it affects your well-being.

Some conflict is minor and short-lived—such as disagreeing with your friends about where to sit in a movie theater or with your sister about whose turn it is to wash the dishes. You can usually resolve minor conflicts easily by talking about them and coming to a compromise or agreement.

Some conflict is serious or ongoing—such as refusing to lie for a friend or disagreeing with a classmate about using animals for medical testing. Serious conflicts often come from conflicting values and may be difficult—or impossible—to resolve. You may not want to compromise your ethics or values. You might have to agree to disagree.

Causes of Conflict

Any disagreement can cause conflict. Sometimes understanding what causes the disagreement can help you resolve the conflict more quickly.

- Differences in values and standards cause conflict. You might want to meet with a study group on a Sunday afternoon instead of on Saturday night, but someone else in the group might spend Sundays with his family.
- Ineffective communication and misunderstandings can cause conflict. If your parents don't tell you that your grandmother is coming to dinner, you might make other plans. Then you are angry when you must cancel your plans.
- Conflict may be caused by personal qualities such as stubbornness or conceit. Your sister might refuse to wear headphones or turn off the radio when you are trying to study.

When you recognize the cause of the conflict, you can take steps to find a solution.

Avoiding Conflict

You cannot avoid conflict. It occurs in all areas of your life.

- Conflict is almost constant in families. You live together and share most resources. You might feel as if you are always fighting with your parents and siblings about something. You might disagree about what to watch on television, how late you can stay up, who gets to use the bathroom first, and the way you dress.
- Conflict with friends occurs often as well. You might disagree about where to sit on the bus, what to do after school, what music to listen to, and who to invite to a party.
- At school, you might have conflict with teachers about homework or other assignments. You might have conflict with coaches about practice schedules or playing time.
- If you work, you might have conflict with co-workers about responsibilities or with your employer about your schedule.
- In your community, you might have conflict with a neighbor who has a barking dog or a kid who teases you.

Sometimes you can walk away from the conflict. More often, you must face the conflict in order to resolve it.

Anger Management

Conflict can make you mad. When you are angry, you might not be reasonable or realistic about the conflict. You might say or do something you will regret later. What if you are too angry to talk to the other person?

- ★ *Take a deep breath.*
- ★ *Count to ten.*
- ★ *Exercise.*
- ★ *Identify your role in the conflict.*
- ★ *Brainstorm solutions.*
- ★ *Consider what you could say to start resolving the conflict.*
- ★ *Ask someone you trust for advice.*

Once you calm down, you will be better able to think critically about what is causing the conflict and how to resolve it. Your brother takes your MP3 player without permission and refuses to give it back. How can you control your anger and resolve this conflict?

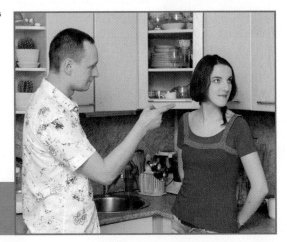

You might feel as if you are always fighting with your family. How can you work together to minimize family conflicts?

Customized Instruction: At-Risk Students

Students will create an "anger log." The log should include the following:

1. What triggered the anger? For example, you did something wrong, or someone took something from you.
2. Location where you got angry, such as home, school, or on the job.
3. Scale that rates how angry you were, such as really angry or a little angry.
4. How you handled your anger: did you yell, or break something, or walk away?
5. End result or outcome, such as good or bad, positive or negative.

Have students enter anger-related incidents in the log for a week. At the end of the week, have them share their logs with the class. For some of those incidents that had a negative outcome, consider having students reenact them but with a result that is positive.

Discuss

Elaborate on the causes of conflict discussed in the text. Remind students that values are things that are important to them, such as family, friends, good grades, or good health. Standards are guidelines for whether or not something meets their expectations, such as the level of support you get from your family and friends. Values and standards vary widely from person to person, which is why they are often a source of conflict.

Discuss barriers to communication. A barrier is something that obstructs the smooth flow of information exchange. Barriers that get in the way of effective communication include distractions, such as the television that prevents one individual from listening to another, or language that prevents one person from correctly understanding another.

Personal qualities and character traits can be a source of conflict. For example, a person who is motivated to get a project done on time might have a conflict with a person who is lazy and fails to contribute to the successful completion of the project.

Anger Management

Students are asked what they would do if their brother takes their MP3 player without permission and refuses to give it back. One solution is to simply remove yourself from the situation. Focus your energies on something that makes you happy. Eventually, your brother will lose interest in the MP3 player. Or, you could calmly explain the situation to a parent and ask him or her to intervene.

Figure Focus

Explain that conflicts at home can invade all other areas of our lives and have a negative impact on our friendships, school work, job performance, and citizenship. To minimize conflict, suggest the following:

1. Respect your family. Without mutual respect, there will always be conflict. People who respect each other can disagree without yelling and getting angry. They can talk calmly and rationally about a conflict. Also keep in mind that your parents are more experienced and knowledgeable than you about some things.
2. Communicate with your family. If you shut them out of your business, they will think the worst. If you share and are open with them, you might find them to be helpful and supportive.
3. Show honesty and responsibility to build your family's trust. When people trust each other, they are less likely to question values and create confrontations.

Fighting with Your Family

Ask students to share their ideas on how to resolve conflicts with family. What is the source of most conflict within their family? Bathroom time? Money? Choosing which TV program to watch?

Vocabulary

Negotiate: Work together to think of a goal that works for everyone.

Discuss

Help students understand basic conflict management skills:

- **Negotiate:** Determine together how to get past or deal with a problem or disagreement.
- **Compromise:** Settle a conflict by agreeing to accept less than what you originally wanted.
- **Resolve:** Find a solution to the conflict.
- **Apologize:** Express remorse or acknowledge that you are sorry for something.

Figure Focus

Students are asked to comment on how an apology reflects your understanding of another person's feelings. When you apologize, you acknowledge that you feel sorry, embarrassed, or guilty about something. A simple apology can go a long way in resolving conflicts. It proves you can admit you are wrong or that your actions caused a negative reaction. But also point out that apologizing just for the sake of "shutting someone up" or getting past the conflict is not an effective way to resolve conflicts. The problem still exists and may get worse over time as people stew about it.

Fighting with Your Family

When you disagree with your friends, you can go home. When you fight with your family, it's hard to get away. Some things that can help you cope with conflicts at home include:

- ✔ *Talking it out*
- ✔ *Agreeing on some rules*
- ✔ *Asking another family member to help*
- ✔ *Respecting each other's right to privacy*
- ✔ *Taking turns instead of sharing*
- ✔ *Going for a walk or a bike ride, or just getting away to your personal space*

Resolving Conflict

There is a problem at the root of all conflict. Recall from Chapter 2 that a problem is something that blocks you from achieving a goal. You can use the problem-solving process to find a solution.

You will be more successful in resolving or minimizing the conflict if you work with the other person or people who are involved in the conflict.

- Together you can identify the disagreement or problem.
- You can **negotiate**, or work together, to think of a goal that works for everyone.
- You can all compromise and select and implement the best solution.

Sometimes you might not be able to get the other person to cooperate. He or she might not want to resolve the conflict or might refuse to admit there is a conflict. Then, you will have to decide whether you need to take action on your own, or just walk away.

Taking Responsibility for Conflict

When you must take steps to solve a conflict, you should try to remain calm and objective. It is easier to focus on the problem if you keep your emotions under control.

- Show respect and understanding for the other person.
- Take responsibility for your own actions and feelings, without blaming anyone else.
- Remember to use the six key factors of effective communication (Chapter 2), including sending a clear, concise message, listening carefully, and using "I" statements to focus on your point of view.
- Insults hurt and cause new conflicts. You can attack the conflict without attacking the other person.

The hardest thing of all might be to apologize. Even if you don't think you caused the conflict or did anything wrong, you can apologize for making the other person feel bad.

Sometimes you have to apologize to resolve conflict. How can an apology show you understand that the other person is hurt or angry?

Team Conflicts

Conflicts in a team can interfere with the team's ability to achieve its goals. Because there are many people involved, the type of conflict can vary:

- Sometimes, the conflict might have nothing to do with the team. One member might have a personal conflict that is getting in his way. For example, your brother might not be helping the family clean the house, because he is on the phone arguing with his girlfriend.
- There may be conflict between two team members. You and your sister may not agree about who should clean the toilet and who should sweep the floor.
- There may be conflict between one team member and everyone else in the team. Your mother might want the whole house clean, but the rest of you want to clean downstairs today and upstairs tomorrow.

To be successful, the whole team should work together to resolve the conflict. Each team member can contribute to identifying the problem and brainstorming solutions.

Unresolved Conflict

When you let conflict go unresolved, it can slowly eat away at a relationship. You might not want to speak up about what is bothering you. You might think it is silly. You might worry the other person will be hurt or angry. When you don't speak up, you can start to **resent** the other person, or blame him for your unhappiness.

Do you expect the other person to know what you are thinking or feeling? You might be annoyed because your friend did not respond to your text message. You might be hurt because you think she is ignoring you. It is possible she did not receive the message. Or that she accidentally hit delete instead of send. Unless you speak up, you will not be able to resolve the conflict and stay friends.

Resolving Team Conflicts

Follow these important steps for resolving conflicts as a team:

- ✔ *Give all team members a chance to express their views.*
- ✔ *Be respectful of all team members.*
- ✔ *Deal with one problem at a time.*
- ✔ *Focus on your common goals.*
- ✔ *Find ways for all team members to be involved in the solution.*
- ✔ *Encourage all team members to take responsibility for their actions — positive and negative.*
- ✔ *Avoid blame.*

Leaving conflicts unresolved can ruin a relationship. How can effective communication help you resolve conflicts?

Resolving Team Conflicts

Have students think of their class as a team. Discuss each of the steps listed in the text and ask students for examples of how this step is executed by the team.

Discuss

Discuss the effects of anger on your health. Studies consistently show those who control their anger get sick less often and feel better emotionally. Feelings of anger put stress on the body and can lead to health-related problems such as high blood pressure, stomach problems, depression, eating disorders, and substance abuse.

Figure Focus

Explain that while it is normal to get angry over conflict, it is usually not effective to *show* your anger or let it control you. The different ways in which people cope with conflict is one of the things that make them unique. But getting angry over something and chalking it up to being "just the way you are" can have negative consequences. It shows that you are rigid and unwilling to see things from another's perspective. Determine ways to control your anger and channel your energies to more positive things.

Customized Instruction: More Advanced/At-Risk Students

Have students work as a team to plan an end-of-quarter class party. Students will create a report that illustrates their team's effort. The report should include:

- The team's name and mission statement (or the goal they want to achieve).
- An outline of the plan or the steps they will take to achieve the goal.
- Assignment of tasks or duties.
- Guidelines for how the team will handle conflict.

If you approve the report, allow the team to execute their plan.

End-of-Chapter Activities

Case Study

Karim is conflicted because he likes his long hair, but he likes his teammates and wants to fit in, too. He always had pride in his hair, but now it is making him feel self-conscious and different.

His relationships with his teammates are affected. It might also affect relationships with his family, if they identify with his long hair, too.

Karim could shave his head to fit in. He could quit the team. He could try to talk to his teammates about why his hair is important to him, and if that does not work, he could decide to keep his hair long and ignore the comments and laughter of his teammates. He could recognize that what they are doing is peer pressure and a form of bullying and that he can stand up for himself and his values.

Sounding Off!

Student answers will vary. Ask students to elaborate on why they do or do not.

FAQ

1. Five characteristics of a healthy personal relationship include respect, trust, honesty, responsibility, and open communication.

2. Ways you can tell if a relationship is unhealthy are:
   - You are unhappy in the relationship.
   - You feel you cannot be yourself.
   - You are afraid the other person will end the relationship.
   - You are afraid the other person will hurt you—physically or emotionally.
   - You do not trust the other person.
   - You are dishonest.
   - You cannot or will not talk about your feelings.
   - You do not respect the other person.
   - You fight a lot.

   Students may think of others.

3. Your parents and siblings are part of your immediate, or nuclear, family. Your aunts, uncles, cousins, and grandparents are your extended family.

4. A good friend is fun, honest, a good listener, flexible, supportive, trustworthy, loyal, understanding, and forgiving. Students may think of other qualities.

5. Peer pressure is when your peers and friends influence you to do something.

Case Study

Karim has always had long hair that he keeps neat in dreadlocks. Jeremy, the captain of the boys' soccer team recently had his head shaved. Now, the other boys on the team are shaving their heads, too. At practice and on the bus to meets, Karim feels as if all the boys talk about is their shaved heads. They say they feel lighter and that it makes them look strong and tough. They laugh and say it makes them play soccer better, too. They tell Karim long hair is for girls. Karim is starting to feel left out and different.

- What conflicts is Karim facing?
- What relationships are affected by the conflicts?
- What can Karim do to minimize or resolve the conflicts?

Sounding Off!

1. Do you tell your parents when you do poorly on a test?
2. Do you tell them when you do well?

F A Q

1. List five characteristics of a healthy personal relationship.
2. List three ways you can tell if a relationship is unhealthy.
3. What is the difference between your immediate family and your extended family?
4. List five qualities of a good friend.
5. What is peer pressure?
6. What is the difference between casual dating and exclusive dating?
7. What are three dating challenges?
8. What is a bully?
9. What is a team?
10. Give an example of a minor, short-lived conflict.

6. Casual dating means you spend time one-on-one with a lot of different people. Casual dating gives you a chance to get to know more than one person. When two people decide they like each other better than they like anyone else, they might choose to be exclusive. Exclusive dating means you make a commitment to your partner and both agree not to date anyone else. It does not mean you cannot have other friends.

7. Dating challenges include communication, breaking up, inappropriate behavior, and pressure to be physical. Students may think of others.

8. A bully is someone who tries to hurt others on purpose, not just once, but over and over.

9. A team is a group that works together to achieve a common goal.

10. An example of a minor, short-lived conflict is disagreeing with friends about where to sit in the movie theater, or with a sibling about chores. Students may think of other examples.

Bullying is a serious problem. In small groups, prepare and perform two skits. The first one should show the negative effects bullying can have on a school or other community if it is not stopped. The second should show the positive steps a school or community can take to stop bullying. With permission, perform the skits for classes in younger grades.

Hot Topics

Have you ever been the victim of a bully? Have you seen someone be a bully? Have you ever been a bully yourself?

Take this opportunity to write anonymously about the problem. Use a word processor so no one recognizes your handwriting. Be honest and open. Put the paper in the class Hot Topics box.

As a class, read the anonymous entries and discuss them.

Web Extra

Use the Internet to locate information about cyber bullies. Research the laws controlling cyber bullies in your state. Make a list of illegal behavior, including the punishments, and post it on your school Web site or in the school library.

Problem Solver

You are a relationship counselor. A mother and daughter have come to you for advice. They say they fight all the time. Sometimes they fight about little things, such as nail polish color. Sometimes they fight about big things, such as eating a vegetarian diet. The daughter is spending a lot of time in her room alone and is communicating with people online. The mother doesn't use the Internet and doesn't understand why her daughter can't spend time with real people.

Individually or in pairs, analyze the relationship between the mother and daughter. Identify things that are positive and things that are negative. Look for conflicts and common bonds. Prepare a presentation or report explaining what you have found and recommending the steps the two should take to build a healthy relationship.

Team Players

Students are to create skits on bullying that they perform for their class or classes in younger grades. One skit should focus on the negative effects of bullying. These include the formation of cliques, increased violence, and divisions between those who know the bully and those who know the person being bullied. The other skit should show the positive steps a school or community can take to stop bullying. These would include written policies or laws against bullying, adults or older kids intervening, and reward programs for those who take a stand against bullying.

Hot Topics

Make sure students understand that they can turn in their papers anonymously. Encourage them to be open and honest about their experiences with bullying.

Web Extra

Students are to locate information about cyber bullies and create a list of illegal behavior and the punishments associated with it.

Problem Solver

Students are asked to prepare a report on the situation of a mother and daughter with an unhealthy relationship. Their reports or presentations should identify the things that are positive and negative in the relationship. For example, the mother and daughter are asking for advice, so they obviously recognize that they have a problem. The negative things include quibbling over unimportant issues, such as nail polish, and refusing to openly communicate about things. Their work should also include steps the mother and daughter can take to build a healthy relationship, such as showing respect for each other's interests and values, making an effort to talk to the other about their lives, and showing honesty and responsibility to build trust in each other.

Write Now

Students are to write a letter to an important person in their life that expresses how they feel about that person. You might suggest students review *Appendix D Language Arts: Grammar and Punctuation Basics*, starting on page 539 of the student text, before they write their letters.

Be Involved!

Students are to plan a project on developing stronger relationships with members of their extended families. They are to treat the project as a goal, with a written action plan for achieving it. They are to keep a journal that details their execution of the plan, and then use the journal entries as the basis for a poster or presentation that illustrates their execution of the plan. Last, they are to write a report on whether or not they were successful in meeting their goal and what they might do differently if they were to start it again.

Social Networking

Students are to create a directory of organizations and agencies in their area that rely on volunteer help. The directory should list the names, addresses, contacts, and a brief description of each group.

Write Now

Knowing how to express your feelings is an important part of any healthy relationship. Think about someone who means a lot to you. Think about the personal qualities he or she has that you admire and the values that you respect. Write a letter to that person expressing how you feel and why.

Be Involved!

www.fcclainc.org

As a class, review the people who are part of your extended family and discuss the benefits of having relationships with your extended family. Brainstorm ways you can develop relationships with members of your extended family. For example, you might visit family members more often, exchange birthday or holiday cards, or add family members to your social networking buddy lists.

Individually, or with your teacher or advisor, use the five-step goal-setting process to plan a project that will help you build a better relationship with your extended family, or with one member of your extended family.

Define the project as a goal, make an action plan for achieving the goal (including a timeframe), assess the plan to make sure it is reasonable and attainable, and then put the plan into action to achieve your goal.

As you work toward your goal, keep a journal to record your progress, and collect documentation that you can use to show what you have achieved. At the end of the set timeframe, use the documentation to make a poster or presentation. Write a report explaining what you learned, whether you were successful or not, and what you would do differently if you were going to start the project all over again.

Social Networking

One way to meet and socialize with new people is to become involved as a volunteer. Opportunities for volunteering depend on where you live and what interests you. There might be food pantries that need help stocking shelves, animal shelters that need help walking dogs, or parks that need help cleaning public areas.

Contact organizations and agencies in your area to find out what kind of help they need. As a class, make a directory that lists the names, addresses, contacts, and type of work. Make the directory available to other classes and clubs in your school.

Part II

Human Development

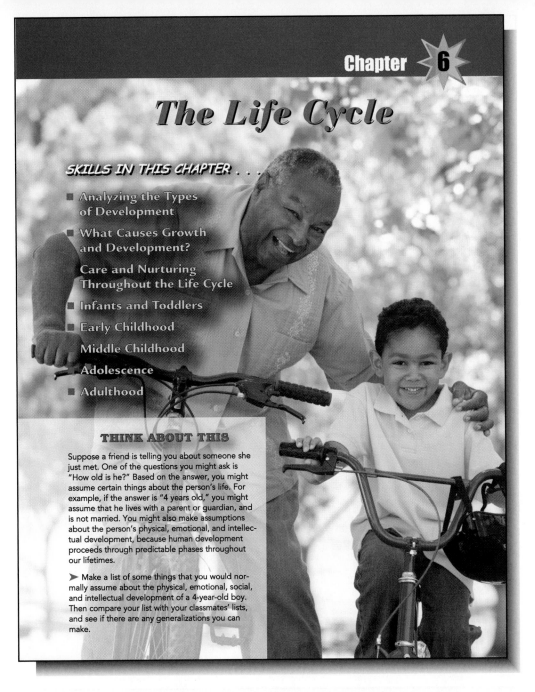

Chapter 6 Overview

This chapter discusses the human life cycle, examining the various stages of development from infancy through adolescence to adulthood.

Analyzing the Types of Development Students explore the physical, emotional, social, and intellectual development during our life cycle.

What Causes Growth and Development? The factors that cause and affect growth and development are discussed.

Care and Nurturing Throughout the Life Cycle Students learn about the nine stages of life and the care and nurturing that characterize them.

Infants and Toddlers This section discusses the physical, social, emotional, and intellectual growth of infants and toddlers. This life stage is from birth to age 3.

Early Childhood The early childhood stage is from age 3 to age 6. In this section, students learn how an individual's sense of self begins to develop.

Middle Childhood This section covers the middle childhood stage, which is from age 6 to age 11. During this stage, many children go through growth spurts in their physical, social, emotional, and intellectual development.

Adolescence Students learn that adolescence occurs between the ages of 11 and 21. During this stage children experience puberty and many other emotional, social, and intellectual changes.

Adulthood This section covers adulthood, which begins at age 21. Students learn that in adulthood, a person gains many freedoms but also takes on many new responsibilities.

Focus and Engage

Bell-Ringer: Think About This

Students are asked to write a list of things they assume about the physical, emotional, social, and intellectual development of a 4-year-old boy. For example: physically, a 4-year-old boy is capable of participating in activities such as running, jumping, swimming, and bicycling. Emotionally, he is focused on how *he* feels about something but not so concerned about how others feel. Socially, he can interact with other kids and adults at home and in other environments, and he understands the difference between right and wrong. Intellectually, he understands shapes, colors, letters, and numbers, and he can formulate questions and express his thoughts. Students are to compare their lists with that of a classmate to determine if they made similar assumptions.

ADVANCE PREPARATION	
Review	*Life Skills for the 21st Century* textbook, Chapter 6.
Prepare	Paper and pencil for some activities. Crayons or markers for drawing. Magazines and newspapers from which students can cut pictures. Yardstick or tape measure. Box labeled "Hot Topics."

CUSTOMIZED INSTRUCTION OVERVIEW				
Less Advanced Students	**More Advanced Students**	**ESOL Students**	**Special Needs Students**	**At-Risk Students**
Pages 114, 123, 125	Pages 120, 128	Pages 117, 132	Pages 123, 125	Pages 114, 127, 131

Introduce the Section

In this section, students are introduced to the types of development we experience in the stages of our life. There are four types of development: physical, emotional, social, and intellectual.

Figure Focus

Explain that physical development refers to the growth and change in your body. Ask students to consider changes in their physical attributes that have occurred naturally over the last few years. They've probably grown taller, added pounds to their weight, and seen changes in their skin and hair growth.

Reinforce and Review

Make sure students can distinguish between the various types of development.

Physical development is how your body grows and changes. This refers to developments that are clearly visible as well as to those that are not, such as your musculoskeletal system, your digestive system, your heart and lungs, and your reproductive organs.

Emotional development is the maturity of your feelings and how you manage them. You have feelings and emotions about everything. Often, biologic factors relating to your physical development have an impact on your feelings and emotions.

Social development is the growth and change in the way you interact with other people and your environment. Your relationships with others and the roles you fill in every area of your life help shape your social development.

Intellectual development is the growth and change in your ability to think, reason, and process information. Research indicates that people have the potential to continue their intellectual development throughout the course of their lifespan.

Analyzing the Types of Development

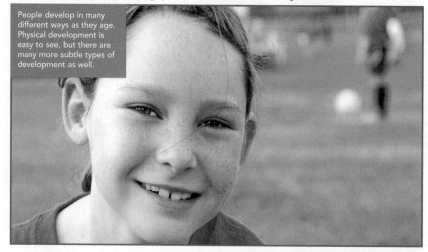

People develop in many different ways as they age. Physical development is easy to see, but there are many more subtle types of development as well.

Even though we are all unique, we pass through the same stages of life from the time we are born until the time we die. We start out as infants—babies—then grow into childhood, adolescence, adulthood, middle age, and old age.

As you progress through these stages, you experience a variety of types of development, which means you mature, grow, or improve. Development occurs in all areas of your life, and affects your physical, emotional, social, and intellectual wellness.

- Physical development is the growth and change in your body from infancy to adulthood.
- Emotional development is the maturity of your feelings and the way you manage them.
- Social development is the growth and change in the way you interact with other people.
- Intellectual development is the knowledge and critical-thinking skills you gain through school and life experience.

In many cases, one type of development depends on another. You don't learn to talk when you're an infant, because physically, your brain hasn't developed enough to process and create speech. And some studies show that the human brain doesn't develop its full capacity for critical thinking until you are 20 to 25 years old!

It's All Connected

Many life experiences contribute to your growth in multiple related ways.

For example, what kind of development happens to you in school? The obvious answer is that you gain skills and knowledge in the classes you take. That's intellectual development.

However, as you go through your school day, you have growth opportunities in other areas, too. For example, gym class helps you develop physically, and your conversations with your friends between classes help your social and emotional abilities.

There are strong relationships between the physical, social, emotional, and intellectual aspects of human growth and development. If one of those areas is lacking, other areas are likely to be affected too. For example, a boy who lags behind in social development might not interact as much with his peers, and so may not have as many opportunities for emotional stimulation and growth. As a result, he may end up isolating himself, spending more time alone in his room and not getting exercise, harming his physical development.

Customized Instruction: Less Advanced/At-Risk Students

As a group, have students prepare a chart that lists and/or illustrates how being part of a team can contribute to their physical, emotional, social, and intellectual development. Their chart should be divided into four sections—one for each type of development. For the physical section, they should focus on the exercise or physical activity they gain from being on a team. For the emotional section, they should focus on the feelings of camaraderie, happiness, or confidence. For the social section, they should focus on the aspects of sharing, cooperation, and support. For the intellectual section, they should focus on the things they learn and gain from others.

Physical Development

Physical development is what most people notice first. Have you ever been apart from a relative for a year or so, and heard "Oh, you've grown so much!" when he or she saw you again? When you develop physically, you:

- Increase in height and weight. Babies start out weighing about 7 pounds and measuring about 18 inches. An adult male might weigh 180 pounds and stand 6 feet tall.
- Mature to look more like an adult. That means your facial features become sharper and more prominent.
- Develop gender-specific body characteristics.

Other changes occur as well. Your reproductive organs mature, your voice changes tone, and you become more coordinated.

What kinds of social skills make someone a good friend? What skills do you value in *your* friends?

Emotional Development

Emotional development refers to the way you grow to understand and manage your feelings. For example, have you ever seen a toddler throw a temper tantrum? (Or do you remember doing that yourself as a child?) A toddler sees everything in very simple terms. He doesn't get a cookie, so he cries and screams. As you grow older, you learn to handle frustrating situations without having a meltdown—most of the time, anyway!

Social Development

As you develop socially, you learn skills for getting along with other people in various situations. For example, you probably speak and act very differently when you are talking to your grandparents than you do with your friends at school. You know the type of interaction that each situation requires because of your social skills. Different people have different levels of social development, regardless of age, but generally speaking, the closer to adulthood you are, the better able you are to navigate social interactions.

"How will working on my intellectual development help me, in and out of school?"

Intellectual Development

Intellectual development refers to two separate traits: the ability to remember facts, and the ability to make good decisions based on logic. As your brain develops physically, it also develops in its capability to do both of those things. Being intelligent is only half of the equation, though: You also have to be taught the facts that you need to remember. That's what your classes are for in school. You also need the opportunity to make decisions and experience their outcomes. You get to make some decisions in school, but a lot of decision-making practice comes from life outside school.

We're All Different

It's perfectly normal to develop faster in one area of your life than you do in another. You might develop faster socially than intellectually, for example, while your brother might excel intellectually but lag behind his peers socially or emotionally. Consider your peers at school; do they all show the same level of development in all areas of life?

✔ *A star athlete has strong physical development.*

✔ *A class leader, such as the class president, has strong social development.*

✔ *A kid who is always getting into fights and having discipline problems has weak social and emotional development.*

✔ *A student with a high grade point average has strong intellectual development.*

Figure Focus

Talk with students about the qualities of a good friend. For example, are friends fun, honest, supportive, forgiving, understanding, and trustworthy? How are these qualities reflected in their social skills? For example, a person who is fun can make people laugh. A person who is trustworthy can be a strong leader. Students are to comment on the social skills they value in a friend. Encourage them to explain why they value these skills.

We're All Different

Most students will recognize that the rate at which we develop varies from person to person, and that applies to all stages of our lives. Ask them to consider at what age they started walking, what age they got their first tooth, what age they learned to ride a two-wheeler, and so on, to illustrate that development occurs at different times for different people.

Figure Focus

Ask students to comment on things they can do to increase their intellectual development. Some ideas are reading more, doing puzzles, brainstorming, and strengthening critical-thinking skills, such as problem-solving, decision-making, and predicting outcomes.

TEAMWORK ACTIVITY

The brain is the control center of the body. It controls the way we think, feel, and move. Working in teams, have students research the brain and how it controls and affects our physical, social, emotional, and intellectual development. They can gather information from the Internet, the library, or other resources. They should prepare a short report that includes an illustration of the brain and identifies its parts. Their reports should cover the following:

- Spinal cord: Carries information to the brain and instructions to other parts of the body.
- Medulla oblongata: Helps control functions such as respiration, digestion, and heart rate. Also acts as a relay station for nerve signals going to and from the brain.
- Pons: Has roles in your level of consciousness and sleep.
- Cerebellum: Mostly deals with movement, posture, and balance.

- Hypothalamus: Linked closely with the pituitary gland to control many of the body's functions, including sleeping and waking cycle, appetite, thirst, and other bodily urges; also plays a role in emotions.
- Thalamus: Relay station for most of the auditory and visual sensory signals.
- Frontal lobe: Responsible for functions such as reasoning, problem solving, judgment, and impulse control as well as higher emotions such as empathy and selflessness.
- Parietal lobe: Involved in processing pain and touch sensation. It's also associated with cognition (including calculating location and speed of objects), movement, orientation, recognition, and speech.
- Temporal lobe: Involved in auditory sensation and emotion, memory, and speech.
- Occipital lobe: Controls visual sensation and processing.
- Broca's area: Part of the cortex that controls speech, language recognition, and facial nerves.

Introduce the Section

The factors that cause and affect growth and development are discussed. Students learn that their development depends on their heredity and their environment.

Vocabulary

Environment: As it relates to an individual's development, the things that happen in a person's life and the surroundings in which they happen.

Genes: Physical descriptors inherited from your parents that are stored in your body's cells and define your body's characteristics.

Inherited traits: Traits that you are born with as a result of your parents' genes.

Figure Focus

Encourage students to discuss the physical traits they have inherited. These might include eye color, body shape, height, and even whether or not they can roll their tongue. They also are to discuss the physical characteristics formed by their environment. Some environmental factors that can affect physical appearance include pollution and sun. An individual's use of substances such as tobacco, alcohol, and drugs during pregnancy can also have an effect on the physical appearance of his or her children.

Reinforce and Review

Remind students that physical development is how your body grows and changes.

What Causes Growth and Development?

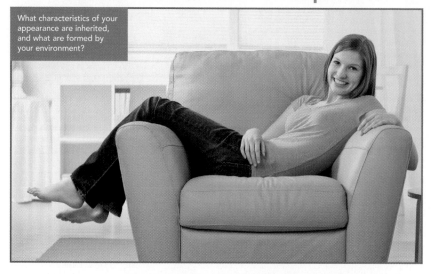

What characteristics of your appearance are inherited, and what are formed by your environment?

Genes are physical descriptors stored in your body's cells, inherited from your parents, that define your body's characteristics. Traits that you are born with as a result of your parents' genes are called **inherited traits**, and the process of inheriting traits is known as **heredity**. Heredity determines many physical characteristics, both the obvious ones you can see at birth—such as hair, skin, and eye color—and the not-so-obvious ones that might not show up until later in life, such as left-handedness, adult height, and shoe size.

Different people have different inherited capabilities when it comes to nonphysical types of growth and development too. For example, if one of your parents is very good at math, you might have inherited that ability. You might find math much easier to understand than most of your classmates do.

Environment—in other words, the things that happen in a person's life and the surroundings in which they happen—plays a role in all types of development. Even though physical development has a strong inherited component to it, environment can also dramatically affect physical growth. For example, a child who eats a nutritious diet and gets lots of exercise is likely to be more physically developed and have more athletic ability than one who eats only junk food and spends all her free time watching TV.

Heredity or Environment?

It isn't always possible to figure out why a person develops in a certain way—that is, whether it is heredity or environment influencing a certain outcome. Often the two are connected.

For example, suppose your parents were both outstanding athletes in high school and college, and are still very interested in sports and fitness. If you seem to naturally excel in sports in your school, why is that?

Some people might say that you have inherited your parents' natural abilities. And that is likely to be a part of the reason. But you also probably have benefitted from growing up in an environment where fitness is a priority, and where the family plays sports and practices athletic skills for fun. Even someone with no "natural talent" for sports might develop into a good athlete in that environment, especially if he or she received praise from parents for working to do so.

Environment also includes the influences of the people around you, such as your parents, your teachers, your siblings, and your friends. All of those people create the environment in which you learn, live, and grow up.

Social Influences

The way other people see you and react to you can influence your growth and development. They might judge you based on your gender, race, ethnicity, and culture, instead of on the person you really are. Some of the factors that may affect the experiences you have include:

- *Gender.* Boys and girls are sometimes treated differently and encouraged to pursue different types of growth experiences. A girl might be discouraged from taking a class in auto mechanics by a parent who grew up in a time when sex roles were more traditional. Girls and boys also have different social experiences. Girls may tend toward friendships based on verbal communication, whereas boys may have more friendships based on activities.

- *Race.* People may make assumptions about you based on the color of your skin, and those assumptions may influence the relationships you have. If you make a new friend who has not spent much time around someone of your race, for example, you may have to do a lot of communicating at first to clear up the stereotypes and misconceptions that person may have.

- *Religion.* People may make assumptions about you based on your religion, and those assumptions may change the opportunities you have. For example, if you belong to a religion that requires you to wear certain types of clothing, other people may look at you differently. In addition, certain religions may place restrictions on their members, and those restrictions might change the experiences you have.

- *Ethnicity and culture.* The national origin or culture of your family may have an impact on your development too. If your family comes from a very traditional culture, for example, the expectations based on gender may be more defined than in U.S. society at large.

Economic and Technology Influences

Growth and development can also depend on your access to money and technology. Although the United States is known as a land of equal opportunity, the playing field is far from level in terms of what resources are available to people.

Some factors that influence people's development environment include:

- *Wealth.* People who have enough money are able to take trips, go to plays and exhibitions, and have other experiences that others who don't have the money for those things can't experience.

- *Social class.* The type of neighborhood you grow up in, and the occupations of most of the people in your neighborhood, can make a difference. For example, people who grow up in environments where education is a high priority are more inclined to spend their time and money pursuing intellectual development.

- *Access to technology.* Having access to the Internet, computers, wireless communications, and other types of technology can affect a person's development.

Overcoming an Environmental Handicap

A person's environment can help or hinder growth in each of the areas.

If you were lagging behind your classmates in a particular subject in school, perhaps due to no fault of your own, what might you do?

- Explain to the teacher that it's not your fault and you should be graded on your effort, not your performance on the tests.

- Copy your answers off the test of a classmate who is known to get good grades.

- Ask your parents or a school counselor to help you get tutoring.

- Ask your teacher for extra help after class, as well as extra homework assignments that will help you learn what you are missing.

"Why are people always judging me?"

Discuss

Remind students that social development is the growth and change in the way you interact with other people and your environment. Your relationships with others and the roles you fill influence your social development. Define the factors discussed in the text:

- **Gender** refers to the sex of a person or organism.

- **Race** refers to a group of humans who share genetic features, such as skin color. For example, you belong to the Caucasian race or the African-American race.

- **Religion** refers to a person's beliefs and opinions about the existence, nature, and worship of a deity and that deity's involvement in the universe and human life. For example, you are of the Catholic religion or the Jewish religion.

- **Ethnicity and culture** refers to a person's cultural, racial, linguistic, or religious heritage that they share with a group. For example, you are of Irish ethnicity or Puerto Rican ethnicity.

Overcoming an Environmental Handicap

Ask students to consider how environmental factors might negatively influence their emotional development. For example, research suggests that the biggest reason why kids misbehave is because their parents are unable to say "no" and constantly give in to their demands. If you have grown up always getting what you want because your parents cannot say no to you, then chances are you will experience emotional meltdowns and feelings of anger and frustration when you are older and having to deal with disappointments on a regular basis. Thus, your parents' behavior has had a negative influence on your emotional development.

Customized Instruction: ESOL Students

Ask students to share the words for "male," "female," "religion," "race," and "culture" in their primary language.

Introduce the Section

In this section, students identify the nine stages of life. The care and nurturing that an individual needs in each stage of life are discussed.

Vocabulary

Life cycle: Progression from one phase of life to another.

Figure Focus

Explain the various life stages:

- Infant: birth–1 year old
- Toddler: 2–3 years old
- Early childhood: 3–6 years old
- Middle childhood: 6–11 years old
- Adolescence: 11–21 years old
- Young adulthood: 20s and 30s
- Middle adulthood: 40s and 50s
- Senior adulthood: 60s and 70s
- Old age: 80s and beyond

STUDENT ACTIVITY

Ask students to name a person they know for each of the various stages of life listed. It's all right if they cannot think of a person for every category. Beside the person's name, students should write an example of how they contribute to that person's quality of life.

Care and Nurturing Throughout the Life Cycle

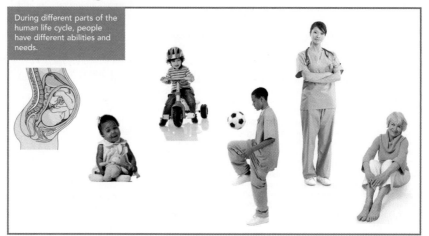

During different parts of the human life cycle, people have different abilities and needs.

The human **life cycle** is the progression from one phase of life to another, beginning with infancy and ending with old age. It is called a cycle, rather than a straight line, because in the middle part of life, humans often reproduce, creating a new cycle with a new baby. The cycle can be interrupted if the person dies before reaching the end, but everyone who stays alive progresses through the same stages in the same order.

At the beginning of the life cycle (infancy and childhood), people are very much dependent on others for their well-being. They become progressively more independent and able to take care of themselves into adulthood, and most people are self-sufficient for most of their adult lives. Then gradually, at the end of life, people become more dependent again on others, as their physical and mental capacities decrease from old age and/or illness. Physical and emotional nurturing and good communication all make dramatic differences in the quality of life in all stages, but especially at those vulnerable ages at the beginning and end.

Life Stages

All humans progress through these stages:

- Infant
- Toddler
- Early childhood
- Middle childhood
- Adolescence
- Young adulthood
- Middle adulthood
- Senior adulthood
- Old age

Stay in School

Studies have maintained that students who drop out of school can expect a lower quality of life thereafter. But findings of a recent study go even further, indicating that people who don't finish high school are at a higher risk of developing Alzheimer's disease than those who graduate and go on to further study. Researchers followed 1,388 participants through middle age and late life and found that those who completed high school had an 80 percent lower risk of developing dementia (a symptom of Alzheimer's disease), than those who had only an elementary school education. Researchers point out that people with less education tend to lead unhealthier lifestyles, which can also contribute to the higher risk of developing dementia and Alzheimer's.

Point out to students the correlation between education and a better quality of life. Stress the importance of formal education and lifelong learning. Encourage them to engage in brain-stimulating activities that are as simple as reading, writing, playing board games, listening to music, and participating in group discussions.

What Is Nurturing?

Nurturing refers to care and concern received from someone else. It can include physical care such as changing a baby's diaper, emotional care such as giving a hug to a crying child, and intellectual care such as teaching someone how to read. Nurturing is a part of the environment that a person exists in, but it pertains specifically to care provided by another person.

At different phases of the life cycle, people have different needs for nurturing. Some things are consistent throughout a person's life, such as the need for physical affection and social interaction. Other things, like physical care, change. Infants and toddlers need a lot of physical care, older children somewhat less, and adults not very much at all. Emotional nurturing is important at all phases, too, but what that consists of changes. Babies are emotionally nurtured through cuddling, touching, and talking to them, but it doesn't matter what you say. Older children, adolescents, and adults are nurtured by positive and encouraging speech, as well as by touch.

Communication needs also change as you move through the life cycle. We all need communication in order to get feedback, and in order to feel connected to other people and the world at large. Infants don't use words, so they receive all their communication through non-verbal cues like facial expressions and sounds. As you grow up and learn to speak, and then to read, you receive more complex messages about your environment and the people in it.

What special issues do you need to be aware of when communicating with an elderly person?

Nurturing People at Different Life Stages

When you are with people of different ages, it's important to understand what kind of nurturing and communication is appropriate for them. Here are some general guidelines:

- Infants need total physical care, but not much communication.
- Toddlers need some physical care, but mostly watchfulness so they do not get into trouble. They need basic rules and discipline, too.
- Young children need physical supervision, opportunities to play, and clear rules to follow.
- Older children need mental challenges, affection, structure, and clear communication.
- Elderly people need companionship, conversation, affection, and allowances made for their increasing physical limitations.

Depending on the individual person, the needs may be different. For example, someone with a disability may need more physical care.

Job Search

As the baby boomers—people born between 1946 and 1964—are reaching retirement age, the average age of a U.S. citizen climbs, creating more and more job opportunities in **geriatric** health care. *Geriatric* means elderly. Some of the positions available include home health care aide, Certified Nursing Assistant (CNA), Licensed Practical Nurse (LPN), Registered Nurse (RN), and physician (M.D.) How many years of post high-school education, if any, do each of those positions require? Do the research

Vocabulary

Nurturing: Refers to care and concern received from someone else.

Figure Focus

Students are asked to comment on the special issues that must be considered when communicating with an elderly person. Some of these include:

- Hearing loss, which makes it harder for them to understand you. You may have to speak louder and slower than you are comfortable doing.
- Vision loss, which may impact their recognition of you and other things in their environment.
- Voice changes, which can affect the loudness or clarity of their speech.
- Memory loss, which might mean that you have to remind them of things in their past.

Emphasize that, first and foremost, communicating with the elderly requires patience and understanding.

Job Search

The text discusses job opportunities in the geriatric health care field. Explain that *geriatric health care* relates to the diagnosis, treatment, and prevention of illness in senior citizens.

- Home health aide: varies by state.
- Certified Nursing Assistant (CNA): high school diploma.
- Licensed Practical Nurse (LPN): varies by state, but schools that train and license LPNs generally prefer high school graduates. Licensing can be obtained through a state-approved training program.
- Registered Nurse (RN): state-approved two-year nursing program and passing grade on a national licensing exam.
- Physician (M.D.): eight plus years post-secondary education and training.

Figure Focus

Students are to suggest reasons why some elderly people do not live on their own. Explain that there are many reasons. The person might be financially unable to live on her own. If he loses a spouse or a source of income, he might not be able to afford his current living arrangement. On the flip side, an older person might be invited to move in to help share in the expenses and daily operations of the household. Another reason older persons do not live on their own is because they are ill or cannot adequately take care of their everyday needs.

 Family Elder Care

Students are asked to consider the proliferation of assisted living facilities and nursing homes and whether they think it is a good trend or bad one. Assisted living facilities and nursing homes provide services, facilities, and varying levels of care tailored to the needs of older people. These facilities have trained staff and access to technologies that help diagnose and treat the illnesses and ailments from which the elderly often suffer. Oftentimes, in-home care provided by family, relatives, and others is not enough or not suitable for the person. It can also be stressful for the caregiver and other family living in the home. In most respects, the trend is good. But there are always concerns about abuse and neglect in such healthcare facilities.

Do you have an older relative that lives with your family? Why do you suppose that person doesn't live on their own?

Care and Nurturing in Other Cultures

In the United States, parents are usually the primary caregivers for their children, either as stay-at-home parents or in combination with daycare (if both parents work). This is not always the case in other places, though. In many countries, grandparents live with the parents and children, and the grandparents do most of the childcare. In some places, older brothers and sisters are expected to care for the younger ones.

Elder care varies between cultures as well. In the United States, nursing homes are very common, providing a home to senior citizens and people with disabilities who need a lot of physical care. Family members often do provide daily care for the elderly, but it is not a cultural expectation. In Asia, Africa, and Latin America, it is expected that family members will live with and support the elderly, so nursing homes are not very common.

When the Child Becomes the Caregiver

As an adolescent, it might seem to you like your parents are invincible and will never need your help. However, at some point in your life, you will probably find yourself taking care of one of your parents, due to:

- Old age
- Disabilities
- Addiction
- Depression

When an adult has to take care of his or her parents, the situation is usually manageable. However, an adolescent may not be up for the challenge of caring for a parent along with completing school, maintaining friendships, and growing up himself or herself. If you find yourself in the situation of being a caregiver to a parent, either temporarily or permanently, don't be afraid to ask for help from other family members, adult friends of the family, and school counselors.

 Family Elder Care

In countries where families are larger and closer (both geographically and emotionally), senior citizens and people with disabilities are more likely to be cared for by relatives. This is especially true in Africa and Latin America, where the majority of the populations are rural and agricultural.

As societies become more modernized and more city-based, we see less in-home care for dependent adults, and more use of assisted living facilities and nursing homes. Why do you think this is so? Is it a good trend or a bad one?

Customized Instruction: More Advanced Students

Have students search for national, state, and county population information on people age 65 and over. They should find statistics on current population as well as projections for 10, 25, and 50 years from now. Students should create graphs that illustrate the information they find. Online resources include the Administration on Aging at www.aoa.gov and the U.S. Census Bureau at www.census.gov.

Caring for an Elderly Person

If a grandparent or other elderly relative lives with you, or visits your home, you may be called on to help make them comfortable and take care of their basic needs. Those needs will depend on the individual, but some of the things you can do to help include:

- Offering to fetch things (food, drinks, books, and so on)
- Helping them stand up or sit down
- Checking medication instructions and dosages
- Reading aloud, if they have a visual impairment
- Speaking loudly and clearly, if they have a hearing impairment
- Being patient and understanding about physical limitations

Some elderly people experience memory problems, and cannot remember whether or not they have told you a particular story, so they may repeat themselves. It is considerate to listen patiently anyway.

Caring for Someone with a Disability

A **disability** is a condition that prevents a person from functioning normally in a certain way. Disabilities can be either mental or physical. Either one can potentially make the person dependent on others for his or her personal care. Physical disabilities can include arm or leg weakness or paralysis, difficulty speaking, difficulty breathing independently, and so on. A **paraplegic** is a person who cannot use their legs, but still has use of their arms. A **quadriplegic** is someone who cannot use both legs and arms.

You should not assume that a person with one type of disability has another type; most people with physical disabilities do not have mental disabilities, for example. When interacting with a person with a physical disability, it is polite to:

- Speak directly to the person, not to a companion they have with them
- Ask if you can be of assistance, rather than jumping in
- Not ask about their disability unless it is directly relevant to an activity you are doing together

Someone with a mental disability may need help making decisions (both large and small), handling money, using transportation, or interacting with other people.

Someone with a physical disability may need help with the things listed above for elderly people. They may need personal care assistance, such as personal grooming, using the restroom, moving from place to place, or picking up dropped items. It is important, though, to ask if you can be of assistance, and not make assumptions.

TECH CONNECT

There are some amazing devices out there to assist people with disabilities, from wheelchairs that can climb stairs to computers that let you control a mouse pointer by moving your eyes. And more new items are becoming available every day.

Using the Internet, find at least three electronic devices that are designed to help someone with a disability function more easily. Share your findings with the rest of the class.

What special issues do you need to be aware of when communicating with a person with a disability?

Discuss

Review the things discussed in the text that students can do to help care for an elderly person. Also review the challenges they might face when dealing with an older person. These include hearing, vision, and memory loss in the older person, as well as impairments and changes to their speech.

TECH CONNECT

Students are to research and find information on devices that are designed to assist someone with a disability. Some examples are voice recognition software, ceiling-mounted electronic lifts that help a person get in and out of bed, screen-readers that translate on-screen text into speech, Braille input devices for keyboarding, etc. Make sure students come up with at least three devices and explain what they are designed to do and who would use them.

Vocabulary

Disability: A condition that prevents a person from functioning normally in a certain way.

Paraplegic: Person who cannot use his legs, but still has use of his arms.

Quadriplegic: A person who cannot use her legs or arms.

Figure Focus

Students are asked to comment on the special issues that must be considered when communicating with a disabled person. Some of these include:

- Avoid asking personal questions about the disability.
- Avoid terms such as "crippled," "defect," "invalid," and "handicapped."
- Do not treat the person as if he is overly special or superhuman.
- Make sure you are facing a hearing-impaired person when you speak.
- Speak directly to the person with the disability, not to her companion or aide.

Introduce the Section

This section discusses the physical, social, emotional, and intellectual growth of infants and toddlers. This life stage is from birth to age 3.

Vocabulary

Developmentally delayed: Slower than average to develop in one or more ways.

Developmentally disabled: Having a problem that prevents normal development in some way.

Infancy: Period of life from birth to approximately 1 year old.

Figure Focus

Ask students to list different ways infants interact with their environment. Explain that at this stage, babies learn about their environment through their senses. They suck their fist or thumb because it feels good; they see an object, such as a toy, and try to grab it; they hear their mother's voice and smile; and so on.

Infants and Toddlers

Infants spend most of their time interacting with their environment to learn and grow.

Infancy is the period of life from birth to approximately 1 year old. You probably don't remember being an infant, because an infant's brain isn't developed enough to record memories the way your brain does now. Even so, your brain and body did a tremendous amount of growth and development during that first year. Babies triple in size from birth to age 1. Can you imagine how large you would be if you continued to grow that much throughout your life?

As an infant, you had two basic desires: to have your physical needs met, and to explore your world. You cried to let your caretakers know that you had unmet needs, such as hunger, thirst, pain, or discomfort (such as a dirty diaper). With those basic needs taken care of, you were curious and eager to focus your attention on objects that interested and comforted you, such as a person, an animal, or a toy.

Most of an infant's waking time is spent learning how to interact with his or her environment. You very quickly learned how to get Mom or Dad's attention by crying, for example. Crying is a very effective communication method at that age.

Delay or Disability?

Different people mature at different rates. A **developmentally delayed** child is slower than average to develop in one or more ways, but there is not necessarily a problem. For example, most children begin talking around age 2, but some children don't talk much until they are 3 or even 4, and they still grow up to communicate normally.

On the other hand, if a person is **developmentally disabled**, he or she has a problem that prevents normal development in some way. Disabilities are more than just delays; they are often permanent conditions. For example, an infant who can't crawl as a result of nerve damage in his legs will probably not be able to move normally later in life either.

As an infant, you also learned how to cause movement. At first, you learned how to move people and objects closer to you by grasping them. As you got a little older, you learned how to crawl and then walk, so you could move *yourself* closer to people and things.

When you started walking, probably somewhere around 1 year old, you became a **toddler**. *Toddle* means to move in short, unsteady steps—which is exactly how a child that age moves when learning to walk. The toddler stage continues until 3 to 4 years of age. Toddlers are curious about their surroundings and are constantly getting into everything they can reach, so they have to be carefully monitored to make sure they do not hurt themselves.

Physical Growth

Infants and toddlers develop physically very quickly, with new physical capabilities happening nearly every week. Here are some typical abilities associated with the various phases of infancy:

- 0 to 3 months: Raises head for a few seconds, makes a fist, touches and tugs own hands
- 3 to 6 months: Rolls over, pulls body up on crib railing, reaches out for objects, puts objects in mouth
- 6 to 9 months: Crawls, grasps and pulls objects, transfers objects between hands
- 9 to 12 months: Sits and stands, walks with help, throws objects, drops and picks up toys
- 1 to 2 years: Walks without help, pushes and pulls objects, scribbles, turns knobs
- 2 to 3 years: Kicks a ball, jumps in place, strings large beads, draws circles

Social and Emotional Growth

Infants are interested in other people almost immediately, and that interest grows as they move into being a toddler. Here are some typical social milestones:

- 0 to 3 months: Shows pleasure at being talked to and touched
- 3 to 6 months: Plays peek-a-boo, laughs out loud
- 6 to 9 months: Responds to speech and gestures, distinguishes family from strangers
- 9 to 12 months: Mimics simple actions
- 1 to 2 years: Imitates adult behavior, helps pick up toys
- 2 to 3 years: Becomes aware of feelings, senses gender identity, participates in group activities such as clapping

Thinking Skills

Newborns begin right away to use the information that their senses provide. Here are some ways infants' and toddlers' minds develop:

- 0 to 3 months: Focuses on and follows moving objects, distinguishes various tastes, sounds, and smells
- 3 to 6 months: Recognizes faces and responds to familiar sights and sounds
- 6 to 9 months: Can tell the difference between inanimate and animate objects, understands that the size an object appears is a clue as to how far away it is
- 9 to 12 months: Knows that an object still exists even when it's not visible, responds to simple questions and directions, understands that pictures represent actual items
- 1 to 2 years: Understands individual words, matches similar objects, distinguishes between "you" and "me"
- 2 to 3 years: Uses objects symbolically in play, like pretending a shoebox is a car; responds to simple directions

Myth Listening to classical music from composers such as Mozart and Beethoven makes an infant smarter.

Truth There is no particular type of music that makes a baby smarter. The child may enjoy the music, though, because classical music tends to be more smooth and soothing than rock or jazz.

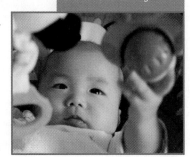
What kinds of items could you give a baby to touch and look at to stimulate thinking?

Customized Instruction: Less Advanced/Special Needs Students

Food is a great stimulant for people at every age, but particularly for infants and toddlers who rely heavily on their senses to learn and grow. Have students research the types of foods you should give a toddler. They will create a small poster that identifies and illustrates the foods. Have students review *Appendix C: MyPyramid Food Group Recommendations*, starting on page 531 of the student text as a starting point.Students' posters should include dairy products, such as milk, cheese, and yogurt; fruits and vegetables, such as bananas, applesauce, green beans, and mashed sweet potatoes; healthy fats, such as eggs, meat, and peanut butter; and whole-grain breads, pastas, and cereals.

Vocabulary

Toddler: Life stage that begins at about age 1 and lasts until 3 or 4.

Myth/Truth

Explain to students that much has been written about the "Mozart Effect," a term coined in the 1990s that refers to the *alleged* increase in brain development that occurs in children under age 3 who listen to the music of Mozart. Although the concept lacks hard evidence to substantiate it, the American public latched onto it with so much fervor that a new industry sprang up almost overnight, selling CDs and music-centered books, toys, and accessories to parents looking for ways to raise smart kids.

Figure Focus

Students are asked what type of things you could give a baby to stimulate thinking. Some examples are:

- Toys with bright, contrasting patterns and colors.
- Crib gyms, with figures and shapes suspended that the baby can reach and grab.
- Rattles or squeaky toys that make noise.

Introduce the Section

The early childhood stage is from age 3 to age 6. In this section, students learn how an individual's sense of self begins to develop.

Vocabulary

Early childhood: Life stage that begins at age 3 and ends at about age 6.

Play age: Early childhood life stage, when children spend the majority of their time playing.

Figure Focus

Ask students to think back to their early childhood years and discuss the things they played, and who and what they played with.

Discuss

Explain to students that during the years between birth and age 6, 75 percent of brain growth is completed. The early childhood years are recognized by many experts as being the most important for a person's success in education and life in general. Many children start preschool at the age of 3 or 4 and then kindergarten at the age of 5.

STUDENT ACTIVITY

Ask students to bring in a few photos of themselves when they were between the ages of 3 and 6. The photos should show them engaged in some type of activity, like the first day of kindergarten, playing in a soccer game, dressing up with a sibling or friend, or simply having fun at a party. They will create a poster with the photos in which they explain how the environment in which the photo was taken contributed to their physical, social, emotional, and intellectual development. Remind students that environment refers to the things that happen in a person's life and the surroundings in which they happen.

If some of your students do not have photographs, have them find pictures of children in magazines or newspapers and describe how what they are doing is contributing to their development in the four areas. Advertising circulars for department stores and toy stores might also be a good source for pictures.

Early Childhood

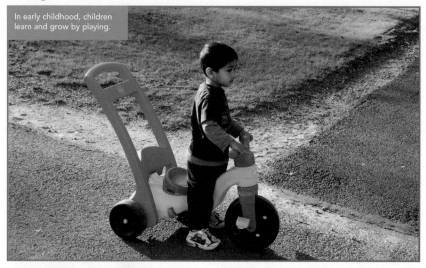

In early childhood, children learn and grow by playing.

In the **early childhood** phase, ages 3 to 6, you began developing a greater sense of yourself, including your likes and dislikes, your talents, and your preferences in everything from food to playmates. By this age, you were not simply "the baby" anymore, but a little person with a uniquely developing personality.

This age range is sometimes called **play age** because that's how children in this age range spend the majority of their time. Play is not just entertainment, though. It serves an essential purpose in helping the child develop in all four of the areas you learned about earlier: physical, emotional, social, and intellectual. Interacting with toys and playmates builds physical coordination, and running or jumping with friends makes for strong muscles, healthy lungs, and good circulation. Figuring out how toys work—and how to make toys do specific things—builds brain power, and negotiating with playmates over toy-sharing and what games to play builds social and verbal skills.

Play Is Important

Even though very young children don't attend school, they still learn lots of lessons every day, with each experience

For example, suppose two 4-year-olds are playing a game where they bounce a big rubber ball back and forth between them. That simple game is as important to their growth as an algebra or history lesson would be for someone older. They are learning in many ways:

- When they decided to play the game and figured out what the rules would be, they used their social skills.
- The physical acts of bouncing the ball, and chasing after it when it goes out of bounds, help them develop physically.
- As they figure out that the ball will go at a different angle depending on how they throw it, they are gaining intellectual knowledge. The whole game is one big physics experiment, in fact!
- If something happens to make the game frustrating, such as the ball going flat or getting lost, both children build emotional maturity by handling their feelings about that outcome.

Physical Changes in Early Childhood

As your body grew larger, it also grew stronger and more coordinated. That means you were able to start participating in "big ball" sports such as kickball and soccer, which use skills like running and aiming a kick. You might also have learned how to pedal a tricycle or push a scooter.

From ages 3 to 6, pencils and crayons are a favorite toy for drawing and for imitating adult behavior by pretending to write. When you were this age, you probably liked playing with coloring books, or drawing on the sidewalk with chalk. You probably also learned how to button and zip your clothes, as well as help with simple household chores such as pouring juice and setting the table.

Intellectual Growth

"Why?" That's a question you asked a lot when you were this age. Why does the sun rise? Why is the grass green? Why does mom or dad have to go to work? Why do older kids get to stay up later? You were constantly gathering data about your environment, and also growing your vocabulary very rapidly. Kids this age also love repetition, because it helps them build memory skills. For example, you might have wanted to watch the same movie over and over, dozens of times. Now that you're older, you can probably imagine how boring your parents thought that was, but at the time you thought it was fascinating.

Social and Emotional Development

At this stage, you were socially very focused on yourself. The world revolved around *you* and *your* needs, as far as you were concerned. Temper tantrums gradually decreased as you learned other coping skills, but there were probably quite a few tears and meltdowns in the process. Sometimes children this age develop new fears. Those fears are not usually permanent; they're just a phase. For example, you might have been terrified of lightning or fire trucks or clowns.

At this age, children also begin learning how to be a good playmate. Most of the group games at this point focus on sharing toys or doing group activities, like singing or clapping; there is not a lot of conversation that does not relate to the activity. Many parents enroll children this age in preschool, day care, or kindergarten, to give them opportunities to practice the social skills that will help them get along with others when they start school.

How would you respond to a toddler throwing a tantrum over not getting her way?

Influences

Young children are very open to the people and things they see and hear. Some of these influences might not be in their best interest, so caregivers must be aware of what's going on. Some influences include:

✔ Playing with other children the same age

✔ Observing the play of older children

✔ Listening to adult conversations

✔ Watching television and movies

✔ Listening to the radio

✔ Finding objects to play with as toys (whether or not they are actually toys)

✔ Exploring nature and the outdoors

✔ Interacting with family pets and other animals

Reinforce and Review

Review with students the physical, intellectual, social, and emotional changes that occur in early childhood years.

■ **Physical:** Between birth and age 3, most children double their height and quadruple their weight. This rapid growth continues in early childhood, and they develop fine motor skills, which means they have good control of pencils, crayons, and scissors. Gross motor skills also develop, where a child learns to skip, hop on one foot, and do simple gymnastics.

■ **Intellectual:** By the age of 5, most children have a vocabulary of about 1,500 words, understand tense, and can put together verbally a five- to seven-word sentence.

■ **Social/Emotional:** In this stage, children form relationships with peers but are still "me" focused. They understand right and wrong, fair and unfair, and openly display emotions which reflect that understanding.

Figure Focus

Students are asked how they would handle a toddler's temper tantrum. Some suggestions are removing the toddler from the situation, distracting the toddler with a different activity, or leaving the toddler alone for a few minutes in a safe place. Explain that most tantrums at this age are caused by the child being tired or hungry. Considering this, you might be able to avoid tantrums altogether just by addressing these basic needs.

Influences

Ask students to give examples of how the influences listed in the text can be positive or negative. For example, watching television and movies can be educational and enhance the child's intellectual and social development, but it can have a negative influence if it shows violence or risky behavior.

Customized Instruction: Less Advanced/Special Needs Students

Ask students to think of something they liked to do in their early childhood years that they still like to do now. For example, did they like to swim, to visit their grandparents, or draw? Then have them draw a picture of themselves doing it then and now.

Introduce the Section

This section covers the middle childhood stage, which is from age 6 to age 11. During this stage, many children go through growth spurts in their physical, social, emotional, and intellectual development.

Figure Focus

Encourage students to think back to their elementary school years. What was the name of their school? What were the names of their teachers? What were the names of their friends? Which was their favorite grade? What kinds of activities do they remember doing? Ask them how those activities contributed to their intellectual development.

Vocabulary

Middle childhood: Stage of life that begins at age 6 and ends at age 11.

Middle Childhood

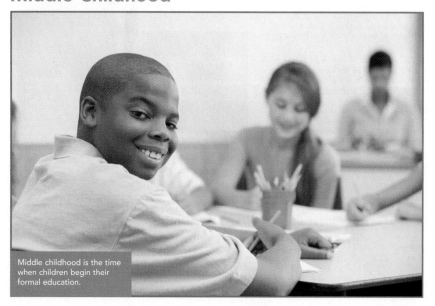

Middle childhood is the time when children begin their formal education.

When you were a very young child, you stuck close to your parents, but around age 6, you started being more adventurous. You were ready to have experiences away from home and family. This is the start of **middle childhood** (ages 6 to 11).

During middle childhood, a child continues to grow physically, socially, intellectually, and emotionally in interconnected ways. The growth in physical coordination makes it possible to write with a pencil and type on a keyboard, and the growth in mental capacity makes it possible to understand and interpret letters and numbers and remember facts. It's time for school!

Most children start school (kindergarten) at age 5 or 6. By this age, they are ready to be away from their parents for several hours at a time and explore the world around them. School provides a perfect environment for this exploration, under the supervision of trained teachers who can set up lessons and activities that will promote growth.

How School Helps

Elementary school is much more than just a place to learn new facts. Kids also learn how to:

■ Make friends with other kids
■ Share ideas and opinions
■ Help others
■ Sit still and listen
■ Express creativity through art
■ Learn about other cultures
■ Listen respectfully
■ Play games and sports on a team

Physical Changes in Middle Childhood

During middle childhood, most children grow 2 to 3 inches in height per year, and they gain about 7 pounds in weight each year. Usually, this physical growth doesn't happen smoothly and consistently. It happens in short start-and-stop bursts that are often called **growth spurts**. Most girls experience a growth spurt around age 9 or 10, and most boys go through one at age 11 or 12.

This is the time when most of you get your adult permanent teeth, and the baby teeth are pushed out by the new set. This is possible because by age 8 or 9, the head and mouth are almost adult sized. The brain reaches near-adult size at this time too.

Sports become fun in middle childhood because the brain and body learn to work together as a team. The brain is able to tell the body to kick or throw in a certain way, and the body is able to obey. For the same reason, middle childhood is often when kids develop an interest in video games that require hand-eye coordination. The body's growth makes playing those games possible.

What types of things do you remember learning when you were eight?

Making and Keeping Friends

What advice would you give someone who wanted to be more popular and have more friends? Middle childhood is also an important time for developing social skills. Children start developing more complex friendships that are centered on the people themselves rather than on toys and games. They start understanding social concepts such as teamwork, fairness, and loyalty, and they learn that there are consequences to their social actions and choices.

Peer pressure to conform to social customs also starts in this age range. For example, in early childhood, a child might pick out whatever clothing he wanted to wear on a particular day—maybe a shirt with a favorite cartoon character on it, for example. When a child is around her peers at school all day, though, she starts comparing her clothes to others and starts becoming conscious of wanting to wear what everyone else is wearing to "fit in."

21st Century Skills

What Happens Next?

Kids whose physical bodies develop strength and coordination early in life have an advantage over others with slower development, because these kids start enjoying and practicing sports earlier. Children who lag behind in physical development may not like playing physical games with other children because they are "no good at it." These children may not get enough exercise and may risk being overweight or obese as adolescents and adults.

Raina is a gym teacher at an elementary school, and she has noticed that one girl in her 5th grade class, Anna, is really struggling because she is not as fast or coordinated as the others. Anna often gets frustrated and quits trying, sitting down on the sidelines. What can Raina do to make gym class more fun for Anna? Using your 21st Century Skills—such as decision making, goal setting, and problem solving—write a story or create a skit showing how Raina could help Anna without making her feel singled out or embarrassed.

Vocabulary

Growth spurts: Physical growth that occurs in short start-and-stop bursts.

Figure Focus

Ask students to consider things they learned both in and out of school during their middle childhood. For example, they might have learned to skateboard or play the piano. Or, they might have learned their multiplication tables and the components of the solar system.

21st Century Skills

What Happens Next?

Students are to write a story or create a skit on what Raina, the gym teacher, can do to make gym class a more positive experience for Anna. Before students start, discuss what gym class typically involves. Is it focused more on team play or individual activities? For this situation, Raina should consider activities that encourage kids to shoot for their personal best rather than competing or trying to keep up with others. Some school districts are experimenting with "alternate" PE equipment, such as unicycles and rock-climbing walls that challenge the individual. Raina should also consider team activities that encourage participation rather than competition; for example, having a team see how many rings they can toss on a cone, or how long they can keep an inflated ball in the air. These involve physical activity as well as critical-thinking and teamwork skills.

Customized Instruction: At-Risk Students

Have students write a letter to an elementary-age student (grade 3, age 8 is ideal) giving them advice on the things to do, and *not* do, to better prepare themselves for middle school. Their letters should cover study habits, classroom and hallway behavior, participation in extracurricular activities, and relationships with other students and teachers.

Introduce the Section

In this section, students learn that adolescence occurs between the ages of 11 and 21. During this stage, children experience puberty and many other emotional, social, and intellectual changes.

Figure Focus

Ask students to comment on the issues they personally face. Are they at the point where they are thinking about a job? Do they need to start thinking about college? Are they concerned about dating?

Teaching Tips

Students may be reluctant to discuss personal issues in class. Encourage them to talk in generalities— what issues do adolescents as a group have to deal with?

Vocabulary

Adolescence: Life stage that starts at age 11 and ends at age 21.

STUDENT ACTIVITY

Have students create a table in which they write how their roles have changed in each area of their lives. Refer them to the shaded box on this page. In the first column, they should write the area. In the second column, they should detail how their roles and responsibilities in that area have changed.

Adolescence

What are some of the issues that an adolescent might face?

Adolescence occurs between the ages of 11 and 21 (between childhood and becoming an adult). This is a time of amazing changes in all four development areas:

- Physically, your body changes from child to adult by growing in size and by releasing hormones that cause sex-based characteristics to develop.
- Intellectually, your skills for thinking critically improve, so you can start making good decisions on your own, and your capacity for remembering facts increases.
- Emotionally, you become more capable of identifying and managing your feelings. And that's a good thing, because the chemical changes in your body due to puberty also cause dramatic shifts in your emotions.
- Socially, you continue learning how to be a good friend and family member, and you start taking on new roles and responsibilities.

Adolescent development progresses through three stages: early (11 to 13), middle (14 to 18), and late (19 to 21). Each period has its own distinct characteristics of growth and development, but the exact time frame varies from person to person. Both heredity and environment can affect the rate at which you develop.

The Roles You Play

As you move from childhood to adolescence, your relationship to the people and groups around you changes, too. Think about how your life changed from age 9 to the present in each of these areas:

- *Family.* What new responsibilities were you given at home? For example, were you asked to help babysit younger brothers and sisters? Or to take care of a family pet?
- *School.* How has your schoolwork increased in difficulty and complexity? What growth in you made that possible?
- *Peers.* How have your relationships with your friends changed? Do you have more friends now? Closer friends? Is what you do together different?
- *Community.* How do people in your community treat you differently now? What contributions do you make to the community that you were not able to make when you were younger?
- *Work.* What type of job do you think you could do now, at your current maturity level? Could you have done that job at age 9? Why or why not?

Customized Instruction: More Advanced Students

Students will prepare a presentation for the class on adolescence. The presentation will be based on a character they create who progresses through the three stages of adolescence (early, middle, and late). They can draw the character at each of the stages or use dolls or figures/figurines to represent the character. At each stage, they will describe the character's environment and how it has shaped the character's emotional, social, and intellectual development.

What Is Puberty?

Puberty is the process of your body's changing into its adult form so that it is capable of reproduction. This includes:

In Boys	In Girls
Growth in height	Growth in height
Growth of pubic hair	Growth of pubic hair
Change and increase in body odor	Change and increase in body odor
Maturity and growth of testicles	Maturity of vagina, ovaries, and uterus
Growth of body and facial hair	Growth of body hair
Deepening of voice	Breast development
Increase in bone mass and muscle density	Menstruation
	Change in body shape and fat distribution

The average age for the **onset** of puberty (that is, the time when you observe the first change in your body) is 9 to 14 for girls, and 10 to 18 for boys. Many factors can influence the timing, though, including:

- *Heredity.* The age of onset is partially inherited from your parents.
- *Nutrition.* Good nutrition lowers the average age of puberty; poor nutrition raises it.
- *Body weight.* Obesity and malnutrition both delay puberty.
- *Diseases.* Some diseases, such as tuberculosis, delay puberty.
- *Environment.* Factors such as emotional stress and exposure to chemical pollutants can bring on puberty sooner.

Puberty is far from an overnight process. For girls, it takes about four years from start to finish. For boys, six years is average. During that time, your body produces **hormones** (chemicals) that trigger the changes to be made, and your body responds to those hormones by producing the changes listed above.

Test **IT** Yourself!

Because girls begin puberty two years earlier than boys, in a typical middle-school classroom the average height of girls is likely to be the same as, or greater than, the average height of boys. This changes in high school, when more boys have completed puberty and are at their adult heights.

To test this, measure the height of everyone in your class, in inches, and find the average height for boys and the average height for girls. To find the average:

1. Measure each person, and record the measurements.
2. Add the measurements separately for males and females.
3. Count the number of people you measured of each sex.
4. For each sex separately, divide the sum of the measurements (step 2) by the number of people you measured (step 3).

Who is taller in your class, on the average, boys or girls? Did the answer surprise you?

Myth People who are short as children and adolescents are likely to be short as adults, too.

Truth There is some relationship, but there are also lots of exceptions. During puberty, many people grow dramatically in height, often in a very short time.

Because people enter puberty at different times, someone who is short in middle school may turn out to be tall in high school and beyond.

"How come all of my friends look older than me?"

Vocabulary

Hormones: Chemicals that trigger the changes to be made in your body.

Onset: In regards to puberty, the time when you observe the first change in your body.

Puberty: Process of your body's changing into its adult form so that it is capable of reproduction.

Discuss

Explain that puberty can have a marked effect on an adolescent's emotions. Hormones can cause emotional highs and lows and even extreme mood swings. Students may find they spend more time wondering what their friends and peers are thinking and doing. They make comparisons between themselves and others and try to determine what makes them unique and what will help them fit in.

Teaching Tips

Be sure to stress to students the importance of asking questions about the changes their bodies are undergoing. Good family communication can help them deal with these changes more easily. Give them other resources they can consult, such as the school nurse, or books from the library.

Test **IT** Yourself!

Students are to find the average height of boys and girls in the class. Be aware that some students may be sensitive about their height. If this is a concern, then you might consider measuring students yourself in a more discrete location, such as outside the classroom in the hallway. Or, assign the measuring to one or two trustworthy students.

STUDENT ACTIVITY

Have students use an online calculator to determine their Body Mass Index. BMI is a tool for determining the healthy weight for your height. Some online resources are:

- http://kidshealth.org/teen/nutrition/weight/weight_height.html
- http://www.cdc.gov/healthyweight/assessing/bmi/

Students will need to know their height and weight to use the calculator. Make sure students use calculators specifically for their age group.

Three Levels of Understanding

Ask students at what step in the problem-solving process might the different levels of understanding be exhibited. Review the problem-solving process:

1. Identify the problem.
2. Consider possible solutions.
3. Identify consequences.
4. Select the best solution.
5. Develop a plan of action.
6. Evaluate.

Level 1 would not be exhibited in any of the steps. You fail to identify the problem or that it even exists. Level 2 would be exhibited at step 1. You can identify the problem, but you don't consider solutions to it. Level 3 is exhibited in all six steps.

Figure Focus

Remind students that when their bodies reach a certain age, their brains release a special hormone that starts the changes of puberty. Ask them to comment on the changes in feelings or emotions they might experience.

TEAMWORK ACTIVITY

Form teams of males and females. Have all teams research the following three puberty hormones:

- Gonadotropin-releasing hormone (GnRH)
- Luteinizing hormone (LH)
- Follicle-stimulating hormone (FSH)

Each team should create a chart that lists the hormone and describes the effect it has on a boy's body (for the male teams) or a girl's body (for the female teams).

Students' charts should touch on the following:

- When GnRH reaches the pituitary gland, it signals this gland to release LH and FSH into the bloodstream. In boys, these hormones signal the testes to begin the production of testosterone (the hormone that causes most of the changes in a boy's body during puberty) and sperm (which must be produced for men to reproduce).

- In girls, these hormones signal the ovaries, which contain eggs that have been there since birth, to begin producing the hormone estrogen. This hormone, along with FSH and LH, causes a girl's body to mature and prepares her to reproduce.

Three Levels of Understanding

Depending on your level of intellectual maturity, you might view a problem in different ways.

✔ *Level 1. You don't see the problem. If a situation doesn't affect you personally, you are oblivious to it.*

✔ *Level 2. You see that something is wrong and can explain what it is. This is the stage that most "chronic complainer" type people get stuck in.*

✔ *Level 3. You see what needs to be done to fix the problem and can propose a plan. People who reach this stage are successful at work and home because they can fix problems, not just identify them.*

"Why do I sometimes feel sad or angry for no reason? Could it be hormones?"

Intellectual Development

Have you ever heard the phrase "like a kid in a candy store"? It means someone who sees so many possibilities that they aren't sure which to focus on. That's very similar to what you might go through as you develop your intellect as an adolescent. There are so many interesting subjects available to learn about, now that your brain is developed enough to handle them! You may find yourself bouncing from subject to subject, one week being fascinated by science and the next week wanting to learn all you can about psychology. Adults may ask you "What do you want to be when you grow up?" It's perfectly normal to not have any idea at this point.

As a child, you were able to memorize facts, such as the multiplication tables or the capitals of states, but you did not have very good reasoning skills yet. As an adolescent, your reasoning skills become much more powerful. When faced with a logical problem, you are able to consider the consequences of each possible course of action and make a decision that provides for the best outcome.

One of the reasons that our society doesn't consider someone a legal adult until age 18 is that until late adolescence, people's reasoning skills are not always strong enough to prevent them from making serious mistakes in judgment that could have life-changing consequences. For example, a 12-year-old might lack the intellectual capacity for understanding why it is important not to stay up all night playing video games before a big test, but an 18-year-old can clearly see the consequences of such a choice. (Not all 18-year-olds do the right thing 100 percent of the time, but at least they *know* they are doing something unwise.)

Emotional Changes

Adolescence can be a challenging time emotionally. During puberty, the body's hormone balance changes dramatically, and some of those hormones can cause mood fluctuations and anxiety. The changes going on in your life can also cause you to feel anxious and uncertain.

Some of the emotional challenges you may face as an adolescent include:

- Increased need for separateness from family
- Disagreements with authority figures such as teachers and parents
- Changes in long-time friendships
- Temptation to participate in unhealthy behaviors
- Stress from having too busy a schedule
- Uncertainty about sexuality

As you grow emotionally, you gain the skills you need to deal with these challenges in a mature way. For example, as a young adolescent you might have cried and yelled when your parents told you that you couldn't go to a party you had been looking forward to. As you get older, you learn how to feel the disappointment without lashing out at others.

Social Growth

Adolescence is a time of figuring out who you are, for developing your independence and identity separate from your parents. This period of growth can be intense and unpredictable, as you struggle to find a balance between pleasing your family, pleasing your friends, and—most important—doing what is right for *yourself*.

During early adolescence, many people begin relying heavily on groups of friends for social identity, as they pull away from their mother and father. Your friends understand very well what you are going through on a daily basis as you mature and struggle with the new challenges that maturity brings. The danger of increasing independence, of course, is that instead of relying on parents—who presumably are adults with good judgment and more life experience—you are relying on people your own age who often don't have any better judgment and life experience than you do. That's how some adolescents end up getting involved in destructive behaviors such as smoking, drugs, and alcohol.

During later adolescence, people typically start being more independent and acting as individuals. As you mature, you will probably find that the approval of your friends is not as important to you as your own moral sense of right and wrong. Your own thoughts and opinions will become the guiding force in your life, not the expectations and pressure placed on you externally. For example, older adolescents must decide whether or not to go to college and if so, where to go and what to major in. While parents and friends provide advice and opinions, ultimately it is your own decision, because it's a choice that affects the path of your adult life.

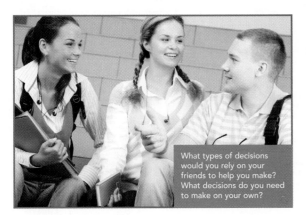

What types of decisions would you rely on your friends to help you make? What decisions do you need to make on your own?

The World of Work

What if you decide to take a part-time job, in addition to going to school?

★ **Money:** If you get a job, you will be able to contribute financially to your family, and you will have money of your own to save and spend on things you want.
BUT…
There may be expenses involved in taking the job, such as money for transportation to or from work or a uniform you must buy.

★ **Friends:** If you work at the same place your friends do, you can earn money while you spend time with them.
BUT…
You might find that working with your friends, you are tempted to goof off and not do your best work. Or you might find that you and your friends don't get along as well in a work environment as you do at play.

★ **The Future:** Having a job while still in high school can provide valuable work experience that future employers will find attractive.
BUT…
Working can cut into the time you have available for studying, which can mean your grades may slip and you may have more trouble getting into college after high school.

Customized Instruction: At-Risk Students

Have students research your school's policies and programs geared toward students who hold jobs. For example, does the school have an early dismissal option for students who have jobs? Does the school have special arrangements with local employers who hire students? Encourage students to set up an appointment with the guidance counselor to discuss these. Have them write a brief summary of what they find and share it with the class.

Discuss

Discuss with students the ways in which their relationships have changed between early childhood years and adolescence. For example, you have a brother who is two years younger and you start to think the things you both used to enjoy doing now seem childish to you. Or, you used to tease and play tricks on the girl down the street, but now you find her attractive and would like to ask her out on a date. Encourage students to talk about relationships with family, friends, and teachers.

Figure Focus

Students are to comment on the types of decisions they rely on their friends to help them make and those they make on their own. Students probably ask their friends to help them make decisions, for example, on the clothes to buy and wear or who to ask to the school dance. But for decisions that require them to choose between right and wrong, good and bad, and positive and negative, they should rely on their own instincts and values.

The World of Work

Landing your first job and making your own money can be exciting and rewarding. Ask students to talk about their first jobs or a job they currently have. Have them comment on any conflicts that may have arisen because of the job. How can the problems discussed in the text be resolved?

■ **Money:** In most instances, the expenses are one-time expenses or do not exceed the income. Before taking a job, make sure you identify additional expenses you will incur and you weigh the pros and cons.

■ **Friends:** If working with friends becomes a problem, you might talk to your manager about working different hours or shifts, or giving you responsibilities that would limit your interaction with friends on the job.

■ **The Future:** Time management is critical when you have both school and work to consider. If being successful at both is important to you, you might have to give up other things, such as hanging out with friends or participating in extracurricular activities, to make sufficient time for both.

Introduce the Section

This section covers adulthood, which begins at age 21. Students learn that in adulthood, you gain many freedoms, but you also take on many new responsibilities.

Figure Focus

Ask students for a show of hands on who is looking forward to adulthood and who is happy in adolescence. For those who are looking forward to it, ask them to explain why. Then, ask them to consider what they might miss about their adolescent years.

Vocabulary

Adulthood: Stage of life that begins at age 21.

Discuss

Discuss the phases of adulthood. Ask students to predict what they will be doing at each phase. Offer to share with them what you were doing or will be doing at each phase of your adulthood.

Adulthood

Adulthood comprises 75% of an average lifespan, from physical maturity to retirement and old age.

The 21 years it takes to reach adulthood may seem like a long time to you now, but in the grand scheme of things, it's only about one-quarter of the average lifetime. The other three-quarters are spent in **adulthood**.

Adults have a lot of freedom. As an adult, you can live anywhere, travel to any location, take on any type of job, have romantic relationships that please you, and so on. With that freedom comes responsibility, though. You need to commit to:

- Obeying the laws so you will stay out of jail and avoid legal trouble
- Supporting yourself so you will not go hungry, be homeless, or be a drain on the social services system
- Being a good person who acts out of personal integrity and kindness, so you will have friends and family who care for and appreciate you

As long as you stick to those three things, you can do almost anything you like. Do you want to be an electrician? A doctor? A pastry chef? Find a school that will teach you the skills you'll need. Have you always wanted to live in the mountains, or on the beach? You can. Just plan a career that involves being in that environment. Go for it!

Adult Roles and Responsibilities

As an adult, you are ready to take on a full set of grown-up responsibilities, such as:

- Voting
- Furthering your education at a college or trade school
- Serving in the military
- Holding a full-time job
- Getting married
- Having children
- Making large purchases such as a home or car
- Making financial investments

Customized Instruction: ESOL Students

Ask students to discuss the ages at which adults in their native country might assume certain responsibilities. For example, at what age can they get a driver's license, hold a full-time job, vote, or serve in the military?

Phases of Adulthood

Adulthood encompasses many decades of life, and just like childhood, there are well-defined phases that people pass through in it. For example:

- Young adulthood (20s and 30s): Completing your education, establishing your career, finding a life partner, having children, buying a house or car
- Middle age (40s and 50s): Reaching the top level of your career, raising children, building financial security, pursuing hobbies and interests
- Retirement age (60s and 70s): Retiring from main career, taking up hobbies or part-time jobs, downsizing to smaller living quarters, spending time with grandchildren, doing volunteer work, traveling
- Old age (80s and beyond): Pursuing hobbies and interests, enjoying family and friends, downsizing living quarters, managing health limitations

Different people may take on specific activities or roles at different rates, but the general progression is the same. For example, not everyone finds their ideal career as a young adult, but most people do eventually find careers they enjoy and are good at before they reach retirement age.

Everybody's Different

Even though adults of all ages have the same rights and responsibilities in our society, their lives can be very different depending on many factors, including age, economic status, education level, sex, race, religion, political affiliation, and even hobbies and interests.

For example, each of the people described below is an adult. Think about how their lives are different from one another.

- An unmarried 22-year-old accounting clerk with a two-year degree in Accounting and one year of work experience, living in a one-bedroom apartment in a large city. She likes to go dancing and take aerobics classes.
- A married 35-year-old mother of three preschool children who stays at home full-time with them in a house in the suburbs of a major city. She likes to do craft projects, go to movies, and meet her friends for coffee.
- A 48-year-old trade school graduate who works as a plumber, is divorced, and lives in his own house in a small town in the Midwest. His hobby is bowling, and he is very good at it. He travels on weekends to tournaments.
- A 61-year-old executive who is soon going to be retiring from his job as a vice-president at a large banking firm. He likes playing golf and is looking forward to traveling with his wife after he retires.
- An 80-year-old widowed retiree, who used to be a hair stylist and who lives in a retirement apartment complex. She enjoys playing cards with her friends, babysitting her grandchildren, and watching daytime TV.

Myth You keep getting smarter throughout adulthood because your brain keeps developing and growing.

Truth The peak of your brain's ability to plan and coordinate tasks and to remember facts occurs from ages 22 to 27. It slowly declines after that for the rest of your life.

That doesn't mean that older people are stupid, though—far from it. Although their brains may not work quite as quickly or efficiently at processing new information, they have a wealth of experiences to draw from, and their abilities to draw wisdom from those experiences keeps building as they age. So the phrase "being older and wiser" is really true!

MONEY MADNE$$

Being able to use the Internet to look up information, take classes, read about world events, and network with other people is an important part of many adults' ongoing growth and development. However, having a computer and Internet access at home is a luxury that many people cannot afford.

Suppose you have an adult relative who wants a computer so he can do word processing and connect to the Internet, but has only $500 to spend. If he gets a laptop, he can use the free online access at his local coffee shop, so that's what he prefers. However, he is concerned that he may not be able to find a laptop in his price range.

Using the Internet, research several brands of laptops, and find one that he can afford and that will meet his needs. Prepare a spreadsheet listing the pros and cons of each of the models you considered.

Myth/Truth

Research indicates that even though the brain's cognitive abilities dwindle with age, you can do things at younger ages to build up your cognitive reserve and, in essence, keep your brain young. Explain to students that lifelong learning and engaging in brain-stimulating activities, such as reading, crossword puzzles, listening to music, and so on, contribute to your cognitive reserve. As brain cells die off during the aging process, the reserve is there to send in replacements.

MONEY MADNE$$

Students are to search for information on laptops and create a spreadsheet that lists the pros and cons of each model. Besides the price, students should consider the following:

- Hard drive speed, which determines how fast you access stored data.
- Memory, which is the amount of space to store data and programs.
- Processor speed, or how fast the computer computes and completes tasks.
- Size. Typically a 14.1-inch screen is considered small. A 17-inch screen is considered big.
- Warranty from the manufacturer covering defective equipment.
- Operating system and applications that come bundled with the laptop.
- Number of ports for connecting devices such as a printer, mouse, flash drive, digital camera, etc.

End-of-Chapter Activities

Case Study

Thomas's frustration is a natural feeling under the circumstances. Thomas does not want to disappoint or disobey his mother, but he also does not want to miss out on this last opportunity to go out with his friend. Thomas's mother's request was reasonable in that she wanted her son to take advantage of a limited opportunity to spend time with this relative. But perhaps she was unreasonable to insist before she had a chance to discuss other options with Thomas. Students should estimate Thomas's age to be early teens. Someone younger might have overreacted and let his emotions control his actions. This would have prevented him from calmly approaching his mother and asking her politely to discuss ways they might work around the problem.

Sounding Off!

Student answers will vary.

FAQ

1. The four areas are physical, social, emotional, and intellectual.

2. Heredity is the traits you have inherited from your parents. Environment refers to the influences you experience after birth.

3. He or she cries or throws a tantrum.

4. A person with access to technology can learn from sources such as the Internet and e-books.

5. A developmental delay is a delay in growth that does not necessarily mean a permanent handicap. A developmental disability is a condition where the person cannot develop at a normal level.

6. Early childhood is called the play age because children learn by playing at this age, rather than by studying in a classroom.

7. Environmental factors can include residence, parents, siblings, school, friends, neighborhood, pets, class, and economics, among others.

8. Boys: growth in height, pubic hair, body odor, maturity and growth of testicles, growth of body and facial hair, deepening of voice, and increase in bone mass and muscle density.

   Girls: growth in height, pubic hair, body odor, maturity of vagina, ovaries, and uterus, growth of body hair, breast development, menstruation, and change in body shape and fat distribution.

Case Study

Thomas is feeling frustrated. He wants to go out for pizza with his friends after his soccer game because one of his friends is moving away, and this will be the last time his friend will get to go out with the team. But Thomas's mother wants him to come home immediately after the game because his Aunt Hazel is visiting. Thomas asks his mother if there is any way he can skip the visit with his aunt, but his mother insists, because Aunt Hazel is only in town once every few of years.

Thomas calmly tells his mother that he feels frustrated, and explains how important it is for him to be with his friends that night. He asks her if they can work together to figure out a way that he can see Aunt Hazel and also spend time with his friends. Together they work out a plan for him to come home and see his aunt for one hour, and then excuse himself to go catch up with his friends.

■ Was it okay that Thomas felt frustrated?
■ Was Thomas's mother's request a reasonable one?
■ Based on how Thomas behaved, how old do you think he is?
■ How might someone younger have behaved, and what might the outcome have been?

Sounding Off!

❶ How has the home environment in which you were raised affected your development?

❷ Which type of development are you the strongest in? Which areas are your parents strongest in—the same as you, or different? Do you think your abilities are due to heredity, environment, or both?

FAQ

1. What are the four areas of development discussed in this chapter?
2. Explain the difference between heredity and environment.
3. How does an infant or toddler express an unmet need?
4. Explain how having access to technology can affect someone's intellectual development.
5. What is the difference between developmental delay and developmental disability?
6. Which phase of development is sometimes called "play age," and why is it called that?
7. List four environmental factors that can influence a young child.
8. List two changes to the male body and two changes to the female body that occur at puberty.
9. Name two social roles or responsibilities that are reserved only for adults.
10. List the four phases of adulthood and a typical activity or trait associated with each of them.

9. Answers may include voting, jury duty, signing legal contracts, and marriage, among others.

10. The four phases are young adulthood, middle age, retirement age, and old age. Answers may include any of the examples from page 132 or others.

Playtime is important for children because it helps them refine their social skills. Through a series of small successes and failures, they learn what behavior will get the approval and what behavior will not.

In small groups, visit local playgrounds, either at your school or at a park, and observe the social interactions between children of various ages. Then write a report or create a presentation that answers the following questions:

- What ages of children did you observe?
- What kind of social interactions happened between them?
- How were conflicts resolved?
- What social lessons were they learning by the games they were playing?
- What would be a good game to suggest for a group of children that age?

Hot Topics

Part of being a responsible parent is sheltering the children under your care from having to deal with adult problems. Unfortunately, some children and adolescents are faced with grown-up problems and challenges before they are prepared to handle them, and such things can take a toll on the child's emotional health.

Take this opportunity to write about a situation where you, or someone you know, had to deal with a problem in your life that a person of that age should not have had to face. How was it resolved? How did it change you, or the person you are writing about? Use a word processing program or write it out on paper, and drop it into the classroom's Hot Topics box. It's anonymous, so you can be honest and open. As a class, read the anonymous entries and discuss them.

> **Web Extra** ▼
>
> In the U.S., people are considered adults at age 18 for most things, including signing legal documents and performing military service. However, for consuming alcohol, the legal age is 21.
>
> Using the Internet, research what the "age of adulthood" is in at least four other countries, and find out what privileges and rights that adulthood gives.

Problem Solver

Schools have a responsibility to help students develop intellectually by educating them in many subjects, including reading, math, science, music, and so on. Some of these subjects are required for all students; others are options you can pick depending on your interests and abilities. For example, most schools have a band, but not everyone is required to be in it. Everyone is required to take Math and English, though.

Suppose you were in charge of developing the curriculum for your grade level. First list all the classes that you are now required to take at your school. Then, alone or with a partner, make a list of all the courses that you think should be required for everyone. Then make another list of the courses that should be made available as electives (options). Compare your lists to those of your classmates. Were there any courses where you disagreed?

Team Players

Students are to observe children at a playground and prepare a report or presentation that answers the questions listed in the text. Remind students to act appropriately in front of the children they are observing. They should not try to engage in conversations or activities with them, as it could lead to unnatural behavior in the kids or concern from the adults who are with them.

Hot Topics

Make sure students understand that they can turn in their papers anonymously. Encourage them to be open and honest about their situation.

Web Extra

Students are to find information on the legal age or age of adulthood in four other countries and determine the privileges and rights people are entitled to when they reach that age. You might consult any ESOL students in the class or in other classes.

Problem Solver

Students are to prepare a list of the current course requirements for their grade level. Then, they should develop a list of the courses they *think* should be required and a list of courses that should be made available for students to choose to take. You might also have students include any electives that are currently available as another list.

Write Now

Students are to write a short story or essay based on a funny or outrageous story told to them by a parent, teacher, or adult friend. Remind students that their piece should have a beginning, middle, and end. The writing should be descriptive and engage the reader through the use of dialogue, imagery, and humor.

Be Involved!

Students are to volunteer to help kids read in an elementary school classroom and then write a report on their experience. Make arrangements ahead of time with a local elementary school for students to visit classrooms. Many schools have a mentoring program in place in which adults from the community meet with students and read together.

Social Networking

Students are to invite a representative from their school or a community program to discuss nutrition and how it affects a child's development. If students have trouble finding a representative to speak, they might contact a local university or college.

Write Now

Almost every adult has a story about something unwise he or she did as an adolescent because of lack of mature judgment. Ask your parents, teachers, and adult friends of the family to tell you about an incident of poor judgment they remember from their teenage years, either something they did themselves or something a friend did. Pick the funniest or most outrageous story you hear, and write it as a short story or essay. Share it aloud with the class.

Be Involved!

www.fcclainc.org

Most children begin to read somewhere around age 6 (first grade), but that's just an average. Some children as young as 3 begin to associate spoken words with the letters on the page, and other children have a hard time catching onto reading until second or even third grade. By that time, those children lag behind their classmates in reading skill and may have difficulty catching up.

Arrange to spend some time being a volunteer reading helper in an elementary school classroom, helping children who need a little extra assistance. If you are doing this as part of a group, talk to the others who are participating in it to see what experiences you had in common. Can you identify any particular difficulty that the children you tutored shared? For example, did they have a short attention span? Did they forget what individual letters were? Did they have trouble sounding out the words? Write an essay or report about the experience.

Social Networking

The physical growth and development of infants and young children is greatly affected by the nutrition they receive. There are government programs aimed at providing low-income families with assistance in giving young children good nutrition, such as WIC and food stamps. Ask a local representative of a food assistance program or the person who runs your school's nutrition program to come to your class and talk about how nutrition affects the ability of children to learn and grow.

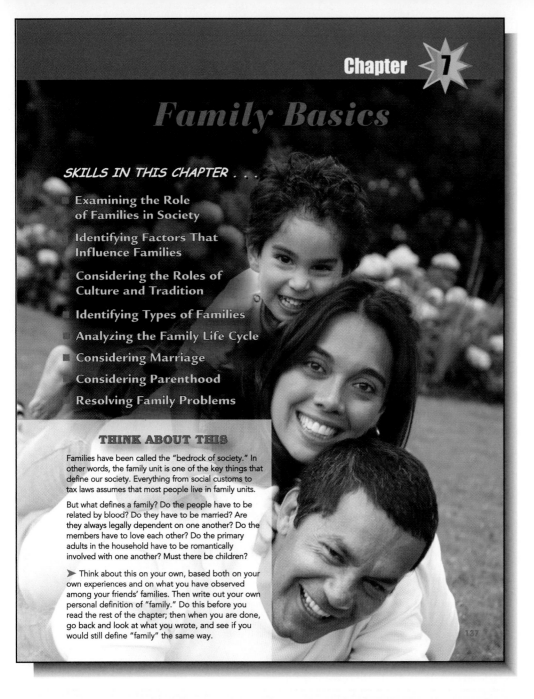

Chapter 7

Family Basics

SKILLS IN THIS CHAPTER . . .

- Examining the Role of Families in Society
- Identifying Factors That Influence Families
- Considering the Roles of Culture and Tradition
- Identifying Types of Families
- Analyzing the Family Life Cycle
- Considering Marriage
- Considering Parenthood
- Resolving Family Problems

THINK ABOUT THIS

Families have been called the "bedrock of society." In other words, the family unit is one of the key things that define our society. Everything from social customs to tax laws assumes that most people live in family units.

But what defines a family? Do the people have to be related by blood? Do they have to be married? Are they always legally dependent on one another? Do the members have to love each other? Do the primary adults in the household have to be romantically involved with one another? Must there be children?

➤ Think about this on your own, based both on your own experiences and on what you have observed among your friends' families. Then write out your own personal definition of "family." Do this before you read the rest of the chapter; then when you are done, go back and look at what you wrote, and see if you would still define "family" the same way.

Chapter 7 Overview

This chapter examines the family dynamic. The different types of families are discussed and the influences of culture, tradition, and society are explored.

Examining the Role of Families in Society
Students learn about the many functions a family serves. For example, a family provides love and support as well as basic environmental needs.

Identifying Factors That Influence Families
The factors that affect a family's interaction with each other and with those outside the family are discussed.

Considering the Roles of Culture and Tradition
The diverse nature of American society can be attributed directly to the cultures and traditions that families value and pass on to generation after generation.

Identifying Types of Families   This section discusses types of families and underscores the importance of recognizing how each type is unique.

Analyzing the Family Life Cycle   The typical stages of the family life cycle are identified and examined.

Considering Marriage   This section covers the concept of marriage. It discusses the benefits of marriage and the factors that two people should consider before getting married.

Considering Parenthood   The joys and frustrations of parenthood are discussed. The section also looks at the sacrifices and added responsibilities an adult takes on when becoming a parent.

Finding Resources for Families   Conflicts and problems are a normal part of family life. When family members cannot resolve a problem on their own, there are many resources to which they can turn for help.

Focus and Engage

Bell-Ringer: Think About This

Students are asked to write out a definition of family. They are to base their definition on their own personal situation as well as on their observations of other families. Encourage students to look beyond the physical makeup of the family; in other words, the number of family members and who they are. They should consider the functions the family fills, such as providing companionship, maintaining the home environment, and contributing to each other's well-being.

ADVANCE PREPARATION

Review	*Life Skills for the 21st Century* textbook, Chapter 7.
Prepare	Paper and pencil for some activities. Crayons or markers for drawing. Box labeled "Hot Topics."

CUSTOMIZED INSTRUCTION OVERVIEW

Less Advanced Students	More Advanced Students	ESOL Students	Special Needs Students	At-Risk Students
Pages 138, 147	Pages 141, 142, 148	Pages 139, 157	Pages 138, 147	Pages 142, 147, 155

Introduce the Section

In this section, students learn about the many functions a family serves. For example, a family provides love and support and helps shape the environment that plays such an important role in every individual's growth and development.

Figure Focus

Explain that a "generation" is defined as all the people who were born at approximately the same time. As a group, a generation usually has shared interests and attitudes. You are most likely the same generation as your cousins. Your parents are the same generation as your aunts and uncles. Your grandparents are probably the same generation as your friends' grandparents. Ask students to think about the different generations in their family. How many different generations are there? What things are shared between generations? For example, is there a home that has been passed from one generation to another? What about a passion for a certain tradition, such as a family vacation at the same location every summer, or even rooting for the same college football team?

Vocabulary

Tradition: A belief or custom passed down from one generation to the next.

Teaching Tips

Help students understand that the functions of a family are varied and diverse and might not always be clear-cut and easy to identify. They should not feel that their family is dysfunctional if they do not provide the things listed in the text.

Examining the Role of Families in Society

Families give people a sense of belonging and stability throughout their lives. A family might include three or even four generations that all keep in close contact.

Families are important because they provide people with many of the basics they need for healthy and happy lives. Families take care of one another's physical, emotional, and financial well-being, and pass on knowledge, values, traditions, and material goods from one generation to another. A **tradition** is a belief or custom passed down from one generation to the next.

Some of the important functions of a family include:

- Making people feel loved and accepted as part of a group
- Helping each other through difficult situations
- Creating a safe and comfortable home environment
- Providing a stable home for children to grow and develop
- Passing on values and traditions
- Helping children understand the expectations of society
- Sharing memories and history
- Passing on wealth and property

Even when a family's structure changes, such as a child growing up and moving out, a family member dying, or a couple getting married or divorced, the basic family structure remains, and continues to provide its members with most of those benefits.

What Does an Extended-Family Household Look Like?

In the United States, we have certain expectations of our families—who they consist of and what roles they will play in our lives. In other countries, though, those expectations may be different.

For example, in some countries it is customary for grandparents and elderly aunts and uncles to live with the younger generations. A typical home might consist of a married couple, their children, one or more grandparent, and perhaps an aunt or uncle and their children.

Some things to think about:

- Why do you think people in the United States are less likely to live in large family units than the people in other countries do?
- What benefits does a family get from having more adults in the household?
- What benefits do children get from living closely with their grandparents?
- What drawbacks might there be to having a large, extended family living together?

Customized Instruction: Less Advanced/Special Needs Students

Have students draw a picture of their family doing something that is considered a family tradition; for example, getting together at a grandparent's house for a holiday dinner. Have students identify the family members in the picture and then list them by generation.

Families Create Stability

Remember your first day of school, when your mom or dad dropped you off at school or the bus stop? Even though you might have been scared, you knew that at the end of the day, there would be someone waiting for you at home to take care of you. One of the purposes of a family is to provide that kind of stability and security that makes it possible for people—both kids and adults—to go out into the world and learn, work, and play.

Families also provide rules and expectations that help everyone get along and that teach children to be good citizens. For example, your family might have a rule against swearing (that is, using bad language) in the house. Following this rule trains everyone in the household to be able to express themselves using nonoffensive language, which can help them succeed outside the home, too.

Your family can also be a place of emotional safety, where you are free to express your feelings among people who love you. A parent or older relative can be the ideal person to confide in about a problem with school or your social life, because he or she has been the same age you are now and can see situations with a broader perspective than you might be able to.

With everyone's busy schedules, it can be difficult to get everyone together for a meal. Why do you think sharing a meal together helps a family stay connected to one another?

Families Help Each Other

Families also exist to make sure everyone is taken care of, especially children and the elderly.

Children and elderly adults rely on the family to provide them with food, clothing, a place to live, a bed to sleep in, and so on. Those are things that, as a student, you probably could not pay for yourself. You depend on your parents, or other adult members of the household, to bring home enough money from their work to meet the family's physical needs.

Families can also help each other out in a wide variety of nonfinancial ways. For example, you might babysit for a cousin who had to go out of town on business unexpectedly, or pick up your father's dry cleaning on the way home from school. Your mother might drive her sister to work when her car is broken down, and your grandfather might help you build a wagon or teach you how to whistle or juggle.

Even more important, your family provides the security, love, recognition, and respect you need to develop a healthy self-concept and personality. Who was there to applaud when you performed in a cardboard cutout of a banana in the first grade Nutrition Pageant? Who was there when you came home crying because you fell off your bicycle? Who will be there for you to celebrate when you finally get your driver's license or get married or get your first job? Your family will.

Call it a clan, call it a network, call it a tribe, call it a family. Whatever you call it, whoever you are, you need one.

— Jane Neville Howard,
Countess of Westmoreland (1533–1593)

Passing It On

Families pass down traditions, stories, and keepsakes from one generation to another. What are some special things your family has passed down from one generation to another? Here are some examples:

✔ *Religious ceremonies and celebrations*

✔ *Menus and recipes*

✔ *Words and phrases with special meaning*

✔ *Traditional games at holiday gatherings*

✔ *Poems or songs*

✔ *Keepsakes or antiques such as jewelry and pottery*

✔ *Pictures and scrapbooks*

✔ *Letters written by ancestors*

Discuss

Discuss with students how their roles and responsibilities at home with family affect their behavior away from home. For example, if you are responsible for putting away your clothes and keeping your house clean, do you automatically put things in their place at school, such as trash in the trash can instead of in your desk? If you are not allowed to play music loudly at home, do you keep the volume low when you are driving? Stress the relationship between family values and students' individual values. Are they more or less the same?

Figure Focus

Much research has been done on the benefits of family meals. Kids who frequently eat meals with family tend to do better in school and have healthier diets, both of which contribute to higher self-esteem and positive attitudes. Family meals also tend to facilitate the productive exchange of ideas, conversation, and feelings among family members. Explain that mealtime can be a good opportunity to reconnect with family and strengthen family ties and traditions.

Passing It On

Ask students to give examples of things their family has passed down from one generation to the next. These can be material things, such as an old quilt or clock, or nonmaterial things, activities, or traditions, such as a story about your ancestors' emigration to America.

"Quote Box"

Jane Neville Howard lived more than 400 years ago. With that in mind, ask students if they think the basic functions of a family have changed much over the centuries.

Customized Instruction: ESOL Students

Ask students to say the words for "family," "generation," "parents," "children," and "cousin" in their primary language.

Introduce the Section

In this section, students identify the factors that affect how family members interact with each other.

Figure Focus

A recent American Religious Identification Survey found that a little more than 75 percent of American adults identify themselves as Christian, with most having a specific religious identity, such as Catholic or Baptist. Ask students to share thoughts on their religious identity and how it influences them and their family.

Vocabulary

Situational: Influences that arise out of temporary conditions around you.

STUDENT ACTIVITY

Have students tear a piece of paper into nine strips. They should write each of the factors listed in the *What Affects You?* text on their strips of paper. Then, have them arrange the factors by order of importance. Which is the most important influence on their family? Have them write a paragraph that explains why they feel this influence is so important.

Identifying Factors That Influence Families

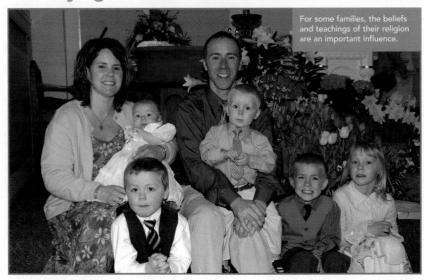

For some families, the beliefs and teachings of their religion are an important influence.

Think about the last time you visited the home of a friend. How was his or her family different from yours? Each family has its own unique dynamic, created by a combination of many influences.

Some of the influences are **situational**, which means they come from the temporary conditions around you. For example, if a large family is living in a small, cramped apartment, there will probably be some tension from the lack of privacy. However, people might be closer emotionally because they are so involved in everything that everyone else is doing. On the other hand, if a family lives in a large house where each person has his or her own room, there might be fewer arguments. However, the family members won't know as much about each other and might not be as close.

Other influences are more enduring (that is, long-lasting), because they have to do with the characteristics, opinions, and interests of the people themselves. For example, in a home where the parents place a high value on higher education, the children are much more likely to want to go to college. And in a family that is very religious, going to events at a place of worship may be something that the whole family does together for fun.

What Affects You?

A family's members and their characteristics, as well as the situations they are in, change the way everyone interacts with one another and with the outside world. Some of the factors that can influence a family include:

- Income and expenses
- Number of working adults
- Education
- Location
- Living environment
- Number of members
- Activity schedules
- Religious practice
- Family hobbies and interests

Which of these are the most important influences on *your* family?

Where You Live Makes a Difference

The region you live in, and size and location of the nearest city or town, can affect your family in many ways.

For example, if you live in an area where real estate prices are very high, your family is more likely to rent their home, and you are more likely to share housing with your extended family. On the other hand, if you live somewhere that has low housing prices, more families can afford to own their homes and can have larger living spaces.

City versus country life also affects the activities that you participate in on a daily basis. If you live in a rural farming community, for example, you might have chores such as feeding livestock or tending a vegetable garden. On the other hand, if you live in a large city, you might have responsibilities such as doing the grocery shopping or running errands on your way home from school. Where you live also affects the activities that you participate in as a family. In a small town, there are likely to be more school-based and religious-based activities; in a large city, families are more likely to visit art exhibits or attend plays.

The type of housing a family lives in can affect the way people deal with one another. What kind of housing do you live in?

Money and Working

Another important influence on a family is the number and amount of incomes. A family where two or more adults have full-time jobs is likely to be more financially stable than one in which there is only one income, so there may be less stress about money. However, there may also be less time to spend together as a family, and you might not always have a parent available when you want one—to give you a ride somewhere or give permission for an activity, for example.

The amount of **expendable income** (that is, money left over after paying for the essentials) that a family has can also be an influence, but it all depends on what the family decides to *do* with the money. A family that has plenty of money for extras might go more places together, such as to plays or movies or on vacations—or, they might spend the money on things that each person does separately, so more money might mean *less* quality time together as a family.

"If I make money at a part-time job, should I offer part of it to my parents to help contribute to the family income? What are the pros and cons?"

A Whole New World

If you live in a large city such as Chicago, New York, or Los Angeles, you may find it hard to imagine living in a different area of the country. What if your parents decided to buy a small dairy farm in rural Wisconsin? Or what if the opposite was true: that your parents were moving from a rural area to a big city?

★ How would your family's type of housing change?

★ Would your family spend more time together, or less?

★ How would your school be different?

★ Is there anything you would be fearful or anxious about?

Customized Instruction: More Advanced Students

Have students research housing and income levels in their community. They will prepare a short report that includes information on the community population, average income per household, and the number of housing units broken down by single-family and multifamily. Online sources of information include www.eachtown.com, www.zip-codes.com, and www.census.gov. They might also contact the city's administrative offices.

Discuss

Discuss with students the ways in which housing, money, and jobs affect their family and how they interact with each other. Have them consider both the positive and negative influences.

Vocabulary

Expendable income: Money left over after paying for the essentials.

Figure Focus

Ask students to share descriptions of the housing in which they live. What do they like most about their homes? What do they like least?

A Whole New World

You might have students in your class who have relocated to places that are drastically different from their previous homes share their stories. Ask them to discuss the differences and what adjustments they and their family had to make.

Figure Focus

Get a show of hands of students who have jobs. Ask if they have any financial responsibilities to their family. Do they have to help pay for gas or transportation costs to get to and from work? Do they have to help with insurance expenses? Do they buy food and groceries?

Introduce the Section

The diverse nature of American society can be attributed directly to the cultures and traditions we all practice and value. This section examines the way culture and tradition shape and influence the family unit.

Figure Focus

Ask students to comment on special meals their family enjoys during holidays or to mark other occasions. If they can't think of one, ask them to suggest one.

Common Cultural Traditions

Discuss the different cultures represented in your classroom. Remind students that "culture" is the beliefs, customs, practices, and social behavior shared by a particular nation or group of people.

Discuss

Ask students about a family tree or family genealogy. Has anyone in their family created a family tree or studied their genealogy? If yes, where are their ancestors from? How long have they lived in America?

STUDENT ACTIVITY

Have students bring in a recipe of one of their favorite dishes served during a holiday or to mark a special occasion. Is the dish served because of family tradition or cultural tradition?

Considering the Roles of Culture and Tradition

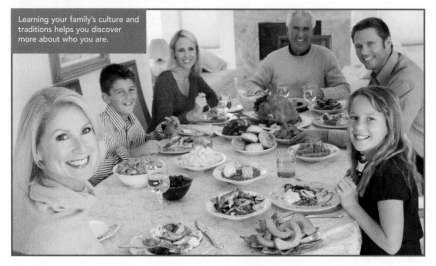

Learning your family's culture and traditions helps you discover more about who you are.

The United States is often called a "melting pot," meaning that almost everyone—or their ancestors—comes from somewhere else, and all the different cultures and ethnicities blend together to create our society. That makes it hard to say definitively that a certain word or custom is "American" while another is not. By definition, American is a blend of outside influences.

Even so, many families carry on traditions from countries and cultures that their parents and grandparents came from, things that are closely associated with those countries and societies. For example, if your family is of Mexican descent, you might celebrate Cinco de Mayo, and families of Chinese descent might celebrate Chinese New Year. The elders in your family may be bilingual, and you may even have grandparents who do not speak much English.

Traditions can also be religious. For example, Christians often celebrate Christmas and Easter with special family dinners, and Jewish people celebrate Passover and other holidays with special meals. In some religious traditions, there are ceremonies for passing from childhood to adulthood; in others, there are rituals performed every day or every week. Many Muslims, for example, say prayers at certain times throughout the day.

Common Cultural Traditions

Does your family have any of these traditions based on their culture, religion, or country of origin?

- Does your family eat the same menu at certain holidays every year?
- Does anyone in your family wear traditional ethnic clothing on a daily basis?
- Are there special rituals or traditions when someone dies, such as covering the mirrors or stopping the clocks in the house?
- Before meals, does someone say a prayer or give a blessing?
- Is it customary to wait until the eldest person at the table has taken a bite to eat?
- Do women and/or men wear head coverings at certain times?
- Are there limitations on what you can do on Sabbath days?
- How do people greet one another? With a handshake or bow? With certain words or phrases of respect?

Customized Instruction: More Advanced/At-Risk Students

Pair up one of your advanced students with an at-risk student to research a common American tradition. Some examples are singing the national anthem before a sporting event, tying a yellow ribbon around a tree to welcome someone home, serving turkey for Thanksgiving dinner, fireworks on the 4th of July, and homecoming games. Students should prepare a short report that explains how the tradition came about and share it with the class.

Ethnic and National Traditions

A family's **ethnicity** (that is, cultural and racial background) and **national origin** (country their ancestors lived in) can determine some of its traditions. Those are not the same thing, and yet they share some overlap. In some countries, there are a variety of ethnicities represented in the population; in other countries, almost everyone is the same ethnicity.

Native American culture, for example, is rooted in ethnicity—that is, a common racial background. Native Americans of various tribes maintain and pass down traditional clothing, ceremonies, values, and spiritual beliefs of their ancestors, and these traditions are an important part of many Native American families.

Ireland is an example of a country with nationality-based culture. Traditional Irish food, dancing, folklore, and customs are all based on the country itself and its history, and not the ethnic background of the citizens.

Does your family have any traditions that are based on its ethnicity or national origin?

Family Traditions, Family History

Family traditions provide a way for family members to feel a sense of belonging—and a way of looking back and connecting with those who have come before. For example, when you help prepare a traditional dish for a holiday meal, you might think about how others who have come before you prepared that same food the same way, and served it to some of the same people. Maybe your grandmother made a certain kind of candy for your dad when he was a little boy, for example, and now you and your mother make it for the young children in your family.

Family history can include not only living traditions, but also photos, scrapbooks, and stories. Is there an eccentric uncle in your family's past whom everyone likes telling stories about? Or a picture of a proud moment in your family history, such as someone meeting the President or winning an award? These too are part of your family's culture and tradition.

 Blending in or Standing Out?

When a family moves to a different country, where the culture is very different, how much should they try to blend in, and how much should they try to preserve their traditions?

It's a difficult balance for many immigrants. Parents want their children to succeed in their new home by fitting in with others, and yet they don't want them to forget where they came from.

If you were a first-generation immigrant to the United States, would you...

■ Speak only English in your home, or speak your native language?
■ Wear clothing that you wore in your home country, or wear typical American clothing?
■ Learn to cook and eat American food, or continue eating the same way you ate in your home country?

Discuss

Make sure students can distinguish between ethnic traditions and national traditions. Ethnic traditions are those centered on your cultural and racial background, whereas national traditions are those centered on the country you live in. For example, Kwanzaa is an ethnic tradition for many African-American families who want to celebrate their African heritage. These same families might also follow the American tradition of setting off fireworks on Independence Day.

Vocabulary

Ethnicity: Cultural and racial background.
National origin: Country your ancestors lived in.

Figure Focus

Ask students to share any ethnic traditions or traditions that are characteristic of their home country. These can range from cuisine, dress styles, and holiday customs to values and beliefs.

 Blending In or Standing Out?

Students are to consider how they would adapt to living in the United States as a first-generation immigrant. Ask students to write down as much as they know about their family roots. What is their country of national origin? Do the language, clothing styles, and cuisine differ that much from those in the United States?

TEAMWORK ACTIVITY

Divide the class evenly into teams of four or five. Each member of the team is to interview a person from a different ethnic group. They can interview anyone except other students in this class. They should ask the person questions about their values, cuisine, customs, dress styles, and traditions. Some ethnic groups to consider include Italian Americans, Irish Americans, Slavic Americans (from Eastern and Central European countries), German Americans, African Americans, American Indians, Hispanics, Amish, and so on. Have students prepare a poster that describes the traditions of each ethnic group represented in their team's interviews. It's all right if more than one team member interviews a person from the same ethnic group. They can just combine their notes. As a class, discuss the different ethnic traditions. How many different ethnic groups did the class obtain information on?

Introduce the Section

This section discusses types of families and underscores the importance of recognizing how each type is unique.

Figure Focus

Families come in all shapes and sizes. Explain that defining "types" of families generally refers to the physical makeup of the family members in relationship to each other, without respect to roles and function. The family structure can take on many forms, as illustrated in the picture. Ask students to define their family type, and also the types in their extended families.

Discuss

Much has been written about the changing face of the American family. Ask students to discuss their ideas of what the traditional family makeup is. Explain that there is no right or wrong family type. An important consideration is how family members relate to each other.

Family Types

Discuss with students types of families portrayed in popular television shows and in movies. Do they think these portrayals are realistic? What do students' families have in common with these families, if anything?

STUDENT ACTIVITY

Go through each of the family types listed in the *Family Types* feature box and ask students to raise their hand for the type that is closest to theirs. Keep a count of each type, adding the category of "other" for students whose family type is not listed. Create a bar chart that illustrates the number of each family type in the classroom. Which is the most common?

Identifying Types of Families

Many different combinations of children and adults can form a family unit.

The stereotypical family that most people think of, and that has been most represented in the media, is one married couple, with or without children. According to 2006 U.S. Census data, though, only 51 percent of families are of that type. The rest include:

- Single-parent households
- Families with multiple generations of adults living together
- Single people living alone
- Friends sharing a home and expenses together

There are many types of families, each with their own unique dynamics and challenges.

Family Types

Which of these family types is closest to yours?

- A married (or otherwise romantically committed) couple and the children they have produced or adopted together. This is sometimes called a *nuclear* or *conjugal* family.
- Two adults who combine their households, each bringing children with them. This is called a blended family.
- A group of biologically related people, such as a single adult living with his or her parents, or two sisters sharing an apartment, with or without children.
- A single mother or father living with one or more of their underage children. This is called *a single-parent* family.
- A pair or group of friends who are not related living together, with or without children. This is sometimes called *collective* living, or a *family of choice*.

Or, is your family a type that is not listed here? How would you describe that type?

How Many Adults Does a Family Need?

The number of adults in the household, and their relationship to one another, makes a big difference in a family. In a family with only one adult, both time and money can be stretched thin because a single person has to take on both the financial and the parenting responsibility. More adults mean more time to spend on children and family projects and activities, and possibly more income as well, if more than one person has a job. When there are multiple adults in the family, there are more people to share the burden. However, there is also more potential for conflict when they don't agree on how the household should be run.

Does a Family have to Have Children?

A family can consist only of adults; children are not required. However, many families do have one or more child. The number of children in a household makes a difference in the atmosphere of the family, and in the way people interact. In a large family with many brothers and sisters, you don't have to look far to find someone to talk to or play with, but privacy and quiet time alone may be scarce. People raised in large families tend to have good social skills with other children, because they constantly practice that. On the other hand, only children have plenty of privacy and quiet time, and tend to be more comfortable talking to adults, but they may sometimes feel awkward around other children because they don't have as much experience being with them.

NUMBERS GAME

According to U.S. Census data, in the year 2003, the U.S. population included 33.5 million people who were foreign-born—that is, they moved to the United States, rather than being born here.

Of those, the breakdown of where they came from was as follows:

Caribbean, 10.1%	Central America, 36.9%
South America, 6.3%	Asia, 25.0%
Europe, 13.7%	Other, 8.0%

How many people are there each of those categories?

Let's do the first one (Caribbean) together:

1. Convert the percentages to decimal numbers by dividing them by 100 (that is, moving the decimal place two spaces to the left). For example, 10.1% becomes 0.101.

2. Multiply the converted percentage by the total (33.5 million). For example, 33,500,000 times 0.101 is 3,383,500. That is the number of foreign-born people who came from the Caribbean.

Repeat this process to determine the number of people from each of the other regions.

Having brothers and sisters can help build a child's social skills. If you have a brother or sister, what is something you have learned from contact with him or her?

Multigeneration Families

How would your life be different if more of your relatives lived with you? For example, what if your grandparents or your aunt and uncle moved in?

★ How would bedrooms or sleeping arrangements have to change?

★ Would your family be better or worse off financially?

★ Would your chores and other responsibilities be greater or fewer?

★ Would you get to spend more time or less time with your parent(s)?

★ Would you have more or less time to be with your friends and do out-of-school activities?

Discuss

Explain that the number of adults and children that make up the family structure varies widely. Ask students to consider the pros and cons of different scenarios; for example, mother and father and ten kids, or mother and father, grandmother and grandfather, adult-age son and his wife, and adolescent daughter. What types of challenges would these types of family units pose? What about benefits?

Figure Focus

Ask students to consider the relationship they have with their siblings. Do they consider them good, or best, friends? Do they look at them as mentors? Do they sometimes fill the role of parent? Students should share their thoughts on something they have learned from a sibling. Stress that you can learn things from siblings of all ages, even a toddler. For example, you might notice that your 2-year-old sister is cranky and tends to throw temper tantrums when she is tired. From this, you learn that not getting enough sleep can make you irritable and impatient.

NUMBERS GAME

The number of people from the other regions is as follows:

- Central America: 12,361,500
- South America: 2,110,500
- Asia: 8,375,000
- Europe: 4,589,500
- Other: 2,680,000

Multigeneration Families

Have students consider the additional resources available to them through multiple generations of family living under the same roof. There are more resources to share in the responsibilities of running the household; there are the knowledge and life experiences of more people; and there are the material resources, such as additional cars, clothing, and money.

Introduce the Section

This section examines the typical stages of the family life cycle. The five stages discussed are independence, coupling, parenting, launching children into adulthood, and retirement.

Figure Focus

Have students discuss the various stages of the family life cycle. Lead the discussion by talking about which stage you are currently in. You might ask other teachers and staff to spend a few minutes speaking with the class about the things that characterize their current stage in the family life cycle. For example, if they are in the coupling stage, they might discuss their and their partner's jobs, home life, and goals.

Teaching Tips

Since most students are not yet in a family life cycle stage, they might not see the relevance of discussing and understanding the stages. Point out that their emotional, social, physical, and intellectual development during childhood and adolescence is preparing them to make the transition into the independence stage of the family life cycle.

STUDENT ACTIVITY

Explain to students that setting career goals now can help them make a smooth transition into the independence stage of the life cycle. Have students list three careers in which they are interested. Have them gather information on various job opportunities within that career and write a short paragraph on each.

Analyzing the Family Life Cycle

Independence   Coupling   Parenting   Launching children into adulthood   Retirement

Do you have any family photos hanging on your walls at home? Those snapshots of moments in time remind you where you've been, but they probably don't accurately represent your family as it is now. Every family changes over time, whether it's the kids growing up or the adults getting older. People leave the family, by growing up or through death or divorce. New people enter the family, through marriage, new relationships, births, and adoptions. Children become adults and move out of the family home. Change happens!

Although every family is different, there is a fairly consistent pattern of development for most nuclear families (that is, families that are created based on the romantic relationship of two adults). The usual cycle is:

1. *Independence.* Young adults move out of their parents' homes, and focus on developing themselves as adults.
2. *Coupling.* Two single adults become a couple, and usually get married. Their focus is on creating a bond with one another.
3. *Parenting children.* The couple adopts or gives birth to children, and focuses on their development.
4. *Launching children into adulthood.* As the children become adults, the parents release responsibility for them and re-focus on their own lives.
5. *Retirement or senior years.* Now mostly free of parental responsibilities, the older adults focus on their retirement.

Independence First!

That first stage—independence—is very important. Before you can be responsible for a family, you have to be responsible for yourself. At a minimum, that means:

- Being fully physically mature (that is, being finished with puberty)
- Having the skills and education needed to make a living
- Possessing the maturity to keep a job and make a stable home
- Being emotionally mature enough to put the needs of others before your own

Shifting the Focus

At each stage of the family life cycle, a shift in focus happens. A young adult striking out on his own for the first time—the first apartment, the first job, and so on—is mostly self-focused, and that's normal. You have to know who you are, and how you fit into the world, before you can build a family.

Once you get comfortable with yourself, you start thinking about pairing up with someone else to form a romantic couple—a two-person family. Your focus shifts from your own needs to the needs of your partner and the needs of your relationship.

After you have become comfortable with being responsible to another adult, the next step is often children. Children require much more care and attention than an adult partner; as a parent, your focus shifts to your children's needs.

Gradually, your children grow up and stop requiring so much of your time and attention. Typically by the time your children reach the legal age of adulthood, they are functioning well enough on their own that you can turn your attention back to your own interests. Many adults have a hard time making this transition from thinking primarily of their children to thinking of themselves again; you may have heard this called **empty nest syndrome**.

Depending on the age at which they had their children, some people have 10 to 20 more working years after their children are grown and moved out, while others may be ready for retirement and life as senior citizens—the final stage of family life. During this stage, the focus is on staying fit and healthy, enjoying family (perhaps including grandchildren), and pursuing hobbies.

Exceptions Happen

As you were reading the stages of the family life cycle, perhaps you were thinking about how this cycle applies to your own family—or doesn't. Real life can be complicated, and there are many exceptions to the pattern. In your own family, there may be different milestones where things change, such as a birth, a death, a divorce, or a change in income, location, or health.

The standard family life cycle also assumes that the family is based on the romantic relationship of a couple—and that the couple will stay a couple, and that both the people will stay alive. That isn't always the case. When a family is based on the romantic relationship of a couple, and that relationship changes, the family structure changes. If the couple divorces, the children may live with one parent or the other, or may split their time between parents, making a home in both places. There may be new step-parents and step-brothers and step-sisters, or half brothers or sisters, to adjust to. If one parent dies, the remaining parent may be faced with life changes that affect the whole family, too, such as moving into a smaller home or moving in with family, getting a job, and re-balancing commitments to work, family, and personal life.

> "If my parents got divorced, or one of them died, how would that change my life?"

Test IT Yourself!

Is the "standard" family life cycle presented in this chapter the norm for the majority of families? Test this theory by conducting an informal poll in your class. Find out from each person you survey:

1. Looking at your grandparents' lives, did their family follow the standard life cycle?
2. Looking at your parents' lives, is theirs following the standard life cycle so far?
3. If either of those does not follow the standard life cycle, in what way does it differ? For example, is the couple no longer still together? (If not, is it due to divorce or death?)

As a class, discuss what you learned from these results. Are families different today than they were when your grandparents were having children? Do the majority of the families in your class fit the standard family life cycle? What are the most common variations?

Customized Instruction: Less Advanced/Special Needs/At-Risk Students

Have students "look into the future" and prepare a timeline that illustrates what they think they will be doing in each of the five stages of the family life cycle. Refer them to the illustration on page 146 of the text to use as an example. They can draw pictures of themselves in the various stages, or they can write a brief description.

Discuss

Explain that in each stage of the family life cycle, you develop and gain new skills that help you work through the changes that challenge families of every type. Discuss with students the challenges that can disrupt the normal family life cycle. For example, you landed a decent-paying job, you've bought yourself a car, and you've moved into your own apartment. But then the company you work for merges with another and a number of positions are eliminated, including yours. Now, you have no income to pay the rent and your monthly car payment. You move back in with your parents, thus disrupting the independence stage of your life cycle and forcing your parents back into the parenting stage of their life cycle. Other things that might disrupt the normal family life cycle include a chronic illness, a death, and divorce.

Figure Focus

Nobody wants to think about losing a parent, and divorce can be hard on every member of the family. But assure students that many resources are available to help them deal with a family crisis. If they feel they need help, a first stop might be the school nurse or guidance counselor. A family doctor or a trusted family friend is also an option. Be sure to emphasize the importance of successfully dealing with disruptions to the family life cycle. This can help prevent disease and emotional or stress-related disorders.

Test IT Yourself!

Students are to survey people in their class about the standard family life cycle. Have students work in teams of two. They should survey each other using the questions listed in the text. As a class, analyze the answers. Total the number of "yes" answers and the number of "no" answers to questions 1 and 2. For the "no" answers, write a list of reasons for why the grandparents or parents did not follow the standard family life cycle. With this information, students should be able to answer the questions in the text.

Introduce the Section

This section covers the concept of marriage. It discusses the benefits of marriage and the factors that two people should consider before getting married.

Figure Focus

Explain that wedding vows traditionally include the concepts of:

- Affection (*promise to love, honor, cherish, and protect*).
- Faithfulness (*forsaking all others*).
- Unconditional love (*for richer or for poorer, in sickness and in health*).
- Permanence (*as long as we both shall live, until death do us part*).

Ask students to comment on these concepts. What do they mean? Can they think of other concepts or notions that wedding vows should address?

Discuss

Discuss the changes and adjustments an individual faces in the coupling stage of the family life cycle. Coupling and marriage require that you reevaluate your personal ideas, expectations, values, and goals in terms of how they relate to those of your partner. For example, in your independence stage, your short-term goal was to make enough money so you could buy a brand-new SUV. But now, you and your partner have determined that you both want to save enough money to buy a house. Ask students to consider what other areas might require a couple to make adjustments. In addition to finances, these would include lifestyle, recreational activities, and relationships with in-laws and friends.

Considering Marriage

Even though many people obsess about having the perfect wedding, a wedding is just one day. The real challenges—and joys—come in the days and years that follow.

About 75 percent of the population in the United States will get married. Marriage is an institution that grants the people a unique set of legal, social, and religious rights and responsibilities.

Legally, marriage is a contract between two people. They agree to combine their lives in many legal and financial ways, such as giving each other the right to inherit property after one of them dies, to manage credit jointly, to file taxes as a couple, and to decline to testify against each other in criminal and civil legal trials.

Socially, marriage is a lifestyle. When people marry, they agree to share their lives in social ways, such as living in the same household, raising children together, getting together with friends as a couple, and so on. They agree to be a family.

Religiously, many people believe that marriage joins the couple in the eyes of their creator. Most religions include a religious-based marriage ceremony in which, the creator is called on for a blessing, and in some cases to join the couple in a spiritual marriage. Some religions teach that a marriage conducted without the church's official blessing is not spiritually valid. (However, it is still valid legally and socially.)

Benefits of Marriage

Marriage gives a couple over 1,400 specific legal rights that unmarried couples do not have, including:

- Joint parenting and adoption
- Status as next-of-kin for hospital visits and medical decisions
- Immigration and residency for partners from another country
- Automatic inheritance of property if there is no will
- Social Security and pension benefits for widowed spouses
- Veterans' discounts on medical care and education for spouses of veterans
- Joint filing of taxes
- Sick leave to care for an ailing spouse
- Legal protection from having to testify against your spouse in court

Customized Instruction: More Advanced Students

Have students research the cost of a wedding. They should assume the wedding will include the following expenses:

- Invitations
- Attire and accessories for the bride and groom
- Location and officiator for ceremony
- Rings
- Flowers
- Photographer and videographer
- Gifts and party favors
- Reception

Have students create a spreadsheet that itemizes the costs of each item. Note that according to *The Wedding Report*, a market research publication, the average American wedding costs almost $29,000.

Who Can Get Married?

A marriage ceremony is both a legal and, in some cases, a religious ceremony. Because church and state are separate, the specifications about who can get married may be different between them.

For a legal marriage (also called a **civil marriage**), the couple must get a **marriage license**. To get a marriage license, you must meet requirements imposed by federal, state, and local regulations and show proper proof of identification. After the wedding ceremony, the couple, the person who officiated (such as a minister or a judge), and the witnesses sign the marriage license and file it with the County Clerk's office in their county of residence. Only then are you legally married.

Different states have different requirements for getting a marriage license, such as:

- *Mental competency.* To get married, you must have the mental capacity required to enter into a legal contract. The exact definition of mental competency varies from state to state.
- *Relationship.* The two people getting married cannot be close blood relatives. The exact restrictions vary from state to state.
- *Age.* You must be 18 to marry without your parents' consent in most states. With parental consent, it is possible to marry younger than that in many states—as young as 14 in some cases.

To be married in a religious sense, the couple must meet the requirements imposed by the denomination of religion under which they are marrying. For example, the Catholic Church requires people being married in a Catholic ceremony to both be of the Catholic faith, but a mixed-faith couple could still be married in another church, or in a civil ceremony at a courthouse.

Marriage and Maturity

Marriage doesn't work if both people aren't emotionally mature enough to put aside their own individual wants for the good of the relationship and the good of the other person. Each person coming into a marriage should already have a healthy sense of who he or she is as a single adult.

Although sometimes marriages do last among very young people, it is more the exception than the rule. That's because throughout your teenage years, you are still going through adolescence, and you are changing rapidly—not only your body, but also your intellect and your emotional self. As you are exposed to new ideas, you change your mind about a lot of things—everything from personal philosophy to what types of books and movies you like. The person that you are most compatible with at 13 is not likely to be the person you will be most compatible with at 21.

A successful marriage also requires two people who know how to resolve conflict in healthy and mature ways. Conflicts and disagreements will always come up, in any relationship. Being able to resolve them in a caring and respectful way is an important part of staying connected as a couple. The more emotionally mature the people involved, the better they are at resolving a tense situation without using angry words or violence that can damage trust.

TECH CONNECT

Suppose you have a cousin who wants to get married to his girlfriend while the family is on vacation in the U.S. Virgin Islands. He is not sure what kind of documentation he and his wife-to-be will need. For example, do they need to show their birth certificates? Or are driver's licenses adequate proof of age and identity?

Use the Web to research this. Find out the address of the office on St. Thomas in the U.S. Virgin Islands where a couple can get a marriage license, and what proof of identity, citizenship, and legal age is needed. Also find out how much the marriage license will cost.

Vocabulary

Civil marriage: A legal marriage.

Marriage license: Issued to couples who meet requirements imposed by federal, state, and local regulations and show proper proof of identification.

Discuss

Discuss the legal requirements regarding marriage. In addition to those covered in the text, some states require a couple to show proof of immunity or vaccination for certain diseases or completion of a general physical examination. In addition, a few states require the couple to have blood tests for venereal disease before a marriage license is issued. Some of these states will not issue a license if one or both people have venereal disease, while others will allow the marriage if the couple knows the disease is present. Some states require a waiting period between the time the license is issued and the time of the marriage ceremony.

Teaching Tips

If the topic of same-sex marriage comes up in your classroom discussion, explain to students that some states allow same-sex couples to marry. However, at this writing, the federal government does not recognize same-sex marriages, so the legal benefits provided by the marriage are limited to what's provided by state and local laws. Not all states recognize same-sex marriages that are performed in other states, so if a married same-sex couple moves to a different state, they may lose some of their marriage rights. This does not happen to opposite-sex couples because of the Full Faith and Credit clause of the U.S. Constitution.

 TECH CONNECT

To get married in the U.S. Virgin Islands, you must submit the following at least eight working days prior to your arrival in the territory:

- Completed marriage license application form (download from the Web).
- Court-certified copies of a divorce or death certificate if applicable.
- A $100 money order or certified cashier's check.
- A letter to the court explaining your arrival and departure dates, the date and location of your ceremony, and the name of your officiate.

The bridal couple must pick up their own marriage license, in person, from the courthouse in St. Thomas prior to their wedding day. Photo ID is also required. The Superior Court is located in the Alexander Farrely Justice Complex on the waterfront in Charlotte Amalie, St. Thomas.

Vocabulary

Arranged marriage: Marriage arrangement in which the parents select the mates for their children.

New relationship energy (NRE) or infatuation: State of being obsessed with someone else and constantly wanting to be with that person.

Figure Focus

Ask students to characterize the behavior of someone who is infatuated with another. Explain that when you are infatuated, you see only the positive qualities of the other person and lose sight of reality. You might be lightheaded or jittery, or you might sweat and be easily excitable. When the infatuation turns to love, your behavior is calmer and more even-keeled. You show more confidence and have a positive attitude.

Reinforce and Review

Ask students how they might determine if they are in love with someone. Some indications are:

- You feel good, not worried, sad, scared, or angry.
- You feel that you are receiving as much from the other person as you are giving.
- You trust the other person with your secrets and, sometimes, even your welfare.

21st Century Skills

What Happens Next?

Students are to write an ending to the story from the perspective of one of the three characters—Daniel, Elsa, or Wendy.

- From Daniel's perspective, a happy ending would mean having the opportunity to talk to Elsa about her behavior toward him and why it makes him angry. Elsa would agree to get to know Wendy better, and Daniel and Elsa would schedule time to continue doing things together.

- From Elsa's perspective, a happy ending would mean being able to tell Daniel that she feels he is neglecting her and to work out a plan that would allow them to continuing doing things together at scheduled times.

- From Wendy's perspective, a happy ending would mean being able to spend time with Daniel and being given the opportunity to get to know his friends better.

In middle school and high school, infatuation is common. How do people behave when they are infatuated? How does their behavior change when infatuation turns to love?

Is It True Love?

In the United States, most people marry for love. In other words, they get married to the person they fall in love with, rather than getting married for financial security or political advantage. That might seem obvious to you, but in many countries, **arranged marriages** are the norm, where the parents select the mates for their children.

Love is different from **infatuation**, which is also sometimes called **new relationship energy** (NRE). Many relationships start out with infatuation, where the people seem almost obsessed with one another, constantly wanting to be together, and constantly wanting to be in physical contact. Have you ever had a friend who had a crush on someone, who spent all of her time texting, talking to, and talking about her crush? That's infatuation. Infatuation is short-term; it usually lasts about 3 to 6 months—until the newness has worn off of the relationship.

Real love is what remains after the infatuation phase is over. Real love is patient and unselfish. Have you ever known someone who made a sacrifice of something he wanted—willingly—because it would help someone else? Your parents, maybe, or a close friend? That's the kind of mature love that marriage is based on.

Some people make the mistake of getting married quickly, while they are still in the infatuation stage. This is a problem because while you are infatuated, you do not have a realistic picture of who the other person is. By waiting until the infatuation has subsided, you can better determine whether or not you feel lasting love for one another that would make marriage work.

21st Century Skills

What Happens Next?

Daniel and Elsa are eighth graders who have been best friends since they were in kindergarten. They both collect comic books and like going to comic book and science fiction events. Their friendship has been strained lately, though, because Daniel now has a girlfriend, Wendy, with whom he spends at least three evenings a week after school. Elsa is feeling neglected, but instead of telling Daniel that, she has been acting like she doesn't care, and even being rude to him when he tries to talk to her. Daniel is angry. He thinks that if Elsa really cared about him, she would be happy for him about Wendy. Wendy doesn't really know Elsa very well, but she feels bad that their friendship seems to be suffering because of her.

Being emotionally mature means being able to resolve personal conflicts where people's fears and insecurities come out. That's an essential skill for marriage, or for any relationship. Pick a person in this situation—Daniel, Elsa, or Wendy—and using your 21st Century Skills—such as decision making, goal setting, and problem solving—write an ending to the story from that person's perspective that shows how the conflict could be resolved for a happy ending. Read it to the class, or form a small group and present it as a skit.

Are You Compatible?

Love is an important part of marriage success, but it is not the only factor to consider. Compatibility is also important. The more ways in which you are compatible with your spouse, the easier it will be to create a home together and have a lifestyle that pleases you both.

Here are some compatibility factors to consider. If you are incompatible in just one or two of these, a happy marriage may still be possible with some compromises on both sides, but if there are serious differences in many areas, you may be in for a difficult time together.

- *Having children.* You agree on whether or not to have children, how many to have, and when to have them. You agree on whether or not you should adopt a child if you cannot bear any biologically.
- *Raising children.* You agree on how discipline, affection, and learning should be handled. For example, you agree on whether or not small children should be spanked when they misbehave.
- *Religious beliefs.* You agree on religious beliefs, on the ideal amount of involvement to have in a faith community, and on the role religion should play in raising children. For example, you agree on whether or not children should go to religious education classes.
- *Level of cleanliness.* You are comfortable with the same level of household cleanliness or clutter; one person does not feel like he or she is constantly picking up after the other.
- *Family involvement.* You agree on how often you should visit your extended families, how long those visits should last, and what you should talk about with them. For example, you agree on whether or not you should spend your vacations with your parents.
- *Pets.* You agree on the types and numbers of pets you should own, where they should sleep, and how they should be disciplined. One person might love cats, for example, and the other person might be allergic to them.
- *Type of home.* You agree on the part of the country you would like to live in, and what kind of home you will have there (old house, new house, apartment, etc.).
- *Spending money.* You agree on how much of your income you should save and how much you should spend on nonessentials. You agree on how credit should be used, and how important it is to have a good credit rating and pay bills on time.
- *Work.* You agree on how much priority work should take in your lives, as opposed to family time. For example, you might agree that you should always work overtime when given the chance for extra money, or that you should come home promptly at quitting time to be with your family.

Compatibility includes not only enjoying each other's company, but having common opinions and goals. Think of an adult couple you know, such as parents or other relatives. In what ways are they compatible?

When a Relationship Ends . . .

Relationship breakups are never easy, but they are a sad fact of life. More than half of all marriages end in divorce. They don't have to end in a nasty way, though; you can end a relationship with the same spirit of love and kindness that you began it.

Suppose you were ending a marriage or other important relationship. What would you do to ease the transition to being apart for both of you?

- 👎 Tell all your friends the details of what your former mate did wrong, so they will be on your side in the breakup.
- 👎 Complain about your former mate's flaws to everyone so they will see that the breakup was not your fault.
- 👎 Keep your anger and hurt stuffed down inside you, where it won't harm anyone but you.
- 👍 Choose one or two trusted friends to confide your feelings in.
- 👍 Consider seeing a psychologist or therapist to help you work through your emotions.
- 👍 Try to be as positive—or at least neutral—as possible when talking about your former mate in public.

Discuss

Explain that compatibility means being able to exist, live, or work together without conflict. Discuss the compatibility factors listed in the text. Ask students for suggestions on other ways to measure compatibility. For example, education, health, and political beliefs might be factors to consider. If your partner supports a candidate for office whom you loathe, how can you deal with it and remain compatible? What about the concept of "opposites attract"? Explain that while opposite personalities can often manage a relationship balanced by each partner's strengths and weaknesses, they also can end up having to deal with a bigger share of friction and conflicts.

Figure Focus

Students are to think of a couple they know and comment on the ways in which they are compatible. Have students refer to the compatibility factors listed in the text, and also consider any of their own measures of compatibility.

When a Relationship Ends...

Students are to consider what they would do to ease the transition from being part of a couple to being alone. In addition to those things discussed in the text, you might suggest the following (which were also discussed in Chapter 5):

- Allow yourself to feel the sadness, anger, or embarrassment of the break-up. Don't try to minimize the importance of the relationship by suppressing your feelings.
- Connect or reconnect with others. They can lend you the support you need to get through a difficult time.
- Consider what you have learned from the relationship as well as from the break-up and how you might apply it to future relationships.
- Try to follow your usual routine, but avoid the things that might bring back painful reminders.
- Reexamine your interests and hobbies and consider developing new ones.
- Do something to help others. Volunteer at a community center or get involved in a volunteer project.

STUDENT ACTIVITY

Explain to students that some people measure compatibility using astrology and signs of the zodiac. Astrology is the study of the positions of the moon, sun, and other planets and how their motions affect human behavior. Have students create a chart that lists and describes the characteristics of the 12 signs of the zodiac (Aries, Taurus, Gemini, Cancer, Leo, Virgo, Libra, Scorpio, Sagittarius, Capricorn, Aquarius, and Pisces). Which sign were they born under? Do they think the description matches their personality? Which sign or signs is their sign supposedly compatible with? Direct them to Web sites such as www.astrology.com and www.astrology-online.com/love.htm.

Introduce the Section

The joys and frustrations of parenthood are discussed. The section also looks at the sacrifices and added responsibilities an adult takes on when he or she becomes a parent.

Figure Focus

Ask students to comment on what joys and frustrations they think a parent might experience. Share with students the following data prepared by the U.S. Department of Agriculture on how much it costs to raise a child. Data is on a child in a family structure that consists of married parents and two children.

- For families with annual before-tax income less than $44,500, the cost ranges from $7,580 per year from birth through age 2, to $8,540 for ages 15 through 17. The total for the 17 years is $143,790.

- For families with annual before-tax income between $44,500 and $74,900, the cost ranges from $10,600 per year from birth through age 2, to $11,660 for ages 15 through 17. The total for the 17 years is $197,700.

- For families with annual before-tax income greater than $74,900, the cost ranges from $15,760 per year from birth through age 2, to $16,970 for ages 15 through 17. The total for the 17 years is $289,380.

Considering Parenthood

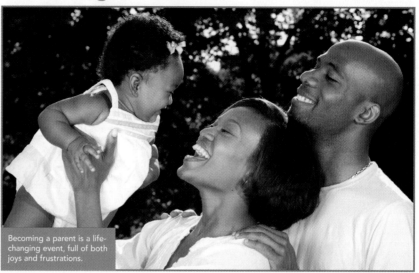

Becoming a parent is a life-changing event, full of both joys and frustrations.

Do you plan to have children someday? It's an important decision, one that will shape the rest of your life in significant ways. Whether or not you are raising children will determine things such as:

- What kind of job you can work at. Your children are your first priority, so you might not be able to take a job that involves a lot of travel or long hours.
- Where you go on vacation. Rather than a romantic get-away, you might opt for a vacation at a family amusement park.
- What your home environment is like. A home with small children is often noisy and chaotic, with toys everywhere.

Children can be a wonderful addition to your life, and growing a family is one of the most rewarding experiences many people have. It's not for everyone, though. When you have children, your time, money, energy, and relationships are not just your own; you must use them in a responsible way for the benefit of your children. That's why it's important not to enter into parenthood lightly—to make sure that you want to have children, and to have them only when you are emotionally, physically, and financially prepared to take good care of them.

Thinking As a Family

When you are a parent, the way you think through a decision must change. You can't just think about what is best for yourself—your first concern must be what's best for the whole family.

For example, suppose you get a $100 bonus at work. What would you spend it on if that happened today? Probably clothes for yourself, cell phone minutes, music, or games. Now fast-forward ahead in life and suppose you have a 6-month-old baby. *Now* what would you spend $100 on? Perhaps diapers, baby food, or a stroller?

Parents must also allocate their time differently from nonparents. For example, suppose you have just worked an 8-hour shift at your job. What might you do next if you do not have children? Perhaps you might run some errands, stop by the mall, or meet friends for dinner out. What if you had preschool-age children? Your evening might consist of picking them up at daycare, feeding them, bathing them, and putting them to bed.

Stay in School

While teen pregnancy accounts for a relatively small percentage of the high school dropout rate, an alarmingly large percentage of students who drop out of school end up becoming pregnant while still in their teens. According to a recent study, girls who drop out of high school significantly increase their risk of becoming pregnant. The study indicated that 40 percent of the female dropouts surveyed gave birth before the age of 20. Among students who stayed in school, on the other hand, only about 15 percent gave birth in their teens.

Explain to students that the negative aspects of dropping out of school—higher unemployment, lower earnings potential, limited access to health care, etc.—present even bigger challenges for female dropouts who have children.

You might consider the following:

- Have your school nurse or other healthcare staff present information on teen pregnancy prevention.
- Partner with community-based organizations to provide information or presentations on teen pregnancy.
- Encourage students to become involved in academics, extracurricular activities, and youth development programs, as participation in these will reduce other risky behaviors.

When Is the Right Time to Have Children?

In an ideal world, only people who were ready to become parents would have children. That means that all parents would be:

- Financially secure, including having a good job
- Finished with their education, so they can focus on family
- Emotionally mature, with a good sense of who they are
- In a stable, committed relationship where both people want to be parents
- Willing and eager to take on parenting responsibilities

Of course, sometimes people who don't meet all those criteria have children. It is still possible to be a good parent if you lack one or more of those qualities, but it is more difficult.

A parent who also has a career has extra challenges in balancing home and work life—plus fitting in any leisure activities that he or she enjoys. A working parent plays several different roles in his or her life—employee, parent, child (if his or her parents are still living), and family member. Each of those roles carries its own responsibilities, and they may sometimes conflict. For example, a parent might have to work late, resulting in the child not being picked up from daycare on time, or resulting in the child missing a piano lesson or soccer game. In many households, though, the alternative—one parent staying home—is not financially possible.

Considering Adoption

Some people who want to be parents, and who meet all the qualifications to be a good parent, are unable to produce children, due to physical limitations, illnesses, injuries, or other factors. For example, some women are **infertile**, which means they cannot bear children at all. Others choose not to bear children because of medical conditions, such as diabetes, that might make pregnancy hard on their body.

Adoption matches up people who want to be parents with children who need parents. Some adoption agencies specialize in matching up children and parents within the United States; others focus on international adoptions. In either case, the main goals of an adoption agency are to make sure that the adults and the children are suited for one another, and that the prospective parents have all—or at least most—of the qualifications for being a good parent.

In many states there are programs that allow someone who has a baby, but feels unprepared to care for it, to safely drop it off at a designated site, such as a fire station or courthouse, without any legal penalty. That facility will then call a social service agency, which will find a good adoptive home for the baby.

Myth If you give a baby up for adoption, you can never see it again.

Truth Some agencies offer open adoption, which means you are able to keep in touch with the adopting parents and even in some cases have occasional visits with the child.

Myth Parents should wait to tell children that they are adopted until they are grown up.

Truth Many psychologists say that adopted children do best if you tell them about the special way they came to be with their families very early. Avoiding talking about adoption may give the impression that there is something wrong with it.

MONEY MADNE$$

Tonya and Mike just had a baby. Up until this point, they both have worked full-time jobs. Mike makes $35,000 a year and Tonya makes $50,000 a year. They would like for one of them to stay home with the baby, but they are not sure they can afford to lose the income. If they both work, they will have to pay $18,000 a year in daycare and babysitting services.

If Tonya goes back to work and Mike stays home, she will have the following work-related expenses:

- Work clothes: $5,000
- Business lunches: $1,000
- Gas and car maintenance from commuting to work: $1,500

If Mike keeps his job and Tonya stays home, they would have these work-related expenses for Mike:

- Work clothes: $1,000
- Gas and car maintenance from commuting to work: $1,200

Is it worth it financially for one of them to stay home? If so, which one should stay home, and why?

Vocabulary

Adoption: Legal procedure in which people who want to be parents are matched with children who need parents.

Infertile: Condition of being unable to bear children.

Myth/Truth

Explain the differences between open, semi-open, and closed adoptions.

- With an open adoption, the birth parent(s) can specify the type of family they consider most appropriate as a placement for their child. The birth parent(s) will meet the chosen family prior to placement and information will be shared by both parties. An open adoption is considered a life-long relationship with on-going contact over the years.

- With a semi-open adoption, the birth parents may specify particular characteristics with regard to the adoptive family. The birth parent(s) may also meet the adoptive parents before the baby is born or after it is placed. After placement, the birth parent(s) may receive pictures and letters from the adoptive family.

- With a closed adoption, the birth parent(s) will have little or no control over the placement of the child. They probably will not have information about their child's health or whereabouts.

Myth/Truth

Explain that once a child reaches the age of majority (age at which the rights and privileges of an adult are legally granted) in their state, they have the option of searching for or being searched for by their biological family.

MONEY MADNE$$

If Tonya works, her income after expenses will be $42,500. If Mike works, his income after expenses will be $32,800. This gives them a combined income after expenses of $75,300. If they subtract $18,000 for daycare and babysitting services, their income drops to $57,300. If one of them were to quit working, it should be Mike because he contributes significantly less to the household income. But without Mike's income, their household income will drop from $57,300 to $42,500, or a total of $14,800 less. Financially, it does not appear to be worth it for one of them to stay home.

Introduce the Section

Conflicts and problems are a normal part of family life. When family members cannot resolve a problem on their own, there are many resources to which they can turn for help.

Figure Focus

Make sure students are aware of the types of assistance discussed in the text. Ask them to share instances in which a member of their family or extended family may have sought help from an outside agency or organization.

Reinforce and Review

Explain that conflicts with family can invade other areas of your life. To minimize conflict, suggest the following:

1. Respect your family. Without mutual respect, there will always be conflict. People who respect each other can disagree without yelling and getting angry. They can talk calmly and rationally about a conflict and figure out together the best way to resolve it.

2. Communicate with your family. If you share and are open with them, you will probably find them to be helpful and supportive. If you shut them out, though, they might automatically think the worst.

3. Show honesty and responsibility to build your family's trust. When people trust each other, they are less likely to create confrontations.

Resolving Family Problems

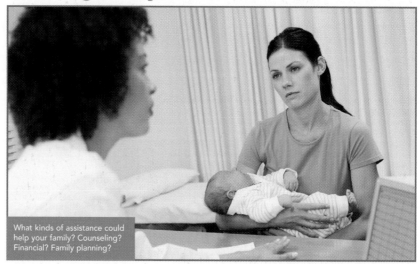

What kinds of assistance could help your family? Counseling? Financial? Family planning?

All families have problems, and some of those problems may even be serious and require outside help. Working through problems together is a natural and normal part of family life.

Because families are such an important building block of our society, there are many programs, benefits, and other resources available to help strengthen them. For example, there are workshops that teach young parents how to care for infants, financial assistance programs that help low-income parents pay for milk and nutritious food for their children, and counselors who can help couples learn to communicate calmly without shouting or becoming physically violent with one another. Many of these programs are free or low-cost, because they are funded with federal, state, and local tax dollars.

Many for-profit businesses also specialize in helping families. Family counselors, therapists, and psychologists work with families, for example, to help them resolve their emotional problems and make better decisions. Family planning clinics help couples who don't want to have children to avoid pregnancy; fertility clinics help couples who want to have babies conceive them; and adoption agencies specialize in matching up prospective parents with children waiting to be adopted.

Who Provides Assistance?

Family assistance programs are available through many different agencies and organizations, including:

- Federal (nationwide) government programs such as Social Security
- State-run facilities such as orphanages and adoption agencies
- County-run programs such as low-cost family immunization services
- Local government programs such as family programs at a library
- Nonprofit charities such as recreation centers and counseling services
- Church programs such as after-school programs for kids whose parents don't get home from work until several hours after school lets out

Types of Problems Families Have

Families can have a variety of problems, from communication difficulties to financial issues. When a problem reaches critical importance, it is called a **crisis**. For example, a family not being able to pay the electric bill would be a problem, but not paying it for so long that it got shut off would be a crisis.

Some of the problem types that families may encounter include:

- *Finances.* The family's expenses are higher than its income, resulting in there not being enough money to pay for the basics they need.
- *Education.* There may not be enough time or money for all the adults in the family to get as much education as they would like.
- *Nutrition.* Not everyone in the family may get proper nutrition on a daily basis. This can stem either from financial problems or from lack of attention.
- *Discipline.* Children may not receive appropriate guidance or discipline from the adults in the family, or an adult may make irresponsible choices for himself or others.
- *Communication.* Family members may not communicate well with each other. They may shut each other out completely, or may say unkind or irrational things out of emotion.
- *Domestic violence/abuse.* Anger and frustration can sometimes erupt into verbal or physical abuse, such as name-calling, hitting, kicking, or throwing things.

The effects of such problems on families can be either mild or severe. When minor problems occur, people might just be temporarily unhappy. When major problems occur and are not addressed, the family might be broken up by someone leaving, by Child Protective Services taking children out of the home, or by someone being arrested and jailed.

Life Cycle–Related Problems

Some family problems occur as a direct result of what phase of the family life cycle they are in. For example:

- When couples first get married, there may be communication problems as they learn how to interact with each other. There may also be financial problems since young couples are often at the beginning of their careers.
- When a couple has a baby, there may be fights about time and money. One or both may not be well-equipped to be a parent, and parenthood might mean that one or both has to postpone education.
- As children grow up, conflicts can occur about discipline. Parents may not agree on what discipline is appropriate, and children may push boundaries and create tense situations in the household.
- Teenagers living in a house with adults may not feel like they are heard or understood, and are under the stress of hormonal changes. They may have verbal or even physical conflicts with other family members.

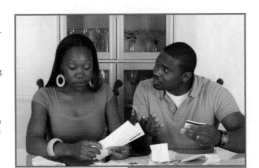

What kinds of problems does your family have? How do they usually resolve them?

"Why don't my parents understand me?"

Vocabulary

Crisis: When a problem reaches critical importance.

Figure Focus

Discuss the types of family problems listed in the text. Ask students to discuss the types of problems their family experiences. Review the following conflict management skills:

- **Negotiate:** Determine how to get past or deal with something that constitutes an obstacle or hazard.
- **Compromise:** Settle a conflict by agreeing to accept less than what you originally wanted.
- **Resolve:** Find a solution to the conflict.
- **Apologize:** Express remorse or acknowledge that you are sorry for something.

APPLY IT

Divide students into six teams. Have each team perform a skit that illustrates one of the six problem types discussed in the text. In the skit, they should reenact the problem and go about resolving it using one of the problem-solving skills discussed above: Negotiate, Compromise, Resolve, and Apologize.

Customized Instruction: At-Risk Students

Obtain a copy of your school's policy on conflict resolution. If your school does not have one, you can download sample policies from different Web sites, including www.cde.ca.gov/ls/ss/se/sample-policy.asp. Give students a copy of the policy and have them modify it so it applies to their family. Have them insert a title for the policy, such as, "The _____ Family's Conflict Management Guidelines."

TECH CONNECT

Students are to go online to find information on the Supplemental Nutrition Assistance Program (SNAP). Explain that the program is offered through the U.S. Department of Agriculture's Food and Nutrition Service (FNS). Students should be able to find information at www.fns.usda.gov/FSP/outreach/map.htm.

Discuss

Discuss ways in which students can take an active role in managing a family crisis. Some suggestions are:

■ Identifying the problem before it evolves into a crisis.

■ Speaking candidly about your concerns at a family meeting.

■ Encouraging other family members to be open about their feelings. If they don't want to speak up, suggest that they write down their thoughts and share them with the family.

■ Speaking directly and one-on-one with the person you think is at the root of the problem.

■ Since it is a "family" crisis, be prepared to take responsibility for the role you might have played in it. Don't put the blame on everyone but yourself.

■ Instilling the desire in all members of the family to resolve the conflict and move on.

Explain the negative effects that stress from a family crisis can have on each member's physical health. It can lead to physical ailments as well as mental and emotional distress.

Figure Focus

Students are asked to consider when a family should seek professional assistance to handle a problem. Many people find the objectivity of an outside expert can be a tremendous help in resolving family problems.

TECH CONNECT

Suppose a friend's family is struggling financially because both parents are unemployed. The parents would like to apply for government food assistance, but they do not know where to go or how to get started. They do not have a computer in their home.

Using your computer, look up information about the Supplemental Nutrition Assistance Program (SNAP) on the Web, and use that information to determine where someone living in your neighborhood should go to apply for the program.

■ When teenagers become adults and move out, the parents may have problem readjusting to life without kids in the house. There may be communication problems between them.

■ As adults reach old age, money may be an issue because they are no longer working. Senior citizens also sometimes do not get adequate nutrition, and can be targets of domestic violence.

How Families Respond to Crisis

Depending on the nature of the problem, and how urgent it is that it be solved, a family may choose to react to a crisis in different ways.

For problem relating to the family's financial security, the adults may choose to handle it themselves, or may choose to involve other relatives or friends. They may work with credit counseling centers, banks, credit card companies, and other institutions to work out a plan. They may also visit food pantries, apply for government assistance such as Supplemental Nutrition Assistance Program (formerly called Food Stamps), or investigate government housing programs.

Discipline or communication problems may involve the entire family, both parents and children. The adults in the family may hold family meetings where the family problems are discussed, or may sit down with individuals separately to talk about behavior problems. They may try to get everyone to talk about their feelings about the conflicts that are occurring, and may impose new rules that will help everyone get along. In some cases, they may involve a therapist, counselor, religious advisor, or other outside person, or attend a group counseling session with other parents or parent-child pairs.

To get more information about problem and crisis management, both parents and children can benefit from doing research. You can find a lot of information about family management and crisis handling online, as well as in books at your local library. You can also find information about each specific problem type there.

What kinds of family problems are best handled with professional assistance?

When Should a Professional Become Involved?

Many families can handle some problems on their own, without outside involvement. However, in critical situations, a professional who is trained in crisis resolution, family counseling, or financial planning can often make the process much easier. Some reasons why:

■ A professional is trained to ask the right questions and make the right suggestions to help your family, whether the problem is personal, financial, or something else.

■ An outside objective opinion can shed new light on a situation. Often people who have an interest in a certain outcome can't be objective without guidance.

■ Sometimes having someone with legal authority is necessary, such as a law enforcement officer or social worker, especially if not everyone involved is cooperative.

Finding Services in Your Area

It can sometimes be challenging to locate an assistance program that matches your need, because so many different organizations and levels of government run the various programs, and each program has its own rules about who and how it serves. Some ways you can find out what's available in your area include:

- *Telephone directory.* Look under *Family Services, Government Services, Family Planning, Counseling,* and other similar headings.
- *Web search.* Use a search engine such as Google, Yahoo, or Bing to look for keywords related to what you want. Make sure you include your city or state name in the search so that you will find local results.
- *Places of worship.* Call the office, or visit the office in person, to find out if they have a list of family services or resources in the area.
- *Local government.* Ask at your local or county government center if there is a list, brochure, or Web site that provides information.
- *Referrals.* Once you have found one organization, ask them if they know of any other organizations that provide related services. Friends may also be able to help by telling you about their own experiences.

Volunteering for Family Services

Family services are not just about what you can get from the system—they're also about what you can give. Most organizations operate on very tight budgets and will gladly accept any donations of time or money. Some things you could offer to do:

- Help young children learn to read and write in a tutoring program.
- Do yard work, such as weeding flowerbeds, for a nonprofit organization.
- Run errands at the business office of a charity.
- Bake cookies or cook a meal for a youth group or soup kitchen.

By volunteering your time to work for an organization that strengthens families, you are contributing to all of society in a meaningful way. You never know how even the smallest kindness and contribution will make a difference.

Job Search

There are many jobs available in family services organizations. Working with families can be a very demanding job, especially emotionally, but can also be very rewarding for those who enjoy making a positive difference in people's lives.

Here are some possible careers to consider:

- *Social worker.* Helps people get access to services, manages foster care and welfare programs, works with at-risk youth. Requires at least a bachelors degree, preferably a master's degree, in sociology, psychology, or social work.
- *Family counselor.* Works with families on their communication skills and relationship issues; helps adults with their parenting skills; counsels children, teens, and adults. Requires a master's degree in psychology or social work.
- *Adoption coordinator.* Helps match up prospective parents with children to be adopted, keeps administrative records, conducts in-home visits to screen applicants. Requires at least a high school diploma; associate or bachelor's degree preferred.
- *Youth program director.* Creates and runs after-school and weekend programs for children and teens. Works directly with both parents and kids to find activities that are safe, fun, and educational. Requires at least a high school diploma; associate or bachelor's degree preferred.

Discuss

Discuss the various resources and services that are presented in the text and how to locate them. Ask students to name specific organizations or groups they are familiar with. Do they or other members of their family volunteer at any such organizations? If yes, ask students to elaborate on what the organization does and what their volunteer duties consist of.

COMMUNITY SERVICE

As a class, develop a list of family services organizations within the community. Students will make contact with each organization and gather information on volunteer opportunities, volunteer duties, and any educational or special training required for volunteers. If the list of organizations is long enough, assign each student to his or her own group. If it is not, then group students into teams. As a class, have students compile the information into a booklet and make a copy for each student.

Job Search

This feature discusses jobs in family services organizations. You might consider inviting people in those careers to speak to the class about their jobs.

Customized Instruction: ESOL Students

Ask students to gather information on volunteering in a family literacy program. They should provide a description of the program, explain who can participate in it, list volunteer opportunities and duties, and describe special training or skills required for volunteers.

End-of-Chapter Activities

Case Study

Brandi's family life will be different in that her family structure will now include a stepmother and two stepsiblings. She will have more room in Julie's large house and maybe more privacy, but she might lose the sense of closeness she had living with her father in their small apartment. By sharing her feelings, Brandi 's father might be able to identify potential problems and help resolve them before they erupt into something more serious. To prepare for the changes ahead, Brandi can visit her new neighborhood and become familiar with where things are and who might be her age and going to the same school she will attend.

Sounding Off!

Student answers will vary.

FAQ

1. Functions include:
   - Making people feel loved and accepted as part of a group
   - Helping each other through difficult situations
   - Creating a safe and comfortable home environment
   - Providing a stable home for children to grow and develop
   - Passing on values and traditions
   - Helping children understand the expectations of society
   - Sharing memories and history
   - Passing on wealth and property

2. Ethnicity is racial and genetic. National origin refers to the country from which your family came.

3. Types of families are:
   - Nuclear or conjugal: A couple and their children
   - Blended: A family where children from two different sets of parents are combined
   - Biologically related people living together
   - A single mother or father living with children
   - A group of unrelated friends living together

4. The five states of the family life cycle are:
   - Independence
   - Coupling
   - Parenting
   - Launching children into adulthood
   - Retirement and senior living

5. Answers will vary, and may include divorce, separation, death, or disability.

Chapter 7 ■ Family Basics

Case Study

Brandi's parents have been divorced for quite a while, and yesterday Brandi's father announced that he and his girlfriend, Julie, are getting married soon. He and Brandi will be moving out of their small apartment in the city, and into Julie's large house in the suburbs, with her 6-year-old son and 4-year-old daughter. Brandi is happy for her father, but she wonders how the upcoming changes will affect her life.

- In what ways will Brandi's family life be different after the move?
- Why would it be helpful for Brandi to talk to her father about her feelings?
- What can Brandi do to prepare for the changes ahead?

Sounding Off!

1. How do the adults in your family manage the balance between work, leisure, and participation in family activities? Do they do a good job of it, or could they be more effective?
2. Describe a holiday that your family celebrates together. Is there one particular family member who is in charge of it? Are there any traditions that are the same every year?

1. List four functions of a family.
2. Explain the difference between ethnicity and national origin.
3. List three types of families and explain what each consists of.
4. List the five states of the family life cycle.
5. Give an example of something that might disrupt the standard family life cycle.
6. Name three rights that are automatically granted to a couple when they get married.
7. List three requirements that a state might impose for a marriage license to be granted.
8. List four factors that contribute to compatibility in a marriage.
9. Describe at least three qualities of a person who is ready to raise children.
10. Name two ways of finding information about family services available in your area.

6. Any three rights from page 148, including:
   - Joint parenting and adoption
   - Status as next-of-kin for hospital visits and medical decisions
   - Immigration and residency for partners from another country
   - Automatic inheritance of property if there is no will
   - Social Security and pension benefits for widowed spouses
   - Veterans' discounts on medical care and education for spouses of veterans
   - Joint filing of taxes
   - Sick leave to care for an ailing spouse
   - Legally protected from having to testify against your spouse in court

7. Requirements include age, mental capacity, and no relation to one another.

8. Compatibility can include agreement about:
   - Having children
   - Pets
   - Spending money
   - Religious beliefs
   - Level of cleanliness
   - Family involvement
   - Raising children
   - Type of home
   - Work

9. Qualities include:
   - Financially secure
   - Finished with education
   - Emotionally mature
   - In a stable, committed relationship
   - Desire to be parents

10. Answers will vary, and may include telephone directory, Web search, places of worship, local government, and referrals.

The family structure, and the roles of families in people's lives, have changed a lot in the past 50 years. What are the most significant changes?

To find out, in small groups interview some people over age 75 about what their family life was like when they were your age. You can choose to interview members of your own families or you can visit a retirement center or nursing home and ask if there are people who would be willing to talk with you. Find out information such as:

■ What relatives besides your parents and siblings lived in your home?
■ What did you and your siblings do for fun?
■ What chores did you have to do?
■ What did your family do for evening entertainment?
■ How many meals a week did the whole family eat together?

Summarize what you learned in a group report, including quotations from the people you interviewed.

Hot Topics

Changes in a family's members, location, income, housing, or other influences can mean big changes in each person's life experience. For example, when a parent divorces or remarries, when a parent loses or gets a job, and when a baby is born or an adult child leaves home, the whole family must adjust to the change.

Take this opportunity to write about a change within your family that was difficult for you to accept at first, and how you dealt with it. Use a word processing program or write it out on paper, and drop it into the classroom's Hot Topics box. It's anonymous, so you can be honest and open.

Then, as a class, read the anonymous entries and discuss them. For each entry, talk about what advice you might give to someone facing a similar situation.

Problem Solver

In an ideal world, everyone who has a child should be able to afford to feed, clothe, house, and educate that child. However, for a variety of reasons, many people who are not able to care for them adequately have children. What are some ways that we as a society could help people who are not financially prepared avoid having more children, while still making sure that all children have the basics of life needed to grow into healthy adults? Brainstorm as a class, and then, working with a partner or in a small group, create a presentation that discusses one of the ideas proposed and its pros and cons.

Team Players

Students are to interview people over the age of 75 about their family life before the stage of independence. Remind students of things they should consider when communicating with an elderly person. Some of these include:

■ Hearing loss, which makes it harder for them to understand you. You may have to speak louder and slower than you are comfortable with.

■ Vision loss, which may impact their recognition of you and other things in their environment.

■ Voice changes, which can affect the loudness or clarity of their speech.

■ Memory loss, which might mean that you will need to repeat your questions or reword them to help jog memories.

Emphasize that, first and foremost, communicating with the elderly requires patience and understanding.

Hot Topics

Make sure students understand that they can turn in their papers anonymously. Encourage them to be open and honest about the change that occurred in their family.

Problem Solver

Students are to brainstorm ideas on how to educate people about the financial responsibilities that come with having a child. They are to work with a partner or in small groups to prepare a presentation on one of the ideas proposed. You might want to review the statistics on p. 152 from the U.S. Department of Agriculture on how much it costs to raise a child. Or, refer students to the Web site www.cnpp.usda.gov/Publications/CRC/crc2007.pdf.

Write Now

Students are to pick a foreign country and write a report on the typical day or week in the life of a family there. Make sure their reports cover the questions in the text.

Be Involved!

Students are to discuss in class the things they have observed parents doing to make their children feel loved and accepted. They are also to discuss mistakes parents have made that harmed a child's self-esteem. Then, they should create a poster or presentation that provides suggestions for first-time parents on how to make their child feel special and build their self-esteem.

Social Networking

Students are to create skits that depict bad communication in dealing with a family problem. After each skit, the class is to discuss how the persons involved could have behaved differently for a better outcome. Review with students suggestions in the teacher text on page 156 on how they can take an active role in managing a family crisis.

Web Extra

Students are to find information on local low-cost events that are suitable for the whole family. They are to bookmark sites and with the rest of the class, compile a list of events in the area. Be sure to distribute a copy of the list to all class members.

Write Now

How are families different in other countries than in the United States? Select a country, and then using the Web or reference books from the library, find out what a typical day or week in the life of a family there consists of. For example, how many children are there in an average-size family? What jobs do the adults have? Do the children go to school? What is the average level of education that people achieve there? What do families do for fun? What is the average life expectancy of an adult? Do grandparents commonly live together with their children and grandchildren? Create a report, including pictures, with the information you find.

Be Involved!

www.fcclainc.org

Nurturing children involves more than just providing food and shelter. It also means giving children the unconditional acceptance and love they need to grow emotionally into healthy adults.

As a class, discuss what kinds of things your parents—or the parents of other people you know—have done that make their children feel loved and accepted. Also discuss any mistakes that you have seen parents make that have harmed children's self-esteem.

Based on this information, create posters or PowerPoint presentations aimed at first-time parents that explain the importance of building a child's self-esteem and some suggestions for ways to accomplish that in daily life.

Social Networking

Many families aren't as close as they might be, because they don't have the communication skills to listen respectfully to each other and to share their own feelings in ways that don't offend. In groups, create a skit that demonstrates bad communication in dealing with a family problem. For example, one group might enact a father confronting his son about a broken taillight in the family car after the son has borrowed it. After each skit is performed, the rest of the class can discuss as a group how each person could have behaved differently for a better outcome.

Web Extra

Use the Internet to locate information about local community events, festivals, concerts, and other free or low-cost activities that a family (adults, teens, and small children) could all attend together. Share your list of bookmarks with your classmates to create a master list of the happenings in your area.

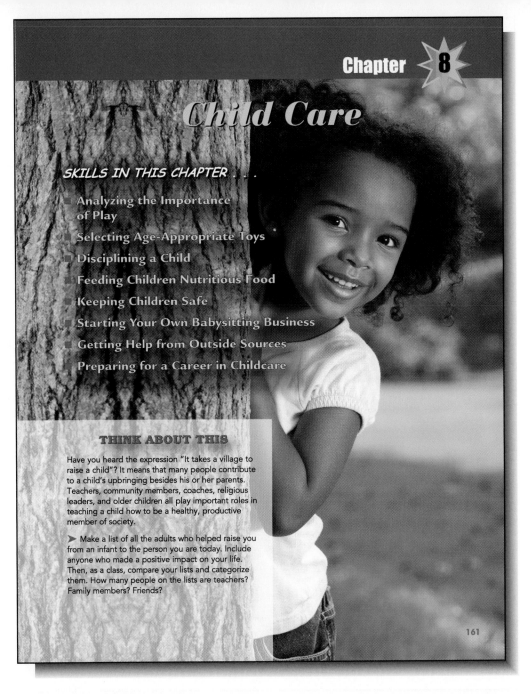

Chapter 8 Overview

This chapter provides an overview of child care. It discusses the guidance and support children need to grow and develop into productive members of society. It also provides information on babysitting and careers in child care.

Analyzing the Importance of Play   Students learn how play strengthens and stimulates a child's physical, social, emotional, and intellectual skills.

Selecting Age-Appropriate Toys   This section identifies the types of toys that are appropriate for children at different age levels.

Disciplining a Child   This section discusses how rules and discipline give children a sense of security, protection, and even accomplishment.

Feeding Children Nutritious Food   The dietary and nutritional needs of children at various age levels are discussed.

Keeping Children Safe   This section discusses the responsibility adults have for keeping children safe at home, at play, and when they are out in public.

Starting Your Own Babysitting Business   This section covers the steps involved in starting and running a successful babysitting business.

Getting Help from Outside Sources   Students learn that child care can be challenging, even for the most experienced providers. Information is provided on sources you can go to for help.

Preparing for a Career in Childcare   This section examines careers and job opportunities available in childcare.

Focus and Engage

Bell-Ringer: Think About This

Students are to make a list of all the adults who helped raise them from birth to today. They should focus on the people who made a positive impact on their life. Some students might want to list friends, but encourage them to think of older children and adults who contributed in some way—big or small—to their growth and development. It might be helpful for students to look through family photo albums or ask their parents about people they might not remember from their early childhood. For that reason, you might want to give students a day or two to complete their lists.

Chapter 8

Child Care

SKILLS IN THIS CHAPTER . . .

- Analyzing the Importance of Play
- Selecting Age-Appropriate Toys
- Disciplining a Child
- Feeding Children Nutritious Food
- Keeping Children Safe
- Starting Your Own Babysitting Business
- Getting Help from Outside Sources
- Preparing for a Career in Childcare

THINK ABOUT THIS

Have you heard the expression "It takes a village to raise a child"? It means that many people contribute to a child's upbringing besides his or her parents. Teachers, community members, coaches, religious leaders, and older children all play important roles in teaching a child how to be a healthy, productive member of society.

➤ Make a list of all the adults who helped raise you from an infant to the person you are today. Include anyone who made a positive impact on your life. Then, as a class, compare your lists and categorize them. How many people on the lists are teachers? Family members? Friends?

161

ADVANCE PREPARATION

Review	*Life Skills for the 21st Century* textbook, Chapter 8.
Prepare	Paper and pencil for some activities. Ball with a bell or noise-maker inside. Crayons or markers for drawing. Box labeled "Hot Topics."

CUSTOMIZED INSTRUCTION OVERVIEW

Less Advanced Students	More Advanced Students	ESOL Students	Special Needs Students	At-Risk Students
Pages 164, 167, 173, 175	Pages 168, 173, 178	Pages 164, 173	Pages 162, 164, 169	Pages 167, 173, 175

Introduce the Section

Play is one of a child's most important education tools. In this section, students learn how play strengthens and stimulates a child's physical, social, emotional, and intellectual skills.

Figure Focus

Remind students that both heredity and environment contribute to a child's physical, social, emotional, and intellectual development.

- **Heredity** is the transfer of genetically controlled traits and characteristics. Much of a person's physical appearance is inherited from his or her parents.

- **Environment** represents the things that happen in a person's life and the surroundings in which they happen. For example, children who get lots of exercise and opportunities to interact and play with their peers are likely to be more physically and socially developed than those who do not.

Vocabulary

Fine motor skills: Small-muscle movement skills, such as arranging tiny objects and using pens and paintbrushes.

Gross motor skills: Big-muscle movement skills, such as running, kicking, and throwing.

TEAMWORK ACTIVITY

Have students partner up with a classmate. They will ball up a piece of scrap paper and then, standing five to seven feet apart, toss the wad of paper back and forth several times. When they are done, ask them how they used their physical, social, emotional, and intellectual skills during the activity.

- Social skills: Interacting with a partner and figuring out how to manage the activity.

- Physical skills: Physically throwing and catching the wad of paper.

- Intellectual skills: Figuring out how fast and at what angle the wad of paper would be coming at them and how to hit their target.

- Emotional skills: Dealing with feelings such as happiness or frustration over the activity and interaction with another person.

Analyzing the Importance of Play

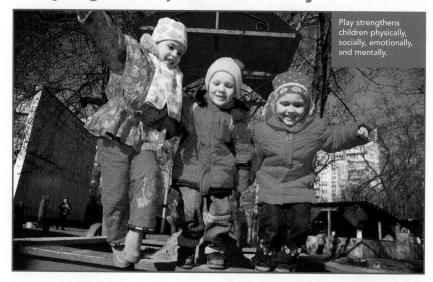

Play strengthens children physically, socially, emotionally, and mentally.

Have you ever tried to learn a new skill by hearing how to do it? Maybe you couldn't picture it or couldn't catch on from what you were told, but when you actually tried it yourself, you understood. Active play is like that for kids. It helps them develop physically, intellectually, emotionally, and socially, and creates personal meaning in a way that facts can't.

Children don't even notice that they are learning from play, but they are. For example, children throwing a ball back and forth are developing hand-eye coordination, and children playing with dolls are practicing child-care skills. Because play isn't usually goal-oriented, children feel free to try new things in a safe, nonthreatening environment, with no fear of failure. Nearly all play is helpful for a child's development—both the games and activities they make up for themselves and the activities that caregivers plan.

Caregivers can suggest play activities and lead structured exercises, but alone, children will also come up with their own activities appropriate to their age and development level.

Play Theory

Why is play so important? Different types of educators and theorists will tell you different things. Among other things, play:

- Provides exercise necessary for physical development
- Teaches children how to handle minor setbacks and frustrations
- Helps children learn social behaviors such as sharing and consideration
- Promotes ego development by providing opportunities for success
- Stimulates intellectual growth by way of critical thinking
- Develops **gross motor skills** (big-muscle movement skills like running, kicking, and throwing)
- Develops **fine motor skills** (small-muscle movement skills like arranging tiny objects and using pens and paintbrushes)

Customized Instruction: Visually-Impaired Students

Provide students with a ball that contains a bell or noise-maker in it when rolled. You can find such toys at pet stores or with pet supplies in grocery or other stores. Have students sit on the ground and roll the ball several times back and forth. Then have them determine how they used their physical, social, emotional, and intellectual skills in the activity. Refer to the *Teamwork Activity* in the left column.

Play Changes As Children Grow Up

Infants and toddlers play in activities that stimulate their senses and develop their motor skills. They like simple, repetitious activities, such as hearing the same song over and over again. Infants engage in **solitary play**, interacting with toys and objects. Although toddlers may play alongside other children (**parallel play**), they usually don't communicate with them; they focus on their own needs, and have no concept of rules.

Preschoolers play with other children (**cooperative play**). They borrow and lend toys, and talk about common activities. For example, preschool children might build a tower together with a set of blocks. They use their imaginations in role-playing games, like pretending to be an animal, a tree, or a fairy. (That's called **imaginative play**.) They also try to re-enact situations they see adults engaging in, such as cooking and talking on the telephone. All of these games are **active play**—that is, play in which the child is actively doing something. Children can also benefit from **passive play**, too, which is play that involves watching or listening.

Primary school children play games that include rules, such as hopscotch and board and card games. This play enhances physical coordination, refines social skills, teaches cooperation and competition, and enables them to demonstrate their skills. Children this age love riddles, number games, and secret codes, which all help with their growing understanding of words and numbers.

In late childhood and early adolescence, play becomes more structured and organized. Sports become a focus, as competition and winning become more important. They choose activities based on their interests, and they may join clubs or sports teams, as well as take on volunteer activities. These activities provide low-risk practice for adult activities and responsibilities, such as serving as president of a club in preparation for being a manager at work as an adult.

How Caregivers Can Help

You don't have to constantly entertain or suggest play activities for a child you are caretaking. Left to their own devices, children will invent age-appropriate games and activities all by themselves.

However, as a caregiver, you are responsible for providing a safe and enriching environment in which children can find their own games and activities. This includes making sure that appropriate toys, materials, and equipment are available for them. For example, you might encourage an 8-year-old child to create a storybook by stapling several sheets of paper together and providing crayons or markers.

It is also important to make sure age-inappropriate materials are *not* available. For example, you would not want a toddler to have a pair of scissors with sharp points on them. You can also help children grow from play by observing them and providing feedback. Telling a toddler "Nice job!" on a building-block tower reinforces his sense of accomplishment and makes the solitary activity into a social one. Observing play can also be useful in redirecting bad behavior, such as suggesting that a child who is getting frustrated and about to have a tantrum should focus on some other toy instead.

Toddlers like toys with big shapes and bright colors. Why do you think they prefer those?

Play or Pass?

If you are being paid for babysitting, are you required to give the child every moment of your attention? What if you were babysitting all day for a very attention-hungry child?

★ She might refuse to play by herself, insisting that you be part of every game and every activity.

★ You might find that you can make her happy by focusing all your attention on her, but this means you cannot do anything else you need to do, like fix dinner or tidy up the house.

★ If there are other children you are responsible for, you might have difficulty giving them adequate attention.

What benefits does getting a lot of attention give a child? What drawbacks might there be to her development, if any, by giving her a lot of attention?

Vocabulary

Active play: Play based on re-enacting real-life situations.

Cooperative play: Playing and interacting through play with other children.

Imaginative play: Play based on imaginative role-playing and fantasy.

Parallel play: Playing alongside other children.

Passive play: Play that involves watching or listening.

Solitary play: Interacting with toys and other objects, but not with other individuals.

Reinforce and Review

Remind students that **infancy** is the period of life from birth to approximately 1 year old. The **toddler** life stage begins at age 1 and lasts until 3 or 4.

Figure Focus

Infants and toddlers rely heavily on their senses to grow and develop. So, big shapes that are in bright and bold colors tend to catch their eye more so than smaller toys in pale or neutral tones.

Play or Pass?

A child who gets a lot of attention normally develops high self-esteem. The constant stimulation provided by the attention can contribute to more rapid intellectual development. However, children who get a lot of attention become accustomed to being the "center of attention," and often find it difficult to share the attention with other children. This can lead to self-conceit or feelings of frustration, disappointment, and even anger toward others.

Introduce the Section

This section discusses toys as learning tools and identifies the types of toys that are appropriate for children at different age levels.

Figure Focus

Discuss ways in which toys promote learning. Figuring out how toys work and how to make them do specific things challenges children to investigate and problem-solve. In fact, toys promote learning at all age levels, including adolescence and adulthood. Encourage students to look around their classroom and identify "toys." Is there a globe that spins on which you can locate different countries and continents? Do other students or your instructors have stress relievers, or rubbery figures that you can squeeze to ease tension? What about magnetic art, brain teasers, puzzles, and board games?

Age-Appropriate Toys

Have students discuss their favorite toys when they were 5 years old and when they were 10 years old. Were the toys similar or quite different? Do they think their favorite toys represent their interests or the things they value now? For example, if your favorite toy when you were 5 was a xylophone and your favorite toy at 10 was an electric guitar, do you now have a passion for music?

Selecting Age-Appropriate Toys

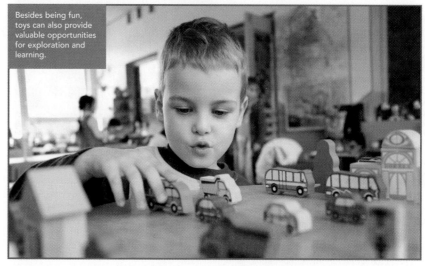

Besides being fun, toys can also provide valuable opportunities for exploration and learning.

There is no such thing as the perfect toy for every child; the ideal qualities a toy should have vary according to the child's age and interests.

What was your favorite toy when you were 5 years old? Think about the qualities of that toy, and how it was appropriate for you at that age. What was it made of? What did it do, if anything? How did it help in your development? Why did you find it so fascinating, and when did you outgrow it?

Now ask yourself the same questions about your favorite toy when you were 10 years old. What are the differences? How did your development between ages 5 and 10 make a difference in the type of toy you most preferred?

The ideal toy also varies from person to person. Compare your answers to those of your classmates; some of you probably chose sports equipment, while others chose art supplies, a board game, or a building set. What might you assume about a person based on his or her choice of toys at a particular age? For example, are people who are athletically gifted more likely to prefer balls and other sports equipment?

Age-Appropriate Toys

Toys—whether they are store-bought or found objects—help children learn and grow. Toys can stimulate the mind and body in various ways. For example, they can:

- Encourage physical activity and exercise
- Teach kids about the world around them
- Foster imagination, creativity, and artistic ability
- Improve hand-eye coordination and fine motor skills
- Teach social skills such as teamwork and cooperation
- Build emotional maturity in accepting wins and losses gracefully
- Encourage kids to imitate adult careers and skills

Customized Instruction: Less Advanced/Special Needs Students

Have students draw a picture of themselves playing with their favorite toy at age 5 and age 10. Make sure they identify the name or type of toy they are playing with. The toys can be the same or different.

Customized Instruction: ESOL Students

Have students draw a picture of themselves playing with their favorite toy at age 5 and age 10. Make sure they identify the name or type of toy they are playing with in their primary language. The toys can be the same or different.

Toys for Babies and Toddlers

For babies and very young children, the primary function of a toy is to stimulate one or more of their senses. For example, mirrors and pinwheels stimulate visually, and rattles make noise and provide something to grasp. At this stage it is important that toys be large enough that they are unbreakable, cannot be swallowed, and have non-toxic surfaces, because babies put everything in their mouths that they can. Toddlers enjoy stacking blocks, touching items of different shapes and sizes, and manipulating objects with their hands (for example, pressing buttons and spinning a wheel). Colors, shapes, and textures all provide important stimulation that will help the child move to the next level of development.

Toys for Young Children

As children grow out of the toddler stage, they begin to enjoy creating and arranging items to create meaning. For example, they may like to put together puzzles or build castles and boats with interlocking plastic blocks. They also may enjoy coloring and creating drawings and other types of art to express themselves. At this age, children are also likely to want to begin mimicking adult behaviors with toys such as tea sets, toy kitchens, and toy toolkits.

Toys for Elementary School Children

School-age children, starting around age 5 or 6, enjoy playing with other kids and are ready to participate in play that includes goals and rules. They enjoy simple board and card games, as well as physical games like jump-rope, hopscotch, and bouncing a ball back and forth.
Games provide an opportunity to practice following rules, competing in a friendly way, and understanding the roles of both luck and skill in competition. Many children also develop a strong interest in arts and crafts starting at this age, and like to paint pictures, string beads, build objects with construction sets, and so on. You can encourage creative play by complimenting a child on his or her artwork and asking simple questions about it.

Toys for Older Children and Adolescents

Older children appreciate games that have a strategic component to them. Board and card games that involve thinking and planning, such as Scrabble®, Monopoly, and Risk are fun at this age. Older children also enjoy team sports with well-defined rules, scoring, and penalty systems, such as soccer, baseball, and basketball, and sports that involve gradual skill-building over time, such as tennis. Video games are also popular at this age, especially those with stories or quests to complete. Balancing sitting activities like playing computer games with active sports and recreation is important, both to get adequate exercise and to build strength and coordination.

"What can I do to amuse a small child for an hour?"

Test **IT** Yourself!

Children don't need expensive toys to learn, or to have a good time. To test this, find several young children, such as younger brothers and sisters, a younger class in your school, or kids from an organization or religious group you are a part of. Then do the following:

1. Assemble a random group of household objects, such as plastic measuring cups and spoons, a small plastic mirror, a towel, a pillow, and a few knick-knacks. Place them on the floor, and have the children sit on the floor with them.
2. Invite the children to examine and use the items in any way they want to. Then casually observe them for 10–15 minutes to see what they do.

Afterwards, write up your findings. Make sure you include information about how old the children were, what they did with the items, how much they interacted with each other, whether they created any rules associated with their games, and so on.

Discuss

Share some of the following fun facts about toys with students. Or, present these as a trivia quiz.

1. The full name of the original Barbie™ doll is Barbara Millicent Roberts.
2. The average child in the United States will wear down 730 crayons by his tenth birthday (or a little more than 11 boxes of 64 crayons).
3. Mr. Potato Head® was introduced in 1953 as a set of parts. He did not come with a body, so children had to swipe one from the potato bin. Mr. Potato Head® was the first toy to be advertised on television with the slogan, "Meet Mr. Potato Head, the most wonderful friend a boy or girl could have!"
4. Twister® was the first game introduced in which players used their bodies as playing pieces. Milton Bradley originally wanted to call the game "Pretzel."
5. The most popular Hot Wheels® vehicle sold is the Corvette.
6. Every year, children spend almost 5 billion hours playing with Lego® bricks. Lego was founded in 1932 in Denmark as a manufacturer of stepladders, ironing boards, and wooden toys.
7. Silly Putty® was discovered by a scientist trying to find a rubber substitute during World War II, when rubber was in short supply.
8. The Teddy Bear was named for U.S. President Theodore Roosevelt who came upon a wounded bear cub during a Mississippi bear hunt. Political cartoonist Clifford Berryman illustrated the event in *The Washington Post*, and thus the Teddy Bear was born.
9. Play-Doh® was originally used as a wallpaper cleaner.
10. The Rubik's Cube® has approximately 43 quintillion configurations, but only one solution. At this writing, the world record for solving the puzzle is 7.08 seconds.

Figure Focus

Have students look around their classroom for appropriate playthings for a young child. Encourage them to use their imagination and to "think like a child." You might even have them crouch down on their knees so they can view the room from a child's perspective. Remind them of safety concerns for small children.

Test **IT** Yourself!

Ask for student volunteers who have easy access to a group of small children to conduct the test described in the text. Or, you might arrange for students to conduct the test at a nearby preschool or in a kindergarten class.

Introduce the Section

This section discusses how rules and discipline give children a sense of security, protection, and even accomplishment.

Figure Focus

Ask students to think of things they have learned from discipline, both at home and in school. For example, if you are grounded for the weekend because you came home after your curfew the weekend before, you should learn that you need to get home on time. Or, you must go to detention after school because you were tardy for class, so you should learn that you need to be in class on time every day.

Vocabulary

Abusive: Discipline or punishment that is too harsh.

Discipline: Process of establishing boundaries and rules that help children learn appropriate behaviors and make good choices.

Punishment: Consists of deliberately placing a child in a temporarily unpleasant or stressful situation as a consequence of bad behavior.

Reinforce and Review

Remind students that children are susceptible to the people and things they see and hear. Some of these influences might not be in their best interest and can contribute to a child's misbehavior. These include:

- Adults or older children arguing or fighting.
- Television shows or movies that involve violence and other risky behaviors.
- Music that uses foul or offensive language.
- Other children who regularly exhibit inappropriate behavior.
- Poor diet.
- Lack of sleep and quiet time.

Disciplining a Child

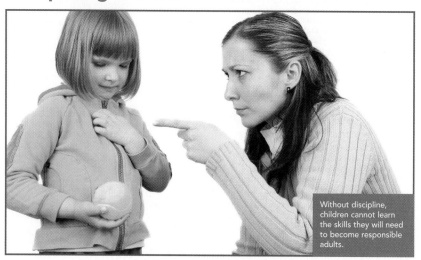

Without discipline, children cannot learn the skills they will need to become responsible adults.

Discipline is the process of establishing boundaries and rules that help children learn appropriate behaviors and make good choices. Discipline teaches self-control, respect for others, respect for self, and responsibility, all of which are important in emotional development.

Children thrive on discipline and boundaries, even though they may not appreciate it in the moment. Having clear rules to follow, and consistent consequences, gives a child a sense of security, protection, and accomplishment in following the rules. Without proper discipline, children are at risk for emotional and behavioral problems.

Discipline is different from **punishment**, although occasionally punishment may be required as a part of discipline. Punishment consists of deliberately placing the child in a temporarily unpleasant or stressful situation as a consequence of bad behavior, such as sitting in "time out" or having a privilege taken away. Punishment can be physical, mental, or emotional, but should never cross the line to being abusive, and should never be done in anger.

Types of Discipline

Some common types of discipline include:

- Imposing rules against doing certain things. For example, you might not allow a child to play in the street or to handle sharp knives.
- Requiring the child to perform a certain task, such as picking up toys.
- Requiring a child to take responsibility and apologize for a mistake.
- Providing clear consequences for behavior choices.

To enforce discipline, sometimes punishment is required, such as:

- Being denied a privilege, such as going to a party or talking to friends on the phone.
- Having a toy or other favorite object taken away, temporarily or permanently.
- Restriction of movement and play, such as sitting alone in a corner.
- Spanking (rarely).

Stay in School

Many students who drop out of school have experienced some form of child abuse. Following are signs that might indicate a child is being abused or neglected:

- Apathy and disinterest or refusal to participate in school activities.
- Aggressive or hostile behavior.
- Withdrawn or antisocial attitude.
- Loss of or change in appetite, such as compulsive or erratic eating, or being hungry much of the time.
- Inappropriate or unsuitable clothes for the weather.
- Continually dirty appearance and clothing, or clothing that is torn, stained, or bloodied.
- Showing up early or staying late at school.
- Suspicious bruises, burns, or fractures.

- Refusal to undress for physical education or sports.
- Exaggerated interest in sex or "acting out" sex with other children.
- Unusually seductive behavior.
- Fear of intimate contact (hugging or sports)

Make sure students know their rights. Nobody, including parents, can:

- Hit you hard enough to cause an injury.
- Leave you by yourself for a long time.
- Force you or tell you to have any kind of sex with anyone else.

If you suspect that one of your students is the victim of abuse, contact school or local authorities, or call the ChildHelp National Child Abuse Hotline at 1-800-4-A-CHILD.

Age-Appropriate Discipline

Have you ever tried to reason or plead with a baby not to cry? It's a hopeless cause. Babies can't be disciplined or reasoned with. They don't have the brain development needed to understand the relationship between their behavior and the consequences, so you can't control them that way. All you can do is meet their needs and keep them away from harm.

A toddler who understands basic language, on the other hand, can respond to very basic, clear instructions. For example, you can tell a toddler to pick up his toys, drink his milk, or stop chasing the cat. And if he does not obey, you can impose consequences.

When possible, phrase the consequences as a positive, rather than a negative. For example, suppose you wanted to say that the child can't go to the park until he picks up his toys. You might say "Pick up your toys, and then we will go to the park" instead of the more negative "If you don't pick up your toys, you can't go to the park." It is also best to make simple, direct orders, rather than giving the child an option. For example, instead of saying "Would you please brush your teeth?", say "Go brush your teeth now."

As children get older, they become better able to follow complex directions and understand delayed consequences. For example, if you are babysitting an 8-year-old and you want her to go to bed at a certain time, and she doesn't want to go, reminding her that her parents may take away privileges when they get home might be effective. What works for one child may not work for another. If a discipline technique is not effective, try another tactic.

Tips for Effective Discipline

Here are some tips for disciplining children effectively:

- *Be a good role model.* Demonstrate behaviors you want the children to mimic.
- *Reward, but don't bribe.* A reward is something the child receives *after* he has done something good. A bribe is given *beforehand*, to try to motivate the child to do what you want. Don't overuse rewards, though; that can backfire because the child may start to expect them.
- *Be consistent.* Make sure the child understands that the same action will get the same result every time. If the child asks for something repeatedly, and you keep saying no, don't suddenly change to yes just because you are tired of hearing it.
- *Redirect a child who is fixed on something.* For example, if a child is throwing a tantrum because he wants a piece of candy, you might encourage him to look at an interesting billboard or ask him where one of his toys is.
- *Stay calm when a child misbehaves.* Avoid yelling and screaming, since that can teach the child that it is all right to lose control when she doesn't get her way.
- *Avoid being too critical.* Make sure that the child understands that you still love him, even though you disapprove of his behavior.
- *Give positive reinforcement for behaviors that you want to see continue,* such as tidying up the bedroom without being asked or willingly sharing a toy with another child.
- *Avoid physical punishment.* Spanking is seldom more effective than other types of punishment, and may make the child more aggressive and angry. Only a child's parents should make the decision to spank.

Why is time-out an effective punishment for a child?

Myth You should teach children courtesy from a young age by phrasing instructions to them as polite questions rather than orders.

Truth Young children do not understand indirect speech. You have to tell them very clearly what you want, and not make it optional. For example, do not say "I would really like it if you would pick up your toys, okay?" Instead say, in a calm, firm voice, "Pick up your toys now."

Vocabulary

Neglect: Not enough discipline; failure to give the proper or required care and attention.

Teaching Tips

If you think your class would benefit from a discussion on child abuse and neglect, you might share some of the following facts:

- Child abuse is harm to a child by another person, whether adult or child, and it can be physical, emotional, verbal, or through neglect.
- Every day, about five children die in the United States because of abuse or neglect, most of them babies or toddlers.
- Neglect is the most common form of child abuse, accounting for more than 60 percent of all cases.
- Physical abuse accounts for between 15 and 20 percent of documented child abuse cases each year.
- Abused children are more likely to abuse alcohol and become addicted to drugs, and one-third will later abuse their own children.
- Close to 85 percent of prison inmates were abused as children.

Figure Focus

Time-out is effective because it removes the child from an environment where he or she was receiving attention and stimuli. In other words, time-out is boring, and if the time-out location is a step or stool, it can be uncomfortable. Most children will not want to go back to time-out if the punishment is carried out effectively.

Myth/Truth

Emphasize that being direct and clear in your instructions leaves little room for a child to negotiate, bargain, or make demands.

Customized Instruction: Less Advanced/At-Risk Students

Have students create a poster that lists ten things a person can do when he or she feels himself or herself getting angry with a child. Here are some suggestions you might offer.

- Take deep breaths and remind yourself that you are the caregiver.
- Splash cold water on your face or take a long drink of cold water.
- Close your eyes and imagine you are hearing what the child is about to hear, or receiving the same punishment.
- Put the child in time-out. Or put yourself in time-out to figure out if you are really angry with the child or about something else.
- Call a friend to talk about it.
- If someone else can watch the child, go out for a walk.
- Turn on some music and sing or hum along.
- Write down a list of positive, happy words or things and refer to it when you are frustrated.

Hang students' posters in the room or elsewhere in the school, if appropriate.

Introduce the Section

The dietary and nutritional needs of children at various age levels are discussed.

Figure Focus

Review the major food groups with students:

- Grains and breads
- Fruit and vegetables
- Milk and dairy foods
- Meat, fish, and poultry

Reinforce and Review

Nutrition is nourishment and represents the connection between food and health. Explain that in addition to the nutrients listed in the text, the body needs water, which is the most important nutrient. The body cannot survive for more than a few days without water. Many foods have high water content, such as watermelon and celery. Carbohydrates are the next most important nutrient, as they provide the fuel for the heart and brain to function.

Teaching Tips

You might want to refer students to the information in *Appendix C: MyPyramid Food Group Recommendations* beginning on page 531 of the student text. Dietary needs for people of all ages are covered.

Feeding Children Nutritious Food

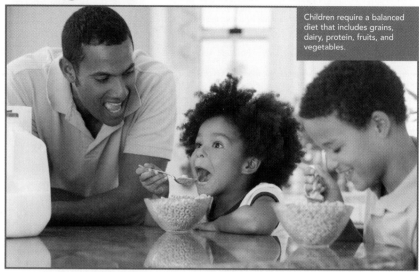

Children require a balanced diet that includes grains, dairy, protein, fruits, and vegetables.

What was your favorite food when you were a young child? Whatever it was, your parents probably didn't let you eat all of it you wanted, did they? As responsible adults, they knew that you needed a balanced diet, so they encouraged you to eat a variety of foods.

What a child wants to eat is not necessarily what is good for him or her. As a caregiver, you are responsible for planning and serving nutritious, balanced meals that give children the vitamins, minerals, and other nutrients that will give them energy, help their bodies grow strong, and prevent diet-related diseases.

A nutritious diet—as opposed to one full of junk food and sugar—can also help children maintain a healthy weight, neither too thin nor too fat. You should never force a child to eat. They will eat when they are hungry. Many obese children were forced as babies or toddlers, and now have a habit of overeating.

Energy-Producing Nutrients

A healthy diet consists of these nutrient types:

- *Carbohydrates:* The main fuel the body needs for energy. Found in bread, pasta, rice, fruit, vegetables, and sugars.
- *Protein:* Foods that provide amino acids that help the body build and maintain muscle. Found in most animal products (beef, pork, chicken, fish, eggs, and dairy), as well as in soy products and beans.
- *Fat:* Oils that make food taste better, deliver fatty acids the body needs, and carry fat-soluble vitamins (that is, vitamins that dissolve only in fat, such as A and D). Found in dairy products, nuts, meats, and many cooked foods.
- *Vitamins and minerals:* Compounds that help the body maintain itself by working with enzymes and hormones. Minerals also promote strong bones and teeth. Present in small amounts in the foods you eat, and also in vitamin/mineral supplement pills.

Each of these is covered in more detail in Chapter 20.

Customized Instruction: More Advanced Students

Have students work in pairs to research a diet-related disease or illness. These include cancer, diabetes, high blood pressure, high cholesterol, obesity, anorexia nervosa, osteoporosis, and gum disease. They should determine how diet can cause the disease, the symptoms of the disease, and how you can change your diet to rid yourself of the disease or minimize its effects. Have students create a presentation of their findings to give to the class.

Nutrients for Growing Children

Nutrient requirements vary depending on the age of the child. Here are some general guidelines for what infants, toddlers, and elementary-school children should eat each day:

Age 0 to 12 months:
- 8 to 16 ounces of baby formula or breast milk

Age 12 to 24 months:
- 16 ounces of whole or 2% milk, or baby formula or breast milk
- 1½ ounces of meat/protein
- 1 cup fruit
- ¾ cup vegetables
- 2 ounces of grains
- Additional calories from carbohydrates, to make 900 calories

Age 2 to 3 years:
- 16 ounces of fat-free milk
- 2 ounces of meat/protein
- 1 cup fruit
- 1 cup vegetables
- At least 3 ounces of grains
- Additional calories from carbohydrates, to make 1,000 calories

Age 4 to 8 years:
- 16 ounces of fat-free milk
- 3 to 4 ounces of meat/protein (3 for girls, 4 for boys)
- 1½ cups fruit
- 1 to 1½ cups vegetables (1 for girls, 1½ for boys)
- 4 to 5 ounces of grains (4 for girls, 5 for boys)
- Additional calories from carbohydrates, to make 1,200 for girls or 1,400 for boys

Age 9 to 13 years:
- 24 ounces of fat-free milk
- 5 ounces of meat/protein
- 1½ cups fruit
- 2 to 2½ cups vegetables (2 for girls, 2½ for boys)
- 5 to 6 ounces of grains (5 for girls, 6 for boys)
- Additional calories from carbohydrates, to make 1,600 for girls or 1,800 for boys

Babies drink milk or formula from bottles, and very young infants get all their nutritional needs met from breast milk or formula. To prepare a bottle, carefully pour the liquid into a clean bottle and attach a nipple to the top. Heat the bottle just enough that the liquid is room temperature to slightly warm, either in the microwave or by placing it (standing up) in a pan of water on the stove. One way to test the temperature of the liquid is to drip a few drops on your wrist; if it is uncomfortably hot there, it is too hot for the baby to drink.

For toddlers and young children, solid food should be cut up into bite-sized pieces, so they do not have to use a knife to cut it. Foods that they can eat with their fingers are great, like carrot sticks, chicken nuggets, and apple slices. So is soft food eaten with a spoon, like oatmeal.

TECH CONNECT

Suppose you wanted to track a family's nutrition using a computer, including number of servings per day of protein, milk, fruit, vegetable, and grain for each person. You can do this on a computer, either by using a Web-based application such as www.fitday.com, or by creating your own spreadsheet in a program such as Excel.

Using a spreadsheet program, design a simple layout that could be used to track your family's food intake.

Easy Snacks

What if you were babysitting for three children, ages 2, 4, and 9, and you wanted to feed them a healthy snack that was easy to fix and easy to eat?

★ What would a good grain-based snack be, and how much of it would you give to each child?

★ What kinds of dairy-based snacks would create a minimal amount of mess to clean up?

★ If you were going to give fruit as a snack, what form would be the easiest for all the children to eat? Would you serve raw whole fruit? Slices? Canned fruit?

★ How could you make a snack of raw vegetables appealing and fun?

Customized Instruction: Special Needs Students

Ask students with food allergies to discuss the foods they cannot eat and what happens if they do eat them.

Reinforce and Review

As you discuss the nutrient guidelines in the text, review food measuring units. You might consider having measuring cups or spoons and a scale on hand, along with some food items, such as cereal, pieces of fruit, and a liquid such as water or milk, to demonstrate volume, mass, and weight. Some useful conversions of measuring units are:

- 1 cup = 250 ml
- 1 cup = 8 ounces
- 1 tablespoon = 15 ml
- 4 tablespoons = ¼ cup
- 1 pound = about 450 grams
- 1 ounce = 28 grams
- 1 ounce = 2 tablespoons
- 5 ounces = approximately ⅓ pound

 TECH CONNECT

Students are to design a spreadsheet that could be used to track their family's food intake. Their spreadsheets should have columns for the date, meal (breakfast, lunch, dinner, snack), food (for itemized list of each thing they eat), calories (for each item), carbohydrates (usually measured in grams), and cells for totaling calories and carbohydrates. Some students might also want to track sugar, protein, fat, and sodium intake.

Easy Snacks

- A good grain-based snack would be baked tortilla chips and salsa, goldfish crackers or pretzels, or mini bran muffins.

- Cheese strings and yogurt or pudding cups create a minimal amount of clean up.

- Softer sliced fruit and canned fruit are suitable for young children and those missing teeth. Whole fruit such as apples, pears, peaches, plums, and grapes are ideal for older children.

- Make vegetables bite size and serve with a low-fat dip or dressing.

Introduce the Section

This section discusses the responsibility adults have for keeping children safe at home, at play, and when they are out in public.

Figure Focus

Discuss safety guidelines that are in place at home and in school. Ask students to comment on rules at home regarding safety. For example, are the doors to be locked at all times? Is there a smoke detector on every floor of the house? Does their family have a fire escape plan? Do you know what to do when someone knocks at the door? Are you allowed to take a shower or bath if you are home alone? Do you know how to call for help if you need it?

APPLY IT

Students will create a list of safety guidelines for home. The guidelines should cover four areas: Building Safety, Personal Safety, Outside Safety, and Travel Safety. Under each area, they should list safety-related guidelines. For example, under Building Safety, they might list installation of smoke detectors; under Personal Safety, they might list wearing a bicycle helmet; under Outside Safety, they might list keeping the grill away from the house and trees; for Travel Safety, they might list wearing a seatbelt. Encourage them to be creative in how they present the guidelines. Also, make sure the guidelines are written or illustrated so that family members of all ages can understand them.

Keeping Children Safe

It is the responsibility of adults to keep children safe, both at home and away from home.

One of the most important parts of childcare is keeping the children safe from harm. Potential dangers are everywhere, and most children don't have the attention span or critical thinking skills to identify and avoid them. That means you, as the caretaker, are responsible!

Keeping children physically safe is one of a caregiver's most important responsibilities. Physical safety can include protection from injuries, making sure you know where the children are at all times, being careful when allowing children to interact with dogs and other pets, imposing rules about where and what to play, and insisting that the children use safety equipment such as biking helmets and car seats.

Emotional safety is important too. Children will experience a certain amount of disappointment and frustration in everyday life, and that's normal. But as a caregiver, it is your responsibility to make sure that they aren't exposed to cruelty, bullying, harsh criticism, or name-calling that could harm their self-esteem.

What Every Child Should Know

From a very early age, children should be coached in safety basics, so they will know what to do in case of a problem. A child as young as age 5 should:

- Know that he should keep away from swimming pools except when adults are actively supervising
- Be able to give her name, address, and phone number to a police officer
- Know to run away from strangers who try to take them or get the child to go with them
- Be able to dial 911 on a telephone, and understand when to do it
- Know not to play with fire, and understand the difference between fire that is okay (like a candle or a gas stove) and fire that is a danger
- Know that she should roll on the floor—and not run—if her clothing is on fire
- Know where to go in the house or in school when there is an earthquake or tornado (or other weather emergency common to his region)

Safety in Public

Keeping a child safe in a public place can be a challenge because you don't have control of the environment. It's hard to anticipate what threats there may be, so you have to keep your eyes and ears open. For example, make sure you know where the child is at all times. Small children should remain within your sight; older children can, if the situation permits, be allowed to leave your sight for short periods of time. Public places may also pose a risk of injuries, because children like to play with things that are not necessarily designed to be played with. For example, a child might think it is fun to swing on a flimsy railing that could give way, or to pick up and throw stones at people or animals.

Occasional minor injuries are a normal part of childhood.

Safety at Home

Your home is supposed to be your safety zone, right? In most cases, home *is* safe, if you observe normal precautions. Unfortunately, children sometimes don't have a sense of those normal precautions, so you must watch them carefully.

In the home, the main safety concerns are physical: trip-and-fall hazards, electrical outlets, hot cooking surfaces, poisons, and so on. Warn children to stay out of the way as you are using the stove, and do not let them play near kitchen knives or other sharp objects. In addition, babies and toddlers like to put things in their mouths, so you need to keep small objects that would fit in their mouths away from their reach. You should also keep poisonous chemicals out of kids' reach; in a household that includes children under age 5 or 6, hazardous materials should never be stored under sinks or in lower cabinets unless there is a way to lock the cabinets.

Safety at home can also involve being careful of intruders. This includes making sure that children understand the importance of not answering the door when no adults are around, not letting strangers in, and keeping doors and windows secured.

Safety at Play

Kids sometimes get minor cuts and scrapes while playing, and it's no big deal. You probably got several yourself as you were growing up! A little soap and water, some antiseptic, and an adhesive bandage, and most kids are fixed up and back in the game.

The more important safety hazards encountered in play are those where the child can suffer more serious injuries. For example, a child who falls off a bicycle without a helmet might suffer a concussion (a type of head injury). Protective equipment such as knee and elbow pads, helmets, and sturdy shoes can help keep children safe while they are doing activities like biking, roller skating, and skateboarding.

Emotional Safety

Safety applies to children's minds too, not just their bodies.

✔ *Give constructive, gentle corrections, not harsh criticism.*

✔ *Encourage toy sharing and cooperation.*

✔ *Do not allow one child to overpower or intimidate another.*

✔ *Monitor what kids watch on television, and use parental controls as needed.*

✔ *Control Internet access with safe surfing utilities or by personally monitoring computer use.*

Emotional Safety

Also discuss that children can experience stress. Some of the signs of stress are:

■ Crying more than usual or having more temper tantrums.

■ Regressive behaviors, such as thumb sucking, bedwetting, rocking, and biting.

■ High sensitivity or overreaction to sudden or loud noises.

■ Physical ailments, such as stomach aches and headaches.

■ Sleep or appetite problems.

■ Stuttering.

■ Grinding their teeth, picking their noses a lot, or biting their nails.

■ Behavioral changes, such as lying, bullying, being disruptive, expressing anger, and defying authority.

Discuss

Discuss street safety with students. If they go out with a child or on their own, they should consider the following:

■ Walk or travel in a group.

■ Make sure you know exactly where you are going. Walk with purpose to give the impression that you are in charge.

■ Stay on main streets and thoroughfares. Avoid walking by abandoned or empty buildings, and do not take shortcuts.

■ If you see someone doing something wrong or you feel threatened, go the other way and find a public place, such as a store or business, where you can get help.

■ Follow the same routes to go to school, the store, or the park, and make sure your parents and the parents of other children with you are familiar with the routes.

■ Avoid distractions, such as headphones, cell phones, and handheld gaming devices. You need to focus on your immediate surroundings and who and what is a part of it.

■ And, of course, never talk to strangers.

Figure Focus: Enrichment Activity

Have students prepare a list of the basic items in a first-aid kit. These include:

■ Antiseptic ointment or spray

■ Gauze pads

■ Scissors

■ Adhesive tape

■ Elastic bandage

■ Cold pack

■ Adhesive bandages

■ Latex gloves

■ Tweezers

■ Sting and bite treatment

■ Ipecac for inducing vomiting if a poisonous substance is ingested

■ Cotton swabs or balls

■ Medication for allergic reactions

You might also encourage students to put together a first-aid kit for their home if they don't already have one.

Introduce the Section

This section covers the steps involved in starting and running a successful babysitting business.

Vocabulary

Babysitting: Taking care of other people's children for pay.

Entrepreneurship: Self-started business.

Figure Focus

Ask for a show of hands of students who have had babysitting jobs. Ask students to elaborate on how often they babysit, how many kids at a time they babysit, what their duties are as a babysitter, and how much they get paid.

TEAMWORK ACTIVITY

Have students work in teams to develop a list of fictional characters from books or TV who they think would make good babysitters. They should review the list of qualities listed in the text and be able to explain which qualities the characters they list possess.

Starting Your Own Babysitting Business

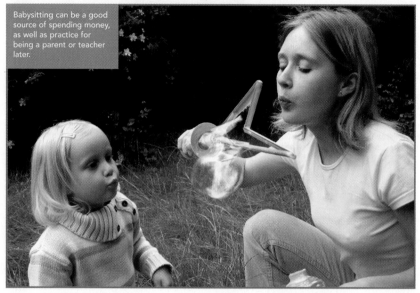

Babysitting can be a good source of spending money, as well as practice for being a parent or teacher later.

Babysitting—that is, taking care of other people's children for pay—is one of the main ways for young teens to make money and get childcare and **entrepreneurship** (self-employment) experience.

Because you are babysitting for private families, rather than an agency, you don't have to be any certain age (in most places) to take on babysitting jobs. Many people consider 12 as the minimum age to be a babysitter, but that varies depending on the area of the country, the maturity and responsibility level of the babysitter, the ages of the children being watched, and the duration of the job. For example, a 12-year-old might do a great job watching a toddler while her mother was cleaning in another part of the house, but might not be ready to be alone in the house taking care of a newborn infant.

Qualities of a Good Babysitter

Age is only one measurement of how ready someone is to babysit. It is more important that the babysitter have certain qualities, including:

- Decision-making skills
- Responsibility
- Punctuality (that is, the ability to be on time)
- Trustworthiness
- Patience
- Love of children
- Awareness of safety
- Clear thinking, especially in an emergency

If that sounds like you, then maybe you would make a good babysitter.

What Does a Babysitter Do?

At the very basic level, a babysitter is in charge of making sure nothing bad happens to the children that he or she is watching, either physically or emotionally. As a babysitter, it is your job to:

■ Prevent the children from getting hurt by steering them clear of hazards such as stove burners, electrical outlets, and high places

■ Prevent them from damaging anything, keeping them away from fragile and expensive items in the home

■ Keep the children on their usual schedule as much as possible (bedtime, mealtime, and so on)

■ Make sure the children obey any rules that the parents have set, such as watching only certain television channels, eating only certain foods, etc.

■ Supervise any activities that the children need help with, such as teeth brushing, changing into pajamas, operating the microwave, or pouring drinks

Depending on the parents' requests, the ages of the children, and your willingness to "go the extra mile," you might also take responsibility for:

■ Suggesting and playing games with them, or even bringing games with you

■ Helping them with their homework

■ Providing hands-on educational activities, such as looking at plants and flowers together, doing Web searches, or letting them help with cooking

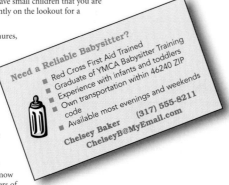

What kind of care would you expect to give to an infant that you were caring for?

How to Find Babysitting Jobs

Word of mouth is a very common way of getting babysitting jobs. Ask your parents and family friends to tell their friends who have small children that you are available for babysitting. Most parents are constantly on the lookout for a responsible babysitter.

You can be your own ad agency by creating brochures, flyers, or business cards advertising your services. Make sure you include your full name, phone number, and e-mail address so people will be able to find you. Include the services you offer, any special training or certification you have (such as graduation from a YWCA babysitting course or first aid training), and the days and hours you are available to work. For safety's sake, do not put your age on your advertising materials if they are going to be available to the public; you can discuss your age after someone has expressed an interest in your services. Also for safety, you may want to confine your advertising to people you know and trust, such as your parents' friends or members of your religious community.

Need a Reliable Babysitter?

■ Red Cross First Aid Trained
■ Graduate of YMCA Babysitter Training
■ Experience with infants and toddlers
■ Own transportation within 46240 ZIP code
■ Available most evenings and weekends

Chelsey Baker   (317) 555-8211
ChelseyB@MyEmail.com

Customized Instruction: Less Advanced/At-Risk Students

Have students design a flyer or advertisement about their babysitting services. Refer them to the sample in the text. Encourage them to be creative.

Customized Instruction: ESOL Students

Have students design a flyer or advertisement in their primary language about their babysitting services. Refer them to the sample in the text. Encourage them to be creative.

Customized Instruction: More Advanced Students

Have students develop a list of babysitting classes and CPR and first-aid training programs offered in your area. The list should include the name of the class, where it is offered, who can enroll, cost (if any), and date and times. Post the list in your classroom and elsewhere in the school, if appropriate.

Discuss

Discuss some babysitting dos and don'ts with students.

DO:

■ Know the phone number or numbers where parents can be reached, and all emergency numbers, including the local police and fire department.

■ Follow the parents' instructions on snacks, TV time, bedtime, and other activities.

■ Ask parents about any food allergies, conditions, or behavioral quirks the kids might have.

■ Play age-appropriate games or activities.

■ Know where the first-aid kit is kept.

■ Know the family's fire escape plan.

■ If there is a pool, make sure the gate is secured from young children.

■ Check doors and windows to make sure they are locked.

■ Give full attention to the children you are supervising.

■ Clean up and put things back where you found them before the parents return home.

■ Make sure small children are in a safe place (such as a playpen or crib) if you are preparing a meal in the kitchen.

DO NOT:

■ Talk or text on the phone, even if the parents say it's all right. Try to use the phone only for emergencies.

■ Invite friends over.

■ Leave children alone, and check on them often once they've gone to bed.

■ Open the door unless you are familiar with who's knocking.

■ Identify yourself to phone callers as the babysitter. Simply ask to take a message for the person being called.

■ Watch TV, do homework, or cram for a test while kids are still awake.

■ Light candles or the fireplace.

Figure Focus

Remind students that infancy starts at birth and ends at about age 1. Infants have two basic desires: to have their physical needs met and to explore their world. As a caregiver, you must be able to identify when they are hungry, thirsty, tired, or in pain or discomfort.

Explain to students that being prepared is of utmost importance when interviewing for any job. You will be at a disadvantage if you do not know the standard rate of pay for the job, the typical responsibilities, and the hours you are expected to work. Without this information, you have no grounds to negotiate if you are dissatisfied with what the customer offers. Refer students to online babysitter pay calculators, such as www.care.com/child-care-p1140-babysitter-pay-calculator.html.

Discuss

Share some of these negotiating tips with students:

- Find out the current minimum wage for hourly workers in your state. This might provide a good starting point. At the time of this writing, the federal minimum wage was $7.25 an hour.

- Determine the pay you want and simply ask for it. If you *don't* ask, you probably won't get it.

- Toot your own horn. In other words, don't be afraid to elaborate on your experience and qualifications for the job.

- Have the names and numbers of references readily available.

- Set an hourly rate that you will not go below. You don't want to go into a job begrudgingly, or feel like you're getting paid less than what you're worth. That can lead to resentment and hard feelings between you and the customer.

Reinforce and Review

Review with students the six-step process for communicating effectively:

1. **Be clear.** Your customer is more likely to get your message if you deliver it in a way he or she can understand.

2. **Be personal.** Use the other person's name. Use an "I" statement to indicate you are taking responsibility for your thoughts and feelings.

3. **Be positive.** Say what you want, not what you don't want.

4. **Get to the point.** Follow the "I" statement with an explanation of how or why you feel or think a certain way.

5. **Actively listen to the response.** Pay attention and make sure you hear the response.

6. **Think before you respond.** Make sure you understand the message. Ask the customer to repeat it if necessary, and ask questions for clarification.

It's important to come to an agreement about the hours and pay of a job before you commit to it. What might happen if you went into a babysitting job without knowing those things?

Negotiating the Job

Once you have someone interested in your babysitting services, then what? The next step is to negotiate—to agree on—the details. Negotiating your fee, the hours, and the services you provide before you arrive for the job can prevent misunderstandings and hard feelings if you and your customer have different expectations.

You should let your customer know how much you charge before you arrive. The amount to charge varies depending on the area of the country, the hours, and the ages and number of the children you are watching. In general, prices are higher on the East and West Coasts, and lower in the center of the country. The younger the children and the more children you are watching, the higher the price should be. Ask other people who babysit in your town how much they charge. Think also about whether you are going to charge extra after a certain number of hours, after a certain time of day, or if the parents are late getting back compared to what time they told you. Make sure that the customer is aware that you expect to be paid—in cash, or with a personal check if you know the client well—at the end of the evening.

Make sure that you understand the scope of the job as well—that is, the number of hours you are committing to, the start and end times, and the duties that will be required of you. Some customers merely want you to keep their children safe, and you can amuse yourself with television, Internet, or talking on the phone as you do that. Other parents expect you to interact with the children the whole time, or even do light housekeeping such as cleaning up the kitchen.

When You Arrive

When you arrive at your babysitting job, there's a lot to do before the parents leave—but you may need to do it fairly quickly, because they may be in a hurry. It may be helpful to arrive early, or meet with the parents beforehand. You'll need to:

- Introduce yourself to the children. Learn their names and ages.
- Find out about food. Do you need to prepare a meal for the children? Is there food that you can eat yourself? Do any of the children have food allergies? Is there any food that is off-limits to the kids?
- Get written instructions for any medicines you need to give the children.
- Find out about bedtime. What time do the children need to go to bed? Do they need to take baths first? What other hygiene routines should they follow? Where are their pajamas kept? Which bed belongs to which child?
- Learn where the emergency contact information is located. Who should you call if there is a medical emergency? Or a problem with the home, such as a water leak or air conditioner outage?
- Ask about restrictions, such as television limits, certain areas of the house that are off-limits, and so on.

MONEY MADNE$$

If you plan on charging different rates for different times and durations, plan on doing a bit of math to calculate the final amount you are owed.

For example, suppose you charge $8.00 an hour for the first 2 hours, and $5.00 an hour after that, up until midnight. After midnight, the hourly rate jumps to $10.00 an hour. You arrive at the customer's home at 5 p.m., and stay until 1:30 a.m. How much will your pay be?

MONEY MADNE$$

Your pay would be $56. You get $8 an hour for the first two hours between 5 and 7 p.m. ($8 + $8 = $16). You get $5 an hour for the hours between 7 p.m. and midnight ($5 × 5 = $25). You get $10 an hour for the hours between midnight and 1:30 a.m. ($10 + $5 = $15). So the total is: $16 + $25 + $15 = $56.

■ Greet any family pets, especially dogs, while the adults are still there, so that if there's a problem with an aggressive animal, the adults can help resolve it. Find out the pets' names and whether you need to provide any food or water, let the pets in or out, or keep the pet confined to certain areas.

■ Confirm the time that the adults are expected home, and ask for a cell phone number to call if they are late. It may also be a good idea to confirm the pay that you charge, and how that pay will change if they are late getting home.

In Case of a Problem

Most babysitting jobs are routine, and any problems are minor. In a real emergency, though, would you know what to do? It's important to prepare for the worst, so if it should come, you won't panic.

1. First, is it an emergency requiring you to call 911? That is, do you urgently need an ambulance, firefighters, or the police? If so, that's your first step.

2. Next, stabilize the situation if you can. If someone is hurt, use your first-aid skills to apply a temporary fix—bandage, splint, antiseptic, etc. If an appliance is smoking, turn it off and unplug it. Do whatever makes sense.

3. Next, call the parents, or whatever family contact number you have been given, and calmly inform them about the situation.

4. Finally, reassure the children, stay with them, and wait for help to arrive.

Wrapping Up

When the parents arrive at home, your job is still not quite over. There are a few administrative matters to tend to before you can leave.

First, give the parents a brief status report. What did the kids do? What did they eat? When did they go to bed? Were there any discipline problems? And if so, how were they handled? Any emergencies or injuries? Did anything get broken? Were there any visitors? Any phone calls, or messages?

In most cases, you will want to collect your pay before leaving. Some customers may ask if they can pay you later, and if it is someone you trust, that's okay, but some babysitters have a hard time getting the money out of the customer if they wait until later for it.

Finally, end your stay by thanking them for using your services, and by telling them something you enjoyed about each of the children. This leaves a positive impression about both you and your relationship to the children, and encourages them to call you again.

Collecting Your Pay

Some people who babysit have a hard time collecting their pay, either because they are too timid to ask for it or because the customer is evasive or difficult to approach. If the customer doesn't offer to pay you as you are leaving, what could you do?

👎 Don't say anything about the money, because you don't want to seem rude or pushy.

👎 If they say they can't pay you now, get angry and demand payment, refusing to leave until they pay you.

👎 Say nothing, but then tell your parents that they didn't pay, so your parents can handle it.

👍 Politely inform them of the amount due, and ask "Will you be paying by cash or check?" to let them know that payment is expected now.

👍 If they say they can't pay you now, get a clear commitment in writing about how much is owed and when it will be paid.

NUMBERS GAME

Suppose you have been asked to babysit for a family with three children, ages 2, 5, and 6, for thirty hours each week over the summer. How much should you charge? You want to be competitive, but also not shortchange yourself.

First, find out the average hourly rate in your area for one child. Then think about how much discount you want to give, in exchange for the commitment of 30 hours of steady work a week for the whole summer. Having a steady job like that is a real benefit.

Next, think about whether you want to multiply that amount by 3, because there are three children, or give a discount because they are all in the same family and it will not really be three times the work to care for them.

Create an estimate for the job based on these figures, including a detailed breakdown of how you arrived at your final weekly charge.

Reinforce and Review

Review the steps to take in case of a problem or emergency as described in the text. Stress the importance of properly managing the situation instead of worrying about how the parents will react when they hear about it. Explain that accidents happen and how the caregiver handles them is most important.

Collecting Your Pay

One other tip you might pass on to students is to turn down requests from a customer who does not pay promptly.

NUMBERS GAME

In determining the estimate, students should also consider other things. Will the customer provide meals and snacks for the babysitter, as well as money for activities and recreation, such as going to the pool or the movies? What about transportation costs, if any?

Customized Instruction: Less Advanced/At-Risk Students

Many single people and working couples often need someone to check on their pets during the day. Ask students to consider how much they would charge a customer to walk her dog 20 minutes and give it food and fresh water once a day. If you did this five days a week for 50 weeks of the year, how much money would you make?

Introduce the Section

Students learn that child care can be challenging, even for the most experienced providers. Information is provided on sources you can go to for help.

Figure Focus

Ask students to share other resources that could provide help on proper child care. What about your pediatrician? Encourage students to recall things they've seen and heard while in the doctor's office.

APPLY IT

Have students write down the list of questions from the text and use them to interview their parents or other caregivers. Have them share the answers with the class.

Getting Help from Outside Sources

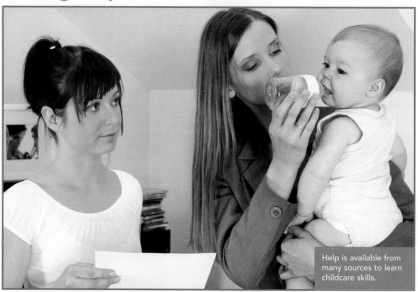

Help is available from many sources to learn childcare skills.

If you are new to child care, it might seem pretty overwhelming at first. There's a lot to know about child development, nutrition, safety, and appropriate toys, as well as the nuts and bolts of babysitting jobs. Fortunately, you don't have to go it alone! Many resources are available to help you learn more about child care, including:

- Books from your local library or bookstore
- Parenting and childcare magazines
- Web sites
- Classes (classroom or online)
- Family and friends
- Observing other childcare providers

Ask Your Parents

One free resource is very close at hand: your own parents or family members who raised you. They know all about how to take care of babies and toddlers—they took care of you, after all—and have first-hand experience in everything from diapers to discipline. Ask them some of these questions, and see what response you get!

- What's one thing you wish someone had told you about childcare when you started?
- What is the biggest mess one of your kids ever made?
- What do you like the most about being around kids?
- What is one thing that you think you could have done better as a caregiver?
- What is one thing that you think you did (and are doing) pretty well?

Training Courses

Many organizations offer babysitting courses you can take, inexpensively or for free, that will help you become a better childcare provider. Taking such a course can also help you get more babysitting business, because it demonstrates that you are serious about wanting to do a good job. A babysitting course covers many of the same topics as this chapter, including safety, play, nutrition, and discipline, but in more detail.

To find a babysitting course in your area, check out the local 4H, American Red Cross, Boys and Girls Clubs, community centers, hospitals, libraries, and other organizations. Some schools may also offer summer or spring break noncredit classes in babysitting. An in-person class is best, if you can find one, because it offers hands-on experience, group discussion, and multiple modes of learning.

If you can't find a local class to attend, look for an online babysitting course. Many are available. They vary quite a bit in both the price and the level of instruction. To find them, do a Web search for the words *babysitting course*.

If you don't know much about first-aid, consider taking a first-aid course, such as one offered by the Red Cross. You will learn, for example, how to clean and sterilize minor wounds, stop bleeding, and figure out when medical help is needed. Visit www.redcross.org to find out about first-aid training in your area.

Free Online Childcare Resources

The Web contains a wealth of free childcare advice, everything from diagrams of how to put on a diaper to healthy snacks for preschool children. If you don't mind taking the initiative to teach yourself, you can gather at least as good an education through free resources online as you can get in most babysitting courses.

Do Web searches on the specific topics you want to know about, or on general topics such as babysitting and childcare. Here are a few sites to get you started:

■ A Guide to the Business of Babysitting
http://urbanext.illinois.edu/babysitting
■ Children's Safety Zone: Guide for Babysitters
http://www.childrensafetyzone.com/safety/babysitters.tips.html
■ How to Change a Diaper
http://www.wikihow.com/Change-a-Diaper
■ Kids Games
http://www.gameskidsplay.net

How can training in first aid or CPR increase your value as a childcare provider?

21st Century Skills

What Happens Next?

Sarah is babysitting a four-year-old named Tyler for an evening while his parents are at a movie. Tyler refuses to do anything Sarah says. He won't pick up his toys, he won't put on his pajamas, and he won't go to bed. Sarah has talked to him sternly, and warned him that his parents will take away privileges when they get home if he does not obey the rules, but Tyler doesn't seem to care. Sarah is frustrated and at the end of her rope with him.

Suppose you are Sarah's friend that she has called for advice. What would you tell her? Using your 21st Century Skills—such as decision making, goal setting, and problem solving—brainstorm as a class some ideas you could give Sarah for coping with the situation. Then have teams of people act out some of the solutions proposed, with one person playing Saran and one playing Tyler.

CPR and first-aid training not only teaches you about basic care and cardiopulmonary resuscitation, it also helps prepare you to "think on your feet." If someone stops breathing or another emergency arises, you have the critical thinking skills to better manage the situation. In addition, by undergoing this type of training, you prove that you are motivated and eager to learn.

21st Century Skills

What Happens Next?

Tyler is acting obstinate and is not responding to Sarah's requests. She could put him in time-out except based on his behavior and attitude, it's unlikely this will be effective. Sarah might consider a variation on time-out by allowing Tyler to do something quietly by himself, such as look through a picture book. She should not allow him to watch TV, play video games, listen to music, or drag out more toys. She also should avoid interacting with him, and just sit in the same room to keep an eye on him. After a while, he may tire or get bored and do what he's been asked on his own. Or, Sarah might prod him again. If he still refuses, then Sarah should let him continue playing quietly and discuss her problems with Tyler's parents when they arrive home. Students' ideas may vary, but they should not advise letting Tyler do what he wants, calling the parents, or trying to forcefully make Tyler do as he is asked.

Introduce the Section

This section examines careers and job opportunities available in childcare.

Vocabulary

Daycare: Taking care of children on a regular basis while the parents are at work.

Figure Focus

Ask students to comment on family members or friends who have jobs related to childcare. What is their job title? Where do they work? Then, ask them to name people (other than their parents or babysitters) who provided childcare for them when they were younger.

STUDENT ACTIVITY

Assign each of the 11 jobs listed in the text to a team of students. Each team should research the job assigned to them and then prepare a "Help Wanted" ad for the job. The ad should include a description of the job, education requirements, experience desired, and salary.

Preparing for a Career in Childcare

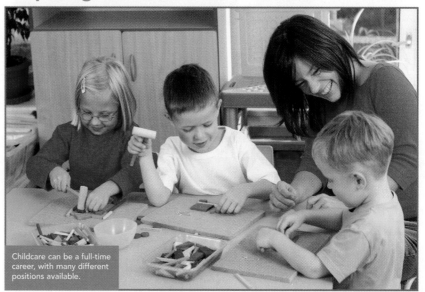

Childcare can be a full-time career, with many different positions available.

Casual babysitting is a good occasional source of extra income when you are a teenager, but childcare can also be a full-time career to consider. Many different jobs in childcare are available, with varying degrees of education and experience required. No matter what level of education you plan to attain, there are positions available that will allow you to positively impact the lives of children.

When babysitting is more than an occasional thing, it goes by different names. When you take care of children on a regular basis while the parents are at work, it is called **daycare**. Daycare can consist of a private individual adult taking in children in his or her home during the day, a commercial facility that cares for children, or something in-between. Daycare centers need teachers and classroom assistants who have at least a high school diploma and who have experience in babysitting. In time, you might get promoted to be a manager of a daycare facility, or own the facility yourself.

Jobs That Involve Children

If you like working with children, you might consider one of these jobs:

- Day care worker or manager
- Academic tutor
- Teacher's aide
- Elementary or middle-school teacher
- Social worker
- Guidance counselor
- Psychologist
- Religious school teacher
- Sports coach
- Nanny
- Pediatric nurse or doctor

Customized Instruction: More Advanced Students

Economists and other experts believe the demand for daycare services will continue to increase. Have students research this trend and prepare a short presentation on what factors are driving it. They should also report on the steps a person might take if they are thinking about starting a daycare business.

When a babysitter works full-time in the child's home, the sitter is called a **nanny** or **au pair.** Some nannies live in the home with the parents and children; others report for work every day, just like a regular job. A nanny typically has only one client at a time, but that client might have several children to tend to, of various ages. There is no specific educational requirement for a nanny, but most parents prefer to hire someone with at least a high school diploma.

International Childcare

Especially in big cities, many nannies and au pairs are from other countries. Young adults from Europe, for example, are often eager to take live-in childcare jobs in the United States so they can see the U.S. first-hand inexpensively.

Jobs in Education

Many careers in education involve working with children in some way. Some of these jobs, such as preschool teacher, religious education teacher, or private tutor, do not specifically require a college degree. However, most formal education jobs (that is, jobs associated with a public or private school, such as an elementary school teacher, school principal, or guidance counselor) require at least a bachelor's degree, and most prefer a master's degree in education. Some people who work in education work with mainstream classes and students; others specialize in a particular type of student, such as gifted, learning disabled, developmentally delayed, or with some physical, emotional, or mental handicap.

"I really like spending time with my little sisters. Maybe I should become a teacher..."

Jobs in Health Care

Most jobs in the health care field have specialties related to children. For example, doctors who specialize in children are called **pediatricians**. Some other medical specialists can also focus on children's health, too. For example, a doctor who treats cancer patients (an oncologist) can specialize in the treatment of cancer in children (a pediatric oncologist).

Some dentists and optometrists (eye doctors) also work with children. A dentist who specializes in straightening teeth, usually with braces or retainers, is called an orthodontist.

Many nurses also work mainly with children, both in hospital and physicians' offices. There are many levels of nursing training, ranging from Licenced Practical Nurse (LPN) to Nurse Practitioner.

Youth-focused social workers and child psychologists deal with the mental and emotional health of children. They can make sure that children are being taken care of at school and at home, and can help children heal from emotional traumas they have faced.

Job Search

Suppose you want to prepare for a job as a junior high school guidance counselor, helping students plan the coursework they should take and advising them on any personal issues they may have. Use the Internet to research the answers to the following questions:

- What positions are available in this field within a 100-mile radius of your home or school?
- What education level do those positions require?
- What level and type of previous experience is required?
- Approximately how much does such a job pay?

Vocabulary

Nanny or au pair: Babysitter who works full-time in the child's home.
Pediatrician: Doctor who specializes in children.

International Childcare

Explain that an au pair is a young foreigner who does domestic work for a family in exchange for room and board and a chance to learn the family's language. What benefits might there be to children under the care of an au pair?

Figure Focus

Explain to students why enjoying children is so important to becoming a teacher.

Job Search

Guidance counselors must have a bachelor's degree in a discipline, such as counseling, social work, education, behavioral sciences, or the social sciences. Many schools prefer a master's degree. Other requirements vary but can include a school counseling certification from the state, licensure to a teacher certificate, and teaching experience. According to the Bureau of Labor Statistics, the median annual earnings of an elementary or secondary school counselor is $53,750.

End-of-Chapter Activities

Case Study

It is not okay for Brandon's friends to come over. He did not get his aunt's permission to have friends over, and they would distract Brandon from focusing his attention on his cousin. Brandon's aunt has hired him to babysit, so he is obligated to commit his time and attention to his cousin, not to his friends or video games.

Sounding Off!

1. Student answers will vary but should mention telling the child clearly that using swear words is against the rules and making him aware of disciplinary measures you will take—such as time-out or telling his parents—if he uses them again.

2. Student answers will vary, but for an infant who has cried that long, the first phone call should be to the parents.

FAQ

1. Play improves physical coordination, promotes creative thinking, and enhances social skills.

2. Answers will vary and may include building with blocks, coloring, or imitating adult behavior.

3. Rules give children practice disciplining their emotions to follow along with the game, such as not cheating or giving up and being a gracious winner and loser.

4. Ways that toys help children learn and grow are:
   - Encouraging physical activity and exercise.
   - Teaching kids about the world around them.
   - Fostering imagination, creativity, and artistic ability.
   - Improving hand-eye coordination and fine motor skills.
   - Teaching social skills such as teamwork and cooperation.
   - Building emotional maturity in accepting wins and losses gracefully.
   - Encouraging kids to imitate adult careers and skills.

5. Answers will vary and might include sports equipment or a board or card game.

6. Punishment is designed to create a negative association with the activity. Discipline is designed to correct bad behavior and instill new, better habits.

7. Toddlers do not understand indirect speech and will think that they have a choice if you phrase the request as a question.

8. Answers will vary and may include fruits, vegetables, low-fat milk products, and bread.

9. Answers will vary and may include picking up items that could be easily broken, picking up items that could be a choking hazard, creating barriers around electrical outlets, and moving items with sharp corners that the child could run into.

10. Qualities of a good babysitter are:
    - Decision-making skills
    - Responsibility
    - Punctuality
    - Trustworthiness
    - Patience
    - Love of children
    - Awareness of safety
    - Clear thinking

Case Study

Brandon is babysitting his 2-year-old cousin on Saturday afternoon at his aunt's house and is getting paid for it. Three of his friends want to come over and play video games with him while he is there. Brandon has not received advance permission to have guests while he is babysitting.

- Is it okay for Brandon's friends to come over? Why or why not?
- Would Brandon still be able to do a good job babysitting if his friends were there?
- Would he be able to do a good job babysitting while he is playing video games?
- What are Brandon's obligations to his aunt in this situation?

Sounding Off!

1. How would you handle discipline if a small child you were babysitting used bad language (swear words)?

2. Suppose you are babysitting an infant who has been crying non-stop for three hours. You are at the end of your rope with stress, and are not sure you can continue the job. Who would you call for help?

FAQ

1. List three ways that play helps children develop.
2. Describe a type of play that a young preschooler might enjoy.
3. Explain how games with rules help children emotionally and socially.
4. List four ways that toys help children learn and grow.
5. Name a toy that a group of older children would enjoy playing with together.
6. Explain the difference between punishment and discipline.
7. Describe why asking instead of telling a toddler to do something can backfire.
8. List three healthy snacks you could give to a child you were babysitting for.
9. Describe how you can make a room safer for a toddler to play in.
10. Name three qualities that a good babysitter possesses.

To be successful at any business, you have to find out what your customers want and then deliver it to them consistently and well. That's true with service jobs like babysitting just as much as jobs where you sell a product.

Interview at least four sets of parents to find out the following:

- What type of person would be your ideal babysitter?
- What is one thing a babysitter has done that has really impressed you?
- What is something a babysitter has done that you thought was inappropriate?
- What is one thing that you wish all babysitters knew?

As a team, compile your interview results into a report to share with the class.

Hot Topics

Sometimes you might see a parent disciplining his or her child harshly in public and wonder whether you should keep out of it, or say something either to the parent or to some other adult who can intervene.

Take this opportunity to write about a situation where you disagreed with the way a parent was disciplining a child, how you handled that situation, and why you made that choice. Use a word processing program or write it out on paper, and drop it into the classroom's Hot Topics box. It's anonymous, so you can be honest and open.

Then as a class, read each one and discuss a better way to handle the discipline. For each one, talk about what advice you might give to someone facing a similar situation.

```
Web Extra  ▼
```

Many infants die or are brain-damaged every year from Shaken Baby Syndrome, where a frustrated caregiver shakes a crying baby to try to make it be quiet. Use the Internet to gather information about Shaken Baby Syndrome, including statistics about how common it is, the damage it does, and the symptoms you might notice in a baby that has been harmed by it.

Problem Solver

There are well-established guidelines for the amounts of various food types that children should eat every day. However, for many reasons, lots of children don't get the right foods. As a class, talk about the reasons for poor nutrition in children, and brainstorm some ways that private or government agencies could help make sure that more children get the food they need to learn and grow.

Team Players

Students are to interview four sets of parents to get their views on babysitters and then compile a report to share with the class. Make sure their reports cover the four questions listed in the text.

Hot Topics

Make sure students understand that they can turn in their papers anonymously. Encourage them to be open and honest about the situation and how they handled it.

Web Extra

Students are to find information on Shaken Baby Syndrome. When a baby is shaken, the brain is bounced back and forth inside the skull cavity, injuring or destroying brain tissue. The blood vessels feeding the brain can be damaged, leading to bleeding around the brain and behind the eyes. Shaking a baby can result in cessation of breathing and heartbeat, which can lead to death. The baby might also experience seizures, limp arms and legs, decreased levels of consciousness, extreme irritability, and vomiting. Other symptoms include not being able to lift or move head, blood pooling in the eyes, bulging or misshapen forehead, and unresponsiveness. In addition to blindness and seizures, lasting damage includes paralysis, mental disabilities, and growth and development problems. Some reports indicate that about 3,000 infants a year are diagnosed with Shaken Baby Syndrome, with 25 percent dying from it and 60 percent sustaining permanent damage.

Problem Solver

Students are to brainstorm ideas on how private and/or government agencies could help make sure children get the food they need. Encourage students to contact their school nutritionist and agencies in their community to discuss efforts in this area.

Write Now

Students are to pick a foreign country and write a report on the types of games and toys children of different ages play.

Be Involved!

Students are to think of clubs or special interest groups they could form for people interested in babysitting or other types of child care. They are to follow these steps:

1. Create a survey to determine the level of interest.

2. Distribute the survey to potential members.

3. Analyze the survey results.

4. Create an action plan for starting a club, including a timeframe, location for meetings, assignment of tasks, etc.

5. Determine a topic for the first meeting.

6. Hold the meeting.

7. Evaluate how successful the first meeting was and determine any changes that should be made for future meetings.

Social Networking

Students are to create skits that depict a situation in which a babysitter has to deal with a problem child. Encourage students to review the tips for effective discipline discussed on page 167 of the text.

Write Now

What games do children play in other countries, and how are they the same or different compared to the games that children in the United States play? Select a country, and then using the Web or reference books from the library, find out about games and toys there for children of several different ages. Create a report, including pictures, with the information you find.

Be Involved!

www.fcclainc.org

Each childcare provider learns a lot as they go, from on-the-job experience. You can learn from other people's experiences, too, though; you don't have to make every mistake and learn every lesson personally yourself. One great way of learning from others' experiences is to join or form an organization.

Working together as a class, brainstorm what types of club or special interest group you might create for people interested in babysitting or other types of childcare. Think about what you might do at meetings, and who might be interested in joining (for example, what ages of people).

First, create a survey to determine whether there is enough interest to start a club. Distribute the survey to people within the age groups you think might want to participate, and analyze the results of the survey to assess how popular the club would be. This will determine the choices for meeting location, because different size groups require different meeting spaces.

Create a plan for starting a club. If there is information that needs to be researched to make decisions, such as finding out if a particular location is available for use, assign the tasks of gathering that information to team members. Write out an action plan, including a timeframe, for the steps involved in planning the club.

Next, determine a topic for your first meeting, and assign an individual or small group the task of facilitating that first meeting's discussion.

Finally, hold the meeting, including the activity or discussion that was planned. After the meeting, work as a team to assess how successful it was and what changes should be made for future meetings.

Social Networking

Some babysitting jobs can be a real challenge because of behavior problems in the children. What would you do with a "problem child" who became violent or abusive to you? Or one who refuses a direct order involving his safety, or throws a tantrum? In groups, create a skit in which a small child is behaving very badly, and show how a mature, confident babysitter can use effective discipline to bring the child under control. After each skit is performed, the rest of the class can discuss as a group how each person could have behaved differently for a better outcome.

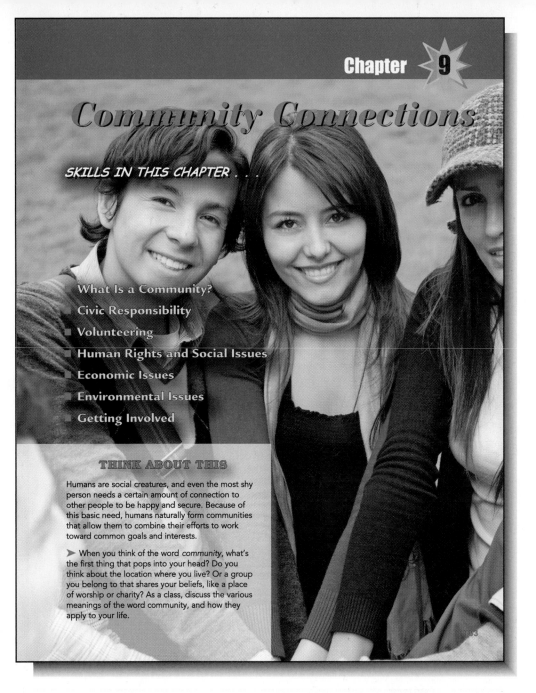

Chapter **9**

Community Connections

SKILLS IN THIS CHAPTER . . .

- What Is a Community?
- Civic Responsibility
- Volunteering
- Human Rights and Social Issues
- Economic Issues
- Environmental Issues
- Getting Involved

THINK ABOUT THIS

Humans are social creatures, and even the most shy person needs a certain amount of connection to other people to be happy and secure. Because of this basic need, humans naturally form communities that allow them to combine their efforts to work toward common goals and interests.

➤ When you think of the word *community*, what's the first thing that pops into your head? Do you think about the location where you live? Or a group you belong to that shares your beliefs, like a place of worship or charity? As a class, discuss the various meanings of the word community, and how they apply to your life.

Chapter 9 Overview

This chapter examines the concept of community and explores how a community's youth can make positive contributions. The chapter also discusses the social, economic, and environmental issues that affect all members of a community.

What Is a Community? Students explore how communities are formed and what factors can bring people together.

Civic Responsibility Serving your community is an integral part of being a good citizen. Students learn what the responsibilities are and explore opportunities to give back to the community.

Volunteering Students learn how to search for opportunities to make a positive difference in the community while gaining experience.

Human Rights and Social Issues The rights of people differ among nations. Students explore their own rights compared to others.

Economic Issues Money can affect people's lives in important ways. Tips on how to change your economic situation are provided.

Environmental Issues Students find out what environmental factors may be affecting their communities, and how to become environmentally sensitive.

Getting Involved Creating a positive change in the community is simple if you know where to start. Students learn how easy it is to volunteer.

Focus and Engage

Bell-Ringer: Think About This

You might help students by asking them to write down the names of three groups they take part in. These can range from a group of friends to a sports team to an organized club or even their class. Ask them to specify how many people are in the group and what connects the people. Explain that communities often form because of a common struggle or a shared sense of purpose. Can they identify the reason their groups were formed?

ADVANCE PREPARATION	
Review	*Life Skills for the 21st Century* textbook, Chapter 9.
Prepare	Paper and pencil for some activities. Poster board and colored markers or pencils. Box labeled "Hot Topics."

CUSTOMIZED INSTRUCTION OVERVIEW				
Less Advanced Students	More Advanced Students	ESOL Students	Special Needs Students	At-Risk Students
Pages 184, 188, 195	Page 187	Page 191	Pages 184, 188, 195	Pages 184, 186, 197

Introduce the Section

In this section, students explore what a community is and why people join together to form one.

Types of Communities

Recognize that the classroom is an example of a community. The common purpose is for students to learn and to better themselves. You lead the community, and the students must join together to help in class discussions. Also, each individual's contribution on topics helps others to understand the lessons better.

Vocabulary

Community: A group of people who have a common goal.

Figure Focus

What obvious characteristics do the students notice about the group in the photo that could lead them to believe it is a community? The group is in a circle, which shows unity; they seem happy, which means they share common interests; and they are dressed casually, which may mean they have created an informal group.

Reinforce and Review

In Chapter 1, students learned to identify their roles and responsibilities. A community is an example of where students can develop new and challenging roles. For example, they might step into a leadership position in which they rally other members to affect change.

What Is a Community?

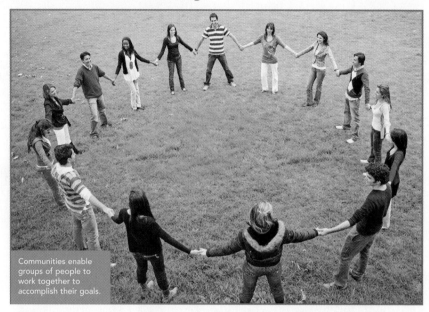

Communities enable groups of people to work together to accomplish their goals.

A community is a group of people who have a common goal. The people might be physically near each other, such as living in the same neighborhood, or they might be spread out all over the world, and connected to each other through the Internet. The people might be very similar to one another, or might have very little in common other than the one interest that draws them together.

Most communities are held together by a shared sense of purpose. That purpose can either be to explore or protect a personal interest (like a club based around a certain hobby), or to work for a larger cause that the members believe in (like an international immunization program). A community can have a personal scope, or a local, regional, national, or global one.

Types of Communities

Communities can include:

- Residential neighborhoods
- Small towns
- Religious groups
- Charitable organizations
- Political action groups
- Volunteers for a cause
- Internet message boards and chat rooms
- Girl Scout and Boy Scout troops
- Music, dance, or art-based groups
- Friends who share common interests
- Schools

Customized Instruction: Less Advanced/Special Needs/At-Risk Students

Have students create a three-column table on the various communities in which they are involved. In the first column, they write the name of the community; in the second column, the common interest that holds the community together; and in the third column, their role in the community. For example, the community might be the animal shelter staff; their common interest is helping animals; and the student's role is walking the dogs so they get exercise and undergo training that will help them be more adoptable.

Communities Based on Personal Interests

Some communities develop because people have an interest in supporting or protecting something in which they have a personal involvement. They get involved to benefit themselves, either directly or indirectly.

For example, if you are interested in camping and the outdoors, you might join a club such as the Boy Scouts or Girl Scouts that focuses on that. As part of the scouting community, you might do some charitable work, but you are participating primarily for your own enjoyment and personal growth.

Adults do this, too. In a neighborhood of houses, for example, home owners have a common interest in preventing property values from declining. If the neighborhood goes downhill, everyone loses money. Therefore, the neighbors work together to protect that interest by helping each other keep up their houses and yards—borrowing and lending tools, pitching in to help each other, and so on. They may even form a neighborhood association that sets upkeep rules everyone must follow. Similarly, neighborhood crime watch programs help reduce crime in an area, so residents may volunteer their time to create and maintain one.

Communities Based on Public Good

Communities also form around public causes that people believe will make the world a better place. For example, people who are passionate about reducing air pollution might get together to discuss bills related to pollution control coming up for vote in Congress and to plan events to educate the public. They might meet in-person locally, or by phone, e-mail, or online chat.

Not everyone agrees on what is in the public's best interest; some causes have enthusiastic believers on both sides of the issue. For example, some people believe that government should pay for food and housing for everyone who cannot afford it. Others believe our society would be better off with less government involvement. Both sides believe that they are acting in the best interest of the majority, and not out of any selfish interest for themselves.

Some causes nearly everyone agrees are in the public's interest, such as feeding the hungry, housing the homeless, and educating children. Different groups emerge, however, when there are disagreements as to how best to achieve those goals. For example, one group might think that the best way to reduce homelessness is to build lots of low-cost housing; another group might think that raising the minimum wage would be a better way to ensure that everyone can pay for housing.

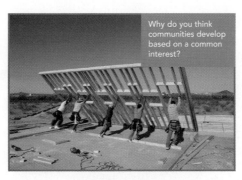

Why do you think communities develop based on a common interest?

MONEY MADNE$$

Sometimes a small investment of money and time in a community can pay big rewards. For example, suppose you and four friends decided to create a community vegetable garden in your neighborhood. To get started, you will need $15.00 each ($75.00 in total) for seeds, tools, and fertilizer. If all goes well, you hope to be able to raise 40 pounds of tomatoes, 20 pounds of zucchini, and 30 red bell peppers (approximately 1/3 of a pound each), to split among the five families.

Go to your local grocery store and find out the prices for tomatoes, zucchini, and red bell peppers. Use that data to determine:

■ What is the worth of the share of the crop that each family will receive?

■ What is the return on investment (ROI) percentage of the $15.00 initial buy-in compared to the value of the vegetables received?

To calculate ROI, divide the value of the crop by 15. So, for example, if the value of the vegetables received were $50, the ROI would be 3.33. To convert that to a percentage, multiply by 100, for 333%. That's a pretty good return on your money!

APPLY IT

Have students think of a person they know who is a member of a community-based group. It could be a teacher, a coach, or a family member or neighbor who volunteers. Ask students to write a paragraph about the person, the community-based group the person belongs to, and why this person is important to the community. Once students are finished, have them read their paragraph to the class.

Discuss

List examples of why communities are created; for example, to reduce pollution or to help the homeless. Engage students in a conversation about what makes a community work. What roles and responsibilities do people have to fulfill for a community to succeed?

Figure Focus

The picture represents teamwork—a group of men working together to achieve a common goal. Ask students to comment on the roles of individual members of a building team. The carpenter, roofer, and plumber are distinct in the organization but must work as a team to complete a project. What would happen if the plumber was unable to work on the house?

MONEY MADNE$$

Answers will vary, depending on the prices found at the local grocery. But, as an example, assume tomatoes are $1.78 a pound, zucchini is $1.59 a pound, and peppers are $.79 a pound.

■ Tomatoes: At $1.78 a pound, their value would be $71.20. Their ROI would be $71.20 ÷ 15, which equals 4.75, multiplied by 100 equals 475%.

■ Zucchini: At $1.59 a pound, their value would be $31.80. Their ROI would be $31.80 ÷ 15, which equals 2.12, multiplied by 100 equals 212%.

■ Red bell peppers: At $.79 a pound, their value would be $23.70. Their ROI would be $23.70 ÷ 15, which equals 1.58, multiplied by 100 equals 158%.

■ Total: The total value of the vegetables is $126.70 ($71.20 + $31.80 + $23.70). If you divide by 5, the value to each family is $25.34, divided by 15 equals 1.69 or an ROI of 169%.

This means that the $15 put up by each of the five families was a profitable investment.

Introduce the Section

This section discusses what being a good citizen means, and the rights and responsibilities that come with the freedoms granted by our government.

Figure Focus

Ask students what rights and responsibilities come to mind when they see the American flag. Most people equate it with freedoms of speech, assembly, religion, etc. Emphasize the importance of recognizing rights as well as civic responsibilities. We can limit our own free speech if we choose not to stand up for what we believe in or choose not to vote.

Discuss

Explain that civic responsibility is the services that you owe your community as a citizen. It could be as simple as throwing your trash or recycling in the proper receptacle, or trying to find the owner of a lost dog. Or, it could be a bigger commitment, such as running for a political office or helping to build affordable housing for low-income families.

Civic Responsibilities

Share this fact with students: In the 2008 U.S. presidential election, only 51 percent of citizens of voting age exercised their right to vote. In national elections in Japan and Germany, close to 90 percent of eligible voters cast a ballot. Much has been written about voter apathy in the United States. Explain the importance of voting and how it should be viewed as a civic responsibility.

Civic Responsibility

Being a citizen of a certain country, state, or region involves both rights and responsibilities.

A s a citizen of your local community, your state, and the United States, you have certain rights and responsibilities. The service that you owe to location-based communities is sometimes called **civic responsibility**.

Some civic responsibilities are dictated by law, such as paying taxes and not littering. Others, like voting, are not required, but are still part of being a good citizen. There are also many things you can do to go the extra mile as a citizen, actively working to make your world a better place. These can include volunteering for worthy causes, serving in local leadership positions such as those on a school or zoning board, picking up litter along the roadside, or donating money or food to local food banks.

Serving your community is not just a nice thing to do; it can also positively impact your own life. Anything you can do to make your community more safe and pleasant will also make your *own* life more safe and pleasant within that community.

Civic Responsibilities

Some civic responsibilities include:

- Obeying laws
- Serving in the military, if drafted—required by the government
- Serving on a jury if summoned to do so
- Paying taxes
- Deciding whether and how to vote for elected officials
- Casting informed votes on ballot issues
- Performing community service

Customized Instruction: At-Risk Students

Ask students to write down three laws that pertain specifically to citizens under the age of 21. Laws on underage drinking, possession of tobacco, driving age, marriage, and even tattoos all pertain to those under 21.

Legal Requirements of Citizenship

As the saying goes, "Freedom isn't free." Federal, state, and local laws and regulations can require you to do—and not do—certain things. Obeying these laws is part of your civic responsibility. That includes everything from driving the speed limit on highways to not hitting anyone when you are angry.

Some laws dictate that you serve the community in certain ways, such as registering with Selective Service, the system that controls the process of drafting citizens into the armed forces. Although there is currently no draft in the United States, all males between the ages 18 and 25 must register in case the country needs to have a draft in the future.

If you register to vote, you may be called to serve on a jury. (Juries are assembled from voter registration rolls.) If summoned for jury duty, you are required by law to go, or to report to the court system why you cannot. You may or may not receive a small amount of pay for serving on a jury, depending on the area you live in.

It is also your duty as a citizen to pay taxes according to both federal laws and the laws of your state and county. Federal income tax is due on most income you make, and most states also have a state income tax as well. You must file a tax return each year even if you do not owe anything.

Being a Good Citizen

In addition to fulfilling the bare minimum of citizenship requirements, many people choose to give more to their communities. Some ways that you can serve your community include:

- Serving in leadership roles, such as being on a school board or neighborhood association board
- Volunteering for neighborhood crime watch, trash pick-up, or other duties that make your neighborhood safer and more beautiful
- Voting in federal, state, and local elections
- Educating yourself about the issues and candidates before elections, and spreading the word about them to others
- Giving money and/or time to charitable organizations that benefit society
- Monitoring political leaders and government agencies, and pointing out when they are not doing their jobs as they should

Did that last point surprise you? As a citizen, you are not required to accept everything that any government organization or official does. In fact, you are serving your community by speaking up, via public speeches, newspaper editorials, protest marches, and other nonviolent acts of disagreement (**civil disobedience**). Many of the most important changes in American society have happened because of people who disagreed with the status quo (that is, the way things were at the moment).

What are some ways that people show support and allegiance to their country?

 The Power of Protest

One of the basic rights of every American citizen, as guaranteed by the Constitution, is the right to assemble peacefully. This means that the government cannot stop citizens from peaceful protests.

What protests have you witnessed, and for what causes? Did the protestors' actions end up helping or hurting their causes? Under what circumstances do you think protests are the most effective way to promote change?

 TECH CONNECT

Which states have no state income tax? Use the Internet to find out.

Discuss

Ask students how ordinary individuals have impacted change in the United States. Give the example of Rosa Parks' refusing to move from her bus seat for a white person and setting off a chain of events that ignited the civil rights movement. Push students to think about ways they can impact change in their communities; for example, volunteering for a political campaign, being elected to student counsel, or being environmentally aware and active.

Figure Focus

People can show loyalty to their country by being knowledgeable on issues when casting a ballot. Some states are instituting "motor voter" laws, which enable voters to register by mail, fax, or online. Explain that registering to vote is as simple as showing a government-issued ID (driver's license or passport are acceptable) to your local elections official.

 The Power of Protest

Explain how protests have affected dramatic changes in the American political, social, and economic landscape. For example, in the early twentieth century, women protested about being denied the right to vote; around mid-century, Vietnam protesters sent a loud message to politicians about their aversion to the war in Vietnam. If citizens are respectful, coordinate their activities with the local police, and assemble peacefully, they can be effective. The right to protest is a freedom that not all countries have, including China, North Korea, and Iran.

TECH CONNECT

The states with no income tax are Alaska, Florida, Nevada, South Dakota, Texas, Washington, and Wyoming. Additionally, New Hampshire and Tennessee limit their state income taxes to dividend and interest income only.

CRITICAL THINKING ACTIVITY

As a class, brainstorm issues the students may have with their community. Ask the class to vote on which is the most important. After a majority of students have voted for the most important issue, create a plan of action to create change. Would they call people to educate them about the problem, form a protest, or write letters to their state representative?

Customized Instruction: More Advanced Students

Have students stage a mock protest over a school or community issue they feel strongly about. For example, maybe they are unhappy with a curfew imposed by local law enforcement officials. What would be the most effective way to protest this?

Vocabulary

Volunteering: Doing work to contribute to the community and gain experience without pay.

Figure Focus

People who volunteer tend to have a positive attitude and high self-esteem. Explain that volunteering can help build character and focus your attention and energies on your strengths and the things you value. There are literally millions of nonprofit organizations in the United States that depend largely on volunteers to support them.

What Volunteers Do

Some students may believe that donating money is the only way to give back to their community. Explain that while monetary donations help every community effort, simple contributions, such as planting a tree or helping a homeless person, can go a long way, too. Explain that the most important part of volunteering is finding the activity that expresses your values and effectively gives back to the community.

Reinforce and Review

Ask students how volunteering can contribute to their personal wellness. The positive interactions with other volunteers and with those you are helping can relieve stress. You devote more of your time to positive activities rather than ones that might involve risky behaviors. Volunteering can help you focus on aiding others instead of dwelling on your own problems.

Volunteering in Your Community

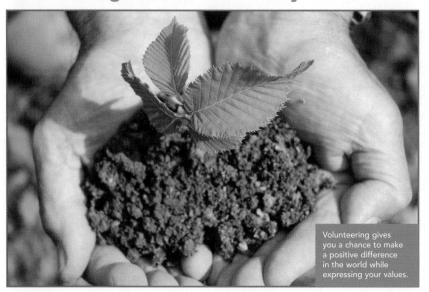

Volunteering gives you a chance to make a positive difference in the world while expressing your values.

Volunteering—in other words, doing work without pay—is a great way to contribute to the communities you care about and gain valuable work experience.

You have probably done a lot of volunteer activities in your life so far, perhaps without realizing that's what you were doing. For example, when a teacher asked for someone to run an errand or hand out supplies, have you ever raised your hand and been chosen to do it? That's volunteering for your classroom community. Volunteering is part of being a good citizen. When everyone pitches in to help, tasks get done more quickly and easily, freeing up the entire group to focus on what's important.

Volunteering also gives you a chance to express your values—in other words, to show what is important to you. For example, if you are passionate about improving the quality of life for children, you might volunteer at an after-school reading program; if your primary interest is the environment, you might volunteer for a conservation group that plants trees.

What Volunteers Do

Nonprofit organizations use volunteers for almost every aspect of their operations, so there is sure to be something that matches your interests and abilities. For example, volunteers can:

- Staff information booths at fairs and trade shows
- Tutor children in reading, math, and other subjects
- Help elderly or disabled people with daily activities
- Do physical labor such as cleaning, yard work, and moving
- Create flyers, brochures, and other printed materials
- Provide childcare
- Collect and distribute donations of food, clothing, or money
- Give presentations and speeches that promote the group
- Entertain groups of people with music, dance, acting, or other creative arts

Customized Instruction: Less Advanced/Special Needs Students

Have students research volunteer opportunities in the classroom and in the school. Have them create a list that describes the opportunity, the duties of a volunteer, and how to become involved. For example, does your class need a volunteer to handle paper recycling?

Who Needs Volunteers?

Many types of organizations welcome volunteers, including schools, religious groups, environmental protection groups, social services organizations, and political action groups. All of these thrive on the work of many volunteers and are likely to have well-established programs set up that make it easy to contribute your time.

Some organizations have restrictions on volunteer work because of insurance liability, laws, or medical privacy issues. For example, some medical facilities may require that everyone who provides care to patients be paid employees, so there may be limits on the things you can do for residents there. When you go through volunteer orientation/training at such facilities, the limits will be explained to you.

Nonprofit Organizations

A **nonprofit organization** (also called a **not-for-profit organization**) is an organization where the profits are not distributed to shareholders or individual owners, but instead rolled back into the business itself, so it can continue or expand its work. A nonprofit is not the same thing as a charity; some nonprofits promote special interest groups, like trade unions or political parties. Others, however, do have charitable missions.

The government grants certain types of nonprofit organizations special status. They are exempt from paying certain taxes, and people who donate to them can deduct those donations on their tax returns. In return for this special status, the organizations agree to follow certain rules, such as not doing political lobbying, not allowing any individual members to profit from its activities, and so on.

Section 501(c) is the part of the U.S. tax code that specifies what types of organizations are exempt from paying taxes. Different organizations are defined in that section of the tax code. The most common one is **501(c)3**, which is defined as "Religious, Educational, Charitable, Scientific, Literary, Testing for Public Safety, to Foster National or International Amateur Sports Competition, or Prevention of Cruelty to Children or Animals Organizations." If you donate time or money to a 501(c)3 organization, you may be able to deduct your donation on your taxes, decreasing the amount of income tax that you have to pay.

How does it make you feel to do things for other people without expecting anything in return?

 Never doubt that a group of thoughtful, committed people can change the world. Indeed, that is the only way it has ever been done.

— *Margaret Mead, American Anthropologist*

21st Century Skills

What Happens Next?

Tamara's best friend, Becky, has asked her to participate in a fund-raiser for an organization that she enthusiastically supports, and Tamara initially agreed to do it. However, after looking at the organization's mission and goals statements on their Web site, Tamara began to have some hesitation about participating because she didn't agree with some of the goals and positions of the organization.

What should she do? Should she go ahead and participate anyway, because she said she would? Or should she back out of the event? Should she tell Becky why? Using your 21st Century Skills—such as decision making, goal setting, and problem solving—discuss your answers in small groups. Then prepare a short skit in which group members role-play a conversation between Tamara and Becky about the event.

Vocabulary

Nonprofit organization: An organization that uses profits to expand its purpose of promoting an issue rather than for personal gain.

Figure Focus

Ask students to share their feelings on helping others. How does it make them feel? How do they think it makes the other person feel? Discuss the concept of "random acts of kindness," or just doing something nice for the heck of it. Ask students to think of instances when they did a random act of kindness, or when they were the recipient of such an act.

"Quote Box"

Margaret Mead was a world-renowned anthropologist who wrote many books on the importance of childrearing to a society's development. Her quote points to the idea that there are no barriers to creating change if you are committed to achieving the desired outcome.

21st Century Skills

What Happens Next?

Students are to consider the situation between Tamara and Becky. Remind students of the importance of valuing others. When you value others, you show that you recognize and appreciate the role they play in your life and that you respect their opinions and feelings. In this case, Tamara needs to show that she values Becky as a friend, but she also needs to stay true to her own values, or what is important to her. Students should prepare skits that demonstrate Tamara's respect for her friend's beliefs, as well as her own commitment to the values and standards that are important to her.

Teaching Tips

Emphasize the difference between a charitable organization and a nonprofit organization. Both bring people together for the common cause of the organization. However, charitable organizations use their funds to help the needy, while nonprofits roll their profits back into the organization to expand its work.

Introduce the Section

The rights of people differ among nations. Students explore their own rights compared to others.

Figure Focus

Ask for a show of hands of who regularly watches news programs, reads the newspaper, or goes online to keep up with current events. What social issues are currently in the news? Do students have an opinion on these issues?

STUDENT ACTIVITY

Have students identify their state representative and the representative's mailing address. Ask students to write a letter to the representative about an issue that concerns them. Examples of issues are pollution, housing, health care, war, or immigration. Ask for volunteers to read their letters to the class.

What Rights Do People Have?

Some countries do not agree on common rights that Americans take for granted. For example:

- North Korea does not allow free speech.
- Saudi Arabia and Vatican City do not allow women to vote.
- Chinese law allows for citizens to be arrested for a peaceful protest.

Teaching Tips

Explain that human rights are a citizen's fundamental rights in which the government does not interfere.

Human Rights and Social Issues

Keeping up on national and international news enables you to talk confidently about human rights and social issues.

As a volunteer, you might choose to become involved in human rights and/or social issues. Working for nonprofit organizations that support human rights and social justice can benefit both large and small groups of people, as well as improve the lives of individuals you touch.

In the United States, it is easy to take basic freedoms for granted and forget that not everyone has the same rights we do. For example, in some countries, women and men are not treated equally under the law, and in some regions, people of certain ethnicities or national origins are restricted as to where they can live or travel. The newspapers are full of stories every day about unfair situations around the world.

Even within the United States, not everyone has equal opportunities. For example, on the average, women make substantially less money than men do for performing the same work, some people are discriminated against because of their ethnicity, and not every American has access to affordable health care.

There are many nonprofit organizations that work to correct social injustice like those, and most of them welcome volunteer support as well as money contributions.

What Rights Do People Have?

Each nation has its own constitution (or equivalent) that spells out the rights that citizens can expect in exchange for being citizens. It's a slightly different set in each country, but here are some general things that many countries agree on:

- Freedom to speak about controversial issues
- Ability to vote in elections, for a voice in government
- Freedom to travel within the country and outside it
- Freedom to assemble in groups without government interference

In addition, in some countries, there are social welfare systems in place that give every citizen a right to basic food, shelter, and health care if they are elderly, disabled, or unable to support themselves.

Stay in School

Many students drop out of school because they are struggling academically and assume they probably won't graduate anyway. Discuss with students the school and community-based resources that can offer support. For example:

- Tutors who work one-on-one with students in certain subject areas.
- Teachers who are willing to work individually with students before and after school, or at designated times during the school day.
- Homework assistance centers where students can go to get help with homework assignments and studying.
- Literacy programs and translation services that are designed to help students with a primary language other than English.
- Youth leadership and development organizations, such as Big Brothers Big Sisters, 4-H, YMCA, and Family, Career and Community Leaders of America (FCCLA).
- School-based clubs, groups, and sports teams.
- Community-based youth programs, which offer counseling, mentoring, work force preparation, and recreational activities.

Human Rights and Political Action

Human rights issues are those things that affect people's basic needs, such as food, clothing, shelter, freedom, and protection from abuse. Nobody should expect a "free ride" in life, of course, but when social systems prevent people from helping themselves, the systems need to be changed for the good of everyone.

Private charities and nonprofits can help feed, clothe, and shelter people in the short term; however, long-term change usually comes from societies and governments changing their priorities and policies. Because of this, getting involved in politics is often the most effective way to promote human rights.

Some of the ways that you can help:

- Read newspapers, news magazines, and Web sites that publish international and national news stories, so you will know what the key issues are.
- Share with your friends and family what you have learned about the issues, to raise their awareness and to get them interested in telling others.
- Keep up on legislation coming up for votes that will affect human rights, such as United Nations resolutions and Congressional bills, and write letters to elected officials letting them know how you would like them to vote.
- Volunteer for organizations that support the political actions you think are necessary to promote human rights. As a volunteer for one of these organizations, you might be asked to do office tasks, collect signatures on petitions, and so on.

When you reach adulthood, there is even more you can do, such as voting for candidates that support your political views and even running for public office yourself.

Social Issues

Social issues are those that affect the opportunities and restrictions placed on people in a certain culture or society. Some social issues affect the entire population. For example, some nations do not have free and fair elections; instead, their leaders are appointed, or rise to power through military force or corruption.

Other social issues involve the targeting of specific segments of society for unfair treatment, such as racism or sexism. When someone makes internal judgments about someone else on the basis of a characteristic such as race or sex, it is called **prejudice** (which, literally means to *pre-judge*). When someone treats someone else differently because of prejudice, it is called **discrimination**.

In the United States, there are laws that prevent employers and landlords from discriminating against employees or renters based on race, color, religion, sex, or national origin. Individual people sometimes do still discriminate, however, and some institutions find loopholes around the laws to do so as well.

One way you can contribute to your community is to educate yourself about any unfair situations you see going on around you, and to speak out against them. At a national and global level, you can work for social justice by supporting politicians and laws that favor the types of policies you think will bring about positive changes. You can also volunteer for organizations that fight for the social justice issues that are important to you.

How do organizations like the United Nations ensure human rights on a global level?

Discuss

Discuss the following terms with students:

- Human rights issue: Matters that affect a person's basic needs, such as food, shelter, freedom, and protection from abuse.
- Social issues: Opportunities or restrictions that affect people's lives in a certain culture or society.
- Discrimination: When someone treats a person differently because of a prejudice.
- Prejudice: A negative judgment or opinion formed about a person or group without knowledge of the facts; often based on race, age, or gender.
- Assumptions: Conclusions based on limited knowledge of the facts.
- Scapegoating: Holding one person or group responsible for all the community's problems. Isolating or rejecting a person or group.

Figure Focus

The United Nations is headquartered in New York City and was formed to promote international peace and human rights for citizens around the world. Countries meet to work together on issues such as international law and world hunger, which cannot be solved by one country alone.

Customized Instruction: ESOL Students

Ask students what the word for discrimination is in their primary language. Some students might be comfortable talking about instances in which they or a family member were discriminated against because of language differences.

Figure Focus

Review the basic human needs of food, water, shelter, and clothing. What factors might cause a family to go without these basic human needs? Some factors include loss of a job, death in the family, or a natural disaster that wipes out the home and possessions.

Vocabulary

Economic issues: Those issues that have to do with money and one's ability to buy necessary items such as food, shelter, health care, and clothing.

Money Changes Everything

Share some of these statistics about the costs of living:

- The monthly cost to feed a family of four ranges from about $500 (thrifty) to $1,100 (liberal).

- The average cost of a home is more than $200,000.

- The average yearly tuition at a public university is about $6,500. This does not include fees and room and board.

- The average household spends about $650 per person on clothes and shoes in a year.

STUDENT ACTIVITY

Ask students to comment on their family budget and monthly living expenses. Write on the board the different things their family spends money on in a typical month. Make sure they consider mortgage or rent, utilities and cell phones, food and clothing, entertainment, transportation, insurance, and other fees.

Economic Issues

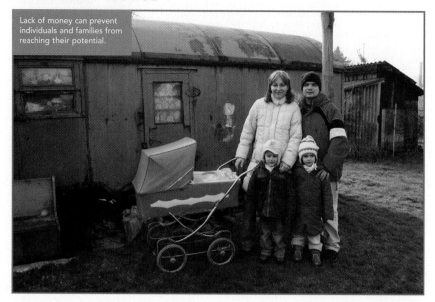

Lack of money can prevent individuals and families from reaching their potential.

Economic issues are those having to do with money. *Money can't buy happiness*, as the saying goes, but it can buy food, shelter, health care, clothing, and education, all of which people need to reach their potential as productive members of society. One important way you can serve your community is to volunteer for organizations that work to ensure that all families and individuals have enough money to take care of their basic needs.

Economic issues are closely related to social issues because they have some of the same causes and effects. For example, a woman applying for a high-paying job might be passed over in favor of a male candidate because of sexism. Social prejudice like that is part of the reason why female-headed households tend to have lower income. Multiple causes and effects of poverty build upon each other; a poor family has less money to send children to college, so the children don't have the education they need to get good jobs that will enable them to send *their* children to college.

Money Changes Everything

In American society, money—or lack of it—affects people's lives and experiences in important ways, including:

- Good nutrition, which can result in better physical and mental performance
- Comfortable and safe place to live
- Higher education opportunities such as college, workshops, and seminars
- Appropriate clothing for work and play
- Access to online services for data gathering, learning, and entertainment
- Access to cultural experiences like music and dance

Working for Economic Justice

Once someone becomes poor, it is hard for him or her to get out of that position because most things that would correct the problem require money. For example, suppose you are trying to get a job, but you don't have appropriate clothes to wear to the interview. If you had money, you could buy clothes, go to the interview, get the job, and have money. The same goes for transportation. Someone who doesn't have a car may find it harder to get to work, so he may be frequently late for his job, which makes his boss unhappy, which makes it impossible for him to get a promotion to make more money to buy a car.

Government programs and private charities can provide short-term help for people who want to break the cycle of poverty. They can provide willing people with money, transportation, clothing, child care, and whatever else may be needed for them to get and keep jobs.

Volunteering for a nonprofit organization that provides people with the tools they need to get started down the path to economic success can be very rewarding! For example, Goodwill is an organization that takes donations of clothing and household items and makes them available for sale very inexpensively at thrift stores. You could volunteer at a Goodwill center to sort incoming donations, price items, or even run the cash register at a thrift store.

Education Is Power

The single best way of empowering someone to be more financially independent is to provide them with an education. Studies have shown that people with four-year college degrees earn, on the average, over a million dollars more in their lifetime than people without one. Education doesn't just mean college, though; it can include general literacy (that is, ability to read and write), general knowledge, and life skills.

There are lots of volunteer opportunities in education. You can:

- Volunteer for an after-school reading or tutoring program
- Be a classroom assistant for workshops or seminars, collecting and handing out papers and doing other errands
- Volunteer to help with programs at your local library
- Read to younger children, or listen to them while they read
- Help friends or family who may have difficulty reading or writing when they need help with employment applications and other written material

Job Search

Adult literacy programs help people learn to read and write who, for whatever reason, did not learn those skills very well when they were children. Suppose you wanted to be a teacher in an adult literacy program. What kind of education and training would you need? What classes would you take in school to prepare?

What skills do you have that you could pass on to a younger child to help him or her succeed in school?

Job Search

Most literacy programs require teachers to have at least a bachelor's degree. Most states require teachers in government-run programs to have some form of licensure as well, such as a license for adult education. Teachers in these programs instruct adults and out-of-school youths in reading, writing, speaking English, and performing elementary mathematical calculations.

To prepare, you might take foreign language classes and classes on computer technology, writing, and sociology. It might also be useful to know about citizenship and the naturalization process, as well.

Figure Focus

Ask students to consider the skills they could pass on to a younger child to help him or her succeed in school. There are many opportunities to tutor, mentor, and coach young children. For example, if you play soccer, you could volunteer to coach a children's soccer team or referee games. If you enjoy reading, you could volunteer to read to young kids. If you enjoy nature and being outdoors, you could volunteer at a local park that offers children's camps and programs.

TEAMWORK ACTIVITY

Have each team research a community-based agency or program that accepts volunteers their age. They should find out volunteer responsibilities and any training or education requirements. Have each team share their information with the class. Encourage team members to volunteer with the group they researched.

Introduce the Section

This section covers the topic of the environment. Students find out what environmental factors may be affecting their communities, and how to become environmentally sensitive and aware.

Figure Focus

Point out that preserving clean waterways is integral for human survival. Water pollutants make it impossible to drink, swim, or fish in many lakes and rivers. Mercury in the water can cause nervous disorders, and sodium can cause cardiovascular disease. An estimated 19.5 million Americans become ill each year from waterborne parasites, bacteria, viruses, and animal waste.

Discuss

Discuss ways in which students are environmentally friendly. For example, do they pick up trash when they see it lying on the ground? Do they and their family recycle? Do they participate in Earth Day activities or "planting parties"? Do they walk or ride a bike instead of getting in the car?

Vocabulary

Environment: The air, water, minerals, and conditions that surround and affect a person.

Environmentalists: People who take part in the environmental conservation social movement; they favor the environment above conflicting economic and political concerns.

Types of Environmental Issues

Americans have been dealing with environmental issues for a long time. Consider this: In colonial days, people simply dumped their waste in the street. That was until Benjamin Franklin petitioned to end the practice and started the first street cleaning service.

Environmental Issues

Preserving the environment for future generations is an important part of being a good citizen.

The **environment** is the natural world—the soil, the water, the air, and the plant and animal life. Volunteering for organizations that promote a healthy environment can pay off in creating a world for yourself—and others—where plants and animals flourish and the air, land, and seas are free of pollutants and toxins.

Sometimes the best thing for the economic health of a local, national, or global community conflicts with the best thing for the environment. For example, drilling for oil in a wildlife area might create hundreds of jobs, bring in millions of dollars to the local community, and provide inexpensive oil to the nation, but oil drilling might also disturb the habitat of several types of animals, which then might decrease in population enough to become endangered species.

When such conflicts occur, it is up to the citizens (and their elected representatives) to decide how they should be resolved. To what extent should environmental protection dictate what people can and can't do? And what activities are most likely to make a positive or negative impact on the environment? There are many environmental and economic organizations, clubs, agencies, and lobbying groups, each of which supports and promotes a different opinion about those answers.

Types of Environmental Issues

Environmentalists are people who favor the environment above conflicting economic or political concerns. Through a combination of public education, political lobbying, protest demonstrations, and special events, they support issues such as:

- Global warming awareness and prevention
- Planting trees to re-grow forests that have been cut down
- Setting limits on how much pollution companies can release into the air and water
- Protecting the habitats of endangered species
- Working with auto makers to reduce air pollution from vehicles, and supporting the development of alternative fuels
- Cleaning up landfills, dumps, roadsides, and other areas
- Promoting the use of recycling programs and recycled paper and plastics

What You Can Do

There are many simple things you can do to help preserve the environment in your community and beyond, and most of them don't require a great deal of time or money. Here are some ideas:

- Get literature from local conservation groups to learn what environmental programs are active in your area and how you can participate in them.
- Volunteer after school and on weekends for organizations that do local environmental clean-up activities such as picking up trash along a river or road, clearing out invasive plants, and planting trees.
- If your school or religious institution does not recycle, do research to find out what the costs and benefits would be, and present that information to decision-makers in the organization.
- Educate your friends and classmates about the importance of minimizing the waste that goes into landfills, especially plastics that do not break down quickly.
- Encourage family and friends who drive automobiles to consider fuel-efficient models such as gas/electric hybrids.
- Conserve electricity at home by shutting off lights and turning off appliances.

How does raising awareness of ecological and conservation issues, such as recycling, help the environment?

Supporting Environmental Organizations

Environmental issues, like social ones, can be temporarily helped by the work of individuals performing good works. Larger-scale changes, however, require the work of organizations with the resources to buy land, hire lawyers, network with politicians, and organize conferences.

As with social programs, different organizations may have conflicting ideas about the best way to achieve common goals. For example, one organization might lobby Congress for harsher penalties for companies that violate air pollution limits; another organization might lobby for tax incentives for companies that create lower-pollution manufacturing processes. When picking an environmental organization to support, you should research their ideas and find the one that matches your own.

NUMBERS GAME

Over 26 tons of new plastic is created in the United States each year, and only 5.8% of that is later recycled, according to the Society of Plastics Engineers.

Suppose everyone in the United States started recycling plastics more, so that the percentage of recycling rose to 10%. How much less new plastic would need to be manufactured each year?

- First, figure out the percentage of the reduction: 10% − 5.8% = 4.2% reduction
- If you have a 4.2% reduction, the remaining amount is 95.8% of the original total: 26 tons × .958 = 24.9 tons
- Subtract the new amount from the old amount: 26 − 24.9 = 1.1 tons

Increasing recycling by 4.2% in the United States would result in 1.1 fewer tons of plastic being created each year.

Customized Instruction: Less Advanced/Special Needs Students

Have students create a poster that is divided in half with pictures of good environmental practices on one side, and bad environmental practices on the other side. They can draw pictures or cut them from newspapers and magazines.

Discuss

Explain to students that lobbying means to urge or influence lawmakers on the passage of bills or action on an issue.

Figure Focus

Educating and advocating environmental conservation can motivate people to create a more sustainable lifestyle.

NUMBERS GAME

Discuss with students the recycling number system used for plastics. The symbol is a triangle containing a number between 1 and 7. The numbers indicate the following:

- **Number 1:** These are the easiest and most common plastics to recycle. Examples include soda and water bottles and medicine containers. These can be recycled into fiber fill for winter coats, sleeping bags and life jackets; bean bag fill; rope; car bumpers; tennis ball felt; combs; cassette tapes; sails for boats; furniture; and other plastic bottles.

- **Number 2:** Examples of number 2 plastic containers include those that hold laundry detergents and bleaches as well as milk, shampoo, and motor oil. These are often recycled into toys, piping, plastic lumber, and rope. Both 1 and 2 plastics are widely accepted at recycling centers.

- **Number 3:** Examples of number 3 plastics are plastic pipes, shower curtains, medical tubing, and vinyl dashboards.

- **Number 4:** Examples are plastic wrap, grocery bags, and sandwich bags.

- **Number 5:** Examples are plastic storage dishes and pitchers. Items with 3, 4, and 5 are not highly recyclable and are typically not accepted by recycling centers.

- **Number 6:** Examples are polystyrene items such as coffee cups, disposable cutlery, meat trays, packing "peanuts," and insulation. These can be recycled into many items, including cassette tapes and foam insulation. These are widely accepted at recycling centers.

- **Number 7:** These items come from combinations of various other plastics or unique plastic formulations not commonly used. These are the most difficult to recycle and are not normally collected for recycling, although more environmentally conscious consumers can return them to the manufacturer and put the burden on the makers to recycle or dispose of the items properly.

Emphasize that volunteering is an ideal way to make new friends and meet people who have the same interests as you. Explain that being an active citizen in the community is essential to personal wellness.

Find Out What's Going On

Explain that being a volunteer can often open the door to job and career opportunities. For example, volunteering can lead to jobs as a(n):

- Fundraiser
- Nonprofit event planner
- Translator
- Counselor
- Human rights lobbyist
- Children's advocate
- Environmental specialist

Discuss

Explain that anyone who volunteers must also consider the following:

- **Transportation:** How will you get where you need to go? Is it within walking distance? Or will you need transportation? Can you carpool?
- **Schedule:** Make sure you prioritize your activities. You have to balance your volunteer duties with other commitments and activities.
- **Mission:** Understand the mission of the group you are volunteering for. Is the mission in line with your values and standards?
- **Credibility:** Research the group or organization in depth before volunteering to work with them.
- **Adult permission:** While you may be determined to volunteer for a specific organization, your parents might feel differently. Discuss your ideas and intentions with your parents before taking any action.

Getting Involved

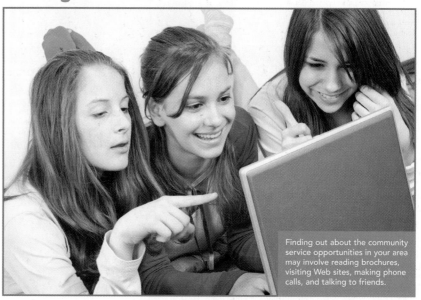

Finding out about the community service opportunities in your area may involve reading brochures, visiting Web sites, making phone calls, and talking to friends.

Are you ready to get involved in community service? You can have a positive impact on the lives of others, including children, the elderly, families, and communities, by participating in volunteer opportunities.

You won't be able to support every worthy cause, of course, so you will need to make some decisions. Here are some things to think about as you begin the process.

- What social and human rights issues are most important to you personally?
- How strongly do you feel about environmental protection?
- How important is it to you to help others get on good financial footing?
- What do you think is the biggest problem facing your local community?
- Would you rather help people close to home, or people in far-away countries?
- Are you interested in animal rights causes or anticruelty issues?

Find Out What's Going On

To find out what organizations exist and what kinds of help they need, think about the types of people who might be interested in that kind of organization, and determine where people like that usually gather. For example, to get information about environmental groups, you might look at a specialty market that sells organic and vegetarian foods. Some other places you can look for community involvement bulletins include:

- College campuses
- Alternative bookstores
- Food co-ops
- Child care centers
- Gardening supply stores
- Youth centers
- Libraries
- Places of worship
- Web sites

Finding Community Service Information on the Web

Almost all organizations have a Web site that publishes contact information, a mission statement, and a schedule of activities and events. Some sites also list requests for volunteer help and application forms for getting started with them. You may need some training or skills development, such as first aid, CPR, child care, or computer training, in order to participate in some programs.

If you know the name of an organization that you want to check out, a simple Web search will probably turn up its Web site. If not, search for keywords representing the general category of organization. You may want to include your city or state name in the search to narrow the results to offices in your own area.

Here are a few sites of popular nonprofit organizations that encourage community involvement.

- American Red Cross: www.redcross.org
  Prepares volunteers to help in emergencies by providing CPR and first aid training, crisis management training, and more
- Habitat for Humanity International: www.habitat.org
  Organizes volunteers to build homes for people who could not otherwise afford them
- The Heifer Project: www.heifer.org
  Helps families earn a livable income by providing them with livestock to care for, breed, raise, and sell
- Greenpeace: www.greenpeace.org/usa
  Organizes volunteers and resources to work for various environmental protection initiatives involving plants, animals, oceans, and toxins
- The Nature Conservancy: www.nature.org
  Promotes nature conservation efforts such as reducing climate change and working for healthy oceans and ecosystems

TECH CONNECT

Think of a community service issue that you care a lot about. It can be anything, from an environmental issue to a human rights issue.

Using the Web and other online resources, such as social networking sites like Facebook or MySpace, identify at least three ways you could connect to other people who also care passionately about the same issue. Share your results with your classmates, comparing the issues that you picked and the types of sites you found.

Why would first aid training be useful to someone who was interested in community service?

Evaluating a Nonprofit Organization

As you are looking for a worthwhile nonprofit organization to work for, consider these factors:

✔ How important is the issue to you that the organization focuses on?

✔ How effective has this organization been in the past? What is their track record?

✔ What percentage of the money the organization takes in goes directly toward fulfilling its mission, and what percentage goes toward the expenses of running the organization (overhead)?

✔ How well does the organization's mission statement match your own beliefs?

✔ What kinds of volunteers does the organization need? Is there anything they need that you can do?

Figure Focus

CPR and first-aid training not only teaches you about basic care and cardiopulmonary resuscitation, it also helps prepare you to "think on your feet." If someone stops breathing or another emergency arises, you have the critical thinking skills to better manage the situation. You are better prepared to assess an injury and decide quickly on the best course of action to take. Many experts believe even minimal knowledge of first aid can be invaluable in any situation, but consider how handy it would be if you were on a nature hike with a local conservationist group and somebody got hurt.

TECH CONNECT

Ways in which you can connect online include online organizing, electronic advocacy, or E-campaigning. Political campaigns mobilize and fundraise on their own home pages. You can react to news by responding to articles on news sites or by blogging. You may send mass e-mails informing people on an issue or e-mail petitions.

Evaluating a Nonprofit Organizations

Explain that in addition to the considerations listed in the text, you should be wary of charities or nonprofits with any of the following characteristics:

- Changed telephone number or no phone at all.
- Fees to participate or fees to the people they help.
- Abusive treatment, verbal and otherwise, toward volunteers and those they are supposed to be helping.
- Post office box as its headquarters.
- Inability to provide detailed explanation of how it is funded and where donations go.

Customized Instruction: At-Risk Students

Have students research resources within your community that offer support for abused or homeless people. They can research on the Internet, contact local government offices, or visit centers that are listed in the phone book. Have students create a brochure that lists the name of the resource and how to contact it, including a street address, Web address, phone number, and contact person, if available.

End-of-Chapter Activities

Case Study

Tony can learn more about the protest by researching the subject online, asking friends if they know anything about it, watching the local news or checking the local newspaper, or by calling local law enforcement to find out if the protesters have organized the protest through them.

In addition to the questions listed on page 197 in the "Evaluating a Nonprofit Organization" feature, Tony should find out if the protesters have an organized and safe protest planned and ask his parents if it is okay for him to go.

Sounding Off!

Student answers will vary.

FAQ

1. A community is a group of people who have a common goal. They may be geographically together or not. They may be very similar or may just have one thing in common.

2. Civic responsibility is the service that you owe to your location-based community, such as obeying laws, serving in the military if drafted, and paying taxes.

3. Legal responsibilities include:
   - Obeying laws.
   - Serving on a jury if summoned.
   - Serving in the military if drafted.
   - Paying taxes.

4. Answers will vary and may include protest marches or sit-ins.

5. Answers will vary and may include errand-running, office work, making signs, staffing booths, tutoring, planting trees, doing physical labor, taking care of children, and providing entertainment.

6. A nonprofit organization is one where the profits are not distributed to shareholders or individual owners, but instead rolled back into the business itself.

7. Answers will vary and may include racial equality, sexual equality, and efforts to help people who are hungry or homeless.

8. 501(c) is the section of the U.S. tax code that specifies what types of organizations are exempt from paying taxes. A 501(c) corporation is one that fits the description in that section of the tax code, such as a charity.

Environmental issues are very important to Tony. He has just found out that some woods that contain an owl habitat are scheduled to be cleared to make room for a shopping mall. Tony has heard that there is a protest scheduled for Saturday morning. However, the information he got about it was very brief and sketchy; he is not even sure what kind of owls they are.

- How could Tony get more information about the planned protest?
- What would be some of the questions Tony should ask to decide whether or not to attend?

Sounding Off!

1. Which of these causes do you think would do the most good in your local community: a program that provided nutritious lunches to home-bound senior citizens, or a program that provided elementary school children with free reading and math tutoring? Why did you choose as you did?

2. Do you think that doing volunteer work is required in order to consider yourself a "good citizen"? Why or why not?

1. Describe the characteristics of a community.
2. Define civic responsibility.
3. List three legal responsibilities that come with citizenship in the United States.
4. Give an example of an act of civil disobedience.
5. List three types of volunteer work that someone your age could do.
6. Explain the characteristics of a nonprofit organization.
7. Give two examples of social equality issues.
8. Explain what a 501(c) organization is.
9. Give two examples of environmental issues.
10. Describe how to get information about a nonprofit organization online.

9. Answers will vary and may include clean water, clean air, anti-littering, anti-pollution standards, and preserving plant and animal life.

10. To get information about a nonprofit online, do a Web search for its name.

Being the leader of a community organization can be challenging. Budgets are typically very low, and volunteers can be hard to manage because you can't use pay as an incentive. It takes a person with very good management skills to do it effectively.

In small teams, interview the leaders of local nonprofit groups, and ask questions like these:

- What do you most enjoy about your job?
- What would you like everyone to know about your organization?
- What is the hardest part about managing a nonprofit?
- Are there volunteer opportunities in your organization for people our age? What would we do?

Write up the information in a report or presentation and share it with your classmates.

Hot Topics

Many laws specific to a local community are designed to prevent nuisances that negatively impact people's lives. For example, a community might have an antilittering ordinance, laws regulating how much noise can be made at night, and so on. Such laws help everyone get along with one another.

Have you ever broken such a law, or witnessed someone else breaking one? For example, have you ever thrown a piece of trash out the window of a car? How do you view such acts? What do you think of a person who does them? Are there any special cases where you think it is okay to break such laws? Use a word processing program, or write out your answers on paper, and drop them into the classroom's Hot Topics box. It's anonymous, so you can be honest and open. Then as a class, read the anonymous entries and discuss them.

Problem Solver

Many residential communities have neighborhood associations that are designed to keep property values high by enforcing certain standards of appearance for the outside areas of the houses and condos. However, some neighborhood associations go too far (at least in the perception of some residents), and try to stifle individuality.

Suppose your grandfather just moved into a neighborhood where the association specifies that owners cannot put up fences. He has a dog and can't let it outside without a fence, so he has to go stand outside with it several times a day—a problem because of his arthritis. What could he do? Brainstorm all the possible actions he could take, and what the outcome of each one would likely be.

Team Players

Students are to interview leaders of local nonprofit organizations using the questions in the text and prepare a report or presentation to share with the class. Emphasize the importance of preparing *before* the interview. Questions should be written out and team members should be assigned duties. For example, who will ask the questions, who will take notes, and who will write up the report? Remind them to dress appropriately and behave professionally.

Hot Topics

Make sure students understand that they can turn in their papers anonymously. Encourage them to be open and honest about the topic and their opinions. During the class discussion, ask students to consider how these experiences generally have a negative impact on the community.

Problem Solver

Some options include:

- Explaining the issue to the local community board and asking them to make an exception.
- Organizing a protest.
- Identifying other neighbors who might support elimination of the fence restriction and preparing a petition to present to the board.
- Putting the dog out on a line instead of accompanying the dog each time it has to go out.

Write Now

Student research should find that Habitat for Humanity uses volunteers to do many things other than building and construction. For example:

- Educating children about the group's mission and its accomplishment
- Translating
- Recruiting other volunteers
- Maintaining and updating databases
- Performing basic clerical tasks
- Assisting with video production

Their letters should discuss volunteer opportunities like those listed above that the friend might feel more comfortable doing.

Be Involved!

Groups should come up with a list of three to five skills they think would benefit their community. They should decide on one skill and then develop a plan on how to make training in the skill available to community members. In addition to the examples in the text (computer and Web development skills and CPR and first-aid certification), some programs that would be useful to a community include those that train on childcare, literacy, and conservation or horticulture.

Web Extra

Students are to create a Web page about their community. Make sure their Web pages illustrate the positive aspects of the community, including housing, schools, and services, such as police and fire protection. Students who do not know how to create a Web page can create a poster instead.

Social Networking

Review with students the following steps for resolving conflicts:

- Give all parties involved a chance to express their views.
- Be respectful of all opinions and views.
- Deal with one problem at a time.
- Focus on the common goals of the community.
- Find ways for all parties in the conflict to be involved in the solution.
- Encourage all parties to take responsibility for their actions, whether they are positive or negative.
- Avoid blame.

Write Now

Many people don't do community service work because they don't feel they have anything to offer. Suppose you have a friend who would like to get involved with Habitat for Humanity (which builds houses for low-income people), but she isn't sure she would be useful because she has a tremor in her hands that makes it difficult for her to hold and use tools. Write a persuasive letter to her, encouraging her to become involved and suggesting some ways that she could benefit the program. Use the Web to research Habitat for Humanity (www.habitat.org) to get any facts you need.

Be Involved!

www.fcclainc.org

To serve your community effectively, you may need to develop some additional skills. For example, if you want to create a Web site for a charity group, you will need computer and Web development skills.

Brainstorm what skills would be valuable for potential volunteers in your community to have, and make a list of three to five types of training that would benefit the community. For example, a community might benefit from having low-cost CPR or first-aid training offered to all teenagers and adults who are interested in being trained.

Pick one of the suggestions, and create a plan for offering it to the community. Divide up the project into several major areas of responsibility, and assign a team of students to each area. Some areas to consider include:

- Finding an instructor to lead the training
- Renting or getting a donation of space to hold the training
- Raising money for the supplies needed
- Tracking the budget and expenses
- Recruiting and organizing volunteers
- Monitoring the schedule and keeping everyone on-task

Carry out the project, with each team doing their part. After the project is over, meet as a class and discuss what went well and what could have been improved.

Using any Web page creation software you like, create a simple Web page to provide information about your community to someone who might be thinking of moving there.

Use other Web sites to collect facts and pictures, and assemble them into a page of your own design. Make sure you appropriately cite the source from which you get the pictures and text.

If you don't know how to create a Web page, use the information that you find to create a poster.

Social Networking

Wherever there are communities of people, there are differences of opinions that lead to conflicts. For example, noise might be a problem; one neighbor might want to have a party, while another one wants it to be quiet so he can sleep.

Make a list of three to five conflicts that neighbors might have who live in a crowded apartment building. Pick a few of them to brainstorm as a class. How could such a conflict escalate into a major problem? How could it be resolved in the early stages peacefully? What could be done if it did get to a point where the residents were very angry at each other? If time permits, choose one of the conflicts to act out as a skit, along with several different resolutions for it.

Part III

Consumer Awareness

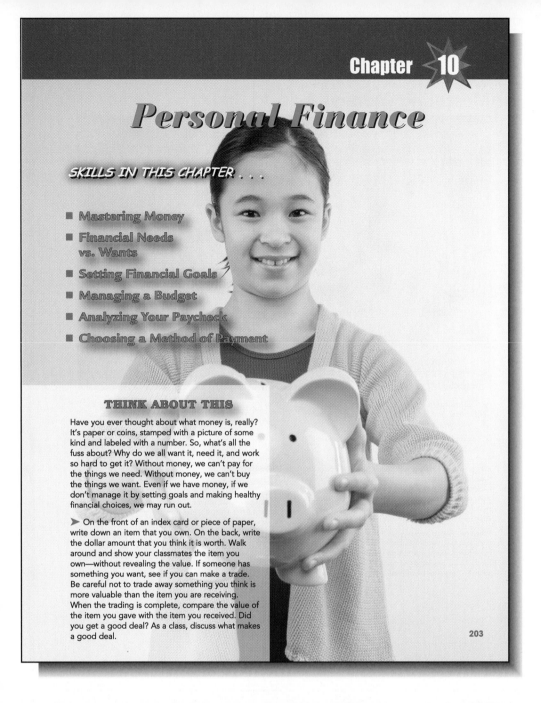

Chapter 10

Personal Finance

SKILLS IN THIS CHAPTER . . .

- Mastering Money
- Financial Needs vs. Wants
- Setting Financial Goals
- Managing a Budget
- Analyzing Your Paycheck
- Choosing a Method of Payment

THINK ABOUT THIS

Have you ever thought about what money is, really? It's paper or coins, stamped with a picture of some kind and labeled with a number. So, what's all the fuss about? Why do we all want it, need it, and work so hard to get it? Without money, we can't pay for the things we need. Without money, we can't buy the things we want. Even if we have money, if we don't manage it by setting goals and making healthy financial choices, we may run out.

➤ On the front of an index card or piece of paper, write down an item that you own. On the back, write the dollar amount that you think it is worth. Walk around and show your classmates the item you own—without revealing the value. If someone has something you want, see if you can make a trade. Be careful not to trade away something you think is more valuable than the item you are receiving. When the trading is complete, compare the value of the item you gave with the item you received. Did you get a good deal? As a class, discuss what makes a good deal.

203

Chapter 10 Overview

This chapter provides an overview of personal finance. It explores the principles of personal finance, which include budgeting, investing, and managing financial tools, such as checking and savings accounts, credit cards, loans, investments, and taxes. The chapter also addresses the ways in which a person obtains and spends monetary resources.

Mastering Money Students learn to identify their personal financial assets and explore the value of money.

Financial Needs vs. Wants This section distinguishes the differences between financial needs and financial wants. It also covers the financial decision-making process.

Setting Financial Goals This section discusses the two main types of financial goals: spending goals, which are buying things you need and want; and saving goals, which are for saving money for the future.

Managing a Budget In this section, students identify the components of a budget (income and expenses). They learn how to prepare a budget and use it to help them manage their money.

Analyzing Your Paycheck This section provides information on paychecks, detailing how they are issued and processed.

Choosing a Method of Payment This section covers various methods of paying for products and services. These include cash, check, and debit and credit cards.

Focus and Engage

Bell-Ringer: Think About This

Students are to write down something they own on one side of a piece of paper and the amount of money they think it is worth on the other side. Then they are to make a trade with another classmate. Students should write down something of significant value to them, such as a purse, MP3 player, or video game. Explain that the goal of this exercise is for students to trade their item for something of equal or greater value.

ADVANCE PREPARATION

Review	*Life Skills for the 21st Century* textbook, Chapter 10.
Prepare	Paper and pencil for some activities. Newspapers and advertising circulars. Calculators. Box labeled "Hot Topics."

CUSTOMIZED INSTRUCTION OVERVIEW

Less Advanced Students	More Advanced Students	ESOL Students	Special Needs Students	At-Risk Students
Pages 205, 211, 214	Pages 212, 215	Pages 206, 216	Pages 205, 211, 214	Pages 209, 216

Introduce the Section

Students learn to identify their personal financial assets and explore the value of money.

Vocabulary

Assets: Property that is owned by a person and to which a value can be assigned.

Denomination: Unit in a scale of value.

Face value: The number printed or stamped on money.

Federal Reserve: Government agency responsible for creating and tracking all of the money in the United States.

Finances: Resources in the form of money.

Figure Focus

Ask students to estimate how much money they typically spend in a week. This would include money for food they buy at school or elsewhere, money for entertainment such as going to the movies or the Friday night football game, and money for gas if they drive. Write the amounts on the board and determine the high, low, and average. Research indicates that teens spend an average of $74 a week, which includes their own and other people's money.

Discuss

Ask students what money-related games they play. Board games, such as Monopoly, Game of Life, and Payday are popular, as are online money games, such as Piggy Bank and Change Maker. Ask them what types of things they learn from these games.

Mastering Money

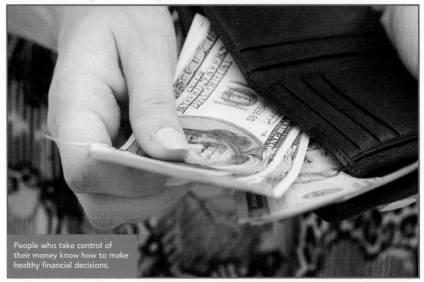

People who take control of their money know how to make healthy financial decisions.

Finances are **assets**, or resources, in the form of money. Your personal finances include the money you earn, spend, and save.

Some people live "hand-to-mouth," or "paycheck-to-paycheck," which means they spend whatever they earn. They may have trouble earning enough to cover their bills, they may not be willing to put their financial needs before their financial wants, or they may not understand money and personal finances enough to make the financial decisions they need to plan ahead. People who live "hand-to-mouth" tend to have a lot of stress, because they are always worrying about not having enough money.

When you take control of your finances, you set financial goals and make healthy financial decisions. You understand how to make sure you have enough money to pay for the things you need and want. Managing your money contributes to your overall well-being.

The Face Value of Money

The **face value**—or **denomination**—of money is the number printed or stamped on it. If you have a bill in your pocket that has a 5 on it, then its face value is 5 dollars. If you have a coin stamped with 25, then its face value is 25 cents.

Face value is determined by the **Federal Reserve**, which is the government agency responsible for creating and tracking all of the money in the United States. The Federal Reserve decides how many $5.00 bills to print, and how many $0.25 coins—quarters—to mint.

Obviously, money is worth more to exchange than the paper and metal it is made from. You know what you can get in exchange for the money, because prices are set by people with goods or services to sell.

- The butcher prices a pound of ground beef at $3.59, so you know you can exchange $3.59 for one pound of ground beef.
- The department store prices a sweater at $19.99, so you know you can exchange $19.99 for that sweater.

Stay in School

The significant difference between a high school graduate's lifetime earnings and that of a high school dropout has been well documented. While education can be the key to higher earnings, it is also linked to the accumulation of assets. Researchers at the University of Michigan have found that, on average, households headed by a high school graduate accumulate ten times more assets than those headed by a high school dropout. So, for every $500 in assets in a household headed by a dropout, there is $5,000 in a household headed by a graduate. Explore with students the opportunities available to them to learn more about personal finance:

- Courses offered at school on personal finance and related topics, such as accounting, economics, and business.
- Local youth development organizations that often provide personal finance workshops and programs. Some of these groups are 4-H, Junior Achievement, and the Jump$tart Coalition for Personal Financial Literacy.
- School-based groups such as Future Business Leaders of America (FBLA); Family, Career and Community Leaders of America (FCCLA); and student councils.
- Community-based banks or credit unions that offer seminars and workshops on personal finance. Some provide savings accounts designed specifically for students.

What Is Money?

Money is anything you exchange for goods or services. In the United States—and most of the world—the money we handle and carry around in our wallets is cash. **Cash** is the money made out of paper—dollar bills—and metal—coins.

Money could be made out of anything. Native Americans used shells. Maasai tribes still use cattle. In most countries now, money is made out of paper and metal because these materials are readily available, easy to work with, and convenient for people to carry.

Cash is not the only type of money we use. We transfer **electronic funds** from one account to a different account using online banking software or a **debit card**. We use **credit cards** to buy something and pay for it later. We write **checks**, which are written orders to a bank to transfer funds from our account to someone else's account. (You will read more about these types of money later in the chapter.)

Before money, people **bartered**, or traded, to get things they needed or wanted. If a farmer had a bushel of tomatoes and needed a roll of barbed wire to build a fence, he would trade with someone who had a roll of barbed wire and needed tomatoes. If he couldn't find someone who needed tomatoes and had barbed wire, he wouldn't be able to make the trade.

To make the exchange easier, people created money. They assigned a specific value to the money, so everyone knew what they had and what it was worth. The farmer could sell his tomatoes to any one with money, and then use the money to buy the barbed wire.

The Real Value of Money

The real value of money is what it is worth to you. How will you spend it? What do you want to get in exchange? The decisions you make about spending your money show your values.

Different people will spend $5.00 in different ways.

- Your mother might exchange it for a loaf of bread and a gallon of milk.
- Your brother might rent a video game.
- You might download five songs for your MP3 player.
- Your friend might save it, because she wants the sweater that costs $19.99. She must wait until she earns an additional $14.99 to purchase the sweater.

Spending Decisions

People make financial decisions based on how much money they have, what they need, and what they want. What if you have $25.00 in your pocket to spend?

★ *You could buy something you need.*

★ *You could buy something you want.*

★ *You could save it for something you might need or want in the future.*

★ *You could donate it to charity.*

★ *You could loan it to a friend.*

What would you do with $25.00?

> If the bill in your pocket has the number 5 on it, then it is worth $5.00. What would you do with $5.00?

International Currency

In the United States our **currency**—type of money—is the dollar. Other countries have different currencies. For example, Mexico uses the peso and India uses the rupee. Some countries call their currency dollars, but these dollars are not the same as U.S. dollars. For example, Canada, Singapore, Australia, and New Zealand all use dollars.

It can get confusing if you travel, because each type of currency has a different value, and the values change all the time. For example, today one U.S. dollar might be worth the same as 48 rupees, but tomorrow it might be worth 50 rupees. In Europe, the countries formed the European Union (EU) and adopted a standard currency—the Euro—to make it easier for people to travel and trade throughout the region.

Use books or the Internet to learn more about the types of currency used around the world. See if you can find pictures and information about the value compared to the U.S. dollar. Create a brief presentation about one country's currency, and present it to the class.

Customized Instruction: Less Advanced/Special Needs Students

Have students take a close look at the money they have in their pockets or wallets. Ask them to list the denominations and to describe the symbols and words that appear on it. You might want to share the following about the $1 bill: The front of the bill features the picture of George Washington. The U.S. Treasury seal is to the right of Washington's picture and contains the balancing scales of justice and 13 stars to represent the original 13 colonies. The Federal Reserve Seal to the left of the picture contains a letter that indicates the issuing Federal Reserve bank. On the back of the bill is the pyramid, which signifies strength and duration, and the eagle, which signifies freedom and independence.

Vocabulary

Barter: Exchange or trade of goods or services.

Cash: Money made out of paper (dollar bills) and metal (coins).

Checks: Written orders to a bank to transfer funds from your account to someone else.

Credit card: A card used to pay for something on credit; buy now and pay later.

Currency: System of money used in a country.

Debit card: A card issued by a banking institution that allows the holder to electronically access his or her funds at any time and at any location that accepts the card.

Electronic funds: Money that is transferred from one bank account to another without any paper money or coins ever changing hands.

Money: Anything you exchange for goods or services.

Spending Decisions

Students are to consider what they would do with $25. Ask for a show of hands of students who have a savings account. Explain how to open a savings account:

- Find a bank where you'd like to open your account.
- Tell the bank what you would like to accomplish with your savings account. Most banks offer a variety of accounts and will be able to suggest the one that will help you meet your goals.
- Bring a photo ID and your Social Security card.
- Some banks require a minimum deposit when you open an account, so you'll need money to place in the account.
- Be sure to ask about any fees.

Figure Focus

Note that the coin denominations currently in circulation in the United States are the cent, nickel, dime, quarter, half dollar, and dollar. The notes are $1, $2, $5, $10, $20, $50, and $100. Production of $500, $1,000, $5,000, and $10,000 denominations stopped during World War II with distribution ending in 1969. The notes are still legal and some are still in circulation, but Federal Reserve banks destroy them as they are received.

International Currency

Students are to research different types of currency used around the world and prepare a brief presentation about one country's currency. Their presentations should indicate the value of the currency as compared to the U.S. dollar, discuss the denominations, and include pictures of the currency.

Introduce the Section

This section distinguishes the differences between financial needs and financial wants. It also covers the financial decision-making process.

Figure Focus

Remind students that a need is something you cannot live without. It is instrumental to your well-being.

A want is something you desire. On the surface, it might *appear* to be instrumental to your well-being but in reality, it only enhances your well-being.

Vocabulary

Financial freedom: Flexibility you have knowing there is money available when you want it.

Financial need: Thing you must buy in order to survive, including food, shelter, and water.

Financial security: Comfort and peace of mind you have knowing there is money available when you need it.

Financial want: Thing you want to buy that will help you maintain a certain standard of living.

Standard of living: Measure of how comfortable you are based on the things you own.

Financial Needs vs. Wants

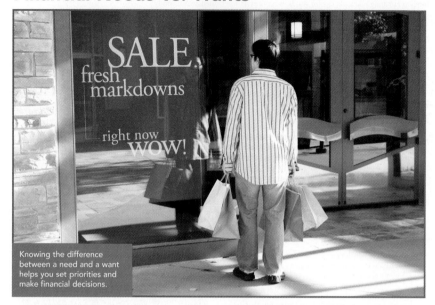

Knowing the difference between a need and a want helps you set priorities and make financial decisions.

Recall from Chapter 1 that a *need* is a fundamental requirement, such as food, oxygen, and water, and a *want* is something that you don't need, but really desire.

Your **financial needs** and **financial wants** cost money. For example, your financial *needs* are the things you must buy in order to survive, including food, shelter, and water.

Your financial *wants* are the things that will help you maintain a certain standard of living. A **standard of living** measures how comfortable you are based on the things you own.

- If you want a standard of living that includes expensive things, such as a big house, fancy car, and designer clothes, then you will spend a lot of money on your wants.
- If you want a standard of living that includes an apartment, used car, and casual clothes, then you will spend less money on your wants.

When you understand the difference between financial needs and wants, you can make healthy choices about what to buy and when to buy it. You can think critically about your options and choose the option that is best for you.

Financial Motivation

Back in Chapter 1, you read that wanting or needing something can be a powerful motivator. When you need money in order to get what you want or need, you are motivated to earn or save. These are two positive motivations, and they can be very good for your happiness and well-being. Both contribute to a positive self-image. Both let you feel proud of your accomplishments and show others that you are responsible.

When you earn money, you have control over it. You get to decide what to buy, how much to spend, and how much to save.

When you save money, you have financial security and financial freedom. **Financial security** is the comfort and peace of mind you have knowing there is money available when you need it. **Financial freedom** is the flexibility you have knowing there is money available when you want it.

Customized Instruction: ESOL Students

Have students list the denominations of money in their country of origin by spelling out the names and writing in currency format; for example, 1 yen and ¥1; 5 yen and ¥5; 10 yen and ¥10; and so on.

Do You Want and Need the Same Things As Your Parents?

Financial needs and wants are different depending on your stage of life. The way a child uses money is not the same as the way a teen, young adult, or adult uses money.

- Children and teens can spend what money they have on their wants; their parents pay for their needs. Children want small items such as snacks and toys. Teens might want more expensive things, such as electronic gadgets or special clothes.

- Young adults are responsible for their own needs and wants. They must use their own income to pay for needs, such as food, shelter, water, electricity, and transportation, as well as for the things they want.

- Adults are responsible for their own needs and wants, as well as for the needs and wants of their family members. They must use their money to provide for the needs of their spouse, children, and sometimes parents. They may not have much left over to buy things they want.

Making Financial Decisions

A financial decision is a decision about how to manage your money. A basic financial decision might be what you should buy for lunch. A more complicated financial decision might be how much money to save for college. To make healthy financial decisions, you must consider your financial needs and wants, as well as how much money you have available.

You can use the decision-making process (Chapter 2) for financial decisions. For example, your bicycle might not be working very well. How can you decide what to do about it?

1. *Identify the decision to be made.* Do you need a new bicycle? Do you need to have your old bicycle repaired?

2. *Consider all possible options.* You could buy a new bike. You could buy a used bike. You could have your old bike fixed. You could use your brother's bike. You don't need a bike.

3. *Identify the consequences of each option.* If you buy a new bike, you will spend a lot of money. You will have less money available for other things. It will cost less to buy a used bike, and less than that to have your old bike fixed. If you have your old bike fixed, it might just break again.

4. *Select the best option.* You decide to have your old bike fixed.

5. *Make and implement a plan of action.* You call a few bike shops to find out what they charge for repairs and how long it will take. You select a shop and take your bike there.

6. *Evaluate the decision, process, and outcome.* Your old bike is working fine. You are happy that you have a bike. You are happy that you spent some money, but not too much.

"I'd really like a new hat, but do I need it?"

Factors to Consider

Things to consider when making a financial decision include:

✔ *Do I have enough money to pay for it?*

✔ *Do I need it?*

✔ *Do I need it now?*

✔ *Do I want it?*

✔ *Why do I want it?*

✔ *Is there something less expensive that would be as good?*

✔ *If I buy it, will I have money left for something else?*

Discuss

Discuss with students the wants their parents normally buy for them and the things they are expected to buy for themselves. For example, do your parents give you money to buy lunch at school, but expect you to pay for food or snacks you want to buy when you are out with your friends? How do students earn their own money? List the ways on the board.

Figure Focus

Ask students to comment on the things that influence their spending decisions. Do they weigh the pros and cons or are they impulse buyers who buy something spontaneously or on impulse and without considering the pros and cons? How could impulse buying negatively affect your financial well-being?

Vocabulary

Financial decision: A decision about how to manage your money.

APPLY IT

Think of an item that you would like to replace in your classroom or maybe even an item that you'd like to see the school replace. Determine ahead of time about how much it will cost to replace the item. As a class, go through the six-step decision-making process to help you make this financial decision.

Factors to Consider

Have students think of one thing they'd really like to buy for themselves and to estimate the price of the item if they don't already know it. Then, have them write answers to the questions listed in the text. For the first question ("Do I have enough money to pay for it?"), students should determine how long it would take them to earn enough money if they don't currently have it.

Introduce the Section

This section discusses the two main types of financial goals: spending goals, which are buying things you need and want; and saving goals, which are for saving money for the future.

Figure Focus

Ask students why setting financial goals will help them focus on what they want to achieve. Explain that setting goals gives us direction. By nature, most humans strive to achieve—financial stability, good health, personal security, loving relationships, and so on. The goals you set for yourself shape the decisions you make and the actions you take.

Vocabulary

Financial goals: The plans you have for using your money.

Discuss

Explain to students that pursuing what we want is conducive to setting goals and going the extra mile to achieve them, but have them consider instances where a person's achieving his goal turned out to be his downfall. For example, you finally saved enough money to buy the video game system you've always wanted. This leads you to play video games for hours a day, which means less time on homework and studying, which results in lower grades at school, which provokes your parents to take away your gaming system until your grades improve and you demonstrate that you've learned how to better manage your time.

Setting Financial Goals

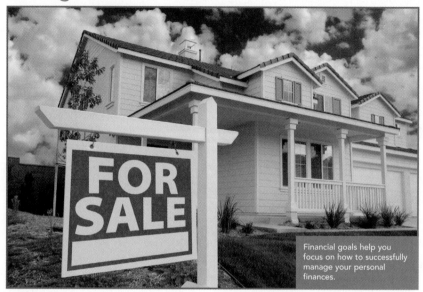

Financial goals help you focus on how to successfully manage your personal finances.

Financial goals are the plans you have for using your money. Like other goals you read about in Chapter 2, financial goals help direct your actions and guide your decision-making. They give you something to work toward. When you set financial goals, you show that you are responsible with money and that you understand the importance of planning for your financial future.

There are two main types of financial goals:

- Spending goals are for buying things you need and want.
- Saving goals are for saving money for the future.

Setting financial goals helps you focus on how you want to use the money you have available. You can decide what you need and want now, and what you will need and want in the future. Then, you can make and implement an action plan for achieving the goal.

Setting Financial Priorities

Money is a limited resource. You have a set amount available, and once you use it, it is gone until you earn more. This means that if you pay for one thing, you may not have enough money left to pay for something else.

For example, you might have $4.00 in your pocket. You need $1.50 to pay for the bus home from school. You need $3.50 to buy a snack. What happens if you buy the snack before you pay for the bus?

When you set financial priorities, you have guidelines to help you make the best decisions about how to manage your money. Setting priorities means that you make a decision about which goal is more important, and you make sure you achieve that goal first.

- You might think it is more important that you have money for the bus, so you put off buying the snack, or you buy a less-expensive snack.
- Your friend might think it is more important to buy the snack, so she walks home from school.

Short-Term and Long-Term Financial Goals

You can use both short-term and long-term goals to manage your finances. Recall from Chapter 2 that short-term goals are for the near future, and long-term goals are for the more distant future.

- You might set short-term financial goals to make sure you have enough money to go to the movies on Saturday night, or to buy a birthday gift for a friend.
- You might set long-term financial goals so you can buy a car when you get your driver's license, go to college after high school, or have money in a retirement account.

You might feel overwhelmed by the thought of setting financial goals. You probably don't even have very much money of your own right now. Breaking long-term financial goals into a series of intermediate goals makes it easier.

For example, your goal might be to have $90.00 to go to the prom. That seems like a lot of money all at once. But, saving $5.00 each month for a year and half seems much more realistic.

Spending Goals and Saving Goals

When you set financial goals, you will probably think first about what you need or want to buy. These are your spending goals. Most of your spending goals right now are short-term, such as an ice cream on the way home from school, or a day at an amusement park. You might have some long-term spending goals, such as the prom.

It's harder to set saving goals. Saving money is not as much fun as spending. It's also hard to think about what you are going to need and want in the future, and how much those needs and wants might cost.

- Will you need to pay for college?
- Will you want to rent an apartment?
- How much will you spend on a car?

Luckily, you don't have to be specific about what you are saving for. Your goal might be to buy a car—but you don't have to know exactly which car, or what it will cost.

Better yet, you can set a goal to save money without having a specific purpose in mind. Your goal might be to save $5.00 each month, not to save $90.00 specifically for the prom. This type of saving goal is open-ended and flexible. It gives you the freedom to know that when you need the money, it will be there.

Tips for Setting Financial Goals

The steps for setting financial goals are similar to those for setting any goal. Some guidelines include:

✔ *Writing down your goals*

✔ *Setting realistic, attainable goals*

✔ *Putting a plan into action*

✔ *Evaluating your progress*

Myth Pennies are worthless.

Truth Coins are money! A handful of pennies might seem worthless, but if you combine the pennies with a handful of quarters, some nickels, and a few dimes, you might be able to buy something.

Try saving your coins in a jar. When the jar is full, take it to your bank or anyplace that has a change-counting machine. You'll be surprised how quickly those coins add up.

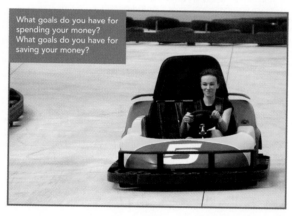

What goals do you have for spending your money? What goals do you have for saving your money?

Teaching Tips

Make sure students distinguish between short-term and long-term goals. Short term means accomplishing the goal in a relatively short period of time, while long term means a time long into the future.

Tips for Setting Financial Goals

Review with students the steps to a goal.

1. Identify the goal and write it down with as much detail as possible.

2. Assess whether the goal is something you really want. Or, is it what someone else wants for you or something you *think* you want because someone else has it?

3. Make a plan for achieving the goal. What resources will you need?

4. Write down your action plan for achieving the goal, being as specific as possible.

Myth/Truth

Ask students if they have seen penny dishes at the checkout counters of stores or restaurants. These are pennies that people donate for others to use if they are a penny short in paying for their purchase. These people think pennies are quite useful.

Figure Focus: Activity

Have students consider both their short-term and long-term spending and saving goals. They should create a table with two columns for short-term and long-term spending goals and two columns for short-term and long-term saving goals. Define short-term goals as those they want to achieve within the next year. Define long-term goals as those they want to achieve within the next two to ten years.

Customized Instruction: At-Risk Students

Have students generate a list of jobs that kids their age can do to earn money. For each job, have them estimate how much they would earn in a week, month, and year. Some examples are babysitting, lawn care, raking leaves, shoveling snow, pet care, refereeing and umpiring youth sporting events, and housework.

Introduce the Section

In this section, students identify the components of a budget (income and expenses). They learn how to prepare a budget and use it to help them manage their money.

Vocabulary

Budget: A plan for spending and saving money.
Expenses: The money that goes out or that you spend.
Income: The money you earn or that comes in to you.

Figure Focus

Explain that people who spend more than they have are "in debt," which means they owe money to someone or some institution. Debt is created when you put off paying for something, as when you charge something on a credit card, or borrow money from your brother. The assumption is that you will eventually make the payment to complete the transaction, but until you do, you are indebted to the other party involved in the transaction. Explain that budgeting can help you avoid debt.

Discuss

Explain the difference between fixed expenses, which are those that tend to be the same each month or each time they're incurred, and variable expenses, which tend to vary. A fixed expense would be rent or the cable bill, while a variable expense would be clothing or entertainment.

Managing a Budget

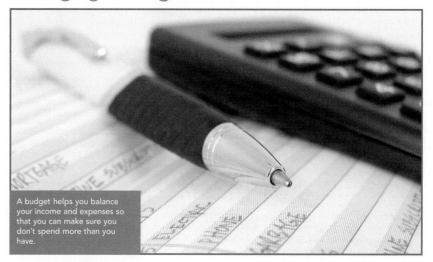

A budget helps you balance your income and expenses so that you can make sure you don't spend more than you have.

A **budget** is a plan for spending and saving money. It helps you manage your money and make healthy financial decisions.

When you make a budget, you keep a record of your **income**, which is the money that comes in to you, and you keep a record or your **expenses**, which is the money that goes out. The goal is to balance the budget—which means making sure that income equals expenses—or to have more income than expenses.

A budget gives you a clear picture of where your money comes from and where it is going. You can use a budget to keep track of the ways you actually use your money, and to set goals and priorities for how you might use your money in the future.

What's in a Budget?

Every budget has two main parts: income and expenses. All the money that comes in to you is income. Income includes:

- Wages and tips you take home from working
- Gifts you receive for birthdays, holidays, and special occasions
- An allowance your parents give you on a regular basis
- Interest that you earn on money in the bank

Expenses are all the ways you use your money. Expenses include:

- Purchases, including needs and wants
- Savings
- Charitable donations

You can set up a budget for any length of time, such as week, or a year. Most budgets are set up for a month, so you can track your income and expenses for one month at a time. A month is convenient because you pay many expenses on a monthly basis, such as rent, telephone, and cable bills, and you often receive income on a monthly basis, as well.

Estimating Is Okay

In theory, setting up a budget is easy. You list your income in one column, your expenses in another, and then subtract your expenses from your income.

In practice, setting up a budget is not quite that easy. Some income and expenses are **fixed**, which means you know what they are each month. But some are **flexible** or **variable**, which means they change from month to month.

- Wages and allowance are fixed income. Gifts and tips are flexible.
- Rent or a lunch card is a fixed expense. Snacks, entertainment, and clothes are flexible.

You can easily enter your fixed income and expenses in a budget, but what do you do about the flexible items? The answer is to estimate. An **estimate** is a guess based on past knowledge or facts. If you know you spent $25.00 on food each of the past two months, you can estimate that you will spend $25.00 this month, too.

The best way to estimate is to look at records of your past income and expenses. For example, a record of how much money you deposited in the bank after your last birthday will give you a good idea of how much you will receive as birthday gifts this year. Receipts from restaurants will give you a good idea of how much you spent last month eating out.

You can use the estimated amounts when you set up your budget, and then go back and adjust them each month by entering the actual amounts you earned or spent.

Setting Up a Budget

The best way to set up a budget is to use a table or spreadsheet. That way you can keep your numbers in neat, organized columns and rows. You list categories of income and expenses in one column, actual amounts in the next column, and estimated amounts in the third column.

There are four basic steps for setting up a budget.

1. *List the categories or types of your monthly income.* For example, list Wages, Allowance, and Gifts. If you know the amounts, enter them in a column to the right of the category. If you don't know the amount, enter an estimate, or guess, in the third column.

2. *List the categories of your regular expenses.* Include things you spend money on each month, such as transportation to and from school, cell phone, club dues, movies and other entertainment, school supplies, clothing, and food. Don't forget to include a category for saving and one for charity. Also include a category called Miscellaneous that you can use for unexpected or one-time purchases. Again, if you know the actual amounts, go ahead and enter them in the column to the right of the category. If not, enter an estimated amount.

3. *Balance your budget.* At the end of the month, go back and replace the estimates with the actual amounts that you spent.

4. *Do the math!* Add your total income and your total expenses, then subtract your total expenses from your total income. If the result is zero or more than zero, congratulations! You have a **surplus**, which means you earned more money than you spent. If the result is less than zero, you have a **deficit**, which means you spent more than you earned.

"I'm not sure how much I'm going to spend on that. Is it okay to guess?"

Monthly Budget

	Actual	Estimated
Income		
Wages	$ 150.00	
Allowance	$ 40.00	
Gifts		$ 20.00
Subtotal	**$190.00**	**$ 20.00**
Total Income		**$210.00**
Expenses		
Bus	$ 30.00	
School Supplies		$ 10.00
Food		$ 45.00
Phone	$ 9.99	
Entertainment		$ 25.00
Clothes		$ 25.00
Dues	$ 5.00	
Miscellaneous		$ 50.00
Charity	$ 5.00	
Savings	$ 5.00	
Subtotal	**$ 54.99**	**$155.00**
Total Expenses		**$209.99**

Vocabulary

Deficit: Spending more than you earned.
Estimate: A guess based on past knowledge or facts.
Fixed expense: One that is the same each month.
Flexible or variable expense: One that fluctuates or varies from month to month.
Surplus: Earning more money than you spent.

Figure Focus

While it is appropriate to estimate variable expenses, stress the importance of realistic estimates. For example, if you know you will need to buy a new pair of sneakers, check out prices advertised in newspapers or online or visit the store where you plan to shop for them ahead of time. If you underestimate, you could end up with expenses that exceed your income.

APPLY IT

Have students set up their own personal budgets using the steps described in the text and the example provided. Encourage them to look through newspapers or circulars that might advertise items on which they can base their estimates of items such as clothes, shoes, or entertainment. Or, they might go online to research costs. Allow them to use calculators to total income and expenses. How many students ended up with a surplus? How many with a deficit?

Customized Instruction: Less Advanced/Special Needs Students

Have students create a budget for a class party. Assume each student will donate $2 for party supplies, snacks, and drinks. The expenses include decorations; paper plates and cups; napkins; drinks; store-bought snacks such as cupcakes, cookies, popcorn, and pretzels; and a party favor for each student and the instructor. If students need help estimating the costs of items, here are some guidelines.

- Decorations (balloons, streamers, etc.): $5–$7
- Plates: $1 for 50 paper plates
- Cups: $2.25 for 24 count
- Napkins: $2 for 100 count
- Drinks: $1.25 per 2-liter container
- Cupcakes or large bakery-type cookies: $3 per dozen
- Popcorn, pretzels, chips: $3 per 14- to 16-oz. bag, assuming 1 oz. serving size
- Party favor: $.50 per person

Encourage them to come up with a *balanced* budget or one that results in a surplus.

Ways to Increase Income

Ask students to comment on the skills or talents they have that they could use to start a business. For example, do you know how to play an instrument, such as the piano or guitar, and could you offer lessons? Are you a sports enthusiast and could coach or umpire/referee youth sporting events? Also, consider your interests and hobbies. Maybe you love dogs so you've cooked up a dog treat for your own pet that you could sell to other dog lovers.

Vocabulary

Unexpected expenses: Purchases you have not planned.

Figure Focus

Emphasize that having a written budget to refer to can help you make decisions about the things you want. If an item costs more than what you estimated, you can check your budget to see if money can be reallocated from another expense category.

MONEY MADNE$$

Two video games at $3.50 each equal $7.00. Add the $7.00 to $8.50 for the movie ticket to get a total of $15.50 spent on entertainment so far. Subtract $15.50 from $25.00 and you have $9.50 left to spend.

Ways to Increase Income

It can be hard for a teen to find income, let alone find a way to earn more. Most states have laws regulating how many hours a teen can work. Many employers don't want to hire anyone younger than 16. What if you want to increase your income?

★ *Could you work more hours?*

★ *Could you ask for a raise?*

★ *Could you find a different job?*

★ *Could you work more than one job?*

★ *Could you ask your parents for a larger allowance?*

One way teens can earn more money is to start a business of their own. You might be able to mow lawns, babysit, or shovel snow. You might be able to fix computers for your neighbors, or sell jewelry you make yourself. What skills or talents do you have that you could use to start your own business?

What Does It All Mean?

After you set up your budget, you can see exactly how you are spending your money. This might come as a surprise. Did you realize you spent so much money on food and entertainment? Are you shocked by how little you save?

To get the most out of your budget, take the time to make it work for you. Look it over. Highlight the flexible income and expense categories. Identify areas where you might be able to make changes.

■ What are your priorities? You might see that you spend a lot on clothes, but very little on charity. Maybe you could spend $5.00 a month less on clothes, and donate $5.00 more a month to charity.

■ What are your financial goals? You might see that you spend a lot of money on the bus. Could you walk to school, or ride your bike? If so, you could save that money instead of spending it on the bus.

Unexpected Expenses

Remember that Miscellaneous category you included in your budget? It's very important. It's the money you use to pay for **unexpected expenses**, such as when you need to pay your brother back for losing his basketball, or when you have to replace a flat tire on your bike.

Unexpected expenses are purchases you have not planned. They are not covered by the money in one of the regular expense categories. If you leave them out of your budget, you might not be able to pay for them when you need to.

When adults forget to budget for unexpected expenses, they can find themselves in financial trouble. The car might need a new transmission. A toothache might require oral surgery. If they don't have the money in the budget somewhere, they might be forced to use savings they wanted for something else, or cut back spending in another category, or charge the expense on a credit card to pay for later.

"It costs more than I planned. Should I buy it anyway?"

Of course, you might decide to use your miscellaneous expense money for something other than an emergency. You might use it to buy a special piece of clothing, or to pay for admission to a museum.

What could you do with money you budgeted for miscellaneous expenses if you don't use it?

MONEY MADNE$$

> Each month you budget $25.00 for your entertainment expenses. This month, you already went to the movies once and rented two video games. Your friends want you to go with them to an arcade. If a movie ticket costs $8.50, and the video games cost $3.50 each, how much money will you have to spend at the arcade?

Customized Instruction: More Advanced Students

Have students select one of the expense categories they listed in the personal budgets they prepared earlier. If they did not prepare a budget, have them select one of the categories shown in the Monthly Budget on page 211 of the text. Have them estimate their expenses in that category month by month for a year.

Staying on Budget

Staying on budget means using your money according to your plan to achieve your financial goals. It doesn't mean you have to earn exactly the amount you entered as income in your budget. It doesn't mean you have to spend exactly the amount you entered as expenses. There's room for flexibility.

You might notice halfway through the month that you already spent the entire amount you budgeted for entertainment. Now, you have choices:

- Do you stop spending on entertainment?
- Do you use money you have budgeted for something else to pay for entertainment?
- If so, which money do you use? Savings? Charity? Food? Miscellaneous?

If you find that your budget is very different from your actual income and expenses every month, you might want to make some changes. You can evaluate your budget to decide if you need to adjust the amounts. Maybe you were being unrealistic when you set the budget amount for entertainment at $25.00. Maybe you really only need $30.00 a month for food.

Lose the Deficit

If you have a deficit, it means you are spending more money than you are earning every month. You might get away with a deficit for a month or two, but eventually you will run out of money.

To have enough money to achieve your financial goals, you'll have to eliminate the deficit. That means making the tough choices. Are there expenses you can reduce or eliminate? How much can you save if you:

- Watch free movies on demand instead of going to the theater
- Bring snacks to school instead of buying them
- Use your computer for e-mail instead of texting from your cell phone
- Drink tap water from a refillable bottle instead of buying bottled water

You might also be able to increase your income. If you have more money to spend, you might be able to cover the expenses the way you have them now, without a deficit.

Job Search

If you think you are good at planning budgets, and you enjoy giving people advice on how to save and spend, you might want to look for a career as a certified financial planner. A financial planner, or personal financial planner, helps people manage their finances by advising them on how to budget, spend, and save.

Certified financial planners must pass a series of certification exams such as those offered by the Certified Financial Planner Board of Standards. Most study financial planning at the college level, as well.

Use the Internet, library, or your school's guidance resources to learn more about a career in financial planning. Write a job description, including the educational requirements, career pathway, and potential salary range.

"How can I adjust my budget so I don't run out of money before the end of the month?"

What Happened to My Surplus?

You set up your budget and it shows that your expenses are less than your income. You should have a surplus, but instead you find yourself running out of money before the end of the month. What's going on?

- 👎 You are not being honest about how much you are spending.
- 👎 You left an expense category out of the budget.
- 👎 You are using estimated amounts instead of filling in the actual amounts.
- 👍 You had more than one unexpected expense in the month. It's a one-time occurrence and you'll be back on track next month.

Being honest about your spending is important. Remember, budgets are flexible. If it's not working, figure out what you need to make it work, and then take action to fix it. What steps can you take to turn a deficit into a surplus?

Reinforce and Review

Review the terms surplus and deficit. When you earn more money than you spend, you end up with a surplus. When you spend more than you earn, you end up with a deficit.

Figure Focus

Ask students to share ideas on how to pare down their expenses. Do you "comparison shop" to find the lowest cost? The most effective way to comparison shop is to check three or four different sources for the same product. Do you check the paper for coupons, sales, and other purchasing incentives? Can you defer a purchase to a later date?

What Happened to My Surplus?

Emphasize the importance of keeping receipts and accurately recording your expenses. Suggest that students store receipts in a marked envelope and keep a log handy where they can record expenses for which they do not have a receipt.

Job Search

Students are to write a job description for a financial planner. The education requirements vary. To be a certified financial planner (CFP), you must pass an exam administered by the Certified Financial Planner Board of Standards. Candidates who take the exam must have a bachelor's degree plus additional coursework in financial planning areas, such as retirement or estate planning. After passing the exam, you must demonstrate that you have experience working in the financial planning field. In addition, you must adhere to the CFP code of ethics, and you are required to complete certain continuing education requirements on an on-going basis in addition to paying a licensing fee every two years. Although a CFP designation is not required to work as a financial planner, most employers desire it, and it is helpful for advancement. Many financial planners advance to positions of greater responsibility or opt to open their own businesses. At the time of this writing, the median annual salary for a financial planner was $67,700.

Introduce the Section

This section provides information on paychecks, detailing how they are issued and processed.

Figure Focus

Explain that cashing a paycheck is easiest if you have your own bank account. If you do not, you can take the check to the bank it was written from. The bank will normally cash the check, but you will need at least one photo ID (sometimes they'll request two, plus a credit card). If the issuing bank does not have a branch conveniently located for you, you can go to a check-cashing service, but they normally charge a fee and might require a contract.

Discuss

Explain that most paychecks have two parts. The paycheck itself is the part you take to a bank to exchange for cash or to deposit in an account you have with the bank. The pay stub provides information on deductions applied to your gross pay, such as those for taxes and Social Security, to derive your net pay, which is how much you "take home." Deductions from pay can be voluntary or involuntary. Examples of voluntary deductions include contributions to retirement through a 401(k) plan; insurance premiums for medical, dental, or eye care; and child care. Examples of involuntary deductions include Social Security, Medicare, and income taxes.

Vocabulary

Deduction: An amount that your employer withholds from your earnings to pay for things such as taxes or insurance; also referred to as *withholding*.

Direct deposit: Arrangement in which your employer directly deposits your paycheck in your account instead of giving you a paycheck.

Pay period: The number of days for which you are being paid.

Discuss

Make sure students can distinguish between hourly and salaried employees. At the time of this writing, the federal minimum wage was $7.25 an hour, although many states set their own minimum wage rates.

Analyzing Your Paycheck

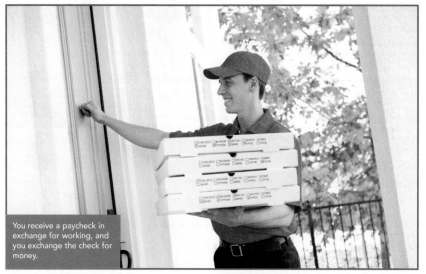

You receive a paycheck in exchange for working, and you exchange the check for money.

The way most people get income is by working. Up to now, most of the jobs you had probably paid you in cash. When you work for a business, however, you receive a paycheck. Your paycheck is a written document that tells your employer's bank how much money to give to you. It is your payment for working.

Most paychecks have two parts: the paycheck itself and the pay stub. The paycheck is the part you take to the bank to exchange for cash or to transfer funds into your account. The pay stub provides information about your pay, including how much you have earned and how much your employer has deducted from your pay. A **deduction**—which is sometimes called withholding—is an amount that your employer withholds from your earnings to pay for things such as taxes or insurance.

Many employers directly deposit your paycheck in your account instead of giving you a paycheck. Even if you have a **direct deposit** arrangement, you will receive a pay stub so that you know how much you earned and how much was deducted.

What's a Pay Period?

A **pay period** is the number of days for which you are being paid. You receive a paycheck for every pay period. Pay periods are different depending on the employer. Common pay periods are one week, two weeks, or one month. Most people receive a paycheck every two weeks or once a month. When you are considering a job, one of the things to think about is how often you will get paid.

- If you are an *hourly employee*, you are paid based on the number of hours that you work. The amount of your paycheck might change from pay period to pay period, depending on how many hours you work.
- If you are a *salaried employee*, you are paid a fixed amount, which is usually set for a year and then divided equally among the pay periods. The amount of your paycheck will be the same each pay period, no matter how many hours you work.

Customized Instruction: Less Advanced/Special Needs Students

Make enlarged copies of the paycheck shown at the top of the next page and pass out to students. Have them label the parts of the check as follows:

- Name and address of employer
- Check number
- Date of check
- Recipient or payee
- Amount of check in (1) number format and (2) spelled out
- Authorized signature representing employer

Using a Paycheck

A paycheck looks like a personal check you might write. Most paychecks include:

- Your employer's name and address in the upper-left corner
- A check number
- The date of the check
- Your name as the recipient, or payee
- The amount of the check written in numbers and spelled out
- The signature of a person authorized by your employer in the lower-right corner

Your paycheck is just a piece of paper until you deposit it or cash it. You must endorse—sign—the back of the check to make it valid. It's a good idea to sign it at the bank, because once you sign it, anyone can cash it or deposit it.

There are two types of endorsements:

- A *blank endorsement* is when you just sign your name. The check can be cashed or deposited by anyone, for any purpose.
- A *restrictive endorsement* is when you sign your name, and below it write how the check should be used. For example, you can write "For Deposit Only," if you want the check to be deposited, or you can write "Pay to the Order of Jack Smith" if you want the check to be used by Jack Smith.

If you lose your paycheck, you will have to follow your company's procedure for canceling it and issuing a new one.

Using a Pay Stub

A pay stub is attached to the paycheck and provides a lot of information about the money you earned. It has no cash value, and you cannot exchange it for money at the bank. Most pay stubs have four sections.

- Personal information about the employee. This usually includes the check number and date, the starting and ending dates of the pay period, your name, and your employee number.
- Information about earnings. This usually includes the number of hours you worked, your hourly wage, and the amount you are being paid this pay period.
- Information about deductions. Employers withhold state and federal taxes, as well as **FICA**, which is social security. They may also withhold local taxes. (There's more about taxes in Chapter 12.) The amount of these deductions is based on a percentage of how much you earn. You might have other deductions such as contributions to a health care plan or to a savings account.
- Information summarizing earnings and withholdings for the current pay period and the year-to-date (**YTD**), which is since January 1 of the current year. In this section, you can see your **gross income**, which is your pay before withholdings, and your **net income**, which is your pay after withholdings. Some people call net pay "take-home pay," because it is the amount you actually take home.

It is important to look closely at your pay stub to make sure the information is correct, particularly the number of hours worked. If there are any errors, you will have to follow your company's procedure for correcting them.

Vocabulary

Endorse: To sign the back of a check to make it valid.

FICA (Federal Insurance Contributions Act): Act that requires an employer to withhold a set percentage of an employee's pay each pay period and contribute that money to the federal Social Security Trust Fund, which provides income, disability insurance, health care, and other benefits to retirees.

Gross income: Pay before withholdings.

Net income: Pay after withholdings.

Figure Focus

Help students distinguish between gross pay and net pay. Gross pay is total pay before any deductions are applied. Net pay is what you take home after deductions are applied. Here are the standard deductions applied to most employees' paychecks:

- Federal income tax: The amount depends on how much you make. Tax rates currently range from zero to 35%.
- FICA (includes Social Security and Medicare tax): This is currently at 7.65%.
- State income tax: These vary by state and range from none to 9.5% at the time of this writing. Some states also deduct for unemployment and disability taxes.
- Municipal income tax: An earnings tax is applied to employees who work in the municipality.

Customized Instruction: More Advanced Students

Have students use a calculator to figure out their gross annual pay if they work 100 hours for each of nine months at $9.25 an hour, and 140 hours for each of three months at $9.25 an hour. Then, have them calculate their net annual pay using the following deductions:

- Federal income tax: 10%
- FICA: 7.65%
- State income tax: 5.5%
- Municipal income tax: 2.1%

To calculate gross annual pay:

- $100 \times 9 = 900$ hours $\times$ $9.25 = $8,325
- $140 \times 3 = 420$ hours $\times$ $9.25 = $3,885
- $8,325 + $3,885 = $12,210

To calculate federal income tax:

- $12,210 \times 10\% (.10) = $1,221

To calculate FICA:

- $12,210 \times 7.65\% (.0765) = $934.07

To calculate state income tax:

- $12,210 \times 5.5\% (.055) = $671.55

To calculate municipal income tax:

- $12,210 \times 2.1\% (.021) = $256.41

To calculate net annual pay:

- $12,210 − ($1,221 + $934.07 + $671.55 + $256.41)
- $12,210 − $3,083.03 = $9,126.97

Introduce the Section

This section covers various methods of paying for products and services. These include cash, check, and debit and credit cards.

Figure Focus

Ask students how they pay for things. How many use cash for all purchases? How many use their own debit cards or credit cards?

Discuss

Explain that in general, an individual must be at least 18 years of age to obtain a debit card, apply for a credit card, or open a checking account.

- Banks will sometimes issue debit cards to customers between the ages of 16 and 18 if an adult signs as the joint owner of the account.

- The legal age in the United States to obtain a credit card is 18, although you can obtain one through your parents or legal guardian, which means they are ultimately responsible for your account.

- In most states, you must be 18 years old to open a checking account (in others, it is 21 years of age). But some banks will open checking accounts for minors if, for example, their parents are good customers. Community-based banks or credit unions might also be willing to open the account, especially if a parent will co-sign.

Choosing a Method of Payment

The method of payment you choose depends on the type of purchase, how much it costs, and convenience.

You use money to pay for expenses. At the beginning of this chapter, you read that there are many types of money including cash, checks, credit cards, debit cards, and electronic funds. The type of money you use to make a payment depends on many things, including the type of purchase.

- For a purchase you make in person, you might use cash, a debit card, or a credit card.
- For a payment you send in the mail, you might use a check.
- For a payment you make over the Internet, you might use a debit card, credit card, or electronic funds.

Other factors include the amount of the purchase and convenience. For example, if something costs a lot of money, you might choose to use a credit card because you can pay for it later. A debit card might be convenient because you do not have to keep going to the bank for more cash.

Benefits and Drawbacks

Each method of payment has benefits and drawbacks. You can use your decision-making skills to consider each option before choosing a method of payment.

- When you use cash, you know you can afford what you are buying. But, if you lose your cash, or it is stolen, there is no way to get it back.
- Sending a check through the mail is safer than sending cash, but the mail might be late, making the payment late.
- A debit card is convenient, but if someone steals it, he might be able to use all the money in your bank account.
- A credit card is useful, but it might end up costing you a lot more than the original purchase price if you do not pay off the credit card charges each month.

Customized Instruction: At-Risk/ESOL Students

Pair up an ESOL student with one of your at-risk students. The at-risk student will be the bank teller; the ESOL student will be the bank customer. Have the ESOL student approach the "teller" to:

1. Open a savings account
2. Make a withdraw from a savings account
3. Make a deposit to a savings account
4. Cash a check

The focus of this instruction should be on the ESOL student's correct pronunciation and understanding of basic banking transactions.

When Should I Use Cash?

Between debit cards, check cards, electronic funds, and credit cards, it almost seems as if no one uses cash anymore. But cash is a good option for most purchases.

- When you use cash, you know you have enough money to pay for the purchase. You don't have to worry about whether there is enough money in your bank account to cover a check or a debit, or if you will have enough money to pay a credit card bill in the future.
- Some businesses give you a discount for paying with cash. Gas stations often charge less per gallon for cash. In some stores, you may be able to negotiate a lower price if you pay with cash.
- Cash is useful if you need to buy a drink from a vending machine, pay for a parking meter, or pay a toll. You may also need it to tip for service.

The biggest drawback to using cash is that it can be lost or stolen. There is very little chance you will recover cash once someone else has it. It can also be inconvenient to keep going to the bank or Automated Teller Machine (ATM) to withdraw cash so you have it when you need it.

What's a Check?

When you write a check, you are **authorizing**—giving permission to—your bank to transfer money from your account to the account of the **payee**—the person whose name you write on the check. In order to pay by check, you must have a checking account with a bank, and you must have enough money in the account to cover the amount of the check (there's more about checking accounts in Chapter 11).

Paying by check can be convenient, because:

- You do not have to carry cash.
- You can send a check through the mail.
- If a check is lost or stolen, your bank can stop payment, or cancel the check so that it cannot be exchanged for money.

If you use a checking account, it is important to keep the account **balanced**. That means you must keep track of how much money is in your account, as well as the amounts of all the payments you have made. If you make more payments than you have money, your account will be **overdrawn**—in deficit. Most banks charge a large fee if you overdraw your account.

When do you think it is a good idea to pay with a check?

Drawbacks to Paying by Check

Some drawbacks to paying by check include:

✔ *You must have a check with you in order to use it.*
✔ *Most banks charge you to buy checks.*
✔ *Banks may charge a fee for every check you write.*
✔ *Not every business accepts checks.*
✔ *Some businesses accept a check only if you can show a valid photo identification, such as a driver's license.*
✔ *Some businesses will not accept a check from a bank in a different city or state.*
✔ *Checks take time to clear—go through the process of verification so your bank will transfer the funds to the other person's bank.*
✔ *If there is not enough money in your account, the check will bounce, which means the payment will not be made. You will be responsible for repaying the original bill along with penalty fees.*

Vocabulary

Bounce: Caused when there are insufficient funds in an account to cover the amount of the check.
Clear: The process of check verification so that your bank will transfer the funds to the other person's bank.

Reinforce and Review

Review the following terms and definitions with students:

- **Cash:** Your dollar bills and coins.
- **Electronic funds:** Money that is transferred from one bank account to another without any paper money or coins ever changing hands.
- **Debit card:** A card issued by a banking institution that allows the holder to access his or her funds electronically at any time and at any location that accepts the card.
- **Credit card:** A card used to pay for something on credit; buy now and pay later.
- **Checks:** Written orders to a bank to transfer funds from your account to someone else.

Vocabulary

Authorizing: Giving permission to your bank to transfer money from your account to the payee.
Balanced: Keeping track of how much money is in an account and how much has been paid out.
Overdrawn: When you have made more payments than you have money in an account to cover them.
Payee: The person who receives a payment.

Figure Focus

Discuss with students the instances in which they have seen their parents pay for something with a check. Do they write out checks to pay for school-related fees, such as yearbook photos or spirit wear? Do they write checks to pay the mortgage or rent, utilities, and credit card bills?

Drawbacks to Paying by Check

Explain to students the importance of carefully reviewing the monthly statement most banks provide to account holders. These statements provide a summary of all transactions that occurred during a given period of time. They list the checks you have written, including the date the check cleared, the number of the check, and the amount; the method by which the checks have been processed (electronic fund transfers vs. regular check transactions); deposits, including the date of the deposit and the amount; and any transactions involving the use of an ATM (automated teller machine) and debit card. In addition, the statement will show your balance at the beginning of the period and at the end, and it will also list any interest earned (if applicable).

21st Century Skills

What Happens Next?

Students are to write or prepare a skit on the ending to the story. Alisha is facing a number of problems. Where will she get the money to pay off the credit card bill? Will she have to borrow from her family and friends? Will she have to pay it off in increments and pay interest and other fees on top of what she already owes?

Review with students the steps to solving a problem.

1. Identify the problem.
2. Consider possible solutions.
3. Identify consequences.
4. Select the best solution.
5. Develop a plan of action.

Vocabulary

Interest: Borrowing charge that is normally a percentage of the purchase price.

Personal identification number (PIN): Password assigned to a debit card identifying that the person who entered it is authorized to use the card.

I Lost My Debit Card!

Explain to students that debit cards fall under the Electronic Fund Transfer Act. Under this act, if a card is lost or stolen, any loss you might suffer is limited to $50 if you notify the bank within two business days. The loss could be as high as $500 if you wait more than two business days. If you fail to report the loss within 60 business days, you risk unlimited loss on transfers made after the 60-day period. In other words, you could lose all the money in the account, plus you would be responsible for paying overdraft fees, or those an account holder owes the bank because more has been withdrawn from the account than has been credited to it.

With a check, you normally don't have to worry about someone stealing it and cashing it or using it to somehow access your checking account. Most institutions will not cash a check without a valid ID. But check writing is not as quick and convenient as debit cards. Offer these safety considerations:

- Use a PIN-only debit card instead of just a signature-based card.
- Be on the lookout for "shoulder surfers" when you are entering your PIN number.
- Don't keep your PIN number with your debit card.
- Don't respond to unsolicited e-mail requesting account numbers or passwords.

---

218 Chapter 10 ■ Personal Finance

21st Century Skills

What Happens Next?

Alisha received a preapproved credit card in the mail. She started using it right away to buy clothes and jewelry and to take her friends out for lunch. It was very convenient because she didn't have to carry money. She bought things she didn't need and things she would never use. She bought gifts for her family and friends. She felt rich.

When the first bill arrived, Alisha owed $1,250.00! At first she thought the bill was wrong, but when she added up everything she had bought, she realized it was correct.

Alisha started to panic. She knew she didn't have that much money in her bank account. She did not know what to do.

What problems and choices are facing Alisha? Did she make mistakes? Can she find solutions? Using your 21st Century Skills—such as decision making, goal setting, and problem solving—write an ending to the story. Read it to the class, or form a small group and present it as a skit.class, or form a small group and present it as a skit.

I Lost My Debit Card!

Losing a debit card is not quite as bad as losing cash. Another person can use it only if he knows your PIN. What if you lose your debit card?

★ *Report the lost card to your bank immediately.*

★ *Go back to the places you shopped to see if they found your card.*

★ *Check your bank account to see if there are any unauthorized transactions.*

Your bank will cancel the card and issue you a new one. You may be responsible for unauthorized transactions. Do you think using a debit card is safer or riskier than using checks?

I Have a Debit Card

A debit card is just like cash except it is more convenient. You must have a bank account in order to use a debit card, and there must be enough money in the account to cover your purchases. Most cards will be declined if there is not enough money in the account to cover the expense.

When you use a debit card, the money is automatically and immediately transferred out of your bank account, just as if you withdrew it as cash.

Most debit cards require you to enter a **personal identification number (PIN)** before each use. By entering the PIN, you prove that you are the person authorized to use the card.

The biggest risk of a debit card is that if someone else gets hold of your debit card and knows your PIN, he or she can use it to access your money.

Because they are just like cash, debit cards are accepted for payment almost everywhere you can buy something, including stores, restaurants, and online.

I Have a Credit Card

A credit card lets you use **credit**—a loan—to buy now and pay later. Every time you use a credit card, you are borrowing money from the business that issued the card, such as the bank, store, or credit card company. The business pays for the purchase, and then you repay the business by paying your credit card bill. (There's more about credit in Chapter 12.)

"I'm pretty sure I have enough money to pay for this. What if I don't?"

Credit cards may be convenient, because you do not have to have enough money to pay at the time you make the purchase. You can also make a lot of purchases, and then pay them all at once with a single check by paying your credit card bill. However, if you don't pay your credit card bill in full each month, you can end up spending a lot more than the original purchase price.

- If you do not pay your credit card bill in full each month, you must repay the original amount of the purchase plus **interest**—a percentage of the purchase price.
- If you pay your credit card bill late—past the due date—or if you pay less than the minimum amount due, you must pay a late fee.
- If you only pay the minimum amount due, you may never be able to pay off the balance, which will keep getting larger as the interest adds up.
- Most credit card businesses charge an annual fee for using the card.

Figure Focus

Review with students the importance of reviewing their bank statements every month. They can also check balances on accounts through ATM machines and through online access.

218 Chapter 10 ■ Personal Finance

How Can I Use Electronic Funds?

You use electronic fund transfers (EFT) to transfer money from one bank account to another. To use an EFT, you must have electronic access to your bank account and enough money in your bank account to cover your purchases. There are three common methods of using EFT:

- A debit card. When you use your debit card, the money is transferred from your account to the seller.
- Online banking. If your bank account is set up for online banking, you can use the bank's online banking system to transfer money from your account to other accounts. You can make the transfer from your home computer or from a bank machine. You can transfer the money to almost any other account, so you can pay bills such as utilities, credit cards, and even taxes.
- Online payment services. Many online retailers such as eBay have their own online banking system that you can use to transfer funds electronically. You must set up an account and make sure you have money available to cover your purchases.

What Is Layaway?

Years ago before credit cards were popular, some retailers offered layaway plans. A **layaway plan** lets you pick out an item you want to buy and then make small payments over time. When you have paid for the item in full, you can take it home. Layaway plans have seen a resurgence due to tight economic times.

- A layaway plan is convenient if you do not have enough money to buy the item all at once, but know that you can afford to pay a little bit at a time.
- It is inconvenient because you cannot take the item home until you have paid for it completely, which might be a while.

Not all retailers offer layaway plans. Those that do may have their own rules and regulations. Before committing to purchasing something on layaway, make sure you understand the rules. Can you get your money back if you change your mind? Can you skip a payment? What is the longest amount of time you have to pay in full? Does the store charge a fee?

Single Transfer

✕✕ Citizens Bank

Home | Manage Accounts | Pay Bills | Transfers | Service Center

Transfer Funds | Manage Other Transfer Accounts

Summary | Single Transfer | Repeating Transfer | Multiple Transfers | External Accounts | S

Single Transfer

Shortcuts...

You can save transfer instructions for future use.

Select Saved Transfer:* [Select... ▾]

OR

From Account:* [Circle Savings - xxxxx1075 Bal. $3,337.82 ▾]

To Account:* [Circle Checking - xxxxx5002 Bal. $758.56 ▾]

Amount:* [100.00]

Date:* [09/16/2012]   Make Repeating

Memo: [car insurance]

Learn more about your fees and limits for Transfers Outside the Bank

* indicates a required field

[SEND TRANSFER]   [SAVE TRANSFER]   [CANCEL]

What do you think are the benefits and drawbacks of electronic fund transfers?

TECH CONNECT

A **secure Web site** uses **encryption**—codes—and authentication standards to protect online transaction information. That means your personal information including debit card numbers and PINs are safe when you shop online.

You can tell that you are viewing a secure Web site because the letters "https" display to the left of the Web site name in the Address bar of your browser. On an unsecured site, there is no "s." Also, a small lock icon displays in your Web browser's status bar. You can double-click the lock icon to display details about the site's security system.

Why do you think it is important to use a secure Web site when you are shopping or banking online?

Vocabulary

Layaway plan: Plan offered by retailers that allows a customer to make small payments over time on an item and to take the item home once it is paid for in full.

Figure Focus

Explain that most people find EFTs to be convenient and effective. In most cases, it costs nothing and can often be done from your computer as long as you have an account number and the authority to conduct the transaction.

On the downside, people tend to think an automated system is infallible, but in truth, errors occur. You have to check your account statements diligently. Also, funds are usually released much quicker from your accounts than when using a paper system, so you must be sure sufficient funds are in the account to cover the transaction. On the other hand, if you use EFTs to pay bills, there is often a two- to four-day processing period. So, if you don't initiate the payment early enough, this could result in a late payment and a late fee.

TECH CONNECT

Much has been written about identity theft and computer hackers who illegally access consumer credit card and other financial information. Using a secure site to conduct online shopping or other financial transactions reduces the risk of outsiders accessing your personal financial information. When transactions go through a secure server, account numbers are encrypted, or scrambled, so no one can recognize them. The coded information is transmitted directly to the financial institution responsible for paying the vendor where it is decrypted, or unscrambled.

STUDENT ACTIVITY

Have students locate an article from a newspaper or magazine or from an online resource on personal finance. They should write three to four sentences summarizing the article.

End-of-Chapter Activities

Case Study

Michael's parents bought him a skateboard that fit their budget and their values. It was one they could afford. Even if they could afford more, they may have decided that $100.00 was too much to spend on a birthday present. They may have decided that Michael would be just as good a skateboarder on a $50.00 board as on a $100.00 board.

Michael is being unreasonable. He may be disappointed, but he should consider his parents' circumstances and recognize that they bought him a new board that fits their budget.

The family should discuss the situation. Michael's parents should explain their financial situation to Michael and help him understand why a $100.00 board is unreasonable, both from a financial point of view and from a values point of view.

Sounding Off!

Student answers will vary, but in answer to the second question, it is important for teenagers to understand the concept and value of saving money. Learning early the importance of saving will help teens grow into responsible adults, money-wise.

FAQ

1. The Federal Reserve is the government agency responsible for creating and tracking all of the money in the United States.

2. Money is anything you exchange for goods or services.

3. In the United States, the currency is the dollar.

4. Factors to consider are:
    - Do I have enough money to pay for it?
    - Do I need it?
    - Do I need it now?
    - Do I want it?
    - Why do I want it?
    - Is there something less expensive that would be as good?
    - If I buy it, will I have money left for something else?

5. A budget is a plan for spending and saving money.

6. Types of income include:
    - Wages and tips you take home from working.
    - Gifts you receive for birthdays, holidays, and special occasions.
    - An allowance your parents give you on a regular basis.
    - Interest that you earn on money in the bank.

7. Flexible expenses include snacks, entertainment, and clothes. Students may think of more.

Case Study

Michael wants a new skateboard for his birthday. He has a skateboard, but it is two years old, and Michael thinks he needs a new one to do the types of tricks he sees other boarders doing at the skatepark. He has picked out the board he wants—a pro grade model that costs about $100.00.

Michael's mother works at a factory and earns about $25.00 per hour. She had been working 35 hours each week, but recently business has slowed, and her hours have been cut back to 30 each week.

Michael's parents buy him a skateboard for his birthday, but it costs $50.00—half the cost of the one he had picked out. He gets angry, accuses his parents of not loving him, and then locks himself in his room.

- Why do you think Michael's parents bought him the less expensive board?
- Do you think Michael is right to be angry?
- What do you think the family should do to resolve the conflict?

Sounding Off!

1. Do you think teens should have to do chores in exchange for an allowance?

2. Do you think it is important for teenagers to save money?

FAQ

1. What is the Federal Reserve?
2. What is money?
3. What currency do we use in the United States?
4. List four factors to consider when you make a financial decision.
5. What is a budget?
6. List three types of income.
7. List three types of flexible expenses.
8. What is the difference between a deficit and a surplus?
9. List three things that are printed on a pay stub.
10. List three drawbacks to paying by check.

8. A surplus is when you earned more money than you spent. A deficit is when you spent more than you earned.

9. Things that are printed on a pay stub include personal information, such as the payee's name and address; information about earnings, such as the number of hours worked and hourly wage; information about deductions, such as how much is being withheld for taxes; and information summarizing earning and withholdings.

10. Drawbacks to paying by check are:
    - You must have a check with you in order to use it.
    - Most banks charge you to buy checks.
    - Banks may charge a fee for every check you write.
    - Not every business accepts checks.
    - Some businesses accept a check only if you can show a valid photo ID, such as a driver's license.
    - Some businesses will not accept a check from a bank in a different city or state.
    - Checks take time to clear—go through the process of verification so your bank will transfer the funds to the other person's bank.
    - If there is not enough money in your account, the check will bounce, which means the payment will not be made. You will be responsible for repaying the original bill along with penalty fees.

Divide into teams of four or five. Spend 10 to 15 minutes thinking of and writing down five questions about personal finances, such as "What is the definition of expense?" When all teams are done, take turns asking the other teams questions. If the other team knows the answer, it gets a point. If they don't know the answer, your team gets a point. If a team thinks of a question that none of the teams has written down, that team gets two points. When all the questions have been asked, the team with the most points is the winner.

Hot Topics

Are you satisfied with your current lifestyle—the quality of your life and the things you own? Do you wish you had more money to spend on your wants? Do you think your family spends too much on luxuries and not enough on savings? Do you think your family uses a budget to help make financial choices? Do you use a budget?

Take this opportunity to write anonymously about the problem. Use a word processor so no one recognizes your handwriting. Be honest and open. Put the paper in the class Hot Topics box.

As a class, read the anonymous entries and discuss them.

Web Extra

Earning money can be challenging for teens. Use the Internet to locate information about the child labor laws in your state. Research the minimum age requirements as well as the time and hour restrictions, necessary work permits. Write a paragraph explaining the laws and post it on your school Web site or in the school library.

Problem Solver

A young adult is having trouble paying her bills each month. She earns a net hourly wage of $18.50—after all deductions—and usually works 35 hours each week. She pays $550.00 a month for rent, $35.00 for utilities—including electricity, heat, and water—and $99.00 for cable, Internet, and phone service. She spends $40.00 a month for her bus pass, and makes a monthly education loan payment of $135.

Individually, or in pairs, set up a budget for this young adult. Include all the expense categories you think are necessary, estimating the amounts if necessary. If possible, use a spreadsheet program such as Microsoft Excel to create the budget, or set it up in a table. Do your best to balance the budget so that there is no deficit. When you are finished, compare your budget with those prepared by your classmates. Discuss the differences.

Team Players

Teams will quiz each other with questions on personal finance. Encourage teams to review the vocabulary terms defined in chapter. Remind them of any activities and class discussions they participated in during the class period(s) in which you taught the chapter.

Hot Topics

Make sure students understand that they can turn in their papers anonymously. Encourage them to be open and honest about their opinions on their family's spending and saving habits and their contribution to them.

Web Extra

Students are to research their state's child labor laws. In the United States, child labor laws apply to minors, or those under the age of 18. As a general rule, the federal Fair Labor Standards Act sets 14 years of age as the minimum age for employment and limits the number of hours worked by minors under the age of 16. In addition, the act identifies minimum ages for jobs that have been determined to be particularly hazardous, as well as those that are not. There are also exceptions to some of these requirements.

Problem Solver

Students should first calculate the woman's monthly income ($18.50 × 35 hours a week × 4 weeks in a month, which equals $2,590 per month). Next, they should calculate her fixed expenses, which total $859 a month. Have them refer to the Monthly Budget illustrated on page 211 of the text to come up with an estimate for her variable expenses, such as food, entertainment, clothes, charity, and savings. Stress to students that the goal is to have a balanced budget, or one with a surplus.

Write Now

Students are to write a personal essay about their future self's personal finances. Remind students that a personal essay is written in the first person. It should have a beginning, a body of information (middle), and a conclusion (end). Stress the importance of descriptive writing and using the active voice. Because this is a personal essay, they should write in a tone that reflects their emotions or feelings.

Be Involved!

Students are to use the FCCLA planning process to prepare a budget for a fundraising event. The FCCLA planning process is:

- Identify the project.
- Set the goal.
- Form a plan.
- Act.
- Follow up.

Students can obtain more information on the FCCLA planning process from the organization's Web site, www.fcclaing.org , or by referring to *Appendix B: Joining a Career Technical Student Organization*, beginning on page 525 of the student text.

Social Networking

Students are to contact a local food pantry to find out what they can do individually and as a class to help. If there is more than one in your community, you might split students into teams and have each team focus on a specific pantry. Have students prepare a list of individual volunteer opportunities at the pantry and then organize a class activity to assist the pantry.

Write Now

Can you imagine how you will be spending money fifteen years from now? Will you have an income? What type of lifestyle will you have? What types of expenses will you have? Will you have achieved any of the financial goals you have now? Will you have new goals? Will you have the same needs and wants that you have today? Will you have found financial security? How about financial freedom?

Use the questions in the previous paragraph as a guide for writing a personal essay about your future self's personal finances. Share your essay with the class.

Be Involved!

www.fcclainc.org

As a class, use the FCCLA planning process to plan a budget for a fundraising event to raise money for an FCCLA activity.

Start by selecting the FCCLA activity and determining how much money you will need. Will you need a bus? Are there participation or entrance fees? How many students will attend? Your goal is to raise enough money to cover as many of the expenses as possible.

Next, brainstorm ideas for fundraising events. For example, you might want to have a bake sale, a talent contest, or a cake auction. Consider how much money you will have to spend on each possible event, and whether you have the resources available for it. Will you have to pay for anything up front? Do you need to rent a space to hold the event? After considering all possible options, select the event that you think will be the best one for achieving your goal.

Make an action plan for achieving your goal. Include a timeframe, make sure the plan is realistic and attainable, and then put the plan into action. You may want to organize teams within the class to handle specific responsibilities, such as volunteer management and publicity.

As you work toward your goal, keep a class journal to record your progress, and collect documentation that you can use to show what you have achieved. After the fundraising event, evaluate your success. Did you raise as much money as you expected? Was your budget accurate? Prepare an article about the event and send it to the school or community newspaper. You might also want to send it to your FCCLA chapter so they can publish it in their newsletter.

Social Networking

Many people do not have enough money to pay for needs as basic as food. Contact the food pantry in your community and ask what you can do to help—as a class and as an individual.

For example, as an individual, you might volunteer to stock the food pantry shelves. As a class, you might hold a food drive at school to collect non-perishable food items in cans, plastic containers, and boxes. You can deliver the goods to the food pantry.

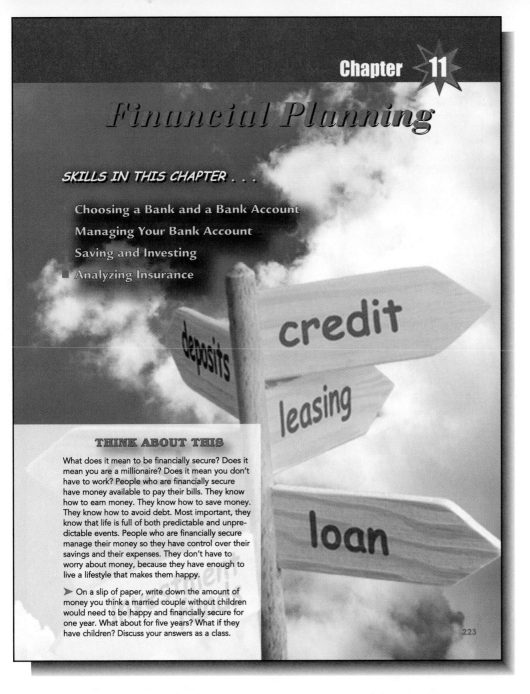

Chapter 11

Financial Planning

SKILLS IN THIS CHAPTER . . .

Choosing a Bank and a Bank Account

Managing Your Bank Account

Saving and Investing

☐ Analyzing Insurance

THINK ABOUT THIS

What does it mean to be financially secure? Does it mean you are a millionaire? Does it mean you don't have to work? People who are financially secure have money available to pay their bills. They know how to earn money. They know how to save money. They know how to avoid debt. Most important, they know that life is full of both predictable and unpredictable events. People who are financially secure manage their money so they have control over their savings and their expenses. They don't have to worry about money, because they have enough to live a lifestyle that makes them happy.

➤ On a slip of paper, write down the amount of money you think a married couple without children would need to be happy and financially secure for one year. What about for five years? What if they have children? Discuss your answers as a class.

deposits · credit · leasing · loan

223

Chapter 11 Overview

In this chapter, students learn more about personal finance and how to manage their money and accounts. It provides information on banking services, investment options, and insurance considerations.

Choosing a Bank and a Bank Account The different types of banks are introduced. Students also learn about different types of bank accounts, how to open one, and the fees and interest income that are associated with them.

Managing Your Bank Account In this section, the importance of diligent recordkeeping and tracking your money is stressed. Students learn how to identify deposits, withdrawals, and other transactions that are detailed on a bank statement. They also learn what it means to balance an account.

Saving and Investing This section discusses the basic types of savings accounts and how they accumulate interest. It also provides an overview of investing in options such as mutual funds, individual retirement accounts, and employer savings plans.

Analyzing Insurance This section covers the basics of insurance. An overview of the different types of insurance is provided. Many important insurance terms and definitions are discussed.

Focus and Engage

Bell-Ringer: Think About This

Students are to write down the amount of money they think a married couple without children would need to be happy and financially secure for a year, for five years, and if they had kids. Review with students the discussion on budgeting in Chapter 10. This will help them estimate expenses. Encourage them to revisit the personal budgets they created. If they did not create one, then have them take another look at the Monthly Budget on page 211. Make sure they understand that this is a budget example for a single person still in school, so they will have to make adjustments to all income and expense categories.

ADVANCE PREPARATION	
Review	*Life Skills for the 21st Century* textbook, Chapter 11.
Prepare	Paper and pencil for some activities. Calculators. Box labeled "Hot Topics."

CUSTOMIZED INSTRUCTION OVERVIEW				
Less Advanced Students	More Advanced Students	ESOL Students	Special Needs Students	At-Risk Students
Pages 227, 233, 234	Page 224	Page 224	Pages 227, 229, 234	Pages 227, 233, 234

Introduce the Section

This section introduces the different types of banks and the basic products and services they offer. Students learn about different types of bank accounts, how to open one, and the fees and interest income that are associated with them.

Figure Focus

Ask students why a bank is considered a safe place to keep money. While many students might envision all their money being safely stored in a steel vault, explain that banks are safe because money deposited with them is insured by the Federal Deposit Insurance Corporation (FDIC), which is an independent agency of the U.S. government. The FDIC insures deposits in accredited banks and thrifts (or savings and loans). Explain that the FDIC was established to help restore consumer confidence in the national banking system after the bank failures during the Great Depression in the late 1920s and early 1930s.

Vocabulary

Bank: Financial institution that stores and manages money for individuals and businesses.

Banking: Doing business with a bank.

Credit union: Customer- or member-owned nonprofit bank that offers basic banking services.

Mortgage: Loan agreement for a home between a borrower and a lender.

Online bank: Retail bank whose services and products are available via the Internet only.

Retail bank: Bank that provides basic services, such as checking and savings accounts; credit cards; and education, car, and home loans.

Choosing a Bank and a Bank Account

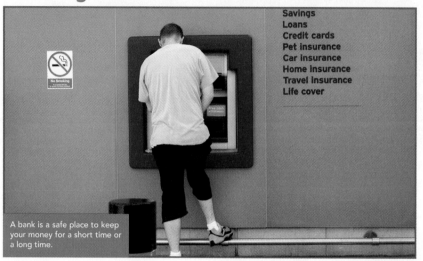

Savings
Loans
Credit cards
Pet insurance
Car insurance
Home insurance
Travel insurance
Life cover

A bank is a safe place to keep your money for a short time or a long time.

A **bank** is a **financial institution**, which is a fancy way of saying a business that stores and manages money for individuals and other businesses. The bank invests that money or loans it to people and other businesses. **Banking** is doing business with a bank.

There are basically two reasons to put your money in a bank.

■ To keep it safe. When your money is in a bank account, it cannot be lost or stolen.

■ To earn interest. For some types of accounts, the bank pays you for using your money. That means you earn money just by having a bank account.

There are many types of banks and bank accounts. Understanding the differences helps you choose the one that is right for you.

Types of Banks

Do you have a savings account or a debit card? If you do, it's probably at a retail bank. Most of the banks that offer basic banking services to individuals are called **retail banks.** They provide services such as checking and savings accounts, credit cards, education loans, car loans, and home loans—**mortgages.** Some retail banks also provide resources for online banking.

You might have a credit union account. **Credit unions** also offer basic banking services. They are nonprofit banks that are owned by the customers, or members. Nonprofit means their goal is not to earn money for the business, but to earn money for the customers. Credit unions are formed by a group of people with something in common, such as employees of the same company or residents of the same town. New members must be part of the same group.

If you use the Internet to do all of your banking, you might have an account at an online bank. **Online banks** are retail banks that operate only on the Internet. They do not have buildings where you can go to talk to a banker or make a deposit. You do all of your banking using electronic funds.

Customized Instruction: More Advanced Students

Ask students to name the banking institutions in their community. These include retail banks, commercial banks (primarily for businesses), savings and loans, and credit unions. Help them identify and categorize the different types of banks.

Customized Instruction: ESOL Students

Ask students to say and write out the vocabulary words in their primary language.

Which Bank Should I Use?

Most communities have several banks that offer personal accounts and other services. You might also be able to use a bank in a different community by using the Internet. So, how do you decide which bank is best for you? If the bank has a **branch**—local office—nearby, you can go in and talk to the manager to learn more about the bank. You can also look online at a bank's Web site. Consider the following when choosing a bank:

■ *Convenience.* You want a bank that is easy to get to and open when you need it. Does the bank have a branch nearby? Is it open in the evenings or on Saturdays? Does the bank have ATMs in convenient locations?

■ *Services.* Different banks offer different services. Does the bank offer the type of account you need? Are there age limits for getting a debit card or ATM card? Does it offer online banking?

■ *Interest rates.* Interest rates vary from bank to bank, and so does the way the bank credits the interest into your account. Does the bank offer the highest interest rate? How does the bank credit the interest? If monthly, the interest is added to your balance at the end of each month. If quarterly, interest is added to your balance at the end of every three months.

What About Fees?

All banks charge fees—that's one way they make money. Before you choose a bank, you can compare the fees each bank charges for common services and transactions.

■ Monthly service fees   ■ Check fees
■ ATM transaction fees   ■ Check printing fees

Some banks waive the monthly service fees if you maintain a minimum balance or sign up for direct deposit of your paycheck. Some allow you to use a certain number of ATM or check transactions for free each month. Most banks charge a fee if you use a different bank's ATM. Some banks also have low-fee or no-fee accounts for students.

NUMBERS GAME

How much should you save? Many financial experts recommend that you save 10% of your income—which is all the money that comes in to you, including wages and gifts.

The word *percent* means *by the hundred*. Each percent represents one part of 100. 100 percent equals the whole or all of something—no matter how much is in the whole.

To find the percentage of a number:

1. Change the percentage to a decimal by replacing the percent sign with a decimal point and moving the decimal point two spaces to the left.

2. Multiply the decimal by the number. For example, to find 20% of 150:

   20% = .20   150 × .20 = 30

If you receive $75.00 for your birthday, how much is 10%?

   10% = .10   75.00 × .10 = $7.50

What if your income is $205.00?

Types of Banks

There are banks that provide services to individuals, businesses, organizations, and even governments.

✔ *Retail banks provide services such as checking and savings accounts, credit cards, car loans, and mortgages to individuals and families.*

✔ *Credit unions offer services similar to retail banks, but they are nonprofit organizations owned by members.*

✔ *Commercial banks are like retail banks, except they provide services to businesses.*

✔ *Investment banks help businesses and other organizations raise money by issuing stocks and bonds. They provide consulting services when one business wants to buy another business.*

✔ *A central bank is an organization responsible for managing banking activity. In the United States, the Federal Reserve is the central bank. Other countries have their own central banks.*

Myth The bank will pay a check even if I don't have enough money in my account.

Truth Every bank has its own rules, but most will "bounce" the check, which means the bank sends the check back to the payee without paying. The bank charges you an overdraft fee, which is a fee for spending more than you have in your account. It may also charge a fee for returning the check. The payee may also charge you a fee for the returned check, and you will still have to pay the original amount. Bouncing a check can end up being very expensive.

Myth/Truth

You might also explain that with the increased use of electronic fund transfers, banks often tend to release funds quicker from your accounts than when using a paper system. So, you should not count on a delay or processing time, and you should be sure sufficient funds are in the account to cover the check at the time you write it.

Vocabulary

Branch: Local office of a bank.

Types of Banks

In addition to reviewing the definitions of types of banks with students, you might review the role of the Federal Reserve. It is a government agency responsible for creating and tracking all of the money in the United States. Most consumers do not interact with the "Fed," as it is commonly called. Instead, it works behind the scenes to supervise the nation's banking system and to protect consumers who have a stake in it.

TEAMWORK ACTIVITY

Assign teams to gather information from a specific bank in the community on the fees they charge on (1) savings accounts and (2) checking accounts. They can call or visit the bank, or obtain information online. As a class, discuss the fees charged by different banks. Ask students to comment on the bank they think offers the best deals.

NUMBERS GAME

Students are to calculate 10% of $205:

■ 10% = .10

■ 205 × .10 = $20.50

Remind students that to set up a decimal multiplication problem, you do not line up decimal points as you do in addition and subtraction. Instead, set up the problem as though it were a whole number problem and then multiply. To place the decimal point in the answer, count the total number of decimal places in both factors. Then, insert a decimal point in the answer so that it has the same total number of decimal places as both factors.

Vocabulary

Balance: The amount of money in a bank account.

Bank account: Record of the transactions between a bank and its customer.

Joint account: Bank account owned by more than one person, such as a parent and child.

Reinforce and Review

Review the terms *deposit* and *withdrawal*. A deposit is money you add to your account. A withdrawal is money you take out of your account. You can deposit and withdraw money in person at the bank, through an ATM, and online if you have access to an online account.

Am I Old Enough?

Students are asked to consider the benefits and drawbacks of having a joint account. The benefit is that the ultimate responsibility for the account lies with two people instead of one. The drawback is that both parties can be held liable for overdrafts and bounced checks. Also, some transactions may require both parties' signatures in order for them to be processed.

Discuss

Explain that when you decide upon a bank in which you want to open an account, you should tell the bank what you would like to accomplish with your account. Most banks offer a variety of accounts and will be able to suggest the one that will help you meet your goals. You might also ask about special accounts for students. Many banks offer a higher interest rate or waive fees for students.

TECH CONNECT

Students are to research personal money management software programs. In addition to Microsoft Money and Quicken, students might investigate Visual Money, Moneydance, YNAB (You Need A Budget), mvelopes, and Mint. Features to consider are ease of use and installation, operating system, online money management capabilities, budget planning, and investment management tips and strategies.

Am I Old Enough?

Some banks have a minimum age requirement for opening an account. For example, you might have to be 16 to open a checking account or have a debit card. What if you are not old enough to open an account?

★ *An adult such as your mom or dad can co-sign the account, which means he or she will sign the signature card, too.*

★ *You may be able to open a savings account instead of a checking account.*

★ *If your parents have an account at the bank, you may be able to open an account that is linked to their account.*

★ *Consider a different bank with different age requirements.*

If an adult co-signs on the account, the account will have your name and the adult's name on it—a joint account. *You can both make transactions. What are benefits to having a joint account? What are drawbacks?*

Types of Bank Accounts

Banks keep track of the money you deposit and withdraw by using a **bank account**. A bank account is not a wallet or safe where the actual cash is stored. It is a *record of the transactions between you and the bank.*

■ When you *deposit* money, the amount is added to your current bank account balance.

■ When you *withdraw* money, the amount is subtracted from the balance.

The most common types of personal bank accounts are checking accounts and savings accounts.

■ Checking accounts are set up so that you can access your money by writing checks. You can also sometimes use a debit card or automated teller machine (ATM) card. You must have enough money in the account to cover all of the checks and debit transactions. Most people use checking accounts so they can pay for things without carrying cash. For example, you can write a check to pay for groceries, or use your debit card to buy movie tickets.

■ Savings accounts are not linked to checks or debit cards, although you may be able to deposit or withdraw money using an ATM card. Savings accounts earn interest, which means the bank pays you a percentage of your **balance**—the amount of money in the account. People use savings accounts to save money for future use. Because you earn interest, the balance grows over time; the longer you leave the money in the account, the more money there will be.

Opening An Account

You open an account by going to a branch, filling out some forms, and making a deposit. Each bank has different rules, but usually you meet with a manager or assistant manager to show a picture I.D., such as a student I.D., a driver's license, or a passport. You may also need a birth certificate or Social Security card. Then you will:

■ Fill out a signature card that the bank will keep on file. A signature card helps keep your account safe, because it identifies the person authorized to use the account. Make the first deposit into the account when you open it. You may deposit cash or a check, or you may be able to transfer the money electronically from a different account. Some banks have a minimum deposit requirement, so it's a good idea to ask ahead of time how much money you will need.

■ Fill out forms for ordering personalized checks, if you are opening a checking account. Personalized checks have your name and address printed in the upper-left corner and your account number printed across the bottom. The cost of the checks is automatically subtracted from your account balance.

■ Select personal identification numbers (PIN) for any debit or ATM cards, or for your online banking access, if available.

TECH CONNECT

You can buy a personal money management software program to keep track of your bank account balances. Microsoft Money and Intuit Quicken are popular products that let you track your income and expenses, monitor your investments, and balance your bank accounts electronically. You set up the accounts and enter the information.

These types of programs simplify the process, because the software does the math for you; you just have to remember to enter all of your transactions. If you don't have a personal money management program, you can achieve the same results using a spreadsheet program such as Excel.

Research personal money management programs. Compare the features and costs, and select one you might like to buy. Explain your decision to the class.

Using a Checking Account

A check is a piece of paper that tells the bank how much money to take from your account and put in someone else's—the payee's—account. A debit card—sometimes called a check card—authorizes an electronic transfer from your account to someone else's. It is important to keep enough money in the account to cover the amounts of every check or debit transaction you make. Otherwise, the check will be returned—and you will have to pay fees—or the debit card will be denied.

When you open a checking account, the bank sends you personalized checks. Each check has printed information on it, including your personal information such as name and address in the upper-left corner, the check number in the upper-right corner, and your bank information such as the bank name and your account number across the bottom.

Each check also has blanks for you to fill in the following:

- Date
- Payee
- Amount in numbers
- Amount in words
- Your signature
- A memo line for noting what the check is for

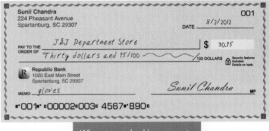

Why open a checking account instead of a savings account?

Each time you write a check, you can record the transaction details in your **account register**, which is a book the bank provides along with your personalized checks. The register has spaces where you can enter the date, check number, payee, and amount. Then, you subtract the amount from your current balance, so you can see how much money is left in the account.

Can I Use a Debit Card?

If you have a debit card linked to your checking account, you can use it instead of writing a check. The card comes with your name and account number stamped on it. Some have your picture on it, too. There is a place on the back for your signature.

To use the card, you run it through a machine at the store. You then punch in your PIN to authorize the transaction. The money is immediately transferred out of your account, so it is important to know that your account balance is great enough to cover the transaction, or your card will be denied for insufficient funds. To keep track of debits so you do not run out of money, record debit transactions in your checking account register the same way you record checks.

Banking Terms

Understanding banking is easier if you understand banking terms. Some common banking terms include:

✔ *Deposit: Putting money in an account*

✔ *Withdrawal: Taking money out of an account*

✔ *Interest: A fee paid for using someone else's money*

✔ *Loan: A sum of money borrowed from a bank*

✔ *Transaction: An exchange between the bank and a customer*

Write the Right Check!

It is important to fill out a check properly to avoid fraud and so that the bank can process it.

★ *Write neatly so the bank can read it.*

★ *Use a pen, not a pencil, so the information cannot be erased and changed.*

★ *Do not cross out mistakes.*

★ *Remember to fill in all blanks, including the date.*

★ *Make sure the numerical dollar amount matches the written dollar amount.*

★ *Remember to sign the check in script—no printing!*

If you make a mistake, tear up the check and write a new one. In your account register, enter the torn-up check as VOID, which means it is not available for use. What are some benefits of paying by check? What are some drawbacks?

Vocabulary

Account register: Book provided by a bank in which transaction details are recorded.

Deposit: Putting money in an account.

Interest: A fee paid for using someone else's money.

Loan: A sum of money borrowed from a bank.

Transaction: An exchange between the bank and a customer.

Withdrawal: Taking money out of an account.

Banking Terms

In addition to the terms defined in the text, explain to students what an account register is. This is a book provided by a bank in which you record the details of your banking transactions, such as checks you've written, deposits you've made, and money you've withdrawn.

Reinforce and Review

Remind students that a check is a written order to a bank to transfer funds from your account to someone else. Also discuss that a debit card allows the holder to electronically access their funds at any time and at any location that accepts them.

Figure Focus

Students are asked why they would open a checking account instead of a savings account. Two reasons are (1) you can write checks for purchases with a checking account and (2) you can also obtain a debit card with a checking account, which eliminates the need to carry cash and write checks.

Write the Right Check!

Students are to comment on the benefits and drawbacks of paying by check. The benefits include:

- You do not have to carry cash.
- You can send a check through the mail.
- If a check is lost or stolen, your bank can stop payment, or cancel the check so that it cannot be exchanged for money.

The drawbacks are:

- You must have a check with you in order to use it.
- Most banks charge you to buy checks.
- Banks may charge a fee for every check you write.
- Not every business accepts checks, and some only accept them if you show a valid photo ID.
- Some businesses will not accept checks from a bank in a different city or state.
- If there is not enough money in your account, the check will bounce and you will be responsible for repaying the original bill along with penalty fees, which can include an overdraft fee or a bounced check or "insufficient funds" fee. In addition, the party you wrote the check to might charge you a "returned check" fee.

Customized Instruction: Less Advanced/Special Needs Students

Create a mock blank check using the figure on this page as a guide. You can also download "pretend" checks from various Web sites, including www.dltk-kids.com/crafts/miscellaneous/mcheck.html or www.galaxy.net/~k12/checks/check.shtml. Provide students with the information to use in filling out the check. You can also have students go to www.themint.org/kids/writing-a-check.html where they can practice filling out an electronic version of a check.

Customized Instruction: At-Risk Students

Pose the following problem to students: You have $78 in your checking account. On Monday, you withdraw $25 from an ATM. On Friday, you use your debit card to buy $20 of tokens at the arcade. On Saturday, you buy a pair of shoes for $38 and pay with a personal check. The following week, you receive a notice from your bank that you have overdrawn your account and you will be assessed a $15 overdraft fee. Then, you receive a bill from the store where you bought your shoes claiming that your check was returned because of insufficient funds and that you now owe them the $38 for the shoes, plus a penalty charge of $25 for the returned check. Ask students to calculate how much they were overdrawn ($78 − ($25 + $20 + $38 = $83) = $5 in the hole. Then have them calculate how much the new shoes really cost: $38 + $15 + $25 = $78. How could this have been avoided?

Introduce the Section

In this section, the importance of diligent record-keeping and money tracking is stressed. Students learn how to identify deposits, withdrawals, and other transactions that are detailed on a bank statement. They also learn what it means to balance an account.

Figure Focus

Explain how accurate recordkeeping can help you budget. By tracking each deposit and each withdrawal, you are, in essence, itemizing your income and expenses. Income and expenses are the two components of a budget.

Reinforce and Review

Review these steps for managing a bank account.

1. Save receipts for all banking transactions. These include canceled checks, deposit receipts, ATM receipts, withdrawal receipts, and receipts for purchases that you paid for with a debit card or check.

2. Record each banking transaction in your account register or in a software program if you use one for personal banking.

3. Balance your account. When you receive your bank statement (usually once a month), check it against your account register to ensure that your records match those of the bank.

Managing Your Bank Account

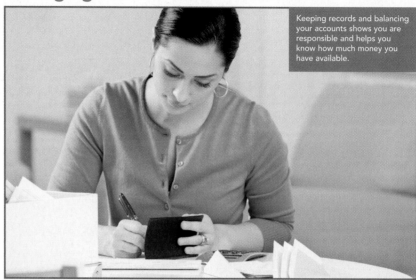

Keeping records and balancing your accounts shows you are responsible and helps you know how much money you have available.

There are two important parts to managing your bank account:

■ Keeping records of every transaction
■ Making sure you and the bank enter each transaction correctly

The first step in keeping complete and accurate records is to save every receipt that details a bank transaction. The second step is to enter the transactions in your account register by hand, or in a software program on your computer.

To make sure you and the bank enter each transaction correctly, you balance your account. Balancing your account involves comparing your records to the bank's records to make sure they match.

Managing your bank accounts gives you control over your money. It allows you to make healthy financial decisions and to achieve your financial goals, because you know where your money is and how you are using it.

Save the Slips!

Banking involves a lot of slips of paper. Bank records include canceled checks, bank statements, deposit receipts, ATM receipts, receipts for purchases you make using a check or debit card, and basically every other piece of paper that details a banking transaction.

After any transaction—deposit, withdrawal, debit card or check purchase—you receive a receipt that shows the transaction details. Save the receipt! You can use it to make sure the transaction is correct, and then save the receipt to compare to your bank statement. If you ever find an error on your bank statement, you can show the bank your receipt, and it can correct the information.

Take the time to organize your paperwork so you can find it if you need it. Set up folders for your checking account statements and your savings account statements. Set up additional folders for debit card receipts and deposit receipts.

Balancing Your Account

Every month or so, the bank sends you a **bank statement**, which is a list of all the transactions for your bank account. The statement may come in the mail, the bank may send it via e-mail, or you may be able to access it online.

When you receive your statement, you can compare it to your account register and your transaction receipts to see if your information matches the bank's information. This is called *balancing your account*, or *bank reconciliation*. When the information matches, you know exactly how much money you have in your account. If you keep complete and accurate records, you will be able to balance your account correctly with each statement.

The bank statement shows your starting balance, which is the amount you had at the beginning of the month, and your ending balance, which is the amount you have at the end of the month. It also shows:

- Deposits and credits added to your balance
- Withdrawals and fees subtracted from your balance

For checking accounts, the bank statement lists each transaction that has cleared, including the date, check number or debit location and amount, and sometimes the payee. Most banks also send a picture of every check that has been processed. Checking account statements usually come once a month.

For savings accounts, the statement shows the interest that is credited to your account. Savings account statements may come once a month or quarterly.

Using an ATM

An ATM is a machine that lets you perform bank transactions without going to a branch office and waiting for a teller. Banks put ATMs in convenient locations, such as on street corners, at the shopping mall, in grocery stores, and outside the bank. You can use an ATM to:

- Deposit cash or checks
- Withdraw cash
- Transfer money from one account to another
- Check your account balance

To use an ATM, you need an ATM card that is linked to your bank account. The card has your name and account information stamped on it. It might also have your picture on it for security. When you apply for the ATM at the bank, you choose a PIN. Every time you use the card, you must enter your PIN. If you enter the wrong PIN, the card will not work.

After you enter the PIN, you follow the instructions on the ATM screen to choose a transaction type and your account. Most ATMs use touch screens, so you just touch the option you want. You can also use the keypad to make your selections. Most ATMs also have instructions for hearing- and visually-impaired customers.

You must have enough money in your account to make a withdrawal at an ATM. Remember to record the transaction in your account register and to adjust the balance by subtracting a withdrawal or adding a deposit. Some banks charge a fee each time you use an ATM, or if you use an ATM owned by a different bank. Subtract the fee from your account balance, too. It is also a good idea to consider your own safety when you use an ATM. Criminals target ATM machines, and know people leaving an ATM usually have cash. Visit your ATM at a time and place where there are other people around.

My Account Doesn't Balance!

There are a number of reasons your account might not balance with your bank statement.

- You forgot to record a transaction.
- You forgot to record bank fees or credits.
- You recorded the incorrect amount.
- You made a math error adding a deposit or subtracting a withdrawal.
- The bank made a mistake.
- You carefully reviewed the bank statement and your records and found that the account does balance.

If the account still doesn't balance after you check it again, take your receipts and the bank statement to the bank and ask a manager or assistant manager to review it with you. If the bank is responsible for the error, they will correct it. What steps can you take to make sure your account will balance with your bank statement?

Vocabulary

Bank statement: A summary or list of all the transactions for your bank account, provided by the bank.

My Account Doesn't Balance!

Following are some steps to take to make sure your account will balance with your statement:

- Record each transaction when it occurs. When you write a check, enter the information in your account register immediately. Do the same when you withdraw money from an ATM.
- Save receipts for purchases you make with a debit card or check.
- Identify any fees that are assessed to your account and log them in your register.
- Check your account register against the itemized listing on your monthly bank statement *every* month.

Discuss

Discuss the advantages and disadvantages of using an ATM. The biggest advantage is convenience. You can conduct transactions from an ATM at any time of the day, any day of the week. ATMs are located all over the place, so no matter where you travel, you can usually find an ATM to use. On the other hand, use of some ATMs might cost you a fee per transaction. In addition, security and fraud are concerns for ATM users. There's been a significant increase in the number of thefts and physical assaults on ATM users as well as fraudulent use of ATM cards to illegally obtain cash from and information on an individual's account.

Customized Instruction: Special Needs (Visually- and Hearing-Impaired) Students

Ask students to share ideas on how ATMs could be more user-friendly to customers with a visual or hearing impairment. For example, many ATMs have Braille labels indicating the function of buttons. Some banks are starting to roll out audio-assisted ATMs, which have an audio component that relays the information on the screen. For hearing-impaired users, some type of mirror or reflective surface could add another level of security. Many ATMs are equipped with security cameras and even police alert buttons, but for the person who does not hear someone approaching, a mirror can be a helpful tool.

Introduce the Section

This section discusses the basic types of savings accounts and how they accumulate interest. It also provides an overview of investing in options such as mutual funds, individual retirement accounts, and employer savings plans.

Figure Focus

Ask students what "wealth" means to them. Wealth can be defined as an abundance of material possessions or resources. These possessions include cash, cars, homes, jewelry, and stocks you own, among other things. How does saving and investing increase wealth? When most people open a savings account or invest money, they do so assuming they will earn interest on their savings or increase the value of their investment.

Vocabulary

Return on investment (ROI): Amount of money you earn compared to the amount of money you invest.

Reinforce and Review

Remind students that financial security is the comfort and peace of mind you have knowing there is money available when you need it. Financial flexibility is the flexibility you have knowing there is money available when you want it.

Saving and Investing

Saving and investing provide opportunities to increase your wealth, leading to financial security and freedom.

When you have money in your pocket, what's the first thing you think of doing? Buying a snack? Buying new clothes? Renting a video game? How about paying yourself?

Paying yourself is one way to think about saving money for the future. Saving money is one of the most important steps toward financial security and financial freedom. You put the money someplace safe—such as a bank or a credit union. You don't have it in your pocket to spend right now, but it's still yours. It will be available when you need it for an unexpected expense (such as medical bills), a planned expense (such as education), or for retirement. As a bonus, the bank will pay you just for leaving the money in your account. The longer it stays in your account, the more money you will have to spend later.

Once you achieve your savings goals, you might decide to invest some of your savings. Investing is riskier than saving, but it also provides an opportunity to earn more money or to increase your savings at a faster rate.

Saving vs. Investing

When you save, you deposit money in a savings account, a checking account, or a certificate of deposit (CD) on a regular basis. When you invest, you take a portion of your savings and purchase a product such as stocks, bonds, or mutual funds.

Savings are usually guaranteed by the Federal Deposit Insurance Corporation (FDIC) or the National Credit Union Administration (NCUA), which are government agencies responsible for insuring bank deposits. Investing is riskier than saving, because the deposit is usually not insured, and your **return on investment** (ROI)—the amount of money you earn compared to the amount of money you invest—is not guaranteed. It is possible that you will lose all of the money you invest, but you have the chance to earn more from an investment than from savings.

Most financial experts advise that you use a combination of saving and investing. The amount you save and the amount you invest depend on your financial goals, your financial resources, how old you are, and how much risk you are willing to take.

Stay in School

Ask students what they think it means when people say education is an investment in your future. How is an education the same as an investment in, say, a company's stock or a bond? When you invest your money in a company, you do so with the expectation that it will benefit you in the form of profits or increased income (return on investment). Likewise, when you stay in school and pursue your education, you do so for many reasons, one of which is the expectation that you will in some way benefit from it in the future. Ask students to consider a graduate's "return on investment."

■ The average annual income for a high school graduate is about $9,000 more than that of a high school dropout and about $250,000 to $300,000 more over the course of their lifetime.

■ The average annual income for a typical college graduate is about $35,000 more than that for a dropout and $1.6 million more over the course of his or her lifetime.

Consider these losses for a high school dropout.

■ High school dropouts are twice as likely as graduates to live below the poverty line.

■ Dropouts are three times more likely to be unemployed than a college graduate.

■ Dropouts are severely limited in their career options and the number of jobs available to them. Many employers will not allow those without a high school diploma to even *apply* for a job.

Understanding Savings Accounts

The safest, most reliable, and most convenient way to save is to deposit your money in a savings account at a retail bank or credit union. The money will earn a small amount of interest and be available when you need it. It is insured by the Federal Deposit Insurance Corporation (FDIC) or National Credit Union Administration (NCUA). If you make regular deposits, your savings will increase.

To start saving, you open a savings account at a retail bank or credit union. When considering a savings account, you want to know:

- What is the interest rate?
- Is the interest simple or compounded? **Simple interest** is calculated based on the principal balance only. **Compounded interest** is calculated based on the principal plus interest that has already been earned. (See Chapter 12 for more information on simple and compound interest.)
- How often is interest calculated?
- How often is the interest credited—added—to your account?
- Are there service fees?
- Can you withdraw your money at any time?

Interest may be compounded daily, monthly, quarterly, semiannually, or annually. But, just because it is compounded doesn't mean it is credited. Some banks might compound the interest daily, but credit it quarterly. If you withdraw money before interest is credited, you may not receive the interest on the full amount.

Types of Savings Accounts

There are three basic types of savings accounts.

- *Passbook accounts* are the standard type of savings account. They earn a small amount of interest but are flexible, so you can withdraw your money at any time. A passbook account is a good way to get started saving. Once you accumulate a specific amount, you may want to move it into a time account.
- *Time accounts* are savings accounts that require you to leave the money untouched for a set amount of time—or **term**. Usually, the longer the term, the higher the interest rate. If you withdraw the money before the end of the term, you may have to pay a penalty, or fee. Certificates of deposit (CDs) are an example of a time account. Many time accounts have a minimum deposit. For example, you may have to deposit $500.00 or $1,000.00.
- *Money market accounts* offer a higher interest rate than a passbook savings account. They usually have a minimum balance requirement and may limit the number of times per month that you can withdraw money. Many offer check-writing or debit card services. They are insured by the FDIC. You might hear of mutual fund money market accounts. These are similar to money market accounts in terms of services, but they are not insured by the FDIC. You might consider saving in a money market account if you have enough money to meet the minimum balance, and you want to be able to access your money using checks or a debit card.

Investment Terms

- ✔ *Bond: A debt security issued by corporations, governments, or their agencies, in return for cash from lenders and investors*
- ✔ *Commodity: An item such as gold, wheat, or coal that can be traded, processed, and sold*
- ✔ *Dividend: The amount of a corporation's after-tax earnings that it pays to its shareholders*
- ✔ *Liquidity: The ability of an investment to be easily converted into cash with little or no loss of capital and a minimum of delay*
- ✔ *Portfolio: All of the investments and accounts an investor owns*
- ✔ *Return: The money received annually from an investment*
- ✔ *Securities and Exchange Commission (SEC): The government agency that regulates the securities industry*
- ✔ *Stock: A share of ownership in a corporation*
- ✔ *Risk: The measurable likelihood of loss or less-than-expected returns*
- ✔ *Security: An asset that has financial value and that can be traded*

Job Search

There are many careers for people who enjoy working with money. From bank teller to stockbroker to certified public accountant, if you have an aptitude for finance, there is a job for you.

Use the Internet, library, or school's guidance resources to learn more about careers in finance. Pick one job and write a cover letter you might send if you were applying for the job. In the letter, state why you are qualified for the job, including your education and interests. Discuss the career path you envision for yourself and the salary you would like to earn.

Job Search

Students are to research a career of their choice in the field of finance. Career areas include bookkeeping, loans, investor relations, financial analysis, accounting, auditing, financial planning, stockbroker, management consulting, and many more.

Vocabulary

Compounded interest: Interest calculated on the principal plus interest that has already been earned.

Simple interest: Interest calculated on the principal balance only.

Term: Set amount of time.

Reinforce and Review

Review the concept of interest. Interest is the fee paid for the use of someone else's money. The rate of interest paid on a savings account varies from bank to bank. Explain that the higher the interest rate, the more money you make.

Investment Terms

You might want to further explain some of the terms as follows.

- Bonds are commonly issued by municipalities to finance large projects, such as a professional sports stadium. A city sells bonds to investors, and then it pays interest on the bonds to the investors, using proceeds from the stadium's operations. At the end of 20 or 30 years, the bonds mature and the investors are paid back their original investment.
- Commodities such as oil are sold either under contracts for future delivery or on what is called a "spot market" for immediate delivery. Power companies, for example, often contract for the oil, natural gas, or coal they'll need months in advance so they can assure their customers of adequate power. Then they buy any additional commodities on the spot market based on current demand for power.
- Dividends are typically cash payments that corporations make to their shareholders. Some companies pay high dividends. Dividends give investors some assurance of a return on their investment.
- Stocks of large publicly traded corporations such as Microsoft are generally considered highly liquid. Their share prices tend to be relatively stable, and individual investors can buy or sell shares without affecting the market price. Shares of smaller companies and many other investments are less liquid because there are fewer shares and fewer buyers and sellers.
- Since they represent ownership in a company, stocks entitle their owners to a share of a business's assets and profits. But the market value of a share of stock also depends on the perceived value of those assets and future profits. If profits begin to slip, the market value of its stock can decline. Stocks are risky in that there's no guarantee that investors will get their money back when they sell their shares.
- Securities come in many forms, including shares of stock, bonds, preferred shares, convertible bonds, and other hybrids. They can offer various risks and potential rewards, depending on their particular terms. Stocks of large, publicly traded companies such as Wal-Mart and General Electric Co. have to conform to detailed rules and regulations, and they are easily bought and sold. Bonds and other securities can be less easy to buy and sell for individual investors.

Vocabulary

Equity investment: Money that is invested in a firm by its owner(s) or stockholders and which is recovered when the stocks are sold to other investors.

Liquidity: Stocks or other assets that can easily be sold and converted into cash.

Mutual fund: Pool of money collected from many investors and then used to buy stocks, bonds, and other securities.

ROI (return on investment): Amount of money you earn compared to the amount of money you invest.

Stock: The share of a company held by an individual investor.

Learning About Investments

Explain to students that companies and organizations which sell securities in the United States must be registered with the Securities and Exchange Commission (SEC). The registration requires:

- A description of the company's properties and business.
- A description of the security to be offered for sale.
- Information about the management of the company.
- Financial statements certified by independent accountants.

Registration statements and prospectuses (official document with details about the security offered for sale) become public shortly after filing with the SEC. Those registrations filed by U.S. domestic companies are available on the EDGAR database accessible at www.sec.gov. Most publicly traded companies also post these documents on their corporate Web sites under an "Investors" or "Investor Relations" link or tab.

Explain that not all offerings of securities must be registered with the SEC. Some exemptions include:

- Private offerings to a limited number of persons or institutions.
- Offerings of limited size.
- Intrastate offerings.
- Securities of municipal, state, and federal governments.

Learning About Investments

The more you know about an investment, the better prepared you will be to decide whether the risk is worth the reward. What if you save $2,500.00 and want to invest it to earn a higher return on investment? How can you find the information you need to make a healthy investment decision?

★ *Ask people you trust how they invest.*

★ *Ask your bank what types of investments they offer.*

★ *Read the business pages of a newspaper or Web site.*

★ *Read a company's annual report.*

★ *Use the decision-making process.*

ROI is not the only thing to consider when researching investments. Investments all have fees, including fees for buying and selling, maintenance fees, and expense fees. Some fees are flat rates and some are a percentage of your investment. How can knowing the fees help you decide whether an investment is worthwhile?

Understanding Investments

Once you achieve your savings goals, you may decide to invest a portion of your savings to see if you can earn a higher **ROI**—return on investment. You may not be able to acquire investments on your own until you are 18 years old. You can ask a parent or other trusted adult to help you set up a joint investment.

Learning as much as possible about an investment before you commit money will go a long way toward minimizing your risk. Still, all investments involve risk, so it is a good idea to invest only as much as you are willing to lose. Here are two basic types of investments:

- **Equity investments,** in which you purchase **stock**—or ownership—in a company. Your ROI depends on the stock price. If the stock goes up—increases in value—you gain. If it goes down—decreases in value—you lose. Stock prices change by the minute. They are affected by how much money a company makes, as well as by other factors such as the economy, the industry, even the personal lives of the managers. You do not actually earn any money until you sell your stock.

- **Fixed income investments,** in which you lend money to a business or government agency in exchange for a bond. A **bond** is a security that provides fixed interest payments for a set period of time. The business or government agency uses your money for the term of the bond.

A fixed income investment is safer than an equity investment. You are guaranteed a specific rate of return, and most bonds are insured. However, equity investments provide greater opportunity to earn money.

What About Mutual Funds?

A **mutual fund** is a pool of money collected from many—maybe thousands—of investors, and then used to buy stocks, bonds, and other securities. If you buy shares of a mutual fund, you become a part owner of all the securities owned by the fund. The success of a mutual fund is not dependent on a single company, the way a stock is. Some of the assets in the fund might decrease in value, but if overall the assets increase in value, then the fund increases in value. This diversity helps minimize your risk over time.

Micro Loan Investments

One trend in banking is the use of micro loans to help people around the world escape from poverty. A micro loan is a very small loan—usually less than $3,500.00. Individuals and microfinance companies—companies that help match micro lenders with people in need—look for someone who would use the loan to start or grow a business. As the business grows, the borrower is able to repay the loan and begin earning income. For example, a borrower might need $500.00 to buy an oven for baking bread which she call sell. Without the oven, she has no way of earning money. With the oven, she can start and run a successful business. Micro loans have been very successful in developing countries such as Bangladesh, Ghana, and Vietnam, but they are also in use in the U.S.

Using the Internet or your library, research and report on micro loans and micro financing companies. Try to learn about the countries where micro loans have been most successful, and the types of businesses they fund. What type of business would you start with a micro loan?

Benefits to investing in a mutual fund include diversity, **liquidity**, which means you can sell your shares for cash at any time, and the fact that a professional manager makes the decisions about the assets to buy. Some mutual funds are available for a relatively small investment, possibly as low as $500.00.

Micro Loan Investments

Students are to research micro loans, the companies that offer them, and how they have been put to use. Mention to students that in the United States, the U.S. Small Business Administration (SBA) manages a micro loan program in which it makes funds available to nonprofit community-based lenders (such as a credit union) which, in turn, make loans to eligible borrowers. The maximum amount of the loan is $35,000. According to the SBA, the average loan size is about $13,000.

TEAMWORK ACTIVITY

Have teams of students brainstorm ideas for a business they would like to start up. Once they decide on the business, they should prepare a proposal to present to a micro loan company. The proposal should address the following:

- Name of the company.
- Product or service to be sold.
- Description of customers who will buy it.
- Explanation of how it will be produced, sold, and delivered.
- Estimation of the costs to produce, sell, and deliver it.

Have students read their proposals to the class. Have the class vote on whether or not they would grant a loan to the team.

Planning for Retirement

Retirement is the stage of life after you stop working, when you can relax and have time to do the things you enjoy. Of course, you need money to pay for your needs and wants, even though you have stopped earning wages. That's why it is important to start saving for retirement as soon as possible.

You can use regular savings and investment accounts to save for retirement. There are also some types of accounts designed specifically for retirement savings. Called **tax-deferred savings plans**, they have tax benefits that encourage people to save. The two most common tax-deferred savings plans are individual retirement accounts and 401(k) plans for private company employees and 403b for public employees.

- An **individual retirement account (IRA)** is a personal savings plan that allows you to set aside money for retirement, usually up to $2,000.00 per year. You do not pay taxes on the money you deposit into the IRA. You can start withdrawing from your IRA when you are 59½ years old. The withdrawals are taxed. A Roth IRA is a type of IRA with slightly different rules. You pay taxes on the money you deposit, so you can then withdraw it tax-free once you are 59½. For all IRAs, there are penalties for withdrawals made before age 59½.

- A **401(k)** or **403(b) plan** is a savings plan offered by an employer to an employee. The employee contributes a percentage of his or her earnings to the 401(k)/403(b) account each pay period. You do not pay income tax on the amount of the contribution. You pay taxes on the money you withdraw, starting at age 59½.

What's Social Security?

In Chapter 10, you read that one of the deductions from your paycheck is FICA. FICA is a tax used to fund the Social Security system. Social Security is a government program that pays monthly benefits to workers in the United States who pay the Social Security tax (FICA). It also pays benefits if you become disabled and cannot work, and to the spouse and children of workers who die before they retire. The benefits are based on the amount of Social Security tax you pay during your working life and the age when you retire.

Social Security provides a welcome income to many retirees, but it is usually not enough to cover living expenses, let alone provide for extra spending money.

- Experts estimate that for most people, Social Security benefits add up to about 40% of the yearly income you earned while you were working, but that you need about 70% to maintain your standard of living.

- You will need savings and investments to make up the 30% difference.

Some people think the Social Security system may run out of money before all of the people who have been contributing are able to collect benefits. The government often discusses ways to change the system to make sure benefits can be paid. Still, when you plan for retirement, you may want to think about the possibility that you may not ever collect any Social Security benefits, even if you paid your share of FICA.

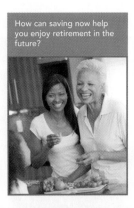

How can saving now help you enjoy retirement in the future?

21st Century Skills

What Happens Next?

Marilyn has been putting money in a savings account for five years, saving money to help pay for college. She has $2,200.00. The savings account earns about 2.5% interest. She thinks she has enough saved now that she might be able to earn more interest if she puts the money in a different type of account, or invests it.

The bank manager recommends putting $1,000.00 or $1,500.00 in a CD for 12 months at 3.8% interest. Marilyn is considering the CD, when her older brother offers to set up a stock trading account online for her. He recommends buying shares of the company where he works. The current stock price is $10.00 per share, so she has enough money to buy at least 200 shares, as well as pay the fees. He guarantees her the stock will go up.

Use the decision making process to help Marilyn. What choices does Marilyn have in front of her? What are the pros and cons of each choice? What information does she need to make the best choice? What factors should she take into consideration? Are there problems she might have to face? Using your 21st Century Skills—such as decision making, goal setting, and problem solving—write an ending to the story. Read it to the class, or form a small group and present it as a skit.

Vocabulary

401(k) or 403(b): Savings plan offered by an employer to an employee, in which the employee contributes a percentage of his or her pre-tax earnings to the account each pay period; the employee does not pay taxes on the money until he or she withdraws it. Employees can start making withdrawals at age 59½. They normally have to pay a penalty for withdrawals made before that age.

Individual retirement account (IRA): Personal savings plan that allows you to set aside money for retirement on which you do not have to pay taxes. Most IRA accounts allow you to deposit $2,000 maximum per year.

Tax-deferred savings plans: Retirement savings account that provides tax benefits which encourage people to save during their younger years.

Figure Focus

Ask students to comment on family members who are retired. Where did they retire from? Where do they live now? What do they do? What are their spending habits? Explain that financial experts agree you should start saving for retirement as soon as you land your first job after graduating from school. Consider this: If you put $2,000 a year (or about $166 a month) into savings beginning at age 25 and continue for 40 years, and you assume a 6 percent annual earnings rate, you will end up with about $310,000. If you wait until you're 35 to start saving and put away the same amount each year for only 30 years, you end up with just under $160,000, or only about half the money.

21st Century Skills

What Happens Next?

Students are to prepare an ending on how Marilyn should invest her savings. Have students review the description of a CD on page 231 of the text. They might also want to review the definitions of various investment terms presented on that same page. Their endings should consider the pros and cons of both options. The CD guarantees an ROI, but you also cannot touch the money for a specified time period unless you want to pay a penalty on your withdrawal. Stocks may provide a better ROI, but they are riskier because their prices depend on market fluctuations and the actions/reactions of other investors.

Customized Instruction: Less Advanced/At-Risk Students

Have students calculate how much money they would have at the end of five years if they saved $2 a week.

- $2 × 52 = $104
- $104 × 5 = $520

Ask students what they would buy with their savings.

Introduce the Section

This section covers the basics of insurance. An overview of the different types of insurance is provided, along with the definitions of common insurance terms.

Figure Focus

Explain that most lending institutions require mortgage customers to have homeowner's insurance. Ask students to discuss examples of when you might need homeowner's insurance. Damage caused by natural disasters, such as floods, tornadoes, and storms are usually covered by insurance policies. Most policies also cover damage from fire; theft; and heating, air-conditioning, and plumbing system malfunctions. In addition, damage due to vandalism, malicious mischief, and civil commotion or rioting is normally covered under a standard homeowner policy.

Vocabulary

Claim: Request for payment to cover a loss.

Deductible: Set amount the beneficiary must pay toward a claim before the insurance company pays any money.

Insurance: Investment that protects you financially against everyday risks.

Insurance agent: Someone who sells insurance.

Insurance policy: Contract issued by the insurance company.

Premium: Amount of money paid by the policy holder; may be paid all at once or at regular intervals.

Analyzing Insurance

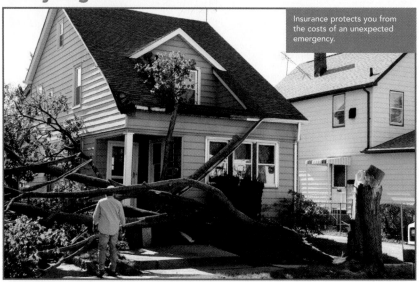

Insurance protects you from the costs of an unexpected emergency.

Another way to plan for your financial future is to buy insurance. **Insurance** is an investment that protects you financially against everyday risks. You can buy insurance to cover to almost anything, including your health, car, home, belongings, and even life. If you suffer an accident or loss in any of the covered areas, you can collect money to pay for the loss or to repair the damage.

Some insurance you use a lot, such as health insurance which helps pay for doctor's visits, prescription medications, and emergency medical care. Some insurance you hope you never need, such as life insurance you purchase for a child, which would pay you money if the child dies.

Insurance can be hard to understand. You pay money to protect yourself against something you hope never happens. If you are lucky, you pay for insurance your whole life, and never collect anything from it.

Insurance Terminology

Understanding insurance starts with understanding the terminology.

- The **insurance policy** is the contract issued by the insurance company.
- The **insurance agent** is someone who sells insurance. Some agents work for one insurance company, but some sell policies from many different companies.
- The **premium** is the amount of money paid by the policy holder. Premiums may be paid all at once, or at regular intervals. For example, you might pay a monthly premium for your car insurance, or your employer might withhold a health insurance premium from each paycheck.
- A **claim** is a request for payment to cover a loss. For example, if you break your leg, you put in a claim with your health insurance provider to cover the cost of the emergency room and orthopedic doctor.
- The **deductible** is a set amount the beneficiary must pay towards a claim before the insurance company pays any money.

Customized Instruction: Less Advanced/Special Needs/At-Risk Students

Explain that people buy health insurance to protect themselves against the high costs of health care. Ask students to make a list of measures they can take to prevent illnesses and injuries that would require expensive treatments. Some suggestions are eating healthy; avoiding risky behaviors that involve smoking, drinking alcohol, or using drugs; exercising safety, such as wearing a helmet and protective elbow, knee, and wrist pads for certain activities; and practicing good hygiene, such as brushing and flossing their teeth regularly. Have them share their lists with the class.

Life Insurance

Life insurance pays a benefit—called a *death benefit*—to your survivors if you die. It is important for a working parent to have life insurance, so that if the parent dies, the family will continue to have money to pay bills. There are two basic types of life insurance policies:

■ **Term insurance** provides protection for a specific dollar value. For example, you could buy a $350,000.00 term life insurance policy. If you die, the insurance company pays the **beneficiary**—the person who collects money if there is a claim—$350,000.00. Most term policies are renewable, which means you pay an annual premium and the policy is good for as long as you pay. The premiums may increase as you age, or if your health fails.

■ **Permanent—or cash-value—insurance** lets you save or invest money in the policy over time. You pay regular premiums that the insurance company puts in a saving account, or investment. The amount in the savings account is called the **cash value** of the policy; before you die, you can cancel the policy and withdraw the money. You can also borrow part of the cash value, or convert it into a retirement account. If you maintain the policy, when you die your beneficiary receives the death benefit, but not the cash value.

There are many variations of these two basic types of life insurance policies. You can learn more by talking to an insurance agent.

Health Insurance

The cost of health care can be overwhelming. Health insurance protects you against the high cost of health care. Some health insurance policies cover basic medical care, such as doctor's visits and hospital stays. Other policies cover major medical care, including long illnesses and rehabilitation.

Currently in the United States, many employers offer health insurance policies to employees. Large employers may be able to pay a portion of the premiums, or to negotiate lower, group rates. The government makes health coverage available to retirees and some disabled citizens. You can also purchase private insurance from an insurance company.

Every health insurance policy is different. Some pay a percentage of the bill, some have a deductible, and some are very specific about what is covered and what is not covered. They also vary in terms of the doctors you can use. For example, a fee for service policy lets you choose any doctor, while a preferred provider policy has a list of doctors from which you can choose.

MONEY MADNE$$

> **Y**ou twisted your ankle at soccer practice, and the coach thinks it might be broken. You go to the emergency room for x-rays. The x-rays cost $855.00. Your mother has health insurance that covers 80% of the cost of x-rays. How much will the insurance cover? How much will you have to pay?
>
> Hint: Calculate 80% of $855.00, then subtract that amount from $855.00.

Other Types of Insurance

✔ *Home owner's insurance, which protects your home from theft or damage. Most lenders require you to have home owner's insurance before they will loan you money for a mortgage.*

✔ *Renter's insurance, which protects your property from theft or damage if you rent an apartment.*

✔ *Auto insurance, which protects your automobile from theft or damage. Most states require you to have auto insurance before they allow you to register your car.*

✔ *Travel insurance, which protects you if you have to cancel or cut short a trip or vacation.*

✔ *Disability insurance, which protects your income if you are too ill or hurt to work. Your employer may offer some disability.*

✔ *Dental insurance, which protects you against the cost of dental care. Some employers offer dental coverage.*

How might the high cost of medical care impact a family's budget?

Vocabulary

Beneficiary: Person named in an insurance policy who collects money if there is a claim.

Cash value: Amount of money saved in the insurance policy account.

Permanent or cash-value insurance: Life insurance policy that lets you save or invest money in the policy over time.

Term insurance: Life insurance policy that provides protection for a specific dollar value.

MONEY MADNE$$

To calculate 80% of $855, multiply $855 by .80. This is $684. To determine the out-of-pocket expense, subtract $684 from $855, which equals $171.

Figure Focus

Explain that even with health insurance, medical expenses incurred to treat a prolonged illness or one that requires extensive or experimental treatment can multiply exponentially and at a rapid rate. Medical expenses such as these are often unexpected. Many families might not budget enough for them or budget anything at all.

Teaching Tips

Most students will not be involved in buying insurance. You might want to quiz students on the different types:

■ **Life:** Pays a death benefit to your survivors.

■ **Health:** Protects you against the high cost of health care.

■ **Dental:** Protects you against the cost of dental care.

■ **Homeowners:** Protects your home and possessions.

■ **Renter:** Protects your possessions if you rent.

■ **Auto:** Protects you and others from financial ruin in the event of a car accident.

■ **Travel:** Protects you from problems that might occur when you travel, such as emergency evacuations, trip cancellations, and medical emergencies or illness.

■ **Disability:** Protects your income if you cannot work due to illness or disability.

End-of-Chapter Activities

Case Study

It may not have balanced because there may have been fees for using the ATM at the arcade, or for writing a check.

Keshawn could have made sure he knew about all the fees for all types of transactions. He could have planned ahead for the arcade by withdrawing money from his usual ATM.

Once Keshawn knows the amount of the fees, he can subtract them from his account, and his statement should balance. Keshawn can ask someone at the bank to help him review his statement to see where he made an error. He can make a list of the locations of ATMs that will not charge fees—those affiliated with his credit union—so he can find one if he needs it. He can make sure there is extra money in his account so if he ever needs to write a check or use an "out-of-network" ATM again, he will have enough money for the fees.

Sounding Off!

Student answers will vary.

FAQ

1. The two basic reasons are to keep it safe and to earn interest.

2. A credit union is a nonprofit organization owned by the members.

3. You fill out a signature card when you open an account. A signature card helps keep your account safe, because it identifies the person authorized to use the account.

4. When you balance your account, you know exactly how much money you have in your account.

5. Investing is riskier than saving, because the deposit is usually not insured, and your return on investment (ROI)—the amount of money you earn compared to the amount of money you invest—is not guaranteed. It is possible that you will lose all of the money you invest.

6. Simple interest is calculated based on the principal balance only. Compounded interest is calculated based on the principal plus interest that has already been earned.

7. Tax-deferred savings plans are an IRA, 401(k), and 403(b).

Case Study

When Keshawn turned 16, his parents agreed that he could get a checking account with a debit card from the local credit union. The first few months, Keshawn was very careful. He used his debit card to buy things only if he knew he had enough money in his account. When he needed cash, he always used the ATM at the credit union branch where he opened the account. He never wrote checks. Every month he compared his withdrawals and deposits to his bank statement to make sure they matched.

One day, Keshawn used an ATM at an arcade to get money for the games and concessions. A few days later, he tried to use the ATM at the mall, but his card was denied. He borrowed the money from a friend, and wrote his friend a check to pay for it.

When Keshawn received his bank statement, the account did not balance. The bank said he had less money than he thought. All of the purchases, deposits, and withdrawals were the same. He checked his math, and it was correct. He didn't know what was wrong.

- Why do you think Keshawn's account did not balance?
- Did Keshawn make the best decisions?
- What should he do to fix the problem?

Sounding Off!

① Do you think it is the government's responsibility to provide retirement income such as Social Security to everyone?

② Do you think you and your peers need life insurance? Why or why not?

FAQ

1. What are the two basic reasons for putting your money in a bank?
2. What type of bank is a nonprofit organization owned by the members?
3. What is the purpose of a signature card?
4. Why is it important to balance your bank account?
5. Explain which is riskier, saving or investing?
6. What is the difference between simple interest and compound interest?
7. List two tax-deferred savings plans.
8. What is insurance?
9. List four things for which you might buy insurance.
10. What is an insurance premium?

8. Insurance is an investment that protects you financially against everyday risks.

9. Things include health care, automobile, home, apartment or rental unit, life, dental, disability, and travel.

10. The premium is the amount of money paid by the policy holder for the insurance.

Divide into teams of four or five and play a version of the Stock Market Game. Each team will have the same amount of money to invest. Research different companies and select those in which you want to invest. Consider mutual funds or other types of investments. Decide what you want to buy, and commit to your investments.

Keep records of your purchases, including the purchase price, the number of shares, and any fees you have to pay. You may want to set up a spreadsheet to track your investments. Follow your portfolio for at least one week. At the end of the week, sell everything. The team that has the greatest profit wins.

Discuss your experience as a class. How did you pick your investments? How did you assess your risk? Did you make smart choices? Could you have done anything?

Hot Topics

Do you worry about money? Do you understand your family's financial situation? Do you have questions or concerns about where your money comes from, how it is spent, and whether there is enough for the future?

Take this opportunity to write anonymously about your concerns. Use a word processor so no one recognizes your handwriting. Be honest and open. Put the paper in the class Hot Topics box.

As a class, read the anonymous entries and discuss them.

Web Extra ▼

There are many government Web sites designed to provide consumers with information about finances and other money issues. Some, such as USA.gov, has a section specifically for teens. Use the Internet to locate useful government Web sites, and make a directory of the sites. Include a brief description of the information available on the site. Post the directory on your school Web site, or make it available in your school library.

Problem Solver

Working in pairs, discuss your requirements for a bank account with your partner. Tell each other why you need a bank account, how you plan to use the account, and what you are looking for in a bank.

Together, research the banks in your community to learn about the types of accounts and services they offer. Use information you find in advertisements or on the Internet to compare interest rates, locations, fees, and other factors. If possible, visit a branch of each bank and talk to a manager or assistant manager about accounts for people your age.

When you have completed your research, prepare a report for your partner, recommending a bank and bank account. It might be a written report, an oral presentation, or a graphic presentation. Explain why you chose the bank and account, how it meets your partner's requirements, and why it might be better than some of the other options. Present your report in front of the class.

Team Players

Students can go to www.stockmarketgame.org to play the game. Make sure they prepare a report or chart that lists the names of their investments, the price at which they started, and the price at which they ended.

Hot Topics

Make sure students understand that they can turn in their papers anonymously. Encourage them to be open and honest about their concerns regarding their family's financial situation.

Web Extra

Students are to research government Web sites that provide information on finances and other money issues. They should create a directory that describes each site and make it available on the school's Web site and in your school library. Students should search for sites with addresses that end in .gov or .org.

Problem Solver

Students are to work in pairs. They are to find out what their partner is looking for in a bank account. Encourage students to question each other on their goals for the account. Do they want to save for college? Or, do they want to have a place to safely store money that they can easily access through an ATM or by using a debit card? Each is to recommend a bank within the community that offers the type of bank account they think is most suitable for their partner. They should prepare a report or presentation on their recommendation.

Write Now

Students are to write an essay on their opinion about minimum age requirements on opening a checking account. Remind students to state their opinion in the first paragraph and then provide two to three supporting arguments for their opinion, and to end with a conclusion.

Be Involved!

Students are to identify a savings goal. Review the steps to a goal.

1. Identify the goal and write it down with as much detail as possible.

2. Assess whether the goal is something you really want. Or, is it what someone else wants for you or something you *think* you want because someone else has it?

3. Make a plan for achieving the goal. What resources will you need?

4. Write down your action plan for achieving the goal, being as specific as possible.

Encourage students to open a savings account if they don't already have one. Review how to open a savings account.

- Find a bank where you'd like to open your account.

- Tell the bank what you would like to accomplish with your savings account. Most banks offer a variety of accounts and will be able to suggest the one that will help you meet your goals.

- Bring a photo ID and your Social Security card.

- Some banks require a minimum deposit when you open an account, so you'll need money to place in the account.

Follow up at the end of the term to see if students achieved their goal. If they did not, ask them to determine why.

Social Networking

Students are to organize the collection of items for senior citizens. They are to solicit donations from the school community and others as is deemed appropriate, and deliver the donations to a local senior center or assisted living facility.

Write Now

Do you think banks should have a minimum age requirement for people opening a checking account? Write an opinion essay about the topic. State your thesis, and then support it with facts. The essay should be at least four paragraphs in length, including an introduction and a conclusion. Read your essay to the class, and discuss it.

Be Involved!

www.fcclainc.org

As a class, discuss the importance of saving as a way to achieve financial goals. Share financial goals, or brainstorm goals together. Some goals might be to save for a trip, education, clothes, computer, or car. Other goals might be to save to buy a gift for someone or make a charitable donation.

Individually or with your teacher or advisor, identify a realistic savings goal for yourself. Use the five-step goal-setting process to define the goal. Determine how much you will need to save each month and where you will deposit the money. Set a start date and specify the term—how long you will save in order to achieve your goal.

If you do not have a savings account, contact banks in your community to learn about no-fee student accounts. Open an account and start working toward your goal.

With your parent or guardian's permission, you may enroll in an online savings partner such as youthsaves.org for support and assistance in achieving your goal. You can enroll online at youthsaves.org.

As you work toward your goal, keep a journal to record your progress, and collect documentation that you can use to show what you have achieved. At the end of the term, evaluate your success. Did you save as much money as you expected? Were you able to achieve your goal? Use your experience to organize an America Saves campaign in your community to encourage other people to save and achieve their financial goals, too.

Social Networking

Many senior citizens rely on their Social Security checks for their income. After they pay their living expenses, they may not have much money left over for extra purchases.

As a class, organize a Senior Special drive to collect items seniors might appreciate, such as special toiletries, warm socks and blankets, fancy tea, and books with large print. Advertise the event, and invite the school community and others to participate. Donate the items you collect to your community senior center or to an assisted living home in the area.

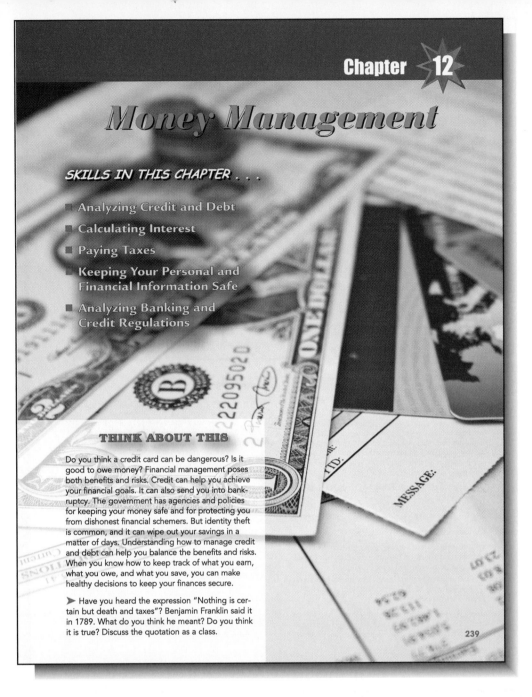

Chapter 12

Money Management

SKILLS IN THIS CHAPTER . . .

- Analyzing Credit and Debt
- Calculating Interest
- Paying Taxes
- Keeping Your Personal and Financial Information Safe
- Analyzing Banking and Credit Regulations

THINK ABOUT THIS

Do you think a credit card can be dangerous? Is it good to owe money? Financial management poses both benefits and risks. Credit can help you achieve your financial goals. It can also send you into bankruptcy. The government has agencies and policies for keeping your money safe and for protecting you from dishonest financial schemers. But identity theft is common, and it can wipe out your savings in a matter of days. Understanding how to manage credit and debt can help you balance the benefits and risks. When you know how to keep track of what you earn, what you owe, and what you save, you can make healthy decisions to keep your finances secure.

➤ Have you heard the expression "Nothing is certain but death and taxes"? Benjamin Franklin said it in 1789. What do you think he meant? Do you think it is true? Discuss the quotation as a class.

239

Chapter 12 Overview

This chapter provides an overview of credit and debt and how to responsibly manage both. Tax basics are covered, and students also learn how to safeguard their financial resources.

Analyzing Credit and Debt   This section discusses sources of credit and the obligations you accept when you borrow money.

Calculating Interest   Students discover that understanding types of interest and how it is calculated can lead to healthy decisions concerning their borrowing and saving practices.

Paying Taxes   Students learn why they are taxed, how to calculate taxes, and the importance of filing income tax returns.

Keeping Your Personal and Financial Information Safe   Discovering techniques to keep personal information safe is an important part of understanding financial responsibility and preventing identity theft.

Analyzing Banking and Credit Regulations Students analyze laws and regulations that apply to financial and banking activities. These laws are designed to protect consumers and promote financial responsibility.

Focus and Engage

Bell-Ringer: Think About This

Students are asked to consider the quote from Ben Franklin. The quote is meant to make a comparison between the inevitability of death and the inescapable burden of paying taxes. Students probably have not felt the "inescapable burden" of paying taxes yet, so you might want to explain generally the taxes that adults are responsible for paying (income, consumption/sales, and asset taxes) and how that tax money is used by the government.

ADVANCE PREPARATION	
Review	*Life Skills for the 21st Century* textbook, Chapter 12.
Prepare	Paper and pencil for some activities. Calculators. Box labeled "Hot Topics." Poster board for the *Social Networking* activity.

CUSTOMIZED INSTRUCTION OVERVIEW				
Less Advanced Students	More Advanced Students	ESOL Students	Special Needs Students	At-Risk Students
Pages 242, 248	Page 241	Page 251	Page 246	Pages 242, 246

Introduce the Section

This section explores what credit means, and identifies both the positive and negative impacts it can have on an individual's financial wellness.

Figure Focus

Ask students if their parents ever complain about the mail or phone calls they get with offers for credit cards. Explain that credit cards are issued by banks, savings and loans, retail stores, and other businesses as a means for the cardholder to repeatedly borrow money or buy products and services on credit. How many students have a credit card, or one their parents allow them to use?

Vocabulary

Credit: Money that you borrow and promise to pay back.
Creditor: The person or organization that loans money.
Debt: Money that you borrowed and owe.
Debtor: The person that owes money.

Teaching Tips

Have students bring in credit offers they or their parents have received in the mail. As a class, read the offers as well as the conditions of the deal in the small print. Discuss why you would have a credit card and why you would choose to have one credit card over another. For instance, if students shop at only one store, it may be beneficial to have a credit card with that store in order to receive discounts and buy things on credit. However, having a credit card with each of seven stores may become overwhelming and tempt you to spend more than you budgeted for.

Analyzing Credit and Debt

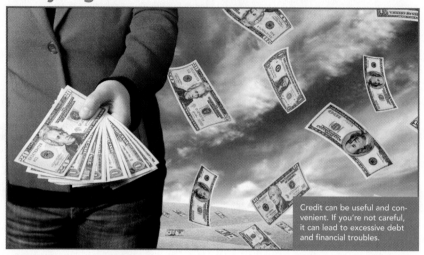

Credit can be useful and convenient. If you're not careful, it can lead to excessive debt and financial troubles.

Credit is money that you borrow and promise to pay back. **Debt** is the money that you borrowed and owe. If you owe money, you are a **debtor**. If you loan money, you are a **creditor**.

When you use credit responsibly, it can be very convenient, because you can use it to buy things now and pay for them later. You might use a credit card to pay for a shirt, because you know your grandmother is going to give you money for your birthday next week. When you receive the money, you can pay the credit card bill.

When you use credit irresponsibly, you might wind up with so much debt that you can never pay it back. What happens if you buy a shirt that costs more than your grandmother gives you? How will you pay the credit card bill?

There are two basic types of credit:

■ Cash credit lets you borrow money. You can get cash credit from a bank, an insurance company, some retailers, and from credit card companies.

■ Sales credit lets you buy things. You can get sales credit from businesses, such as stores that want you to buy their merchandise.

Managing credit and debt responsibly shows that you are trustworthy, you understand the difference between needs and wants, and you can make healthy financial decisions.

Paying It Back

A loan is a transaction in which the lender agrees to give the borrower money and expects to be repaid in full. If the lender does not expect the money back, then it is a gift, not a loan. You can get a loan from a bank, business, credit company, insurance company, relative, or friend.

Most loans have terms that are written in a contract that both the lender and the borrower sign. For example, you might agree to repay the loan by a certain date, and you might agree to pay a specific rate of interest.

A contract protects both the lender and the borrower. It spells out all the conditions so everyone involved knows what to expect. If there is no contract, there may be misunderstandings between the borrower and the lender.

Generally speaking, borrowing more money than you can repay is not good for your well-being. Your credit history will suffer, you will be unable to get new loans, and personal relationships with the lender will suffer. You are likely to suffer stress.

Likewise, if you lend money to a friend or family member who does not pay you back, you may become angry, hurt, and resentful. Your relationship will suffer.

Stay in School

In recent years, the unemployment rate for high school dropouts has soared, with some reports claiming it to be as high as 33 percent. That means that roughly one in three students who did not graduate from high school is unemployed. Explain to students that without a job or steady source of income, many people are unable to establish credit. Without credit, it is extremely difficult to obtain a loan for a car, home, or college education, or even to start up a business. In addition, you might not be able to find a landlord to rent you an apartment. Emphasize the importance of a high school diploma to an individual's financial future. High school graduates have many more career options and job opportunities, make about 35 percent more in income than a dropout, and have better opportunities to establish and maintain good credit ratings.

Should I Have a Credit Card?

A credit card is useful and convenient. It lets you make a bunch of purchases and then pay for them all at the same time by writing a single check, or making a single electronic funds transfer. A credit card can come in handy in an emergency, such as paying for repairs or towing if your car breaks down. If you use it responsibly, it helps you establish credit so you can get loans in the future.

"I better use this card—I think I'm close to my credit limit on the others."

Responsible credit card use means:

- Paying the entire balance by the due date each month
- Only using it to buy items that you can afford
- Using your credit card sometimes, but also using cash, checks, or your debit card
- Saving all receipts and checking your statement carefully for errors each month

Having too many cards can cause problems for you in the future, even if you don't use them all, or if you pay your bills on time. Potential lenders assume you will *max out*—or use all of the available credit—on every card you own. If they believe you have too much credit, they will reject a loan application. You might not be able to borrow money for education or to buy a car.

Credit Card Woes

A credit card can get you into financial trouble if you aren't careful. If you use it to buy more than you can afford, and if you fail to pay your bill in full each month, you may end up deep in debt. The information will become part of your credit report. Banks, landlords, and even employers will doubt your ability to make responsible decisions and repay loans.

Credit card companies are in business to make money. Each card comes with a set of terms and conditions that states the fees, penalties, and other charges that the company can impose. Common terms and conditions include:

- *Credit limit:* the maximum amount of purchases you can charge to the card
- *Annual percentage rate:* the interest you pay on your outstanding balance
- *Annual fee:* the yearly charge for using credit
- *Grace period:* the length of time from when you make a purchase to when you start accumulating interest
- *Late fee:* the fee charged when you make a payment past the due date
- *Over-limit fee:* the fee you pay when you charge an amount over your credit limit
- *Minimum payment:* a percentage of the outstanding balance that must be paid each month

The only way to avoid paying additional fees and charges is to pay your balance in full and on time every month. If you don't, the fees and charges are added to your balance, which continues to grow, even if you don't make any new purchases. If you only pay the minimum amount required you will be paying that same bill for many years. In fact, you may never pay it off.

Can I Borrow 20 Bucks?

Borrowing from friends and family can help you achieve certain financial goals. You might be able to get a loan from a relative even if you don't qualify at the bank. But, it's still a loan, and you still have to pay it back. Acting responsibly as a borrower will keep your relationship intact. Taking advantage of a friend or relative by ignoring your responsibilities is likely to hurt your relationship.

👎 You skip payments

👎 You use the money for frivolous wants

👎 You borrow for something you can afford on your own

👎 You forget to put the terms in writing

👍 You make all payments on time and in full until the loan is repaid

A loan from a friend or relative adds to your debt. If you already have high credit card bills, or other outstanding loans, you might find yourself in over your head, which means you do not have enough income to pay all of your bills. What can you do to avoid excessive debt?

Figure Focus

Explain that a credit limit is the maximum amount of credit a credit card company will extend to you at any given time. The limit varies and depends on how much money you have been able to repay in the past, the company's general standards, whether you pay your bills on time, and if you have requested a higher limit.

Can I Borrow 20 Bucks?

To avoid excessive debt, you can:

- Pay for purchases in cash or with a debit card so you are aware of exactly how much you have to spend.
- Leave your credit card at home instead of carrying it with you. You won't be tempted to buy something if you don't have the card with you.
- Avoid applying for more credit cards than you need.
- Seek help if you feel you are not in control of your finances or don't understand why your credit card bills are as high as they are.
- Keep a personal budget and retain receipts for all financial transactions.

Discuss

Explain to students the ramifications of paying only the minimum payment on their credit card. Use the following example: If you have a credit card balance of $1,000 with an annual interest rate of 18%, the interest that will be applied each month is 1.5% (divide 18% by 12 monthly payments). Most banks require that you pay a minimum of 2.5% of your balance. Assuming you make the minimum payment, your first month's payment will be $25 ($1,000 × 2.5%). Considering the card's interest rate, $15 of the $25 you paid will go toward the interest alone with only $10 being deducted from your credit card balance.

Customized Instruction: More Advanced Students

Pose this problem to students: You borrowed $1,000 from your parents to help pay for a car. They have asked you to come up with a plan on how you will pay it back. They would like you to make payments on the loan every month. They will not charge any interest for the first six months, but after that, they are tacking on an additional $10 "in interest" to each month's payment. You earn $4,000 a year at your after-school job. Have students prepare a plan on how they would go about paying off the loan.

Reinforce and Review

Discuss with students the measures they can take to establish and maintain a strong credit history. One of the most important things they can do at a young age is to avoid overdrafts, or writing checks for which they do not have sufficient funds to cover. A bounced check can be a black mark on your credit history for a long period of time. Having a steady job and source of income is also a plus.

Ways to Protect Your Credit

Discuss with students the issue of identity theft. Roughly 750,000 Americans fall victim to identity theft each year. To protect yourself from identity theft on your computer:

- Keep anti-virus and anti-spyware software up to date.
- Shop only on secured sites that say they are encrypted and have locked graphics.
- Check your credit report periodically.
- Never enter your Social Security number on a Web site.
- Be sure that you are on the site you intend to be on. Many bogus sites are intentionally designed to look like Web sites for legitimate businesses.

 The World Bank

Students are to report on a project for which the World Bank provided a loan or credit. Examples of areas the World Bank supports include:

- Reduction of greenhouse gases.
- Improving the sanitation and water supply of communities.
- Relieving the debt burden of impoverished people.

Vocabulary

Credit report: A report summarizing your credit history.

Credit score: A three-digit number that ranks your likelihood of paying loans.

Ways to Protect Your Credit

You can keep your credit safe by making sure your credit information does not get into the hands of an unauthorized person. To keep your credit safe:

✔ *Keep a list of your account numbers in a safe, secure place.*

✔ *Keep a list of the contact information for your banks and lenders.*

✔ *Keep your credit, debit, and ATM cards in a safe place.*

✔ *Report lost or stolen cards immediately.*

✔ *Do not give anyone who calls, texts, or e-mails you your account number.*

✔ *Do not give anyone your PIN.*

✔ *Shred documents that have your account number on them.*

How Do I Establish Credit?

At some point in your life, you will need a loan. You might need an education loan to go to college, an auto loan to buy a car, or a mortgage to buy a house. You might apply for a credit card to use to pay for purchases.

Before a bank or retailer will give you a loan or issue you a credit card, it checks your credit history to find out if you know how to manage money and make healthy financial decisions. Landlords check your credit history before they rent you an apartment. Specifically, lenders check whether you have money in a bank account, whether you already have debt, and whether you pay your bills on time.

It takes time to establish credit, but it is worth the effort. Positive steps for establishing credit include:

- Maintaining bank account balances
- Earning a paycheck
- Paying bills on time
- Paying rent

Having a credit card is also a good way to establish credit. Most credit cards have age restrictions, but when you are old enough, you can ask a parent or other adult to co-sign for the card. Both of your names will be on the account, but it gives you the opportunity to make payments and learn how to use the card responsibly.

What's a Credit Report?

A **credit report** is a summary of your credit history—usually for the past 7 to 10 years. If you have a good credit history, lenders will loan you money. If you have a poor credit history, they won't. For example, if you have a few loans and credit cards, and you pay all of your bills on time every month, banks, landlords, and other lenders will believe you are responsible. If you have many credit cards with high outstanding balances, and you regularly miss payments or pay late, the lenders will believe you are irresponsible.

A credit report lists:

- All of the loans you have received, including all credit cards
- Your outstanding balances—the money you owe
- Whether you have paid your bills on time
- The names of agencies or companies who have recently requested copies of your credit report
- Your **credit score**, which is a three-digit number that ranks your likelihood of repaying your loans

The information is collected by a credit bureau, or consumer credit reporting company, and sold to banks and other lenders. For example, a landlord might request your credit report to see if you can be trusted to pay your rent on time.

> **The World Bank**
>
> The World Bank is not really a bank at all. It is a part of the United Nations called a specialized agency. It includes two organizations—the International Bank for Reconstruction and Development and the International Development Association. Together, they support efforts to improve the lives of people in developing countries by providing low-interest loans, interest-free credit, and grants. The funds are used in a wide range of areas such as agriculture, water supply, science and technology, and education.
>
> Using resources in your library or on the Internet, research the World Bank and the areas that it supports. Select a project for which it provided a loan or credit and report on it to your class.

Customized Instruction: Less Advanced/At-Risk Students

Present the following scenario to students: If you spent more than your credit card limit, could not pay the balance, and had to borrow money from your parents, how would it impact the relationship you have with them?

There are three nationwide consumer credit reporting companies in the United States: Equifax, Experian, and TransUnion.

By law, you can obtain one copy of your credit report for free, once a year, from each of the three credit bureaus. Looking over your credit report gives you the opportunity to see if there are any mistakes that might hurt your chances of getting a loan. It also lets you see if any unauthorized people have been trying to get credit in your name. If you find an error, notify the reporting agency immediately. It must investigate the problem and correct it, if necessary.

How Do I Avoid Debt?

Some debt is inevitable over the course of your life. As long as you make your payments in full and on time, you are managing your debt responsibly. The problems come when debt grows to the point where you do not have enough money to pay your debt. The costs of the debt—fees, penalties, and finance charges—continue to accumulate, and you are unable to meet your obligations.

Excessive debt may be caused by irresponsible use of credit cards and loans, but it can also be caused by unexpected expenses such as medical bills. Using a budget, saving, and setting financial goals will help you keep your debt in control.

■ Pay all of your bills in full and on time every month.

■ Keep accurate records, so you always know how much you have and how much you owe.

■ Do not purchase more than you can afford.

How Do I Get out of Debt?

When debt grows to the point that you cannot pay more than the monthly minimum, or maybe not even that, it will affect your well-being. It is not easy, but you can get out of debt.

■ Figure out how much you owe.

■ Stop using your credit cards.

■ Analyze your budget and cut out all nonessential expenses.

■ Set aside as much as possible to paying your bills.

The last straw is when you have spent all of your money and cannot pay any of your bills. At that point you may be faced with bankruptcy. **Bankruptcy** is a process in which you declare yourself legally unable to pay your outstanding debts. A judge approves your request, and most of your debts, including those owed to credit card companies and doctors or hospitals, are cleared so you can start over. Bankruptcy negatively affects your credit report, making it very difficult to get credit again for a long time.

"If I miss a payment, what will happen to my credit score?"

21st Century Skills — What Happens Next?

As soon as Miguel turned 21, his bank issued him a credit card. It had an introductory annual percentage rate (APR) of 9.9%, and no annual fee for the first year. Miguel charged about $300.00 worth of purchases each month. He was out, bought new clothes, and upgraded the stereo system in his car. He made payments every month, but never quite managed to pay off the balance.

When he turned 22, Miguel graduated from college with a degree in computer science. He had $35,000.00 in education loans. He was hired for an entry-level programming job and earned $22.00 an hour. He planned to live with his parents until he saved some money and could afford his own apartment. He traded in his old car for a new, used car. The car payments were $185.00 per month.

Miguel's parents decided to move to a retirement community. They told him to start looking for another place to live. Miguel put in applications at three apartments, but they all rejected him as a tenant.

Use the decision-making process to help Miguel. What choices does he face? What are the consequences of each option? What obstacles are in his way? How can he solve his problems. Using your 21st Century Skills—such as decision making, goal setting, and problem solving—write an ending to the story. Read it to the class, or form a small group and present it as a skit.

21st Century Skills

What Happens Next?

Discuss Miguel's financial situation:

■ He charged about $3,600 on his credit card in the first year he had it.

■ When he graduated from college, he had $35,000 in student loans to pay off. The monthly payment on student loans varies widely, but assume he's paying about $200 a month.

■ He has a $185 per month car payment, which amounts to $2,220 per year.

■ At $22 an hour and 40 hours a week, Miguel's gross income (before taxes) is about $45,000 per year.

Miguel must come up with a plan to improve his credit rating. He is employed and has a steady income, which will help. He should decrease his credit card purchases and put extra income toward paying off his credit card debt. He should pay his student loan on time every month, and pay more on it if he can manage it. By establishing a good credit rating, he will have a better chance of being accepted as a renter. He might also consider an arrangement in which he shares an apartment with a roommate who has good credit. Sharing expenses could be beneficial to both of them.

Figure Focus

Explain that your credit score is a quick method for lenders to determine if you are creditworthy.

■ Your payment history constitutes around 35 percent of your score, so if you consistently pay credit card bills late, it will hurt your score. Not paying your bills at all will force the bank to assume your account is a charge-off and close it without your permission. If your account is sent to collections, creditors, or a third party, it can substantially lower your credit score in addition to added late fees.

■ The second most important part of your credit score is your level of debt. If you have high credit card balances or have exceeded your card limit, you will see a significant drop in your credit score.

Vocabulary

Bankruptcy: A process in which a judge approves your request to clear all of your debts because you are legally unable to pay your outstanding debts.

Discuss

In 2008, more than 1 million bankruptcies were filed in U.S. courts. Filing for bankruptcy can have a negative and lasting effect on your credit rating. Your credit score will be lowered and, subsequently, credit card companies will charge a higher interest on your account, banks can refuse to give you a loan for a home or vehicle, and it may be more difficult to find a landlord to rent to you.

Emphasize to the class that declaring bankruptcy does not mean all of your debt is wiped away.

■ Those who file for Chapter 7 bankruptcy must demonstrate that there is no hope of paying off debts and that they earn less than the state median income. If you are eligible, a trustee is appointed to ensure that your creditors are paid as much as possible of what you owe them. The more of your assets the trustee is able to recover for your creditors, the more the trustee is paid.

■ Under Chapter 13 bankruptcy, you remain in control of your assets but must create an approved plan to repay your creditors. Some of the debt may be erased depending on your income, but the substantial debt owed still has to be paid.

TEAMWORK ACTIVITY

Divide the class into teams. Have each team contact a bank or retailer and learn more about the credit card it offers. Students should find out how to apply for the card, who can apply, any annual fees, the interest rate, and the minimum payment required. Have each team share their information with the class.

Introduce the Section

This section provides an overview on interest rates, what they are applied to, and how they are calculated.

Figure Focus

Explain that in simple terms, you want to avoid paying interest but you want to look for opportunities to earn interest.

Reinforce and Review

- A **loan** is a sum of money borrowed from a bank or other party.

- **Credit** is money you borrow and promise to pay back.

- **Debt** is money that you borrowed and owe.

- **Interest** is the fee paid for using someone else's money.

- **Principal** is the account balance or loan amount.

- **Simple interest** is calculated on the principal balance only.

- **Compounded interest** is calculated on the principal plus interest that has already been earned.

- **Term** is the set amount of time for a loan.

- **Annual percentage rate (APR)** is the annual interest without compounding or other added charges.

- **Annual percentage yield (APY)** is the annual interest including compounding.

Calculating Interest

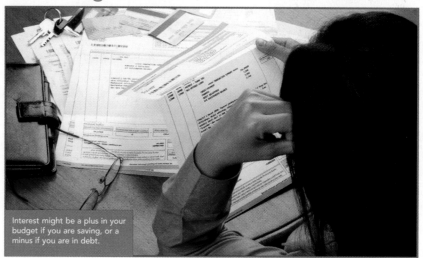

Interest might be a plus in your budget if you are saving, or a minus if you are in debt.

Recall that interest is a fee paid for using someone else's money. It is calculated as a percentage of the principal—the account balance or loan amount. You might have realized that interest works in two ways.

- You *earn* interest on savings and investments. When you deposit money in an account, the bank pays you interest because they use your money.

- You *pay* interest on debt. When you borrow money, you pay the lender interest because you are using its money.

Understanding the types of interest and how interest is calculated will help you make healthy decisions about borrowing, saving, and lending money. You will know how to include interest in your budget, which will make it easier for you to achieve your financial goals.

Interest Terminology

Banks and lenders use some confusing terms to advertise the interest rates on loans and investments. To really know how much interest you will earn or owe, it's important to understand the following:

- The annual percentage rate (APR) is the annual interest without compounding or other added charges. Credit card companies usually advertise this rate using large, bold type, because it makes the amount of interest you will be charged seem smaller than it really is.

- The annual percentage yield (APY) is the annual interest including compounding. Banks usually advertise this rate in big numbers, because it makes the amount of interest you will earn seem greater than it really is.

When you compare offers, make sure you are comparing APR to APR, and APY to APY. For example, you might get an offer for credit card with a 13% APR. If you do the math, that equals a 13.8% APY. Likewise, you might see an ad for a CD with a 4.5% APY. That's really a 4.4% APR. Look carefully in the small print to find the truth.

Calculating Simple Interest

Simple interest is calculated based on the principal amount only. Most student loans use simple interest. So do many certificates of deposit (CDs).

To calculate simple interest: Multiply the amount of Principal (P) times the Interest Rate (r) times the number of Time (t) periods that make up the duration of the loan.

For example, if you deposit $500.00 in a savings account that earns 2% annual interest, at the end of one year, you will earn $10.00 of interest:

$500.00 × .02 × 1 = $10.00

Calculating Compound Interest

Compound interest is calculated based on the principal and on any interest that has already been added to the principal. Credit cards, auto loans, mortgages, and investments use compound interest.

To calculate compound interest, you calculate the simple interest for the time period, add it to the principal, and then calculate the simple interest for the next time period on the new principal balance, add it to the principal, and so on for the duration of the loan.

For example, if you deposit $500 in a savings account that earns 2% annual interest, compounded quarterly, at the end of one year you will earn $10.07. Remember to use the compounding time period in your calculation—in this case quarterly, which is ¼ or 0.25.

Quarter 1: $500.00 × .02 × .25 = $2.50
Quarter 2: $502.50 × .02 × .25 = $2.51
Quarter 3: $505.01 × .02 × .25 = $2.52
Quarter 4: $507.54 × .02 × .25 = $2.54

The total interest for the year, $10.07, might not seem like much, but if you borrow $150,000.00 to buy a home, or invest $5,000.00 in a CD with a 6% APR compounded quarterly, you will soon see that compound interest adds up much faster than simple interest!

MONEY MADNE$$

"Why is it more fun calculating interest I earn than it is calculating interest I owe?"

On the day you were born, your parents opened a savings account in your name with an initial deposit of $200.00. Every month since then, they deposited $25.00 in the account. You just celebrated your fourteenth birthday. How much have your parents deposited? Hint: Multiply $25.00 times 12 to find the total deposit for each year, and then multiply that by 14.

If the account earned 2% APR without compounding, how much would be in the account? What if the account earned 2% compounded quarterly? Hint: Use a spreadsheet program to set up the calculations.

Using an Average Daily Balance

Most credit card companies use an average daily balance as the principal amount when they calculate how much interest you owe. To get your average daily balance, you total the balance from each day in the billing cycle, and then divide the sum by the number of days in the billing cycle. What if you charge $200.00 for gifts on December 15?

★ *December 1–14, you had a daily balance of $0.00.*

★ *December 15–31, you had a daily balance of $200.00.*

★ *To get your total balance for 31 days you add $0.00 for each of the first 14 days, and $200.00 for each of the last 17 days. The total is $3,400.00.*

★ *Divide $3,400 by 31, the number of days in December.*

★ *Your average daily balance is $106.68.*

The credit card company uses the following formula to calculate your interest: (Average Daily Balance × APR × Number of Days in Billing Cycle) ÷ 365. If your APR is 13%, your interest for December would be $1.18: ($106.68 × .13 × 31) ÷ 365 = $1.18. How can you avoid being charged interest on credit card purchases?

Using an Average Daily Balance

Review with students responsible credit card use.

- Pay the entire balance by the due date each month.
- Only use your credit card to buy items that you can afford.
- Use your credit card sometimes, but also use cash, checks, or your debit card.
- Save all receipts and check your statement carefully for errors each month.
- Limit yourself to one or two credit cards.

Discuss

You might also discuss fixed rate and floating or adjustable interest rates. A fixed interest rate is one that does not change for the duration of the loan. A floating interest rate is one that changes on a periodic basis. The change is usually tied to another rate, such as the prime interest rate. You might opt for a fixed rate loan when interest rates are low. This would allow you to lock in the low rate and not be concerned with fluctuations. You might opt for a floating rate when interest rates are high on a consistent basis. This would allow you to benefit when the rates eventually fall. At that point, some lenders allow you to switch to a fixed rate loan.

MONEY MADNE$$

To calculate how much money you would have on your fourteenth birthday:

$200 + ($25 × 12 months per year × 14 years) = $4,400

To demonstrate simple interest, have students calculate 2% APR on the accumulated principal in the account at the end of each year. For example, there is $500 in the account at the end of the first year, so the simple interest would be $10. At the end of the second year, the accumulated principle (not including interest) would be $800 ($500 + $300), so calculate 2% interest on $800, which equals $16, and so forth. At the end of 14 years, they would have earned a total of $686 in simple interest. Added to $4,400 of accumulated principle, they'd have $5,086. You might note that in real-world situations, the total would be less, because a bank would normally calculate interest on the average balance over the year rather than on the total principle at the end of the year. We used the end-of-the-year amounts to keep the calculations simpler.

With quarterly compounding, assume that you are depositing $75 per quarter in the account and you are calculating quarterly interest by multiplying the principal by 2% and then by .25%. The total in the account will be $5,121.71.

Introduce the Section

This section explores why we pay taxes, how to calculate them, and where the tax money goes.

Figure Focus

Some of your students may already be paying income tax if they hold jobs. Ask them to share the amount or percentage of their pay that is taken out for taxes. Where do they think this money goes? Ask them to provide examples of how the government spends taxpayer money. Does their community have a municipal tax? What services does their city government provide? What government service would you like to see cut if it meant a decrease in the taxes you pay? Some options to consider are:

- Medicare/Medicaid
- Medical research
- Public school funding
- Defense funding
- Social Security
- Public roadways
- Police and fire protection
- Public parks
- Unemployment benefits
- Air traffic controllers
- Job training
- Public libraries

Vocabulary

Tax: Money paid to the government, which is then used for public resources.

Who Gets the Taxes?

Explain that state income and sales taxes vary widely. Some states do not have an income tax, while others have rates ranging from 4 to 9 percent. California currently has the highest sales tax with 8.25 percent, while Alaska, Delaware, Montana, New Hampshire, and Oregon have no state sales tax. If you bought a shirt in California for $20, it would cost $21.65 with tax. You may have heard of people who travel across state lines to buy certain things because the taxes are lower.

Paying Taxes

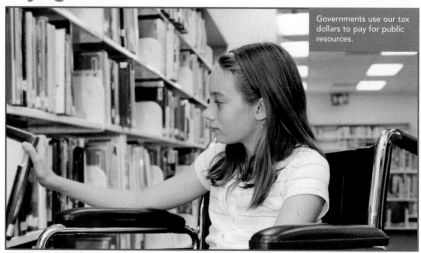

Governments use our tax dollars to pay for public resources.

A **tax** is money we pay the government. The government uses the money to pay for public resources. People complain about taxes all the time, but if we didn't pay them we wouldn't have things like streets, sidewalks, parks, schools, and libraries. The government wouldn't be able to run programs to help citizens in need, pay for the military, conduct medical research, or send astronauts into space.

There are three basic categories of taxes:

- Income taxes are based on wages and other earnings.
- Consumption taxes are based on things we buy, such as computers or gasoline.
- Asset taxes are based on things we already own, such as houses or cars.

Forgetting about taxes can wreck a budget. You must leave a percentage of your income to cover taxes. You must include sales tax when you set a financial goal. For example, you might want a bicycle that costs $350.00. If you live in a state with a 5% sales tax, you will need to save $350.00 plus 5%, for a total of $367.50, in order to buy the bike.

Who Gets the Taxes?

In Chapter 10, you saw how income taxes and Social Security taxes are withheld from a paycheck. We pay a lot of other taxes, too, including sales tax on things we buy, gas tax on gasoline, and property tax on buildings or homes that we own. Most taxes are calculated as a percentage of something. For example, basic income tax is a percentage of the amount of money you earn in a year. Sales tax is a percentage of an item's purchase price.

- Some taxes we pay to the federal—national—government. Federal taxes are the same for everyone, no matter where you live. We all pay income tax, Social Security tax, and federal fuel tax for gasoline.
- Some taxes we pay to the state government. State taxes are different depending on where you live. Some but not all states have income and sales taxes. Most states have a fuel tax—that's in addition to the federal fuel tax! Each state sets its own rates, so one state might have a 5% sales tax, while another state might have an 8% sales tax.
- Some taxes we pay to the local government—the community where we live. Some communities have property taxes. Each community sets its own tax rates, although it may have to get state approval.

Customized Instruction: At-Risk Students

While tax avoidance is legal, tax evasion is illegal and carries penalties with it, such as fines or jail time. Ask students whether the following actions are tax avoidance or tax evasion:

- Keeping a log of business expenses. *Answer:* Tax avoidance
- Not reporting earnings from a summer lawn mowing job. *Answer:* Tax evasion
- Not reporting interest earned on savings account. *Answer:* Tax evasion
- Keeping a log of contributions to charity. *Answer:* Tax avoidance
- Not reporting tips from waiting tables. *Answer:* Tax evasion

Customized Instruction: Special Needs Students

Have students look through a newspaper or magazine to find an article or editorial on taxes. They might look for keywords such as *tax levy, taxpayer, government spending, tax credit, tax bill, earnings tax, income tax, IRS,* etc. They should cut out the article and write a two- to three-sentence summary of it.

How Much Income Tax Do I Owe?

Income tax is a percentage of your income that you pay to the government. The federal government collects income tax, and most—but not all—state governments do, too. Income tax is automatically withheld from your paycheck by your employer (see Chapter 10).

Of course, paying income tax is a lot more complicated than just withholding a percentage of your wages. The United States has a *progressive tax system*, which means the more you earn, the more you pay. Income is categorized into levels, called **tax brackets**. If your income falls into the lowest tax bracket, you pay 0%. If it falls in the next tax bracket, you pay 10%. Currently, the highest tax bracket pays 35%. The government changes the levels and percentages as necessary to keep up with economic changes, such as salary levels and the cost of living.

Your tax bracket is based on your **taxable income**, which is not the same as your annual salary. To calculate your taxable income, you add up all of your income and then subtract **tax deductions**, which are expenses that you are allowed to deduct from your income, such as contributions to charities and interest you pay on a mortgage. The remainder is your taxable income.

Once you know your tax bracket, you can calculate the amount of actual tax you owe. From that, you may be able to subtract **tax credits**, which are expenses you are allowed to subtract from your actual tax payment. Some typical tax credits include expenses for college and child care.

Filing Income Tax Returns

Each year, you must file income tax returns for the income you earned the previous year. You must file the income tax returns by April 15th or the date specified by the government if the 15th is on a weekend or holiday. (That means on April 15, 2012, you file a return for the income you earned in 2011.) **Income tax returns** are forms on which you calculate the amount of income tax you owe. You file federal tax returns to the Internal Revenue Service (IRS), the agency responsible for collecting federal taxes, and you file state tax returns with your state's revenue department.

The minimum amount you have to earn to file a tax return changes every year, and depends on your age and whether or not you are married.

Once you calculate the amount you owe based on your tax bracket, you subtract the amount that your employer withheld throughout the year. If it is more than the amount you owe, the government sends you a refund check. If it is less than the amount you owe, you must send the government a check for the difference.

> I like to pay taxes. With them, I buy civilization.
>
> — Oliver Wendell Holmes, Jr.,
> U.S. Supreme Court Justice

Myth Wealthy people don't pay their fair share of taxes.

Truth Experts believe that the top 25% of the wealthiest Americans pay about 99% of the income taxes. Think about it: The more you earn, the higher your tax bracket. The higher your tax bracket, the higher the percentage you pay.

Some people think wealthy people are able to hide income, or use complicated tax rules to reduce their taxable income. Even so, they still pay most of the income taxes collected in the United States.

What Do You Get for Your Tax Dollars?

Property taxes can be much higher in one community than they are in the community right next door. Usually, if the taxes are higher, it means the community provides more public services. Local taxes pay for resources such as:

✔ *Teachers and schools*

✔ *Firefighters*

✔ *Police officers*

✔ *Trash collection and recycling*

✔ *Street plowing and cleaning*

✔ *Parks*

✔ *Public celebrations*

Vocabulary

Taxable income: Total income minus tax deductions.

Tax brackets: The levels in which income is categorized.

Tax credits: Expenses you are allowed to subtract from your tax payment.

Tax deductions: Expenses that you are allowed to deduct from your income.

Myth/Truth

Explain that everyone, including wealthy people, pay the following taxes.

■ Driver's license fee, which varies from state to state.

■ Personal property tax calculated on property value.

■ Personal income tax based on a person's income.

■ Hunting and fishing license fees, which vary from state to state.

■ Estate taxes imposed upon death and based on the value of the estate.

What Do You Get for Your Tax Dollars?

State and local revenues to pay for the services listed come from a variety of taxes imposed on residents. Below is an example breakdown of where states get their money to operate.

■ 24% from property tax

■ 29% from individual income tax

■ 24% from general sales tax

■ 6% from corporate income

■ 3% from motor fuel sales tax

■ 2% from motor vehicle licenses

■ 1% from tobacco product and alcoholic beverage sales taxes

■ 11% from other services and miscellaneous taxes

"Quote Box"

Explain that taxes help fund the groups, organizations, and systems that are the framework of our communities. Ask students to consider what their community would be like without tax money. Would you have police and fire protection or trash and recycling services? Would you have a public school, library, or park? How would your arts and cultural centers operate? How accessible would flu shots and vaccines be for your community's citizens?

Discuss

Explain that the United States uses a progressive tax system, which means the more you earn, the more you pay in taxes. Ask students if they think that's a fair system. Do they have suggestions for a better tax system?

Introduce the Section

In this section, students learn that being financially responsible means taking measures to keep personal information safe and protect themselves from identity theft.

Figure Focus

Reinforce the idea that most businesses and other organizations use personal information legitimately. We give out personal information probably more often than we realize. We supply information when we go to the doctor's office, when we accept a job, when we start at a new school, and so forth. Emphasize that asking why certain information is needed is a good habit to get into. Also, be wary of giving personal information out online, such as on social networking and shopping sites where the information may not be encrypted and secured.

Identity Theft Is Big Business

Explain to students just how inconvenient and time consuming it is for a victim of identity theft to re-establish credit.

- Victims spend an average of 330 hours repairing damage.

- Around 30 percent of victims have to spend a period of four to six months dealing with identity theft issues.

- Victims typically spend between $800 and $1,400 on expenses related to identity theft.

- Nearly 50 percent of victims claim they had trouble getting credit or a loan because of the identity theft.

Keeping Your Personal and Financial Information Safe

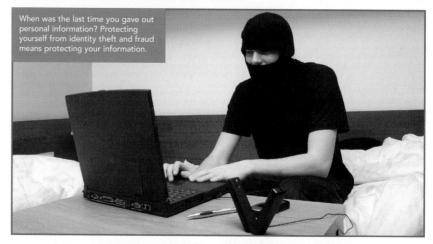

When was the last time you gave out personal information? Protecting yourself from identity theft and fraud means protecting your information.

Personal information includes your name, address, phone number, and e-mail address. It also includes your birth date, Social Security number (SSN)—the number assigned to you by the U.S. government to track your income and employment history—bank and credit card account numbers, medical and insurance records, and your mother's maiden name—her original family name.

Most businesses use your information legitimately.

- Your bank uses it to maintain your bank accounts.
- The supermarket uses it to offer you coupons and special deals.
- An online retailer uses it to process your order.

Some criminals use the information to commit fraud.

- They might steal your credit card information and make unauthorized purchases.
- They might steal your bank account information and withdraw your money.
- They might sell your information to someone else.

Keeping your personal and financial information safe is an important part of financial responsibility. You can minimize your risk by understanding how criminals trick you into providing your information, and how they use it once they get it.

Identity Theft Is Big Business

Experts believe that identity theft is one of the fastest growing crimes in the United States. The Federal Trade Commission (FTC)—the government agency responsible for protecting consumers—estimates that as many as 9 million Americans have their identities stolen each year.

It occurs when someone steals your personal information and uses it to commit fraud. The crook might open new charge accounts, rent an apartment, buy stuff, and take out loans. He might get a job using your Social Security number, or apply for a driver's license or passport. She might obtain medical care using your insurance information.

You might discover you are a victim by checking your credit report. You might not even know you are a victim until you apply for your own credit, and find out someone with your name and Social Security number is not paying credit card bills and is skipping loan payments. Credit collection agencies might come after you for debts you didn't know you had. Your credit history is ruined, and you have to spend time and money to prove that you are the real you and that the imposter—who no one knows—is a thief.

Customized Instruction: Less Advanced Students

Ask students to role-play ways to prevent someone from shoulder surfing (looking over their shoulder) while they are paying for something at a store using their debit or credit card.

Protect Your Records

Identity thieves will do almost anything to get their hands on your personal, financial, and medical records. They'll go through your trash, bribe clerks, and peek over your shoulder when you use your computer. It is important to keep track of these documents and make sure they are stored safely.

What types of documents should you secure?

■ Personal records such as a birth certificate and Social Security card

■ Medical records showing when you had immunizations

■ School records showing what school you attend, how you do on report cards and standardized tests, and your student I.D.

■ Financial records such as bank statements, credit and debit card numbers, and loan information

■ Copies of tax returns, pay stubs, and insurance records

■ Driver's license, marriage certificate, and passport

You can keep these items in a safe, or in a **safe deposit box**, which is a box in a fireproof vault that you can rent from your bank. The information will be safe from thieves, and you will know where to find it when you need it.

I Lost My Wallet!

Think about the stuff you carry in your purse or wallet: cash, credit and debit cards, insurance card, driver's license or student I.D., cell phone, receipts, and keys. What could a thief do with all of that?

If you lose your wallet or purse, you should assume it will be found by a criminal. Immediately take steps to protect your identity and your finances. If your wallet or purse is missing:

■ File a report with the police immediately and keep a copy.

■ Report the loss to the fraud department at your bank and other financial institutions.

■ Cancel your credit, debit, and ATM cards immediately.

■ Apply for new cards with new account numbers.

■ Call the fraud departments of the three major credit reporting agencies.

■ Ask each agency to put out a fraud alert on your accounts. A fraud alert is like a red flag on your accounts that shows your information may be in the hands of an unauthorized person.

■ Review your credit reports regularly and have them corrected when necessary.

■ Report a missing driver's license to your state's department of motor vehicles.

■ If your keys are missing, change the locks on your home and car.

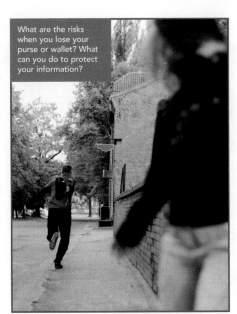

What are the risks when you lose your purse or wallet? What can you do to protect your information?

How the Thieves Do It

How do thieves collect personal information? They:

✔ Rummage through trash to find bills, account statements, and other documents

✔ Set up mechanical devices at ATM machines and places where you swipe a credit or debit card

✔ Phish online by pretending to be a legitimate business or your bank

✔ Send in change-of-address forms so your account statements and other mail are sent to them instead of to you

✔ Steal your purse, wallet, or mail

✔ Read personnel records or medical records

Introduce the Section

In this section, students take a look at the laws and regulations that apply to their financial and banking activities and identify ways to protect their financial resources.

Figure Focus

Explain the importance of knowing your legal rights as a borrower. Borrowers are protected by laws that forbid creditors from threatening them with violence, jail, a lawsuit, or loss of wages. In addition, collectors are not allowed to harass borrowers with phone calls; specifically, they are not to call after 9 p.m., before 8 a.m., or at the borrower's place of work.

Who Regulates the Banks?

You might also briefly discuss the Truth in Lending Act. This law requires banks to tell you how much it will cost to borrow money so you can compare the terms to those of other lenders.

STUDENT ACTIVITY

Most states have laws in place to protect consumers from a wide range of criminal activity. For example, states have laws on telemarketing, mortgage fraud, home improvement scams, privacy protection, lemon car sales, phony investment schemes, and so on.

Have students research three of their state's consumer protection laws and create a brochure that describes the laws, what they are designed to protect the consumer from, where to learn more about them, and how to lodge a complaint if they feel that the law has been violated.

Analyzing Banking and Credit Regulations

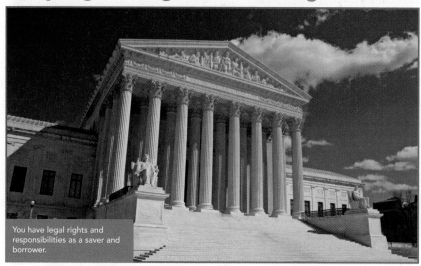

You have legal rights and responsibilities as a saver and borrower.

Both your state and the U.S. government want to keep your money safe. They depend on you to:

- Spend, which helps companies stay in business
- Save, which gives banks money to loan
- Pay taxes, which gives the government money to use to support public resources

So, they have passed many laws and regulations designed to protect you and your money. They have set up agencies such as the FDIC—Federal Deposit Insurance Corporation—to provide insurance for your deposits, and the FTC—Federal Trade Commission—to make sure businesses treat you fairly. They allow you to report problems, such as lenders that discriminate based on your race, and to ask questions, such as "What's my credit score?"

It might be difficult to learn all of the banking and credit laws and regulations, but you can become familiar with a few. Knowing your rights and responsibilities can help you make healthy financial decisions and use your financial resources wisely.

Who Regulates the Banks?

Banks must be chartered to operate in the U.S. A bank charter is an agreement that controls how the bank operates. The agency that charters the bank is responsible for making sure the bank follows all rules and regulations.

Each state has a regulatory agency responsible for regulating state-chartered banks. It's usually called the Banking Commission, or the Department of Banking and Finance. There are three federal agencies that regulate banks:

- The Office of the Comptroller of the Currency (OCC) (www.occ.treas.gov), part of the Treasury Department, generally makes sure the bank complies with all laws and regulations.
- The Federal Reserve Board (www.federalreserve.gov), which supervises and regulates banks not subject to the OCC's supervision.
- The FDIC (www.fdic.gov), which examines and supervises financial institutions that are not members of the Federal Reserve System.

All of these agencies have consumer protection departments. You can contact them with questions or problems at any time.

What About Investments?

Investment accounts are not insured by the government the way savings accounts are. One of the best ways to minimize the risks of investing is to make sure you have as much information about the security you are investing in as possible. The Securities and Exchange Commission (SEC) is a government agency responsible for supervising and regulating companies to protect investors.

The SEC monitors companies to make sure they disclose meaningful financial and other information, so you have access to the information you need to make healthy investment decisions. The SEC requires the information to be accurate, but it does not guarantee it. It will prosecute companies that knowingly withhold information or distribute incorrect information, and it gives consumers rights to sue if the information is incomplete or inaccurate.

Protecting Credit

Consumer credit laws are designed to help consumers and creditors meet their legal responsibilities. Some of the most important federal acts regulating credit include:

■ *The Fair Credit Reporting Act.* This act is enforced by the Federal Trade Commission (FTC). It promotes accuracy and ensures privacy of the information used in consumer reports such as your credit report. For example, you have the right to know what's in your credit report, and you have the right to challenge errors you find in your credit report.

■ *The Equal Credit Opportunity Act.* This act protects you from discrimination by creditors for any reason other than your creditworthiness. Creditors cannot ask your race, sex, country of origin, religion, or age.

■ *The Fair Credit Billing Act.* This act sets rules for when credit card bills are mailed and payments are credited, as well as procedures for settling billing errors. For example, creditors must mail a bill at least 14 days before the date a finance charge will be added so that you can pay the bill by the due date.

■ *Truth in Lending Act.* This law is designed to make sure you have all of the information you need to make a healthy decision about borrowing money. It lists the information that a creditor must disclose before lending you money, such as the APR, APY, all fees and charges, and the term of the loan.

New laws and regulations are passed when the government thinks they are necessary, such as the Credit Card Act of 2009. This act restricts credit card issuers from raising interest rates without warning, charging excessive fees for late payments, and raising the minimum age for obtaining a credit card to 21.

Monitor Your Own Accounts

You have responsibilities as a borrower. You cannot assume the banks and lenders and regulatory agencies are always going to know what is going on with your accounts. What if you notice an unauthorized charge on your credit card statement?

★ *Notify the credit card company by phone and in writing immediately.*

★ *Check your other statements to see if there are any other unauthorized charges.*

★ *Check your credit report to see if there are any signs of fraud.*

★ *Pay the undisputed charges in full and on time.*

What would you do if you found an error on your credit report? What if you suspect you were denied credit because of your race?

TECH CONNECT

Phishing is a scam designed to steal your personal and financial information over the Internet. Criminals use e-mail messages and fake Web sites to trick you into entering the information, which they can sell or use themselves. You can protect yourself by being wary.

■ Never reply to an e-mail message, text message, or pop-up browser window that asks for your personal information, even if the message looks like it comes from a bank or credit card company you use.
■ Never call a phone number included in an e-mail message or text to contact your bank or credit card company. Use the phone number on the back of your account statements or credit card.
■ Keep your antivirus and antispyware software up to date, and use a firewall.

What should you do if you suspect you have received a phishing e-mail?

Monitor Your Own Accounts

Explain the measures you can take if you find an error on your credit report.

■ You can file a complaint with the Federal Trade Commission, which enforces rules on credit bureaus, at www.ftc.gov.

■ You can file corrections with the credit bureau.

■ You can contact an attorney who might be able to send a letter to the credit bureau.

■ You can speak to your bank or lender about using another credit bureau that has accurate information on your credit.

■ You should keep all of your credit report copies, letters you have sent about the mistake, copies of the newer reports, as well as the correct credit reports from other bureaus to show to your lender.

If you feel you were denied credit because of your race, you can send a complaint letter to the Federal Trade Commission. The Equal Credit Opportunity Act prohibits credit discrimination on the basis of race, color, religion, national origin, sex, marital status, age, or because you receive public assistance.

 TECH CONNECT

Explain that some phishing messages ask that you update or confirm your account information, while others threaten extreme consequences if you do not respond. Emphasize that if you suspect you have received a phishing e-mail, you should not reply or open any attachments because they could have viruses in them. You should report it immediately to www.ftc.gov/idtheft.

Discuss

Ask students why they believe the minimum age for obtaining a credit card was raised to 21. Do they agree or disagree with this change?

Customized Instruction: ESOL Students

Ask students what the words for credit and debt are in their primary language.

End-of-Chapter Activities

Case Study

Chelsea's personal information is at risk. So is her personal security. A criminal can use the information in her wallet to identify her and find her at school or at home. The criminal even has the keys to her house!

Chelsea should file a police report immediately. She should notify her banks immediately and cancel her debit card. She should notify her health insurance company. She should change the locks on her house—and her car if her car keys were stolen, too. She should begin to monitor her bank statements and credit report immediately so if anyone tries to access her accounts or use her information, she will know right away.

Chelsea should take steps to make sure she keeps track of her purse in the future. If she had been able to get to the mall as soon as she realized she had left her purse behind, she might have found it. Or, she might have been able to call security at the mall, or the places where she might have left the purse to have them check for it.

Sounding Off!

Student answers will vary.

FAQ

1. Credit is money that you borrow and promise to pay back.

2. You should pay the entire balance off by the due date.

3. The minimum age for credit card ownership is 21.

4. A credit limit is the maximum amount of purchases you can charge to a credit card.

5. Positive steps for establishing credit include maintaining bank account balances, earning a paycheck, paying bills on time, paying rent, and using a credit card responsibly.

6. The three nationwide consumer credit reporting companies are Equifax, Experian, and TransUnion.

7. The annual percentage rate (APR) is the annual interest without compounding or other added charges.

8. You must file the income tax returns by April 15th or the date specified by the government if the 15th is on a weekend or holiday.

Case Study

Chelsea, Alisha, and Deanna spent Saturday afternoon at the mall. When they got home, Chelsea realized she had left her purse behind. Her mother drove her to the mall that evening and they looked everywhere for it. It wasn't in any of the stores where the girls had shopped. It wasn't in the food court. It wasn't at the Lost and Found.

Chelsea made a list of everything that was in her bag. She had lost a makeup kit, her datebook, and her house keys. Luckily, her cell phone had been in her pocket. Unluckily, her wallet had been in her purse. She thought she had about $18.00 in her wallet, along with her debit card, her health insurance card, her library card, and her student ID.

- What are the risks and problems facing Chelsea?
- What action do you think Chelsea should take?
- Do you think Chelsea could have avoided the situation?

Sounding Off!

❶ Do you agree with the minimum age requirement for credit card ownership?

❷ Why do you think identity theft is more common now than when you parents were young?

1. What is credit?
2. How can you avoid credit card finance charges?
3. What is the minimum age for credit card ownership?
4. What is a credit limit?
5. List four positive steps for establishing credit.
6. What are the three nationwide consumer credit reporting companies?
7. What is APR?
8. By what date each year do you have to file your tax return?
9. List five resources paid for by local taxes.
10. What is the purpose of consumer credit laws?

9. Resources paid for by local taxes include:
   - Teachers and schools
   - Firefighters
   - Police officers
   - Trash collection and recycling
   - Street plowing and cleaning
   - Parks
   - Public celebrations

   Students may think of others.

10. The purpose of consumer credit laws is to help consumers and creditors meet their legal responsibilities.

Divide into teams of four or five and play Name that Agency. As a team, think up five questions about the agencies and organizations responsible for regulating the banking and credit systems. Write the questions down on a piece of paper.

Take turns asking the other teams your questions. Teams get one point for each correct answer. Each team also gets a point if they ask a unique question—one that no other team has written down to ask. The team with the most points at the end of the game wins.

Hot Topics

What would you do if you received a credit card offer in the mail? Would you respond, hoping to receive the card? Would you tell your parents? Would you throw it away?

Take this opportunity to write anonymously about your thoughts regarding credit and debt. Use a word processor so no one recognizes your handwriting. Be honest and open. Put the paper in the class Hot Topics box.

As a class, read the anonymous entries and discuss them.

Web Extra ▼

There are Web sites such as webmath.com that have automatic interest calculator features. Make a set of interest calculation math problems, and then use an online interest calculator to solve the problems. Swap problems with a classmate and solve them using a different calculator.

Problem Solver

The state just announced it will reduce the payment it gives your community for the coming year by $150,000.00. That means there will not be enough money to fund the entire budget. There seem to be two options: cut services or raise taxes.

Working in pairs, develop a plan for solving your community's problem. Present your plan to the class.

Team Players

Divide students appropriately into teams. They are asked to answer questions about agencies and organizations that regulate the banking and credit systems. Students should review those organizations and laws listed on pages 250–251 of the text.

Hot Topics

Make sure students understand that they can turn in their papers anonymously. Encourage them to be open and honest about their opinions on opening a credit card account and their concerns about credit and debt.

Web Extra

Explain to students that at www.webmath.com, they can go to "Quick jump to math help" and choose "Interest, Simple" or "Interest, Compound." You might get students started with a sample problem such as this: You owe $1,200 in credit card bills with a 6.8% simple interest charged per month. How much would you owe after 6 months, and then after a year? The interest at the end of six months is $40.80, and at the end of one year is $81.60.

Problem Solver

Students are to work with a partner or in small groups to develop a presentation on whether they would cut services or raise taxes to solve the difference in their community's budget. Make sure they find real solutions to the issue. If they are going to cut the budget, where exactly will they do it and what will the effects be? If they want to raise taxes, how will they gain support for their proposal?

Write Now

Students are asked to create a brochure comparing responsible uses of credit in different stages of life. When creating the brochures, students should think about the consequences of their use of credit, their roles and responsibilities at different stages of life, and their goals at the various stages of life.

Be Involved!

The class develops a list of prospective speakers to present information about credit and debt. Review the steps to meeting a goal.

1. Identify the goal.
2. Assess whether the goal is realistic and the speaker is suitable for the topic to be covered.
3. Make a plan for achieving the goal.
4. Prepare an action plan for achieving the goal.
5. Evaluate the outcome.

Social Networking

Students are asked to create posters that illustrate their community's total revenue and total expenses. Students should be able to gather this information from their community's government offices. Emphasize the importance of presenting the information clearly and accurately. Ideally, the posters will be on display around the community and will positively reflect on the students and their school.

Write Now

Create a three-part brochure or comparison table explaining responsible use of credit for people in different stages of life. In part 1, discuss credit for teens and college-age students. In part 2, discuss credit for young and middle-aged adults. In part 3, discuss credit for older adults and seniors. Explain how credit might be useful at each stage of life, and how credit problems at one stage might affect you in a different stage. Provide information about how to avoid credit card trouble and excessive debt, and how to protect your credit throughout your life. Share your brochure with the class.

Be Involved!

www.fcclainc.org

As a class, make a list of people in your community who are knowledgeable about the risks and benefits of credit and debt. For example, you might include bank managers, loan officers, real estate professionals, and credit counselors on the list. With your teacher or advisor, identify one person you think would be able to provide useful information about credit and debt to students at your school, and plan an event.

Start by writing a letter inviting the person to visit the school and speak to your class, or to a larger audience. If the person is not available, select a different person from the list.

When you have found someone interested in speaking to you, organize the event. Select a location and a date that is mutually convenient. Make the necessary arrangements with the school, teachers, and students. If necessary, set up a budget for things such as refreshments. Notify your local media about the event, and arrange for the school newspaper or Web site to cover it as well.

As you work toward your goal, keep a journal to record your progress, and collect documentation that you can use to show what you have achieved. After the event, evaluate your success. How many students attended? Was the speaker informative? Did you achieve your goal? Write a report about the experience.

Social Networking

People might feel better about paying taxes if they knew about how the money is used. As a class, or in groups, contact the government body for your community and ask for information about where revenue—income—comes from and how it is spent. For example, if you live in a city, contact the mayor or city councilors. If you live in a town, there might be a town manager. Ask how much of the community's budget income comes from taxes, and how much comes from other sources, such as money from the state, from grants, or from the sale of bonds. Also ask how the tax revenues collected from the citizens are used. How much goes to the schools, how much to public safety, and so on.

Create posters of two pie charts that illustrate the information. The first chart will represent total revenue, with slices for each source (taxes, state, grants, etc.). The second chart will represent total expenses, with slices for each service (education, police, water, parks, etc.).

Display your posters in the government building—such as city hall—or in another public building such as a senior center so citizens can learn more about how the community uses tax money.

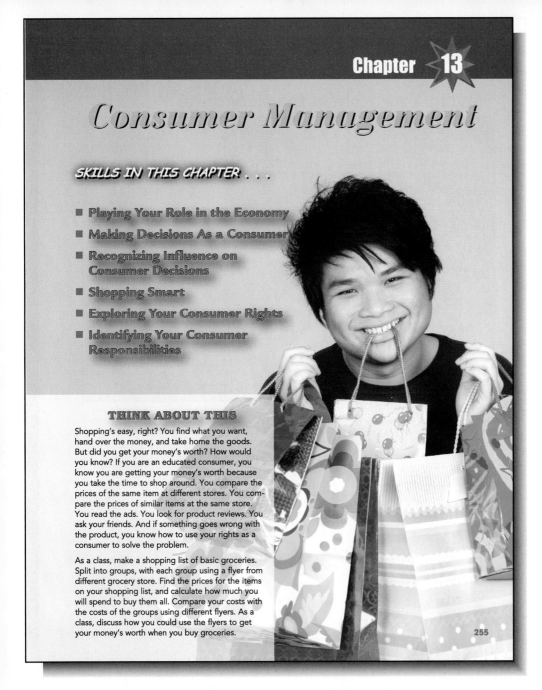

Chapter 13 Overview

This chapter discusses factors that affect consumer purchasing and provides an overview of the impact of consumer buying habits and patterns on the economy. It reviews the principles of decision-making and how they apply to purchasing. It also identifies consumer rights and responsibilities.

Playing Your Role in the Economy   In this section, students explore how consumer purchasing activities impact the local, national, and international economy. The terms "goods" and "services" are also defined.

Making Decisions As a Consumer   This section identifies the considerations behind a wise purchasing decision. It also covers how to use the decision-making process in purchasing.

Recognizing Influences on Consumer Decisions   This section discusses the main influences on consumer purchasing decisions. These include individual values, family, past experiences, stage of life, and advertising.

Shopping Smart   Students learn the difference between impulsive buying and thoughtful shopping. Tips on where and how to shop and the benefits of comparing options are discussed.

Exploring Your Consumer Rights   This section provides information on the consumer's right to safety, to be informed, and to choose among competing brands. It also covers the various agencies and laws designed to protect consumers.

Identifying Your Consumer Responsibilities   This section covers the responsibilities involved in shopping. These include acting respectful to store employees, reading and following directions, and identifying infringements on consumer rights.

Focus and Engage

Bell-Ringer: Think About This

The class is asked to develop a list of basic groceries, then break into groups and calculate how much the groceries will cost, using flyers and advertisements from different stores. Remind students to list *basic* groceries, such as meats, produce, milk, juice, and eggs. If their lists get too specific, they might have difficulty finding prices in a store's advertisements. As a class, the groups will discuss why using grocery store flyers can help them make wise purchasing decisions that will save them money. Ask them to discuss other considerations in choosing a grocery store. Should its proximity to your home or place of work matter? What about food quality and customer service?

Consumer Management

SKILLS IN THIS CHAPTER . . .

- Playing Your Role in the Economy
- Making Decisions As a Consumer
- Recognizing Influence on Consumer Decisions
- Shopping Smart
- Exploring Your Consumer Rights
- Identifying Your Consumer Responsibilities

THINK ABOUT THIS

Shopping's easy, right? You find what you want, hand over the money, and take home the goods. But did you get your money's worth? How would you know? If you are an educated consumer, you know you are getting your money's worth because you take the time to shop around. You compare the prices of the same item at different stores. You compare the prices of similar items at the same store. You read the ads. You look for product reviews. You ask your friends. And if something goes wrong with the product, you know how to use your rights as a consumer to solve the problem.

As a class, make a shopping list of basic groceries. Split into groups, with each group using a flyer from different grocery store. Find the prices for the items on your shopping list, and calculate how much you will spend to buy them all. Compare your costs with the costs of the groups using different flyers. As a class, discuss how you could use the flyers to get your money's worth when you buy groceries.

255

ADVANCE PREPARATION

Review	*Life Skills for the 21st Century* textbook, Chapter 13.
Prepare	Paper and pencil for some activities.
	Newspapers and advertising circulars from local stores.
	Box labeled "Hot Topics."

CUSTOMIZED INSTRUCTION OVERVIEW

Less Advanced Students	More Advanced Students	ESOL Students	Special Needs Students	At-Risk Students
Pages 257, 265	Page 267	Page 270	Pages 257, 265, 269	Pages 259, 261

Introduce the Section

This section introduces basic economic terminology. Students learn how consumer buying habits impact the economy, and how consumer laws and policies in the United States differ from those in other countries.

Vocabulary

Economics: The study of the choices people and communities make regarding the way they produce and purchase goods and services.

Economy: Activity related to the production and distribution of goods and services.

Figure Focus

Ask students if they've heard or read news reports about teen spending power. American teens spend approximately $150 billion annually, representing a powerful force in the U.S. economy. Market research indicates that video games dominate teen budgets with electronics coming in second. Further, research indicates that teenagers are becoming more fickle about their icons which, in turn, is making it more difficult for marketers to target their preferences. This has spurred growth of a new class of consumers called "tweens," or those between the ages of 8 and 14 years old. Their annual spending is at $43 billion and growing.

Playing Your Role in the Economy

Your actions as a consumer affect the economy in your community, the United States, and even the world.

The economy's a pretty big thing. You hear the president talk about it. It's in the news. Your parents might worry about it. But, what does it have to do with you?

The **economy** is activity related to the production and distribution of goods and services.

- *Goods* are things you can see, touch, buy, and sell. Clothing and food are goods.
- *Services* are work that one person does for other people, in exchange for payment. Doctors, hairstylists, bus drivers, and lawyers are people who provide services.

You participate in the economy because you buy goods and services. Every time you make a decision to buy a pack of gum, download a song, or hop on the subway, you have an impact on the economy.

Do your actions make a difference? Yes.

What's Economics?

Economics is the study of the choices people and communities make regarding the way they produce and purchase goods and services. Specifically, economists are interested in how people use their resources to achieve their needs and wants. For example, if you are cold, how do you use your economic resources—money—to get warm?

- Do you buy a sheep so you can use the wool to knit a sweater?
- Do you buy a sweater made by someone else?
- Do you buy a blanket?
- Do you move to a city where it is warm all year?
- If you do not have enough money to buy a sheep, sweater, or blanket, or to move, does your community spend economic resources to help you stay warm?

Stay in School

High school graduates are seven times more likely to own a home than a high school dropout, and less likely to be on public assistance. Many say the best economic stimulus is a high school diploma. Students who drop out often feel financial pressure because of lack of opportunity.

To help students understand the financial and economic ramifications of graduating vs. dropping out, consider contacting the following to come speak to the class:

- A local university career adviser who might speak about the types of skills and experience employers are currently looking for in graduates.
- A community-based bank or credit union, which might offer workshops on personal finance and establishing credit.
- A representative from a college or university's student financial aid office, who can explain the steps to take to apply for financial aid and scholarships.

Your Impact on the Economy

Around the world, businesses—and some individuals—produce goods and provide services that they think people will buy.

- If you buy, then the business does well. It can hire more employees, pay higher wages, and purchase supplies from other companies. This puts money into the economy and causes economic growth.
- If you don't buy, the business does not do well. It may have to lay off employees, pay lower wages, and stop purchasing supplies. Less money goes into the economy, causing an economic slowdown.

The decisions you make about what to buy impact the economy. When you buy a pack of gum:

- The store earns money and orders more gum from the gum manufacturer.
- The gum manufacturer earns money, buys new supplies, and makes more gum.

The type of gum you buy makes a difference, too. If you buy bubblegum, that's what the gum manufacturer will make. If no one buys spearmint gum, the gum manufacturer stops making it. This is called **supply and demand**, because companies supply goods and services that consumers demand.

Types of Economies

In most countries, the government makes laws and policies that impact the way people earn and spend money. The laws and policies regulate the economic system in that country. Three major economic systems are:

- *Capitalism.* Citizens are free to own property and goods and to start and own businesses. They have freedom of choice to make financial decisions on their own. Competition between businesses is encouraged.
- *Socialism.* The government owns and operates most businesses and is heavily involved in promoting the well-being of citizens. Citizens are free to make most decisions, but the government provides many jobs, education, and health care.
- *Communism.* The government owns the land and almost all industries. Citizens make very few decisions and rely on the government to provide income, education, and health care.

Most countries have economies that combine elements from more than one of the three major systems. For example, the United States, which is capitalist, has socialist programs such as Social Security and unemployment benefits. China, which is communist, now allows some capitalism, such as ownership of property and the ability to make some independent purchasing decisions.

"If I don't buy this, will the store go out of business?"

Economic Terminology

✔ *Recession: An economic slowdown that lasts for six months or more*
✔ *Depression: A long, severe economic recession, usually marked by deflation and high unemployment*
✔ *Competition: Two or more businesses that sell the same goods or services*
✔ *Monopoly: A single business that sells all, or nearly all, of one type of goods or services*
✔ *Inflation: A general increase in the price of goods and services*
✔ *Deflation: A general decline in the price of goods and services*

 The Global Economy

How does the economy in Asia affect you in the United States? Nations around the world are linked through trade and the flow of goods and services. Toys made in China are sold in the United States; American companies such as Nike have factories in Indonesia. Companies can save money by moving manufacturing to countries where supplies cost less and workers earn less. The savings mean the companies can charge you less for each item. Companies can also increase sales by expanding internationally.

Look at the labels on items such as clothing, shoes, electronics, and appliances to see where they are made, and record the results in a table. Make a graph or chart showing the results. As a class, discuss the benefits and drawbacks of a global economy.

Economic Terminology

You might discuss these additional terms.

- Fiscal deficit: When a government entity spends more money than it takes in.
- Fiscal policy: Use of government spending and tax revenue to influence the economy.
- Exports: The selling of goods and services to other countries.

Customized Instruction: Less Advanced/Special Needs Students

Have students take a close look at the tags on their clothing, shoes, coats, bags, and other items in the classroom. They should write down the names of the countries in which these items were made. (Note: If students completed the activity at the end of *The Global Economy* feature on this page, they may use the graph or chart they created for this activity as well.) They should also write down the name of the store in which they purchased the item, if they can remember it. Have students locate these countries on a map or globe.

Discuss

Explain the following terms and identify countries that operate under such economic systems.

- **Capitalism:** Citizens are free to own property and goods, to start their own businesses, and to make financial decisions on their own. Competition between businesses is encouraged. Examples of capitalist economies are the United States, Great Britain, and Canada.

- **Socialism:** Government owns and operates most businesses and provides many jobs, education, and health care to its citizens. Examples of socialist economies are North Korea, Cuba, and Vietnam.

- **Communism:** Government owns the land and almost all industries, leaving citizens little freedom to make their own financial decisions. They rely on the government for income, education, and health care. An example of a communist economy is China.

Figure Focus

Explain that stores go out of business for many reasons. Of course, the ability to sell products and make a profit is the cornerstone for a successful business. But every business also has overhead expenses, such as rent, utilities, and insurance. If a business chooses to locate in a high-rent area, it may not be able to weather slow economic times, when consumer purchasing is down.

 The Global Economy

Students are asked to look at labels in clothing, shoes, electronics, and other household products, and write down the countries they were made in. They should create a table that lists the name of the item and where it was made. As a class, discuss the results.

Further, explain the concept of "globalization." Globalization refers to the integration of national economies through trade, foreign investment, migration, and the spread of technology. Benefits of globalization include:

- Introduction of technology to depressed regions of the world.
- Increased awareness of other cultures.
- Improvement of the economic and social status of minorities around the world.
- Strengthening and infusing much-needed resources in poorer economies.

Drawbacks include:

- Proliferation of sweatshops (workplace with overworked and underpaid employees).
- Deterioration of a country's natural resources along with a loss of culture and traditions.

Introduce the Section

This section identifies the considerations behind a wise purchasing decision. It also covers how to use the decision-making process in purchasing.

Figure Focus

Remind students that a need is something you cannot live without. It is instrumental to your well-being. A want is something you desire. On the surface, it might *appear* to be instrumental to your well-being, but in reality, it only enhances it. As a consumer, you must sharpen your decision-making skills to determine the difference.

Vocabulary

Consumer: Someone who buys goods and services.

What Is a Wise Consumer?

Explain impulsive shopping as a form of purchasing that's based on emotion rather than logic. Some impulsive purchases are harmless. For example, you grab a candy bar as you're waiting in line to pay for groceries. But many impulsive purchases prove to be unwise decisions. Suggest students ask themselves the following questions when they are considering a purchase.

- Can I live without this?
- Would it be OK to wait?
- Can I buy it cheaper elsewhere?
- Is there a cheaper alternative?
- Am I buying this for me or competing with someone else?

If they answer "yes" to any of these, then it could be an impulsive purchase.

STUDENT ACTIVITY

Bring in three to five different types of popcorn, making sure you know the price for each one. You can choose another snack, such as crackers or pretzels, if desired. Have students compare the brands of popcorn to determine which tastes the best, the price per serving, and the health benefits and drawbacks of each. Ask students which popcorn brand they think represents the best deal. What was the most important factor in their decision: the taste, the cost, the presentation of it, or something else?

Making Decisions As a Consumer

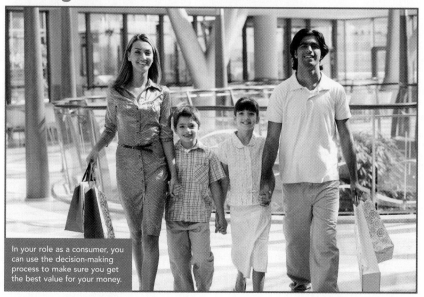

In your role as a consumer, you can use the decision-making process to make sure you get the best value for your money.

A consumer is someone who buys goods and services. Even if you don't have a lot of money to spend, you are already a consumer. Right now, most of the things you buy are wants. Your parents or guardians take care of your needs.

We live in a world that offers many consumer options. Just selecting something as basic as shampoo can be overwhelming. Do you want curls? Do you want sleek and shiny? Do you want volume? Do you have dandruff? You can choose a product based on an endless list of options, such as brand, hair type, scent, or price.

Understanding how to use the decision-making process can help you make healthy consumer decisions, which makes you a wise consumer.

What Is a Wise Consumer?

A wise consumer makes healthy decisions about what to buy, where to buy it, and when to buy it. If you are a wise consumer, you:

- Understand the difference between what you want and what you need
- Learn as much as possible about an item before you buy it
- Know how to compare prices
- Spend only what you can afford

For example, before buying a cell phone or other hand-held device, you might:

- Read customer reviews online so you know which gadget other people recommend
- Compare prices at different stores so you know where to shop
- Consider whether you need to save your money for something else

---

What's a Healthy Consumer Decision?

A healthy consumer decision contributes to your well-being. When you make a healthy consumer decision, you:

- Are confident you bought the best product at the best price
- Feel proud about your ability to manage your economic resources
- Understand your rights and responsibilities as a consumer
- Achieve your goals as a consumer

When you make an unhealthy consumer decision, you:

- Feel disappointed, cheated, or angry
- Waste your economic resources, leaving you without money for other needs and wants
- Are dissatisfied with a product that doesn't meet your expectations

Six Steps to a Purchase

No matter what you are buying—shampoo, a computer, or a membership at a health club—you can use the six-step decision-making process to help you choose the item that is right for you.

1. *Define your decision as a goal.* Exercising regularly might be the goal; buying a membership at a health club might be the decision.

2. *Consider all possible options.* Determine how many health clubs are in your area, and the types of memberships they offer. Also, consider other options that might help you meet your goal, such as buying exercise equipment or a bicycle, walking to school, or running with a friend.

3. *Identify the consequences of each option.* For a consumer decision, this means comparing the costs and benefits of each option. Which option will best help you achieve your goal? Which option is the best use of your money? Which option has worked for other people you know?

4. *Select the best option.* When you have all the information, you can make your decision.

5. *Make and implement a plan of action.* Do you have enough money for the purchase? Do you need an adult's approval? Take the steps necessary to make the purchase a reality.

6. *Evaluate the decision, process, and outcome.* Did you use your resources wisely? Did you achieve your goal? Are there things you might have done differently? Are you satisfied with your purchase?

"Did I consider all possible options?"

 TECH CONNECT

Supermarkets and other stores are always looking for technology that makes shopping easier, more convenient, and more fun. Some have introduced self-checkout registers where consumers can scan and bag their own items instead of waiting for a cashier. The systems use a touch-screen monitor with voice commands to interact with consumers.

A newer option is a handheld scanner that consumers carry with them through the store. They scan each item before placing it in their bag or cart. Before leaving, the consumer simply prints the receipt and pays. Stores can offer special deals through the scanner, and consumers spend less time checking out.

As a class, discuss the benefits and drawbacks of handheld scanners. Can you think of other ways stores use technology to make shopping easier for consumers?

Introduce the Section

This section discusses the main influences on consumer purchasing decisions. These include individual values, family, past experiences, stage of life, and advertising.

Figure Focus

Explain that wise consumers know how to apply critical-thinking skills to their purchasing decisions. You look objectively at information and understand that you don't have to believe everything you hear or read. Critical thinking can help you evaluate your options. And this is very important as retailers and marketers use all types of methods and strategies, including peer pressure, to get teens to spend their money.

Ask students to identify how different clothing stores advertise and market themselves to teens. Do they try to categorize young men as the "big man on campus," or "red-blooded boys"? Do they label young women as "jockettes," or "in-style socialites"? How do they try to appeal to an individual's self-image?

Values

It is estimated that by the time a teenager turns 16 years old, he or she will have seen 6 million advertisements. Ask students how advertising affects their purchasing decisions. One recent survey found that most teens distrust marketing ploys and will research the product on the Internet or in magazines before going out to shop for it.

Recognizing Influences on Consumer Decisions

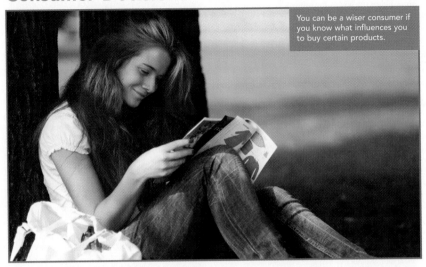

You can be a wiser consumer if you know what influences you to buy certain products.

Recall from Chapter 1 that an influence is something that affects the way you think and act. In your role as a consumer, many things influence what you buy and where you shop. First and foremost, you are influenced by your economic resources and your financial goals. How much money do you have to spend? Are you saving for a car, education, home, or retirement?

Other influences are the same things that influence the decisions you make in other roles of your life. For example:

- You are influenced by your values. If you value quality, you might choose a product because it has a reputation for being well-made. Your friend who values convenience might choose a less well-made product because it is easier to use.
- You are influenced by your past experiences. If you bought a pair of jeans in a store where the sales people were helpful, you might shop there again. If the sales people were unfriendly, you might go to a different store.

Recognizing the things that influence your consumer decisions can help make you a wise consumer. You can think critically about the influence factor and consider it when you are comparing the costs and benefits of each decision.

Values

When something is important to you, it has value. Your values are a major influence on your consumer decisions. You might also benefit from understanding how the values of other consumers influence their buying decisions.

- You buy things you value. For example, if clothes are important to you, you choose to spend your money on clothes. If music is important to your sister, she chooses to spend her money on MP3 downloads or concert tickets.
- You also buy things that reflect your personal values. For example, if protecting the environment is important to you, you choose to buy organic products. If curing cancer is important to your friend, he chooses to shop at a store that donates money to cancer research.

Family Influences

Consumer decisions are often influenced by your family members and by your family situation. Family values, income, the number of family members, and the ages of family members all affect consumer decisions. They affect the decisions of the individuals within the family as well as the family as a whole.

■ A family with a higher income can choose to spend more money on wants than a family with a lower income. For example, a family in which both parents earn wages may have more money than a family in which only one parent earns wages. The single-earner family may have to spend more of its money on needs, such as housing and food.

■ A family with more members may have to spend more money on needs than a small family. For example, a family with four children may have to spend more money on food, clothes, and medical care than a family with one child.

■ The wants of one family member may have to wait until the needs of the other family members are met. One child may want a new bike, but the family may have to spend money on housing, transportation, and food instead.

Stage of Life Influences

The stage of a family in the family life cycle also affects consumer decisions. A young family makes different choices than a retired couple; a single young adult has very different economic resources and financial goals than a divorced single mom with teenagers.

■ A young couple may be saving money to buy a house, so they try not to eat out very often, and they drive an older car. Or, they may spend freely on vacations and luxuries, because they do not have to spend money on children.

■ A family with young children may be saving money for college tuition. They also have to spend money to meet the needs of all family members.

■ An older couple may no longer have to support children, but they may need to support their aging parents. They may choose to help their children and grandchildren financially. They may still be saving for retirement.

■ After retirement, a family usually has to adjust their spending depending on the amount they saved and their remaining income.

Fitting In

Are your consumer decisions influenced by peer pressure?

👎 Do you buy an expensive shirt because that's what the other kids are wearing?

👎 Do you eat junk food because that's what the other kids are eating?

👍 Do you listen to the recommendation of a trusted friend before buying a new video game?

How can you take your peers' opinions about fashion and trends into consideration and still make wise, healthy consumer decisions?

How are the consumer decisions of a single adult different from those of a family?

Discuss

Make sure students distinguish between their own values and what advertisers want them to value. Students should analyze what their wants and needs are now and realize they will have different wants and needs in futures stage of life.

Fitting In

Students are asked how they can take their peers' opinions under consideration without feeling peer pressure. The popular phrase "keeping up with the Joneses" refers to the common tendency to compare one's self to one's neighbors. In recent years, the phrase has morphed to "keeping up with the Joneses' kids."Ask students to comment on peer pressure and how it influences the way they spend their money. Do they feel pressured to shop at certain stores or feel embarrassed if they are seen shopping somewhere else? Can they really recognize the difference between a pair of $85 jeans and a pair costing $25?

Figure Focus

A single adult will make different consumer decisions compared to those of a family. A single adult has only himself or herself to consider when making purchasing decisions, whereas a family must consider purchasing decisions that will benefit all members of the family. A single person, for example, might purchase a certain model car simply because it's the one she has always wanted, but when a parent purchases a car for the family, he might have to consider how many people it will seat, how safe it is, its gas mileage, etc.

Customized Instruction: At-Risk Students

Have students create a list of how they spent their money in the last week. For each expenditure, ask them to determine if it was a need or a want. If it was a want, ask them to explain what influenced their decision to make the purchase.

Negative Consequences

Some life skills a family can use to avoid stress or conflict include:

- Discussing the decision to be made and keeping the lines of communication open.
- Encouraging everyone to share ideas and give opinions.
- Listening respectfully and keeping a positive attitude.
- Examining the family budget to determine the feasibility of the purchase.

Figure Focus

Ask students what the difference is between these two questions:

1. "Will I be cool if I buy this?"
2. "Will I look cool if I buy this?"

The first question implies that a material possession can somehow change your personality or character. The second question implies that a material possession can have an impact on your image and physical appearance. Ask students if they think it's OK to make a purchasing decision based on the answer to either question.

Discuss

Explain the difference between an individual's values and those values that advertisers use to motivate a person to buy an item. Advertisers may appeal to an individual's insecurities, images of success and beauty, and fear of inadequacy in order to portray their values as yours.

Negative Consequences

Consumer decisions can cause stress and conflict if family members spend money on wants without discussing it first. Even purchases that benefit the whole family might cause conflict if there is no communication. What if one parent surprises the family with a new television?

★ *A family vacation might be delayed.*

★ *The family may have to use a credit card to pay for necessary car maintenance.*

★ *The family may have to skip a few months of saving for tuition or retirement.*

The negative consequences of the decision might outweigh the enjoyment the family would get from the new television. What life skills could a family use to avoid stress and conflict when making consumer decisions?

"Will I be cool if I buy this?"

Managing Resources for Consumer Decisions

Your consumer decisions are also influenced by your available resources. Money, of course, is one resource you use to buy goods and services. The way you manage your money has a direct effect on what you buy, where you shop, and when you buy.

- Skill and talent are resources that are valuable for a consumer. You might be able to use your skill or talent to obtain goods and services. For example, if you can sew or knit, you can create your own clothes instead of buying them in a store. If you are handy, you can repair a broken item instead of buying a new one or hiring someone else to fix it.
- Knowledge is a valuable resource for a consumer. The more you know about a product or service before you buy, the better prepared you will be to make a wise decision.
- Education is another valuable resource. The more education you have, the more income you are likely to earn. The more income you earn, the more money you have to spend. For example, if you graduate from college, you are likely to have greater economic resources than if you drop out of high school.
- Time is always a consideration. You might be willing to spend a lot of time comparing prices at many stores and reading many product reviews. Your brother might prefer to save time by shopping online and reading one or two reviews.

Advertising Influences

Businesses use advertising to convince you to buy their products. Although they must be truthful when they advertise, businesses use different techniques to influence you. Knowing how to recognize these techniques helps you identify the important information in the ad while ignoring the influence factor. You are better able to make informed, healthy consumer decisions. Some common advertising techniques include:

- *Lifestyle ads.* These ads portray an appealing lifestyle. They try to convince you that the people who use the product are special, and that if you use the product you will be special, too.
- *Celebrity ads.* These ads use famous people to sell products. They are sometimes called testimonial ads, because they include a recommendation from a famous person. Like lifestyle ads, they try to convince you that you can be like the celebrity if you use the product.
- *Values ads.* These ads appeal to personal values, such as patriotism or courage. They try to convince you that using the product is one way to demonstrate your own values.
- *Emotional ads.* These ads appeal to various emotions, such as fear or happiness. They try to convince you that using the product will somehow affect your emotions. For example, you might be happier if you drive a certain car, or less fearful if your car has a certain type of tires.
- *Comparison ads.* These ads compare one product directly to a similar product made by a different company. They try to convince you that one product is significantly better than the other.

Test **IT** Yourself!

Different people are influenced by different factors when they make consumer decisions. Some look for convenience. Some look at cost. Some look for quality. Use the following experiment involving lemonade to see what influences your classmates.

1. Divide into four teams. One group will make lemonade from scratch, one will make lemonade from frozen concentrate, one will make lemonade from a powdered mix, and one will use ready-made lemonade in a bottle or carton.
2. Each team will keep track of how much money and time it spends to assemble the tools and ingredients they need and then to prepare enough of their type of lemonade for the whole class.
3. Each student will rate each type of lemonade on five criteria: cost, time, convenience, enjoyment, and quality, using a scale of 1 to 5. The class will use the data to chart the results.
4. Individually, each classmate will choose the type of lemonade he or she would make in the future, and explain why. Is it quality? Is it convenience? Is it cost?

Sales are often advertised in the form of discounts, such as *10% off*. You must know the exact amount of the discount in order to know the sales—or discounted—price of an item. This information can help you comparison shop and make wise consumer decision.

To calculate a discounted price, you calculate the percentage, and then subtract it from the original price. Suppose an item's original price is $25.00 and it is on sale for 10% off. How much will it cost?

Recall the steps for finding the percentage of a number:

1. Change the percentage to a decimal by replacing the percent sign with a decimal point and moving the decimal point two spaces to the left.
2. Multiply the decimal by the number: $25.00 × .10 = $2.50
3. Subtract the percentage from the original price: $25.00 – $2.50 = $22.50

If a pair of jeans originally priced at $43.99 is on sale for 20% off, what will they cost?

What is a better deal—a shirt originally priced at $18.99 marked down to $14.99, or a shirt originally priced at $18.99 on sale for 20% off?

Speak Out

Some stores try to take advantage of young people and teens. The manager or sales person might think you don't know your rights, or will be too afraid to speak out. What can you do if you purchase a defective product, but the store won't replace it, repair it, or refund your money?

👎 Nothing.

👎 Yell at the sales person or manager.

👎 Spend money to buy a new product.

👍 Write a formal letter of complaint to the manager or the store owner.

👍 Ask a parent or other adult to come to the store to help you seek compensation.

👍 Contact your state's division of consumer affairs to ask for assistance.

After you receive compensation—payment or a new replacement product—what steps could you take as a consumer to show the store that its actions were wrong, and possibly illegal?

Test **IT** Yourself!

Student groups will make different types of lemonade. Students are to individually rate the type of lemonade they prefer. Emphasize to students that they should consider all the variables in their decision-making process: quality, taste, convenience, and cost. They can also consider additional factors such as the health value of the lemonade, if the lemonade is organic or is free of pesticides, and if it is made locally. Record each student's choice and then, as a class, discuss which lemonade got the most votes.

STUDENT ACTIVITY

For the "Test It Yourself!" activity, have each team of students create an advertisement for the lemonade that got the most votes. Encourage students to think of strategies advertisers have used to convince them to buy beverages.

Speak Out

Some of the steps you can take against the store are:

■ Contact the local Better Business Bureau.

■ Call action lines of local newspapers, TV, and radio stations.

■ File a complaint with the Federal Trade Commission (www.ftc.gov).

NUMBERS GAME

If a pair of jeans costs $43.99 with a 20% discount, they will cost $35.19:

■ 20% = .20

■ $43.99 × .20 = $8.80

■ $43.99 – $8.80 = $35.19

If a shirt was originally $18.99 and is 20% off, it would cost $15.19.

■ 20% = .20

■ $18.99 × .20 = $3.80

■ $18.99 – $3.80 = $15.19

The shirt marked down to $14.99 is a better deal.

Introduce the Section

This section distinguishes between impulse buying and thoughtful shopping. Tips on where and how to shop are provided, and the benefits of comparing options are discussed.

Figure Focus

Emphasize that having a written budget to refer to can help you make decisions about the things you want. However, you may be able to afford more of your wants if you shop smart and find good deals on the products you need.

Vocabulary

Impulse buying: When you see something and buy it without any thought or consideration.

Warranty: A written statement or guarantee that the product will work as expected for a set length of time.

Impulse vs. Thought

Retailers try to capitalize on impulsive shopping behavior with ploys such as:

- Prominently displaying candy, gum, and chocolate in the checkout area.
- Offering "Buy One, Get One Half Off" discounts.
- Placing "Quick-Click" links on Web sites to encourage purchasing an item online.
- Displaying the "Others who bought this, also bought this" sales pitch online.
- Using in-store demonstrations on customers to inspire you to "live in the moment."
- Playing in-store video or audio clips, such as popular music or testimonials, which appeal to your senses.
- Placing merchandise displays so that the shopper has to circle the entire store. Grocery stores, for example, place common products such as eggs, milk, and bread on the outside lanes of the store and spread them out so the shopper has to move from one end of the store to the other, with the hope being that he or she will pop in and out of aisles along the way.

Shopping Smart

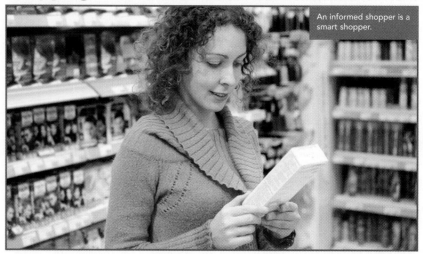

An informed shopper is a smart shopper.

Does your mother always shop at the same grocery store? It might be convenient, but does it have the best prices?

Do you always buy the same brand of athletic shoes? They might be fashionable, but do they have the best fit?

A smart shopper is an informed shopper. You are a smart shopper if you know all of your options before you buy. That includes:

- Understanding the product
- Knowing all the places where you could shop
- Recognizing the difference in prices between products and stores
- Understanding the store's return policy

If you know all your options, you may still decide to sacrifice fit in order to wear the coolest shoes. But, at least you considered a different, better fitting shoe.

Impulse vs. Thought

Have you ever walked into a store to buy a new shirt and walked out with a shirt, a pair of jeans, and a sweater? **Impulse buying** is when you see something and buy it, without giving it any thought or consideration. Stores actually try to get you to make impulse buys, by setting up irresistible displays near checkout lines.

Impulse buys can be fun, and you might end up with an item you really enjoy. They can also be a waste of money. You might get home and realize you are now the proud owner of something you didn't really need or want, like a marshmallow shooter. You can avoid impulse buys by being an informed shopper.

- Research a product before you go to the store. Look up information online or in consumer magazines. Talk to people who have used the product before. Ask if they like the product. Would they buy it again? Is it worth the price?
- Before you buy, read the product labels or tags. What is it made out of? Where is it made? Does it come with a **warranty**—a written statement or guarantee that the product will work as expected for a set length of time—that provides you with some protection?

TEAMWORK ACTIVITY

Have student teams visit a local grocery or other store and prepare a list of advertising ploys. They should look for what is placed near the checkout, what is displayed in the show windows, how shoppers move through the store (or flow of the store), and environmental factors such as lighting, music, and the temperature in the store. As a class, discuss each team's observations. Ask students how being aware of these ploys can help you be a smart shopper.

Deciding Where to Shop

As a consumer, one of the decisions you must make is where to shop. Your decision will be influenced by many things, including price, convenience, return policies, and the available **merchandise**—products. It may also be influenced by other factors such as loyalty, values, and the quality of the sales help.

Different stores offer different merchandise. They also offer different shopping environments.

- Do you like shopping in your pajamas? Shop online or from catalogs.
- Do you like attentive sales help? Shop at a specialty store.
- Do you like hunting for bargains? Check out a thrift shop.

Have you ever shopped at a price club store? How can you know if the prices are really less than at a regular grocery store?

Types of Stores

Before you make a decision about where to shop, it is helpful to know all of your options. Some common shopping options include:

- *Internet shopping.* You can find most products online. Web sites display pictures and list details so you know what you are buying. Some major stores have online shopping, while many shopping sites exist only on the Web and have no physical stores. Internet shopping is fast and convenient for buying, but it may be inconvenient if you need to return an item.
- *Department stores.* You can find a variety of items such as clothing, shoes, household items, and electronics in a department store. A department store is convenient when you need to buy different things but don't want to go to different stores. Department stores are often located in or near a shopping mall.

> Being a smart shopper is the first step to getting rich.
>
> — Mark Cuban, Owner Dallas Mavericks NBA

- *Specialty stores.* Smaller than a department store, a specialty store carries one type of merchandise, such as women's clothing, children's toys, shoes, sporting goods, or toiletries.

Bargain Hunting

Some stores are set up specifically to offer lower prices or bargains. If your main shopping goal is to save money, consider the following:

✔ *Price clubs. Warehouse price clubs sell merchandise in bulk—large quantities for lower prices. The merchandise may vary but often includes everything from seasonal items such as outdoor furniture to food and electronics. Customers pay a membership fee.*

✔ *Outlets and discount stores. Factory outlets and discount stores often sell items that were overstocked or left over from past seasons. They might sell damaged or irregular items, such as a shirt with inconsistent stitching.*

✔ *Thrift shops. Stores that sell used merchandise are called thrift shops. People sell or donate items they don't want any more to the store, which then sells those items at bargain prices to you.*

Figure Focus

A price club store is one that usually sells a variety of merchandise and which requires customers to pay annual membership fees in order to shop. The stores offer products in bulk, which may be attractive to bargain hunters. If you are comparing a price club to your local grocery store, look online, call, or visit to find out about the annual membership fees, membership cancellation fees, the quality of produce and merchandise, and whether the brands that you like are in stock.

Vocabulary

Merchandise: Products in stock at a store.

Bargain Hunting

Emphasize the importance of keeping receipts and learning more about return policies before purchasing items at bargain prices. Many times, discounted items will have limited warranties or cannot be returned.

"Quote Box"

According to Mark Cuban, the best return you can earn is on your own spending. Emphasize to students to save wherever they can, no matter how little, because it can add up quickly in their bank accounts.

Discuss

Ask students to discuss the positives and negatives of shopping at a department store, specialty store, and online. For example, shopping at a specialty store may provide unique merchandise and give you the opportunity to support a local business, but it might be more expensive and have a less flexible return policy.

Figure Focus

Explain the following regarding the return of an online purchase:

- Most sites offer full refunds, but others may charge restocking fees if the goods are not defective.
- Know how long you have to return the product ahead of time and add the return shipping time into that timeframe.
- Remember that many stores charge both shipping and return fees.
- Assume refunds will take 30 to 60 days to appear on your credit card.
- Check on whether you can return the item to a local retail outlet instead of shipping it back to the warehouse.

Sales, Rebates, and Coupons

Some other suggestions for learning about sales offers are:

- Get your name added to the retailer's mailing or e-mailing list.
- Look online for special promotions.
- Ask an employee to add you to her client book, and call you with any promotions.
- Join a frequent shopper program to gain access to pre-sale events.

21st Century Skills

What Happens Next?

Students are to prepare an ending to Justin's story. Justin is facing the decision of whether or not he should purchase a workout system that he has not researched and which costs a significant amount of money. Factors that may be influencing his decision include his desire to make the football team and to find a quick way to become stronger and bigger. Students' endings should consider Justin's financial state, whether his parents would approve of such a large purchase, and how he defines his needs and wants.

What If I Want to Take It Back?

Return policies vary from store to store. Make sure you understand the policy before you buy. Always save your sales receipt as a proof of purchase. You may need it for a warranty or a return.

Most states have a law that requires a store to display its return policy where consumers can see it. Some common return policies include the following:

- Returns or exchanges are allowed at any time, as long as you have the original sales slip.
- Returns or exchanges are allowed for a limited amount of time from the purchase date.
- Refunds may be full, or a store may charge a restocking fee—which means they keep a percentage of the purchase price and give you back the rest.
- Some stores will not refund your money, but will give you a store credit that you can use to buy something else.
- Some stores will not accept any returns or exchanges at all.

Comparing Your Options

Not only does a wise consumer compare prices, but he or she also compares the quality of construction, features, warranties, and service options. For example, if you are thinking about buying a camera, you might compare the cost, picture quality, zoom level, ease of use, and warranty.

Some people are willing to pay a higher price for higher quality. Sometimes a higher price indicates additional features. A computer will cost more if it has a larger monitor or a faster processor. Do you need the larger monitor? Do you want the faster processor?

Sometimes a higher price indicates a brand-name product. Many stores sell generic versions of brand-name products for a much lower price. You get the same features and quality, without the high cost.

These heels are higher than they looked on the Web site! How can I return an online purchase?

Sales, Rebates, and Coupons

When you compare costs, don't forget to consider sales, coupons, and rebates—cash back from the manufacturer. What if you see the camera you want to buy on sale at a store far from home?

- ★ *If the price is a lot less, it might be worth traveling.*
- ★ *You can ask the local store if they will match the sale price offered at the other store.*
- ★ *You might decide the sale price is not worth the drive.*

What sources can you use to learn about special sales offers?

21st Century Skills

What Happens Next?

Justin is thinking about going out for the football team. He is smaller than some of the other kids, and he thinks he would have a better shot at making the team if he were bigger and stronger. His dad suggests that he start a regular exercise routine, including running and weight lifting, but Justin has trouble sticking to a schedule.

One night, Justin sees an ad on television for a total body workout system. The people in the ad are all slim and muscular. The announcer says it takes only 15 minutes three times a week to build up muscle using the total body workout system. He also says that if you order right now, it will only cost four easy payments of $45.99 each.

What choices are facing Justin? What factors might influence his decision? What can he do to make a wise, healthy decision? Using your 21st Century Skills—such as decision making, goal setting, and problem solving—write an ending to the story. Read it to the class, or form a small group and present it as a skit.

Discuss

Ask students why they think people spend more money on a brand name compared to a generic product. Are brand-name products always better than generic ones? Someone might prefer brand-name drugs versus generic ones because he or she considers them safer. On the other hand, clothes and shoes may not be of any better quality but may hold more value to the person wearing them.

What's a Warranty?

Some products have warranties. A **warranty** is a written statement that promises the product will work for a set amount of time. Warranties are usually offered for electronics and other products that have motors or working parts. For example, an electric razor might have a warranty. So might a computer. Even a car comes with a warranty.

When you buy a product that has a warranty, you may have to fill out a warranty card and mail it to the manufacturer, or fill out a form online. You may also have to save your sales receipt to show as proof of purchase.

Note that a warranty is usually offered by the manufacturer, not the store where you bought the product. If you need the item repaired or replaced, you may have to send it to the manufacturer.

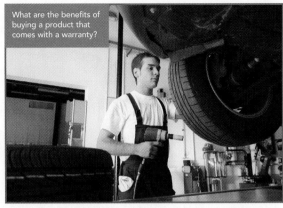

What are the benefits of buying a product that comes with a warranty?

What's a Service Contract?

Many stores will offer to sell you a **service contract** when you buy electronics or other products that might break, such as household appliances. A service contract is an agreement that the store—or manufacturer—will provide repair or replacement services if the product breaks or fails. Service contracts are usually available for different amounts of time. The longer the contract, the more you will pay.

- Read the contract carefully before buying it to see what is covered. The manufacturer's warranty might already cover the same things.
- Consider the cost of replacing or repairing the original item compared to the cost of service contract. The service contract might cost more.

Sometimes, a service contract is a good idea. For example, a service contract for a new computer might make it easier and cheaper to have the system fixed. Sometimes, a service contract is a waste of money. For example, it is probably less expensive to buy a new printer than it is to pay for a service contract.

MONEY MADNE$$

You purchased a DVD player at an electronics store for $99.00. When you got home, you saw the same player advertised on sale at a department store for $89.00. The electronics store charges a 10% restocking fee for returned items. Is it worth it to return the player to the electronics store and buy it at the department store? What if you paid $110.00 for the player at the electronics store?

Where to Get Product Information

When you research a product, it's important to use objective, reliable sources of information. The manufacturer and retailer will provide subjective information, because they want you to buy the product. Some useful sources include:

✔ *Family and trusted friends*

✔ *Government agencies, such as the Consumer Product Safety Commission (CPSC) and the Better Business Bureau*

✔ *Reports published by consumer protection organizations, such as Consumer Reports, which is published by Consumers Union, or Consumer's Research, which is published by Consumer's Research, Inc.*

Customized Instruction: More Advanced Students

Pair up students and have them role-play a sales associate at a shoe store and a customer. The customer is returning the shoes because of a defect in the heel. The sales associate earns a commission on each sale and will lose the commission if the cost of the shoes is refunded. Students should consider how to resolve the situation so that both the customer and the sales associate are satisfied.

Vocabulary

Service contract: An agreement that the store or manufacturer will provide repair or replacement services if the product breaks or fails.

Warranty: A written statement that promises a product will work for a set amount of time.

Figure Focus

Explain that warranties may be helpful in increasing the overall value of the product, protect you from paying for replacements or repairs, and give you peace of mind if you are a first-time buyer.

Where to Get Product Information

Discuss the "sales pitch" with students. Have they had to deal with a salesperson either on the phone or in person? Offer these tips to students for when they are dealing one-on-one with a salesperson.

- Get everything in writing.
- Do not sign contracts without reading them.
- Obtain the salesperson's name, title, business phone number, and business license number before making the purchase.
- Ask questions about warranties. If it says that it is free for repairs, then there should be no costs associated with it.
- Beware of extra charges for repairs or returns of defective products.
- Don't rush into a purchase because it's being offered at a certain price for a limited time only.

MONEY MADNE$$

Calculate the restocking fee on the player: 10% of $99.00 is $9.90. If you add that to the $89.00 the player costs at the department store, you get $98.90. You would save 10 cents by returning the item, paying the restocking fee, and buying the item on sale at the other store. It probably is not worth it. However, if you pay $110, the restocking fee of 10% would be $11.00. Adding that to $89, you get $100, so you would save yourself $10 by returning it. Whether it is worth it or not depends on your values.

Introduce the Section

This section provides information on the consumer's right to safety, to be informed, and to choose among competing brands. It also covers the various government agencies and laws designed to protect consumer rights.

Figure Focus

Ask students how knowing their rights can help them make better buying decisions. Explain that most stores put in writing their policies for returning or exchanging products sold. Sometimes these will be posted on signage in the store or printed on receipts. You should be familiar with these policies before you make your purchase.

Unlawful Trade Practices

Explain other measures you can take to protect yourself.

- Sign up with the National Do Not Call Registry at www.donotcall.gov to minimize sales calls to your home or cell phones.
- Check product recalls before making a purchase. You can do this through the U.S. Consumer Product Safety Commission's Web site at www.cpsc.gov.
- Contact your state Department of Agriculture, Trade & Consumer Protection to verify a business's licensing.

Vocabulary

Bait and switch tactics: Advertising one product and then selling a different product.

Exploring Your Consumer Rights

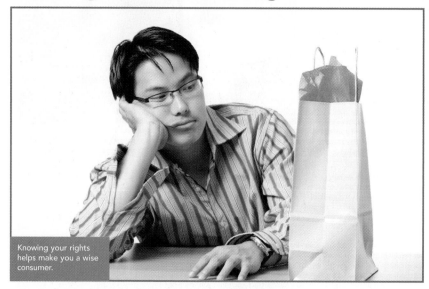

Knowing your rights helps make you a wise consumer.

Have you ever bought a product that broke almost as soon as you got it home? Or opened a food item such as cheese or pudding that was moldy? Did you take it back? Did you throw it away?

As a consumer of goods and services in the United States, you have certain rights that are protected by law. That means there are federal and state government agencies looking out for your safety and best interests.

Understanding your consumer rights can help you be a wise consumer. You will be better prepared to make informed decisions about where to shop and what to buy. You will also know who to contact and what to do if you buy something that does not work the way you expected.

Unlawful Trade Practices

Many states have laws that prohibit deceptive or misrepresentative behavior by vendors, such as the Unlawful Trade Practices Act in Oregon. These laws are designed to stop sellers from lying or hiding the truth about their products, and to force them to disclose all important information. Some common violations include:

- Lying about the characteristics, benefits, and qualities of the product or services
- Making false or misleading statements about prices
- Falsely claiming that a person or organization endorses or recommends the product
- Saying that used or altered goods are new
- Advertising goods that are not available, or are available in only a very limited quantity
- Using **bait and switch tactics**, which means advertising one product, and then selling you a different product
- Offering free items, and then charging you for service, handling, or other associated costs

The Right to Safety

You have the right to be safe from unreasonable risk of injury caused by consumer products. Three government agencies responsible for your right to safety include the following:

- The Consumer Product Safety Commission (CPSC) is responsible for the safety for consumer products, such as toys and clothing.
- The Food and Drug Administration (FDA) is in charge of the safety of processed food, drugs, medical devices, and cosmetics.
- The National Highway Traffic Safety Administration (NHTSA) sets highway safety standards and monitors safety-related motor vehicle defects, such as brakes that fail or engines that catch fire.

The Right to Be Informed

You have the right to truthful information about the goods and services you are buying. Laws at both the federal and state level help ensure that you receive the information you need to make a thoughtful, responsible buying decision.

- The Federal Trade Commission (FTC) is responsible for making sure that advertising and labels are not false or misleading.
- The federal Fair Packaging and Labeling Act requires that packages are labeled truthfully with basic facts such as the quantity and the ingredients.
- Most states have unit pricing laws that require grocery stores to display the cost of an item per pound, quart, or count so that shoppers can compare the cost of different sizes of products. Many states also require that perishable foods display an expiration or a sell-by date.

The Right to Choose

The FTC and the U.S. Department of Justice are responsible for enforcing laws that protect competition and your right to choose among a variety of goods, services, and vendors.

When there is competition, each vendor wants you to choose its product—not the one sold by someone else. So, vendors work to make a better product and to offer a fair price.

The Right to Be Heard

If you experience a problem as a consumer, you have the right to speak out or complain, and to seek **compensation**—payment or a replacement item—or **redress**—have a wrong corrected. For example, if you buy a remote control car that does not work, you have the right to ask for a refund, replacement, or repair. Although you can complain by telephone or in person, you should always put your complaint in writing, as well. Putting it in writing provides proof of your complaint, and preserves your rights as a consumer. Include specific information about the purchase and the problem, including dates, prices, and the store location. Keep a copy of the letter for yourself as proof that you made the complaint.

Many government agencies and consumer protection groups are available to help you seek compensation. For example, the Better Business Bureau (BBB) is a non-profit organization that will try to help you settle a consumer complaint. The Consumer Information Center and the FTC can provide information about how to make a formal complaint. If a business or manufacturer refuses to cooperate, you have the right to sue in court. Small claims courts are available for resolving disputes for amounts up to $3,000.00.

Other Safety Agencies

Other federal agencies responsible for protecting your safety as a consumer include:

✔ The Environmental Protection Agency (EPA). The EPA protects the land, air, and water systems. For example, it monitors noise levels, radiation levels, the quality of water for drinking and recreation, and the disposal of hazardous waste.

✔ The United States Department of Agriculture (USDA). The USDA is responsible for monitoring nonprocessed food, such as meat, dairy products, fruit, and vegetables. It sets standards of quality, provides nutritional information, and inspects products.

✔ The Federal Aviation Administration (FAA). The FAA enforces safety regulations in the manufacture, maintenance, and operation of commercial aircraft.

✔ The National Institute of Standards and Technology (NIST). The NIST establishes performance criteria for many consumer products.

✔ The Federal Reserve System, Federal Home Loan Bank Board, Federal Deposit Insurance Corporation, National Credit Union Administration, and the Comptroller of the Currency share responsibility for overseeing operations of banks, credit unions, and savings and loan associations.

Other Safety Agencies

Discuss additional consumer protection laws.

- The Consumer Product Safety Act gave the Consumer Product Safety Commission the ability to develop safety standards and force recalls of hazardous products.
- The Federal Trade Commission Act created the Federal Trade Commission to prevent deceptive acts and unfair competition as well as regulate trade.
- The U.S. National Do Not Call Registry law allows people to have their telephone numbers removed from telemarketing call lists.

Discuss

Discuss with students the benefits of food and drug labeling as required by the Food and Drug Administration. The FDA requires all food and drugs to be labeled with the following:

- Name of the product
- Net quantity
- Serving size
- Nutrition facts
- Ingredient list
- Name of manufacturer or distributor

Food labeling is designed to protect the health of consumers. Consumers who have food or drug allergies as well as those who have special dietary needs rely on this information to plan their meals and eliminate the risk of adverse reactions. Because of new forms of bioengineering and the introduction of new pesticides, labeling regulations are constantly changing to keep consumers informed.

Vocabulary

Compensation: Payment or a replacement for a loss or injury.
Redress: Having a wrong corrected.

Customized Instruction: Special Needs (Allergies) Students

Ask students to share information about their allergies. How do they identify foods that contain allergens?

Introduce the Section

This section covers the responsibilities involved in shopping. These include acting respectful to store employees, reading and following directions, and identifying infringements on consumer rights.

Figure Focus

Ask students if they read the labels on packaging and instructions for using products, such as toys or electronics, before unpacking and using them. What are the risks of not reading the labels and instructions? For example, did you know you can damage video game cards by storing them in extreme hot or cold temperatures? Did you know that people with epilepsy or a history of seizures can have an adverse reaction to the flashing lights and patterns that are prominent in video games? Could not reading the labeling and instructions for use have an effect on your ability to return the product?

Be Honest and Polite

Ask the class how being honest and polite can affect not only your attitude but those of the people with whom you interact. For example:

- It can make someone's day better.
- You might receive a free product or extra product testers.
- Someone might go out of his way to help you find an item.
- You might feel better about yourself.

Discuss

Discuss with students the irresponsibility of returning merchandise that has been used or damaged after the purchase. More than 50 percent of retailers say this is a common occurrence. Retailers must absorb the cost of damaged goods. This, in turn, makes their operating costs higher and forces them to either charge higher prices to consumers or cut costs elsewhere. In extreme cases, some companies are forced out of business, which has a negative effect on consumers because fewer stores mean less competition, which almost always results in higher prices.

Identifying Your Consumer Responsibilities

One of your consumer responsibilities is to heed the manufacturer's instructions and warnings.

In exchange for your protected rights, you have responsibilities as a consumer. Recall that a *responsibility* is something people expect you to do, or something you must accomplish.

Many of your consumer responsibilities are the same responsibilities you have in other roles of your life. For example, you are responsible for being polite and honest. Other responsibilities are unique to you as a consumer. For example, you are responsible for making informed buying decisions, for being aware of product recalls and dangers, and for seeking compensation when you are sold a defective product.

When you live up to your responsibilities as a consumer, you show others that you are mature and that you can make healthy decisions. You also help other consumers and support your economy. For example, when you notify the Better Business Bureau that a store uses deceptive advertising, you are helping to stop the unlawful actions and to inform other consumers.

Be Honest and Polite

Honesty and courtesy are two positive personal qualities. You can show these qualities as a consumer in various ways.

- Do not steal. Shoplifting is a crime, and you will be caught and punished.
- Inform the sales clerk if you are overcharged or undercharged. If you are overcharged, the store should refund your money. If you are undercharged, you should point out the error and pay the correct price.
- Return extra change. Most stores count the money in the cash register after a clerk's shift. If money is missing, they take it out of the clerk's paycheck, or fire the clerk for stealing.
- Be polite to the workers in the store and the other customers. That means waiting your turn for a sales clerk or in line to check out.
- Shop ethically. Buy products that reflect your values. Shop at stores that are honest and reputable.

Customized Instruction: ESOL Students

Ask students if their purchasing decisions are influenced by the availability of product labeling and instructions in their primary language.

Read and Follow Directions

Most products come with documentation, such as instructions for use, assembling instructions, maintenance schedules, and warnings. As a consumer, you have a responsibility to read and follow the manufacturer's documentation.

- Some instructions might be printed in a multipage booklet. For example, you might buy a desk that you have to assemble.
- Some products have very simple instructions. For example, even shampoo and toothpaste have directions for use printed on the package.
- Accidents and even death occur when consumers fail to pay attention to the manufacturer's warnings. One of the best-known warnings is the one on cigarette packages warning of the risks of smoking.
- If a manufacturer supplies a recommended maintenance schedule, you are responsible for following it. For example, a manufacturer might recommend that you change the batteries in your smoke detector twice a year, or replace the filter in an air conditioner.

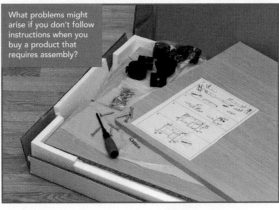

What problems might arise if you don't follow instructions when you buy a product that requires assembly?

Protest When You Are Wronged

Not only is it your right to complain and to seek compensation when you are wronged, it is also your responsibility. As a consumer, you have the power to influence which products manufacturers build and which stores stay in business.

- If you walk away from a defective product without reporting it, the vendor will continue to sell it, and the manufacturer will continue to produce it.
- If you report a defective product, the vendor will stop selling it, and the manufacturer will design and produce a better product.
- If you continue shopping at a store that uses deceptive or unlawful sales practices, the store stays in business, and other consumers suffer.
- If you stop shopping at a dishonest store, it will lose business, and possibly fail.

When you are old enough, you can vote for representatives who support consumer rights. Voting gives you power to affect laws and policies.

Myth You can always return an item and get your money back.

Truth Return policies vary from store to store. You have the right to compensation if a product is defective or not as advertised, but compensation does not necessarily mean a refund. You may have to accept a replacement, a repair, or a store credit.

End-of-Chapter Activities

Case Study

Maria's problem is that she bought a product she did not want. She thought she was buying perfume but instead bought scented hand lotion. She has a right to truthful and accurate information and labeling. The product was labeled as perfume. She has a right to compensation or redress. However, she gave the item as a gift; her grandmother might want to keep it. In that case, it is still Maria's responsibility to notify the store that the item was mislabeled. They can check to make sure the remaining items are labeled correctly.

Sounding Off!

Student answers will vary.

FAQ

1. Goods are things you can see, touch, buy, and sell. Clothing and food are goods. Services are work that one person does for other people, in exchange for payment. Doctors, hairstylists, bus drivers, and lawyers provide services.
2. A consumer is someone who buys goods and services.
3. Things that influence consumer decisions are economic and other available resources, financial goals, values, past experience, opinions of family members, family values, family income, the number of family members, the ages of family members, the stage of a family in the family life cycle, peer pressure, and advertising. Students may think of others.
4. Types of advertisements are:
   - Lifestyle ads. These ads portray an appealing lifestyle. They try to convince you that the people who use the product are special, and that if you use it you will be special, too.
   - Celebrity ads. These ads use famous people to sell products. They are sometimes called testimonial ads, because they include a recommendation from a famous person. They try to convince you that you can be like the celebrity if you use the product.
   - Values ads. These ads appeal to personal values, such as patriotism or courage. They try to convince you that using the product is one way to demonstrate your own values.
   - Emotional ads. These ads appeal to various emotions, such as fear or happiness. They try to convince you that using the product will somehow affect your emotions. For example, you might be happier if you drive a certain car.
   - Comparison ads. These ads compare one product directly to a similar product made by a different company. They try to convince you that one product is significantly better.

Case Study

Maria was shopping for a birthday gift for her grandmother. She found a bottle of her grandmother's favorite perfume at a specialty beauty store. It cost $24.99, and came prepackaged in a decorative box with a ribbon around it.

When Maria's grandmother opened the box, she found that it contained the wrong item. Instead of her favorite perfume, it held a bottle of hand lotion scented with the perfume.

- What problem is Maria facing?
- As a consumer, what are her rights and responsibilities?
- What do you think Maria should do?

Sounding Off!

1. Do you think you are a wise consumer? Why or why not?
2. Do you express your values as a consumer? If so, how? If not, why not?

FAQ

1. What is the difference between goods and services?
2. What is a consumer?
3. List three things that influence consumer decisions.
4. List five types of advertisements.
5. What is impulse buying?
6. What is a warranty?
7. What type of store carries one type of merchandise only?
8. List four types of unlawful trade practices.
9. List four consumer rights.
10. List three consumer responsibilities.

5. Impulse buying is when you see something and buy it, without giving it any thought or consideration.
6. A warranty is a written statement or guarantee that the product will work as expected for a set length of time.
7. A specialty store carries one type of merchandise only.
8. Types of unlawful trade practices are:
   - Lying about the characteristics, benefits, and qualities of the product or services.
   - Making false or misleading statements about prices.
   - Falsely claiming that a person or organization endorses or recommends the product.
   - Saying that used or altered goods are new.
   - Advertising goods that are not available, or are available in only a very limited quantity.
   - Using bait and switch tactics, which means advertising one product, and then selling you a different product.
   - Offering free items, and then charging you for service, handling, or other associated costs.
9. Consumer rights are:
   - The right to safety.
   - The right to be informed.
   - The right to choose.
   - The right to be heard.
10. Consumer responsibilities include:
    - To be honest and polite.
    - To read and follow directions.
    - To protest when you are wronged.

The text inside the book page box:

In small groups, prepare and present skits that demonstrate how you would return a product in different circumstances. For example, you might present a skit about returning an item when the clerk is unhelpful, or returning an item that you purchased online. Use the skits to show the correct and incorrect way to interact with sales clerks and other consumers.

Hot Topics

Do you think your classmates pay too much attention to who has the trendiest, newest, and coolest stuff? Do you think you do, too? Is it a problem?

Take this opportunity to write anonymously about the situation. Use a word processor so no one recognizes your handwriting. Be honest and open. Put the paper in the class Hot Topics box.

As a class, read the anonymous entries and discuss them.

Web Extra ▼

Some agencies and organizations responsible for protecting consumers have complaint forms on their Web sites. You can use the forms to submit complaints online, or print the form to mail.

Use the Internet to locate consumer complaint forms. Print them and make a book for your class, or compile a list of Web sites where classmates can find the forms. Include information about consumer rights, and when they might need to use such a form.

Problem Solver

A friend tells you he received money as a gift from an uncle, and he is going out to buy a new bike. You suggest that a bike is a big purchase, and maybe he should think about it for while. Individually or in pairs, make a plan for the friend who wants a new bike. Use reliable sources to collect information about different bikes. Identify places where he could buy a bike, and investigate the prices of the available models. Use the decision-making process to help the friend consider all options, assess the costs and benefits, and make a decision.

Prepare a presentation or report explaining the steps you used and the decision you made.

Team Players

Teams will create skits on how to interact during the return of an item. Review with students the keys to effective communication.

- Be clear, speak slowly, and make eye contact.
- Be personal. Use the other person's name if you know it.
- Be positive. Phrase your message in positive terms. Say what you want, not what you don't want.
- Get to the point. Explain why or how you feel a certain way.
- Actively listen to the other person. Pay attention and make sure you understand him or her.
- Think before you respond. Ask questions for clarification, if necessary.

Hot Topics

Make sure students understand that they can turn in their papers anonymously. Encourage them to be open and honest about their opinions regarding competition among students over who has the trendiest or coolest stuff.

Web Extra

Students are to research how to submit a consumer complaint online, and when they might need to use such a form. A consumer can file a complaint if a company has lied about the qualities of a product, made misleading statements about prices, advertised goods that are not used, and offered free items and then charged you a fee, to name a few. To learn more, students can begin their research by going to www.ftccomplaintassistant.gov.

Problem Solver

Students are asked to use the decision-making process to help a friend determine the type of bike to buy. Review the process, if necessary.

1. Define the goal: Purchasing an affordable and high-quality bike.

2. Consider all possible options: Check different bike models, new versus used, mountain versus racing, and trick bikes versus standard ones.

3. Identify the consequences of each option: Some bikes are more expensive and may require a payment plan. Others may be cheaper but not as high quality. The answer depends on your friend's values.

4. Select the best option for the bike: Compare costs, preferences, and quality.

5. Make and implement a plan of action on how to pay for the bike.

6. Evaluate the decision, process, and outcome of choosing the bike. Will your friend regret listening to you or will he appreciate your input?

Write Now

Students are to write a letter to an advertiser, explaining why they are disappointed with a product. Remind students that a letter is written in the first person. Review with students the parts of a letter: dateline, letter address, salutation, body, complimentary close, and writer's name and title. The body of the letter should have a beginning, middle, and end. Because this is a persuasive letter, they should write in a tone that appeals for change.

Be Involved!

Students are to use the FCCLA planning process to prepare some form of a presentation on how to be a wise consumer. The FCCLA planning process is:

- Identify the project.
- Set the goal.
- Form a plan.
- Act.
- Follow up.

Students can obtain more information on the FCCLA planning process from the organization's Web site, www.fcclainc.org or by referring to *Appendix B: Joining a Career Technical Student Organization* beginning on page 525 of the student text.

Social Networking

Students are to gather information on local consumer protection organizations. You might split students into teams and have each team focus on an organization. In addition to gathering pamphlets and other materials, have students research volunteering opportunities with the organizations.

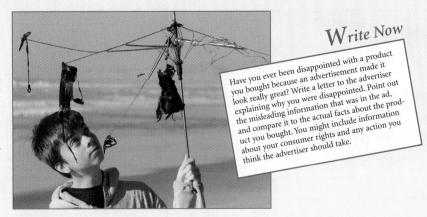

Write Now

Have you ever been disappointed with a product you bought because an advertisement made it look really great? Write a letter to the advertiser explaining why you were disappointed. Point out the misleading information that was in the ad, and compare it to the actual facts about the product you bought. You might include information about your consumer rights and any action you think the advertiser should take.

Be Involved!

www.fcclainc.org

As a class, brainstorm ways you could educate other students about the importance of consumer clout and being a wise consumer. For example, you might organize a comparison shopping trip, prepare a presentation about consumer decision-making, or create a booklet or Web site about consumer rights and responsibilities.

Individually, or as a group, meet with your teacher or advisor and use the FCCLA planning process to select and plan a project that will let you educate your peers about consumer management.

Define the project as a goal, make an action plan for achieving the goal (including a timeframe), assess the plan to make sure it is reasonable and attainable, and then put the plan into action to achieve your goal.

As you work toward your goal, keep a journal to record your progress, and collect documentation that you can use to show what you have achieved. Contact local newspapers or other media outlets for publicity, if appropriate.

At the end of the set timeframe, use the documentation to make a poster or presentation. Write a report explaining what you learned, whether you were successful or not, and what you would do differently if you were going to start the project all over again.

Social Networking

As a class, identify organizations in your area that work to protect the rights of consumers. Contact the organizations to request materials such as pamphlets and posters. Use the materials to decorate a bulletin board near your classroom.

If possible, consider inviting a representative of one of the organizations to visit your class to discuss what the organization does.

Part IV

Career Management

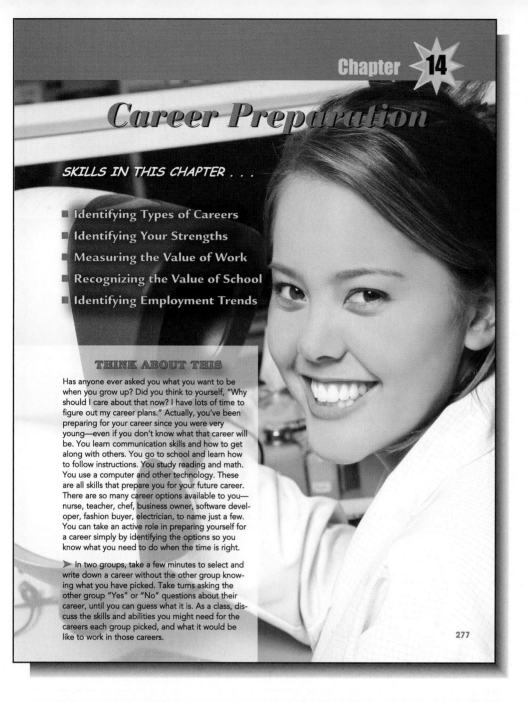

Chapter 14

Career Preparation

SKILLS IN THIS CHAPTER . . .

- Identifying Types of Careers
- Identifying Your Strengths
- Measuring the Value of Work
- Recognizing the Value of School
- Identifying Employment Trends

THINK ABOUT THIS

Has anyone ever asked you what you want to be when you grow up? Did you think to yourself, "Why should I care about that now? I have lots of time to figure out my career plans." Actually, you've been preparing for your career since you were very young—even if you don't know what that career will be. You learn communication skills and how to get along with others. You go to school and learn how to follow instructions. You study reading and math. You use a computer and other technology. These are all skills that prepare you for your future career. There are so many career options available to you— nurse, teacher, chef, business owner, software developer, fashion buyer, electrician, to name just a few. You can take an active role in preparing yourself for a career simply by identifying the options so you know what you need to do when the time is right.

➤ In two groups, take a few minutes to select and write down a career without the other group knowing what you have picked. Take turns asking the other group "Yes" or "No" questions about their career, until you can guess what it is. As a class, discuss the skills and abilities you might need for the careers each group picked, and what it would be like to work in those careers.

277

Chapter 14 Overview

This chapter introduces students to types of careers. They identify job opportunities that might utilize their strengths and talents, and they explore strategies on acquiring the education and skills that will help them meet their career goals.

Identifying Types of Careers   This section looks at the different resources that help students identify types of careers.

Identifying Your Strengths   Recognizing your strengths and talents can steer you toward a career that will further develop and strengthen them.

Measuring the Value of Work   In this section, students learn about the emotional, educational, and financial benefits of work.

Recognizing the Value of School   Education is an investment in the future, and in this section, students learn to identify the many resources available through school. If used effectively, these resources can put students on the path to career success.

Identifying Employment Trends   This section discusses the economic, demographic, and technological factors that contribute to job outlooks and industry trends.

Focus and Engage

Bell-Ringer: Think About This

Split the class into two groups and have each group select a career. Each group will try to guess the other group's selected career by asking "yes" and "no" questions. Instruct students to select a career that they are somewhat knowledgeable about. For example, they should have a general understanding of education requirements for those who choose that career, types of jobs within the career, and types of businesses that offer those jobs.

ADVANCE PREPARATION	
Review	*Life Skills for the 21st Century* textbook, Chapter 14.
Prepare	Paper and pencil for some activities. Current newspapers or magazines. Box labeled "Hot Topics."

CUSTOMIZED INSTRUCTION OVERVIEW				
Less Advanced Students	**More Advanced Students**	**ESOL Students**	**Special Needs Students**	**At-Risk Students**
Pages 281, 284, 286, 288	Page 279	Page 278	Pages 281, 286, 288	Pages 283, 284

Introduce the Section

This section distinguishes between careers and jobs. It also identifies the different resources that help students identify types of careers.

Figure Focus

Help students understand the difference between a career and a job. A career or occupation is a chosen field of work, whereas a job is an activity, such as a trade or profession, which you do for pay. For example, you might have a career in education and hold a job as a high school teacher. Ask students about the jobs they or other members of their family have. What career do these jobs fall under?

Vocabulary

Career: Chosen field of work in which you try to advance over time by gaining responsibility and earning more money.

Job: Any activity you do in exchange for money or other payment.

STUDENT ACTIVITY

Have students prepare a list of their hobbies, special talents, and interests. This could be anything from playing the piano to collecting trading cards to drawing pictures. Then, have them identify one or two of those things they enjoy most. At this point, you can have students come up with career ideas that match their top interests on their own or have the class come up with ideas.

Identifying Types of Careers

Identifying different types of careers helps you decide which career will be right for you.

A career is a chosen field of work in which you try to advance over time by gaining responsibility and earning more money. Another word for *career* is occupation.

A job is any activity you do in exchange for money or other payment. A job does not necessarily lead to advancement.

The career you choose has a major impact on the kind of life you will lead. Your career determines the type of training and education you will need. It might impact where you live and even who you will marry.

Your career choice affects how much money you earn and how you spend most of your time. Most workers in the U.S. spend between 40 and 50 hours each week at work!

■ Where will you be? In a large office, a hospital, or on a construction site?

■ Who will you be with? Will you work alone or have co-workers? Will you be supervising children, helping animals, or caring for the elderly?

Even if you have no idea what career you want in the future, you can start now to identify different types of careers. Learning about careers now will help prepare you to choose the career that is right for you.

Reasons for Choosing a Career

Most people work because they need money to pay for their needs and wants. Money is a good reason to choose a career, but it is not the only reason. People who are happy with their careers usually do something they enjoy. They choose a career because it gives them satisfaction, uses their skills and talents, and gives them a role in the community.

■ Do you enjoy being with animals? You might want a career as a veterinarian, zoologist, or animal shelter manager.

■ Do you have a talent for arranging furniture in rooms and making homes look beautiful? You might want a career as an interior decorator or movie set designer.

■ Do you get satisfaction from balancing a budget? You might want a career as a financial planner.

Customized Instruction: ESOL Students

Ask students about career and job opportunities for people who are bilingual. Being bilingual is a huge plus for those considering a career in travel and tourism. In health care, there is a need for bilingual nurses and nursing aides. Banks and other financial institutions as well as marketing companies need bilingual employees at almost every level. Teachers who know a foreign language— even if they do not teach that language—are considered an asset to a school system. Many government offices look for bilingual counselors, social workers, and caseworkers.

Career Clusters

There are an overwhelming number of career opportunities. How can you identify the ones that might be of interest to you?

The U.S. Department of Education organizes careers into 16 clusters. A **cluster** is a grouping of similar things. Career clusters help you sort the career possibilities into 16 manageable groups.

The careers in each cluster are in related industries or business areas. They require a similar set of skills and the same core training and education. For example, the Hospitality and Tourism career cluster includes the food service industry, the hotel industry, the recreation industry, and the travel industry.

Within each cluster, there are different pathways. A pathway leads to a specific career. For example, pathways in the Hospitality and Tourism career cluster include:

■ Restaurants and Food and Beverage Service, leading to careers such as chef, restaurant manager, or banquet manager

■ Lodging, leading to careers such as hotel manager, concierge, or housekeeping

■ Travel and Tourism, leading to careers such as travel agent, public relations representative, trip organizer, or tour guide

■ Recreation, Amusements, and Attractions, leading to careers such as club manager, resort instructor, or festival planner

■ You can learn more about the 16 career clusters and pathways in Appendix A.

Resources for Identifying Careers

You have many resources to help you identify types of careers, starting with your school guidance and career counselors. Your counselors have books, computer programs, videos, and lists of useful Web sites that provide information about types of careers.

School clubs and organizations may also have information about types of careers. A business club might invite someone to speak about his or her occupation. An organization such as FCCLA has career-related projects and activities.

You can schedule an **informational interview** to talk directly to someone who works in a career that interests you. The person can answer questions about job responsibilities and the work environment.

The U.S. Bureau of Labor Statistics (BLS) is a government agency responsible for tracking information about jobs and workers. Its Web site has a section specifically for students (www.bls.gov/audience/students.htm). It includes information on more than 60 occupations, including descriptions of responsibilities, education requirements, salary ranges, and job outlook. A **job outlook** includes statistics and trends about whether the job is in an industry that is growing or shrinking.

The BLS also publishes the Occupational Outlook Handbook (OOH) in printed and online editions (www.bls.gov/oco/). The OOH describes more than 200 occupations, including responsibilities, working conditions, education requirements, salary ranges, and job outlook.

A career counselor or librarian can help you find resources for identifying careers. Why do you think it is important to research careers while you are still in school?

Nontraditional Occupations

A nontraditional occupation is any job that a man or woman does that is usually done by someone of the other gender. For example, nurse is an occupation usually done by women, so it is nontraditional for men. Construction worker is an occupation usually done by men, so it is nontraditional for women. Some other nontraditional careers include:

Men	*Administrative assistant*
	Flight attendant
	Hair stylist
	Child care
	Elementary school teacher
Women	*Auto mechanic*
	Detective
	Architect
	Chemical engineer
	Pilot

Try not to rule out a nontraditional career because you associate it with one gender or another; it might be a good match for your skills and abilities.

Figure Focus

Students are to consider why it is important to research careers while they are still in school. Experts believe that you should start the process as early as the eighth and ninth grades. Explain that the earlier you start researching, the more time you have to gather information and determine your likes and dislikes. Stress the importance of experience. As students progress through their high school years, they should take a variety of elective classes, participate in extracurricular activities, and take on part-time jobs. These experiences will help them identify possible career paths that might interest them.

Teaching Tips

Refer students to *Appendix A: Career Clusters*, which starts on page 513 of the student text. This section defines the career classification system established by the U.S. Department of Education. A description of each career cluster is provided, along with job, industry, and occupation types (referred to as "pathways") and samples of occupations.

Nontraditional Occupations

Nontraditional occupations as defined by the U. S. Department of Labor are any occupations in which men or women comprise 25% or less of its total employment. Ask students to think of nontraditional occupations in addition to those listed in the text.

For women:	For men:
■ Bellhop	■ Cashier
■ Bricklayer	■ Dental hygienist
■ Electrician	■ Elementary school teacher
■ Exterminator	
■ Funeral director	■ Restaurant host
■ Plumber	■ Librarian
■ Religious leader	■ Maid or housekeeper
	■ Physical therapist

Customized Instruction: More Advanced Students

Have students define the term "job shadowing" and research companies or organizations in their community that they'd be interested in contacting about job shadowing opportunities. Ask students to explain why they are interested in those companies. Job shadowing enables students to learn about a job or company by experiencing it in the "shadow" of a working professional. It gives students exposure to the workplace in an occupational area of interest to them.

Introduce the Section

Recognizing your strengths and talents can steer you toward a career that will further develop and strengthen them.

Vocabulary

Skill: An ability or talent; something you do well.
Strengths: Positive qualities and skills.

Figure Focus

Ask students what they think is more important in a job: liking what they do or making a lot of money. Have students share reasons for why they answered the way they did.

Reinforce and Review

In Chapter 3, students learned how to recognize their own character qualities, both negative and positive. They also learned that positive character qualities can be developed. Simply doing the things that make you feel good about yourself is one way to develop them. Ask students to name some positive character traits they would see in a person who is happy in his work. Some traits are enthusiasm, thoughtfulness, compassion, tolerance, kindness, fairness, and citizenship. Then ask them to name traits they might see in a person who was unhappy in her work. These include laziness, indifference, dishonesty, intolerance, meanness, and stubbornness. Finally, ask them which employee—the one with positive traits or the one with negative traits—will probably advance quicker and make more money.

Identifying Your Strengths

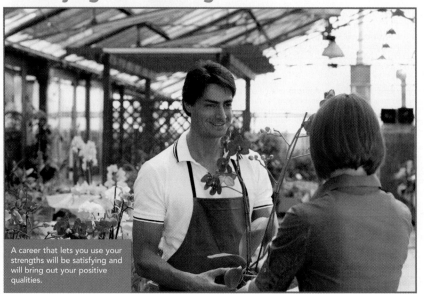

A career that lets you use your strengths will be satisfying and will bring out your positive qualities.

If you are like most people, you will spend half your life or more working. So, choosing a career that will bring you satisfaction makes good sense. How can you know what will bring satisfaction? One way is to choose a career that gives you a chance to use and develop your strengths.

Your **strengths** are your positive qualities and skills. Your personal qualities are the characteristics and traits that make you unique (Chapter 3). A **skill** is an ability or talent—something you do well.

- You might have a talent for growing flowers.
- You might understand how machines work.
- You might speak multiple languages.

Being able to identify your strengths will help you choose a career that is right for you. It will also help you set realistic educational and career goals. (In Chapter 15, you use a career self-assessment worksheet to connect your strengths with possible career opportunities.)

Personal Qualities and Your Career

Recall from Chapter 3 that everyone has positive and negative personal qualities. When you start looking for a career, it helps to understand the situations that bring out both types of qualities.

- Are you happy working alone, or would you get lonely and sad?
- Do you enjoy talking on the phone, or would you prefer to meet with people face to face?
- Are you relaxed sitting at a desk for a long time, or would you rather be outdoors and active?
- Do you enjoy the excitement of having to meet a deadline, or does it cause you to feel stress?

You will spend a lot of time and energy at work. The best work environment will bring out your positive personal qualities.

Discovering Your Interests

Often, people have strengths that relate to their interests. **Interests** are subjects or activities that attract your attention and that you enjoy doing or learning about. You can have interests in the different areas of your life.

- At home, you might have interests in cooking, gardening, sewing, or design.
- At school, you might have interests related to your class subjects, athletics, and clubs.
- With peers, you might share interests in movies, music, and sports.
- In your community, you might have interests in volunteer activities, politics, and public services.

Many of your interests are probably related to activities such as sports, arts, and entertainment. These interests may be useful in your career, or they may be things you do outside of work for fun. (There's more about doing things outside work for fun in Chapter 18.)

For example, if you are interested in music, you might consider a career such as a music teacher, a disc jockey, an agent for a musician, an owner of a club that hosts performers, or a radio host. You might consider performing with a band for fun.

Don't Forget Your Values!

Knowing what you value is key to choosing an occupation that is right for you. Recall from Chapter 1 that when you value something, it is important to you. Your values can help you determine career decisions.

- If you value adventure, you might consider a career in tourism or recreation management.
- If you value **job security**—knowing you will have your job for a long time— you might consider a career in government.

Of course, values can change. When you are young, you might value the opportunity to travel and meet new people. You might consider a career as a flight attendant.

As you get older, you might value job security and a steady salary. You might consider a career in hotel management.

Multilingual Employees

Are you bilingual? Bilingual means that you can communicate in more than one language. It is an ability that is an advantage to anyone looking for a career.

Many businesses have offices in countries all around the world. Even those that have offices in only one country have customers who speak different languages. Employers are eager to hire qualified candidates who can speak multiple languages. If you understand different cultures and are interested in living internationally, that is an advantage as well.

What languages do you think are spoken by the most people around the world? Use the Internet or the library to find the answer. Make a poster showing how you might use multiple languages to succeed in a career.

Interests and Careers

You don't have to be an expert in something to have an interest in it. An interest might be a favorite activity or something you just like to do. For example, you might not be a star basketball player, but you can still seek a career that satisfies your interest in basketball and also uses your other skills and abilities. What if you are interested in basketball but know you do not have the talent to be a professional player?

★ *If you have an ability for communications, you might consider a career as a sports journalist.*

★ *If you have an ability for food and nutrition, you might consider a career as a sports nutritionist.*

★ *If you have an ability for marketing, you might consider a career in public relations, sales, or marketing for a sports team.*

What interests and abilities do you have that you think might relate to a career?

Myth There is one perfect job for everyone.

Truth Trying to find one perfect job limits your opportunities. There are many occupations that can satisfy your career goals, and most people will have several jobs and careers throughout life.

Vocabulary

Interests: Subjects or activities that attract your attention and that you enjoy doing or learning about.

Job security: Knowing that you will have a job for a long time.

Interests and Careers

Students are asked to consider their interests and abilities that relate to a career. You might have students do an online interest inventory or obtain one from your school guidance counselor. Free online resources include www.learnmoreindiana.org and www.self-directed-search.com.

Myth/Truth

Explain that people often make job and career changes. Sometimes, they decide for themselves to make the change; other times, someone or something else inspires them to change. For example, a textbook publisher is developing a series of economics books and hires an economist currently working in a bank's research department to serve as editor of the series. The economist has made a change from a career in finance to one in education and training. Making such changes often involves additional schooling and training. For some job or career changes, you might have to take college credit courses or undergo vocational training. Sometimes, the employer hiring you will provide on-the-job or other specialized training.

 ## Multilingual Employees

The most common languages spoken are:

- Mandarin Chinese
- Hindi (language of India)
- English
- Spanish
- Arabic

Students are to create posters that illustrate how you might use multiple languages to succeed in a career.

Customized Instruction: Less Advanced/Special Needs Students

Pair students up and have them interview each other, asking questions about hobbies, interests, and abilities as well as character traits and personality strengths. Based on the answers, have each student suggest a career they think would be suitable for the student they interviewed.

Introduce the Section

In this section, students learn about the emotional, educational, and financial benefits of work.

Reinforce and Review

Remind students that "well-being" is the feeling and understanding that everything is going right in your life. It is when you have a positive outlook about yourself and the people and things around you. You are happy, healthy, confident, and satisfied. Often, well-being has a lot to do with how well you meet your responsibilities.

Figure Focus

Ask students who have or have had jobs to discuss the positive effects of work. These might include learning a new skill or strengthening an existing one; making new friends or expanding their network of contacts; earning money to buy things they want; and feeling a sense of responsibility and accomplishment. Then, ask them to discuss any negative effects of work, or work-related issues that got in the way of their well-being. For example, personality clashes with other employees or supervisors; physical ailments, such as fatigue or stress; lower grades owing to less time for studying; and personal relationships that have suffered because of less time for socializing. Do the positives outweigh the negatives?

Vocabulary

Productivity: Amount of work an employee accomplishes.

Measuring the Value of Work

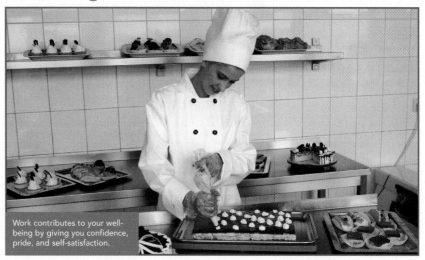

Work contributes to your well-being by giving you confidence, pride, and self-satisfaction.

Value is a measure of the quality or importance of something. (Recall that if you value something, it is important to you.) So, how do you measure the importance of work? Start by defining the word *work*. Work has different meanings in the different areas of your life.

- In terms of a career, work refers to the way you spend your time in order to earn an income.
- At home, it might mean the chores you do around the house.
- At school, it might mean homework, tests, or class projects.
- With your peers, it might mean the effort you put into friendships.
- In your community, it might mean the time you spend volunteering.

In this part of the book, the focus is on careers and the work you do to earn an income. When you recognize the value of work as a career, you might discover that the ideas and concepts are valid for the other areas of your life, as well.

The Economic Value of Work

If you have a job now, you probably know the economic value of work. You work, and you are paid for it. When you receive a paycheck, you can use the money to buy things you want and need. You can contribute to your family's finances. You can save for the future.

The economic benefits of work are greater than just putting cash in your pocket. When you work, you contribute to the success of the economic system around you.

- The economy measures the value of work in terms of the flow of goods and services. Work produces the goods and services that people need and want. People who work are able to buy the goods and services. The stronger the economy, the more jobs there are, and the more people work.
- Employers measure the value of work in terms of **productivity**—the amount of work an employee accomplishes. When workers are productive, the employer is successful.
- The community measures the value of work in terms of taxes. When you earn an income, you pay taxes that support your local community, your state, and the federal government.

Stay in School

Everyone benefits from increased graduation rates.

- High school graduates themselves earn higher wages and experience a better quality of life. A high school graduate earns between $250,000 and $300,000 more than a dropout over the course of their lifetime.

- Municipalities, states, and the nation benefit from graduates' increased purchasing power and higher income tax receipts. For example, if the students who dropped out of the class of 2007 had graduated, the nation's economy would have benefited from an additional $329 billion in income over their lifetimes.

- When more students graduate, government spends significantly less on social programs.

- Employers benefit from a more skilled workforce and higher worker productivity.

Furthermore, recent government data shows 90 percent of the U.S. economy's fastest growing jobs require education or training beyond high school. And, at the current high school dropout rate, there will be a shortfall of 7 million college-educated workers by 2012.

The Emotional Value of Work

Some days you might think your job is not worth your paycheck. Your friends might be playing Guitar Hero while you are stocking shelves at the market. Or they are watching videos while you are babysitting.

Luckily, the benefits of work include more than just money. Every job has responsibilities. When you meet your work responsibilities, you can be proud of your accomplishments. Working contributes to your self-image and self-esteem.

- Your employer appreciates your efforts.
- Your customers respect your knowledge.
- Your co-workers enjoy working with you.
- Your family recognizes that you can achieve goals and make healthy decisions.

The Educational Value of Work

Jobs you have when you are still in school provide the opportunity to gain knowledge that will be valuable as you begin to plan and search for a career. You can discover more about the workplace and about the types of jobs you enjoy.

- As a data entry clerk, you might realize that you have a knack—ability—for computer programming.
- As a landscaping assistant, you might realize that you get satisfaction from working outdoors.

Throughout your life, work is valuable because it provides an opportunity to learn new skills and information.

- A waiter learns how to take orders and serve food.
- A child care assistant learns how to clean up after snack time and monitor children in a play area.
- An office assistant learns how to answer phones, manage inventory, and use the office computer.
- A sale representative learns about new products and services.

Can you think of skills you have developed in school that will help you succeed in a future career?

21st Century Skills

What Happens Next?

J.T. is looking for a summer job. His friend Alex is a lifeguard and works at the town pool. He tells J.T. that lifeguarding is fun. The pay is good, he gets to be outside all day, the other guards are nice, and the girls all think the lifeguard is cool.

J.T. applies for the job. The town's recreation manager explains that the town will pay for the lifeguard training and certification as long as J.T. works all summer. If he quits, he will have to repay the cost of the training.

The training is harder than J.T expected. He does not enjoy learning first aid and CPR. However, he completes the course and is certified. The recreation manager schedules J.T. to work 5 days a week, for 6 hours a day.

The job is not as much fun as J.T. expected. Little kids are constantly asking for band aids. J.T. has to clean the bathrooms at the end of the day. His brother wants to go camping for the weekend, but J.T. is scheduled to work on Saturday. After one week, J.T. is regretting his decision to become a lifeguard. He is thinking about quitting.

What problems are facing J.T.? Can he find solutions? Did he make the best decisions while looking for a summer job? What could he have done differently? Using your 21st Century Skills—such as decision making, goal setting, and problem solving—write an ending to the story. Read it to the class, or form a small group and present it as a skit.

Figure Focus

Students should consider not only skills they've acquired through the classroom, but also in their extracurricular activities. These can range from subject-specific skills (such as keyboarding, algebra, writing, or a foreign language) to critical-thinking skills (such as decision-making, problem-solving, communicating, and resource management).

21st Century Skills

What Happens Next?

Students are to prepare an ending to the story on J.T. and his summer lifeguarding job. J.T. is facing a number of problems. If he quits, he will have to repay the town the cost of his lifeguard training and certification. He does not have another job lined up. He runs the risk of offending his friend Alex, who helped him get the job.

J.T. could have avoided the problems by researching the job requirements and duties on his own rather than relying solely on Alex's opinion. That would have helped him decide if lifeguarding was a job he would like or not.

Customized Instruction: At-Risk Students

Have students write the name of each of their classes on a separate strip of paper. They should order the strips from the class they enjoy most to the class they enjoy least. Ask if their preferences indicate their interests, talents, or "strong suits," and what careers someone with those interests might pursue.

Introduce the Section

Education is an investment in the future, and in this section, students learn to identify the many resources available through school that, if used, can put them on the path to career success.

Figure Focus

Remind students that their school is a community. It is a group of people who have a common goal and have a shared sense of purpose. Ask students what they think the common goal is for their school community.

Teaching Tips

You might help students better understand the multitude and diversity of resources available through school by providing them with some basic facts on the following.

- Number of students enrolled in your school district at the high school level (grades 9–12) and the middle school level (grades 5–8).
- Number of teachers employed by your school district.
- Number of nonteaching employees in your school district.
- Number of courses offered at each grade level.

Recognizing the Value of School

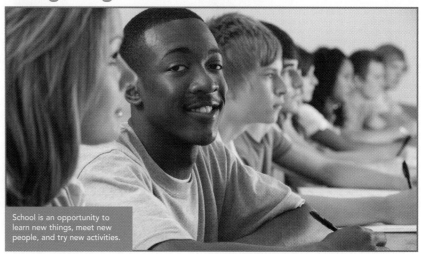

School is an opportunity to learn new things, meet new people, and try new activities.

Finishing school is an investment in your future. Most companies will not hire an employee who has not graduated from high school, and many will not hire an employee who has not graduated from college. If a company does hire dropouts, it usually pays them less than it pays graduates.

School also provides an opportunity to prepare for a career. Core subjects such as reading, writing, and math are vital for the career search process. Science, social studies, music, art, technology, family and consumer sciences, and sports all help you gain knowledge and build skills you will need to succeed at work, such as teamwork, leadership, and problem-solving. School clubs and organizations also help you build skills for future success.

- How will you find a job if you cannot read the job description?
- How will you prepare a cover letter if you cannot write a paragraph?
- How will you compare salaries if you cannot do basic math?

Classes for Careers

Most of the classes you take in school are required. But, as you move into higher grades, there will be more opportunity to take electives—classes you choose because you are interested in the subject—and advanced level courses.

Electives allow you to explore new subjects outside the standard core courses. Advanced courses can help you learn more about a subject and prepare for college.

- You might take a foods and nutrition elective and discover that you would be interested in a career as a dietitian.
- You might take a drafting elective and learn that you have a talent for architectural drawing.
- If you are interested in health care, you might take advanced biology and earn college credit.
- If you are interested in public policy, you might take government or politics.
- If you are interested in business, you might take accounting.

The number and type of electives vary from school to school. Your school counselor can help you select the courses that match your career goals.

Customized Instruction: Less Advanced/At-Risk Students

Have students create a written "learning plan" for an upcoming test. The components of the plan might be:

1. Topic of the test, with a list of subtopics or key points it will cover.
2. Dates and times set aside for studying. Students should list two to three minimum.
3. Organization of the material to study. This might be in list format, in pictures, or in a graphic organizer of some sort.
4. Method or methods for remembering what is studied. For example, some students retain information if they read it aloud to themselves, or if they write it out repeatedly.
5. Self-testing tool, such as answering review questions in the text, or having a friend or family member quiz them on the material.

Encourage students to use the plan and evaluate its effectiveness.

Developing Communications Skills

Almost every employer wants workers who can read, write, and speak effectively. For example, you might need to write an order for supplies, or explain the features of a product to a customer. Communications skills are the tools you need to share information with others.

In school, Language Arts classes help you develop communications skills. You learn to organize written information, understand the things you read, and speak out loud in front of an audience.

Clubs and organizations also help you build communications skills. You can join the debate team to learn how to argue politely and effectively. You can write for the school newspaper or Web site. You can perform with the drama club.

Building Math Skills

Basic math skills such as addition, subtraction, multiplication, and division are vital for success in careers ranging from nursing to inventory control. Most schools require students to pass a basic math test in order to graduate.

■ If you are a nurse's aide, you count a pulse for 10 seconds, and then multiply the number by 6 to find a patient's heart rate.
■ If you are installing drywall, you measure the square footage of a room to determine how much building material to buy.

You might benefit from a business math class if you are interested in a career in business. Business math covers topics such as accounting, tax management, reading and creating charts and graphs, and personal finance.

You will need advanced math skills for a career in technology, business, engineering, or science. Advanced math includes subjects such as advanced algebra, calculus, and trigonometry.

Study Strategies for Success in School

People who do well in school usually work very hard. They know how to use study **strategies**—careful plans and methods—that improve their ability to remember new things. You can make study strategies part of your academic plan.

■ *General strategies.* Sit near the front of the class so you pay attention; take notes; set a daily study goal, such as completing your homework.
■ *Strategies for memory.* Study your notes soon after class; make flash cards with a key idea on one side and a definition or explanation on the other side.
■ *Strategies for listening and note-taking.* Listen for clues that the speaker is giving a key point; underline or star the main points; use abbreviations for commonly used words.

Developing Useful Skills

Every job you have—for wages and as a volunteer—provides an opportunity to develop skills that will help you succeed in the present and in the future.

✔ *Showing respect to employers, customers, and co-workers*
✔ *Dressing appropriately for the workplace*
✔ *Arriving on time*
✔ *Making healthy decisions*
✔ *Solving problems*
✔ *Setting and achieving goals*
✔ *Working as part of a team*

TECH CONNECT

The Internet provides many resources for locating jobs online.

■ Job search engines such as Indeed, LinkUp, and Simply Hired search Web sites that list job openings for positions that meet your criteria.
■ Job search Web sites such as Monster.com and Careerbuilder.com list available positions, or let you upload your resume so potential employers can find you.
■ Social networking sites such as LinkedIn, Facebook, and Twitter let you connect with potential employers.
■ Company Web sites often have a page listing employment opportunities and contact information.

Do you think using the Internet is an effective way to locate and apply for jobs? What are some of the benefits? What are some of the drawbacks?

TECH CONNECT

The benefits are:

■ You can more easily and quickly find jobs in other cities, other states, and other countries.
■ You can find background and financial information on potential employers through corporate Web sites as well as government (www.sec.gov, for example), media, and other independent Web sites.
■ You can submit an application or resume on a timely basis.

Some drawbacks are:

■ The quality of job information available on the Internet is not always current, accurate, or complete.
■ The multitude of people who use the Internet to search for and apply for jobs means employers are burdened with sorting through the flood of applicants and resumes submitted online.
■ The security of personal information you supply in an application or resume may be jeopardized.

Reinforce and Review

Review the following communications terms with students.

■ **Verbal communication** is the exchange of messages by speaking or writing. We talk face to face or on the phone. We send text messages, e-mails, and instant messages. We write blogs, pass notes, and letters.
■ **Nonverbal communication** includes visual messages, such as a smile, tone of voice, and the language you use when speaking or writing.
■ **Active listening** is a sign of respect and shows you are paying attention to the speaker and making sure you hear and understand the message.

Ask students to comment on how their school experiences have helped them strengthen their communications skills.

Discuss

Discuss the importance of math skills not only to career pursuits but also to general, everyday activities. You use math skills constantly to track time, make purchases, take measurements, and even to determine if you've written enough words for your English essay!

Developing Useful Skills

Encourage students to think of "jobs" they have at home or in school, and the skills they have acquired or strengthened by doing them. For example, at home, you might have the job of doing your family's laundry. You are able to determine at what point in the week you need to do the laundry, thus strengthening your time management skills. You learn to calculate the amount of laundry to wash in each load and how much detergent is needed, thus strengthening your ability to manage resources.

Vocabulary

Strategies: Careful plans and methods.

What's a Personal Academic Plan?

A **personal academic plan** is a document that you use to set goals for the things you want to accomplish while you are in school. Explain that a personal academic plan might also include a list of all the courses you have taken, when you took them, and your final grade. Some plans ask you questions about your academic strengths and the areas in which you need support, your study habits, and the important relationships in your life.

Vocabulary

Postsecondary education: School after high school, including college, military training, and apprenticeships.

Job Search

Students are to write a job description for a job in the communications field. To get students started, you might refer students to the Arts, Audio-Visual Technology & Communications cluster and the Marketing cluster described in *Appendix A: Career Clusters* starting on page 513 in the student text.

MONEY MADNE$$

You will earn $2,200 at the day camp job for the eight weeks. You will earn $2,364 at the daycare center (30 hours per week at $9.85 per hour × 8 weeks). So, you should take the job at the daycare center.

What's a Personal Academic Plan?

A *personal academic plan* is a document that you use to set goals for the things you want to accomplish while you are in school. Some schools call it a personal career plan. It serves as a map that helps you achieve your educational goals. You create a personal academic plan with help from your school counselor. Some things that you might put in your plan include:

✔ *Goals beyond high school*
✔ *Assessment of your skills, knowledge, and experience*
✔ *Assessment of factors that will contribute to your success*
✔ *Assessment of factors that might interfere with your success*
✔ *Basic skills assessment*
✔ *Graduation requirements*
✔ *Plan for achieving graduation*
✔ *Plan for achieving goals beyond high school*

- *Strategies for planning and organization.* Keep a calendar, schedule, or to-do list; write assignments and due dates in an assignment notebook and on a calendar; prioritize your responsibilities and tasks; break a large project into smaller steps, and set a deadline for each step.
- *Strategies for tests.* Ask your teacher what the test will cover and what type of questions it will include; don't wait until the night before to study—study a little bit each evening in the days leading up to the test; read test directions carefully; check your answers; skip questions you are unsure of and go back to them after you have completed the others.

Setting Goals for Postsecondary Education

Is a high school diploma enough education to land you the career of your choice? If not, you will want to start thinking about **postsecondary education**, or school after high school. For most people, postsecondary education means college, but it can also include military training and apprenticeships.

You may enroll in a program to earn a professional certificate for a career such as master electrician or nurse's aide. Many careers require a minimum of an associate's degree—two years after high school—and many require a bachelor's degree—four years post high school. Professions such as doctor, lawyer, and teacher require additional education. Planning for postsecondary education involves:

- Selecting a school or program
- Making sure you have the necessary qualifications
- Applying for admission
- Obtaining financial aid

Goal-setting skills can help you manage the process from start to finish. It can help you stay focused on the educational objectives that you need to achieve your career goals.

Job Search

If you enjoy using reading, writing, and speaking skills to share information, you might want to look for a career in communications. Although all careers use communications skills, careers in the field of communications fall into industries such as advertising, public relations, technical writing, film-making, journalism, teaching, and speech therapy.

The educational requirements depend on the type of career and specific occupation; for example, advertising and public relations may require a bachelor's degree in a related area such as Journalism or Marketing. A speech therapist may require a master's degree in speech-language pathology, as well as certification by a state board. Use the Internet, library, or school's guidance resources to learn more about a career in communications. Write a job description, including the educational requirements, career pathway, and potential salary range.

MONEY MADNE$$

You have been offered two jobs for the summer. They are both in child care, which is a field that interests you, and they have similar responsibilities. You have decided to choose the one that offers the best wages.

The first position is as a counselor at a day camp. It pays $2,200.00 for working 8 weeks. The other is a position as an assistant at a day care center. It pays $9.85 per hour, and you are expected to work 30 hours a week for 8 weeks. Which position should you accept?

Customized Instruction: Less Advanced/Special Needs Students

Ask students about the benefits of taking advanced placement (AP) courses in high school. Three benefits are:

- If you can apply AP college credits you earn in high school to your college general education requirements, then you can skip these classes in college, saving yourself some tuition money.

- Getting ahead in meeting your general education requirements might mean you can graduate early.

- By taking AP courses, you demonstrate that you are motivated and committed to academic achievement.

Researching Colleges

You can find information about different postsecondary opportunities online, in your school guidance center, and at the library. As you research the programs, ask yourself the following:

■ Does it offer a degree in my field of interest?

■ Where is it located? Will I live at home or on campus? Is it in a city or a small town?

■ How many students are there? Will I be more comfortable in a small school or a large school?

■ How much does it cost? What is the annual **tuition**—cost of education? How much is **room and board**—the cost of a dorm room and meals? Are there additional fees?

■ Am I qualified for admission? Does my grade point average meet the school standards? Are my **ACT** or **SAT** scores high enough? Do I have the right extracurricular activities?

Most careers require education you can only get after you graduate from high school.

Which College Is Right for Me?

There are more than 3,500 colleges in the United States. They range from technical colleges that award certification for a specific job or career, to universities that grant bachelors' and graduate degrees. Use the following chart to compare postsecondary programs.

	Technical College/ Vocational School	Community College/ Junior College	Four-Year College	University
Focus of program	Specialized training for particular occupation	Two-year degree in career area or academic course credit that transfers to a four-year college	Four-year degree; general academic courses plus focus on major	Four-year degree plus graduate programs
Length of program	Nine months to two years	Two years	Four years or more	Four years or more

Things You Need to Apply to College

A college application form asks for information about yourself and your family. It has space for listing your extracurricular activities and for a personal essay that tells the college about you, your goals, and your abilities. In addition to the application form, you will also need:

■ An official **transcript**, which is a record of the courses you took in high school and the grades you earned

■ An official score report, which gives the results of the standard college entrance exam, such as the Scholastic Aptitude Test (SAT) or American College Test (ACT)

■ Recommendations, which are forms that you ask one teacher and one counselor to fill out, describing your qualities as a student and a person

■ Financial aid forms, which provide information about your ability to pay

Things to Do on a College Visit

You can take virtual college tours online, but the best way to get a sense of whether you would be happy at a college is to visit. You can:

✔ Tour the campus

✔ Talk to students

✔ Stay overnight in a dorm

✔ Sit in on a class

✔ Talk to a professor

✔ Attend an information session

Vocabulary

Room and board: Fee charged for a dorm room and meals at a school or university.

Transcript: Record of the courses taken in high school and the grades earned.

Tuition: Fee charged for instruction at a school or university.

Figure Focus

Remind students that most companies will not hire an employee who has not graduated from high school, and many will not hire an employee who has not graduated from college. Furthermore, employers that do not require a college degree tend to look for applicants with some form of on-the-job training and experience.

TEAMWORK ACTIVITY

Divide the class into teams and have each team identify a school in your area that offers a postsecondary education program like those listed in the table on this page. Each team should contact the school and ask them to send a brochure or packet that describes the focus of its program. Students might also be able to obtain this information from your school's guidance counselor.

Things to Do on a College Visit

In addition to those things listed in the text, students might want to check out a dining hall, the campus health center, on-campus gym or athletic facilities, the bookstore, and social areas outside of the dorms. In addition to talking to a professor, you might arrange brief meetings with an admissions counselor and the department chair of the major you're considering.

Introduce the Section

This section discusses the economic, demographic, and technological factors that contribute to job outlooks and industry trends.

Vocabulary

Job outlook: Forecast or prediction about trends affecting a job.

Unemployment rate: Percentage of unemployed people looking for jobs.

Figure Focus

Explain how employment opportunities are driven largely by population trends. Changes in population influence the demand for goods and services. Ask students to identify changes in population that would affect employment trends. Some answers are:

- **Age distribution.** Baby boomers, or those between the ages of 55 and 64, now make up the largest age group of the population.

- **Ethnic diversity.** Minorities and immigrants continue to make up a growing share of the U.S. population, with the number of Asians and people of Hispanic origin growing much faster than other racial and ethnic groups.

- **Gender.** There will continue to be between 3 and 5 percent more females than males in all regions of the country, except in the West, where the numbers are just about equal.

Identifying Employment Trends

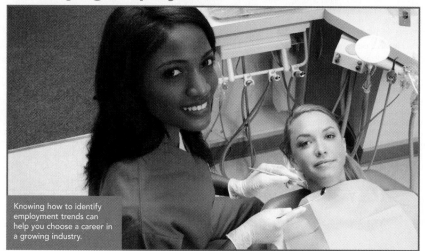

Knowing how to identify employment trends can help you choose a career in a growing industry.

Will there be jobs for construction workers when I get out of school? Will California be hiring music teachers? Is the salary for transportation managers increasing or decreasing? One way to learn the answers to these questions is to look at employment trends. A *trend* is a general move in a certain direction. An employment trend is one way the job market is changing over time. Sometimes trends in a specific field or industry are called the **job outlook**, which means it is a forecast or prediction about trends affecting that job.

Employment trends include things such as the number of jobs in a certain industry. For example, experts see a growing need for health care workers and educators, but a shrinking need for assembly line workers. Other employment trends include where the jobs are. For example, are businesses opening offices in the Midwest and closing them in the Northeast?

Employment trends are influenced by trends in other areas of life. Three major factors include:

- The economy
- Technology
- Lifestyle trends

Knowing how to identify employment trends can help you choose a career with a positive outlook.

Economic Trends

The economy impacts employment in many ways. The **unemployment rate** is the percentage of unemployed people looking for jobs. The economy affects the unemployment rate, and the unemployment rate affects the economy.

- When the economy is strong, there is demand for goods and services. Businesses hire workers, so the unemployment rate is low.
- When the economy is weak, there is less demand for goods and services. Businesses cannot afford to pay wages. The unemployment rate is high.
- When the unemployment rate is low, many people are working and earning income. They have money to spend, which increases the demand for goods and services and boosts the economy.
- When the unemployment rate is high, many people are out of work. They have little money to spend, which decreases the demand for goods and services.

Customized Instruction: Less Advanced/Special Needs Students

Have students look through current newspapers or magazines to find an article on an economic or employment trend. Have them write a two- to three-sentence summary of the article.

Impact of Technology

Technology has a strong influence on employment and job outlook. It creates new jobs, replaces old jobs, and changes the way some people perform their existing jobs.

- The development of new technology such as mobile phones and handheld devices creates new jobs in areas such as application development, sales, and research and development.
- The trend toward smaller computers has shifted the manufacturing of systems from desktops to notebooks and e-books.
- Improvements in robotics have made it possible to use robots in positions that people once held, such as on automobile assembly lines.
- Electronic recordkeeping in fields such as healthcare has changed the way medical professionals enter patient information, order prescriptions, and access patient records.
- The trend toward storing information and applications on the Internet instead of on local computers has eliminated the need for some information technology managers at large companies.
- The trend toward using video conferencing instead of traveling to meetings impacts travel agents, hotel workers, and people who work in restaurants where travelers might eat.

Changing Lifestyles

Lifestyle trends affect employment. For example, the trend toward dual-income families—both parents working outside the home—and the trend toward divorce both cause an increase in demand for child care workers. Many companies are adding on-site day care centers to provide child care in the same building where parents work. Other lifestyle trends that affect employment include:

- The number of children in a family
- Where a family lives
- How a family chooses to spend and save money

Improved health also impacts employment. When people have an increased **lifespan**—live longer—job are affected. People may retire at an older age, so there are fewer jobs for younger workers. There is more demand for senior housing, health care, and activities for senior citizens, and therefore more jobs in those areas. The government must pay more Social Security, which can reduce resources for other groups.

A trend to a more flexible lifestyle is impacting employment. In your grandparent's generation, many people worked at the same job their entire life. Now, people are willing to change careers to find a better workplace environment, higher salary, or more responsibility.

People also want careers that let them spend time with their families, or doing leisure activities that they enjoy. They may want to work from a home office, have flexible hours, or even *job-share*, which means share the responsibilities for one job with another person.

Shifting Populations

Trends in population impact employment trends. Where people live, the number of people in a community, and lifespan, affect the number of jobs, the type of jobs and the level of pay. For example, new businesses often open where there are a lot of people. In the rural areas:

- ★ *There are fewer people available to work in agricultural careers. Farmers might have to pay high wages to hire farm hands.*
- ★ *Businesses in rural towns might not have enough customers.*
- ★ *The towns will not collect enough taxes to support community programs and services.*
- ★ *In the cities, there will be more competition for existing jobs. Employers might be able to pay lower salaries.*
- ★ *New businesses will open in the cities to provide goods and services for the many residents.*
- ★ *City services such as trash collection and schools may be overwhelmed by demand.*

Why do you think employers might have to pay higher wages when there are fewer job applicants and lower wages when there are more applicants?

Can you think of current lifestyle trends that might affect careers?

Shifting Populations

Fewer job applicants means the pool of candidates from which an employer can select is smaller, which in turn tends to indicate that fewer applicants will have the desired qualifications. So, the employer might have to increase wages to make the job offer more appealing to the ideal candidate. More applicants, on the other hand, mean the opposite for the employer. The more applicants, the likelier it is that more of them will have the desired qualifications. The employer can offer lower wages because there is more competition among applicants for the job and odds are favorable that one of them will accept the job for lower wages.

Figure Focus

Some other lifestyle trends that affect careers include telecommuting, where the employee works from home and is electronically linked to the office. Stay-at-home dads are also a lifestyle trend that affects both parents' careers.

Vocabulary

Lifespan: Expected length of life.

Teaching Tips

You might share some of the following employment projections from the U.S. Bureau of Labor Statistics.

- Service-providing industries are expected to account for approximately 15.7 million new wage and salary jobs generated over the 2006–2016 period, while goods-producing industries will see overall job loss.
- Of the service-providing industries, the education and health services industry will see the most growth. More than 3 out of every 10 new jobs created during the 10-year period will be either in the healthcare and social assistance or in the public and private educational services sectors.
- Employment in general in the goods-producing industries will decline. This includes construction, manufacturing, natural resources and mining, and agriculture, forestry, and fishing.
- Some industries within the goods-producing sector will increase employment. These include pharmaceutical and medicine manufacturing and support activities for agriculture and forestry, which include farm labor contractors and farm management services.
- With the continued growth of service industries, demand will increase for workers in professional and related occupations. Over the 2006–2016 period, a 16.7 percent increase in the number of professional and related jobs is projected, which translates into nearly 5 million new jobs. The majority of these jobs will be in computer and mathematical occupations; healthcare practitioners and technical occupations; and education, training, and library occupations.
- Workers in service occupations also will be in demand. Duties of service workers range from fighting fires to cooking meals. Employment in service occupations is projected to increase by 4.8 million jobs. Food preparation and serving-related occupations as well as healthcare support occupations and personal care and service occupations are expected to account for 2.1 million new jobs.

End-of-Chapter Activities

Case Study

Casey can identify his skills, interests, and abilities. He can research the career clusters to identify industries that match his skills, interests, and abilities, and then look at the companies at the job fair to see which are in the industries that interest him.

To prepare for the job fair, he can talk to his career counselor to get help and suggestions. He can research the companies so he can talk about them to the company representatives. He can make sure he has clean, neat clothes to wear. He can prepare a resume.

Casey's parents are being helpful to a point. They could take the time to help Casey identify his skills, interests, and abilities, instead of just making random suggestions.

Sounding Off!

Student answers will vary.

FAQ

1. A career is a chosen field of work in which you try to advance over time by gaining responsibility and earning more money.

2. A job is any activity you do in exchange for money or other payment.

3. People choose a particular career because it:
   - Supplies money.
   - Gives them satisfaction.
   - Uses their skills and talents.
   - Gives them a role in the community.

4. Resources for identifying types of careers are guidance and career counselors, school clubs and organizations, informational interviews, and the U.S. Bureau of Labor and Statistics.

5. A nontraditional occupation is any job that is usually done by someone of the other gender.

6. A skill is an ability or talent; something you do well.

7. An interest is a subject or activity that attracts your attention and that you enjoy doing or learning about.

8. You can measure the economic, emotional, and educational value of work.

Case Study

Casey is preparing to attend a job fair to find part-time work. He is not sure what type of job he wants. His mother suggested he consider a position as a bank teller. His father thinks he might want to be a landscape assistant.

Casey has a list of the companies that will be at the fair. There are more than 50! He is not sure if he will be able to visit every booth, and he is worried he might miss the one that has the best opportunity for him.

- What can Casey do to narrow the list of companies he should visit at the job fair?
- What else can Casey do to prepare for the job fair?
- Do you think Casey's parents are being helpful with their suggestions?

Sounding Off!

1. When do you think teens should start thinking about career options?
2. What do you think is the most important thing to consider when looking for a career?

1. What is a career?
2. What is a job?
3. List three reasons people choose a particular career.
4. List four resources for identifying types of careers.
5. What is a nontraditional occupation?

6. What is a skill?
7. What is an interest?
8. List three areas in which you can measure the value of work.
9. List three ways school contributes to your career preparation.
10. List three factors that influence employment

9. School contributes to your career preparation in the following ways:
   - You can take electives or advanced courses to explore new subjects outside the standard core courses.
   - You can develop communications skills in language arts class, or as a member of a club or organization such as the debate team, drama club, or school newspaper.
   - You can build math skills.
   - You can be on a team or part of a club to develop leadership, teamwork, and problem-solving skills.

10. Factors that influence employment trends are the economy, technology, lifestyle trends, and population shifts.

Individually, select one of the 16 career clusters that interest you. You can go to www.careerclusters.org to learn more about the career clusters. Then, divide into teams of four or five classmates interested in the same cluster. Using available resources, research the industries in the selected cluster. Select one pathway and make a presentation about the occupations and opportunities in the pathway. Include information about the qualities, interests, and skills a person considering that pathway might need. Also include information about classes someone thinking about that pathway might want to take in school, and about other educational requirements. Show your presentation to the class.

Hot Topics

Are you taking advantage of the opportunities available in school to prepare for a future career? Have you met with a guidance counselor? Do you have a personal academic or career plan? Do you think you are taking courses that will help you identify your interests and abilities? Have you joined clubs that provide the opportunity to explore career options?

Take this opportunity to write anonymously about whether you feel that school is providing you with the opportunities you need to prepare for a career. If not, include thoughts and suggestions about how your school could make more opportunities available. Use a word processor so no one recognizes your handwriting. Be honest and open. Put the paper in the class Hot Topics box.

As a class, read the anonymous entries and discuss them.

Web Extra ▼

There are many job Web sites that include sections specifically for teens, such as groovejob.com and myfirstpaycheck.com.

Use the Internet to identify the sites that you think might be the most useful for your peers. Make a directory of the sites, including the Web site address and a brief description. Post the directory on your school Web site or in your school career center or library.

Problem Solver

Sometimes it is difficult to identify your own interests, skills, and abilities. Working in pairs, spend 15 minutes talking to your partner about the things you like to do. Discuss the things you think you are good at, your favorite subjects in school, and the clubs or organizations you have joined. Take notes so you will remember what your partner tells you.

When you have finished talking, look over your notes and select a career that you think suits your partner's interests, skills, and abilities. Write a letter of recommendation to a potential employer on behalf of your partner, explaining why you think this would be the right career match.

Team Players

Student teams are to gather information on a selected career cluster. Refer students to *Appendix A: Career Clusters*, beginning on page 513. Students can obtain additional information for their presentations at www.careerclusters.org. Student presentations should include information on skills and suggested plan of study for the pathway.

Hot Topics

Make sure students understand that they can turn in their papers anonymously. Encourage them to be open and honest about their school's efforts and programs to prepare them for a career.

Web Extra

Students are to research Web sites that provide useful information on jobs and careers for teens. They are to prepare a directory of the sites that includes a description of each and post it in the school career center or library.

Remind students that a reliable Web site usually publishes the name of the author or organization that sponsors it and the date the content was created or last updated in a fairly obvious location, such as at the top or bottom of the page or on the home page. The site is usually organized with headings and an obvious navigation system. A reliable site clearly states its purpose and any affiliations. You should also look for accuracy in spelling and grammar.

Problem Solver

Students are to interview a partner on his or her interests, skills, and abilities. Based on the notes they take during the interview, they should select a career they think suits their partner. Then, they should write a letter to an employer, recommending their partner and why they think he or she would be a suitable employee. Review with students the parts of a letter: dateline, letter address, salutation, body, complimentary close, and writer's name and title.

Write Now

Students are to write a want ad for a nontraditional occupation. You might refer students to the following Web sites:

- www.workplacesolutions.org/about/jobs.cfm
- www.bls.gov

Be Involved!

Students are to prepare a career portfolio. In addition to the information and documents discussed in the text, students might also include letters of recommendation from teachers, coaches, and community leaders as well as any employers. Other examples of achievement might include certificates, newspaper articles about the achievement (including those for sports and other group activities), and awards.

Social Networking

Students are to organize a career information day for their class. You might encourage students to develop a form letter that they can send out to people in different occupations. Assist them with scheduling the date and time. On the day of the event, make sure to remind them of the importance of making a good impression and how their behavior and attitude not only reflect upon the individual, but also the entire class and school.

*W*rite Now

Can you picture yourself in a nontraditional occupation? Many employers actively recruit males for traditionally female careers, and females for traditionally male careers. Spend some time researching different types of nontraditional occupations, so you can understand the benefits or drawbacks they might provide.

Write a want ad for a nontraditional occupation that you think might appeal to the underrepresented gender—men for a traditionally female career or women for a traditionally male career. Share your ad with the class.

Be Involved!

www.fcclainc.org

A career portfolio can help you stay focused and organized as you explore career options and develop a career plan. A portfolio is a collection of information and documents. A career portfolio includes information and documents that show the progress you make in school and in your career plan. It helps you stay on track to achieve your educational and career goals. You can also bring it to job interviews and job fairs, so you have the information you need to fill out applications, and the documents you want to show to potential employers.

As a class, discuss the types of information and documents you might include in a career portfolio. For example, you might include a list of skills, interests and abilities, a personal academic plan, a resume, and a sample cover letter. You might also include examples of achievement, such as a brochure you designed, artwork, or writing samples, as well as report cards or other assessments.

On your own, set up a career portfolio. It might be a paper folder or an electronic folder. For the first document, make a list of the documents and information you plan to include in the portfolio. As you collect the items, you can cross them off the list.

Social Networking

One way to learn about different types of careers is to talk to people who have jobs. They can tell you what it is really like at work, what training or education they needed, and why they enjoy what they do.

Organize a career information day by inviting people from different occupations in your community to come to school to speak to your class. If they cannot come in person, they may be able to write a description and send it in for you to present. With the visitors' permission, create a video of the speeches and make it available on your class Web site.

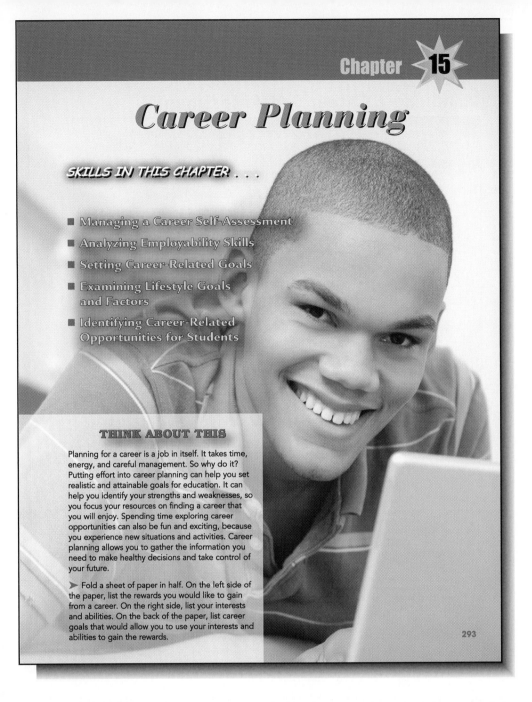

Chapter 15

Career Planning

SKILLS IN THIS CHAPTER . . .

- Managing a Career Self-Assessment
- Analyzing Employability Skills
- Setting Career-Related Goals
- Examining Lifestyle Goals and Factors
- Identifying Career-Related Opportunities for Students

THINK ABOUT THIS

Planning for a career is a job in itself. It takes time, energy, and careful management. So why do it? Putting effort into career planning can help you set realistic and attainable goals for education. It can help you identify your strengths and weaknesses, so you focus your resources on finding a career that you will enjoy. Spending time exploring career opportunities can also be fun and exciting, because you experience new situations and activities. Career planning allows you to gather the information you need to make healthy decisions and take control of your future.

➤ Fold a sheet of paper in half. On the left side of the paper, list the rewards you would like to gain from a career. On the right side, list your interests and abilities. On the back of the paper, list career goals that would allow you to use your interests and abilities to gain the rewards.

293

Chapter 15 Overview

This chapter provides students with an overview of career planning. It examines tools for assessing skills and interests, and stresses the importance of setting realistic career and lifestyle goals.

Managing a Career Self-Assessment The step-by-step process for assessing career interests, skills, and abilities is detailed in this section.

Analyzing Employability Skills Identifying the skills, attitude, and qualities you need to get and keep a job are an effective measure of an individual's employability.

Setting Career-Related Goals In this section, students learn more about setting realistic goals to help them focus on the things that will lead to career success.

Examining Lifestyle Goals and Factors The lifestyle you envision for yourself at different life stages and the career you choose are interconnected in many ways. This section explores the factors an individual should consider when setting career and lifestyle goals.

Identifying Career-Related Opportunities for Students This section discusses volunteer positions, apprenticeships, internships, and other opportunities from which students can gain career-related experience.

Focus and Engage

Bell-Ringer: Think About This

Have students write about rewards, interests and abilities, and career goals as directed in the text. If they need prompting, you might suggest rewards such as financial stability, a feeling of accomplishment, learning new skills, and meeting new people. For their interests and abilities, have students review the "Identifying Your Strengths" section on pages 280–281 in Chapter 14 as well as the *Problem Solver* activity on page 291. For career goals, encourage students to list the career(s) they're interested in, their idea of the perfect job in that career, and the desired annual salary when they start the job and 5 to 10 years into the job.

ADVANCE PREPARATION

Review	*Life Skills for the 21st Century* textbook, Chapter 15.
Prepare	Paper and pencil for some activities. Colored pencils or markers. Current newspapers. Box labeled "Hot Topics."

CUSTOMIZED INSTRUCTION OVERVIEW

Less Advanced Students	More Advanced Students	ESOL Students	Special Needs Students	At-Risk Students
Pages 295, 297, 301, 302	Pages 298, 303	Pages 297, 303	Pages 295, 301, 302	Pages 295, 297, 302

Introduce the Section

The step-by-step process for assessing career interests, skills, and abilities is detailed in this section.

Vocabulary

Self-assessment: A process by which you learn more about your career-related skills, interests, values, and abilities.

Figure Focus

Explain that a self-assessment is a tool designed to help you recognize your strengths and talents as well as your weaknesses. It is a tool that can provide you with a balanced and objective view of the jobs you might be suitable for and those that might not be as appropriate.

Reinforce and Review

Review the discussion of values in Chapter 1:

- Values are the things that are important to you.
- Your personal values are thoughts, ideas, and actions that are important to you. You use them to gauge or evaluate the people and things in your life.
- Something has instrumental value if it is important for acquiring something else. For example, a good salary has instrumental value because you can use it to buy the things that help you meet your lifestyle goals.
- Something has intrinsic value if it is important in and of itself. For example, job security and prestige have intrinsic value.
- You show your values by the way you act and the choices you make in life.

Managing a Career Self-Assessment

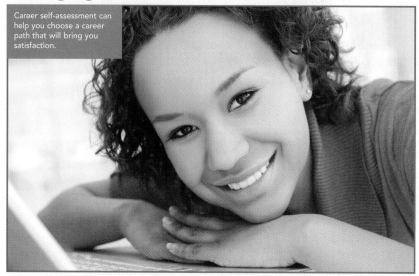

Career self-assessment can help you choose a career path that will bring you satisfaction.

A career **self-assessment** is a process by which you learn more about your career-related skills, interests, values, and abilities. To perform a career self-assessment, you examine your strengths and weaknesses honestly and objectively.

It might be difficult to think critically about your strengths, interests, and abilities.

- You might have trouble identifying your interests. You enjoy riding your bike. Is that an interest that relates to job skills?
- You might feel self-conscious talking about your strengths. You are embarrassed when people praise your love of animals or your patience with toddlers.
- You might not want to admit that you enjoy a subject such as math, because you worry that your peers will tease you.

Taking a close look at yourself can be hard, but rewarding. Knowing your abilities helps you choose a job that you will be good at. Knowing your interests helps you choose a career that you will enjoy.

What Are Work Values?

Work values are the things important to you that relate to work. Identifying your work values can help you choose a career that you will enjoy. Some common work values include:

- *Creativity:* Being able to express yourself or use your imagination
- *Physical activity:* Being able to move around and be active at work
- *Independence:* Being your own boss, an entrepreneur
- *Good salary:* Being paid well for your work
- *Job security:* Having a steady, long-term job
- *Work environment:* Working in a space where you are comfortable, such as outside, or in an office
- *Leadership opportunities:* Directing or managing the work of others
- *Prestige:* Having a job that commands the respect and admiration of others
- *Challenge:* Having the opportunity to perform difficult or important tasks
- *Work safety:* Being able to work in a predictable job, or in a job where there is risk

The Self-Assessment Process

There are many ways to assess your career interests, skills and abilities. One way is to use a six-step process to help you complete an objective career self-assessment. The result will be a worksheet that you can use to set academic and career goals.

1. *List your two favorite school subjects.* Usually—but not always—these are the subjects you do well in. They might be core subjects, such as science or social studies, or they may be electives, such as woodworking or art.

2. *List at least four specific skills you have acquired in your favorite subjects.* For example, if you chose Spanish, your skills might include reading or speaking Spanish or understanding Spanish culture, or even cooking Spanish food. If you chose science, your skills might include understanding chemical properties, using a microscope, or valuing peer review.

3. *List at least four achievements in your favorite subjects.* Your achievements are the things you have earned based on your performance. They might include good grades, awards, or acknowledgements. For example, for Language Arts, you might list a poem that was published in the school literary magazine. For Music, you might list a solo in the Fall concert.

4. *List at least four abilities—the things you do well, or your talents.* You can list specific abilities, such as playing guitar or repairing machines. You can also list qualities that help you succeed in many areas, such as being a good listener or having good time management skills. (Refer to the list at the side of the page for categories of abilities.)

5. *List at least two interests.* Again, you can list specific interests, such as working with animals or photography, or you can list interest areas. Six common interest areas include the arts, business, crafts, office work, science, and social services.

6. *List at least four work values.*

Using Your Career Self-Assessment Worksheet

 Once you have completed your career self-assessment, you can look through the information to find connections that might point to a possible career path. Then, complete the worksheet by listing your top two preferred career clusters—the clusters that best match your skills, interests, and abilities. (It might help to have a list of the career clusters in front of you. You'll find one in Appendix A.)

Every career self-assessment worksheet will be unique, because you are unique. You might share interests with a friend, but you might have different abilities or work values. What career path might you consider if your self-assessment profile includes the following?

■ Subject: Technology
■ Skill: Computer programming
■ Achievement: Award for Web page design
■ Ability: Artistic
■ Interest: Business
■ Work value: Independence

You might look at the Information Technology career cluster and the Web and Digital Communications pathway, or you might consider the Business Management and Administration career cluster and the Business Information Management pathway. Can you think of other career opportunities that might appeal to someone with the profile above?

How Abilities Relate to Careers

In this list, the ability in bold is useful for the careers that follow it:

Artistic *Graphic designer, photographer, fashion designer, interior decorator*

Clerical *Medical records technician, administrative assistant, public safety dispatcher, bookkeeper*

Interpersonal *(the ability to relate to other people)* *Customer service representative, flight attendant, home health aide, retail salesperson*

Language *Editor, translator, social worker, speech therapist*

Leadership *Educational administrator, lawyer, chef, firefighter*

Manual *Carpenter, animal caretaker, auto mechanic, conservation worker*

Mathematical/Numerical *Software engineer, financial analyst, pharmacist, network administrator*

Musical/Dramatic *Musician, actor, producer, director, music or drama educator*

Organizational *Air traffic controller, nurse, travel agent, computer systems analyst*

Persuasive *Lawyer, psychiatrist, retail salesperson, advertising executive*

Scientific *Agricultural inspector, dental assistant, dietitian, chemical engineer, physical therapist*

Social *School counselor, recreational worker, social worker, home health aide*

Visual *Carpenter, landscaper, mechanical engineer, architect, dentist*

Technical/Mechanical *Airline pilot, electrician, master mechanic, auto mechanic*

Customized Instruction: Less Advanced/Special Needs/At-Risk Students

Help students identify their skills, achievements, and abilities if they are struggling with these. Their skills can be as simple as knowing the multiplication tables or being able to identify the seven continents. Their achievements can be passing a big test or getting their homework done on time. Their abilities can range from taking care of a younger sibling to running errands for an elderly relative. If you think it's appropriate, ask the teachers of their favorite subjects to assist in identifying skills and achievements.

Introduce the Section

Identifying the skills, attitude, and qualities you need to get and keep a job are an effective measure of an individual's employability.

Figure Focus

Ask students to think of a store, restaurant, bank, or other business they have visited within the last week and to recall one employee they interacted with. What qualities do they remember about that employee? What was his attitude toward customers? Did he exhibit any particular skills? Ask students if they think other employers would want to hire the worker.

Vocabulary

Employability: Having and using skills and abilities to be hired and stay hired.

Discuss

Ask students to comment on basic work responsibilities, or those that you would have at any job regardless of the type of work. These would include:

- Punctuality, or being on time.
- Adhering to company policy on working hours, sick leave, dress code, safety, confidentiality, and more.
- Respecting the employer's property and that of other employees.
- Performing to the best of your ability.

Reinforce and Review

Review with students the keys to effective communication:

- Be clear, speak slowly, and make eye contact.
- Be personal. Use the other person's name if you know it.
- Be positive. Phrase your message in positive terms. Say what you want, not what you don't want.
- Get to the point. Explain why or how you feel a certain way.
- Actively listen to the other person. Pay attention and make sure you understand him or her.
- Think before you respond. Ask questions for clarification, if necessary.

Analyzing Employability Skills

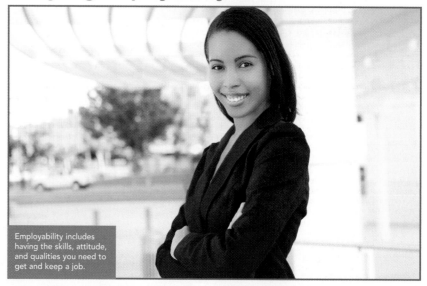

Employability includes having the skills, attitude, and qualities you need to get and keep a job.

You might graduate from college with a bachelor's degree in design, but if clients think you are unfriendly, or if they question your confidence, they are unlikely to hire you. Attitude and confidence are part of employability. **Employability** means having and using your life skills and abilities to be hired and stay hired. It is more than just meeting the qualifications for a position. It also means knowing how to:

- Present your positive qualities to an employer
- Communicate effectively with employers, co-workers, and customers
- Meet your responsibilities at work

Having employability skills will give you an advantage when you are ready to apply and interview for a position, no matter what career you choose.

What Are Employability Skills?

Employability skills include the knowledge for a specific career—such as wiring for an electrician, or engine repair for an auto mechanic. They also include the life skills you use in your roles at home, in school, with peers, and in your community.

- *Decision making* shows you know how to evaluate options. A truck driver may need to choose between different routes.
- *Problem solving* shows you know how to take a leadership role to find positive solutions. A hairstylist may need to find a way to satisfy a client.
- *Goal setting* shows you know how to set up a plan to achieve specific goals. An administrative assistant may need to make a filing system more efficient.
- *Critical thinking* shows you know how to be objective. A nurse may need to assess which patient should see the doctor first.
- *Communicating effectively* shows you know how to work with others. An architect may need to effectively explain the client's opinions to a design team.

Employability Characteristics

There are certain personal qualities that help make you employable. Positive qualities such as honesty, tolerance, patience, and responsibility show a potential employer that you are someone who will not only get the work done, but be good to have around the workplace. You can develop other positive qualities to improve your employability:

- A positive attitude shows that you enjoy your work. You do not complain or criticize others.
- Being cooperative shows that you respect your employer, co-workers, and customers. You meet your responsibilities, value other team members, and help others when it is necessary.
- Accepting and using **criticism**—advice about how to make positive changes in your actions or behavior—show that you want to improve and are willing to learn.
- Flexibility shows that you can accept change and adapt to new situations.
- Leadership shows that you are capable of making decisions and solving problems. It shows that others respect you and want to work with you.

Employers want to see that you are generally happy and easy to work with. Developing positive personal qualities and showing these qualities to an employer improves your chances of finding and keeping a job.

How Can I Build Employability Skills?

Recall from Chapter 3 that you develop character qualities over time as you come to understand what is important to you. You can also work to develop character qualities by taking active steps. For example, you can make an effort to be more cooperative in school, or more flexible with your family. You can also emulate—copy—someone who shows qualities that you admire.

You can build employability skills that will appeal to an employer by practicing them in all areas of your life.

- At home, you can practice conflict-resolution. Look for ways to fight less with your siblings and to communicate more effectively with your parents.
- At school, you can set academic goals and work with a teacher or counselor to create a plan for achieving them.
- With your peers, you can practice leadership by standing up against bullies or becoming active in a club or organization such as FCCLA.
- In your community, you can practice problem solving by looking for ways to support public resources. You might look for ways to reduce trash or to improve safety.

Myth Once I choose a career, I am stuck with it.

Truth Most people change careers at least three times in their lives, and many change more than that. Skills that you develop in one job can be used in a different line of work. Attending school or training programs at night or on the job may lead you in a different direction. Your goals are likely to change over time. You can change careers, too.

What to Look for in a Job Description

When you research career opportunities, consider the following:

✔ *What are the responsibilities?*

✔ *What kind of education or training is required?*

✔ *What is the pay range?*

✔ *What is the work environment?*

✔ *Where is the job?*

How Long Is Your Work Week?

A work week is the number of hours you work per week. How do you think the length of a work week affects your lifestyle? How might it affect the employer's business or the economy?

In the United States, the number of hours an employee works is set by the employer and agreed to by the employee. Typically, a full-time employee works 8 hours a day, 5 days a week, which equals a 40-hour work week.

In France, most employees work a 35-hour work week. In South Korea, they work 44 hours per week.

Make a chart comparing the typical work week hours in three or four countries around the world. Use the Internet or the library to find the information. You might also include information about other lifestyle factors, such as vacation time.

 How Long Is Your Work Week?

Students are to create a chart that compares the typical work week hours in three or four different countries. You might direct students to the map at the following Web site: www.billshrink.com/blog/working-around-the-world/.

Vocabulary

Criticism: Advice about how to make positive changes in your actions or behavior.

Reinforce and Review

Ask students to name positive character qualities that enhance their employability. These include:

- **Enthusiasm:** Having a passionate interest in or eagerness to do something.
- **Thoughtfulness:** Treating people in a kind and considerate way.
- **Compassion:** Sympathy for the suffering of others with a desire to help them.
- **Trustworthiness:** Reliability.
- **Tolerance:** Acceptance of others with differing views.
- **Kindness:** Showing sympathy or compassion.
- **Fairness:** Being just or impartial.
- **Respectfulness:** Showing consideration and thoughtfulness.
- **Citizenship:** Being a dutiful and responsible member of a community.
- **Friendliness:** Affectionate and helpful toward others.

Myth/Truth

Explain that for older generations (people who are now at retirement age), it was common for employees to work at the same job their entire life. But with the trend to a more flexible lifestyle, people are now willing to change careers to find a better workplace environment, higher salary, more responsibility, and bigger challenges. Making such a change often involves additional schooling and training. For some career changes, you might have to take college credit courses or undergo vocational training. Sometimes, the employer hiring you will provide on-the-job or other specialized training.

What to Look for in a Job Description

In addition to those things listed in the text, explain to students that they might also want to explore job benefits other than salary. For example, what kind of health care and employee savings plans does the employer offer? What about sick leave, holidays, and vacation pay? Does the employer reimburse for continuing education?

Introduce the Section

In this section, students learn more about setting realistic goals to help them focus on the things that will lead to career success.

Figure Focus

Stress the importance of setting realistic goals that are specific and have a timeframe in which you will meet them.

Teaching Tips

Have students refer to the career self-assessments they did earlier in this chapter. Using the career path(s) they identified, instruct students to write two to three realistic goals related to the career. For example, if their career cluster is Arts, Audio-Visual Technology & Communications, they might set a goal of getting a job as a reporter for a newspaper or as an editorial assistant for a magazine publisher within one year of graduating from college in a location within driving distance to family.

Stay in School

History proves that students who drop out of high school will most likely move from job to job without the benefits of health insurance, paid vacations, retirement benefits, and the like. Some level of postsecondary education is becoming a necessity for 90 percent of new high-growth, high-wage jobs, according to the U.S. Department of Labor. But without a high school diploma, you cannot access a postsecondary education.

Many students believe that if they drop out, they can simply take the GED (General Education Development Test) to get their diploma at their convenience. The GED is not a diploma, but simply a certificate that shows the holder has the skill levels of an average high school graduate. The test was developed for those who do not obtain a high school diploma.

Most colleges accept a GED, although they require GED holders to take the SAT or ACT, and many require additional letters of recommendation. Some four-year colleges will not accept a GED certificate until the applicant has earned a specified number of college credits from a community college or other postsecondary institution. Although employers accept applicants with a GED, the certificate is commonly considered a lower form of a high school diploma.

Emphasize that a far better course would be to stay in school in the first place.

Setting Career-Related Goals

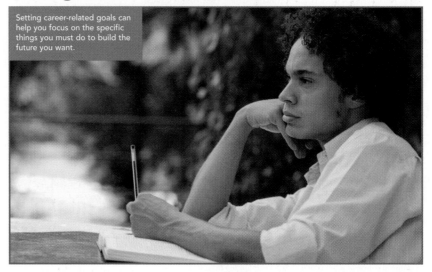

Setting career-related goals can help you focus on the specific things you must do to build the future you want.

The five-step goal-setting process can help you set realistic and attainable career-related goals (look back at Chapter 2 for the goal-setting process). There are two types of career-related goals.

- Some goals help you succeed in your career by directing your actions and guiding your decision-making once you are already working. There's more about this type of career-related goal in Chapter 18.
- Some goals help you achieve the career of your choice. These goals, which are covered in this section, direct your actions and guide your decision-making while you are preparing and planning for a career.

Both long-term and short-term goals can help you develop a career plan. They can help you identify obstacles and solve problems so that you can attain the career you want.

What Are Realistic Career-Related Goals?

A career goal needs to be realistic. You might dream of being a famous actor or a superstar athlete. When you perform your self-assessment, however, do you realistically believe you have the skills and abilities to achieve those goals?

A realistic career goal is one that:

- You can plan for and achieve.
- You have the resources to accomplish.
- Uses your skills and abilities.

Career goals should also be specific. They should describe exactly what you want to accomplish and when. They might even include where.

- *Working in Alaska* is not a specific career goal. It does not identify the type of career you want. It does not give a time frame.
- *Working as a tour guide in Denali National Park within five years* is a specific career goal. It identifies a job, a location, and a time frame.

Customized Instruction: More Advanced Students

Have students research a person they think is successful in their career. This could be a famous person, such as a professional athlete, an author, an actor, a businessperson, or a politician, or even someone in their family or community who they know personally. They should gather information on how these persons got started in their chosen career and the path they followed to get where they are now. Have them present the information in an interesting format, such as a slide show, poster, or report with pictures.

Academic Goals Are Also Career-Related Goals

If you do not complete high school, your chances of finding a meaningful, satisfying, well-paying career are very small. Most careers require a post secondary degree from a college or technical school, and you cannot attend college or technical school if you do not complete high school. (See Chapter 14 for more about educational opportunities after high school.)

Setting academic goals will help you focus on the things you need to do to successfully complete your education. You can work with your teachers or school counselors to create a personal academic plan in which you identify and set long-term and short-term academic goals.

- You might set a long-term goal of graduating from high school.
- You might set short-term goals of not being absent, passing your core subjects, and choosing electives that interest you.

Beyond high school, you can take advantage of educational opportunities to gain the skills you need to succeed in your chosen career. You can set goals for:

- Attending college
- Attending a career or vocational training center
- Enlisting in the military
- Working as an apprentice or intern

Mapping out a Career Plan

 Recall that part of the goal-setting process is to make a plan for achieving the goal. When you are setting career-related goals, that means creating a career plan. A **career plan** is a map that shows you the way to reach your goal. You can develop a career plan on your own, or with help from your parents, teachers, or school counselor.

Start your career plan by writing a statement that describes your long-term ultimate career goal. For example, write: *I will be an occupational physical therapist in California by the time I am 30 years old.*

Add short-term career goals that define how you will gain the skills, knowledge, and experience that you need to achieve your ultimate career goal. Include a timeline for achieving each one. For example, add:

- Get an A in health class this semester
- Volunteer at a physical rehabilitation center this summer
- Research colleges and universities in California that offer physical therapy degrees by the end of the school year

When you write your career plan, make it realistic and attainable. You want to feel confident that you can put the plan into action and achieve your goals.

Keep in mind that your career plan will probably change over time. Your goals might change, or your available resources might change.

But I Haven't Chosen a Career!

How can you use career-related goals to help identify a career that matches your interests and abilities? What if you are unsure about the career path you will follow?

★ Set goals for academic achievement
★ Set goals for volunteering
★ Set goals for researching different types of career
★ Set goals for building skills and abilities
★ Set goals for earning and saving money

Can you think of career-related goals you can set right now? Make a list and discuss it with the class.

NUMBERS GAME

Paid vacation time is a job benefit that affects your lifestyle. The amount usually depends on the job and the length of time you have been an employee.

Many employees **accrue** vacation, which means it builds up over time. For example, you might accrue 1/12 of your annual vacation time each month. That means you accrue 1/12 of the time in the first month, 1/12 of the time in the second month, and so on. By the end of the year—if you have not taken any vacation—you will accrue 100% of your annual vacation time.

To find out how much time you accrue each month, divide your annual vacation time by 12. For example, if your annual vacation time is 80 hours, you will accrue 6.67 hours per month ($80 \div 12 = 6.67$).

Do the math: How many hours will you accrue each month if your annual vacation time is 90 hours?

How many months will you have to work to accrue enough for a 10-day vacation?

NUMBERS GAME

To determine how many hours you will accrue each month if your annual vacation time is 90 hours, divide 90 by 12, which equals 7.5. You will accrue 7.5 hours per month. To determine how many months you will have to work to accrue enough for a 10-day vacation, you must first calculate how many work hours there are in a 10-day vacation. If there are 8 hours in a workday, you would multiply 8×10, which equals 80 hours in a 10-day vacation. Next, divide 80 by 7.5, which equals 10.6. So, you would have to work about 11 months to earn 80 hours of vacation.

Vocabulary

Career plan: Map that shows you the way to reach your goal.

APPLY IT

Have students create a career plan as explained in the text. If your state has a career plan document that students need to complete, point them to that document. They should start out by writing a statement that describes their long-term ultimate goal. This should be followed with short-term goals that define how they will gain the skills, knowledge, and experience they will need to achieve the ultimate career goal. For example, if their ultimate career goal is to be a magazine editor in New York City, then short-term goals might be:

- Get A's in English and creative writing classes in high school.
- Research colleges that offer journalism programs, with specialized sequences in magazine journalism.
- Obtain internship(s) during college or after graduation with a New York City-based magazine publisher.

But I Haven't Chosen a Career!

Students are to suggest career-related goals they can set now, even if they have not chosen a career. Some of these are:

- Research postsecondary education options and determine application dates and requirements for those institutions that interest you the most.
- Become familiar with the location in which you'd like to live and work, if it's different from where you currently live.
- Identify employment trends to determine which industries will see increased job growth and which occupations will see an increased demand for workers.

Introduce the Section

The lifestyle you envision for yourself at different life stages and the career you choose are interconnected in many ways. This section explores the factors an individual should consider when setting realistic career and lifestyle goals.

Figure Focus

Discuss lifestyle goals with students. Explain that "lifestyle" refers to your manner of living or the way you think and behave every day. Ask students how they envision their future—10 years from now, 15 years from now, and 20 years from now. What will their family situation be? Where will they live? What type of work will they be doing? What will they be doing for fun?

Reinforce and Review

Remind students that their wellness largely affects their lifestyle. Wellness is when all of the areas of your life are working together to make you healthy, happy, and confident. Wellness happens when you make healthy choices about the way you live your life. Review the six areas of wellness.

- **Physical.** Being physically fit and well makes you alert and energetic.

- **Emotional.** Being emotionally healthy makes you confident and enthusiastic. You can think clearly and critically, set realistic goals, and make healthy choices.

- **Social.** Being socially fit makes you comfortable and relaxed. You can communicate effectively with others and have fun with your friends.

- **Personal.** Being personally fit makes you happy and satisfied with yourself. You understand your own strengths and weaknesses, and you recognize the things that influence you.

- **Intellectual.** Being intellectually fit helps you be open-minded about other people and new situations. You can think critically and make reasonable decisions.

- **Environmental.** Being environmentally fit ensures that you feel safe in your community. You have respect for the natural environment, and you appreciate your own home and neighborhood.

Examining Lifestyle Goals and Factors

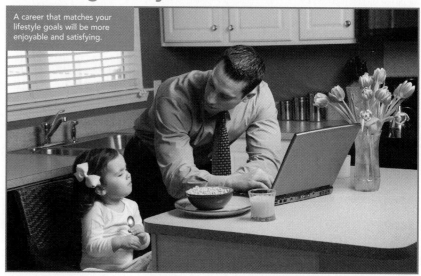

A career that matches your lifestyle goals will be more enjoyable and satisfying.

Does a clinical laboratory technician earn enough money to afford a vacation home? How many hours a week does an agricultural inspector spend on the job? Is a hotel clerk expected to work nights and weekends? Does a sales representative travel a lot?

The career you choose helps determine the lifestyle you will achieve, and your lifestyle might impact the career you choose.

- An attorney working 60 hours a week has less time to spend with her family than a bookkeeper working 40 hours a week.

- A flight attendant has more opportunity to visit international cities than an organic farmer.

You can consider lifestyle factors such as location, salary, education, time, and environment when you choose a career. You can also set goals for the way you want to live your life and the things you want to have in life as part of your career plan.

Setting Lifestyle Goals

Lifestyle goals are the things you want in life such as a family, where you want to live, how much money you have, and how much free time you have for friends, sports, and other activities that you enjoy.

- You might want to live in the mountains and spend as much time as possible out of doors. You might consider a career in recreation.

- You might want to have children and be available in the afternoons when they get home from school. You might consider a career in education or part-time sales.

- You might want to have enough money to travel, even if it means working many hours between trips. You might consider a career such as corporate lawyer or surgeon.

Selecting a career path that gives you the opportunity to achieve your lifestyle goals will make you a happier, more satisfied person.

What Are Lifestyle Factors?

The things about your job that affect the way you live your life are **lifestyle factors**. There are five basic lifestyle factors you might want to consider when you are making decisions about the career that will be right for you.

- *Location.* Where do you want to live? Do you want to be near your family? Do you want to live in the mountains or near the ocean? Do you prefer a city, the country, or the suburbs?
- *Salary.* How much money do you think you must earn to pay for your needs and wants? Are you willing to work for less money to achieve other goals, such as more free time or less work-related stress?
- *Education.* How many years are you willing to spend in school? Would you be happy taking classes at night while you work during the day? Would you be willing to earn less money while you train on the job?
- *Time.* How many hours a week do you want to spend at work? Would you work at night or on weekends? Would you mind being on-call, which means being available at any time to cope with emergencies? Do you want to work part-time, even if it means earning less money?
- *Environment.* What type of people do you want to work with? What type of space do you want to be in? Do you like sitting at a desk? Do you want to be outdoors? Do you need windows in your office? Do you like to dress in a suit or do you prefer casual clothes?

Making Trade-Offs

When you make decisions about your lifestyle and career plans, you may have to make trade-offs. A **trade-off** is a compromise, or giving up one thing in order to get something else.

You might want to be a social worker helping young adults in New York City. You might also want to live in a house with a backyard. Houses in New York City are very expensive, and social workers typically do not earn very high salaries. What trade-off could you make?

- You could choose to rent an apartment in the city, and put off the goal of living in a house with a backyard.
- Or, you could choose to live in a less expensive community outside the city. You would have a long commute to work, but you would be able to afford a house with a backyard.

Focusing on the things that are most important to you and setting priorities can help you make the best decisions. You can use the decision-making process to consider all possible options and the consequences of each option, and then choose the option that helps you achieve your career goals and your lifestyle goals.

Are Your Lifestyle Goals Realistic?

Like career-related goals, lifestyle goals should be realistic. While it might be useful to aim high, it is important to have attainable goals.

- 👎 Marry a supermodel and cruise around the world on a 300-foot yacht
- 👎 Work 10 hours a week and earn a $1,000,000.00 salary
- 👎 Live in a mansion and be the NBA's most valuable player for three years in a row
- 👍 Study hard to become a doctor and open your own practice
- 👍 Join the Air Force, learn to fly jets, and then travel the world as a commercial pilot
- 👍 Attend cosmetology school and get a job as a stylist at a salon in a city

Knowing you can achieve your lifestyle goals will help you work hard and stay on track. What lifestyle goals do you have that might influence your career plans?

TECH CONNECT

Technology has made the option of working at home a reality for many employees.

- E-mail, instant messaging, and voice over Internet protocol (VOIP) make it easy to communicate.
- Applications and documents stored on Internet servers let workers collaborate on projects no matter where their desks are.
- Video conferences make it possible to meet face to face—even when you are miles apart.

Many employees think working from home offers an ideal lifestyle. Benefits include less time commuting, flexible hours, and more time for family and friends. Many employers find that it saves money and increases employee productivity.

Would you like a career that lets you work from home? What might be some benefits and drawbacks? What technology do you think would be most useful? Write an essay that answers these questions.

Customized Instruction: Less Advanced/Special Needs Students

Have students draw a picture of themselves doing their ideal job. You might refer them to the long-term ultimate career goal they identified in their career plan (see page 299 of the student text).

Vocabulary

Lifestyle factors: The things about your job that affect the way you live your life.

Trade-off: A compromise, or giving up one thing in order to get something else.

Are Your Lifestyle Goals Realistic?

Remind students that lifestyle goals should take into account family, where you want to live, how much money you have, and how much free time you have for the things you enjoy. When determining lifestyle goals, you might suggest that students come up with their long-term ultimate goal, just as they did for their career plan (refer to page 299 in the student text). Then, identify short-term goals that define how they will gain the resources they need to achieve the ultimate goal. Emphasize the importance of a timeline for every goal.

TECH CONNECT

Students are to write an essay on the benefits and drawbacks of telecommuting. Some of the benefits they should touch on in their essays are:

- Reduces travel time and cost.
- Expands opportunities for work. Workers are not limited to the available work within a certain distance of their home.
- Minimizes the need to relocate. With telecommuting, it's not necessary to pack up and move if you're assigned to a different job or project.
- Allows for more time for family or home life. Because of less time traveling to and from an office, the telecommuter gains time at home.
- Provides flexible hours. Being able to work at your "peak" times leads to higher productivity.

Some of the drawbacks are:

- Less motivation. Some employees are not organized or motivated enough to work on their own, away from a structured office routine.
- Unproductive work environment. Some homes are not equipped for telecommuting, and there is an increased risk for distractions, such as family and other social and community factors.
- Inability to manage. For employees who are responsible for managing others, telecommuting can pose communication problems and the inability to oversee and track employee performance and progress on tasks.
- Ineffective support system. Many tasks are executed best in a team environment, where the input of and constant contact with others contribute to the success of the business.

Introduce the Section

This section discusses volunteer positions, apprenticeships, internships, and other opportunities from which students can gain career-related experience.

Figure Focus

Discuss career-related opportunities with students. These include part-time jobs, volunteering, job-shadowing, mentoring, and involvement in school- and community-based organizations. Ask students to share the career-related experiences they've gained from jobs, volunteering, and memberships in various clubs.

Reinforce and Review

Review with students the benefits of volunteering. People who volunteer tend to have a positive attitude and high self-esteem. Explain that volunteering can help build character and focus your attention and energies on your strengths and the things you value. There are literally millions of nonprofit organizations in the United States that depend largely on volunteers to support them. Explain that being a volunteer can often open the door to job and career opportunities. For example, volunteering can lead to a job as a(n):

- Fundraiser
- Nonprofit event planner
- Translator
- Counselor
- Human rights lobbyist
- Children's advocate
- Environmental specialist

Identifying Career-Related Opportunities for Students

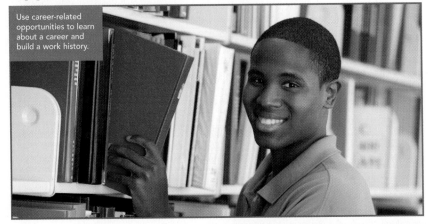

Use career-related opportunities to learn about a career and build a work history.

Employers like to hire people who have experience. But, most teens don't have much work experience. Some states have laws restricting the number of hours a teen can work, and many companies won't even hire people under 16.

In addition to part-time jobs, career-related opportunities such as volunteer positions, apprenticeships, and internships help you gain job experience. Gaining job experience is an important part of developing a career plan. Experience serves two main purposes.

- It gives you the opportunity to learn about a career first-hand. While you are working, you can find out if you enjoy the environment, feel comfortable with the responsibilities, and see a future for yourself in the industry.
- It gives you the opportunity to build a work history that you can include on job and school applications. A **work history** is a list of jobs you have held from the past through the present, showing your experience as an employee.

You can explore career-related opportunities with the help of your parents, teachers, or school counselor. They can show you how to identify opportunities that relate to your skills, interests, and abilities, and how to apply for positions.

Are You An Entrepreneur?

Many teens use entrepreneurial skills to create first jobs for themselves. An **entrepreneur** is a person who organizes and runs his or her own business. Being your own boss has advantages, such as independence, flexibility, and the pride and excitement that comes with ownership. It also has disadvantages, such as no regular salary, an unpredictable work schedule, and the risk of losing everything if the business fails.

Entrepreneurs usually start out with an idea for a product or service that they think other people will buy. If you have a skill or ability that other people will pay for, you can be an entrepreneur.

- Are you patient, responsible, and good with kids? You can babysit.
- Do you love animals and exercise? You can walk dogs.
- Can you play the guitar? You can teach others.
- Are you comfortable working in a kitchen? You can wash dishes or serve at parties.

Entrepreneurs usually have a lot of self-confidence. They believe in themselves and the product or service they are selling. They are not afraid of making decisions and they are willing to take risks.

Customized Instruction: Less Advanced/Special Needs/At-Risk Students

Have students look through help wanted ads in their local newspaper or online. They should search for a job they think would give them experience in the career(s) they identified on their career self-assessment worksheet (see page 295 in the student text). Have them cut out or print the ad and write a sentence or two on why that job represents a good opportunity for them.

What Is An Internship?

An **internship** is a temporary job, usually for students. Internships may or may not pay a salary, but they provide other, useful benefits. You have the opportunity to work in a field that interests you and to build skills. You meet people who might act as **references**—people who will provide a recommendation for you when you apply for jobs or school in the future.

- An internship might be part-time after school. For example, you might intern at a law office two afternoons a week.
- Many internships are in the summer. You might intern full-time at a television station during summer vacation.
- Some internships are for a specific project, or time period. You might intern at a company to develop a Web site, or to digitize records. When the project is complete, the internship ends.

Usually you apply for an internship using a process similar to applying for a job. Your school counselor can help you find internship opportunities.

Volunteer!

Do you think volunteering is for goodie-goodies? It's true that many volunteers are looking for ways to help others and contribute to their communities. But volunteering is also an opportunity to gain career-related experience.

Volunteers are unpaid workers. Many volunteer positions are in service organizations, such as homeless shelters, health clinics, animal shelters, and food pantries. These organizations are usually short on money to pay workers, so they depend on volunteers to perform a full range of responsibilities. They need people to do everything from answering telephones to maintaining mailing lists to communicating directly with clients.

- If you are interested in the arts, you might volunteer as a **docent**—guide—at a museum.
- For health career experience, you might volunteer as a receptionist in a hospital, clinic, or nursing home.
- If you are considering a career in communications, you might volunteer as a production assistant at a public access cable station, public television station, or public radio station.
- If you are thinking about a career in recreation, many nature centers and state parks hire volunteers to clean, lead tours, and answer visitor's questions.

The opportunities for volunteering are nearly endless. Select an organization that interests you, and ask what positions are available. The organization may even offer training.

Other Ways to Gain Experience

Some other ways to gain career-related experience:

✔ Mentoring programs pair experienced workers with students or less-experienced employees. The mentor acts as an advisor, providing advice, job contacts, and tutoring.

✔ Apprenticeships allow a worker to learn a trade by working with someone who has already mastered that trade. An apprenticeship combines on-the-job training and classroom education. Some trades require apprenticeships in order to qualify for certification.

✔ Job shadowing allows you to follow an experienced worker through his or her work day to see the specific responsibilities and tasks required on the job.

✔ School clubs and organizations offer opportunities to gain management and leadership skills.

21st Century Skills

What Happens Next?

Julio's favorite subject in school is biology. He loves watching medical shows on television. He thinks he is quick to react and solve problems. He thinks he might be interested in a career in health care—specifically as an emergency medical technician. He knows he will need money for an education, so he starts looking for his first job.

His mother works as a dispatcher for the local emergency service center. She says they need temporary office help to catch up on filing. If Julio is interested, she can set up an interview with the office manager.

Julio thinks office work is boring. He would like to find a part-time job that relates directly to emergency medical care. He visits the hospital to see what part-time openings they have, but they tell him they don't hire anyone under 17. He contacts a medical clinic, but they say he needs training and experience.

What problems are facing Julio? What decisions does he have to make? Using your 21st Century Skills—such as decision making, goal setting, and problem solving—write an ending to the story. Read it to the class, or form a small group and present it as a skit.

Vocabulary

Docent: Guide working in a museum, cathedral, or other tourist site.

Internship: Temporary job, usually for students.

References: People who will provide a recommendation for you when you apply for jobs or school in the future.

Volunteers: Unpaid workers.

Other Ways to Gain Experience

Discuss the ways to gain work-related experience as outlined in the text. If possible, have your school guidance counselor make a presentation to the class about the programs offered through your school.

In addition, review the following opportunities for volunteers:

- Staff information booths at fairs and trade shows.
- Tutor children in reading, math, and other subjects.
- Help elderly or disabled people with daily activities.
- Do physical labor such as cleaning, yard work, and moving.
- Create flyers, brochures, and other printed materials.
- Provide childcare.
- Collect and distribute donations of food, clothing, or money.
- Give presentations and speeches that promote the group.
- Entertain groups of people with music, dance, acting, or other creative arts.

21st Century Skills

What Happens Next?

Students are to prepare an ending to Julio's dilemma. He wants to work in the health care field, but he is too young to get the type of paying job he'd like. Julio should consider opportunities through his mother's office, where he can gain experience in the health care field. Employers in the health care field, as he has found, are looking for employees with experience. Students' endings should explore opportunities for Julio to gain work-related experience. In addition to the job with his mother's office, he should investigate volunteer opportunities in the health care field.

Customized Instruction: ESOL Students

Have students look through help wanted ads in their local newspaper or online. They should search for a job they think would give them experience in the career(s) they identified on their career self-assessment worksheet (see page 295 in the student text). Have them cut out or print the ad and then rewrite it in their primary language.

Customized Instruction: More Advanced Students

Have students look through help wanted ads in their local newspaper or online. They should search for a job they think would give them experience in the career(s) they identified on their career self-assessment worksheet (see page 295 in the student text). Have them cut out or print the ad and identify three short-term goals that define how they will gain the skills, knowledge, and experience needed to get the job, including a timeline for achieving each one.

End-of-Chapter Activities

Case Study

Answers to the first bullet will vary. Some will think he is reasonable, because they understand he does not want to move far from his friends and school. Others will think he is unreasonable because he has the opportunity to go with his family and enjoy a more affluent lifestyle.

Ari's parents are excited because they will have more money to save and spend on wants. They will be able to live a more expensive lifestyle. Ari's dad may also be excited because he is getting a promotion. He is being rewarded for his hard work, which contributes to his self-esteem and well-being. They may also welcome the move to North Carolina, where the weather may be better than in Pittsburgh.

Trade-offs for all family members include moving away from extended family, friends, and their usual routine in order to take advantage of the promotion. Ari's mom will have to find a new job. She will work part-time, which may impact her ability to continue to achieve in her career. Ari's siblings will have to start at a new school, which may be stressful.

Students may think of other answers.

Sounding Off!

1. Student answers will vary.
2. People who set unrealistic goals struggle more with staying focused on what they want to achieve. Knowing you can achieve your goals helps you work hard and stay on track. If you set unrealistic goals, you set yourself up for disappointment, which can lead to low self-esteem and a negative attitude.

FAQ

1. Answers will vary, but should include three of the following:
   - Creativity
   - Independence
   - Job security
   - Prestige
   - Work safety
   - Leadership opportunities
   - Physical activity
   - Good salary
   - Work environment
   - Challenge

2. The six steps in the career self-assessment process are:
   - List your two favorite school subjects.
   - List at least four specific skills you have acquired in your favorite subjects.
   - List at least four achievements in your favorite subjects.
   - List at least four abilities—the things you do well, or your talents.
   - List at least two interests.
   - List at least four work values.

3. Employability means having and using your life skills and abilities to be hired and stay hired.

Case Study

Ari is 15. His father works as a financial analyst for a large company. His mother is a bank teller. Ariel has one sister and two brothers. They live in a three bedroom apartment in Pittsburgh, Pennsylvania.

One day Ari's parents say they have good news. The family is moving to Charlotte, North Carolina. The company has offered Ari's dad a promotion, with more responsibilities and a much larger salary. The family will be able to buy a house, and Ari's mom will be able to work part-time so she can be home more.

Ari is angry. He does not think it is good news at all. His friends are all in Pittsburgh. His school is in Pittsburgh. He demands to stay behind and live with friends.

- Do you think Ari is being reasonable?
- Why do you think Ari's parents are happy about the move?
- What trade-offs are facing each member of the family?

Sounding Off!

1. Do you think it is more important to employers if an applicant has the appropriate education and training or if the applicant is happy, friendly, and cooperative?
2. Why do you think having unrealistic career goals might create problems?

FAQ

1. List three work values that are important to you.
2. List the six steps in the career self-assessment process.
3. What is employability?
4. List four positive qualities that might improve your employability.
5. List two ways you can build employability skills at school.
6. Describe the two types of career-related goals.
7. What is a career plan?
8. List five lifestyle factors.
9. What is an entrepreneur?
10. List three types of career-related opportunities for students.

4. Positive qualities that might improve your employability include honesty, tolerance, patience, responsibility, a positive attitude, being cooperative and respectful, and flexibility. Students may think of others.

5. At school, you can set academic goals and work with a teacher or counselor to create a plan for achieving them. You can stand up against bullies and become active in a club or organization such as FCCLA. Students may think of others.

6. The two types of goals are:
   - Goals that help you succeed in your career by directing your actions and guiding your decision-making once you are already working.
   - Goals that help you achieve the career of your choice. These goals direct your actions and guide your decision-making while you are preparing for a career.

7. A career plan is a map that shows you the way to reach your goal.

8. Lifestyle factors include location, salary, time, education, and environment. Students may think of others.

9. An entrepreneur is a person who organizes and runs his or her own business.

10. Types of career-related opportunities for students include entrepreneurship, internship, apprenticeship, volunteering, after-school job, and summer job.

Divide into teams of four or five. As a team, brainstorm ways you might be entrepreneurs and start a business. Discuss your skills, interests, and abilities. Consider things you can offer that other people might be willing to pay for. Select one idea and write a plan or presentation, or create a skit that shows how you would put the plan into action. Include information about the risks and benefits of starting this business.

Share your plan with the other teams. Individually, vote for the idea that you think is the most realistic and attainable. The team whose idea earns the most votes wins.

Hot Topics

Do you have a career or lifestyle goal you are shy about discussing? Maybe you think your peers will laugh at you, or your family won't take you seriously.

Take this opportunity to write anonymously about your career and lifestyle goals. Be realistic and specific. Use a word processor so no one recognizes your handwriting. Be honest and open. Put the paper in the class Hot Topics box.

As a class, read the anonymous entries and discuss them.

Web Extra ▼

Find links to free and fee-based career assessment tools and worksheets on many Web sites, such as www.quintcareers.com and www.rileyguide.com.

Use the Internet to identify the sites that you think might be the most useful for your peers. Make a directory of the sites, including the Web site address, a brief description, and whether the site is free or has a fee. Post the directory on your school Web site or in your school career center or library.

Problem Solver

Maya is interested in a career in recreation management. She was offered a volunteer position at a professional golf tournament at a golf course in her area. She would work as an assistant to the Volunteer Coordinator. The position would be part-time for three months, and then full-time for the week of the tournament. It does not pay any wages. In fact, Maya would have to pay $50.00 to buy a uniform! She has asked you to help her decide whether she should accept the position or not.

Working alone or in pairs, use the decision-making process to help Maya decide what to do. Analyze the situation, look for all possible options, and consider the consequences of each option. Write a report that explains your advice to Maya. Be specific about the reasons for your decision.

Team Players

Student teams are to select a business they would like to start up and prepare a plan that explains how they would go about launching it. Their plans should address the following:

- Name of the company
- Product or service to be sold
- Description of customers who will buy it
- Explanation of how it will be produced, sold, and delivered
- Estimation of the costs to produce, sell, and deliver it

Hot Topics

Make sure students understand that they can turn in their papers anonymously. Encourage them to be open and honest about their career and lifestyle goals.

Web Extra

Students are to research Web sites that provide career assessment tools and worksheets. They are to prepare a directory of the sites that includes the address, a description of each, and whether or not the assessment is free or has a fee, and then post it in the school career center or library.

Remind students that a reliable Web site usually publishes the name of the author or organization that sponsors it and the date the content was created or last updated in a fairly obvious location, such as at the top or bottom of the page or on the home page. The site is usually organized with headings and an obvious navigation system. A reliable site clearly states its purpose and any affiliations. You should also look for accuracy in spelling and grammar.

Problem Solver

Student pairs are to use the decision-making process to determine if Maya should take the volunteer position. In their reports, students should clearly identify the steps to a decision:

1. **Identify the decision.** Should Maya take the volunteer position at the golf course?
2. **Consider options.** Maya can accept the job without pay. Maya can reject the position. Maya can try to negotiate some type of compensation for her work, or reimbursement for her expenses. Maya can look for other volunteer opportunities in recreation.
3. **Identify consequences.** Students should list the pros and cons of each option identified in step 2.
4. **Select the best option.** The team should vote on the best option.
5. **Develop a plan of action.** Students should determine how they will implement the decision made.

Write Now

Students are to prepare a career assessment worksheet for an imaginary student. Then, they are to trade papers with a classmate and analyze the classmate's worksheet to identify two career clusters that match the assessment information. Students should write a letter recommending the clusters, along with possible pathways and specific jobs. Their letters should discuss why they chose the particular clusters and why they think they are a good match.

Be Involved!

As a class, students are to develop and design a campaign to educate other students and families about the different clubs and organizations at their school. Students are to follow the FCCLA planning process:

- Identify a concern.
- Set a goal.
- Form a plan (who, what, when, where, how, cost, resources, and evaluation).
- Act.
- Follow up.

Remind students that a successful team relationship depends on all team members working together. Make sure they take steps to delegate responsibilities, communicate effectively, and manage conflicts or disagreements.

Social Networking

Students are to create a directory of organizations and agencies in their area that rely on volunteer help; specifically, volunteers from the school. The directory should list the name, address, contact name, and a brief description of each group. Students should categorize the agencies according to career cluster or pathway. Refer students to *Appendix A: Career Clusters*, starting on page 513 of the student text.

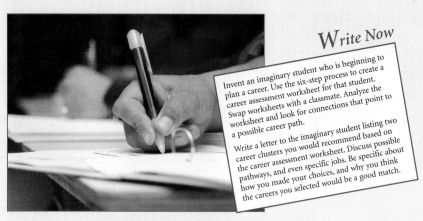

Write Now

Invent an imaginary student who is beginning to plan a career. Use the six-step process to create a career assessment worksheet for that student. Swap worksheets with a classmate. Analyze the worksheet and look for connections that point to a possible career path.

Write a letter to the imaginary student listing two career clusters you would recommend based on the career assessment worksheet. Discuss possible pathways, and even specific jobs. Be specific about how you made your choices, and why you think the careers you selected would be a good match.

Be Involved!

www.fcclainc.org

Participating in school clubs and organizations can provide valuable opportunities to gain career-related experience. As a class, brainstorm ways you can inform students and families about the different clubs and organizations at your school. For example, you might publish a booklet, design a Web site, or organize an Activity Fair.

Working together, select one idea that will let you educate students and families about the clubs and organizations available at school. Use the FCCLA planning process to plan it and make it happen. Define the project as a goal, make an action plan for achieving the goal (including a timeframe), assess the plan to make sure it is realistic and attainable, and then put the plan into action to achieve your goal. You may want to organize teams within the class to handle specific responsibilities. For example, if you choose to publish a booklet, you might need some people to report and write the descriptions, some people to do the layout and design, and some to handle distribution. You might want someone to handle publicity—inviting the local media to cover an Activity Fair, or to advertize your booklet or Web site.

As you work toward your goal, keep a class journal to record your progress, and collect documentation that you can use to show what you have achieved.

When the project is complete, evaluate your success. Did you achieve your goal? Did you create a useful product? Did the students and families find it useful and informative? Did you run into any obstacles? If so, how did you overcome them? Did you have to make any trade-offs? Write a report explaining what you learned, whether you were successful or not, and what you would do differently if you were going to start the project all over again.

Social Networking

Most community service organizations welcome volunteers of all ages. Contact organizations in your community and ask them if they have positions for volunteers from your school. Create a directory of volunteer opportunities. Categorize the positions according to career cluster or pathway. Make the directory available in your classroom, library, or career center, or post it on the school Web site.

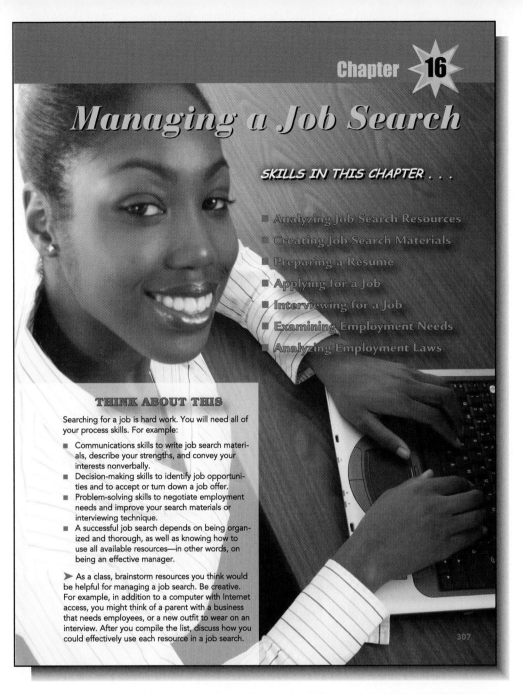

Chapter 16

Managing a Job Search

SKILLS IN THIS CHAPTER . . .

- Analyzing Job Search Resources
- Creating Job Search Materials
- Preparing a Resume
- Applying for a Job
- Interviewing for a Job
- Examining Employment Needs
- Analyzing Employment Laws

THINK ABOUT THIS

Searching for a job is hard work. You will need all of your process skills. For example:

- Communications skills to write job search materials, describe your strengths, and convey your interests nonverbally.
- Decision-making skills to identify job opportunities and to accept or turn down a job offer.
- Problem-solving skills to negotiate employment needs and improve your search materials or interviewing technique.
- A successful job search depends on being organized and thorough, as well as knowing how to use all available resources—in other words, on being an effective manager.

➤ As a class, brainstorm resources you think would be helpful for managing a job search. Be creative. For example, in addition to a computer with Internet access, you might think of a parent with a business that needs employees, or a new outfit to wear on an interview. After you compile the list, discuss how you could effectively use each resource in a job search.

307

Chapter 16 Overview

This chapter provides students with an overview of career planning. It examines tools for assessing skills and interests and stresses the importance of setting realistic career and lifestyle goals.

Analyzing Job Search Resources This section identifies the tools you can access to help you find job leads and employment opportunities.

Creating Job Search Materials The primary elements you will need in a job search are a cover letter, resume, and list of references.

Preparing a Resume This section provides helpful tips on designing, writing, and formatting a resume.

Applying for a Job This section explores the job application process and explains how a successful application leads to the job interview.

Interviewing for a Job In this section, students learn how to prepare for a job interview and how to conduct themselves during an interview. The importance of follow-up is also discussed.

Examining Employment Needs Employee compensation, benefits, and other needs are all part of the job package. Before you accept a job, you need to ensure your needs and expectations will be met.

Analyzing Employment Laws Many laws and regulations are in place to protect a worker's rights and responsibilities. This section provides an overview of the major laws designed to protect employees.

Focus and Engage

Bell-Ringer: Think About This

Students are to suggest resources that would be helpful in managing a job search. Encourage students to think broadly about this. For example, in addition to using the Internet, you could look through local newspapers for jobs. You could also visit local community centers, which often post job openings, particularly those with local companies that prefer to hire local employees. You will need a supply of stationery and envelopes on which to print cover letters and resumes. If you do not have access to a computer and printer, you might be able to use library equipment or your school's computer lab. If you land a job interview, you will not only need the proper attire, but also a means for getting to and from the interview. Can you drive or walk, or will you need to take public transportation?

ADVANCE PREPARATION	
Review	*Life Skills for the 21st Century* textbook, Chapter 16.
Prepare	Paper and pencil for some activities.
	Colored pencils or markers.
	Current newspapers.
	Box labeled "Hot Topics."

CUSTOMIZED INSTRUCTION OVERVIEW

Less Advanced Students	More Advanced Students	ESOL Students	Special Needs Students	At-Risk Students
Pages 308, 313, 318, 320	Pages 308, 318	Pages 308, 321	Pages 308, 313, 320, 323	Pages 308, 314, 320

Introduce the Section

This section identifies the tools you can access to help you find job leads and employment opportunities. These include networking, online resources, want ads, career counselors, employment agencies, and job fairs.

Figure Focus

Remind students of the career self-assessment they did in Chapter 15. A career self-assessment is a process by which you learn more about your career-related skills, interests, values, and abilities. Were their self-assessments useful in narrowing their career focus?

Vocabulary

Job leads: Opportunities for employment.
Job search resources: Tools designed to help you find job leads.

Discuss

Ask students if they have used one of the job search resources discussed in the text. What about word of mouth? Explain that going through formal job search channels can be effective, but personal contacts can also be a valuable resource for job leads. Often, existing employees know about job openings before they are posted or advertised. Furthermore, you often hear people say, "I'll put in a good word for you." Knowing someone who works for a company that's hiring can be an advantage. If an existing employee in good standing with the company refers you for a job, it might give you an edge over other candidates. The important thing to consider is that you have the skills and qualifications to do the job.

Analyzing Job Search Resources

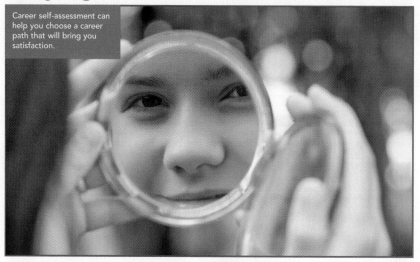

Career self-assessment can help you choose a career path that will bring you satisfaction.

The first step in applying for a job is finding out what jobs are available. How can you find opportunities that meet your needs and fit your strengths? You can use **job search resources**—tools designed to help you find **job leads**—to identify opportunities for employment.

You can use a variety of resources to identify available jobs. You will probably need to use more than one of the following resources.

- Networking uses people you know to help you find opportunities.
- Online resources let you access information and job listings on the Internet.
- Want ads are a traditional source for job listings.
- Career counselors help you identify jobs that match your skills, interests, and abilities.
- Employment agencies work to match employers with employees.
- Job fairs provide an opportunity to introduce yourself to many different employers.

Knowing how to make the most out of available job search resources is critical for finding a job.

How Long Does It Take to Find a Job?

Surveys show that the average time it takes to find a job is between 12 and 24 weeks—that's 3 to 6 months! In a down economy with a high unemployment rate, it can take longer than that. Knowing that it can take a long time to find a job helps keep you from becoming discouraged, or giving up.

Some experts recommend that you begin an active job search 6 to 9 months before the date you hope to start working. During that time, you can work at a job to earn money, or volunteer to gain experience.

If you treat your job search like a job itself, you know you are actively working to achieve your career goals. How much time would you spend working each day if you had the job you want? Try to spend that time working on your job search.

You might not be earning an income, but you can meet your responsibilities by developing your employability skills, creating and improving job search materials, and exploring resources that might lead to job prospects—the possibility of employment.

Customized Instruction: More Advanced Students

Have students role-play a job seeker calling a contact to set up an appointment for an informational interview. The job seeker should make a personal introduction, identify the purpose for setting up the appointment, and suggest possible appointment dates and times.

Customized Instruction: Less Advanced/Special Needs/At-Risk Students

Have students use index cards or note-size paper to create a directory of contacts. They should include teachers, coaches, current or past employers, friends, neighbors, etc., who they consider a resource for job leads. For each contact, they should write the person's name, occupation, mailing address, phone number, e-mail address, and a brief note on how they know the person.

Customized Instruction: ESOL Students

Have students do the same thing as directed above for Less Advanced/Special Needs/At-Risk students, except have them write the brief note in their primary language.

What Is Networking?

Some studies show that nearly 80 percent of all job openings are never advertised. How can you find out about a job if it isn't advertised? Network!

Networking in a job search means sharing information about yourself and your career goals with personal contacts—people you know already, or new people you meet in any area of your life. Hopefully, one of the contacts works for a company that is hiring, or knows someone at a company that is hiring. The contact recommends you for the position. Employers like to hire people who come with a recommendation from someone they know and trust.

Here's how it works:

1. You see a cousin at a family party and tell him that you are trying to find a job as a paralegal—someone who works in a law office assisting lawyers with legal paperwork.
2. Your cousin is bowling with friends and mentions that you are looking for a position as a paralegal.
3. One of the bowling buddies tells his mother, who is a lawyer, about you.
4. The law firm where she works is looking for a paralegal. She invites you to apply for the job.

How Do I Network?

The first step in networking is to tell everyone you know that you are looking for work. Be specific about your career goals. Tell your family, friends, classmates, and teachers. If you volunteer, tell the people at the volunteer organization. If you are a member of a club or organization, tell the other members.

Stay in touch with your contacts through regular calls or e-mails. Set up a networking file to keep track of each contact. Set up the file using index cards or a computer program. In the file, include:

■ The name, occupation, mailing address, phone number, and e-mail address of each contact.

■ A reminder of how you know the contact. Is it a personal friend? Did you meet through someone else? Did you meet through a club or organization?

■ Notes about each time you communicate with the contact.

The first time you call a contact, explain who you are and why you are calling. Do not ask for a job. Instead, ask for:

■ Job leads

■ Information about occupations and companies, such as what trends are affecting a certain industry

■ Introductions to people who might become part of your network

Remember to give the contact your phone number and e-mail address so he or she can reach you. Always be polite, speak clearly, and say thank you.

"I wonder if this person will be a good contact?"

Job Search. Career Research. What's the Difference?

You completed a career self-assessment worksheet. You picked two careers that match your interests, skills, and abilities. Why isn't anyone asking you for an interview?

👎 You are spending only a couple of hours a week on your job search.

👎 You are applying for positions that require more skill and training than you currently have.

👎 You do not have personal recommendations for the positions.

👎 You are applying for the same job that hundreds of other candidates are applying for, too.

👍 You are continuing to spend time building a network of contacts.

👍 You keep your job search materials organized to make it easy to apply to any new job opening.

👍 You use all available job search resources to increase your chances of finding a job.

Remember, career research helps you identify types of careers that match your skills, interests, and abilities. A job search identifies specific job openings and opportunities for employment. How can you use your career research to help you in your job search?

Figure Focus

It's important to stress to students that networking is a two-way street in which both parties are working to build relationships. You benefit from contacts who refer you, and they need to know that they may benefit from your referrals of them. As the saying goes, "what goes around comes around," meaning that when you share ideas about a job opportunity that you cannot take advantage of, you improve your chances of someone in your network doing the same for you.

Vocabulary

Networking: In a job search, the means for sharing information about yourself and your career goals with personal contacts.

Discuss

Discuss the dynamics of networking. According to data from the U.S. Department of Labor, close to 50 percent of job seekers obtain their jobs by networking. Students have probably engaged in networking without even realizing it. For example, has a friend ever referred you to a parent who needs a babysitter? What about an uncle whose grass you mowed and who then told his neighbors about you?

Explain that the important thing about networking is building up the pool of specific individuals in your network. You can get names through the following:

■ Teachers, friends, neighbors, relatives, and their friends.

■ Members of school- or community-based organizations, clubs, and associations.

■ Community and public service agencies, such as resource center directors, librarians, and chambers of commerce.

■ Human resource directors, public relations officials, or public information specialists at local businesses.

■ Charities and other volunteer-run groups and the fundraising events they sponsor.

■ Past employers.

■ Your school's alumni group.

Job Search. Career Research. What's the Difference?

Your career research helps you identify a broad field in which you would like to work. It gives you insight to the areas in which you might effectively apply your personal interests, skills, and abilities. Knowing this will help you narrow your search to jobs within that field. Once you gain experience, you will be able to further narrow your job search to certain positions and certain types of employers.

Reinforce and Review

Review with students the benefits and drawbacks of using online resources to locate and apply for jobs. Some of the benefits are:

- You can more easily and quickly find jobs in other cities, other states, and other countries.
- You can find background and financial information on potential employers through corporate Web sites as well as government (www.sec.gov, for example), media, and other independent Web sites.
- You can submit an application or resume on a timely basis.

Some drawbacks are:

- The quality of job information available on the Internet is not always current, reliable, accurate, or complete.
- The multitude of people who use the Internet to search for and apply for jobs means employers are burdened with sorting through the flood of applicants and resumes submitted online.
- The security of personal information you supply in an application or resume may be jeopardized.

Government Job Search Resources

Explain that in addition to the Web sites listed in the text, many states, cities, and other municipalities sponsor online job boards. The human resources office within the state or city government is typically responsible for posting job openings.

21st Century Skills

What Happens Next?

Students are to prepare an ending on Glenna and Jane's job searches. Their endings should demonstrate that Glenna's job search has effectively utilized a number of resources, including online research, newspapers and magazine advertisements, a career counselor, and networking. By setting up an informational interview with the lawyer, she has gained the opportunity to further build her network of contacts and learn more about the career in which she's interested. Jane, on the other hand, has not treated her job search like a job itself. She has relied on others (those to whom she has sent her resume) to act on her behalf. She may have been more successful if she delivered her resume in person to hotels in the area, or followed up her resume with a phone call.

Government Job Search Resources

Some Web sites that link to government job search resources include:

✔ Federal:

www.usajobs.opm.gov
www.allthegovernmentjobs.com
www.jobsfed.com/
www.studentjobs.gov/

✔ Texas:

www.twc.state.tx.us/jobs/job.html

✔ New York:

www.labor.state.ny.us/
lookingforajob.shtm

✔ California:

www.ca.gov/Employment/Jobs.html

21st Century Skills — What Happens Next?

Jane is looking for a summer job. She is considering a career in hospitality, so she would like to work in a hotel.

Glenna is also looking for a summer job. She is considering a career in law, so she would like to work in a law office.

Jane goes online and starts looking through want ads. She sends out her resume to a few hotels in the area, but does not hear back from any. She goes to the library and looks through the want ads in newspapers and magazines. She sends out more resumes, and still gets no response. She is beginning to think she will never find a job.

Glenna also looks online and in newspapers and magazines. She makes an appointment with a career counselor at school, who helps her compile a list of offices in the community. The counselor gives Glenna the name and phone number of a lawyer she knows. Glenna makes time one afternoon to personally drop off her resume at a few of the local law offices. She calls the lawyer and asks if she can come in for an informational interview. She feels that her chances of finding a job she wants are pretty good.

What is different about the way the two girls are approaching their job searches? Which girl do you think has a better chance of finding a summer job? Using your 21st Century Skills—such as decision making, goal setting, and problem solving—write an ending to the story. Read it to the class, or form a small group and present it as a skit.

Using Online Resources

The Internet is a great tool for finding career prospects and job leads. You can even use it to make contacts for networking. Some of the more effective online resources include:

- *Company Web sites.* You can learn a lot about a company from its Web site, including what they do, the backgrounds of the people who work there, and who to contact in each department. Most sites also have a page listing job openings, with information on how to apply. Even if there are no openings that interest you, you can contact the human resources department to try to set up an informational interview.
- *Government sites.* Like corporations, government agencies list information and job openings. There are also government Web sites that provide job listings.
- *Industry sites.* Many industries and industry associations have Web sites that list job opportunities. For example, if you are interested in a career as a social worker, you could look for positions on www.socialworkjobbank.com.
- *Online job agencies.* Companies such as Monster.com or CareerBuilder.com list job openings and let you upload your resume for employers to look at. You can search these sites for jobs in a field or career that interests you. Some of these sites charge fees.
- *Social networking sites.* You can use social networking sites such as Facebook or LinkedIn to meet contacts and learn about jobs. There are groups for people in certain careers, or who work for specific companies. Employers join these sites, as well. They look for potential employees based on the personal profile you create. That's an important reason for only posting information that would be appropriate for a potential employer to see!

Using a Career Center

A career center is an excellent place to start a job search. Your school might have a career center that you can use free of charge. Career centers have job listings, research resources, and counselors who will help you identify jobs that match your skills and interests. They can also introduce you to former students who are now employed—giving you more opportunities for networking.

Employment offices are similar to career centers. Some are sponsored by the state or local government. They provide job search resources and assistance free of charge.

Private employment agencies charge a fee to match employees with employers. Sometimes you pay the fee, and sometimes the employer pays the fee. Sometimes you pay even if you don't find a job. They all have different policies, so be sure to ask before you sign a contract.

Temporary employment agencies are hired by a company to fill temporary jobs. For example, a company might need temporary data entry help to complete a large project, or help to fill in for a worker on vacation or on a leave of absence. Temporary jobs can lead to a permanent position. They are also a good way to build skills, gain experience, and meet people in the industry.

What About Want Ads?

Another resource used by job seekers are help wanted ads. Help wanted ads—which are sometimes called classified ads—are printed in newspapers and magazines, and posted online at newspaper and magazine Web sites.

Usually, there are many ads listed alphabetically. They may be organized into general categories, such as Medical, Professional, and Education. For example, if you are looking for a teaching position, you would look at the listings under Education.

Help wanted ad listings usually include a job title and a very brief description of the responsibilities and experience required. Sometimes they include information about wages and hours. There may be a phone number or e-mail address to contact for more information or to apply, or a mailing address where you can send a resume.

Managing Your Job Search Resources

Keeping your job search resources organized will help you follow up every possibility. When you are actively looking for work at many companies, it is easy to forget who you spoke to and even what you spoke about. An employer might not look favorably on someone who repeats the same conversation, or cannot remember who referred her in the first place.

"I wonder how many kids are going to apply for the same job?"

- Keep a to-do list of tasks you want to accomplish each day, such as people you want to contact, resumes you have to send out, and thank-you notes to write. Cross off each item you complete, and add new items as they come up.
- Contact some people in your network every day. Make brief phone calls, or send brief e-mail messages to let them know you are looking for work, and to ask for assistance finding job opportunities.
- Follow up on all leads. Keep a record of the people you contact, including phone numbers, e-mail addresses, and mailing addresses. Include the dates and times, the method of communication, and the result. Did they invite you in for an interview? Did they refer you to someone else?
- Set up folders for storing documents that relate to your job search. Use the folders to keep track of information you send to each contact or potential employer, and the response you get back. The folder might include copies of the cover letter and samples of achievement you sent. It might also include notes you took during a phone call or interview, a brochure about the company, and a printout of an e-mail message you received.

Is It Too Good to Be True?

Do not fall for employment scams, such as a job ad that promises income of thousands of dollars a week and requires no experience or education. If a job description sounds too good to be true, it probably is. Be wary of any job that:

✔ *Asks you to pay for something up front*

✔ *Asks for a scan of your passport or other personal information*

✔ *Offers a part-time, work-from-home job that earns a large salary*

✔ *Includes money transfers or money transactions in the job description*

✔ *Comes from an agency representing a cruise ship*

Job Search

If you enjoy researching careers, and matching skills, abilities, and interests with jobs, you might want to consider a career in human resources. Most companies have a human resources department—or a personnel department. People who work in human resources review job applications, advise employees on work- and career-related issues, and manage employee records.

The educational requirements depend on the specific job, but usually require a bachelor's degree. Use the Internet, library, or your school's guidance resources to learn more about a career in human resources. Write a job description, including the educational requirements, career pathway, and potential salary range.

Job Search

Students are to research a career in human resources and prepare a job description. Refer students to the Business Management & Administration career cluster discussed on page 516 in *Appendix A*. Human resources management focuses on the staffing activities that involve planning, recruitment, selection, orientation, training, performance appraisal, compensation, and safety of employees. In their job descriptions, make sure students include educational requirements for the job they chose, previous experience, and salary range.

Discuss

Explain that many local and regional employers rely on help wanted ads in local media for two reasons:

1. They want to avoid the flood of applications they typically receive when posting an opening on a major job site, such as Monster.com.

2. They want locally based applicants so they don't have to pay relocation fees.

Help wanted ads are suitable for finding local jobs; often, applicants are familiar with the company posting the job. However, you might share with students that data from the U.S. Department of Labor indicates that a small percentage of job seekers obtain jobs through help wanted ads. That's why many career management consultants believe that a job search that targets only advertised job openings will likely miss more opportunities than it uncovers. Stress the importance of using various job search resources.

Is It Too Good to Be True?

According to the National Council of Better Business Bureaus, some of the more common employment scams are:

- Assembly work at home, where victims buy supplies and spend many hours assembling projects, but after completing the work, the company rejects it and refuses to pay.

- Processing medical claims, where victims are pressured to buy software or computers at exorbitant prices. But, because of privacy concerns, this service is rarely utilized by doctors and dentists.

- Job leads, where consumers pay for lists of free government Web sites, or of business opportunities requiring further investment.

Employees' rights and laws that are designed to protect workers are discussed later in this chapter.

Figure Focus

In recessionary times, job applicants should expect intense competition for just about any type of job. Explain to students that effectively using your job search tools and developing an organized network of resources can give you an edge over the competition.

Introduce the Section

The primary elements you will need in a job search are a cover letter, resume, and list of references. This section defines each item.

Vocabulary

Cover letter: Introduces you to a potential employer and highlights the qualities that make you suitable for a certain position.

List of references: Names and contact information of people who know you and your qualifications and who are willing to speak about you to potential employers.

Resume: Written summary of work-related skills, experience, and education.

Figure Focus

Ask students how their cover letter, resume, and list of references reflect upon them personally.

For example, the cover letter is typically your first chance to make a good impression. In addition to telling the employer about the skills and abilities you can bring to the job and why the employer should consider you a qualified candidate, it represents your chance to highlight your individuality and personality. You do this not only through *what* you write, but also *how* you write it. Even the typeface (or font) and stationery you select can influence an employer's preconceptions about you.

The organization and physical appearance of a resume also can influence an employer. Is it neat and organized? Is the information clearly presented? Is the paper on which it's printed free of smudges or dirt?

Your list of references can impress upon the potential employer your ability to establish professional relationships and build a network of resources.

Do I Need a Portfolio?

Many younger students will not have samples of current work to put in a portfolio. You might suggest they include the following.

- Letters of recommendation from teachers, coaches, and community leaders.
- Certificates that recognize good grades or participation in or completion of an activity, special course (such as CPR or first-aid training), or program.
- Awards for achievements in academics and athletics.
- Newspaper articles about achievements.

Creating Job Search Materials

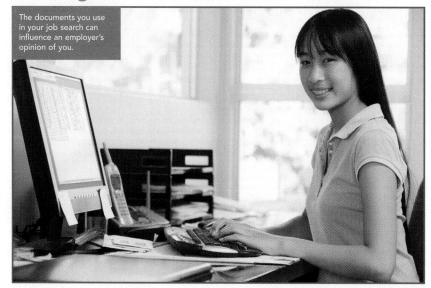

The documents you use in your job search can influence an employer's opinion of you.

Employers often consider tens or even hundreds of candidates for every job opening. Sometimes they shuffle through stacks of letters, or field multiple phone calls. How can you make a positive impression and show you are serious and qualified for the job?

You can prepare professional, accurate job search materials, including a resume, cover letter, and list of references.

- Your **resume** may be the most important job search document. It is a written summary of your work-related skills, experience, and education. It is so important, it has its own section, starting on page 314.
- A **cover letter** is sent along with your resume. It introduces you to a potential employer and highlights the qualities that make you suitable for the position you want.
- A list of references includes the names and contact information of people who know you and your qualifications, and who are willing to speak about you to potential employers.

Do I Need a Portfolio?

If you are looking for a position in a creative career, such as photography, graphic design, or journalism, a portfolio that includes samples of current work, such as clips of published articles or samples of artwork. is an important part of your job search materials. It lets you show potential employers your abilities and achievements.

It is a good idea to have the original sample in the portfolio if possible, and to have copies available to give to potential employers. Artists sometimes create slides of their artwork to include in a portfolio.

Everyone looking for work should keep a career portfolio for storing documents such as a resume, cover letters, personal data sheet, and list of references. You can use a career portfolio as a resource when you are applying for jobs or going to an interview. For example, if you have your reference list with you when you are filling out a job application, you do not have to worry about remembering names and contact information.

Why Do I Need a Cover Letter?

When you include a cover letter with your resume, you make a better impression on the employer than if you send the resume alone. Including a cover letter shows that you have taken the time to match your qualifications with a specific job.

A cover letter should be short and to the point. Direct it to the person who is responsible for hiring. If you do not know the person's name, title, and address, call the company and ask.

You can customize the cover letter to the job opening you are applying for. Use it to tell the employer why you are interested in that job, and why you are qualified to do the work.

Even when you send a resume electronically, it is important to send a cover letter. For example, you can write the cover letter in an e-mail message, and include the resume as an attachment.

When you write a cover letter, ask yourself these questions:

- Have I identified the job title for the job I want?
- Have I stated where I learned about the position?
- Have I listed the skills I have that make me qualified for the position?
- Have I thanked the reader for his or her time and consideration?
- Have I checked for and corrected all spelling and grammatical errors?

How Do I Choose a Reference?

A *reference* is someone who knows you well and is willing to speak to employers about your qualifications. A good reference knows your positive work qualities and values, understands your abilities and interests, and can describe how you behave in a work environment.

Create a reference list to include in your career portfolio, and make sure you have it available to give to employers when they ask. Put your name and contact information at the top, and use the heading "References."

Select at least three people, and ask them for permission to use them as a reference. On the list, include each person's full name, occupation, mailing address, e-mail address, and daytime telephone number.

Some people who make good references include former or current employers, coaches, club advisors, and teachers. A relative or best friend is not usually a good choice for a reference because relatives and friends may not be objective about you and your strengths and weaknesses.

> What message do you think spelling errors in a cover letter sends about your qualifications as an employee?

October 3, 2012

Ms. Helen White
MNO company
4671 Highland Avenue
Palatine, IL 60067

Dear Ms. White,

I am writing in response to the job posting for a human resources assistant that I saw on your Web site. I am enclosing my resume for your review.

For the past two years, I have worked as an account assistant at Employ Action, LLC., an employment agency. In that time, I have learned a great deal about employment options and opportunities. I am a hard worker who is looking for new challenges.

I would welcome the opportunity to speak with you personally about the human resources assistant position. You can contact me by phone or e-mail using the information below.

Thank you for your time and consideration,

Sincerely,

Thomas Leslie

Thomas Leslie
2323 McCloud Street
Palatine, IL 60067
555-555-5555
thomasleslie@mail.net

MONEY MADNE$$

> **C**an you save money by submitting your resume and cover letter electronically? How much does it cost to send a first class letter using the U.S. Postal Service? How many resumes are you going to send out?
>
> Say it costs 52 cents for each resume, and you plan to send out 20 resumes. How much will it cost? What if you send out 55 resumes? Write a paragraph explaining why the cost of mailing a resume and cover letter is worth it, or not, and what alternative methods of delivery you might use instead.

Discuss

Explain that employers highly regard the cover letter as a good measure of the applicant's ability to express thoughts in writing. In addition, the use of appropriate grammar, correct spelling, and neat formatting demonstrates a candidate's attention to detail and willingness to invest time and energy to make a good first impression.

Figure Focus

Explain that typos and poor formatting signal an applicant who failed to take the time to make a good impression. Ask students to identify negative character traits that you might associate with a person who fails to take the time to do something right. These include laziness, disinterest, lack of enthusiasm, and apathy.

MONEY MADNE$$

If you send out 20 resumes at 52 cents each, the cost would be:

$0.52 \times 20 = 10.40.

To send out 55 resumes, the cost would be:

$0.52 \times 55 = 28.60

When you send your resume and cover letter by mail, you can see how they will look to the employer. It shows the employer that you took the time and made the effort to create and print the documents. Some employers request that resumes be sent electronically only, or by mail only. You should always do what the employer requests. Delivering the resume electronically saves the postage and the printing costs.

Customized Instruction: Less Advanced/Special Needs Students

Make a copy of the cover letter shown on this page for each student. Using a different color pencil or marker for each item, have them underline the following:

- Job title for the job the applicant is seeking. (*human resources assistant*)
- Where the applicant learned about the position. (*Web site*)
- List of the skills that qualify the applicant for the position. (*account assistant at an employment agency; "learned a great deal about employment options and opportunities"*)
- Thank you to the reader for her time and consideration. (*"Thank you for your time and consideration"*)

Introduce the Section

This section provides helpful tips on designing, writing, and formatting a resume.

Vocabulary

Resume: Document that summarizes you, your skills, and your abilities; statement of who you are, what you have done in your life, and what you hope to do next.

Templates: Sample documents.

Figure Focus

Ask students to explain what they think "snapshot image of your qualifications" means. "Snapshot image" implies that a resume captures in brief your qualifications, skills, and abilities. Explain that it's not uncommon for an employer to spend less than a minute reading a resume. In fact, if an employer has dozens of resumes to review, you can bet the ones that are long and overcrowded get tossed without much more than a glance. Explain the importance of being clear and concise and avoiding superfluous information. Remind students that it's a resume, not an autobiography.

Discuss

You might discuss with students some tips on sending resumes via e-mail.

- If you are responding to an advertisement, follow any special instructions for addressing the e-mail. For example, the employer might specify you use the job title or job code in the subject line. If you are "cold calling," briefly state your objective in the subject line.

- The body of the e-mail should be a brief cover letter that introduces you and describes how you meet the needs of the employer.

- Include your resume in the body of the e-mail message instead of as an attachment. Otherwise, the person may decide not to open the attachment and your chance to make contact is gone. Also, some e-mail systems reject messages with attachments, so this will eliminate that risk.

- Make sure your resume is formatted for e-mail. It might look different on someone else's screen than it does on yours, so play it safe and use shorter text lines and adequate spacing between sections.

Preparing a Resume

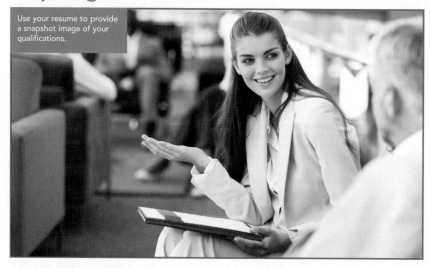

Use your resume to provide a snapshot image of your qualifications.

A resume is a document that summarizes you, your skills, and your abilities. It is a statement of who you are, what you have done in your life, and what you hope to do next. Your resume may be the first communication between you and a potential employer. You will make a positive impression if your resume is:

- Neatly printed on white paper
- True and accurate
- Free of any typographical, grammatical, or spelling errors
- Direct and to the point

You want your resume to describe you in a way that makes the employer want to meet you. A well written resume will help you to get an interview.

How Should I Format My Resume?

There are many ways to organize or format a resume. Most word processing programs come with resume **templates**—sample documents. You can also find sample resume designs in books and on the Internet.

Choose a format that highlights your experience and skills so they stand out to someone who might just glance at the resume quickly. Other factors to consider include:

- Make it easy to read. Leave space between lines so it is not crowded or overloaded.
- Use one font, and apply different font styles and sizes for emphasis.
- Bullets are effective for making lines of text stand out.
- Use proper spelling, punctuation, and grammar.
- Keep it to one page, if possible; two pages at the most. (If you use two pages, be sure to put your name in the header or footer on page 2, in case it becomes separated from page 1.)

Sometimes you will mail your resume in an envelope with a cover letter. Sometimes you will send it electronically by e-mail. Make sure it looks professional when it is printed, and when you view it on a computer.

Customized Instruction: At-Risk Students

Tell students to think of a resume as a personal brochure. Using an 8½- by 11-inch piece of plain white paper folded in half, have them create a brochure about themselves. They can draw pictures or write about themselves or both. They should focus on their academic, community, and employment-related activities; for example, the subjects they take in school and their achievements in those subjects, extracurricular or volunteer activities, and any part-time jobs they've had. The front page or cover should include their name, address, and contact information. The inside should include their personal information, and the back can include names of important people in their lives.

What to Include on Your Resume

A typical resume has four main sections.

- *Contact information.* Include your full name, address, telephone number, and e-mail address at the top of the page. This gives the employer all the information necessary to get in touch with you.

- *Objective.* An objective describes your career goal. It should be short and clear. You can have a general, long-term goal as your objective, or you can customize your resume for a specific position by using a short-term goal. For example, a general objective might be "*To work in fashion sales.*" A customized objective might be "*To work as a part-time sales associate in a fashion clothing store.*"

- *Education.* If you have little work experience, it is important to highlight your education. List the name, city, and state of every school where you earned a degree, starting with high school (or the last school you attended). Include the years you attended the school, the degree you earned, and any special courses or certificates that relate to your career. You might want to include your grade point average, as well.

- *Work experience.* Include all full-time and part-time jobs, internships, apprenticeships, and volunteer experience, starting with the most recent experience first. Include employment dates, job titles, company names, city, and state. Briefly describe your main responsibility, and list your duties and accomplishments. Be specific. If you have work experience, you might want to put this section before Education.

You may also include a Skills section for listing jobs skills such as your ability to use computers or speak a foreign language. You might also want to include Personal Information, such as extracurricular activities, awards, and honors. You can list all clubs and organizations of which you are a member, and things you do in your school or community.

Use Action Words!

Action words are verbs that describe your actions in a way that makes them stand out to the reader. When you use action words to describe your responsibilities and skills in a cover letter or on your resume, it will bring your actions to life.

- Instead of *Made lunch,* try *Cooked healthy lunches for 50 people.*
- Instead of *Filed papers,* use *Organized customer files alphabetically.*
- Instead of *Took pictures,* try *Photographed school events and functions for use on Web site and in newspaper.*
- Instead of *Know CPR,* try *Certified by the American Red Cross in cardiopulmonary resuscitation (CPR).*

> Why do you think it is important to include extracurricular activities on your resume?

Clyde Duggan
2556 Granger Avenue
Palatine, IL 60067
(555) 555-5555
clydeduggan@mail.net

Objective	To work as a part-time sales associate in a fashion clothing store.
Education	Currently enrolled in Wickham High School; expect to graduate in June 2013.
Work Experience	
9/10–present	Fashion consultant, HH Shelter for Women and Children, Palatine, IL • Select and coordinate outfits for women preparing for job interviews.
5/09	Fashion show organizer, Wickham High School, Palatine, IL • Proposed, planned, and managed fashion show of student designs to raise funds for the HH Shelter for Women and Children.
Skills	• Sewing • Clothing coordination and fit • Basic math skills • Fluent in Spanish
Extracurricular Activities	Family, Career and Community Leaders of America (FCCLA); member since 2008; chapter treasurer 2010–present

---

Other Action Words to Consider

Use a thesaurus—reference book of definitions and synonyms—to find action words to replace common verbs, such as go, have, or get. Some attention-getting action words for resumes include:

✔ Created	✔ Operated
✔ Supervised	✔ Prepared
✔ Built	✔ Produced
✔ Published	✔ Planned
✔ Coached	✔ Improved

Figure Focus

Explain that employers look for a number of skills and experiences in a job applicant no matter what the industry or job. These include time management, loyalty, honesty, responsibility, and the ability to work on a team. Being involved in extracurricular activities typically indicates that a student is motivated, can work successfully as part of a team, and has the desire to learn and achieve more. To the potential employer, this type of involvement is a strong indication that a candidate possesses basic workplace skills.

Other Action Words to Consider

Have students suggest sentences that use each of the words listed in the text. These should be sentences that might go on a resume. Write the sentences on the board, underlining the action word used. Ask if there is a better word that could be used instead.

Students will gather and organize information to be included in their resume. Give each student eight index cards or sheets of paper. They should title each with the following headings and then fill in the appropriate information:

- **Personal.** Include name, address, phone, and e-mail address.

- **Education.** List names and locations of schools from which you graduated or are currently enrolled, along with dates attended, diploma or degree earned, and any special courses or certificates you received.

- **Activities.** List all extracurricular and volunteer or community activities in which you are involved.

- **Interests.** List hobbies or personal interests.

- **Work Experience.** Include all part-time and full-time jobs you have held, including the name of the employer, the dates you were employed, your position, and your duties.

- **Honors and Awards.** These include academic, athletic, and other awards you have received.

- **Skills and Abilities.** List job-related skills and abilities.

- **References.** List the name, job title, employer name, and contact information for job references.

Have students use the resume shown in the text as an example. Using the information they gathered in the activity above, have them create their resume. For the objective, they can enter one or two sentences that describe their career goal, or they can leave it blank and customize it for specific jobs. Their goal should be a one-page resume, with references listed on a separate sheet. *Note:* Students are asked to create their resume, cover letter, and list of references in the *Write Now* activity at the end of this chapter.

Introduce the Section

This section explores the job application process and explains how a successful application leads to the job interview.

Vocabulary

Candidate: Possible employee.

Figure Focus

Explain to students that a job application is a form document that employers use for two reasons.

1. To find out information about you, your education, and your work experience.
2. To determine your ability to follow directions, work neatly, spell correctly, and provide accurate and complete data.

Ask students for a show of hands of those who have completed a job application. Have them share with the class the types of questions that were asked and the information they supplied. Were they able to supply everything they needed? Was there any additional information they wished they had brought with them?

Applying for a Job

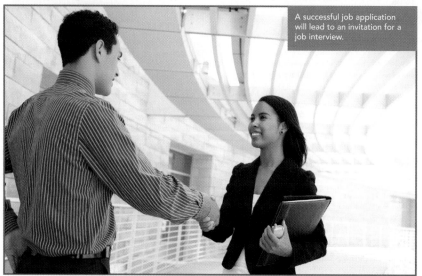

A successful job application will lead to an invitation for a job interview.

When you find a job you think you want, you apply for it. Applying means that you present yourself as a **candidate**—possible employee—for the position. Applying usually starts with sending in your resume and a cover letter. Sometimes you can improve your chances of landing an interview by applying in person.

- In a small company, that means speaking directly with the owner or manager. For example, if you are applying for a position in a local restaurant, you would speak with the manager.
- In a large company, applying in person might mean going to the human resources department. Employees in the human resources department often meet job applicants first to decide whether they meet the qualifications for the position.

Be sure to bring a few copies of your resume and reference list to hand out when you apply in person. Also, ask for business cards from the people you meet so you know how to contact them.

Tips for Applying

When you apply for a job, your short-term goal is to get invited for an interview. There are a few things you can do to improve your chances and to make your application stand out from the crowd.

- Use a professional e-mail address. A cutesy address such as suzieq, lonewolf, daredevil, or wildgrrl828 is not likely to impress a potential employer.
- Even when you are asked to fill out a standard job application form, submit a resume as well.
- Be polite and professional to everyone you meet. Whether you apply in person or are speaking on the phone, be courteous and respectful to everyone.
- When you submit a resume online, ask whether you must use a specific format. Some companies want resumes in plain text format, others accept files created using a word processing program.
- Customize your resume for a specific job. You can customize the objective, or rearrange your experience and skills to highlight the information you think is most appropriate for the position.

Stay in School

Explain to students that it is very common for an employer to get hundreds of applications for a single job. For example, one school system reported receiving 700 applications for a single janitorial position! If you're a high school dropout, how would your application, along with your other job search materials, stand out among those submitted by high school graduates?

- Do you have the writing skills to write a cover letter and resume?
- Do you have the reading skills to properly fill in an application?
- Do you have letters of recommendation, certificates of achievement, awards, and samples to present in a portfolio?
- Do you have the math skills to compute pay and benefits?
- Do you have technology skills to fill out applications and send materials electronically?
- Do you have a list of former employers, teachers, coaches, or community leaders who will give you a good job reference?

High school dropouts will find it difficult to make their job search materials stand out in today's competitive job market. Furthermore, some employers won't even let you fill out an application if you don't have a high school diploma.

Filling out a Job Application

A **job application** is a standard form you will fill out when you apply for a job. You might fill it out in person when you visit a potential employer, or you might fill it out online. It requires a lot of the same information that you put on your resume, such as your contact information, as well as details about your education and work experience. It may ask for your Social Security number.

Filling out an application form may seem simple, but a lot of people make mistakes, or forget important information. A messy or incomplete job application will not make a positive impression on the employer.

- Read the form before you start filling it out.
- Follow all instructions.
- Be truthful and accurate.
- Write neatly.
- Enter N/A for not applicable if there is a question that does not apply to you.
- Check your spelling and grammar.
- If you make a mistake, ask for a new form and start again.

You might find it helpful to bring a personal information card with you when you apply for a job. A personal information card is an index card on which you write the information you might need, such as your Social Security number and the contact information for your past employers.

So That's Why I Have a Career Portfolio!

You can use the documents you have in your career portfolio to help fill out a job application. Your resume includes facts you will need about your previous employers. Your reference list includes the names and contact information of your references.

If you do not want to bring your entire career portfolio with you, write key facts on index cards, or print this information on a piece of paper:

- Your Social Security number
- The names and addresses of your previous employers, including dates, and the amount you were paid
- The names and addresses of schools where you earned a degree, including dates
- The names and addresses of your references

"Oh, no! I can't remember my Social Security number! What should I do?"

TECH CONNECT

Careers in the field of technology range from software programming and game development to hardware installation and maintenance.

However, almost every job in every field requires experience with technology. Office workers use computer applications to create business documents, databases, and spreadsheets. Graphic designers use programs to create artwork. Even jobs such as construction or animal care benefit from an understanding of how to use technology to communicate with others, plan a schedule, and store customer information.

How are your technology skills? Do you have experience keyboarding? Have you used a presentation graphics program? Do you know how to write a program, install an app on a cell phone, or add memory to your PC? Make a list of your technology skills and experience. Write a paragraph explaining how these skills and experience might be useful at work.

What's Important About a Business Card?

A business card lists contact information such as name, title, phone number, and e-mail address. What if you attend a job fair and meet representatives from 10 companies? If you collect business cards, you can:

★ *Contact each representative using the correct title and address.*

★ *Copy the information from each business card into an electronic database or contact manager.*

★ *File the business cards in a business card organizer for future use.*

★ *Write notes on the card to help you remember details about the people you meet.*

What problems might arise if you forget to collect business cards from contacts that you meet?

Vocabulary

Application: Standard form you fill out when you apply for a job.

What's Important About a Business Card?

Students are to comment on problems that might arise if you forget to collect business cards from contacts. The most obvious is that you might not remember how to contact the person. Second, you will have to rely on your memory for the correct spelling and accuracy of the contact's information. Business cards are particularly useful to pick up at job fairs. A job fair allows you to meet with representatives from a variety of companies—sometimes hundreds of them. Most representatives provide information about the company and its job opportunities, along with their business card. As you collect cards, you might jot notes on them to remind you of your initial reaction to the representative, what he or she looked like, any special topics you discussed, or anything else that will help you remember the meeting.

Figure Focus

Discuss the idea of providing a Social Security number on a job application. Identity theft is a much-talked-about crime, and most employers are aware of the concerns that people now have about sharing their Social Security numbers. Often, the employer will wait until an individual is hired before requesting the information. If an application requests your Social Security number and you are uncertain about sharing the information, you might write in that it is available upon a job offer.

TECH CONNECT

Students are to list their technology skills and experience and write a paragraph explaining how these skills and experience might be useful at work. In addition to the skills listed in the text, students might be experienced in online research, word processing, graphic design, and working with digital photographs.

Introduce the Section

In this section, students learn how to prepare for a job interview and how to conduct themselves during an interview. The importance of follow-up is also discussed.

Figure Focus

Ask students what factors about a job might make them decide it is not right for them. For example, does the work schedule interfere with school and other responsibilities? Are the job duties different from what you expected? Is the pay lower than you can afford to work for? Does it require that you put in time with no pay for training or that you buy your own uniform?

Telephone Interviews

Suggest the following tips for phone interviews:

- If the call comes in at an inconvenient time, ask if you can set up the interview for another time. Do not try to conduct the interview while you are driving or in a noisy, public setting. Make sure you get the caller's name and phone number and the date and time for the callback.

- Keep your resume and cover letter handy so you can "follow along." The person calling will most likely have them in front of him or her as well. You should also have paper and pen for taking notes.

- If you have call-waiting, turn it off. Also, consider using a land line if you have concerns about losing callers on your cell phone. Turn off your cell phone if you are not using it.

- Conduct the interview in a quiet place, with no stereo or television noise.

- Don't eat, drink, or chew gum while you're on the phone.

- Speak slowly and clearly and do not use slang.

- Do not call the person by a first name unless he or she asks you to.

- When the interview comes to an end, thank the interviewer and ask what the next step in the process will be.

Interviewing for a Job

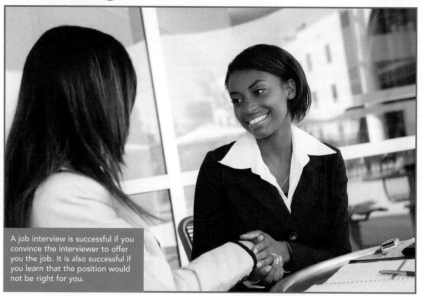

A job interview is successful if you convince the interviewer to offer you the job. It is also successful if you learn that the position would not be right for you.

What happens when an employer reads your cover letter and resume and thinks you have the qualifications she is looking for? She invites you for a job interview. A job interview is a meeting between a job seeker and a potential employer—the interviewer. A job interview helps you and the interviewer make important decisions:

- The interviewer decides if the job seeker is the best person for the position.
- You decide if the position is one you really want.

Both you and the interviewer can use the job interview to get to know each other. You learn information that you cannot learn from a cover letter or resume. For example, the interviewer learns whether or not you make eye contact. You learn if people at the company are friendly.

Telephone Interviews

Many companies use telephone interviews to *screen*—make a first decision about—potential employees. They might be interested in you based on your cover letter and resume, but want to see how you present yourself during a conversation before they invite you for a face-to-face interview.

- Some employers will call or e-mail to schedule a telephone interview. Then, you can prepare for the call the same way you would prepare for a face-to-face interview (see the next page).
- Some employers will call out of the blue. This lets them learn how well you handle stress, and if you are able to communicate effectively without preparation.

You can prepare for surprise calls by practicing with a friend or relative. You can also make sure you are always prepared to talk about a company you apply to, the position, and yourself.

Customized Instruction: Less Advanced/More Advanced Students

Think of a job in your classroom that all students would be qualified to do; for example, teacher assistant or classroom maintenance manager. Briefly describe the job duties to students. Have a less advanced student pair up with a more advanced student. They should prepare a list of questions that an interviewer would ask an applicant for the job. When they are done, have them role-play the interview for the class.

Preparing for a Job Interview

A test is always easier if you are prepared. A job interview is like a test—if you pass, you are offered the job. Use these four steps to prepare for a job interview.

1. *Research the company or organization where you are going for the interview.* Talk to someone who works there. Visit the company's Web site.
2. *Make a list of questions an interviewer might ask you.* Common questions include, "Tell me about yourself.", "Why do you want to work here?", "Do you have the skills to get the work done?", and "Why should I hire you?".
3. *Prepare answers to the questions.* Be specific. Emphasize your strengths, skills, and abilities. Explain how you solved a problem, made an important decision, or showed responsibility. Mention your goals, and how you plan to achieve them.
4. *Make a list of five to ten questions you can ask the interviewer.* Ask about the company, the work environment, and the position. Common questions include "What kinds of projects or tasks will I be responsible for?", "Is there opportunity for advancement?", "What are the hours?", "What is the salary range?", and "When will you make a hiring decision?".

> How can practicing for an interview help you perform better in an actual interview?

Practicing for a Job Interview

A job interview is stressful. You are trying to make a good impression. You want to look and sound your best. You want the interviewer to like you and to respect you. Practicing for the interview by rehearsing your behavior and answers to questions helps give you confidence.

Working with a partner is probably the best way to practice. You can take turns being the interviewer and the job seeker. If you are alone, practice in front of a mirror. If possible, record your practice so you can watch yourself.

Test **IT** Yourself!

Does practicing really make a difference in your ability to answer questions? Conduct an experiment to find out:

1. Think of ten questions, type them in a word processor, and print six copies. Start with easy questions, such as "When is your birthday?", and progress to questions that require more and more thought, such as "What is your favorite color?", "When is your mother's birthday?", or "On what continent is the country of France?".
2. Assemble 10 volunteers and split them into two groups.
3. Give the list of questions to the five volunteers in the first group (keep one copy for yourself).
4. One at a time, out of earshot of the others, ask each volunteer in the second group—the group that has not seen the questions—each question. Rate how quickly and accurately they answer each question on a scale of 1 to 10, with 10 being the best.
5. One at a time, out of earshot of the others, ask each volunteer in the first group to answer each question. Rate their responses based on speed and accuracy.
6. Analyze the results. Which group ranked higher in terms of how quickly and accurately they answered the questions? Did the group who had a chance to prepare do better?
7. Write a paragraph explaining the results. Use a chart or graph to illustrate your results.

Tips for Practicing for a Job Interview

Practicing your interview will help you feel comfortable and prepared. Use the time to rehearse your words and actions for the actual interview. Here are some tips for practicing:

✔ *Be truthful.*

✔ *Pronounce your words in a strong, clear voice.*

✔ *Keep your answers brief and to the point.*

✔ *Use positive nonverbal communication, such as eye contact, relaxed arms, and good posture.*

✔ *Dress as you would for an actual interview.*

✔ *Avoid fidgeting or playing with your hair.*

✔ *Ask someone to critique your interviewing skills and use their comments to improve your technique.*

Discuss

Discuss further the four steps to prepare for a job interview.

1. Explain the importance of making yourself familiar with the company and its business as well as its competitors. Know the industry buzzwords, and research general trends that are affecting the industry. You should also have an understanding of the company's structure. Does it have one office, or many? What are the main departments? Who is the president of the company and the manager of the department for which you would be working? Who would you be reporting to?

2. In addition to the questions in the text, you might be asked about previous employers listed on your resume. Some questions include, "Why did you leave?" "What did you like or dislike about the job?" "What was your biggest accomplishment?" "What do you expect from a supervisor?"

3. Be specific in your answers to questions. It is also important to give actual examples that demonstrate your skills and abilities.

4. In addition to those questions in the text, you might also ask why the position is open, how long it has existed, how many people have held it in the last year or two, what specific projects or assignments you will be working on, and what the work environment is like.

Figure Focus

As with any activity or task, practicing will help you perform better. You will learn how to anticipate typical interview questions, how to react to questions on which you are unsure how to answer, and how to effectively present and express yourself.

Tips for Practicing for a Job Interview

Review with students how context can affect their communication with an interviewer. Context refers to the tone, facial expressions, and body language that accompany verbal communication. Suggest that students practice for a job interview in front of a mirror. They should watch for posturing, facial expressions, and hand and arm movements. They should listen for tone and instances where they tend to use slang; for example, many people use "you know" or "like" as a transition from one sentence to another.

Test **IT** Yourself!

Have students conduct the experiment in class. For their charts, they will probably find a column chart most useful in illustrating the test results, with the question numbers along the horizontal axis and the rating scale on the vertical axis. See the example below.

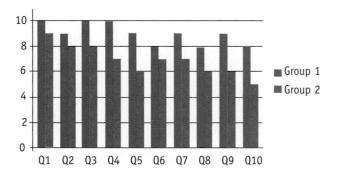

Looking Your Best for an Interview

Review with students the factors that demonstrate a positive attitude and contribute to a good first impression.

- Making eye contact.
- Neat, clean appearance.
- Good posture, both standing and sitting.
- Smiling and shaking hands.

Myth/Truth

Students should understand that the type of job and the employer's line of business will greatly influence the types of questions you are asked in an interview. For example, the manager at a fast-food restaurant might ask you questions regarding your familiarity with cooking equipment and food service operations, whereas the manager at the local swimming pool might ask you questions regarding your swimming skills and ability to work under pressure.

Figure Focus

Ask students what their next step would be in either scenario. If you get the job, your first step might be to ask for the offer in writing, along with a description of benefits, start date, schedule, and job duties. If you don't get the job, your first step might be writing a note thanking them for the opportunity, or you might want to find out the reason why you weren't selected.

Looking Your Best for an Interview

Some tips for presenting a professional appearance:

✔ Wash, dry, and comb your hair.

✔ Trim and clean your fingernails.

✔ Use deodorant.

✔ Brush your teeth.

✔ Avoid products such as perfume or body spray that have a strong odor.

✔ Wear small, neat jewelry.

✔ Wear clean, neat clothes that are appropriate for the work environment.

✔ Avoid bright or contrasting colors that might distract the employer.

✔ Avoid revealing too much skin.

✔ Arrive early enough so you have time to visit the restroom to check your appearance and freshen up.

Myth Interviewers all ask the same questions.

Truth Most interviewers ask questions that relate to the job opening, the company, and the individual candidate. A good interviewer will know how to ask questions that encourage you to describe your own strengths and weaknesses.

Making the Most of the Job Interview

Many interviews are 10–15 minutes long. How can you best use that time to get a job offer?

- Dress neatly and professionally. Your clothes should be clean and appropriate for the workplace.
- Be clean. Comb your hair, brush your teeth, and wear deodorant. Avoid using body products that have a strong odor.
- Arrive ten minutes early.
- Be polite and respectful to everyone you meet.
- Shake hands with your interviewer.
- Listen carefully, using positive body language. For example, smile and lean forward slightly when the interviewer is talking.
- Use proper English when you speak; no slang.
- Avoid chewing gum, cell phone calls, and texting.
- At the end of the interview, shake hands again, and thank the interviewer. Ask for a business card, so you have the interviewer's contact information.

A neat appearance, positive attitude, and confidence will make a good impression. In fact, studies show that interviewers judge job seekers first by appearance, next by behavior, and third by what they say.

After the Interview

The interview is over. Now what? Start by writing a thank-you note.

A thank-you note reminds the interviewer that you are serious about wanting the job. You can use a thank-you note to restate your interest in the job and your qualifications, and to thank the interviewer for spending time with you. Refer to something specific that you discussed during the interview. Address the note to the person who interviewed you—that's why you asked for the business card! Send the note within 24 hours of the interview.

"Wow. I got the job!"

"I didn't get the job. Did I do something wrong?"

Customized Instruction: Less Advanced/Special Needs/At-Risk Students

Have students prepare a "first-impression" checklist for an interview. The checklist should include personal hygiene and what they will wear to an interview. They should also include any materials they will take with them to the interview, such as their resume and portfolio.

What's Taking So Long?

During the interview, you asked how long it would be before the interviewer made a decision. If you do not hear from the interviewer within that timeframe, you can call or send an e-mail. Ask if he or she has made a decision, and say again that you are interested in the position.

Sometimes, one interview leads to another. The first interviewer might like you for the job, but not be authorized to make hiring decisions. Or, he or she wants to see how other employees react to you. Being called back for a second interview is a good thing. It means you passed the first test.

What If You Get the Job?

If you are offered the job, you have reason to celebrate. But, before you accept the offer, make sure you have all the information you need to make the best decision. You should not have to accept or reject the offer immediately. If possible, ask to talk to someone in the human resources department who can explain the company policies to you. For example, you might want to ask:

- What is the salary?
- What benefits—health insurance, vacation time—come with the position?
- When does the job start?
- What are the hours?
- When do you need an answer, because I would like to put thought into my decision?

Do not automatically turn down the offer if the salary and benefits are lower than you expected. You may be able to negotiate—reach a compromise—with the employer (see the next section, *Examining Employment Needs*). When you have all the information you need, use the decision-making process to decide whether to accept the position or not.

- If you accept the offer, thank the employer and ask when and where you should report to work. You may have to sign a formal letter of acceptance.
- If you reject the offer, thank the employer anyway.

What If You Do Not Get the Job?

If you do not get a job offer, it is okay to be disappointed. It will be very helpful if the interviewer can explain why you were not selected for the job. When you are feeling calm:

- Call the interviewer and politely ask what you could have done differently to get the job.
- Listen carefully—take notes, even. The information will help you succeed at your next interview.
- Say thank you at the end.
- Ask the interviewer to keep you in mind for other opportunities.

Some interviewers will not want to talk to you. Do not be discouraged. Remind yourself that the interviewer thought highly enough of you to invite you for an interview. Sooner or later, you will find the right position, and you will get the job.

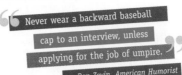
> Never wear a backward baseball cap to an interview, unless applying for the job of umpire.
> — *Dan Zevin, American Humorist*

I Thought It Went Well, But...

You showed up on time. Your hair was neat. Your tie was clean. But, you didn't get the job. You asked the interviewer why. She said you came across as uninterested. What actions might affect an interviewer's opinion of you?

👎 You don't shake hands.

👎 Your cell phone buzzes during the interview.

👎 You are chewing gum.

👎 You don't make eye contact.

👎 You ask no questions.

👍 You are knowledgeable about the company.

👍 You ask lots of questions.

👍 You smile and lean forward to listen when the interviewer talks.

👍 You follow up immediately with a thank-you note.

How can you use the information an interviewer gives you about your behavior during an interview to improve your chances of getting a job offer in the future?

"Quote Box"

Ask students what they think the quote from Dan Zevin means. Most people understand it to mean that you should dress appropriately for the position that you are applying for. For example, if you're applying for a job as a data entry clerk, don't wear low-rise pants, a belly-baring midriff, and flip-flops. On the other hand, this attire might be appropriate if you're applying for a job as a salesperson at a retail store that sells that type of clothing.

I Thought It Went Well, But...

Discuss again with students the importance of a positive attitude and making a good first impression. Some studies indicate that an interviewer's impression of an interviewee is influenced most by the way they act in the interview rather than what they say. So, knowing that, you should pay special attention to your body language, tone of voice, posturing, and general attitude when you go to future job interviews.

Customized Instruction: ESOL Students

Pair up students and have them prepare a list of questions they would ask someone who wants the job of translator in the student's primary language. Some of the questions they might ask include:

- Are you a native speaker of the language?
- Are you familiar with the culture of the native country?
- Do you have experience in being a translator?
- What writing and language courses have you taken?
- Are you a member of any professional or translation-related clubs, associations, or organizations?
- What experience do you have dealing with people from other cultures?

Once they have completed their list of questions, have them role-play the parts of interviewer and interviewee.

Introduce the Section

Employee compensation, benefits, and other needs are all part of the job package. Before you accept a job, you need to ensure your needs and expectations will be met.

Vocabulary

Benefits: Things other than wages that have value.

Compensation: Wage and benefits paid by an employer to employees.

Subsidy: Cash payment toward a specific work-related need.

Figure Focus

Ask students how they define work needs, other than compensation. For example, do you need to limit the number of hours you work on school days? Do you need time off for a planned vacation? Do you need a certain type of chair to help alleviate back pain? Make sure students understand that their specific work needs are not always the same as the benefits provided by their employer. For example, you might need a week off for a planned vacation, but your employer might not provide you with the benefit of a *paid* vacation.

Discuss

The benefits offered by employers vary widely. Explain to students that employers offer benefits as a way to attract employees and then to retain and motivate them. Employers generally provide benefits at no or low cost to employees. Otherwise, many employees would have to do without them because they can be very costly to the individual. At some companies, benefits can comprise 35 to 40 percent of a worker's annual compensation. That means that if your annual salary is $40,000, the value of the benefits you receive represents an additional $15,000 or so. Discuss some of the more common benefits offered by employers.

- **Time benefits.** Includes paid vacation, sick leave, personal days, and holidays.

- **Family and Medical Leave Act.** This applies to employers with 50 or more employees within a 75-mile radius, and provides for up to 12 weeks of unpaid time off annually to care for a child, ill family member, or one's own illness.

- **Health insurance.** Provides employees with insurance to protect them from the high cost of health care. In addition to medical, these plans might also include dental insurance, counseling and mental health benefits, vision care, and a prescription drug plan.

Examining Employment Needs

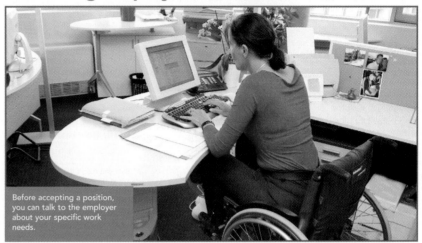

Before accepting a position, you can talk to the employer about your specific work needs.

Recall that needs are things you require. Employment needs are the things you require to be successful in your job. When you receive the job offer you have been working for, it's time to think about your employment needs. Employment needs range from compensation—wages and benefits—to recognition; from training to accommodations for disabilities.

Employers provide compensation to employees in exchange for work. You may be satisfied with the first offer from the employer. It may meet your requirements. However, if you believe that the company could pay more, or offer different benefits or accommodations, knowing how to negotiate for the things you need will help you make sure the exchange is fair.

What Are Benefits?

Benefits are things other than wages that have value. Most companies offer some type of benefits, although smaller companies may not. Some benefits, such as unemployment insurance, are required by law. Some types of benefits include:

- Health insurance
- Retirement plan
- Life insurance
- Vacation time
- Disability insurance
- Education benefit to pay tuition for work-related classes

Some companies offer benefits in the form of a **subsidy**, which is a cash payment toward a specific work-related need. For example, a company might offer a child- or elder-care subsidy to use to pay a caregiver, or a transportation subsidy to use for travel or parking expenses.

There is a trend toward flexible—or cafeteria style— benefits. With flexible benefits, an employee can choose the benefits that are appropriate. For example, a single adult might choose an education benefit instead of a child-care benefit.

- **Child/elder care benefits.** Some employers provide benefits for child care and/or the care of an elderly person.

- **Employee discounts.** Many employers offer free or reduced cost on their products or services; for example, stores and restaurants provide discounted or free products to employees, and airlines might offer free travel.

- **Wellness benefits.** These include free or low-cost check-ups and immunizations, screening tests, or an on-site fitness center or program.

- **401(k) plan.** Many employers provide retirement benefits such as a 401(k) plan in which employers often match employee contributions by a specified percentage.

- **Employee assistance programs.** Some employers provide assistance and counseling on retirement planning, personal finance, and crisis management.

- **Flex-time and telecommuting.** Some employers allow for flexible work arrangements to accommodate working parents.

How to Negotiate Your Compensation

Negotiating is a bit like problem solving. The employer makes you an offer. You point out the things about the offer that you think are problems. You work together to find solutions that make you both happy.

For example, you might think the salary is too low. Your employer might not be able to offer you more money, but maybe he can offer a benefit that has value to you, such as free parking, or a flexible schedule. Or, he may be able to offer you a raise if you meet expectations for three months.

When you negotiate, always be polite and positive. State your goals clearly so your employer knows what you are trying to achieve. Be prepared to compromise. Remember, you want the job.

Do You Need Accommodations?

A disability might get in the way of you performing a task the same way a nondisabled person would. For example, if you use a wheelchair to move around, you might not be able to access a storage room that is down a flight of stairs.

An **accommodation** makes it possible for a disabled employee to perform his or her job responsibilities in a safe and accessible work environment. By law, employers who are aware of an employee's disability must make accommodations, if the accommodations do not impose an extreme hardship on the business. (See the next section for more about employment laws.) Tell your employer if you need an accommodation to do your job. Not all disabilities are visible—your employer may not know that you have one.

Negotiating is like problem solving. How can you use the problem-solving process to negotiate employment needs?

NUMBERS GAME

Some salespeople are paid a commission in addition to or in place of a salary. A **commission** is a payment calculated as a percentage of total sales. Earning a commission encourages sales people to sell more, because the more they sell, the more they earn.

Commonly, expensive items such as cars, boats, recreational vehicles, houses, and furniture are sold on commission.

If you are a real estate agent earning a 7% commission, how much would you earn by selling a house for $195,000.00?

Multiply $195,000.00 by 7%: $195,000.00 × .07 = $13,650

What if you sell a house for $242,900.00?

What if you sell cars and earn 8% on your total monthly sales. In one month, you sell one car for $13,955.00, one for $15,495.00, and one for $14,455.00. How much commission will you earn for that month?

Typical Accommodations

Examples of accommodations include:

✔ Making nonwork areas such as cafeterias and lounges accessible by installing wheelchair ramps or elevators

✔ Modifying work schedules

✔ Replacing equipment

✔ Changing exams, training materials, or policies

✔ Providing sign-language interpreters for the hearing impaired

Vocabulary

Accommodation: Modification to a physical space or object that makes it possible for a disabled employee to perform his or her job responsibilities in a safe and accessible work environment.

Commission: Payment calculated as a percentage of total sales.

Figure Focus

Explain that when you negotiate, you attempt to come to an agreement on something through discussion and compromise. You and the other party determine how to get past or deal with something that constitutes an obstacle. You can use the problem-solving process to: 1) identify the obstacle or the point of contention between you and the employer; 2) consider all options from both your point of view and the employer's; 3) identify the consequences or ramifications of each option; 4) select the best option; and 5) determine how to execute the solution.

Typical Accommodations

Ask students to consider any accommodations that have been made in their classroom and school for disabled employees and students.

NUMBERS GAME

If necessary, refer students to the "Working with Decimals and Percentages" section on page 557 of *Appendix E: Math Review*. To determine the commission on a home sale of $242,900:

$242,900.00 × .07 = $17,000.03.

To determine 8% commission on a month's car sales, first add up the sales:

$13,955 + $15,495 + $14,455 = $43,905. Then, multiply that by 8%:

$43,905 × .08 = $3,512.40

Customized Instruction: Special Needs Students

Have students refer back to the career self-assessment they did in Chapter 15. In the preferred careers or specific jobs they identified, ask them to discuss what accommodations they would provide if they were the employer hiring an employee like them.

Introduce the Section

Many laws and regulations are in place to protect a worker's rights and responsibilities. This section provides an overview of the major laws designed to protect employees.

Vocabulary

Fair Labor Standards Act (FLSA): Government regulation that sets the rules for workers under the age of 18.

Figure Focus

You might discuss with students some of your rights and responsibilities as a teacher. In addition, explain that basic employee rights include:

■ The right not to be discriminated against because of your race, national origin, skin color, gender, pregnancy, religious beliefs, disability, or age (and in some places, marital status, sexual orientation, gender identity, or other characteristics).

■ The right to a workplace free of harassment.

■ The right to fair pay (at least the minimum wage, plus an overtime premium for any hours worked over 40 in one week or, in some places, over eight hours in one day.)

■ The right to a safe workplace.

■ The right to take leave to care for your own or a family member's serious health condition, or following the birth or adoption of a child.

■ The right to some privacy in personal matters.

Youth Labor Laws

You might refer students to the *Web Extra* activity they did on page 221 of Chapter 10 in which they were to research their state's child labor laws.

Analyzing Employment Laws

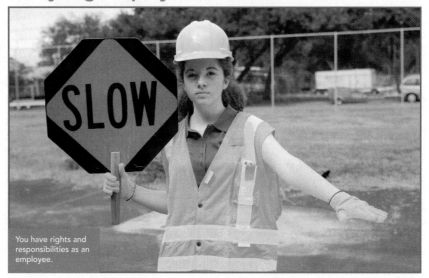

You have rights and responsibilities as an employee.

What would you do if an employer did not pay you for two months? What if an employer expected you to use a dirty bathroom, or work in a building without smoke detectors?

As a worker in the United States, you have rights that are protected by law. Federal and state agencies are responsible for making sure your employer treats you fairly and obeys the law. Your employer is responsible for:

■ Paying you on time
■ Providing you with safe working conditions
■ Allowing you to leave to care for your family
■ Preventing discrimination against you

Understanding your rights as a worker will help you make decisions about where to work, and what type of career to choose. You will also be better prepared to negotiate for your needs.

Youth Labor Laws

The government protects the rights of children as workers. The **Fair Labor Standards Act (FLSA)** sets the rules for workers under the age of 18.

■ An employee must be at least 16 years old to work in most nonfarm jobs and at least 18 to work in nonfarm jobs declared hazardous by the Secretary of Labor.

■ Youths 14 and 15 years old may work outside school hours in various nonmanufacturing, non-mining, nonhazardous jobs under the following conditions:
  ● No more than 3 hours on a school day or 18 hours in a school week
  ● Eight hours on a nonschool day or 40 hours in a nonschool week
  ● Work may not begin before 7 a.m. or end after 7 p.m., except from June 1 through Labor Day, when evening hours are extended to 9 p.m.

Different rules apply for young people working in an agricultural occupation. For more information, visit the YouthRules! Web site at www.youthrules.dol.gov.

The Right to Safe Work

The Occupational Safety and Health Act (OSHA) is the main federal law governing safety at work. As a worker, you have the following rights and responsibilities:

How does the Family and Medical Leave Act promote equal employment opportunities for men and women?

- *Right to know.* You have the right to know about hazards in your workplace, as well as the right to training to learn how to identify workplace hazards and what to do if there is an incident.

- *Right to refuse unsafe work.* If you have reasonable grounds to believe the work you do or the piece of equipment you use is unsafe, you can stop this work immediately. You cannot be laid off, suspended, or penalized for refusing unsafe work if you follow the proper procedures.

- *Responsibility to follow safety rules.* It is your employer's responsibility to teach you the safety rules; it is your responsibility to follow the rules.

- *Responsibility to ask for training.* If you feel that you need more training than your employer provides, it is your responsibility to ask for it.

- *Responsibility to speak up.* It is your responsibility to report incidents and unsafe work practices as well as unsafe conditions.

Other Types of Worker's Protection

Workers with disabilities are protected by the **Americans with Disabilities Act (ADA)**. The ADA prohibits employers from discriminating against qualified individuals with disabilities in all aspects of employment. States also have anti-discrimination laws. Some of the state laws are stronger than the federal laws.

The **Family and Medical Leave Act (FMLA)** provides certain employees with up to 12 weeks of unpaid, job-protected leave per year. The leave must be used for family or medical reasons, such as the birth of new baby or to care for an ailing parent. The law also requires that the employee's health benefits continue during the leave.

According to the government, FMLA is designed to help employees balance their work and family responsibilities. It also promotes equal employment opportunity for men and women.

Who Made Your Sneakers?

Laws protect workers in the United States. Workers in other countries might not be as fortunate.

Many of the pieces of clothing sold in the United States are made in Southeast Asia. In countries such as Thailand and Cambodia, workers have very few rights, and very few opportunities. Sweatshops—unsafe factories—are common. Children as young as 7 may work, and wages for everyone may be very low.

Do you own clothes made in Southeast Asia? How do your own buying habits impact sweatshops in Southeast Asia? How do the sweatshops impact the economy of the United States? Use the Internet or the library to learn more about working conditions in other parts of the world. Write an essay on the topic, "Should We Care About Workers in Other Countries?"

Putting Others at Risk

You have the right to a safe workplace, but you also have responsibilities to do your part to keep yourself, co-workers, and clients safe. How might your actions affect the safety of others?

- 👎 You fail to report a worn-out electrical cord.

- 👎 You do not request training on a new piece of equipment.

- 👎 You do not report that a new co-worker does not know how to use the equipment.

- 👍 You participate in your company's safety committee.

- 👍 You request safety inspections.

- 👍 You keep your safety training current.

What careers do you think have the riskiest work environments? Does risky work appeal to you?

Vocabulary

Americans with Disabilities Act (ADA): Prohibits employers from discriminating against qualified individuals with disabilities in all aspects of employment.

Family and Medical Leave Act (FMLA): Provides certain employees with up to 12 weeks of unpaid, job-protected leave per year. The leave must be used for family or medical reasons, such as the birth of a new baby or to care for an ailing parent.

Figure Focus

History has shown that women have held the main responsibility for taking care of family and that this responsibility has affected the workplace roles of women more than men. Explain that the FMLA was designed to minimize the potential for gender-based employment discrimination by making leave from a job available to both male and female employees.

Putting Others at Risk

Students are asked what careers have the riskiest work environments. You might share the list of the ten most dangerous jobs below from the U.S. Bureau of Labor Statistics:

- Timber cutters
- Fishers
- Pilots and navigators
- Structural metal workers
- Drivers-sales workers
- Roofers
- Electrical power installers
- Farm occupations
- Construction laborers
- Truck drivers

Most of these fall into the Agriculture, Food & Natural Resources; Architecture & Construction; Manufacturing; and Transportation, Distribution & Logistics career clusters.

Who Made Your Sneakers?

Students are to write an essay entitled, "Should We Care About Workers in Other Countries?" You might refer students to *Appendix D: Language Arts: Grammar and Punctuation Basics* beginning on page 539 of the student text for a review of sentence structure, word choice, and other writing tips. Student essays should discuss working conditions in a sampling of countries or regions around the world. They should include a brief explanation on the impact, if any, that U.S. consumption has on these conditions. Their essays should conclude with their opinion on whether or not we should care about workers in other countries.

End-of-Chapter Activities

Case Study

Claude did a good job matching his skills and interests with companies in his area that hire summer interns. He did a good job calling the human resources department to ask about the position. He did a good job by sending in his resume with a cover letter. Claude probably should not have printed his cover letter on yellow paper, or put his picture on his resume. He could have found ways to make his documents stand out by using active verbs, or formatting such as bold, italics, and bullets. He could have contacted the other companies at the same time, instead of limiting his job search to one company.

Now, Claude should learn from his mistakes. He should ask the human resources department why they turned him down. He should contact the other companies to see if they are still accepting applications. He should redo his resume and cover letter. In case Claude is not able to find an internship, he may want to try to identify companies or organizations that are accepting volunteers.

Sounding Off!

1. Equal pay for equal work means that individuals doing the same work should receive the same pay regardless of their sex, race, sexuality, nationality or anything else.

2. Student answers will vary, but in general, they should answer yes, that employees have some responsibility for making their workplace safe. They should follow all company policies regarding safety, and report co-workers who do not. They should participate on safety committees and request safety inspections. They should keep their safety training current.

FAQ

1. Types of job search resources are job fairs, help wanted ads, networking, employment agencies, career counselors, and online resources.
2. Networking in a job search means sharing information about yourself and your career goals with personal contacts—people you know already, or new people you meet in any area of your life.
3. A resume is the most important job search document.
4. The purpose of a cover letter is to introduce you to the employer and highlight your qualifications.
5. The four main sections of a resume are the contact information, objective, education, and work experience. Optional sections include skills and abilities and extracurricular activities.

6. Types of information are your Social Security number, contact information for your references, your contact information, and details about your education and work experience, including dates.
7. Four steps for preparing for a job interview:
   1. Research the company or organization where you are going for the interview.
   2. Make a list of questions an interviewer might ask you.
   3. Prepare answers to the questions.
   4. Make a list of five to ten questions you can ask the interviewer.
8. Things you can do to make a good impression at a job interview include:
   - Dress neatly and professionally.
   - Be clean.
   - Arrive ten minutes early.
   - Be polite and respectful to everyone.

- Shake hands with your interviewer.
- Listen carefully, using positive body language.
- Use proper English when you speak.
- Avoid chewing gum, cell phone calls, and texting.
- At the end of the interview, shake hands again, and thank the interviewer.
- Ask for a business card, so you have the interviewer's contact information.

9. Benefits include health insurance, retirement plan, life insurance, vacation time, disability insurance, education benefit to pay tuition for work-related classes, transportation subsidy, and child/elder care subsidy.
10. An accommodation makes it possible for a disabled employee to perform his or her job responsibilities in a safe and accessible work environment.

326   Chapter 16 ■ Managing a Job Search

Case Study

Claude is hoping to land an internship at a company where he can use his skills in computer programming. He researches companies in his community and identifies five that hire student interns. He picks the one that is closest to his home and calls the human resources department. The assistant tells him to send in a resume and cover letter, along with a school transcript.

Claude wants his application to stand out from those of the other students who apply. He inserts his class photo at the top of his resume. He prints his cover letter on neon yellow paper.

Two weeks after sending in his information, Claude receives a letter telling him that he will not get the internship.

- What do you think Claude did well in his job search?
- What do you think Claude could do to improve his job search?
- What do you think Claude should do next?

Sounding Off!

1. Have you heard the phrase "equal pay for equal work"? What do you think it means? Do you think that there is any instance where unequal pay for equal work happens? Do you think it is right?
2. Do you think employees should be responsible for safety in the workplace?

1. List five types of job search resources.
2. What is networking when searching for a job?
3. What is the most important job search document?
4. What is the purpose of a cover letter?
5. What are the four main sections of a resume?
6. List four types of information you are likely to need to complete a job application.
7. List four steps for preparing for a job interview.
8. What are four things you can do to make a good impression at a job interview?
9. List six types of benefits.
10. What is the purpose of an accommodation in the workplace?

As a class, brainstorm for specific jobs that might be available to students in your community. Divide into teams of four or five. As a team, randomly select one of the jobs. Set a timeframe, such as one week. Using a variety of job search resources, locate as many openings for the selected job as you can, within the set timeframe. For example, you might find classified advertisements, or online listings, or you might know someone in the business who is hiring. Keep a record of every resource you use. At the end of the timeframe, compare the results of each team. The team with the most job leads wins.

Hot Topics

Are you concerned that you have a disability that might interfere with achieving your career goals?

Take this opportunity to write anonymously about your concerns. Be specific about why you think disability might be an issue. Use a word processor so no one recognizes your handwriting. Be honest and open. Put the paper in the class Hot Topics box.

As a class, read the anonymous entries and discuss them.

There are Web sites for teens that provide useful information about managing a job search. For example, www.gotajob.com has a section on resume-writing tips and links to sample cover letters.

Use the Internet to identify the sites that you think might be the most useful for your peers. Make a directory of the sites, including the Web site address, a brief description, and whether the site is free or has a fee. Post the directory on your school Web site or in your school career center or library.

Problem Solver

Practicing is an excellent way to prepare for a job interview. With a partner, write a job description for a specific job at a specific company. Prepare for an interview by researching the company and thinking up questions and answers. Take turns acting as the interviewer and the job seeker. If possible, videotape the practice. Analyze the interview carefully and find ways to improve your interviewing skills.

Team Players

Student teams are to select a job that would be available to students in their community. They are to find as many openings for the selected job as they can within a set timeframe. Remind students to select jobs for which teens would be hired, such as those with restaurants, city recreation departments and services, lawn care, and retailers.

Hot Topics

Make sure students understand that they can turn in their papers anonymously. Encourage them to be open and honest about their disability and the concerns they have about it interfering with their career plans.

Web Extra

Students are to research Web sites that provide information on managing a job search. They are to prepare a directory of the sites that includes the address, a description of each, and whether the site's services are free or come with a fee, and then post it in the school career center or library.

Remind students that a reliable Web site usually publishes the name of the author or organization that sponsors it and the date the content was created or last updated in a fairly obvious location, such as at the top or bottom of the page or on the home page. The site is usually organized with headings and an obvious navigation system. A reliable site clearly states its purpose and any affiliations. You should also look for accuracy in spelling and grammar.

Problem Solver

Student pairs are to write a job description for a specific job at a specific company. They might consider companies they are familiar with, such as where their parents or another relative or friend works. Then, they should think up interview questions and answers and take turns acting out the roles of interviewer and interviewee. Encourage students to critique each other's performance as the interviewee, paying special attention to attitude, body language, tone of voice, and gesturing.

Write Now

Students are to prepare a resume, cover letter, and list of references that they could realistically submit for a job in a career that interests them. Have students review the sections, *Creating Job Search Materials* and *Preparing a Resume* presented earlier in this chapter

Be Involved!

As a class, students are to develop and design a booklet or presentation to inform other students about the careers available in family and consumer sciences careers. Students might want to focus on the career clusters presented in *Appendix A* that relate to education, arts, retail, hospitality and tourism, and human services. Students are to follow the FCCLA planning process.

- Identify a topic.
- Set a goal.
- Form a plan (who, what, when, where, how, cost, resources, and evaluation).
- Act.
- Follow up.

Remind students that a successful team relationship depends on all team members working together. Make sure they take steps to delegate responsibilities, communicate effectively, and manage conflicts or disagreements.

Social Networking

Students are to create a bulletin board display that includes information on types of accommodations that might be needed for people with different disabilities. In addition to contacting agencies and organizations in their area, students might talk to their school administration about accommodations made for students and faculty and staff with disabilities.

Write Now

Use job research tools to identify a job in a career that interests you. Prepare job search materials that you could use to apply for the job.

- Develop a resume. Be complete and accurate. Include an objective specific to the job for which you plan to apply. Use action words to describe your experience and skills. Use formatting that is professional and easy to read.
- Write a cover letter to submit with your resume. Customize it for the specific job. Keep it brief and to the point.
- Develop a list of references. Try to include at least three people who are willing to speak on your behalf. Ask them for permission to include them on the list.

Ask a classmate, teacher, or advisor to review the materials and offer comments and suggestions. Use the comments and suggestions to improve the documents. Add the documents to your career portfolio.

Be Involved!

www.fcclainc.org

The field of family and consumer sciences (FACS) includes a wide variety of career opportunities. As a class, review the FACS career cluster and pathways. Individually or in small groups, develop a booklet or presentation to inform other students about FACS careers.

Before you begin, use the FCCLA planning process to define the project as a goal, make an action plan for achieving the goal (including a timeframe), assess the plan to make sure it is realistic and attainable, and then put the plan into action to achieve your goal.

If you are working in a group, assign roles and responsibilities for each member. For example, one person may be responsible for writing job descriptions, another for illustrating the jobs, and a third for designing the finished product. As you work toward your goal, keep a class journal to record your progress, and collect documentation that you can use to show what you have achieved.

When the project is complete, evaluate your success. Does the finished product match your expectations? Will other students find it useful? Did you run into obstacles? If so, how did you overcome them? Write a report explaining what you learned, whether you were successful, and what you would do differently if you were going to start the project all over again.

Social Networking

By law, employers have to make accommodations for employees with disabilities only if they are aware of the disability. Think about your classmates, neighbors, or friends who have disabilities. How can you raise awareness in your community about the importance of protecting the rights of all people, and making sure that opportunities are available for everyone?

Contact an agency or organization in your area that watches out for people with disabilities and request information. Use the information to make a bulletin board about the types of accommodations that might be needed for people with different disabilities.

Chapter 17 Overview

This chapter provides insight on what you can expect when you start a new job and discusses the dynamics of the workplace environment. Students will also learn how to handle workplace conflicts and identify acts of discrimination and harassment.

Beginning a New Job This section discusses the things to expect when you start a new job. It also looks at what others expect of you as a new hire.

Building Work Relationships Students identify the traits of a successful employee and explore how ethics, teamwork, and leadership affect workplace relationships.

Applying Time-Management Techniques in the Workplace This section provides tips and identifies tools to help you better manage your time at work.

Managing Workplace Conflict In this section, students learn that the critical thinking, problem-solving, and leadership skills they've acquired in other areas of their life can also be applied to resolving conflicts at work.

Overcoming Discrimination and Harassment This section provides information on how to identify discrimination and harassment, and your rights as an employee to stand up against them.

Focus and Engage

Bell-Ringer: Think About This

Students are asked to list five personal qualities they can develop in school and then apply in the workplace. If students need prompting, you might suggest that some of the qualities employers say they desire most in prospective employees include good communication skills, initiative, teamwork, leadership, technical skills, problem-solving, and interpersonal skills. Students should be able to write examples of how they can further develop their personal qualities in school. For example, participating in extracurricular activities helps students build communication, teamwork, and interpersonal skills. Organizing activities such as class parties or spirit days helps build leadership and initiative skills. And taking computer classes or assisting in the computer lab helps build technical skills.

ADVANCE PREPARATION	
Review	*Life Skills for the 21st Century* textbook, Chapter 17.
Prepare	Students will need paper and pencil for some activities. Box labeled "Hot Topics." Poster board for the "Be Involved!" activity.

CUSTOMIZED INSTRUCTION OVERVIEW				
Less Advanced Students	**More Advanced Students**	**ESOL Students**	**Special Needs Students**	**At-Risk Students**
Pages 332, 334	Pages 333, 338	Page 334	Pages 332, 341	Pages 332, 334

Introduce the Section

This section discusses how to prepare for a new job and how to get acclimated to the work environment. It also looks at what others expect of you as a new hire.

Figure Focus

Explain to students that the first day of a new job usually involves filling out forms, meeting new people, and undergoing some type of training or orientation. Suggest the following tips for preparing for the first day.

■ Read the newspaper or search online for any new information regarding the company since you last interviewed with them. You don't want to be the one in the dark about any publicized changes.

■ Contact the supervisor a day or two before starting to review what is expected of you on the first day.

■ Dress appropriately. If you have been issued a uniform, make sure it fits properly and is clean. If you will be using other gear, make sure it is in working condition and ready for use.

■ Write down questions about benefits and responsibilities to ask during orientation.

The First Day

You might offer students the following tips to help avoid stress on the first day of a new job.

■ Do your best to get a good night's sleep. Avoid caffeine and do not overeat.

■ Choose an outfit that is clean and press it the night before.

■ Memorize the names of any employees you met during the interview process.

■ Bring a book or magazine and a simple lunch.

■ Figure out the traveling route and approximately how long it will take you.

■ Give yourself extra time for unexpected delays. You should aim to be early in order to make a good first impression.

Beginning a New Job

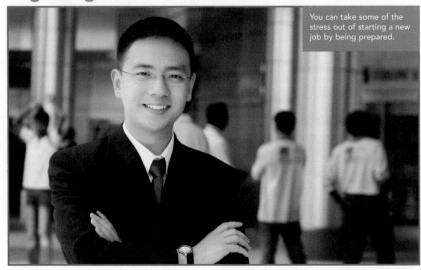

You can take some of the stress out of starting a new job by being prepared.

Starting a new job can be stressful, like starting a new school year. You will have to make changes in your routine. You will have to meet new responsibilities.

■ Will you arrive on time?
■ Will people be friendly?
■ Will you know what to do?

Keep in mind that your employer hired you. He or she is confident that you have the skills and attitude to be a successful employee; you should be confident, too.

To make the first days less stressful, it helps to be prepared. Knowing what to expect can give you confidence.

The First Day

Do you know where to go on your first day of work? Do you know who to report to? The first day—even the first week or month—is full of new information and new experiences. It can be overwhelming. One of the best ways to avoid feeling confused is to speak up and ask questions. Do not wait until you make a mistake.

■ Asking questions is the best way to get the information you need.
■ Asking questions also shows your employer and co-workers that you want to learn.

Most employers expect you to bring proof of residency and all necessary work permits with you on the first day—if not before. If your employer does not tell you what to bring, call and ask, so you have the right documents ready. Be prepared to bring:

■ Your birth certificate or passport, or resident card, if you are not a U.S. citizen, proof that you can legally work in the United States
■ Your Social Security card
■ A work permit or employment certificate, if necessary

Stay in School

Share some of the following facts about high school dropouts and employment.

■ More than 30 percent of high school dropouts were unemployed a short time after dropping out.

■ Fewer than half of high school dropouts who are in their late 30s or older have a job.

■ At age 55, less than 40 percent of high school dropouts are employed.

■ High school dropouts are much more likely to be unemployed during economic downturns. In July 2009, for example, the dropout unemployment rate was 15.4 percent whereas the rate for high school graduates was 9.4 percent. Furthermore, when they are employed, high school dropouts earn about 35 percent less than graduates.

What Are All These Forms?

Your first day will probably include time for filling out forms. One of the first forms you will fill out is a W-4—the Employee's Withholding Allowance Certificate. It is a form employees fill out to provide information the employer needs to calculate how much money to withhold from wages to pay taxes. You can follow the instructions on the form to fill it out correctly, or ask someone in human resources to help you.

You may also have to fill out a state tax withholding form and complete the Employment Eligibility Verification form, which proves you are a U.S. resident or are authorized to work in the United States. Other forms depend on your employer. They may include:

- Authorization to deposit your paycheck directly into your bank account.
- An application for an identification card.
- Benefits selection forms. For example, you may have to make decisions about things like the type of health insurance plan you want. Some employers will give you information to read first, and let you fill out the forms at home, or on another day.

Making the Most of Orientation

Do you have an assembly at the beginning of the school year? When you start a new job, you may have an **orientation**—welcome—session your first day, or within the first few days. It may be led by someone from human resources, or it may be an online presentation. Orientation will answer most of your questions and provide the information you need to get started. When you meet other new employees, you may realize that you are not the only one who is nervous about being in a new situation.

At orientation, you are likely to receive an **employee handbook**, which is like a student handbook. It is a written document that describes all the company policies and procedures, such as how to request vacation time, and the different benefits that are available. Someone may review the handbook, or you may have an opportunity to read it and ask questions.

Many companies provide new-employee training on the first day, or within the first few days. Some training may be for all new employees. For example, you may receive training about safety procedures, or about harassment policies (there is more on harassment later in this chapter).

Some training may be specific to your job. For example, if you are a cashier, you may receive training on how to use the cash register. Make sure you pay attention during training, and ask questions.

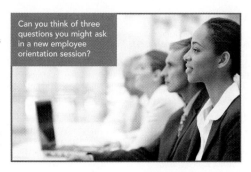

Can you think of three questions you might ask in a new employee orientation session?

"Should I read this handbook now, or wait until I have questions?"

I Was Asked to Join a Union!

A *trade* or *labor union* is an organization of people who do similar work. Some are called *guilds*. The purpose of a union is to work together to ensure fair treatment of the members. What if you are asked—or required—to join a union?

★ Unions hold elections to choose representatives.

★ Representatives negotiate for workers' salaries and benefits.

★ They speak up for workers' rights, such as safe working conditions.

★ Unions charge a membership fee or dues.

Why do you think an organization of many workers may be better able to negotiate than one worker alone?

Figure Focus

Students are asked to think of three questions to ask during a new employee orientation session. These might include:

- What are my specific duties with the team?
- How am I evaluated?
- What are the organization's goals for me?
- Who is my direct supervisor?
- What is the dress code?
- What are the expected work hours?
- What is the company's policy on time off for doctor or dental appointments?

Vocabulary

Employee handbook: A written document that describes all of the company's policies and procedures.

Orientation: A welcome session within the first few days of starting a job to answer questions and provide information to get started.

Trade or labor union: An organization of people who do similar work and ensure the fair treatment of all of the members. Some are called guilds.

W-4: A form employees fill out so an employer can calculate how much money should be withheld from wages for taxes.

I Was Asked to Join a Union!

Unions that are recognized by employers can negotiate on behalf of its members for better or improved working conditions. The agreements negotiated are binding on both the union members and on the employer. Because the union represents a significant portion of the employer's labor force, it has more leverage and bargaining power than a single employee.

Figure Focus

Explain that many employers require new hires to sign a form acknowledging that they have read and understood the employee handbook. The employee handbook explains procedures, such as how to put in for overtime or submit vacation requests, and states the company's policy on discrimination, harassment, and other workplace issues. Reading the handbook and being familiar with its contents help employees gain a better understanding of their rights and responsibilities.

Odors in the Office

Remind students that a consequence is simply the result of the choice you make. When students choose to communicate respectfully with co-workers about differences they have, they will experience more positive outcomes than if they disregard people's feelings. Personal behaviors that might interfere with a co-worker's job performance include:

- Cell phone ringing and usage.
- Speaking loudly.
- Flagrant disrespect for the appearance of common areas, such as the office lunchroom, lobby, and restrooms.
- Gossiping.
- Forwarding spam to co-workers.
- Bothering others when they have deadlines to meet.

Vocabulary

Probation period: A set amount of time during which you and your employer have the chance to make sure you are both happy with the situation.

MONEY MADNE$$

Buying ingredients to make a sandwich for five days (or more) costs $5.75 + $1.25 + $3.15 = $10.15. If you divide by five, you find that it costs $2.03 a day to bring a sandwich from home.

Buying a sandwich for five days costs $4.25 × 5 = $21.25.

Cost is an important factor, and if you are on a tight budget, it may be the only important factor. Other factors include getting along with your co-workers and fitting in. Eating different food each day might be important, too. There might be other options you can consider. The cafeteria might serve salads, fruit, and yogurt, or hot meals.

Odors in the Office

The co-worker who sits at the next desk wears very strong cologne. It gives you a headache, and makes it difficult for you to concentrate. How can you solve the problem?

- Take lots of ibuprofen to make your headache feel better.
- Sit at your desk and complain about it in a loud voice, hoping he will overhear you.
- Leave an anonymous note about it on his desk.
- Buy him a brand of cologne that you like.
- Ask to speak with him privately, explain the situation, and see if you can work together to find a solution.
- Ask your supervisor to speak with him about changing his behavior.
- If he will not change his behavior, request a different desk.

Does wearing strong cologne show respect for your co-workers? What other personal behaviors might interfere with a co-worker's ability to do her job?

MONEY MADNE$$

You like a turkey sandwich on whole-wheat bread with lettuce for lunch. At the supermarket, the sliced turkey costs $5.75 per pound. A head of lettuce costs $1.25. A loaf of whole-wheat bread costs $3.15. You can use the items to make more than enough sandwiches for a whole week.

Your co-workers eat in the cafeteria. They buy freshly made sandwiches for $4.25.

How much does it cost you to bring a sandwich for lunch five days a week? How much does it cost to buy a sandwich for five days? Which option do you think you should choose? Is cost the only thing to consider? Write a paragraph explaining your decision to your co-workers.

What's Probation?

Some employees have a **probation period**, which is a set amount of time during which you and your employer have the chance to make sure you are both happy with the situation. Probation varies in length depending on the company. It may be one month, three months, six months, or even longer!

While you are on probation, your employer expects you to prove you are right for the job. You must meet your responsibilities, get along with your co-workers, and fit into the routine of the workplace. You will receive training and earn your wages.

Probation is also a chance for you to decide if you like the job or not. Is it what you expected? Are you happy and comfortable in the workplace? At the end of probation, you will have an opportunity to meet with your supervisor and discuss your performance.

- If your employer is pleased with your work, you will continue in the job, and probation will end.
- If your employer is not satisfied with your work, he or she may agree to extend the probation period to see if you improve, or you may be dismissed, or let go.
- If you are not satisfied with the job or the work environment, you may decide that you want to leave and look for a different job someplace else.

Problem Solving at Work

You will experience many new situations when you start a new job, just like beginning a new school year. You will meet new people, perform new tasks, and spend time in a new environment. It is likely that you will run into problems and obstacles that you have not encountered before. Recall from Chapter 2 that a problem is a difficulty you must resolve before you can make progress.

- Should you bring a lunch, plan to eat out, or is there a cafeteria?
- Do you know the right person to speak to about ordering supplies?
- What should you do if a co-worker wants to gossip about your supervisor?

You can use your problem-solving skills at work the same way you use them in other areas of your life.

- Identify the problem.
- Consider all possible solutions.
- Identify the consequences of each solution.
- Select the best solution.
- Make and implement a plan of action.

Taking responsibility for your problems and working to find solutions shows you are independent and capable. Your employer will respect you for it.

Customized Instruction: Less Advanced/Special Needs/At-Risk Students

Networking is about connecting with people who have common interests and building mutually beneficial relationships. Ask students to write down three ways they can network that could potentially lead to an internship, apprenticeship, or job position. Answers will vary but may include:

- Conduct informational interviews to learn more about a company and available positions.
- E-mail friends of the family, and ask if they would be willing to forward your resume to the human resources department at their place of work.
- Thank contacts in writing for their support.
- Send holiday cards to remind contacts of your relationship.
- Connect online through professional or social networking sites.

Your Role in a Small Enterprise

If you work in a small enterprise—business or organization—will your first day be the same as at a large corporation? Some things will be the same—you will meet new people, fill out forms, and learn your way around the office. But some things will be different.

A **small enterprise** is one that is privately owned and operated, has a small number of employees, and earns a relatively small amount of money. Working in a small enterprise can be very different from working in a large office or company.

- *Flexibility is important.* Employees in a small enterprise often *wear many hats*, which means they may have to handle the responsibilities for more than one job. You might be hired as a receptionist, but you may also be responsible for scheduling meetings and ordering office supplies.

- *Responsibilities in a large company are often strictly defined.* In a small enterprise, you may have the opportunity to develop your own routines and responsibilities as you go along.

- *Decisions in a small enterprise may be made quickly, by the people most affected.* In a large business, decisions often require many meetings, analysis, reports, and approval.

On your first day at a small enterprise, be prepared to get right to work. There may not be a human resources department—your supervisor will give you the forms you need, and expect you to start working. If you have questions, speak up.

Communicating in a Small Enterprise

At a small enterprise, you work with a small number of people, and it is important that you are able to communicate effectively with everyone. The work environment at a small enterprise is likely to be less formal than at a large company. Likewise, relationships at a small enterprise are much more personal than at a large corporation.

- If you work in a family-owned pizza shop, you might spend all day working side by side with the shop owner and his son.

- If you work in a small Web page design firm, the person at the next desk might be the company founder and president.

Small business owners and top managers are more involved in the day-to-day operations than those at a large company. They interact with their employees on a regular basis, giving you greater opportunity to make a real contribution to the company, to see how your contribution affects the company's success, and to be noticed by the top management.

Is a Small Enterprise Right for You?

There are advantages and disadvantages in working for a small company:

Possible advantages:

✔ *More responsibility*
✔ *More flexibility*
✔ *Less formality*
✔ *Independence*
✔ *Opportunity to experience many aspects of the business*
✔ *Opportunity to be noticed by the boss*

Possible disadvantages:

✔ *Fewer benefits*
✔ *Longer work weeks*
✔ *Less opportunity to meet new people*
✔ *Less job security*
✔ *Fewer available resources*
✔ *Opportunity to be noticed by the boss*

NUMBERS GAME

At your job, you may have to choose how much you want to deposit in a retirement plan, such as a 401(k). Many companies offer a matching contribution for retirement plans. They often state the contribution as a ratio, such as 2:1 or 1:1.

A **ratio** is a proportional relationship between two numbers or quantities. For example, if there is one teacher in your class and 24 students, the ratio of teachers to students is 1 to 24, which is written as 1:24.

A 2:1 ratio means that for every $2.00 you contribute, the company will contribute $1.00. A 1:1 ratio means that for every $1.00 you contribute, the company will contribute $1.00.

If you contribute $100.00 a week into your 401(k), and your employer makes a 2:1 matching contribution, how much is deposited into your account each week?

Your contribution	$100.00
Employer contribution	$100.00 ÷ 2 = $50.00
Total contribution	$100.00 + $50.00 = $150.00

Do the math: How much is contributed if your employer makes a 1:1 contribution and you put in $500 a month? How much is deposited each week if you contribute $125.00?

Customized Instruction: More Advanced Students

Divide the students into teams. Have each group contact a local small business owner and interview him or her about the business's hiring process and what he or she is looking for in new hires. Students should prepare questions on the type of business, number of employees, types of positions for which they hire, and qualifications of employees. A good resource for names of small businesses is the local chamber of commerce. Have each team write a short report on the interview and present it to the class. Have them discuss whether or not they would like to work for a small business like the one they interviewed.

NUMBERS GAME

If you contribute $500 per month and there is a 1:1 contribution, your employer also puts in $500 per month, for a total of $1,000 per month.

If you contribute $125 a month and there is a 1:1 ratio, your employer also puts in $125 per month for a total of $250 per month. To determine the weekly contribution, multiply $250 × 12, which equals $3,000, divided by 52, which equals $57.69 per week.

Vocabulary

Ratio: A proportional relationship between two numbers or quantities.

Small enterprise: A privately owned and operated company that has a small number of employees and earns a relatively small amount of money.

Is a Small Enterprise Right for You?

Explain that a small business often relies on employees to take on tasks that in a larger company would be delegated to another position. For example, a small business employee might be expected to have the following in addition to specific job-related skills and abilities:

- Basic understanding of office machinery, such as a copier or fax machine, and how to operate and maintain it.

- Basic understanding of office procedures, such as sending out business mailings, scheduling deliveries, and even ordering coffee or water for the water cooler.

- Knowledge of computer operations, maintenance, and troubleshooting.

- Advanced multitasking and organization skills.

- An understanding of business law and those government laws and regulations that apply to the specific business.

Discuss

Discuss the importance of effective communication in a small business environment. Offer the following tips on communication in the small business office:

- Make an effort not to cut people off when they are speaking.

- Make it obvious that you are listening and understanding what people are saying by making eye contact and using gestures and verbal indicators.

- Be consistent in your values and what motivates you.

- Be direct about what you envision for your position.

- Be responsive to others' requests.

- Ask for regular feedback to understand how you are doing.

- Discuss sensitive or delicate matters in person rather than in e-mails that could be misinterpreted.

Introduce the Section

Students identify the traits of a successful employee and explore how ethics, teamwork, and leadership affect workplace relationships.

Figure Focus

Ask students who have had a job or currently have one to discuss the challenges of work relationships. If you think it is relevant, you might discuss some of the challenges you've faced in previous jobs. Share with students the following suggestions on how to build strong work relationships.

- If you feel the need to discuss a problem over a work relationship, be prepared to offer suggestions for solving it.
- Avoid alienating others by placing the blame on everyone but yourself.
- Use positive verbal and nonverbal skills. For example, do not use sarcasm or roll your eyes. Instead, listen carefully, ask questions, and make sure both parties understand exactly what the problem is.
- Follow through on the things you commit to doing.
- Share credit for accomplishments and ideas.
- Compliment others' talents, skills, and experience.

Vocabulary

Professionalism: Ability to show respect to everyone around you while you perform your responsibilities as best you can.

Traits of a Successful Employee

Explain to students that it is important to make a good impression on supervisors as well as colleagues. Ask students to comment on the qualities and actions that speak to an employee's professionalism. Some of these are:

- Arriving early to meetings.
- Using proper language and avoiding slang.
- Stating your opinions confidently and speaking clearly.
- Dressing in a professional manner.
- Avoiding talk about personal matters.

Building Work Relationships

Cooperating with co-workers makes it easier to achieve your common goals.

Recall from Chapter 5 that you have relationships with people in all five areas of your life. Relationships you build at work—like relationships you build at school—can have a major impact on your overall well-being.

- You have relationships with your co-workers and your supervisor. As a team, you work together to achieve common goals. For example, you might work as a flight attendant. The other members of the flight crew are on your team. You work together to make sure that you depart on time and arrive safely.
- You may also have relationships with customers or clients. You work to provide them with goods or services that satisfy their needs. The passengers are your customers. You work to provide them with information about the flight, drinks or snacks, and other things to make them comfortable.

You may have relationships with other people in your work environment, such as the baggage handlers and cleaning crew. Knowing how to get along and avoid or solve conflicts is an important part of your career success. You can start building these skills today by how you build relationships with other students and teachers in your school or how you relate to family members.

Traits of a Successful Employee

The qualities that make you successful in other areas of your life, make you successful at work, too. Have you ever heard someone say that a worker exhibits *professionalism*? Maybe a sales clerk is calm and friendly while dealing with an angry customer. Maybe an emergency dispatcher talks a frantic mother through the steps necessary to stop her child's bleeding while waiting for the ambulance. Maybe a busy waiter takes the time to help you select a meal, and feel comfortable.

Professionalism is the ability to show respect to everyone around you while you perform your responsibilities as best as you can. It includes a basic set of personal qualities that make an employee successful—no matter what job or career he or she has. The personal qualities that combine to create professionalism include:

- Integrity
- Honesty
- Courtesy
- Responsibility

When you show professionalism, you will earn the trust and respect of your supervisor, co-workers, and customers. You will contribute to your own well-being, because you can feel good about the way you treat others, and the way you meet your work responsibilities.

Customized Instruction: Less Advanced/At-Risk Students

Have students write a definition for each of the four personal qualities listed in the box: Integrity, Courtesy, Honesty, and Responsibility. They can use a dictionary, or you might encourage them to write what they think the terms mean. Following are dictionary definitions for each.

- Integrity: Quality of adhering to high moral principles or professional standards.
- Courtesy: Polite or considerate behavior.
- Honesty: Quality or characteristic of being fair and truthful.
- Responsibility: Being accountable to somebody or for something.

Customized Instruction: ESOL Students

Have students do the same activity as your less advanced and at-risk students, except have them write the terms in their primary language. The definitions should be in English.

Being Ethical at Work

Recall from Chapter 1 that *ethics* are a set of beliefs about what is right and what is wrong. **Work ethics** are beliefs and behaviors about what is right and wrong in a work environment. When you behave ethically at work, others will trust and respect you.

Most work ethics are the same ethics from other areas of life that you apply to your workplace. For example:

- Always try to do your best.
- Respect the authority of your supervisor.
- Respect your co-workers.
- Respect company property.

How are ethics in the workplace similar to ethics in school and other areas of your life?

Not everyone behaves ethically at work. When you are in a situation where others are acting in a way that you know is unethical, you will have to use your decision-making skills to choose how to respond.

- You might see someone taking office supplies home for personal use, which is stealing.
- You might hear co-workers gossiping about a customer or manager, which is disrespectful.
- Someone might leave early and ask you to lie about it to your supervisor, which is dishonest.

Teamwork and Leadership

People who can work successfully as part of a team—whether as a leader or a team member—are valued in the work environment, just as they are valued in school, the community, and at home. As a team member, you can:

- Use active listening to make sure you understand the needs and opinions of others
- Show cooperation in order to achieve your common goals
- Compromise when necessary
- Complete your tasks and responsibilities on time, and to the best of your ability

As a leader, you can:

- Help build cooperation among team members
- Show *initiative*, which means you take charge to accomplish a task that needs to be done
- Make healthy choices at work
- Respect the diverse opinions of others
- Be assertive, but not aggressive

Team members recognize that each person on the team has different ideas and skills. They use these differences to achieve their common goals.

> "You are only as good as the people you hire."
>
> — *Ray Kroc, Founder of McDonald's*

Peer Pressure at Work

You spend a lot of time with your co-workers, customers, and supervisors. Your thoughts and actions are likely to be influenced by their thoughts and actions. Is peer pressure at work positive or negative?

- 👎 Co-workers convince you to leave work early to go to the movies.
- 👎 Your supervisor asks you to tell an angry customer that he is out, when you know he is in the office.
- 👎 A vendor says she will pay you cash on the side if you buy office supplies from her.
- 👍 Co-workers encourage you to exercise during lunch.
- 👍 Your supervisor invites you to join a professional organization that can help your career.

How can recognizing peer pressure at work help you make healthy decisions and achieve your career goals?

Introduce the Section

This section provides tips and identifies tools to help you better manage your time at work.

Figure Focus

Explain to students the importance of managing their time at work, school, and home. Ask students to share their time-management techniques. Do they use a calendar or daily planner? Do they use an electronic version of either? Do they prioritize? Have they ever used the two-minute rule, in which you identify the tasks that will take only a couple minutes to complete and then do them one after the other? On the flip side, maybe they do the most important or most time-intensive task first. Once you have that task out of the way, you feel a sense of accomplishment and the motivation to complete the rest.

Respecting Time at Work

Explain to students that lost productivity because of personal Internet usage, phone calls, and texting can have a huge impact on a company's bottom line. In fact, a Nielsen study found that the average employee spends 18 hours per week on personal Internet usage. Another survey found that almost 60 percent of all online purchases were made during regular work hours. Emphasize how this type of irresponsible behavior has negative effects on the entire company and its employees. Lower workplace productivity commonly leads to less revenue, which, in turn, can force a company to take measures to cut costs. These measures can include reductions to wages, benefits, and even the workforce.

Review and Reinforce

Applying time-management skills in school can make it easier to transition to a new job. Review the term *procrastination*, which means to delay action until an opportunity is lost. How does procrastination get in the way of achieving goals at school and at work? What are the negative effects of procrastination?

Applying Time-Management Techniques in the Workplace

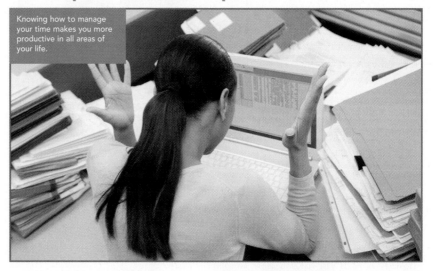

Knowing how to manage your time makes you more productive in all areas of your life.

You arrive at your work as a marketing assistant at 8:50 a.m. You look at your to-do list. It has ten tasks on it. You get started on task 1.

The phone rings. Your supervisor asks you to reschedule an appointment. Then, a co-worker needs help preparing a mailing that has to go out today. Your sister calls. She's in the area and wants to meet for lunch. After lunch, a customer calls to inquire about a new product. Then, your supervisor wants you to sit in on a meeting. You look at your watch and it is 5:05. None of the ten tasks on your to-do list have been completed. In fact, there are now four new tasks on the list! Where did the day go?

Chapter 4 discussed time-management techniques. You read about how to set goals and manage your schedule to make the most out of your available time. Time management is a critical skill for succeeding at work. To achieve your career goals, you will have to manage your time effectively and set *priorities*—decide which tasks must be completed first.

Respecting Time at Work

Would your friends be happy if you said you'd meet them at 4:00 but you didn't show up until 4:45? Employers and co-workers expect you to honor and respect time in the workplace, too. You can expect the same thing from them. That means:

- Showing up on time
- Showing up every day—except vacations and holidays
- Leaving for lunch and breaks at the scheduled time—not before—and returning promptly—not late
- Staying until the end of the work day
- Meeting your deadlines, which means completing all work before it is due
- Taking care of personal business on your own time, not during work hours

Respecting time at work shows that you respect your co-workers. It demonstrates to your supervisor that you take your responsibilities seriously. It is one way you prove you are ready for new challenges such as those that might come from a promotion.

Tools for Managing Time at Work

You can use many of the same time-management tools you use at home and at school to manage your time at work. Schedules and goal-setting can keep you focused on the tasks at hand. Computer programs can help you organize and meet your responsibilities.

- *Set realistic and attainable goals using daily, weekly, and monthly schedules.* Different schedules can help you identify tasks that must be accomplished within a specific timeframe. For example, you may have to call a customer today, but you may have to submit a report sometime this week. You may have to request vacation time before the 1st of next month, and you may have to attend a safety training session before Wednesday.
- *Make use of the calendar program on your computer or handheld.* You can enter schedules, phone calls, and appointments. Use the tasks list feature to record and prioritize the things you need to accomplish. Set the program to display a message or make a sound to remind you of deadlines.

Tips for Managing Time at Work

Learn to say no. Some people may ask for too much of your time. They may expect you to take on more responsibility than you can handle. It is OK to say no. Be polite and respectful, but explain that your schedule is full.

Ask for help. If you are having trouble completing tasks that are part of your assigned responsibilities, you will need to find a way to get them done. Ask your supervisor, a co-worker, or someone in human resources to help you learn how to organize your time, or find ways to be more efficient so you can get more work done.

Notify your supervisor if you are late. Most people try to be **punctual**—on time. They don't intend to be late for work or meetings. But things come up to delay them.

- Your morning bus is late because of traffic.
- You are called to a family emergency an hour before your shift ends.
- You receive an unexpected phone call just as you are heading for a conference.

All of these things take up time and can make you late, or absent. When possible, call to notify your employer that you will be late, or request the time off for unplanned absences. If you are gone without an explanation, you appear disorganized, irresponsible, and unreliable.

"How can I avoid being late?"

Myth Working too many hours causes stress.

Truth Working too much might cause stress, but so can working too little. The number of hours you work has less to do with stress than how you feel about your work. If you feel stress, take a long look at what you are doing. Are you unhappy? Is your work boring? Identify the stressor, and then take steps to remove it, or reduce the stress it causes.

TECH CONNECT

Most employers want to know when an employee arrives and leaves. Some ask employees to fill out a time sheet, or table with cells for entering the time in, time out, and total hours at work.

Some use time clocks to record employee hours. A **time clock** is a machine that automatically records the time you *clock-in*—arrive—and the time you *clock-out*—leave. With older, mechanical, time clocks, you actually insert a card in the machine and the current time prints on the card.

Newer time clocks are computerized. The current time is recorded when you swipe your ID card or punch in a code. **Biometric time clocks** use a fingerprint or handprint to record when an employee comes and goes.

Why do you think employers want to track their employees' hours? Can you think of any advantages to using a biometric time clock? Draw a poster advertising a time clock product.

Figure Focus

Ask students what measures they take to be on time to school, to work, to social engagements, etc. Some examples you might discuss are:

- Examine the morning routine to see which activities can be done the night before.
- Assemble your outfit, lunch, and even your breakfast menu the night before.
- Delegate chores that might be making you late, such as walking the dog or taking out the trash.
- Maintain your car so you don't have to fill the gas tank at inopportune times and to avoid an unexpected breakdown.
- Set two alarms, and don't use the snooze button.
- Use a calendar to write down varying schedules or when you need extra time in the morning to prepare.
- Set your clock forward 15 minutes to get yourself going earlier.

Myth/Truth

Stress can be caused by a number of internal factors, such as not enough sleep, disorganization, eating junk food, drinking too much caffeine, and a negative attitude. Explain that one way to minimize stress is to address the things over which you have control; for example, your diet, your social commitments, and your attitude. How might you change those in order to relieve work-related stress?

Vocabulary

Biometric time clock: A machine that uses a fingerprint or handprint to record when an employee comes and goes.

Time clock: A machine that automatically records the time you clock-in (arrive) and the time you clock-out (leave).

 TECH CONNECT

Employers track employee hours to determine punctuality and hours worked, and also to track how much time an employee spends on certain tasks or projects. For companies that bill customers based on the hours spent on a task or project, such as law firms, this information is invaluable in identifying those tasks or projects (or clients) that are profitable and those that are not. Advantages of biometric time clocks include decrease in timecard fraud, elimination of badges, and the ability to monitor who enters the employer's premises, thus enhancing security.

Introduce the Section

In this section, students learn that the critical thinking, problem-solving, and leadership skills they've acquired in other areas of their lives can also be applied to resolving conflicts at work.

Figure Focus

Discuss how the types of work relationships you have can influence how you resolve workplace conflicts. For example, if you have a good relationship with your supervisor, then it's easier for you to work together to find a resolution to a conflict. If your relationship is unhealthy, then the conflict might go unresolved and interfere with your well-being. This, in turn, can lead to stress, anger, depression, and resentment.

Reinforce and Review

Emphasize that you will be more successful in resolving or minimizing a conflict if you work with the other person or people who are involved in it. Together, you can identify the conflict. Together, you can figure out a solution that works for everyone.

Communicating

Explain that workplace conflicts often arise over the negative feedback an employee gets on his or her work. Nobody wants to hear that he's not doing his job right, but it's important to learn how to use the feedback constructively. Discuss with students the following tips for dealing with negative feedback.

- Control your emotions and avoid going on the defense.
- Remain objective and listen carefully to what is being said.
- Do not make judgments about the person supplying the feedback.
- If necessary, repeat what the person has said to make sure you understand his or her feedback.
- Ask questions to clarify points you don't understand.
- Ask for examples of where you are underperforming and what you need to improve upon.
- Ask for suggestions on how to improve.
- If you feel the negative feedback is not justified, take time to make your case, identifying specific examples of how your performance does measure up to your employer's expectations. Then, set up a specific time to discuss the matter with the appropriate person.

Managing Workplace Conflict

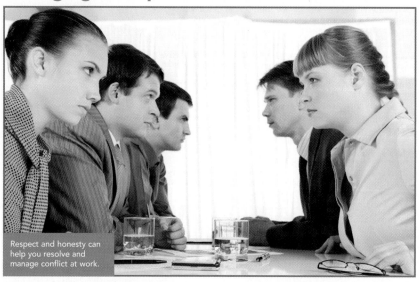

Respect and honesty can help you resolve and manage conflict at work.

Recall from Chapter 5 that *conflict* is a disagreement between two or more people who have different ideas. Conflict occurs in all areas of your life and can cause stress and interfere with your well-being if it is not resolved.

Conflict at work can interfere with your career goals. It can make you angry and cause you to resent the other people at work. If it is left unresolved, conflict can make it difficult or even impossible to successfully complete your tasks and responsibilities.

- Some workplace conflicts are small, such as a disagreement about who gets to use the printer first.
- Some workplace conflicts are more significant, such as a disagreement over who will be the manager of a new project.

As in other areas of your life, managing workplace conflict does not always mean eliminating the conflict completely. It means that you are able to recognize what is causing the conflict, and that you can cope with it in an honest and respectful way.

Communicating

Knowing how to use communication skills to manage workplace conflict will help you earn the respect of your supervisor and co-workers. It will make you a valuable member of your work team.

Review the steps for effective communication from Chapter 2:

- *Be clear.* Use words and body language that the other person can understand, and that send a clear message.
- *Be personal.* Address the other person by his or her name or title. Use "I" statements to show that you take responsibility for your role in the conflict.
- *Be positive.* State your message in positive terms directed at how to achieve your common goal.
- *Get to the point.* Explain why you feel or think this way.
- *Use active listening* to be sure you hear the response.
- *Think before you respond.* Use critical thinking instead of emotions.

Customized Instruction: More Advanced Students

Have students prepare a skit on the positive resolution to a conflict between one employee who repeatedly talks down to and dismisses the ideas of another employee during a team meeting with the department manager. Students should come up with a list of possible scenarios. For example, the business could be a city newspaper, the meeting could be for reporters and the editor, and one reporter's ideas for stories include one on a large donation to an animal shelter, another on the purchase of city buses that run on biofuel, and a third on the opening of a hair salon run by a group of senior citizens. Make sure students address how the reporter and/or the editor might resolve the conflict with a solution that benefits everyone. Have the students act out the skit in front of the class.

Valuing Differences

You will encounter people with different backgrounds and experiences in your workplace. You are also likely to encounter people from different cultures. Sometimes, these differences can cause conflict.

- You might think the food a co-worker eats in the lunchroom stinks, even though it is common in her native country.
- You might be frustrated trying to understand an order placed by a customer who speaks English as a second language.
- You might become impatient waiting for a disabled co-worker to complete a task you know you could do faster.

Recall from Chapter 3 that understanding the differences between people makes it easier to communicate, and that it helps if you can find common bonds. At work, focusing on the common goals you and your teammates share will help you see past the differences to resolve conflicts.

Coping with Workplace Barriers

Barriers in the workplace are obstacles that interfere with your ability to achieve your goals. Barriers often cause conflict, but they may be caused by conflict, too.

- You might not understand your responsibilities.
- You might find your supervisor is not helpful or supportive.
- You might not feel that you have received adequate training.
- You might think a co-worker is not pulling his or her weight on the job.

You can knock down a lot of barriers by maintaining a positive attitude. A negative attitude can quickly cause conflict and result in the loss of respect and support from the rest of your team.

Effective communication is one of the best ways to avoid barriers at work. Be respectful and polite. Show that you value the opinions of others, and present your point of view in a clear and positive way.

What Time Is It in London?

The earth is divided into 24 different **time zones**—geographic regions that use the same standard time. When you cross from one time zone into another, the time is different.

When you work in an office that does business with people living in different time zones, it is important to know the **local time**—time in the time zone where the other people are located.

For example, if you work in Miami, FL, you are in the U.S. Eastern Standard Time Zone. A client in London, England, is 5 hours later, in the Western European Time Zone. When it is 9:00 a.m. in Miami, it is 2:00 p.m. in London.

Can you think of jobs that might have problems due to changing time zones? Write about a work problem caused by time zones. Be specific about the job, the problem, and the time zones. Describe how you would solve the problem.

Is the Conflict Your Fault?

Your co-workers are angry at you. They have been "forgetting" to tell you about meetings. They do not listen to your suggestions or ideas. How can you earn their respect and support?

👎 Make excuses to cover up your mistakes.

👎 Blame your co-workers for your errors.

👎 Take credit for other's work.

👍 Find ways to cooperate and compromise.

👍 Show appreciation for their efforts.

👍 Take responsibility for your work.

How can unhealthy relationships with your co-workers interfere with your career success?

Myth   Only bad employees cause conflict.

Truth   While negative attitudes and inflexible opinions can cause conflict, there are lots of other causes, too. Very good employees can cause or contribute to conflict if they don't understand how to use effective communications, teamwork, leadership, and problem solving to manage and solve conflict when it occurs.

Is the Conflict Your Fault?

Unhealthy relationships with co-workers may interfere with your career success if you:

- Provide personal information to untrustworthy colleagues.
- Disrupt meetings with side conversations or spend too much time socializing.
- Develop a reputation for gossiping by listening to a friend who enjoys doing it.
- Give a friend preferential treatment.
- Openly act rude to a co-worker with whom you have had difficulties.

Vocabulary

Local time: The time in the time zone where people are located.

Time zones: Geographic regions that use the same standard time.

What Time Is It in London?

Time changes may affect someone who travels for her job, companies that transport their materials to different regions, or companies that outsource several different tasks for one project. Answers will vary for a work problem involving time zones. As a software consultant, a person might have to travel to several clients' offices in only a few days' time. It could become easy to confuse meeting times if you are on Eastern time in the morning and then travel to the West coast, where you are on Pacific time in the afternoon.

Myth/Truth

Ask students how they define a "good" employee. What qualities and character traits does a good employee have? A good or successful employee is honest, courteous, responsible, and has high professional standards. But consider a good employee who is so diligent in doing good work that it causes him or her to sometimes miss a deadline or to be late to a meeting. How could that contribute to conflict?

Introduce the Section

This section provides information on how to identify discrimination and harassment, and your rights as an employee to stand up against this type of behavior.

Figure Focus

Discuss with students how workplace harassment and discrimination can affect an employee's well-being. Some ways are:

- Loss of self-confidence and self-esteem.
- Physical symptoms such as headaches, stomach aches, nightmares, and anxiety attacks as well as emotional stress and depression.
- Poor attendance to or disinterest in family and social activities and events.
- Inability to concentrate.
- Increased inclination to act out or engage in risky behavior.
- Suicidal behavior.

Vocabulary

Discrimination: Unfair treatment of a person or group based on age, gender, race, or religion.

Harassment: Unwanted, repeated behavior or communication that bothers, annoys, frightens, or stresses another person.

Privacy in the Workplace

Discuss with students the following examples of inappropriate employer monitoring.

- Surveillance practices that are being used to discriminate or retaliate against workers.
- Use of the information gained through monitoring to embarrass or harass employees.
- Electronic workplace monitoring that extends to an employee's private life.

Discuss

Discuss ways in which you can avoid privacy problems with an employer. These include refraining from instant messaging with friends or downloading video games on a business computer, walking outside to take personal phone calls, and refusing to gossip or talk about personal matters in the office.

Overcoming Discrimination and Harassment

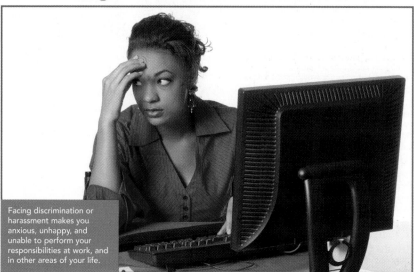

Facing discrimination or harassment makes you anxious, unhappy, and unable to perform your responsibilities at work, and in other areas of your life.

Have you ever felt that you were treated differently from others because of a quality or characteristic that you cannot control? Maybe girls did not want you walking home with them because you are a boy. Maybe a teacher did not choose you to narrate a class presentation because you have an accent.

If you thought the treatment was unfair, you were right. In fact, it was discrimination. **Discrimination** is unfair treatment of a person or group based on age, gender, race, or religion. Discrimination is usually because of prejudice, or negative opinions, that are not based on fact.

Sometime, instead of discriminating, employers or co-workers harass others. **Harassment** is unwanted, repeated behavior or communication that bothers, annoys, frightens, or stresses another person. Harassment at work is also against the law.

Learning how to cope with and overcome discrimination and harassment at work can help you achieve success at work.

Privacy in the Workplace

Would you be angry if you found out your supervisor was reading e-mails from your mother that you received at work? Maybe, but your supervisor did not break the law. Employers have the right to check on their employees to make sure they are being honest and productive. They may:

- Read e-mail messages and personal computer files stored at work
- Listen to telephone conversations that take place at work
- Monitor Internet usage, including tracking the sites an employee visits while at work
- Video employees using hidden cameras, if they suspect them of illegal or unethical behavior

Employers own the computer and telephone systems in the workplace. Most systems save e-mails and voice mail messages even after an employee deletes them. You will avoid problems by assuming that your employer is able to read or hear everything that passes through your computer and telephone at work.

Your Right to Fair Treatment

You have the right to be treated fairly in the workplace, and to be safe from harassment. The Civil Rights Act of 1964 states that employers may not use race, skin color, religion, sex, or national origin as a reason to promote, not promote, hire, or **fire**—dismiss—an employee. Newer laws such as the Americans with Disabilities Act (ADA) make it illegal to discriminate based on age or physical disability. If you believe you are facing discrimination or harassment at work:

■ Keep a careful written record of every incident. That means writing down what people say or do, including the date, time, and names of all the other people who were there. If you receive written threats or offensive documents such as letters, texts, or e-mails, save them and print them.

■ Get a copy of your company's policy on discrimination and harassment. It may be online, or in the employee handbook.

■ Follow the procedure in the company policy for reporting illegal behavior. If there is no procedure, meet with someone in human resources to report it.

■ If the company is not responsive, you can report directly to the Equal Employment Opportunity Commission (EEOC), the federal agency responsible for investigating charges of discrimination against employers.

Encouraging a Productive Environment

Sometimes co-workers put up barriers that interfere with the ability of one person, or an entire group of people, to succeed in the workplace. These barriers cause conflict. They distract employees from their responsibilities.

■ Co-workers might complain when a Muslim employee takes time from his desk for his daily prayers.

■ An office manager might resent that he must rearrange the workspace to accommodate a worker's wheelchair.

■ Employees might think it is funny to put inappropriate jokes on the company bulletin board.

The workplace will be more a productive environment if all employees are happy and comfortable. You can encourage a more productive environment by developing qualities such as tolerance, cooperation, respect, and understanding.

What can you do if your employer does not make accommodations for your disability?

Are You a Harasser?

Harassment can take many forms. You might think you are funny, but a co-worker might feel harassed. Avoid any behavior that might threaten others, or make them uncomfortable:

✔ *Commenting on someone's appearance*

✔ *Telling inappropriate jokes, such as insulting an ethnic group*

✔ *Touching a co-worker, except for a handshake*

✔ *Hanging up inappropriate pictures*

✔ *Asking a co-worker on a date, after he or she already said, "No thanks"*

✔ *Using crude or inappropriate language*

21st Century Skills — What Happens Next?

Eduardo works at a restaurant, handling take-out orders over the phone. He works hard. He takes extra shifts when his manager needs him. He covers for co-workers who want time off. He likes the work environment. He gets along well with his co-workers and managers.

When a waiter quits, her job becomes available. Eduardo applies. He has the necessary qualifications. He is familiar with the restaurant, the menu, and the procedures. Someone who had never worked in the restaurant is offered the job.

Eduardo is one of the few Latino people who work at the restaurant. He thinks he did not get the job because of his cultural background. Do you agree with Eduardo? Are there other reasons he might not have been hired? Use your problem-solving and decision-making skills to help Eduardo decide what to do next. Using your 21st Century Skills—such as decision making, goal setting, and problem solving—write an ending to the story. Read it to the class, or form a small group and present it as a skit.

Customized Instruction: Special Needs Students (with Allergies)

Ask students what accommodations an employer could make to ensure the safety of employees with food allergies. Some of these are:

■ Allow the employee to eat at his desk or in his office.

■ Allow flexible scheduling so the employee has time to go home to eat, to work from home, or to work when fewer people are present so as to decrease possible exposure to the allergen.

■ Relocate the employee's workspace to reduce the possibility of exposure to the allergen.

■ Post signs around the facility alerting other employees about food allergies and their side effects.

21st Century Skills

What Happens Next?

Students are to prepare an ending to Eduardo's dilemma. Before they prepare their endings, they must first decide if they agree with Eduardo's assessment on why he didn't get the job as waiter. You might discuss reasons why he didn't get the job. For example, maybe his employer wanted to keep him in his current position because he does such a good job at it. Eduardo's next step should be to calmly talk with his employer on the reasons why he was denied the job.

Figure Focus

Explain that under the Americans with Disabilities Act (ADA), employees have a right to ask for reasonable accommodations for a disability. Some common types of accommodations for people with disabilities include:

■ Physical changes such as installing a ramp or modifying a workspace.

■ Providing a quieter workspace for those with a mental disability.

■ Training someone in an accessible format such as Braille or audiotapes.

Explain that the ADA provides for persons with disabilities who feel their rights have been violated to lodge a complaint with the nearest Equal Employment Opportunity Commission (EEOC) office. Emphasize to students that there are time limitations for filing a complaint depending on the state. There is no fee to file a charge, and many times the EEOC will suggest mediation as a way to resolve the conflict. If a conflict is not referred to mediation or if mediation is unsuccessful, the EEOC will decide if you were discriminated against. For more information, visit www.eeoc.gov.

Vocabulary

Fire: To dismiss an employee.

Are You a Harasser?

Explain that an employee who harasses might also engage in bullying behavior, which can be just as serious as harassment. Some examples of workplace bullying are:

■ Shouting at someone whether in private or in front of others.

■ Name calling.

■ Belittling or insulting someone and making him the butt of jokes.

■ Excessive monitoring or checking up on what another is doing.

■ Constantly criticizing and being overly critical on minor or trivial matters.

■ Deliberately embarrassing someone.

■ Overloading someone with work or giving her no work at all.

■ Setting someone up to fail or withholding information that the person needs to do his job.

■ Forming cliques and excluding someone from casual workplace conversations or gatherings.

■ Making remarks or asking intrusive questions about someone's private life.

End-of-Chapter Activities

Case Study

Amanda stole the soccer ball. Stealing is illegal. Lucy has a problem because she knows Amanda stole the ball. It is also her responsibility to make sure all equipment is put away. If—or when—someone notices the ball is gone, Lucy will be responsible and may lose her job. If she tells, Amanda will be mad at her. If she doesn't tell, it will seem as if she thinks it is OK to steal.

Lucy should discuss the problem with Amanda and see if she can convince her to return the ball. If Amanda refuses, Lucy should discuss the situation with her supervisor.

Sounding Off!

1. Benefits of "friending" co-workers and supervisors on social networking sites include identifying common ground and building your network of contacts. However, problems might arise if personal photos or personal information is exchanged on the site.

2. Emphasize to students that speaking out against sexual harassment is important. Belittling comments about being "too sensitive" are harmful and can be used as a manipulation tactic.

FAQ

1. The W-4 (Employee's Withholding Allowance Certificate) is a form employees fill out to provide information the employer needs to calculate how much money to withhold from wages to pay taxes.

2. An employee handbook is like a student handbook. It is a written document that describes all of the company policies and procedures.

3. A probation period is a set amount of time during which the employee and employer have the chance to make sure both are happy with the situation.

4. Professionalism is the ability to show respect to everyone around you while you perform your responsibilities as best you can.

5. Personal qualities that are part of professionalism are integrity, honesty, courtesy, and responsibility. Students may think of others.

6. Work ethics are beliefs and behaviors about what is right and wrong in a work environment.

7. Examples of unethical behavior include gossiping, stealing, blaming others for your mistakes, lying, and showing disrespect. Students may think of others.

Case Study

Lucy and Amanda work at an afterschool recreation program for elementary school kids in their town. The program uses the gym at the middle school. The girls give the kids snacks and help them do their homework. Then they play games using the middle school gym equipment. At the end of the day, Lucy and Amanda are responsible for making sure all the equipment is locked up in the storage room.

One day, Amanda takes a soccer ball home with her instead of locking it in the closest. Lucy notices, but doesn't say anything. She hopes Amanda will bring it back the next day. Lucy never sees the soccer ball again.

■ What do you think of Amanda's actions?
■ Can you identify a problem or challenge facing Lucy?
■ What do you think Lucy should do next?

Sounding Off!

① Should you "friend" your co-workers on your social networking account? What about your supervisor or manager? What benefits could there be? What problems might arise?

② Do you think harassment is a serious issue or are some people just too sensitive?

1. What is a W-4 form?
2. What is an employee handbook?
3. What is a probation period?
4. What is professionalism?
5. List four personal qualities that are part of professionalism.
6. What are work ethics?
7. Give two examples of unethical behavior at work.
8. List four ways you can respect time in the workplace.
9. What is a time zone?
10. What is discrimination?

8. You can respect time in the workplace by coming to work on time and every day except vacation, holidays, or when you're sick; staying until the end of day; leaving for lunch and returning at the correct times; notifying your supervisor if you will be late or absent; meeting deadlines; and taking care of personal business on personal time. Students may think of others.

9. A time zone is a geographic region that uses the same standard time.

10. Discrimination is unfair treatment because of prejudice, specifically based on age, gender, race, or religion.

Divide into teams of four or five. Act as the human resources department of a company, and develop an employee handbook. Include information about the company policies, procedures, and benefits. Write the handbook, and publish it using a publishing software program, or by hand. Share the publication with the other teams in your class.

Hot Topics

Have you ever felt discriminated against or harassed?

Take this opportunity to write anonymously about your experience, how it made you feel, and what you did about it. Use a word processor so no one recognizes your handwriting. Be honest and open. Put the paper in the class Hot Topics box.

As a class, read the anonymous entries and discuss them.

Web Extra ▼

The nonprofit organization Workplace Fairness provides workers with information about many issues, including employee rights. Use its Web site—www.workplacefairness.org—to learn about issues facing workers today.

Pick an issue that you find interesting, and write a summary explaining how it affects workers, why you think it is important, and how workers can deal with it.

Problem Solver

You are the owner of a small pet supply store. Your business is growing, and you are having trouble keeping your business records organized.

Use the Internet to research the types of simple small business records that are most important for the success of a small enterprise. Try to find examples, such as a sample transaction journal, or accounts payable and accounts receivable records. Then set up samples for your pet supply store.

Team Players

Student teams are to write an employee handbook. Students can search the Internet to find examples of employee handbooks. You might also refer them to *Language Arts: Grammar and Punctuation Basics* in *Appendix D* starting on page 539 of the student text.

Hot Topics

Make sure students understand that they can turn in their papers anonymously. Encourage them to be open and honest about their experience with discrimination or harassment. In the class discussion, offer concrete solutions that students can realistically apply.

Web Extra

At the Workplace Fairness Web site, students should click the "Issues" link at the top of the page to jump to the various issues on which information is provided. Make sure students' summaries identify the issue and why they think it is important, explain how the issue affects workers, and offer examples of how workers can deal with the issue.

Problem Solver

Students are to develop a presentation on important records for a small business to keep, and set up examples of them for a pet supply store. In addition to those mentioned in the text, some records to keep are:

- Sale records
- Year-end financial statements
- Inventory lists
- Invoices from vendors
- Payroll summaries
- Employment applications and personnel records

Write Now

Students are asked to compare and contrast the skills and roles they will use in their home, school, and work environments. Have students review the *Recognizing Roles and Responsibilities* section in Chapter 1. As a writing prompt, have them create a three-column table in which they characterize their roles and responsibilities in their home environment in one column, those of school in the second column, and those of work in the third column. Or, they might create a Venn diagram consisting of three overlapping circles with the similar roles and responsibilities listed in the center and each environment's unique characteristics listed in the outer part of the circles.

Be Involved!

Students are to create posters that promote anti-harassment and anti-discrimination in school. Students might review the section *Overcoming Discrimination and Harassment* in this chapter as well as the *Coping with Bullies* section in Chapter 5 to refresh their memory on bullying behavior, its effects, and how to deal with it. Remind students to be persuasive in their message, and to design their posters so that students of all ages will understand their message.

Social Networking

Students are asked to find a homeless shelter or women's shelter that collects business clothing for residents to wear to job interviews. They are to organize a clothing drive to collect this type of apparel to then donate to the shelter. Make sure students select appropriate clothing from the donations received. Those items not deemed appropriate might be donated to another organization, such as Goodwill Industries.

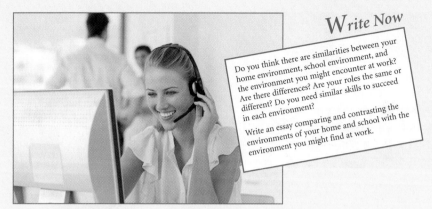

Write Now

Do you think there are similarities between your home environment, school environment, and the environment you might encounter at work? Are there differences? Are your roles the same or different? Do you need similar skills to succeed in each environment?

Write an essay comparing and contrasting the environments of your home and school with the environment you might find at work.

Be Involved!

www.fcclainc.org

Students have the right to be free of harassment and discrimination in school, just like employees in the workplace. As a class, discuss the ways harassment and discrimination occur in school. Brainstorm ideas for an anti-harassment and discrimination theme and slogan.

Individually, create a poster that educates people about harassment or discrimination, using the theme and slogan selected by the class. Display the posters in your classroom, or on a bulletin board in a common area of the school. Invite members of your school community to vote on the poster they think best represents the theme and slogan. Notify your local media about the display. They may want to publish examples of the posters in print or online.

Social Networking

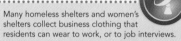

Many homeless shelters and women's shelters collect business clothing that residents can wear to work, or to job interviews.

Contact organizations in your area to see if they would welcome donations. Then, sponsor a clothing drive at school to collect clothing appropriate for a workplace. You might give prizes to the class that collects the most items. Deliver the collected items to the organization, or request a pick-up.

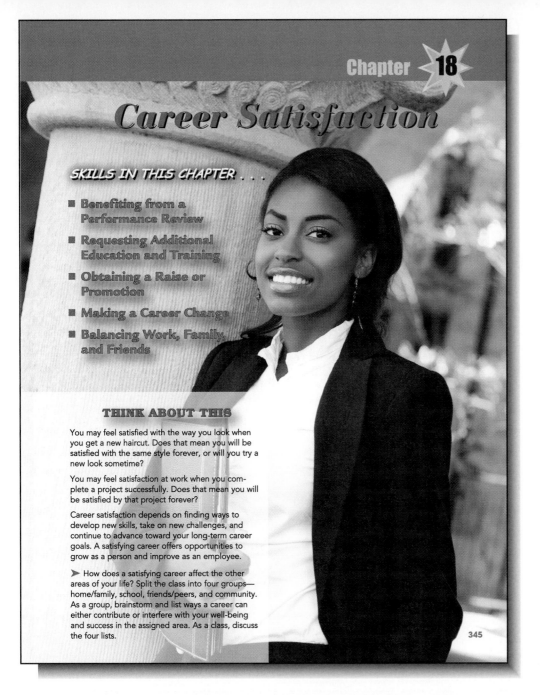

Chapter **18**

Career Satisfaction

SKILLS IN THIS CHAPTER . . .

- Benefiting from a Performance Review
- Requesting Additional Education and Training
- Obtaining a Raise or Promotion
- Making a Career Change
- Balancing Work, Family, and Friends

THINK ABOUT THIS

You may feel satisfied with the way you look when you get a new haircut. Does that mean you will be satisfied with the same style forever, or will you try a new look sometime?

You may feel satisfaction at work when you complete a project successfully. Does that mean you will be satisfied by that project forever?

Career satisfaction depends on finding ways to develop new skills, take on new challenges, and continue to advance toward your long-term career goals. A satisfying career offers opportunities to grow as a person and improve as an employee.

➤ How does a satisfying career affect the other areas of your life? Split the class into four groups—home/family, school, friends/peers, and community. As a group, brainstorm and list ways a career can either contribute or interfere with your well-being and success in the assigned area. As a class, discuss the four lists.

345

ADVANCE PREPARATION	
Review	*Life Skills for the 21st Century* textbook, Chapter 18.
Prepare	Paper and pencil for some activities. Box labeled "Hot Topics."

CUSTOMIZED INSTRUCTION OVERVIEW				
Less Advanced Students	More Advanced Students	ESOL Students	Special Needs Students	At-Risk Students
Pages 346, 350	Page 348	Page 348	Page 350	Page 346

Chapter 18 Overview

This chapter explores how on-the-job experiences contribute to your roles, responsibilities, and well-being in other areas of your life. It also discusses ways to optimize performance reviews and negotiate pay raises and promotions.

Benefiting from a Performance Review It's normal to be nervous about a performance review, but knowing what to expect and how to apply the feedback to improve your performance can put you closer to meeting your career goals.
Requesting Additional Education and Training Much of an individual's career success depends on his or her ability to strengthen existing skills and develop new ones through continuing education and on-the-job training.
Obtaining a Raise or Promotion This section provides tips on how to earn a raise or promotion and discusses how they are an important part of career success and satisfaction.
Making a Career Change This section discusses the common reasons for making a career change and how to manage the transition from one job to another.
Balancing Work, Family, and Friends This section explores the career and lifestyle choices that influence your well-being, satisfaction, and happiness.

Focus and Engage

Bell-Ringer: Think About This

Student teams are to list the positive and negative ways a career affects an individual's well-being and success in the assigned area of life: home/family, school, friends/peers, and community. Some ideas are:

- In the home/family area, the most obvious positive effect is financial security. Others include high self-esteem for family members and increased opportunities to acquire more resources, such as education. The most obvious negative effect is the demands on your time, leaving less time for family.
- In the school area, the positive effect is the development of important skills that you can apply in school, such as time-management, leadership, and teamwork. The negative effect is the time it can take away from studying, school work, and the pursuit of additional education.
- In the friends/peers area, the positive effects are making new friends with whom you share a common interest and developing stronger interpersonal skills. The negative effect is having less time to focus on friends and your social network.
- In the community area, the positive effects are the employee's increased purchasing power, tax revenues, and higher productivity. The negative effect is less time to volunteer or be involved in the community.

Introduce the Section

This section discusses performance reviews. It's normal to be nervous or anxious about a performance review, but knowing what to expect and how to apply the feedback to improve your performance can put you closer to meeting your career goals.

Vocabulary

Peer reviews: Type of performance review in which co-workers rate an employee's performance.

Performance review or job review: A report that rates how well an employee does his or her job.

Self reviews: Type of performance review in which an employee rates his or her own performance.

Figure Focus

Explain that a performance review is also an opportunity for you to share ideas about your future with the company. Ask students who have gone through a performance review what they gained from the process. If you think it is appropriate, discuss your own experiences in performance reviews.

Benefiting from a Performance Review

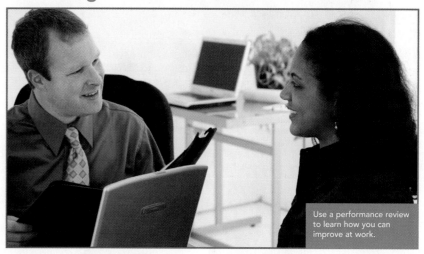

Use a performance review to learn how you can improve at work.

How do you know when you are doing well in school? Do you receive a report card? Do you have a conference with your teacher to discuss your progress?

When you are an employee, you receive a **job review** or **performance review**—a report that rates how well you do your job. A performance review evaluates you in different areas, depending on your job. For example, if you are a carpenter, it might evaluate you on your ability to use tools or follow safety procedures. Some common areas for evaluation include:

- Job performance
- Attendance
- Attitude
- Ability to communicate with customers
- Relationships with co-workers
- Relationship with manager

A performance review is a resource that helps you understand how your supervisor views your ability to manage your work-related tasks. You can use the information to improve and advance in your career.

What to Expect

Most companies schedule performance reviews on a regular basis. Your supervisor or a representative from human resources should tell you the schedule, or you might find it in your employee handbook.

Many companies use an assessment form, similar to a report card. Your supervisor will rate your performance in different areas. Ask your supervisor to explain the performance standards, so you know what is expected of you.

Some companies use **peer reviews**, in which your co-workers rate your performance, or **self reviews**, in which you rate your own performance. In any case, when it is time for the performance review, you will sit down with your supervisor to discuss your scores.

- You might receive a score of Meets Standards for your ability to complete your responsibilities on time.
- You might receive a score of Exceeds Standards because you often help others complete their tasks.
- You might receive a score of Needs Improvement if you are frequently late for work.

Following your meeting, your supervisor may ask you to sign the assessment form. Read it to make sure you understand it before you sign.

Customized Instruction: Less Advanced/At-Risk Students

Have students do a self-review of their classroom performance during the last week. Have them rate the following:

- Attendance (includes being on time for class)
- Performance on tests or quizzes
- Completion of homework assignments
- Attitude
- Relationship with classmates
- Relationship with teacher

They can use the following scale or another one you prefer:

3 – Exceeds Expectations

2 – Meets Expectations

1 – Needs Improvement

Making the Most of Your Performance Review

What does it mean if you receive a score of "Needs Improvement" on a performance review? Does your supervisor hate you? Will you lose your job?

The information in your performance review is intended to help you succeed at work. Use the time in the meeting to discuss with your supervisor ways you can make the most of your strengths at work, as well as how you can improve on the areas where you may be underperforming—or not living up to expectations. Use these tips to make the most out of your performance review:

- Listen attentively to all your supervisor says.
- Take notes highlighting the areas in which your supervisor expects you to improve.
- Be prepared to talk about yourself and your role at work.
- Accept criticism calmly; it is meant to help you improve.
- Ask questions so you fully understand what is expected of you.

Your performance review is also a good time to discuss the goals you have achieved and to set new goals for the coming year. You can discuss things that are on your mind, such as requesting training or asking about opportunities for new responsibilities. You can exhibit qualities of a successful employee, which will help establish a positive relationship with your supervisor and also show that you are committed to your career.

Requesting a Performance Review

In a supportive work environment, your supervisor and co-workers offer praise and guidance every day. There are regularly scheduled performance reviews to help guide your career growth and progress.

Sometimes, a supervisor forgets to schedule the review. He or she may be busy, or might not enjoy the process. If that happens, you will have to speak up.

Be polite but assertive when you request a performance review. Remind your supervisor that it is time for the review, and that you would welcome information that will help you succeed at your job.

If your supervisor continues forgetting to schedule the review, you may have to use problem-solving skills to find a way to arrange one.

- In a larger company, you can contact the human resources department for help scheduling a meeting with your supervisor.
- In a small company, performance reviews may be less formal; you may have to politely remind your supervisor that it would benefit both of you to schedule the time.

What can you do during a performance review to show your employer that you are committed to your career?

Don't just work for the money. That will bring you only limited satisfaction.

— Kathy Ireland, American Model and Actress

Do You Meet Performance Standards?

Here are three reasons employees might not meet performance standards, and actions you can take to improve.

✔ *Not enough training. If you do not know the proper procedure, it is difficult to perform up to expectations. Ask for training so that you can improve.*

✔ *Distractions. Problems in the workplace can interfere with performance. For example, you might be bothered by noise, conflict with co-workers or customers, lack of air circulation, poor lighting, or equipment that does not work. Politely discuss the problems with your supervisor, and use the problem-solving process to find solutions.*

✔ *Lack of motivation, or encouragement. You may be bored or tired, or feel as if your work is not valued by your supervisor or co-workers. It is hard to be positive if you are not motivated. Politely discuss your feelings with your supervisor to see if there are steps you can take to improve conditions.*

Introduce the Section

Much of an individual's career success depends on their ability to strengthen existing skills and develop new ones through continuing education and on-the-job training. This section discusses types of education and training opportunities for employees.

Figure Focus

Ask students to comment on any special training or courses they have taken for work or which their employers have offered. What type of training was it? What did they learn and what skills did they acquire from it? You might discuss any continuing education or additional training you have undergone in your career.

Discuss

Some reports estimate that American businesses spend in excess of $2 billion a year on employee education. Changing technology is one reason employers are investing in employee education. Another is the fact that workers are increasingly forced to wear many hats, so there is a greater need to cross-train employees. Discuss how the employer benefits from providing employees with additional education and training opportunities. Many companies that offer education benefits report an increase in productivity and significantly higher employee retention rates.

Requesting Additional Education and Training

Education and training help you develop skills to advance your career.

You have been in the same job for over a year. Your performance review is "Meets Expectations" in all categories. You like your workplace and your co-workers. You get along well with your supervisor. So, why are you feeling frustrated and a little bored?

To keep up with changes in the workplace, you may need to develop new skills. Some careers such as those in health care require that you update your certification on a regular basis. For other careers, it is up to you to make sure you stay up to date on changes and advancements.

- A computer technician must keep up with changes in technology.
- A tax accountant is responsible for knowing about changes to tax policy and regulations.
- A travel agent may want to keep up with world events so she can recommend safe vacation spots to her clients.

It is up to you to seek out opportunities for education and training, and to make sure you are prepared for changes and advancement that come your way.

Why Should You Develop New Skills?

There are two basic reasons for developing new skills:

- Keeping up with changes that affect your current job. You might work in a doctor's office where you must change from a paper filing system to a digital filing system. You must learn to use the digital filing system, or you will not be able to meet your responsibilities.
- Preparing for new career opportunities. You might have a job as a bank teller, which you started after high school graduation. To advance to a position as a branch manager, you must earn a bachelor's degree.

Customized Instruction: More Advanced Students

Have students work as a team to develop a list of your school's clubs and groups. For example, the Spanish Club, the Drama Club, FCCLA, Future Business Leaders of America, and the Yearbook Staff. Have them talk to the club's adviser to find out what types of education and training members might obtain or have access to. Have the team present their findings to the class.

Customized Instruction: ESOL Students

Ask students to share their thoughts on how ESOL training and programs would benefit a company. In general, an important workplace skill is effective communication—with other employees, with supervisors and managers, and with customers. ESOL training would help workers build and strengthen their "employability" skills.

How Can You Develop New Skills?

There are many ways to develop new skills. Co-workers and supervisors often provide on-the-job training simply by showing you how to improve the way you do your regular tasks, or teaching you new skills. For example, a co-worker at a restaurant might show you a faster way to prep salads or a more efficient way to load the dishwasher.

Your company might also offer other opportunities for education and training:

- Specialized courses, such as a seminar about customer service for sales representatives, or a session on how to use Web-based storage for data management employees.
- **Professional development**—training in your chosen career. Teachers are usually required to participate in professional development to learn about new trends in education and advancements in their area of expertise, or to prepare for certification exams.
- Tuition reimbursement programs—which means that if you take a class your company will pay the tuition costs. You can take classes at a local college on nights or weekends to earn a degree or certification, or simply to learn material that might help you advance.

Developing new skills prepares you for new responsibilities and helps you achieve career, academic, and life goals. Even if your employer does not offer these opportunities, you can take steps to continue your education and training on your own by taking classes or reading books. It makes you a more valuable worker and helps you grow as a person.

Benefits of Joining a Professional Organization

A **professional organization** is an association of people who are all employed in the same field or industry. Usually, the goals of a professional organization include providing education and training and acting as a source of information about the industry. It is similar to a student organization, such as FCCLA, or Future Business Leaders of America.

There are professional organizations for just about every career you can imagine—sometimes more than one. Benefits of joining a professional organization include:

- Opportunities to meet people in the industry. You can increase the number of contacts you have for networking and make friends who share similar interests.
- Access to the most current news and trends affecting the industry. Professional organizations publish Web sites and newsletters to make sure members have the latest information.
- Access to training. Organizations hold meetings, sponsor speakers and seminars, and offer classes for members.
- Leadership opportunities. Organizations are run by members. You can participate in meetings, volunteer for community events, or run for an office, such as president or treasurer of your local chapter.

Some companies will pay for membership in a professional organization, but you may have to pay the dues yourself. Joining helps you expand your career opportunities and improve your career-related skills. It also shows your employer that you are serious about your career.

TECH CONNECT

Do you think it is possible to take a college course without ever leaving your home? Welcome to the world of online education. Many colleges offer online courses that you access using your computer and the Internet. The instructor posts video lectures, notes, and assignments on a Web site. You log in and participate as if you were on campus. Sites often have tools that allow students to communicate in real time so they can study together, or work on group assignments.

Some companies provide online training, too. You might be able to complete a course in ethics online, or use a simulation training program to learn how to use new equipment.

Use the Internet to research the online courses offered by colleges in your area. Do they lead to a degree? What requirements must you meet to enroll? Make a presentation about the benefits and drawbacks of taking a course online.

Education and Training in All Areas of Your Life

Education and training is not limited to learning new skills for the workplace. You might also want to consider educational opportunities to enrich your life at home, with friends, and in your community.

- ✔ *Take a class to learn a new hobby, such as quilting or woodworking.*
- ✔ *Join an exercise program, such as karate, golf, or fitness.*
- ✔ *Enroll in a community college to improve your personal finance skills.*
- ✔ *Join a book club to expand your reading skills and social group.*
- ✔ *Attend a seminar at your bank about starting your own business.*

Education and Training in All Areas of Your Life

Stress the importance of lifelong learning and how it can help keep your brain young. Some medical experts believe that lifelong learning and stimulating educational activities help build your cognitive reserve, which is a complex network of neural connections that enable the brain to maintain function in spite of damage or the dying-off of brain cells due to aging. The bigger the reserve, the more cells you'll have to stave off memory loss and stay sharper. Emphasize that at the very least, you should engage in lifelong learning and take advantage of training and education opportunities to enhance your quality of life.

Vocabulary

Professional development: Training in your chosen career.

Professional organization: An association of people who are all employed in the same field or industry; goals include providing education and training and acting as a source of information about the industry.

TECH CONNECT

Students are to research online courses offered by colleges in their area and create a presentation about the benefits and drawbacks of taking a course online. Some of the benefits are:

- Flexible scheduling. You can log on to complete coursework at your convenience.
- Self-paced. You can learn at your own pace, as long as your work is completed by the due date.
- No transportation hassles or cost. Because you work from your computer, you do not spend time traveling to and from a physical location nor do you incur transportation or parking costs.

Some of the drawbacks are:

- No face-to-face interaction. You will not meet classmates in person.
- No immediate answers or clarification. If you have a question about the course content, you have to send the question to the instructor and then wait for his or her response.
- No set schedule. Because an online course is designed to fit around your schedule, you have to be motivated and organized and utilize good time management skills.

Discuss

Discuss different types of continuing education. These include:

- On-the-job learning.
- In-house course work.
- Professional association credits.
- Seminars and certificates offered by universities.
- Customized education programming offered on-site in collaboration with a university.

Introduce the Section

This section provides tips on how to earn a raise or promotion and discusses how they are an important part of career success and satisfaction.

Vocabulary

Bonus: Pay in addition to your regular salary.
Promotion: An advance in your career that includes a new job title and additional responsibilities.
Raise: An increase in pay.

Figure Focus

Explain that pay raises and promotions are typically linked to how you rate on your performance review. In most occupations, an employer is not required to give you a raise or promotion. In others, pay raises are standardized and promotions are based on your performance on a written test.

Discuss

In addition to pay raises and bonuses, discuss other financial rewards. These include:

- Donating to the employee's favorite charity or his children's school.
- Sharing a percentage of the company's profits.
- Granting more paid time off.
- Offering tuition reimbursement or opportunities for training and continuing education.

Also discuss nonfinancial ways employers can reward employees. These include:

- Providing more flexible work arrangements such as telecommuting, part-time employment or job-sharing, or hours that accommodate an employee's other interests.
- Assigning a special project to manage.
- Granting more autonomy or freedom in work duties and responsibilities.
- Giving bonuses in the form of tickets to a sporting event or concert, a weekend getaway, or junkets (expense-paid trips).

Obtaining a Raise or Promotion

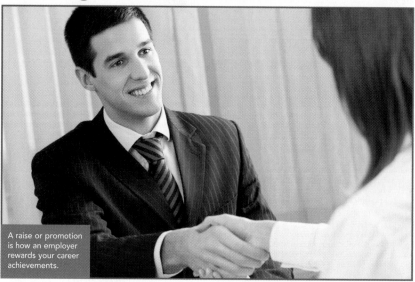

A raise or promotion is how an employer rewards your career achievements.

A raise or a promotion might be career goals you have set for yourself. A **raise** is an increase in pay. A **promotion** is an advance in your career that includes a new job title and additional responsibilities. Both are ways that a company recognizes and rewards your achievements.

So, how do you achieve a raise or promotion? One way is to work hard, excel at your job, and show your supervisor that you have the skills, interests, and abilities to take on more responsibility. Another way is to work at the same company for a long time.

Earning a raise or promotion is an important part of career success and satisfaction. They are proof that your employer appreciates your contributions to the company. They contribute to your well-being by enhancing your self-image, providing new challenges, and—of course—giving you more money to spend on your needs and wants.

The Importance of Advancement

You might feel satisfied in your current position, or happy that you don't have more responsibility. It might seem as if earning a promotion is too much . . . well, work. So, why bother?

Recall from Chapter 14 that a *career* is your chosen field of work in which you try to advance over time by gaining responsibility. Without advancement and added responsibility, a career is just work.

Obviously, a promotion is likely to come with more money. It might also come with added benefits, such as an end-of-year **bonus**—pay in addition to your regular salary. Promotions are also important because:

- Your self-esteem is enhanced by your success.
- Accepting new challenges is exciting.
- Being recognized and rewarded brings career satisfaction.
- Achieving certain goals allows you to set new goals for the future.

Customized Instruction: Less Advanced/Special Needs Students

Ask students to list the rewards they get at home and at school for a job well done. At home, these might include an allowance, new clothes or video games, a later curfew, or more freedom to do what they like. At school, these might be homework passes, spirit wear or gift items, and special achievement awards and certificates.

How Can You Earn a Raise?

How long does it take to earn a raise? The answer depends on your job and on company policies. There are two basic types of raises:

- An *annual raise* is awarded to all employees on a regular basis—usually once a year. It may be based on **seniority**—how long you have worked for the company——or on how successful the company has been. You will be notified of the increase a few weeks in advance. It is usually a percentage of your current pay.
- A *merit raise* is based on your performance. If you are exceeding expectations, or if you are promoted to a new job or assume new responsibilities, you might earn a merit raise. A merit raise can be awarded at any time.

How Can You Earn a Promotion?

What does it take to earn a promotion? You must prove to your supervisor that you are ready for more responsibility. Then, there must be an opportunity.

- You might earn a promotion if someone with more seniority leaves. For example, your supervisor might retire, or a co-worker with more responsibility might take a job in a different department.
- Another way to earn a promotion is if the company grows. Companies that do well might expand into new areas of businesses. They will need employees to take on the new tasks and responsibilities.
- A third way to earn a promotion is to create a new job for yourself. You might see an opportunity for something new in your department. For example, you might work in a restaurant. You suggest to your manager that you could expand business by offering home delivery. Your manager might put you in charge of the new home delivery service.

NUMBERS GAME

Area measures the amount of space taken up by the surface of a shape. Some jobs and hobbies depend on knowing how to calculate area. For example, a gardener may need to know the area of a flower bed. A farmer may need to know the area of a field he plans to plant. A painter may need to know the area of a wall in a room she is going to paint.

To find the area of a surface, multiply the length by the width. For example, if the flower bed is 14 feet long by 8 feet wide, the area is $14 \times 8 = 112$.

- What is the area of a wall in a room that is 13.75 feet long and 8 feet high?

Hint: Draw a picture of the wall and label it with the measurements.

- If the room is 12 feet wide, what is the area of each of the other three walls?
- What is the total area of all the walls in the room?

Hint: Add the area of each of the four walls.

"If I take a leadership role on this project, will I earn a merit raise?"

But I Deserve It!

You have been at the company a few years. You have no scores of Needs Improvement on your performance assessment. You earn an annual raise every year. What can you do to earn a promotion?

- 👎 Start acting like you were promoted and boss your co-workers around.
- 👎 Be disrespectful to your supervisor.
- 👎 Pass up opportunities for developing new skills.
- 👍 Join a professional organization.
- 👍 Propose new projects or suggest ways to improve productivity.
- 👍 Meet with your supervisor to discuss opportunities in your department, or in other departments.

How could you advance in your career if there are no opportunities for a promotion available?

Vocabulary

Annual raise: Raise awarded to all employees on a regular basis, usually once a year.

Area: Amount of space taken up by the surface of a shape.

Merit raise: Raise based on your performance; can be awarded at any time.

Seniority: How long you have worked for the company.

NUMBERS GAME

To calculate the area of a wall in a room that is 13.75 feet long and 8 feet high, multiply 13.75 by 8; this equals 110 square feet. For the other wall that is 12 feet wide and 8 feet high, multiply 12 by 8; this equals 96 square feet. One other wall is also 96 square feet, and you know from the first calculation that two of the walls are 110 square feet each. So, the total area of walls is 96 + 96 +110 + 110, which equals 412 square feet.

Figure Focus

In addition to taking a leadership role, ask students to suggest other ways an employee might earn a merit raise. Some examples are meeting goals, improving your performance, helping the company save money, and helping the company make more money.

But I Deserve It!

You can advance in your career without a promotion by expanding your responsibilities, cross-training in other areas, and taking on more challenging duties or projects.

Stay in School

Explain to students that the jobs available to high school dropouts tend to be unstable, to pay low wages, and to provide little opportunity for advancement. Even if you stay with the same job for several years, the payoff is only modest for those with little education. For example, one study found that among women who stay with the same employer, those without a high school diploma see annual wage increases of less than 1 percent; those with a high school diploma see about twice that; and those with a college degree see their wages grow five times as fast. Furthermore, if a less-educated worker decides to leave an existing job, he or she is more likely to end up unemployed rather than in a new job.

Introduce the Section

This section discusses the common reasons for making a career change and how to manage the transition from one job to another.

Figure Focus

Discuss with students the reasons listed in the text for making a career change. Ask if they can think of others. Then, discuss the possibility of making a career change for the wrong reasons. For example:

- You confuse hating your job with hating your career. You might be unhappy with your job, but that doesn't necessarily mean you'd be unhappy in a different job within the same career.

- You see that the career you are currently in does not provide the higher salary levels and benefits that other careers do.

- Your parents, friends, or significant other pressure you to change careers.

- You have friends or relatives who are successful in their career so you think it could also be a good choice for you.

Discuss

Explain the importance of conducting ongoing career assessments. Before making a career change, you should reassess your likes and dislikes, interests, and abilities. You should take inventory of the skills, education, and experience you've acquired in the career in which you've been working. You should revisit your career plan, which defines your ultimate career goal and the short-term goals you've set to achieve it.

Making a Career Change

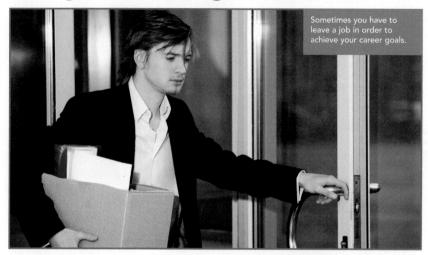

Sometimes you have to leave a job in order to achieve your career goals.

How do you know when it is time to change jobs? That depends on whether it is a decision you make for yourself, or one that your employer makes for you.

- You might feel that you have reached your potential, and that there is no more room for advancement.
- Your family might move to a different city, making the commute to your current job impossible.
- You might just want to try something new.

Or,

- Your employer might not be satisfied with your performance.
- Your job may be eliminated.
- Your company might go out of business.

Changing jobs is stressful, just like changing schools or starting a new grade. It means leaving a familiar situation. It means beginning your job search all over again. It is also an opportunity to think critically about your career, and to set new career goals. Looking at a job change as an opportunity for something new instead of the loss of something old can lead to greater career satisfaction and positive well-being.

Leaving the Company

Even when you are the one who makes the decision to leave, changing jobs can be confusing and depressing. Some things you can do to make process easier for yourself and your employer include:

- *Give plenty of notice.* Giving notice means telling your employer you are leaving. You should be clear about the date you plan to stop working. Most companies ask you to give notice two weeks before your last day. That gives them time to look for your replacement.
- *Create a job folder for your replacement.* The folder should contain lists of the responsibilities, procedures, and resources needed for the job. It will help your replacement settle in and become productive.
- *Meet with human resources to discuss your benefits, including what to do with your 401(k) or other retirement account.* This may be part of your **exit interview**—a meeting with your supervisor or human resources to discuss why you are leaving.

Leaving on good terms is important. You want to maintain positive relationships with your supervisor and co-workers. You may want them as references for future jobs or as contacts for networking, or you may want to work for the company again someday.

Coping with a Layoff

At some point, through no fault of your own, you may be **terminated**—lose your job. You might be working hard and doing everything right. But, you and your co-workers could be out of work because of a **layoff**. A layoff is a job loss caused when a company has no work for certain employees for a period of time. Some layoffs are short—you might work at a factory that receives no orders for new products for six months, but when new orders come in, you are called back to work. Some layoffs are permanent. The factory might shut down and never reopen.

Losing your job can make you angry or depressed. It seems unfair. You lose your income. You lose your daily routine. You may even lose friends. Steps for coping with a job loss include the following.

- Make sure you understand the reason for your termination.
- Ask for letters of recommendation.
- Analyze the terms of your **severance package**—which is compensation you receive because you are being terminated. It may include wages, training, career counseling, and temporary continuation of medical insurance.
- File for unemployment benefits as soon as you are eligible. **Unemployment benefits** are money and career counseling services that are available to unemployed workers while they are looking for new jobs.

Finding a New Job

The best time to look for a new job is while you still have the old one. If you make the decision to resign, or if you know a layoff is coming, you can update your resume and start your job search before you are unemployed.

The process for finding a new job is basically the same as for finding a first job. Assess your skills, abilities, and interests; research job opportunities; and send out your resume.

- One advantage finding a new job has over finding a first job is that you have experience. Make sure your resume highlights your most recent job description.
- Another advantage is that you can focus your networking on the contacts you have developed in the industry. Get in touch with people you met through work, including customers and clients, members of professional organizations, and even your competition. Let them know you are looking for work.

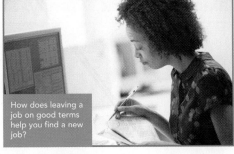

How does leaving a job on good terms help you find a new job?

Loss or Opportunity?

Being unemployed may be an opportunity to expand your knowledge and skills. What if your company closes permanently?

★ *You might decide to open your own sandwich shop.*

★ *You might retrain in an industry that is growing, such as education.*

★ *You might move to a part of the country that has low unemployment.*

★ *You might take a temporary job while you decide what to do next.*

What skills and resources can you use to turn a job loss into an opportunity for advancement?

What Is Outsourcing?

An employment trend that has led to layoffs in the U.S. is outsourcing. **Outsourcing** is when one business pays another to perform a task that the first business could do itself.

For example, a U.S clothing manufacturer that hires fabric cutters and stitchers in Mexico is outsourcing the work. The American fabric cutters and stitchers who used to do the job are laid off.

Some people think outsourcing is bad, because people lose their jobs. Others think it contributes to lower costs and prices, and that the employees who lost their jobs can retrain for new, better jobs.

Use the Internet to research outsourcing and how it has affected the economy in the United States and in other countries. Divide the class in two, and hold a debate on whether outsourcing is good or bad.

Vocabulary

Layoff: Job loss caused when a company has no work for certain employees for a period of time.

Outsourcing: When one business pays another to perform a task that the first business could do itself.

Severance package: Compensation you receive because you are being terminated.

Terminated: To lose your job.

Unemployment benefits: Money and career counseling services that are available to unemployed workers while they are looking for new jobs.

Figure Focus

Ask students why they think it's important to leave a job on good terms. It's important because prospective employers will most likely ask you questions about your most recent job or they might want to contact your previous employers to verify information you have provided on your resume. Leaving a company on good terms adds to your employability skills. It is a good indicator of a positive attitude, the ability to communicate effectively with supervisors and co-workers, and responsibility in doing the job right.

Loss or Opportunity?

Ask students to think of skills and resources they could tap in order to turn a job loss into a job opportunity. Skills will vary by student. Resources would include your network of contacts, online resources (such as company Web sites, online job agencies, and social networking sites), a career center at school or within your community, employment agencies, job fairs, and help wanted ads.

 What Is Outsourcing?

The class is to debate the topic of outsourcing. Some of the positive effects are:

- Lowers the expenses of the company, which means, theoretically, that lower costs will be passed on to the consumer.
- Lower prices on products increase consumer spending power.
- When consumers buy more, companies will need to increase production and hire more employees.
- Provides jobs for workers in less-developed countries, which improves the countries' economies, which should lead to improved trade between those countries and the United States.

The negative effects include:

- Loss of jobs for U.S. workers.
- Without a job, workers lose their income and their spending power is decreased.
- Decreased spending power means consumers buy less, and companies see sales decrease.
- When sales decrease, companies decrease production and have fewer jobs available.
- Jobs that are outsourced do not always benefit workers in other countries where working conditions can be poor and even abusive.

Introduce the Section

This section explores the career and lifestyle choices that influence your well-being, satisfaction, and happiness.

Figure Focus

Ask students to think about the number of hours they spend in a typical week on their roles in the five main areas of their life:

- At home
- With peers
- In school
- At work
- In the community

Encourage them to be as precise as possible, breaking down the hours they spend each day in each area. Then, discuss in which areas they spend the most time and the least time. Do they feel they are balancing their roles in each area?

Reinforce and Review

Review the concepts of values and standards. You develop values by figuring out what is important to you. Some things have monetary value because they cost money. Some have sentimental value because they are important for emotional reasons. Your personal values are the thoughts, ideas, and actions that are important to you. You use values to set standards. When you have high standards, it shows you value something a lot. Setting a lower standard means you don't value something so much.

Balancing Work, Family, and Friends

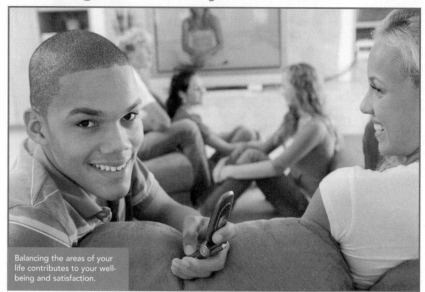

Balancing the areas of your life contributes to your well-being and satisfaction.

How much time do you want to spend at work? How much time do you want to spend at home? Do you need time to volunteer? When will you see your friends?

- An attorney works 80 hours a week. She earns enough money to host her extended family for one month each summer at her vacation beach home.
- A chef works nights and weekends, but he is available during the day to volunteer at his child's school.
- A truck driver is frequently out of town, but calls home every night to talk to his family before bed.

Your career impacts the way you perform your responsibilities in other areas of your life. Balancing work with the other areas of your life will help you achieve overall satisfaction.

Career Choices and a Balanced Lifestyle

The choices you make in your career impact your relationships with your family, friends, and community. Using your values and standards to make choices will help you keep the areas of your life in balance.

- Do you pursue a high-paying career because it enables you to provide your family with the things they need and want, and you can make cash contributions to charities?
- Do you work in human services because you enjoy helping others and think it sets an important example for your family?

Your values and standards are likely to change over time. You may benefit from reconsidering your choices on a regular basis to make sure they still support your values.

Lifelong Learning

Lifelong learning is more than just developing new skills and maintaining old ones. It means being aware of changes that occur around you, and adapting your roles and responsibilities, as necessary. Setting goals for lifelong learning can help you achieve your career goals and find career satisfaction.

By taking the time each day to read news online or watch it on television, you can keep up with current events. You will be prepared to identify trends that might affect your career, family, or community. Other ways to pursue lifelong learning include the following.

- Continuing your education will contribute to your self-esteem and improve your qualifications for achieving career success. It will help you adapt to changing roles in your family. For example, you may shift from a dependent to a provider.
- Developing hobbies and interests will help you maintain your role as a friend. You will meet new peers and find new ways to enjoy time with old friends.
- Contributing to your community lets you show your values while supporting shared resources. It enhances your self-esteem, develops new skills and abilities, and earns you respect and friendship.

Enjoying Leisure Activities

One hundred years ago, it was common for people in the United States to work 6 days a week, 12 hours each day. They had very little time for **recreation** or **leisure**—fun—activities outside of work. Now, most people value leisure activities and vacation as a necessary part of balancing work with the other areas of their lives. Leisure activities contribute to your well-being in many ways.

- They improve your emotional well-being by helping you cope with stress.
- They improve your social well-being by giving you time with family and friends.
- Some forms improve your physical well-being by providing exercise.
- They improve your personal well-being by helping you develop new skills and interests.

Leisure activities can range from reading a book to playing sports, to taking a hike. The ones that are most satisfying match your interests and values. You might want to volunteer for the Special Olympics, go bird-watching, or attend a concert.

Leisure is an opportunity to relax and enjoy yourself, and to take time off from your work responsibilities. Finding time for leisure activities may seem difficult. Use goal-setting strategies to incorporate them into your daily schedule.

Events That Can Change Career Plans

Be prepared for the unexpected! Flexibility, problem solving, and decision making will help you cope with events that might disrupt your career plans, including:

✔ *Marriage*
✔ *Parenthood*
✔ *Divorce*
✔ *Sickness or disability*
✔ *Layoffs*
✔ *Relocation to a new city*

Myth Balancing work and family is a women's issue.

Truth Once, traditional roles meant men were responsible for earning money and women were responsible for taking care of the home and family. Now, the responsibilities are more evenly shared, and both men and women are concerned with balancing work and family.

21st Century Skills — What Happens Next?

Malik looks forward to Sundays. He and his family have always spent Sundays at his grandmother's house. His aunts, uncles, and cousins often come, too. There may be 20 relatives there—eating dinner, playing games, and having a good time.

Malik is considering a career as a personal trainer. He has a part-time job at a fitness club. He collects towels from the locker room, wipes down equipment, and keeps the floors clean and dry. He usually works on Tuesdays and Thursdays from 3:30 until 6:00, and on Saturdays from 6:00 a.m. until noon.

An instructor offers Malik the opportunity to help out with a weekly class. She needs someone to demonstrate proper form and to show people the right way to use the equipment. Malik is very excited, until she explains that the class is on Sundays.

Malik is faced with a decision that impacts his roles at work and at home. Use your decision-making skills to help Malik analyze the situation, identify the problems, and make a choice. Using your 21st Century Skills—such as decision making, goal setting, and problem solving—write an ending to the story. Read it to the class, or form a small group and present it as a skit.

Vocabulary

Recreation or leisure: Fun or relaxing activities outside of work.

STUDENT ACTIVITY

Have students list the things they do for fun or in their leisure time and then write a sentence about how the activity contributes to their lifelong learning.

Events That Can Change Career Plans

Discuss with students the things you can do to remain focused on your career goals. These include:

- Staying in touch with important contacts and developing new ones.
- Keeping up with news, events, and trends that affect your industry and/or employer.
- Engaging in continuing education and lifelong learning activities.

Myth/Truth

Ask students to share ideas on how to balance work and family. Encourage them to provide examples from their immediate and extended families.

21st Century Skills

What Happens Next?

Students are to prepare an ending to Malik's dilemma. He must decide if he wants to take on additional responsibilities at the fitness club, which would mean missing the Sunday gatherings at his grandmother's house. Malik should first determine how much time he must commit to the new class. He might be able to help out and still join the family gathering on Sundays. If the scheduling is a conflict, he will need to decide if the opportunity is worth giving up the Sunday visits that he values greatly.

End-of-Chapter Activities

Case Study

Answers will vary, but students should think Leah did not handle herself appropriately. She became defensive, blamed others for her mistakes, interrupted her supervisor, and complained that her work was too easy, making it sound as if she didn't like her job.

She could have listened politely to her supervisor, and then accepted responsibility for misfiling records. She could have asked for training in records management or for suggestions on how she can become more organized. She could have told her boss how much she likes the job, and how she wants to improve so that she can contribute to the success of the office.

Now, Leah has to decide if she wants to continue working in this office. If she does, she should immediately apologize for her outburst, and then take the opportunity to do all the things mentioned in the previous paragraph. If she wants to leave, she should still apologize, but explain that the job is not turning out as she expected and that she is giving her two weeks' notice.

Sounding Off!

Student answers will vary.

FAQ

1. Areas that are commonly evaluated on a performance review form include:
   - Job performance.
   - Attendance.
   - Attitude.
   - Ability to communicate with customers.
   - Relationships with co-workers.
   - Relationship with manager.
2. Tips for making the most of your performance review include:
   - Listen attentively to all your supervisor says.
   - Take notes highlighting the areas in which your supervisor expects you to improve.
   - Be prepared to talk about yourself and your role at work.
   - Accept criticism calmly; it is meant to help you improve.
   - Ask questions so you fully understand what is expected of you.
3. Reasons for developing new skills are to keep up with changes affecting your job and to prepare for new career opportunities.
4. Benefits of joining a professional organization include:
   - Opportunities to meet people in the industry.
   - Access to the most current news and trends affecting the industry.

Case Study

Leah has been working as an assistant in a medical office for three months. At her first performance review, her supervisor praised her for having a perfect attendance record. However, she received a score of Needs Improvement for organization, because she often filed patient records incorrectly.

Leah did not like the Needs Improvement score. She interrupted her supervisor to say that she thought it was one of the other assistants who made the errors. She said that filing was too easy, anyway, and that she needed something more challenging to do.

Leah's supervisor replied that if Leah was not happy with her role in the office, maybe the job was not right for her. Leah was stunned. Was she being fired?

■ Do you think Leah handled herself appropriately at her performance review?
■ What could she have done differently?
■ What decisions does Leah have to make now?
■ How should she respond to her supervisor?

Sounding Off!

1. Would you want your performance review to be completed by a peer or co-worker? Why or why not?
2. Do you think you would quit a job you like if you applied for a promotion but someone else got the job?

FAQ

1. List five areas that are commonly evaluated on a performance review form.
2. What are five tips for making the most of your performance review?
3. What are two reasons for developing new skills?
4. List four benefits of joining a professional organization.
5. List and explain the two types of raises.
6. List three ways to earn a promotion.
7. What is a layoff?
8. Explain at least one cause of layoffs.
9. How can lifelong learning contribute to your self-esteem?
10. How do leisure activities improve your social well-being?

- Access to training.
- Leadership opportunities.

5. An annual raise is awarded to all employees on a regular basis—usually once a year. It may be based on seniority—how long you have worked for the company—or on how successful the company has been. You will be notified of the increase a few weeks in advance. It is usually a percentage of your current pay. A merit raise is based on your performance. If you are exceeding expectations, or if you are promoted to a new job or assume new responsibilities, you might earn a merit raise. A merit raise can be awarded at any time.

6. You might earn a promotion if someone with more seniority leaves. Another way to earn a promotion is if the company grows.

A third way to earn a promotion is to create a new job for yourself.

7. A layoff is a job loss caused when a company has no work for certain employees for a period of time.

8. You might work at a factory that receives no orders for new products for six months, so manufacturing is stopped. Students might think of others, including a poor economy or outsourcing.

9. Learning new skills and gaining knowledge about subjects that interest you improve your self confidence. They prepare you for career advancements. You meet new people. You contribute to your community.

10. They improve your social well-being by giving you time with family and friends.

One goal of a professional organization is to distribute information about the industry. Most organizations have publications such as Web sites, newsletters, or magazines.

Working in teams of three or four, select an industry and create a two-page publication for its professional organization. Use the Internet to research current trends, policies, or events affecting the industry. Give the publication a suitable name, and write three or four articles that the members would find useful. Include pictures if appropriate. When your project is complete, print it to share with the class, or publish it on your class Web site.

Hot Topics

Has anyone in your family lost a job? Maybe a parent was hurt by layoffs. Maybe a sibling was fired. How did it affect your family?

Take this opportunity to write anonymously about your experience, how it made you feel, and how you dealt with it. Use a word processor so no one recognizes your handwriting. Be honest and open. Put the paper in the class Hot Topics box.

As a class, read the anonymous entries and discuss them.

Web Extra ▼

Each state has its own system for handling unemployment benefits. Use the Internet to research the procedure for your state. You might start at www.doleta.gov, the site for the U.S. Department of Labor.

Summarize the information in a report, and include links to important information for your state. Publish the summary on your school Web site, or make it available in your career center or library.

Problem Solver

You are the personnel director at a vacation resort. The manager of housekeeping services is looking for new ways to evaluate the performance of her staff. She has asked you to help her develop a performance review form.

Working alone or in pairs, research the careers and jobs in housekeeping services. Use the Internet to look up sample performance review forms. When you have enough information, create a performance review form that the manager could use to evaluate her employees.

Team Players

Student teams are to select an industry and create a two-page publication for its professional organization. Students will need access to the Internet for researching and a desktop publishing program in which to design their publication. They should come up with a name for the publication and identify who it is published for and its purpose somewhere within the publication. It should include three or four articles. Optional items are photographs, clip art, and charts or tables that help illustrate the content.

Hot Topics

Make sure students understand that they can turn in their papers anonymously. Encourage them to be open and honest about the job loss and how it affected their family.

Web Extra

Students are to research their state's system for handling unemployment benefits. In addition to the U.S. Department of Labor Web site listed in the text, students might search their state's official Web site for an office of unemployment compensation. They are to summarize the information in a report, and then post it in the school career center or library.

Problem Solver

Students are to research the careers and jobs in housekeeping services and prepare a performance review form for the manager of housekeeping services at a vacation resort. Jobs include housekeeping supervisor, laundry manager, guest room attendant, and public area attendant. The performance review form should include sections on accomplishments, areas in which to improve, and goals.

Write Now

Students might find it easier to complete this activity if they can interview someone they know who has been dissatisfied in a job. Encourage them to talk with friends and family to identify a possible "case study" candidate.

Be Involved!

As a class, students are to brainstorm ways they can help support working parents of their school community. They are to use the FCCLA planning process outlined below to develop, execute, and evaluate their efforts.

- Identify the topic.
- Set a goal.
- Form a plan (who, what, when, where, how, cost, resources, and evaluation).
- Act.
- Follow up.

Remind students that a successful team relationship depends on all team members working together. Make sure they take steps to delegate responsibilities, communicate effectively, and manage conflicts or disagreements.

Social Networking

Students are to contact a local senior center or daycare center to find out about volunteer opportunities. They should focus on volunteering for leisure time and recreational activities, such as making crafts or assisting in art, music, or dance classes.

Write Now

Can you think of reasons why someone might become dissatisfied with a job that he or she used to enjoy? Is it because of changing values? Changing goals? Could changes in other areas of life affect his or her job satisfaction?

If you were a career counselor, how would you advise someone who is dissatisfied with work? Write a report describing the person. Include information about the job and the person's career history, such as how long he or she has had the job, what responsibilities there are, and the quality of his or her relationships with co-workers. Describe the reasons the person is dissatisfied. Explain how you would recommend he or she approach the problem and find solutions.

Be Involved!

www.fcclainc.org

Sometimes working parents need help to successfully balance work and family. Busy parents may not have time to attend teacher conferences. They may not have resources to hire babysitters so they can participate in parent-teacher meetings, or volunteer in the community.

As a class, brainstorm ways you might be able to support the working parents of your school community. For example, could you provide babysitting services during school events such as teacher conferences or meetings? Could you create a booklet listing community resources that provide support?

Select one idea that uses the abilities and skills of all classmates. Use the goal-setting process to plan it and make it happen. Define the project as a goal, make an action plan for achieving the goal (including a timeframe), assess the plan to make sure it is realistic and attainable, and then put the plan into action to achieve your goal. You may want to organize teams within the class to handle specific responsibilities. For example, if you choose to publish a booklet, you might need some people to report and write the descriptions, some people to do the layout and design, and some to handle distribution. If you choose babysitting, you might want someone to handle advertizing the service so parents know it will be available.

As you work toward your goal, keep a class journal to record your progress, and collect documentation to show what you have achieved.

When the project is complete, evaluate your success. Did you achieve your goal? Did you create a useful product? Did the students and families find it useful? Did you run into any obstacles? If so, how did you overcome them? Did you have to make any trade-offs? Write a report explaining what you learned, whether you were successful or not, and what you would do differently if you were going to start the project all over again.

Social Networking

Recreation and leisure activities are important to people of all ages. Contact a local senior center and ask if you could volunteer to lead an activity. The senior center may need help with regularly scheduled events, such as bingo callers, or you may be able to suggest something that interests you, such as playing music or teaching a craft. If you prefer working with children, contact a daycare center or kindergarten.

Practical Living

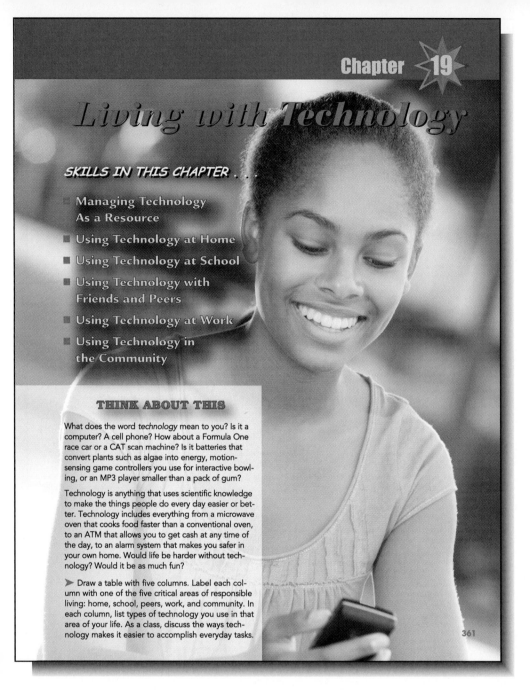

Living with Technology

SKILLS IN THIS CHAPTER . . .

- Managing Technology As a Resource
- Using Technology at Home
- Using Technology at School
- Using Technology with Friends and Peers
- Using Technology at Work
- Using Technology in the Community

THINK ABOUT THIS

What does the word *technology* mean to you? Is it a computer? A cell phone? How about a Formula One race car or a CAT scan machine? Is it batteries that convert plants such as algae into energy, motion-sensing game controllers you use for interactive bowling, or an MP3 player smaller than a pack of gum?

Technology is anything that uses scientific knowledge to make the things people do every day easier or better. Technology includes everything from a microwave oven that cooks food faster than a conventional oven, to an ATM that allows you to get cash at any time of the day, to an alarm system that makes you safer in your own home. Would life be harder without technology? Would it be as much fun?

➤ Draw a table with five columns. Label each column with one of the five critical areas of responsible living: home, school, peers, work, and community. In each column, list types of technology you use in that area of your life. As a class, discuss the ways technology makes it easier to accomplish everyday tasks.

361

Chapter 19 Overview

This chapter explores the role of technology in the five main areas of life. It provides an overview of how we use technology at home, in school, with friends and peers, at work, and in the community.

Managing Technology As a Resource This section discusses the benefits and drawbacks of technology. It also defines common types of technology that we use in our daily life and which can have a significant impact on our well-being and quality of life.

Using Technology at Home Technology contributes to the comfort level, safety, and entertainment we experience in our homes. This section takes a look at smart homes, high-tech homes, and trends in home technology.

Using Technology at School Students, parents, and teachers all use technology to research, learn, and educate. This section identifies common technological tools used in today's classroom.

Using Technology with Friends and Peers Technology helps people stay in touch and communicate. The technologies that affect relationships and social well-being are discussed.

Using Technology at Work Technology automates many routine tasks within the workplace. This section explores technology's impact on worker productivity.

Using Technology in the Community This section explores the role of technology in bringing neighbors together, improving public safety, and giving a community access to resources.

Focus and Engage

Bell-Ringer: Think About This

Students are to create a five-column table for the areas of their life: home, school, friends/peers, work, and community. They are to list the ways in which they use technology in each area. Some ideas are:

- **Home:** appliances, cell phones, computers, entertainment systems, air-conditioning and heating systems, and home security systems.
- **School:** computers and Internet access, cafeteria order and payment systems, air-conditioning and heating systems, and alarm and security systems.
- **Friends/peers:** cell phones and texting capabilities, digital cameras, video games, MP3 players, and social networking sites.
- **Work:** automated order entry systems, handheld scanners, automated cash registers, copy and facsimile machines, phone systems, personal digital assistants (PDAs), and local area networks.
- **Community:** neighborhood- or community-based Web sites, 911, traffic control, and other public safety technologies, computer access to public services and information, and community-wide wireless networks.

ADVANCE PREPARATION

Review	*Life Skills for the 21st Century* textbook, Chapter 19.
Prepare	Paper and pencil for some activities.
	Plain white paper or poster board and colored pencils or markers.
	Box labeled "Hot Topics."

CUSTOMIZED INSTRUCTION OVERVIEW

Less Advanced Students	More Advanced Students	ESOL Students	Special Needs Students	At-Risk Students
Pages 365, 369	Pages 366, 372	Page 367	Pages 363, 372	Pages 365, 367, 369

Introduce the Section

This section discusses the benefits and drawbacks of technology. It also defines common types of technology that we use in our daily lives and which can have a significant impact on our well-being and quality of life.

Figure Focus

Ask students to think of technologies they use now or commonly see being used by others that they didn't see five years ago. Some examples include cell phone texting, digital cameras, handheld video game systems, GPS devices, netbooks, personal digital assistants (PDAs), high-definition television, hybrid and alternative fuel cars, and satellite television and radio.

STUDENT ACTIVITY

Have students interview a parent or older relative about the changes they've seen in technology over their lifetime. Specifically, they should ask questions about telephones, television, kitchen appliances, automobiles, methods for listening to music, and entertainment/recreation.

Managing Technology As a Resource

Technology is a resource that makes everyday life easier, more fun, and more rewarding.

Technology is a varied resource that impacts all areas of your life. Recall that a *resource* is something you use to achieve something else. Technology is varied, because it is used in many different ways, to accomplish many different goals.

- At home, you use technology for tasks as diverse as cooking and watching movies on demand.
- At school, technology provides different ways to learn, share, and present information, from looking up your homework on your class Web site to displaying a math problem on an interactive white board.
- With your friends and peers, you might purchase movie tickets online, share music on your cell phones, or upload photos to your social networking page.
- At work, you meet with colleagues by video conference, prepare documents using software programs, and receive your paycheck via direct deposit.
- In your community, you voice your opinion on a television Web site, check the weather on your cell phone, and find your lost dog thanks to a microchip embedded under her skin.

Using Technology Wisely

As with any resource, knowing when and how to use technology can help you be more productive. Using technology just because it's there or seems cool might be fun; it can also end up wasting other resources, such as time, energy, or money. For example:

- The Internet is a technology we use all the time. It can provide many benefits when you use it wisely. You can find information to complete a homework assignment, communicate with friends, or shop when it is convenient.
- If you don't use the Internet wisely, you might waste time looking at Web sites that provide incorrect or misleading information. You might spend so much time online that you put your real relationships at risk. Or, you might accidentally send personal information to identity thieves.

Critical thinking can help you recognize how best to use technology in your own life. You can decide whether technology will be a solution to a problem you are facing, or if it will cause new problems.

Benefits and Drawbacks of Technology

Is it always better to use technology? There are obvious benefits to using technology, but there are also drawbacks. Most new technologies have both positive and negative effects.

- Technology makes it possible to complete tasks faster. Manufacturing is faster when you use assembly lines, robots, and automated management systems, than when you build products by hand. But, manufacturing processes may release chemicals into the environment, causing pollution.
- Water filtration systems, access to electricity, and advancements in medical care are a few ways technology has improved health and the quality of life. Technology also creates ethical dilemmas, such as testing medical products on animals, or genetically modifying food products.
- Jet engines make it possible for people to travel quickly and easily. But, passengers on airplanes can rapidly transmit disease from one country to another.
- Computers provide access to information and keep people connected. They also store personal information that can lead to invasions of privacy or identity theft.

Some newer technologies can help reverse problems caused by older technologies. For example, pollution caused by technology brought some animals to the brink of extinction. Genetic technology is helping animal breeding programs to restore the animal populations. Understanding the positive and negative effects can help you make choices about how best to use technology.

Types of Technology

Technology can be classified into many different categories. You might use or encounter the following common types of technology.

- *Information technology* is likely to be the type of technology you use and that impacts your daily life the most. It refers to the use of computers to collect, store, and distribute information. For example, you use information technology to write, edit, and print a letter, or to store a name and address in a computerized contact list. You also use information technology to search the Internet or read a news story online, or for online shopping.
- *Communications technology* is part of information technology. It refers to the use of technology to make communication easier and more efficient. It includes cell phones, as well as video conferencing, voice over Internet protocol (VoIP), and social networking.
- *Agricultural technology* is the use of technology to control the growth and harvesting of animal and plant products. It includes a wide range of areas, such as soil preparation, harvesting and planting techniques, and the use of chemicals for growth or pest control.
- *Medical technology* is the use of technology to improve the management and delivery of health care. It includes areas such as medical imaging technology, nuclear medicine technology, and veterinary medical technology.
- *Banking technology* also stems from information technology. It includes areas such as software for managing online banking, controlling access to accounts, and technology for automated teller machines, as well as debit and credit card readers.

Does Everyone Use Technology?

Even if you don't have a cell phone or computer, you use technology if you ride a bus, drive a car, or even write with a ball-point pen. What if you don't want to use technology?

★ You could remove electricity and indoor plumbing from your home.
★ You could only go places that are within walking distance.
★ You could communicate with people only if you are face to face.
★ You could sit and tell stories with friends and family for entertainment.

Can you think of other ways you could remove technology from your life?

Myth Putting more computers into schools will directly improve learning.

Truth Computers can enhance education, but are not enough on their own to directly improve learning. They are tools that can be used to provide access to information, engage the attention of students, and help motivate students to achieve.

Job Search

Careers in technology range from software programmers to aircraft mechanics. The skills, abilities, and interests required are just as broad.

Use the Internet, library, or your school's guidance resources to learn more about careers in technology. Make a list of five industries that offer careers in technology, and then list five types of jobs in each industry. Select one job that interests you. Write a job description, including the educational requirements, career pathway, and potential salary range.

Discuss

Ask students to share their thoughts on the benefits and drawbacks of technology they use in their everyday lives. Select one or two technologies and write pros and cons on the board.

Does Everyone Use Technology?

Students are asked to think of ways to remove technology from their lives. For example, could they do without a microwave oven or cable television? What about vending machines in the school cafeteria or debit cards that enable them to make purchases with a swipe of their card? What about online research for school projects? Ask students to suggest how they might accomplish or obtain the same things if they did get rid of these technologies.

Myth/Truth

Discuss specific ways students use computers in your school. Have students make a list of the courses they are currently taking. Have them place a checkmark beside each course in which they use a computer, and then explain what they use the computer for; i.e. to gather information or conduct research, to engage in a learning activity, or to complete an assignment.

Job Search

You might suggest that students review *Appendix A: Career Clusters* before conducting their research. This will give them ideas on careers and where to start their search. They might also refer to *Chapter 15, Career Planning*, where they completed their career self-assessment worksheet and developed their career plan.

Customized Instruction: Special Needs Students

Some students might be willing to discuss assistive technologies that help them with everyday functions, such as voice recognition software, motorized wheelchairs, voice simulation software for the visually impaired, and captioning technologies for the hearing-impaired.

Introduce the Section

Technology contributes to the comfort level, safety, and entertainment we experience in our homes. This section takes a look at smart homes, high-tech homes, and trends in home technology.

Figure Focus

Ask students to comment on how technology at home helps their family:

- **Conserve resources.** For example, digital controllers attached to water heaters and clothes dryers monitor energy usage.
- **Communicate.** For example, cell phones and wireless technology make staying in touch quick and easy.
- **Have fun.** For example, record shows and movies to watch later or listen to music through the computer.
- **Stay safe.** For example, automatic garage door openers and car locking devices keep vehicles secure, and home security systems can automatically alert authorities when there's a security breech or fire.

Enrichment Information

Discuss with students the concept of home automation, sometimes referred to as *domotics* (domestic robotics). The use of domestic robots for common household chores may sound like something from a science fiction novel, but it's becoming more prevalent in today's technology-minded society. For example, there are robotic mops and vacuum cleaners on the market, as well as robots to mow the lawn and clean out the swimming pool. Even robots for cleaning out the cat's litter box are in development! Have students think of a household chore for which they'd like to use a domestic robot. Then, have them design a model of the robot, either by drawing it on paper or poster board or by building a 3-D model of it. Have them share their models with the class.

Using Technology at Home

Technology at home helps families conserve resources, communicate, have fun, and stay safe.

Your first thought about using technology at home might be updating your social networking page on your computer. But there is a lot more to home technology than computers. For example:

- Appliances use technology to save time, money, and energy. Families can spend more time together and less time performing routine household chores.
- Cellular phones and computers provide access to voice mail, text messaging, instant messaging, and e-mail.
- Entertainment systems use technology to enhance sound and video to make gaming, television, and movies more fun and realistic.
- Keyless entry systems provide you with secure access to your home or car.

Knowing how to use technology in your home can help you develop skills and abilities, keep you safe, and contribute to positive relationships with your family.

Smart Homes vs. Standard Homes

What's a Smart Home? It's a home that uses technology to improve or enhance a family's lifestyle. A Smart Home incorporates advances in the areas of energy, communications, health, environment, and entertainment.

Not all homes are Smart Homes. But, most homes have some level of technology in place to improve the family's quality of life. Some traditional technologies include the following.

- *In the kitchen:* Dishwasher, microwave oven, ice maker, self-cleaning oven
- *Outside:* Automatic garage door openers, built-in sprinkler system
- *Security:* Security system linked to the police or fire department, smoke detectors, carbon monoxide detectors
- *Environment:* Air conditioning, thermostats for adjusting the temperature
- *Communications and entertainment:* Computer with Internet access, telephone, on-demand videos, digital television, games console

What other technologies do you use in your home?

Entertainment

Over the years, technology has had a major impact on entertainment in your home. Your grandparents might remember when televisions first started showing color! Now, there are high-definition, wide-screen plasma displays that make it seem as if you are in the action when you watch a movie or play a video game.

- You use your computer to play games and communicate with friends. You can watch videos and television shows online, buy and download music, and share digital pictures with family and friends. You can also create your own content—including Web pages, videos, music, and artwork.
- You use your television to watch shows and movies. You can record content to watch later. You might have your television linked to a video game console or to a DVD player so you can watch movies or listen to music.
- Even our telephones provide entertainment. Cell phones have built-in cameras for capturing videos and still photos. They store and play music. They have built-in games.

You and your family can enjoy many types of high-tech entertainment in your home. You can also still enjoy low-tech games and activities. You might like to play board games, go for a walk, or just sit around and talk.

Trends in Home Technology

What does the future hold for home technology? Most trends come from improvements in existing technologies. For example, there's a trend toward centralizing control of different devices. That means having one remote or computer screen that lets you access everything from your television to your heating system.

Other trends include:

- The integration of environmentally friendly technology to conserve resources or minimize the impact of homes on the environment. For example, floors and carpets can be made from recycled materials, and systems can automatically monitor usage of resources such as energy and water to promote conservation.
- Building materials that use technology to resist damage from pests and weather, and to minimize the effects of construction on the environment.
- Remote-controlled security systems that let you enter your home without using a key. Future developments might include systems that are activated using finger scans instead of a punch code.
- Virtual reality that may be integrated into everything from gaming to home buying. You could use virtual reality programs to visit cities in other countries, to play interactive games, to try out redecorating ideas, or to tour a house for sale.
- Global positioning systems (GPS) built into telephones and cars that parents can use to track the location of their children.

High-Tech Homes

Does your home have any of the following?

✔ *A touch-screen controlled home-automation system that operates temperature, lighting, and entertainment features.*

✔ *Remote-controlled energy settings that let you automatically adjust the home environment to conserve energy. For example, selecting a "hibernation" mode lowers window shades, turns off lights, and adjusts the temperature to when the family is gone.*

✔ *Sensors that monitor activity and automatically turn off lights, the television, and music when no one is in a room.*

✔ *An energy monitoring system that tracks electricity and water usage on a real-time basis. Linked to the energy provider utility, it can display current costs and savings information.*

✔ *Alternative energy sources such as wind turbines, solar panels, or geothermal heat pump.*

✔ *A refrigerator that senses when it is time to order groceries.*

TECH CONNECT

One Laptop per Child is a nonprofit organization with a goal of creating educational opportunities for the world's poorest children by giving them laptop computers they can use to access and share information.

To achieve its goal, the organization developed a low-cost, rugged laptop called the XO. It has built-in wireless communications and a screen that can be read even in bright sunlight—so it can be used outdoors.

Use the Internet to learn more about One Laptop per Child and the XO. Why does the XO need to be rugged? How can providing children with laptops help solve problems associated with poverty and the lack of education? Can you think of other solutions that might work? Discuss the topic as a class.

Discuss

Discuss the risks of technology on a family's "togetherness." How can advances in video and voice communication undermine in-person contact among family members?

High-Tech Homes

If you have students who answer yes to having any of the home automations listed in the text, ask them to elaborate and explain how the technology has improved their family's quality of life.

TECH CONNECT

Students are to research the One Laptop per Child organization and its XO laptop computer. The laptop needs to be rugged because it is designed especially for children living in remote locations in countries with extreme climates and environmental conditions. Often, these children are taught in an outdoor classroom. Laptops are considered an interactive learning tool, enabling students to be active and involved in their learning. The more active and involved they are, the more likely they are to remain interested in their education and pursue higher levels of it. Educators and social scientists inarguably point to the fact that the more educated a person is, the less likely it is that he or she will live below the poverty line.

Customized Instruction: Less Advanced/At-Risk Students

On a piece of plan paper or poster board, have students create a floor plan of their home. The basic idea is to draw a space for each room. Then, in each room, they should list or draw the things that represent the use of technology.

Introduce the Section

Students, parents, and teachers all utilize technology to research, learn, and educate. This section identifies common technological tools used in today's classroom.

Figure Focus

Besides personal computers and laptops, ask students to discuss other forms of technology they use in school. For example, do you use calculators in math, microscopes in science, or digital and video cameras in art and social studies?

Technology As a Teaching Tool

Most of your students will probably be enthusiastic about a discussion on their use of video games, computer simulations, and social networking sites. But steer the discussion toward the educational opportunities they represent. For example:

- Video games provide opportunities to use critical-thinking skills, such as decision-making, problem-solving, and conflict management. They also require students to understand and follow rules and to devise strategies for achieving goals.

- Computer simulations challenge students to recreate a modeled or modified version of a real-world situation or scenario. Students exercise creativity and also use problem-solving and decision-making skills.

- Social networking sites engage students in topics of conversation with others who have the same interests. A recent report published by the National School Board Association found that 96 percent of youths between the ages of 9 and 17 have used social networking tools at some time, and the average time spent on them is 9 hours a week. Interestingly, the study found that the most common topic of conversation at these sites is education, with 60 percent of the students surveyed indicating they use the sites to talk about education topics and more than 50 percent using it to talk about specific schoolwork.

Using Technology at School

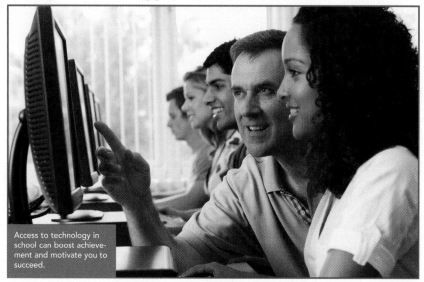

Access to technology in school can boost achievement and motivate you to succeed.

Do you look forward to the opportunity to use computers in school? Do you think it makes classes more interesting or fun? Do you think you learn more? Technology is a resource that can benefit the entire school community—including teachers, students, administrators, and parents. For example:

- Computers and the Internet make it possible to access current information from the classroom or computer lab.
- Teachers can use technology to create flexible lesson plans to reach different levels of learners.
- Parents stay connected using the school's Web site.
- Parents can monitor student's grades through home access to the teachers grade book.
- Administrators can use software to maintain student records and improve scheduling.
- Even the cafeteria benefits from automated payment systems.

Do you need technology to learn? Maybe not. Can technology be used to enhance the school environment, making it more effective? Probably yes.

Technology As a Teaching Tool

The main reason for using technology in school is to teach. Computers, projectors, interactive whiteboards, and other devices help students and teachers access and share information.

- When you access information in online reference books such as dictionaries and encyclopedias, it is probably more complete and up-to-date than the information in your school library.
- You, your teacher, and your classmates are likely to be motivated by the ability to use technology such as slide shows, videos, and Web pages to communicate knowledge.
- E-mail and wiki or social networking-like Web sites let you use technology to collaborate with your classmates, communicate with your teachers, and reach out to peers in other schools or even other countries.
- Specialized technology can help you integrate into a classroom if you have a disability. For example, voice recognition software lets you generate assignments even if you cannot write.

Customized Instruction: More Advanced Students

Have students prepare a computer inventory for your school. They should visit individual classrooms, as well as common areas, such as the computer lab or library, and get a count of the number of computers in each. Then they should briefly interview the instructor in each class on how students use the computers. Have them prepare a table that identifies the classroom, the number of computers, and the types of tasks for which the computers are used.

Benefits and Drawbacks of Technology in School

One main benefit of using technology regularly in school is that it prepares you for the workplace. Most jobs require at least some knowledge of technology.

- When you use technology in school, you have the opportunity to develop skills and interests using computers, programs, and the Internet.
- Some technologies reduce costs in schools. Many classic books used in Language Arts classes can be read online instead of purchased for each student. Communicating with parents by e-mail saves printing and mailing costs.

There are drawbacks to technology in school, too. For example, not all information online is accurate. Anyone can post a blog, or edit a **wiki**—a collaborative Web site. Many organizations have Web sites to promote their own point of view, even if it is not supported by facts. There are other drawbacks as well.

- The Internet makes plagiarism easy, because you can copy and paste text from a Web page into a document. **Plagiarism** is when you copy someone else's work and pass it off as your own. It is illegal. Many teachers use software programs designed to identify plagiarism, so they can be certain students do not cheat.

- Technology can save time, but it can also waste time. It is easy to spend hours browsing from one Web page to another instead of using the time to gather and process information. You might also spend more time choosing fonts and colors for a report or presentation than you do researching and organizing the content.

- A significant problem with technology in school is that not all students have the same access to the same technologies. Some school districts can afford to buy computers for every student; other districts may need the money for teacher salaries or building maintenance.

Trends in Education Technology

In education, trends in technology seem to tend toward reducing costs, improving equal access to information, and encouraging collaboration. For example, schools can lower costs by using technology to handle administrative tasks. Other trends include:

- Online or virtual classrooms that let students take courses that might not be offered at their own school.
- Digital textbooks that can be customized to meet the needs of school districts.
- Interactive whiteboards, devices, and programs that enable students and teachers to enter information and receive immediate feedback.
- Increased use of wikis, blogs, and other tools that promote collaboration and teamwork.

"Did I spend more time on the research or on the animation effects?"

Will Technology Help Me Get an A?

You spent a lot of time on a project. You used the Internet to find information. You created a slide presentation to display your results. Will your teacher approve?

👎 You used information you found on unreliable Web sites.

👎 You copied and pasted from Web pages instead of writing original content.

👎 You dressed up your presentation with transitions, animations, and graphics instead of developing the content.

👍 You double-checked that your sources and facts were correct.

👍 You thought about the information you learned and used it to develop a thoughtful and original presentation.

👍 You cited your sources correctly, including the author's name, the title of the article, the name of the Web site, the date the article was published, the date you accessed the article, and the URL.

How can you use technology in school to improve achievements?

Test IT Yourself!

Is it faster or more accurate to use the Internet for research or to use reference books in the library? Conduct an experiment using two researchers—or two teams—to find out.

1. Select a research topic.
2. Have one student or team go to the library to use reference books such as an encyclopedia.
3. Have the other student or team use a computer with Internet access.
4. At the same time, have both students or teams start their research.
5. At the same time, have both students or teams end their research.
6. Compare the quality and quantity of information collected by each team. Was one method faster? Was one more complete? Write a report explaining the results.

Customized Instruction: ESOL Students

Have students say and write the words for "computer," "laptop," "software," "World Wide Web," and "Internet" in their primary language.

Customized Instruction: At-Risk Students

Have students prepare a demonstration that they could give to elementary-age students on how to find information on the Internet. Have them choose a topic of interest and then write the steps for conducting a search. Their steps should discuss the use of keywords for searching, how to navigate a Web site, and how to identify relevant information.

Vocabulary

Plagiarism: Copying someone else's work and passing it off as your own.

Wiki: A collaborative Web site.

Will Technology Help Me Get an A?

Ask students how they can use technology in school to improve their work and achievements. Make sure students recognize that the Internet is a tool through which anyone can acquire information and learn new things. It expands upon traditional education resources, providing quick and easy accessibility to information, which can sometimes be limiting factors in a school setting.

Figure Focus

Discuss strategies for staying focused on the requirements of a project or assignment and achieving the desired end result. It's easy to be distracted by the bells and whistles of a computer application, and once you've figured out how to use them, you want to "show off" your expertise. Suggest the following tips for staying on course:

- Keep the project or assignment requirements handy and reread them often.

- Create an outline or use a different type of graphic organizer to determine the information that must be included in the project.

- Make the content your priority. Find the information that fulfills the requirements and present it in the appropriate format.

- When you have met the content requirements, then you can take time to enhance the project or assignment using the software's formatting, graphics, and other special features.

Test IT Yourself!

Students are to conduct a test to determine the quality and quantity of information collected through reference books in the library vs. the Internet. Help students select a topic of interest on which information is readily available from both sources. For example, they might research the habitat of a certain animal or a past president of the United States.

Make sure each researcher or team is given the same amount of time to conduct their research. Students are to compare the information collected by each researcher or team and write a report explaining the results.

Introduce the Section

Technology helps people stay in touch and communicate. The technologies that affect relationships and social well-being are discussed.

Figure Focus

Ask students to discuss the ways in which they and their friends use technology. Encourage them to be open and honest about how much they use their cell phones for talking and texting; the amount of time they spend on social networking sites, such as Facebook and MySpace; the types of gaming devices they own and how much time they spend playing games; and their level of interest in online music and videos.

Vocabulary

Anonymous: Unnamed; unknown person at the other side of a conversation.

Are There Risks?

Discuss some of the drawbacks and dangers of "social" technology.

- **Cell phones:** Distracted driving because of cell phone use is a serious and prevalent problem. You are four times more likely to be in a crash when you are talking on your cell phone than when you are not. Also, troubling photos and videos can be captured with cell phones and then posted on the Web for the world to see. And you can receive messages from anyone who has your number, including spammers, scammers, identity thieves, online predators, and cyberbullies.

- **Online music and videos:** Many teens report that they have viewed drug-related videos online. These videos and popular music lyrics can make drug use seem accepted and even cool. The ability to download music from illegal music-sharing sites still exists. When you download music from such a site, you are violating the artist's intellectual property rights.

- **Video games:** In addition to the risk of addiction, much has been written about video game violence, bloodshed, and debauchery. Many studies have been done on their effects on users, reporting that kids who start playing early in their lives are more likely to suffer from depression, sadness, and low self-esteem as compared to those who engage in other activities, such as sports and social events.

Using Technology with Friends and Peers

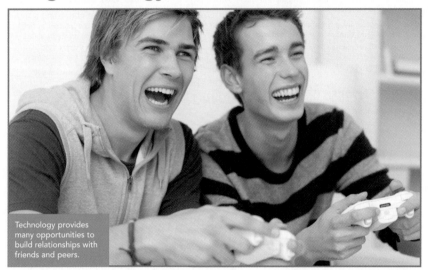

Technology provides many opportunities to build relationships with friends and peers.

How do you use technology with your friends? Do you text? Do you tag pictures for each other's social networking pages? Do you play video games? Do you share MP3s? Do you Tweet? Technology plays an important role in your social well-being.

- It lets you stay in touch with friends.
- It keeps you up-to-date on what your peers are doing, wearing, and saying.
- It provides entertainment.
- Technology is a resource that you can use to build friendships and maintain healthy relationships.

Are There Risks?

Technology of all kinds has both positive and negative effects. Using technology with friends and peers can lead to misunderstandings, bullying, and even identity theft. (Chapter 4 discusses the risks of cyberspace, and Chapter 5 covers coping with online bullies.) Are there other risks?

- Technology can be **anonymous**, which means you don't always know who is at the other side of the conversation. Anonymity can be positive—you might feel safe discussing personal problems or giving advice. It can also be negative. You can't hear the voice of the person sending you a threatening text message, or see who is uploading a picture of you.
- Gaming is fun, and can even develop skills and interests that will help you choose a career. It can also be addictive. Recall from Chapter 4 that an addiction is a compulsion or uncontrollable urge to do something. If you spend 24 hours a week or more playing video games, it might be a problem. Are you unhappy unless you are playing games online? Are you lying about how much time you spend at it? Are you losing friends because you have no time for other activities?

Social Networking

Technology is ideal for enabling communication. You can have multimedia conversations that use text, voice, photos, music, and video. You can talk to one friend at a time, or open yourself up to the entire cyber universe.

You can use technology to define your relationships. Do you communicate differently with friends and peers than you do with parents or teachers?

■ You might have separate e-mail accounts—one for school or work and one for friends and family.

■ You might use different ring tones to identify a call from a close friend and a call from your sister.

■ You might allow your friends more access to your social networking page than you allow a casual acquaintance.

You can use technology to build a safe and judgment-free community of friends and peers. Do you show trust and respect online?

■ Are you honest and open when you communicate?

■ Do you take advantage of anonymity to spread rumors or tell lies?

■ Are you tolerant and respectful of others' values and opinions?

■ Do you take risks you might not take if you were meeting face to face?

Trends in Technology for Friends and Peers

The trends in technology that you use with your friends and peers are all about communication and having fun. Your phone might not get smaller, but it will get a better camera for photos and videos, the network will become faster and more reliable, and the screens will become more interactive and easier to use. Other trends include the following.

■ Technology will keep track of your location and automatically notify your friends of what you are doing and where. You'll receive alerts about activities where you are, such as sales in the store you are passing.

■ Movies and videos will go 3-D— three-dimensional. You won't need to wear silly glasses to feel like you are in the action, because monitors will be designed to display 3-D images.

■ You'll watch television on your computer, not your television.

How do you think trends in technology might affect your relationships with others?

Myth You have no privacy on a social networking site.

Truth You have as much privacy on a social networking site as you want. You control the information in two ways: You should only post information you want to share, and you can set filters or blocks to control who can view your profile.

21st Century Skills

What Happens Next?

Janine and Holly are best friends. They are about to start seventh grade when Holly tells Janine that her parents have decided she should switch to a private school. The private school is about 45 minutes away. Holly will leave the neighborhood early in the morning every day and not get home until late. She will not have much time to spend with Janine anymore.

Janine is afraid of losing her best friend. She asks her parents if she can switch schools, too, but they are happy with her neighborhood school and think the private school would be a waste of money. Janine's mother says that there are lots of ways that Janine and Holly can keep their friendship strong, even if they cannot see each other as often as they used to.

Can Janine and Holly stay friends? What obstacles might be in the way? What resources can they use to overcome the obstacles to build and maintain their relationship? Using your 21st Century Skills—such as decision making, goal setting, and problem solving—write an ending to the story. Read it to the class, or form a small group and present it as a skit.

Customized Instruction: Less Advanced/At-Risk Students

As a group, have students create a short directory of the acronyms and abbreviations teens commonly use when texting or e-mailing. Make sure they understand that the directory should contain terms appropriate for the classroom.

Discuss

Discuss some of the drawbacks and dangers associated with social networking sites. Many sites have age requirements, but some teens have learned to get around them and find themselves in an adult world that is not suitable for them. Many teens feel empowered by having "their space" on the World Wide Web, but that often means they give out too much personal information to online strangers. Some teens post inappropriate content, such as photos and videos from parties and even more private activities. And then there are cyberbullies, who send threatening or harassing messages, spread rumors, distribute someone else's personal information, and create hurtful Web sites.

Figure Focus

Ask students to discuss the ways in which they communicate with their friends. Can they break down the time they spend interacting with friends according to their methods, such as face-to-face contact, talking on the phone, texting, e-mailing, and social networking? Which is the most often-used method?

Teaching Tips

You might obtain a copy of your school's policies on cell phone use and read it to the class. Ask students to comment on what school would be like without such a policy.

Myth/Truth

Ask students to discuss the safeguards they have in place to protect their privacy on a social networking site. Many of these sites have been pressured to develop new technologies that enable them to verify a user's age and enact measures that would make the default setting "private" for younger users, set a quicker response time to complaints of improper content, and more easily identify online predators.

21st Century Skills

What Happens Next?

Students are to prepare an ending for Janine and Holly's dilemma. The girls can remain friends, but they will have to make the effort now to schedule time to see each other. They could also explore other means for keeping in touch, such as regular phone calls and e-mails. In their endings, students might discuss the qualities of a healthy relationship (respect, honesty, trust, and open communication) and the importance of having shared interests and values.

Introduce the Section

Technology automates many routine tasks within the workplace. This section explores technology's impact on worker productivity.

Figure Focus

Ask students to consider how their use of technology at home and with friends and peers can help them adapt to technology used in the workplace. Will they have an edge because they inherently understand how to use online resources? Will they instinctively know how to use a PDA? Will they have the skills to train other workers on using technology?

Stay in School

Explain to students that the supply of workers in unskilled labor categories far exceeds the demand for their services. Instead, technology and global competition have raised the skill level that employers are now requiring of prospective employees. In virtually every industry and along every career path, employees will be expected to use technology. An office worker, for example, needs to have a basic understanding of computer operations and software applications, keyboarding skills, and the ability to use tools such as modems, personal digital assistants, facsimile machines, and voice mail. Today's auto mechanic must have knowledge of computers, electronics, and high-tech mechanical systems. The retail sales clerk must know how to use bar code scanners, computers, and sophisticated cash registers. Furthermore, higher-paying, high-tech jobs require advanced mathematical and science skills, communications skills, problem-solving skills, and the ability to work in a team.

Stress to students the importance of staying in school and taking advantage of opportunities to develop and strengthen their technology skills. Encourage them to explore courses on computer science, desktop publishing, multimedia, video technology, Web mastering, business information systems, telecommunications, and networking. Of equal importance are extracurricular activities focused on technology, such as a computer programming or robotics club, business and professional development clubs, and community-based clubs and organizations that provide educational and networking opportunities for those interested in technology.

Using Technology at Work

Recognizing the value of technology can help you achieve your career goals.

Can you think of a job that does not require you to use technology? Telephones, computers, printers, copy machines, and facsimile machines are standard equipment in almost every office. Even entry-level positions that require no previous work experience often require some use of technology.

- Restaurant workers use automated order entry systems.
- Supermarket stock workers use handheld scanners.
- Ice cream scoopers use automated cash registers.

Technology is a tool that can help you meet your responsibilities at work. The type of technology you use might depend on the type of job you have, but all employees can benefit from technology that gives them tools to be more productive, solve problems, and meet their work responsibilities.

A Productivity Tool

In Chapter 14, you read that *productivity* is the amount of work an employee accomplishes. The more productive an employee is, the more value he or she has to the company. Technology is a tool that, when used wisely, can make you more productive at work. Some common technologies can improve productivity. For example:

- Information technology can improve your ability to manage data ranging from client records and weekly schedules to legal documents and accounts payable. It can make you faster and more accurate.
- Communications technology allows you to maintain contact with co-workers, no matter where you are located. It makes it easy to collaborate with team members, hold virtual meetings, and complete projects successfully.

Technology can also negatively impact productivity. For example, if you must spend time learning to use the technology, or if you are distracted by the technology, you may be less productive. A handheld device might make it easier for you to communicate while you are traveling, but if you are constantly responding to instant messages or texts, you might not be able to complete your work.

Technology on the Road

Road warrior is a term used to describe an employee who travels frequently on work-related business. In the past, travel time was unproductive. Without a notebook computer and a **personal digital assistant** (PDA)—handheld computing and communications device—there was little you could do while you were away from the office.

Now, technology has equipped the road warrior so that employers expect productivity at all times. Some useful tools include:

- *Netbook computers:* Small, lightweight computers designed specifically for working online.
- *PDAs:* Handheld devices that combine cell phone features with tools for scheduling, using e-mail, searching the Web, and even working with simple documents.
- *Wireless adapters:* Devices that allow you to connect computers, PDAs, or cell phones to an available cellular or broadband network.
- *Synchronization software:* You can synchronize—match up—data from one device with another, keeping all information current and available. For example, after a business trip, you can synchronize the data on your netbook with your desktop computer at work.
- *Online storage:* The ability to store data and programs on Web-based systems allows road warriors to access the information they need from any location.

Trends in Workplace Technology

In Chapter 14, you read about the way technology impacts the economy and jobs. Technology creates new jobs, replaces old jobs, and changes the way some people perform their existing jobs. Some technology trends that affect employment are listed on page 289. Here are some additional trends in technology that are likely to impact the workplace.

- Cloud computing—technology allowing data and applications to be stored on Internet servers—that makes information accessible from any device connected to the Internet.
- Collaboration technologies that encourage employees to work in teams. These include Web sites such as wikis that allow co-workers to work on a project simultaneously; video conferencing, which enables face-to-face meetings across distance; and standard communications technologies, including cell phones and e-mail which make communication easier.
- Collaboration technologies that encourage nonemployees to participate in the development and review of products and services. Businesses can invite customers and others to contribute thoughts and ideas using collaborative Web sites. For example, a restaurant might invite customers to create a video advertisement, which would run on its Web site. An automobile designer might invite parts suppliers to suggest ways of improving design.
- Advances in specialized areas that will affect certain industries. For example, digital medical records will improve the quality of health care.

Does Technology Make Me More or Less Productive?

Technology is a tool or resource. It doesn't do your work for you. It doesn't make decisions. It is your responsibility to use technology wisely at work. Will a new PDA make you more productive?

- You don't know how to use it.
- You receive messages from friends during work hours.
- You download and play games without anyone noticing.
- When you are at your desk, you receive the same e-mails on your work computer that you receive on the PDA.
- You use it to communicate with your supervisor while you are traveling.
- You use it to access your work e-mail when you are away from your desk.
- You use the calendar application to stay organized.
- You turn it off when it is time to focus on a task.

How can you use technology responsibly to achieve your career goals?

MONEY MADNE$$

Your parents pay the monthly charge for your prepaid cell phone, but you pay for your text messages. The plan charges you for messages you send and receive. You have been buying 1,000 messages per month for $9.99. There is an additional charge of $0.05 for every text message over the limit. The phone company recently added an unlimited text option for $19.99 per month. How many messages over the 1,000 limit would you have to exchange each month in order to make the unlimited option worth the $19.99 cost?

MONEY MADNE$$

First, calculate the difference between the cost for 1,000 messages and the cost for unlimited messages:

$19.99 − $9.99 = $10.00

Then, calculate how many messages you would have to exchange at $0.05 each to spend $10.00.

$10.00 ÷ $0.05 = 200

You would have to exchange 200 messages over the 1,000 limit to make it worth the $19.99.

Vocabulary

Cloud computing: Technology allowing data and applications to be stored on Internet servers.

Personal digital assistant (PDA): Handheld computing and communications device.

Reinforce and Review

Review with students the influence of technology on employment and job outlook.

- Mobile phones, handheld devices, and other new devices create new jobs in areas such as application development, sales, and research and development.
- Developments in robotics have made it possible to automate many repetitive tasks and, thus, eliminate the need for the workers who once did those tasks.
- Electronic recordkeeping in fields such as healthcare has affected the management of patient records and information and prescription orders.
- The trend toward video conferencing and collaboration technology means fewer people traveling, which impacts travel agents, airlines, and other workers in the hospitality industry.

Does Technology Make Me More or Less Productive?

Stress the importance of professionalism and performing your job responsibilities as best you can. This includes taking care of personal business on your own time, not during work hours. Explain that many employers have adopted policies on employee use of technology in the workplace and take measures to enforce these policies. The main reasons such policies are implemented are:

- Lower productivity that often results from employees who do personal Web surfing, shopping, blogging, texting, etc., on company time.
- The loss of confidential information; for example, sensitive information about the company's internal operations appearing on a social networking page.
- The increased vulnerability to viruses from employees who are careless about e-mailing and downloads.

Introduce the Section

This section explores the role of technology in bringing neighbors together, improving public safety, and giving all community members access to resources.

Figure Focus

Remind students that a community is a group of people who have a common goal. Almost all communities have a Web site that publishes contact information for public offices and officials, emergency phone numbers, and a schedule of activities and events. Ask students to discuss the ways technology impacts the residents of their community. Does your community have a public transportation system that enables students and workers to get where they need to go? Does your community have a weather alert system? Does it use police surveillance systems in higher-crime areas?

Using Technology in the Community

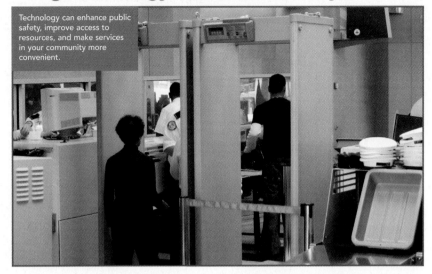

Technology can enhance public safety, improve access to resources, and make services in your community more convenient.

Have you ever seen an electronic road sign warning of construction ahead? Do you know someone who has used 911 to call for help? These are just two ways that you use technology in your community.

Technology can bring neighbors together, improve public safety, and help make shared resources available for all. For example:

- Neighborhoods can set up Web sites to share information about local news and events.
- Police can use reverse 911—a system that automatically sends a recorded telephone message to all residents—to notify a community about a safety hazard, such as dangerous weather conditions.
- The department of public works can monitor usage to determine if a ban is necessary to conserve water resources.

Technology can help governments protect citizens. It can also help citizens find ways to work together to build strong communities.

Public Safety

Public safety officials have long relied on technology. From criminal database systems to tornado sirens, governments use technology in communities to protect citizens. How do you benefit from technology in public safety?

- You can call 911 for help in an emergency.
- You can push a traffic light button to stop traffic so you can cross the street.
- You can pull a fire alarm in a public building to call the fire department.
- You can tune your television or radio to a weather alert system.

Information might be the government's most valuable resource in protecting people. At the federal, state, and local level, agencies have developed systems for collecting and distributing information that can help keep you safe. For example, you can use the Food and Drug Administration's Web site to learn about policy regarding food safety, and the Federal Trade Commission's Web site to learn about consumer safety issues.

Customized Instruction: More Advanced Students

Have students visit their community's Web site and prepare a summary of the information published on it. Their summaries should be organized according to the main pages or site map.

Customized Instruction: Special Needs Students

Have students research their community's demographics. They should find the population total and breakdowns by age groups and gender. Have them illustrate the data in a chart.

Access to Community Resources

Your community uses technology to provide and protect access to community resources. Recall from Chapter 1 that community resources are services that the government provides, such as public parks, libraries, and police and fire departments.

- Do you use your local library? You can use the computerized catalog to find a book, and the computerized check-out system to borrow it. Your library probably also has computers available for you to use, and provides free Internet access.
- Technology can help you access community recreation resources. You can make reservations for campsites in state and national parks online. Some parks that have entrance fees sell passes online at discounted rates. You may be able to purchase licenses for hunting, fishing, boating, snowmobiling, and other activities online.
- Communities use technology to monitor the quality of water used for drinking or swimming. They track contamination and issue reports and warnings. You can usually find information about water quality online, and many communities send information to citizens via e-mail or regular mail.
- Technology comes in handy for collecting tolls on highways. Unmanned booths use transponders to register when a car passes through. The transponders are linked to customer debit accounts for easy payment.

Trends in Technology for the Community

Trends in technology that might impact the community focus on public safety. Many communities are looking for ways to provide security, such as installing surveillance cameras and metal and explosive detection systems in public areas. Some of the technologies raise concerns about citizen privacy rights. For example, is it legal to install surveillance cameras?

Other trends include:

- Citizen journalism, which empowers people to report on news and events that they may witness. They may upload videos, photos, and text to news Web sites or blogs. Citizen journalism helps people feel connected to their community, and encourages them to build relationships and protect resources.
- Community-wide wireless networks, which provide Internet access to citizens who might not have it otherwise. Many communities are installing the technology to provide free or low-cost Internet access.
- Electronic notifications let public safety officials send out warnings and announcements to large numbers of people all at once. College campuses have pioneered efforts to use cell phones and text messages to reach people who are not home, or who do not have a landline telephone.

Cell Phone Etiquette

Have you ever been annoyed by someone nearby talking loudly on a cell phone? Here are some tips for making sure you are never annoying.

✔ *Do not use your phone in any way while you are doing something else. That includes activities such as driving, eating, visiting relatives, and riding your bike.*

✔ *Turn your phone off in school, meetings, and public places such as movie theaters, restaurants, libraries, elevators, museums, cemeteries, dentist or doctor waiting rooms, places of worship, or public transportation.*

✔ *Use vibrate mode for incoming calls and messages.*

✔ *If you receive an important call or text, find someplace where you can respond in private.*

✔ *Never shout or speak loudly into your cell phone. If the connection is not very good, call back.*

 Can Cell Phones Reduce Poverty?

In many developing countries around the world such as parts of India and Uganda, people consider a cell phone to be a tool that will help them climb out of poverty. People are willing to make sacrifices in other areas of life in order to afford a cell phone. They believe the cell phone will lead to increased opportunities in the future.

Cell phones can provide a link to information. Farmers can check weather reports. Entrepreneurs can make arrangements to sell or buy goods at a specific location. Cell phones provide access to banking services such as loans and money transfers. They can even be rented to others to generate income.

Use the Internet to research how cell phones can be used to combat poverty in developing countries. Do you think it is a trend that will be successful? Do you think there might be other factors influencing poverty that a cell phone cannot address? Create a poster showing how a cell phone might increase economic opportunities in these countries.

Cell Phone Etiquette

Suggest to students that the same rules of etiquette for cell phone use also apply to their use of hand-held video game systems in public.

Discuss

Discuss the concept of community-based blogs. A blog is a type of Web site usually maintained by an individual with regular entries of commentary, descriptions of events, and other material. An important feature of many blogs is the ability for readers to enter their own comments and responses to content posted on the site. Ask students if they know of any community-centered blogs. Do they know who writes them? What is the primary focus? Do they think these sites are beneficial to the community?

Can Cell Phones Reduce Poverty?

If students need prompting, you might share the list below of the ways cell phones help people living in poverty:

- Farmers and business owners can simply call a market to find out the price it will pay for goods and commodities instead of relying on sometimes unscrupulous middlemen.
- In the same respect, consumers can call a store or market to find out the availability of products instead of wasting the time and money to physically travel there.
- Cell phones eliminate the need for a land line, which in some countries takes months and even years to obtain, and then is more costly to maintain than a cell phone.
- They provide access to the Internet and other important services, such as electronic banking; healthcare and medical advice; and public service messages, alerts, and warnings.

End-of-Chapter Activities

Case Study

Answers will vary. Some students will think his mother is being unreasonable to make a complete ban. Others will think she is reasonable because she is going to let him earn back his privileges if his grades improve.

Answers will vary about Peter's suggestions. Some will think they are great—and probably do these things themselves. Others will think the suggestions are sneaky and dishonest.

Some will think George should listen to Peter's advice, and some will think not. Other options include talking calmly to his mother to reach a compromise, or working harder so his grades improve.

If George's mother catches George being dishonest and breaking her rules, she will get angry and impose a worse or longer-lasting punishment. She might take away his video games completely and move the computer into the room where she spends most of her time so she can monitor his computer use. She might stop him from seeing Peter. She might tell Peter's parents, and get him in trouble, too.

Sounding Off!

1. Student answers will vary.
2. If you haven't already, take the opportunity to discuss your school's policy on cell phone use with students.

FAQ

1. Information technology is likely to impact your daily life the most.
2. Medical technology is the use of technology to improve the management and delivery of healthcare.
3. Types of technology that improve home security are keyless entry systems, security system linked to the police or fire department, smoke detectors, and carbon monoxide detectors. Students may think of others.
4. Technology can improve building materials so they resist damage from pests and weather.
5. When you use technology in school, you have the opportunity to develop skills and interests using computers, programs, and the Internet. Some technologies reduce costs in schools. Students may think of others.
6. Plagiarism is when you copy someone else's work and pass it off as your own. It is illegal.

7. Anonymity can be positive—you might feel safe discussing personal problems or giving advice. It can also be negative. You can't hear the voice of the person sending you a threatening text message, or see who is uploading a picture of you.
8. Technology can negatively impact productivity at work if you must spend time learning to use the technology, or if you are distracted by the technology.
9. Cloud computing is technology allowing data and applications to be stored on Internet servers.

10. Ways in which communities can use technology to provide or protect resources include:
   - At the library to provide access to books and information.
   - Online to find information about recreation and other public resources, or to apply for licenses, make reservations, or pay fees.
   - To monitor water and air quality and distribute information about it.
   - To collect tolls on highways.

Case Study

George was having trouble keeping up in school. His mother decided that he would not be allowed to watch television, play video games, or use his computer for anything except school work until his grades started to improve. George complained, but his mother would not give in. She said that he could get his screen privileges back if he put effort into his studies.

George's friend Peter said George shouldn't worry. Peter knew lots of ways to use the computer to have fun, while pretending to do school work. He could tell George Web sites for watching television shows and playing online games. He suggested that George tell his mother that they were working together on a research project and that they would have to spend a lot of time collaborating online. Then, she wouldn't bother him when he was using the computer.

- Do you think George's mother is being reasonable?
- What do you think about Peter's suggestions?
- Do you think George should listen to Peter's advice, or are there other options that might have a better result?
- What might happen if George's mother finds out George is following Peter's advice?

Sounding Off!

❶ Do you think parents should use GPS in phones and cars to track the movements of their children?

❷ Why do you think cell phones are supposed to be off in school? What problems might arise from using your phone during class?

FAQ

1. What type of technology is likely to impact your daily life the most?
2. What is medical technology?
3. List two types of technology that improve security in a home.
4. How can technology improve building materials?
5. What is one benefit of using technology regularly in school?
6. What is plagiarism?
7. Explain how being anonymous online can be positive and negative.
8. Explain two ways technology can negatively impact productivity at work.
9. What is cloud computing?
10. List three ways communities can use technology to provide or protect resources.

Information technology has a significant impact on consumers. Advertising on television and the Internet influences our buying decisions, access to online shopping affects how and where we shop, and access to information helps us compare and evaluate products and stores before we shop.

Working in teams of four or five, research the influence technology has on products and services, and how it impacts consumer decision-making. Organize the information into a presentation that you can deliver to the class.

Hot Topics

Do you feel that you have access to all of the technology you need? How does that affect your self-image and well-being?

Take this opportunity to write anonymously about how access to technology affects your well-being. Use a word processor so no one recognizes your handwriting. Be honest and open. Put the paper in the class Hot Topics box.

As a class, read the anonymous entries and discuss them.

Web Extra ▼

There are many educational Web sites that provide reliable and accurate information for students, including www.math.com, www.howstuffworks.com, and www.sciencemadesimple.com.

Use the Internet to locate some sites that you think might be useful for your peers. Make a directory of the sites, including the Web site address, a brief description, and whether the site is free or has a fee. Post the directory on your school Web site or in your school career center or library.

Problem Solver

You are a counselor at a career center. A woman has come in looking for help finding a job. She is older than most people who come in. She says her husband recently passed away, and she is lonely. She would like a job to fill some of her time, and to help her meet new people. Income would be nice, she says, but it is not very important. You ask her to list her skills and abilities. She has a lot of volunteer experience, and has strong people skills—which means she works well with others. But, you are more surprised by the skills she lacks than the skills she has. She has never used a computer. She does not know what a cell phone is. She does know how to use the copy machine. Will you be able to help her find a job?

Working alone or in pairs, assess the problems facing the woman. List the obstacles that she faces, and the possible solutions. Consider her strengths and her weaknesses. Analyze the solutions to select the best one, and develop a plan of action that might help her achieve her goal of finding a job.

Team Players

Student teams are to prepare a presentation on the influence of technology on consumer behavior and buying patterns. Their presentations will most likely touch on the Internet and how it enables consumers to order everything from groceries to furniture to automobiles online. You can also order takeout food and movie tickets online. Consumer decision-making can also be influenced by advertising and marketing geared specifically to them. Using records of your debit card and credit card purchases, marketers and retailers can customize coupons and special discounts to target customers. The proliferation of in-store handheld scanners that enable shoppers to keep a running total of their purchases influences consumers in that they can more quickly and easily compare prices among brands.

Hot Topics

Make sure students understand that they can turn in their papers anonymously. Encourage them to be open and honest about their feelings on how technology affects their well-being.

Web Extra

Students are to research educational Web sites and compile a directory of those they deem reliable and accurate. The directory should include the Web site address, a brief description, and whether the site is free or fee-based. Have them post the directory in the school career center or library.

Problem Solver

Students are to use the problem-solving process to develop a plan of action for the woman. The obstacles she faces include her age and her lack of technological skills. But she has significant experience volunteering and has strong skills dealing with people. Students should focus on jobs in which customer service and interaction with others is a primary responsibility. These include jobs in sales, restaurants, and recruiting others for jobs. It will be difficult to find a job that does not require some use of technology, so their plan of action might include a course on computer basics and technology. Since the woman is looking for something to fill her time, she might like the opportunity to meet new people and develop her technology skills.

Write Now

Students are to write an essay about Web-based information and the importance of verifying its reliability and accuracy. Their essays should point out that a reliable Web site usually publishes the name of the author or organization that sponsors it and the date the content was created or last updated in a fairly obvious location, such as at the top or bottom of the page or on the home page. The site is usually organized with headings and an obvious navigation system. A reliable site clearly states its purpose and any affiliations. You should also look for accuracy in spelling and grammar.

Be Involved!

As a class, students are to develop a project for applying technology to address a concern or problem, provide education, or improve a situation related to family and consumer sciences. They are to use the FCCLA planning process outlined below to develop, execute, and evaluate their efforts.

- Identify the topic.
- Set a goal.
- Form a plan (who, what, when, where, how, cost, resources, and evaluation).
- Act.
- Follow up.

Encourage students to review the chapter and how technology is used in the five main areas of their life.

Social Networking

Students are to research organizations in their community that accept cell phone donations for redistribution to those who need them. They are to work with the agency to organize a cell phone drive in their school and in other public areas around the community. Their efforts should include an advertising campaign for the drive and the actual collection of the cell phones.

Write Now

How do you know if the information you find on a Web site is reliable and accurate? How can you tell if someone is presenting an opinion as fact, ignoring facts, or changing facts? One way is to use Web sites with a .gov or .edu domain extension. Another way is to find the information on at least two different sites.

Write an essay about the risks of believing everything you read on the Internet. Include information about how you might know if information is false or misleading, and how you might know if it is reliable. Use examples that you find online, if possible.

Be Involved!

FCCLA
www.fcclainc.org

Develop a project for applying technology to address a concern, solve a problem, provide education, or improve a situation related to Family and Consumer Sciences. For example, you could create an electronic community for sharing healthy recipes, or organize a fitness program for senior citizens or young children using active video games such as DanceDanceRevolution™ or Wii™ bowling. The project should integrate and apply content from academic subjects, as well, such as language arts, math, and science.

Use goal-setting and problem-solving skills to develop a plan for your project. Assess the plan to make sure it is realistic and attainable, and then put the plan into action to achieve your goal. As you work toward your goal, keep a journal to record your progress, and collect documentation for a portfolio that you can use to show what you have achieved. Notify your local media to see if they will provide publicity for your project, before, during and after it is complete.

Prepare an oral presentation of up to 15 minutes in length explaining your project, and deliver it to your class. Use your portfolio and other visual aids to support your presentation.

When the project is complete, evaluate your success. Did you achieve your goal? Were you able to apply technology to address a concern, solve a problem, provide education, or improve a situation related to Family and Consumer Science? Did you run into any obstacles? If so, how did you overcome them? Did you have to make any trade-offs?

Social Networking

Old technologies can create environmental problems. For example, cell phones thrown in the trash may leak pollutants such as lead or mercury into the ground. Some devices, including cell phones, can be recycled. There are organizations that accept the phones and redistribute them to senior citizens or military troops. Investigate such organizations in your community, and then work with them to sponsor a cell phone drive. Set up collection centers in your school and in other public areas, advertise the collection, and then donate the items.

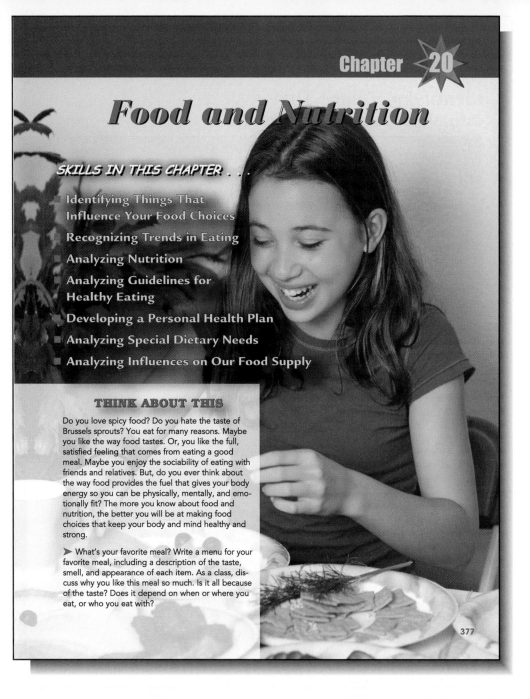

Food and Nutrition

SKILLS IN THIS CHAPTER . . .

- Identifying Things That Influence Your Food Choices
- Recognizing Trends in Eating
- Analyzing Nutrition
- Analyzing Guidelines for Healthy Eating
- Developing a Personal Health Plan
- Analyzing Special Dietary Needs
- Analyzing Influences on Our Food Supply

THINK ABOUT THIS

Do you love spicy food? Do you hate the taste of Brussels sprouts? You eat for many reasons. Maybe you like the way food tastes. Or, you like the full, satisfied feeling that comes from eating a good meal. Maybe you enjoy the sociability of eating with friends and relatives. But, do you ever think about the way food provides the fuel that gives your body energy so you can be physically, mentally, and emotionally fit? The more you know about food and nutrition, the better you will be at making food choices that keep your body and mind healthy and strong.

▶ What's your favorite meal? Write a menu for your favorite meal, including a description of the taste, smell, and appearance of each item. As a class, discuss why you like this meal so much. Is it all because of the taste? Does it depend on when or where you eat, or who you eat with?

377

Chapter 20 Overview

This chapter provides information on nutrition and trends associated with physical wellness that contribute to a healthy diet and lifestyle.

Identifying Things That Influence Your Food Choices This section discusses the factors that can influence your eating preferences, including personal taste, convenience, culture, and advertising.

Recognizing Trends in Eating Students identify the culture and customs associated with eating, and how healthy eating patterns contribute to personal wellness.

Analyzing Nutrition Nutrients are the building blocks of a healthy diet. This section discusses good nutrition and how you can use it to prevent disease and stay fit.

Analyzing Guidelines for Healthy Eating This section provides tips on how to read food labels and discusses the guidelines for a healthy diet and nutrition.

Developing a Personal Health Plan Students learn the importance of setting diet and exercise goals for themselves through a personal health plan.

Analyzing Special Dietary Needs This section discusses the effects of an unhealthy diet on a person's physical and emotional wellness. It also provides tips on how to manage your health and wellness.

Analyzing Influences on Our Food Supply Global politics, policies, and laws impact the quality of our food supply and the food choices we are able to make. The section provides an overview of those influences.

Focus and Engage

Bell-Ringer: Think About This

Students are asked to write a menu for their favorite meal and explain the factors that influence their preference. Then, students are to discuss in class the reasons they like the meal so much. You might hear responses that point to the availability of the food, their routines, marketing and advertising of food, cultural and social meanings of the food, their family or living situations, their feelings, and knowledge of how the food will affect their nutrition. By discussing their reasons in class, they gain a clearer understanding of the factors that influence their eating habits and can more easily identify unhealthy eating practices.

ADVANCE PREPARATION	
Review	*Life Skills for the 21st Century* textbook, Chapter 20.
Prepare	Paper and pencil for some activities. Poster board or plain white paper. Magazines and newspapers. Box labeled "Hot Topics."

CUSTOMIZED INSTRUCTION OVERVIEW

Less Advanced Students	More Advanced Students	ESOL Students	Special Needs Students	At-Risk Students
Pages 380, 384, 386	Page 382	Pages 381, 386	Pages 380, 384	Page 384

Introduce the Section

This section discusses the factors that can influence your eating preferences, including personal taste, convenience, culture, and advertising.

Figure Focus

Explain that food choices can be influenced by a number of factors. Good eating habits as a young person can lead to personal wellness in adulthood. Emphasize that you don't have to eliminate foods you love, but eat them in moderation. Suggest the following tips.

- Eating healthy does not mean eating "boring" foods, but cutting down on portion size and adding foods with nutritional value.
- Eat smaller portions of fast food, and switch sugary, low-nutrient beverages for healthier ones such as milk or water.
- Remember to read food labels.
- Always jump-start the body with breakfast. Skipping meals can cause lethargy and lead to binge eating.
- Incorporate exercise into your daily routine— 30 to 60 minutes most days of the week is recommended.

Individual Choice

You might share with students how McDonald's restaurants address the importance of individual choice.

- Hinduism, which is the major religion in India, reveres cattle. McDonald's restaurants in that country, therefore, offer chicken/mutton burgers rather than beef sandwiches.
- Chinese McDonald's restaurants offer a seasonal New Year meal that includes a grilled chicken burger, fries, and a horoscope for the 12 animals in the Chinese Zodiac.
- All meat served at Israeli McDonald's restaurants is kosher.
- Regular menu items in Japan include shrimp burgers and French fries with barbecue, seaweed, or Italian basil flavors.

Identifying Things That Influence Your Food Choices

Food choices are influenced by many factors, including taste, cost, convenience, culture, and advertising.

What's on your lunch menu today? How did you decide what to eat?

- Do your friends eat the cafeteria food, or bring a lunch from home?
- Are you trying to bulk up or slim down to make a team?
- Did you decide to spend your lunch money to buy a report cover at the school store?

You probably have a variety of eating choices every day. Each choice has consequences. Some are positive, such as the health benefits of choosing an apple instead of a bag of potato chips. Some are negative, such as being teased for eating something the other kids think is weird. Understanding the things that influence your food choices can help you make healthy decisions about what—and how much—to eat.

Individual Choice

Your individual values, culture, and religion impact your food choices. So does where you live in the world.

- *Personal taste*: You might like chocolate ice cream while your sister prefers rocky road.
- *Values*: You might be a vegetarian while your parents enjoy eating meat.
- *Location*: In America, we eat a lot of foods that are made with wheat and corn. In Asia, families eat less bread and more rice.
- *Culture*: Is your family culture Hispanic? You might eat tamales, fajitas, and frijoles. If your heritage is Greek, you might eat spinach pie—spanakopita—and lamb on skewers—souvlaki.
- *Religion*: Some religions have dietary restrictions, which means their members cannot eat certain foods. For example, Buddhists and Hindus are often vegetarian, Mormons avoid alcohol and caffeine, and Muslims and Jews do not eat pork.

Stay in School

Explain to students that nutrition is known to be directly linked to a person's ability to learn and perform, whether in school or on the job. Going without food has emotional consequences such as depression, aggression, anxiety, and poor social skills. Furthermore, limited access to nutritious food can cause a weaker immune system, stomach aches, headaches, and fatigue.

Emphasize the importance of a healthy diet and proper nutrition. If you think it is relevant, you might invite a school administrator or dietitian to discuss your school's free and reduced-cost meal plan, emphasizing the physical as well as emotional benefits of nutritious eating. You might also consider contacting a local food bank to learn about programs for students, such as food backpacks for weekends and holidays, after-school meals, and summer food programs.

Some Things That Influence Food Choices

Recall from Chapter 1 that an *influence* is something that affects the way you think and act. Lots of things influence the way we eat and drink. First of all, there's taste. We all prefer to eat the things we think taste good. Other major influences include:

■ *Availability*: You can't eat what's not there. You might want pizza, but if it's not available, you'll have to settle for something else.

■ *Cost*: You are likely to choose the foods that you can afford. Foods that are common and easy to produce, such as beans, rice, eggs, milk, and bread, are typically less expensive than luxury or rare foods, such as steak, caviar, and some fancy desserts. Cooking a meal at home is usually less expensive than eating in a restaurant.

■ *Convenience*: You might choose food because it is convenient, even if it costs more. If you have little time to shop, you might grab something from a restaurant to-go. If you have little time to cook, you might choose foods that you can prepare quickly in a microwave oven.

■ *Advertising* has a major impact on the food we buy and eat. It can be helpful in informing you about new products, but it can also influence your buying decisions. Recall from Chapter 13 that businesses use advertising to convince you to buy their products. When you recognize the advertising influence, you are better able to make a healthy food decision.

■ *Health* also influences your food choices. In addition to choosing nutritional foods, you might have allergies caused by eating certain food, such as peanuts or shellfish. You might have a condition such as a celiac disease, which gets worse if you eat wheat products that contain gluten.

More Things That Influence Food Choices

What else influences your food choices? Have you ever bought or eaten something just because you saw a commercial for it? Have you left a lunch in your locker because your friends eat cafeteria food? Do you avoid bananas because one made you sick last year?

■ *Your friends* influence what you choose to eat. You might be embarrassed to eat ethnic food in front of them, or you might want to eat what they eat so you fit in. Recall that peer pressure can have positive and negative influence. If your friends encourage you to try new foods and eat a healthy, balanced diet, the influence is positive. If they laugh at your food choices, or force you to eat a diet you know is unhealthy, the influence is negative.

■ *Your state of mind* impacts your ability to make healthy food choices. Stress and depression often cause people to eat more or less than usual. A negative body image or low self-esteem might affect your eating patterns. You might develop an eating disorder such as anorexia nervosa or bulimia nervosa. (Read more about stress, depression, and eating disorders in Chapter 4.)

■ *Fun and sociability* influence your food choices. Eating is frequently part of leisure activities. You might snack while you play video games or bake cookies with your friends on a rainy day. You choose foods according to the activity: sandwiches and potato salad for a picnic at the lake, or popcorn for movie night.

Are You a Super-Taster?

The number of taste buds on your tongue determines how sensitive you are to the taste of food.

✔ *Super-tasters are extra-sensitive. They have a lot of taste buds, and may be very sensitive to bitter flavors. They are generally pickier eaters, and want sauces and dressings on the side.*

✔ *Non-tasters have very little sensitivity to taste. They have fewer taste buds and are more likely to prefer food that is very sweet.*

✔ *Tasters fall somewhere in the middle. They generally have positive feelings about food. Many chefs are tasters.*

Look in the mirror and stick out your tongue if you want to see your taste buds! The more there are, the more sensitive a taster you're likely to be.

TECH CONNECT

Technology and science have made a big difference in the American diet over the past 100 years. For example, foods that were previously available for only a short season each year, such as fresh apples or green beans, are now available year-round thanks to improvements in refrigeration, preservation, and transportation. Changes in agricultural practices have made it possible to grow crops in areas where they never grew before. Genetic research has led to the development of varieties of foods that resist disease, drought, pests, and spoilage.

Use the Internet to investigate a technology that has had an impact on your food choices, such as irradiation, which keeps food fresher, longer; refrigeration, which allows food to be shipped over long distances; or medical technology used to promote growth in animals raised for food. Prepare a presentation about the subject, including how it impacts you personally, as well as the positive and negative consequences.

Are You a Super-Taster?

Explain that many parts of your body work together when you eat. You might share the following with students.

■ The nose has olfactory receptors that send messages to the brain about whether the smells will lead to a good taste or not.

■ The bumps on the tongue, which are called papillae (*puh-pih-lee*), contain around ten-thousand taste buds and are replaced every two weeks.

■ The taste buds are built from microscopic hairs that send messages to the brain about the tastes.

■ Saliva dissolves chemicals in the food so that the tastes can be detected by the taste buds.

Discuss

A recent study published in the American Journal of Clinical Nutrition reported that friends often act as "enablers" for an adolescent's food intake. Ask students if their peers have an influence on their eating habits. Do students find it difficult to say no to unhealthy foods they are served during athletic banquets and pre-game meals? What about at sleepovers or parties? When their friends are buying candy or desserts during lunch, do they feel compelled to do the same?

TECH CONNECT

Students are asked to investigate technology that has had both positive and negative consequences on our food choices. Another example of technology affecting our food choices is milk, a cornerstone of the American diet. Unless you buy organic milk, you will most likely be purchasing milk that has been processed with chemicals. Cows are fed antibiotics that leave residues in the cow's milk. Also, cows are given steroids to boost their milk production. Once the milk is produced, enzymes are added to extend its shelf life. While the processing of milk has increased milk production and shelf life, many experts argue that it has had negative consequences that include increased chances of cancer, difficulty digesting lactose, and increased allergies.

Introduce the Section

Students identify the culture and customs associated with eating and learn how healthy eating patterns contribute to personal wellness.

Figure Focus

Ask students how many of them feel rushed or stressed when they eat. School, work, family, and social obligations might have them feeling crunched for time, which often affects eating patterns. Share these statistics with students and ask them if they think these have positive or negative effects on their diet.

- McDonald's is the source of 10 percent of family meals.
- The average American's lunch hour is 29 minutes.
- Americans spend more than 40 percent of their food budgets on meals outside the home.
- The average restaurant meal has about 60 percent more calories than a homemade meal.

Family Eating Patterns

Many families find it challenging to change their eating patterns when some members are picky eaters. Suggest the following ideas to help a picky eater develop more food tolerance:

- Challenge your taste buds with foods you remember disliking. If it has been years since tasting the food, try it a second time.
- Try different forms of foods that you dislike. Flavors, textures, and colors of vegetables cooked could have completely different results than if they are raw.
- Change the flavor of foods you dislike with new ingredients and herb mixtures.
- Look for different variations of fruits and vegetables, such as white grapefruit instead of red or pink grapefruit.
- If you find that a food you usually dislike actually tastes really good to you at a restaurant, ask the chef how it was made.
- Add nutritious foods to others you love; for example, mix in broccoli with your macaroni and cheese.

Recognizing Trends in Eating

Recognizing trends in eating can help you understand the role food plays in all areas of your life.

You can tell a lot about a person from his or her eating habits. Does she like to eat with friends, or alone in front of the television? Does he enjoy dining in restaurants, or cooking at home? Individuals and families develop patterns of cooking and eating that help define their relationships.

- Your family might eat dinner together every night.
- Your friend's family might eat together only on Fridays.
- Your mother might do all the cooking.
- Your friend's parents might enjoy planning and preparing meals together.

Recognizing trends and patterns can help you understand the choices people make about food and meals. For example, a family with a stay-at-home parent might eat at home more than a family where both parents work outside the home. Eating at home usually costs less than eating out. It also requires time spent shopping, cooking, and cleaning up.

Family Eating Patterns

Fifty years ago in the United States, families ate meals at home. Today, busy lifestyles make it difficult for many families to eat at the same time each night. They set shopping, cooking, and eating priorities that meet their unique family needs.

- A family might eat take-out or prepared meals so they can spend less time shopping and cooking and more time eating together.
- A mother might shop for fresh food and prepare a meal for her children, and then eat later with her spouse after the children have finished.
- A father might buy the children dinner at a fast-food outlet on the way home from soccer practice.

A regular pattern can help you consume the nutrients you need. For example, starting the day with breakfast gives your body a boost of energy and nutrition to keep you alert and full of energy. If you skip breakfast, you might get a headache or feel sleepy or irritable. Eating meals at regular times instead of snacking can help you feel full and satisfied, maintain a healthy weight, and consumer all the nutrients you need.

Customized Instruction: Less Advanced/Special Needs Students

Ask students to choose a meal they like, but which may not have high nutritional value. It can be homemade or from a restaurant. Have them determine ways to make the meal healthier. For example, can they substitute ingredients, add ingredients, or reduce portions? On a plain sheet of paper or poster board, have them draw a picture of the meal before and after its modifications.

Food Customs and Cultures

You already know that culture affects the choices you make when it comes to buying and eating food. It also affects the rituals, customs, and habits surrounding your meals.

■ In Pakistan and Japan, it is polite to "clean your plate" to show how delicious the food was, whereas in Russia it is polite to leave a bite or two to show that the host served more than enough to satisfy the guest.

■ In some Asian countries, it is good manners to leave a friend's house immediately after a meal; if you linger, it indicates you did not get enough to eat. In India, Europe, and the Americas, it is rude to "eat and run," because it indicates you came for the food, not the company.

■ In France, both hands should be visible above the table at all time. In the United States, it is considered polite to keep your left hand in your lap while you eat with your right hand (reverse for lefties).

■ In India, it is rude to talk during a meal. In the United States, it is polite to talk with the other people at the table.

■ In Japan, it is acceptable to make a slurping noise when you eat noodles. In the United States, slurping is considered rude.

■ In Mediterranean European countries, Latin America, and Sub-Saharan Africa, it is normal to arrive 30 minutes late for a dinner invitation. In Germany and the United States, arriving late is considered rude.

Food on Occasions and Holidays

Eating is often used as a way to meet and spend time with other people. It might be a social event that helps bind families and friends together. It might be a business event such as a meeting, performance evaluation, or even a job interview.

Food is also symbolic of many family and cultural traditions and occasions. How do you celebrate holidays and occasions?

■ On your birthday, do you enjoy cake and ice cream?

■ On Thanksgiving, do you eat roasted turkey, mashed potatoes, and pumpkin pie?

■ Do you celebrate the 4th of July with hotdogs, hamburgers, and watermelon?

Dining with other people provides an opportunity to communicate in a relaxed and enjoyable environment. It can contribute to your overall well-being by letting you connect with others at the same time that you fuel your body.

How does your family use food to celebrate holidays and special occasions?

21st Century Skills

What Happens Next?

Penny Cho and Michelle Stein were classmates assigned to work together on a science project. They agreed to meet Saturday afternoon at Penny's house.

While they were working, Michelle noticed an unfamiliar smell coming from the kitchen. Penny said her mother was cooking Doenjang Chigae, a Korean stew made with bean paste and seafood. She invited Michelle to stay for dinner.

Michelle didn't know what to do. The smell of the stew made her a little queasy—sick to her stomach. She thought bean paste sounded gross, and her family never ate shellfish. But she liked Penny, and she was hoping they could become good friends.

What are Michelle's options? What type of consequences does each option have? Use your decision-making skills to help Michelle choose a plan of action. Using your 21st Century Skills—such as decision making, goal setting, and problem solving—write an ending to the story. Read it to the class, or form a small group and present it as a skit.

Respecting Others' Food Traditions

The way people eat, the food they eat, and what they consider polite behavior varies depending on factors such as country of origin, culture, and religion. What if you have a Japanese foreign-exchange student eating dinner with your family?

★ *You could ask her to tell you what a family dinner would be like at her house.*

★ *You could discuss your own family dinner traditions.*

★ *You could all eat with chopsticks.*

★ *You could all remove your shoes.*

★ *You could sit at a low table on the floor.*

★ *You could say "Itadakimasu" which means "I am about to eat" before you start eating.*

★ *You could end the meal by saying "gochisousama deshita" which means "It was a feast."*

If you were eating dinner with a Japanese family, how might they act to make you feel comfortable?

Respecting Others' Food Traditions

If you were eating with a Japanese family, they could make you feel more comfortable by learning basic English terms and terms for the foods being served, making a traditional American meal, using a fork instead of chopsticks, and by discussing the differences between American and Japanese traditions.

21st Century Skills

What Happens Next?

Students are to prepare an ending on what Michelle should do when asked to eat an unfamiliar dish at Penny's house. Students' endings will vary. Emphasize that if Michelle chooses to stay, being polite will offset her potential dislike of the food. You might discuss the following tips on good manners when eating at someone else's home:

■ Try the food before passing judgment. If you don't like it, avoid making negative comments about it.

■ Never serve yourself first.

■ Do not put anything on the table, such as a cell phone.

■ Ask politely to pass food and thank the person.

■ Chew with your mouth closed, and do not talk with your mouth full.

■ Offer to help with the clean-up.

■ Thank the host for inviting you.

Figure Focus

Ask students to comment on the foods that are served during their family holiday and other celebrations and traditions. Do they consider these foods healthy and nutritious? Ask students to discuss tips for enjoying these foods while maintaining a healthy diet. Some tips are:

▨ Focus on weight maintenance rather than weight loss.

▨ Be physically active every day, even during holidays and special occasions.

▨ Eat light snacks before going to parties; going hungry makes it easier to overeat.

▨ Make a plan. Know what your personal triggers are and how you can minimize them during social situations.

▨ Reduce the calories and fat in holiday and traditional recipes by substituting lower-fat and lower-calorie ingredients.

▨ Choose your beverages wisely by knowing which ones have sugary, high-calorie ingredients. Remember that water is always an option.

▨ Enjoy being with friends and family rather than focusing on celebrating with food.

▨ If you do overeat, maintain your perspective. It takes several occasions of overeating before you gain weight. Return to your usual eating plan without guilt or despair.

Introduce the Section

Nutrients are the building blocks of a healthy diet. This section discusses good nutrition and how you can use it to prevent disease and stay fit.

Figure Focus

You might expand upon the topic of good nutrition and a person's ability to perform in sports and recreational activities. Discuss the following:

- Avoid eating simple sugars such as candy or high-fructose drinks because these can cause a quick rise and fall in blood sugar, resulting in lethargy.

- Avoid too much fat or protein because it takes longer to digest.

- Eat around 200 to 300 calories if eating within an hour of the activity.

- Stay hydrated. The American College of Sports Medicine recommends that you drink about 16 ounces of water two hours before working out.

- Avoid exercising on an empty stomach as it lowers stamina and endurance.

Vocabulary

Diet: Food you eat.
Nutrients: The parts of food that your body needs.
Nutrition: A science that studies the way the food you eat nourishes your body.

What Is a Healthy Diet?

One in three kids in the United States is obese or overweight, with young people eating on average 8 percent more than they did less than 30 years ago. Emphasize to students that their daily eating habits are important to their well-being. Poor nutrition during adolescence can impair their development and increase the likelihood of weight-related disease and impairment in their adulthood.

Analyzing Nutrition

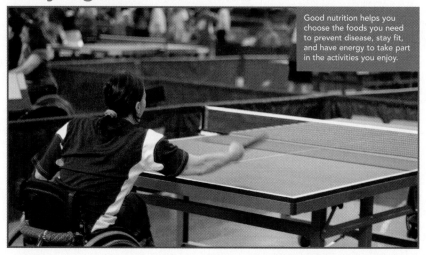

Good nutrition helps you choose the foods you need to prevent disease, stay fit, and have energy to take part in the activities you enjoy.

Do you know the difference between diet and nutrition? **Diet** is the food you eat. **Nutrition** is a science that studies the way the food you eat nourishes your body.

- If you miss a meal, do you feel tired?
- If you eat too much sugar, do you get a headache?

When you have good nutrition, your body is getting all the nutrients it needs to work at its best level. Your main way to get good nutrition is to eat a healthy diet. Different foods contribute different **nutrients**—the parts of food that your body needs. Recognizing that food is a resource you can use to stay healthy and happy can help you choose the foods and food combinations that provide what your body needs.

What Is a Healthy Diet?

A healthy diet is one that gives your body balanced nutrition. Like a car, if you give your body the right fuel, it will run great and last a long time. If you give it the wrong fuel, it might break down. To achieve a balanced diet, you can eat a variety of foods from the different food groups. Other basic guidelines include:

- Eating a variety of fruits and vegetables, including dark green vegetables, orange vegetables, and beans
- Eating foods that are rich in calcium, such as low-fat milk, cheese, and yogurt
- Eating whole grains
- Eating lean meats and poultry, such as skinless chicken
- Limiting amount of fats, salts, and sugars that you eat
- Drinking plenty of water, to maintain your body's proper temperature and keep your internal organs working correctly

A healthy diet also balances the amount of food you take in with your physical activity. Think of *food* as energy that comes into your body, and *activity* as energy that goes out. A healthy goal is to have the same amount of energy in as energy out. That way you can maintain a healthy weight and obtain all the nutrients your body needs to function properly.

Customized Instruction: More Advanced Students

Have students make a food journal of what they have consumed and the quantities for one day. Then have them refer to *Appendix C: MyPyramid Food Group Recommendations*, starting on page 531 of the student text to compare their diet with the daily recommendations for all of the food groups. Did they meet those requirements? Ask that they summarize and reflect on their findings.

Nutrient Basics

Technically, your whole digestive system is a long, hollow tube, with openings at both ends. Food goes in one end; waste comes out the other. Between these two points, your body breaks down the food and takes the nutrients. There are six essential nutrients that your body needs to stay healthy.

- **Proteins** build and renew body tissues, generate heat and energy, and provide **amino acids**—the basic building blocks of proteins. Sources of protein include meat, fish, eggs, and legumes such as peas and beans.
- **Carbohydrates** generate heat and energy and provide fiber, which helps with digestion. Sources include pasta, bread, and sugar.
- **Fats**—also called *lipids*—provide fatty acids your body needs for growth and development. They generate heat and energy and carry fat-soluble vitamins—vitamins that dissolve in fat—to cells. Sources include butter, oil, and nuts.
- **Minerals** regulate the activity of the heart, nerves, and muscles. They build and renew teeth, bones, and other tissues. You get minerals from many sources. For example, calcium comes from dairy foods and green leafy vegetables, iron comes from red meat, and potassium comes from bananas, spinach, melon, and orange juice.
- **Vitamins** assist your body in processing food and aid in growth and body development. They also help prevent certain diseases. Like minerals, vitamins come from different sources. For example, you get vitamin A from liver, milk, and sweet potatoes. You get vitamin B2—riboflavin—from liver, wheat bran, eggs, meat, milk, and cheese.
- **Water** carries other nutrients through the body. It regulates body temperature and helps the body eliminate waste. You drink water, and you also absorb some from foods such as fruits and vegetables.

Nutrition for All Ages

One size does not fit all when it comes to nutrition. Your nutritional needs change depending on factors such as age, sex, physical activity level, and health.

- An infant needs only 900 **calories** a day, while a 14-year-old boy needs 2,200 calories a day. A calorie is a unit of measurement that describes how much energy the food you eat delivers to your body.
- Teen age girls need more iron than teen age boys, and adult women need more iron than teen age girls.
- Pregnant women need almost twice as much iron as women who are not pregnant. They also need **folate**—a B vitamin that helps prevent malformations in a developing fetus—and calcium, which helps build bones and teeth. Pregnant women should also avoid certain foods, including alcohol and caffeine.
- Senior citizens must eat nutrient-dense food so they can absorb the nutrients they need without extra calories that might cause them to gain weight. They often have health issues that require a specific diet, such as high blood pressure (low-sodium diet) or heart disease (low-fat diet).

Nutritionists and dietitians use this information to develop personalized diet plans for their clients. You can use the information to adjust your own diet depending on your current circumstances. For example, you might need more calories in the summer because you are more active than in the winter.

What's Malnutrition?

Malnutrition refers to any type of poor nutrition. It can be a **deficiency** (not enough nutrients) or an **excess** (too many nutrients). The symptoms depend on what's missing or in excess. Some diseases caused by malnutrition include:

✔ *Anemia:* Low red blood cell count caused by vitamin B6, B9, B12, or iron deficiency, or possibly vitamin E deficiency in infants.

✔ *Rickets:* Softening of the bones in children, caused by vitamin D deficiency.

✔ *Scurvy:* Paleness, depression, spongy gums, bleeding from mucous membranes, caused by vitamin C deficiency.

✔ *Osteoporosis:* A loss of bone mass resulting in bones that are fragile and break easily. It is caused by a variety of genetic, dietary, hormonal, exercise, and lifestyle factors, including calcium deficiency.

✔ *Tooth decay:* Cavities caused by excessive refined white sugar.

Myth Eating a very high protein diet helps an athlete gain muscle mass quickly.

Truth Eating extra protein does not build extra muscle. Once the body gets the protein it needs, the extra is burned for energy or stored as fat. Muscle is gained by exercise, not by eating certain foods.

Myth/Truth

Discuss with students the following tips for gaining muscle mass.

- Aim to eat about 1 gram of protein per pound of body weight each day.
- Limit workouts to less than 45 minutes, and increase their intensity.
- Isolate the muscle groups in each session to get the most out of your workout; for example, focus on your upper body in one session and the lower body in another.
- Change your routine every four to six weeks.
- Train your entire body to avoid injuries and increase flexibility.
- Allow your body to recover by sleeping seven to eight hours per night, and take at least one day off from working out per week.

Vocabulary

Amino acids: The basic building blocks of proteins.
Calories: The units of measurement that describe how much energy the food you eat delivers to your body.
Carbohydrates: Sources that generate heat and energy and provide fiber that helps with digestion.
Deficiency: Not enough nutrients.
Excess: Too many nutrients.
Fats: The substances that provide fatty acid the body needs for growth and development (also known as lipids).
Folate: B vitamin that helps prevent malformations in a developing fetus.
Malnutrition: Any type of poor nutrition, whether it is a deficiency or an excess of nutrients.
Minerals: Elements that regulate the activity of the heart, nerves, and muscles.
Protein: The plant or animal tissue rich in molecules that builds and renews body tissues, generates heat and energy, and provides amino acids.
Vitamins: Substances that assist your body in processing food, aid in growth and body development, and prevent certain diseases.
Water: Fluid that carries other nutrients through the body, regulates body temperature, and eliminates body waste.

What's Malnutrition?

In addition to the diseases listed in the text, you might discuss those caused by excess nutrients or obesity.

- **Hypertension:** Disease of the arteries in which chronic high blood pressure is the main symptom.
- **Diabetes:** Inadequate production or use of insulin.
- **Osteoarthritis:** The most common form of arthritis with the chronic breakdown of cartilage in joints that causes pain, stiffness, and swelling.
- **Sleep apnea:** The temporary pausing of breathing occurring repeatedly during sleep from an obstruction in the breathing tract.
- **Heart disease:** An abnormality of the blood vessels supplying the heart because of lipids.

Introduce the Section

This section provides tips on how to read food labels and discusses the guidelines for a healthy diet and nutrition.

Figure Focus

Explain that reading labels is an important part of understanding nutrition. Fats are nutrients to build tissue, and calories measure how much energy food provides the body. Food labels list fat and calories according to the serving size. Students may be surprised by how many calories and fat they are eating when they do the math. To read a label:

1. Read the serving size.
2. Find how many calories or fat are in one serving.
3. Multiply the number of calories or fat in one serving by the number of servings you are eating.

Vocabulary

Dietary guidelines: Guiding principles about the benefits of food and exercise that can help you develop a diet that is right for you.

Dietary Guidelines for Americans: A set of guidelines for people two years and older about how good dietary habits and physical activities can promote health and reduce the risk of disease.

STUDENT ACTIVITY

Have students create a menu for a healthy lunch. The menu should include the name of the item and portion size. When they are done, have them exchange their menus with a classmate. The classmate should evaluate the nutritional value of the meal, using *Appendix C: MyPyramid Food Group Recommendations* starting on page 531 of the student text. You might also review food measuring units. Have measuring cups or spoons and a scale on hand, along with some food items such as cereal or pieces of fruit and a liquid such as water or milk, to demonstrate volume, mass, and weight. Some useful conversions of measuring units are:

- 1 cup = 250 ml
- 1 cup = 8 ounces
- 1 tablespoon = 15 ml
- 4 tablespoons = ¼ cup
- 1 pound = about 450 grams
- 1 ounce = 28 grams
- 1 ounce = 2 tablespoons
- 5 ounces = approximately ⅓ pound

Analyzing Guidelines for Healthy Eating

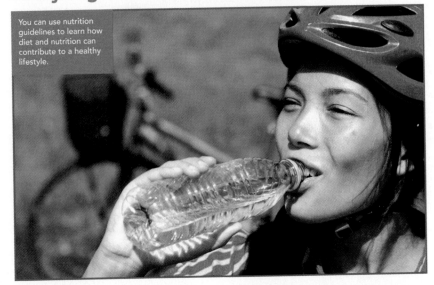

You can use nutrition guidelines to learn how diet and nutrition can contribute to a healthy lifestyle.

Do you eat foods that contribute to a healthy lifestyle? Do you exercise regularly to keep your body physically fit? How can you know if you are eating the right amount of nutrients to fuel your body? How do you know the right combination of food and activity to maintain a balanced diet?

Several government and private organizations have published clear, easy-to-follow **dietary guidelines**, which are guidelines about the benefits of food and exercise that can help you develop a diet that is right for you. Specifically, they help you identify how to:

- Achieve your best health and well-being
- Manage your weight
- Prevent diseases, such as diabetes and heart disease

The guidelines help you understand the role diet and exercise play in your overall wellness, so you can incorporate healthy eating into your daily routine.

Dietary Guidelines for Americans

Every five years, the U.S. Department of Health and Human Services (HHS) and the U.S. Department of Agriculture (USDA) publish the **Dietary Guidelines for Americans**, a set of guidelines for people two years and older about how good dietary habits and physical activity can promote health and reduce risk for major chronic diseases. You can download the publication for free at www.health.gov/DietaryGuidelines, or see Appendix C.

The publication is intended for policymakers, healthcare providers, nutritionists, and nutrition educators, but it can provide useful information for individuals as well. Key points include:

- The importance of eating fewer calories, being more active, and making wise food choices
- The importance of meeting nutrient needs by eating food, not by taking dietary supplements
- The importance of developing eating patterns that integrate dietary recommendations into a healthy lifestyle, rather than using weight-loss diets

---

Customized Instruction: Less Advanced/Special Needs/At-Risk Students

Ask students to brainstorm three healthy breakfast meals that have nutrients from all of the following groups: fruit, dairy, grain, and protein. Have them divide a plain sheet of paper or poster board in three columns and draw pictures of their meals in each column. Also, have them title the poster with a slogan for why they should eat breakfast such as, "Do Better in School" or "Kick-Start Your Brain" and post them around the classroom.

Is the Food Label Right?

You've seen the labels on packages of food: how many calories per serving, how much fat, how much vitamin A, and so on. They're called Nutrition Facts labels, and they are required by law. Nutrition Facts labels list the serving size, servings per container, and nutrition information per serving.

The information on a Nutrition Facts label uses a standard called Daily Values (DV). Food labels are a good source of nutritional information for all people. They provide general guidelines. You can use them to evaluate the content of packaged foods and to make healthy food choices. Keep in mind, though, that there are other more customized guidelines available such as MyPyramid—covered later in this chapter—that can help you make personal choices that are right for you as an individual.

Packaged foods all have a Nutrition Facts label. How can you use the label to develop a healthy diet?

What About Nutrient Density?

It's 3:00 p.m. You want a snack. Do you grab an apple or a donut?

■ The apple has about 80 calories, and lots of vitamins and fiber. The fiber and water fill your stomach and keep you feeling full until dinner time. The apple is nutrient dense.

■ The donut has about 200 calories, but not much else. It won't keep you feeling full, so you might even grab another one—or two—before dinner. The donut is nutrient poor.

Nutrient density is a measure of the nutrients a food provides compared to the calories it provides. Foods low in calories and high in nutrients are **nutrient dense**. Foods high in calories and low in nutrients are **nutrient poor**, or **energy dense**. You can identify the nutrient density of foods by reading the Nutrition Facts label and by comparing the number of calories per serving to the amount of nutrients.

A healthy diet includes nutrient-dense foods that provide the fuel your body needs, without extra, empty calories. If you eat mostly nutrient-poor foods, such as soft drinks, candy, and potato chips, you will take in plenty of calories, but not enough nutrients to successfully fuel your body.

Good Fats or Bad Fats?

Fats are a rich source of energy, but some types can increase your risk of heart disease. Nutrition Facts labels list values of many types of fat. How can you know if you are eating the "right" kinds of fats?

👎 Saturated fat increases your risk of heart disease. Find it in meat, poultry, seafood, eggs, dairy products, lard, butter, and coconut, palm, and other tropical oils.

👎 Trans fat molecules can collect in clumps in your bloodstream, increasing your risk of heart disease. Find it in partially hydrogenated vegetable oils, shortening, and margarine.

👍 Polyunsaturated fat may help balance cholesterol levels in the blood. Find it in vegetable oils such as safflower, corn, sunflower, soy, and cottonseed.

👍 Monounsaturated fat may help balance cholesterol levels in the blood. Find it in olive oil, peanut oil, canola oil, avocados, nuts, and seeds.

👍 Omega-3 fatty acids are a type of polyunsaturated fat thought to be very good at preventing heart disease. Find it fish and dark-green leafy vegetables.

How can you make healthy choices about the types of fats you include in your diet?

Discuss

Explain the following terms to students:

■ **Nutrition Facts labels:** Labels on packages of food required by law, which include serving size, servings per container, and nutritional information per serving.

■ **Daily values (DV):** Percentages based on the amount of nutrients recommended each day based on a 2,000-calorie diet for a person age 18 years or older.

■ **MyPyramid:** A tool designed by the U.S. Department of Agriculture for consumers to personalize their nutritional plan.

Vocabulary

Nutrient dense: Foods low in calories and high in nutrients.

Nutrient density: Measure of the nutrients a food provides compared to the calories it provides.

Nutrient poor: Foods high in calories and low in nutrients, also known as energy dense.

Good Fats or Bad Fats?

Explain that when choosing between foods with different types of fat, you don't need to eliminate all fats but rather eat them in moderation. Unsaturated fats (monounsaturated and polyunsaturated fats) are the healthiest types. Many fast foods such as French fries, cheeseburgers, and fried foods have the bad types of fat. By reducing your fast food intake and reading food labels, you can reduce your risk of heart disease.

Should I Take Vitamins?

While dietary supplements can complement your diet if you have difficulty getting enough nutrients, explain that whole foods provide you with nutrients that dietary supplements cannot.

- Foods such as oranges provide you with micronutrients, including vitamin C, beta carotene, and calcium.

- Fruits and vegetables contain protective substances such as phytochemicals, which protect against disease and provide antioxidants that slow cell and tissue damage.

Dietary supplements may be necessary if you have a medical condition in which your body doesn't absorb nutrients normally, such as chronic diarrhea, food intolerance or allergies, and diseases of the liver, pancreas, intestines, or gallbladder.

Figure Focus

Explain that dietary supplements can be used to build muscle mass. However, there is evidence that over-the-counter supplements can cause heart palpitations, loss of consciousness, heart attacks, and even death. Many supplements contain caffeine or ephedrine, which increases your metabolism, heart rate, and blood pressure. Substituting protein supplements with a balanced diet that incorporates protein (chicken, lean meats, eggs, fish, dairy, beans, nuts, soy, etc.) is recommended. Also, too much protein can actually be harmful because it can cause dehydration, bone calcium loss, and kidney damage.

MONEY MADNE$$

If cost is the only factor, the packaged cookies are the best deal, but there are other factors. You might consider the ingredients—do the packaged cookies contain saturated fat or trans fat? What about preservatives in the packaged cookies and the dough? Other factors include convenience, taste, sociability, and fun. You might want to bake cookies because it is fun and sociable. You might want to use packaged cookies because you have other things to do, and the package is convenient. You might like the flavor and taste of home-baked cookies better than packaged, or you might want a type of cookie you can only get in a package. You might want to compromise by baking cookies using the refrigerated dough. Another consideration is food allergies. Packaged cookies might contain peanuts, and one of your friends might have an allergy. (Costs are rounded up.)

- Cost per cookie for the package: $3.80/40 = approximately $0.10

- Cost per cookie for the dough: $3.80/24 = approximately $0.16

- Cost per cookie made from scratch: $4.50/24 = approximately $0.19

(Reproduced student page)

386 Chapter 20 ■ Food and Nutrition

Should I Take Vitamins?

Taking a multivitamin pill once a day is not harmful. Risks come from using supplements to replace a healthy diet. What if you skip your daily servings of fruits and vegetables and take a vitamin pill instead?

★ *A pill can't provide everything, so you still won't get the right balance of nutrients for your body.*

★ *There's no dietary fiber in the pill.*

★ *If you take in more fat-soluble vitamins such as vitamin A and vitamin D than your body can use, the vitamins build up in your system, causing health problems over time.*

★ *You'll get hungry and eat more than you need to be healthy.*

★ *You'll spend money on supplements that you don't really need.*

Your doctor can give you information about whether dietary supplements are right for you. Can you think of a well-balanced meal that would provide a variety of nutrients to fuel your body?

MONEY MADNE$$

You are having a sleepover party for five friends. You want to have chocolate chip cookies for a late night snack. You could buy a package of 40 cookies for about $3.80. You could buy an 18-ounce log of refrigerated dough to make 24 cookies for about the same price—$3.80. Or you could make a batch of 24 cookies from scratch, which would cost about $4.50.

Which option should you choose? (Hint: Determine the cost per cookie.) Is cost the only factor? What else might influence your decision?

Evaluating Dietary Supplements

Most people do not need vitamin and mineral supplements if they eat enough nutritious food, in the proper balance. Nutrition guidelines advise people to use proper diet to take in the necessary nutrients.

There may be special situations when dietary supplements are necessary. For example, doctors and nutritionists may recommend supplements for:

- Senior citizens who do not consume enough nutritious food
- People on restricted diets who might not eat a variety of foods, such as vegetarians, who may not take in enough protein due to the lack of meat in their diets.
- Pregnant women who need more vitamins and minerals than can be obtained from food alone
- Athletes who are on calorie-restricted diets

"I wonder if this dietary supplement will help me build muscle mass?"

Be wary of advertising for supplements that promise to deliver quick and easy results for muscle growth, weight loss, or energy boosts. As with all advertising, the businesses are trying to sell you a product, and they may not be disclosing the whole truth.

Dietary Reference Intakes

You can use *dietary reference intakes* (DRI) guidelines to determine the best amount of each nutrient to eat. The DRI provide information for groups of people with similar characteristics, such as age, sex, and activity level. For example, the DRI for an active male adolescent are not the same as for a middle-aged overweight female. The DRI guidelines for most nutrients are made up of four parts:

- *Estimated Average Requirement (EAR):* The EAR is the average amount of a nutrient you should eat every day.
- *Recommended Dietary Allowance (RDA):* The RDA is also an average amount of a nutrient you should eat each day, but it's a recommendation, not just an average.
- *Adequate Intake (AI):* Some nutrients cannot be adequately measured to create an RDA or EAR value. In that case, scientists make an educated guess, and call it the AI.
- *Tolerable Upper Intake Level (UL):* The UL is the highest level of a nutrient that you can eat without risk of negative effects.

There are separate guidelines for protein, carbohydrate, and fat. The *Estimated Energy Requirement (EER)* is the average amount of energy you should eat to maintain a healthy weight. The *Acceptable Macronutrient Distribution Ranges (AMDR)* are the percentage of each category you should eat: 45% to 65% carbohydrate; 10% to 35% protein; and 20% to 35% fat.

Customized Instruction: ESOL/Less Advanced Students

Have students prepare a food pyramid booklet. They should use different color construction paper for the front and back covers and insert six sheets of notebook paper between the covers for each of the food groups. Have students label each page with the food pyramid group, the daily recommended serving, and what it provides for their age group. Then, have the students cut out examples of the food group from magazines and newspapers and paste them on the pages. Refer students to Appendix C.

Evaluating Sources of Dietary Information

Your friend tells you she heard it's really healthy to eat only grapefruit for breakfast and lunch. You saw an article online that claims a raw food diet—eating only uncooked food—makes you live longer. You saw a different article online that claims MyPyramid is no good, because it's influenced by politics and not by science.

How do you know what to believe? Not all sources of information are equally reliable. When you evaluate nutrition claims, consider the following:

- *Expertise*: Is the person a known expert in the field of nutrition, or someone with a relevant degree? A classmate of yours might post a Web site about nutrition for a class project. Is it more or less reliable than a Web site sponsored by an organization such as the American Dietetic Association?
- *Objectivity*: Is this source seeking to sell you something or to make money from you? Nutrition Web sites sponsored by companies that sell vitamins might overstate the value of nutritional supplements. Web sites sponsored by the government are usually reliable because they are not selling anything, and because they are usually written or monitored by professionals in the field.

Where to Find Nutritional Information Online

Government agencies and industry organizations that provide accurate and reliable nutrition information include:

- The Center for Nutrition Policy and Promotion, an organization of the United States Department of Agriculture (USDA), www.MyPyramid.gov
- Centers for Disease Control (CDC), www.cdc.gov
- National Health and Nutrition Examination Survey (NHANES), www.cdc.gov/nchs/nhanes.htm
- The National Institutes of Health (NIH), www.nih.gov
- American Dietetic Association (ADA), www.eatright.org
- American Society for Nutrition (ASN), www.nutrition.org
- The Society for Nutrition Education (SNE), www.sne.org
- The American College of Sports Medicine (ACSM), www.acsm.org

Test IT Yourself!

Did you know that acids, such as vinegar, remove calcium carbonate from compounds such as bones? You can test this using the so-called "Rubber Chicken Experiment." You'll need a chicken drumstick, a glass jar with a lid that is large enough to hold the drumstick bone, and a quart of white vinegar.

1. Roast a chicken drumstick and remove as much meat from the bone as possible. Try to bend the bone. You can't because the calcium keeps the bone strong and firm.
2. Put the bone in the jar, fill the jar with enough vinegar to cover the bone, and put on the lid.
3. After two days, remove the bone and try to bend it again. It should be more flexible. (If it's not, dump out the vinegar and replace it with fresh vinegar.)
4. Put the bone back in the jar, and test it again every few days. By the end of the week, most of the calcium will be removed from the bone, and it should flop around like it's made out of rubber!

What does this experiment prove about bones and calcium? Make a list of foods that you can eat to ensure your bones remain strong and firm.

What's a Serving Size?

Nutrition Facts labels list information about a particular serving size. You can use a food scale to measure the exact amount of food you eat, or you can use estimates provided by a reliable organization, such as the National Center on Physical Activity and Disability.

✔ *One ounce is the size of an average adult thumb or four dice.*

✔ *Three ounces is about the size of a deck of playing cards.*

✔ *Two tablespoons is the size of a golf ball.*

✔ *A half-cup of cooked beans is the size of a light bulb.*

✔ *A cup of cooked rice, cereal, or pasta is the size of a tennis ball.*

✔ *A cup of chopped fruits or vegetables is the size of a baseball.*

✔ *A medium apple or orange is the size of an average woman's fist.*

✔ *A medium potato is the size of a computer mouse.*

Test IT Yourself!

Explain that vinegar is a mild acid that is strong enough to dissolve calcium in bones. Once the calcium is gone, there is no substance to keep the bone tissue hard. Calcium and phosphorus are the building blocks of strong bones. Lack of calcium is a danger for women in particular because it causes osteoporosis, which is the thinning of bones. To reverse bone calcium loss, you should increase your daily calcium intake with milk, cheese, yogurt, almonds, sesame seeds, broccoli, spinach, and turnips.

What's a Serving Size?

In addition to finding the correct serving size, explain that it is important to avoid common mistakes when reading food labels.

- Reduced fat or sodium means that fat or sodium is reduced by 25% from the original product. This doesn't mean the food is low in fat or sodium.
- "%DV" for fat or percent of daily recommended fat doesn't mean that 15% of the calories come from fat. You are using 15% of all the fat you need for the day with the one serving, based on 2,000 calories per day.
- When the amount of sugar is on the label, it does not mean it is an additive. Some foods such as milk have natural sugars. If foods are made with high-fructose corn syrup or other similar ingredients, it means they contain refined sugar, which you should eat in moderation.
- Don't assume that small items such as vending machine foods contain only one serving. Read the label.

Discuss

The U.S. Food and Drug Administration requires that food labels use standardized phrasing and terminology. Some of the more common terms and their meanings are:

- No fat or fat-free: Contains less than ½ gram of fat per serving.
- Lower or reduced fat: Contains at least 25% less per serving than the reference food.
- Low fat: Contains less than 3 grams of fat per serving.
- Lite: Contains ⅓ the calories or ½ the fat per serving of the original or similar product.
- No calories or calorie free: Contains less than 5 calories per serving.
- Low calorie: Contains ⅓ the calories of the original or similar product.
- Sugar-free: Contains less than ½ gram of sugar per serving.
- Reduced sugar: Contains at least 25% less sugar per serving than the original food.
- No preservatives: Contains no preservatives.
- No preservatives added: Contains no added chemicals to preserve the product.
- Low sodium: Contains less than 140 mg of sodium per serving.
- No salt or salt-free: Contains less than 5 mg of sodium per serving.
- High fiber: Contains 5 grams or more per serving.
- Good source of fiber: Contains 2.5 to 4.9 grams per serving.
- More or added fiber: Contains at least 2.5 grams more per serving than the original product.

Introduce the Section

Students learn the importance of setting diet and exercise goals for themselves through a personal health plan.

Figure Focus

An important thing to remember when developing a personal health plan is knowing how many calories are burned during physical activity and how that correlates to calorie intake. The USDA recommends that Americans do a minimum of 30 minutes of moderate exercise every day. In some instances, 60 minutes of moderate physical activity may be needed to prevent weight gain, and 50 to 90 minutes of exercise are recommended for weight loss.

Setting Goals for Nutrition and Wellness

In addition to tracking calories and nutrients, encourage students to consider their sodium intake. Consuming unhealthy amounts of sodium can cause high blood pressure. Some tips for reducing sodium intake are:

- Eat fewer processed foods, including chips, bacon, sausage, hot dogs, and canned foods.
- Avoid adding salt to food because most foods already contain sodium.
- Read labels to find out how much sodium the food contains.
- Be aware that sodium can come in several forms including sodium benzoate, sodium nitrate, and sodium ascorbate.
- Remember that condiments and seasonings also contain sodium. Reduce the amount or replace it with an herb mixture that does not contain sodium.
- Limit brined or pickled foods because they are usually soaked in a sodium-based solution.
- Look for "low sodium" or "reduced sodium" foods containing 140 mg or less per serving.

Developing a Personal Health Plan

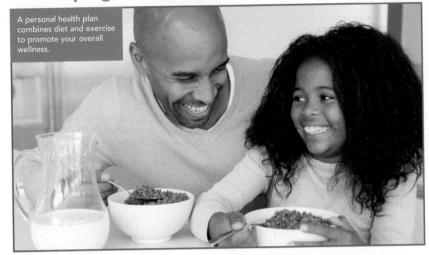

A personal health plan combines diet and exercise to promote your overall wellness.

Do you need the same number of calories a day as your dad? Should you drink whole milk, or fat-free? How much fiber is enough? Every person has different nutritional needs, depending on factors such as age, sex, height, weight, health, and physical activity. You can use available nutrition and diet planning resources such as MyPyramid.gov to develop a personal health plan that is right for you. Components of a health plan might include:

- A diet that includes the proper amounts of foods your body needs to function
- A pattern of regular exercise so that the amount of energy you take in is balanced with the amount of energy you give out
- Recreation and leisure activities that you enjoy
- Educational activities to develop skills and abilities
- Positive social relationships

A personal health plan contributes to all areas of your well-being: physical, emotional, personal, and social.

Setting Goals for Nutrition and Wellness

How can you develop a healthy diet? Do you want to eat more fruit and less sugar? Do you want to increase your physical activity to help balance your energy output with your calorie intake? Setting goals for nutrition and wellness can help you achieve a balanced personal health plan.

A good first step is to start a food journal. A food journal is simply a list of everything you eat in a day. You can keep track of food items, and then use the Nutrition Facts label to record the calories and nutrients. This information will help you identify ways to improve your eating habits. You can also include physical activity in the journal, so you can identify ways to improve your energy output.

You can refer to MyPyramid (www.mypyramid.gov) for useful information on customizing an eating plan for your own personal needs. Other resources that can help you include your school or local library, your school nurse, and nutritional Web sites such as www.fitday.com that provide free journals for tracking the nutrients you eat as well as your daily intake of essential vitamins and minerals.

STUDENT ACTIVITY

Ask students to research how many calories they burn during everyday activities, such as walking home from school, playing sports, climbing stairs, and yard work. As a class, discuss ideas on how to burn more calories. For example, you might find a longer route to follow for your walk home from school, or you might take a break from studying by riding your bicycle for 10 minutes or by jumping rope.

Climbing MyPyramid

The U.S. Department of Agriculture (USDA) wants to help you select the foods that are right for you—not for someone else. As a result, it developed a nutrition guide called MyPyramid (www.MyPyramid.gov). The USDA states that MyPyramid can help you make smart choices from every food group, find balance between food and physical activity, get the most nutrition from the calories you eat, and stay within your daily calorie needs.

At first glance, the MyPyramid logo does not look much like a food guide. It has no pictures of foods, and the food groups are represented by colored bands. Its goal is to encourage individuals to use the information to create a personal eating plan that combines healthy diet and physical exercise.

- *Activity* is represented by a figure climbing the steps of the pyramid.
- *Moderation* is represented by the way the colored bands of each food group become narrower as they approach the top.
- *Personalization* is represented by the person on the steps, and the name: MyPyramid.
- *Proportion* is shown by the different widths of the food group bands, indicating you should eat more of the foods in the wider bands—grains and vegetables.
- *Gradual improvement* is encouraged by the steps, which suggest that you can improve your diet and lifestyle one step at a time.

The USDA recommends that everyone use the MyPyramid.gov Web site to create a personalized pyramid based on your own age, weight, gender, and activity level.

What Color Is Your Food Group?

Many nutritionists and dietitians recommend eating a *rainbow of foods* to achieve a healthy diet. That means that if you eat foods of different colors, you are likely to take in a balance of nutrients that will contribute to your health and wellness.

When you eat different colors—such as red apples, green spinach, yellow squash, and orange carrots—you are eating a variety of healthy, nutrient-rich foods. The USDA tries to symbolize variety, and a rainbow of foods, on MyPyramid by using colored bands to represent each of the different food groups (refer to Appendix C to see how much of each group you should eat daily):

- Orange: Grains
- Green: Vegetables
- Red: Fruits
- Blue: Milk
- Purple: Meat and Beans
- Yellow: Fats and Oil

MyPyramid.gov
STEPS TO A HEALTHIER YOU

USDA U.S. Department of Agriculture
Center for Nutrition Policy
and Promotion
April 2005 CNPP-16

USDA is an equal opportunity provider and employer.

GRAINS | VEGETABLES | FRUITS | OILS | MILK | MEAT & BEANS

How can you use MyPyramid to develop a personal eating plan?

What's Wrong with My Diet?

You have trouble waking up in the morning. You can't concentrate in class. You feel sick to your stomach working out with the team after school. You get plenty of exercise and eat three meals a day. Is there a problem with your diet?

👎 You eat a breakfast cereal that is loaded with sugar.

👎 You only eat vegetables at dinner.

👎 You drink carbonated soft drinks.

👍 You switch to low-fat or fat-free milk.

👍 You choose whole-wheat bread for your sandwiches.

👍 You have fruit and vegetables with every meal.

👍 You substitute water for sports drinks and soft drinks.

Are there other changes you can make to improve your diet?

Figure Focus Activity

Have students go to www.mypyramid.gov. At the site, they should click on "MyPyramid Plan" on the left side menu. Have them fill in answers for the questions on age, gender, height, weight, and amount of physical activity and then submit it. A personalized set of recommendations will display. Allow students to print their summary and then encourage them to analyze how they can incorporate the recommendations in their daily diet and exercise routine.

What's Wrong with My Diet?

Some additional tips for improving diet include:

- Replace white rice with brown rice.
- Substitute air-popped corn for sugary or high-sodium snacks.
- Try oatmeal or whole grain breakfast cereals.
- Use vegetable oils for cooking instead of margarine, lard, or butter.
- Sprinkle vinegar and oil or lemon juice onto salads instead of dressings.
- Drink 100% fruit juice instead of high-fructose drinks or sodas.
- Purchase 90 to 95% lean ground beef.
- Try salsa or fruit chutney on meats instead of sauces or gravies.
- Broil, grill, or roast meats and fish instead of frying them.

Introduce the Section

This section discusses the effects of an unhealthy diet on a person's physical and emotional wellness. It also provides tips on how to manage your health and wellness.

Teaching Tips

Be aware that some students might be sensitive to a discussion on BMI, dieting, and obesity. If you sense this, keep the discussion focused on proactive things you can do to maintain a healthy weight and diet.

Figure Focus

Obesity is a serious issue facing Americans. You might share these facts from the Centers for Disease Control and Prevention:

- Eighty percent of children aged 10–15 years who were overweight became obese adults at age 25.
- One in seven low-income, preschool-aged children is obese.
- Obesity is highest in western and southern California, Texas, the central and northeastern seaboard, and some Appalachian states.

Vocabulary

Obesity: The condition of being extremely overweight.

Nutrition and Weight Loss

Discuss the consequences of obesity. These include psychological disorders, cardiovascular disease, and other health conditions. Many things contribute to obesity. Discuss with students the factors and triggers involved in their daily lives that could put them at risk of obesity.

- Genetic factors, which are passed on to a person by his or her parents. However, prevalence of obesity has tripled among school-aged children in the last three decades, which cannot be explained solely by genetics.
- Behavioral factors, such as energy intake, physical activity, and sedentary behavior. A recent study reported children ages 8 to 18 spend more than three hours per day watching TV and movies.
- Environmental factors, such as parent-child interactions, child care, and school interactions.

Analyzing Special Dietary Needs

In some circumstances, you might need a special diet to achieve your nutrition and wellness goals.

An unhealthy diet can contribute to various health problems and disease, including **obesity**—the condition of being extremely overweight—diabetes, high blood pressure, heart disease, eating disorders (see Chapter 4), and even cancer. Special diets can help people cope with health problems. For example, people with diabetes eat a diet low in carbohydrates; people with high blood pressure eat a diet low in sodium. It is important for people on special diets to read food labels so they know what they are eating.

Understanding special diets helps you manage your health and wellness. For example, someone who wants to adjust energy intake to lose body fat must still take in proper nutrients.

Nutrition and Weight Loss

The first step in a healthy weight loss plan is to talk to a doctor. A doctor can confirm if weight loss is necessary and help you develop a safe plan that you can sustain—keep going for a long time—without returning to unhealthy habits. The plan will probably include cutting down on calorie intake, increasing physical activity, and improving nutrition.

A safe and sustainable weight loss program has the following qualities:

- *Moderation*: It reduces overall caloric intake by a reasonable amount, such as 15%.
- *Balance*: It provides a balance of nutrients, such as 20% to 35% fats and the rest split evenly between carbohydrates and proteins.
- *Flexibility*: It allows for healthy eating choices in a variety of situations, including dining at home with friends and family, dining out, picking up fast food, and eating special occasion dinners.

Discuss

Ask the class to name a few of the fad diets they have heard about in the news. About 50 percent of women and 25 percent of men have reported trying a fad diet, according to one study. People eat strange combinations of food, drastically reduce their calories, or crash diet to lose weight quickly. However, these "miracle" diets can be dangerous. Many times, people gain the weight back immediately after stopping the diet, gain more weight, or worse. Explain that the best way to lose weight is using a balanced diet high in nutrients and a regular exercise regimen.

Energy In

Calories are the only source of energy that you take in. Proteins, carbohydrates, and fats all produce energy, which means that they contain kilocalories. A **kilocalorie** (kcal) is a unit of measurement that describes how much energy the food you eat delivers to your body. When you see a food label that lists the number of **calories** in a serving, it is actually listing the number of kilocalories.

A kilocalorie is the amount of heat—energy—required to raise the temperature of one kilogram of water by one degree on the Celsius temperature scale. Proteins and carbohydrates deliver 4 kcal per gram. That means for every gram you digest, your body receives 4 kcal of energy. Fats deliver 9 kcal per gram.

When you *count calories*, you pay attention to the number of calories you are taking into your body. The easiest way to identify the number of calories in a food item is to look at the nutrition information on the food label.

"Will I gain weight if I balance my energy in with my energy out?"

Energy Out

There are many ways for your body to expend energy—or burn calories. Three of the main ways of buring calories are sitting around, being physically active, and eating:

■ Your basal metabolic rate (BMR) is the number of calories you use just to rest. About 60% to 70% of the calories you consume each day are used for your BMR. Everyone has a different BMR, based on factors such as amount of muscle in the body, height, age, and sex.

■ You use about 20% to 35% of your calories on physical activity. Activities that use more muscles and larger muscles burn more calories.

■ Your body burns calories processing food. Called the *thermic effect of food* (TEF), it is usually 5% to 10% of the number of calories that you eat. So, if you eat something that contains 100 calories, 10 of those calories go toward processing the food. The TEF value varies depending on the nutrient type. For example, fat takes very little energy to process, but carbohydrates can take up to 25% of calories.

You can calculate the number of calories in a meal that combines different foods by adding the calories in each food.

For example, a hot dog might have 110 calories and the bun might have 130 calories. To find out how many calories you take in if you eat the hot dog in a bun, add 110 + 130 = 240 total calories.

If a hamburger has 240 calories and a hamburger bun has 130, how many calories will you take in if you eat the hamburger in a bun?

A typical 12 ounce can of cola has about 136 calories. How many calories will you take in if you eat the hot dog and bun, and drink a can of cola?

What if you eat the hamburger, bun, and can of cola?

How Much Energy Am I Using?

You can use online calculators to look up how many calories you burn doing different activities, such as running, biking, or walking. They take into consideration your age, height, and weight. Here are some standard numbers for common activities. The value is the number of calories burned per minute, for a person who weighs 120 pounds.

Sitting still	1.4
Walking slowly	2.2
Walking briskly	4.75
Bicycling	3.8
Running slowly	7.6
Running moderately	9.45
Running fast	13.2
Yoga	2.4

Vocabulary

Calories: The number of kilo-calories that measures how much energy the food you eat delivers to your body.

Kilo-calorie (kcal): Unit of measurement that describes the amount of heat or energy that is required to raise the temperature of 1 kilogram of water by 1 degree Celsius.

Figure Focus

By balancing the amount of calories you consume with how many your body burns, you should not gain weight. Share the following with students:

■ High-fat foods containing more calories per serving can increase the likelihood of weight gain.

■ Patterns of eating can make you gain weight if you consume all of your calories before periods of rest.

■ Frequent binge-eating or food restriction can contribute to weight problems.

■ Losing muscle mass will decrease your weight but hurt your overall well-being.

■ Excess fat in the stomach area can increase the risk of high blood pressure, diabetes, early heart disease, and cancer.

■ Smoking tobacco and drinking too much alcohol can increase the risk for diseases related to obesity.

How Much Energy Am I Using?

Explain that physical activity should be moderate or vigorous and should be done at least 30 to 60 minutes each day. The USDA recommends moderate exercises such as:

■ Walking briskly (about 3½ miles per hour)

■ Hiking

■ Gardening/yard work

■ Dancing

■ Golf (walking and carrying clubs)

■ Bicycling (less than 10 miles per hour)

■ Weight training (general light workout)

Examples of vigorous physical activities include:

■ Running/jogging (5 miles per hour)

■ Bicycling (more than 10 miles per hour)

■ Swimming (freestyle laps)

■ Aerobics

■ Walking very fast (4½ miles per hour)

■ Heavy yard work, such as chopping wood

■ Weight-lifting (vigorous effort)

■ Basketball (competitive)

NUMBERS GAME

■ 240 + 130 = 370 calories
when you eat a hamburger in a bun.

■ 240 + 136 = 376 calories
for the hot dog, bun, and cola.

■ 370 + 136 = 506 calories
for the hamburger, bun, and cola.

Calorie Content of Some Common Snack Foods

"Eating smart" does not mean you cannot eat your favorite foods. However, stress to students that it's important to pay attention to foods that nourish your body while tasting good. Remember to take time to chew your food slowly and savor it. Avoid stress while eating because it can interrupt your digestion and cause heartburn. Also, try not to eat while working, driving, or watching television, as this might be "comfort eating" or not paying attention to what you are consuming. Listen to your body and know when you are satisfied. Always eat breakfast to jump start your body and eat small, healthy snacks often to minimize lethargy and prevent binge eating.

Vocabulary

Body Mass Index (BMI): A height and weight ratio used for evaluating the body condition.

Figure Focus

Explain that BMI is designed to help people understand whether they are classified in a "healthy" weight class. A high BMI can help students understand their risk of becoming obese, and the conditions and diseases related to obesity. However, it does not provide information on body composition such as muscle mass, bone mass, and fat. For example, a person who lifts weights and has a lot of muscle mass can be considered obese while an inactive person with too much fat but less weight may be considered healthy.

Calorie Content of Some Common Snack Foods

You can read the Nutrition Facts label to find out how many calories are in an item. You can also look up the information online. Here are the counts for some common snack foods:

✔ *8 oz potato chips:*
1242 kcal, 749 from fat

✔ *1 cup microwave popcorn*
164 kcal, 42 from fat

✔ *1 oz slice-and-bake chocolate chip cookies*
138 kcal, 57 from fat

✔ *1 medium apple*
95 kcal, 3 from fat

✔ *1 medium banana*
105 kcal, 3 from fat

✔ *6 oz nonfat fruit yogurt*
161 kcal, 3 from fat

✔ *1 slice cheese pizza*
192 kcal, 89 from fat

✔ *1 slice pepperoni pizza*
432 kcal, 200 from fat

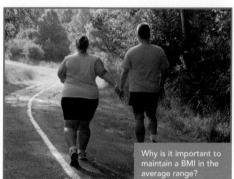

Why is it important to maintain a BMI in the average range?

How Many Calories Should I Eat?

There is actually a calculation you can use to figure out how many calories you should take in to maintain a healthy body weight. Multiply your body weight in kilograms (kg) by your BMR by the additional calories you expend in physical activity—called an activity multiplier.

1. Multiply your weight in pounds by 0.453 to get your weight in kilograms.
2. (a) If you are male, multiply your weight in kg by 1.0 kcal, and then multiply that result by 24 to get your BMR.
   (b) If you are female, multiply your weight in kg by 0.9 kcal, and then multiply that result by 24 to get your BMR.
3. Use a chart to identify the high and low values of your activity multiplier. You can find the chart online or in a medical or fitness reference book, or you can ask your school nurse for one.
4. Multiply your BMR by the low activity multiplier and then add the result to your BMR to get the minimum number of calories you need.
5. Multiply your BMR by the high activity multiplier and then add the result to your BMR to get the maximum number of calories you need.

To maintain your weight, you want to take in somewhere between the minimum and maximum number of calories. To gain weight, take in more than the maximum. To lose weight, take in less than the minimum.

What About BMI?

The **Body Mass Index** (BMI) is a height-weight ratio measurement used for evaluating body condition. The lower your BMI, the leaner you are. A BMI of less than 19 is considered underweight; 19 to 25 is considered average; 25 or greater is considered overweight; 30 or greater is considered obese.

■ If you have a BMI of less than 19 you are at risk for having a weakened immune system, slow wound healing, respiratory problems, and malnutrition.

■ If you have a BMI over 25, you might be at risk for health problems such as heart disease, high blood pressure, diabetes, strokes, gallbladder disease, sleep apnea, and breathing problems.

BMI can be misleading in people who have higher than normal amounts of muscle, such as athletes. They might register a higher BMI than average, when in fact they have a low percentage of body fat. You can look up your BMI in a BMI chart that you find online or in a medical or fitness reference book, or you can ask your school nurse for one.

Nutrition and Athletics

Physical activity is a part of any healthy diet plan. Athletes—people who pursue physical activity as a hobby, passion, or career—have different dietary needs. Diet affects athletic performance in many ways. It might provide a burst of energy for a sprinter or endurance for a marathoner.

Athletes generally need more calories than an average person. However, that does not mean athletes should eat density-poor foods in order to take in more calories. It is important for athletes to eat foods that are high in nutrition.

Athletes need carbohydrates to produce glucose, which supplies energy. Most nutritionists recommend that an athlete's diet consist of 50% to 60% whole grain carbohydrates such as whole grain pasta, brown rice, and whole-grain bread.

Water is the most important nutrient for an athlete. Vigorous exercise can cause your body to lose several liters of water by sweating. You must replace that water by drinking.

> I had a back injury and followed a good nutrition program to help speed up my recovery. I focused on exercise and staying healthy in order to get back out on the ice.
>
> — *Sasha Cohen, Olympic Figure Skater*

Managing Food Allergies and Intolerances

Have you ever felt your nose itch after you eat a new food? Have you noticed that you get a stomachache every time you eat a certain type of cheese? You might have a food allergy or intolerance.

- A food allergy causes your body to react when you eat a certain food. Physical symptoms include swelling, difficulty breathing, skin rashes, upset stomach, or vomiting. Severe allergies can result in anaphylactic shock, which is a condition in which blood pressure drops and breathing becomes shallow. It can result in death.
- A food intolerance is when your body does not digest a certain food properly. Lactose intolerance—an intolerance for milk and other types of dairy products—is a common food intolerance. Gluten intolerance—an intolerance for gluten, which is a protein in wheat, rye, barley, and oats—is less common.

Being aware of food allergies and intolerances can help you understand why someone might refuse to eat certain things. It can also help you plan and prepare meals for a variety of people.

Job Search

If you are interested in food and you enjoy helping people improve their health and physical well-being, you might want to consider a career in nutrition. Careers in nutrition range from nutritionists, who might work in a weight-loss center or health club, to registered dietitians, who usually work in institutions such as medical centers or extended care facilities.

Registered dietitians must earn a bachelor's degree in nutrition, complete a 9- to 12-month internship, and pass a certification examination. A nutritionist generally has less education and training.

Use the Internet, library, or your school's guidance resources to learn more about a career in nutrition and wellness. Write a job description, including the educational requirements, career pathway, and potential salary range.

Does It Contain Peanuts?

Peanut allergies are very common and can pose a serious health risk. Obviously, if you have a peanut allergy, you should not eat peanuts, but peanuts are sometimes hiding in other foods, such as packaged cookies or processed ice cream. What if you have a peanut allergy?

- ★ *Read the list of ingredients on all packaged foods.*
- ★ *Look for an allergy warning label indicating the presence of peanuts on all packaged foods.*
- ★ *Do not share your friend's food.*
- ★ *Explain your allergy to your friends so they do not give you food containing peanuts.*
- ★ *Check with restaurant staff to make sure that there are no peanuts in the food served to you.*
- ★ *Have medicine available to use to counteract the effects of peanuts if you do have a reaction.*

Why is it important to understand food allergies even if you do not have one yourself?

Does It Contain Peanuts?

The most prevalent food allergens include milk, eggs, peanuts, tree nuts, fish, soy wheat, and shellfish. It is important to understand food allergies, even if you don't have one, for several reasons. Discuss the following:

- You'll understand why someone may be refusing certain foods.
- You'll know how to prepare foods for someone with a food allergy.
- You'll recognize that the person may experience the effects of a food allergen hours or even a day or two before symptoms appear.
- You'll be able to determine when someone may be suffering from anaphylaxis and cannot breathe.
- You'll be able to determine if symptoms you develop yourself might be from an allergic reaction to something you've eaten.

Job Search

Examples of careers in nutrition and wellness include:

- Dance/aerobics/yoga Instructor
- Health or physical education teacher
- Drug and alcohol abuse counselor
- Social worker
- Corporate wellness director
- Various careers in sports medicine
- Emergency medical technician
- Nurse
- Spa/health club manager
- Physician's assistant
- Genetic counselor
- Physical therapist
- Athletic trainer
- Mental health services
- Rehabilitative services
- Acupuncturist
- Camp counselor

Introduce the Section

Global politics, policies, and laws impact the quality of our food supply and the food choices we are able to make. The section provides an overview of those influences.

Figure Focus

Discuss agricultural subsidies, which are government funds paid to farmers to supplement their income and keep them in business. Some people argue it would be much cheaper to import fruits and vegetables rather than subsidize farmers in the United States. Ask students why they believe the government continues to subsidize agriculture. Some responses might include:

- Jobs would be lost.
- Domestic farming would be weakened and unable to compete against foreign competition.
- The country would be more vulnerable to trade pressures and global food shortages.
- Imported foods could be tainted or used as a threat.
- Subsidies preserve local agricultural traditions and customs.
- Subsidies encourage the production of bio-fuels and green space.

The Impact of Global Politics

Explain that in many other countries, farmers must withstand years when agriculture products are worth less because of lack of demand or market volatility. Therefore, the cost is driven down and many small farmers do not have a living wage. You might discuss the concept of "Fair Trade Coffee." This refers to the partnership between consumers in North America and producers in Asia, Africa, Latin America, and the Caribbean which guarantees that poor farmers in the organization receive a minimum price of $1.26 per pound of coffee regardless of the market worth. Ask students to look for Fair Trade Certified coffee when they visit local coffee shops and the grocery store.

Analyzing Influences on Our Food Supply

In the United States, we have a huge selection of food to choose from in any supermarket. It might seem like we are making those choices completely independently, but many influences are constantly in effect, and constantly changing.

What does a trade agreement between the United States and Mexico have to do with the food on your supermarket shelves? How can a drought in Africa affect the supply of wheat in the United States? The cost and availability of food in the United States is impacted by many factors locally and around the world, including:

- Politics
- Trade
- Environmental conditions
- Economics
- Law
- Conflict

Recognizing the influence of global factors on our food supply can help you prepare for changes and disruptions. You can also identify ways that your choices influence the global food supply.

The Impact of Global Politics

Governments impact the flow of goods and services from one country to another.

- Trade agreements set policies for **importing** (bringing in) and **exporting** (sending out) products, including food. For example, the United States might agree to buy rice from Asia, making rice plentiful in the U.S.
- Governments can apply taxes—or **tariffs**—on foreign products, and even prohibit certain products from being sold. For example, the United States might impose a tax on cheese from France, making French cheese more expensive, thereby making American-made cheese comparatively less expensive.
- Governments also impact the availability of food by waging war. If there is a war in a country that produces bananas, it might be harder for the farmers there to harvest and ship the fruit. Bananas would become scarce and more expensive in the U.S.
- War might destroy crops or grazing land, making it difficult or impossible for farmers to produce food in those areas.

Vocabulary

Exporting: To send out products to foreign countries.

Importing: To bring in products from a foreign country.

Tariffs: Government taxes on imported foreign products.

U.S. Government Policies and Laws

From the federal level to your local city council, government cares about what you eat. Agencies such as the Food and Drug Administration and the U.S. Department of Agriculture monitor the quality and safety of food.

- The USDA might shut down a processing plant that is not clean, impacting the availability of that product.
- The USDA might require a company to recall a product that has made people sick.

The federal government also sets policies to protect the food distribution system. For example, to protect the number of fish in the oceans, the government sets limits on when commercial fishers can catch certain species, and how many days they can work. To control the cost of certain crops, the government might provide payments—called subsidies—to some food producers. They might pay farmers not to grow wheat, or pay dairies to produce more milk.

States can also set laws that impact your access to food. They might require additional inspections to ensure that products are safe, or impose taxes on products from somewhere else.

Can Your Food Choices Influence Others?

Does your choice of snack have an impact on the food supply? Recall from Chapter 13 that you play a role in the economy. Every food choice you make has an effect on a food-producing company. Choose an apple for a snack and you are supporting the apple industry. Choose cheese and you are supporting the dairy industry.

Here are some ways that your food choices impact the economy—locally and around the globe:

- You may choose to buy foods produced by companies that use fair labor practices. For example, you might buy from a company that pays workers a fair wage, so they can earn a living and contribute to their economy.
- You may choose to buy food produced in the United States to support the U.S. economy.
- You may choose to buy foods that are grown in your community in order to support your local economy. Buying locally also minimizes the cost and negative environmental effects of transporting foods long distances.
- You may choose to support farms that use *sustainable agriculture*, which means that they minimize the impact of farming on the environment by using environmentally-friendly methods.

What's a Food Additive?

A food additive is something natural or man-made that is added to food to make it taste better, look better, or last longer. Some common food additives include the following.

- ✔ *Spices and herbs are added to food to enhance flavor.*
- ✔ *Glutamates are flavor-enhancing chemicals, such as monosodium glutamate (MSG).*
- ✔ *Food coloring is added to most processed foods to make products look more appealing.*
- ✔ *Texturizers are chemicals that improve the texture of food.*
- ✔ *Stabilizers help products maintain texture or color over time.*
- ✔ *Emulsifiers help keep fat evenly distributed through food.*
- ✔ *Vitamins and minerals are added to enrich certain foods, such as pasta, white rice, and white bread. Vitamin C and vitamin E are natural preservatives, and are added to make food stay fresh longer.*

How Does the Global Environment Affect Your Food Supply?

How does a freeze in Florida affect the availability of lemons in Detroit? Why does a drought in Australia cause the cost of lamb in New York to skyrocket? Weather and natural disasters affect the growth and harvesting of crops and food animals. They can also disrupt the supply chain used to transport products.

- *A typhoon in Hawaii might destroy the crop of pineapples.*
- *A flood in Colombia might wash out the road used to transport coffee beans to the airport.*
- *A wildfire in New Zealand might destroy apple orchards.*

Use the Internet to research the effects weather or natural disasters have on the U.S. food supply. Are some areas more susceptible than others? Are some types of food at greater risk? Prepare a presentation explaining what you have learned.

Discuss

Discuss the ways in which an individual might use sustainable agriculture. These include growing vegetables in your garden, keeping a hen to lay eggs, and using a compost pile.

What's a Food Additive?

While food additives give products a longer shelf life and a more attractive appearance, buying organic foods is a growing trend. Discuss some of the reasons for this:

- Long-term effects of additives are unknown.
- Additives can trigger allergies.
- Some chemicals can increase nausea and diarrhea.
- Sodium chloride can lead to kidney failure, hypertension, and heart attacks.
- Sodium nitrite is used to preserve, color, and flavor meat but has been linked to certain types of cancer.
- Trans fats can cause heart disease, stroke, heart attacks, kidney failure, and vascular diseases.
- Artificial food colorings such as Blue 1 and 2, Red 3, Green 3, and Yellow 6 are considered low risk but have been linked to cancer in mice.

How Does the Global Environment Affect Your Food Supply?

Students are to prepare a presentation on the effects of weather and natural disasters on the country's food supply. For enrichment purposes, you might discuss the importance of preparing for natural disasters and tips for keeping food safe during emergencies. These include:

- Meat, poultry, fish, and eggs must be refrigerated below 40 degrees. A refrigerator can keep food safely cold for about four hours if it is unopened.
- Purchase dry or block ice if there will be an extended period without energy.
- Always have boxed or canned milk and other canned goods, water, and pet foods available.
- Consider storing food safely on higher shelves if you live in a location affected by floods or in basements if you are affected by tornadoes.
- Do not eat foods that have come in contact with flood waters.
- If you do not have bottled water, boil water to make sure it is safe.
- If your home has been on fire, discard all foods because chemicals from fighting the fire, heat, and smoke fumes could have tainted it.

End-of-Chapter Activities

Case Study

Answers will vary, but students should decide that the diets do not sound sensible. Cutting out an entire form of a food element is never a good idea. It is much better to eat a balanced diet. The supplement diet is likely just a gimmick by a company trying to make money. The diets Marissa finds online are fads, and while they might work in the short term, they will not work in the long term, and might cause health problems.

Marissa might not need to lose weight at all. She might just be feeling insecure about changing schools, and putting too much emphasis on her appearance instead of on her personality.

She should consult her doctor or school nurse to discuss how to measure her body mass index to see if she is at a healthy weight. A professional can also advise her on healthy eating habits and how to use proper diet and exercise to maintain a healthy body and self-image.

Sounding Off!

Student answers will vary, but in answer to the second question, eating can be seen as a social activity in respect to customs and cultures, occasions, and holidays, and family dynamics such as eating dinner together each night.

FAQ

1. Factors that influence your food choices are taste, availability, cost, convenience, advertising, health, peer pressure (friends), state of mind, fun and sociability, values, location, culture, and religion. Students may think of others.

2. Nutrition is a science that studies the way the food you eat nourishes your body.

3. The essential nutrients are proteins, carbohydrates, fats, minerals, vitamins, and water.

4. The three key points of the Dietary Guidelines for Americans are:

   ■ The importance of eating fewer calories, being more active, and making wise food choices.

   ■ The importance of meeting nutrient needs by eating food, not by taking dietary supplements.

   ■ The importance of developing eating patterns that integrate dietary recommendations into a healthy lifestyle, rather than using weight-loss diets.

5. Things you can find on a label include serving size, servings per container, number of calories per serving, amount of fat per serving, amount of vitamins per serving, amount of minerals per serving, amount of cholesterol per serving, number of carbohydrates per serving, and amount of protein per serving. Students may be more specific, listing items such as vitamin A, sodium, calcium, etc.

6. Nutrient density is a measure of the nutrients a food provides compared to the calories it provides.

7. Dietary supplements might be necessary for:

   ■ Senior citizens who do not consume enough nutritious food.

   ■ People on restricted diets who might not eat a variety of foods, such as vegetarians, who may not take in enough protein owing to the lack of meat in their diets.

   ■ Pregnant women who need more vitamins and minerals than can be obtained from food alone.

   ■ Athletes who are on calorie-restricted diets.

8. The colored bands symbolize the food groups.

9. Obesity is the condition of being extremely overweight.

10. Qualities of a safe and sustainable weight loss program are moderation, balance, and flexibility.

396   Chapter 20 ■ Food and Nutrition

Case Study

Marissa is 15 years old. She has moved to a new town and starts a new school in September. She is worried about fitting in. She thinks she will make friends more quickly if she loses a few pounds.

Marissa uses the Internet to look up diets that will help her lose weight fast. She finds one that suggests eating only cabbage soup, and another that says to eat only grapefruit. One diet guarantees she will lose 10 pounds in 10 days. Another requires using an expensive weight-loss supplement drink.

Finally, Marissa finds a diet that she thinks sounds sensible. It says she can eat whatever she wants as long as it contains no fat. She prints the suggested menus and starts the diet immediately.

■ What are some of the problems with the diets Marissa found online?
■ Do you think Marissa should even be looking for a diet?
■ What are some of the factors influencing Marissa's decision to start a diet?
■ How can Marissa find out if she really does need to lose weight, and if so, how to do it in a safe and healthy way?

Sounding Off!

❶ What is more important to you when you make food choices—cost, convenience, taste, or nutrition?

❷ Do you think eating is a social activity?

1. List ten factors that influence your food choices.
2. What is nutrition?
3. List the six essential nutrients that your body needs to stay healthy.
4. What are the three key points of the Dietary Guidelines for Americans?
5. List four things you can find on a Nutrition Facts label.
6. What is nutrient density?
7. List three special situations when dietary supplements might be necessary.
8. What do the colored bands on MyPyramid symbolize?
9. What is obesity?
10. What are the three qualities of a safe and sustainable weight loss program?

In small groups, work together to create a brochure, flyer, or poster about the health benefits and risks of different types of oils and fats. Research the nutritional value of the items and use the information you locate in your document. Use pictures to illustrate your document. When the document is complete, print it. With permission, distribute it at a local elementary school, daycare center, or senior center.

TEAM PLAYERS

Hot Topics

Do you feel that you personally eat a diet that contributes to your health and well-being? Are there changes you would like to make to your personal health plan? Are there obstacles or challenges in your way?

Take this opportunity to write anonymously about how your diet affects your well-being. Use a word processor so no one recognizes your handwriting. Be honest and open. Put the paper in the class Hot Topics box.

As a class, read the anonymous entries and discuss them.

Web Extra ▼

There are many Web sites that provide reliable and accurate information about nutrition specifically for teens. For example, www.kidshealth.org has a section on food and fitness for teens, and so does the FDA, at www.fda.com.

Use the Internet to locate some sites that you think might be useful for your peers. Make a directory of the sites, including the Web site address and a brief description. Post the directory on your school Web site or in your school career center or library.

Problem Solver

You are having friends over to celebrate New Year's Eve. One friend is a vegetarian, one is lactose intolerant, and one is allergic to peanuts. What factors must you consider when you make choices for the food and drink you plan to serve?

Create a menu for dinner and snacks for the party. Write a paragraph explaining your choices.

Team Players

Teams will work together to create a brochure, flyer, or poster about the health benefits and risks of different types of oils and fats. Encourage teams to review the following sections in the chapter: *Analyzing Nutrition*, *Analyzing Guidelines for Healthy Eating*, and *Developing a Personal Health Plan*. You can also refer them to the *Oils* section on page 538 of Appendix C.

Hot Topics

Make sure students understand that they can turn in their papers anonymously. Encourage them to be open and honest about their diet and how it contributes to their health and well-being.

Web Extra

Students are to research health and fitness Web sites designed specifically for their age group and create a directory. Students should be wary of sites trying to sell products and those that require lengthy registration or contain more opinions than facts. Encourage students to make their directories creative and eye-catching.

Remind students that a reliable Web site usually publishes the name of the author or organization that sponsors it and the date the content was created or last updated in a fairly obvious location, such as at the top or bottom of the page or on the home page. The site is usually organized with headings and an obvious navigation system. A reliable site clearly states its purpose and any affiliations. You should also look for accuracy in spelling and grammar.

Problem Solver

Student menus will vary but should take into consideration the following:

- A vegetarian usually eats vegetables, fruits, grains, seeds, and generally eggs and dairy products, but not meat or fish.

- Someone who is lactose-intolerant does not have the ability or has insufficient ability to digest lactose, which is a sugar found in milk and milk products.

- Someone who is allergic to peanuts cannot eat anything containing nuts, peanut oil, or peanut flour.

Write Now

Students are to write a news article about a hypothetical incident in which a major crop of grain is destroyed and the effects of this disaster on the food supply. Remind students that a news article is in the third person. It should have the most important information first and an eye-catching headline. Stress the importance of basing the information in the article on statistics and facts.

Be Involved!

Students are to use the FCCLA planning process to help educate others about the importance of nutrition and wellness. The FCCLA planning process is:

- Identify the project.
- Set the goal.
- Form a plan.
- Act.
- Follow up.

Students can obtain more information on the FCCLA planning process from the organization's Web site, www.fcclainc.org. If students work in groups, remind them that a successful team relationship depends on all team members working together. Make sure they take steps to delegate responsibilities, communicate effectively, and manage conflicts or disagreements.

Social Networking

Students are to investigate nutrition programs available through agencies and organizations in their community. You might have students work in teams with each team focusing on a specific program. Have students prepare a list of volunteer opportunities with the organization, and then organize a team effort to assist the organization.

Write Now

What would happen if a disease kills the rice crop in Asia, or a drought destroys the corn crop in North America? How would such an event affect the food supply?

Write a news article about an incident in which a major crop of grain is destroyed. Include information about who would be affected, how, and why.

Be Involved!

www.fcclainc.org

As a class, brainstorm ways you can help educate others about the importance of nutrition and wellness. For example, you might consider creating a Web site for sharing healthy recipes with your peers, printing a cookbook of healthy recipes for senior citizens, organizing a health and fitness workshop for your community, or volunteering to prepare healthy snacks with the children at a day-care center.

In groups or individually, select a project relating to educating others about nutrition and wellness. Use the FCCLA planning process to develop a plan for your project. Assess the plan to make sure it is realistic and attainable, and then put the plan into action to achieve your goal. As you work toward your goal, keep a journal to record your progress, and collect documentation for a portfolio that you can use to show what you have achieved. Notify your local media to see if they will provide publicity for your project, before, during, and after it is complete.

When the project is complete, write a report about it. Evaluate your success, and analyze things you could have done differently. Did you achieve your goal? Were you able to educate others about the importance of nutrition and wellness? Did you run into any obstacles? If so, how did you overcome them? If you were going to start the project over again, what would you do differently?

Social Networking

Many communities have programs to help make sure groups that might be at risk for poor nutrition have access to healthy meals. For example, Meals On Wheels delivers nutritious food to home-bound senior citizens. Summer lunch programs distribute healthy meals to underserved school-aged children. State agencies administer the Women, Infants, and Children (WIC) program—a nutrition program that helps pregnant women, new mothers, and young children eat well and stay healthy. Investigate the nutrition programs in your community. Find out how you can become involved.

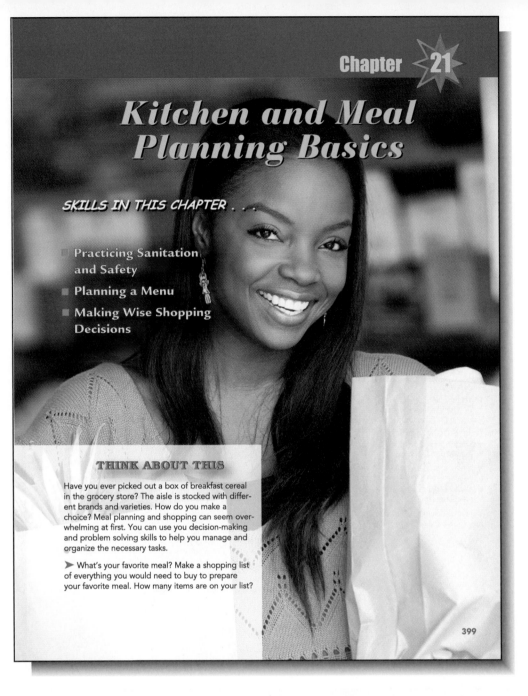

Chapter 21

Kitchen and Meal Planning Basics

SKILLS IN THIS CHAPTER . . .

- Practicing Sanitation and Safety
- Planning a Menu
- Making Wise Shopping Decisions

THINK ABOUT THIS

Have you ever picked out a box of breakfast cereal in the grocery store? The aisle is stocked with different brands and varieties. How do you make a choice? Meal planning and shopping can seem overwhelming at first. You can use you decision-making and problem solving skills to help you manage and organize the necessary tasks.

➤ What's your favorite meal? Make a shopping list of everything you would need to buy to prepare your favorite meal. How many items are on your list?

399

Chapter 21 Overview

In this chapter, students are introduced to the basics of kitchen operations and organization. Guidelines on kitchen safety and sanitation are provided. In addition, students learn how to plan and execute a menu, and they discover the importance of being a discerning and conscientious shopper in the grocery store.

Practicing Sanitation and Safety Accidents on the highway are in the news all the time, but accidents that occur at home rarely make the headlines, even though they occur much more often. This section identifies hazards in the kitchen and provides tips on safe food-handling, proper clean-up, and basic housekeeping.

Planning a Menu There's more to planning a menu than meets the eye. In this section, students explore the steps involved in planning, preparing, and serving a well-balanced and appetizing meal.

Making Wise Shopping Decisions This section takes a look at the different types of stores where consumers shop for groceries. It also discusses tips for identifying the best quality items and ingredients and provides insight on making cost-conscious purchasing decisions.

Focus and Engage

Bell-Ringer: Think About This

Students are to make a shopping list of everything they would need to prepare their favorite meal. Make sure they account for each dish that comprises the meal, including, beverages, appetizers, and desserts. If they are unsure of the ingredients that a dish requires, encourage them to research recipes on the Internet or to look through cookbooks that might be available in your classroom, library, or school dietician's office. The goal is to make the list as complete as possible so that students gain a real understanding of the time and money that goes into planning and preparing a meal.

ADVANCE PREPARATION

Review	*Life Skills for the 21st Century* textbook, Chapter 21.
Prepare	Paper and pencil for some activities.
	Markers or different color pencils.
	Poster board or plain white paper.
	Newspapers and advertising circulars from local grocery stores.
	Box labeled "Hot Topics."

CUSTOMIZED INSTRUCTION OVERVIEW

Less Advanced Students	More Advanced Students	ESOL Students	Special Needs Students	At-Risk Students
Pages 401, 403, 405	Pages 400, 408	Page 405	Pages 401, 405, 411	Page 403

Introduce the Section

Accidents on the highway are in the news all the time, but accidents that occur at home rarely make the headlines, even though they occur much more often. This section identifies hazards in the kitchen and provides tips on safe food-handling, proper clean-up, and basic housekeeping.

Figure Focus

Explain that the term *sanitation* refers to cleanliness and hygiene. Ask students to discuss what they do during the course of a day that contributes to good sanitation. Some responses might be:

- Wash hands regularly.
- Put food away and do not leave anything sitting out on counters or tables.
- Wash dirty dishes or rinse off and place in the dishwasher.
- Clean microwave, stovetop, and oven.
- Avoid handling or preparing food for others when you are ill.

Vocabulary

Pathogens: Living organisms that exist in or on food, including bacteria, viruses, parasites, and fungi.

Sanitation: Methods of keeping clean.

Practicing Sanitation and Safety

Good sanitation helps keep you and your guests safe and healthy.

The last thing you want is for guests to leave your home feeling sick after eating. Although the food supply in the United States is generally safe, there are many ways food can become unhealthy.

- Safe foods are foods that won't make you sick or hurt you when you eat them.
- Unsafe foods have been contaminated by hazardous materials or organisms and can make you sick.
- An illness that you get from eating unsafe food is called a foodborne illness.

You can use **sanitation**—methods of keeping clean—to make sure you don't serve unsafe foods.

What Can Turn Your Food Into a Hazard?

There are three basic types of hazards associated with foods: biological, physical, and chemical:

- *Biological hazards*—**pathogens**—are living organisms that exist in or on foods. They include bacteria, viruses, parasites, and fungi.
- *Physical hazards* are actual things you might find in your food, such as hair, a piece of food packaging, or a piece of glass. Physical hazards can damage your mouth or digestive tract. For example you might break a tooth biting on a piece of metal, or cut your gums on a piece of glass.
- *Chemical hazards* include things people use around food, such as cleaning compounds, bug sprays, food additives, and fertilizer, as well as toxic metals such as mercury and cadmium that find their way into the food supply through the environment. For example, some types of fish contain levels of mercury that might be harmful to children, senior citizens, and pregnant women.

Customized Instruction: More Advanced Students

Have students write definitions for the pathogens listed in the text: bacteria, viruses, parasites, and fungi. You might also ask them to provide an example of each.

- **Bacteria:** Single-celled, often parasitic microorganisms that typically live in soil, water, and organic matter, various species of which are responsible for many plant and animal diseases. Examples are *E. coli* and *Salmonella*.

- **Viruses:** Parasitic particles that can only replicate within a host cell and are not considered independent living organisms; can cause various diseases and sicknesses. A well-known example is viral gastroenteritis, commonly referred to as the stomach flu.

- **Parasites:** Plants or animals that live on or within another host organism in a way that harms or is of no advantage to the host. An example is a tapeworm.

- **Fungi:** Organisms that reproduce by spores and live by absorbing nutrients from organic matter. Fungi include mildews, molds, rusts, and yeasts.

How Does Your Food Become Hazardous?

Food can become contaminated by **direct contamination**—coming directly into contact with a hazard—or by **cross-contamination**, which happens when an uncontaminated food comes in contact with something already touched by contaminated food.

Cross-contamination usually happens when hazards in raw food are transferred to food that has already been cooked or is ready to be served. For example, if you cut raw chicken on a cutting board, and then use the same knife and cutting board to slice bread, the bread may become contaminated with bacteria from the chicken.

You can contaminate food if you are not clean, well-groomed, or healthy. If you are dirty, the dirt might fall off you into the food. If you are sick, you might pass your illness through the food. If you are not well-groomed, your hair might fall into the food.

Biological hazards live and multiply at the *danger zone*—temperatures between 40°F and 140°F. If you properly refrigerate food at a temperature lower than 40°, and then cook it to 140°, most bacteria will not survive. Follow these guidelines to keep food out of the danger zone:

- Keep cold food at temperatures lower than 40° in refrigerators, coolers, or on ice.
- Keep hot food in ovens, heated chafing dishes, preheated steam tables, warming trays or slow cookers.
- Throw out any food left in the "danger zone" more than 2 hours.

Wash Your Hands!

The most important and effective way to make sure you are not responsible for cross-contaminated food during preparation is to wash your hands a lot. Washing cleans the dirt off your hands, and removes bacteria that might be present. Specifically, you should wash your hands:

- When you arrive in the kitchen
- After using the restroom
- After you sneeze or cough
- After touching your hair, face, or clothing
- After you eat or drink
- Before you handle food that will not be cooked again prior to serving
- After handling garbage
- After handling dirty equipment, dishes, or utensils
- After touching raw meat, poultry, or fish
- After caring for or touching animals

When you work in a commercial kitchen, you must wear disposable gloves to keep your bare hands from coming into contact with food. Wearing gloves does not mean you don't have to wash! Wash before you put on gloves, and change your gloves if you touch foods or surfaces that might be contaminated.

Foodborne Illnesses

Food poisoning is a general term that people use to describe all types of foodborne illnesses. Here are some common types of foodborne illnesses.

- ✔ *Salmonella poisoning is caused by the Salmonella bacterium. It is often present in raw chicken and raw eggs. Symptoms include fever, diarrhea, and stomach cramps.*

- ✔ *E. coli infection is caused by the E. coli bacterium usually found in cattle, and in water that cattle have infected. Symptoms include bloody diarrhea and painful stomach cramps.*

- ✔ *Norovirus spreads from one infected person to another, so if a kitchen worker has the virus and touches food, everyone who eats that food is at risk of infection. Symptoms include vomiting.*

- ✔ *Botulism is caused by the presence of Clostridium botulinum bacteria that create a toxin—or poison—in the food. The toxin can cause severe illness and even death. It is very rare in the United States, but can be caused by improperly canning foods.*

Many foodborne illnesses make you sick, but are only deadly if you are very young, very old, or have a condition that makes you more sensitive than average.

Vocabulary

Cross-contamination: Contamination that occurs when an uncontaminated food comes in contact with something already touched by contaminated food.

Direct contamination: Contamination that occurs when food comes directly into contact with a hazard.

Toxin: Poison.

Discuss

Students may be aware of the controversy surrounding antibacterial soaps and hand sanitizers. These products contain triclosan, which has been shown to disrupt hormone production in bullfrogs and which some theorize could also have negative effects on early childhood brain development. Furthermore, many critics believe that the pervasive use of antibacterial products could lead to the development of "super" bacteria that are resistant to modern antibacterial products and medicines.

Foodborne Illnesses

Discuss ways to avoid the risk of contracting a foodborne illness:

- Do not use wooden cutting boards or spoons, which are porous and can be difficult to sanitize.
- Do not put cooked meats on the same platter they were on when they were raw.
- Use separate towels for wiping your hands and washing dishes. Better yet, use disposable towels for your hands.
- Do not use sponges to clean up. They're extremely porous and basically a breeding ground for bacteria.
- Be meticulous in cleaning kitchen appliances and equipment used for cooking and food preparation.
- Wash your hands often.
- Follow proper food storage guidelines.

Customized Instruction: Less Advanced/Special Needs Students

On a plain sheet of paper or poster board, have students list the guidelines for when to wash hands (see the list in the text) and the proper way to do it. Encourage them to be creative in the design of their guidelines. If possible, post their work in appropriate locations around the school. The proper way to wash hands is to:

1. Use very warm, running water and soap.
2. Vigorously rub both sides of the hands for 20 to 30 seconds, paying close attention to under the fingernails.
3. Rinse well with very warm, running water.
4. Dry hands with a disposable paper towel.

Figure Focus

Explain that meticulous cleaning of kitchen surfaces will help eliminate germs and bacteria. A detergent with chlorine bleach or a solution of diluted bleach can accomplish this and is suitable for most surfaces. Stress the importance of thoroughly rinsing a surface after it has been sanitized in order to remove all traces of the cleaning product.

Vocabulary

Hazard Analysis Critical Control Point (HACCP): Process for monitoring food safety.

Sanitize: To clean in a way that kills bacteria and other hazards.

Discuss

While the HACCP system was developed primarily for institutional settings, you might discuss how some of the guidelines could be applied in the home. For example:

■ Conduct a hazard analysis. Identify areas in your kitchen where pests might get in, or where food particles and water might collect and go unnoticed. Check the temperature settings on your refrigerator and freezer, and check for cleanliness in all compartments. Ensure that the microwave, stove, and oven are operating properly. Check the sink and ensure that it is draining properly.

■ Determine Critical Control Points, or those locations and times of kitchen use where you can prevent or eliminate hazards.

■ Establish critical limits. Check expiration dates on all foods before eating or preparing them.

■ Establish monitoring procedures. Set up a schedule or system for checking expiration dates on foods.

■ Identify corrective actions. With your parents, determine what should be done with foods that have expired.

Why is it important to use a detergent to clean surfaces in a kitchen?

EEEWWW! Bugs!

Kitchens attract pests, including rodents (mice and rats), flies, and other insects such as roaches and ants. Can you keep the pests out?

👎 Leave crumbs on the counters and floors.

👎 Forget to cover food containers in the cupboards and cabinets.

👎 Keep full garbage cans loosely covered in the kitchen area.

👍 Wipe up spills and sweep up crumbs.

👍 Store food in airtight containers.

👍 Store garbage cans off the ground and use tight-fitting lids.

Pests come for the food, so make it as hard as you can for them to find it. What problems might arise from pests in the kitchen?

Keeping Your Kitchen Clean

Everything that comes into contact with food must be clean—including your hands, utensils, and work surfaces such as countertops. At home, you might clean and rinse your utensils and surfaces, and sweep the floor. In a commercial kitchen, you also **sanitize** surfaces, which means you clean them in a way that kills bacteria and other hazards.

1. Clean by washing with a detergent such as a dishwashing liquid, or a product made for a specific purpose, such as for cleaning a glass-top stove.
2. Rinse thoroughly with fresh water, removing all traces of the cleaning product.
3. Sanitize using either heat or chemicals. You can use hot water—180°F or hotter—or a chemical sanitizer such as chlorine or iodine.

Towels might be a source of cross-contamination. At home, you can use a towel you know is clean and dry—or use paper towels. In a commercial kitchen, let items air dry before you put them away.

The HACCP System

HACCP is a process for monitoring food safety. It stands for Hazard Analysis Critical Control Point, and is pronounced HAS-sup. HACCP is used in restaurants and institutions that serve food, such as your school cafeteria. There are seven steps in the HACCP process:

1. Conduct a hazard analysis to identify potential areas where contamination might occur.
2. Determine Critical Control Points (CCP), which are places or times where you can prevent, eliminate, or reduce a hazard.
3. Establish critical limits for factors such as how long food can be stored before cooking. Critical limits are usually set by the local health department, or based on the recommendations from the FDA.
4. Establish monitoring procedures for ensuring that the critical limits are maintained, such as a schedule for checking temperatures.
5. Identify corrective actions to take if a problem occurs. For example, what should an employee do if he finds that eggs have been stored for longer than the specified critical limit?
6. Establish procedures for record-keeping and documentation, such as a chart for recording temperatures, and a log book for recording corrective actions.
7. Develop a verification system so that supervisors and inspectors make sure that employees follow all required steps in the process.

EEEWWW! Bugs!

Explain that bugs and other household pests represent a real health danger. Share the following:

■ Rodents such as mice and rats bring other pests including fleas, mites, ticks, and lice indoors. They can contaminate food with droppings that might contain *Salmonella* bacteria and hantaviruses.

■ Cockroaches spread many kinds of bacteria, parasitic worms, and other types of human pathogens. Cockroach droppings and their shed skins can lead to allergen accumulation that can trigger asthma attacks, especially in children.

■ According to the Centers for Disease Control, West Nile virus, a disease spread by mosquitoes, resulted in more than 1,300 human cases and 43 fatalities in 2008.

■ All types of pests can do physical damage to a home. Ants are capable of building nests that damage walls, floors, and even the motors of appliances, which they find warm, inviting spots to set up their homes. Rodents can chew through plumbing to get to a source of water.

Kitchen Safety

There are five common types of kitchen injuries: burns, cuts, falls, electric shocks, and strains or sprains. Keeping your kitchen clean and organized and being aware of all risks can help you avoid these accidents. Some tips for staying safe in the kitchen include the following precautions.

■ Do not use loose area rugs in the kitchen, because you might trip on one and fall.
■ Use an oven mitt or pot holder when you touch a hot pot or pan.
■ Keep electrical cords away from water.
■ Be aware of sharp objects such as knives.

Fires are a danger in the kitchen because of the heat and flames you use to cook. There are four important aspects to fire safety.

■ *Prevent fires* by being careful about heat sources, including flames, ovens, stoves, appliances, and wiring.
■ *Detect fires* if they happen by installing working smoke detectors.
■ *Extinguish fires* by making sure equipment such as fire extinguishers and sprinklers (in commercial kitchens) are installed and maintained properly.
■ *Train* everyone who uses the kitchen in how to operate the fire extinguishers and how to put out a fire if a fire extinguisher is not available.

Using Equipment Safely

If you work in a commercial kitchen, the Occupational Safety and Health Administration (OSHA) is the federal agency responsible for protecting your safety. It publishes standards for safely using and maintaining kitchen equipment. Your employer is required to provide you with the information and training you need to be safe at work.

At home, you are responsible for your own safety. Here are a few tips for using kitchen equipment safely.

■ Read all instructions and warnings that come with kitchen equipment and appliances.
■ Use the proper equipment for a task.
■ Be aware of sharp blades and hot surfaces.
■ Learn how to use knives properly.

Fire Extinguishers

A fire extinguisher is a canister with pressurized contents that can put out fires. There are three types:

✔ *Water-based fire extinguishers douse the fire with water. They are labeled Fire Class A and are used for fires burning paper, wood, cloth, or plastic.*

✔ *Foam-based fire extinguishers use foam to smother the fire. They are labeled Fire Class A and B and are used for fires burning paper, wood, cloth, plastic, grease, oil, or liquid stored under pressure.*

✔ *Dry chemical fire extinguishers use chemicals to stop the fire. They are labeled Fire Class A, B, or C and are used for fires burning paper, wood, cloth, plastic, grease, oil, liquid stored under pressure, electrical equipment, outlets, cords, circuits, motors, switches, or wiring.*

"Am I doing everything I can to avoid an injury in this kitchen?"

21st Century Skills

What Happens Next?

Elijah has a cold. His mother suggests that he stay home from school, but his Family and Consumer Sciences class is baking muffins, and Elijah does not want to miss it.

Elijah goes to school. He has a headache, his nose is running, and he is coughing a lot. Elijah's FACS teacher hears him coughing and asks if he feels well. Elijah hesitates for a minute. If he says he has a cold, his teacher might not let him bake the muffins. If he says he is fine, he might transmit his cold to others.

Use your decision-making skills to help Elijah make a decision. Consider all options, and the consequences of each option, and then choose a plan of action. Using your 21st Century Skills—such as decision making, goal setting, and problem solving—write an ending to the story. Read it to the class, or form a small group and present it as a skit.

Discuss

In addition to food safety issues already discussed in this chapter, you might talk about other safety precautions, such as:

■ Keeping all cleaning products out of the reach of children and away from food.
■ Using good-quality, well-balanced pots and pans, and keeping handles turned in so they cannot be bumped.
■ Using appropriate potholders, not dishtowels, to handle hot dishes.
■ Wiping up spilled or splashed grease, water, and food immediately.

You might take extra time to discuss knife safety:

■ Don't point a knife at anyone.
■ Always cut away from yourself.
■ Don't test the knife's sharpness on your finger.
■ Don't use a knife as a screwdriver or a pry bar.
■ Use the right knife for the right job. A knife with a serrated edge is good for slicing bread or cake; a paring knife should be used to chop vegetables.
■ Keep knives sharp. With a dull knife, you need to apply more pressure, which increases the risk of your hand slipping and causing injury.

Fire Extinguishers

You might discuss what to do in case of various types of fire emergencies in the kitchen.

■ **Oven or broiler fire:** Turn off the heat, close the oven door, and keep it closed.
■ **Stove or grease fire:** Turn off the heat, cover with a metal lid, or throw salt or baking soda at the base of the flames. Do not pick up the pan or appliance or throw water on it.
■ **Electrical fire or smoking:** Unplug the appliance or disconnect all electricity and call the fire department.

21st Century Skills

What Happens Next?

Students are to prepare an ending to Elijah's story. Elijah must decide if he should lie about being ill and take the risk of contaminating the muffins that he and his class will be baking, or admit to his teacher that he is sick and risk her not allowing him to bake the muffins. Students' endings should have Elijah deciding to tell his teacher that he has a cold and taking the necessary precautions to reduce the risk of spreading his cold to others.

Customized Instruction: Less Advanced/At-Risk Students

Ask students to make a list of all the appliances and equipment in their home kitchens. These will include microwave ovens, conventional ovens, stoves, food processors, blenders, mixers, electric can openers, electric knives, toasters, coffee makers, dishwashers, and garbage disposals. Have them place a check beside those items they use and operate on their own.

Introduce the Section

There's more to planning a menu than meets the eye. In this section, students explore the steps involved in planning, preparing, and serving a well-balanced and appetizing meal.

Vocabulary

Menu: List of foods for one or more meals you plan to prepare.

Figure Focus

Ask students for a show of hands of those who have planned, prepared, and served a meal, whether for family or friends. Have them share details on what they served, how many people they served, and how the meal turned out.

Discuss

Discuss with students the types of meals they have for breakfast, lunch, and dinner in a typical week. Encourage them to be specific. You might have your school's lunch (and breakfast, if applicable) menu handy for those students who buy in the cafeteria. For meals they eat at home, ask students if they typically eat alone or with other family members. Do they eat in front of the television? How often do they eat food from a restaurant?

Planning a Menu

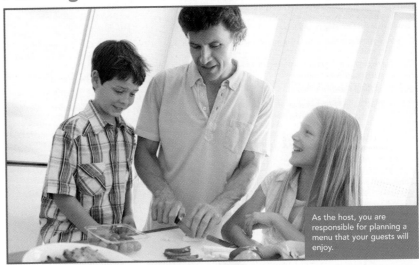

As the host, you are responsible for planning a menu that your guests will enjoy.

A menu is a list of foods for one or more meals you plan to prepare. It can include one single dish, but usually includes all the dishes you plan to serve.

- Should you serve your favorite foods?
- Do any of your guests have special dietary requirements, such as vegetarian, low-sodium, or low-fat diets?
- Is there a magic combination of ingredients which will ensure that everyone likes the food and leaves satisfied?

As the host, you get to plan the menu. You might ask for input from your friends and family, but you are the one responsible for selecting dishes that your guests will find appealing, tasty, and nutritious.

Types of Meals

Is a meal you eat in a restaurant different from a meal you eat at home? Is your lunch menu different from your breakfast menu? Your decision about what meal to plan and prepare can be influenced by many factors, including time of day, special occasions, your budget, and your taste.

- On a busy Tuesday night, your Dad might pick up ready-to-serve food from the grocery store, or reheat frozen food or leftovers.
- On a Sunday morning, your Mom might make scrambled eggs, toast, and bacon.
- On Mother's Day, you might dine at a restaurant.
- When you're at the mall with friends on a Saturday, you might grab a fast-food lunch at the food court.

Different situations call for different meal choices. You might plan a sit-down dinner, a buffet—which is a meal where you put all the food on one table, and guests help themselves—or pot-luck, which is a dinner where you ask your guests to bring a dish to contribute to the meal. Recognizing the situation can help you plan a delicious, nutritious, and enjoyable meal for you and your guests.

What Should I Serve?

You chose a date. You invited guests. Now, what are you going to serve? Deciding on a menu can be overwhelming—there are so many options. Selecting the food can also be a big part of the fun of entertaining. You are the host; you get to choose. How do you know what foods to choose? Considering the following factors can help you decide.

- *Time of day.* What meal are you serving? Is your menu for breakfast, lunch, brunch, dinner, or snacks?
- *Occasion.* Is it someone's birthday, a team party, or a holiday? Or is it just a nice meal with friends? Some special occasions require specific food, such as cake on a birthday.
- *Cost.* Do you have a budget so you know how much you want to spend? You don't want to plan a menu, and then find out that you can't afford all of the ingredients.
- *Nutrition.* Are you including something nutritious from each of the main food groups? Do you have protein, vegetables, fruit, grain, and dairy?

How Much Food Do I Need?

Do you have a relative who always serves enough food to feed twice the number of people who are eating? Or maybe you ate at a friend's house once, and went home hungry because the portions were so small. It can be hard to judge the amount of food you need to serve.

- Prepare too much and you might be eating the same leftovers for the entire week.
- Prepare too little and your guests leave the table unsatisfied.

As you gain experience planning and cooking meals, you begin to know how much food you will need. When you are just starting, you have to use problem-solving to make a best guess. How many people are eating? How many dishes are you serving? How much do you think each person will eat?

Consider how many people you are feeding. This tells you the number of servings you need. For example, if there are four people, and you are serving spinach salad, grilled chicken breasts, whole-grain rice, and asparagus, you will need four servings of each item. You can estimate the amount of each serving, or use the Nutrition Facts label on the product packaging.

Of course, you may want to include extra. Someone might want seconds, you might want to plan for leftovers, or there might be a surprise guest.

Other Meal Planning Factors

In addition to time of day, cost, occasion, and nutrition, the following factors might influence your menu:

✔ *Courses. Will you serve a main course only, or will you include appetizers, side dishes, and dessert? Sometimes you might provide the main course, and ask your guests to bring the other items. Sometimes you will be responsible for providing the full meal.*

✔ *Balance of foods. Can you include a variety of textures, flavors, temperatures, and colors? Variety makes the meal interesting and enjoyable, and makes it easier to include balanced nutrition.*

✔ *Equipment. What type of kitchen equipment do you have for storage, preparation and cooking? Do you want to invest in new equipment, or can you make do with what you have?*

✔ *Theme. Do you want to plan a menu around a theme such as a Mexican Fiesta or Hawaiian Luau?*

 Pasta Around the World

Pasta means "dough" in Italian. It is a grain product that is made in many shapes and in many varieties across the world:

- Lo mein noodles made from wheat in China
- Soba noodles made from buckwheat in Japan
- Bee hoon noodles made from rice in Malaysia
- Gnocchi dumplings made from flour and potato in Italy

Working individually, in pairs, or in small groups, use the Internet to select a country and research how they make and eat pasta. What type of flour do they use, what shapes do they make, when is it served, and what name do they give the dish? Prepare a presentation about your topic, including nutritional information, and share it with your class.

Customized Instruction: ESOL Students

Ask students how pasta is served in their country of origin. Ask them to say and write the names of favorite or traditional pasta dishes in their primary language.

Customized Instruction: Less Advanced/Special Needs Students

On a plain piece of paper, have students draw shapes of the different pastas they eat and label them. If possible, you might let them visit the Web site www.ilovepasta.org/shapes.html, which identifies some of the more common shapes.

Discuss

Discuss the use of recipes in meal planning. Recipes not only include ingredients and cooking/baking time, but they also indicate the number of servings, identify calories and other nutrition information, and often provide recommendations on accompaniments or other dishes that would complement or complete the meal. In addition, recipes will usually indicate if the dish or a portion of it can be prepared ahead of time. This allows you to better balance your time in the kitchen with the time spent entertaining your guests.

Other Meal Planning Factors

In addition to those factors listed in the text, discuss with students the basics of table-setting. For most occasions, you'll need:

- Plates
- Glassware
- Flatware (knives, forks, and spoons)
- Napkins

Offer these guidelines for the basic place setting:

- Place the dinner plate in the center of the place setting.
- The flatware is arranged around the plate in the order in which it will be used. The fork is on the left; the knife is on the right with the cutting edge toward the plate; and the spoon goes to the right of the knife.
- Glassware is placed above the knife.
- Napkins can be placed under the forks or on the plate for a casual setting.
- If you're serving salad, place salad bowls or plates to the left of the fork.

 Pasta Around the World

Students are to select a country and research how they make and serve pasta. As a prompt, you might want to discuss the following fun facts about pasta.

- October is National Pasta Month.
- It is believed that the Chinese were the first to eat pasta, beginning in 5,000 B.C.
- Thomas Jefferson is credited with introducing macaroni to the United States.
- The first American pasta factory was opened in Brooklyn, New York, in 1848 by a Frenchman.
- One cup of cooked spaghetti has about 200 calories.
- The average person in North America eats about 15½ pounds of pasta a year. The average person in Italy eats about 51 pounds a year.
- There are more than 600 pasta shapes produced worldwide.

Subtract 1¼ hours from 12:15. The start time is 11:00 a.m.

Vocabulary

Impulse buys: Making a spur-of-the-moment decision to buy something you don't need.

Meal time plan: Schedule to help manage meal preparation.

Can I Get this Ready in Time?

One of the biggest challenges in preparing a meal is having everything ready to serve when your guests take their seats. Share the following time management tips with students:

- Read through your recipes ahead of time to ensure that you have the ingredients and the appropriate cookware and utensils.

- Make a list of dishes you will serve and their preparation time. Most recipes provide this. Under each item, list the tasks involved in preparing the dish. For example, if the item is spaghetti sauce, the tasks might include browning the meat, chopping onions and tomatoes, and mincing the garlic.

- Identify the things you can or should prepare ahead of time. For example, you might need to marinate chicken for six hours before grilling it. Or, you might be able to chop vegetables ahead of time that will go in the salad you're serving. Many desserts can be made ahead of time, too.

- Using the list, prepare a schedule for when you need to start each task. Don't be tempted to prepare your dishes in the order they will be eaten. Start with the dish that will take the longest to prepare.

- Set up any necessary equipment (food processor, blender, mixer, etc.), as well as cooking dishes and utensils.

- Clean up as you go. Put spices and other ingredients away when you are done using them, throw away trash immediately, and keep the number of dirty dishes sitting in the sink or on the counter to a minimum. This will keep you organized and give you the counter space you need to prepare your serving dishes.

When you schedule an event such as a dinner, you can use the clock to determine what time you must start your meal preparation.

You must know the time of the event, and the amount of time you need to prepare. Then, you subtract the preparation time from the event time to get your start time.

If you plan to serve dinner at 6:00 p.m. and need 45 minutes to prepare, you would subtract 45 minutes from 6:00 p.m. to get 5:15 as your start time.

You do the math: You invite guests to a lunch beginning at 12:15 p.m. You need 1¼ hours to prepare. What time should you start your preparations?

Time Management

When you plan a menu, take into consideration how much time you have to spend on the meal. A **meal time plan**, or schedule, can help you manage your meal preparation. Once you have selected your menu, you can set goals and create a schedule for completing each task based on the amount of time it will take, and when you want to serve. If you don't have a lot of time, you might want to keep your menu simple. If you have lots of time, you might want to try a new recipe, or prepare an extra dish. Take the following into consideration when you make a meal time plan:

- When will you do the shopping?
- When will you prepare your house for guests and set the table?
- How long will it take to prepare all the dishes?
- Will you be able to cook so everything is ready to serve at the right time?

Use a Shopping List

Have you ever come home from the supermarket only to realize you forgot to buy something important? Or that you bought a lot of expensive, unhealthy snack items instead of the ingredients for the meal you planned to make for dinner?

The best way to make sure you remember to buy what you need and avoid **impulse buys**—making a spur of the moment decision to buy something you don't need—is to use a shopping list—a written list of the items you need to buy. You can create a shopping list for one meal, a few days, or a whole week.

- You might shop for one meal if it is a special occasion, you are inviting friends for dinner or lunch, or if you are hosting a meeting at your home.
- You might shop for a few days if you are spending the weekend at a vacation cabin or campsite.
- You might shop once a week if you want to take care of your shopping all at once.

Can I Get this Ready in Time?

Using a schedule makes it much easier to get a meal ready and on the table on time. What if you have 1 hour to prepare and serve a dinner of oven barbecued chicken breasts, brown rice, asparagus, and baby spinach salad?

Time	Task	Action
6:00–6:10	Prepare rice	Measure water and rice into a sauce pan according to directions. Place on stove burner over high heat until boiling. Cover tightly, lower heat, and simmer for 45–50 minutes.
	Prepare chicken breasts	Wash chicken and pat dry with paper towels. Season with salt and pepper. Place in baking dish and cover with barbeque sauce. Cover pan with foil and bake in oven at 350° F for 45–50 minutes.
6:10–6:25	Prepare salad	Wash baby spinach and arrange in bowls.
6:25–6:35	Set table	Set table and organize service plates and utensils.
6:35–6:40	Prepare asparagus	Wash asparagus and break or cut off woody stems. Add water to saucepan with steamer insert. Place asparagus in steamer, cover, and cook on stovetop over high heat for 7–10 minutes.
6:40–6:50	Clean up kitchen and monitor cooking	Wash dishes and wipe off counters. Check chicken, rice, and asparagus for doneness. Place salad and dressing on table.
6:50–5:55	Prepare beverages	Fill water glasses with ice and water.
6:55–7:00	Plate dishes	Remove rice and asparagus from the stove and chicken from the oven. Put on serving dishes and put serving dishes on table.

What Goes on My Shopping List?

A shopping list includes the ingredients you need for the meals you have planned, as well as items you might need to keep your kitchen well-stocked.

It can be helpful to keep a running shopping list in an obvious location, such as stuck to the refrigerator door. Then everyone in the family can add items to the list. For example, if you eat the last orange, you can add *oranges* to the list. If you plan to bake brownies for an FCCLA bake sale, you can add the ingredients for brownies to the list.

When you create a shopping list, take into consideration:

■ **Non-perishable**—food that does not spoil—kitchen or pantry staples, which are basic items you like to keep available, such as flour, vegetable oil, and sugar.

■ Fresh or **perishable** foods—items that will spoil—you like to keep in the house, such as fruit and vegetables for snacking, fruit juice, milk, eggs, and cheese.

■ Ingredients for the meals you have planned between this shopping trip and the next. Look at your recipe to make sure you write down everything you need.

■ The amounts of each item that you need.

■ Specific information about each item. You could write "beans," or you could write "1 16-ounce can of black beans." Which description would be more useful?

Storing Food

Once you return from the market, you have to put everything you bought away. Properly storing your food prevents cross-contamination and spoilage. It also helps preserve nutrients and flavor. The three basic places to store food include:

■ *Refrigerator.* Your refrigerator should be between 35° and 40°F.

■ *Freezer.* Frozen foods should be kept at 0°F or lower.

■ *Storage closet or cabinet.* Most dry goods such as pasta and grains should be kept in tightly closed containers, in a cool, dry environment—below 85°F.

Here are some general guidelines for properly storing food.

■ Canned and boxed items can be stored in a cabinet or pantry.

■ Most fruits and vegetables should be stored in the refrigerator. Exceptions include onions and potatoes, which should be stored in a cool, dry place.

■ Raw meat, poultry, and fish should be stored on a plate in the refrigerator, separate from other foods to avoid cross-contamination, or packed and frozen for future use.

■ Frozen foods such as ice cream, frozen fruits or vegetables, or prepared meals should be placed in the freezer as soon as possible.

Fridge Storage Tips

Different areas in your kitchen fridge might have different temperatures. For example, the shelves on the door might be warmer than 41°F, while the crisper bins are probably nice and cold. Here are some tips for properly storing items in your kitchen fridge.

✔ *Use the door compartments for things that do not spoil easily when warmer than 41°, such as mustard, ketchup, and soft drinks.*

✔ *Do not keep eggs, milk, and cheese in the door.*

✔ *Store all meats on the bottom shelf, above the drawers—not in the drawers. This is likely to be the coldest spot in the fridge.*

✔ *Place raw meat, fish, and poultry on a plate so they do not drip on shelves or on other foods.*

✔ *Use the top shelf for dairy, leftovers, or other precooked foods.*

✔ *Use wraps or airtight containers to cover and protect food.*

Job Search

If you have an interest in food safety, you might consider a career as a food inspector, a food scientist, or an organic farmer. If meal planning and shopping sounds like fun, you might consider a career as a dietitian, planning menus for people on special diets or you might look into a career as a grocery store manager or buyer.

Each job in food service requires different abilities and interests. Education requirements and working environments vary as well. A food scientist requires a PhD in chemistry, biology or a related field and works in a laboratory. A farmer might need a degree in agriculture, and would also benefit from knowledge of accounting, and business management and entrepreneurial skills.

Use the Internet, library, or your school's guidance resources to learn more about a career in food service. Select a job that appeals to you, and write a job description, including the educational requirements, career pathway, and potential salary range.

Vocabulary

Non-perishable: Food that does not spoil, such as flour, vegetable oil, and sugar.

Perishable: Food that will spoil, such as fresh fruit and vegetables, milk, juice, eggs, and cheese.

Fridge Storage Tips

In addition to the tips covered in the text, you might share the following suggestions on freezing and refrigeration:

■ Leftover cooked dishes should be refrigerated as soon as possible after their preparation. Allow for a minimal amount of time for cool-down before placing a warm or hot dish in the fridge.

■ Divide leftovers into smaller portions and place them in shallow, airtight containers. You can also wrap cooked meat, poultry, and fish in plastic wrap or aluminum foil, which helps to prevent them from drying out.

■ Do not overcrowd the refrigerator; this can prevent proper circulation of cold air.

■ Keep similar items grouped together so they are easy to find.

■ Place small items and those that are frequently accessed at eye level and at the front of the shelves.

■ The safest way to defrost frozen foods is to place them in the refrigerator.

■ The temperature of the freezer should be 0° or colder.

■ Make sure food that you freeze is tightly wrapped or sealed so that no air or water can get in.

■ Foods, particularly meat products, can become rancid if left in the freezer for an excessive amount of time. If it has an odor or is discolored when defrosted, it's best to throw it away.

Job Search

Students are to research a career in food service and write a job description about a position that appeals to them. There is a wide variety of jobs in the food service industry, ranging from food production and manufacturing to distribution to service to marketing and sales. To get students started, refer them to *Appendix A: Career Clusters* starting on page 513.

Introduce the Section

This section takes a look at the different types of stores where consumers shop for groceries. It also discusses tips for identifying the best-quality items and ingredients and provides insight on making cost-conscious purchasing decisions.

Figure Focus

Ask students how they define a wise shopper. Is it someone who studies the grocery store flyers or newspaper inserts to determine what's on sale at which store? Or is it someone who buys only store-brand or generic-brand items? Or is it someone who shops at markets that specialize in certain products?

Reinforce and Review

Review with students the characteristics of a wise consumer:

- You understand the difference between what you want and what you need.
- You learn as much as possible about an item before you buy it.
- Likewise, you learn as much as possible about the store in which you plan to buy an item.
- You know how to compare prices.
- You spend only what you can afford.

Discuss

Discuss with students the "visual merchandising" strategies that grocery stores often employ to capitalize on the consumer's impulse to buy. One strategy is to place merchandise displays so that the shopper has to circle the entire store. For example, the grocer might place common products such as eggs, milk, and bread on the outside lanes of the store and spread them out so the shopper has to move from one end of the store to the other, with the hope being that they will pop in and out of aisles along the way. Grocers also prominently display candy, gum, and chocolate in the checkout area. Many also offer samples of foods to shoppers. Ask students if these strategies have compelled them to make a purchase that they had no intention of making when they walked in the store.

Making Wise Shopping Decisions

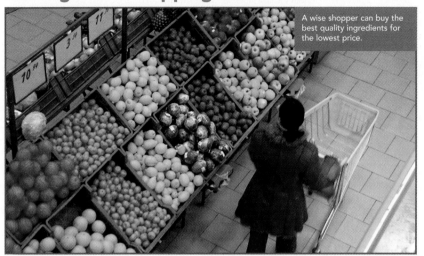

A wise shopper can buy the best quality ingredients for the lowest price.

Grocery stores in the United States are overflowing with food options. In one aisle alone, you might find ten brands of salad dressing in twenty different flavors. Some are labeled lite, some are low-fat, all-natural, or organic. Bottles come in many sizes and many prices, ranging from $0.99 to $4.19. Which one should you buy?

The concepts of being a wise consumer covered in Chapter 13 are as true when you shop for groceries as when you shop for clothes, cars, or cell phones. You should educate yourself about the products, compare prices, and pay close attention to quality.

Being an educated consumer and using your decision-making skills can help you choose nutritious, delicious food. It can also help you save money.

Interpreting Sale Prices

When a department store has a sale, they usually advertise items at a discount. For example, sweaters might be 15% off. (Refer to Chapter 13.) When a grocery store has a sale, they usually do one of three things.

- *Drop the price of selected items.* For example, your favorite breakfast cereal might regularly cost $3.49, but be on sale this week for $2.99.
- *Apply volume pricing,* which means the price is lower if you buy more of an item. For example, this week your cereal might be advertised as "two for $6.00." At this price, each box costs $3.00, about the same as the sale price.
- *Offer a buy one-get one price.* For example, if you buy one box of cereal this week at the regular price—$3.49—you get a second box free. At this price, each box costs $1.75, which is a good deal.

It is important to calculate the actual price you will pay for an item when evaluating sales pricing. It is easy to be influenced by signs and advertising. There may be considerations other than price, as well, such as whether you can use multiple items before they spoil, or whether you have room to store them.

Customized Instruction: More Advanced Students

Have students pair up. Give the teams a sample meal for which they will shop. If you completed the *Teamwork Activity* on page 404 of the teacher text, you might use one of the meals on the team menus. Have the teams create a grocery list of items they will need to prepare the meal. Then, using their lists, have them "shop" for the best deals on each item. They can do this by looking through newspaper or magazine advertisements, by researching online, or by visiting their local grocery store(s). Each team should report back on the best prices they found for items on their list, the stores in which they found them, and the grand total. *Note:* Students should not be expected to purchase the items.

Advertising Flyers and Coupons

Most markets prepare advertising flyers once a week to tell the prices of common items and indicate products that are on sale. You can use the information to plan your menus, estimate your shopping budget, and add sales items to your shopping list. The flyers might come to your home in the mail, you might be able to get them online, or you can pick them up in the store.

You can find savings coupons in the advertising flyers, in newspapers and magazines, and online. Coupons list a specific item and a savings amount. For example, you might have a coupon to save $1.00 off the price of a particular brand of yogurt. Coupons usually have an expiration date; you must use the coupon before the expiration or it is not valid.

If you use coupons, keep them neat and organized. Check your coupons when you make your shopping list, and bring the ones you need with you to the market. Putting a "c" next to an item on your list will help you remember to use the coupon when you are checking out.

Should I Buy Brand-Name Products?

You can save money by buying store-brand or generic products instead of brand names.

- A **brand-name product** is a product that you associate with a particular company. A company spends a lot of resources to label and advertise brand-name products. Their goal is to convince you that their brand-name product is the best, and that it is the only one you should buy.
- A **generic brand** is a product that is not identified with a particular company. Generic products usually cost less than brand-name products.
- A **store-brand product** is a type of generic. It is labeled with the name of the store where it is sold. It is usually less expensive than a brand-name product but may be more expensive than a generic.

Many store brands and generics are almost exactly the same as the brand-name equivalent. You can read the ingredients and Nutrition Facts labels to compare the contents to see how close they really are. You can also try the generic or store-brand product to judge the quality for yourself.

Test **IT** Yourself!

You can look for bacteria on items in your kitchen lab or classroom. Ask your science teacher if you can borrow a microscope, or collect the objects and use the microscope in the science lab. Look for the bacteria on:

- A sponge that you used to wipe the countertops.
- A plastic wrapper from packaged food.
- A cutting board.
- Your own fingernail.

What areas have the most bacteria? Were you able to identify the type of bacteria?

Where Should I Shop?

Many different types of stores sell groceries, each with their own strengths and weaknesses.

✔ *Grocery stores. Grocery stores are usually the most convenient place to shop. They generally offer a variety of products and brands. Prices are competitive with other grocery stores in the area.*

✔ *Online shopping. Many local and national chains offer online service. You place your order using the Internet, and then it is delivered to your home, or you go to the store to pick it up. Online shopping can be convenient if you do not have time to go to the market, if you are ill, or if you are disabled. There may be a delivery or service charge added to the cost of the items, and you do not have the opportunity to look for in-store specials, or to evaluate the quality of items such as meat or produce.*

✔ *Deep-discount grocery stores. These stores don't offer much service—you might need to bag your own purchases—but the prices are lower than in other stores.*

✔ *Warehouse clubs. These stores offer good values on items available in large quantities. There may not be a wide selection of brands, and the selection may change from week to week. Sometimes you must pay a membership fee.*

✔ *Convenience stores. These are small markets that offer mostly packaged products, such as snacks, toiletries, and soft drinks. They have a small selection of grocery items, and usually have very high prices.*

Vocabulary

Brand-name product: Product that you associate with a particular company.

Generic brand: A product that is not identified with a particular company.

Store-brand product: A type of generic labeled with the name of the store where it is sold.

Where Should I Shop?

Ask students to name stores in their community that fit under the types of stores listed in the text. Are they or their families regular customers of these stores? Do they have a preference? If yes, why do they prefer that store?

Test **IT** Yourself!

Explain that bacteria have certain attributes that help in their identification. One is their shape.

- Bacteria that resemble spheres are called *cocci* (plural of *coccus*).
- Those that look like rods or tubes are called *bacilli* (plural of *bacillus*).
- Those that look like spiral corkscrews are called *spirilla* (plural of *spirillum*).

Another attribute by which bacteria are identified is their cluster formation. The following prefixes are used to identify the cluster.

- *Diplo* means the cells form groups of two.
- *Strepto* means the cells form long chains.
- *Staphlo* means the bacteria form large clumps.

These prefixes are combined with the shape to help name the bacteria. For example, a round-shaped bacterium that clusters into a long chain would be a *streptococcus*.

Another way to identify bacteria is through use of a Gram stain, which is a common method used in school science labs. This technique uses a dark purple stain and a light pink stain. Gram-positive bacteria will retain the dark purple stain. Those that don't will let the purple wash off and retain the pink stain. These are Gram-negative bacteria. The composition of their cell walls distinguishes between positive and negative. Gram-positive bacteria have a two-part cell wall while Gram-negative bacteria have a stronger, three-part cell wall. Gram-positive bacteria do not cause disease; Gram-negative bacteria can cause disease because their cell walls provide a stronger defense against the human immune system.

Are Convenience Foods Worth It?

Ask students about the types of convenience foods they eat. Do they prefer these over homemade foods? Do family, friends, or circumstances influence why or when they eat them?

Vocabulary

Bulk: Buying large quantities of an item.
Unit price: Cost of an item per standard unit, such as ounce, pound, or quart.

Figure Focus

Explain that the biggest benefit of buying in bulk is saving money, but that's not such a big benefit if you end up throwing away half of what you buy because it's gone bad. When buying in bulk, it's important to consider an item's expiration date or shelf life, your storage capacity, and the possibility of becoming bored with eating the same thing over and over again.

MONEY MADNE$$

- Cheese 1 costs $4.99 for 16 ounces. $4.99/16 = $0.31 per ounce.

- Cheese 2 costs $4.79 for 12 ounces. $4.79/12 = $0.40 per ounce.

Based on cost alone, cheese 1 is a better value. Other factors to consider include amount, brand, and sell-by date. Other foods to put on the tray include fruit, such as grapes in different colors, or dried fruit such as apricots. Cut vegetables such as carrots or celery sticks add variety of color and texture. Crackers in different shapes and flavors can also dress up the tray.

Are Convenience Foods Worth It?

Convenience foods are foods that are convenient to prepare, serve, or both. They can save you time in the kitchen, but may cost more than preparing the same food yourself. Should you use convenience foods?

- 👍 Convenience foods may have high fat, sugar, sodium and caloric content.

- 👎 Convenience foods may cost more than cooking from scratch.

- 👎 Convenience foods may not provide enough servings of fruits and vegetables.

- 👍 Convenience foods save time, so you can spend more time with family and friends.

- 👍 Convenience foods can be kept on hand and prepared quickly.

- 👍 Convenience foods may be easier for seniors, children, and disabled persons to prepare.

What type of convenience foods do you enjoy? What makes them more appealing than preparing the same food from scratch?

MONEY MADNE$$

> A few friends are meeting at your house so you can all go to the play at school together. You want to have a tray of cheese and crackers to serve while you wait for everyone to arrive. At the market, you find one brand of cheddar cheese priced at $4.99 per pound. Another brand is on sale for $4.79 per 12-ounce package. Which cheese is the better value? What else might you serve on your cheese tray to add variety of color, texture, and nutrition? Hint: Calculate the cost per ounce.

Buying in Bulk

Sometimes you can save money by buying in **bulk**—buying large quantities of an item. Usually, the unit price on large quantities is less than the unit price on small quantities. The **unit price** is the cost of an item per standard unit, such as ounce, pound, or quart.

For example, how can you tell if the $35.00 price on a 25-pound bag of rice is a better deal than the $2.07 price on a 1-pound bag? In this example, the standard unit is pounds. To calculate the unit price, divide the price by the number of units. In this case:

$2.07 ÷ 1 = $2.07 per pound

$35.00 ÷ 25 = $1.40 per pound

The unit price for the 25-pound bag is much lower than the unit price for the 1-pound bag. In this case, it is a better deal to buy in bulk.

More About Unit Pricing

There might be considerations other than price when you buy in bulk, such as convenience and safety.

- Can you use 25 pounds of rice before it gets moldy?
- Do you have a place to properly store 25 pounds of rice?

Sometimes bulk is convenient even if it is not less costly. If you use a lot of ketchup, you might want to buy it in bulk. It is convenient to have it in your pantry when you need it.

Unit pricing can also be handy for comparing the cost of different brands of the same item, and deciding whether a sale price is really a good deal. Most foods must be labeled with a unit price. The label is usually on the shelf below the item. You can quickly check the unit price and compare it to the unit price of a different product to see which one is a better value.

> "This was cheap, but will I be able to eat all of these peaches before they spoil?"

Stay in School

High school dropouts face a much greater risk of living in poverty than high school graduates. A recent study reports that between 35 and 40 percent of high school dropouts live in poverty. The result is that a dropout will be seriously challenged to provide adequately for him- or herself, much less provide for a family.

Ask students to consider how much they or their families spend on food in a week. The USDA's Economic Research Service reports that Americans spend about 10 percent of their disposable income on food. Now, consider the poverty guidelines issued by the U.S. Department of Health and Human Services. Based on 2009 guidelines, a single person whose annual income is below $10,830 is considered to be living in poverty. The poverty level for a family of four is $22,050.

Have students do the math. Assume their income is $10,000. Calculate 10 percent of that, which is $1,000 to spend on food in a year. How much would that give them to spend in a month? (*Answer:* about $83.) In a week? (*Answer:* about $19.)

Ask students if they think they could buy the foods they need *and* want for $19 a week.

Reading and Interpreting Food Labels

When you compare two products, you can find a lot of useful information on the labels. You read about Nutrition Facts labels in Chapter 20. You can also use the ingredients list, the quantity information, the grade labeling, and the product description to help you decide which product to buy.

How can information on a food label help you make a wise shopping decision?

- The ingredients list includes all items that are contained in the product. The ingredient that makes up the largest percentage is listed first, followed by the next largest percentage, and so on. The last ingredient is used in the smallest amount. For example, a can of pork and beans that lists beans and then pork has more pork in it than one that lists beans, corn syrup, and then pork.

- Quantities are listed on all packages, and on unit pricing labels, too. Quantities are usually measure in **net weight**, which is the total weight, minus the weight of the packaging. For example, one box of breakfast cereal might contain 12 ounces, and another might contain 13.15 ounces. The boxes might look the same size, but one contains more cereal, by weight.

- Some products have grades based on standards set by the USDA. Some grades are letters; grade A milk is higher quality than B or C. Some are names; Prime beef is higher quality than Choice or Select.

- You can learn a lot by reading the description of the product on the packaging. Is the chicken free-range and hormone free? Is the cheese real or processed? Is the orange juice from concentrate or freshly squeezed?

What About Expiration Dates?

Have you ever taken a bottle of salad dressing out of the cabinet and noticed the date on it was two months ago? Additional important information that you can find on products is expiration and best-by dates.

Some companies stamp a date on products to help you determine if the item is fresh and healthy. There are four basic types of dates:

- *Use by* or *Expiration dates* indicate the last date on which the product should be eaten. After that date, the food is not safe, and you should throw it out. Stores are supposed to remove expired products from their shelves, but may miss some.

- *Best If Used By* is a recommendation that indicates a time frame when the product has the best flavor, texture, and quality. You can safely eat the food after the date.

- *Sell By* or *Pull By* dates tell grocers when to remove the item from the shelf. Usually, you can safely eat the product for up to five days past this date.

- *Closed* or *coded dates* are strings of mysterious numbers that do not seem to mean anything at all. These numbers usually indicate when and where a product was packaged, and are used for identification and inspection purposes.

Does This Milk Smell Funny?

You can often judge the quality of food by the way it looks or smells and by its texture. For example, fish should smell sweet, not fishy. If it smells fishy, it probably isn't fresh.

✔ Fruits and vegetables in general should have good color, with no signs of bruising or mold. They should have a sweet smell.

✔ Meat should have good color and texture. If the meat is coarse, very dark in the lean area, and has yellow fat, it is not good quality.

✔ Poultry should have intact skin, with no tears or punctures. There shouldn't be holes in the wrapper, either, and the grade should be on the label.

✔ Shellfish such as clams and mussels should have a sweet smell and be tightly closed. If the shells are open, they are dead, and unsafe to eat.

✔ Fresh herbs and spices should be soft and the leaves should be intact. If they are dry, brittle, stale, bruised or wilted, and smell musty, they are not fresh, and may be moldy.

✔ Bread should be soft. If it is hard or moldy, it is not fresh.

Myth You can't eat food after the sell-by date stamped on the label.

Truth The sell-by date is the last date a product should be sold. If it is stored properly in the refrigerator, it should remain safe for five to ten days past the sell-by date.

Vocabulary

Net weight: Total weight minus the weight of the packaging.

Figure Focus

Read the food labels on an item or two you have in the classroom or that students might volunteer to share from their lunch containers. You could use a bottle of soda, a candy bar or pack of gum, a bag of pretzels, etc. Identify the ingredients and the quantity or net weight. What other information is on the packaging that would help you decide if you wanted to eat it or not?

Does This Milk Smell Funny?

Since most fresh foods are not stamped with "use by" or expiration dates, it is important to be able to recognize their quality and freshness. If you are unsure, ask a store clerk or the manager in the produce, meat, or bakery departments. They should be able to tell you the exact date when the products were put on the shelf.

Myth/Truth

On the other hand, you shouldn't put complete trust in a sell-by date. For example, you might buy milk before the sell-by date and when you get it home, you discover that it's curdled. As a responsible consumer, you should return the milk to the store where you bought it and alert the store manager to the problem. It's quite possible that other containers of milk that came in the same shipment are spoiled as well.

Customized Instruction: Special Needs (Food Allergies) Students

Have students discuss any ingredients they must be on the lookout for in the foods they eat. Is it easy for them to find this information on food labels?

End-of-Chapter Activities

Case Study

The bread spoiled. It got moldy. The team should not eat the bread. Some types of mold can be very toxic. Vicki could have taken the bread home and put it in the freezer so it stayed fresh.

Sounding Off!

Student answers will vary.

FAQ

1. Hazards that can cause foodborne illness are biological, physical, and chemical hazards.

2. Cross-contamination happens when an uncontaminated food comes in contact with something already touched by contaminated food.

3. Common types of kitchen injuries are burns, cuts, falls, electric shocks, and strains or sprains.

4. Factors to consider are time of day, occasion, cost, and nutrition. Also, number and type of courses, balance of foods, available equipment, and theme should be considered.

5. Non-perishable means food that does not spoil.

6. Examples of perishable foods are milk, eggs, cheese, fresh fruit, fresh vegetables, meat, fish, and poultry. Students may think of others

7. Your refrigerator should be between 35° and 40°F.

8. A generic brand is a product that is not identified with a particular company. Generic products usually cost less than brand-name products.

9. The unit price is the cost of an item per standard unit, such as ounce, pound, or quart.

10. "Sell by" or "pull by" dates tell grocers when to remove the item from the shelf. Usually, you can safely eat the product for up to five days past this date.

Case Study

Vicky is on her school's debate team. They have an all day event scheduled on Saturday from 8:00 a.m. until 5:00 p.m. Each team member is responsible for bringing food for the team, and Vicky is assigned to bring the bread for sandwiches.

Vicky buys two loaves of packaged whole wheat bread on Friday. It snows overnight and the event is postponed until the following week. Vicky leaves the bread in her locker all week, and then brings it to the debate. When she takes it out at lunch time, it is hard around the edges has had dark green spots.

- What do you think happened to the two loaves of bread?
- Should the team eat the bread anyway?
- What steps could Vicky have taken to keep the bread from getting hard and spotty?

Sounding Off!

1. What is the grossest thing you ever ate? What made it gross?

2. What do you think is the most important factor in planning a meal? Is it cost? Is it convenience?

1. What are three basic types of hazards that can cause foodborne illness?
2. What is cross-contamination?
3. List five common types of kitchen injuries.
4. List four factors to consider when you are deciding on a menu.
5. What does non-perishable mean?
6. List three examples of perishable food.
7. What is the proper temperature range for your kitchen refrigerator?
8. What is a generic product?
9. What is a unit price?
10. What is the sell-by date?

As a class, plan a meal for a particular occasion. Select the occasion and decide how many people will be invited. Think of five dishes you want to serve—an appetizer, a main dish, two side dishes, and a dessert, and assign a budget for each dish.

Divide the class into five groups, and randomly select one of the dishes for each group. As a group, find a recipe for the assigned dish, keeping in mind the occasion, the budget, and the number of guests. If necessary, adjust the yield for the recipe so you make the right amount for your guests.

Make a shopping list. Be specific about the types and amounts of each ingredient you need to buy. Consider extra items such as garnishes to make the dish look appealing, as well. If possible, include the cost of each item, so you know your budget. When the shopping list is complete, make a meal time plan or schedule for preparing the dish. If possible, prepare the dish.

Make copies of the recipe—using the adjusted yield, if necessary—for your class. Include nutritional values, tips, and suggestions. Make copies of your shopping list and meal time plan, as well.

Hot Topics

Do you have any food secrets? Maybe you have allergies or intolerances you don't like to discuss. Maybe you have a health condition that requires a special diet, or a cultural or religious dietary restriction. Maybe you just don't like the taste or smell of a particular food.

Take this opportunity to write anonymously about your food secrets, and why you feel you have to keep them to yourself. Use a word processor so no one recognizes your handwriting. Be honest and open. Put the paper in the class Hot Topics box.

As a class, read the anonymous entries and discuss them.

Problem Solver

A friend is hosting a party for her hockey team. There are 15 members of the team, and each is contributing $5.00 to the party. Your friend is not sure what to serve. Using advertising flyers from different grocery stores in your area, help your friend develop a menu that includes a variety of healthy choices and stays within the team's budget.

Write the menu out along with a shopping list, indicating which store is selling each item for the best price. Include the quantities.

Team Players

Divide the class into five teams and assign a dish to each team. Have students review the information presented on pages 405–406 in the chapter. You might also refer them to *Appendix C: MyPyramid Food Group Recommendations*. Their end result should consist of a copy of the recipe, tips and suggestions for preparing and serving the dish, and a summary of the dish's nutritional value.

Hot Topics

Make sure students understand that they can turn in their papers anonymously. Encourage them to be open and honest about their food secrets.

Problem Solver

Students are to develop a menu for a large number of people on a budget of about $75. They will research prices for menu items using advertising flyers from local grocery stores. The goal is for students to provide a well-balanced and nutritious menu that would be appealing to all guests.

Write Now

Students are to prepare an invitation to a special occasion meal. The invitation should specify the time, place, and menu that will be served. Students should strive to be creative in the format and design of their invitations. If they have access to computers, encourage them to use their desktop publishing skills.

Be Involved!

As a class, students are to brainstorm ways they can educate their peers about the importance of food and kitchen safety. They are to use the FCCLA planning process outlined below to develop, execute, and evaluate their efforts.

- Identify the project.
- Set a goal.
- Form a plan (who, what, when, where, how, cost, resources, and evaluation).
- Act.
- Follow up.

Remind students that a successful team relationship depends on all team members working together. Make sure they take steps to delegate responsibilities, communicate effectively, and manage conflicts or disagreements.

Web Extra

Students are to create a directory of Web sites that offer discount coupons. The directory should include the Web site address and a brief description of the site.

Remind students that a reliable Web site usually publishes the name of the author or organization that sponsors it and the date the content was created or last updated in a fairly obvious location, such as at the top or bottom of the page or on the home page. The site is usually organized with headings and an obvious navigation system. A reliable site clearly states its purpose and any affiliations. You should also look for accuracy in spelling and grammar.

Students should post the directory in their school career center or library.

*W*rite *Now*

Write an invitation to a special occasion meal. Include information about the occasion, the time and place, and the menu you will serve. Make the invitation decorative to match the occasion.

Be Involved!

www.fcclainc.org

As a class, use the FCCLA planning process to plan a project to educate your peers about the importance of food and kitchen safety. You might write articles for your school or local newspaper, create a presentation, video, or brochure, organize a panel discussion, or invite representatives from your local health department to speak at a meeting. Set a goal and brainstorm projects and activities. After considering all possible options, select the project that you think will be the best one for achieving your goal.

Make an action plan for achieving your goal. Include a timeframe, make sure the plan is realistic and attainable, and then put the plan into action. You may want to organize teams within the class to handle specific responsibilities, such as volunteer management and publicity.

As you work toward your goal, keep a class journal to record your progress, and collect documentation that you can use to show what you have achieved. After the project is complete, evaluate your success. Did you achieve your goal? Were you able to get the message out about the importance of food and kitchen safety? Are there things you could have done differently? Prepare an article about the event and send it to the school or community newspaper. You might also want to send it to your FCCLA chapter so they can publish it in their newsletter.

Web Extra ▼

You can find discount food coupons for products at corporate Web sites and at Web sites for many grocery chains.

Use the Internet to locate some helpful and trustworthy Web sites that offer discount coupons. Make a directory of the sites, including the Web site address and a brief description. Post the directory on your school Web site or in your school career center or library.

Social Networking

There is a lot of information you can learn from a food label. Make a poster showing a label from a common food item. On the poster, explain how to read the label, and what the information in each section tells you. Hang the posters on a bulletin board or in an area of your school where other students will see them, such as a hallway or the cafeteria.

Social Networking

Students are to create a poster of a food label from a common food item. They are to identify the different types of information you find on a food label. Refer students to page 385 in Chapter 20 and page 411 in this chapter for a review of the various types of information on a food label. Their labels should include Food Nutrition facts (serving size, servings per container, and nutrition information per serving). It should also include a list of ingredients, quantity, and grades, if applicable.

Cooking Basics

SKILLS IN THIS CHAPTER . . .

- Following a Recipe
- Utilizing Basic Ingredients
- Serving a Meal
- Identifying Basic Kitchen Equipment

THINK ABOUT THIS

Fish, chicken, pasta, and pastries! What tastes good to you? Does it taste better if you cook it yourself, buy it ready-to-eat, or enjoy it as a guest in someone else's home? Preparing food can be a fun and satisfying experience, whether you are cooking at home for yourself, or in a restaurant kitchen for hundreds of paying guests. But, do the ingredients just appear in your cabinets? Do recipes just pop into your head? There's a lot of work involved in organizing and managing a meal. You must be prepared to make choices, set goals, and solve problems at every step of the way.

➤ On a piece of paper, make a table with three columns (or just fold the paper into thirds). In the first column, make a list of five foods you like to eat, such as hamburger, strawberries, or potatoes. In the second column, write where you think the food item comes from, such as "grows on a tree," "part of a cow," or "from the ocean." Using books or the Internet, research where the item really does come from, and write it in the third column. How many did you get right?

415

Chapter 22 Overview

In this chapter, students are introduced to the basics of cooking. The parts of a recipe are identified, and basic food preparation and cooking terms and methods are defined. Students also learn tips and techniques for serving a fun, relaxing, and satisfying meal.

Following a Recipe   In this section, the parts of a recipe are identified. Common terminology and abbreviations used in recipes are explained. Students also learn about different techniques for preparing and cooking food.

Utilizing Basic Ingredients   This section discusses basic ingredients used in cooking. Tips on selecting and storing ingredients are provided. Students also learn to differentiate among the different forms and variations of foods.

Serving a Meal   Students explore dining etiquette in this section. The proper way to set a table, present the meal, and use good table manners are discussed.

Identifying Basic Kitchen Equipment   This section provides an overview of kitchen equipment and when and how it is used. Information is provided on utensils such as cutting and measuring tools, types of appliances, and pots and pans.

Focus and Engage

Bell-Ringer: Think About This

Students are to make a list of five foods they like to eat. Next to each food item, they are to list where they think the food comes from. Then, they should research using books or the Internet to find out where the item really does come from. For simplicity's sake, make sure students list a single food item as opposed to a meal. For example, they should list pepperoni instead of pepperoni pizza or cheese instead of macaroni and cheese.

ADVANCE PREPARATION	
Review	*Life Skills for the 21st Century* textbook, Chapter 22.
Prepare	Paper and pencil for some activities.
	Markers or different color pencils.
	Poster board or plain white paper.
	Newspapers and advertising circulars from local grocery stores.
	Box labeled "Hot Topics."

CUSTOMIZED INSTRUCTION OVERVIEW				
Less Advanced Students	**More Advanced Students**	**ESOL Students**	**Special Needs Students**	**At-Risk Students**
Pages 416, 422	Pages 416, 421, 423	Pages 416, 422	Pages 416, 418, 422, 427	Pages 418, 423

Introduce the Section

This section identifies the parts of a recipe and explains common terminology and abbreviations used in recipes. Students also learn about different techniques for preparing and cooking food.

Figure Focus

Ask students to share recipes they have "in their head." For example, do they make hot chocolate or popcorn in a certain way? Do they mix different beverages to create a favorite drink concoction? Do they have a favorite sandwich they made up on their own, or a special snack that only *they* can make? Encourage them to talk about unique recipes they have tried or would like to try.

Vocabulary

Recipe: Written set of directions for making a certain dish.

Discuss

Discuss the places where you can find recipes. Some resources are:

- **Family and friends.** Does your grandmother make world-famous chocolate chip cookies? How about your friend's mother whose lasagna is unrivaled?

- **Cookbooks.** Libraries usually have scores of cookbooks with recipes you can copy. You can also buy cookbooks in bookstores and other stores that have book departments.

- **Online.** The Internet has many recipe and cooking sites from which you can download recipes for free. You also can search for a specific recipe to find many variations of it.

- **TV cooking shows.** In addition to specific cooking shows, many news and talk shows have their own cooking segments.

- **School.** Students might find cookbooks in your school library or through cooking classes.

- **Magazines and newspapers.** Many newspapers have daily or weekly sections on cooking that include recipes.

- **Grocery stores.** Grocers often post recipes that use store brands. Check at the meat, produce, and fish counters.

- **Food packages.** Recipes are often printed on food packages and containers or provided inside the packaging. These recipes use the product, but you can easily substitute a different brand if you find one you like better or which costs less.

Following a Recipe

A recipe provides all the information you need to prepare a dish properly.

A **recipe** is a written set of directions for making a certain dish. You use a recipe so you know the food will come out properly every time. You can find recipes in cookbooks, magazines, and online. Some of the best sources for recipes are your family and friends.

Some recipes are very simple and others can be quite complicated.

- A simple recipe usually has three or four ingredients and does not take a long time to prepare.
- A complicated recipe may have 12 to 15 ingredients, require a lot of time to organize, use lots of equipment, and take a long time to prepare.

Just because a recipe is complicated does not mean it will taste better than a simple recipe. When you are learning to cook, or when you do not have a lot of time, use a simple recipe to prepare a tasty dish. When you have more experience as a cook, or if you have a lot of time to experiment, you might have fun trying a more complicated recipe.

Parts of a Recipe

Most recipes include the following information:

- *Title*: A descriptive name for the dish.
- *Yield*: **Yield** is the measured output, such as the number of servings, or the serving size.
- *Preparation time*: The average amount of time it takes to prepare and cook the recipe.
- *Ingredient list*: A list of the items and quantities you will need to make the recipe.
- *Method*: The step-by-step directions you follow to prepare the recipe.
- Some recipes also include a list of the equipment you will need, the nutrition facts per serving, and tips or hints to help you prepare and serve the dish.

Customized Instruction: More Advanced Students

Have students develop a recipe organization system. This could be a box, binder, or notebook with divider tabs. They should determine the main categories of recipes, such as "Breakfast," "Salads," "Soups and Stews," "Fish and Chicken," "Meat," and "Desserts." Have them find five to ten recipes of foods they like and place them under the correct category.

Customized Instruction: Less Advanced/Special Needs Students

Have students write up a recipe for one of their favorite dishes. They can copy it from a cookbook or other resource. Then, have them draw a picture of it, explaining how important a good photograph is to the appeal of a recipe.

Customized Instruction: ESOL Students

Ask students to bring in a recipe that's written in their primary language. Have them translate the recipe into English.

Reading a Recipe

In order for a recipe to work, you have to follow the instructions. Reading the recipe more than once helps you make sure that you know the tools and ingredients you need and that you understand the directions.

- The first time you read a recipe is usually before you shop. You determine the ingredients you need and add them to your shopping list.
- The next time you read a recipe is before you start preparing the dish. You can take out the ingredients and equipment you need and make sure you understand the directions.
- The third time you read a recipe is while you are cooking. You follow the instructions to ensure that the dish comes out the way it should.

Measuring Ingredients

Every recipe includes a list of ingredients and the quantity of each ingredient you will need. There are three ways to measure ingredients.

- *Dry volume* measures dry ingredients such as flour and sugar. Use a dry measuring cup or measuring spoon. These usually come in a nested set. Overfill the measuring container, and then level off any excess from the top with a flat object, such as the straight edge of a spatula.
- *Liquid volume* measures liquid ingredients such as water or oil. Use a clear liquid measuring cup with measuring lines on it. Set it on a flat surface, fill to the desired mark, and read it at eye level for accuracy.
- *Weight* measures both dry and liquid ingredients. Set an empty container on a scale and adjust the scale to zero to account for the weight of the container. Fill the container until the scale shows the desired weight. This type of measuring is common in Europe and in large volume cooking such as a school cafeteria.

Substituting Ingredients to Enhance Nutrition and Meet Special Dietary Needs

Although the point of a recipe is to make sure the dish turns out the way it is supposed to every time it is made, sometimes you can make changes to improve the nutrition. For example, you can lower the fat, sugar, or sodium in many recipes by substituting ingredients.

- Use 1 cup of applesauce instead of 1 cup of butter, shortening, or oil in baked goods.
- Use light or fat-free cream cheese instead of regular cream cheese.
- Use two egg whites instead of one whole egg.
- Use a sugar substitute instead of regular granulated sugar.
- Use low-sodium ingredients, such as low-sodium chicken stock.
- Use herbs and spices such as garlic and pepper in place of salt.

Why is it important to use a dry measuring cup to measure dry ingredients?

Common Recipe Abbreviations

Recipes use abbreviations to indicate the quantities of ingredients. Here are some common abbreviations and equivalent measurements:

tsp or t	teaspoon
tbsp or T	tablespoon
oz	ounce
fl oz	fluid ounce
c	cup
pt	pint
qt	quart
gal	gallon
lb	pound
mL	milliliter
L	liter
g	gram
sq	square
f.g.	few grains
#	pounds
°F	degrees Farenheit
°C	degrees Celsius

Common Equivalents:

2 c = 1 pt	2 pts = 1 qt
4 qts = 1 gal	16 T = 1 c
3 t = 1 T	16 oz = 1 lb
8 oz = 1 c	1 stick butter = ½ c

Figure Focus

The reason for using a dry measuring cup is that it makes it easier to scoop dry ingredients and then level them off. It also allows for a more accurate measurement. If you were to use a liquid measuring cup, you tend to shake the ingredient until it is level with the line of measure and that can cause settling. So, you end up adding more of the ingredient than you need, resulting in an inaccurate measure.

Common Recipe Abbreviations

In addition to the abbreviations listed, you might want to review some common conversions.

- 1 liter = 4.23 cups
- 5 milliliters = 1 teaspoon
- 1 ounce = 28 grams
- 350° Fahrenheit = 177° Celsius

Discuss

You might want to discuss some other common ingredient substitutions.

- 1 cup buttermilk = 1 teaspoon lemon juice or vinegar plus milk to measure 1 cup
- ¾ cup cracker crumbs = 1 cup bread crumbs
- 1 clove garlic = ⅛ teaspoon garlic powder
- 1 cup half-and-half cream = 1 tablespoon melted butter plus enough whole milk to equal 1 cup
- 1 cup honey = 1¼ cups sugar plus ¼ cup liquid called for in recipe
- 1 teaspoon lemon peel = ½ teaspoon lemon extract
- 1 small onion chopped = 1 teaspoon onion powder or 1 tablespoon dried minced onion
- 1 cup sour cream = 1 cup plain yogurt
- 2 cups tomato sauce = ¾ cup tomato paste plus 1 cup water

Orange-Blueberry-Banana Smoothie

Discuss the different types of smoothies.

- **Fruit smoothie:** Probably the most common type of smoothie, these use ingredients such as strawberries, pineapple, raspberries, bananas, blueberries, and sorbet. They usually contain between 300 and 400 calories.

- **Post-workout smoothie:** Sometimes referred to as a recovery shake, these are usually higher in calories and often contain peanut butter, honey, whey protein powder, and milk or soy milk, along with fruit if desired. They contain 350 to 500 calories and often have a 4 to 1 carbohydrate to protein ratio.

- **High-protein smoothie:** These contain milk or water plus protein powder. These are consumed mostly by people on a high-protein diet.

- **Dessert smoothie:** These usually contain ice cream, chocolate or other flavored syrup, peanut butter, and a variety of other add-ins, such as crushed nuts, cookies, or candy bars. These contain a high number of calories; it's not uncommon for them to exceed 750 calories.

Discuss ways to vary the flavor of the smoothie recipe in the text. These include using frozen fruit instead of fresh, fruit-flavored yogurt instead of vanilla, milk instead of yogurt, or other fruits or fruit juices.

Vocabulary

Dry heat: Method of cooking that uses hot air, hot oil, or a hot pan to cook foods. Methods include grilling, frying, broiling, roasting, and baking.

Moist heat: Method of cooking that uses water or another liquid to slowly cook the foods in a covered container. Methods include braising, poaching, stewing, steaming, and boiling.

Figure Focus

Explain the importance of carefully reading a recipe and determining the number of servings it will yield. If you are doubling a recipe or increasing the quantity of ingredients by another amount, you also need to make sure that the dishes you plan to cook or bake the recipe in can accommodate the larger quantity. Otherwise, you might have overflow that makes for a nasty mess to clean up.

Orange-Blueberry-Banana Smoothie

Would you want to try the smoothie? Here's the complete recipe:

Yield: 2 cups   **Serving Size:** 2 cups

Ingredients

- ★ 1 cup vanilla low-fat yogurt
- ★ 1 cup blueberries, washed and patted dry
- ★ ½ banana, peeled
- ★ ½ cup orange juice
- ★ ½ cup ice

Method

1. Combine all ingredients in a blender.
2. Process on high speed until smooth.
3. Serve immediately.

Nutrition

- ★ Calories   380
- ★ Protein   13 g
- ★ Fat   4 g
- ★ Carbohydrates   72 g
- ★ Sodium   9 mg
- ★ Cholesterol   15 mg

Can you think of ways to vary the flavors in this recipe?

What If I Need More?

If you need to adjust a recipe *yield*—the amount of food or servings you get from the recipe—you may have to increase or decrease the quantity of ingredients. The important thing is to adjust the quantities for all ingredients by the same amount. For example, if you want twice the yield, you must double the quantities for all ingredients. If you want half the yield, you must halve the quantities for all ingredients.

To the left, you have the recipe for an orange blueberry banana smoothie. You have two friends coming over tomorrow, and you want to buy enough ingredients to make three smoothies, so you must triple the yield—multiply the amounts of each ingredient by 3.

"Uh oh. Is this going to make enough to serve all my guests?"

Cooking Terms and Techniques

What's the difference between baking and roasting? Is deep-frying the same as sautéing? If a recipe says to simmer but I boil, will the dish come out all wrong?

The two basic methods of cooking include moist heat and dry heat:

- **Moist heat** methods use water or another liquid to slowly cook the foods in a covered container. Braising, poaching, stewing, steaming, and boiling are moist heat methods.
- **Dry heat** methods use hot air, hot oil, or a hot pan to cook foods. Grilling, frying, broiling, roasting, and baking are dry heat methods.

Here are descriptions of some of the common types of cooking techniques.

Bake	A dry heat technique in which food is cooked by hot air trapped inside an oven.
Boil	Cook food directly in hot liquid over high heat.
Braise	A cooking method that combines dry and moist heat techniques. Food is seared and then gently cooked in flavorful liquid.
Broil	A dry heat technique in which the food is placed on a rack for cooking, and the heat source is located above the food.
Brown	Cook food until the outside turns brown.
Deep-fat fry	Cook food by submerging it in hot oil.
Grill	A dry heat method in which food is placed on a rack for cooking, and the heat source is located below the rack.
Pan fry	Cook food in hot oil in a pan. There should be oil as deep as half the thickness of the food.
Poach	Cook food directly in hot liquid over low heat.
Preheat	Heat the oven to a specified temperature before cooking. Not a cooking technique, but an important step in cooking preparation.
Roast	Almost the same as baking, although the cooking temperature may be higher, and the item being cooked is usually whole or large.
Sauté	Cook uncovered in a small amount of fat in a pan over high heat.

Customized Instruction: At-Risk/Special Needs Students

Using the example recipe in the text, have students create their own smoothie recipe. Have them draw a picture to accompany the recipe.

Scald	To heat to just below the boiling point.
Simmer	Cook food directly in hot liquid over medium heat.
Steam	Cook food in a closed pot or steamer over a small amount of liquid.
Stew	Cut food into small pieces and cook in enough liquid to cover.
Stir fry	Sauté in a wok, a pan with a round bottom and high sides.

Food Preparation Techniques

Is slicing the same as dicing? If you chop an onion instead of mincing it, will the dish taste bad? Here are descriptions of some of the common types of food preparation techniques.

Beat	Stir a mixture until smooth.
Blend	Mix ingredients until smooth and uniform.
Chill	Lower the temperature of a food that was just cooked to 40° F.
Chop	Cut into small pieces. Sometimes the recipe specifies a size for the pieces such as fine (small) or coarse (large).
Combine	Mix ingredients together.
Core	Remove the center or core, usually from a fruit.
Curdle	Separate a mixture into a liquid with solid particles.
Cream	Rub, whip, or beat with a spoon or mixer until soft and fluffy.
Dice	Cut into square cubes of even size—usually about ¼ inch on each side.
Dissolve	Mix a dry substance into a liquid.
Fold	Gently combine ingredients using a spatula or whisk.
Glaze	Cover with a thin, sugary syrup or melted fruit jelly.
Grate	Shred or flake, using a grater.
Knead	Work and press dough with the heels of your hands so the dough becomes stretchy.
Marinate	Let food stand in a liquid mixture.
Mince	Chop into very small pieces.
Mix	Stir until ingredients are thoroughly combined.
Peel	Remove the skin, usually from a fruit or vegetable.
Puree	Blend or strain finely to create a paste or liquid.
Scramble	Stir or mix food gently while cooking, such as eggs.
Shred	Cut into slivers or slender pieces.
Sift	Put dry ingredients through a fine sieve, or strainer.
Slice	Cut into slices.
Stir	Mix with a spoon or fork until ingredients are blended.
Temper	Combine hot and cool ingredients in a way that prevents them from breaking down. For example, warm a mixture of cream and egg yolks so the yolks will not cook when added to a simmering liquid.
Toss	Tumble ingredients lightly with a lifting motion.
Whip	Beat rapidly in order to incorporate air and expand the volume.
Whisk	Beat ingredients with a fork or wire whisk to mix, blend, or whip.
Zest	Finely grate the colored peel of a fruit, usually a lemon, orange, or lime.

Tropical Fruit Salad

A fruit salad is a healthy dish that can be served as an appetizer, side dish, or dessert. You can make it using almost any kind of fruit. What if you want to serve a tropical fruit salad? Here's a complete recipe:

Yield: 10 cups   *Serving Size:* 3½ oz

Ingredients

★ 1 cup mango, diced
★ 1 cup pineapple, diced
★ 1 cup melon, diced
★ 1 cup papaya, diced
★ 3 fl oz orange juice
★ 1 cup banana, sliced
★ ¾ cup unsweetened shredded coconut

Method

1. Toss the mango, pineapple, melon, and papaya together with the orange juice.
2. Keep chilled until you are ready to serve.
3. Arrange the fruit salad in a serving dish or on individual plates.
4. Top with the bananas and sprinkle with the coconut. Serve at once.

Nutrition

★ Calories   70
★ Protein   1 g
★ Fat   2 g
★ Carbohydrates   12 g
★ Sodium   5 mg
★ Cholesterol   0 mg

Can you think of ways to vary the flavors in this recipe?

Tropical Fruit Salad

Ask students to share ideas on other types of fruit salad they have eaten or would like to eat. Discuss some creative ways to serve fruit.

■ Scoop out a watermelon half and use it as a bowl to hold other fresh fruit, such as cantaloupe, strawberries, blueberries, and pineapple.

■ Put fresh fruit chunks, such as kiwi, melon, strawberries, pineapple, and mango, on skewers.

■ Dip strawberries and banana chunks in chocolate that hardens when refrigerated.

Teaching Tips

Refer to the types of cooking techniques table and ask students to provide examples of foods they could prepare using the specific techniques. Do the same for the food preparation techniques.

Introduce the Section

This section discusses basic ingredients used in cooking. Tips on selecting and storing ingredients are provided. Students also learn common methods for preparing and serving them.

Figure Focus

Explain that basic ingredients are categorized by the food groups. Refer students to *Appendix C: MyPyramid Food Group Recommendations*.

Vocabulary

Produce: Fruits and vegetables.

Discuss

Discuss with students the different forms or variations of ingredients or foods they regularly eat. For example, beans come in many shapes, sizes, and colors. Some types of beans are string, wax, pinto, kidney, garbanzo, navy, and lima. Another example is apples, which include Gala, Fuji, Golden Delicious, Granny Smith, Jonathan, McIntosh, and Red Delicious varieties. You might also discuss commonly used recipe ingredients, such as flour (all-purpose, bread, buckwheat, pastry, rice, self-rising, etc.), oil (canola, coconut, corn, olive, sesame, peanut, soybean, etc.), and salt (iodized, kosher, sea, rock, etc.).

STUDENT ACTIVITY

Have students select a food or ingredient and create a poster of its different types or variations. They can use a plain sheet of paper or poster board. They should label each type or variation.

Utilizing Basic Ingredients

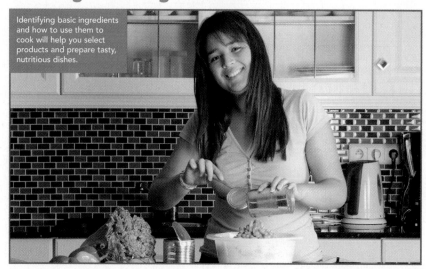

Identifying basic ingredients and how to use them to cook will help you select products and prepare tasty, nutritious dishes.

A salad recipe calls for lettuce—do you use iceberg, bibb, or romaine? You want to grill a chicken—should it be a fryer, roaster, or will a package of thighs do? Selecting the right ingredients can be overwhelming.

The more experience you have working with basic ingredients, the better you will become at knowing the type to buy and the cooking techniques to use.

Basic ingredients can be divided into categories, roughly aligned with the food groups. They include fruits, vegetables, protein (meat and beans), milk or dairy, grains, and fats. Within each group, foods share common qualities, such as nutritional value and storage requirements. Recognizing the similarities among basic ingredients can help you understand how to use them when you cook.

Fruits and Vegetables

Fruits and vegetables—called **produce**—come in a rainbow of colors, flavors, shapes, and textures. They are loaded with vitamins, minerals, fiber, and antioxidants, which help protect against cancer, heart disease, and Type 2 diabetes. Fruit is often served as an appetizer or dessert, or eaten as a snack. Vegetables are usually served as a side dish, but may be used as an ingredient in many dishes such as soups and casseroles. Vegetarians eat vegetables as a main dish.

Once it was only possible to have fresh fruit and vegetables in season—meaning in the season when they grow locally—but modern transportation, packaging, refrigeration, and farming technologies make it possible to have them fresh year round. Processed fruit and vegetables come in cans, dried, or frozen.

Most fresh fruit and vegetables should be stored in the refrigerator. Tropical fruits such as bananas should be kept in a cool, dry location. Many fresh fruits and vegetables can be served raw or cooked lightly. Wash them well using running water and a brush designed for cleaning fruits and vegetables to remove dirt and hazards.

Protein: Meat, Poultry, Eggs, and Legumes

Meat, poultry, eggs, and legumes are full of protein and other nutrients. Meat generally contains more fat than poultry. Poultry is often used as a protein source in a low-fat diet. These items are typically used for the main dish in a meal, but may be served as a side dish or appetizer.

- Meat raised for food includes beef and veal from cattle, pork from pigs, and lamb from young sheep.
- Poultry is any bird raised as food, including chicken, geese, and turkey.
- Eggs and legumes—plants such as peas and beans—provide protein when meat is scarce or as an alternative for vegetarians.

Fresh meat and chicken are packaged and sold in grocery stores and butcher shops. You can also purchase ready-to eat or ready-to cook meats and chicken, such as canned beef stew or frozen chicken nuggets.

Store fresh meat and chicken in the refrigerator. Cook them to make them more tender, to kill bacteria, and to make them taste good. Both moist and dry heat methods can be used. Cook meat and poultry until the internal temperature registers at least 165° F.

Most eggs sold in the United States are from chickens. Most nutrients are in the **yolk**—the yellow part of the egg—including protein, vitamins A and D, and iron. The yolks also contain cholesterol. The whites of the eggs—called **albumen**—are made of protein and water.

Eggs come in different sizes. Unless it says otherwise, recipes use large eggs. Store eggs in the refrigerator and do not use them if the shell is cracked or broken.

Job Search

There are many types of jobs in the food service industry, including chefs, cooks, caterers, private chefs, banquet managers, restaurant owners, food writers, food critics, food photographers, and food stylists. Each job requires different abilities and interests. For example, a food writer must combine writing and communications skills with a strong, basic knowledge of food and cooking. A caterer must be a creative chef who can plan and price a pleasing menu and deal with a variety of clients.

Education requirements and working environments vary as well. A chef must have a culinary degree and would benefit from knowledge of nutrition, accounting, and business management. A restaurant owner might need a business degree and entrepreneurial skills.

Use the Internet, library, or your school's guidance resources to learn more about a career in food service. Select a job that appeals to you, and write a job description, including the educational requirements, career pathway, and potential salary range.

Tuna Salad

Tuna in a can or pouch is a convenience food. It's packaged and ready for use in any recipe. What if you want to serve tuna salad for lunch? Here's a complete recipe:

Yield: 3 servings
Serving Size: about 2.5 oz

Ingredients

- ★ 1 7-oz can solid white tuna packed in water
- ★ ¼ cup mayonnaise
- ★ 1 tbsp sweet pepper relish

Method

1. Drain the tuna and place in a small bowl.
2. Add the mayonnaise and relish and mix well.

Nutrition

- ★ Calories 142
- ★ Protein 16.7 g
- ★ Fat 5.9 g
- ★ Carbohydrates 4.4 g
- ★ Sodium 240 mg
- ★ Cholesterol 26 mg

Can you think of at least two ways to serve this tuna salad?

Myth Poultry labeled "free-range" is healthier and more nutritious than regular poultry.

Truth According to the USDA, any poultry with access to the outdoors can be labeled "free-range" even if they don't go outdoors and are raised using methods similar to those used to raise regular poultry.

Vocabulary

Albumen: White part of an egg.
Yolk: Yellow part of an egg.

Discuss

MyPyramid recommends that girls and boys between the ages of 9 and 18 eat 5 to 6 ounces of food each day from the meat and beans food group. Ask students what types of foods from this group they eat. Do they eat something from this group every day?

Tuna Salad

Ask students to suggest different ways to serve tuna salad. Following are some suggestions:

- On sandwich bread with lettuce, tomato, and onion.
- In pita bread with chopped lettuce, tomato, and onion.
- Rolled in a soft tortilla and sprinkled with hot sauce.
- On a bed of lettuce with cottage cheese.
- Baked on French bread with melted cheese.
- Stuffed in a hollowed-out tomato.
- Served with pasta and sprinkled with Italian or herb dressing.
- Served with fresh vegetables, such as avocado slices, carrots, celery, and cucumber.
- Mixed with beans and onions and sprinkled with vinaigrette.

Job Search

Students are to write a description of a job in the food service industry. Refer students to *Appendix A: Career Clusters* to help them get started. You might suggest they focus on the Agriculture, Food & Natural Resources; Hospitality & Tourism; and Science, Technology, Engineering & Mathematics clusters as these list sample occupations related to food services.

Myth/Truth

Explain that "free-range" refers to food that comes from animals that are raised out of confinement or free to roam outdoors as opposed to being confined indoors or in a contained feedlot.

Hard Cooked Eggs

Explain that if you do not cook eggs long enough, their yolks will be gooey instead of firm. Following are some additional tips on boiling eggs:

- Make sure none of the eggs are cracked.
- Fresher eggs tend to be more difficult to peel, so buy eggs three to five days before you plan to cook them.
- Bring eggs to room temperature before cooking them. This reduces the chance of them cracking during the boiling process.

Vocabulary

Fats: Substances such as butter, lard, shortening, and margarine that are solid at room temperature.

Oils: Liquid fat, such as vegetable oils and oil blends.

Pasteurized: Process in which milk and milk products are heated to destroy pathogens.

Figure Focus

Ask students what type of milk they drink. You might also discuss the type(s) of milk served in your school cafeteria. Explain that the percentages indicate the amount of fat in the milk. For example, in whole milk, about 4% of total content is fat; 2% milk has 2% fat; low-fat or 1% milk has 1% fat; and fat-free or skim milk contains no fat. All types of milk have essentially the same amount of vitamins and minerals, including vitamin D and calcium; however, those with a higher percentage of fat also are higher in calories.

Hard Cooked Eggs

Eggs are one of the most versatile foods. You can simmer, poach, fry, or scramble them. You can combine them with other ingredients to make omelets, French toast, or baked goods. What if you want to use hard cooked eggs to garnish a salad? Here's a complete recipe:

Yield: 6 servings   *Serving Size:* 2 eggs

Ingredients
★ 12 large eggs

Method
1. Place the eggs in a pot.
2. Fill the pot with enough cold water to cover the eggs by 2 inches.
3. Bring the water to a boil and immediately lower the temperature to a simmer.
4. Simmer the eggs for 15 minutes.
5. Place the eggs under running water to cool.

Nutrition
★ Calories   149
★ Protein   13 g
★ Fat   10 g
★ Carbohydrates   1 g
★ Sodium   132 mg
★ Cholesterol   425 mg

What do you think would happen if you didn't cook the eggs long enough?

Protein: Fish

Fish is low in calories and saturated fat, and high in protein, vitamins, and minerals. Many types of fish, including salmon, trout, mackerel, herring, and sardines contain omega-3 fatty acids which are said to promote heart health. There are two basic categories of fish:

- Finfish such as trout, salmon, and haddock have scales and fins.
- Shellfish such as clams, scallops, or lobster are enclosed in a hard shell.

Most fish can be cooked using a variety of techniques, including grilled, broiled, baked, roasted, or steamed. Fish can spoil very quickly, even when it is stored properly. Only buy fish that has a clean, sweet smell and is stored at 40° F or less. Cook fish until the internal temperature registers 145° F.

Dairy

Dairy products such as milk and cheese are a major component of most diets. You can eat them alone—such as a glass of milk—with other foods—such as milk in cereal—or use them as an ingredient in a huge number of recipes.

Dairy products include foods made from milk, such as yogurt, butter, cream, ice cream, and cheese. They are full of nutrients, including calcium and vitamin D, which promote the growth of strong bones and teeth. Milk and milk products are **pasteurized** to insure safety, which means they are heated to destroy pathogens—bacteria. Milk is homogenized, which means it is processed so that the fat does not separate and rise to the top, which creates cream.

Milk and cheese contain protein. If you cook dairy at a high heat, the proteins break down. Fresh milk spoils quickly. Store it in the refrigerator and throw it away five days after the Sell by date stamped on the label.

"I wonder if fat-free milk tastes the same as this low-fat milk?"

Fats and Oils

Fats and oils play an important role in making food taste good, giving foods a specific texture, and even making some foods stay fresh longer. They provide energy, and help your body absorb nutrients. Fats such as butter, lard, and margarine, which are made from animal products contain cholesterol. Some types of cholesterol contribute to heart disease and other health problems. Use fats sparingly to avoid unnecessary health risks.

- **Fats** are solid at room temperature. Common types of fats include butter, lard, shortening, and margarine.
- **Oils** are liquid at room temperature. Common types of oils include vegetable oils and oil blends, made from canola, corn, and safflower oils, and flavored oils made from nuts and olives.

You can store oils made from vegetable products at room temperature, but fats made from animal products, such as butter, and margarine should be kept in the refrigerator.

Customized Instruction: Special Needs (Lactose-Intolerant) Students

Students may be willing to discuss what it means to be lactose intolerant and how it affects their eating habits and diet. Ask them to discuss the types of dairy foods they can and cannot eat and what they look for on food labels.

Customized Instruction: Less Advanced Students

Have students create an ad for their preferred type of milk. They can do this on a plain sheet of paper or poster board. The ad should include an illustration and nutrition facts.

Customized Instruction: ESOL Students

Have students do the same activity as the one above for less advanced students, except their ad should be in their primary language.

Grains

Grains are the seeds of cereal grasses. Different types of grasses grow all over the world, so different types of grains are eaten in different countries. Some grains have been eaten since ancient times.

Grains are relatively inexpensive, filling, tasty, and highly nutritious. You can prepare them in different ways to create a wide variety of main dishes, side dishes, appetizers, and desserts. On a global scale, grains provide people with more nutrients and calories than any other food source.

Grain products include items made from grain, such as breads, cereals, pasta and rice. You make grains tender enough to eat by boiling or steaming them in liquid. For example, you cook cereal such as oatmeal by stirring the grain into simmering liquid. You must stir constantly to keep it smooth and free of lumps.

Grains may also be ground into flour and used to make items such as pasta, bread, or pastry. Bakeries and grocery stores sell fresh baked bread or packaged loaves. Packaged bread stays fresh longer than fresh bread. Throw all bread away five days after the Sell by date, or if it has mold growing on it.

- Yeast breads are breads that rise because the dough contains yeast. They take longer to prepare because you must wait for the dough to rise and you usually must knead the dough. You usually use yeast breads for making sandwiches. Sandwiches combine bread with a filling. Once considered a quick, portable lunch, sandwiches are now served at every meal.
- Quick breads are made from batter that contains baking soda or baking powder. They are often sweet or contain add-ins such as fruit, vegetables, or even chocolate. Muffins are a type of quick bread. Quick breads do not have to rise before baking, and do not require kneading. They are usually easier and faster to prepare than yeast breads.

Spices and Herbs

Spices and herbs are natural seasonings you can add to food to enhance its flavor and add color. Spices have been used since ancient times for everything from money to medicine. Some were used as food preservatives, cosmetics, and perfume. Spices and herbs have little or no nutritional value, but they have the power to turn a plain meal into something special.

- Spices are sweet-smelling natural ingredients. They might be the seeds, bark, roots, stalk, buds, fruit, and even flowers from a variety of plants. Some common spices include cinnamon, cloves, dill, ginger, pepper, and vanilla. Most are sold dried and packaged, either whole or ground into a powder.
- Herbs are the leaves, stems, and flowers of plants. They are sold fresh or dried. Some common herbs include basil, bay leaves, cilantro, mint, garlic, oregano, parsley, sage, rosemary, tarragon, and thyme.

Herbs and spices should be used according to your recipe. Store them in a cool dry place. They will lose their flavor and smell over time. Most dried herbs are more concentrated then fresh. If you want to substitute dried herbs for fresh in a recipe use one-third the amount of the fresh herb.

International Grains

Rice is a primary source of nutrients and calories for most people in Asia. Millet is common in countries in Northern Africa. You might be served sorghum in Australia.

Working individually, in pairs, or in small groups, use the Internet to select a country and research the type of grains common in that country. Discover how the grain grows, and how it is prepared. Prepare a presentation about your topic, including nutritional information, or find a recipe using the grain, and share it with your class.

Types of Grains

There are many types of grains grown all around the world. *Whole grains* are minimally processed so they keep their dietary fiber as well as vitamins and minerals. Most processed grains have vitamins and minerals added so they provide nutrients. Some common types of grains include:

Wheat	Rice
Oats	Corn
Rye	Buckwheat
Barley	Couscous
Tabula	Quinoa
Amaranth	Brown rice
Flaxseed	Millet
Spelt	Wheat berries
Wild rice	Bulgur (cracked wheat)

What kind of grain is your favorite breakfast cereal made from?

Vocabulary

Whole grains: Grains that are minimally processed so they keep their dietary fiber as well as vitamins and minerals.

Discuss

According to MyPyramid, boys and girls between the ages of 9 and 18 should eat 5 to 7 ounces of grains each day, and about half those grains should be whole grains. Explain that one slice of bread is about 1 ounce, as is 1 cup of dry cereal, and a half cup of cooked rice or pasta. Ask students to name the grains they typically eat every day.

International Grains

Students are to select a country and research the types of grains common in that country. Suggest to students that once they have selected the country, they should research the country's crops or agriculture to find information about grains. Students should prepare a presentation about their country's grains, including nutritional information and/or a recipe that uses the particular grain.

Types of Grains

Students are asked to name the type of grain their favorite cereal is made from. If your school cafeteria serves cereal for breakfast, you might ask to borrow boxes to identify grains. Or, you might have students look through magazines or advertising circulars from grocery stores or research on the Internet to find this information.

Customized Instruction: At-Risk Students

Using the following equivalents as a guide, have students develop a breakfast, lunch, and dinner menu for a day that includes 5 to 7 ounces of grains.

- 1 ounce = one slice of bread
- 1 ounce = one cup of dry cereal
- 1 ounce = a half cup of cooked rice or pasta

Customized Instruction: More Advanced Students

Have students pick a spice and research its origin, history, and uses. Have them write a one-page report on the spice.

Introduce the Section

Students explore dining etiquette in this section. The proper way to set a table, present the meal, and use good table manners are discussed.

Figure Focus

Ask students to comment on the things, aside from the menu, that can influence the dining experience. For example, does the use of a tablecloth and candles have an impact? How does music or TV noise in the background affect the ambience? What about the dishes, flatware, and glassware used? Do the personalities of your dining guests have an influence?

This Is Not a Barn!

Without naming names, ask students to comment on the good and bad table manners they see while eating in their school cafeteria. Discuss the opinions you might form about a person based on his or her table manners. For example, you might think a person with good table manners is respectful, polite, conscientious, and confident. You might think a person with bad table manners is lazy, disrespectful, and has low self-esteem.

TEAMWORK ACTIVITY

Does your school have guidelines on table manners or proper cafeteria behavior? Divide the class into four to five teams and give each team a piece of poster board. They should create a set of "Dining Guidelines" that can be posted in your school cafeteria. If guidelines already exist, have teams restate them in their poster, but embellish them with illustrations or a clever slant that will catch the attention of their peers. If appropriate, hang the team posters in the cafeteria or hallways.

Serving a Meal

You can enhance any meal by creating an appealing dining environment.

Have you ever eaten a meal standing up at the kitchen counter, or in the car on the way to school? You were probably in a rush, and enjoying a pleasant meal was not important at the time.

When you prepare a meal for your family or guests, however, you want them to relax, have fun, and appreciate the experience. You can achieve this by setting an attractive table, serving appealing food, and encouraging social conversation during the meal.

This Is Not a Barn!

Do you know someone who talks with her mouth full of food? Have you tried to enjoy a meal with someone who practically shovels the food into his mouth? Eating politely can make a meal much more pleasant for everyone.

In general, follow your host's lead when it comes to etiquette. Sit when she sits. Start eating when she starts eating. Use the utensil she uses. Here are some other guidelines:

- Turn off your cell phone before sitting at the table.
- Keep your napkin in your lap, moving it only when you need to wipe your mouth or hands.
- Sit up straight and bring the food to your mouth, not your mouth to the food.
- Keep your elbows off the table.
- Do not stuff your mouth. Take small bites, and chew with your mouth closed.
- Do not talk if you have food in your mouth. If you must, cover your mouth with your napkin.
- Say please and thank you.
- Be neat. Do your best to keep the food on your plate or in your mouth, not on the table, chair, or floor.
- At the end of the meal, place your utensils on your plate and return your napkin to its original spot—to the left of the plate.

Stay in School

Hispanic students have a significantly higher dropout rate than their white and African-American counterparts. Researchers have identified a number of reasons for this, including limited cultural understanding and support of Hispanic students in the school environment.

Have your class plan a meal that celebrates Hispanic culture. They should research traditional foods such as enchiladas, tamales, tortillas, burritos, and others. Have them find recipes and develop a shopping list. They should determine traditional dining or meal etiquette. They should identify types of decorations and party favors with a Hispanic flavor. They should find music that would complement the Hispanic theme. They should learn the Spanish names for meals (breakfast, lunch, dinner) and the dishes they will serve.

You might want to divide the class into teams, with one to three teams focusing on the meal preparation, one on the dining and meal etiquette, and one on the music and decorations. Make sure your Hispanic students are split up among the teams and that every team member contributes to the effort. It would be ideal if the class could prepare and enjoy the meal together, but if not, then have each team create a presentation on their efforts that they can share with the class.

Setting the Table

When you set the table for a sit-down meal, every guest gets a place setting. A **place setting** includes the plates, utensils, glasses, and napkin. There are many ways to arrange the place settings, usually based on how formal the meal will be. A formal dinner will have more plates, glasses, and utensils than a simple family meal. Some general guidelines for setting a family table include the following.

- The dinner plate goes in the middle of the place setting.
- The fork goes to the left of the dinner plate and the knife goes to the right, with the blade toward the plate.
- If there is a spoon, it goes to the right of the knife.
- A folded napkin goes to the left of the fork.
- The water glass should be placed just above the tip of the knife.
- You do not have to put out more utensils, plates, or glasses than you will use.

You might also decorate the table with flowers, a centerpiece, candles, a tablecloth, or placemats. The goal is to present an attractive arrangement that makes the diners feel comfortable and happy to be present.

Serving Appealing Food

Of course, you want the food you serve to be delicious, but taste is only one way that you make food appealing. You want it to look and smell good, too. Here are some guidelines for preparing and serving a meal that appeals to all of your guests' senses.

- *Vary the colors.* If all the food on the table is the same color, the meal looks boring. If the main dish is brown, serve an orange or green vegetable as a side.
- *Vary the textures.* Serve soft noodles with crisp vegetables, or crunchy salad with a smooth grain.
- *Vary the temperatures.* Serve a cold salad with a hot main dish, or a dessert that combines cold ice cream with a hot sauce.
- *Vary the flavors.* Serve a spicy side dish with a mild main dish, or a sweet vegetable with a savory—not sweet—main dish.
- *Vary the shapes.* Serve spaghetti with round meatballs, or long thin asparagus with a fish filet.
- *Add a garnish.* A garnish is an edible ingredient that adds color, flavor, and texture to a dish. You can top a dessert with mint leaves, or place a lemon twist on a dish of sorbet.

Who's Cleaning Up?

The meal's not over just because everyone has finished eating. What if you go to bed without cleaning up?

★ *Your kitchen might attract pests because you didn't clean up crumbs and spills.*

★ *You might waste food by not wrapping it and storing it properly.*

★ *You'll have to wash the dishes when you wake up in the morning.*

★ *The dirty dishes will be harder to clean, because the food will have hardened on the dishes.*

★ *Your kitchen floor might be sticky or slippery from spills you didn't wipe up.*

What tools or techniques can you use to make cleaning up faster and more enjoyable?

Test **IT** Yourself!

Use the following experiment to compare the cost, time, nutritional value, and convenience of buying ready-made cookies and baking cookies with a mix, refrigerated dough, and from scratch.

1. Divide into four teams. One group will make cookies from scratch, one will make cookies from refrigerated dough, one will make cookies from a mix, and one will simply buy a box or bag of ready-made cookies.
2. Each team will keep track of how much money and time it spends to assemble the tools and ingredients they need and then to prepare enough of their type of cookies for the whole class.
3. Each student will rate each type of cookie on six criteria: cost, time, nutritional value, convenience, enjoyment, and quality, using a scale of 1 to 5. The class will use the data to chart the results.
4. Individually, each classmate will choose the type of cookies he or she would serve in the future, and explain why. Is it quality? Is it convenience? Is it cost?

Vocabulary

Place setting: An individual table setting that includes a plate, eating utensils, glassware, and napkin.

Who's Cleaning Up?

Students are to discuss the tools and techniques they can use to make cleaning up faster and more enjoyable. Some suggestions are:

- Clean up as you go. Put away cooking ingredients when you are done using them. Throw away garbage immediately. Wash up dishes and utensils or load them in the dishwasher as you finish using them.
- If you have a dishwasher, make sure it is unloaded before you start to prepare your meal.
- Soak pots and pans on which food has hardened. This will loosen the food residues and make them much easier to clean up after the meal.
- Plan ahead of time how and where you will store leftovers. Do you have the right size airtight containers or aluminum foil and plastic wrap? Is there room in your refrigerator or freezer for them?
- Start cleanup when everyone is done eating. The longer you let dishes and utensils sit, the more difficult they will be to rinse and clean.
- Delegate work. It's OK to let a good friend or family member help you with some basic cleanup, such as removing dishes from the table, rinsing plates and placing them in the dishwasher, or drying dishes that you've washed.

Test **IT** Yourself!

Divide the class into four teams. They are to compare the cost, preparation time, nutritional value, and convenience of cookies prepared in different ways. Make sure the teams are preparing the same type of cookie. You might suggest sugar or oatmeal cookies because you can buy these ready-made as well as in the packaged mix and refrigerated dough forms. Also, be sure to consider any of your students with food allergies who might be sensitive to the ingredients used. Each team should have enough cookies for all students in the class. Students should do individual ratings. For the class to create a chart, you should first compile the individual ratings for each cookie on each of the six criteria. For example, collect each student's rating for the "Cost" of the ready-made cookie. Then, calculate the class average for that criterion and cookie. You might end up with a table of data that looks like the following table.

Class Average for Each Criterion

	Store	Mix	Dough	Scratch
Cost	3	4	2	5
Time	5	4	4	3
Nutrition	3	3	3	4
Convenience	5	4	4	3
Enjoyment	3	3	2	4
Quality	3	3	2	5

Then, you might illustrate the data in a bar chart similar to the following:

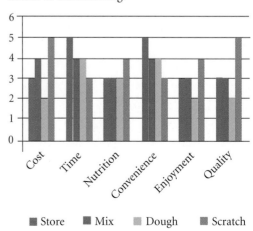

■ Store ■ Mix ▪ Dough ■ Scratch

Introduce the Section

This section provides an overview of kitchen equipment and when and how it is used. Information is provided on utensils such as cutting and measuring tools, types of appliances, and pots and pans.

Figure Focus

Ask students what kitchen equipment they use on a regular basis. Review some basic safety guidelines.

- Pots and pans should never have their handles sticking out where they can be knocked.

- Do not leave dish towels, paper towels, or other paper products near the open flame on a stove.

- Do not leave sharp knives and scissors lying out where small children can reach them; never put them in a dishpan filled with water; place them in the dishwasher blade down.

- Use a pair of oven mitts or potholders to handle hot dishes, not a dish towel.

- Place hot dishes on a potholder or trivet to avoid damage to countertops and tabletops.

- Properly clean and disinfect all kitchen equipment you use to avoid contamination and the spread of germs.

Vocabulary

Utensils or smallware: Hand tools used in the kitchen. These include cutting tools; mixing tools; cooking tools; straining, draining, and processing tools; and measuring tools.

STUDENT ACTIVITY

Ask students to find a tool or gadget in their kitchen at home that they've never used and are not familiar with. Ask the class to provide ideas on what the item could be used for. You might allow students to search sites, such as The Cook's Thesaurus at www.foodsubs.com/FGEquip.html, which lists kitchen tools and equipment by category and includes photos.

Identifying Basic Kitchen Equipment

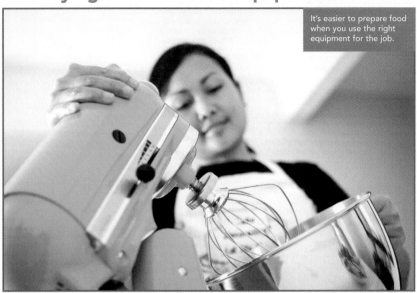

It's easier to prepare food when you use the right equipment for the job.

Have you ever tried to cut a tomato using a butter knife? How about blend a smoothie with a spoon? Kitchen equipment comes in all shapes and sizes.

- There is large equipment, such as a refrigerator or a dishwasher.
- There is small equipment such as a knife or a whisk.
- Some equipment is high tech—such as a microwave or a convection oven for baking and roasting.
- Some is very low-tech, such as a colander for straining pasta.

When you can identify the equipment in your kitchen, you are able to choose the best resource to accomplish the task at hand.

Utensils

Hand tools that you use in the kitchen are called **utensils**, or **smallware**. You use utensils such as forks, knives, and spoons to eat and to prepare food. Some categories of utensils include:

- *Cutting tools*, such as a vegetable peeler, apple corer, scissors, and garlic press
- *Mixing tools*, such as a whisk, spatula, and spoon
- *Cooking tools*, such as tongs, skimmer, and a long-handled fork
- *Straining, draining, and processing tools*, such as a colander, sieve, and a funnel
- *Measuring tools* such as a scale, thermometer, measuring cups, mixing bowls, and measuring spoons

Cutting Tools:	Mixing Tools:	Cooking Tools:	Straining Tools:	Measuring Tools:

Large Equipment

Your kitchen has large equipment and appliances including a refrigerator, oven, and stove-top or range. You might have a dishwasher and a trash compactor, too.

- A refrigerator keeps food cold. Yours may have special features, such as a water dispenser, or built-in freezer with an automatic ice-maker.
- A dishwasher cleans and sanitizes dishes and glassware, and sometimes pots and pans, using high heat and detergent.
- You use an oven to bake, broil, or roast food. Some ovens have a stove-top with burners for heating food in pots and pans. There are three basic types of ovens:
  - A conventional oven uses electric or gas heat to increase the temperature from the bottom up. It may have a broiler for applying heat from the top down.
  - A convection oven uses fans to circulate the hot air in the oven, so the food cooks more evenly. Convection ovens cook food a bit faster than conventional ovens.
  - A microwave oven uses microwave radiation to cook food. Microwave ovens cook much faster than conventional and convection ovens. When you cook in a microwave oven, be sure to use a microwave-safe plate. Never put anything with metal on it—such as an aluminum pie plate or metal mixing bowl—in the microwave or you may start a fire, ruin the microwave, or both.

Pots and Pans

Cookware is another name for pots and pans, the containers you use to hold food while you cook it in the oven or on the stove-top. What's the difference between a pot and a pan? A **pot** is typically deep with straight sides and two handles. A **pan** is shallower and has curved sides and a single handle. Pans include most cookware that goes in the oven. Pots include most cookware that goes on the stove-top.

When you are choosing a piece of cookware for a task, consider the following:

- *Size.* The food should fit comfortably without crowding. Make sure there's space so liquid doesn't overflow. For stove top cooking make sure the pan is the right size for the burner. Too small might cause a fire and too large will not get good heat distribution.
- *Material.* Cookware comes in a variety of metals, including stainless steel, cast iron, aluminum, and glass. Handles come in different materials, such as plastic or silicone. A plastic handle will melt in a hot oven.
- *Coating.* Some pots and pans have a nonstick coating that prevents the food from sticking. Some recipes and cooking techniques call for nonstick pans; others require a pan without a coating. Note that a pan with coating will last longer if you use non-abrasive utensils and cleaners.
- *Heat tolerance.* Some cookware can withstand high heat and can be used in an oven. Some can only be used on the stove-top. Some are designed for use in the oven, and might break or warp if you use them on the stove-top.
- *Side shape.* Some cooking techniques work best in a pan with sloped sides, such as a wok. Others work better in straight-sided pots or pans.

What's the Difference Between a Mixer and a Blender?

An appliance is an electrical or mechanical device that you use to accomplish a specific task. In the kitchen, you use appliances for everything from making coffee and opening cans to toasting bagels and blending smoothies. Some common small kitchen appliances include the following.

✔ *Food processor has interchangeable blades for shredding, chopping, and slicing.*

✔ *Mixer has a bowl with beaters or other attachments for mixing and blending batters, dough, and other combinations of food.*

✔ *Blender has a fixed blade for mixing, chopping, and liquefying.*

✔ *Toaster has heating coils for toasting one or both sides of toast and other items.*

✔ *Toaster oven can be used for toasting, baking, or broiling.*

TECH CONNECT

The kitchen is full of technology, such as microwave and convection ovens, that makes cooking faster and easier.

Automatic appliances with timers add convenience to everyday tasks such as making coffee. Methods for processing and preserving food have improved convenience foods so they are easier to store and cook, tastier, and more nutritious.

Use the Internet to research a technology that has had an impact in the way we prepare food. Create a presentation about the technology including pictures and deliver it to your class.

Vocabulary

Cookware: Containers used to hold food that is cooked in the oven or on the stove-top.

Pan: Cooking container that is shallower and has curved sides and a single handle.

Pot: Cooking container that is typically deep with straight sides and two handles.

What's the Difference Between a Mixer and a Blender?

Discuss the differences between food processors, blenders, and mixers, and when to use each. A food processor has interchangeable blades and is ideal for foods in which you'd like to maintain texture, such as salsas, smoothies, and pie dough. Blenders have only a single blade but different settings. They are ideal for pureeing foods and chopping ice. Mixers are suitable for mixing batters and dough for baking. Quality food processors typically cost $200 plus; blenders run about $100 or more; and mixers are between $35 and $60.

TECH CONNECT

Students are to research a technology that has impacted the way we prepare food. They are to create a presentation they will deliver to the class. Make sure students' presentations include information on energy-saving or "green" features of the technology.

Customized Instruction: Special Needs Students

Students may be willing to discuss modifications made to their kitchens at home that provide easier access, mobility, and use of kitchen equipment; for example, varied heights of kitchen counters, sinks, and appliances; oven doors that open sideways instead of down; water taps with levers or no-touch infrared controls; talking thermometers and microwaves; and frying pans with Braille controls.

End-of-Chapter Activities

Case Study

Answers will vary. The girls should not complain, but could discuss their opinions with their mother. They should calmly and politely explain that they are tired of eating convenience foods and simple meals such as cereal and eggs.

Their mother is leaving a variety of foods, but she is not including fresh fruit and vegetables.

She could leave fresh fruit and vegetables. She could also prepare a meal such as a soup or casserole ahead of time that the girls could reheat in the microwave. She could leave salads that the girls could just add dressing to. They could look for simple, easy-to-prepare recipes together. She could practice the recipes with the girls on days she is not working, so she would feel comfortable about their safety when she is not around. She could also look for more nutritious and varied prepared or convenience foods. They might cost a little more, but it might be worth it for her peace of mind.

Sounding Off!

Student answers will vary.

FAQ

1. A recipe is a written set of directions for making a certain dish.

2. The recipe yield is the measured output, such as the number of servings, or the serving size.

3. Ingredients include flour, sugar, rice, baking powder, baking soda, and corn starch. Students may think of others.

4. Ingredients include water, milk, oil, juice, and vinegar. Students may think of others.

5. You could substitute 1 cup of applesauce.

6. Examples of moist heat methods of cooking are braising, poaching, stewing, steaming, and boiling.

7. Examples of dry heat methods of cooking are grilling, frying, broiling, roasting, and baking.

8. Foods that are full of protein include meat, fish, poultry, legumes, and eggs.

9. Dairy products include milk, yogurt, cream, cheese, ice cream, and butter. Students may think of others.

10. A garnish is an edible ingredient that adds color, flavor, and texture to a dish. You would use one to make a dish more appealing. You can top a dessert with mint leaves or place a lemon twist on a dish of sorbet.

Case Study

Sasha's mother recently accepted a job where she has to work the evening shift three days a week. On those days, Sasha is responsible for preparing dinner for herself and her younger sister.

Sasha's mom doesn't want to worry about Sasha having a cooking accident when she is not around. She stocked the freezer with pizza and hot dogs. She bought boxes of macaroni and cheese dinners, and keeps milk, cereal, and eggs in the house at all times. She thinks this should be enough to get the girls through the nights when she is not home.

After two weeks, Sasha's sister starts to complain about the dinners.
- Do you think the girls are right to complain?
- Do you think the meals their mother leaves are healthy and well-balanced?
- Can you think of a ways she could provide a wider variety of foods without worrying about their safety in the kitchen?

Sounding Off!

1. Who does the cooking and cleaning up in your house? Is one person responsible or are the tasks shared? Is the system fair?

2. What's your favorite meal? Why?

FAQ

1. What is a recipe?
2. What is recipe yield?
3. List two ingredients you would measure using a dry measuring cup.
4. List two ingredients you would measure using a liquid measuring cup.
5. What could you substitute for 1 cup of butter to lower the fat in a cake recipe?
6. List five examples of moist heat methods of cooking.
7. List five examples of dry heat methods of cooking.
8. List four types of food that are full of protein.
9. List four dairy products.
10. What is a garnish and why would you use one?

A small but growing number of people believe that drinking **raw milk**—which is unpasteurized—from grass-fed cows is healthier than drinking pasteurized milk. For safety reasons, however, the Food and Drug Administration (FDA) advises consumers to use only pasteurized milk and dairy products.

Divide the class into teams of four. Research the topic of raw milk to discover why some people think it is beneficial and some people think it is dangerous. After completing the research, select either a pro viewpoint in favor of drinking raw milk or a con viewpoint against drinking raw milk. Conduct a debate in class between the two sides. Classmates who watch the debate can select a winner.

Hot Topics

Do you like to cook? Do you wish you never had to set foot in a kitchen? Do you think cooking is a waste of time? Do you wish you had more opportunity to try new recipes?

Take this opportunity to write anonymously about your feelings about cooking. Use a word processor so no one recognizes your handwriting. Be honest and open. Put the paper in the class Hot Topics box.

As a class, read the anonymous entries and discuss them.

Web Extra ▼

Many Web sites provide recipes for free. Some—such as www.epicurious.com—collect recipes from various magazines and other Web sites, and some—such as www.allrecipes.com—let readers submit their own recipes to share.

Use the Internet to locate some recipe sites. Test a few recipes to see if they might be useful for your peers. Make a directory of the sites, including the Web site address and a brief description. Post the directory on your school Web site or in your school career center or library.

Problem Solver

A friend needs your help planning a dinner menu. He is serving broiled salmon as the main dish, with a tossed salad. He wants to serve potatoes as a side dish but is not sure how to prepare them. One of his guests is on a low-fat diet due to heart disease. Use cookbooks, magazines, and the Internet to locate a selection of heart friendly potato recipes. Make a booklet that includes at least four potato recipes, along with nutritional information, and a brief explanation of why the recipe is suitable for someone on a low-fat diet.

Team Players

Divide the class into four teams. Each is to research the benefits and drawbacks of raw milk. Once the teams have completed their research, they are to choose a viewpoint. If you find that all the teams have the same viewpoint, then encourage two of them to argue the other viewpoint. The teams can select a person or two to debate the issue.

Some people think raw milk is beneficial because:

- It contains all the essential amino acids.
- It is a rich source of calcium.
- It contains vitamins, including A, B, and C.
- It contains enzymes and antibodies that make milk less susceptible to harmful bacteria.
- Farmers who supply raw milk tend to take better care of their animals and rarely use hormones and chemicals.

It is thought to be dangerous because:

- There is no scientific evidence to back up the claims of raw milk's health benefits.
- There are risks of infection from *Salmonella*, *E. coli*, and *Listeria* bacteria and the number of reported illnesses stemming from unpasteurized milk is on the rise.
- It is very low in vitamin D; pasteurized milk is fortified with this vitamin.

Hot Topics

Make sure students understand that they can turn in their papers anonymously. Encourage them to be open and honest about their feelings about cooking.

Web Extra

Students are to create a directory of Web sites that provide recipes for free. The directory should include the Web site address and a brief description of the site.

Remind students that a reliable Web site usually publishes the name of the author or organization that sponsors it and the date the content was created or last updated in a fairly obvious location, such as at the top or bottom of the page or on the home page. The site is usually organized with headings and an obvious navigation system. A reliable site clearly states its purpose and any affiliations. You should also look for accuracy in spelling and grammar.

Students should post the directory in their school career center or library.

Problem Solver

Students are to develop a booklet containing a minimum of four potato recipes that are suitable for someone on a low-fat diet. Students should search for recipes that combine potatoes with other low-fat ingredients, such as skim milk, low-fat cheese, and fat-free sour cream and yogurt.

Write Now

Students are to write a persuasive essay on their favorite breakfast cereal. Review with students the components of a persuasive essay. It has an introduction that states the topic and grabs the reader's attention; a body consisting of at least three paragraphs in which the argument is developed; and a conclusion that restates what the reader is to believe.

Be Involved!

As a class, students are to plan a project that combines food preparation with fund raising. You might have students check out the Share Our Strength® organization's Great American Bake Sale at http://gabs.strength.org, which uses bake sales to raise money to feed the hungry.

Students are to use the FCCLA planning process outlined below to develop, execute, and evaluate their efforts.

- Identify the project.
- Set a goal.
- Form a plan (who, what, when, where, how, cost, resources, and evaluation).
- Act.
- Follow up.

Remind students that a successful team relationship depends on all team members working together. Make sure they take steps to delegate responsibilities, communicate effectively, and manage conflicts or disagreements.

Social Networking

Students are to visit a senior center or nursing home to find out what elderly people consider their "comfort" foods. If possible, students should find recipes for the comfort foods and assemble a cookbook to give to the centers or homes they visited.

Write Now

What's your favorite breakfast cereal? Why? Write a persuasive essay to convince your classmates that they should choose your favorite cereal, too. Include information about the cost, the nutritional value, the ingredients, and the taste.

Be Involved!

www.fcclainc.org

As a class, use the FCCLA planning process to plan a project that combines food preparation with fund raising. Start by brainstorming project ideas. You might consider a bake sale to raise money for FCCLA activities or a cake auction to raise money for a community organization in your area, or you might run a food concession at a school event to benefit a student activities fund.

Consider how much money you will have to spend on each possible event, and whether you have the resources available for it. Will you have to pay for anything up front? Do you need to rent a space to hold the event? After considering all possible options, select the event that you think will be the best one for achieving your goal.

Make an action plan for achieving your goal. Include a timeframe, make sure the plan is realistic and attainable, and then put the plan into action. You may want to organize teams within the class to handle specific responsibilities, such as volunteer management and publicity.

As you work toward your goal, keep a class journal to record your progress, and collect documentation that you can use to show what you have achieved. After the fundraising event, evaluate your success. Did you raise as much money as you expected? Was your budget accurate? Prepare an article about the event and send it to the school or community newspaper. You might also want to send it to your FCCLA chapter so they can publish it in their newsletter.

Social Networking

Comfort foods are basic, familiar dishes such as soups and casseroles that give diners a sense of warmth and wellbeing. Comfort food may help cheer up people who are lonely or sad. Organize a visit to a senior center or nursing home. Ask the residents about their favorite recipes and comfort foods. If possible, after the visit look up recipes for the foods they discusses, and make a "Comfort Food" cookbook.

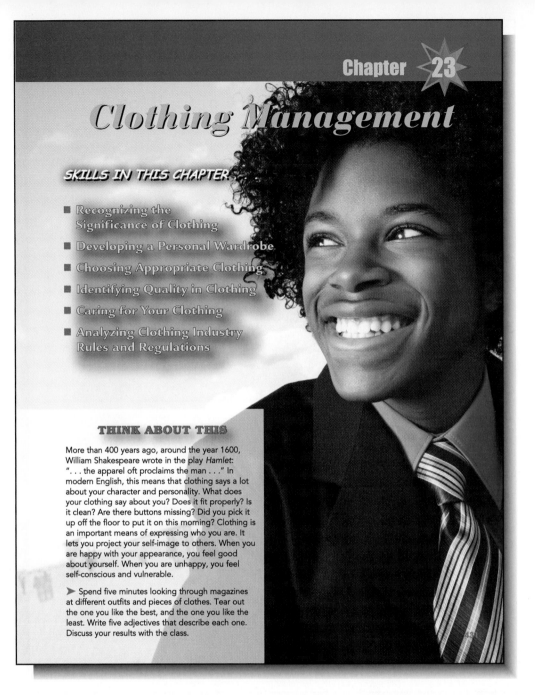

Chapter 23
Clothing Management

SKILLS IN THIS CHAPTER . . .

- Recognizing the Significance of Clothing
- Developing a Personal Wardrobe
- Choosing Appropriate Clothing
- Identifying Quality in Clothing
- Caring for Your Clothing
- Analyzing Clothing Industry Rules and Regulations

THINK ABOUT THIS

More than 400 years ago, around the year 1600, William Shakespeare wrote in the play *Hamlet*: ". . . the apparel oft proclaims the man . . ." In modern English, this means that clothing says a lot about your character and personality. What does your clothing say about you? Does it fit properly? Is it clean? Are there buttons missing? Did you pick it up off the floor to put it on this morning? Clothing is an important means of expressing who you are. It lets you project your self-image to others. When you are happy with your appearance, you feel good about yourself. When you are unhappy, you feel self-conscious and vulnerable.

➤ Spend five minutes looking through magazines at different outfits and pieces of clothes. Tear out the one you like the best, and the one you like the least. Write five adjectives that describe each one. Discuss your results with the class.

Chapter 23 Overview

This chapter provides an overview on clothing, a basic need that many people also use to make a personal statement and develop their self-image. It identifies the factors that influence clothing decisions. It also provides tips on choosing appropriate clothing pieces and caring for clothing.

Recognizing the Significance of Clothing This section discusses the factors that can influence your clothing choices. These include wants, values, standards, and the different roles you play.

Developing a Personal Wardrobe Students learn how to manage their clothing resources and determine how to make wise decisions based on their clothing needs.

Choosing Appropriate Clothing The decision-making process is an important tool for selecting and buying clothing. A good first step in shopping for clothing is making a shopping plan.

Identifying Quality in Clothing Students learn how to identify quality in the fabric type, construction, and label information of clothing.

Caring for Your Clothing In this section, students learn the importance of reading the care instructions on clothing labels. Information also is provided on different laundry products and storage requirements for clothing.

Analyzing Clothing Industry Rules and Regulations There are many rules and regulations governing the textile and garment industry. This section takes a look at those for textile and garment labeling, care, and flammability.

Focus and Engage

Bell-Ringer: Think About This

Students are to tear out a picture from a magazine of an outfit they like and one they don't like. Then they are to write down five adjectives that describe each outfit.

Ask students to discuss how their clothing can emphasize their different roles, values, financial standards, and overall well-being. Ask how peer pressure influences their clothing choices. Do they feel pressure to keep up or stay ahead of fashion trends? Does clothing represent a significant portion of their spending? It can be expensive (and exhausting) to keep up with the latest styles. Explain the logic behind choosing conventional pieces of clothing that withstand changing trends and styles. For example, consider popular styles in the 1950s: Girls wore blouses, cardigans, and jeans; boys wore jeans, white t-shirts, and leather jackets. Both styles have survived through the decades and are still being worn today.

ADVANCE PREPARATION

Review	*Life Skills for the 21st Century* textbook, Chapter 23.
Prepare	Students will need paper and pencil for some activities.
	Magazines and advertisements from which students can tear pictures.
	Box labeled "Hot Topics."

CUSTOMIZED INSTRUCTION OVERVIEW

Less Advanced Students	More Advanced Students	ESOL Students	Special Needs Students	At-Risk Students
Pages 434, 436, 447	Page 440	Pages 438, 447	Page 436,	Pages 434, 438

Introduce the Section

This section discusses the factors that can influence your clothing choices. These include wants, values, standards, and the different roles you play. Students also learn how clothing can impact first impressions.

Figure Focus

Recent studies show that girls are more active shoppers than boys; however, both genders are more clothes-conscious than previous generations. Many believe the teenage years are for pushing limits and finding ways to make a personal statement. Many schools, however, have found it necessary to rein in some of the more flamboyant clothing and accessories that students use in making their personal statements. Ask students to share comments on the benefits and drawbacks of a school dress code.

Clothing Needs vs. Wants

Remind students that a need is something you cannot live without. It is instrumental to well-being.

A want is something you desire. On the surface, it might **appear** to be instrumental to well-being but in reality, it only enhances well-being. When you are out shopping, you must use decision-making skills to determine the difference between them. Following are some simple questions you can ask yourself to help you identify clothing you need vs. clothing you want.

- Can I live without this?
- Would it be OK to wait?
- Can I buy it cheaper elsewhere?
- Is there a less-expensive alternative that will serve me just as well?
- Am I buying this for me or competing with someone else?

Recognizing the Significance of Clothing

Clothing is a basic need that also lets you make a personal statement.

How much time do you spend thinking about what you are going to wear? Do you choose a shirt because of the color? Because the fabric is warm in winter or cool in summer? Because it's easy to keep clean?

Your clothing is a resource that helps you meet your needs and wants, make a personal statement, and develop self-esteem.

- Clothing fulfills a basic need. It protects you from the sun, wind, cold, and rain.
- Clothing reflects your values and standards. You use it to express your character and your individuality.
- Clothing helps you associate with your different roles in life. You can dress like your friends in order to fit in, or wear a uniform to school or work.

When you recognize the significance of clothing, you are better able to make decisions about how to manage it as a resource in all the areas of your life.

Clothing Needs vs. Wants

Recall from Chapter 1 that a *need* is something you can't live without; a *want* is something you desire. Clothing is a basic need. It is also something you want.

- You need a jacket when it is cold outside.
- You want the jacket you saw your favorite performer wearing at the Teen Choice Awards.

Some people are satisfied with clothing that meets their basic needs. Your brother might pull a T-shirt and jeans out of the drawer each morning and head off to school. Most people want clothing that reflects their character and personality and projects an image.

Stay in School

According to a recent survey, 80 percent of teens said they consider education to be essential to future success. By contrast, surprisingly, only 56 percent of adults surveyed said they felt that education was essential to future success.

More and more young people are recognizing education as an important cornerstone of the coming-of-age process. According to the survey, 62 percent of teens aged 14 through 19 believe it is important to save their money for college.

Ask students for their input on the importance of higher education. How will it contribute to an individual's personal, physical, social, emotional, and intellectual well-being? Discuss how to set short-term goals related to gaining a higher education. Review the importance of a personal academic plan or personal career plan. You might invite your school counselor to discuss the components of this type of plan. These include:

- Goals beyond high school.
- Assessment of your skills, knowledge, and experience.
- Assessment of factors that will contribute to your success.
- Assessment of factors that might interfere with your success.
- Graduation requirements.
- Plan for achieving graduation.
- Plan for achieving goals beyond high school.

Finding Your Own Style

When you are young, your parents might select the clothing you wear. You want to be comfortable, but you don't think very much about style. **Style** is a particular look. It comes from the characteristics that make one **garment**—piece of clothing—or **accessory**—a nonessential item that you wear or carry, such as a belt, handbag, or scarf—different from another.

As you get older, you begin to notice that there are different styles of clothing. You see celebrities wearing the latest **fashion**—the current and most popular style of the moment. The kids at school all take on the latest **fad**—fashion that lasts for a very short amount of time. You develop likes and dislikes and start choosing clothes that you want, not just clothes that you need. The styles you choose are very personal.

- You might like peasant blouses, long skirts, and ballet flats.
- Your sister likes peasant blouses, but wears them with short skirts and boots.

You might be comfortable with one style, but you might want to try different styles. Your style might change when your values and standards change. You might have a different style for different areas of your life. For example, you might have a uniform for school, sweats for hanging around with your family, and the latest fashions for when you are with your friends.

Clothing Sends a Message

No matter what your style, the clothing you wear contributes to the first impression you make on others. Recall from Chapter 3 that a *first impression* is the opinion someone forms about you the first time you meet.

- When you dress in clean, neat clothing that fits correctly, you let others know you are responsible because you care for your things.
- Dirty, torn, or wrinkled clothes send the message that you don't value yourself, your appearance, or your possessions.

Fashion fades. Only style remains the same.
— Coco Chanel, French Designer

MONEY MADNE$$

A department store is running a sale of 15% off your entire purchase. You selected a shirt for $19.99, a pair of pants for $32.99, and a pair of boots for $89.99. What is the total cost before the discount? What is the total cost after the discount? How much do you save?

International Fashion

Most countries have costumes, or clothing, that *represent traditional cultures. For example, in Japan the* **kimono** *is the official costume. It is a long, patterned robe made of silk and tied with a sash called an obi. In Scotland, traditional clothing is made from a plaid fabric called a tartan, which is woven in a plaid that identifies a family, or clan. Tartan is used to make kilts (traditional dress of men and boys in the Scottish highlands worn by men) and plaids (sashes worn thrown over the shoulder).*

International costumes also usually include accessories, such as belts and shoes, and may include specific hairstyles or makeup.

Select a country and use the Internet to research its traditional costume or clothing. Investigate the history and influence factors. Determine whether the costume is worn by men, women, children, or all three. Prepare a presentation that includes illustrations, and deliver it to your class.

Accessorize!

Accessories are the extra items that help complete an outfit, such as shoes, belts, hats, gloves, jewelry, ties, and scarves. You can use accessories to change the style of an outfit or to make an outfit work for a different occasion. What if you have a white shirt and black pants that you like to wear a lot?

- ★ *Wear a tie to make the outfit more formal.*
- ★ *Use a scarf for a belt to add color and style.*
- ★ *Wear boots for a casual look.*
- ★ *Wear sandals for an even more casual look.*
- ★ *Wear delicate jewelry for a classic look.*
- ★ *Change to bold, clunky jewelry for a modern look.*

Can you think of other ways to use accessories to change or update your clothing?

Accessorize!

Other ways to use accessories to change or update your style include:

- Varying the ways you wear a scarf, such as folding a square scarf into a triangle and draping it over your chest or around your shoulders, tying it around your neck as a choker, or tying it around your wrist to wear as a bracelet.
- Incorporating trendy accessories, such as printed shoes, a bright clutch, colorful or textured stockings, or a unique hat.
- Transforming a shirt by cutting and sewing sleeves and necklines.
- Using layering, such as a cardigan or pullover sweater for cooler weather or different color tank tops or shirts under or over another shirt.
- Wearing colorful bands, ribbons, and scarves in your hair.

Vocabulary

Accessory: A nonessential item that you wear or carry, such as a belt, handbag, or scarf.

Fad: Fashion that lasts for a very short amount of time.

Fashion: The current and most popular style of the moment.

Garment: A piece of clothing.

Kimono: The official costume that represents the traditional culture of Japan.

Style: A particular look.

International Fashion

Students are to select a country and prepare a presentation about its traditional costume or clothing. As a prompt, you might discuss costumes or clothing associated with the United States. While we do not have an official national costume, Olympic athletes often wear cowboy costumes in opening and closing ceremonies. Discuss costumes representing regions of the United States. For example, elaborate hoop skirts are often symbolic of the South; cowboy hats and chaps represent Texas and the West; and hula skirts are often associated with the Hawaiian Islands.

"Quote Box"

Ask students to comment on the meaning of the quote from Coco Chanel. The implication is that "style" is a personal thing or the way you express yourself. Unlike fashions, it is not subject to the whims, tastes, and decisions of others. You might share the following information on Coco Chanel. She was born into poverty and lived seven years in an orphanage, where she learned the trade of seamstress. In the early 1900s, she got her start in the clothing business as a designer of hats. From there, she went on to sportswear. Chanel's trademark is clothing that projects comfort, confidence, and independence.

MONEY MADNE$$

The total cost before discount is:

$19.99 + $32.99 + 89.99 = $142.97

The cost after the discount is

$142.97 × .15 = $21.45

$142.97 − $21.45 = $121.52

You save $21.45.

Explain that a wardrobe analysis should take into consideration basic items that are always good to have on hand. These include:

- A suit for special occasions, job interviews, or a funeral.
- White blouses or button-down shirts to wear to more formal events.
- For girls, all-occasion black dress.
- For boys, all-occasion neutral sport jacket and tie.
- Jeans that are fitted and can be worn to school or to social events.
- Undergarments such as tanks, t-shirts, or camisoles.
- Black pants.
- Dress shoes or heels that can be worn for long periods of time.
- Tennis shoes to exercise or wear to school.
- Nice purse, wallet, or billfold.

Vocabulary

Personal wardrobe inventory: Managing your clothing resources by identifying the clothing and accessories you already own.

Wardrobe: All the clothing you own and wear.

What's Missing?

Discuss the "1, 2, 3" method for analyzing your clothes. Put clothing that you love and do not want to live without in the "1" pile. This pile is also for the items that are of the best quality and in good condition. Put functional and essential pieces, such as a white shirt or blouse, nice pants, professional wear, and undergarments in the "2" pile. Place items that you might have impulsively purchased and things you've worn for too long, or which have tears or stains that you cannot remove, in the "3" pile. You might have a fourth pile in which you put clothes you need, but only on certain occasions, such as for doing yard work, or when you lose that last ten pounds.

With the "1, 2, 3" method, you should seriously consider getting rid of most of the "3" pile. Then, determine what your "2" pile is missing. Analyze the "1" pile to determine the fashions that hold high value to you and which you might consider investing more money in.

Developing a Personal Wardrobe

Analyzing the clothing you own will help you make decisions about garments you need and garments you want.

Your **wardrobe** is all the clothes you own and wear. You change your wardrobe by acquiring new clothes and discarding clothes you don't wear anymore. What's in your wardrobe? Most people don't really know.

Managing your clothing resources starts with a **personal wardrobe inventory**. That means identifying the clothing and accessories you already own.

You can sort the items into categories to identify how useful and important they are. Then, you can donate, recycle, or throw away the garments that don't fit or that you don't need, and organize the remaining items so you get the best use from them. Finally, you will see what items you could acquire to complete your wardrobe.

The information you gain from a personal wardrobe inventory will help you make wise decisions about your clothing needs. You will be better prepared to develop a wardrobe that expresses your style and personality for all occasions.

What's Missing?

Analyzing the clothes you have lets you identify your *wardrobe gaps*—the articles of clothing missing from your wardrobe—and your *wardrobe overstock*—types of clothing you have too much of.

- You might have 25 T-shirts but only one pair of gym shorts.
- You might have five pairs of athletic shoes but no summer sandals.

You can donate the overstock to a charity, or have a clothing swap with your friends. When you shop for new clothes, you can consider the garments you already own. You know the types of garments you wear most often, and those that you rarely wear. You can buy items that enhance or coordinate with garments you already have, or that fill in the gaps.

Customized Instruction: Less Advanced/At-Risk Students

Using the photo of the five youths at the top of the page, have students select one of the kids pictured and describe on a piece of paper what they like or do not like about the clothes he or she is wearing.

What Clothes Do You Have?

It's time to count. The only way to find out what's in your wardrobe is to go through it piece by piece. Start by sorting garments and accessories into basic categories, such as shirts, sweaters, pants, and shoes. Next, sort each category into three groups:

- *It needs alteration or repair.* Can you fix it or recycle it into something else? You may be able to make a garment wearable by sewing on a button, stitching a seam, or removing a stain. Ask yourself if you have the skills, time, and interest to spend on the garment. Also consider the cost of repair. If you decide not to alter or repair it, you do not need to keep it. If it is in good condition, give it away. If not, throw it away.
- *I wear it a lot.* These are your favorite garments. They help you define your personal style. Ask yourself why you like to wear these items. You can use the information to make wise decisions when you look for new clothes.
- *I wear it rarely, or not at all.* Before you recycle these garments, think about why you don't wear these items. Are they uncomfortable? Did they go out of fashion? Do they no longer match your personal style? If you had a different **coordinate**—an item you could combine with the garment to make a new look or outfit—would you wear the garment more often?

What Clothes Do You Wear?

Do you wear the same outfit every day? Do you wear the same thing to exercise that you wear to the movies? You wear different clothes depending on your current role and the area of your life. Recognizing the reasons you wear certain garments, and how often you need an outfit, can help you set priorities for your personal wardrobe and choose clothing that is appropriate for the occasion.

- As a student, you might wear a uniform or clothes that meet a **dress code**—rules about what you can or cannot wear.
- Are you an employee? Again, you may need a uniform or specific clothing such as comfortable shoes if you work on your feet, a suit if you work in an office, or stylish clothes if you work in a boutique shop.
- Relaxing with your family, you might wear clothes that are comfortable, such as sweats or pajamas.
- When you do chores around the house, you might wear old clothes that you can get dirty.
- As an athlete, you might need a team uniform, or gear for a particular activity. What would you wear for a yoga class or for swimming?
- What do you wear on holidays or special occasions with your family? Are there socials or dances at school that require you to dress up? Do you need a suit and tie or a semi-formal dress? Is one outfit enough?
- You might need seasonal clothing—garments that you wear in one season but not in another, such as a ski parka for winter, or shorts for hot weather.

You can make a list of activities for which you need clothes, and compare it to your inventory. Analyzing the two lists can help you identify wardrobe gaps and overstocks.

What can you learn from identifying garments you bought but rarely wear?

Make Your Wardrobe Last

Clothing can be expensive. Here are some tips for making the most out of your wardrobe.

- ✓ *Take care of your clothes.*
- ✓ *Learn how to make alterations and repairs.*
- ✓ *Invest in good-quality items that will last.*
- ✓ *Invest in items that you can mix and match—wear in different combinations for variety.*
- ✓ *Wear the appropriate outfit for the occasion.*

Vocabulary

Coordinate: An item that can be combined with another garment to make a new look or outfit.
Dress code: Rules about what you can or can't wear.
Mix and match: Items that you can wear in different combinations for variety.

Figure Focus

Discuss with students what motivates them to make a clothing purchase. For example, was it on sale for next to nothing? Did it look good on the mannequin or model? Did you think you would buy something else to go with it but never got around to it? Did you convince yourself that it would fit properly once you lost a little weight? Identifying the reason you bought a piece of clothing can help you make more-informed decisions the next time you shop. Suggest the following tips:

- Price is important, but just because something is priced very inexpensively does not mean you should add it to your closet. Make sure it's something you will wear.
- Only buy clothes that don't gap, pull, or need to be altered before you wear them.
- Buy durable, easy-care fabrics.

Make Your Wardrobe Last

Discuss how impulsive buying can lead to a shorter lifespan for your clothing (or a shorter amount of time it appeals to you). Impulse buying is when you see something and buy it, without giving it any thought or consideration. Sometimes, it can be fun. But, other times, it might turn out to be a waste of time and money. Suggest the following tips for avoiding impulsive buying:

- Review your budget, including credit card and banking statements, so you have a clear and accurate understanding of how much you can afford to spend.
- Use your personal wardrobe inventory to identify exactly what you need and where you need to wear it.
- Stick to your plan and don't be tempted by deals such as, "buy two, get one free."
- Resist the urge to buy consolation items when you cannot find what you are looking for.
- Give yourself plenty of time to browse and shop so you can make sure the pieces fit and match correctly.
- Buy items that will be part of a specific outfit rather than random pieces that don't match anything in your closet.
- Buy the right size for yourself, even if you have to go up or down a size. Telling yourself that you will lose or gain weight is not practical.
- Check the labels to find out the cleaning instructions, the type of fabric, and the price before trying on something.
- Avoid buying anything before trying it on. It may fit differently even if you often buy from the same store and usually are a certain size and fit.

Introduce the Section

The decision-making process is an important tool for selecting and buying clothing. A good first step in shopping for clothing is making a shopping plan. This helps you recognize your shopping habits and also helps you stick to a budget.

Figure Focus

Discuss the popularity of celebrity clothing lines. In 2006, sales of celebrity-licensed products reached about $3.5 billion annually. While sales dipped during the recession, these lines are still big business. Specifically:

- Singer Jessica Simpson's collection, which includes items ranging from shoes to hair extensions, brought in $300 million in 2008.
- Hip-hop and rap artist Jay-Z's brand, Rocawear, earns about $700 million annually.
- Actresses Ashley and Mary-Kate Olsen run two successful fashion labels—in 2008, they earned $15 million from the businesses.

A Shopping Plan

Ask students to comment on the things that influence their spending decisions. Do they weigh the pros and cons or are they impulse buyers? Discuss how clothing is a form of self-expression. Ask students to name characteristics, qualities, and even interests that clothing can convey about a person. Some responses are:

- Wealth and social status
- Professionalism
- Confidence
- Mood
- Individuality
- Subcultures (gothic, preppy, jock, etc.)
- Political allegiances (liberal, conservative, green, etc.)
- Social causes

Choosing Appropriate Clothing

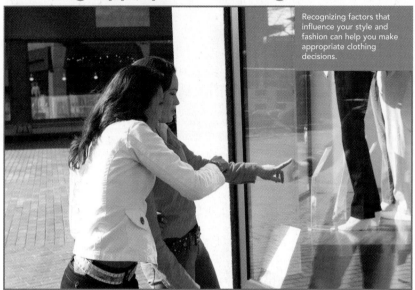

Recognizing factors that influence your style and fashion can help you make appropriate clothing decisions.

Selecting and buying clothing is an important decision.

- When you make a wise decision, you end up with an item that enhances your wardrobe. It makes you feel good when you wear it.
- When you make an unwise decision, the item ends up unused; taking up space at the back of your closet.

You might want to review Chapter 13, which covers making consumer decisions. You can apply the information to your clothing choices. Recognizing that you can use the decision-making process to choose new clothing and accessories can help you take control and manage your clothing responsibilities.

A Shopping Plan

A good first step in making wise clothing decisions is to have a shopping plan. A shopping plan includes:

- A budget for how much money you will spend
- The method of payment you will use
- Where you will shop
- What you will buy

Having a plan helps you avoid *impulse buys*—seeing something and buying it, without giving it any thought or consideration. Your parents or other adults can help you make a wise shopping plan.

Customized Instruction: Special Needs/Less Advanced Students

Ask students to interview their parents or grandparents to determine the types of clothing they wore during their teenage years. Have students prepare the questions in advance. They should ask about styles, costs, types of fabrics used, and places where they shopped most often. Have students summarize their interviews for the class.

Traditional Sources for Clothes

Where do you get your clothes? Do you shop online, use department stores, or enjoy the personal experience you get at a specialty store? Traditional sources for new clothes include department stores, discount stores, online stores, and specialty stores (refer to Chapter 13).

■ You might have a favorite store where the sales clerks know you, and you are always able to find something appropriate.

■ Your brother might prefer shopping online because he can easily compare prices without spending a lot of time.

■ Your friend might like to browse every store in the mall.

When you shop at a traditional source for new clothes, you usually feel confident you will find something appropriate that fits and looks good.

Nontraditional Sources for Clothes

Traditional clothing stores are certainly the most obvious place to look for new clothes and accessories. Have you ever considered an alternative source?

■ You might have a relative or friend who gives you **hand-me-downs**—garments that he or she no longer wears.

■ You and your friends might trade or swap clothes.

■ You might have the skills to make your own clothes and accessories.

■ You can shop in your own closet. Try a different combination of garments or accessories to create a new outfit or look using items you already own, or use sewing and design skills to embellish an existing garment.

"I wonder if anyone will recognize this old thing once I dress it up?"

Second-Hand Savings

Second-hand and consignment shops sell previously-owned clothes that are in good condition. What if you shop at a second-hand store?

★ *You might find designer clothes for a fraction of the original cost.*

★ *You might find one-of-a-kind items for a unique look or style.*

★ *You might find vintage accessories to give your wardrobe a retro look.*

★ *You might find fabrics you can recycle or alter to make your own designs.*

Why do you think it is important to try on and closely inspect second-hand clothing before you buy?

21st Century Skills

What Happens Next?

Lindsay was invited to her friend Camille's quinceanera party—a celebration of her 15th birthday. The party was scheduled for 6:30 Saturday night at a local restaurant. Lindsay had never been to a quinceanera party before, and she was not sure what to expect.

At noon on Saturday, Lindsay called Camille to ask what she should wear. Camille's brother said Camille was out getting her hair styled and nails polished. Lindsay called another friend, Elizabeth. Elizabeth said she had bought a new dress.

Lindsay started feeling nervous. She began looking through her closet to see what she had to wear. She hadn't worn her one party dress in almost six months. Lindsay pulled it out and saw right away that it had a big stain on the front. She ran downstairs, told her mother she did not want to go to the party, then went back to her room and slammed the door.

Can you identify areas where Lindsay made decisions that caused negative consequences? What problems and choices are facing her now? What life skills can she use to find solutions and make positive decisions going forward? Using your 21st Century Skills—such as decision making, goal setting, and problem solving—write an ending to the story. Read it to the class, or form a small group and present it as a skit.

Vocabulary

Hand-me-downs: Garments that a person no longer wears and gives to another person.

Figure Focus

Discuss vintage clothing. This term refers to clothing originating in an earlier era. While you can find authentic vintage clothing in second-hand stores or at garage sales and flea or antique markets, some designers are creating new clothes that look as if they're vintage. Vintage clothing has been popularized by celebrities, such as Julia Roberts and Kate Moss, and by the increased interest in environmental sustainability. Other reasons for its popularity are:

■ It is unique and sometimes a one-of-a-kind find.

■ Pieces tend to be made from good-quality fabric, which is one of the reasons they have lasted so long.

■ Likewise, many fabrics used are no longer being manufactured or are now more expensive to make.

■ Garments tend to be lower priced, even though they're high quality.

Second-Hand Savings

It is important to try on and inspect second-hand clothing before buying it because:

■ Sizing of older garments may differ from that of more contemporary ones.

■ You can determine the overall condition of the garment by closely inspecting the stitching of the seams, buttons and buttonholes, hems, and fabric quality.

■ You can identify the cleaning requirements and determine if any stains can be treated and removed.

21st Century Skills

What Happens Next?

Students are to prepare an ending to Lindsay's dilemma. Lindsay overreacted because of her fear of embarrassment over wearing the wrong outfit to the quinceanera. If she were to use her decision-making skills, she could sit down with her mother and go over her possible options and goals for the party. Her mother may be able to help remove the stain. Lindsay could also borrow a dress, buy a new dress, find out what another friend will be wearing, or research common outfits worn at a quinceanera party on the Internet to see if she might have an alternative outfit in her closet.

Figure Focus

Discuss the impact of fashion trends on clothing opinions. Explain that in general, a fashion trend is a simple cycle that lasts about a year. According to the American Marketing Association, a trend has the following phases:

1. **Distinctive phase.** This is the period following the item's introduction or first "public appearance" (for example, in a fashion show or worn by a celebrity on an awards show). The item is highly sought after.

2. **Emulation phase.** This is the period when everyone wants to be part of the trend. The item is seen frequently in the media and is often available in high-end retail stores only.

3. **Saturation phase.** During this period, the item is sold at lower prices and is widely available in all types of stores. It might also have many knock-offs at this point.

Why'd I Buy This?

Following are some options on what to do with something that you decide you don't need or want:

- Give the item to a local homeless shelter.
- Sell it to a second-hand store.
- If you still have the receipt and you have not worn the item, return it for a refund or exchange.

What do you think has the strongest influence on your clothing opinions?

Why'd I Buy This?

You spent money on a pair of shoes you never wear. How can you make sure you buy clothes that are useful and enhance your wardrobe?

- 👎 Buy a garment only because it is on sale
- 👎 Buy something without trying it on
- 👎 Buy a style that doesn't suit you
- 👎 Buy a garment that is not appropriate for any of your roles or activities
- 👍 Buy a garment that fills a gap in your wardrobe
- 👍 Buy something that fits well and is comfortable
- 👍 Buy a garment that coordinates with items you already own

What steps can you take if you buy something and then decide you don't really need or want it?

Clothing Influence Factors

Your opinions about style and clothing are influenced by many factors. Recall that an *influence* is something that affects the way you think and act. You might choose a style because you admire your classmates who wear it, or because it makes you feel like you fit in. Some common clothing influence factors include:

- *Your values.* Your choice of clothing is influenced by your personal values. Recall that *values* are things that are important to you. If you value fashion, you wear the latest styles. If you value comfort, you wear comfortable clothes.
- *Your friends and peers.* The way your friends and peers dress, and how they react to your clothing, have a strong impact on your choices. If your friends admire your outfit, you will feel confident when you wear it. Their opinions contribute to your positive self-image. If your peers tease you because of the clothes you wear, you might feel self-conscious and be influenced to try a different style.
- *The media.* Advertising and the media influence your clothing choices. You see styles and outfits in the pages of magazines and on television and the Internet. These ads make the people wearing the clothes look beautiful and happy, which appeals to you.
- *Celebrities.* Celebrities may wear the latest fashion, sell their own clothing brands, or adopt a personal style. You might like the image the celebrity projects, so you are influenced to wear the same styles.

Selecting Clothing, Part 1

What factors do you consider when you look for new clothes? Some people think only about style, and some only about cost. There are people who look for clothes only when they need a particular garment, and some who consider clothes shopping a hobby or social activity.

Here are some things to think about when you are selecting clothes.

- *Cost.* Is the item a good value? Clothing prices vary from store to store and from season to season. Unless you must have something immediately, take your time to compare prices at different stores and online. Look for coupons or sales that can save you money. (Read more about being a wise consumer in Chapter 13.)
- *Style.* Is the item an appropriate style that fits your personality? Fads such as plastic clogs are fun and fashionable, but spending too much money on fads that you wear for a short time is not wise. Some styles are **classic**, which means they do not change from year to year. When you choose a classic style, you can be confident you will be able to wear your clothes for a long time. A white shirt with blue jeans is a classic style. So is a blue blazer and khaki or gray slacks.
- *Quality.* Is the item well-made? Well-made items use a durable fabric. They have straight, smooth seams. Closures such as buttons and zippers are attached properly. Sometimes well-made items cost more, but they generally last longer, as well. If you buy an item of poor quality, it may rip or stain or lose its shape. Even if it is less expensive, it might not be worth the cost.

Customized Instruction: ESOL/At-Risk Students

In pairs, have students perform a mock shopping exercise for the class. Have one student act as the sales associate and the other as a customer. The student acting as the customer should ask three questions about concerns he or she has about the cost, quality, and fashion of a garment. The salesperson avoids answering the questions, focusing instead on persuading the customer to buy the garment. The goal of the exercise is to emphasize why you cannot always trust salespeople and should rely on your own values, instincts, and decision-making skills when making purchasing decisions.

Selecting Clothing, Part 2

Here are some other factors to consider when you are looking for new clothes.

- *Fit.* Does the item fit you? Even the least expensive garment in the store is not a good value if it doesn't fit properly. Try every item on before you buy it to make sure it is comfortable, fits properly, and looks good.
- *Age.* Does the garment make you look younger or older than you really are? Selecting clothing that is age-appropriate is always a wise decision. Age-appropriate means it was designed for someone your age, so the style, colors, and fabric suit you.
- *Occasion.* When will you wear the garment? Is it appropriate for school or work? Will you wear it for a special occasion or when you are out with friends on the weekend? Maybe the garment will fill a gap in your wardrobe?
- *Climate.* Do you live in an area that has seasonal weather? Is the garment suitable for the current season, or will you save it for a different season?

Six Steps to a New Shirt

Recall from Chapter 13 that you can use a six-step decision-making process to help you make buying decisions. Use the process when you are choosing new clothing.

- *Define your decision as a goal:* A job interview might be your goal; buying an appropriate shirt for the occasion might be the decision.
- *Consider all possible options:* Determine where you might be able to buy a new shirt. Also, consider other options that might help you meet your goal, such as borrowing a shirt, making a shirt, or wearing a shirt you already own.
- *Identify the consequences of each option:* Compare the costs and benefits of each option. Can you afford a new shirt? Will you wear it more than once? Does the borrowed shirt fit you well? Do you have the ability to make a shirt?
- *Select the best option:* When you have all the information, you can make your decision.
- *Make and implement a plan of action:* Take the steps necessary to make the purchase a reality.
- *Evaluate the decision, process, and outcome:* Did you use your resources wisely? Did you achieve your goal? Are there things you might have done differently? Are you satisfied with your purchase?

Job Search

Are you interested in fashion? Do you have talent for putting together an eye-catching outfit? Then a career in clothing management might be right for you. There are different areas within the industry, including retail, marketing, and merchandising. Jobs range from fashion consultant and retail sales, to personal shopper and window dresser. If you are entrepreneurial, you might run your own retail clothing store or a dry cleaner business.

Use the Internet, library, or your school's guidance resources to learn more about a career in clothing management. Select a job that appeals to you, and write a job description, including the educational requirements, career pathway, and potential salary range.

Should I Buy This?

Some questions to ask yourself before you select a garment:

✔ *Does it look good on?*

✔ *Does it fit?*

✔ *Is it comfortable?*

✔ *Can you afford it?*

✔ *When will you wear it?*

✔ *Does it coordinate with items in your wardrobe?*

✔ *Do you already have something similar?*

✔ *What are the care requirements?*

"Did I make a wise choice wearing shorts and sandals in the middle of winter?"

Introduce the Section

Students learn how to identify quality in the fabric type, construction, and label information of clothing.

Figure Focus

Discuss with students the designer and brand name fashions that are currently popular. Do they buy these clothes? What do they like about them? Stress the importance of comparing costs as well as quality when you buy clothes, regardless of who makes them. If designer clothing and brand names are important to you, consider the following advice:

- Designer clothing is often made for a slender frame and may not be sized by common standards.

- Search for designer garments in second-hand and consignment stores or find local designer factory stores or outlets.

- Research cheaper lines available in department stores that are designed by high-end fashion designers.

- Become familiar with designer item price ranges by looking at magazines and researching online.

- Make sure designer clothing is "wearable" and does not have complicated and costly cleaning and care requirements.

- You can buy high-quality clothing and accessories at some stores, even if they are not designer clothes.

Vocabulary

Construction: The way a garment is put together.

Brand Names

Discuss "knock-offs," which are unlicensed copies of something intended to be sold at a lower price than the original. Brand counterfeiting makes up 5 to 7 percent of global trade, or $450 to $550 billion. The most commonly counterfeited designer brands include Louis Vuitton, Kate Spade, Christian Dior, Prada, Gucci, and Burberry.

Identifying Quality in Clothing

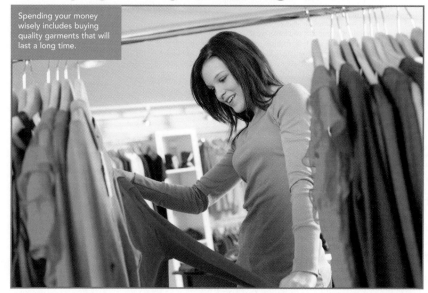

Spending your money wisely includes buying quality garments that will last a long time.

Have you heard the phrase "You get what you pay for"? It means that in general, you pay more for quality products. Sometimes, quality clothing and accessories cost more. They almost always last longer. Sometimes it may not be worth the extra expense. Is it necessary to spend a lot of money on a shirt you might wear for one special occasion, or that only coordinates with one pair of pants? Sometimes you may want to spend more for quality. For example, you may need a pair of shoes you want to last a long time.

To judge the quality of clothing, consider the following.

- Who is the manufacturer? Some manufacturers have a reputation for producing high-quality items.

- Is it made from quality fabric? There are many types of fabrics, and some last longer and wear better than others.

- Is the construction—the way the garment is put together—solid and technically correct? A well-constructed garment will fit better and last longer.

Recognizing quality in clothing will help you make wise decisions when you are looking for new garments and accessories.

Brand Names

Brand names, items made by a known manufacturer and associated with a particular logo or name, usually cost more, so many people assume that they are well-made. Brand names cost more because manufacturers spend money on promotion and advertising. For example, you are likely to pay more for athletic shoes made by Nike. Some people don't care if the products are well-made. They want the brand because of the image it reflects.

In clothing, some brand names are associated with a particular designer, such as Calvin Klein. Often designer products are well-made, because the designer has a reputation to uphold. If designer products do not last long, the designer's reputation will suffer.

Customized Instruction: More Advanced Students

Working in pairs, have students select a clothing item, such as jeans, and research the differences between a designer product and a knock-off. Students should analyze the differences and report back to the class about the distinctions, the downside of buying knock-offs, and penalties for selling knock-offs.

Fabric

Fabric—the material used to make a garment—has a lot to do with the quality. Some fabrics are more **durable**—they last longer. Some hold their shape better over time. Some are more suitable for a particular clothing style. Each fabric has positive and negative characteristics. Experience will help you recognize quality fabrics.

Fabrics are made from **fibers**, tiny strands that are twisted into yarn, which is woven or knit into fabric. Usually, higher quality fabrics use more yarn to create a tighter weave or knit.

- **Natural fibers** are made from plant and animal products. Cotton, linen, silk, bamboo, ramie, and wool are natural fibers.
- **Man-made fibers**, which are also called synthetic or manufactured, are made from materials such as wood pulp and chemical products such as coal, petroleum, and natural gas. Rayon, nylon, spandex, polyester, and polypropylene are types of man-made fibers. Usually, fabrics made from synthetic fibers cost less and require less care than natural fibers.
- A **blend** is when two or more types of fibers are combined.

A **finish** is a treatment or process that alters the appearance, feel, or performance of a fabric. Some finishes enhance the quality of the fabric, some affect the durability, and some affect the style.

- Dyeing and printing are finishes that change the color of the fabric.
- Waterproofing and permanent press change the performance.
- Polished cotton is finished with chemicals to appear shiny.
- Organdy—a type of thin, transparent cotton—is finished to be very crisp.

Read the Label

Every garment has a fiber content label required by federal law. The label shows:

- The percentage of each fiber in the garment
- The name of the manufacturer
- The country where the garment was made

You can use the information on the fiber content label to determine the quality of the product. For example, you might believe a product that has a higher percentage of natural fiber lasts longer and is more comfortable to wear. You might have purchased clothes made by a particular manufacturer in the past, and found them to be well-made. You may prefer clothes made in the United States to clothes made in Southeast Asia.

Construction

The way a garment is constructed indicates quality. A high-quality item will be well-stitched along all seams and hems. If a hem curls or puckers, the quality of construction is not very high. The zippers should be straight and even. They should move up and down easily, and not catch or snag on the fabric. Raw edges will be finished with binding or overcast stitching that prevents them from unraveling.

Well-constructed clothes are cut on the grain, which means that the threads run straight up and down and straight across. When the grain runs on a diagonal or slant (unless the garment is intentionally cut on the *bias*, or at an angle to the grain), it indicates a problem with the quality of the construction. Fabric in clothes that are off-grain is likely to pull to one side or the other, instead of hanging straight.

Did you ever have a pair of jeans where the leg twisted after you washed it? The fabric was off grain when the jeans were cut and sewn. During washing, the fabric tries to correct itself and ends up twisted.

Quality or Not?

Tips for checking garment quality:

✔ *Hold the fabric up to the light. A tight weave lets less light through than a loose weave.*

✔ *Patterns such as plaids should line up at the seams. If they don't, it indicates cheaper, or shoddy, construction.*

✔ *Check for loose or undone threads, ripped seams, or tears.*

✔ *If the fabric has beads or sequins, make sure they are securely attached.*

✔ *Verify that all the buttons are sewn on tight and buttonholes are well constructed and not unraveling.*

✔ *Crumple heavier fabric such as wool to see if it resists wrinkling. It should bounce back to its original condition.*

✔ *Turn the garment inside out to check the quality of construction on the inside. It should match the quality on the outside.*

✔ *Check the label on cotton and cotton blends to see if the item is pre-shrunk If not the fit and style may change with wash and care.*

Myth   Man-made fibers cost less than natural fibers.

Truth   Some man-made fibers cost less and some cost more. Factors such as fabric design, quality of fiber and manufacturing, exclusivity and type of fabric contribute to the cost of a fabric, and therefore to the cost of the garment made from the fabric.

Vocabulary

Blend: When two or more types of fibers are combined.

Durable: Fabrics that last longer.

Fabric: The material used to make a garment.

Fibers: Tiny strands that are twisted into yarn, which is woven or knit into fabrics.

Finish: Treatment or process that alters the appearance, feel, or performance of a fabric.

Man-made fibers: Synthetic or manufactured fibers.

Natural fibers: Fibers that are made from plant and animal products.

Quality or Not?

Additional tips for finding quality clothing include:

- Seams inside the garment should have little excess material at the sides. If there is excess material, the seams may easily rip out or stretch.
- Where possible, seam lines should blend with the pattern and grain of the fabric.
- Inconsistent coloring may indicate more color fading after washing.
- Well-made jackets should have lining throughout the entire interior.
- Jeans should have double stitching around the seams and stress points.

Myth/Truth

You might discuss synthetic fibers and their use in clothing. These are made artificially by chemical processes so as to resemble a natural product. Some scientists and interest groups believe the following fabrics may be detrimental to your health and the environment:

- Acrylic fabrics may be carcinogenic.
- Nylon and polyester are made from petrochemicals, which produce nitrous oxide, a greenhouse gas.
- Rayon is made from wood pulp that has been treated with chemicals.
- Dyes in fabrics can come from heavy metals and pollute waterways.
- Formaldehyde is often used for flame-retardant fabrics or to prevent wrinkles.

Introduce the Section

In this section, students learn the importance of reading the care instructions on clothing labels. Information also is provided on different laundry products and storage requirements for clothing.

Figure Focus

Review with students the definition of self-concept or self-image. It refers to the way you see yourself. It includes your physical appearance, as well as how you see your character, abilities, values, feelings, and beliefs. It also includes what you think other people see when they look at you.

Discuss how neat and clean clothing influences a person's self-image. Ask students why it is important to take pride in how their clothing looks. Some responses might include:

- It shows that you are conscientious and attentive to details, both of which are positive character qualities.
- You might receive better service.
- You will be taken more seriously.
- You will feel more confident and self-assured.
- It promotes good hygiene.

The Care Label

Care labels provide useful information, but they don't always tell you how to remove common stains from a garment. Discuss with students what kinds of things can easily stain their clothing; for example, ink, grass, mud, blood, and red or dark-colored foods and liquids. Then, ask students what methods they or their parents use to remove stains. For example, to remove a mustard stain:

1. Blot or sponge the stain immediately with cool water; do not rub it.
2. Gently work a mild detergent into the stain and scrub.
3. Rinse the garment in cool water.
4. Apply a laundry stain remover.

Caring for Your Clothing

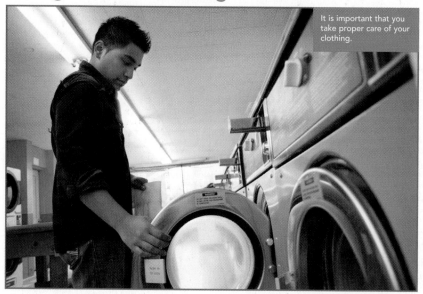

It is important that you take proper care of your clothing.

There is much more to looking your best than just knowing what to wear. You might buy expensive, high-quality garments, but you send a negative message about yourself by:

- Wearing clothes that are dirty or stained
- Wearing clothes that look like you slept in them
- Wearing clothes that are ripped at the seams or missing buttons

When you wear clothes that are clean, neat, and in good repair, you send the message that you respect yourself, that you value your appearance and image, and that you can assume responsibility for your belongings. Knowing how to care for your clothing means that not only will the garments be clean, but they will also continue to look their best, remain in good repair, and last for a long time.

The Care Label

Each garment requires specific care, depending on its fabric content. By law, every garment must have a care label that provides instructions on the type of cleaning, drying, and ironing methods to use to properly care for the item. (See the next section for more about rules and regulations.) Most care labels are sewn into the collar, side seam, or waistband of the garment. A new practice is to stamp the information directly on the fabric.

The care information may be written, shown with universal symbols—which are standard symbols used by all clothing manufacturers in the world—or both. (See page 443.)

Always check the care label before you wash a garment. If you do not use the recommended procedures, you might permanently damage the item. For example, if you wash and dry a sweater labeled *Dry Clean Only*, you are likely to shrink it. If you wash a pair of blue jeans labeled *Machine wash with like colors* with white socks, you may end up with blue socks.

Using a Washing Machine

Most of the time, you will use a washing machine to clean your clothes. Use the following guidelines to make sure your clothes come out clean and in good condition, and that you do not waste resources such as water and energy:

■ *Check the care label* to find out the recommended water temperature, wash cycle, and special instructions such as whether it is safe to use bleach.

■ Sort clothes according to the care labels. For example, put all clothes together that require the same water temperature, wash cycle, and special instructions—such as no bleach or color-safe bleach only.

■ *Empty all pockets.* Items left in a pocket, such as a pen or lipstick, can permanently damage clothes. Tissues tend to shred and stick to garments. A wash cycle is likely to ruin a wallet and anything made from paper. (Cash is 25% fiber, so it does not fall apart in the wash!)

■ *Pretreat stains* using a stain remover. Apply the stain remover directly to the stain as soon as possible, and leave it on according to the product directions.

■ *Set the water temperature.* Most clothing can be washed and rinsed in cold water, unless the care label states a specific temperature.

■ *Set the load size.* The load size sets the amount of water used. Using too much water is a waste of resources.

■ *Add the detergent.* Many detergents are concentrated, which means you only need a small amount. Check the directions on the detergent container, and use only the amount you need. Using too much may damage clothes if they do not rinse thoroughly.

■ *Add the clothes.* Make sure you add the amount that matches the load size you selected. Overloading the washer will prevent your clothes from getting clean.

■ *Start the cycle.* Choose the cycle that matches the care instructions, such as delicate or permanent press.

Drying and Ironing Your Clothes

Check the care label before putting your clothes into an automatic dryer. Some fabrics will shrink when they are exposed to heat, or even melt or lose their finish. Some items, such as sweaters and other knits, must be laid flat to dry so they do not lose their shape. All laundry can be dried on a clothesline, although it may be best to avoid direct sunlight. A clothesline saves energy.

Ironing removes wrinkles from fabric. Even permanent press and wrinkle-free garments usually need some ironing to make them look sharp and pressed. Check the care label to find out what temperature to use. Some fabrics may be damaged by an iron that is too hot, even melting onto the surface of the iron. Most irons have heat settings that correspond to fiber types. For example, a high setting might indicate use for cotton or linen.

Some common care symbols that you might see on labels, and their meanings.

Normal	Cool/Cold	Do Not Wash	Do Not Bleach	Iron Low
Hand Wash	Warm	Dry Clean	Dry Flat	Tumble Dry Low

Set a Clothing Care Schedule

Some clothing care should be done daily in order to keep your garments clean and in good repair. Some clothing care can be done less often. Use these guidelines to help you set up a clothing care schedule:

✔ *Daily   Check the clothes you wear for stains and damage. Treat stains and repair damage as soon as possible.*

✔ *Weekly   Do your standard laundry tasks, such as washing, drying, and ironing.*

✔ *Monthly   Take clothes to the dry cleaner.*

✔ *Seasonally   Rotate your wardrobe based on the season, making sure the items for the season that has ended are clean and properly stored. Check the items for the season that is starting to make sure they are clean and in good repair. Try them on for fit and style, and decide if you want to keep them or give them away.*

Discuss

Ask students why personal hygiene, clean clothing, and a neat appearance are required by many employers. Some responses include:

■ A messy appearance can signal you are unprepared or unable to manage all parts of your life.

■ Professional attire can give you additional confidence.

■ Tattoos and body piercings may signal difficulty in complying with rules and common practices.

Set a Clothing Care Schedule

Explain that a clothing care schedule should also include the proper sorting of clothes. If they are not properly sorted, clothing can fade onto other articles of clothing; it can become discolored; or it might be torn or snagged by hardware on other clothing. Tips for sorting include:

■ Sort clothing by color so that white, darks, and bright colors are separated.

■ Separate man-made fabrics such as polyester from natural fibers. Man-made fibers can attract the oils released from the natural ones during washing.

■ Wash dirty or heavily soiled items separately from lightly soiled clothing.

■ Separate delicate, loose-knit fabrics from heavier fabrics such as jeans and items with clasps, zippers, or other hardware that might snag delicate fabrics.

■ Keep clothing that produces lint, such as fleece and towels, separate.

■ Add a half cup of white vinegar to the initial washing of clothing to keep dyes from running.

Figure Focus

Clothing labels usually will provide guidelines on whether to dry and iron garments. Offer the following tips for drying and ironing clothing:

■ When taking items out of the washer, lightly shake them before placing them in the dryer.

■ Use the tumble dry or permanent press setting on the dryer for items that specify it in the directions.

■ Take delicates out while damp and immediately hang or fold them. Brush out wrinkles with your hands.

■ Keep the lint filter cleaned to decrease drying time and save money spent on electric and gas bills.

■ Keep the iron and ironing board clean to avoid permanently pressing dirt into clothing.

■ Do not iron clothing with dirt or stains on them because heat will set the stains.

■ Keep the iron constantly moving to avoid damaging fabrics.

Figure Focus

Dry cleaning is often necessary for garments that are difficult to wash, such as suits and delicate fabrics. But note that dry cleaning can sometimes damage garments or decrease their lifespan. Dry cleaning costs more because dry cleaners have overhead costs, such as purchasing and operating dry cleaning machinery, employees, and rent and utilities, that they pass on to the customer. You might discuss some techniques for washing clothes at home that can eliminate or minimize dry cleaning expenses.

- Hand-wash knits with a mild soap in warm water to guarantee the softness and quality of the fabric.

- Machine-wash and hang-dry dress shirts. If you are dry-cleaning, ask that the shirt be hand-ironed rather than machine-pressed and starched to extend the life of the garment.

- Dry clean suits only once a season and clean any stains or spots by hand-washing them with mild soap and warm water.

- Use a steamer to remove wrinkles and regain the original shape of clothing.

- Avoid using a dry cleaner if the clothes fit differently, look shiny, or have indents because of improper techniques.

It's Still Dirty!

Share this fact with students: Economists examined the impact that appearance had on a person's earnings and found that people with an above-average appearance tended to earn 5 percent more per hour than an average-looking person, while people with a below-average appearance earned 9 percent less per hour than an average-looking person.

Vocabulary

Dry cleaning: A special method that uses chemicals instead of water and detergent to remove dirt.

TECH CONNECT

Students are to research new fiber and fiber technology. Following are examples of man-made fibers:

- **GORE-TEX®** was engineered to be breathable in addition to being waterproof and windproof.

- **Kevlar** is a material that is five times stronger than the weight of steel, does not rust, and is used in bulletproof vests. The material also can be used in parachutes, boats, and vehicles.

- **Spandex** is an elastic fiber that is stretchy, stands up to frequent washing, and is used in undergarments and hosiery.

Why do you think dry cleaning costs more than washing clothes at home?

It's Still Dirty!

You washed your favorite shirt, but it still looks dirty. How can you make sure your clothes come out of the washer looking clean?

👎 Use the wrong water temperature

👎 Overload the washing machine

👎 Wash whites and colors together

👍 Follow the instructions on the care label

👍 Pretreat stains

👍 Use the appropriate laundry products, including detergent and bleach.

Why should you take care to wear clothes that look clean and neat?

Hand Washing

If a product is labeled Hand Wash Only, it will likely be damaged if you put it into the washing machine. Many delicate items such as undergarments, stockings, and clothing that includes delicate fabrics such as lace benefit from the care of hand washing.

You can wash items by hand in a large sink or tub. Follow the instructions on the detergent container, or use these guidelines.

1. Fill the container with warm water and mild detergent, and add the clothes.
2. Gently squeeze the soapy water through the garments without twisting. Let the garments soak according to the directions.
3. Drain the water from the container and refill it with clean water. Repeat until all the soap is rinsed from the garments.
4. Wrap the garment in a dry towel to remove excess water, and then hang it or lay it flat to dry.

Dry Cleaning

If a product is labeled Dry Clean Only, it may be damaged if you wash it in the washing machine or by hand. **Dry cleaning** is a special method that uses chemicals, instead of water and detergent, to remove dirt. It is done by a trained professional cleaner. Some dry cleaners use environmentally-friendly—or "green"—cleaning techniques that do not involve dangerous chemicals.

When you drop off your clothes at the dry cleaner, point out any stains and tell them whether you applied a stain remover. When you pick up the item, look it over carefully. If the stain is still there, they may be willing to try to clean it again, for free. Dry cleaning can be expensive. Before you purchase an item labeled Dry Clean Only, consider how often you will have to pay to have it cleaned. Some items you might clean once a year, such as a woolen winter coat. Some items you might clean more often, such as your favorite wool sweater.

Some people choose to have items such as men's shirts dry cleaned, even though shirts can usually be safely washed in a machine. They may prefer the way the item looks when it is professionally pressed, or they may not want to be bothered ironing it themselves. They consider the convenience of the dry cleaner to be worth the cost.

TECH CONNECT

From the spinning wheel and the loom to processes for creating man-made fibers from chemicals, technology has always had an impact on fabrics and clothing. One recent development is sun-protective clothing, which claims to block the sun's ultraviolet (UV) rays. Another new fiber claims to kill bacteria and prevent body odor.

Clothing made from these high-tech fibers is usually more expensive than similar garments without the protection. They may lose their protective quality over time, through washing and wear. Sun-protective clothing is usually more expensive than similar garments without the protection. It may lose its protective quality over time, through washing and wear.

Use the Internet to research new fibers such as these. What are the benefits? What are the drawbacks? Present your findings to the class.

Laundry Products

The store shelves are filled with laundry products. They come in every scent from fresh linen to spring air. Some claim to be **hypoallergenic**, which means they don't cause allergic reactions. Some detergents are designed for use in front-loading machines or high-capacity machines. Some fabric softeners are for the washer, and some for the dryer. The choice is dizzying. How do you know which one to use?

Use your consumer decision-making skills (Chapter 13) to analyze the cost of various products. You may also want to ask people you trust for recommendations or buy small sizes at first until you find a product you like.

Most laundry products can be classified into the following categories.

- *Soaps and detergents*: Soaps are natural products, whereas detergents are synthetic or man-made. Detergents are more common. Some detergents also include fabric softeners and bleach.
- *Bleaches*: Bleaches are used to whiten fabrics or to remove stains. There are two types of bleach: chlorine and oxygen. Chlorine bleach is the stronger of the two and is designed to remove color. Oxygen bleach, also called nonchlorine bleach, is safe for most fabrics, including colors.
- *Fabric softeners*: Fabric softeners can be purchased in either liquid form or in the form of dryer sheets. These products make clothes softer, and they help reduce wrinkles and static cling from drying.
- *Starches and fabric finishes*: These products are used to give body to fabrics. They also help the fabric resist stains and soil. These come in both liquids and sprays.

Storage

The floor of your room or closet is not the best place to store your clothes. Proper storage helps to prevent wrinkles and other damage, and can help your clothes last for a long time.

After you wear a garment, look it over. Treat stains with a spot remover and make repairs such as sewing on a loose button or stitching a torn hem or seam. Empty the pockets and remove accessories such as jewelry or belts. If the item needs cleaning, put it in a hamper or in the laundry room. If it is clean, store it properly so it will be ready when you need it again.

Here are some guidelines for storing your clothes properly.

- All clothes should be stored someplace dry.
- Hang items such as blouses, dresses, jackets, and pants on hangers. Take the time to empty the pockets, close zippers, and fasten buttons so the items hang straight.
- Fold items such as sweaters and store them flat in a drawer, on a shelf, or in a storage container.
- Clean and dry seasonal clothing when the season ends. For example, pack away winter clothes when warm weather approaches, and store your bathing suits and sandals when the summer ends.
- Clothes that are not worn frequently, such as special-occasion suits and dresses, can be covered in plastic to keep them from collecting dust.

Removing Stains

Here are some tips for removing common stains.

- ✔ *Blot or scrape carefully to remove as much of the stain as possible.*
- ✔ *Avoid using heat, including hot water, unless the stain remover indicates otherwise.*
- ✔ *Select a stain remover designed for the fabric type.*
- ✔ *If the stain causer contains grease, use detergent and warm water.*
- ✔ *Apply the stain remover from the back or inside of the fabric.*
- ✔ *Rub gently, and then rinse with cold water (except for grease).*
- ✔ *Allow the garment to air dry because the heat in the dryer can set the stain.*
- ✔ *Repeat until the stain is gone.*

Test **IT** Yourself!

Do you think stain removers really work? Try an experiment to find out. You will need five white cotton napkins or cloths; five packets of ketchup; and four types of stain remover, such as liquid laundry detergent, Spray 'N Wash®, Shout®, and OxiClean®.

1. Divide into five teams. Team 1 will be the control. The other four teams will each test a different stain remover to try to remove a ketchup stain from a cotton napkin.
2. Each team will use one ketchup packet to make one stain on its cotton napkin.
3. Once the napkin is stained, team 1 will wash its napkin without any other treatment.
4. The other teams will treat the ketchup stain according to the directions on the stain remover package.
5. Analyze the results. Compare the quality of the stain removal, the cost, and the ease of use of the different products. Which product would you want to have in your laundry room? Why do you think some products worked better than others? What other factors might influence the end result (for example, time or water temperature)?

Vocabulary

Hypoallergenic: Fibers that are designed to reduce or minimize an allergic response.

Removing Stains

You might also want to discuss tips for identifying and treating unexplained stains:

- Oil or grease stains may smell rancid but appear dry.
- Cosmetics can cause a rusty-looking stain, similar to those caused by tea, coffee, and caramel.
- Soak garments in cold water for at least 30 minutes to see if the stain lightens.
- Look for perspiration stains under arms and around collars.
- Keep stain removers, such as stain pens, odor eliminators, gels with fabric brushes, and bleach on-hand.

Test **IT** Yourself!

Discuss additional factors that might influence the end results of spot removal. These include how vigorously you rub the stain, the severity of the stain, and the color density and type of fabric. If students are concerned about using chemicals when removing stains, recommend the following natural stain removers:

- Use borax instead of bleach.
- Put moist salt on a small, damp coffee stain.
- Remove mildew with equal parts of vinegar and salt.
- Rub white chalk into an oil stain before laundering.
- Use baking soda to remove perspiration spots.
- Club soda, lemon juice, and salt are common spot removers.

Introduce the Section

There are many rules and regulations governing the textile and garment industry. This section takes a look at those for textile and garment labeling, care, and flammability.

Figure Focus

Discuss how product labeling rules and regulations on the clothing industry benefit consumers. Ask students if their purchasing decisions are influenced by such rules and regulations. For example, you might discuss the Fur Products Labeling Act. This act requires:

- Identification of the animal(s) from which the fur came.
- Identification of bleaches, dyes, or artificial colors applied to the fur.
- Explanation of the fur's composition; i.e., composed in whole or in part from paws, tails, bellies, or waste fur.
- The name or identification issued or registered by the Federal Trade Commission.
- The name of the country of origin.

Wool Product Labeling Act

Students may not know where wool comes from and the variety of animals it comes from. Some types of wool and the animals they come from include:

- Alpaca fleece comes from an alpaca, a long-haired South American animal of the camel family.
- Angora wool comes from an angora rabbit and is used for sweaters and mittens.
- Camel hair is from soft, fine fur from the undercoat of the camel. It can be used for coats or sportswear.
- Cashmere comes from cashmere goats. The soft hair is woven or knit into fibers.
- Vicuna is a soft fiber that comes from the vicuna, a rare, wild animal in the llama family.

Analyzing Clothing Industry Rules and Regulations

Knowing the rules and regulations that control the clothing industry can help you be a wise clothing consumer.

There are many rules and regulations that are related to the textile and garment industries. The Federal Trade Commission (FTC) is responsible for enforcing these rules and regulations, which are designed to protect consumers by preventing untruthful or unfair business practices. The rules and regulations are also designed to keep consumers informed about industry business practices.

Becoming aware of these rules and regulations can help you be an educated consumer of clothing and accessories. You will be better prepared to make wise clothing decisions.

Wool Product Labeling Act

Wool sometimes has other fibers added to it to make it less costly to produce, or to make it last longer. This act requires labeling that names the wool fiber content and source. Fibers from sheep, rabbits (angora), goats (angora, cashmere), and certain other animals can be classified as wool. The garment label must also include the country of origin. The FTC also categorizes the types of wool as follows:

- *Wool:* New wool or wool fibers coming from knit scraps, threads, etc.
- *Recycled wool:* Scraps of new wool or fibers that were felted, shredded, and used again to create fabric
- *Virgin wool:* Wool that has never been used in any way

Textile Fiber Products Identification Act

This act covers all fibers except wool. It does not require that a label be sewn into a garment, but the label must be available to the consumer when the article is purchased. The fiber content of a garment or article is required on the label and is often included as part of the care instructions.

The following information must be included in English on the label of most textile items, including towels, bedding, furniture coverings, and clothing.

- The percentage of each fiber, listed in order of weight, beginning with the fiber that comprises the largest amount.
- The name of the manufacturer, or the company's identification number.
- The first time a trademark appears on a label, it must be associated with the name of the family of fibers it comes from. For example, Kevlar is a trademarked name of a synthetic fabric.
- The country of origin, which means the country where the garment was finished.

Permanent Care Labeling Regulation

This law requires apparel and certain fabrics to provide a permanently attached label that provides care requirements such as washing instructions. These labels must be located where the consumer can find them. For example, many shirts have a label located at the center back of the neckline or along a side seam.

These care instructions can either be in writing or they can incorporate standard symbols. If a garment is made in another country and sold in the United States, it must also meet these care label requirements. There are exceptions to this rule for some items, such as fur garments, leather goods, and belts, which must be labeled with the type of animal source and the country of origin.

Flammability Fabrics Act

This act is designed to protect the consumer from materials that are dangerously flammable. It is overseen by the Consumer Product Safety Commission. Any children's sleepwear sizes 0–6x and 7–14 must meet these flammability standards. Also included in this act are carpets, rugs, mattresses, and mattress pads. There are voluntary standards for upholstered furniture.

N U M B E R S G A M E

Front-loading washing machines are supposed to save you money and be better for the environment because they use less water and energy than top-loading washers. On average, a front-loading washer uses about 45% less water than a top-loading washer. To calculate the difference, multiply the amount of water used by a top-loading machine by 45%, and then subtract the product. For example, if a top-loading washer uses 40 gallons of water per load:

$40 \times .45 = 18$ $40 - 18 = 22$

The front-loading washer uses 22 gallons per load.

On average, front-loading washers use about 55% less energy. If a top-loading washer uses 800 kWh per year, how much does a front-loading washer use?

$800 \times .55 = 440$ $800 - 440 = 360$

The front-loading washer uses 360 kWh per year.

You do the math: If a top-loading washer uses 32 gallons of water and 725 kWh of electricity per year, how much does a front-loading washer use?

Returning a Garment

Most—but not all—stores let you return a garment for a refund or store credit. Here are some guidelines for making a return successfully:

✔ *Read the store's return policy before you buy.*

✔ *Do not remove the store tags until you are certain you are keeping the garment.*

✔ *Do not wash or wear the garment until you are certain you are keeping it.*

✔ *Return the garment as soon as possible*

✔ *Take the garment and the receipt to the store.*

✔ *Go to customer service and politely explain why you want to make the return, and what you expect in terms of a refund or exchange.*

✔ *If there is a problem or defect, point it out when you return the garment.*

✔ *If you cause the problem or defect by improper care or cleaning, do not expect the store to accept the return.*

Returning a Garment

Discuss with students the irresponsibility of returning merchandise that has been used or damaged after the purchase. More than 50 percent of retailers say this is a common occurrence. Retailers must absorb the cost of damaged goods. This, in turn, makes their operating costs higher and forces them to either charge higher prices to consumers or cut costs elsewhere. In extreme cases, some companies are forced out of business, which has a negative effect on consumers because fewer stores mean less competition, which almost always results in higher prices.

Explain that recent data indicate "return fraud and abuse" costs the retail industry millions of dollars a year. Some retailers are implementing methods to identify "bad returners." These include development of abuser lists, exception reports, fraud detection computer systems, and video surveillance.

N U M B E R S G A M E

About 95 percent of the energy used in both the front-loading and top-loading washing machines comes from heating the water. While the front-loading washing machine uses less water, it may also be helpful to use hot water sparingly to save money. Always use cold water for the rinse cycle and try using warm water instead of hot water whenever possible. Front-loading may also be better for the lifespan of your clothing considering the front-loader gently tumbles your clothing instead of jerking it in a circular motion with an agitator.

The front-loading washer uses 17.6 gallons of water per load:

$32 \times .45 = 14.4$

$32 - 14.4 = 17.6$

It uses 396.26 kWh of electricity per year.

$725 \times .55 = 398.75$

$725 - 398.75 = 396.25$

End-of-Chapter Activities

Case Study

Aidan was influenced by his friend Paul. He was also influenced by the advertising of a clearance sale and by the brand name. Aidan ignored some pretty serious problems, including the fact that the shoes don't fit, and that it is a final sale. Aidan certainly did not make the best decision. He bought shoes that don't fit and that he cannot return. A pair at the department store fit just right and cost the right amount of money. If he didn't want that pair, he could have continued shopping to see if he could find a better-fitting pair someplace else.

Sounding Off!

Student answers will vary.

FAQ

1. A garment is a piece of clothing.

2. Accessories include belts, scarves, shoes, hats, gloves, jewelry, and ties. Students may think of others.

3. Fashion is the current and most popular style of the moment.

4. A fad is fashion that lasts for a very short amount of time.

5. A wardrobe is all the clothes you own and wear. (It is also a piece of furniture for storing clothing, similar to a closet.)

6. Nontraditional sources for clothes include swapping clothes with your friends, hand-me-downs, creating your own clothes, and shopping in your closet to create different combinations or accessories.

7. Factors that influence your choice of clothing are values, peer pressure, the media, celebrities, cost, style, quality, fit, age, occasion, and climate. Students may think of others.

8. Things to consider include construction, manufacturer, and fabric.

9. Natural fibers are made from plant and animal products. Man-made fibers, which are also called synthetic or manufactured, are made from materials such as wood pulp and chemical products such as coal, petroleum, and natural gas.

10. Ironing removes the wrinkles from the fabric.

Case Study

Aidan has two pairs of athletic shoes, a pair of dress shoes, and flip-flops. The weather is getting cooler, and he wants casual shoes to wear instead of his flip-flops. His dad gives him $50.00 and drops him at the mall with his friend, Paul.

Aidan starts shopping in a department store. There are two pairs of shoes that cost less than $50.00. He tries them on. One pair is too small, but the other pair fits just right. Paul says they aren't very stylish. The boys head to a shoe store that has a sign up advertising a clearance sale. On a rack marked "Final Sale," they see a brand-name pair of shoes in Aidan's size, marked down from $110.00 to $49.99. Aidan tries them on; they are just a bit too big. Paul says they look great—really cool. He thinks Aidan's feet will grow. Aidan buys the shoes.

- What influenced Aidan's decision to buy the shoes?
- What problems did Aidan ignore?
- Do you think Aidan made the best decision?

Sounding Off!

❶ What do you think about adults wearing clothes designed for teens or young adults? Is it a good idea?

❷ What is your opinion of some of the current clothing fads in your school?

1. What is a garment?
2. Give three examples of an accessory.
3. What is fashion?
4. What is a fad?
5. What is a wardrobe?
6. List four nontraditional sources for clothes.

7. List seven factors that influence your choice of clothing.
8. List three things to consider when assessing the quality of clothing.
9. What is the difference between natural and man-made fibers?
10. What is the purpose of ironing clothes?

Divide the class into teams of four or five. Each team should use the Internet—or examples from their own wardrobes— to identify fabrics that have different care labeling. Team members should then look through magazines or store advertising flyers to identify five garments that would require different methods of care. At least one garment should be Dry Clean Only.

As a team, make a chart comparing the steps, costs, and convenience of cleaning each of the five garments. Include information about the fabric and how care might affect the garment. Share your chart with the other teams.

Hot Topics

Are you happy with your personal style? Do you feel as if you fit in or stand out? Does your style make a positive impression on others? Do you feel as if your style does not reflect your personality?

Take this opportunity to write anonymously about your attitude toward your personal style, and the positive or negative affects it has on your self-esteem and well-being. Use a word processor so no one recognizes your handwriting. Be honest and open. Put the paper in the class Hot Topics box.

As a class, read the anonymous entries and discuss them.

```
Web Extra  ▼
```

Many Web sites that provide clothing and fabric care information, such as www.fabrics.net and www.fabriclink.com.

Use the Internet to locate some clothing and fabric care sites that you think might be useful for your peers. Make a directory of the sites, including the Web site address and a brief description. Post the directory on your school Web site or in your school career center or library.

Problem Solver

Your grandparents are celebrating their anniversary with a big family party. Your cousin texts you to say she is tired of wearing the same clothes to every party, but she has no money to buy something new. Can you think of ways you and your cousin might be able to work together to come up with new outfits without spending money? Use the problem-solving process to define the problem as a goal, and to come up with as many possible solutions as you can. Create a list of ideas you can text back to your cousin, and put a star next to the one you think would be the best. Explain your choice in writing.

Team Players

Teams will work together to research different care labels. These can be from their own wardrobe and the Internet. Then, they should look through magazines or store advertising flyers to identify five garments that require a different method of care, including one that should be dry-cleaned only. They should create a chart that illustrates and compares the steps, costs, and convenience of cleaning each of the five garments.

Hot Topics

Make sure students understand that they can turn in their papers anonymously. Encourage them to be open and honest about their personal style, whether they feel that they fit in, and what first impression they believe they make on others.

Web Extra

Students are to research fabric care Web sites and make a directory of them for their peers. The directory should include the Web site address and a brief description of the site.

Students should be wary of sites trying to sell products or that require a lengthy registration. Remind students that a reliable Web site usually publishes the name of the author or organization that sponsors it and the date the content was created or last updated in a fairly obvious location, such as at the top or bottom of the page or on the home page. The site is usually organized with headings and an obvious navigation system. A reliable site clearly states its purpose and any affiliations. You should also look for accuracy in spelling and grammar.

Students should post the directory in their school career center or library.

Problem Solver

Some ideas might include swapping clothes with her cousin or other friends, modifying old outfits with accessories, and shopping in her closet to come up with different combinations or ensembles.

Write Now

Students are to write an opinion essay on school dress codes and uniform policies. Review with students the components of an opinion essay. It has an introduction that states the writer's opinion on the topic; a body consisting of at least three paragraphs in which the writer supports his or her opinion with facts and details; and a conclusion that restates and summarizes the writer's opinion.

Be Involved!

Students are to use the FCCLA planning process to organize an event that would make clothing available to members of the community. The FCCLA planning process is:

- Identify the project.
- Set the goal.
- Form a plan.
- Act.
- Follow up.

Students can obtain more information on the FCCLA planning process from the organization's Web site, www.fcclainc.org, or by referring to *Appendix B: Joining a Career Technical Student Organization* starting on page 525 of the student text.

Social Networking

Students are to contact a community organization that sponsors activities that use fabric. If there is more than one organization in your community, you might split students into teams and have each team focus on a specific program. Students are to organize a collection of fabric remnants or swatches and deliver donated items to the organization.

Write Now

Does your school have a dress code or require students to wear uniforms? Do you think such rules controlling what students can and cannot wear in school are a good idea? Write an essay expressing your opinion on the topic. Consider the benefits and drawbacks of dress codes and uniforms in school. Consider situations when uniforms are standard, such as for sports teams or some employees. Use specific information to support your opinion.

Be Involved!

www.fcclainc.org

As a class, use the FCCLA planning process to organize an event that would make clothing available to members of your community. Set a goal and brainstorm projects and activities. You might sponsor a clothing drive for a specific purpose, such as to collect winter clothing, children's clothing, or jeans for teens. You might organize a Prom Swap where teens could exchange formal and semiformal clothes for school dances, or organize a sports swap where athletes could swap gear such as cleats, hockey skates, or dance shoes. After considering all possible options, select the project that you think will be the best one for achieving your goal.

Make an action plan for achieving your goal. Include a timeframe, make sure the plan is realistic and attainable, and then put the plan into action. You may want to organize teams within the class to handle specific responsibilities, such as volunteer management and publicity.

As you work toward your goal, keep a class journal to record your progress, and collect documentation that you can use to show what you have achieved. After the project is complete, evaluate your success. Did you achieve your goal? Were there things you could have done differently? Prepare an article about the event and send it to the school or community newspaper. You might also want to send it to your FCCLA chapter so they can publish it in their newsletter.

Social Networking

Many community organizations run activities that use fabric, such as quilting bees at senior centers or craft projects at a daycare center or women's shelter. Contact organizations in your area to find out if they welcome donations of fabric remnants or swatches. Then, sponsor a collection. You can ask students, teachers, and family members to bring in the fabrics, and you can also contact businesses in your area that might have fabric, such as a tailor shop or curtain store. Make sure the donated items are clean, and then deliver them to the organization in need.

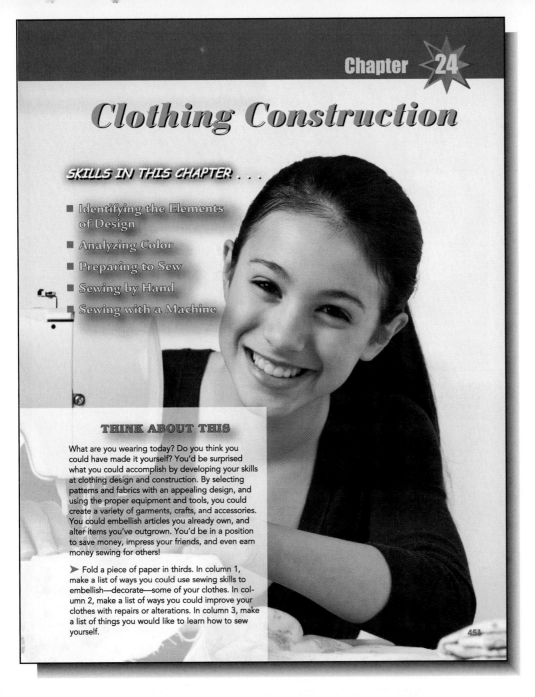

Chapter **24**

Clothing Construction

SKILLS IN THIS CHAPTER . . .

- Identifying the Elements of Design
- Analyzing Color
- Preparing to Sew
- Sewing by Hand
- Sewing with a Machine

THINK ABOUT THIS

What are you wearing today? Do you think you could have made it yourself? You'd be surprised what you could accomplish by developing your skills at clothing design and construction. By selecting patterns and fabrics with an appealing design, and using the proper equipment and tools, you could create a variety of garments, crafts, and accessories. You could embellish articles you already own, and alter items you've outgrown. You'd be in a position to save money, impress your friends, and even earn money sewing for others!

➤ Fold a piece of paper in thirds. In column 1, make a list of ways you could use sewing skills to embellish—decorate—some of your clothes. In column 2, make a list of ways you could improve your clothes with repairs or alterations. In column 3, make a list of things you would like to learn how to sew yourself.

451

ADVANCE PREPARATION

Review	*Life Skills for the 21st Century* textbook, Chapter 24.
Prepare	Paper and pencil for some activities.
	Markers or different color pencils.
	Poster board or plain white paper.
	Box labeled "Hot Topics."

CUSTOMIZED INSTRUCTION OVERVIEW

Less Advanced Students	More Advanced Students	ESOL Students	Special Needs Students	At-Risk Students
Pages 452, 455, 457, 459, 463	Page 454	Pages 452, 455	Pages 452, 455, 459, 463	Pages 452, 457

Chapter 24 Overview

This chapter provides an overview of designing, sewing, and constructing clothing. Students learn about the principles of design, basics of sewing, and techniques for embellishing and altering their clothing.

Identifying the Elements of Design This section defines the elements and principles of design. Students learn to identify the characteristics of clothing that lend to its quality and style.

Analyzing Color Most people rely heavily on color to help them choose the clothing they will buy or wear. This section discusses the characteristics of color and provides tips on selecting and mixing colors.

Preparing to Sew Being able to sew and alter your clothing is a valuable skill. This section provides an overview of sewing tools and techniques. Students also learn about patterns and types of fabrics and sewing notions.

Sewing by Hand Students learn the basic tools and equipment used for hand sewing. They also are introduced to types of stitches and are given tips on threading a needle and sewing on a button.

Sewing with a Machine The basic parts of a sewing machine are detailed in this section. It also covers the steps for using a sewing machine and how to take proper care of the machine.

Focus and Engage

Bell-Ringer: Think About This

Students are to fold a piece of paper in thirds so that it resembles a three-column table. In column 1, they are to list ways they could use sewing skills to embellish some of their clothes. In column 2, they are to list ways they could improve some of their clothes with repairs or alterations. In column 3, they are to list things they would like to learn to sew themselves.

If students need prompting for their column 1 items, you might suggest sewing decorative beads or appliqués on jackets or purses, replacing plain buttons on a shirt or blouse with fancier ones, or cutting off a pair of pants and hemming them to wear as shorts.

For the column 2 list, you might suggest hemming a pair of pants that are too long, letting the hem out of a pair of pants that are too short, or sewing a torn seam.

Introduce the Section

In this section, the elements and principles of design are defined. Students learn to identify the characteristics of clothing that lend to its quality and style.

Figure Focus

Explain that the basic elements of design are line, color, and texture. Other elements to consider in regards to clothing construction include shape and value. You might ask students to give definitions for each element.

- **Line:** Path between two points.
- **Color:** Property of an object that depends on the light it reflects.
- **Texture:** Actual or simulated tactile quality; feel of a surface.
- **Shape:** Form of something, or perceivable area.
- **Value:** Lightness and darkness of an object.

Vocabulary

Elements of design: Qualities that help define the style of a garment or outfit.
Principles of design: Qualities that describe the way the elements of design work together.

Reinforce and Review

Review the basic principles of design with students.

- **Balance:** Relationship between sections of a garment. Symmetrical balance is when both sides of a garment are identical; asymmetrical balance is when the sides are different.
- **Repetition:** Repeating an element over and over again.
- **Emphasis:** Focal point(s) within a design.
- **Proportion:** Relationship between the sizes of objects within a design.

Identifying the Elements of Design

You can use the elements of design to create a style or look that emphasizes your personal characteristics.

The **elements of design** are qualities that help define the style of a garment or outfit. The basic elements of design are line, color, and texture. (Other design elements, which are covered in Chapter 26, include space and shape.)

Using the elements of design when you choose clothes and accessories will help you develop an appealing personal style. The items in your wardrobe will work well together because they will represent similar qualities of design.

When you consider the elements of design, you will be able to select clothing that highlights your positive features and sends an appropriate message to the people around you.

Principles of Design

The **principles of design** are the qualities that describe the way the elements of design work together—in this case, the line, color, and texture of clothing. Some basic principles of design include balance, repetition, emphasis, and proportion. (Other principles are covered in Chapter 26.)

- *Balance* is the relationship between sections of a garment. *Symmetrical balance* is when both sides of a garment are identical. *Asymmetrical balance* is when one side is larger or has more or different colors, shapes, or patterns than the other side.
- *Repetition* is when certain elements of a garment occur over and over again. For example, a line, pattern, or color might be repeated across a neckline or skirt.
- *Emphasis* gives the eye a series of focal points within a design. It directs the eye across the garment. For example, a splash of color might attract the eye and give emphasis to a scarf.
- *Proportion* is the relationship between the sizes of objects within a design. A garment with good proportion has a pleasing scale of sizes between sleeves, collar, bust, and waist.

Customized Instruction: ESOL Students

Have students say and write the terms *line, color, texture, balance, repetition, emphasis,* and *proportion* in their primary language.

Customized Instruction: Less Advanced/At-Risk/Special Needs Students

Have students work in pairs to identify the principles of design in a piece of clothing worn by their partner. They should determine the type of balance (symmetrical or asymmetrical); repetition of lines, colors, or patterns; point of emphasis; and proportion.

Line

Line is the element of design that defines the shape, angles, and outline—*silhouette*—of a garment. *Structural lines* include features such as seams, pleats, pockets, or drapes. *Decorative lines* might be stripes or plaids in the fabric pattern or texture, or embellishments such as trims and ruffles. Lines can affect the way you look in a garment and can create a mood or send a message:

■ Wear vertical lines to make a body look taller and thinner, or horizontal lines to make a body look shorter and wider.

■ Straight lines usually make a garment look stiff and formal, while curved lines give a garment a graceful, softer appearance.

Texture

Texture is the look and feel of the surface of the fabric. For example, a cashmere scarf has a soft texture and a silk blouse is shiny and smooth. Texture comes from the fibers, yarn structure, and finish used to create the fabric. Like lines, texture can affect the way you look.

■ Stiff fabrics such as crisp cotton can hide the shape of a body, while soft, loose fabrics might cling and show the body shape.

■ Bulky fabrics such as heavy knit sweaters add mass to a body.

■ Shiny textures such as silk and satin reflect light, which makes a body look larger than it really is, and dull textures can make a body look smaller.

What type of lines would you recommend to someone who wants to look taller?

What Happens Next?

Melanie does not know Andrea very well, but she admires Andrea's sense of style. She likes the way Andrea combines colors and lines. She thinks Andrea uses accessories to make her outfits stand out and to give her look a personal touch.

Melanie takes note of how Andrea dresses. She starts looking in her wardrobe to find color combinations that Andrea wears. She tries to pick out designs that Andrea wears, and even accessories similar to Andrea's. Melanie begins to feel more confident about her appearance.

Andrea starts notice how Melanie is dressing. She thinks there is something oddly familiar about the outfits Melanie is wearing to school. She soon realizes that Melanie is copying her style. Andrea gets angry.

Use your decision-making skills to help the girls recognize the problems they are facing. Consider actions they might take, and the consequences of each action. Using your 21st Century Skills—such as decision making, goal setting, and problem solving—write an ending to the story. Read it to the class, or form a small group and present it as a skit.

Optical Illusion

An optical illusion tricks your eyes into seeing something that isn't really there. You can use the elements of design to create optical illusions.

✔ *To appear taller: A-line skirts and dresses, boat or V-necklines, button down or full zip fronts, neutral colors, pinstripes*

✔ *To appear shorter: cuffed pant legs, white or light-colored shoes, pleated slacks*

✔ *To appear smaller: dark colors, straight-leg pants, dull textures, smooth textures*

✔ *To appear larger: bright colors, bold patterns, shiny textures, bulky textures*

Vocabulary

Line: Element of design that defines the shape, angles, and outline (or silhouette) of a garment.

Texture: Look and feel of the surface of the fabric.

Figure Focus

To appear taller, wear items with vertical stripes, lines, and seams. These would include A-line and princess line (vertical seams that shape) garments, those with vertical pleats, and those that use designs of vertical striping or patterns.

Optical Illusion

Ask students to share their own tips on optical illusions that result in a more flattering look. Some ideas are:

■ Garments with princess and A lines can make you look slimmer.

■ Sleeveless garments or those with short or cap sleeves call attention to the arms. Avoid these if you're worried about arms that are too thin or too heavy.

■ To make a short body look longer, wear solid colors, vertical lines, and narrow V-lines.

■ To make a long body look shorter, contrast colors in tops and bottoms and wear big, bold prints.

■ Wide collars and padded shoulders give the illusion of wider shoulders.

■ Raglan sleeves and those set into a wide armhole can make the shoulders look narrower.

■ Loosely woven fabrics help hide bulges.

■ Thin, unobtrusive belts can make the waist look smaller.

■ Turtlenecks and fancy collars can make a long neck look shorter.

■ Single-breasted jackets can have a slimming effect.

21st Century Skills

What Happens Next?

Students are to prepare an ending to the situation between Melanie and Andrea. Their endings should address Melanie's attempt to copy Andrea's style. Melanie needs to understand that "style" is the way in which you express yourself personally. It's not something you should try to copy from another. While there's no harm in admiring another person's style, you should strive to develop your own. Andrea should be flattered that Melanie is trying to emulate her style. Since she has a flair for combining colors and accessories, she might suggest to Melanie how she can use her wardrobe elements to create her own style.

Introduce the Section

Most people rely heavily on color to help them choose the clothing they will buy or wear. This section discusses the characteristics of color and provides tips on selecting and mixing colors.

Figure Focus

Ask students to discuss the color or colors that dominate their wardrobes. Do these same colors appear in other areas of their environment, such as their bedroom, or even school supplies? Do they wear clothes with these colors on certain occasions?

Vocabulary

Color value: Lightness or darkness of a color.

Hue: Name of a color, such as red or blue, which defines its characteristics and distinguishes it from another color.

Intensity: Brightness or dullness of a color.

Shades: Darker color values made by adding black to a color.

Tints: Lighter color values made by adding white to a color.

STUDENT ACTIVITY

Have students create a table with two to four columns. They should write their favorite colors as the column headings. Under each color, they should list adjectives that describe the color and the feelings or emotions it evokes for them. Students should come up with at least five adjectives for each color.

Analyzing Color

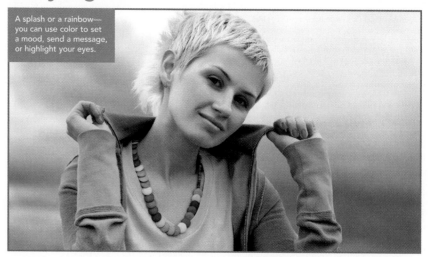

A splash or a rainbow—you can use color to set a mood, send a message, or highlight your eyes.

If you're like most people, the first thing you notice when you look at clothes is the color. You might love the style of a sweater, but if you don't like the color, you won't buy it.

- Color can send a message about personality or mood. Are you wearing gray? People might think you are sad. Are you wearing yellow? People might think you are happy.

- Color is symbolic, too. Think about stop signs, fire engines, and orange cones in construction zones. They all use bright color to command your attention. What colors do you associate with Thanksgiving or the Fourth of July? What color balloons would you give to the parents of a new baby boy?

Analyzing the relationships among different colors can help you use color to create a style or look, and to emphasize your positive features.

How Do I Describe Color?

- **Hue** is the name of a color, such as blue or red. Hue describes the characteristics of a color that distinguish it from another color. For example, when you compare two orange scarves and notice that one is a more reddish orange and the other is a more yellowish orange, you are seeing the difference in the hue.

- **Color value** refers to the lightness or darkness of a color. Lighter values are called **tints** and are made by adding white to a color. For example, adding white to red makes pink. Darker values are called **shades** and are made by adding black to a color. For example, adding black to blue makes navy blue. When you dress, you can make an outfit more interesting by using different—or contrasting—values. For example, wearing a pale blue shirt with gray pants and black shoes makes a very different statement from wearing a brown shirt, brown pants, and brown shoes.

- **Intensity** is the brightness or dullness of a color. Bright colors contain the most color and are the most vivid. Examples of bright colors are jewel tones such as emerald green and ruby red. Dull colors are softer and more subdued. Colors become duller if gray or their complement is added to them.

Customized Instruction: More Advanced Students

Have students research the connection between an individual's favorite color and his or her personality type. For example, red is considered the color of strength, health, and vitality. It is often the favorite color of those who are outgoing, ambitious, and aggressive. Students should create a chart that illustrates their findings and then share it with the class.

What Is Color?

Color is the way our eyes see light. You can use a color wheel to explore the relationships among colors.

- **Primary colors** are red, yellow, and blue. You can mix the primary colors in different combinations and amounts to create all the other colors.
- **Secondary colors** are made by mixing equal amounts of two primary colors. Mix red and yellow to get orange, red and blue to get violet, and blue and yellow to get green.
- **Intermediate colors** are made by mixing a primary color and the secondary color that's next to it on the color wheel. Examples of intermediate colors are red-violet, blue-violet, blue-green, yellow-green, yellow-orange, and red-orange.
- **Complementary colors** are the colors opposite each other on the color wheel. Red and green are complementary. So are violet and yellow.
- **Analogous colors** are next to each other on the color wheel. For example green, blue-green, and blue are analogous.
- **Neutral colors** are black, white, and gray.

How Do I Select Color?

Even before you choose colors for your clothes, you have a color scheme to work with. Your hair, eyes, and **complexion**—skin tone—all have color. When you choose to wear colors that enhance your natural features, you will look and feel your best.

Color affects the appearance of everything around it. Light, bright, and warm colors attract more attention than dull colors. They jump out at the viewer. Dark and dull colors blend in with the background more.

Warm colors, such as red, orange, and yellow, are associated with fire and the sun. They send a message of energy and excitement. Cool colors, such as blue, green, and violet, are associated with water, sky, and grass. They send a calm, soothing message.

When you choose a color for yourself, consider what you want the color to do.

- Do you want to stand out from the crowd? Select a bright, intense color.
- Do you want to look calm and relaxed? Select blues, greens, and violets.

What is the relationship between complementary colors on a color wheel?

Harmonize!

A **color harmony** or **color scheme** is a combination of colors that look good together. You can use them as a guideline for selecting colored clothing and accessories. The five most common color harmonies are described below.

Monochromatic: A color harmony that uses only one color. This harmony can include different values of one color or include neutrals.

Analogous: A color harmony that includes two or more colors that are next to each other on the color wheel. An example is orange, yellow-orange, and yellow.

Complementary: A color harmony that uses two colors that are direct opposites on the color wheel. An example is yellow and violet.

Split-complementary: A color harmony that uses one color and the two colors on either side of its complement. An example is red, blue-green, and yellow-green.

Triad: A color harmony that uses three colors that are an equal distance from each other on the color wheel. An example is the three primary colors, red, blue, and yellow.

Discuss

Explain the concept of a color wheel. It is an arrangement of hues around a circle showing the relationship of primary, secondary, intermediate, complementary, and analogous colors.

Figure Focus

Complementary colors are opposite each other on the color wheel. They contrast, enhance, and intensify each other. They are often used together to create an aesthetically pleasing presentation. Discuss your school colors with students. Are they complementary colors? What about those of other schools in your region?

Vocabulary

Analogous colors: Colors next to each other on the color wheel.

Color harmony or color scheme: Combination of colors that look good together.

Color: Property of something that determines the way our eyes see light.

Complementary colors: Colors opposite each other on the color wheel, such as red and green.

Complexion: Skin tone.

Intermediate colors: Colors made by mixing a primary color and the secondary color next to it on the color wheel.

Neutral colors: Colors of black, white, and gray.

Primary colors: Colors of red, blue, and yellow.

Secondary colors: Colors made by mixing equal amounts of two primary colors.

Harmonize!

Have students look around the classroom and at each other's clothing to find examples of items that use the harmonies described in the text.

Customized Instruction: ESOL/Less Advanced Students

Companies often use complementary colors in the branding of their products. Have students bring in a grocery store product from home or one found in the classroom. Have them determine the colors used and identify the color harmony it most resembles.

Customized Instruction: Special Needs (Visually Impaired) Students

Students might be willing to discuss special aids and assistive technology they use to identify colors.

Introduce the Section

Being able to sew and alter your clothing is a valuable skill. This section provides an overview of sewing tools and techniques. Students also learn about patterns and types of fabrics and sewing notions.

Figure Focus

Ask students to think of crafts and projects they have worked on that involved sewing or other clothing construction techniques. Maybe they recall stuffing old socks and then applying faces to them to create puppets, or sewing the outline of clothes on cards punched with holes, or making a homemade costume for Halloween. Discuss ways that sewing skills can be used to create art.

What's in Your Sewing Basket?

In addition to the items listed, discuss other sewing basket essentials:

- Full-size spools of white, beige, and black threads and smaller size spools of other colors, such as blue, green, brown, and yellow. You might also want heavier-gauge spools of black and white on hand.
- Needle-threader.
- Safety pins.
- Packets of snaps, hook-and-eye fastenings, and buttons.

Preparing to Sew

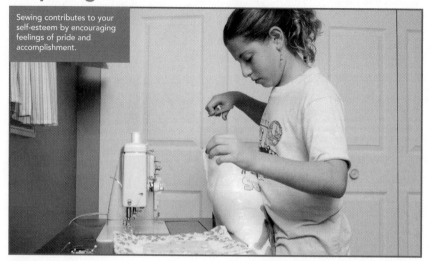

Sewing contributes to your self-esteem by encouraging feelings of pride and accomplishment.

When you sew, you stitch items together using a needle and thread. You can sew to create something new, to repair something damaged, or to enhance—or embellish—something that might benefit from new features.

- You might sew a new shirt, a pillow, or a tote bag.
- You might sew a button back on a shirt, or stitch a ripped seam.
- You might add decorative patches to a pair of jeans, beads to a sweater, or ribbons to a hat.

Sewing lets you express your creativity and personality while you develop a useful skill. You can prepare to sew by organizing the tools and information you will need to complete a project.

What's in Your Sewing Basket?

A sewing basket is any container in which you store your sewing tools. Specially made sewing baskets are designed to store sewing equipment, but you can use any container that has a cover. The basic tools you will use include:

- *Measuring tools* such as a flexible tape measure and a seam gauge, which is a 6-inch ruler with a movable marker for measuring and marking seams, hems, and other features
- *Sewing tools*, including straight pins, a pin holder, a seam ripper for removing stitches and loose threads, a thimble for protecting your fingertip, and hand and sewing machine needles in various sizes
- *Cutting tools* such as small scissors for clipping threads and dressmaker shears for cutting fabrics
- *Marking tools* such as a nonpermanent marker that you can use to transfer the pattern lines onto your fabric
- *Pressing tools* including an iron and an ironing board

Keep your tools organized and in good repair. Throw away broken or bent pins and needles. Remember to return any sewing tool to its proper place in the box. Then, you can easily check to see if anything is missing.

What Is a Pattern?

A **pattern** is a guide for making a project. It includes paper shapes of all the pieces, and instructions for sewing the pieces together. The pattern envelope or guide sheet provides a lot of information, including:

■ What the finished project will look like

■ A drawing of each piece with construction details such as seams

■ Fabric recommendations

■ A table of measurements to help you select the correct size

■ A chart for figuring out how much fabric you will need, based on the selected size

■ A list of notions—things you need other than fabric such as thread, zippers, or buttons

■ Layouts, which are diagrams showing how to place the patterns on the fabric

How Do I Choose a Pattern?

You want a pattern that suits your needs. Your teacher will usually select an appropriate project for you in school. When you choose a pattern, ask yourself these questions.

■ *What is the pattern for?* Select a pattern for a project you want to complete. You might want to make a garment, a decorative item such as a pillow or draperies, or a specialty item, such as a locker organizer or laundry bag. It might be for yourself or a gift for someone else.

■ *How hard is it to complete?* The more pieces and seams there are, the more difficult the pattern will be. Select a pattern that matches your skills and abilities.

■ *How long will it take?* A complicated pattern with features such as zippers, buttonholes, and pleats might require more time than you have. In school, you may only be able to use the sewing lab on certain days or at certain times.

■ *What materials do I need?* The pattern might require special tools that might not be available in the sewing lab, or notions that are difficult to find.

■ *How much will it cost?* Some patterns are expensive, and some are free. Select a pattern that fits your budget.

"How can I use the information on a pattern to choose a project that is right for me?"

I'll Never Finish This!

It's November 1 and you're planning to sew a holiday gift for your best friend. What steps can you take to make sure you finish the project on time?

👎 Select a pattern that has many pieces and seams

👎 Select a print fabric that must be matched at the seams

👎 Assume you will have time in class to work on the project

👍 Select a pattern that suits your abilities

👍 Select a fabric that is easy to work with

👍 Make a schedule so you can manage your time

What are some sewing projects that would make good gifts for your family and friends?

Test **IT** Yourself!

Can you really make every color starting with blue, red, and yellow? Use food coloring and water to see how many colors you can come up with. You will need blue, red, and yellow food coloring, clear plastic cups, and water. As you progress, have one or two students work together to keep a chart of the color combinations.

1. Select three primary-color students—one to be red, one to be yellow, and one to be blue.
2. Each will put about an ounce of water into a cup and add a few drops of either red, blue, or yellow food coloring.
3. Select secondary-color students. Each will take an empty cup, and choose two primary color students to dump their water into it, making a secondary color. The primary-color students will repeat step 2 to refill, as necessary.
4. Continue as long as you want, with new students selecting colors to combine in his or her cup.
5. Examine the color chart. How many colors did you make? Could you control the shade or tint?

Vocabulary

Notions: Items used in sewing, such as thread, zippers, and buttons.

Pattern: Guide for making something.

Figure Focus

Discuss the types of information available on a pattern. If possible, hold up a sample pattern and point out the types of information. You can use the information to determine the difficulty level of the project and how long it will take to complete. Based on the fabric and other supplies and materials you will need, you can determine how much the project will cost.

I'll Never Finish This!

Students are to comment on sewing projects that would make good gifts for family and friends. Some ideas are:

■ Cloth bags and totes that you've personalized and decorated.

■ Dolls and toys.

■ Basket liners.

■ Aprons.

■ Scarves.

■ Flags and banners.

■ Holiday-related decorations and accessories, such as placemats, hand towels, and window hangings.

Test **IT** Yourself!

Students are to use red, blue, and yellow food coloring to create as many different colors as possible. Make sure students use equal amounts of each primary color to create their secondary color. If you have more than one team of students doing this experiment, suggest the different teams compare their primary and secondary colors. It might be interesting to students to compare the reds, greens, purples, etc.

Customized Instruction: Less Advanced/At-Risk Students

Have students use 8½- by 11-inch paper to create a pattern for a T-shirt that would fit an infant. Students should include information or a guide sheet similar to that described in the text. This includes a drawing of the finished product, a drawing of each piece and how they will all fit together, and the type of fabric to use.

Fabric Types

Review the fabric types with students. You might have them look at their clothing labels to determine which fabric is most common.

You might also discuss weaves and knits. A weave is a fabric whose fibers are manipulated on a loom to create the finished product. Types of weaves are:

- Broadcloth, which is a standard over-under-over-under pattern that can be made in most fabric types.

- Twill, which is similar to broadcloth, but the horizontal thread skips over more than one vertical thread at regular intervals, producing diagonal ridges in the fabric .

- Satin, which uses multiple layers of thread, with a tightly-woven back but long threads lying on the front of the fabric, allowing for a smooth look and feel.

- Gauze, which is also similar to broadcloth, but the threads are not pulled tight, leaving a light and airy feel.

- A knit is a fabric whose fibers are looped together in rows. Examples of knits are:
  - Interlock, characterized by interconnected stitches.
  - Rib knit, which has a vertically ridged pattern.
  - Jersey, which is a plain knit fabric without a distinct rib.

Figure Focus

Factors that affect fabric choices include durability, cost, washing instructions and care requirements, ability to maintain shape, wrinkling, grain, and colorfastness and fading.

Fabric Types

Here is a list of some common types of fabric.

✔ *Cotton is a natural fiber made from the cotton plant. It is used in a wide variety of clothing and home furnishings. Cotton is cool and absorbs moisture.*

✔ *Linen is a natural fiber made from the flax plant. It is very strong, and the fabric is cool and absorbent but wrinkles easily.*

✔ *Nylon is a synthetic fabric that is strong and lightweight. Nylon is easy to wash and take care of. It resists absorbing moisture and dries easily, so it is often used for swimwear and activewear.*

✔ *Polyester is a strong, durable man-made fabric. It dries quickly and resists wrinkles.*

✔ *Rayon is a synthetic fiber made from cellulose. It is a soft, absorbent, and comfortable fabric. It can shrink.*

✔ *Silk is a natural fiber made from silkworm cocoons. It is soft and versatile and can be dyed many colors.*

✔ *Wool is a natural fiber that comes from the coat of various animals, including sheep, goats, and alpaca. Wool fabrics are resilient, resist wrinkles, and provide warmth.*

Which Fabric Is Best?

The fabric you choose depends on the project. Start by reading the fabric recommendations on your pattern envelope. Then, consider the following factors.

What factors might influence your choice of fabric?

- *Purpose.* Think about the project you are making and how it will be used. A shirt that you will wash a lot needs a different fabric than a decorative pillow you will leave on your bed. A winter scarf needs a different fabric than a summer T-shirt. Depending on the project, you might want a special finish, such as wrinkle-resistance or flame retardant.

- *Ease of use.* Some fabrics are easier to work with than others. For example, woven fabrics may be easy to sew, but they tend to unravel unless finished with a strong seam. Knits and textured fabrics are harder to sew and might require specialty threads and stitching. Fabrics that require a nap layout, such as velvet or corduroy which have a raised, fuzzy surface and one-way prints and plaids that must be matched at all seams, usually require extra fabric.

- *Cost.* You buy fabrics by the yard. If you are making a small pillow, you might be able to afford more expensive fabric than if you are making a blanket or dress.

How Do I Choose Notions?

Notions are all the things you need to complete a sewing project other than the fabric. Select your notions after you select a pattern and fabric. The pattern envelope or guide sheet lists all the notions you will need. Common notions include:

- *Thread.* Choose thread the same color or a little darker than the fabric. Look for good-quality thread that is strong and smooth.

- *Fasteners.* Your pattern will list the types of fasteners you will need, such as zippers, buttons, and snaps.

- *Elastic.* Elastic might be used in a pull-on waistband or sleeve band. Choose the type and size of elastic listed on the pattern envelope or guide sheet.

- *Trims, tapes, and bindings.* Tapes and bindings reinforce seams or cover raw edges. Trims are decorative coverings for edges. Select items that match or coordinate with your fabric in terms of color and texture.

- *Linings and interfacings.* Linings are fabrics used to finish the inside of a project, such as to line a skirt. You might be able to see a lining, so you want a color that matches or coordinates with your outer fabric. Interfacing is not visible. It is fabric that is sewn between two pieces of outer fabric to add support body and prevent stretching in areas such as collars and cuffs.

Preparing Your Fabric and Pattern

Before you begin your project, follow these steps to prepare your fabric and pattern:

1. Wash the fabric according to the fabric care label to preshrink it.
2. Press the fabric to remove all wrinkles.
3. Straighten the grain—the direction that the yarns run—to make sure the finished project will hang straight and even. For example, pull a thread across the width of the fabric near the top, and then cut along the pulled thread line to create a straight top edge.
4. Read the pattern guide sheet and examine the pattern diagram to identify all the pattern pieces.
5. Cut the pieces apart, leaving extra pattern tissue around each one so you can make alterations, if necessary.
6. Press the pattern pieces flat using a dry iron set to a low temperature.
7. Layout the pattern pieces using the layout guide, and pin them into place.

Lab Procedures

The *clothing and textile lab* is the room in school where you will do your sewing. It has the tools and equipment you need. It is your responsibility to respect the equipment and your classmates to keep the lab a safe and fun place. Your instructor will go over proper procedures before you use the lab. Some common guidelines include the following.

- Be prepared by organizing the equipment and supplies you will need.
- Read all instructions before you start a project. If you are unsure what they mean, ask your teacher.
- Be considerate of your classmates. You may be sharing equipment and supplies.
- Use a pincushion to hold your pins and needles.
- Keep your work area and supplies neat and organized.
- Stand up the iron on its end when you are not using it to press.
- Turn the sewing machine off and lower the presser foot when you are finished using it.
- Allow yourself enough time to clean up your work area and put away all of your supplies before the end of class.

N(U)M(B)E(R)S G(A)M(E)

Measuring with a ruler or tape measure is an important skill for sewing. An inch ruler or tape measure is divided into inches, and each inch can be divided into 16 parts. Marks on the ruler indicate the parts: the shortest lines mark 1/16, the next shortest mark 1/8, then 1/4 and 1/2. Each inch line is marked with a number (refer to the above illustration).

To measure, you line up an inch mark at the edge or point where you want to start measuring, use the lines to count off the length, and draw a line to indicate the spot. (If you are using fabric, you make the line using chalk.) For example, to measure 3/8 from the edge of fabric, you line up the edge with the inch mark, count three 1/8 inch marks, and draw a line. To measure 5/8 from the edge—a standard seam allowance—you line up the edge, count five 1/8 inch marks, and make a line.

Using a blank piece of paper and a ruler, tape measure, or the illustration, measure 1/4 inch from the left edge of the page. Write the measurement next to the line that you draw.

Measure 5/8 from the right edge. Write the measurement next to the line that you draw.

Measure 1 1/8 from the top edge. Write the measurement next to the line that you draw.

Lab Safety

The clothing and textile lab is full of sharp, hot objects. Use safety:

✔ Close scissors when not in use.
✔ Pass scissors and other sharp tools with the handle—not the sharp end—pointing toward the other person.
✔ When you use a sewing machine, sew at a slow, even speed.
✔ Keep your fingers to the sides of the presser foot and clear of the sewing machine needle.
✔ Keep your attention on the needle area while you sew.
✔ When you are not sewing, keep your foot off the pedal.
✔ When you are finished sewing, be sure the needle and presser foot are in the down position.
✔ Keep pins and needles out of your mouth.
✔ Keep your hands away from the hot surface of the iron.
✔ Unplug all electrical cords when you are finished using electric equipment.

1/8 inch mark
1/4 inch mark
1/16 inch mark   1/2 inch mark

0 inch   1   2

Lab Safety

You might discuss other safety issues with students:

- Pin back long hair to keep it away from sewing equipment.
- Remove dangling jewelry and scarves.
- Roll up and secure loose or baggy shirt and jacket sleeves.
- Observe good housekeeping practices, such as throwing away trash and cleaning up as you go.
- Do not eat or drink when working around sewing equipment and fabrics.
- Follow all written and verbal instructions carefully.

N(U)M(B)E(R)S G(A)M(E)

If students have rulers, instruct them to find the same measurements that are labeled on the figure in the text before they start measuring on their papers. You might also have them measure clothing-related things, such as the hem in their pants, the distance between buttons, or the depth of the cuff on a shirt or blouse sleeve.

Customized Instruction: Less Advanced/Special Needs Students

Working in teams, have students create a poster that lists safety guidelines for your school's clothing and textile lab. If guidelines already exist, students can restate them, but they should embellish them with attention-grabbing colors and illustrations.

Introduce the Section

Students learn the basic tools and equipment used for hand sewing. They also are introduced to types of stitches and are given tips on threading a needle and sewing on a button.

Figure Focus

Discuss situations in which hand-sewing skills would be more useful than using a sewing machine. For example, a seam on a bedspread has ripped and it would be easier to hand-sew it while it's still on the bed rather than take it off and try to manipulate it on a sewing machine. Or, you're at a party and you somehow rip a hole in the knee of your leggings. Using your emergency sewing kit, you can mend the hole instead of returning home or, worse yet, walking around with an embarrassing tear in your clothing. Or, you might want to put an appliqué on a backpack, which is too bulky to sew on a machine.

Discuss

If time allows, you can share some of the following fun facts about sewing:

- Native Americans used porcupine quills and animal sinew (tendons) for sewing and needlework.

- The expression "the whole nine yards" is believed to have originated in early 1700s England as a way to describe the amount of fabric needed to make the fanciest coat for a man of fashion.

- The first sewing needles were made from bone.

- Villages in Japan have a shrine dedicated to broken sewing needles. Villagers believe that the needle has performed its task well and has "passed on" while in active service. So, broken needles are laid to rest on a soft bed of tofu.

- The Bible states that Adam and Eve sewed fig leaves together to make coverings for themselves (Genesis 3:7).

- A seamstress is a woman who makes clothes or sews for a living; a tailor can be either a man or a woman who makes or repairs clothes.

Sewing by Hand

Sewing by hand lets you develop sewing skills that will help you complete large and small projects.

When you sew by hand, you use a needle and thread to stitch two items together. It is usually slower than sewing with a machine, but costs less—you don't have to buy a sewing machine.

Although you can complete an entire project sewing by hand, usually you will use hand-sewing techniques for small projects, or for parts of a larger project. In fact, some tasks are easier to do by hand, or actually come out neater, including:

- Sewing buttons
- Finishing hems
- Joining edges

Sewing by hand is a good way to start developing your sewing skills. You can start with smaller projects that will help you gain confidence and prepare you for sewing with a machine.

Equipment for Sewing by Hand

One tool you use when sewing by hand that you don't use when sewing by machine is a **thimble**—a small cap for one finger—when you sew by hand. It protects your fingertip from needle and pin pricks, and gives you a brace for pushing the needle through the fabric.

Needles come in different types. Use sharps for general sewing. Needles also come in different sizes. For hand-sewing, the sizes are numbered from 1 to 12, with 1 being very heavy and 10 being very fine. The hole in the end of the needle is called the eye. The smaller the number, the larger the eye and length. You thread the needle through the eye.

- Use a lower number needle for heavy or dense fabrics.
- Use a higher number for light fabrics.
- Use a middle number for most hand-sewing projects.

Keep your tools in a secure, organized location, such as a sewing basket or box. Keep pins and needles in a pincushion or in a special book or box. You will know where to find them when you need them.

Hand-Sewing Stitches

There are many types of stitches you can use when you sew by hand. Here are some of the most common and useful.

■ *Backstitch* is a strong, general-purpose stitch used to repair seams, fasten the ends of thread at the beginning and end of stitching, and fasten pieces of fabric together. Technique: Push the threaded needle through the fabric and make a small forward stitch. Go back to the middle of the previous stitch and push the needle through again. Repeat, overlapping each stitch. The front looks like a dotted line, and the backside looks like it was retraced.

■ *Running stitch* is a simple stitch used to join fabric for gathering and mending. Technique: Pass the threaded needle in and out of the fabric in one direction. Both sides will look like a dotted line.

■ *Basting*—also called tacking—is a long, temporary stitch used to hold fabric together until a more permanent stitch is applied. Technique: Pass the threaded needle in and out of the fabric to create a loose running stitch.

■ *Slipstitch* is an almost invisible stitch used for pockets, hems, linings, and trims. Technique: Pass the threaded needle inside the folded edge and fabric and then out, catching a bit of the under layer of fabric, then back into the folded edge for the next stitch.

■ *Blanket or buttonhole stitch* is used to reinforce the edge of thick fabric, or as a decorative edging. Technique: Pass the threaded needle from the back, bringing the point of the needle out at the edge of the fabric. Loop the thread behind the point of the needle. Pull the threaded needle through the fabric, allowing the edge thread to loop on the edge of the fabric.

■ *Hem stitch* is used to create hems. Technique: Working from right to left, pull the threaded needle through the hem on a diagonal, catching a bit—two threads—of the fabric above the folded edge.

Backstitch   Running stitch

Basting   Slipstitch

Blanket stitch   Hem stitch

Steps for Sewing by Hand

Basic guidelines for sewing by hand:

1. Cut the thread about 14 inches long.
2. Thread the needle. Use your thumb and forefinger to hold the needle firmly while pushing the thread through the needle eye.
3. Make a knot with the thread. After pulling the thread through the eye of the needle, find the appropriate place to knot it. Using the cushion of your forefinger, wrap the thread over it and hold it with your thumb. Twist the thread between your forefinger and thumb and pull to make the knot.
4. Make a double backstitch: Push the needle through the fabric and make a small forward stitch. Go back to the first insertion point and push the needle through again. Do this two or three more times to make sure that the thread is firmly in place.
5. Sew.
6. Finish the stitching with another double backstitch.

Hand-Sewing a Button

One of the most common types of button is called a sew-through, because it has two or more holes in the center that you sew through to attach the button to the fabric. To attach a sew-through button:

1. Mark the spot where you want to place the center of the button.
2. Pull the threaded needle through the fabric from the back—wrong—side and up through one hole in the button. Take a stitch or 2 to anchor the thread to the fabric.
3. Center the button over the placement mark.
4. Push the needle back into another button hole, and pull it through to the back side of the fabric.
5. If the button is shankless, place a pin or toothpick under the thread between the holes. This allows room for the buttonhole to go around the button.
6. Stitch through each hole pair at 5 or 6 times.
7. End with the needle on the wrong side.
8. Pull out the pin or toothpick and push the needle back to the front of the fabric, but not through the button's holes. Wind the thread around the threads you have sewn to attach the button several times. This creates the shank.
9. Pull the needle through to the back side of the fabric and fasten off or knot the thread.

Teaching Tips

You might want to provide students with fabric remnants or ask them to bring in some from home. You also will need thread and needles. Have them practice each of the stitches described in the text. Refer them to the guidelines for sewing by hand at the bottom of the page.

As an option, you might also allow them to practice hand-sewing buttons onto their remnants. Refer them to the instructions at the bottom of the page.

Stay in School

A recent study reported that nearly half of the ninth graders in the 50 largest U.S. cities do not graduate with their class in four years. Those students who end up dropping out altogether often encountered severe academic problems in the ninth grade.

Ninth grade is a year of transition from middle school to high school. The transition can be difficult for students of all social backgrounds and in all educational environments. But it has been well-documented that the transition is especially tough for those who are struggling academically.

Researchers have identified a set of early warning signs that teachers can look for to gauge whether a student is off track and at risk of dropping out. These include:

■ **Delayed promotion from ninth to tenth grade.** Research indicates that failure to move from ninth grade to tenth grade on time is highly predictive of whether a student will graduate or not.

■ **Insufficient accumulation of required high school credits.** Dropouts earned fewer credits than did on-time graduates during each year of high school. The gap between each group's cumulative credits increased with each year.

■ **Poor attendance.** Students who are frequently absent, especially in ninth grade, are at greater risk of dropping out than students who attend regularly.

■ **Behavior issues.** Students with a history of behavior problems in school tend to have a higher likelihood of dropping out.

Introduce the Section

The basic parts of a sewing machine are detailed in this section. It also covers the steps for using a sewing machine and how to take proper care of the machine.

Figure Focus

Ask students if they've ever bought something and thought to themselves, "This would look really great on me if it were a little more fitted through the waist," or "if the collar had a different shape," or "if the hemline was a little shorter." Have students discuss how they would like to alter a piece of clothing to make it fit just right. If possible, share an example of your own.

Discuss

You might discuss some tips on buying a sewing machine:

- Consider buying from a local dealer instead of from an online supplier. You can test the machine beforehand, and most usually have an on-site repair department. Many also offer classes on sewing.

- Research machines ahead of time and make sure you know all the names for parts of the machine.

- Prepare a list of the types of sewing projects you do so you can find the machine that's best suited to your needs.

- When you visit a dealer, take remnants and swatches of the fabrics you work with most, as well as samples of the types of things you sew.

- Use your samples to test the machine. Do buttonholes and look for even stitching. Also pay attention to seam guides.

Sewing with a Machine

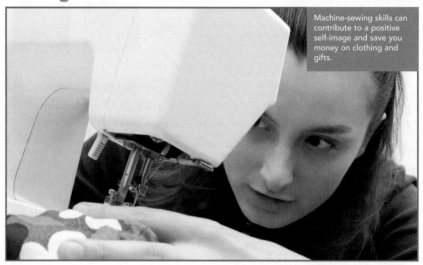

Machine-sewing skills can contribute to a positive self-image and save you money on clothing and gifts.

Using a sewing machine makes the process of completing a sewing project faster and easier. It has other benefits as well.

- You gain access to many stitch types.
- You can use special stitch types that provide decorative touches or professional finishing options, such as zigzagging, buttonholing, and hem stitching.
- You can create seams that are sturdier and more professional-looking.
- You gain options for controlling the stitch length for purposes such as basting or to suit a specific type of fabric.

You can earn money doing all these things for other people. You can help others by donating your skills to people in need. Your skills could even lead to a career in fashion or design.

Sewing Machine Basics

Most sewing machines work in the same basic way: When the needle moves up and down through the fabric, thread from the needle and thread from the bobbin—a small spool of thread loaded in the bobbin case below the presser foot of the sewing machine—interlock to create a stitch.

There are many types and brands of sewing machines, and they offer a wide variety of features and functions. A basic sewing machine is perfectly appropriate for most general projects. It might offer anywhere from two to ten built-in stitches and a basic buttonhole feature, but not much else. A loaded, computerized sewing machine might offer 50 or more built-in stitches, an automatic needle-threader, drop-in bobbin, adjustable presser feet, adjustable feed dogs, and a hard case.

Prices can vary from a $100.00 or less to more than $2,000.00. If you are thinking about buying a sewing machine, consider the type of sewing you will be doing, and the features you will need. For example, if you are planning to mend clothes, you probably do not need a computerized machine that costs $2,000.00.

Parts of a Sewing Machine

Most sewing machines have the same basic parts, but they are often located in different places. Your instructor will explain your machine before you begin sewing.

- Power switch for turning the machine off and on
- Light for making it easier to see the work area.
- Display screen (computerized machines only) or diagrams for selecting stitch settings and other options
- Tension adjustment dials (**A**) (noncomputerized) for adjusting the upper thread tension
- Presser foot (**B**) for holding the fabric
- Stitch selection (width (**C**) and length knobs (**D**)) may be computerized or manual
- Spool pins (**E**) for holding the thread
- Bobbin winding spindle (**F**) for winding thread onto the bobbin
- Bobbin case (**G**) for holding threaded bobbin
- Needle which may have adjustable positioning
- Feed dog (**H**) for moving the fabric under the presser foot
- Manual controls—hand wheel (**I**), reverse feed button (**J**)
- Throat plate (**K**) to cover the feed dog
- Presser foot lifter (**L**) for raising and lowering the presser foot
- Thread controls—top thread guide (**M**), front thread control, and take-up lever (**N**)

TECH CONNECT

Elias Howe, the American inventor who patented the first sewing machine in 1846, might be amazed at the newest models. Most high-end models today have built-in computers and small display screens.

The computer controls the speed and movement of the needle and the feed dogs so precisely that you can create hundreds of different stitches. It can store your favorite settings in memory. Some sewing machines even connect to your personal computer so you can download patterns from the Internet!

Use books or the Internet to learn more about the difference between a conventional and a computerized sewing machine. Then, make an advertisement for a sewing machine that offers the features you think are the most important.

Caring for a Sewing Machine

A sewing machine is a pretty big investment. Your instructor will advise you on how to care for the machines in the clothing lab. If you have a machine at home, you can take steps to keep it clean and in good working order:

✔ Before you buy a machine, check the warranty—the written statement or guarantee that it will work as expected (see Chapter 13) so you know what to do if there is a problem.

✔ Read the instruction manual for information about your specific machine.

✔ Before you perform any maintenance, unplug the machine from the electrical outlet.

✔ Remove lint after every project. Lint can build up in unseen areas of your machine, such as under the bobbin case.

✔ Unless your machine is self-lubricating, apply sewing machine oil to lubricate all moving parts, prevent wear, and reduce the risk of rust.

✔ Tighten loose screws whenever necessary.

✔ Check wires for wear and other damage.

Customized Instruction: Less Advanced/Special Needs Students

Ask students to consider products other than clothing that are made through the use of a sewing machine. They should draw a picture of such a product that they use on a regular basis. Some products include carpeting and rugs, shoes and boots, books, and furniture.

STUDENT ACTIVITY

Make copies of the student page, covering up everything except the picture of the sewing machine and the letters pointing to each part. Pass out copies to students and quiz them on the names of the parts.

Caring for a Sewing Machine

Discuss the following additional tips on sewing machine maintenance:

- Use *only* oil that's made for use on sewing machines. Do not use other household sprays or lubricants. Refer to your owner's manual for the proper spots to oil.
- After oiling the machine, do some test stitches on scraps of fabric. This eliminates the chance of any oil residue getting on your next project.
- If you find that some screws are missing, don't assume you can replace them with any household screws you have lying around. This can affect the machine's timing. Instead, take the machine to a repair shop.
- Do not try to repair worn or damaged wires yourself. Take the machine to a professional repair shop.

 TECH CONNECT

Students are to research the differences between conventional sewing machines and those that are computerized. Then, they are to create an advertisement for a sewing machine that offers the features they think are most important. Some of the features their ads might include are:

- Responsive foot pedal.
- Easy-to-reach and easy-to-read controls.
- Sufficient space to the right of the needle.
- Lightweight and easy to store.
- Automatic needle threader.
- Easy-to-load bobbin.
- Automatic buttonholer.

Press As You Go

Equipment for pressing includes:

- Steam iron or iron with a thermostat.
- Adjustable ironing board.
- Press mitt, which is a padded cushion that's useful for curved garment pieces, such as sleeve caps.
- Sleeve board, which is useful for pressing narrow garment sections, such as sleeves and pants legs.

Job Search

Students are to write a description of a job in textile or clothing production that interests them. You might suggest that they look through help-wanted ads in their local newspaper before going online, as there are thousands of these types of jobs posted. Reviewing a smaller sampling might help students focus on a particular job.

Figure Focus

The most effective way to ensure a straight hem is to use seam guides. On a sewing machine, these are commonly etched on the throat plate. If your machine does not have a seam guide, you can use household items, such as masking tape and note paper with a sticky back.

Press As You Go

Pressing is an up and down motion to lock stitches together usually with steam. Ironing is a gliding back and forth motion to remove wrinkles What if you don't press regularly while you are constructing a project?

★ *The seams might not lie flat.*

★ *It might be difficult to stitch seams that cross each other.*

★ *It might be difficult to match seams.*

★ *Your finished project will look crumpled.*

What equipment do you need to properly press seams as you sew?

Basic Steps for Using a Sewing Machine

1. If necessary, wind the thread from the spool to the bobbin, and insert the threaded bobbin in the bobbin case.
2. Thread the machine. The steps will vary depending on the type of machine you are using. (Check http://www.sewusa.com/Sewing_Machine_Threading_Diagrams.htm for diagrams showing how to thread different machines.) If a machine is not threaded correctly, it will not operate correctly.
3. Select the stitch type.
4. Select the stitch length.
5. Position the fabric under the presser foot.
6. Lower the presser foot.
7. Turn the handwheel to lower the needle into the fabric.
8. Begin sewing.
9. Backstitch at the beginning and end of a seam to secure the thread.

Stitching a Seam

The basic stitch for most sewing projects is the straight stitch. It is formed by the interlocking threads from the bobbin and the needle, but you can use it in different variations for different purposes.

- Use a straight stitch with a length of 2.0 mm to 2.5 mm for sewing seams, or 10 to 12 stitches per inch.
- Adjust the length up to 6 mm for gathering and basting.
- Set the length to 0 to sew straight up and down and anchor a seam at the beginning or end of the stitching line.

You can also use a straight stitch for topstitching, edge stitching, and decorative stitching.

What techniques can you use with a sewing machine to make sure you get a straight hem?

Job Search

If you like to work with your hands, get satisfaction from completing a project, and have an eye for design, then a career in textile or clothing production might be right for you. There are many types of jobs in the industry, including fashion and fabric designer, pattern maker, tailor, and family and consumer sciences teacher. The jobs might seem different, but they all combine an interest in design with a creative talent.

Education requirements and working environments vary depending on the job. Most require math and computer skills, as well as an ability to be organized and pay attention to detail.

Use the Internet, library, or your school's guidance resources to learn more about a career in textile or clothing production. Select a job that appeals to you, and write a job description, including the educational requirements, career pathway, and potential salary range.

Steps for a Straight Seam

To straight stitch a seam:

1. Place the two fabrics together, usually with the right sides on the inside, and line up the edges so they are even. (If you are following a pattern, make sure the markings and notches match.)
2. Pin the two pieces together, placing the pins perpendicular to the edge of the fabric.
3. Select the correct settings on your machine.
4. Place the fabric under the sewing machine's presser foot, lining up the fabric edge with the appropriate mark on the throat plate. For example, line up the fabric edge with the 5/8 inch mark on the throat plate to allow 5/8 inch between the seam and the edge of the fabric.
5. Backstitch 2 or 3 stitches to anchor the seam, and then start your straight stitch seam.
6. Let the feed dogs move the fabric. You guide the fabric along in a straight line without pushing or pulling, keeping the edge of the fabric lined up along the ⁵/₈ inch mark as it moves.
7. Pause sewing as you come to each pin and pull the pin out before you sew over it.
8. At the end of the seam, backstitch 2 to 3 stitches to anchor the seam.

What's a Serger?

A **serger**, sometimes called an **overlock machine**, is a special machine that stitches, trims, and finishes off the edges of a seam all in one step. There are several differences between a serger and a conventional machine.

- A serger does not have a bobbin. It has loopers that form the stitches and knives that trim the fabric.
- A serger uses from three to five threads depending on the serger. Threading a serger is very different from threading a conventional machine.
- A serger is faster than a regular or conventional sewing machine.

A serger cannot replace a conventional machine. There are some things a serger cannot do, such as make buttonholes, but it is very useful and makes your garments look more professional.

MONEY MADNE$$

Y ou want to give your mother a tote bag for Mother's Day. You saw one in the store for $34.99. Your friend has a sewing pattern for a tote bag. It requires 1 yard of fabric for the bag, ½ yard of fabric for lining and an inside pocket, and a 22-inch zipper. The bag fabric costs $13.00 per yard. The lining and pocket fabric costs $7.50 per yard. The zipper costs $2.25. You already have the thread, needles, and bobbin. How much will you save by making the bag? What other benefits or drawbacks might there be to making the bag yourself?

A serger is a specialized machine for stitching, trimming, and finishing edges all at once. Would you choose a serger or a sewing machine to have at home?

Sergers Can...

✔ Finish seams and edges
✔ Sew stretch seams
✔ Embellish with decorative thread
✔ Embellish with flatlock, chainstitch, or coverstitch
✔ Reduce puckering and rippling on hard-to-sew fabrics
✔ Apply elastic and other trims
✔ Hem sheer and lightweight fabrics without puckering
✔ Hem garments with coverstitch
✔ Edge-finish reversible items
✔ Execute rolled hems
✔ Finish with decorative edgings
✔ Gather fabric

Sergers Cannot...

✔ Baste
✔ Sew in reverse
✔ Install zippers
✔ Make buttonholes
✔ Embroider

Vocabulary

Serger or overlock machine: Special machine that stitches, trims, and finishes off the edges of a seam all in one step.

Figure Focus

Explain that a serger is most useful for sewing seams, which you can also do with a conventional sewing machine. A serger cannot make buttonholes or sew in reverse, so it's more limited in its capabilities than a conventional machine.

Sergers Can... Sergers Cannot...

If necessary, review some of the terms used on the lists:

- **Stretch seam:** Special stitching for knit fabrics that incorporates stretch.
- **Flatlock:** Stitch used to create a seam where the seam allowance lies flat against the garment instead of hanging loose from it.
- **Chainstitch:** Sewing and embroidery technique in which looped stitches form a chain-like pattern.
- **Coverstitch:** Double or triple needle stitching you see on the hems of most ready-to-wear garments.
- **Baste:** To sew fabric with long loose stitches in order to hold pieces of material together temporarily.
- **Embroider:** To sew decorative needlework.

MONEY MADNE$$

First, total the costs of materials: $13.00 + $3.75 + $2.25 = $19.00

Subtract the cost of materials from the cost of buying the bag in the store: $34.99 − $19.00 = $15.99

You will save $15.99 if you make the bag yourself.

Other benefits include the satisfaction of making the bag yourself. Your mother may appreciate the gift more knowing that you made it yourself.

Drawbacks include the fact that the bag might not be as perfect as one you buy in the store. You also have to shop for the materials and schedule the time to make the bag. It might be hard to surprise your mother if you are doing the work at home.

End-of-Chapter Activites

Case Study

Matthew's parents might think sewing is for girls. They might think it is a waste of time. They might prefer Matthew to be involved in sports.

Answers to the second bullet might vary. Some will think Matthew should look for a more masculine hobby. Others will think he should do what he likes best and develop his talent for clothing construction.

If Matthew wants to convince his parents, he should discuss it with them calmly and politely. He should explain that it is important to him, and that developing talents and interests might lead to a career. If they are still against it, he may want to talk to his guidance or career counselor for advice, or to his FACS teacher. They might be able to help him convince his parents that he should continue sewing.

Sounding Off!

Student answers will vary.

FAQ

1. Elements of design are line, color, and texture. Students may mention shape and space.

2. Principles of design are balance, repetition, emphasis, and proportion. Students may mention rhythm, unity, and scale.

3. A tint is a lighter color value, made by adding white to a hue; a shade is a darker color value, made by adding black to a hue.

4. Complementary colors are opposite each other on the color wheel. Red and green or violet and yellow are complementary.

5. You can sew to create something new, to repair something damaged, or to enhance—or embellish—something that might benefit from new features.

6. Categories are:
   - Measuring tools such as a flexible tape measure and a seam gauge, which is a 6-inch ruler with a movable marker for measuring and marking seams, hems, and other features.
   - Sewing tools, including straight pins, a pin holder, a seam ripper for removing stitches and loose threads, a thimble for protecting your fingertip, and hand and sewing machine needles in various sizes.

Case Study

In clothing lab, Matthew discovers he has a talent for clothing construction. He understands the way the patterns work, and he has a good eye for selecting fabric and colors. Other students like his designs. One girl asked if she could buy a pillow he made.

Matthew tells his parents about it. He says he is thinking about buying a sewing machine. He thinks he can develop his skills and make some money selling his work. His parents do not think it is a good idea. They tell him to look for a different hobby.

- Why do you think Matthew's parents don't want him to continue sewing?
- Do you agree that he should look for a different hobby?
- What can Matthew do to convince his parents that sewing is right for him?

Sounding Off!

❶ What colors do you like to wear? Why?

❷ What do you think is the most essential piece of sewing equipment? Why?

F A Q

1. What are three basic elements of design?
2. What are four principles of design?
3. What is the difference between a tint and a shade?
4. What are complementary colors? Give an example.
5. List three reasons for sewing.
6. List five categories of sewing tools, and give one example of each.
7. What is a pattern?
8. What are notions?
9. List six types of hand stitches.
10. What is a serger?

- Cutting tools such as small scissors for clipping threads and dressmaker shears for cutting fabrics.

- Marking tools such as a nonpermanent marker that you can use to transfer the pattern lines onto your fabric.

- Pressing tools including an iron and an ironing board.

7. A pattern is a guide for making a project. It includes paper shapes of all the pieces and instructions for sewing the pieces together.

8. Notions are all the things you need to complete a sewing project other than the fabric, such as thread, zippers, and elastic.

9. Types of hand stitches are backstitch, running stitch, basting, slipstitch, blanket or buttonhole stitch, and hem stitch. Students may think of others.

10. A serger, sometimes called an overlock machine, is a special machine that stitches, trims, and finishes off the edges of a seam all in one step.

Divide the class into teams of four or five. As a team, design and plan a quilt block that you can create by combining individual pieces of fabric that each team member prepares. Select a theme, and discuss how each individual piece will represent the theme. Determine the size and shape of each piece, and assign one piece to each team member.

As individual members of your team, use your sewing skills to create your assigned piece. Honor the theme and plan you agreed on as a group, but use your own skills and creativity to personalize the piece.

As a team, work to combine the pieces to complete the project. Display the quilt blocks in your classroom, or in a public area of the school.

Hot Topics

Do you care if your clothing design elements emphasize your positive features or hide your negative features? Do you just like to "wear what you like"?

Take this opportunity to write anonymously about your opinions regarding using design to enhance the way you look. Use a word processor so no one recognizes your handwriting. Be honest and open. Put the paper in the class Hot Topics box.

As a class, read the anonymous entries and discuss them.

Web Extra ▼

There are many Web sites that provide sewing patterns and project ideas for free. Some—like www.sewtrendy.com—are even designed specifically for teens.

Use the Internet to locate some pattern and project sites that you think might be useful for your peers. Make a directory of the sites, including the Web site address and a description of some of the types of projects on the site. Post the directory on your school Web site or in your school career center or library.

Problem Solver

You are a tailor and clothing designer. You are opening a new shop. You want to be ready to serve your clients by delivering garments that suit their taste, style, and needs, and also make them look great. Develop a list of at least ten questions you can ask each client to help you determine his or her clothing needs.

Exchange lists with a classmate, answer the questions, and exchange the lists back. Take your classmate's answers and design a garment or outfit for him or her. Write a paragraph explaining the elements, colors, and features you would use in the design. You may draw an illustration, too.

Team Players

Teams are to design and plan a quilt block. The team members should agree on the quilt's theme and general design and each team member is charged with contributing his or her own piece.

Remind students that a successful team relationship depends on all team members working together. Make sure they take steps to involve each team member, communicate effectively, and manage conflicts or disagreements.

Hot Topics

Make sure students understand that they can turn in their papers anonymously. Encourage them to be open and honest about their feelings about using design to enhance the way they look.

Web Extra

Students are to create a directory of Web sites that provide sewing patterns and project ideas for free. The directory should include the Web site address and a brief description of the site.

Remind students that a reliable Web site usually publishes the name of the author or organization that sponsors it and the date the content was created or last updated in a fairly obvious location, such as at the top or bottom of the page or on the home page. The site is usually organized with headings and an obvious navigation system. A reliable site clearly states its purpose and any affiliations. You should also look for accuracy in spelling and grammar.

Students should post the directory in their school career center or library.

Problem Solver

Students are to pretend they are a tailor or clothing designer just opening a new shop. They are to prepare a list of questions to ask a client that would help them understand his or her clothing needs. Examples of questions are:

1. What are the dominant colors of your wardrobe?
2. Is the clothing for a special occasion?
3. What do you like best about your figure?
4. What do you consider your biggest figure flaw?
5. What is your budget?
6. Are you allergic to or does your skin become irritated by certain fabrics or fibers?
7. What essential wardrobe elements do you already have?
8. How would you describe your personal style?
9. When do you need the clothing?
10. What time of year do you want to wear the clothing; i.e., cool weather, summer time, winter, etc.

Students are to exchange their lists with a classmate and then design an item or outfit based on the classmate's answers to their questions.

Write Now

Students are to write an advertisement for a selected fabric. They should review the fabric types on page 458 of the text. Make sure they use descriptive words in their advertisements.

Be Involved!

As a class, students are to plan a project that uses sewing to bring their peers and senior citizens together. Some ideas are a craft fair, quilting bee, or production of an instructional video.

Students are to use the FCCLA planning process outlined below to develop, execute, and evaluate their efforts.

- Identify the project.
- Set a goal.
- Form a plan (who, what, when, where, how, cost, resources, and evaluation).
- Act.
- Follow up.

Remind students that a successful team relationship depends on all team members working together. Make sure they take steps to delegate responsibilities, communicate effectively, and manage conflicts or disagreements.

Social Networking

Students are to contact a local hospital to find out what types of crafts or sewing projects they might accept to comfort or assist patients. If the hospital does not have such a program, students should investigate what they could do to launch one. The goal is to have students use their sewing skills to make items that could be donated to hospital patients.

Write Now

Write an advertising flyer for a fabric of your choice. Include information about the history of the fabric, how it is made, and what qualities it has. Describe how it is used and how to care for it.

Be Involved!

www.fcclainc.org

Many senior citizens have sewing skills that they could share with the younger generation. As a class, use the FCCLA planning process to organize a project that uses sewing to bring senior citizens and your peers together. Set a goal and brainstorm projects and activities. You might invite the seniors to class to show you their technique, or organize a trip to the senior center. You might create an instructional video starring the seniors, that you can upload to a class or school Web site. You might organize a craft fair to showcase the projects completed by both senior citizens and your peers.

After considering all possible options, select the project that you think will be the best one for achieving your goal.

Make an action plan for achieving your goal. Include a timeframe, make sure the plan is realistic and attainable, and then put the plan into action. You may want to organize teams within the class to handle specific responsibilities, such as volunteer management and publicity.

As you work toward your goal, keep a class journal to record your progress, and collect documentation that you can use to show what you have achieved. After the project is complete, evaluate your success. Did you achieve your goal? Were there things you could have done differently? Prepare an article about the event and send it to the school or community newspaper. You might also want to send it to your FCCLA chapter so they can publish it in their newsletter.

Social Networking

Many hospitals welcome crafts and sewing projects that comfort or assist patients. For example, they might accept blankets and teddy bears for children, hats and scarves for cancer patients, and totes and organizers for beds, wheelchairs, and walkers. Contact a hospital in your area and ask if they have a program in place, or if you could start one. Then select a project, locate a pattern, and get to work! Recruit your friends and relatives to participate, too.

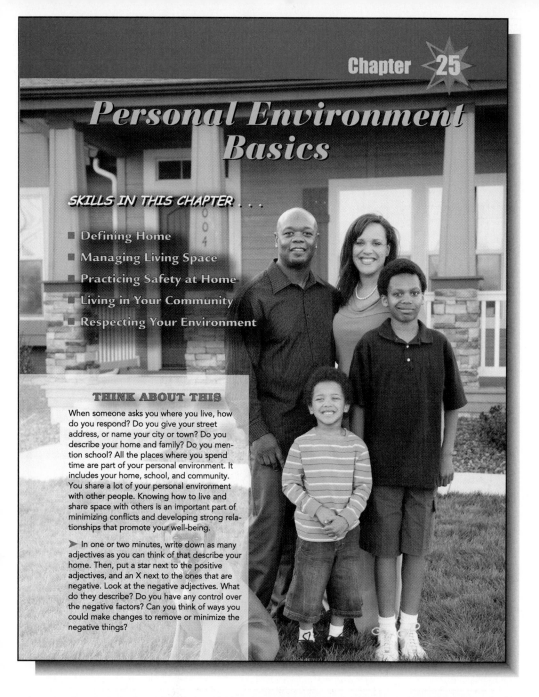

Chapter 25

Personal Environment Basics

SKILLS IN THIS CHAPTER . . .

- Defining Home
- Managing Living Space
- Practicing Safety at Home
- Living in Your Community
- Respecting Your Environment

THINK ABOUT THIS

When someone asks you where you live, how do you respond? Do you give your street address, or name your city or town? Do you describe your home and family? Do you mention school? All the places where you spend time are part of your personal environment. It includes your home, school, and community. You share a lot of your personal environment with other people. Knowing how to live and share space with others is an important part of minimizing conflicts and developing strong relationships that promote your well-being.

➤ In one or two minutes, write down as many adjectives as you can think of that describe your home. Then, put a star next to the positive adjectives, and an X next to the ones that are negative. Look at the negative adjectives. What do they describe? Do you have any control over the negative factors? Can you think of ways you could make changes to remove or minimize the negative things?

Chapter 25 Overview

This chapter discusses the many factors that define an individual's personal environment. These include your home or dwelling, the school you attend, and the community in which you live.

Defining Home In this section, different types of dwellings are identified. Students also learn how they can contribute to a happy, healthy home environment.

Managing Living Space The values and standards of you and your family help make a home livable. This section discusses how to organize living space so all family members feel safe and comfortable.

Practicing Safety at Home This section explores ways you can make your home safe. Tips are provided on fire safety and basic first aid. Students also learn what steps they can take to prevent accidents in the home as well as prevent crime.

Living in Your Community This section explains how your quality of life and living standards extend to your roles and responsibilities at school, at work, and in the community.

Respecting Your Environment This section discusses the importance of being environmentally aware. Students explore methods for conserving resources and disposing of and managing waste.

Focus and Engage

Bell-Ringer: Think About This

Students are to write down as many adjectives as they can think of to describe their home. Give students one to two minutes to do this, although if you see that some are struggling, you can allow another minute or two.

When they are done, they should put a star beside the positive adjectives and an X beside the negative ones. You might encourage students to share their list of adjectives with the class. Ask students if they think other family members would list similar adjectives. For example, a student might think their house is disorganized and messy, but their siblings think it is fine the way it is. Ask students for ideas on how to manage different living styles and preferences.

ADVANCE PREPARATION

Review	*Life Skills for the 21st Century* textbook, Chapter 25.
Prepare	Paper and pencil for some activities.
	Colored pencils or markers and plain white paper.
	Box labeled "Hot Topics."

CUSTOMIZED INSTRUCTION OVERVIEW

Less Advanced Students	More Advanced Students	ESOL Students	Special Needs Students	At-Risk Students
Pages 470, 477, 480	Pages 472, 474	Pages 470, 477	Pages 470, 477, 480	Pages 471, 474

Introduce the Section

In this section, different types of dwellings are identified. Students also learn how they can contribute to a happy, healthy home environment.

Figure Focus

Ask students to describe their homes. Do they live in a single-family house or an apartment? How many rooms and bathrooms does the home have? Do they have their own bedroom or share one? What type of common living areas, such as kitchen, living room, and basement, does it have?

Vocabulary

Dwellings or residence: Buildings where people live.

Defining Home

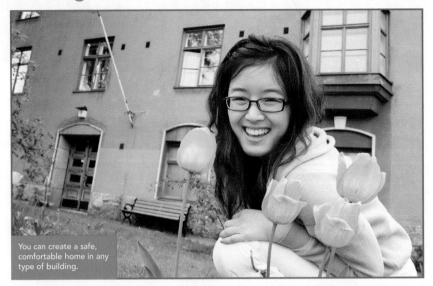

You can create a safe, comfortable home in any type of building.

Where do you call home? For some people, home is the place where they live. For others, it is the town where they grew up. Some call the planet Earth home. For others, home is any place they feel safe and loved.

There are many types of **dwellings**—buildings where people live. Another word for dwelling is **residence**. You might live in a single-family house or a high-rise apartment. You might live in a condominium or a mobile trailer. Any building can meet your basic need for shelter, but that does not make it a home.

A home provides more than just shelter. It provides safety and comfort. It gives you space to store your belongings, and space to take part in activities alone or with family and friends. A home reflects your lifestyle—the quality and style of life you lead—and your values.

Recognizing the way a home meets your needs, and the needs of your family, can help you contribute to the development of a happy, healthy, home environment.

Homes Meet Many Needs

The place you live can meet many basic needs, including physical needs, such as shelter; psychological needs, such as security; and functional needs, such as a closet for your clothes.

- A healthy and comfortable home provides shelter from heat, cold, wind, and rain. It offers a place where you can eat and sleep.
- A safe and secure home provides protection from danger and intruders. It might have smoke detectors, as well as strong doors and locks, and be well lit inside and out.
- A comfortable home is a place where family provides love and support. It lets you grow and develop with a strong, positive sense of self, and an understanding of your values.
- A functional home provides accessible space. It can be customized to meet special needs, such as wheelchair ramps, wide hallways, and easy grip door handles. It might have flashing lights to indicate the ring of a phone or doorbell.

Customized Instruction: Less Advanced/Special Needs Students

Have students draw a picture of their house or the building in which their home is. They should write the address underneath and also list the names of all the people living in their home.

Customized Instruction: ESOL Students

Have students draw a picture of their house or the building in which their home is. They should write the type of dwelling it is (refer to the list on page 471) in their primary language and also list the names of all the people living in their home.

Your Role at Home

How do you fit in at home? Are you a son or daughter? Are you a brother or sister? Do you share your home with one person, with a group of unrelated individuals, or with a large family?

■ If you are an only child, you might have a lot of private space, including your own bedroom and bathroom. You share common areas such as the kitchen and living room. You do not disturb anyone if you turn the bedroom light on in the middle of the night, or set your alarm clock for early in the morning. Does that mean you can leave a wet towel on the bathroom floor?

■ If you live with a lot of people, you might share space. You take turns in the bathroom and store your clothes in a shared closet. Does that mean you can wear your brother's sweatshirt without asking?

You show that you are mature and responsible by respecting your home, the people who live there, and their belongings.

What About Responsibilities?

What are your responsibilities at home? Do you let others clean and cook? Do you stay alone in your room or spend time with your family? Are you just a **resident**—someone who lives there—or are you an active participant—someone who cooperates with the other people to create a healthy home for all?

■ You can contribute to care for the shared space by keeping your personal belongings in your own space.

■ You can take responsibility for your own belongings and personal space by keeping your toys, books, and gadgets neat and organized.

■ You can share responsibility for common areas and shared belongings by leaving the television remote where everyone can find it, sticking to a bathroom schedule, and asking permission before using something that belongs to someone else.

■ You can use communication skills as well as the qualities of patience, tolerance, and good humor to minimize and avoid conflicts.

"If I help in the kitchen, will my parents think I am responsible?"

Dwellings in Other Countries

Not everyone in the world lives in homes that look like homes in the United States. A *yurt* is a portable, felt-covered dwelling called home by many people in Mongolia. A *bulla* is a straw, dome-shaped hut called home by the Atr tribe in the country of Eritrea.

Select a country and then use books or the Internet to research their traditional styles of homes. Discover how the homes were constructed and whether they are still in use today. Did factors such as climate or lifestyle influence the style and material? Write a real estate listing for one of the homes.

Where Do You Live?

Housing comes in many shapes and sizes. Here are a few types of places where people live.

✔ *Apartment: One of three or more dwellings in a common building. Apartments are rented or leased by the residents, not owned.*

✔ *Boarding house: A facility that offers single rooms for rent and provides meals.*

✔ *Condominium: An apartment that you own. Your ownership extends inward from your interior walls, floors, and ceilings. You share ownership in common areas and exteriors with the other owners in the complex.*

✔ *Co-op: An apartment building or other type of dwelling owned by all of the residents.*

✔ *Duplex or 2-family: Two dwellings in a common building. The dwellings may be apartments or condominiums.*

✔ *Mobile home: A house trailer that can be connected to utilities such as electricity and water, parked in one place, and used as permanent housing.*

✔ *Single-family home: A dwelling that sits on its own piece of land that is not attached to anyone else's dwelling.*

✔ *Townhouse: A dwelling that is attached to one or more other houses, but which sits directly on a parcel of land that you also own.*

✔ *Group home: A family-style living arrangement run by state or local governments.*

✔ *Shelter: A temporary living arrangement run by state or local governments for people who have no where else to live.*

Reinforce and Review

Review with students the concepts of roles and responsibilities. A role is the way you behave, or your function, in a specific situation. A responsibility is something you are expected to do or accomplish in the roles you fulfill. Ask students to comment on their specific roles at home. They should be able to list several, such as older brother, younger sister, son or daughter, grandson or granddaughter. Have them consider other roles they might fulfill, such as mentor to a younger sibling or caretaker to an elderly or ill relative.

Vocabulary

Resident: A person who lives in a place permanently or for the long term.

Figure Focus

Ask students to discuss their responsibilities at home. Encourage them to be specific. Ask them what impact it would have on their home environment if they did not take care of their responsibilities.

Where Do You Live?

You might read through the list of housing types and have students raise their hands for the type in which they live. What's the most common?

 Dwellings in Other Countries

Students are to select a country and research its traditional styles of homes. They are to find information on how the homes are constructed and what factors influence the styles and materials used. Using the information collected, they should write a real estate listing for one of the homes. You might have students read through real estate listings online or in your local newspaper to get a better idea of the type of information to include; for example, the general size and construction of the home, the number of rooms, availability of utilities, and other amenities.

Customized Instruction: At-Risk Students

Have students divide a piece of paper into two columns. In the left column, they should list the pros of living in the home they do; in the right column, they should list the cons. Then, have them pick one item listed as a con and discuss how it could be transformed into a pro.

Introduce the Section

The values and standards that are important to you and your family help make a home livable. This section discusses how to organize living space so all family members feel safe and comfortable.

Figure Focus

Ask students who do not have their own room at home to discuss creative ways to get privacy. Here are some tips:

- Find a room or space that others won't be walking through.
- Define the space with a personal item, such as a beanbag chair, a poster, or a wall hanging.
- Create coziness or comfort by adding a lamp or favorite blanket.
- Soundproof the space with a rug or piece of carpeting and pillows.
- If possible, use a screen, tall plants, bookcase, or other piece of furniture to partition off the space or mark its boundaries.
- Add personal accents, such as photos, favorite books, or artwork.

Vocabulary

Living space: Includes the rooms and areas in a home where you spend time.

Managing Living Space

You can manage your living space so that you have a place to be alone and a place to be with others.

A home does not have to be large in order to accommodate—or fit—the needs of the people who live there. More important than the size is the organization of the living space. **Living space** includes the rooms and areas in your home where you spend your time.

- *Common areas*, such as the kitchen, family room, or yard, are where you spend time with other people.
- *Personal areas*, such as a bedroom or bathroom, are where you spend time alone.

If a home is organized so that the people in the home can access the space they need, then it can be a comfortable environment for everyone.

What Makes a Home Livable?

A livable home is one in which you feel safe and comfortable. It reflects your lifestyle choices, goals, and values.

In addition to organized living space, factors that make a home livable include the location, the condition, and the services that are available. For example, you might think a home is livable because you have lots of friends in the neighborhood. You might think a home is not livable because the roof leaks. You might think a home is livable because the city picks up trash and recycling.

Not everyone agrees on what makes a home livable. It depends on your values and standards. It depends on the goals you have for your own personal environment.

- If you value luxury, you might set a goal to have a home in a neighborhood with large, new, single-family houses.
- If you value security, you might set a goal to have a home with an alarm system wired to the police station.
- If you value conserving resources, you might set a goal to have a home built from recycled material and designed to use a minimal amount of energy.

Customized Instruction: More Advanced Students

Have students create a list of the top ten things that make their homes livable. They should list them in the order of importance to them personally. Have them compare their lists with a classmate.

Organizing Living Space

When you organize living space, keep two basic categories in mind: space for activities and space for storage. For example, you need space in your kitchen for activities such as cooking and eating, but you also need space for storing food and equipment.

Also, most living areas serve more than one purpose. A kitchen is for cooking and eating, but you might also use the kitchen table for homework, crafts, and socializing with family and friends.

- In your bedroom, you might need storage space for clothing and accessories, books, games, and electronics. You might need activity space for sleeping, reading, studying, and listening to music.
- In the bathroom, you might need storage space for towels, toilet paper, and shampoo. You might need activity space for taking a shower, brushing your teeth, and fixing your hair.
- In the family room, you might need storage space for a television, DVDs, video games, computer, board games, and blankets. You might need activity space for watching television, playing games, taking a nap, socializing, or listening to music.
- Outside, you might need storage space for a car, bicycles, outdoor games, and equipment for caring for the yard. You might need activity space for grilling, playing games, and socializing.

Creating Privacy

Most homes are bustling with activity. On any evening, one person might be getting ready for a game or practice, another might be cooking or eating. Someone might be practicing a musical instrument, and someone might be trying to get work done. There is noise and commotion everywhere.

At times, even when you live with only one other person, your home can seem crowded. You might feel as if you have no space to yourself; nowhere quiet where you can be alone.

Privacy—having space and time to yourself—is an important need. Everyone needs time to relax away from the demands of roles and responsibilities.

If you have your own room, you can escape to it whenever you want. If not, you can work with your family to find a solution to the problem. You might be able to:

- Arrange a schedule of times when you can have a room to yourself
- Use noise-canceling headphones to block out the commotion around you
- Go outside for a walk or bike ride
- Go to the library
- Discuss guidelines for when family members should knock on a closed door

Leave Me Alone!

You feel tired and worn out from school and activities and just want to be alone to listen to music or chat with friends. How can you make a case for privacy?

👎 Sulk and slam doors

👎 Lock yourself in your bedroom or the bathroom

👎 Sneak out of the house without telling anyone

👍 Discuss your concerns in a calm and reasonable way

👍 Express privacy as a positive goal, such as needing time to think, grow, and be yourself

👍 Prove through your actions that you are responsible and can be trusted

How can you share resources such as the bathroom and computer with your family and still manage to respect everyone's privacy?

Why is it important to find privacy in a busy, active household?

Discuss

Ask students to discuss living space and storage space in their homes. Where do they typically store their personal belongings, such as clothing and shoes, recreational items (bicycles, rollerblades, skateboards, etc.), and personal hygiene items? Do they have a system of organization for their belongings?

Vocabulary

Privacy: Having space and time to yourself.

Leave Me Alone!

Explain that privacy and having "your own space" is a common source of conflict for many families. Conflicts like these can invade other areas of your life. To minimize conflict with family members, suggest the following steps:

1. Respect your family. Without mutual respect, there will always be conflict. People who respect each other can disagree without yelling and getting angry. They can talk calmly and rationally about a conflict and figure out together the best way to resolve it.

2. Communicate with your family. If you share and are open with them, you will probably find them to be helpful and supportive. If you shut them out, though, they might automatically think the worst.

3. Show honesty and responsibility to build your family's trust. When people trust each other, they are less likely to create confrontations.

Figure Focus

Ask students to comment on why they value privacy. Does it allow them to concentrate better on schoolwork? Or do they value it because nobody can judge them or make demands on them when they are alone and in private? Is it easier to relax and unwind in private? Do they seek privacy when they are upset or angry over something?

Introduce the Section

This section explores ways you can make your home safe. Tips are provided on fire safety and basic first aid. Students also learn what steps they can take to prevent accidents in the home as well as prevent crime.

Figure Focus

Ask students to discuss the security measures that are in place at home. Do they practice security by keeping doors and windows locked? Does their home have a security system? Do they know how to contact the local police if there is a security problem? Does their family have a plan of action in place in case of an intruder?

Discuss

Discuss neighborhood factors that contribute to the safety and security of a home. For example, does the neighborhood have sidewalks and green space? Are lawns well-kept and litter-free? Is the neighborhood well-lit? Are traffic and pedestrian signs clearly visible? Ask students to comment on the neighborhoods in which they live and how their upkeep and maintenance affect individual home security.

Practicing Safety at Home

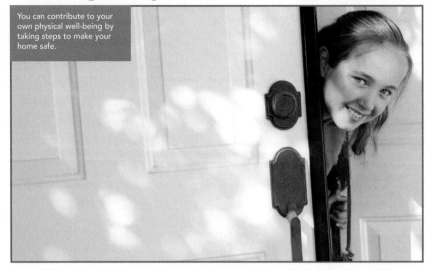

You can contribute to your own physical well-being by taking steps to make your home safe.

Do you feel safe at home? There are two factors to consider regarding home safety: preventing injuries and accidents and keeping out intruders who might steal or cause harm to people or property.

Preparation is the first step for keeping your home safe and coping with emergencies. For example, you can have a first aid kit ready in case you need to treat an injury. You can create an emergency escape plan in case you must get out of your home quickly. You can prepare for weather emergencies, such as hurricanes or tornadoes by storing emergency food and equipment such as flash lights, and planning an escape route.

Stopping Crime

Some neighborhoods might have more crime than others, but any home in any neighborhood can be a target for thieves and others interested in doing harm. You can put security systems in place to prevent crimes.

- To keep unwanted visitors out, check that all doors and windows have locks that work. Keep your doors locked, even when you are home. Open the door only if you know the person who is knocking.
- Intruders avoid homes with bright outside lights, alarm systems, and dogs. You can notify your community's department of public works if street lights are not working. You can install bright bulbs in your outdoor light fixtures. You can even install motion-sensitive lights that turn on automatically when something—or someone—moves near them.
- Thieves look for places where no one is home. To make your home looked lived in, stop the mail delivery, leave a radio playing, or put lights on a timer to turn on and off in different rooms at different times.
- You can organize a neighborhood watch, where people keep an eye out for unusual or suspicious activity.

Customized Instruction: At-Risk/More Advanced Students

Pair up one of your more advanced students with an at-risk student. Have them research a neighborhood crime prevention program. This can be one that already exists in the community or one that has been started in other cities. Students should find out the focus and mission of the group, how they operate, how their efforts are coordinated with local law enforcement, and the levels of success they've experienced. Students might also research the steps involved in organizing such a group. Have them prepare a short report or presentation on the group that they can share with the class.

Preventing Falls

Studies show that more injuries happen at home than in any other place. Most injuries that happen in homes result from falls. You can take steps to lower the risk of falls by following these guidelines.

- Safe stairways are well lit, in good repair, and free of litter. Handrails and carpeting help limit falls on stairs. Installing **nonskid** strips or pads can also prevent falls on stairs. Nonskid strips or pads are made of rubber, plastic, or another material that provides traction—gives your shoes something to grip.
- People can slip or trip on spilled food or objects left on the floor. You can prevent this by cleaning up spills as soon as they happen and by keeping toys and clothes off the floor.
- Area rugs are safer if they have nonskid backing to keep them from moving. Bathtubs can have nonskid mats or stickers and grip bars.
- People sometimes stand on wobbly chairs, boxes, or tables to reach high places. This is dangerous because you can easily lose your balance and fall. Use a sturdy stepladder or step stool.

Fire Safety

House fires can start from many sources, including careless use of space heaters, candles, stoves, grills, and fireplaces.

- Cigarettes are one of the most common causes of death in home fires. Most cigarette fires start when a lighted cigarette is dropped onto a bed, furniture, or clothing. The best way to avoid a cigarette fire is to not smoke.
- Electrical fires are caused by overheated wires and problems with electrical outlets. One way to prevent an electrical fire is to make sure you do not overload an outlet by plugging in too many appliances or appliances that use more electricity than the outlet can produce. Another way to prevent electrical fires is to make sure all electrical cords are in good repair.

Smoke detectors provide warning if there is a fire, giving you time to escape. Check the number and placement of smoke detectors in your home. There should be at least one on every level, near the kitchen, and outside bedrooms.

Can you think of types of equipment you can install in your home to improve safety?

TECH CONNECT

Many homes are now being equipped with keyless entry security systems, which let authorized people enter by punching in a code, swiping a card, or touching a fingerprint pad. Keyless entry offers many benefits.

- It is faster and easier for an authorized person to enter the home.
- It is more difficult for an unauthorized person to gain entry.
- It is easier for someone with a motion or vision disability to use a keyless entry system.

Use books or the Internet to learn more about keyless entry systems. Then, make a poster that demonstrates one way a keyless security system can make a home safer or more livable.

We've Been Robbed!

You come home from vacation to find that thieves have ransacked your house and stolen all your valuables. How can you protect your home when you are away?

- Leave a note on the door, away message on your e-mail or social networking page, or on your voice mail saying that you are away
- Leave all lights off
- Let newspapers and mail pile up in front of the house
- Set timers on lamps to turn on and off at usual times, so people think you are home
- Ask a trusted friend or neighbor to collect your mail and newspapers, and keep an eye on the house
- Activate an alarm system

Can you think of other problems that might come up while you are away from home, and steps you can take to avoid them?

Discuss

Discuss with students the safety precautions they take at home. In addition to the measures discussed in the text, you might talk about the following:

- In the kitchen, keep cleaning supplies in locked or tightly secured cabinets. Never mix cleaning materials. Wipe up spilled grease, water, and other liquids. Keep pot and pan handles turned inward, away from stove edges. Use a sturdy step stool for reaching things at higher levels.
- In the bathroom, use rubber mats or strips in the tub or shower. Never use electrical appliances around water.
- In the stairways and halls, install sufficient lighting and keep these areas picked up and free of toys, shoes, and other items. Make sure banisters and handrails on stairways are tightly secured. Use rug pads under rugs to keep them from sliding.
- In the basement, garage, and storage areas, make sure flammable or combustible products are stored properly away from sources of heat and out of the reach of children. Throw out oily rags and combustible piles. Do a regular maintenance check on furnaces, water heaters, and chimneys.

Figure Focus

Other types of safety equipment include:

- **Smoke detectors.** These devices identify the products of combustion in their earliest stages, thereby setting off a warning alarm. Often, the smoke will be invisible to the eye.
- **Heat detectors.** These devices are for areas where smoke alarms are not recommended, such as kitchens and garages. They activate an alarm when the temperature reaches a specific point.
- **Sprinkler systems.** These operate on the same principle as heat detectors. When the temperature at a sprinkler head reaches a certain level, water is released and an alarm is sounded.
- **Carbon monoxide detectors.** These detect the presence of carbon monoxide, which is a harmful gas that can be released from faulty heating and gas appliances as well as unvented or poorly vented heaters, barbecues, and motorized vehicles.
- **Radon detectors.** These detect the presence of radon gas, which is a naturally occurring, odorless, and colorless gas produced by the breakdown of uranium in soil, rock, and water. It can seep into buildings through openings or cracks in the foundation and then be inhaled by the building's inhabitants. Inhalation of radon has been linked to lung cancer.
- **Mold detection devices.** These can be in the form of tape lifts, swabs, or petri dish mold kits. They are designed to identify mold, which at certain levels can be toxic and harmful to humans.

We've Been Robbed!

Other problems that might come up while you are away from your home include burst water pipes; power outages that knock out timers on lamps; power surges that cause an electrical fire or damage to electronics; and problems resulting from severe weather, such as fires from lightning strikes, water damage from heavy rains and floods, and downed trees and exterior damage caused by high winds.

TECH CONNECT

Students are to research keyless entry systems and create a poster that illustrates how such a system can make a home safer and more livable. Keyless locks are designed to be "bump-proof," unpickable, and hacksaw-proof. Lock "bumping" is a lock-picking technique for opening a standard key lock using a specially-crafted bump key. One bump key will work for all locks of the same type.

Job Search

Students are to write a description of a job in architecture or construction, urban planning, or community development that interests them. Refer them to the Architecture & Construction and Science, Technology, Engineering & Mathematics career clusters in *Appendix A* of the student text as a starting point. You might also have them search help wanted ads in newspapers, magazines, and online to see descriptions of jobs in these industries.

Vocabulary

Carbon monoxide: Colorless, odorless gas that can be deadly. Faulty furnaces, gas ovens, and motor vehicles can produce or leak carbon monoxide.

Electrical shock: Flow of electricity through the body.

Electrocution: Death by electrical shock.

Fumes: Gas in the air.

Poison: Substance that causes injury, illness, or even death when it enters the body.

APPLY IT

Have students prepare an emergency escape plan for their home. You might want to give them a day or two to complete it so they can include their family's input. They should create a poster that outlines the plan and presents the information in a suitable format for family members of all ages.

Job Search

If you have an interest in housing, there are many different careers that you might like. If you enjoy working with your hands, you might consider a career in construction. If you like to draw, you might consider a career in architecture. If you are interested in the way people live in different communities, you might consider a career in urban planning or community development.

Careers in the architecture and construction career cluster include pathways in design, construction, and building maintenance. Education requirements and working environments vary depending on the job. Most require math and computer skills, as well as an ability to be organized and pay attention to detail.

Use the Internet, library, or your school's guidance resources to learn more about a career in architecture and construction, or in urban planning or community development. Select a job that appeals to you, and write a job description, including the educational requirements, career pathway, and potential salary range.

Emergency Escape Plan

How would you get out of your home if there was an emergency such as a fire? Follow these guidelines to make an emergency escape plan.

1. Discuss with your family the importance of being prepared for an emergency.

2. Draw a floor plan of your home. Mark two or more escape routes from each room that you could use in an emergency.

3. Choose an emergency meeting place for your family to gather once you are all out of the home.

4. Hang up the floor plan where every family member can see it.

5. Write the names and phone numbers of two neighbors where you can go in case of an emergency.

6. Have regular emergency drills with all family members.

Prevent Poisoning

A **poison** is a substance that causes injury, illness, or even death when it enters the body. Some household plants are poisonous if you eat them. Most household cleaning products such as laundry detergent, bathroom cleaner, and glass cleaner are poisonous if you swallow them. Medicine taken in the wrong dosage, or for the wrong condition, can also be poisonous. Alcohol can be poisonous.

Children and babies are at high risk of poisoning because they put things in their mouths and cannot read warning labels. It is important to store all poisons out of the reach of children and babies or in a locked cabinet.

Some poisons can be spread by **fumes**—gas in the air. If you breathe poisonous fumes, you become sick. Some household cleaners must be used in a room with ventilation—fresh air—or outside to avoid breathing in too many dangerous fumes. Some household cleaners such as bleach and ammonia create a poisonous, deadly gas when they are combined.

Carbon monoxide is a colorless, odorless gas that can be deadly. Faulty furnaces and gas ovens can leak carbon monoxide. Motor vehicles produce carbon monoxide. You can install carbon monoxide detectors in your home to sound a warning if there is carbon monoxide in the air.

Prevent Electrical Shock

An **electrical shock** is a flow of electricity through the body. Electrical shock may cause serious burns; injuries to internal organs, such as your heart; and even death. Death by electrical shock is called **electrocution**. Shocks can happen when electrical appliances such as hair dryers, coffeemakers, and power tools are wet or are not working properly. Here are some ways to prevent electrical shock or electrocution.

- Never use an electrical appliance if the floor, your body, or your clothes are wet.
- Pull the plug, not the cord, when you disconnect a lamp or appliance.
- Cover electrical outlets with safety plugs in homes with small children.
- Do not put anything other than a plug into an electrical outlet.
- Unplug electrical appliances that do not seem to be working correctly. Have them repaired or replace them.
- Avoid above-ground and buried power lines.

Getting Help

Often, the first thing to do in an emergency is call for help. The 911 emergency telephone system notifies emergency responders that you are in danger. You can use 911 to report crimes, accidents, medical emergencies, and fires. If 911 is not available in your area, you can call the police or fire department directly. When you call, calmly provide information, answer questions, and follow directions until you are told to hang up.

It can be helpful to have the names and phone numbers of family and friends entered in your cell phone, so you can call them in an emergency. It is also a good idea to enter an emergency number in your cell phone number directory or address book. Name the entry *Emergency* and enter the phone number of someone such as your parents or guardian who you would want the police to call if you were in trouble and needed help.

When there is a fire, leave your home immediately. Follow these guidelines.

- Do not stop for belongings.
- Drop to the floor and crawl to a door. Stay close to the floor where there is more air to breathe, and less smoke.
- Carefully touch the door or doorknob before leaving or entering a room. If it is hot, take a different route out, such as a window.
- Meet your family outside of the house in a safe place, and call 911.

Basic First Aid

You may be able to treat minor injuries at home using basic first aid. **First aid** is the first care you give to someone suffering from an injury, illness, or accident.

- To treat bleeding, press a clean, soft cloth against the wound, and raise the injured body part up higher than the heart.
- To treat a cut or wound once the bleeding has stopped, clean the area with warm water. Wipe away dirt and debris with warm soapy water. Apply an antibiotic cream and a clean bandage.
- To treat a mild burn, put it under cool water immediately to stop the burning process. When it is cool, apply a burn ointment or spray to ease the pain. Do not apply any type of oil, grease, or butter.
- To treat a minor sprain or strain, remove all weight from the injured body part, rest the body part, apply ice or cold compresses several times a day to relieve swelling, and apply an elastic bandage or splint.

If someone stops breathing, you should call 911. The proper action is to administer **cardiopulmonary resuscitation** (CPR), which can keep the heart pumping and air entering the lungs. You can do more harm than good if you do not know the correct way to perform CPR. You can become certified in CPR by taking a course from your local Red Cross or hospital.

MONEY MADNE$$

> **Y**our family is moving into a new home. You need to install three smoke detectors and two carbon monoxide detectors. The smoke detectors cost $17.99 each. The carbon monoxide detectors cost $32.99. How much will all of the detectors cost?

A First Aid Kit

A safe home has a first aid kit, which is a container with a lid that you can store in a handy location. Stock your first aid kit with the following items.

- ✔ *Exam gloves to wear when helping someone else*
- ✔ *Pain reliever tablets such as ibuprofen*
- ✔ *Tweezers for removing splinters*
- ✔ *Alcohol wipes*
- ✔ *Antiseptic hand cleaner*
- ✔ *Medical adhesive tape*
- ✔ *Sterile gauze*
- ✔ *Elastic bandages*
- ✔ *Several sizes of adhesive bandages*
- ✔ *Insect bite swabs*
- ✔ *Triple-antibiotic ointment*
- ✔ *Hydrogen peroxide*
- ✔ *Bandage scissors*
- ✔ *Triangular bandages*
- ✔ *Instant cold packs*

Myth The first step to stop a nosebleed is to lean your head back.

Truth Leaning back actually causes the blood to drip down into your throat, which can cause you to throw up. The correct action is to lean forward and pinch the nose just below the bridge for at least five minutes. Repeat two or three times, and if the bleeding does not stop, call 911.

Vocabulary

Cardiopulmonary resuscitation (CPR): Emergency procedure to revive somebody whose heart has stopped beating that involves clearing the person's airways and alternating heart compression with mouth-to-mouth respiration.

First aid kit: Container with a lid in which you can store items with which to administer first aid treatment.

A First Aid Kit

Ask students if their family keeps a first aid kit at home or in the car. Does it contain the items that are listed in the text? Which ones are missing? Does it have items in addition to these?

Discuss

Discuss some of the following first aid remedies with students. Or, you might consider inviting your school nurse to the classroom to discuss basic first aid. Be sure to emphasize that first aid is temporary help you give a person until professional medical assistance can be provided.

- **Insect bites and stings.** Unless a person is allergic, most insect bites and stings are not serious. Remove a stinger with tweezers and apply a soothing cream or a paste of baking soda and water.
- **Fainting.** If someone says he feels as if he is going to pass out, have him sit down and lower his head between his knees or lie down with the head lower than the rest of the body. If a person does faint, lay her flat on the back, elevate the feet, and loosen any tight clothing.
- **First-degree burns.** Apply cold water to the affected area.
- **Blisters.** Wash the affected area and apply a sterile dressing and bandage. Do not pop a blister.
- **Sprains.** Elevate affected limb or appendage and apply cold compresses.
- **Cuts or scrapes.** Clean affected area, blot dry, and cover with antibiotic ointment and bandage. For deeper wounds that are bleeding, apply pressure on the wound to stop bleeding.
- **Frostbite.** Rewarm person slowly in room temperature. Cover frozen part with your hand or place in warm water.
- **Animal bites.** Rinse the wound under running water for several minutes. Apply an antibiotic and cover with sterile gauze.
- **Heatstroke or sunstroke.** Move person to a cool place. Remove extra clothing and cover with cold cloths, or place person in a tub of cool water.

MONEY MADNE$$

Smoke detectors: $3 \times \$17.99 = \$53.97$
Carbon monoxide detectors: $2 \times \$32.99 = \$65.98$
Total cost: $\$53.97 + \$65.98 = \$119.95$

Myth/Truth

You might discuss some other common mistakes people make in administering first aid. For example, you should not put butter or grease on a burn; you should not rub frostbitten toes or fingers with snow or ice; and you should not give someone who has swallowed a poisonous substance milk or water in hopes of diluting it.

Customized Instruction: Less Advanced/Special Needs Students

Have students role-play various emergency situations or instances where one person needs to administer first aid to another. For example, have them act out what they would do if another person twisted his or her ankle; what they would do if someone got a fairly deep cut; or what they would do if someone got a nose bleed.

Customized Instruction: ESOL Students

Have students role-play a situation in which they must call 911 to report that a family member is choking. The goal is to have them speak clearly in English to provide the necessary information, such as the reason for the call and their address.

Introduce the Section

This section explains how your quality of life and living standards extend to your roles and responsibilities at school, at work, and in the community.

Figure Focus

Ask students to consider how rules and ethics help define their behavior at school, at work, and in the community. For example, does the school have rules regarding the clothes you wear and the way you act in the cafeteria or hallways? Are you expected to be honest and respectful of others? Discuss how following rules and a code of ethics contribute to a feeling of safety and security within the school, work, and community environments.

Living in Your Community

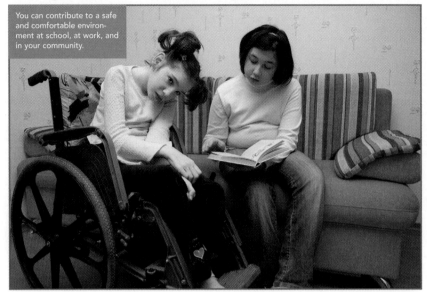

You can contribute to a safe and comfortable environment at school, at work, and in your community.

Your life is not limited to the space inside your home. You might not sleep at school, the local library, or at work, but they are part of your living space.

- You share space at school with teachers, administrators, and peers.
- You share space in the community with neighbors, public service workers, and business owners.
- You share space at work with co-workers, customers, and supervisors.

Recognizing that you can contribute to a positive lifestyle for the people in all areas of your life helps you build strong relationships, avoid conflict, and develop a positive self-image.

Living at School

You spend a lot of time at school. Feeling safe and comfortable in your school community is important for all aspects of your well-being. How can you help develop a strong community in school? You can:

- Show up on time and be prepared for class
- Respect your classmates and teachers
- Participate in afterschool activities
- Join organizations such as FCCLA
- Speak up for yourself and others
- Treat the school building and property with the same respect you show to your own belongings

---

Stay in School

Researchers have found that an individual's level of involvement in his or her community is closely tied to education. A recent report released by the National Conference on Citizenship found that high school dropouts are less likely to vote, to go to places of worship, and to do volunteer work than better-educated Americans. In 2004, for example, only about 30 percent of high school dropouts voted compared to 62 percent of those with a college degree.

Furthermore, you might explain that those with a high school diploma contribute significant fiscal benefits to their community over their lifetime. In addition to the payment of taxes and their purchasing power, they are less likely to commit crimes, rely on government health care, or tap other public services.

Being a Good Neighbor

Does the cashier at the local market know your name? Do you pick up trash in front of your home? Do you keep an eye on the other kids at the bus stop, or walking to and from school?

You can take steps to be a **citizen**—or active member of the community—by becoming involved and interested in the welfare of the other citizens who live there, too. You can:

- Introduce yourself to neighbors and business owners
- Show respect for police, firefighters, and other public-service employees
- Volunteer for a community organization
- Keep your neighborhood clean
- Treat public buildings and resources with respect
- Obey community laws and regulations

Living at Work

If you have a job, the time you spend at work should contribute to your well-being and the well-being of your co-workers, customers, and employers. You can take action to help make your work environment a comfortable living space. You can:

- Show up on time
- Have a positive attitude
- Respect your co-workers, customers, and supervisors
- Keep your workspace neat and organized
- Respect the privacy and personal space of others
- Use honest and open communication to avoid and resolve conflicts

How can being a good citizen contribute to your well-being?

21st Century Skills

What Happens Next?

One evening in August, Derek and his friends were playing soccer on the field outside the local high school. As they were leaving, one boy, Cody, found a can of spray paint lying near the field. He picked it up and started shaking it. It was full. Cody sprayed his name on the grass at the edge of the field.

Derek told Cody to throw the can in the trash, but the other boys wanted to spray their names. Cody started running towards the school building. He sprayed a line along the path as he ran. The other boys ran after him.

Use your decision-making skills to help Derek, Cody, and the other boys recognize the problems they are facing and make wise decisions. Consider actions they might take, and the consequences of each action. Using your 21st Century Skills—such as decision making, goal setting, and problem solving—write an ending to the story. Read it to the class, or form a small group and present it as a skit.

Finding Ways to Help

Volunteering is one of the best ways to become involved in your community (refer to Chapter 9). It helps you develop skills and interests that may lead to career goals. It encourages you to build relationships with different types of people. It contributes to your well-being and positive self image. What if you want to volunteer, but do not know where?

- ✶ *Ask your FCCLA advisor for information about volunteer opportunities.*
- ✶ *Meet with your career or guidance counselor to discuss possibilities.*
- ✶ *Contact your community's youth commission or community service association.*
- ✶ *Look for a volunteer Web site in your area where organizations list openings.*
- ✶ *Directly contact an organization that matches your skills and abilities.*
- ✶ *Create your own opportunities by thinking of ways you can organize others to benefit your community.*

Finding Ways to Help

Suggest students ask themselves the following questions to help them determine suitable ways to get involved:

- What social and human rights issues are most important to you personally?
- How strongly do you feel about environmental protection?
- How important is it to you to help others get on good financial footing?
- What do you think is the biggest problem facing your local community?
- Would you rather help people close to home or people in far-away countries?
- Are you interested in animal rights causes or anticruelty issues?

Vocabulary

Citizen: Active member of the community.

Reinforce and Review

Review the term "civic responsibility." This refers to the services or duties you provide as a conscientious citizen of your community. It could be as simple as throwing your trash or recycling in the proper receptacle, or trying to find the owner of a lost dog. Or it could be a bigger commitment, like running for a political office or helping to build affordable housing for low-income families.

Figure Focus

Explain that being an active citizen in the community is essential to personal wellness. People who are active and do volunteer work tend to have a positive attitude and high self-esteem. Being involved can help build character and focus your attention and energies on your strengths and the things you value rather than on activities that might involve risky behaviors. The positive interactions with others who are involved and who volunteer can relieve stress and broaden your network of quality contacts.

CRITICAL THINKING ACTIVITY

Discuss with students the idea of "paying it forward." Benjamin Franklin wrote in a letter to his friend Benjamin Webb that instead of paying back the sum of money Webb borrowed, he could repay him by lending the sum to another "honest man in similar distress." The expression "pay it forward," which has been popularized more recently in books and movies, stems from the idea of asking that a good turn be repaid by having it done to others instead.

Ask students to consider acting on this concept. Can they think of recent circumstances in which they could have paid it forward? Discuss in class or have students write about it.

21st Century Skills

What Happens Next?

Students are to prepare an ending to the situation with Derek, Cody, and the other boys. Students' endings should focus on Cody and the other boys' disrespectful attitude toward the environment and the property of others. Not only can the spray paint damage the grass, but the boys are violating laws designed to protect property owners from vandals and trespassers.

Introduce the Section

This section discusses the importance of being environmentally aware. Students explore methods for conserving resources and disposing of and managing waste.

Figure Focus

Review some of the environmental problems that are of concern to the general population. Discuss ways in which people can support efforts to address these problems. Some responses are:

- Global warming awareness and prevention.
- Planting trees to re-grow forests that have been cut down.
- Setting limits on how much pollution companies can release into the air and water.
- Protecting the habitats of endangered species
- Working with auto makers to reduce air pollution from vehicles, and supporting the development of alternative fuels.
- Cleaning up landfills, dumps, roadsides, and other areas
- Promoting the use of recycling programs and recycled paper and plastics.

Vocabulary

Ecosystem: Community of living things.

Respecting Your Environment

You can make decisions that will help protect and preserve the environment for future generations.

*E*nvironment has a lot of meanings. It can be any area where you spend time, such as your kitchen environment, or your classroom environment. It can also be a mood or feeling in a particular space. You might think your grandmother's house is a comfortable environment or that a hospital emergency room is a scary environment.

Environment also refers to an **ecosystem**, or community of living things. Using that definition, our environment includes all the natural resources on the planet Earth. Recall from Chapter 1 that *natural resources* are things that exist in nature and are available for everyone. Natural resources include air, water, wildlife, minerals, and plants, and all the things that live in our environment.

People share a responsibility for protecting the health and safety of our environment (refer to Chapter 9). We also share a responsibility for conserving our natural resources so that they remain available for you, your children, and your grandchildren, for generations to come.

Environmental Awareness

The environment is pretty big. There is a whole government agency—the Environmental Protection Agency (EPA)—responsible for making policies and laws controlling the environment. You are just one person. How can your actions make a difference?

Every person lives in our environment. Every person has an impact on our environment. The way you live and the decisions you make can have positive or negative consequences on our environment and our natural resources. Being aware that your actions can affect the environment can help you make decisions with positive consequences.

- Plastic pollutes our environment with trash and can harm animals that eat it or get tangled in it. You can recycle plastic and use refillable water bottles.
- Automobiles produce air pollution and harmful gases. You can take public transportation, ride, or walk, and you can encourage adults to purchase cars that have lower emissions.
- Chemicals in household products seep into the soil and water, poisoning plants and animals. You can read labels to identify and select products without harmful chemicals, and encourage adults to do the same.

Customized Instruction: Less Advanced/Special Needs Students

Have students write a definition for "ecosystem" and then list a type of ecosystem. Have them identify resources provided by the ecosystem that help humans live and thrive.

An ecosystem is defined as an interdependent group of natural elements and organisms that exist in a particular environment. Ecosystems can be categorized into two major types: terrestrial (land-based) and aquatic (water-based). The main biomes within the two categories are forest, arctic, grassland, desert, tundra, urban, littoral (seaside), lake, river, swamp, and ocean.

Conserving Resources

How much clean air is enough? How much water will we need in the future? Believe it or not, natural resources might not last forever. Some are nonrenewable, which means when they are gone, they are gone forever.

People might produce so much pollution that the air becomes poisonous. We might use so much coal, natural gas, and petroleum that we have none left to produce energy for electricity or gasoline for cars. The damage we do to the environment might cause animals such as polar bears to become extinct—cease to exist, never to return.

You can **conserve**—save—natural resources by using less of them. There are many opportunities in the areas of your life to conserve resources. Here are a few suggestions:

- At home, you and your family can save energy by turning off lights when you leave a room and by wearing sweaters instead of turning the temperature up on the thermostat. You can save water by fixing leaky faucets and taking showers instead of baths.
- At school and work, you and your peers can collect paper for recycling. You can ask to keep the heat lower in cold months and higher in warm months. You can ask to install energy-efficient light bulbs and to use reusable trays in the cafeteria.
- In the community, you and your neighbors can plant trees to absorb carbon dioxide and produce oxygen, which helps keep the air and climate healthy. You can educate others on the importance of recycling. You can put out rain barrels to collect rain for watering lawns and gardens.

Managing Waste

Waste has two meanings. It is the trash we produce that cannot be used for another purpose. For example, when you use a paper towel to wipe your hands, then throw it away, you create waste. Waste is also excess or unnecessary use of resources. When you leave the water running while you brush your teeth or comb your hair, you are wasting water.

How can you make decisions that reduce the amount of waste? By using the three R's of conservation: Reduce, Reuse, and Recycle.

- *Reduce* is the first step in conservation. It means reducing the amount of resources you use in order to reduce the amount of waste you produce. For example, you and your family could use cloth napkins instead of paper napkins. You can purchase energy-efficient appliances.
- *Reuse* an item instead of throwing it away and buying something new. Alter clothing so you can continue wearing it. Repair broken appliances. Use old towels and sheets for cleaning rags or for washing a car. Carry reusable cloth grocery bags instead of getting paper or plastic at the store. Use broken glass or pottery to create artwork such as a mosaic. You can even buy products made from recycled material.
- *Recycle* your trash instead of throwing it away. You can recycle paper, cardboard, most types of plastic, aluminum cans, and glass. If your community does not have a recycling program, take steps to get one started. Recycle books and clothing that are in good repair by giving them to charity.

> "Wait! I wonder if I could get more use out of these before I throw them away?"

Waste Disposal

How do people get rid of trash?

- We bury it in landfills. Some landfills are turned into parks or recreation centers. But often, when trash is buried, it leaks poisonous chemicals into the water and soil. Landfills can smell bad and attract rodents.
- ✔ We burn it in incinerators. When trash is burned, it can produce poisonous gases that pollute.
- We dump it at sea. The oceans are filling up with trash at an alarming rate. It harms the plants and animals. Chemicals such as mercury become part of the food chain, which means that when we eat fish that have eaten mercury, we are eating the mercury, too. High concentrations of mercury can be toxic.
- ✔ We recycle. Recycling is the most environmentally friendly way to dispose of trash, because it turns waste into products that can be used for a new purpose.

What alternatives can you think of instead of throwing away food and trash?

TEAMWORK ACTIVITY

Have the class develop a school recycling program. You can suggest they follow the steps below:

1. Determine what can be recycled.
2. Select an organizer, or main point of contact, for the program.
3. Identify recycling handlers that will collect recyclables.
4. Determine the type of recycling containers you will need.
5. Decide how to collect and store the recyclables.
6. Educate students and teachers about the program.

Vocabulary

Conserve: To save.

Figure Focus

Discuss items that can be donated for reuse. These include:

- Cell phones, which can be donated, recycled, and distributed to people in underdeveloped countries.
- Computers and electronics, whose parts are recycled and then used in other machines.
- Eyeglass lenses and frames, which are recycled or refitted for needy persons who cannot afford them.
- CDs, which you can donate or trade in at music stores.
- Holiday cards, which you can cut up to make unique and individual gift tags.
- Household items, clothing, toys, and furniture, which you can donate to charities or other non-profit organizations.

Waste Disposal

Share the following definitions with students:

- **Landfill:** Area containing buried waste.
- **Solid waste:** Garbage that has a definite firm shape and volume.
- **Pollutants:** Harmful substances in air and water.

Figure Focus

Discuss with students how common items can be recycled into other common items. For example:

- Old newspapers become new newspapers.
- Old corrugated boxes become new corrugated boxes.
- Old paper becomes new writing paper and stationery, and paper used for books, magazines, and brochures.
- Scrap paper becomes paper towels, tissues, and egg cartons.
- Old grocery bags become dog food bags and wrappings for mailed catalogs and magazines.
- Toy boxes and shoe boxes become new cereal boxes, pizza boxes, and soft drink cartons.

End-of-Chapter Activities

Case Study

Answers will vary, but most students will recognize that Marianna is angry because she had made plans, and had certain expectations about what her life would be like when Rose moved out, and those plans are not going to happen. Also, they may believe she is angry because her mother did not discuss the situation with her ahead of time, so she was surprised and caught off guard.

Most will think Marianna's mother did not handle the situation well. She should have taken Marianna into consideration from the start, because Marianna is directly affected by the change. She did not show Marianna the respect Marianna deserves.

Marianna faces the challenge of living with a new person. She will not get the privacy she was counting on, or the extra space. She will have to adjust to the habits and patterns of her cousin.

Marianna should try to make the best of the situation. She should talk to her mother about ways she can find more privacy and space in their home. She should also talk to KiKi about how they can share space happily. KiKi might want to help with the redecorating. She might be able to sew or create storage containers for the room. She also might be willing to take up less storage space in order to give Marianna more.

Sounding Off!

Student answers will vary.

FAQ

1. A dwelling is a residence or building where people live.
2. You can contribute to creating a healthy home in the following ways.
   - You can contribute to the care of shared space by keeping your personal belongings in your own space.
   - You can take responsibility for your belongings and personal space by keeping your toys, books, and gadgets neat and organized.
   - You can share responsibility for common areas and shared belongings by leaving the television remote where everyone can find it, sticking to a bathroom schedule, and asking permission before using something that belongs to someone else.
   - You can use communication skills as well as the qualities of patience, tolerance, and good humor to minimize and avoid conflicts.
3. Common areas in the home are kitchen, family room, living room, and backyard. Students may think of others.
4. The personal area is space where you spend time alone, such as a bedroom or bathroom.
5. Factors that contribute to making a home livable include the location, the condition, and the services that are available.
6. Privacy is having space and time to yourself.
7. You can protect your home from crime by:
   - Making sure doors and windows have locks that work.
   - Keeping your doors locked at all times, and only open them to let in people you know.
   - Installing bright outside lights or notify the police if streetlights are not working.
   - Installing an alarm system.
   - Making your home look lived in even if you are away. Do not let newspapers and mail pile up. Set up timers to turn lights on and off, or leave a radio playing.
   - Organizing a neighborhood watch. Students may think of others.
8. The best way to avoid a cigarette fire is to not smoke.
9. Ways to conserve resources at home include:
   - Taking showers instead of baths.
   - Fixing leaky faucets.
   - Turning off lights when you leave the room.
   - Installing low-energy light bulbs and appliances.
   - Wearing sweaters instead of using more heat.
   Students may think of others.
10. The three R's of conservation stand for reduce, reuse, and recycle.

Student edition page 482

Chapter 25 ▪ Personal Environment Basics

Case Study

Marianna and her sister Rose share a bedroom. Marianna is looking forward to September, when her sister Rose will move out to live in a dorm at college. Marianna is excited to have more space for her clothes and other belongings. She is planning to sew new curtains, a bedspread, and pillow covers from a fabric she picks out herself. She can already picture herself living in a room of her own.

The week before Rose leaves, their mother calls Marianna into the kitchen to talk. She says that Marianna's younger cousin, KiKi, is going to come live with them. KiKi will arrive the day after Rose leaves, and will move into Rose's place in the shared bedroom. Her mother says she expects Marianna to make KiKi feel welcome. Mariana is stunned and angry. She runs to her bedroom and slams the door.

- Why do you think Marianna is so angry?
- Do you think Marianna's mother handled the situation well?
- What challenges are now facing Marianna?
- What options do you think Marianna should consider?

Sounding Off!

1. Do you share a room with anyone? If you do, how do you make it work?
2. Do you think your parents and grandparents meet their responsibilities for protecting and preserving the environment? Why or why not?

FAQ

1. What is a dwelling?
2. List four ways you can contribute to creating a healthy home for yourself and your family.
3. List three common areas in your home.
4. What is a personal area in a home?
5. List three factors that contribute to making a home livable.
6. What is privacy?
7. List four ways you can protect your home from crime.
8. What is the best way to avoid a cigarette fire?
9. List four ways you can conserve resources at home.
10. What do the three R's of conservation stand for?

482 Chapter 25 ▪ Personal Environment Basics

As a class, make a list of natural resources. Divide the class into teams of three or four. Randomly select one of the natural resources. As a team, take two minutes to write down as many ways as you can think of to conserve the selected resource. Repeat the exercise with the remaining natural resources. Compare your answers with the other teams. Your team gets a point for every unique idea—an idea that none of the other teams came up with. The team with the most points wins.

Hot Topics

Do you feel safe and comfortable in your home? Why or why not? Have you discussed your concerns with anyone?

Take this opportunity to write anonymously about your feelings toward your home environment. Use a word processor so no one recognizes your handwriting. Be honest and open. Put the paper in the class Hot Topics box.

As a class, read the anonymous entries and discuss them.

```
Web Extra   ▼
```

The Internet is full of information about how you can conserve resources and suggestions for ways to reduce, reuse, and recycle.

Locate some credible and helpful Web sites that you think might be useful for your peers. Make a directory of the sites, including the Web site address and a description of the site. Post the directory on your school Web site or in your school career center or library.

Problem Solver

Adults are always complaining that the electric bill is too high. They get angry when you take a long shower, because water costs money, too. How can you and your family work together to conserve resources in your home?

Keep a resource log for one week to track how you and your family use resources such as water, electricity, and gas. Include information about how much trash and waste you create. At the end of the week, use your problem-solving and decision-making skills to analyze your habits and look for ways you might be able to conserve. Write an action plan for your family.

Team Players

Student teams will compete to see which team can come up with the most ideas on how to conserve a natural resource. Natural resources include air, water, wildlife, minerals, and plants. Make sure you allow only two minutes for teams to come up with their ideas for each resource.

Hot Topics

Make sure students understand that they can turn in their papers anonymously. Encourage them to be open and honest about their feelings concerning the safety and comfort of their home environment.

Web Extra

Students are to create a directory of Web sites that provide useful information on conserving resources and helpful tips on reducing, reusing, and recycling. The directory should include the Web site address and a brief description of the site.

Remind students that a reliable Web site usually publishes the name of the author or organization that sponsors it and the date the content was created or last updated in a fairly obvious location, such as at the top or bottom of the page or on the home page. The site is usually organized with headings and an obvious navigation system. A reliable site clearly states its purpose and any affiliations. You should also look for accuracy in spelling and grammar.

Students should post the directory in their school career center or library.

Problem Solver

Students are to keep a log for a week that documents how their family uses resources, such as water, electricity, and gas, and the amount of waste that is generated in that same time period. Students might find it helpful to place "usage" sheets near the bathroom tub or shower, sink, and kitchen sink, as well as on major appliances, such as the washer and dryer, dishwasher, and stove/oven. They should have each family member fill in the time for when they started their usage and when they stopped. If possible, they should also record the gas and electric meter readings at the beginning of the week and at the end of the week. Their parents might be able to help them determine the cost of electricity and gas per unit, or they could contact the local utility company.

Write Now

Students are to write a one-page biography of a person who has succeeded in a career in environmental protection or resource conservation. They might find potential candidates through their parents, relatives, neighbors, teachers, church, and community organizations. Remind students that a biography is an account of a person's life and is based on fact. It can include direct quotes from the person as well as from other people who know the person.

Be Involved!

As a class, students are to plan a project that educates their peers about the negative consequences of vandalism. This might be articles for the school newspaper, a presentation or video, a panel discussion, or a presentation by a law enforcement or other community leader to the school.

Students are to use the FCCLA planning process outlined below to develop, execute, and evaluate their efforts.

- Identify the project.
- Set a goal.
- Form a plan (who, what, when, where, how, cost, resources, and evaluation).
- Act.
- Follow up.

Remind students that a successful team relationship depends on all team members working together. Make sure they take steps to delegate responsibilities, communicate effectively, and manage conflicts or disagreements.

Social Networking

Students are to create a directory of the government agencies with offices available in their community. It should include the address, phone number, Web address, and a description of the services the agency provides. Students should also be encouraged to include information on if and how each agency uses volunteers. An optional item for the directory is a map identifying the buildings in which the agencies are housed as well as other historical sites or points of interest within the community.

Write Now

Many people work in jobs to protect the environment and conserve resources. There are waste management engineers, environmental analysts, and chemical engineers. There are lawyers who work for environmental agencies, architects who design energy-efficient buildings, and community activists who organize recycling programs.

Write a one-page biography of someone who succeeds in a career in environmental protection or resource conservation. Use books or the Internet to investigate the career. Include information about the interests, abilities, and characteristics that helped the person succeed, as well as the type of education required, and his or her career path.

Be Involved!

www.fcclainc.org

Vandalism is the willful destruction or defacing of property. It is against the law. It costs communities a lot of money, and makes them unattractive and unsafe. As a class, use the FCCLA planning process to organize a project that educates your peers about the negative consequences of vandalism. You might write articles for your school or local newspaper, create a presentation, video, or brochure, organize a panel discussion, or invite representatives from the community to speak to an assembly. Set a goal and brainstorm projects and activities. After considering all possible options, select the project that you think will be the best one for achieving your goal.

Make an action plan for achieving your goal. Include a timeframe, make sure the plan is realistic and attainable, and then put the plan into action. You may want to organize teams within the class to handle specific responsibilities, such as volunteer management and publicity.

As you work toward your goal, keep a class journal to record your progress, and collect documentation that you can use to show what you have achieved. After the project is complete, evaluate your success. Did you achieve your goal? Were you able to get the message out about the negative consequences of vandalism? Are there things you could have done differently? Prepare an article about the event and send it to the school or community newspaper. You might also want to send it to your FCCLA chapter so they can publish it in their newsletter.

Social Networking

Being a good citizen means learning how to live and work as an active member of your community. Help others learn about the government agencies available in your community. Working in small groups, or as a class, make a directory of the main government buildings in your community. Include the address, phone number, Web address, and a description of the services available, and even how community members might be able to get involved as a volunteer. For example, you might include your city hall, county courthouse, police station, fire station, hospitals, schools, and libraries. If possible, include a map showing the location of each. Expand the directory to include historical or other points of interest. Make the directory available in your school library or on your Web site.

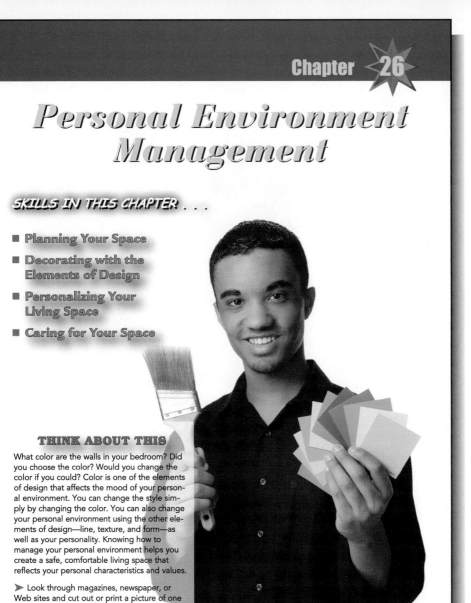

Chapter 26

Personal Environment Management

SKILLS IN THIS CHAPTER . . .

- **Planning Your Space**
- **Decorating with the Elements of Design**
- **Personalizing Your Living Space**
- **Caring for Your Space**

THINK ABOUT THIS

What color are the walls in your bedroom? Did you choose the color? Would you change the color if you could? Color is one of the elements of design that affects the mood of your personal environment. You can change the style simply by changing the color. You can also change your personal environment using the other elements of design—line, texture, and form—as well as your personality. Knowing how to manage your personal environment helps you create a safe, comfortable living space that reflects your personal characteristics and values.

➤ Look through magazines, newspaper, or Web sites and cut out or print a picture of one piece of furniture or a home accessory that you would like in your living space. Explain what appeals to you about the object.

485

Chapter 26 Overview

This chapter provides tips and information on how to make your personal living space functional, comfortable, and uniquely yours. It also discusses how to organize, decorate, personalize, and care for your space.

Planning Your Space   Students learn the importance of organizing their personal space in order to maximize comfort as well as functionality. Students also learn how to create and use a floor plan.

Decorating with the Elements of Design   This section explores further the elements and principles of design and how to apply them to personal space. Tips are provided on home decorating and selecting quality furniture.

Personalizing Your Living Space   In this section, students learn how to express their personal style in the way they decorate and accessorize their living space.

Caring for Your Space   This section explains the importance of maintaining a neat and clean home. Basic maintenance as well as the tools and resources used to clean a home are covered.

Focus and Engage

Bell-Ringer: Think About This

Students will need magazines and newspapers or access to the Internet for this exercise. They are to find a picture of a piece of furniture or a home accessory that they would like to have in their living space. Discourage students from selecting entertainment or recreational types of items, such as stereos, TVs, or video game consoles. They should focus on items that would contribute to the comfort and functionality of their living space. Ask students to share with the class why they chose the item they did.

ADVANCE PREPARATION	
Review	*Life Skills for the 21st Century* textbook, Chapter 26.
Prepare	Paper and pencil for some activities.
	Colored pencils or markers and plain white paper.
	Graph paper.
	Newspapers and magazines (preferably related to interior design, home decorating, or architecture).
	Box labeled "Hot Topics."

CUSTOMIZED INSTRUCTION OVERVIEW

Less Advanced Students	More Advanced Students	ESOL Students	Special Needs Students	At-Risk Students
Pages 487, 492, 493, 494	Page 489	Pages 487, 495	Pages 492, 493, 494	Pages 487, 492

Introduce the Section

Students learn the importance of organizing their personal space in order to maximize comfort as well as functionality. Students also learn how to create and use a floor plan.

Figure Focus

Help students distinguish between functional and comfortable. *Functional* means to have a practical application or serving a useful purpose, such as a kitchen table. *Comfortable* refers to something that makes you feel physically relaxed, like a chair with soft, fluffy cushions. Ask students to name a functional item in their homes, a comfortable item, and an item that is both functional and comfortable (such as a bed).

Vocabulary

Barrier-free living space: Space that is organized and designed so everyone can use it.

TEAMWORK ACTIVITY

Divide the class into teams and have them research the idea of barrier-free parks and playgrounds. These are springing up around the country to give disabled children and adults the same opportunities to socialize and enjoy recreational activities as others. Some of the things you find at a barrier-free playground or park include:

- Wider paths with safe, smooth surfaces.
- Swings with high backs and straps.
- Elevated sandboxes that are wheelchair height.
- Climbing apparatus equipped with special grips and hand holds.
- Adjustable basketball hoops and backstops.

As part of their research, have students identify barrier-free parks and playgrounds in their community. If there is no such facility, ask them what they could do to get their community to develop one.

Planning Your Space

You can plan your living space to be functional and comfortable.

Your home living space includes the areas you share with other people, such as the kitchen and family room, and your personal space, such as your bedroom. It also includes the objects and items within that space.

- A functional living space meets the needs of everyone who uses it. It has chairs and sofas for sitting, desks for studying, and mirrors for showing one's reflection.
- A comfortable living space reflects the lifestyle, values, and standards of the people who use it. The chairs and sofas are comfortable, the desks are in a quiet location with good light, and the mirrors are at the right height.

Usually, adults will plan and organize the common areas of a home. If the home is a rental—you pay rent to live there and do not own it—there may be restrictions to what you can and cannot change. However, there are ways you can use your own creativity to organize and design your personal space so it reflects your interests, personality, and style.

Barrier-Free Space

Barrier-free living space is space that is organized and designed so everyone can use it—even people with disabilities. Some barrier-free accommodations, such as wheelchair ramps, wide hallways, and shower safety bars, require construction or remodeling. However, there are many things you can do to make a home accessible and barrier-free with some organization and planning.

- You can remove area rugs that might trip or block someone who is mobility-impaired.
- You can improve lighting for someone who is vision-impaired.
- You can install easy grip door knobs and handles.
- You can organize closets so clothing hangs low enough for someone in a wheelchair to access.
- You can organize study space so someone with a learning disability can focus without distractions.

Organizing a Functional Living Space

A major goal of organizing living space is to make it functional. When you plan and organize your space, consider the purpose of the space, as well as the habits and preferences of the people who will use it. **Traffic flow**, which is the way people move through a room, is a key consideration. For example, is it important to keep a pathway clear so people can walk through the room? Is it important to group seating so people can socialize?

■ Keep in mind that space that functions for one person might not function for someone else.
■ You might like to study sitting in a straight-backed chair at a desk.
■ Your brother might concentrate better lounging in a bean-bag chair with his books on a lap desk.

Organizing a Comfortable Living Space

A second goal is to make your space comfortable. A comfortable living space takes the functional elements and makes them convenient and comfortable to use. For example, would you put an overstuffed easy chair at your kitchen table?

Like function, convenience and comfort depend a lot on who will be using the space.

■ A low chair might not be comfortable for a tall adult.
■ A young child may not be able to reach items in the top drawer of a dresser.

Living space works best if it is functional and comfortable. How can you make sure your space meets your needs and reflects your personality?

Job Search

There are many careers in personal environment management. If you have a knack for organizing objects and colors in pleasing arrangements, you might be interested in a career in interior design. Interior designers work to develop and create homes and business environments that satisfy the needs and wants of their clients. They might work for large companies or have their own small businesses. You might also be interested in closet or home organization jobs, drapery and accessory manufacturing, or working in a retail shop that specializes in home décor.

You might prefer a job in maintenance. Building and home maintenance careers include jobs cleaning homes or offices, trades such as electrician or plumber, and roofers.

Use the Internet, library, or your school's guidance resources to learn more about a career in personal environment management. Select a job that appeals to you, and write a job description, including the educational requirements, career pathway, and potential salary range.

My Room Is Uncomfortable!

Your room has everything in it you need, including a bed, chair, and desk, but it feels cold and unwelcoming. What can you do to make your living space functional and comfortable?

👎 Paint all the walls bright white
👎 Use the same furniture you have had since you were five years old
👎 Let family members tell you how to decorate
👍 Display objects that have personal meaning
👍 Select furniture and accessories that fit your needs
👍 Cooperate with family members to decorate the room

What other steps can you take to make a room functional and comfortable?

Vocabulary

Floor plan: Map of a room that shows the shape of the space looking down from above, and how objects fit inside it.

Figure Focus

A floor plan is helpful because it enables you to determine what objects will fit in certain areas before you actually go to the trouble of moving furniture. It also identifies the location of doors, windows, closets, sinks, tubs, toilets, and heating registers or ventilation ducts, which are important to consider when designing and organizing a space. For example, you would not want to place a couch over top of a heating and air conditioning floor vent.

Scaling Your Bedroom

Other professions that might use scaled drawings include:

- Builder
- Architect
- Engineer
- Carpenter
- Artist
- Pipefitter
- Electrician
- Construction worker

MONEY MADNE$$

First total the cost of all supplies.

- Paint: $22.95
- Paint rollers: $3.25 × 2 = $6.50
- Paint trays: $1.79 × 2 = $3.58
- Paint brushes: $1.82 × 4 = $7.28
- Drop cloth: $3.15

The total is $43.46. Then divide the total by 2. Your share will cost $21.73.

Scaling Your Bedroom

You can use a floor plan to see if you want to rearrange the furniture in your bedroom, but you must first adjust the scale so you can draw the plan on a sheet of paper. What if your bedroom is 12 feet long by 10 feet wide? What if your bed is 6½ feet long by 3½ feet wide?

★ *If you choose 1 inch to equal 1 foot: You would draw the room 12 inches long by 10 inches wide, and the bed 6 ½ inches long by 3 ½ inches wide*

★ *If you choose ½-inch to equal 1 foot: You would draw the room 6 inches long by 5 inches wide and the bed 3¼ inches long by 1¾ inches wide.*

★ *If you choose ¼-inch to equal 1 foot: You would draw the room 2½ inches wide by 3 inches long and the bed 1⁵/₈ inches long and ⁷/₈ inch wide.*

An interior designer uses scale drawings to make floor plans to help clients see what a room might look like. What other professions might use scaled drawings?

MONEY MADNE$$

You share a room with your sibling. You both want to paint the room chocolate brown. Your parents give permission, but they say you must pay for the painting supplies yourselves.

You will need the following supplies: one gallon of paint for $22.95 per gallon; two paint rollers for $3.25 each; two paint trays for $1.79 each; four paint brushes in assorted sizes, for $1.82 each; one drop cloth for $3.15.

You are going to split the cost of supplies evenly. How much will your share of the supplies cost?

Using a Floor Plan

A **floor plan** is a map of a room that you use to organize the objects in the room. It shows the shape of the space looking down from above, and how objects fit inside it. You can use the floor plan to try different arrangements until you find the one that is functional, livable, and appealing.

How does a floor plan help you plan and organize your space?

Because it is not practical to draw a map the actual size of the room, you scale a floor plan to make it smaller. Recall from Chapter 22 that *scale* means to adjust measurements equally by the same amount. When you adjust the measurements equally, the proportions remain the same relative to the space and other objects.

To draw a floor plan to scale, you select a measurement unit you want to use to represent 1 foot. For example, you might choose 1 inch to equal 1 foot, or ½-inch to equal 1 foot. Then, you adjust all measurements using the selected measurement unit.

You can draw a floor plan on graph paper by scaling down the width and length of the room, and then scaling down the size of the objects you want to place in the room.

TEAMWORK ACTIVITY

Divide the class into three or four teams. Each team will need one or two tape measures and sheets of graph paper. Each team is to draw a floor plan of your classroom. They should get the measurements of the room first and then those of the movable furniture in the room, including desks, chairs, bookcases, cabinets, etc. Their floor plans should identify any partitioned areas of the room as well as windows, doors, and closets. Refer students to the floor plan illustrated on this page of the student text.

Making Do with What You've Got

Whether you have a room to yourself or share with others, chances are you wish you had more space. Here are some tips for making even a crowded living space feel open and comfortable.

- *Eliminate clutter.* That means organizing storage for all your stuff—from papers and schoolwork to games and electronics to clothes and shoes.
- *Choose the right color.* Paint the walls a soft cool color to make the room appear larger than it really is.
- *Select furniture that lets you use the most space.* Plan for bunk beds or a loft to make floor space available for other uses. Hang shelves for storage off the floor
- *Allow for light.* Make the most of the natural light from windows, and use lamps to highlight specific areas such as a desk or reading area.
- *Use mirrors.* Hang a mirror so it reflects as much space as possible. For example, hang it to reflect out the window, the door into the room, or artwork.

Sharing a small space can be difficult. What can you do to minimize conflict when you share living space with others?

NUMBERS GAME

You want to replace the carpet in your bedroom. How much carpet do you need?

Carpet is measured and sold in square feet. To calculate how many square feet you need, you calculate the area. The formula for calculating the area of a rectangle is length (l) × width (w) = area (A)

- If your room is 11 feet long and 8 feet wide, how much carpet do you need?
- If your room is 12½ feet long and 9¼ feet wide, how much carpet do you need?

If you take up the carpet and find a beautiful hardwood floor, you might decide you would like a round area rug instead of wall-to-wall carpet. How do you calculate the area of a round rug?

The formula for calculating the area of a circle is radius (r) × radius (r) × pi (π) = area (A).

The radius is the length of a straight line from the center of the circle to any point on the circle, or half the diameter (d). The diameter is the distance across a circle through its center. Pi equals 3.14.

What is the area of a round rug that is 5 feet in diameter?

- Divide 5 by 2 to find the radius: $5 \div 2 = 2.5$
- Multiply the radius by the radius and the product by pi: $2.5 \times 2.5 \times 3.14 = 19.625$.

The round rug has an area of 19.63 square feet.

You do the math! What is the area of a round rug that is 4½ feet in diameter?

21st Century Skills

What Happens Next?

Jayden lives with his mother and two brothers. Recently, the landlord raised the rent on their apartment, so Jayden's mother started working a second job. She is very busy, and she expects the boys to help out with chores around the house.

The boys know they have a responsibility to help their mother, but they do not like to clean. They usually wash their dishes after meals, but they never sweep the floor. They hang up their towels after they shower, but they never clean the toilet. They forget to take out the garbage until it starts to smell.

One evening, Jayden is studying in his room. He hears his mother come in the house. She drops her keys on the kitchen counter, and then she screams. The boys race into the kitchen. Their mother is standing on a chair. She says she saw a mouse run through the room when she turned on the light.

What challenges are facing the family? What behaviors have brought them to this point? Consider actions they might take, and the consequences of each action. Using your 21 Century Skills—such as decision making, goal setting, and problem solving—write an ending to the story. Read it to the class, or form a small group and present it as a skit.

Ask those students who share a bedroom to comment on how they manage differences they might have with their "roommate." For example, do they consult with each other on decorating and design changes? Do they have equal storage space? Do they respect each other's need for quiet and privacy?

NUMBERS GAME

If your room is 11 feet long and 8 feet wide, you multiply length by width:

$11 \times 8 = 88$ square feet

If your room is 12½ feet long and 9¼ feet wide, convert the measurements to decimals and then multiply:

$12.5 \times 9.25 = 115.63$ square feet

To find the area of a round rug that is 4½ feet in diameter:

$4.5 \div 2 = 2.25$

$2.25 \times 2.25 \times 3.14 = 15.9$ square feet

21st Century Skills

What Happens Next?

Students are to prepare an ending to the situation with Jayden and his family. Their endings should address the cause of the problem, which is the boys' irresponsible housekeeping. They could solve the problem by coming up with a list of cleaning chores that the boys can take turns doing, such as mopping the kitchen floor, cleaning the toilet, and taking out the trash. If they share in the work, it will not seem like such a chore and they will end up with a cleaner, safer, and more comfortable home.

Customized Instruction: More Advanced Students

Have students research a design style, such as contemporary, traditional, country, art deco, retro, Southwest, Victorian, etc. They should find a picture of a room that represents the style and write a summary of the style's characteristics. Have them share with the class.

Introduce the Section

This section explores further the elements and principles of design and how to apply them to personal space. Tips are provided on home decorating and selecting quality furniture.

Figure Focus

Remind students that the basic elements of design are line, color, texture, space, and shape. The principles of design include balance, repetition, emphasis, and proportion. Have students discuss the elements and principles of design evident in the photo. For example, the colors are bright and bold; the fuzzy covering on the headboard provides texture and also serves as a point of emphasis; and the straight lines of the bedspread and headboard contrast with the round shapes on the wallpaper, helping to provide balance.

Discuss

Discuss with students types of multifunction furnishings. For example, sleep sofas and futons, beds with under-bunk drawers or cubby shelves and bookcase headboards, chairs that recline and have built-in drink holders or magazine racks, bookcases and entertainment centers that can be reconfigured in a variety of ways, a table that doubles as a desk, and baskets that serve as side tables. Ask students to discuss clever ways they've converted household items into room furnishings.

Decorating with the Elements of Design

You can use design to create a pleasing living space.

You decorate your living space by arranging furniture and home accessories. Home accessories include objects such as pillows, curtains, picture frames, and souvenirs.

The elements and principles of design that were introduced in Chapter 23 for constructing clothing are also useful for designing and furnishing your living space. They give you the tools you need to design a space that creates a mood or feeling, reflects a style, and has a pleasing appearance.

You can identify the ways that the elements and principles of design impact your living space. Then, you can select and arrange accessories and furniture to create a pleasing, comfortable, and functional home.

How Do I Select Furniture?

Furniture makes a room comfortable. It defines the purpose of the room, and makes a room functional. You choose furniture based on a number of factors.

- *Function.* You want a piece of furniture that is functional. A chair that tips over when you sit in it is not functional, even if it looks really cool. A bed that is too small is not functional.
- *Personal taste.* There are many styles of furniture. You want a piece that you like to look at. You might find the sleek lines of a modern desk appealing. Your friend might prefer the romantic look of a French Provincial table.
- *Cost.* Furniture comes in a wide range of prices. You want furniture that fits your budget.
- *Quality.* Good-quality furniture will last longer than lesser-quality pieces. Look for sturdy pieces that don't wobble. Other characteristics depend on the type of furniture. For example, high-quality wood furniture will not have staples and glue holding the parts together. High-quality upholstery should use a durable fabric.

Stay in School

Some studies show that twice as many high school dropouts are unemployed and living in poverty than those with a high school diploma.

Ask students what they think it is like to live in poverty. Many might imagine destitution, where the home has scant furnishings and might even lack utilities, such as running water and heat. Others might imagine it as having only the basic necessities, such as adequate housing, decent nutrition, and sufficient clothing. Still others might envision it as just the average way of life, where you live in a house, have a car, watch TV, and eat three meals a day. Living conditions for those in poverty vary widely, but one thing that remains constant for poor people is real material hardship. Even with public assistance in the form of low-income housing, food subsidies, and health care, people in poverty do without many extras, including the things that make their living space comfortable and functional.

Ask students to consider what their personal living space might be like if they could not afford extras. What would they have to do without? How would that make them feel?

Elements of Design in Home Decorating

Recall that the basic elements of design are line, color, and texture. When you design a living space, it is good to also consider **form**, which is the shape of a three-dimensional object, and the space around it. For example, the form of a wooden rocking chair is different from the form of an upholstered easy chair.

- Lines in a room can be structural, such as the frame around a door. They can be decorative, such as a pattern on a carpet. Use vertical lines to make objects look taller or ceilings look higher. Use horizontal lines to make things look wider. As in clothing, straight lines are clean and strong. Curved lines are soft and graceful.

- Texture is the look and feel of surfaces. Texture can set a mood or make a room look interesting. Use shiny surfaces such as polished marble to make a room look clean and cool. Use soft surfaces such as plush fabric drapes to make a room look warm and cozy.

- Color can set a mood, reflect personality, and make a room look larger or smaller. Use light colors and tints to make a room seem larger, and darker colors and shades to make a room seem smaller. Use warm colors such as orange or yellow to bring energy into a room. Use cool colors such as blue or green to make a room calm and soothing.

- All three-dimensional objects have form or shape. You can arrange objects so their forms look appealing and do not conflict with each other. It is also important to consider the space between objects. Too much space makes a room feel empty. Too little space makes it feel crowded.

Principles of Design in Home Decorating

Recall that the *principles of design* are the qualities that describe the way the elements of design work together—in this case, the way line, color, texture, and form work together to create a functional, comfortable, and appealing living space.

- Use **balance** to make the room feel even. Too many objects on one side of the room, too much color in one spot, or an uneven arrangement of pictures or accessories can create an unbalanced feeling.

- Use **proportion** to manage the size of objects in relation to each other. Use large furniture and accessories in a large room and smaller items in a smaller room.

- **Rhythm** is the way your eyes move through a room or across a design. There are different techniques to control rhythm, including repetition. In repetition, you might use the same color on the walls and in the sofa fabric, or the same shape for pillows and picture frames. Other types of rhythm include **gradation**, which is a gradual change in size or shape, and **opposition**, which is an abrupt change, such as right angles defining a fireplace or bookshelf.

- Use **emphasis** to create a focal point in the room. Emphasis is useful if you have a special object you want to highlight, such as the view out a window or a family portrait.

- **Harmony**—the opposite of conflict—means cooperation and unity. You can create harmony by using a similar element of design in different objects. For example, you might have a similar color in the curtains, pillows, and carpet, even if the textures are different.

Get Organized

It can be hard to see the design potential in a room cluttered with clothes and personal items. What if you want to redecorate, but you have so much stuff that you don't know where to begin?

- ★ *Donate clothes, books, and toys you have outgrown, to make space for new items.*

- ★ *Box up items you want to keep but rarely use, such as old photos, trophies, and toys. Ask your parents if there is a place in the house you can store the boxes, such as the attic or basement, or put them under your bed.*

- ★ *Put up shelves for displaying personal items such as souvenirs or a collection.*

- ★ *Put up more shelves for storing books and electronic gadgets.*

- ★ *Buy or make boxes that fit under your bed for storing clothes that are out of season, such as sweaters in summer or bathing suits in winter.*

What other steps can you take to clean out and organize clutter in your personal space?

Myth Your decorating plan should include the most fashionable colors and accessories.

Truth Fashion comes and goes. If you use your personal style, interests, and values as a guide, you will create an environment that suits your own needs and comforts.

Reinforce and Review

Review the following definitions with students:

- **Line:** Element of design that defines the shape, angles, and outline of a space or object.
- **Color:** Property of an object that depends on the light it reflects.
- **Texture:** Actual or simulated tactile quality; feel of a surface.
- **Shape:** Form of something, or perceivable area.
- **Space:** Area set apart for use.

Vocabulary

Balance: Relationship between sections or areas of a space; makes a room feel even. Symmetrical balance is when both sides are identical; asymmetrical balance is when the sides are different.

Emphasis: Focal point(s) within a design.

Gradation: Type of rhythm in which the change in size or shape is gradual.

Harmony: Unified arrangement of elements such as colors, textures, and lines.

Opposition: Type of rhythm in which the change in size or shape is abrupt.

Proportion: Relationship between the sizes of objects within a design.

Rhythm: The way your eyes move through a room or across a design.

Get Organized

Explain that "organization" means different things to different people. One of the first steps you might take to get organized is to define what organization means to you. For example, does it mean having everything put away in its proper place? Or does it mean a floor full of neatly stacked piles?

Once you've determined what an organized room means, set goals for achieving that state of organization. For example, you might decide that your goal for day one is to organize your music CDs in alphabetical order and clean out your desk drawers.

Use organization methods that are practical for you. For example, if you habitually leave dirty clothes lying on the floor, then consider placing a nice basket in your room in which to toss the dirty clothes.

Myth/Truth

Ask students to comment on the way their grandparents or older relatives or family friends decorate their home, the way their parents decorate, and the way they prefer to decorate. What are the similarities and differences?

Introduce the Section

In this section, students learn how to express their personal style in the way they decorate and accessorize their living space.

Figure Focus

Ask students to discuss the personal style elements that define their living space. For example, you might be a car enthusiast and have model cars displayed on shelves and posters hanging on your walls. Or maybe you like to sew and you have a homemade quilt on your bed along with embroidered pillows and a few dolls you've made. Or maybe you're into computers and electronics and have set up an elaborate shelving system that makes all components easily accessible.

Discuss

Remind students that "style" is a personal thing or the way you express yourself. Unlike a trend or fad, it is not subject to the whims, tastes, and decisions of others.

Personalizing Your Living Space

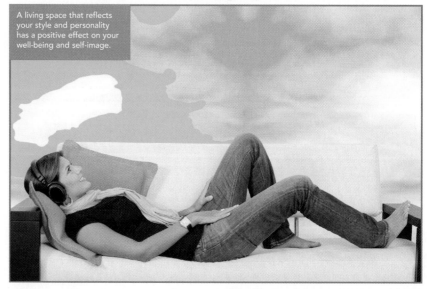

A living space that reflects your style and personality has a positive effect on your well-being and self-image.

Recall from Chapter 22 that style is a particular look. In interior design, style comes from the way objects and design elements combine to create a mood or feeling in a space.

There are standard styles, such as modern, which uses sleek lines and lots of space; English country, which uses lots of floral patterns and dark wood; and southwest, which uses ceramic tiles and blends earth tones with vibrant colors including red, orange, and blue. You can also create a style that reflects your personality, character qualities, and values.

Decorating your space with your own style helps you feel comfortable in your home, which contributes to your well-being. You can be proud of your space, too, which contributes to a positive self-image.

Express Yourself

Your personal taste—the things you like and dislike—will help guide the design choices you make. Your values and standards can also help you make choices for decorating your space.

- Your brother might want a comforter with the logo of his favorite sports team.
- You sister might hang up posters of her favorite television star.
- You might choose bamboo roll-up shades because you are interested in protecting the environment, and they are made from a renewable resource.
- Your friend might choose to use her own handmade accessories in her room, because she is proud of her own creative talents.

Customized Instruction: Less Advanced/At-Risk/Special Needs Students

Have students write a list of five to ten adjectives they think describes their personal style. Then, pair up students and have them write a list of adjectives they think defines their partner's style. They should exchange lists and then compare their partner's list with their own list. Did they use any of the same adjectives? Did they think their partner came up with any adjectives that were more on-target than their own?

Goals for Decorating

You can set goals to help you decorate your space. Think about what you want to accomplish and the resources you have available. Consider all possible alternatives, then select one and make a realistic and attainable action plan.

- Do you need to change everything in the room? That could be expensive and time-consuming.
- Can you create a new look by painting and replacing the artwork? That could be a quick change you can do yourself.
- If you give away clothes, toys, and books that you have outgrown, will you have more space for objects that reflect your current interests and values? That could be an efficient way to emphasize your personality.

It is important to respect the opinions of the other people who live with you. You may need to compromise with siblings if you share the space. Your parents may be more supportive if you discuss your goals with them before you start making changes.

It is also important to think about how you will feel regarding a style in the future. If you buy a trendy shirt that soon goes out of style, you can stop wearing it. If you paint your room a trendy color scheme, you will have to live with it until you are able to paint again.

Make the Most of Your Accessories

Changing or enhancing the accessories in your space may be the easiest way to make a design change and to introduce your personality. *Accessories* include objects such as curtains, pillows, posters, and blankets. They also include personal items such as photographs, souvenirs, trophies and awards, and items you make or decorate yourself.

- Use your sewing skills to make items such as pillows and curtains that reflect your personality.
- Print photos of your friends and family and arrange them on tables and walls.
- Create craft items such as storage containers and wall hangings, or use crafts such as stenciling to decorate walls and furniture.

TECH CONNECT

Green design refers to the use of nontoxic, recycled, or sustainable products in home decoration and design. A **sustainable product** is one that lasts for a long time and has little negative impact on the environment. For example, there are eco-friendly paints that contain no harmful chemicals, carpets made from recycled newspapers, and flooring and window blinds made from bamboo.

Use books or the Internet to learn more about green design. Select one product and make a brochure about it.

How can you use your creativity to personalize your living space?

Decorate on a Dime

Here are tips for personalizing your space without spending much money:

✔ *Rearrange the furniture.*

✔ *Stencil a design on a wall.*

✔ *Paint a mural on a wall.*

✔ *Rearrange the artwork you have on the walls.*

✔ *Hang new photos, posters, or banners.*

✔ *Sew new pillow or comforter covers.*

✔ *Embellish accessories such as lampshades and picture frames by stitching or gluing on trims, paper flowers, buttons, or shells.*

Why is it important to talk to your family members before you make any changes to your room or belongings?

Customized Instruction: Less Advanced/Special Needs Students

Have students research on the Internet, in books, and in design and decorating magazines to come up with a list of decorating DOs and DON'Ts. They should create a poster that attractively illustrates the information. For example, the DOs might include:

- Do sketch out a floor plan first.
- Do recognize your personal style.
- Do identify the room's focal point.
- Do define the room's style (country, contemporary, etc.).
- Do purchase large items first and then choose accessories to coordinate with them.
- Do apply the principles of design.

Some DON'Ts include:

- Don't let someone talk you into or out of something you like.
- Don't paint first; instead, choose furniture, flooring, and curtains first.
- Don't decide on colors in the store. They will most likely look different in your home lighting.
- Don't obstruct natural pathways through a room.
- Don't invest in trendy pieces.

Introduce the Section

This section explains the importance of maintaining a neat and clean home. Basic maintenance as well as the tools and resources you can use to clean a home are covered.

Figure Focus

Ask students what housekeeping chores they have at home. How often do they do them? What chores do other family members take care of? Do they think the assignment of chores is fair? What would their home be like if they or others did not fulfill their housekeeping responsibilities?

Vocabulary

Maintenance: Performing tasks to keep all parts of a home in good working condition.

Caring for Your Space

You can cooperate with family members to care for shared and personal living space.

People have different standards for neatness and cleanliness. You might not mind that you can't see your bedroom floor because it is covered with clothes. Your mother might start cleaning if one crumb falls on the kitchen floor.

No matter what your standards, maintaining a neat and clean home is important. When your home is neat and clean, it is safer and healthier, and it can save you money.

- A neat home has fewer risks of accidents. There is less clutter to trip over and fewer fire hazards.
- A clean home has fewer germs to cause illness, and attracts fewer pests and insects that might cause disease.
- Your home and belongings will last longer if you take care of them, saving you money you might have to spend to repair or replace damaged items.

Keeping a home neat and clean is a shared responsibility. You can work together with your family members to create a comfortable and safe environment.

What About Maintenance?

Maintenance is performing tasks to keep all parts of the home in good working condition. *Preventive maintenance* is when you take steps to solve problems before they occur. For example, you might notice that the stair railing is a little loose. You can fix it right away, before it breaks and someone falls.

Keeping your home neat and clean maintains the living areas. It is important to check and clean all parts of the home, including the roof, chimneys, basement, attic, and systems such as plumbing and electrical. You might:

- Scrape snow off the roof before it causes a leak.
- Have the chimney cleaned before carbon monoxide gas leaks into the house.
- Have the septic system cleaned regularly.
- Treat the home for insects.

If you rent your home, the landlord has a responsibility to maintain the property so it is safe and all parts work properly. Your responsibility is to report all potential problems as soon as possible.

Customized Instruction: Less Advanced/Special Needs Students

Have students create a "Household Chores List." They should create a three-column table. In the first column, they should list "Daily Chores," such as washing dishes, wiping down countertops and tabletops, making beds, and tidying up. In the second column, they should list "Weekly Chores," such as vacuuming floors, dusting furniture, doing laundry, and cleaning bathrooms. In the third column, they should list "Now and Then Chores," such as washing windows, cleaning curtains and draperies, and polishing furniture. Encourage them to write comprehensive lists for each category. Have them put a star or check beside the chores for which they are now responsible. Do they think they could take on more chores in order to help out around the home?

Manage Your Cleaning Resources

Caring for your home is not something you do one day and then never do again. You have to repeat the same tasks over and over on a regular basis in order to keep the dirt from building up and the mess from overtaking the house.

- Some tasks are best done every day, including making your bed, washing the dishes, putting away personal belongings, hanging up damp towels, and sweeping the kitchen floor.
- Some tasks can be done once a week, including doing the laundry, changing the bed linens, washing the kitchen floor, cleaning the bathroom, dusting the furniture, and vacuuming the rugs and floors.
- Some tasks can be done less often, or when necessary, such as cleaning out the refrigerator and kitchen cabinets, cleaning closets, wiping walls and woodwork, and washing draperies.

You and your family can set up a cleaning plan to help you manage cleaning responsibilities. A *cleaning plan* is a schedule of all cleaning tasks that need to be completed. You might assign each family member a set of specific tasks, or you might rotate tasks so each family member has a chance to be responsible for different tasks.

Use a Problem-Solving Approach

How do you know what to clean, when to clean it, and who is responsible? It depends on how much time you have, how many people there are to help, how much space needs cleaning, and the supplies you have to use. You and your family can work together and use a problem-solving approach to manage your home cleaning needs.

1. *Identify the problem and define it as a goal.* List the cleaning tasks you want to accomplish.
2. *Consider all possible solutions.* Think about who will perform each task and how it will be completed. Will you divide the tasks evenly among family members? Will you hire a cleaning service?
3. *Consider the consequences of each solution.* Will a young child do a good enough job to satisfy everyone's needs? Can you afford to pay someone else to clean?
4. *Select the best solution.* Using all the available information, select the solution that will achieve the goal in the quickest and most effective way.
5. *Make a realistic and achievable plan of action.* Identify the tasks that should be completed first, make a schedule for completing all tasks, assign responsibilities for each task, and allocate resources such as supplies or money.
6. *At the end of the allotted time, assess your solution.* Did it work? Were all tasks accomplished to the satisfaction of all? If not, consider how you can change the plan to improve it.

Use the Right Tool for the Job

Using the right tools and supplies makes cleaning easier and faster. Keep the following items available for cleaning.

✔ *Broom and dust pan for sweeping floors*

✔ *Dust cloths or dust wands made from fibers that attract dust for dusting furniture*

✔ *Vacuum cleaner for vacuuming rugs and floors*

✔ *Wet mop and bucket or quick damp mop for mopping kitchen and bathroom floors*

✔ *Sponges, rags, and wipes for washing surfaces such as countertops, tiles, and walls*

✔ *Toilet brush for cleaning the inside of toilets*

✔ *Stepladder for reaching high places*

✔ *Rubber gloves to protect your hands*

 International Design

Have you ever heard of Feng Shui (pronounced fung shway)? It's an Asian philosophy that influences the organization and design of objects in a home.

Other countries have their own design styles and philosophies. For example, Scandinavian designs place an emphasis on function in a simple form.

Use books or the Internet to research the design styles that are common in different countries. Find or draw a picture that illustrates the style, and explain it to your class.

Use the Right Tool for the Job

In addition to the items listed in the text, you might also suggest the following supplies:

- All-purpose cleaner
- Kitchen cleaner or wipes
- Bathroom disinfectant cleaner or wipes
- Scrubbing brush or pads
- Glass cleaner
- Upholstery spot remover
- Leather cleaner
- Bleach
- Silver or metal polish
- Furniture polish or dusting spray

In addition, you might mention the following household products that can be used for cleaning:

- Vinegar: Mix a solution of one part water and one part vinegar in a spray bottle to use as a general cleaning agent for all rooms.
- Lemon juice: This can be used to dissolve soap scum and hard water stains as well as to clean brass and copper.
- Baking soda: This works just like most commercial abrasive cleaners and also helps deodorize.

 International Design

Students are to select a country and research a design style that is common in homes. They should find or draw a picture that illustrates the style and explain it to the class. Students might find it helpful to search for "design philosophy," "traditional home architecture," and "characteristics of a [name of country] home."

Customized Instruction: ESOL Students

Have students draw a picture of a standard or traditional home décor item or accessory you would find in a home in their country of origin. For example, a home in Mexico might have Mexican folk art, Talavera pottery, painted ceramic masks, and Zapotec rugs. Students should write the name of the item in both their primary language and English.

End-of-Chapter Activities

Case Study

Answers will vary. Some students will think Lauren was right, and some will think she was wrong. All should recognize that she should have gone about it differently.

Her family was furious for a number of reasons. Lauren did not talk to anyone about her plan ahead of time. She did not ask permission.

Lauren could have told her family how much she hated the color of the room. She could have communicated her feelings and opinions in a calm way and asked them to help her find a solution to the problem.

She did do at least one thing right—she carefully covered everything to protect it all from paint.

Sounding Off!

Student answers will vary.

FAQ

1. Barrier-free living space is space that is organized and designed so everyone can use it—even people with disabilities.

2. Ways you can remove barriers from a living space include:

   - You can remove area rugs that might trip or block someone who is mobility-impaired.

   - You can improve lighting for someone who is vision-impaired.

   - You can install easy grip door knobs and handles.

   - You can organize closets so clothing hangs low enough for someone in a wheelchair to access.

   - You can organize study space so someone with a learning disability can focus without distractions.

3. Factors that influence choice of furniture are function, personal taste, cost, and quality.

4. Form is the shape of a three-dimensional object.

5. Use cool colors such as blue or green to make a room calm and soothing.

6. Gradation is a gradual change in size or shape.

7. Harmony—the opposite of conflict—means cooperation and unity.

8. Accessories include objects such as curtains, pillows, posters, and blankets. They also include personal items such as photographs, souvenirs, trophies and awards, and items you make or decorate yourself.

9. A neat home has fewer risks of accidents. There is less clutter to trip over and fewer fire hazards. A clean home has fewer germs to cause illness and attracts fewer pests and insects that might cause disease.

10. A cleaning plan is a schedule of all cleaning tasks that need to be completed.

Case Study

Lauren shares a room with her younger sister Mia. Lauren thinks the room is babyish. Everything is pink and white. The curtains are pink and white and the bedspreads are pink and white. The walls are white and the carpet is pink. Even the lampshades are pink and white. Lauren hates to bring friends home, because she is ashamed of the room.

One Saturday, Lauren's parents take Mia to a birthday party, leaving Lauren home alone. She walks to the hardware store and buys a gallon of forest green paint and a roller. She carefully covers everything in the room, and starts painting the walls. When her family comes home, they are furious. Mia cries and her parents yell. They make Lauren paint over the green with white, and ground her for two weeks.

- Do you think Lauren was wrong to paint the walls?
- Why do you think Lauren's family was furious?
- What do you think Lauren could have done differently?

Sounding Off!

1. Do you have chores you are responsible for at home? What are they?
2. Do you think it is important to personalize your bedroom decorations? Why or why not?

1. What is barrier-free living space?
2. List five ways you can remove barriers from a living space.
3. List four factors that influence your choice of furniture.
4. What is form?
5. What colors would you choose to make a room calm and soothing?
6. What is gradation?
7. What is harmony?
8. List four examples of home accessories.
9. Why is a neat and clean home safer and healthier?
10. What is a home cleaning plan?

Divide the class into teams of four or five. As a team, design and plan a bedroom in a space that is 12 feet long by 10 feet wide. Decide who the room is for. For example, is it for a 13-year-old girl, a married couple, or 8-year-old twin boys? Decide on the furniture you will need in the room, and draw a floor plan—or map—of where the furniture will go. Agree on a color scheme and style. Decide on the type and number of accessories you will need in the room, such as floor covering, curtains and lamps, artwork, photos, and other personal items. Have each member of the team draw or create one of the accessories. Present your room to the class, explaining why you made the decisions that you did, and how it will suit the needs and comfort of the person(s) who will live there.

Hot Topics

Are you proud of the look and feel of your personal living space, or does it embarrass you? Have you ever not invited a friend over because you didn't want anyone to see your home?

Take this opportunity to write anonymously about your living space and how it makes you feel. Use a word processor so no one recognizes your handwriting. Be honest and open. Put the paper in the class Hot Topics box.

As a class, read the anonymous entries and discuss them.

Web Extra ▼

There are many Web sites that provide interior design games for teens, children, and adults. The games let you try different designs and colors to create appealing living spaces. Some sites are free, and some charge a fee.

Locate some credible and helpful Web sites that you think might be useful for your peers. Make a directory of the sites, including the Web site address and a description of the site. Give the directory to your teacher to make available in the classroom.

Problem Solver

You have a new classmate. She is physically disabled and uses a type of crutch called a forearm crutch on both arms in order to walk. You want to invite her over to your house, but you think there might be problems or barriers that make it difficult for her to get around.

Use resources such as the Internet, books, and community service organizations to learn about forearm crutches and how they assist people who have trouble walking. Then, use the information to determine if there are things in your home that might create barriers for your new friend. Make a list of the challenges and suggest ways to overcome them, so you can invite your new friend to visit.

Team Players

Graph paper will make this activity easier for students to complete. Student teams are to design and plan a bedroom for a person(s) of their choosing in a space that is 12 feet long by 10 feet wide. Have students review page 488 of the text before they begin. Make sure they understand how to create scaled drawings. Make sure each member of the team is given responsibility for creating at least one of the room's accessories.

Hot Topics

Make sure students understand that they can turn in their papers anonymously. Encourage them to be open and honest about their feelings concerning their personal living space.

Web Extra

Students are to create a directory of Web sites that provide interior design games that let you experiment with room designs and colors. The directory should include the Web site address, a brief description of the site, and whether it charges a fee or is free to use.

Remind students that a reliable Web site usually publishes the name of the author or organization that sponsors it and the date the content was created or last updated in a fairly obvious location, such as at the top or bottom of the page or on the home page. The site is usually organized with headings and an obvious navigation system. A reliable site clearly states its purpose and any affiliations. You should also look for accuracy in spelling and grammar.

Students should post the directory in their school career center or library.

Problem Solver

Students are to research forearm crutches and how they assist people who have trouble walking. This type of walking aid provides balance and support and, because it has a wrist cuff, allows users to use their hands without dropping the crutches.

Ways that you can create a barrier-free space for your friend include:

- Keep stairways and halls picked up and free of toys, shoes, and other items. The same goes for pathways through rooms.
- Remove throw rugs or those that can bunch up or easily trip someone.
- Use pads under rugs to keep them from sliding.
- Make sure all electrical cords are secured along a wall and not strung across a doorway or pathway.
- If you do not have a ground-level entryway into your home, make sure the steps are cleared and the railing or banister is tightly secured so that your friend can scoot up and down the steps.

Write Now

Students are to write a letter to the editor of an interior design magazine or Web site that states their opinion of a selected article. Review with students the elements of a letter to the editor. The letter should include the sender's name, address, e-mail address, and phone number at the top. In the introductory paragraph, state the title of the article and the publication date and issue number, if available, and then identify the reason you are writing the letter. Expand upon your opinion in two or three paragraphs. Summarize your opinion in the conclusion. Make sure their letters touch on the elements and principles of design.

You should also encourage students to check the publication or Web site's guidelines or procedures for submitting letters to the editor.

Be Involved!

As a class, students are to plan a project that educates students and families in their school community on the importance of caring for and cleaning a home.

Students are to use the FCCLA planning process outlined below to develop, execute, and evaluate their efforts.

- Identify the project.
- Set a goal.
- Form a plan (who, what, when, where, how, cost, resources, and evaluation).
- Act.
- Follow up.

Remind students that a successful team relationship depends on all team members working together. Make sure they take steps to delegate responsibilities, communicate effectively, and manage conflicts or disagreements.

Social Networking

Students are to locate a community service organization that could use their volunteer help to manage its interior environment. In addition to the suggestions in the text (senior center, food pantry, and health clinic), students might check with teachers in their school district. For example, elementary school teachers often need help organizing their rooms. Or the librarian might need help improving traffic flow in the library. Or the school secretary might need assistance in managing the mailroom or copy room.

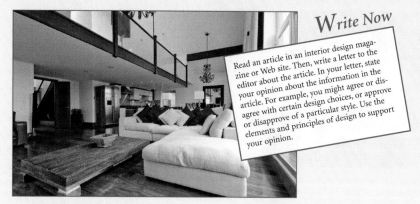

Write Now

Read an article in an interior design magazine or Web site. Then, write a letter to the editor about the article. In your letter, state your opinion about the information in the article. For example, you might agree or disagree with certain design choices, or approve or disapprove of a particular style. Use the elements and principles of design to support your opinion.

Be Involved!

www.fcclainc.org

As a class, use the FCCLA planning process to organize a project that educates families in your school community about the importance of caring for and cleaning your home. Set a goal and brainstorm projects and activities. You might create an educational video, booklet, or presentation, or organize a meeting and invite safety and health professionals to speak.

After considering all possible options, select the project that you think will be the best one for achieving your goal.

Make an action plan for achieving your goal. Include a timeframe, make sure the plan is realistic and attainable, and then put the plan into action. You may want to organize teams within the class to handle specific responsibilities, such as volunteer management and publicity.

As you work toward your goal, keep a class journal to record your progress, and collect documentation that you can use to show what you have achieved. After the project is complete, evaluate your success. Did you achieve your goal? Were there things you could have done differently? Prepare an article about the event and send it to the school or community newspaper. You might also want to send it to your FCCLA chapter so they can publish it in their newsletter.

Social Networking

Contact community services organizations in your area to see if they help with interior environment management. For example, you may be able to help rearrange furniture in a senior center, organize the shelves in a food pantry, or decorate the walls in a children's health clinic. Organize your classmates to help with the project.

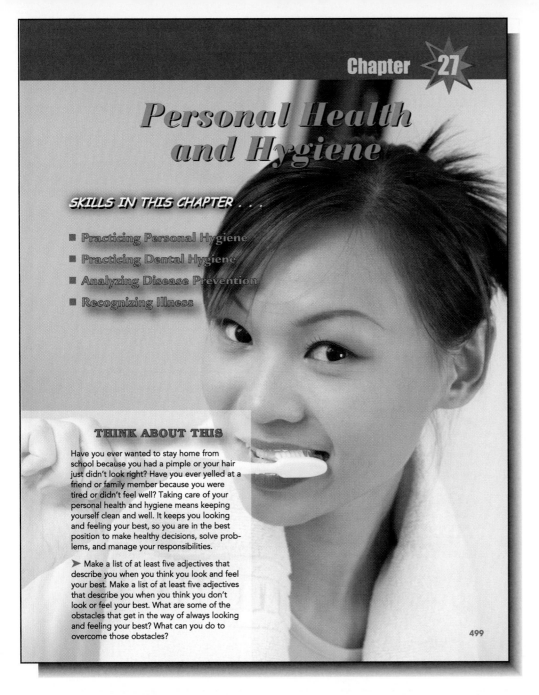

Chapter 27

Personal Health and Hygiene

SKILLS IN THIS CHAPTER . . .

- Practicing Personal Hygiene
- Practicing Dental Hygiene
- Analyzing Disease Prevention
- Recognizing Illness

THINK ABOUT THIS

Have you ever wanted to stay home from school because you had a pimple or your hair just didn't look right? Have you ever yelled at a friend or family member because you were tired or didn't feel well? Taking care of your personal health and hygiene means keeping yourself clean and well. It keeps you looking and feeling your best, so you are in the best position to make healthy decisions, solve problems, and manage your responsibilities.

➤ Make a list of at least five adjectives that describe you when you think you look and feel your best. Make a list of at least five adjectives that describe you when you think you don't look or feel your best. What are some of the obstacles that get in the way of always looking and feeling your best? What can you do to overcome those obstacles?

499

Chapter 27 Overview

This chapter provides an overview of personal health and hygiene with information on hair care, skin care, and dental care. It also discusses disease prevention techniques and how to care for yourself when you're ill.

Practicing Personal Hygiene   In this section, students learn the importance of good grooming. They also learn how good personal hygiene contributes to better physical and emotional health.

Practicing Dental Hygiene   Good dental hygiene involves more than brushing your teeth twice a day. This section discusses basic dental hygiene and also explores how a healthy diet and certain risky behaviors can affect your dental health.

Analyzing Disease Prevention   This section explores common ways to prevent disease. It also looks at how disease spreads from region to region.

Recognizing Illness   This section identifies symptoms of common illnesses and provides tips on how to treat them. Chronic conditions and cancer are also covered.

Focus and Engage

Bell-Ringer: Think About This

Students are to make a list of five adjectives they think describe them at their best and another five that describe them when they're not at their best. For example, adjectives that describe a person at her best would be positive, cheerful, confident, attractive, strong, and outgoing. Adjectives that describe a person not at his best would be depressed, sad, angry, ugly, insecure, and grouchy. Encourage students to think of the adjectives on their own rather than looking them up in a thesaurus.

Discuss with students the obstacles that get in the way of looking and feeling their best. For example, people with sensitive skin often break out in acne or other rashes that affect their appearance. People who don't get enough rest often feel lethargic and worn out and may develop dark circles or bags under the eyes. Using these two examples or those provided by students, discuss ways to overcome obstacles to good health and wellness.

ADVANCE PREPARATION	
Review	*Life Skills for the 21st Century* textbook, Chapter 27.
Prepare	Paper and pencil for some activities.
	Colored pencils or markers and plain white paper.
	Newspapers and magazines (general interest that contain advertisements for personal care products).
	Box labeled "Hot Topics."

CUSTOMIZED INSTRUCTION OVERVIEW				
Less Advanced Students	More Advanced Students	ESOL Students	Special Needs Students	At-Risk Students
Pages 500, 504, 508	Pages 501, 507	Pages 500, 504	Pages 500, 504, 509	Pages 504, 508

Introduce the Section

In this section, students learn the importance of good grooming. They also learn how good personal hygiene contributes to better physical and emotional health.

Figure Focus

Discuss some of the bodily changes experienced by teens that affect their personal hygiene routine. For example, sweat glands become more active during puberty, so they might notice they perspire more and the sweat has a stronger odor; therefore, many teens begin using deodorant or antiperspirant and bathing more often. Hormones increase the amount of oil produced by glands in the hair and skin during puberty, which often results in an oily shine on the face or hair and scalp that become oily quicker than they used to. Hormones also contribute to the growth of hair in new places, and may necessitate that shaving become part of the personal hygiene routine.

Vocabulary

Personal hygiene or grooming: The way you keep your body clean and neat.

Practicing Personal Hygiene

Personal hygiene keeps your body clean and neat so you look and feel your best.

Personal **hygiene**, or grooming, is the way you keep your body clean and neat. Basic personal hygiene includes caring for your skin, hair, teeth, and clothing.

Good grooming contributes to your health because when you keep your body clean, you transmit fewer germs. It contributes to your well-being because you have fewer body smells, and you are pleasant to be around. It also gives you an opportunity to express your personality.

- You might wear your hair in braids or dreadlocks.
- Your friend might paint her fingernails black.

When you take the time for grooming, you show others that you care about yourself and your appearance. It helps you develop a positive self-image and project a positive image to others. When you are clean and neat, you look and feel fresh. You can be proud of yourself.

Setting Up a Hygiene Routine

You can make personal hygiene a part of your routine. Some tasks you can perform daily, some weekly, and some less often. Make a grooming schedule to follow until personal hygiene becomes a standard part of your life.

- Brush your teeth as soon as possible when you wake up, after a meal, and before bedtime.
- Daily tasks include showering with soap and hot water, flossing your teeth, brushing or combing your hair, changing your underwear, and putting on deodorant. You may wash your hair every day, but less often may be enough.
- Weekly tasks include cutting or filing your fingernails and toenails.
- Monthly tasks include getting a haircut.
- Every six months, visit the dentist for a thorough cleaning and checkup.
- Once a year, visit the doctor for a checkup, routine care, and to discuss issues and concerns.

Customized Instruction: Less Advanced/Special Needs Students

Have students create a "Hygiene Checklist" that they can hang or post in their bedroom or bathroom at home. Encourage them to be creative with the format and design of the checklist; however, it should have a section for daily, weekly, monthly, semi-annual, and annual tasks. They should be specific on the tasks for each category and, if possible, include specific dates for when the semi-annual and annual tasks will be carried out.

Customized Instruction: ESOL Students

Have students complete a "Hygiene Checklist" as instructed above, but have them write it in their primary language.

Caring for Your Hair

Hair provides a great opportunity to express your personality. You can cut it, curl it, straighten it, color it, or even shave it off. No matter how you wear it, your hair will stay healthy and look its best if it is clean and neat.

To keep your hair in good condition, wash it with shampoo to remove dirt and oil. If your scalp produces a lot of oil, wash your hair often—even once a day. If your scalp does not produce too much oil, you may have to wash your hair only once a week. Comb or brush your hair at least once a day to remove tangles and knots, and use a conditioner, if necessary.

Most common hair and scalp problems such as dandruff can be treated with good grooming and a healthy diet. Some problems such as the following require special treatment.

- **Lice** are insects that are passed from person to person by sharing hats, combs, and hair brushes. Treat lice with a special shampoo.
- **Ringworm** is not an insect. It is a fungal infection, and it also spreads from person to person by sharing hats, combs, and hair brushes. Athletes can spread ringworm by using unclean sports equipment such as wrestling mats. It must be treated with antifungal medication and shampoo.

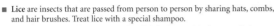

How do you use your hair to express your personality?

> " I'm a hygiene freak. "
> — Kelly Clarkson, First American Idol

Caring for Your Hands and Feet

You use your hands and feet a lot. Keep them clean by washing them with soap and warm water. Dry them thoroughly to help keep bacteria from growing.

Your fingernails protect the tips of your fingers, and your toenails protect your toes. You can keep your nails healthy and strong by following these guidelines.

- Keep them clean and dry to help prevent infection.
- Cut or file them straight across—not to a point. Pointed nails are weaker and break more easily.
- Do not abuse them by biting or picking. Abused nails are more likely to become infected. They are also not very nice to look at.

Job Search

If you are interested in personal hygiene and grooming, you may be interested in a career in personal care services. Personal care services include jobs such as massage therapist, nail technician, hair stylist, cosmetologist, embalmer, and skin care specialist. Personal care also includes personal or home care aides who help the elderly, disabled, or ill to live in their own homes or in residential care facilities instead of in health facilities or institutions. This career path is highly suitable for people with entrepreneurial skills, because it offers many opportunities to manage your own small business, such as a hair salon.

Use the Internet, library, or your school's guidance resources to learn more about a career in personal care services. Select a job that appeals to you, and write a job description, including the educational requirements, career pathway, and potential salary range.

Customized Instruction: More Advanced Students

Have students pick either the hands or the feet. They will research a common ailment that affects them and methods for treating the ailment. They should create a presentation, in the form of a slideshow, poster, or report, to share with the class.

Examples of common hand ailments are:

- Carpal tunnel syndrome
- Arthritis
- Eczema
- Trigger finger
- Ganglion cysts

Examples of common foot ailments are:

- Athlete's foot
- Heel spurs
- Calluses
- Ingrown toenail
- Bursitis
- Corns

Figure Focus

Explain that hairstyles, like clothing styles and decorating styles, help define an individual's personal style. If you're the quiet, conservative type, you might wear your hair in a straight, simple style. If you're outgoing and gregarious, you might opt for a style characterized by waves, spikes, or curls. Ask students to use two to three adjectives to describe their hairstyle. Are any of the adjectives the same as those they came up with to describe themselves when they're feeling and looking their best? (See the Bell-ringer activity on page 499 of the teacher text.)

Discuss

Discuss celebrities or other famous people and fictional characters who are known for their hairstyles. Students will probably come up with a number of examples, but some you might suggest include Donald Trump, Jennifer Aniston, Don King, Shirley Temple, Bart Simpson, Marge Simpson, and Jimmy Neutron. How does the hairstyle help define the person or character's personal style?

"Quote Box"

Some students may not be familiar with *American Idol*. The television show debuted in June 2002 as a reality competition to find new solo musical talent. The program seeks to find talent through a series of auditions held around the country. Contestants are critiqued by a panel of judges and the winner is picked by program viewers through phone voting. Kelly Clarkson was named the first American Idol.

Job Search

Students are to write a description of a job in personal care services that interests them. Refer them to the Health Science and Human Services clusters in *Appendix A* of the student text as a starting point. You might also have them search help wanted ads in newspapers, magazines, and online to see descriptions of jobs in these industries.

Figure Focus

When it comes to skin care, a teen's focus is primarily on his or her face. But emphasize the importance of taking care of all of your skin. The skin on all of your body requires the same basic care.

- **Cleansing:** Shower or bathe once a day using a cleanser suitable for your skin type.

- **Exfoliating:** This process removes dead skin cells and helps renew the living ones. Use an exfoliating scrub and/or special exfoliating sponge. Dry and sensitive skin should be exfoliated once or twice a week while oily skin can be exfoliated more often.

- **Moisturizing:** This helps make the skin soft and smooth and prevents dry, cracked skin. Moisturizers are most effective after washing when they can penetrate through open pores and be absorbed better. It's important to choose a moisturizer suitable to your skin type.

- **Protecting:** Your skin provides you with a lot of protection, so it's very important to protect it from the sun's damaging rays. Use a sunscreen and lip balm before going out in the sun.

Vocabulary

Acne: Common skin disorder caused by clogged pores.

Dermatologist: Skin doctor.

Exfoliate: Remove a layer of dead skin cells.

Noncomedogenic: Type of skincare product that does not clog pores.

What's That Smell?

Figuring out how to tell a friend he or she smells bad can be a dilemma for anyone. The best approach is to consider how you'd like to be told if you were the one with the odor. Be direct but kind. Explain that you don't mean to offend, but you would want a friend to bring the issue to your attention if the shoe were on the other foot. If you are close to the friend's family, you might consider discussing the issue with his or her parents or a sibling as they would probably be more comfortable confronting the person about the problem.

NUMBERS GAME

$15 \times 15 = 225$ minutes (3 hours and 45 minutes)

$15 \times 30 = 450$ minutes (7 hours and 30 minutes)

Your skin covers your entire body. How can you keep your skin looking fresh and clean?

Caring for Your Skin

You can keep your skin clean and healthy by washing at least twice a day with a mild cleanser to remove dirt, oil, and sweat. Other steps include:

- Drinking six 8-ounce glasses of water each day
- Getting plenty of rest
- Exercising regularly
- Eating a nutritious diet that includes five servings of fruits and vegetables
- Wearing oil-free sunscreen with a sun protection factor (SPF) of at least 15 to protect your skin from the sun's harmful rays

What's That Smell?

Have you ever been in a room when someone took off her shoes and the odor made you want to throw up? How can you reduce the chance that your body parts will smell bad?

- 👎 Forget to brush your teeth every day, leading to bad breath
- 👎 Go out after exercising without taking a shower, leading to body odor—"BO"
- 👎 Wear dirty clothes
- 👎 Wear wet shoes and socks
- 👍 Brush your teeth at least twice a day
- 👍 Bathe or shower every day—more often if you exercise or get really hot
- 👍 Wear clean clothes
- 👍 Use antiperspirant or deodorant to combat body odor
- 👍 Use foot powder or spray, and never wear wet shoes or socks

How would you tell a friend that he or she smells bad?

What About Acne?

Pimples are a common skin disorder caused by clogged pores. All teens get some pimples. **Acne** is a severe case and can lead to scaring and painful cysts. If you have severe acne, a **dermatologist**—skin doctor—can prescribe treatment. Use these guidelines to minimize breakouts and keep your skin clean and healthy.

- Wash gently with a mild cleanser. Washing too often or scrubbing too hard can dry out your skin and irritate the pimples, making them worse.
- Exfoliate—remove a layer of dead skin cells—by gently washing with a facial scrub once or twice a week.
- Use oil-free lotions and sunscreens. Look for products that say **noncomedogenic**, which means they do not clog pores.
- Keep your hands off your face. Rubbing your chin or forehead easily transfers dirt or germs from your fingers to your skin.
- Ask your doctor or dermatologist about medications that kill bacteria, and to recommend a routine for cleansing.

NUMBERS GAME

How long can you stay in the sun before you start to burn? It depends on your skin pigment, the intensity of the sun, and the type of sunscreen you are using. Sunscreen protects your skin from the sun's ultraviolet rays, which cause sunburn. Sunscreen is rated using an SPF—sun protection factor, which can range from 2 to 50 or higher. The SPF indicates how much longer you can spend in the sun wearing the sunscreen than if you had no sunscreen on at all.

To calculate how much longer you can stay in the sun using sunscreen, you multiply the SPF by the amount of time you can stay in the sun without sunscreen before you burn. (Use an average time of 10 or 15 minutes.) That means someone who usually starts to burn after 10 minutes without sunscreen won't start to burn for 80 minutes wearing sunscreen with an SPF of 8: $10 \times 8 = 80$.

If you usually start to burn after 15 minutes without sunscreen, and you wear sunscreen with an SPF of 15, how long can you stay in the sun before you burn?

What if you wear sunscreen with an SPF of 30?

Other factors such as the time of day and the altitude and strength of the sun affect how long it takes to burn. Doctors recommend that everyone always wear sunscreen with an SPF of at least 15.

TEAMWORK ACTIVITY

Divide the class into three teams. Have one team research natural sunlight tanning, another research indoor tanning, and the third team research self-tanners and spray-on tans. Each team should prepare a presentation on the considerations and risks of each form of tanning and share it with the class.

Caring for Your Clothes

The way you dress makes a statement about your personality. It also contributes to the impression you make on others. When you wear clothes that are clean and in good repair, you let other people know you respect yourself and your appearance.

Refer to Chapters 23 and 24 for specific information about clothing management. Use these basic guidelines to make caring for your clothes part of your personal grooming routine.

- Wear clean, fresh-smelling clothes.
- Wear clothes that fit.
- Wear clothes that are appropriate for the occasion.
- Treat stains as soon as possible so you have a better chance of removing them completely.
- Store your clothes properly.
- Repair damage such as ripped seams or loose buttons as soon as possible.

Minimizing Bad Smells

The adolescent and adult body has lots of parts that might start to smell if you don't keep them clean. Perspiration mixes with bacteria on your skin and produces an odor. Body odors—"BO"—can be embarrassing. They can negatively impact your self-confidence and self-esteem. You can keep unpleasant odors to a minimum by following these basic guidelines.

- Shower or bathe regularly, washing with soap and hot water.
- Wear clean clothes.
- Brush your teeth at least twice a day to reduce the risk of **halitosis**—bad breath.
- Use deodorant.
- Rinse your mouth with mouthwash.
- Use breath mints.
- Use foot powder or spray.

TECH CONNECT

Some people think that the whiter your teeth, the better you look. There are many products available that claim to whiten your teeth. Some products you can use yourself, and some are applied by a dentist.

Research different teeth-whitening options using magazines, the Internet, or information available from a dentist. Create a chart comparing the different methods, including the cost, time, and safety factors. Would you recommend any of the options? Why or why not? Present your information to the class.

Myth Greasy foods and chocolate make acne worse.

Truth There are lots of things that make acne worse, but not eating French fries or chocolate. Some things that make acne worse include pinching pimples, scrubbing your skin, things that rub your skin such as hats or headbands, cosmetics, creams and hair products that contain oil, hormones, emotional stress, and nervous tension.

What would you do if someone told you that you had body odor?

21st Century Skills

What Happens Next?

Sienna had lots of friends in elementary school. Now she is in middle school, and she feels like she is all alone. No one will sit with her at lunch. The other girls giggle when she walks by. Even her old friends sometimes hold their noses and turn away. Sienna does not understand the problem.

One day, Sienna finds a note stuck on her seat. It says she stinks and has BO. It has a picture of a stick figure with long stringy hair. Sienna feels sick to her stomach. She races to the school nurse's office and starts to cry.

What challenges are facing Sienna? Use your decision-making skills to help her recognize the problems she must solve. Using your 21st Century Skills—such as decision making, goal setting, and problem solving—write an ending to the story. Read it to the class, or form a small group and present it as a skit.

21st Century Skills

What Happens Next?

Students are to prepare an ending to Sienna's situation. They should recognize that Sienna's problem is that her friends have alienated her because she has poor hygiene. Sienna should take steps to develop a personal hygiene routine that includes daily bathing and hair washing, brushing and flossing her teeth, wearing deodorant, and making sure the clothes she wears are clean. Once she has taken this step, she might feel confident enough to confront her friends and tell them how the note and their recent behavior toward her has hurt her feelings and caused her great embarrassment.

 TECH CONNECT

Students are to research different teeth-whitening products and procedures. They can find information on the Internet as well as through a dental office. They should create a chart that compares the different options.

Teeth whitening systems include over-the-counter toothpastes, gels, rinses, strips, and trays, and whitening agents obtained from a dentist. The active ingredient in most is hydrogen peroxide, which helps lighten the color deep in the tooth. Over-the-counter products are cheaper than those obtained through a dentist. Because of the bleaching compound, teeth whitening products can cause soreness and irritation for those with sensitive teeth and gums or those with gum disease. Those allergic to peroxide should not use whitening products.

Myth/Truth

You might discuss some home treatments for acne. These include:

- Washing your face gently at least twice a day.
- Using over-the-counter water-based skincare products such as medicated creams, soaps, lotions, and gels.
- Avoiding products that contain oil, such as milky cleansers, cold creams, lipsticks, and lip gloss.

Examples of the active ingredients you should look for in over-the-counter products to treat acne are:

- Benzoyl peroxide, which unclogs pores.
- Alpha-hydroxy acid, which dries up oily areas and causes the top layer of skin to peel.
- Salicylic acid, which also dries up blemishes.
- Tea tree oil, which kills bacteria.

Figure Focus

Ask students to respond honestly to the question in the figure caption. Students should respond that they would immediately try to identify the cause of the odor and take steps to eliminate it. For example, wearing clean socks and spraying the insides of shoes with a deodorizer can help eliminate foot odor.

Introduce the Section

Good dental hygiene involves more than brushing your teeth twice a day. This section discusses basic dental hygiene and also explores how a healthy diet and certain risky behaviors can affect your dental health.

Figure Focus

Ask students to discuss their daily dental hygiene routine. How many times a day do they brush? What type of toothpaste do they use? What's their method for brushing and how long do they do it?

Explain that dentists recommend you brush your teeth twice a day and floss once a day. Use a toothbrush that has soft, nylon bristles with blunt ends and a toothpaste that contains fluoride. You should brush for a minimum of two minutes each time you brush. Hold your brush at a 45° angle to the gum line and gently brush using short, circular strokes. Brush the inside and outside of the teeth the same way. Stress that brushing your teeth too hard can lead to receding gums, tooth sensitivity, and even loose teeth.

Vocabulary

Plaque: Soft deposit of bacteria that forms on the surface of teeth.

Customized Instruction: At-Risk/Less Advanced/Special Needs Students

Provide each student with an illustration of a set of teeth. If you do not have a school textbook that contains such an illustration, you can search the Web for downloadable images using keywords such as "oral anatomy" or "mouth anatomy." Have students label the names of teeth on the illustration. They only need to label the top and bottom teeth on one side of the mouth.

The top teeth starting with the front and moving to the back are:

- 1 central incisor
- 1 lateral incisor
- 1 canine
- 2 premolars (or bicuspids)
- 3 molars

The bottom teeth starting with the front are:

- 1 central incisor
- 1 lateral incisor
- 1 canine
- 2 premolars (or bicuspids)
- 3 molars

Practicing Dental Hygiene

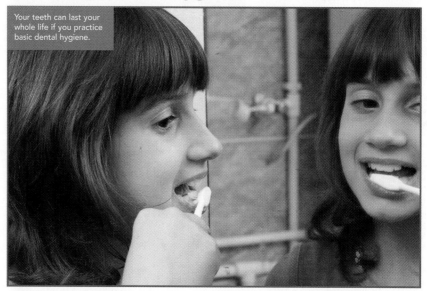

Your teeth can last your whole life if you practice basic dental hygiene.

Basic dental hygiene means taking care of your mouth. It includes brushing and flossing, seeing your dentist and your dental hygienist for regular checkups and cleanings, and eating a mouth-healthy diet.

Some benefits of practicing basic dental care include:

- Shorter dentist appointments because your teeth are clean and in good condition
- Money savings because you will reduce the need for fillings and other costly procedures
- Fresher breath
- Whiter teeth
- Protecting the heart from infection

When you understand the importance of dental hygiene, you can develop good dental health habits that will help you avoid tooth decay, gum disease, and bad breath.

Brushing and Flossing

The most important steps in proper dental hygiene are brushing and flossing. Brushing and flossing remove **plaque**—a soft deposit of bacteria that forms on the surface of teeth—prevent bad breath, prevent infection, and prevent bleeding gums. Here are some guidelines to keep your teeth healthy and clean.

- Brush your teeth in the morning and before bed or after every meal. Brushing removes plaque that causes tooth decay.
- Use toothpaste that contains fluoride, which helps prevent tooth decay and cavities.
- Use a toothbrush with soft, rounded-end bristles and a head that is small enough to reach all parts of your teeth and mouth.
- Replace your toothbrush every three to four months.
- Floss at least once a day to remove plaque from between teeth, and to promote gum health. The type of floss you use is not important. Choose the type and flavor that you like best.

Customized Instruction: ESOL Students

Have students do the same exercise at left but have them write the labels in their primary language.

What's a Mouth-Healthy Diet?

Good nutrition is very important for maintaining healthy gums and avoiding tooth decay. You can learn more about overall nutrition in Chapter 20. Here are some guidelines for eating a mouth-healthy diet:

- Eat a balanced diet that includes whole grains, vegetables, and fruits.
- Avoid foods that are high in saturated fat and sodium, such as snack foods like chips and prepackaged cookies.
- Eat cheese, peanuts (unless you are allergic), yogurt, milk, and sugar-free chewing gum. These help remove sugars from your mouth and protect against plaque.
- Avoid foods that contain a lot of sugar, especially soda and sticky, sweet foods like taffy and raisins. The longer sugar stays in contact with your teeth, the more damage the sugar will do.
- If you snack before bedtime, brush your teeth before you fall asleep. Food left on your teeth at night is more likely to cause decay.

Risky Behavior

There are a number of activities and actions that put your mouth at risk for damage or disease. Follow these guidelines to minimize your risk.

- Do not use tobacco products. Tobacco causes bad breath and stains your teeth and tongue. It significantly increases your risk of developing gum disease as well as cancer in your mouth and lungs.
- Be careful regarding piercings in and around the mouth. Pierced jewelry always increases the risk of infection, and the mouth is especially risky because it contains so much bacteria. Metal jewelry can irritate the gums and cheeks and cause teeth to chip and crack. If jewelry comes loose you might choke on it.
- Limit the amount of sports drinks you consume. They contain acids that can erode—eat away—the enamel on your teeth. The result can be severe tooth damage and even tooth loss.
- Limit the amount of sugary drinks, such as soda, you consume. The sugar promotes tooth decay.
- Wear a mouth guard when you play contact sports. A properly fitting mouth guard will protect your teeth so they are not damaged or knocked out.

Test **IT** Yourself!

How well do you brush? You can use disclosing tablets to check. Disclosing tablets contain a blue or red dye that stains bacteria—including plaque.

1. Ask your dentist for disclosing tablets.
2. Put one tablet in your mouth and chew it. Let it mix with your saliva and swish it around for about 30 seconds.
3. Rinse your mouth with water and spit it out.
4. Examine your teeth in a mirror. Note the areas that are dark. That's where you are not doing a great job removing the plaque.
5. Brush and floss your teeth, and repeat steps 2–3.
6. Examine your teeth again. There should be fewer dark areas.

Write a letter to your dentist thanking him or her for the disclosing tablets. Explain what you learned about proper brushing and flossing.

What's Wrong with My Mouth?

The mouth is susceptible to many types of sores and problems that can damage your teeth, gums, tongue, and lips. Some common mouth problems include:

✔ Canker sores, which are painful sores on the tongue, inner cheek, or inside of the lips. They are not contagious. You can coat them with a liquid medication to reduce the pain and promote healing. They usually heal by themselves within a week to 10 days.

✔ Cold sores or fever blisters, which are clusters of small blisters that form on the lip or outer edge of the mouth. Avoid kissing or sharing food and drink with someone who has a cold sore. They are caused by a virus, are contagious, and are likely to recur. There are medications that might reduce the pain and promote healing. A cold sore usually lasts 7 to 10 days.

✔ Tooth decay, which occurs when bacteria in your mouth creates acids that erode or eat away the protective tooth enamel. The result is a cavity that causes pain and can result in infection or tooth loss. You can prevent tooth decay by properly caring for your teeth. Treatment includes filling the cavity.

Discuss

Ask students who have or have had braces to discuss the reasons they got them. Braces are usually recommended to improve a person's orofacial appearance. They can correct crooked or overcrowded teeth, overbites, underbites, incorrect jaw positions, and disorders of the jaw joints. While many people wear braces for cosmetic reasons only, those who need them but go without them often suffer from headaches; earaches; speaking, chewing, and biting problems; and other mouth problems.

Test **IT** Yourself!

Explain that dental disclosing tablets and rinses are also available without prescription from most pharmacies. If possible, provide each student with an image of a set of teeth. You might download this from sites such as health.allrefer.com/pictures-images/oral-anatomy.html or healthguide.howstuffworks.com/mouth-anatomy-picture.htm.

Students should use the tablets or rinse *after* brushing and flossing and should be sure to follow the instructions on the packaging. Have them shade in the areas on the image that showed up dark. Encourage them to keep the image handy so they know the areas they need to pay closer attention to when they brush and floss.

What's Wrong with My Mouth?

You might also discuss the following mouth problems:

- **Gingivitis:** Gum disease that affects the gums and causes swelling and bleeding.

- **Periodontitis:** When gingivitis goes untreated, this type of gum disease develops, affecting the gums and the bone structure that supports the teeth. Periodontitis causes the gums to pull away from the teeth, leaving deep pockets where bacteria can grow and damage the bone. Gums can also shrink back from the teeth. Teeth may become loose, fall out, or have to be pulled out by a dentist.

- **Halitosis:** Bad breath that can be caused by not brushing, by foods you eat, by dry mouth, by tobacco products, or by another medical disorder.

Introduce the Section

This section explores common ways to prevent disease. It also looks at how disease spreads from region to region.

Figure Focus

Discuss your school's program or efforts to educate students on common diseases and how to prevent the spread of germs. Are signs and information posted in the school? Are brochures and other literature available for students and parents? Does your school nurse or health center staff discuss preventive measures with students? Do students feel as if they are informed on the steps they can take to stay healthy and strong?

Vocabulary

Host: A living environment in which a virus or microorganism can live and reproduce.

Pathogenic: Harmful viruses and microorganisms, such as bacteria and fungi, that cause illness.

Susceptible host: Host that has a low resistance to a pathogen.

STUDENT ACTIVITY

Using the information in the feature box, *How Do Diseases Spread?*, have students create a poster that illustrates how to prevent the spread of disease. For example, they might show a young boy sneezing without covering his mouth and nose and then draw a big X through the illustration. Encourage them to be creative in the format and design of their posters. You might consider hanging finished posters in the classroom or in other common areas of the school.

Analyzing Disease Prevention

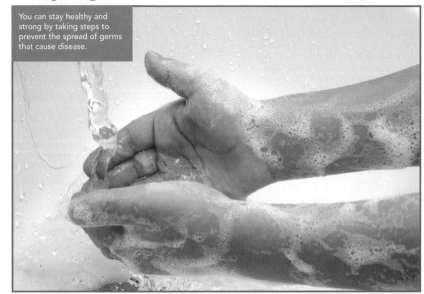

You can stay healthy and strong by taking steps to prevent the spread of germs that cause disease.

Most common illnesses are caused by harmful—pathogenic—viruses and microorganisms, such as bacteria and fungi (the plural of fungus).

For microorganisms or viruses to cause disease or infection, they must have a susceptible host. A **host** is a living environment in which the virus or microorganism can live and reproduce. A **susceptible host** has a low resistance to the pathogen. Low resistance may be caused by poor diet, fatigue, stress, or poor health.

You prevent disease by stopping viruses and microorganisms from spreading. The two basic ways to prevent disease are to avoid exposing yourself to someone who is already sick, and to avoid exposing others if you are sick.

How Do Diseases Spread?

When a pathogen finds a susceptible host, it reproduces, creating more pathogens. Common methods of spreading pathogens to a new host include:

- *Direct contact.* You physically touch the infected person.
- *Indirect contact.* You touch an object that an infected person touched.
- *Through the air.* An infected person sneezes or coughs, releasing drops of moisture that contain the pathogens. A cough or sneeze can spread up to 12 feet!
- *Through the mouth.* You drink contaminated water, eat contaminated food, kiss, or touch your mouth with a contaminated object, such as a shared water bottle.
- *Through pests.* Insects and rodents (mice and rats) carry the pathogens from one host to another.

Stay in School

Education is one of the best predictors of an individual's health. In fact, evidence suggests that it may have an even stronger influence on a person's health than income, occupation, or social status.

Researchers have long maintained that the more schooling a person has, the better his or her health is likely to be. Ask students to suggest reasons why a better-educated person would have better health than a person with less education. Some reasons are:

- The more education a person has, the less likely he or she is to engage in risky health behaviors, such as smoking, drinking alcohol, using drugs, and being overweight.
- The higher the level of education, the more money a person will earn, giving him or her more opportunities to buy healthier food, better medical care, better education, and better homes in safer neighborhoods, all of which are linked to better health.

- Better educated people tend to climb the occupational and social ladders more quickly, empowering them with more responsibility and prestige, which contribute significantly to both physical and mental health.
- Better education provides easier access to a broader range of health-related resources, including specialized health programs and social networks.
- People with a higher level of education have more options in every area of their lives. Being able to choose the best option gives them a sense of control over their lives, which is closely associated with better health.

Wash Your Hands!

The single most important way to stay healthy and stop the spread of germs is to wash your hands. Washing your hands removes pathogens that you may have touched before you can spread them. The U.S. Centers for Disease Control and Prevention (CDC) recommends that you wash your hands:

■ Before and after eating
■ After touching or playing with pets and other animals
■ After sneezing, coughing, or blowing your nose
■ After going to the restroom
■ After touching trash or putting out the garbage
■ Before and after treating a cut or wound

To remove the most germs, use soap and warm water. Rub your hands together vigorously. Wash both the front and the back of your hands, your wrists, and under your fingernails. The longer you wash, the more germs you remove. Some doctors suggest that you start singing the Happy Birthday song when you start washing, and don't rinse until you finish the song twice. Rinse thoroughly and dry using a paper towel. When you cannot wash, use hand sanitizer to kill the germs.

What's a Pandemic?

An **epidemic** is an outbreak of a disease in a local area or community. According to the World Health Organization (WHO) and the CDC, a **pandemic** is a global outbreak of disease that occurs when a new virus infects people. The virus must cause serious illness and spread easily from one person to another. For example, the H1N1 influenza virus—swine flu—became a pandemic in 2009. The flu pandemic of 1918 (Spanish Flu) caused the death of 50 to 100 million people worldwide and infected 500 million people.

What could you do to keep your hands clean if you do not have access to soap and water?

The term *pandemic* refers mostly to the number of people infected, not the severity of the illness. It is used to inform governments that they should take action to prepare for large numbers of infected people. For example, when there is a flu pandemic, governments cooperate to develop a vaccine, to prioritize who gets the vaccine as it becomes available, and to distribute the vaccine. They also inform people how to reduce their risk of becoming infected, how to recognize symptoms, how to prevent the spread of the infection, and how to treat the illness.

Infectious Diseases Around the World

Many deadly diseases that are common in developing nations are spread through insect bites and contaminated water.

■ Malaria and dengue fever are spread by mosquitoes.
■ Sleeping sickness is spread by tsetse flies.
■ Cholera is spread in contaminated water.
■ Hepatitis A is spread by contaminated water or food.

Pick a developing nation and then use books or the Internet to research the most common disease in that area. Look for information on how the disease is spread, as well as symptoms and treatments. Make a poster that shows one way people might be able to slow or prevent the spread of the disease.

Don't Touch My Germs!

Germs spread easily in environments where people are in close contact and there is not a lot of fresh air. That includes schools, locker rooms, and office buildings. What if you want to help prevent the spread of germs in school?

★ Stay home if you are sick.
★ Do not share water bottles, utensils, or other objects that you put in your mouth.
★ Do not share hats, hairbrushes, combs, or hair clips.
★ When you cough or sneeze, cover your mouth and nose with the crook of your elbow instead of in your hand.
★ Dispose of tissues and napkins properly.
★ Wash your hands!

Can you think of other ways to prevent the spread of germs?

Vocabulary

Epidemic: Outbreak of a disease in a local area or community.
Pandemic: A global outbreak of disease that occurs when a new virus infects people.

Infectious Diseases Around the World

Students are to select a developing country and research a common disease that afflicts its population. You might refer students to Web sites such as web.worldbank.org, en.wikipedia.org/wiki/Developing_country#List_of_emerging_and_developing_economies, and www.un.org for a list of developing countries. They might be able to follow links from these sites to information on diseases in the country, or they can simply research diseases using keywords such as "common diseases in [country name]." For example, measles epidemics are common in children in Ethiopia. Make sure student posters illustrate a way people can slow or prevent the spread of the disease.

Figure Focus

If you don't have access to soap and water, you can use commercially available hand sanitizers or wipes.

Don't Touch My Germs!

Some other ways to prevent the spread of germs are:

■ Do not use a toothbrush you used while you were sick.
■ Wash dirty dishes or place them in the dishwasher as soon as you have used them.
■ Launder bedding and bath towels more frequently in the hottest water that can be used for the fabric.
■ Get a flu shot.

Customized Instruction: More Advanced Students

Have students research an epidemic or pandemic. They should prepare a report or presentation that describes the epidemic or pandemic, when it occurred, how it originated (if known), how it was spread, the number of people afflicted, and how it was treated. Have them share their findings with the class.

Introduce the Section

This section identifies symptoms of common illnesses and provides tips on how to treat them. Chronic conditions and cancer are also covered.

Figure Focus

Explain that not everyone experiences the same symptoms for common illnesses. For example, one person might experience a lot of pain from an ear infection while another might notice only a slight loss of hearing. Ask students to discuss the symptoms they experience for common illnesses, such as a cold, flu, ear infection, strep throat, gastroenteritis (stomach flu), or pinkeye.

Vocabulary

Pinkeye (conjunctivitis): Viral or bacterial infection that results in inflammation of the clear membrane that covers the white part of the eye and lines the inner surface of the eyelids.

Strep throat: Sore throat caused by streptococci bacteria.

Symptoms: Signs of an illness.

Recognizing Illness

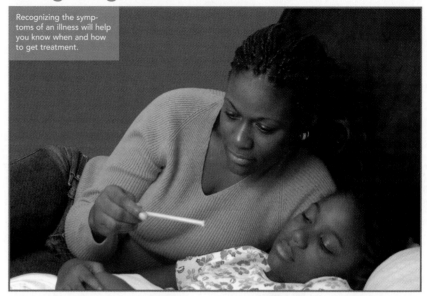

Recognizing the symptoms of an illness will help you know when and how to get treatment.

Sooner or later, everyone gets sick. You might have a sore throat, or a stomach ache. You might even throw up. Should you stay home? Should you go to the doctor? Do you need medicine to get better?

Being able to recognize the **symptoms**—signs—of an illness will help you know when and how to get treatment.

The most common disease in the United States is the cold. A cold is caused by a virus. Symptoms include sneezing, coughing, stuffy or runny nose, and sore throat.

The flu has most of the same symptoms as a cold. You might also have fever, headache, extreme tiredness, aching muscles, *chills*—feeling cold even when you are warm—nausea, vomiting, and diarrhea.

Treatment for colds and the flu are similar. Stay home, get plenty of rest, and drink lots of fluids.

Common Illnesses

There are different strains of the flu, caused by different viruses. Every year, there is a seasonal flu strain. Sometimes there are other strains, such as H1N1, or swine flu. Swine flu is not caused by eating pork. It is a form of the flu virus.

Some common illnesses, such as **strep throat** and **pinkeye** (conjunctivitis), are caused by bacteria and must be treated with antibiotic medication. Symptoms of strep include a sore throat, pain when you swallow, fever, and swollen glands at the back of your throat. Symptoms of pinkeye include red, swollen, itchy eyes that discharge thick yellow pus.

Customized Instruction: Less Advanced/At-Risk Students

Have students define the following common illnesses that often affect children: ringworm, head lice, impetigo, and chicken pox. Their definitions should include symptoms or signs of the illness, how it is treated, and how to prevent it from spreading.

- **Chicken pox:** Contagious disease caused by a virus. Produces itchy, fluid-filled blisters; often accompanied by flu-like symptoms.
- **Ringworm:** Skin infection caused by a fungus (not by a worm) and characterized by a raised, scaly ring pattern. It is contagious and easily spread from person to person.
- **Head lice:** Tiny insects that infest the hair of the scalp and sometimes eyebrows and eyelashes, resulting in intense itching and sometimes red bumps that become crusty and ooze. Easily spreads through close contact with an infected person.
- **Impetigo:** Skin disorder caused by a bacterial infection and characterized by crusty skin lesions. Often, the bacteria infect an open wound or cut. Tiny blisters are usually the first symptom.

Chronic Conditions

A chronic condition is a disease or ailment that lasts a long time or comes back frequently. Chronic conditions are usually treatable, but they may never be cured completely. People with chronic conditions must learn to live with them. Some common chronic conditions include the following.

Do you know anyone with a chronic condition such as asthma? How does it affect his or her well-being?

- *Asthma* is when the bronchial airways—tubes through which air moves to reach the lungs—become swollen or inflamed so air cannot get to the lungs. Symptoms of an asthma attack include coughing, wheezing, rapid breathing, and shortness of breath. An asthma attack may be triggered by things such as cigarette smoke, a cold, or allergens such as cat or dog hair, food, or plant pollen. Asthma is treated by avoiding the things that trigger an attack, and by using medications that reduce the inflammation of the bronchial airways.
- *Diabetes* is a disease in which the body does not produce or properly use insulin, a hormone that converts sugar, starches, and other food into energy. Type I diabetes usually starts in childhood. It is controlled with insulin injections. Type II diabetes is more common. It usually occurs in adults over age 40, and others with an unhealthy lifestyle. It may be controlled through diet, weight loss, and exercise.
- *Arthritis* is a group of diseases that result in swollen and painful joints, such as knees, elbows, and fingers. Rheumatoid arthritis is the most serious type of arthritis. Juvenile rheumatoid arthritis affects children under the age of 16. Arthritis is usually treated with medications that relieve the swelling and the pain.

What Is Cancer?

Cancer is an abnormal and harmful growth of cells in the body. There are screening tests for many types of cancer that help detect the disease before it has a chance to spread. Early detection and advances in treatment mean that the chances of survival have been greatly improved.

The symptoms of cancer vary depending on where the cancer is located. Someone with lung cancer might have a cough that won't go away. Someone with breast cancer might feel a lump.

You can reduce the chance of getting cancer if you avoid risk factors such as:

- Tobacco products, which contain chemicals that cause cancer.
- Sunbathing and tanning booths that provide exposure to harmful sunlight that causes skin cancer.
- An unhealthy lifestyle that increases your risk of cancer. Eat a healthy diet, maintain a healthy body weight, and be physically active to reduce your risk.

You can find more information about cancer on the Web, as well as how to perform self-checks for certain cancers such as skin cancer and breast cancer. Try www.cdc.gov, www.cancer.org, and www.dana-farber.org. Some sites, such as http://kidshealth.org, have information written for kids and teens.

Job Search

If you are interested in health and disease prevention, you might consider a career in the field of health sciences. Nurses, therapists, physician assistants, nurse practitioners, MRI technicians, and doctors have opportunities to work directly with patients. Medical lab technicians work to diagnose injuries or illness. Other options include records and information management, support service jobs such as dietary technicians, and biotechnology research and development positions, such as pharmacist.

Education requirements vary widely, from a technical program certificate for a nurse's aide to four or more years of graduate school for a physician.

Use the Internet, library, or your school's guidance resources to learn more about a career in health sciences. Select a job that appeals to you, and write a job description, including the educational requirements, career pathway, and potential salary range.

Discuss

You might discuss some additional types of chronic conditions that students have probably heard of. These include:

- **Bronchitis:** An inflammation of the lining of the bronchial tubes.
- **Cellulitis:** Inflammation of the skin caused by different types of bacteria.
- **Hypertension:** High blood pressure can be caused by health issues such as kidney problems and hormonal disorders, but you can also inherit the tendency toward hypertension from one or both parents. Other lifestyle factors can increase a person's risk of developing hypertension. These include obesity, lack of exercise, and excessive use of alcohol and drugs.
- **Migraine headaches:** Recurrent headaches that are often accompanied by dizziness, nausea, and sensitivity to noise and light. Common causes are stress, too much caffeine, skipping meals, certain foods, smoking, and changes in hormone levels.

Figure Focus

Explain the importance of being informed on chronic conditions that you, a family member, or a close friend suffer from. Ask students to discuss their experiences with those who have chronic conditions.

Job Search

Students are to write a description of a job in health sciences that interests them. Refer them to the Health Science and Human Services clusters in *Appendix A* of the student text as a starting point. You might also have them search help wanted ads in newspapers, magazines, and online for examples of descriptions of jobs in these fields.

Customized Instruction: Special Needs Students

Students might be willing to discuss chronic conditions or illnesses for which they are being treated. Ask them to share information on what causes or triggers the condition and the measures they take to treat it or alleviate its effects.

End-of-Chapter Activities

Case Study

Answers will vary, but students should identify the sports drinks as the problem.

Wyatt can stop drinking sports drinks. He can brush his teeth more often.

It is important for Wyatt to make dental care part of his daily hygiene routine because the health of his teeth affects his overall health and wellness. Poor dental care leads to problems such as cavities, infection, bleeding gums, and tooth decay. It causes bad breath. Dirty, damaged teeth might interfere with his self-esteem.

Sounding Off!

Student answers will vary.

FAQ

1. Daily tasks include showering with soap and hot water, flossing your teeth, brushing or combing your hair, changing your underwear, and putting on deodorant. You may wash your hair every day. Students may think of others.

2. Lice are insects that are passed from person to person by sharing hats, combs, and hair brushes. Treat lice with a special shampoo.

3. Oil-free or noncomedogenic sunscreen with a sun protection factor (SPF) of at least 15 is useful in preventing pimples.

4. Acne is a skin disorder caused by blocked pores.

5. Halitosis is bad breath.

6. Fluoride helps prevent tooth decay and cavities.

7. Tobacco causes bad breath and stains your teeth and tongue. It significantly increases your risk of developing gum disease as well as cancer in your mouth and lungs.

8. Common methods of spreading pathogens are direct contact, indirect contact, through the air, through the mouth, and through pests.

9. The single most important way to stay healthy and stop the spread of germs is to wash your hands.

10. The cold is the most common disease in the United States.

Case Study

Wyatt loves to work out. He is on the basketball team, and he stays in shape by running and lifting weights. He knows that it is important to eat a healthy diet and to drink plenty of fluids when he exercises.

At his six-month dental checkup, the hygienist spends a lot of time working on Wyatt's front teeth. The dentist looks in Wyatt's mouth. He says there is a problem. There seems to be a lot of erosion—tooth enamel that has been eaten away. He asks if Wyatt drinks sports drinks. He tells Wyatt's mother that he can repair the teeth using a process similar to filling a cavity, but that it will be expensive. He also says that unless they find the cause of the erosion and stop it, it is likely to damage more teeth.

■ What do you think is causing the tooth erosion?
■ What changes can Wyatt make to prevent the erosion from continuing?
■ Why is it important for Wyatt to consider his dental hygiene as part of his overall health and wellness?

Sounding Off!

❶ How important is your hairstyle for your self-esteem? How do you feel when you have a "bad hair day" or get a great new haircut? Why do you think it matters so much?

❷ Do you think it is selfish when someone comes to school with a cold?

1. List five personal hygiene tasks you should perform daily.
2. What are lice? How can you avoid them, and how can you treat them?
3. What type of sunscreen is useful for preventing pimples?
4. What is acne?
5. What is halitosis?
6. What ingredient in toothpaste helps prevent tooth decay and cavities?
7. List three ways tobacco products can interfere with a healthy mouth.
8. List five common methods of spreading pathogens.
9. What is the single most important way to stay healthy and stop the spread of germs?
10. What is the most common disease in the U.S.?

Companies spend a lot of money advertising personal care and grooming products such as shampoo, conditioner, skin cream, and body lotions. In teams of four or five, select an advertisement for a personal care product from a magazine, the Internet, or television and look at it closely. Answer the following questions:

- What product is being advertised?

- What claims does the ad make about the product?

- Can you achieve the same result using something other than the advertised product?

Then, pick a personal-care product, service, or idea and create your own advertisement. It might be a poster, video, presentation, or even a song. Work together as a team to complete the project, using cooperation, compromise, and teamwork to achieve your goal. Present your ad to the class.

Hot Topics

Do you feel as if you are the only one in school who has pimples? Are you self-conscious because of your skin?

Take this opportunity to write anonymously about how your self-image and self-esteem are affected by the condition of your skin. Use a word processor so no one recognizes your handwriting. Be honest and open. Put the paper in the class Hot Topics box.

As a class, read the anonymous entries and discuss them.

Web Extra ▼

There are many Web sites that provide information about the proper way to brush your teeth and floss. Some have step-by-step directions, and some have videos. Some are geared to teens and include information on what to do if you have braces.

Locate some credible Web sites that you think might be useful for your peers. Make a directory of the sites, including the Web site address and a description of the site. Post the directory on your school Web site or in your school career center or library.

Problem Solver

Someone in school has bad breath. You want to let the person know he or she has a problem, but you are not sure how to do it. Individually or in pairs, use your problem-solving and decision-making skills to determine the best course of action. Define the problem as a goal and consider all possible options. Think about the positive and negative consequences and the benefits and drawbacks of each option. When you are ready, select the best possible option and make a realistic and achievable action plan. Include steps for helping the person overcome the problem he or she is facing.

Team Players

Student teams are to select an advertisement for a personal care product. They should review the ad to identify the claims the ad makes about the product and determine if the same result can be achieved with a different product. Then, as a team, they are to select a personal care product, service, or idea and create an advertisement for it. Encourage them to select unusual or unique products that you might not hear about every day or even those they've concocted themselves; for example, a shampoo, facial mask, or nail treatment. These types of advertisements will be more interesting to the rest of the class.

Hot Topics

Make sure students understand that they can turn in their papers anonymously. Encourage them to be open and honest about their feelings concerning the appearance and condition of their skin.

Web Extra

Students are to create a directory of Web sites that provide information and step-by-step instructions on how to brush and floss correctly. The directory should include the Web site address and a brief description of the site.

Remind students that a reliable Web site usually publishes the name of the author or organization that sponsors it and the date the content was created or last updated in a fairly obvious location, such as at the top or bottom of the page or on the home page. The site is usually organized with headings and an obvious navigation system. A reliable site clearly states its purpose and any affiliations. You should also look for accuracy in spelling and grammar.

Students should post the directory on the school Web site and in their school career center or library.

Problem Solver

Students are to use their problem-solving and decision-making skills to determine the best way to tell a person he or she has bad breath. In addition to problem-solving and decision-making skills discussed in Chapter 2, you might want to review effective communication skills:

- **Be clear.** Practice what you will say beforehand and be aware of the messages you might send through body language.

- **Be personal.** Consider how you would feel if you were the one being told you had bad breath.

- **Be positive.** Smile, and demonstrate that you understand how the problem could affect anyone.

- **Get to the point.** Be direct but kind.

Write Now

Students are to write an opinion essay about mouth piercings. Review with students the components of an opinion essay. It has an introduction that states the writer's opinion on the topic; a body consisting of at least three paragraphs in which the writer supports his or her opinion with facts and details; and a conclusion that restates and summarizes the writer's opinion.

Be Involved!

As a class, students are to plan a project that educates children, peers, or families in the school community about the importance of good dental hygiene.

Students are to use the FCCLA planning process outlined below to develop, execute, and evaluate their efforts.

- Identify the project.
- Set a goal.
- Form a plan (who, what, when, where, how, cost, resources, and evaluation).
- Act.
- Follow up.

Make sure students choose the audience or target group before they select the project.

Remind students that a successful team relationship depends on all team members working together. Make sure they take steps to delegate responsibilities, communicate effectively, and manage conflicts or disagreements.

Social Networking

Students are to create a poster for the school community that explains the importance of preventing the spread of disease and illustrates ways to achieve this. You might suggest that students review the section *Analyzing Disease Prevention*, on pages 506–507 of the student text.

Write Now

What do you think about tongue or lip piercings? Do you think they look attractive? Do you think they look gross? Write an opinion essay about mouth piercings, explaining your viewpoint. Include specific information to support your opinion.

Be Involved!

www.fcclainc.org

As a class, use the FCCLA planning process to organize a project that educates children, your peers, or families in your school community about the importance of good dental hygiene. Set a goal and brainstorm projects and activities. For example, you might create a presentation for elementary school children about the risks of too much sugared soda or sports drink, or you might create a video for your peers about the dangers of tobacco products, or you might ask dental health professionals to participate in a panel discussion or presentation about overall dental care for families.

After considering all possible options, select the project that you think will be the best one for achieving your goal. Make an action plan for achieving your goal. Include a timeframe, make sure the plan is realistic and attainable, and then put the plan into action. You may want to organize teams within the class to handle specific responsibilities, such as volunteer management and publicity.

As you work toward your goal, keep a class journal to record your progress, and collect documentation that you can use to show what you have achieved. After the project is complete, evaluate your success. Did you achieve your goal? Were there things you could have done differently? Prepare an article about the event and send it to the school or community newspaper. You might also want to send it to your FCCLA chapter so they can publish it in their newsletter.

Social Networking

Make a poster showing how students, teachers, visitors, and administrators can take action to prevent the spread of germs in school. On the poster, explain why it is important to be aware of how illness spreads and how to stop it. Hang the posters on a bulletin board or in an area of your school where other students will see them, such as a hallway or the cafeteria.

Career Clusters

The United States Department of Education identifies 16 career clusters by classifying specific jobs and industries into similar categories. You can use the information on career clusters to learn about careers while you are in school or any time you are doing career research.

The 16 career clusters can best be described as themes that group specific occupations together. One example of a career cluster is Agriculture, Food, & Natural Resources. Another is Architecture & Construction.

Within each career cluster are job, industry, and occupation types known as pathways. For example, the Architecture & Construction cluster has three pathways: Construction, Design/Pre-Construction, and Maintenance/Operations. The pathways are the building blocks of the16 career clusters. Each pathway offers a variety of careers you might choose. For example, in the Construction pathway, occupations include architect, carpenter, civil engineer, and interior designer.

The clusters and their pathways help job seekers and individuals interested in specific careers to identify professions that best suit their interests and abilities. Through the clusters and pathways, you can learn about the education and skills you will need to be effective in a specific job and career. The clusters and pathways provide you with clear-cut choices and options as you begin your career exploration.

On the following pages you will find a list of the career clusters, their pathways, and specific jobs within each pathway. You can learn more about career clusters at www.careerclusters.org.

The Agriculture, Food & Natural Resources career cluster is for people interested in the production, processing, marketing, distribution, financing, and development of agricultural commodities and resources. Their interests in the field might include food, fuel, fiber, wood products, natural resources, horticulture, and other plant and animal products/resources.

Pathways

■ Agribusiness Systems
■ Animal Systems
■ Environmental Service Systems
■ Food Products and Processing Systems
■ Natural Resources Systems
■ Plant Systems
■ Power, Structural and Technical Systems

Sample Occupations

■ Agricultural Communications Specialist
■ Animal Scientist
■ Embryo Technologist
■ Feed Sales Representative
■ Fish and Game Warden
■ Food Scientist
■ Livestock Buyer
■ Logging Equipment Operator
■ Tree Trimmer and Pruner

Are you interested in a career in Agriculture, Food & Natural Resources? Use your school library or the Internet to research the requirements for a career in this cluster.

People in the Architecture & Construction cluster careers design, plan, manage, build, and maintain the built environment. Take a look around you. The houses across the street, the roads that cars drive on, and the parks that you walk through every day were created or maintained by the people performing jobs in this cluster and its pathways.

Pathways

■ Construction
■ Design/Pre-Construction
■ Maintenance/Operations

Sample Occupations

- Architect
- Architectural and Civil Drafter
- Carpenter
- Civil Engineer
- Civil Engineering Technician
- Code Official
- Computer Aided Drafter (CAD)
- Concrete Finisher
- Construction Laborer
- Cost Estimator
- Drywall and Ceiling Tile Installers
- Pipe Layer

Are you interested in a career in Architecture & Construction? Use your school library or the Internet to research the requirements for a career in this cluster.

Have you ever wanted to design, produce, exhibit, perform, write, and publish anything by making music or creating multimedia visual content? Do you love the performing arts? You could be dreaming of becoming an actress on the stage or television. Or perhaps you would rather be a world-renowned painter. Then again, your interest might be in journalism as the next star anchor of the evening news or a respected blogger, or in communications as a public relations specialist working behind the scenes to guide the careers of the rich and famous. If so, this cluster field is for you.

Pathways

- Audio and Video Technology and Film
- Journalism and Broadcasting
- Performing Arts
- Printing Technology
- Telecommunications
- Visual Arts

Sample Occupations

- Broadcast Technician
- Cinematographer
- Graphics and Printing Equipment Operator
- Publisher, Editor, Journalist or Reporter
- Video Graphics, Special Effects, and Animation Technician
- Video Systems Technician

Are you interested in a career in Arts, A/V Technology & Communications? Use your school library or the Internet to research the requirements for a career in this cluster.

Every business hires individuals to manage its operations. Businesses need office managers and accountants to ensure that the phones get answered and that the books are in order. These businesses can range in size from small convenience stores to large hospitals. They all need employees who ensure that operations run smoothly within the organization. The employees in the jobs and industries of the Business, Management & Administration cluster play this role.

Are you interested in a career in Business Management & Administration? Use your school library or the Internet to research the requirements for a career in this cluster.

Pathways

- Administrative Support
- Business Information Management
- General Management
- Human Resources Management
- Operations Management

Sample Occupations

- Accounting Manager
- Accounts Payable Manager
- Assistant Credit Manager
- Billing Manager
- Business and Development Manager
- Chief Executive Officer
- Compensation and Benefits Manager
- Credit and Collections Manager
- Entrepreneur
- General Manager
- Payroll Manager
- Risk Manager

Much thought and care go into planning, managing, and providing education as well as training and related learning support services. People employed in this field serve children and adults. Workers in this cluster need patience and good customer service skills to be effective in their jobs.

Pathways

- Administration and Administrative Support
- Professional Support Services
- Teaching/Training

Sample Occupations

- College President, Dean, Department Chair, Program Coordinator
- Corporate Trainer
- Curriculum Specialist
- Education Researcher, Test Measurement Specialist/ Assessment Specialist
- Elementary and Secondary Superintendent, Principal, Administrator
- Post-Secondary Administrator
- Supervisor and Instructional Coordinator
- Teacher
- Textbook Author

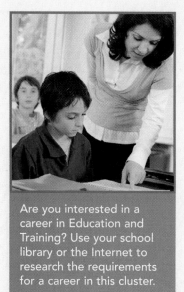

Are you interested in a career in Education and Training? Use your school library or the Internet to research the requirements for a career in this cluster.

Finance is often linked to banking alone, but there are many facets of the industry because there are so many different types of financial institutions. Employees in this field provide services for financial and investment banking, insurance products, business/financial management, and more.

Pathways

- Accounting
- Banking Services
- Business Finance
- Insurance
- Securities and Investments

Sample Occupations

- Brokerage Representative
- Development Officer
- Investment Advisor
- Personal Financial Advisor
- Sales Agent, Securities and Commodities
- Securities/Investments Analyst
- Stock Broker
- Tax Preparation Specialist

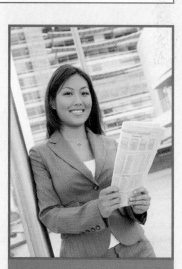

Are you interested in a career in Finance? Use your school library or the Internet to research the requirements for a career in this cluster.

overnment & Public Administration

Local, state, and federal governments need employees to perform functions that include governance, national security, foreign service, planning, revenue flows and taxation, regulation, and management and administration.

Pathways
- Foreign Service
- Governance
- National Security
- Planning
- Public Management and Administration
- Regulation
- Revenue and Taxation

Sample Occupations
- Air Crew Member
- Aircraft Launch and Recovery Officer
- Assessor
- Congressional Aide
- Detective
- Equal Opportunity Representative
- Legislative Aide
- Postal Service Clerk
- President
- Radar and Sonar Technician
- Special Forces Officer
- Transportation Inspector
- Urban and Regional Planner
- Vice President

Are you interested in a career in Government & Public Administration? Use your school library or the Internet to research the requirements for a career in this cluster.

ealth Science

Health Science cluster employees plan, manage, and deliver therapeutic services, diagnostic services, health informatics, support services, and biotechnology research and development to individuals throughout the United States. They work in cities, suburbs, rural areas, and other communities to provide crucial services to a diverse client base.

Pathways
- Biotechnology Research and Development
- Diagnostic Services
- Health Informatics
- Support Services
- Therapeutic Services

Sample Occupations

- Acupuncturist
- Anesthesia Technologist/Technician
- Anesthesiologist/Assistant
- Art/Music/Dance Therapist
- Athletic Trainer
- Audiologist
- Certified Nursing Assistant
- Chiropractic Assistant
- Chiropractor
- Dental Assistant/Hygienist
- Dental Lab Technician
- Dietitian/Nutritionist

Are you interested in a career in Health Science? Use your school library or the Internet to research the requirements for a career in this cluster.

Hospitality and tourism careers comprise the world's largest industry. Its workers manage, market, and operate restaurants and other food services, lodging, attractions, recreation events, and travel-related services. They are very busy people who cater to the needs of individuals that visit your town, city, state, and other countries of the world as tourists.

Pathways

- Lodging
- Recreation, Amusements and Attractions
- Restaurants and Food/Beverage Services
- Travel and Tourism

Sample Occupations

- Animal Trainer
- Baggage Porter and Bellhop
- Catering and Banquet Manager
- Concierge
- Convention Planner
- Kitchen Manager
- Museum Curator
- Restaurant Owner
- Service Manager
- Switchboard Operator

Are you interested in a career in Government & Public Administration? Use your school library or the Internet to research the requirements for a career in this cluster.

Human services careers prepare individuals for employment in pathways that relate to families and human needs. They work in daycare centers, drive the elderly and disabled to their appointments, provide massages in spas, and counsel those in need of emotional support.

Pathways

- Consumer Services
- Counseling and Mental Health Services
- Early Childhood Development and Services
- Family and Community Services
- Personal Care Services

Sample Occupations

- Barber
- Clergy
- Elementary School Counselor
- Embalmer
- Hairdresser/Cosmetologist
- Loan Counselor
- Manicurist and Pedicurist
- Sociologist
- Tailor

Are you interested in a career in Human Services? Use your school library or the Internet to research the requirements for a career in this cluster.

Individuals employed in this cluster build the bridges between people and technology. They design, develop, support, and manage hardware, software, multimedia, and systems integration services that allow you to have access to the Internet, operate your remote control device, and use your iPod.

Pathways

- Information Support and Services
- Network Systems
- Programming and Software Development
- Web and Digital Communications

Sample Occupations

- Administration Associate
- Analyst
- Computer Programmer
- Computer Security Specialist
- Developer
- Modeler
- Network Designer
- Network Developer
- Web Administrator

Are you interested in a career in Information Technology? Use your school library or the Internet to research the requirements for a career in this cluster.

There are individuals who plan, manage, and provide legal, public safety, protective services, and homeland security, including professional and technical support services, in your community. They are police officers, lawyers, security guards, and firefighters, and they deliver the services that make you feel a little safer in times of crisis.

Pathways

- Correction Services
- Emergency and Fire Management Services
- Law Enforcement Services
- Legal Services
- Security and Protective Services

Sample Occupations

- Arbitrator, Mediator and Conciliator
- Correctional Officer and Jailer
- Crossing Guard
- Detective and Investigator
- Dispatchers
- Fire Fighter
- Immigration and Custom Inspector
- Judge
- Lawyer
- Paramedic
- Police Officer
- Social Worker

Are you interested in a career in Law, Public Safety, Corrections & Security? Use your school library or the Internet to research the requirements for a career in this cluster.

Products ranging from plastic bottles to cars are built in factories and developed in manufacturing plants all over the world through specific processes. Those employed in the manufacturing cluster perform the steps that go into intermediate or final products and related professional and technical support activities such as production planning and control, maintenance, and manufacturing/process engineering.

Pathways

■ Health, Safety and Environmental Assurance
■ Logistics and Inventory Control
■ Maintenance, Installation and Repair
■ Manufacturing Production Process Development
■ Production
■ Quality Assurance

Sample Occupations

■ Assembler
■ Automated Manufacturing Technician
■ Bookbinder
■ Calibration Technician
■ Electrical Installer and Repairer
■ Electromechanical Equipment Assembler
■ Extruding and Drawing Machine Setter/Set-Up Operator

Are you interested in a career in Manufacturing? Use your school library or the Internet to research the requirements for a career in this cluster.

Marketing professionals plan, manage, and perform activities to reach organizational objectives. Their work can range from handing out flyers to publicizing an event or working in an office to research consumers' spending habits.

Pathways

■ Marketing Communications
■ Marketing Management
■ Market Research
■ Merchandising
■ Professional Sales

Sample Occupations

- Account Executive
- Fashion Designer
- Key Account Manager
- Market Research Analyst
- Merchandise Displayer and Window Trimmer
- Real Estate Agent
- Sales Representative
- Telemarketer
- Wholesale and Retail Buyer

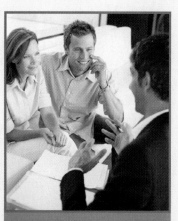

Are you interested in a career in Marketing? Use your school library or the Internet to research the requirements for a career in this cluster.

Can you see yourself planning, managing, and providing scientific research as a career? Are you interested in laboratory and testing services or in research and development? If so, are you also willing to earn the certification or advanced education necessary to work in this career cluster? If your answer is a "yes" to any of these questions, then take a closer look at these pathways and occupations.

Science, Technology, Engineering & Mathematics

Pathways

- Engineering and Technology
- Science and Math

Sample Occupations

- Anthropologist
- Biological Scientist
- Food Science Technologist
- Mathematician
- Microbiologist
- Park Naturalist
- Physicist
- Statistician
- Technical Writer

Are you interested in a career in Science, Technology, Engineering & Mathematics? Use your school library or the Internet to research the requirements for a career in this cluster.

How does food get to your supermarket shelves, or fuel to your local gas station? There is a lot of planning that goes into the transportation and shipping of products around the globe. Many people work behind the scenes to coordinate, manage and move these goods to their final destinations by arranging for their transportation by road, pipeline, air, rail and water. They also oversee the related professional and technical support services that are a part of the process. Here are the pathways and some of the occupations that make up this cluster.

Pathways

- Facility and Mobile Equipment Maintenance
- Health, Safety and Environmental Management
- Logistics Planning and Management Services
- Sales and Services
- Transportation Operations
- Transportation Systems/Infrastructure Planning, Management, and Regulation
- Warehousing and Distribution Center Operations

Sample Occupations

- Dispatchers
- Drivers
- Industrial and Packaging Engineers
- Logisticians
- Storage and Distribution Managers
- Surveying and Mapping Technicians
- Traffic Managers
- Traffic, Shipping and Receiving Clerks
- Urban and Regional Planners
- Warehouse Managers

Are you interested in a career in Transportation, Distribution & Logisitics? Use your school library or the Internet to research the requirements for a career in this cluster.

The Career Clusters icons and definitions are being used with permission of the: States' Career Clusters Initiative, 2009, www.careerclusters.org.

Joining a Career Technical Student Organization

Career technical student organizations (CTSOs) are groups of students who are enrolled in a career and technical education program that engages in career and technical activities as part of the curriculum. There are different CTSOs for different career and technical programs; students join the organization related to the CTE program in which they are enrolled.

CTSOs provide members with a range of individual and group programs and activities. They promote career education and training and provide opportunities for leadership, teamwork, competition, and citizenship. CTSOs offer a unique program of career and leadership development, motivation, and recognition for students in grades 6 through 12. Members benefit from:

- Belonging to a positive and supportive group of their peers
- Examining firsthand the relationship between academics and the world of work
- Identifying career opportunities
- Building confidence and knowledge through competition
- Exercising leadership and teamwork skills
- Practicing personal skills for success
- Developing employability skills
- Recognizing and developing interests and abilities that align with career goals

525

Common Career Technical Student Organizations

There are CTSOs to support every career cluster and pathway. The National CTSOs supported by educators in most states include the following:

- Family, Career and Community Leaders of America (FCCLA) for students in Family and Consumer Sciences programs (www.fcclainc.org)

- Future Business Leaders of America-Phi Beta Lambda (FBLA-PBL) for students in business, government, and public service programs (www.fbla-pbl.org)

- Business Professional of America (BPA) for students in business and marketing programs (www.bpanet.org)

- DECA for students in marketing programs (www.deca.org)

- Health Occupations Students of America (HOSA) for students in health services programs (www.hosa.org)

- National FFA Organization for students in agriculture programs (www.ffa.org)

- National Young Farmer Educational Association (NYFAE) for students in agriculture programs (www.nyfae.org)

- SkillsUSA for students in technical, skills, and service programs (www.skillsusa.org)

- Technology Student Association (TSA) for students in technology, innovation, design and engineering programs (www.tsaweb.org)

For more information on CTSOs at the national level, contact:

U.S. Department of Education
Office of Vocational and Adult Education
Washington, DC 20202
(202) 205-5440
National Website Address: http://www.ed.gov/offices/OVAE

What Is FCCLA?

Family, Career and Community Leaders of America (FCCLA) is a nonprofit national career and technical student organization for students in Family and Consumer Sciences education in public and private school through grade 12. FCCLA is the only CTSO with the family as its central focus. It functions as an integral part of the Family and Consumer Sciences education curriculum and operates within the school system. FCCLA provides opportunities for active student participation at local, state, and national levels.

Since 1945, FCCLA members have been making a difference in their families, careers, and communities by addressing important personal, work, and societal issues through family and consumer sciences education. Today, FCCLA has over 219,000 members in nearly 6,500 chapters active in a network of associations in 50 states as well as in the District of Columbia, the

Virgin Islands, and Puerto Rico. Chapter projects focus on a variety of youth concerns, including teen pregnancy, parenting, family relationships, substance abuse, peer pressure, environment, nutrition and fitness, teen violence, and career exploration. Involvement in FCCLA offers members the opportunity to expand their leadership potential and develop life skills necessary in the home and workplace such as planning, goal setting, problem solving, decision making, and interpersonal communication.

As an FCCLA member, you can:

- Explore career opportunities
- Attend conferences
- Participate in competitions
- Access information about jobs, internships, and scholarships

What Is FCCLA's Mission and Purpose?

FCCLA states that its mission is to promote personal growth and leadership development through Family and Consumer Sciences education. Focusing on the multiple roles of family member, wage earner, and community leader, members develop skills for life through character development, creative and critical thinking, interpersonal communication, practical knowledge, and career preparation.

FCCLA lists its purposes as the following:

- To provide opportunities for personal development and preparation for adult life
- To strengthen the function of the family as a basic unit of society
- To encourage democracy through cooperative action in the home and community
- To encourage individual and group involvement in helping achieve global cooperation and harmony
- To promote greater understanding between youth and adults
- To provide opportunities for making decisions and for assuming responsibilities
- To prepare for the multiple roles of men and women in today's society
- To promote family and consumer sciences and related occupations

Who Can Join?

Any student who has taken a course in Family and Consumer Sciences or courses as determined by the state department of education at the middle or high school level is eligible for active membership in an organized chapter within his or her school. Once the state and national dues are paid, the student will be an official affiliated member. Teachers who are certified to teach Family and Consumer Sciences education as determined by their state department of education can serve as the FCCLA chapter adviser.

What Do FCCLA Members Do?

FCCLA encourages members to participate in a wide range of programs in school, at home, and in the community. Activities may be individual or team oriented, and some are competitive events.

Career Connection   A national program that guides youth to link their options and skills for success in families, careers, and communities. Through individual, cooperative, and competitive activities, members discover their strengths, target career goals, and initiate a plan for achieving the lifestyle they desire.

Community Service   A program designed to help students to develop, plan, carry out, and evaluate projects that improve the quality of life in their communities. Community Service helps young people build skills for family, career, and community roles; provides youth-centered learning experiences related to Family and Consumer Sciences education; and encourages young people to develop the positive character traits of trustworthiness, respect, responsibility, fairness, caring, and citizenship.

Dynamic Leadership   A program designed to help young people learn about leadership; recognize the lifelong benefits of leadership skills; and practice leadership skills through FCCLA involvement.

FACTS—Families Acting for Community Traffic Safety   A national peer education program through which students strive to save lives educating adults and youth about traffic safety and supporting enforcement of local rules and regulations regarding community traffic safety.

Families First   A national peer education program through which youth gain a better understanding of how families work and learn skills to become strong family members. Its goals are to: help youth become strong family members and leaders for today and tomorrow and strengthen the family as the basic unit of society. Members can also experience other cultures and family relationships through Japanese Exchange, sponsored by Kikkoman Corporation. Members who are sophomores or juniors can apply for a Japanese Exchange Scholarship to spend four- to six-weeks as an exchange student with a Japanese host family.

Financial Fitness   A national peer education program that involves youth teaching one another how to make, save, and spend money wisely. Through FCCLA's Financial Fitness program, youth plan and carry out projects that help them and their peers learn to become wise financial managers and smart consumers.

Leaders at Work   A program that recognizes members who create projects to strengthen leadership skills on the job. These skills contribute to success across a broad range of career fields. In conjunction with the Career Connection national program, Leaders at Work motivates students to prepare for career success.

Power of One   A program designed to help students find and use their personal power. Members set their own goals, work to achieve them, and enjoy the results. The skills members learn in Power of One help them now and in the future in school, with friends and family, in their future at college, and on the job.

STAR Events   STAR stands for Students Taking Action with Recognition. STAR Events are competitive events in which members are recognized for proficiency and achievement in chapter and individual projects, leadership skills, and career preparation. STAR Events offer individual skill development and application of learning

STOP the Violence   STOP stands for Students' Taking On Prevention. It is a national program that empowers youth with attitudes, skills, and resources in order to recognize, report, and reduce youth violence.

Student Body   A national peer education program that helps young people learn to eat right, be fit, and make healthy choices. Its goals are to help young people make informed, responsible decisions about their health, provide youth opportunities to teach others, and develop healthy lifestyles as well as communication and leadership skills.

MyPyramid Food Group Recommendations

The United States Department of Agriculture (USDA) developed MyPyramid to provide the information you need to choose a healthy diet. According to the Dietary Guidelines for Americans, a healthy diet:

- Emphasizes fruits, vegetables, whole grains, and fat-free or low-fat milk and milk products
- Includes lean meats, poultry, fish, beans, eggs, and nuts
- Is low in saturated fats, trans fats, cholesterol, salt (sodium), and added sugars

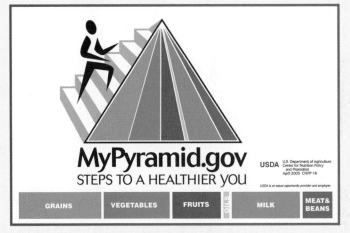

You can use the information from MyPyramid to develop a personalized health plan that includes eating foods from every food group. Of course, every person has different nutritional needs, depending on factors such as age, sex, height, weight, health, and physical activity. Use the tables on the following pages to identify the amount from each food group that is right for you. You can also find the information on the www.MyPyramid.gov Web site.

Note that the amounts are intended for individuals who get less than 30 minutes per day of moderate physical activity, beyond normal daily activities. If you are more physically active, you may be able to eat more while staying within calorie needs.

Also, MyPyramid is not a therapeutic diet for any specific health condition. Individuals with a chronic health condition should consult with a health care provider to determine what dietary pattern is appropriate for them.

(Source: www.MyPyramid.gov)

531

Grains

How Many Foods from the Grains Food Group Do You Need Every Day?

Any food made from wheat, rice, oats, cornmeal, barley, or another cereal grain is a grain product. Bread, pasta, oatmeal, breakfast cereals, tortillas, and grits are examples of grain products.

Most Americans consume enough grains, but few eat enough whole grains. Recall that whole grains have not been processed, so they retain all vitamins and minerals, as well as fiber. At least half of all the grains you eat should be whole grains, such as whole-grain bread, whole-grain cereal, and whole-grain pasta.

		Daily Recommendation for Grains	Daily Minimum Amount of Whole Grains
Children	2–3 years old	3 ounce equivalents	1½ ounce equivalents
	4–8 years old	4 to 5 ounce equivalents	2 to 2½ ounce equivalents
Girls	9–13 years old	5 ounce equivalents	3 ounce equivalents
	14–18 years old	6 ounce equivalents	3 ounce equivalents
Boys	9–13 years old	6 ounce equivalents	3 ounce equivalents
	14–18 years old	7 ounce equivalents	3½ ounce equivalents
Women	19–30 years old	6 ounce equivalents	3 ounce equivalents
	31–50 years old	6 ounce equivalents	3 ounce equivalents
	51+ years old	5 ounce equivalents	3 ounce equivalents
Men	19–30 years old	8 ounce equivalents	4 ounce equivalents
	31–50 years old	7 ounce equivalents	3½ ounce equivalents
	51+ years old	6 ounce equivalents	3 ounce equivalents

Vegetables

How Many Foods from the Vegetables Food Group Do You Need Every Day?

Any vegetable or 100% vegetable juice counts as a member of the Vegetables group. Vegetables may be raw or cooked; may be fresh, frozen, canned, or dried/dehydrated; and may be whole, cut up, or mashed.

Most vegetables are naturally low in fat and calories. Vegetables are important sources of many nutrients, including potassium, dietary fiber, folate (folic acid), vitamin A, vitamin E, and vitamin C.

		Daily Recommendations for Vegetables
Children	2–3 years old	1 cup
	4–8 years old	1½ cups
Girls	9–13 years old	2 cups
	14–18 years old	2½ cups
Boys	9–13 years old	2½ cups
	14–18 years old	3 cups
Women	19–30 years old	2½ cups
	31–50 years old	2½ cups
	51+ years old	2 cups
Men	19–30 years old	3 cups
	31–50 years old	3 cups
	51+ years old	2½ cups

Weekly Recommendations for the Vegetable Subgroups

Vegetables are organized into five subgroups, based on their nutrient content. It is not necessary to eat vegetables from each subgroup daily. However, over a week, try to consume the amounts listed from each subgroup as a way to reach your daily intake recommendation. The five subgroups are:

- Dark green vegetables, such as broccoli, spinach, collard greens, and romaine lettuce
- Orange vegetables such as carrots, pumpkin, sweet potatoes, and butternut squash
- Dry beans and peas, such as black beans, kidney beans, white beans, tofu, and black-eyed peas
- Starchy vegetables such as corn, green peas, lima beans, and potatoes
- Other vegetables such as asparagus, beets, celery, green beans, mushrooms, and onions

Weekly Recommendations for Vegetable Subgroups

		Dark Green Vegetables	Orange Vegetables	Dry Beans and Peas	Starchy Vegetables	Other Vegetables
Children	2–3 years old	1 cup	½ cup	½ cup	1½ cups	4 cups
	4–8 years old	1½ cups	1 cup	1 cup	2½ cups	4½ cups
Girls	9–13 years old	2 cups	1½ cups	2½ cups	2½ cups	5½ cups
	14–18 years old	3 cups	2 cups	3 cups	3 cups	6½ cups
Boys	9–13 years old	3 cups	2 cups	3 cups	3 cups	6½ cups
	14–18 years old	3 cups	2 cups	3 cups	6 cups	7 cups
Women	19–30 years old	3 cups	2 cups	3 cups	3 cups	6½ cups
	31–50 years old	3 cups	2 cups	3 cups	3 cups	6½ cups
	51+ years old	2 cups	1½ cups	2½ cups	2½ cups	5½ cups
Men	19–30 years old	3 cups	2 cups	3 cups	6 cups	7 cups
	31–50 years old	3 cups	2 cups	3 cups	6 cups	7 cups
	51+ years old	3 cups	2 cups	3 cups	3 cups	6½ cups

Fruits

How Many Foods from the Fruits Food Group Do You Need Every Day?

Any fruit or 100% fruit juice counts as part of the fruit group. Fruits may be fresh, canned, frozen, or dried, and may be whole, cut up, or pureed.

Most fruits are naturally low in fat, sodium, and calories. Fruits are important sources of many nutrients, including potassium, dietary fiber, vitamin C, and folate (folic acid).

		Daily Recommendations for Fruits
Children	2–3 years old	1 cup
	4–8 years old	1 to 1½ cups
Girls	9–13 years old	1½ cups
	14–18 years old	1½ cups
Boys	9–13 years old	1½ cups
	14–18 years old	2 cups
Women	19–30 years old	2 cups
	31–50 years old	1½ cups
	51+ years old	1½ cups
Men	19–30 years old	2 cups
	31–50 years old	2 cups
	51+ years old	2 cups

Milk

How Many Foods from the Milk Food Group Do You Need Every Day?

All fluid milk products and many foods made from milk are considered part of this food group. Foods made from milk that retain their calcium content, such as milk, ice cream, yogurt, hard natural cheeses, soft cheeses, and processed cheeses, are part of the group. Foods made from milk that have little to no calcium, such as cream cheese, cream, and butter, are not.

For those who are lactose intolerant, lactose-free and lower-lactose products are available. These include hard cheeses and yogurt. Also, enzyme preparations can be added to milk to lower the lactose content.

Milk products are important sources of many nutrients, including potassium, calcium, and vitamin D. It is wiser to choose fat-free or low-fat milk products to avoid consuming unnecessary fat.

		Daily Recommendations for Milk Products
Children	2–3 years old	2 cups
	4–8 years old	2 cups
Girls	9–13 years old	3 cups
	14–18 years old	3 cups
Boys	9–13 years old	3 cups
	14–18 years old	3 cups
Women	19–30 years old	3 cups
	31–50 years old	3 cups
	51+ years old	3 cups
Men	19–30 years old	3 cups
	31–50 years old	3 cups
	51+ years old	3 cups

Meat and Beans

How Many Foods from the Meat And Beans Food Group Do You Need Every Day?

All foods made from meat, poultry, fish, dry beans or peas, eggs, nuts, and seeds are considered part of this group. Note that dry beans and peas are part of this group as well as the vegetable group.

Fish, nuts, and seeds contain healthy oils, so choose these foods frequently instead of meat or poultry. Meat, poultry, fish, dry beans and peas, eggs, nuts, and seeds supply many nutrients. These include protein, B vitamins (niacin, thiamin, riboflavin, and B6), vitamin E, iron, zinc, and magnesium.

Most Americans eat enough food from this group, but need to choose more lean or low-fat items, and make more varied selections.

		Daily Recommendations for Meat and Beans
Children	2–3 years old	2 ounce equivalents
	4–8 years old	3 to 4 ounce equivalents
Girls	9–13 years old	5 ounce equivalents
	14–18 years old	5 ounce equivalents
Boys	9–13 years old	5 ounce equivalents
	14–18 years old	6 ounce equivalents
Women	19–30 years old	5½ ounce equivalents
	31–50 years old	5 ounce equivalents
	51+ years old	5 ounce equivalents
Men	19–30 years old	6½ ounce equivalents
	31–50 years old	6 ounce equivalents
	51+ years old	5½ ounce equivalents

Oils

How Much Fat and Oil Do You Need Every Day?

Most of the fats you eat should be polyunsaturated (PUFA) or monounsaturated (MUFA) fats. Oils are the major source of MUFAs and PUFAs in the diet. PUFAs contain some fatty acids that are necessary for health—called *essential fatty acids*. Oils are also the major source of vitamin E in typical American diets.

Most Americans consume enough oil by eating foods such as nuts, fish, cooking oil, and salad dressing. While consuming some oil is needed for health, oils still contain calories. In fact, oils and solid fats both contain about 120 calories per tablespoon. Therefore, the amount of oil consumed needs to be limited to balance total calorie intake. Consult the Nutrition Facts label on an oil product for information about the type of fats it contains, so you can make healthy choices.

		Daily Recommendations of Oils
Children	2–3 years old	3 teaspoons
	4–8 years old	4 teaspoons
Girls	9–13 years old	5 teaspoons
	14–18 years old	5 teaspoons
Boys	9–13 years old	5 teaspoons
	14–18 years old	6 teaspoons
Women	19–30 years old	6 teaspoons
	31–50 years old	5 teaspoons
	51+ years old	5 teaspoons
Men	19–30 years old	7 teaspoons
	31–50 years old	6 teaspoons
	51+ years old	6 teaspoons

Language Arts: Grammar and Punctuation Basics

Grammar

Subjects and Verbs

The basic unit of writing is the simple sentence. A simple sentence expresses a complete thought. Every simple sentence must contain two basic building blocks: a **subject** and a **verb**. The subject is the main topic of the sentence—who or what the sentence is about. The verb says what the subject does.

Example of a simple sentence:
Donna bakes cupcakes for the New York Cupcake Café.

Subject: *Who?* <u>Donna</u>

Verb: *What does Donna do?* She <u>bakes</u>.

All sentences are built from subjects and verbs, so understanding how to find them is an important first step in mastering other sentence skills.

Find the Subject

When you write a sentence, you write about someone or something: the subject. To find the subject of a simple sentence, ask who or what the sentence is about. Subjects can be people, places, things, or ideas.

- Maddie eats cheese every day.
  Who? <u>Maddie</u> (person)
- Expensive restaurants intimidate me.
  What? Expensive <u>restaurants</u> (place)

Find the Verb

When writing about someone or something (the subject), to complete the thought you must write what the subject does: the **verb**. A verb often conveys the idea of action. To find the verb, ask what the subject does.

Action Verbs

Verbs often show action. These verbs are called **action verbs**. They tell us what somebody or something *does*.

- Maddie eats cheese every day.
  What does Maddie do? She <u>eats</u>.
- Expensive restaurants intimidate me.
  What do expensive restaurants do? They <u>intimidate</u>.

Linking Verbs

Some verbs, called **linking verbs**, do not show action. Instead, a linking verb connects a noun in front of the verb with a word or group of words that comes after it. In doing so, the linking verb tells something about the subject: what the subject is or was.

Some Common Linking Verbs

am	be	feel
is	become	seem
are		look
was		appear
were		

- Pizza <u>is</u> my favorite food. (connects *pizza* with *favorite food*)
- Your outfit <u>looks</u> good. (connects *outfit* with *good*)

Prepositional Phrases

A **prepositional phrase** is a group of words beginning with a part of speech called a preposition and ending with a noun. Writers often use prepositional phrases to show time or location, as in before the game, during the party, below the table, or inside the box.

Common Prepositions

about	behind	despite	in	onto	until
above	before	down	inside	over	up
across	beneath	during	into	through	upon
after	beside	except	of	to	with
around	between	for	off	toward	within
at	by	from	on	under	without

NOTE
Since not all verbs express action, it is helpful to keep in mind that verbs are also words that change their forms to indicate the tense or time of a sentence.

For example:

Reading is my favorite activity.

What is the verb?

Change to past tense:

Reading was my favorite activity.

Which word has changed?

So what is the verb?

NOTE
Linking verbs sometimes relate to the five senses: sight, sound, taste, touch, and smell.

NOTE
Prepositional phrases often answer the question *when* or *where*.

For example:

When?

before breakfast

Where?

over the fence

The subject never appears within a prepositional phrase, so you should ignore prepositional phrases when looking for the subject of a sentence. In the examples below, the prepositional phrases are crossed out.

■ ~~Through the night~~, we heard a strange tapping sound.

Subject: *Who?* <u>We</u>

Verb: *What did we do?* We <u>heard</u>.

■ The music ~~at the party~~ was boring.

Subject: *What?* The <u>music</u>

Verb: *What about the music?* It <u>was</u>.

Helping Verbs and Verb Phrases

Both action and linking verbs often are accompanied by other special verbs called **helping verbs**. Helping verbs frequently show time. Listed below are some frequently used helping verbs.

Helping Verbs

can	may	shall	will
could	might	should	
have	must	used to	
is	need	was	

Main verbs accompanied by one or more helping verbs are called **verb phrases**. For example, following are some verb phrases formed by adding helping verbs to the main verb learn:

Helping Verbs and Verb Phrases

is learning	has learned	should have learned
was learning	will learn	should have been learned
	had been learning	had learned
	has been learned	should have been learning

Below are sentences that contain verb phrases:

■ Eliza will be moving to Washington next week.

Subject: *Who?* <u>Eliza</u>

Verb phrase: *What about her?* She <u>will be moving</u>.

■ We should have left hours ago.

Subject: *Who?* <u>We</u>

Verb phrase: *What about us?* We <u>should have left</u>.

NOTE
Helping verbs must always accompany (help) another verb.

NOTE
Words like *not, never, always,* and *just* are not considered part of the verb even though they may be in the middle of the verb.

I will not *be going with you today.*

Kate had never *flown on an airplane before*

NOTE
Fragment literally means "a part broken off."

Fragments

A word group that lacks a subject or a verb and that does not show a complete thought is called a **fragment**. Because fragments are incomplete thoughts punctuated as complete ones, they can confuse readers and must be avoided. One key to eliminating fragments from your writing is knowing the difference between two types of word-groups: **phrases** and **clauses**.

Phrases and Clauses

A group of words without a subject/verb unit is called a **phrase**. A group of words with a subject/verb unit is called a **clause**.

■ **Phrase (Fragment):**
   My relatives in Chicago. (no verb)
   Clause:
   My relatives live in Chicago. (contains a subject, *relatives,* and a verb, *live*)

■ **Phrase (Fragment):**
   Rounding the corner. (no subject)
   Clause:
   A red convertible was rounding the corner.
   (contains a subject, *convertible,* and a complete verb phrase, *was rounding*)

Independent and Dependent Clauses

Though clauses contain both a subject and a verb, that does not mean that all clauses are complete sentences. There are two types of clauses: **independent clauses** and **dependent clauses**.

A clause that can stand alone as a complete sentence is called an **independent clause**.

A **dependent clause** cannot stand alone. Dependent clauses always start with a word called a **subordinator**. Words like *although* and *since* are subordinators. Because they are incomplete thoughts, dependent clauses must be attached to independent clauses.

Common Subordinators

after	if	until	wherever
although	in order that	what	whether
as	since	whatever	which
because	that	when	while
before	though	whenever	who
even though	unless	where	whose

For example:

■ Independent Clause:
Dwane likes professional basketball.

Dependent Clause (Fragment):
Although Dwane likes professional basketball.

Correction:
Although Dwane likes professional basketball, he enjoys watching football even more. (attached dependent clause)

■ Independent Clause:
Richard came home for summer vacation.

Dependent Clause (Fragment):
Since Richard came home for summer vacation.

Correction:
Since Richard came home for summer vacation, he has not done a single thing. (attached dependent clause)

Correcting Fragments

Sentence fragments are phrases or dependent clauses punctuated as if they were complete sentences. Fragment literally means a "part broken off." In keeping with this definition, a sentence fragment can usually be fixed by attaching the fragment to a sentence. Thus, the "broken part" is glued back to its original position.

For example:

■ Phrase (Fragment):
Stanley has no patience for people. Especially his sister-in-law Blanche.

Correction:
Stanley has no patience for people, especially his sister-in-law Blanche.

■ Dependent Clause (Fragment):
Because Donna took so long to get ready. We all missed the first act of the play.

Correction:
Because Donna took so long to get ready, we all missed the first act of the play.

Hints on Proofreading for Fragments

Focus on each sentence separately, reading slowly. Do not be tempted to skim over your work.

Try reading out loud when you are trying to decide whether a group of words is complete or incomplete. You can often "hear it" when something is incomplete.

Learn to identify phrases and dependent clauses in writing. If you see a word group that is unattached, you know it must be a fragment.

NOTE
Use a comma after a dependent clause if it comes at the beginning of a sentence:

After I started exercising, I had a lot more energy.

Do not use a comma if the dependent clause comes at the end of a sentence:

I had a lot more energy after I started exercising.

NOTE
Technically, run-ons that have no punctuation to mark the break between complete thoughts are called *fused sentences*.

Run-ons that use only a comma to attempt to join complete thoughts are called *comma splices*.

What Are Run-on Sentences?

While some writers make the mistake of not putting enough information in a sentence, resulting in sentence fragments, others try to cram too much into their sentences. **Run-on sentences** result when two complete sentences (independent clauses) are joined with either no punctuation or only a comma. This construction makes it unclear where one thought ends and the next one begins.

Like fragments, run-ons cause readers to become confused. People often write run-ons when they sense that two thoughts belong together *logically* but do not realize that the two thoughts are separate sentences *grammatically*, as in the following examples.

- **Run-on:**

  Dave and Rhonda are crazy about figure skating they watch it on television constantly.

- **Run-on:**

  Dave and Rhonda are crazy about figure skating, they watch it on television constantly.

- **Correction:**

  Dave and Rhonda are crazy about figure skating. They watch it on television constantly.

Generally, good writers will often join sentences which are logically related to make a more complex point. However, complete sentences *cannot* be joined with just a comma or no punctuation at all.

Correcting Run-on Sentences

Following are three useful ways to correct run-ons:

- Make two separate sentences of the run-on thoughts by inserting a **period and a capital letter.**

  Dave and Rhonda are crazy about figure skating. They watch it on television constantly.

NOTE
If you have trouble recognizing the seven coordinating conjunctions, remember them by the handy acronym "FANBOYS": For, And, Nor, But, Or, Yet, So.

- Use a **comma plus a coordinating conjunction** (*and, but, for, or, nor, so, yet*) to connect the two complete thoughts. Coordinating conjunctions are joining words that, when used with a comma, show the logical connection between two closely related thoughts.

  Dave and Rhonda are crazy about figure skating, *so* they watch it on television constantly.

- Use a **subordinator**. You can also show the relationship between two sentences by using a subordinator (words like *after, because,* and *although*) to change one of them into a dependent clause.

  Because Dave and Rhonda are crazy about figure skating, they watch it on television constantly.

Common Subordinators

after	even though	unless	whenever
although	if	until	where
as	in order that	what	wherever
because	since	whatever	whether
before	though	when	while

Words That Often Lead to Run-on Sentences

Frequently the second sentence in a run-on begins with one of the words in the following list. These words often refer to something in the first sentence or seem like joining words. Beware of run-ons whenever you use one of these words in your writing.

Words That Often Lead to Run-ons

I	we	there	now
you	they	this	then
he		that	next
she			
it			

Making Subjects and Verbs Agree

Being able to identify subjects and verbs is important. But you must also make sure that the subjects and verbs agree in number. This grammatical rule is called **subject-verb agreement**.

■ A singular subject (one person or one thing) is used with a singular verb.
   For example:
   Her <u>habit</u> <u>annoys</u> me. (singular)
   The <u>plane</u> <u>was</u> late. (singular)

■ A plural subject (more than one person or thing) is used with a plural verb.
   For example:
   Her <u>habits</u> <u>annoy</u> me. (plural)
   The <u>planes</u> <u>were</u> late. (plural)

Writers sometimes make mistakes in subject-verb agreement in sentences with more than one subject—a compound subject—or with verbs separated from subjects. It's also common for writers to confuse subject-verb agreement when using pronouns (I, you, he, she, it, we, you, and then), either/or, neither/nor connectors, or "there" sentences. Examples of these follow.

NOTE
The rules of subject-verb agreement apply mostly to *present tense* verbs since the form of a verb changes in the present tense singular.

<u>Present</u>	<u>Past</u>
I write	I wrote
you write	you wrote
he/she *writes*	he/she wrote
we write	we wrote
they write	they wrote

NOTE
The verb *to be* causes agreement problems in the past tense as well as the present because it has many different forms.

<u>Present</u>	<u>Past</u>
I *am*	I *was*
you *are*	you *were*
he/she *is*	he/she *was*
we *are*	we *were*
they *are*	they *were*

You must learn these forms to avoid any agreement problems in your writing.

Compound Subjects

Subjects joined by **and** are typically paired with a plural verb. These are called **compound subjects.** The only exception to this rule would be subjects considered singular because they are they are taken as a single unit, such as *Rock 'n' Roll.*

- For example:

  <u>John and Tina</u> <u>are</u> very close. (plural)

  <u>Corned beef and cabbage</u> <u>is</u> my favorite meal. (singular)

  <u>Hot cocoa and a good book</u> <u>make</u> Sandra happy. (plural)

  <u>Hide-and-seek</u> <u>is played</u> by almost all children. (singular)

Verbs Separated from Subjects

When words, such as prepositional phrases, come between the subject and verb, the interrupting words do not change subject-verb agreement. The verb still must agree with the subject of the sentence.

- For example:

  The <u>coins</u> ~~on the table~~ <u>are</u> mine. (plural)

  The <u>price</u> ~~of the dining room chairs~~ <u>is</u> ridiculous. (singular)

  That <u>woman</u> ~~with plaid bell bottoms~~ <u>seems</u> strange. (singular)

  Those <u>shirts</u>, ~~as well as that coat~~, <u>need</u> a thorough cleaning. (plural)

Punctuation

Commas

Writers use commas to mark slight pauses or breaks in sentences. When used properly, commas clarify meaning in a sentence. When overused, however, commas can interrupt the smooth flow of sentences and cause confusion. Whenever you add a comma to a sentence, you should be conscious of the specific comma usage rule you are applying. All good writers should know the six primary comma rules covered in this topic.

NOTE
Inexperienced writers tend to overuse commas rather than omit them. If you cannot think of a specific reason to use a comma, *leave it out.*

1. Use a comma after an introductory word or word group that leads into the main sentence.

   - Strolling down the nature trail, Zac saw a brown bear.
   - When you have finished eating your broccoli, you may leave the table.

A dependent clause that comes at the beginning of a sentence always needs to be followed by a comma. The second example above illustrates this concept. However, if the dependent clause comes at the end of the sentence, no comma is necessary:

   - You may leave the table when you have finished eating your broccoli.

2. Use commas to enclose a word or word group that interrupts the flow of a sentence.
   - Jane, however, will not be coming tonight.
   - Richard, knowing that it was going to rain, bought a new umbrella.

If you are unsure whether Rule 2 applies to a sentence, try reading the sentence without the interrupting word or words. If the sentence still makes sense without the missing material, set off the interrupting expression with commas. Note how **nonessential information** is set off with commas in the following example:

> **NOTE**
> Nonessential information: information that can be removed from a sentence without changing its meaning.

   - Marty Lasorda, who sat next to me in high school, is now a trader on Wall Street.

The words *who sat next to me in high school* are added information and not needed to identify the subject of the sentence, *Marty Lasorda*. However, in the next sentence the added information is necessary:

   - The guy who sat next to me in high school is now a trader on Wall Street.

The words *who sat next to me in high school* are **essential** to the sentence. Without them, we would have no idea to which *guy* the writer is referring.

3. Use commas to separate items in a series.
   - Steve ordered a large coke, large fries, and a double cheeseburger.
   - Tanya did her laundry, cleaned the bedroom, washed the dishes, and painted the kitchen on Sunday.

Use a comma between descriptive words in a series if *and* sounds natural between them, as in the following:

   - We immediately left the crowded, noisy restaurant.
     (We immediately left the crowded *and* noisy restaurant.)
   - Pablo wore an expensive, well-tailored suit to the party.
     (Pablo wore an expensive *and* well-tailored suit to the party.)

Notice, however, how commas are not necessary in the following sentences:

   - Brenda bit into a juicy red apple.

     Awkward:

     Brenda bit into a juicy *and* red apple.

In the above example *and* does not sound natural between descriptive words, so no comma is used.

4. Use a comma before the conjunctions and, but, for, or, nor, yet, or so when they connect two independent clauses.
   - Dwane thought he had enough money for the movie, but he was fifty cents short.
   - The running back broke through the line for a thirty yard gain, and the home crowd began cheering wildly.

5. Use commas around direct addresses.

When addressing a person, set off the person's name or title with commas. If the direct address comes at the beginning or end of a sentence, only one comma is necessary.

- Ernest, your pants are on backwards.
- Ladies and gentlemen, you are cordially invited to a reception after the show.

6. Use a comma to set off a direct quotation.

A comma separates what is said from who said it.

- "Never tell me the odds," said Han Solo.
- "Seeing the movie version," continued Samantha, "is never as good as reading the book."

Possessive Apostrophes: Singular Nouns

The possessive form of a noun shows ownership—or possession. There are several ways to show ownership without changing the noun itself, such as:

- the sweater belonging to the *girl*
  OR
- the sweater of the *girl*

However, a simpler, more efficient way to show ownership is to change the possessive noun using a punctuation mark called an **apostrophe** ('):

- the *girl's* sweater

Rule 1: To make a singular noun possessive, add an apostrophe and an s ('s).

- the test of the *student* = the *student's* test
- the ending of the *movie* = the *movie's* ending

Be careful: Do not use 's when you are simply forming a plural.

- Incorrect:
  Barbecue short rib's are the specialty here.
- Correct:
  Barbecue short ribs are the specialty here.

NOTE
Commas and end punctuation marks go on the *inside* of quotation marks.

NOTE
When a proper noun (a name) ends in s, you may choose to add either 's or ', depending on your preference in pronunciation.

For example:

Charles's room

OR

Charles' room

Possessive Apostrophes: Plural Nouns

A plural noun names two or more persons, places, things, or ideas. Most commonly a noun is made plural by adding an *s*: one *girl* becomes several *girls*; one *book* becomes several *books*. Making a plural noun ending in s possessive is simple:

Rule 2: To make a plural noun ending in s possessive, place an apostrophe after the s (s').

■ the tests of the *students* = the *students'* tests

■ the endings of the *movies* = the *movies'* endings

Some nouns change their spellings to form the plural: *child* becomes *children*; *woman* becomes *women*, for example. To make this kind of plural noun possessive simply add an apostrophe and an *s* (*'s*).

■ the children's toys

■ the women's self defense class

Contractions

Sometimes writers combine two words to form a single shorter word. Such a construction is called a **contraction**. An apostrophe is added to show where letters have been omitted. For example:

■ I + am = I'm (the apostrophe replaces the missing *a*)

■ you + will = you'll (the apostrophe replaces the missing *w* and *i*)

Here are some other common contractions:

cannot = can't	is not = isn't	they have = they've
did not = didn't	it is = it's	was not = wasn't
do not = don't	let us = let's	we are = we're
he is = he's	she is = she's	we have = we've
I will = I'll	there is = there's	will not = won't

Be careful: The possessive form of the word *it* is *its*. Do **not** add an apostrophe to show possession in this case; *it's* always means *it is* or *it has*.

■ Vlada's car blew out *its* right front tire. (possessive)

■ The plant outgrew *its* pot. (possessive)

■ *It's* been a pleasure to meet you. (contraction: *it has*)

■ I think *it's* time to go home now. (contraction: *it is*)

NOTE

When using an apostrophe to show possession, the owner is always followed by the thing possessed. To determine the owner simply ask, "*To whom does it belong?*" The answer to this question takes the 's or the '.

NOTE

Although contractions are very common in everyday speech, try to avoid them in formal writing.

NOTE

To test if "its" is correct in a sentence, substitute the word "its" with "his."

For example:

Give the dog its bone.

Give the dog his bone.

Other Punctuation Marks

Punctuation is necessary to help make sentence meanings clearer. Commas and apostrophes are the most commonly misused punctuation marks. However, they are not the only marks that give writers trouble. Listed below are the rules for other punctuation marks that are used in writing.

Period

Use a **period** (.) at the end of all sentences except for direct questions and exclamations.

Use a period at the end of any indirect question.

■ **Example:**
   John asked Beth why there were no cookies left.

Use a period after most abbreviations.

■ **Example:**
   Dr.
   Ms.
   Jr.

> **NOTE**
> Before the advent of computers, two spaces were always inserted after a period. However, the current trend is to use only one space after a period.

> **NOTE**
> Do not use periods in acronyms (abbreviations made up of the first letter from a series of words).
>
> Example:
>
> *NATO*

Question Mark

Use a **question mark** (?) at the end of a direct question. But, as illustrated above, do not use a question mark to end an indirect question.

■ **Examples:**
   How cold is it outside?
   When was the Civil War fought?
   John asked Beth, "Why are there no cookies left?"
   "Why are there no cookies left?" asked John.

Exclamation Point

An **exclamation point** (!) is used to at the end of a statement of strong feeling or after an interjection.

■ **Example:**
   Look out for that truck!
   Hey! Somebody stole my wallet!

> **NOTE**
> Never use exclamation points in formal writing. Save them for casual e-mail correspondence and written dialog.

Colon

Use a **colon** (:) to introduce a list. The words that come before the colon must be a complete sentence.

■ **Incorrect:**
   Two things that I hate are: rainy days and Sundays.

■ **Correct:**
   There are two things that I hate: rainy days and Sundays.

A colon is used to help explain the statement that precedes the colon. It is also used to set off an explanation or final word.

- ■ **Examples:**

   There are only two things I like to do on Sundays: go to the movies and have pizza for dinner.

   We all had the same goal: success.

Use a colon after salutations in business correspondence, even if you address the person by their first name.

- ■ **Examples:**

   Dear Ms. Smith:

   Dear Verna:

Semicolon

A **semicolon** (;) is used to separate closely related independent clauses. Often the semicolon is used in place of the word *because*.

- ■ **Example:**

   Sarah was excited about the party; she knew that Greg was going to be there.

Use a semicolon to separate items in a series when the items themselves contain commas.

- ■ **Example:**

   There are four pizza toppings that I enjoy: pepperoni, sausage, and mush-rooms; green peppers, onions, and olives; eggplant, garlic, and anchovies; and spinach, goat cheese, and sun-dried tomatoes.

> **NOTE**
> Do not use semicolons to set off a list; use a colon.

Hyphens

Hyphenating documents has become much easier on the computer since you can automatically hyphenate the document, move the word to the next line, or compress the word to keep it on one line. However, hyphens have other functions, as discussed below.

Use a **hyphen** (-) to combine two nouns when they are acting as a singular, descriptive word. To see if the two words should be hyphenated into one descriptive word, ask yourself "what kind" of noun is being described.

- ■ **Examples:**

   a three-legged dog (What kind of dog? *three-legged*)

   a four-day convention (What kind of convention? *four-day*)

   Incorrect:

   I went to a convention that lasted four-days.
   (Four days does not answer the question "what kind.")

In writing, hyphenate the numbers twenty-one through ninety-nine and all fractions:

- ■ **Examples:**

   thirty-three

   one-half

> **NOTE**
> If you are not sure if you should hyphenate a compound word, try looking the word up in the dictionary. As a rule of thumb, words ending in *ly* are not hyphenated.
>
> Incorrect: *freshly-cut flowers*
>
> Correct: *fresh-cut flowers*

Do not hyphenate three-word numbers.

- **Example:**

  four hundred five

Use a hyphen with the prefix *mid* when referring to time.

- **Example:**

  the mid-sixties

Do not hyphenate the prefix *mid* when referring to other things:

- **Example:**

  midlife crisis

Hyphenate the prefix *re* only for ease of reading.

- **Examples:**

  re-edited

  re-evaluated

  restated (no hyphen needed)

Dashes

Use a **dash** (—) to show a sudden break in thought or to set off parenthetical information. The dash is also called an **em dash** because it is about the width of a capital M.

Use an **em dash** (—) to interrupt a sentence or to add additional information. Em dashes can be used in place of commas to add additional drama to the sentence. Em dashes can also be used to set off contrasting remarks.

- **Examples:**

  The bank robbers—with guns in hand—fired the first shot.

  We plan to revise the book in two—not three—months.

An **en dash** (–) is longer than a hyphen and shorter than an em dash. Its length is about the width of a capital N. Use an en dash to show continuation in time, dates, or other numbers. Think of using an en dash instead of the words *to* or *through*.

- **Examples:**

9:00 AM–5:00 PM	1990–94
March–May	pages 220–284

NOTE

In Microsoft Word you can create an em dash (—) by typing two hyphens (--) with no spaces between them or before or after them. Word will automatically create an em dash for you.

Parentheses

Like dashes or commas, **parentheses** ( ) are used to set off information that is extra or inessential to the meaning of the sentence.

■ Example:

The chapter on medieval art (pages 172–184) is very interesting.

Quotation Marks

Quotation Marks ("") are used to set off someone's exact words. A comma always separates what is said from who said it. Periods and commas go inside of quotation marks.

■ Examples:

"There are too many rules to punctuation," he stated.

The clerk told me, "There are no more bananas today."

Use **single quotes** ('') to enclose titles of poems, stories, movie titles, or other quoted material within quoted material.

■ Examples:

"'Survivor' is my favorite TV show," the teenage girl proclaimed.

"If you call Johnny 'stinky toes' one more time," Mom told Suzy, "you're going to your room."

NOTE
Do not over use parentheses in your writing.

NOTE
Quotation marks always come in pairs.

Math Review

Knowing basic math concepts and knowing when to apply them are essential skills. You should know how to add, subtract, multiply, divide, calculate percentages, and manipulate fractions. This section will help you accurately apply basic math concepts and skills necessary to your success at school, work, and to manage your personal finances at home.

Numbers

Numbers are expressed in different forms:

- Whole numbers, which are the counting numbers and zero. Whole numbers do not contain decimals or fractions. *Examples:* 1, 2, 3, 10, 15, 18, 0. Ignore zeros before whole numbers. For example, 025 is the same as 25.
- Nonwhole numbers, which are numbers that have decimals, such as 6.25 or 9.85.
- Mixed numbers, which are numbers that combine whole numbers and a fraction, such as 6 1/4 or 7 2/3.
- Percentages, which are portions in relation to a whole, such as 65% or 22%.

whole numbers
(HOHL NUHM bers)
Numbers that do not contain decimals or fractions
(e.g., 1, 2, 3).

nonwhole numbers
(non HOHL NUHM bers)
Numbers with decimals
(e.g., 6.25, 9.85).

mixed numbers
(mikst NUHM bers)
Numbers with whole numbers and a fraction
(e.g., 6^1/4, 7^2/3).

percentages
(per SEN tij es)
Portions in relation to a whole
(e.g., 65%, 22%).

Place Value

Numbers that have more than one digit are defined by their place value. Place value is the value of a digit based on where it is in a number. For example, the number 7777 is given the following values:

$$7 \quad 7 \quad 7 \quad 7$$
$$\blacktriangle \quad \blacktriangle \quad \blacktriangle \quad \blacktriangle$$

Place value ⟶ thousands   hundreds   tens   ones

This number is described by saying "seven thousand, seven hundred seventy-seven." Numbers are written with a comma placed to the left of every third digit. The number 7777 is properly written "7,777."

Rounding Whole Numbers

1. Find the place to be rounded.
2. If the digit to the right is 5 or more, add 1 to the place to be rounded. If the digit to the right is 4 or less, leave the place to be rounded unchanged.
3. Change all digits to the right of the rounded place to zeroes.

For example, to round 687 to the nearest ten:

1. The place to be rounded is the number in the tens column.
2. The digit to the right of the tens column is greater than 5, so you add 1 to the digit in the place to be rounded, making it 9.
3. Change the 7 to a zero. The result is 690.

555

Four turtles = 100%.

One turtle or 25% of the turtles are sold.

Three turtles or 75% of the turtles are left.

If there were five turtles in the figure, what percentage would one turtle represent?

Working with Decimals and Percentages

Recall that a percentage is a portion of a whole. 100 percent = the whole or all of something. The symbol for percent is %. In the figure to the right, four turtles = 100% or all of the turtles. One turtle is $1/4$ of the total, or 25%. Two turtles = $1/2$ of the total, or 50%. Three turtles = 3/4 or 75%. Numbers to the left of a decimal are whole numbers. Numbers to the right of a decimal are less than one.

To divide decimals by whole numbers:

$$24.5 \div 4 = 4\overline{)24.5}$$ Place the decimal point in the answer directly above the decimal point in the dividend.

$$
\begin{array}{r}
6. \\
4\overline{)24.5} \\
\underline{24}
\end{array}
\qquad
\begin{array}{r}
6.1 \\
4\overline{)24.5} \\
\underline{24}\!\downarrow \\
5 \\
\underline{4} \\
1
\end{array}
\qquad
\begin{array}{r}
6.125 \\
4\overline{)24.500} \\
\underline{24}\!\downarrow\downarrow \\
5 \\
\underline{4}\!\downarrow \\
10 \\
\underline{8}\!\downarrow \\
20 \\
\underline{20}
\end{array}
$$

Add 0s to carry answer.

Numbers to the right of a decimal point indicate less than one whole. For example, 1.5 is the same as $1^1/2$.

Examples:

Decimal		Percentage		Fraction(s)
0.10	=	10%	=	$^{10}/_{100}$ or $^1/_{10}$
0.25	=	25%	=	$^{25}/_{100}$ or $^1/_4$
6.25	=	625%	=	$6^{25}/_{100}$ or $6^1/_4$

To change a decimal number into a percentage: Move the decimal two places to the right.

Examples:

$0.5 = 0.5\,0. = 50\%$

$30.0 = 30.0\,0. = 3000\%$

$0.04 = .0\,4. = 4\%$

To change a percentage into a decimal number: Replace the percent sign with a decimal and move the decimal two spaces to the left.

To find the percentage of a number:

1. Change the percentage to a decimal.
2. Multiply that decimal by the number.

Examples:

15% of 63 change 15% to 0.15 then multiply $0.15 \times 63 = 9.45$

9.45 is 15% of 63

20% of 100 change 20% to 0.20 then multiply $0.20 \times 100 = 20$

20 is 20% of 100

Addition

Addition is the totaling of two or more numbers. Each number you are adding is called an *addend*. The result is called the *sum* or *total*. For example, 2 computers in the reception area + 3 computers in accounting = a total of 5 computers in the office.

To add:

1. Write the addends in columns, making sure each digit lines up correctly according to its place value. That means putting ones in the ones column, tens in the tens column, hundreds in the hundreds column, and so on.
2. Draw a line under the last addend in the column.
3. Add all the addends above the line and write the total or sum below the line.

Examples:

```
   2      34      <— addends
 + 3     + 4      <— addends
   5      38      <— totals
```

When adding more than one column of numbers, always start adding numbers in the right column—place value ones—first.

Adding by Carrying Numbers

When the numbers in a column add up to more than 10, you must *carry* all digits to the left of the place value ones column. To carry means to move the digits to the top of the next place value column. You then add the carried digits with all the numbers in that column.

For example, to add 81 + 384 + 10 + 9 (refer to the following example):

1. Write the numbers in columns, lining them up according to place value.
2. Add the numbers in the ones column. The total is 14.
3. Write the 4 in the ones column below the total line, and carry the 1 to the top of the tens column.
4. Add the numbers in the tens column, including the 1 you carried. The total is 18.
5. Write the 8 in the tens column below the total line, and carry the 1 to the top of the hundreds column.
6. Add the numbers in the hundreds column, including the 1 you carried. The total is 4.
7. Write the 4 in the hundreds column below the total line. The sum of the numbers is 484.

Example 1:

= 14; leave the 4 in the total row and carry the 1 to the
 top of the tens column.

= 18; leave the 8 in the total row and carry the 1 to top of the
 hundreds column.

= 4; place the 4 in the total row.

Example 2:

= 14; leave the 4 in the total row and carry the 1 to the
 top of the tens column.

= 35; leave the 5 in the total row, carry the 3 to top of the
 hundreds column.

= 12; leave the 2 in the total row, and carry to the 1 to the top
 of the thousands column. 1 is the only number in the thousands
 columns, so you write the 1 in the total column.

Subtraction

subtraction

(suhb TRAK shuhn)
Taking a number away from
another number; the operation opposite of addition.

Subtraction is the opposite of addition. Subtracting numbers means taking one
number—called the *subtrahend*—away from another number—called the *minuend*.
The result is called the *difference*. Write a subtraction problem in columns, just like
you write an addition problem. Put the minuend on top, and the subtrahend below
it. Make sure you line up the digits in the proper place value column.

Subtract the number in the ones column first, and write the difference below the
line. Then, subtract the number in the tens column, then the hundreds column, and
so on.

$$
\begin{array}{ccc}
84 & \longleftarrow \text{minuend} \longrightarrow & 136 \\
-23 & \longleftarrow \text{subtrahend} \longrightarrow & -12 \\
\boxed{61} & \longleftarrow \text{difference} \longrightarrow & \boxed{124}
\end{array}
$$

Check your answer by adding the difference to the subtrahend. If your answer is correct, your total will equal the minuend

For example, you can check your subtraction for the first equation above by adding
61 (the answer) to 23 (the number you subtracted). 61 + 23 = 84, which is the number you started with at the top of the equation. The answer is correct.

Subtracting by Borrowing Numbers

When the number you are subtracting is greater than the number above it in the column, you can borrow a one from the column to the left. Borrowing makes the number at the top of the equation greater, so you can complete the subtraction.

When you borrow the one, you must do two things:

1. Cross out the number in the column to the left, and replace it with a number that is one less than the number that was there. For example, if there is a 3 in the column to the left, you cross out the 3 and replace it with a 2. If there is a 7, you cross out the 7 and replace it with a 6.
2. Write the borrowed 1 to the left of the number that is currently in the column you are subtracting. So, if there is a 5 in the column you are subtracting, you write the borrowed 1 to the left of the 5; the 5 becomes 15. (Refer to the following example.)

Examples:

$^{2}\not{3}\,^{1}5$ 8 is greater than 5, so you can borrow a one from the tens column.
$-\ 1\ \ 8$ Cross out the 3 in the tens column and replace it with a 2.
$\overline{\boxed{1\ \ 7}}$ Write the borrowed 1 to the left of the 5, making it 15.
        Subtract 8 from 15 and write the result(7) below the line in the ones column.
        Subtract 1 from 2 and write the result (1) below the line in the tens column.

Adding and Subtracting Decimals

For decimals, the process of adding and subtracting numbers is similar to the process for adding and subtracting whole numbers. The only difference is how the numbers are aligned in the column. Numbers should be aligned by the decimal point as in the following examples:

$$\begin{array}{r} 12.136 \\ +\ 10.246 \\ \hline 22.382 \end{array}$$

$$\begin{array}{r} 23.453 \\ -\ 10.37\ \ \\ \hline 13.083 \end{array}$$

Adding and Subtracting Fractions

A fraction is made up of two parts: a *numerator*, which is the number on top, and a *denominator*, or the number on the bottom. To add or subtract a fraction, the denominator must be the same. Consider the following examples:

Example 1:

$$\frac{1}{4} + \frac{3}{4} = \frac{1+3}{4} = \frac{4}{4} = \frac{1}{1} = 1$$

Example 2:

$$\frac{1}{5} + \frac{2}{5} + 12\frac{4}{5} = \frac{1}{5} + \frac{2}{5} + \frac{64}{5} = \frac{1+2+64}{5} = \frac{67}{5} = 13\frac{3}{5}$$

numerators
(NOO muh rey ters)
The top numbers of fractions.

denominators
(di NOM uh ney ters)
The bottom numbers of fractions.

Example 3:

$$\frac{2}{3} - \frac{1}{3} = \frac{2-1}{3} = \frac{1}{3}$$

Note that Example 1 shows a simplified fraction, or a fraction that does not have any common factors (other than 1) for the numerator and denominator. Example 2 shows a mixed number, which is converted to a fraction to be added or subtracted.

In some cases, fractions will need to be converted so each fraction being added has a common denominator. Consider the following example:

$$\frac{1}{3} + \frac{1}{2} = ?$$

Step 1: Convert each fraction so they have a common denominator.

The denominators, 2 and 3, are factors of 6, so multiply both the nominator and the denominator of each fraction by the number that makes the denominator equal to 6.

$$\frac{1}{3} \times \frac{2}{2} = \frac{2}{6}$$

$$\frac{1}{2} \times \frac{3}{3} = \frac{3}{6}$$

Step 2: Add fractions.

$$\frac{2}{6} + \frac{3}{6} = \frac{5}{6}$$

For subtraction, follow the same process to make fractions that have the same denominator. Simplify fractions after adding and subtracting as needed.

$$\frac{3}{4} - \frac{1}{4} = ?$$

Step 1: Convert each fraction so they have a common denominator.

$$\frac{3}{4} \times \frac{1}{3} = \frac{3}{12}$$

$$\frac{1}{4} \times \frac{1}{3} = \frac{1}{12}$$

Step 2: Subtract fractions.

$$\frac{3}{12} - \frac{1}{12} = \frac{2}{12}$$

Add or subtract the following:

3.45 + 2.34 + 5.6

$$3\frac{3}{4} + \frac{2}{3} + \frac{4}{5}$$

3.4 − 1.28

$$2\frac{3}{4} - 1\frac{1}{3}$$

What will happen if you don't convert fractions to a common denominator before adding or subtracting them?

Multiplication

Multiplication, the process of finding the product of two factors, is a quick, easy way to add. For example, $9 + 9 + 9 = 27$, but an easier process is $3 \times 9 = 27$.

To multiply numbers easily, memorize the multiplication table.

multiplication
(muhl tuh pli KEY shuhn)
Finding the product of two numbers.

Multiplication Table

	1	2	3	4	5	6	7	8	9	10
1	1	2	3	4	5	6	7	8	9	10
2	2	4	6	8	10	12	14	16	18	20
3	3	6	9	12	15	18	21	24	27	30
4	4	8	12	16	20	24	28	32	36	40
5	5	10	15	20	25	30	35	40	45	50
6	6	12	18	24	30	36	42	48	54	60
7	7	14	21	28	35	42	49	56	63	70
8	8	16	24	32	40	48	56	64	72	80
9	9	18	27	36	45	54	63	72	81	90
10	10	20	30	40	50	60	70	80	90	100

Multiplying Fractions

To multiply fractions:

1. Multiply the first **numerator**—the number above the line in the fraction—by the second numerator. Write the answer as the numerator in the result.
2. Multiply the first **denominator**—the number below the line in the fraction—by the second denominator.

Write the answer as the denominator in the result.

The numerators, or top numbers of the fractions, are multiplied; and the denominators, or bottom numbers of the fractions, are multiplied. For example:

$$\frac{3}{4} \times \frac{12}{15} = \frac{36}{60}$$

If possible, reduce the fraction, which means dividing both the numerator and the denominator by the largest number than goes into both. In the following example, 12 is the largest number that goes into both. 36 divided by 12 equals 3. 60 divided by 12 equals 5. You can reduce the fraction to $3/5$.

$$\frac{36}{60} \quad \text{to} \quad \frac{3}{5}$$

Division

division
(di VIZH uhn)
The process of separating into parts; the operation opposite of multiplication.

remainder
(ri MEYN der)
The amount left over after division that is less than a whole number.

Division is the opposite of multiplication. It is the process of separating a whole into parts. Knowing the multiplication table will help you when dividing. Consider this example: A medical office budget allows $600.00 a year for magazines. Each magazine subscription costs $35.00. How many magazines can you buy? Divide the total budgeted amount—$600.00—by $35.00. The result is 17. You can buy 17 magazine subscriptions. This problem is written as follows:

$600 \div 35$, or $35\overline{)600}$

$$\frac{17}{35\overline{)600}} \text{ magazine subscriptions}$$

To understand how 17 magazine subscriptions can be purchased for $600, review the following division skills:

Dividing three-digit numbers by one-digit numbers:

$812 \div 4$

Divide hundreds	Divide tens	Divide ones
$\boxed{2}$	$\boxed{20}$	$\boxed{203}$
$4\overline{)812}$	$4\overline{)812}$	$4\overline{)812}$
$\underline{8}$	$8\!\downarrow$	8
0	$\overline{01}$} 4 does not divide	$\overline{01}$
	$\underline{00}$ into 1. Place a 0	$00\!\downarrow$
	1 next to the 2 in	$\overline{12}$
	the answer.	$\underline{12}$} Divide 4 into 12.

Glossary

401(k) plan   A savings plan offered by an employer to an employee. The employee contributes a percentage of his or her earnings to the 401(k)/403(b) account each pay period. The money is taken out before taxes are withheld.

501(c)3   An organization defined by U.S. tax code as "Religious, Educational, Charitable, Scientific, Literary, Testing for Public Safety, to Foster National or International Amateur Sports Competition, or Prevention of Cruelty to Children or Animals Organizations." If you donate time or money to a 501(c)3 organization, you may be able to deduct your donation on your taxes, decreasing the amount of income tax that you have to pay.

Accessory   A nonessential item that you wear or carry, such as a belt, handbag, or scarf.

Accommodation   An adjustment that makes it possible for someone to meet a responsibility. In employment, an accommodation enables a disabled employee to perform his or her job responsibilities in a safe and accessible work environment. Also, a place to stay.

Account register   A book you use to record bank account transactions.

Accrue   To build up over time.

Acne   A common skin disorder caused by clogged pores.

ACT   A standardized test used to judge your preparedness for college.

Active listening   An important part of effective communication: When you are an active listener, you pay attention to the speaker, and make sure you hear and understand the message.

Addiction   A compulsion or uncontrollable need for something.

Adolescence   A stage in the human life cycle that occurs between the ages of 11 and 21 (between childhood and becoming an adult).

Adoption   The process of matching up people who want to be parents with children who need parents.

Adulthood   The three-quarters of a human lifespan that occur after reaching maturity.

Aggressive   Being aggressive means that you force your opinions on others. You express your feelings and thoughts in a hostile, or angry, way.

Americans with Disabilities Act (ADA)   A federal law that protects the rights of workers with disabilities.

Amino acids   The basic building blocks of proteins

Analogous colors   The colors that are next to each other on the color wheel. For example green, blue-green, and blue are analogous.

Anonymous   Not attributed to a person. For example, when you use technology you do not always know who is at the other side of the conversation because that person can remain anonymous.

Arranged marriage   The process of parents selecting a mate for a child.

Assertive   Being assertive means that you stand up for yourself. You express your feelings and thoughts with confidence, in a strong, honest, and direct way.

Assets   Resources. For example, finances are assets in the form of money.

563

Attitude   The way you think, feel, or behave, particularly when you are with other people.

Au pair   Someone from another country who comes to live with a family and help take care of their children.

Authorizing   Giving permission to someone to do something.

Average   The sum of two or more quantities divided by the number of quantities.

Baby Boomers   The generation of people born between 1946 and 1964.

Babysitting   Caring for somebody else's child, usually as a paid job.

Bait and switch   An unlawful trade practice in which a vendor advertises one product and then sells you a different—usually inferior—product.

Balance   The amount of money in a bank account. Also, a basic principle of design that describes the visual weight of objects and the way they are arranged.

Balanced account   An account for which the banks' record of transactions matches the account owner's record of transactions.

Bank   A business or financial institution that stores and manages money for individuals and other businesses.

Bank account   An account with a financial institution, recording the financial transactions between the customer and the bank and the resulting financial position of the customer with the bank.

Bank branch   A local office of a bank.

Bank statement   A list of all the transactions for your bank account.

Banking   Doing business with a bank.

Bankruptcy   A legal process in which you declare yourself legally unable to pay your outstanding debts.

Barrier-free living space   Living space that is organized and designed so everyone can use it—even people with disabilities.

Barter   To trade to get the things you need or want.

Beneficiary   The person who collects the money if there is a claim on an insurance policy.

Benefits   Things that have value. In employment, benefits are compensation other than wages.

Biases   Opinions based on something you think you know, not on the truth.

Binge eating   Eating too much, or eating an abnormally large amount.

Binge eating disorder   When someone has the first part of bulimia nervosa—the binge eating—but not the purging part. Individuals who have it tend to be obese—extremely overweight—and may describe their relationship with food as an addiction.

Biometric time clock   A time clock that uses a fingerprint or handprint to record when an employee comes and goes.

Blend   To mix together; to combine.

Blended family   A family that includes members originally from two separate families.

Body image   The opinion you have of your physical appearance is your body image.

Body Mass Index (BMI)   A height-to-weight ratio measurement used for evaluating body condition. The lower your BMI, the leaner you are. A BMI of less than 19 is considered underweight; 19 to 25 is considered average; 25 or greater is considered overweight; 30 or greater is considered obese.

Bond   A debt security issued by corporations, governments, or their agencies, in return for cash from lenders and investors.

Bonus   Something extra. In employment compensation, a bonus is pay in addition to your regular salary, usually paid to reward success.

Bounce a check   If there is not enough money in your account, the check will bounce, which means the payment will not be made.

Brand-name product   A product that you associate with a particular company.

Budget   A plan for spending and saving money. It helps you manage your money and make healthy financial decisions.

Bulk   A large quantity of something. When you buy in bulk you are buying large quantities of an item.

Bully   Someone who tries to hurt others on purpose, not just once but over and over.

Calorie   A unit of measurement that describes how much energy the food you eat delivers to your body.

Candidate for employment   A possible employee.

Carbohydrates   Starches or sugars that generate heat and energy for your body, and provide fiber.

Carbon monoxide   A colorless, odorless gas that can be deadly.

Cardiopulmonary resuscitation (CPR)   A process that can keep the heart pumping and air entering the lungs if a person stops breathing.

Career   A chosen field of work in which you try to advance over time by gaining responsibility and earning more money. Another word for career is occupation.

Career plan   A plan for reaching your career goals, including education, development of employability and practical skills, and job search resources.

Cash   The money made out of paper—dollar bills—and metal-coins.

Casual dating   Spending time one-on-one with a number of different people.

Central bank   An organization responsible for managing banking activity. In the United States, the Federal Reserve is the central bank. Other countries have their own central banks.

Character   The personal qualities or traits that make a person unique. You show your character qualities by the way you act and the things you say.

Checks   Written orders to a bank to transfer funds from your account to someone else's account.

Chronic dieting   A common form of disordered eating, in which the person consistently and successfully follows a diet to maintain an average or below-average body weight.

Citizen   An active and responsible member of the community.

Civic responsibility   The service you owe to location-based communities.

Civil disobedience   Nonviolent acts of disagreement.

Civil marriage   A marriage that is legal according to the laws of the government.

Classic style   A style that does not change from year to year.

Clear a check   The process of verifying that a check is real and valid before a bank will transfer the funds.

Cloud computing   Technology allowing data and applications to be stored on Internet servers, which makes information accessible from any device connected to the Internet.

Cluster   A grouping of similar things.

Color   The way eyes see light. A basic element of design.

Color harmony   A combination of colors that look good together.

Color value   The lightness or darkness of a color.

Commercial banks   Banks that provide financial services to businesses.

Commission   A payment calculated as a percentage of total sales.

Commodity   An item such as gold, wheat, or coal that can be traded, processed, and sold.

Community   A group of people who have a common goal. The people might be physically near each other, such as living in the same neighborhood, or they might be spread out all over the world, and connected to each other through the Internet.

Community resources   Services that the government provides, such as public parks, public schools, libraries, and police and fire departments.

Compensation   Wages and benefits received by an employee in return for his work. As a coping mechanism, compensation is substituting one goal for another. Also, payment to replace a damaged or unusable product.

Complementary colors   The colors opposite each other on the color wheel. Red and green are complementary. So are violet and yellow.

Complexion   Skin tone.

Compound interest   Interest calculated on both the principal and interest previously earned.

Compromise   A solution that satisfies the needs of everyone involved

Conflict   A disagreement between two or more people who have different ideas.

Consequences   The results of your decisions.

Conserve   Save.

Construction   In clothing, the way a garment is put together.

Consumer   Someone who buys goods and services.

Context   Context is the current situation or environment. When communicating, it includes nonverbal communication, such as your tone of voice, expressions, and body language.

Cookware   Pots and pans and other utensils used to prepare food.

Coordinate   To match or align. In clothing, it is an item you could combine with a garment to make a new look or outfit.

Coping skills   Techniques to help you deal with or overcome problems and difficulties.

Courtesy   Behavior that makes other people feel comfortable and appreciated.

Cover letter   A letter you send with your resume to a potential employer. It highlights the qualities that make you suitable for the position you want.

Credit   A loan that allows you to buy now and pay later.

Credit card   A credit card lets you use credit to buy now and pay later. Every time you use a credit card, you are borrowing money from the business that issued the card, such as the bank, store, or credit card company. The business pays for the purchase, and then you repay the business by paying your credit card bill.

Credit history   A record of your credit transactions over the past seven to ten years.

Credit report   A summary of your credit history.

Credit score   A three-digit number that ranks your likelihood of repaying your loans.

Credit unions   Nonprofit banks that are owned by the customers, or members.

Creditor   Someone who loans money.

Critical thinking   The ability to be honest, rational, and open-minded about your options without letting emotions get in the way of choosing the best course of action.

Criticism   Advice about how to make changes in your actions or behavior.

Cross-contamination   When food becomes hazardous by coming in contact with something already touched by contaminated food.

Crush   A strong but short-lived attraction to another person. Usually, the other person is unattainable.

Cultural diversity   An environment that includes people of many cultures.

Culture   The attitudes, values, and behaviors that are common to a particular group of people.

Currency   Money.

Dating   Seeing someone one-on-one so you can get to know each other better without being distracted by other people.

Daycare   A type of childcare service that can consist of a private individual adult taking in children in his or her home during the day, a commercial facility that cares for children, or something in-between.

Debit card   A card linked to a bank account that you use like cash. There must be enough money in the account to cover your purchases.

Debt   Money owed to a lender.

Debtor   Someone who owes money.

Decimal point   The dot between the whole number and the parts.

Decimals   Part of a whole. When you are working with dollars, decimals are parts of a dollar, or cents.

Decision   Making up your mind about something, or choosing one option over another.

Deductible   A set amount the beneficiary must pay towards a claim before the insurance company pays any money.

Deduction   An amount that your employer withholds from your earnings to pay for things such as taxes or insurance. Sometimes called a withholding.

Defense mechanism   A mental process that changes a situation in your mind so that it is easier to deal with.

Deficiency   A lack of something. In nutrition, it refers to a lack of a particular vitamin or mineral.

Deficit   Spending more money than you earn. An account is in deficit when it does not contain enough money to pay all expenses.

Denial   A defense mechanism by which you refuse to recognize the situation.

Denomination   The face value of money.

Deposit slip   A slip of paper you fill out when you make a deposit into your bank account. It includes information about the transaction, such as your name, account number, and the deposit amount.

Dental hygienist   A dental professional who specializes in cleaning the. He or she acts as the patient's guide in establishing a proper oral hygiene program.

Depression   A state of extreme sadness. People who are depressed usually have low self esteem and feel that they are not worthy of anything good.

Dermatologist   A doctor specializing in the care and treatment of the skin.

Developmentally delayed   A person who is slower than average to develop in one or more ways.

Developmentally disabled   A person who has a problem that prevents normal development in some way.

Diameter   The distance across a circle through its center.

Diet   The food you eat.

Dietary guidelines   Guidelines about the benefits of food and exercise published by government and private organizations.

Dietary Guidelines for Americans   Set of guidelines published by the U.S. Department of Health and Human Services (HHS) and the U.S. Department of Agriculture (USDA) for people two years and older about how good dietary habits and physical activity can promote health and reduce risk for major chronic diseases.

Direct contamination   When food becomes hazardous by coming directly in contact with a contaminant.

Direct deposit   Automatically depositing a paycheck into a bank account using electronic fund transfers.

Discipline   The process of establishing boundaries and rules that help children learn appropriate behaviors and make good choices.

Discrimination   When someone treats someone else unfairly because of prejudice, specifically based on age, gender, race, or religion.

Dividend   The amount of a corporation's after-tax earnings that it pays to its shareholders.

Docent   A guide at a museum.

Dress code   Rules about what you can and cannot wear.

Dropout   Someone who leaves school without receiving a degree.

Dry cleaning   A special method of cleaning textiles that uses chemicals instead of water and detergent to remove dirt.

Durable   Long lasting.

Dwelling   A place where people live. Also called a residence.

Dysfunctional   Not working correctly.

Economic issues   Issues having to do with money.

Economics   The study of the choices people and communities make regarding the way they produce and purchase goods and services.

Economy   Activity related to the production and distribution of goods and services.

Ecosystem   An environment or community of living things.

Effective communication   Interactions in which the receiver interprets the message the way the sender intended.

Elapsed time   The amount of time that has passed from one point in time to another. You find the amount of elapsed time by subtracting the earlier time from the later time.

Electrical shock   A flow of electricity through the body.

Electrocution   Death caused by an electrical shock.

Electronic community   A community in which people are connected via the Internet.

Electronic funds   Funds transferred from one account to a different account using online banking software or a debit card.

Elements of design   Qualities that you combine to create a pleasing look or style. The basic elements of design include line, color, texture, space, and shape.

Emotional well-being   The feeling and understanding that everything is going right in your emotional life.

Emphasis   A basic principle of design in which the elements of design are used to highlight or focus attention on a particular object.

Employability   Having and using your life skills and abilities to be hired and stay hired.

Employee handbook   A written document that describes all of the company policies and procedures, such as how to request vacation time, and the different benefits that are available.

Empty nest syndrome   A condition that occurs when parents have trouble coping with the transition when their children are old enough to live on their own.

Emulate   To copy in a respectful manner.

Encryption   Codes that secure and protect information transmission.

Endorse   To sign the back of a check in order to make it valid.

Energy dense   Foods that are high in calories and low in nutrients. Also called nutrient poor.

Entrepreneur   A person who organizes and runs his or her own business.

Environment   The natural world, including the soil, the water, the air, and the plant and animal life. Also, the circumstances surrounding a person's life.

Environmental wellness   When the environment in which you live contributes to your happiness, health, and confidence.

Environmentalists   People who favor the environment above conflicting economic or political concerns.

Epidemic   An outbreak of an infectious disease in a local area or community.

Equity investments   The purchase of stock—or ownership—in a company.

Estimate   A guess based on past knowledge or facts.

Ethics   A set of beliefs about what is right and what is wrong.

Ethnicity   Cultural and racial background.

Excess   Too much of something. In nutrition, it refers to too much of a particular vitamin or mineral.

Excluding   Leaving someone (or something) out.

Exclusive   Limited to a small number, or to only one. Exclusive dating means you make a commitment to your partner and both agree not to date anyone else.

Exfoliate   Remove a layer of dead skin through either mechanical or chemical means.

Exit interview   A meeting with your supervisor or human resources to discuss why you are leaving, when you resign or are terminated from a job.

Expendable income   Money left over after you pay for your needs.

Expenses   Money that you spend.

Exporting   Sending out.

Extended family   Relatives outside your immediate family such as grandparents, aunts, uncles, and cousins.

Fabric   The material used to make a garment.

Face value   The value printed or stamped on a piece of currency.

Fad   A fashion that lasts for a short period of time.

Fair Labor Standards Act (FLSA)   The federal law that sets the rules for workers under age 18.

Family and Medical Leave Act (FMLA)   A federal law that provides certain employees with up to 12 weeks of unpaid, job-protected leave per year for family or medical reasons.

Fashion   The current and most popular style of the moment.

Fats   Foods, made from animal products, that are solid at room temperature. Common types of fats include butter, lard, shortening, and margarine.

Federal Reserve   The government agency responsible for creating and tracking all of the money in the United States.

Fibers   Tiny strands that are twisted into yarn, and used to make fabric.

FICA   Federal Insurance Contributions Act: money withheld from a paycheck that is contributed to Social Security.

Fight-or-flight response   How people react when they are faced with danger; they choose to fight it or take flight—run away from it.

Finances   Assets, or resources, in the form of money.

Financial freedom   The flexibility you have knowing there is money available when you want it.

Financial goals   The plans you have for using your money. Financial goals may be long-term or short-term.

Financial institution   A business, such as a bank or credit union, that stores and manages money for individuals and other businesses.

Financial needs   The things you must buy in order to survive, including food, shelter, and water.

Financial security   The comfort and peace of mind you have knowing there is money available when you need it.

Financial wants   The things you want to buy to maintain a certain standard of living, or level of comfort.

Finish   In textiles and clothing, a treatment or process that alters the appearance, feel, or performance

Fire   Dismiss, terminate, or let an employee go.

First aid   The first care you give to someone suffering from an injury, illness, or accident.

First aid kit   A container with a lid that you can store in a handy location, in which you keep supplies you might need to provide first aid.

First impression   The opinion someone forms about you the first time you meet.

Fixed expenses   Expenses that do not change from budget period to budget period.

Fixed income investments   A form of investment in which you lend money to a business or government agency in exchange for a bond.

Flexible expenses   Expenses that are variable, or change from budget period to budget period.

Flexible standards   Standards that you can adapt to different situations.

Floor plan   A map of a room you can use to design and organize the objects in the room.

Folate   A B vitamin.

Form   The shape of a three-dimensional object. One of the elements of design.

Formula   A rule or method of doing something.

Fumes   Gas in the air.

Functional   Useful.

Future time   The time it will be when you finish something you are working on. You find the future time by adding the time it will take to do something to the current time.

Garment   A piece of clothing.

Generalizations   Assigning one individual character trait to an entire culture or group.

Generation X   The generation that includes people born between 1965 and 1976.

Generation Y   Sometimes called Millennials, this generation includes people born between 1977 and 1998.

Generation Z   Refers to people born in the mid-1990s to late 2000s.

Generational culture   People of similar ages are often part of a generational culture. Generational cultures are shaped by shared music, current events, and experiences.

Generic brand   A product that is not identified with a particular company. Generic products usually cost less than brand-name products.

Goal   A plan to obtain something. Goals help you focus on what is really important to you and what you are willing to work for.

Going out   Dating.

Gradation   A gradual change in size or shape. Also, a type of rhythm used in design

Graduate Successfully complete one level, and move on to the next level. For example, to complete a level of education and earn a degree so you can continue to the next level.

Gross income Your pay before withholdings.

Growth spurt Physical growth that happens in short start-and-stop bursts. Most girls experience a growth spurt around age 9 or 10, and most boys go through one at age 11 or 12.

Guild An organization of people who do similar work, united to work together to ensure fair treatment of the members.

HACCP A process for monitoring food safety. It stands for Hazard Analysis Critical Control Point, and is pronounced HAS-sup.

Halitosis Bad breath.

Hand-me-downs Garments, given to you by a relative or friend, which he or she has outgrown.

Harmony Cooperation and unity. The opposite of conflict. Also a principle of design created by using a similar element of design in different objects.

Healthy self-concept A realistic attitude and opinion about yourself in which you appreciate your strengths and accept your weaknesses.

Heredity The process of inheriting traits from your parents.

Heritage Traditions that are passed down through families.

Home A dwelling or living space where residents feel safe, secure, happy, healthy, and loved.

Honor a confidence To listen to someone's private thoughts without telling anyone else.

Hormones Chemicals produced by your body that trigger changes to be made.

Host A living environment in which the virus or microorganism can live and reproduce.

Hue The name of a color, such as blue or red. Hue describes the characteristics of a color that distinguish it from another color.

Human resources The resources people provide that things cannot. Human resources include knowledge, talent, physical and mental abilities, time, energy, and even personal character.

Human rights Those issues that affect people's basic needs, such as food, clothing, shelter, freedom, and protection from abuse.

Hygiene Practices promoting cleanliness and sanitation.

Hypoallergenic Will not cause an allergic reaction

Ideal self The person you would like to be. Along with the real self and the public self, the three parts of self-concept.

Identification Looking for acceptance from a person or group.

Immediate family Family that is directly related to you. In other words: parents and siblings.

Importing Bringing in.

Impulse buys Unneeded things that you buy based on a spur-of-the-moment decision.

Inappropriate behavior Any behavior in a relationship that makes one person uncomfortable, afraid, or hurt—emotionally or physically. It can range from calling someone an unkind name to hitting or forcing unwanted sexual contact.

Income The money that comes in to you.

Income tax returns Forms on which you calculate the amount of income tax you owe.

Individual retirement account (IRA) A personal savings plan that allows you to set aside money for retirement.

Ineffective communication   A communication exchange in which the receiver misinterprets the message.

Infancy   The first stage of the human life cycle.

Infatuation   An unrealistic attraction to another person.

Infertile   Unable to produce offspring.

Influence   Something or someone that affects the way you think and act. Also, to affect the way someone thinks or acts.

Inherited traits   Traits that you are born with as a result of your parents' genes.

Instrumental value   Worth based on how useful or important something is for acquiring something else. For example, money has instrumental value because you use it to buy other things.

Insurance   An investment that protects you financially from everyday risks.

Insurance agent   A person who sells insurance.

Insurance claim   A request for payment to cover a loss.

Insurance policy   The contract issued by the insurance company that specifies the terms of the agreement.

Insurance premium   The amount of money paid by the policy holder for the insurance.

Intellectual wellness   When the ways that you think and learn make you healthy, happy, and confident.

Intensity   The brightness or dullness of a color.

Interest   A percentage of original value that accrues over time. Also, a fee paid for using someone else's money.

Interests   Subjects or activities that attract your attention and that you enjoy doing or learning about.

Intermediate colors   Colors made by mixing a primary color and the secondary color that's next to it on the color wheel.

Internal Revenue Service (IRS)   The agency responsible for collecting federal taxes.

Internship   A temporary job, usually for students, designed to provide the opportunity to work in a field of interest and to build career skills. Internships may or may not pay a salary.

Intrinsic value   Worth based on how useful or important something is in and of itself. Things with intrinsic value might include emotions or feelings.

Investment banks   Banks that help businesses and other organizations raise money by issuing stocks and bonds.

Job   Any activity you do in exchange for money or other payment.

Job application   A standard form you fill out when you apply for a job.

Job interview   A meeting between a job seeker and a potential employer.

Job leads   Hints and opportunities to help find employment.

Job outlook   Statistics and trends about the future opportunities in a particular job, industry, or field of employment.

Job review   A report that rates how well you do your job.

Job search resources   Tools designed to help you identify opportunities for employment.

Job security   Knowing that you will have a job for a long time.

Joint account   An account with multiple names on it such as a parent and a child. All of the signers on the account are authorized to make transactions.

Kilocalorie (kcal)   A unit of measurement that describes how much energy the food you eat delivers to your body. One kcal is the amount of heat—energy—required to raise the temperature of one kilogram of water by one degree on the Celsius temperature scale.

Kilowatt (kW)   A unit of electrical power equal to 1,000 watts.

Kilowatt hour   The amount of energy drawn by a 1,000-watt load for an hour.

Kimono   The official costume in Japan. A kimono is a long, patterned robe made of silk and tied with a sash called an obi.

Labor union   An organization of people who do similar work, united to work together to ensure fair treatment of the members. Also called a trade union.

Layaway plan   A payment plan that lets you pick out an item you want to buy and then make small payments over time. When you have paid for the item in full, you can take it home.

Layoff   A job loss caused when a company has no work for certain employees for a period of time.

Leader   A type of manager. A leader is someone who unites people to work toward common goals.

Leisure   Time for fun and recreation.

Lice   Insects that are passed from person to person by sharing hats, combs, and hair brushes. Treat lice with a special shampoo.

Lifespan   How long you live.

Lifestyle   The way you live, think, and behave every day.

Lifestyle factors   The things that affect the way you live your life including family, responsibilities, resources, location, salary, education, time, and environment.

Line   The element of design that defines the shape, angles, and outline—silhouette—of a garment.

Liquidity   The ability of an investment to be easily converted into cash with little or no loss of capital and a minimum of delay.

Living space   The rooms and areas in your home where you spend your time.

Local time   Time in the current time zone.

Long-term goal   Something you want to achieve in the more distant future—maybe a year from now, or maybe even more distant than that.

Maintenance   Tasks that keep all parts of something—such as a home or machine—in good working condition

Malnutrition   Any type of poor nutrition.

Manager   Someone who makes decisions, solves problems, and uses resources to achieve specific goals.

Man-made fibers   Man-made fibers are made from materials such as wood pulp and chemical products such as coal, petroleum, and natural gas. Rayon, nylon, spandex, polyester, and polypropylene are types of man-made fibers. Also called synthetic or manufactured fibers

Marriage license   A certificate that proves you are legally able to marry.

Meal time plan   A schedule that can help you manage your meal preparation.

Menu   A list of foods for one or more meals you plan to prepare. It can include one single dish, but usually includes all the dishes you plan to serve.

Merchandise   Products or goods that consumers buy.

Middle childhood   The period from ages 6 through 11 when a child starts being more adventurous and continues to grow physically, socially, intellectually, and emotionally in interconnected ways.

Millennials   Generation Y: includes people born between 1977 and 1998.

Minerals   An element needed in small amounts by the body to regulate the activity of the heart, nerves, and muscles and to build and renew teeth, bones, and other tissues.

Mix and match   To wear clothing in different combinations for variety.

Monetary value   The amount of money that an item is worth.

Money   Anything you exchange for goods or services.

Moral values   Values that help us judge behavior based on what we think is right compared to what we think is wrong.

Mortgage   A loan to buy a house.

Motivator   Something that encourages you to set goals and make decisions that will lead to your happiness and well-being.

Mutual fund   A pool of money collected from many—maybe thousands—of investors, and then used to buy stocks, bonds, and other securities.

Nanny   A baby-sitter who works full-time in the child's home.

National origin   Country one's ancestors lived in.

Natural fibers   Fibers made from plant and animal products. Examples include wool, cotton, silk, and linen.

Natural resources   Things that exist in nature and are available for everyone, such as air, water, wildlife, minerals, and plants.

Need   Something you cannot live without.

Negative attitude   A generally gloomy outlook on life. When you have a negative attitude, you are unhappy, you think life is unfair, and you have little confidence in yourself and others.

Negotiate   Work together to accomplish a common goal.

Net income   The amount of money you earn after all withholdings are subtracted.

Net weight   The total weight of something, minus the weight of packaging.

Networking   Sharing information about yourself and your career goals with personal contacts. In technology, networking is a system of linking computers.

Neutral colors   Black, white, and gray.

New relationship energy (NRE)   Infatuation.

Noncomedogenic   A product that does not clog pores.

Non-human resources   Things, such as money or possessions.

Nonprofit organization   An organization that does not earn money for profit. Also called a not-for-profit organization.

Nonrenewable resources   Natural resources that are available in limited quantities and may one day be used up. Coal is a nonrenewable resource.

Nonskid   Nonskid items such as pads or strips are made of a material that provides traction, giving your shoes something to grip so you do not fall.

Nontraditional occupation   Any job that a man or woman does that is usually done by someone of the other gender.

Nonverbal communication   Exchanging messages without using words. Examples include visual messages that the receiver can see, such as a smile when you are talking, and physical messages, such as a pat on the back.

Not-for-profit organization   An organization that does not earn money for profit. Also called a nonprofit organization.

Notions   Things other than fabric that you need to create a garment or other textile project, such as thread, zippers, or buttons.

Nuclear family   A family unit consisting of one or more parents with or without children. Also called an immediate family.

Nutrient dense Foods that are low in calories and high in nutrients.

Nutrient density A measure of the nutrients a food provides compared to the calories it provides.

Nutrient poor Foods that are high in calories and low in nutrients. Also called energy dense.

Nutrients The parts of food that you body needs to be healthy and strong.

Nutrition The study of how the food you eat nourishes your body.

Obesity The condition of being extremely overweight.

Objective Fair, without emotion, bias, or prejudice.

Occupation Employment, or a career.

Occupational Safety and Health Act (OSHA) The main federal law governing safety at work.

Odometer A device that measures the distance traveled in a vehicle

Online bank A retail bank that operates only on the Internet.

Onset Beginning or start.

Opposition An abrupt change or resistance. Also, a type of rhythm used in design.

Optimist Someone who has a positive attitude.

Orientation A welcome session for new employees or students.

Outsourcing When one business pays another to perform a task that the first business could do itself.

Overdrawn In deficit. A bank account is overdrawn when it does not contain enough money to pay all expenses.

Overlock machine A serger, which is a machine that stitches, trims, and finishes off the edges of a seam all in one step.

Pan A container you use to hold food while you cook it in the oven or on the stove-top. A pan is typically shallower than a pot and has curved sides and a single handle.

Pandemic A global outbreak of disease that occurs when a new virus infects people.

Pathogenic Harmful viruses and microorganisms such as bacteria.

Pathogens Biological hazards in the form of harmful living organisms, such as parasites, bacteria, viruses, and fungi.

Pattern A guide for making a garment or other project. Also, a design on fabric.

Pay period The number of days for which you are paid on a paycheck.

Payee The person to whom money is paid.

Pediatrician A doctor who specializes in caring for children.

Pedometer A small electronic device that counts the number of steps you take.

Peer pressure Influence from your peers and friends to do something.

Peer reviews A process during which co-workers or other peers rate your performance.

Peers People your own age.

Performance review A report that rates how well you do something. In employment, a performance review rates how well you do your job.

Permanent life insurance A policy in which you save or invest money over time. Also called cash value life insurance.

Personal academic plan A document that you use to set goals for the things you want to accomplish while you are in school. Sometimes called a personal career plan.

Personal digital assistant (PDA) A handheld computing and communications device

Personal finances The money you earn, spend, and save.

Personal hygiene Practices that keep you clean and healthy.

Personal identification number (PIN) A code that identifies and authorizes you to use an account.

Personal values The thoughts, ideas, and actions that are important to a person. You use personal values to gauge or evaluate the people and things in your life.

Personal wardrobe inventory A count or assessment of all the clothing and accessories that you own.

Personal well-being The level of satisfaction that comes from your opinion about yourself.

Pessimist Someone who has a negative attitude.

Phishing A scam designed to steal your personal and financial information over the Internet.

Physical needs Basic items you need to survive, such as food, shelter, clothing, and water.

Physical well-being The level of satisfaction that comes from the quality of your health.

Pinkeye Conjunctivitis. An eye condition caused by bacteria. Symptoms include red, swollen, itchy eyes that discharge thick yellow pus. Pinkeye is treated with antibiotic eye drops or ointment.

Place setting The plates, utensils, glasses, and napkin placed on the table for a diner to use during a meal.

Plagiarism Copying someone else's work and passing it off as your own. It is illegal.

Plaque A soft deposit of bacteria that forms on the surface of teeth.

Play age Early childhood, or the stage of development from ages 3–6, when children spend most of their time at play.

Poison A substance that causes injury, illness, or even death when it enters the body.

Portfolio A collection of information and documents. For example a career portfolio is a collection of documents and information that might help you get hired. An investment portfolio is all the investments and accounts you own.

Positive attitude A generally happy outlook on life. When you have a positive attitude, you are happy, you think life is good, and you have confidence in yourself and the people around you.

Postsecondary education School after high school.

Pot A container you use to hold food while you cook it on the stove-top.

Predators Adults who look for ways to mistreat children.

Prejudice A negative bias.

Prestige The level of respect given to a person, usually based on achievement, but also sometimes based on or influence.

Preventive maintenance Taking steps to solve a problem before it occurs.

Primary colors Red, yellow, and blue. You can mix the primary colors in different combinations and amounts to create all the other colors.

Principles of design The qualities that describe the way the elements of design work together. The principles of design include balance, rhythm (repetition), emphasis, proportion, scale and unity.

Prioritize Rank items in order of importance.

Privacy Space and time for yourself.

Probability The chance that something will happen.

Probation period A set amount of time during which you and your employer have the chance to make sure you are both happy with the situation.

Problem A difficulty or challenge that you must resolve before you can make progress

Procrastination   Putting off things you need to do.

Productivity   The amount of work an employee accomplishes.

Professional development   Training in your chosen career.

Professionalism   The ability to show respect to everyone around you while you perform your responsibilities as best you can.

Professional organization   An association of people who are all employed in the same field or industry.

Projection   A defense mechanism in which you blame someone or something else.

Promotion   An advance in your career that includes a new job title and additional responsibilities.

Proportion   A basic principle of design that describes the size and location of an object in relation to other objects.

Proteins   Essential nutrients that build and renew body tissues, generate heat and energy, and provide amino acids

Psychological needs   The things you need to maintain a healthy and positive attitude. Psychological needs are different for everyone. Examples include love, security, acceptance, and respect.

Puberty   The process your body goes through to change into its adult form so that it is capable of reproduction.

Public self   The person other people think you are. Along with the real self and the ideal self, the three parts of self-concept.

Punctual   On time.

Punishment   Deliberately placing a person in a temporarily unpleasant or stressful situation as a consequence of bad behavior.

Purge   To empty or throw away. Also, the part of the bulimia nervosa eating disorder when sufferers vomit or use laxatives to expel food before it is digested.

Radius   The length of a straight line from the center of a circle to any point on the circle.

Raise   An increase in pay.

Ratio   A proportional relationship between two numbers or quantities.

Rationalization   A defense mechanism in which you explain away the situation.

Real self   The person you really think you are. Along with the ideal self and the public self, the three parts of self-concept.

Realistic self-concept   A healthy attitude and opinion about yourself. You see yourself the way others see you and you are honest about your strengths and weaknesses. When the real self, ideal self, and public self are similar, you are likely to have a realistic self-concept.

Recipe   A written set of directions for making a certain dish.

Recreation   Fun activities

Redress   Correct a wrong. For example, repair or replace a faulty product.

References   People who will provide a recommendation for you when you apply for a job or school.

Relationship   Interaction with another person.

Renewable resources   Natural resources that can be recreated in unlimited quantities, such as air and sunlight.

Reputation   The way your peers see you, and their opinion of you.

Resent   Blame someone or something for your unhappiness.

Residence   A place where someone lives. Also called a dwelling.

Resident   Someone who lives in a residence or dwelling.

Resources   Things, ideas, and abilities that you use to get something else. We use resources to achieve our goals

Responsibility   Something people expect you to do, or something you must accomplish.

Resume   A written summary of your work-related skills, experience, and education.

Retail bank   A bank that offers services to individuals.

Return on investment (ROI)   The amount of money you earn compared to the amount of money you invest.

Rhythm   A principle of design characterized by the way your eyes move through a room or across a design.

Ringworm   A fungal infection that spreads from person to person by sharing hats, combs, and hair brushes. It must be treated with antifungal medication and shampoo.

Risk   The measured likelihood of loss or danger.

Risk factors   Characteristics that indicate your chance of risk.

Risky behavior   Any activity that puts your health and wellness in danger.

Roadblock   An obstacle; something that gets in the way and interferes with your progress or your ability to achieve a goal.

Role   The way you behave in a specific situation.

Role model   Someone who shows you how to behave in a specific situation.

Romantic   Based on love.

Room and board   The cost of living and eating at a college or university.

Rule   A written or unwritten statement that defines how something is supposed to be done.

Safe deposit box   A box in a fireproof vault that you can rent from your bank.

Sanitation   Methods of keeping clean.

Sanitize   Clean surfaces in a way that kills bacteria and other hazards.

SAT (Scholastic Aptitude Test)   A standardized test used to judge your preparedness for college.

Scale   A tool for measuring the weight of something. Also, to adjust the amount of something proportionately.

Secondary colors   The colors made by mixing equal amounts of two primary colors. Mix red and yellow to get orange, red and blue to get violet, and blue and yellow to get green.

Secure Web site   A Web site that uses encryption and authentication standards to protect online transaction information.

Securities and Exchange Commission (SEC)   The government agency that regulates the securities industry.

Security   An asset that has financial value and can be traded.

Self review   A process during which you rate your own performance.

Self-assessment   A process by which you learn more about your skills, interests, values, and abilities. A career self-assessment helps you identify a career that matches your skills, interests, values, and abilities.

Self-awareness   Your sense of self. Self-awareness is a combination of factors including self-concept and self-esteem.

Self-conceit   A false or exaggerated pride in your own accomplishments. Also, conceit.

Self-concept   The way you see yourself. Also, self-image.

Self-esteem   The pride and respect you feel for yourself.

Self-image   The way you see yourself. Also, self-concept.

Seniority   How long you have held a position or worked for a company.

Sentimental value Importance based on emotional or personal reasons.

Serger A machine that stitches, trims, and finishes off the edges of a seam all in one step. Also called an overlock machine.

Service contract An agreement that the store or manufacturer will provide repair or replacement services if a product breaks or fails.

Severance package Compensation you receive because you are being laid off or terminated from your job.

Shades Darker values of a color, made by adding black to the color.

Short-term goals Something you can accomplish in the near future.

Silhouette The outline of a garment.

Simple interest Interest calculated on the principal balance only.

Situational Depending on the current situation, or on temporary conditions.

Skill An ability or talent; something you do well.

Small enterprise A business or organization that is privately owned and operated, has a small number of employees, and earns a relatively small amount of money.

Smallware Small utensils used by hand in a kitchen.

Social issues Issues that affect the opportunities and restrictions placed on people in a certain culture or society.

Social well-being The level of satisfaction that comes from the quality of your relationships with other people.

Socializing Getting together with people to have fun and relax.

Standard of living A measure of how comfortable you are based on the things that you own.

Standards Guidelines for whether or not something meets expectations.

Steroids Artificial versions of the hormone testosterone.

Stock A share of ownership in a corporation.

Store-brand product A type of generic product that is labeled with the name of the store where it is sold. It is usually less expensive than a brand-name product but may be more expensive than a generic.

Strategies Careful plans and methods.

Strengths Positive qualities, abilities, and skills.

Strep throat An infection caused by bacteria. Symptoms include a sore throat, pain when you swallow, fever, and swollen glands at the back of your throat.

Stress The way your body reacts to a difficult or demanding situation.

Stressor Something that causes stress

Style A particular or personal look or appearance.

Subjective Affected by existing opinions, feelings, and beliefs.

Subsidy A cash payment toward a specific need.

Substance abuse When you use substances such as alcohol, drugs, and tobacco that are bad for your health and wellness.

Suicide Killing oneself.

Suicide pact An agreement between two or more people to commit suicide.

Supply and demand An economic process by which companies produce, or supply, products that consumers buy, or demand.

Surplus   Having more money than you spend. An account is in surplus when it still contains money after all expenses have been paid.

Susceptible host   A host that has a low resistance to a pathogen.

Sustainable product   A product that can be renewed or replaced easily. Bamboo is an example of a sustainable product because it grows quickly.

Symptoms   Signs of an illness.

Tariffs   Taxes usually associated with imports or exports from other countries.

Tax   Money paid to the government so the government can pay for public services.

Tax bracket   A level of income that determines the percentage of tax you will pay.

Tax credit   Recognition of partial payment already made towards taxes.

Tax deduction   An expense you are allowed to deduct from your income before you determine your tax bracket.

Tax deferred savings plans   Savings accounts set up to encourage people to save for retirement. Taxes are not paid until funds are withdrawn from the account.

Taxable income   The actual income on which you must pay taxes.

Team   A group of two or more people who work together to achieve a common goal.

Technological resources   Technology that we use to achieve something. Examples include computers, automated teller machines, and medical equipment.

Technology   The practical application of science to business and industry.

Templates   Sample documents or models.

Term   A set amount of time.

Term life insurance   A policy that provides protection for a specific dollar value.

Terminated   Let go from your job.

Texture   The look and feel of a surface, such as fabric. A basic element of design

Thimble   A small cap worn on a finger while sewing by hand, to protect the finger tip.

Time clock   A machine that automatically records the time you arrive and the time you leave.

Time zones   Geographic regions that use the same standard time.

Tints   Lighter values of a color, made by adding white to the color.

Tolerant   Willing to consider the opinions of others

Toxin   Poison.

Trade-off   A compromise; or giving up one thing to get something else.

Trade union   An organization of people who do similar work, united to work together to ensure fair treatment of the members. Also called a labor union.

Traffic flow   The way people move through a room during everyday use.

Transcript   An official record of the courses you took in high school and the grades you earned.

Tuition   The annual cost for attending school.

Unemployment benefits   Money and career counseling services that are available to unemployed workers while they are looking for new jobs.

Unemployment rate   The percentage of unemployed people who are looking for jobs.

Unit price   The cost of an item per standard unit, such as ounce, pound, or quart.

Utensils   Tools and containers used for food preparation and serving.

Value   The importance of something. Also to consider something important.

Values   Thought and feelings that you use to judge the importance of things. Also, the relative lightness or darkness of a color.

Vandalism   Destroying property that belongs to someone else.

Verbal communication   The exchange of messages by speaking or writing.

Virtue   Positive character traits

Vitamins   Substances that are required in small amounts to keep your body healthy and strong.

Volunteers   Unpaid workers.

W-4   The Employee's Withholding Allowance Certificate. It is a form employees fill out to provide information the employer needs to calculate how much money to withhold from wages to pay taxes.

Want   Something you desire.

Wardrobe   All the clothes you own and wear.

Warranty   A written statement that promises a product will work for a set amount of time.

Watt   A unit of electrical power

Watt-hour   The amount of power used by a device drawing a 1-watt load for an hour.

Well-being   The feeling and understanding that everything is going right in your life.

Wellness   When all the areas of your life work together to make you happy, healthy, and confident.

Wiki   A Web site that enables people to collaborate or work together, or to exchange ideas and information.

Work ethics   Beliefs and behaviors about what is right and wrong in a work environment.

Work history   A list of jobs you have held from the past through the present, showing your experience as an employee.

Yield   The measured output. For a recipe, yield is the number of servings produced.

Yo-yo dieting   Repeatedly losing and gaining weight.

YTD (year to date)   The period of time between January 1 of the current year and the current date.

Index

Disabled persons *(cont.)*
  developmentally disabled children, 122
  technology and, 121
Discipline, 166–167
  age-appropriate discipline, 167
  crisis, family response to, 156
  effective discipline, tips for, 167
  family problems with, 155
  types of, 166
Discount stores, 265
  grocery stores, 409
Discrimination, 191
  workplace discrimination, overcoming, 340–341
Disease and illness
  cancer, 509
  career plans and, 355
  careers in preventing, 509
  chronic conditions, 509
  common illnesses, 508–509
  foodborne illnesses, 401
  hand-washing and, 507
  international diseases, 507
  malnutrition and, 383
  preventing, 506–507
  puberty and, 129
  recognizing symptoms of, 508–509
  spread of, 506
Dishonesty, 49
Dishwashers, 426, 427
Dishwashing, 425
Dissolving ingredients, 419
Diversity, cultural, 52
Dividends, 231
Divorce
  career plans and, 355
  family life cycle and, 147
  reasons for, 151
  stress and, 67
Docents, 303
Doctors, 119, 509
  pediatricians, 179
Doleta.gov, 357
Dollars, 205
Domestic violence
  child abuse, discipline and, 166–167
  family problems with, 155
Draining tools, 426
Dramatic abilities and careers, 295
Dress codes, 435
Driver's license, protecting, 249
Dropping out, 56–57
  as risky behavior, 77
Drucker, Peter, 71
Drug use, 77
Dry chemical fire extinguishers, 403
Dry cleaning clothing, 442, 444
Dry heat, cooking with, 418
Drying clothing, 443

Dry volume, measuring by, 417
DSM-IV (Diagnostic and Statistical Manual of Mental Disorders), 74
Duplexes, 471
Durable fabrics, 441
Dust cloths, 495
Dust pans, 495
Dyeing of fabrics, 441
Dysfunctional relationships, 85

E

E. coli infection, 401
Early childhood, 124–125
  emotional growth in, 125
  intellectual growth in, 125
  physical growth, 125
  social growth in, 125
Earnings. *See* Income
Eating disorders, 74–75
  causes of, 75
  symptoms of, 74
  treatments for, 75
Economic influences
  on development, 117
Economic issues, 192–193. *See also* Poverty
  education and, 193
  justice, working for, 193
Economics, 256
Economy, 256–257
  employment trends and, 288
  impact on, 257
  terminology of, 257
  types of economies, 257
  work, value of, 282
Ecosystem, 480
Education
  babysitting training courses, 177
  career goals and, 299
  careers, classes for, 284
  careers in, 179
  consumer decisions and, 262
  economic issues and, 193
  employer, requesting education from, 348–349
  employment benefit, tuition help as, 323
  family problems with, 155
  lifelong learning, 355
  literacy programs, 193
  online education, 349
  personal academic plans, 286
  resumes including, 315
  technology and, 366–367
  work, educational value of, 283
Effective communication, 34
Effective managers, 38
Eggs, 421
  Hard Cooked Eggs, 422

Eggs, substituting for, 417
Elapsed time, 71
Elastic, choosing, 458
Elderly persons
  caring for, 121
  children as caregivers for, 120
  culture and care of, 120
  dietary supplements for, 386
  families helping, 139
  geriatric health care, 119
  nurturing, 119
  old age phase of life, 133
Electrical fires, 475
Electrical shock, preventing, 476
Electrocution, 476
Electronic fund transfers (EFTs), 205, 219
Electronic safety notifications, 373
E-mail
  home-based careers and, 301
  job application, address on, 316
  phishing e-mail, 251
Emergencies
  babysitter, contact information for, 174
  help, getting, 477
  home escape plans, 476
  911 system, 372, 477
Emotional ads, 262
Emotional development, 114, 115
Emotional growth
  in adolescence, 128, 130
  in early childhood, 125
  of infants and toddlers, 123
Emotional wellness, 8–9, 62, 63
Emotions
  critical thinking and, 33
  depression, 72–73
  food choice and, 379
  safety, emotional, 170, 171
  stress and, 67
  work, emotional value of, 283
Emphasis
  in clothing design, 452
  in home design, 491
Employability skills, 296–297
Employment. *See also* Babysitting; Job search; Work
  adolescence and, 128
  applications for, 316–317
  barriers in workplace, coping with, 339
  bilingual employees, 281
  changing jobs, 352–353
  compatibility about, 151
  conflict in, 105, 338–339
  differences at work, valuing, 339
  discrimination, overcoming, 340–341
  education or training, requesting, 348–349
  ethics and, 335